Medications *and* Mothers' Milk

A Manual of Lactational Pharmacology

2010

Medications *and* Mothers' Milk

Fourteenth Edition

Thomas W. Hale, R.Ph., Ph.D.

Professor of Pediatrics
Assistant Dean of Research
Texas Tech University
School of Medicine
Amarillo, Texas 79016

HALE PUBLISHING

1712 N. Forest St. Amarillo, Texas 79106

Medications *and* Mothers' Milk
Fourteenth Edition

Hale Publishing, L.P.
1712 N. Forest
Amarillo, TX 79106-7017

www.iBreastfeeding.com

(806)-376-9900
(800)-378-1317

DISCLAIMER

The information contained in this publication is intended to supplement the knowledge of health care professionals regarding drug use during lactation. This information is advisory only and is not intended to replace sound clinical judgment or individualized patient care. The author disclaims all warranties, whether expressed or implied, including any warranty as to the quality, accuracy, safety, or suitability of this information for any particular purpose.

ISBN: 978-0-9823379-9-8

Library of Congress Number: 2010923822

Preface

Introduction

Everyone now agrees that human milk is best for human infants. The benefits to growth and development are obvious and confirmed by many studies. However, the use of medications in breastfeeding mothers is often controversial and steeped in misconception by the medical field. This book is dedicated to reducing some of these misconceptions. The truth is most drugs don't enter milk in levels that are hazardous to a breastfed infant. The problem is which drugs are safe and which are hazardous?

Because so few clinicians understand lactational pharmacology, the number of women who discontinue breastfeeding in order to take a medication is still far too high. Fortunately, many mothers are now becoming aware of the enormous benefits of breastfeeding and simply refuse to follow some of the advice given by their healthcare professionals. They seek out the information on their own and invariably find this book.

Because so many women ingest medications during the early neonatal period, it is not surprising that one of the most common questions encountered in pediatrics concerns the use of various drugs during lactation. Unfortunately, most health care professionals simply review the package insert or advise the mother not to breastfeed without having done a thorough study of the literature to find the true answer. Discontinuing breastfeeding is often the wrong decision, and most mothers could easily continue to breastfeed and take the medication without risk to the infant.

In the last 25 years we have collected a lot of data on many current medications and their use in breastfeeding. This book contains most of this knowledge.

It is generally accepted that all medications transfer into human milk to some degree, although it is almost always quite low. Only rarely does the amount transferred into milk produce clinical doses in the infant. Ultimately, it is the clinician's responsibility to review the research we have on the drugs in this book and make a clear decision as to whether the mother should continue to breastfeed.

Because all package inserts advise against the use of their product for breastfeeding mothers, which is almost always incorrect, perhaps we will soon have regulations from the FDA requiring studies of many products in breastfeeding mothers. Since the PDR basically lists only the pharmaceutical manufacturer's package insert, the standard recommendation is to not take the medication while breastfeeding. Therefore, the PDR is the poorest source for obtaining accurate breastfeeding information.

Drugs may transfer into human milk if they:

- Attain high concentrations in maternal plasma
- Are low in molecular weight (< 500)
- Are low in protein binding
- Pass into the brain easily

However, once medications transfer into human milk, other kinetic factors are involved. One of the most important is the oral bioavailability of the medication to the infant. Numerous medications are either destroyed in the infant's gut, fail to be absorbed through the gut wall, or are rapidly picked up by the liver. Once in the liver, they are either metabolized or stored, but often never reach the mother's plasma.

Drugs normally enter milk by passive diffusion, driven by equilibrium forces between the maternal plasma compartment and the maternal milk compartment. They pass from the maternal plasma through capillaries into the lactocytes lining the alveolus. Medications must generally pass through both bilayer lipid membranes of the alveolar cell to penetrate milk; although early on, they may pass between the alveolar cells (first 72 hours postpartum). During the first three days of life, large gaps between the alveolar cells exist. These gaps permit enhanced access into the milk for most drugs, many immunoglobulins, maternal living cells (lymphocytes, leukocytes, macrophages), and other maternal proteins. By the end of the first week, the alveolar cells swell under the influence of prolactin, subsequently closing the intracellular gaps and reducing the transcellular entry of most maternal drugs, proteins, and other substances into the milk compartment. It is generally agreed that medications penetrate into milk more during the colostral period than in mature milk. However, the absolute dose transferred during the colostral period is still low as the total volume of milk is generally less than 30-100 mL total volume/day for the first few days postpartum.

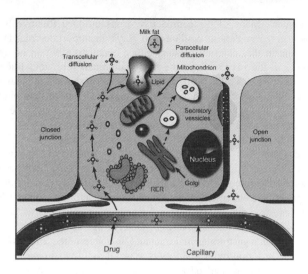

In most instances, the most important determinant of drug penetration into milk is the mother's plasma level. Almost without exception, as the level of the medication in the mother's plasma rises, the concentration in milk increases as well. Drugs enter and exit milk as a function of the mother's plasma level. As soon as the maternal plasma level of a medication begins to fall, equilibrium forces drive the medication out of the milk compartment back into the maternal plasma for elimination. In some instances, drugs are trapped in milk (ion trapping) due to the lower pH of human milk (7.0-7.2). With drugs with a high pKa, the ionic state of the drug changes and stops its exit back into the maternal circulation. This is important in weakly basic drugs, such as the barbiturates (drugs with high pKa). There are a few known pumping systems that use energy to pump drugs into milk. The most important is for iodine. The iodine pump is the same as found in one's thyroid gland. Its purpose is to make sure the infant receives iodine to maintain thyroxine production.

The iodides, such as ^{131}I or any "ionic" form of iodine, concentrate in milk due to this pump. Thus iodides, particularly radioactive ones, should be avoided as their milk concentrations are exceedingly high. Two other physicochemical factors are important in evaluating drugs in breastfeeding mothers - the degree of protein binding and lipid solubility. Drugs that are very lipid soluble penetrate into milk in higher concentrations almost without exception. Of particular interest are the drugs that are active in the central nervous system (CNS). CNS-active drugs invariably have the unique characteristics required to enter milk. Therefore, if a drug is active in the central nervous system, higher levels in milk can be expected; although, the amounts still are often subclinical. Many of the neuroactive drugs produce Relative Infant Doses of >5%. Protein binding also plays an important role. Drugs circulate in the maternal plasma, either bound to albumin or freely soluble in the plasma. It is the free component (unbound fraction) that transfers into milk, while the bound fraction stays in the maternal circulation. Therefore, drugs that have high maternal protein binding (warfarin, many NSAIDs) have reduced milk levels simply because they are excluded from the milk compartment.

Once a drug has entered the mother's milk and has been ingested by the infant, it must traverse through the infant's GI tract prior to absorption. Some drugs are poorly stable in this environment due to the proteolytic enzymes and acids present in the infant's stomach. This includes the aminoglycoside family, Omeprazole, and large peptide drugs, such as Heparin or Insulin. Other drugs are poorly absorbed by the infant's gastrointestinal tract and do not enter the infant's blood stream. Thus, oral bioavailability is a useful tool to estimate just how much of the drug will be absorbed by the infant. Many drugs are sequestered in the liver (first pass) and may never actually reach the plasma compartment where they are active. Absorption characteristics such as these ultimately tend to reduce the overall effect of many drugs in breastfed infants. There are certainly exceptions to this rule, and one must always be aware that the action of a drug in the GI tract can be profound, producing diarrhea, constipation, and occasionally syndromes such as pseudomembranous colitis. One of the more popular methods for estimating risk is to determine the Relative Infant Dose (RID). The RID is calculated by dividing the infant's dose via milk (mg/kg/day) by the mothers dose in mg/kg/day. The RID gives the clinician a feeling for just how much medication the infant is exposed to on a weight-normalized basis. However, many authors calculate the infant dose without normalizing for maternal and infant weight, so be cautious.

Relative Infant Dose

$$RID = \frac{Dose.infant \quad \frac{mg/kg}{d}}{Dose.mother \quad \frac{mg/kg}{d}}$$

Dose.infant = dose in infant
Dose.mother = dose in mother

Key Points About Breastfeeding and Medications

- Avoid using medications that are not necessary. Herbal drugs, high dose vitamins, unusual supplements, etc. that are simply not necessary should be avoided.

- If the Relative Infant Dose is less than 10%, most medications are quite safe to use. The RID of the vast majority of drugs is < 1%.

- Choose drugs for which we have published data, rather than those recently introduced.

- Evaluate the infant for risks. Be slightly more cautious with premature infants or neonates. Be less concerned about older infants.

- Medications used in the first three to four days generally produce subclinical levels in the infant due to the limited volume of milk.

- Recommend that mothers with symptoms of depression or other mental disorders seek treatment. Most of the medications used to treat these syndromes are safe.

- Most drugs are quite safe in breastfeeding mothers. The hazards of using formula are well known and documented.

- Discontinuing breastfeeding for some hours/days may be required, particularly with radioactive compounds. Follow the guidelines in the appendices of this book.

- Choose drugs with short half-lives, high protein binding, low oral bioavailability, or high molecular weight.

Lastly, it is terribly important to always evaluate the infant's ability to handle small amounts of medications. Some infants, such as premature or unstable infants, may not be suitable candidates for certain medications. But remember that early postpartum (and in late stage lactation), the amount of milk produced (30-100 cc/day) is so low that the clinical dose of drug transferred is often low, so even premature neonates would receive only a limited amount from the milk.

Evaluation of the Infant

- Inquire about the infant - always inquire as to the infant's age, size, and stability. This is perhaps the most important criteria to be evaluated prior to using the medication.
- Infant age - premature and newborn infants are at somewhat greater risk.
- Infant stability - unstable infants with poor GI stability may increase the risk of using medications.
- Pediatric Approved Drugs - generally are less hazardous if long-term history of safety is recognized.
- Dose vs Age – the age of an infant is critical. Use medications cautiously in premature infants. Older, mature infants can metabolize and clear medications much easier. Remember the dose of the drug is dependent on milk supply. In mothers in late-stage lactation (>1 year), milk production is often low, so is the dose of drug delivered.
- Drugs that alter milk production – avoid medications that may alter the mother's milk production. See the appendices for lists of such drugs.

General Suggestions for the Clinician

1. Determine if the drug is absorbed from the GI tract. Many drugs, such as the aminoglycosides, vancomycin, cephalosporin antibiotics (third generation), morphine, magnesium salts, and large protein drugs (heparin), are so poorly absorbed that it is unlikely the infant will absorb significant quantities. At the same time, observe for GI side effects from the medication trapped in the GI compartment of the infant (e.g., diarrhea).

2. Review the relative infant dose (RID) and compare that to the pediatric dose if known. Most of the RID were derived from the C_{max} (highest milk concentration of the drug) that were published. In this edition, I've added 'ranges' of RID, so the reader can see the various dose estimates from different studies. The milk/plasma ratio is virtually worthless unless you know the maternal plasma level. It does not provide the user with information as to the absolute amount of drug transferred to the infant via milk. Even if the drug has a high milk/plasma ratio, if the maternal plasma level of the medication is very small (such as with propranolol), then the absolute amount (dose) of a drug entering milk will still be quite small and often subclinical.

3. Try to use medications with shorter half-lives as they are generally eliminated from the maternal plasma rapidly, thus

exposing the milk compartment (and the infant) to reduced levels of medication. This is particularly true with anti-cancer drugs (see Appendix A).

4.   Be cautious of drugs (or their active metabolites) that have long pediatric half-lives as they can continually build up in the infant's plasma over time. The barbiturates, benzodiazepines, and meperidine are classic examples where higher levels in the infant can and do occasionally occur.

5.   If you are provided a choice, choose drugs that have higher protein binding because they are generally sequestered in the maternal circulation and do not transfer readily into the milk compartment or the infant. Remember, it's the free drug that transfers into the milk compartment. Without doubt, the most important parameter that determines drug penetration into milk is plasma protein binding. Choose drugs with high protein binding.

6.   Although not always true, I have generally found centrally active drugs (anticonvulsants, antidepressants, antipsychotic) frequently penetrate milk in higher (not necessarily 'high') levels simply due to their physicochemistry. If the drug in question produces sedation, depression, or other neuroleptic effects in the mother, it is likely to penetrate the milk and may produce similar effects in the infant. Thus, with CNS-active drugs, one should always check the data in this book closely and monitor the infant routinely.

7.   Be cautious of herbal drugs as many contain chemical substances that may be dangerous to the infant. Numerous poisonings have been reported. Prior to using, advise the mother to contact a lactation consultant or herbalist who is knowledgeable about their use in breastfeeding mothers. Do not exceed standard recommended doses. Try to use pure forms, not large mixtures of unknown herbals. Do not overdose, use only minimal amounts.

8.   For radioactive compounds, check Appendix B. I have gathered much of the published data in this field into several new tables. The Nuclear Regulatory Commission recommendations are quite good, but they differ from some published data. They can be copied and provided to your radiologist. They are available from the Nuclear Regulatory Commission's web page address in the appendix.

9.   Use the Relative Infant Dose. The box below shows the calculation. In general, a Relative Infant Dose of < 10% is considered safe, and its use is becoming increasingly popular by numerous investigators.

Most importantly, it is seldom required that a breastfeeding mother discontinue breastfeeding just to take a medication. It is simply not acceptable for the clinician to stop lactation merely because of heightened anxiety or ignorance on their part. The risks of formula feeding are significant and should not be trivialized. Few drugs have documented side effects in breastfed infants, and we know most of these.

The following review of drugs, and even diseases, is a thorough review of what has been published and what we presently know about the use of medications in breastfeeding mothers. I hope that that our knowledge in this field will grow if the FDA promulgates regulations requiring drug studies in breastfeeding mothers. Let us all support this issue.

THE AUTHOR MAKES NO RECOMMENDATIONS AS TO THE SAFETY OF THESE MEDICATIONS DURING LACTATION, BUT ONLY REVIEWS WHAT IS CURRENTLY PUBLISHED IN THE SCIENTIFIC LITERATURE. INDIVIDUAL USE OF MEDICATIONS MUST BE LEFT UP TO THE JUDGEMENT OF THE PHYSICIAN, THE PATIENT, AND OTHER HEALTHCARE CONSULTANTS.

Thomas W. Hale

How To Use This Book

This section of the book is designed to aid the reader in determining risk to an infant from maternal medications and in using the pharmacokinetic parameters throughout this reference.

Drug Name and Generic Name:
Each monograph begins with the generic name of the drug. Several of the most common USA trade names are provided under the *Trade* section.

Other Trades:
This book is used all over the world. Thus many other trade names from other countries are now included in this section.

Uses:
This lists the general use of the medication, such as penicillin antibiotic or antiemetic or analgesic, etc. Remember, many drugs have multiple uses in many syndromes. I have only listed the most common use.

AAP:
This entry lists the new recommendations provided by the American Academy of Pediatrics as published in their document, *The transfer of drugs and other chemicals into human milk* (Pediatrics. 2001 Sep;108(3):776-789.)

Drugs are listed in tables according to the following recommendations:
- Cytotoxic drugs that may interfere with cellular metabolism of the nursing infant;
- Drugs of abuse for which adverse effects on the infant during breastfeeding have been reported;
- Radioactive compounds that require temporary cessation of breastfeeding;
- Drugs for which the effect on nursing infants is unknown, but may be of concern;
- Drugs that have been associated with significant effects on some nursing infants and should be given to nursing mothers with caution;
- Maternal medication usually compatible with breastfeeding.

In this book, the AAP recommendations have been paraphrased to reflect these recommendations. Because the AAP recommendations do not cover all drugs, "Not Reviewed" simply implies that the drug has not yet been reviewed by this committee. The author recommends that each user review these recommendations for further detail.

Drug Monograph:
The drug monograph lists what we currently understand about the drug, its ability to enter milk, the concentration in milk at set time intervals, and other parameters that are important to a clinical consultant. I have attempted at great length to report only what the references have documented.

Pregnancy Risk Category:

Pregnancy risk categories have been assigned to almost all medications by their manufacturers and are based on the level of risk the drug poses to the fetus during gestation. They are not useful in assigning risk via breastfeeding. The FDA has provided these five categories to indicate the risk associated with the induction of birth defects. Unfortunately, they do not indicate the importance of when during gestation the medication is used. For this reason, I have added small comments to indicate that some drugs are more dangerous during certain trimesters of pregnancy. The definitions provided below are, however, a useful tool in determining the possible risks associated with using the medication during pregnancy. Some newer medications may not yet have pregnancy classifications and are therefore not provided herein.

Category A:
Controlled studies in women fail to demonstrate a risk to the fetus in the first trimester (and there is no evidence of a risk in later trimesters) and the possibility of fetal harm appears remote.

Category B:
Either animal-reproduction studies have not demonstrated a fetal risk, but there are no controlled studies in pregnant women, or animal reproduction studies have shown an adverse effect (other than a decrease in fertility) that was not confirmed in controlled studies in women in the first trimester (and there is no evidence of a risk in later trimesters).

Category C:
Either studies in animals have revealed adverse effects on the fetus (teratogenic or embryocidal, or other) and there are no controlled studies in women, or studies in women and animals are not available. Drugs should be given only if the potential benefit justifies the potential risk to the fetus.

Category D:
There is positive evidence of human fetal risk, but the benefits from use in pregnant women may be acceptable despite the risk (e.g., if the drug is needed in a life-threatening situation or for a serious disease for which safer drugs cannot be used or are ineffective).

Category X:
Studies in animals or human beings have demonstrated fetal abnormalities, or there is evidence of fetal risk based on human experience, or both, and the risk of the use of the drug in pregnant women clearly outweighs any possible benefit. The drug is contraindicated in women who are or may become pregnant.

Dr. Hale's Lactation Risk Category:

L1 SAFEST:
Drug which has been taken by a large number of breastfeeding mothers without any observed increase in adverse effects in the infant. Controlled studies in breastfeeding women fail to demonstrate a risk to the infant and the possibility of harm to the breastfeeding infant is remote; or the product is not orally bioavailable in an infant.

L2 SAFER:
Drug which has been studied in a limited number of breastfeeding women without an increase in adverse effects in the infant. And/or, the evidence of a demonstrated risk which is likely to follow use of this medication in a breastfeeding woman is remote.

L3 MODERATELY SAFE:
There are no controlled studies in breastfeeding women; however, the risk of untoward effects to a breastfed infant is possible, or controlled studies show only minimal non-threatening adverse effects. Drugs should be given only if the potential benefit justifies the potential risk to the infant. (New medications that have absolutely no published data are automatically categorized in this category, regardless of how safe they may be.)

L4 POSSIBLY HAZARDOUS:
There is positive evidence of risk to a breastfed infant or to breastmilk production, but the benefits from use in breastfeeding mothers may be acceptable despite the risk to the infant (e.g., if the drug is needed in a life-threatening situation or for a serious disease for which safer drugs cannot be used or are ineffective.)

L5 CONTRAINDICATED:
Studies in breastfeeding mothers have demonstrated that there is significant and documented risk to the infant based on human experience, or it is a medication that has a high risk of causing significant damage to an infant. The risk of using the drug in breastfeeding women clearly outweighs any possible benefit from breastfeeding. The drug is contraindicated in women who are breastfeeding an infant.

Relative Infant Dose:
The relative infant dose (RID) is calculated by dividing the infant's dose via milk in "mg/kg/day" by the maternal dose in "mg/kg/day" (see box above). This weight-normalizing method indicates approximately how much of the "maternal dose" the infant is receiving. Many authors now use this preferred method because it gives a better indication of the relative dose transferred to the infant.   In this edition, I now report RID ranges, which is the RID published by various authors. This gives the reader an estimate of all the relative infant doses published by the various authors.

Please understand, however, that many authors use different methods for calculating RID. Some are not weight-normalized. In these cases, their estimates may differ slightly from this book.   While I often place the 'authors' estimates of relative infant dose, the RID range that I calculate is based on a 70 Kg mother and is weight-normalized in all instances.   So RID may be slightly different according to who calculates it.

Many researchers now suggest that anything less than 10% of the maternal dose is probably safe. This is usually correct. However, some drugs (metronidazole, fluconazole) actually have much higher relative infant doses, but because they are quite non-toxic, they do not often bother an infant. To calculate this dose, I chose the data I felt was best, and this often included larger studies with AUC calculations of mean concentrations in milk. I also chose an average body weight of 70 kg for an adult. Thus, the RIDs herein are calculated assuming a maternal average weight of 70 kg and a daily milk intake of 150 mL/kg/day in the infant. Please note, many authors fail to normalize their data for weight. Others provide a RID for 'each' feeding, not a daily average. Therefore, my values may vary slightly from others simply due to differences in the method of calculation.

Adult Concerns:
This section lists the most prevalent undesired or bothersome side effects listed for adults. As with most medications, the occurrence of these is often quite rare, generally less than 1-10% of the time. Side effects vary from one patient to another and should not be overemphasized, since most patients do not experience untoward effects.

Pediatric Concerns:
This section lists the side effects noted in the published literature as associated with medications transferred via human milk. Pediatric concerns are those effects that were noted by investigators as being associated with drug transfer via milk. In some sections, I have added comments that may not have been reported in the literature, but are

well known attributes of this medication and are useful information to provide the mother so that she can better care for her infant ("Observe for weakness, apnea").

Drug Interactions:

Drug interactions generally indicate which medications, when taken together, may produce higher or lower plasma levels of other medications, or they may decrease or increase the effect of another medication. These effects may vary widely from minimal to dangerous. Because some medications have hundreds of interactions and because I had limited room to provide this information, I have listed only those that may be significant. Therefore, please be advised that this section may not be complete. In several references, I have suggested that due to the large number of interactions the reader consult a more complete drug interaction reference. Please remember that the drugs administered to a mother could interact with those being administered concurrently to an infant. Example: Maternal fluconazole and pediatric cisapride.

Alternatives:

Drugs listed in this section may be suitable alternate choices for the medication listed above. In many instances, if the patient cannot take the medication or it is a poor choice due to high milk concentrations, these alternates may be suitable candidates. WARNING: The alternates listed are only suggestions and may not be at all proper for the syndrome in question. Only the clinician can make this judgment. For instance, nifedipine is a calcium channel blocker with good antihypertensive qualities, but poor antiarrhythmic qualities. In this case, verapamil would be a better choice.

Adult Dosage:

This is the usual adult oral dose provided in the package insert. While these are highly variable, I chose the dose for the most common use of the medication.

T½ =

This lists the most commonly recorded adult half-life of the medication. It is very important to remember that short half-life drugs are preferred. Use this parameter to determine if the mother can successfully breastfeed around the medication by nursing the infant, then taking the medication. If the half-life is short enough (1-3 hours), then the drug level in the maternal plasma will be declining when the infant feeds again. This is ideal. If the half-life is significantly long (12-24 hours) and if your physician is open to suggestions, then find a similar medication with a shorter half-life (compare ibuprofen with naproxen).

PHL=
This lists the most commonly recorded pediatric half-life of the medication. Medications with extremely long half-lives in pediatric patients may accumulate to high levels in the infant's plasma if the half-life is exceeding long (>12 hours). Pediatric half-lives are difficult to find due to the paucity of studies.

M/P=
This lists the milk/plasma ratio. This is the ratio of the concentration of drug in the mother's milk divided by the concentration in the mother's plasma. If high (> 1-5), it is useful as an indicator of drugs that may sequester in milk in high levels. If low (< 1), it is a good indicator that only minimal levels of the drug are transferred into milk (this is preferred). While it is best to try to choose drugs with LOW milk/plasma ratios, the amount of drug which transfers into human milk is largely determined by the level of drug in the mother's plasma compartment. Even with high M/P ratios and LOW maternal plasma levels, the amount of drug that transfers is still low. Therefore, the higher M/P ratios often provide an erroneous impression that large amounts of drug are going to transfer into milk. This simply may not be true.

T_{max}=
This lists the time interval from administration of the drug until it reaches the highest level in the mother's plasma (C_{max}), which we call the peak or "time to max", hence T_{max}. Occasionally, you may be able to avoid nursing the baby when the medication is at the peak. Rather, wait until the peak is subsiding or has at least dropped significantly. Remember, drugs enter breastmilk as a function of the maternal plasma concentration. In general, the higher the mother's plasma level, the greater the entry of the drug into her milk. If possible, choose drugs that have short peak intervals, and suggest mom not breastfeed when the drug is at C_{max}.

PB=
This lists the percentage of maternal protein binding. Most drugs circulate in the blood bound to plasma albumin and other proteins. If a drug is highly protein bound, it cannot enter the milk compartment as easily. The higher the percentage of binding, the less likely the drug is to enter the maternal milk. Try to choose drugs that have high protein binding in order to reduce the infant's exposure to the medication. Good protein binding is typically greater than 90%.

Oral=
Oral bioavailability refers to the ability of a drug to reach the systemic circulation after oral administration. It is generally a good indication of the amount of medication that is absorbed into the blood stream of the

patient. Drugs with low oral bioavailability are generally either poorly absorbed in the gastrointestinal tract, are destroyed in the gut, or are sequestered by the liver prior to entering the plasma compartment. The oral bioavailability listed in this text is the adult value; almost none have been published for children or neonates. Recognizing this, these values are still useful in estimating if a mother or perhaps an infant will actually absorb enough drug to provide clinically significant levels in the plasma compartment of the individual. The value listed estimates the percent of an oral dose that would be found in the plasma compartment of the individual after oral administration. In many cases, the oral bioavailability of some medications is not listed by manufacturers, but instead terms such as "Complete", "Nil", or "Poor" are used. For lack of better data, I have included these terms when no data are available on the exact amount (percentage) absorbed.

Vd=
The volume of distribution is a useful kinetic term that describes how widely the medication is distributed in the body. Drugs with high volumes of distribution (Vd) are distributed in higher concentrations in remote compartments of the body and may not stay in the blood. For instance, digoxin enters the blood compartment and then rapidly leaves to enter the heart and skeletal muscles. Most of the drug is sequestered in these remote compartments (100 fold). Therefore, drugs with high volumes of distribution (1-20 liter/kg) generally require much longer to clear from the body than drugs with smaller volumes (0.1 liter/kg). For instance, whereas it may only require a few hours to totally clear gentamycin (Vd=0.28 l/kg), it may require weeks to clear amitriptyline (Vd=10 l/kg), which has a huge volume of distribution. In addition, some drugs may have one half-life for the plasma compartment, but may have a totally different half-life for the peripheral compartment, as half-life is a function of volume of distribution. I have found that drugs with high Vd also produce lower milk levels. For a complete description of Vd, please consult a good pharmacology reference. In this text, the units of measure for Vd are liters/kg.

pKa=
The pKa of a drug is the pH at which the drug is equally ionic and nonionic. The more ionic a drug is, the less capable it is of transferring from the milk compartment to the maternal plasma compartment. Hence, the drug becomes trapped in milk (ion-trapping). This term is useful because drugs that have a pKa higher than 7.2 may be sequestered to a slightly higher degree than one with a lower pKa. Drugs with higher pKa generally have higher milk/plasma ratios. Hence, choose drugs with a lower pKa.

MW=

The molecular weight of a medication is a significant determinant as to the entry of that medication into human milk. Medications with small molecular weights (< 200) can easily pass into milk by traversing small pores in the cell walls of the mammary epithelium (see ethanol). Drugs with higher molecular weights must traverse the membrane by dissolving in the cells' lipid membranes, which may significantly reduce milk levels. As such, the smaller the molecular weight, the higher the relative transfer of that drug into milk. Protein medications (e.g., Heparin, Insulin), which have enormous molecular weights, transfer at much lower concentrations and are virtually excluded from human breastmilk. Therefore, when possible, choose drugs with higher molecular weights to reduce their entry into milk.

Common Abbreviations

$T\frac{1}{2}$	Adult elimination half-life
T_{max}	Time to peak plasma level (PK)
M/P	Milk/Plasma Ratio
RID	Relative Infant Dose
C_{max}	Plasma or milk concentration at peak
Vd	Volume of Distribution
PB	Percent of protein binding in maternal circulation
PHL	Pediatric elimination half-life
Oral	Oral bioavailability (adult)
µg/L	Microgram per liter
ng/L	Nanogram per liter
mg/L	Milligram per liter
mL	Milliliter. One cc
NSAIDs	Non-steroidal anti-inflammatory
ACEi	Angiotensin converting enzyme inhibitor
MAOI	Monoamine oxidase inhibitors
MW	Molecular Weight
µCi	Microcurie of Radioactivity
mmol	Millimole of weight
µmol	Micromole of weight
X	Times
AUC	Area under the Curve
BID	Twice daily
TID	Three times daily
QID	Four times daily
PRN	As needed
QD	Daily
d	Day

[11]C-WAY 100635 or ^{11}C-RACLOPRIDE	L2

Trade: C-Way 100635, C-Raclopride
Other Trades:
Uses: Diagnostic Agent, Radiopharmaceutical Imaging
AAP: Not reviewed

[11]C-WAY 100635 and ^{11}C-raclopride (sequentially) are used to measure brain serotonin-1A and dopamine- 2 receptor binding, respectively, in depressed and non- depressed postpartum research subjects. In a study of 5 lactating women the [11]C- WAY 100635 injection was followed by 90 min of scanning.[1] Sixty minutes later, ^{11}C-raclopride injection was followed by 60 min of scanning. Approximately 15 min after the conclusion of each scan, study participants expressed their milk for the study. The mean infant age was 9.4 ± 3.4 wk; the range was 4-13 wk.

The mean activity of ^{11}C in breast milk (455 ± 107 Bq/mL) was similar to that in plasma (355 ± 99 Bq/mL) 60 minutes after 526 ± 61 MBq of ^{11}C-WAY 100635 had been injected. For ^{11}C-raclopride, the mean activity concentration of ^{11}C in breast milk (105 ± 32 Bq/mL) was significantly less than that in plasma (913 ± 361 Bq/mL) 60 min after radiopharmaceutical injection (384 ± 24 MBq). Using worst-case scenario, the mean radioactive dose to the nursing infant at 1 h was 2.7 ± 0.6 μSv after ^{11}C-WAY 100635 and 0.6 ± 0.2 μSv after ^{11}C-raclopride injection.

The authors concluded that interruption of breastfeeding was not warranted. A brief interruption of breastfeeding for only 100 minutes would remove all risk to the infant.

Pregnancy Risk Category:

Lactation Risk Category: L2 after brief delay

Adult Concerns:

Pediatric Concerns: Milk levels were equal to or less than maternal plasma levels. However, the half-life of this radioisotope is brief (20.3 min), so only limited exposure would result.

Drug Interactions:

Relative Infant Dose:

Adult Dose:

Alternatives:

T ½	= 20.3 minutes	M/P	=
PHL	=	PB	=
Tmax	=	Oral	=
MW	=	pKa	=
Vd	=		

References:
1. Moses-Kolko EL, Meltzer CC, Helsel JC, Sheetz M, Mathis C, Ruszkiewicz J, et al. No interruption of lactation is needed after ^{11}C-WAY 100635 or ^{11}C-raclopride PET. J Nucl Med 2005 Oct; 46 (10):1765.

5-HYDROXYTRYPTOPHAN | L3

Trade: PowerSleep, Oxitriptan
Other Trades:
Uses: Precursor of serotonin
AAP: Advise not to breastfeed

5-Hydroxytryptophan (5-HTP) is a natural aromatic amino acid which is the immediate precursor of the neurotransmitter serotonin. L-Tryptophan is another amino acid formerly used to treat depression.

L-Tryptophan: L-tryptophan (LTP), once absorbed, is rapidly transported to the liver where some of it is incorporated into proteins, and some passes unchanged into the general circulation. It is a precursor of serotonin. One of the major problems with the use of LTP is that when used at higher doses, metabolism to kynurenine is highly induced, and the majority of LTP is subsequently metabolized rather than converted into serotonin. Even under the best of circumstances, less than 3% of the LTP is likely to be converted to serotonin in the brain. L-Tryptophan crosses the blood-brain barrier only poorly. As the doses increase, the creation of the metabolite kynurenine tends to block entry of LTP into the brain. As the doses of LTP used are extraordinarily high 2000-6000 mg/d cost and adverse effects are significant.[1] Older formulations created with contaminates were responsible for the eosinophilia-myalgia syndrome.

5-HTTP: 5-HTP is rapidly absorbed, and approximately 70% of the dose is bioavailable. The remaining 30% is converted to serotonin by intestinal cells which may lead to some nausea. 5-HTP readily crosses the blood-brain barrier (24% in CSF) and is one step closer to serotonin production. The dose of 5-HTP is much lower, averaging 100-300 mg/d, and some studies have found it equivalent to tricyclic antidepressants[2] and fluvoxamine (an SSRI) in treating depression.[3] Although several cases of eosinophilia-myalgia syndrome have been reported with the use of 5-HTP[4,5], both of these patients had defective metabolic mechanisms for converting 5-HTP.

Unfortunately, there are no data on the transfer of exogenously supplied LTP or 5-HTP into human milk. For instance, it is not apparently known if high maternal plasma levels would produce high milk levels. While it is true human milk contains higher levels of LTP, presumably to stimulate serotonin levels in the infant's CNS, it is not known if high maternal doses would likewise produce high milk levels. Because the infant's neurologic development is incredibly sensitive to serotonin levels, and because we do not know if supplementation with LTP or 5-HTP could produce high milk levels leading to overdose in the infant, this author does not recommend the use of L-tryptophan or 5-HTP supplementation in breastfeeding mothers until we know corresponding milk levels.

Pregnancy Risk Category:

Lactation Risk Category: L3

Adult Concerns: Adverse anorexia, diarrhea, nausea, and vomiting have been reported.

Pediatric Concerns: None reported via milk.

Drug Interactions: Carbidopa may increase absorption of 5-HT. Use with MAOI is potentially dangerous. 5-HT may potentiate the serotonergic effect of selective serotonin reuptake inhibitors (SSRIs).

Relative Infant Dose:

Adult Dose:

Alternatives:

T ½	= 4.3 hours	M/P	=
PHL	=	PB	= 19%
Tmax	= 3-6 hours	Oral	= <70%
MW	= 393	pKa	= 6.96
Vd	= 0.6		

References:
1. Murray MT, Pizzorno JE. 5-Hydroxytryptophan. In: Murray MT, Pizzorno JE, editors. Textbook of Natural Medicine. Churchill Livingstone, 1999: 783-796.
2. van Praag HM. Management of depression with serotonin precursors. Biol Psychiatry 1981; 16 (3):291-310.
3. Poldinger W, Calanchini B, Schwarz W. A functional-dimensional approach to depression: serotonin deficiency as a target syndrome in a comparison of 5-hydroxytryptophan and fluvoxamine. Psychopathology 1991; 24 (2):53-81.

4.   Sternberg EM, Van Woert MH, Young SN, Magnussen I, Baker H, Gauthier S, Osterland CK. Development of a scleroderma-like illness during therapy with L-5-hydroxytryptophan and carbidopa. N Engl J Med 1980; 303 (14):782-787

5.   Michelson D, Page SW, Casey R, Trucksess MW, Love LA, Milstien S, Wilson C, Massaquoi SG, Crofford LJ, Hallett M, An eosinophilia-myalgia syndrome related disorder associated with exposure to L-5-hydroxytryptophan. J Rheumatol 1994; 21 (12):2261-2265

[99m]TECHNETIUM TC SESTAMIBI   L4

Trade: Cardiolite, Sestamibi
Other Trades:
Uses: Imaging agent
AAP: Radioactive compound that requires temporary cessation of breastfeeding

[99M] Technetium sestamibi is a myocardial imaging agent that is also sometimes used as an oncologic imaging agent. The radioactive [99] Technetium ion is chelated to the sestamibi molecule. It is used as an alternative to [201]Thallium imaging.[1] Sestamibi is largely distributed to the myocardium and is a function of myocardial viability.[2]

Technetium is a weak gamma emitter with a radioactive half-life of only 6.02 hours. The biological half-life of this product is approximately 6 hours, but the effective half-life (both biological and radioactive) is only about 3 hours. Transfer of significant amounts of sestamibi into human milk is yet unreported but is rather unlikely as sestamibi binds irreversible to myocardial tissue and does not redistribute to other tissues to a significant degree. Other forms of [99]TC have been reported to enter milk, but entry would be largely determined by the chemical form, not the radioactive agent.[3] For current Nuclear Regulatory Commission breastfeeding guidelines consult table in Appendix B.

Pregnancy Risk Category: C

Lactation Risk Category: L4

Adult Concerns: Dysgeusia, headache, flushing, angina, hypersensitivity, and hypertension.

Pediatric Concerns: It is not known if the sestamibi chelate is transferred into human milk. But Technetium salts in general do transfer. "Pump and discard for 24-30 hours or pump and hold the milk for approximately 24-30 hours prior to feeding."

Drug Interactions:

Relative Infant Dose:

Adult Dose: 10-30 mCi X 1

Alternatives:

T ½	= 6 hours	M/P	=
PHL	=	PB	= <1%
Tmax	=	Oral	= Complete
MW	=	pKa	=
Vd	=		

References:
1. Berman DS. Introduction--Technetium [99m] myocardial perfusion imaging agents and their relation to thallium-201. Am J Cardiol 1990; 66 (13):1E-4E.
2. Berman DS, Kiat H, Maddahi J. The new Tc [99m] myocardial perfusion imaging agents: Tc [99m] sestamibi and Tc [99m] teboroxime. Circulation 1991; 84 ((suppl)):7-21.
3. Maisels MJ, Gilcher RO. Excretion of technetium in human milk. Pediatrics 1983; 71 (5):841-842.

ABATACEPT   L3

Trade: Orencia
Other Trades:
Uses: Antirheumatic
AAP: Not reviewed

Abatacept is a soluble fusion protein that is linked to the a modified portion of human immunoglobulin G1 (IgG1).[1] The apparent MW of abatacept is 92 kilodaltons. Abatacept inhibits T cell activation by binding to CD80 and CD86 receptors which down regulates the T cells which are implicated in inflammation of rheumatic disorders. In vitro, abatacept decreases T cell proliferation and inhibits the production of thecytokines TNF alpha (TNFα), interferon-γ;, and interleukin-2.

There are no data on the transfer of this antibody into human milk. Due to its large MW and unusual structure, it is not likely to enter milk in clinically relevant amounts. But as yet we have not studies to confirm this.

Pregnancy Risk Category: C

Lactation Risk Category: L3

Adult Concerns: The adverse events most frequently resulting in clinical intervention were infections. The most frequent infection listed is upper respiratory tract infecrtions, bronchitis, and herpes zoster. Other side effects include: headache, nasopharyngitis, dizziness, COPD exacerbation, cough, rhonchi, and dyspnea.

Pediatric Concerns: None yet reported in breastfeeding infants.

Drug Interactions: Do not use with other anti TNF products such as adalimumab, etanercept, and infliximab because such combination therapy may increase their risk for infections.

Relative Infant Dose:

Adult Dose: 750 mg (for 60-100 Kg weight) Intravenous

Alternatives: Infliximab, etanercept

T ½	= 13.1 days	M/P	=
PHL	=	PB	=
Tmax	=	Oral	= Nil
MW	= 92,000	pKa	=
Vd	= 0.07		

References:
1. Pharmaceutical manufacturers prescribing information.

ACAMPROSATE   L3

Trade: Campral
Other Trades:
Uses: GABA Agonist / Glutamate Antagonist
AAP: Not reviewed

Acamprosate is a medication used for ethanol dependency. Its mechanism of action is not fully known, however it does increase levels of GABA and decrease levels of glutamate. During use, it reduces alcohol intake without the disulfram-like effects.[1] There are no data available on the transfer of acamprosate to human milk. It is not a sedative and is not additive, and its oral absorption is minimal. Due to the relatively low MW and the lack of protein binding, transfer could be possible. In addition, alcohol-dependent mothers may not be a good risk for breastfeeding. However, this drug poses a minimal risk to infants.

Pregnancy Risk Category: C

Lactation Risk Category: L3

Adult Concerns: Adverse effects seen include diarrhea, insomnia, anxiety, anorexia, weakness, and nausea.

Pediatric Concerns: No data are available one the use of this product in pediatric patients.

Drug Interactions: None reported.

Relative Infant Dose:

Adult Dose: 666 mg tid

Alternatives:

T ½	= 20-33 hours	M/P	=
PHL	=	PB	= Minimal
Tmax	=	Oral	= 11%
MW	= 400	pKa	=
Vd	= 1		

References:
1.   Pharmaceutical Manufacturer Prescribing Information. 2005.

ACARBOSE   L3

Trade: Precose, Prandase
Other Trades: Prandase, Glucobay
Uses: Delays carbohydrate absorption
AAP: Not reviewed

Acarbose is an oral alpha-glucosidase inhibitor used to reduce the absorption of carbohydrates in the management of Type II (NIDDM) diabetics.[1] The reduction of carbohydrate absorption reduces the rapid rise in glucose following a meal; hence, glycosylated hemoglobin (Hemoglobin A1C) levels are reduced. Acarbose is less than 2% bioavailable as an intact molecule.[2] No data are available on the transfer of acarbose into human milk but with a bioavailability of less than 2%, it is very unlikely any would reach the milk compartment or be orally absorbed by the infant.

Pregnancy Risk Category: B

Lactation Risk Category: L3

Adult Concerns: Adverse effects include flatulence, abdominal pain and distention, diarrhea, and borborygmi. Isolated cases of elevated liver enzymes have been reported. Elevated liver enzymes occurred in approximately 15% of acarbose-treated patients and is apparently dose related with doses >300 mg daily.

Pediatric Concerns: None reported via milk.

Drug Interactions: May increase hypoglycemia when used with other antidiabetic medications such as the sulfonylureas.

Relative Infant Dose:

Adult Dose: 50-100 mg TID

Alternatives:

T ½	= <2 hours	M/P	=
PHL	=	PB	=
Tmax	=	Oral	= 0.7- 2%
MW	= 645	pKa	=
Vd	= 0.32		

References:
1. Pharmaceutical Manufacturer Prescribing Information. 1999.
2. Balfour JA, McTavish D. Acarbose. An update of its pharmacology and therapeutic use in diabetes mellitus. Drugs 1993; 46 (6):1025-1054.

ACEBUTOLOL   L3

Trade: Sectral
Other Trades: Monitan
Uses: Antihypertensive, beta blocker
AAP: Drugs associated with significant side effects and should be given with caution

Acebutolol is predominately a beta-1 blocker, but can block beta-2 receptors at high doses. It is low in lipid solubility, and contains some intrinsic sympathetic activity (partial beta agonist activity). It increases cold sensitivity. Studies indicate that on a weight basis, acebutolol is approximately 10-30% as effective as propranolol. It is 35-50% bioavailable orally.[1] After relatively high doses in animal studies, acebutolol does not appear to be overly teratogenic or harmful to the fetus. Acebutolol is well tolerated by pregnant hypertensive women. In a study of seven women receiving 200-1200 mg/day acebutolol, the highest milk concentration occurred in the women receiving 1200 mg/day and was 4123 μg/L.[2] In women receiving 200, 400, or 600 mg/day of acebutolol, milk levels were 286 μg/L, 666 μg/L and 539 μg/L respectively. Acebutolol and diacetolol (its major metabolite) appear in breastmilk with a milk/plasma ratio of 1.9 to 9.2 (acebutolol) and 2.3 to 24.7 for the metabolite (diacetolol). These levels are considered relatively high and occurred following maternal doses of 400-1200 mg/day. When the metabolite is added, the dose may approach 10% of maternal dose. Neonates appear much more sensitive to acebutolol.

Pregnancy Risk Category: B

Lactation Risk Category: L3

Adult Concerns: Hypotension, bradycardia, and transient tachypnea have been reported. Drowsiness has been reported.

Pediatric Concerns: Hypotension, bradycardia, and transient tachypnea have been reported. Drowsiness has been reported.

Drug Interactions: Decreased effect when used with aluminum salts, barbiturates, calcium salts, cholestyramine, NSAIDs, ampicillin, rifampin, and salicylates. Beta blockers may reduce the effect of oral sulfonylureas (hypoglycemic agents). Increased toxicity/effect when used with other antihypertensives, contraceptives, MAO inhibitors, cimetidine, and numerous other products. See drug interaction reference for complete listing.

Relative Infant Dose: 3.6%

Adult Dose: 200-400 mg BID

Alternatives: Propranolol, Metoprolol

T ½	= 3-4 hours	M/P	= 7.1-12.2
PHL	=	PB	= 26%
Tmax	= 1-4 hours	Oral	= 35-50%
MW	= 336	pKa	=
Vd	= 1.35		

References:
1. Drug Facts and Comparisons 1995 ed. ed. St. Louis: 1995.
2. Boutroy MJ, Bianchetti G, Dubruc C, Vert P, Morselli PL. To nurse when receiving acebutolol: is it dangerous for the neonate? Eur J Clin Pharmacol 1986; 30 (6):737-739.

ACETAMINOPHEN   L1

Trade: Tempra, Tylenol, Paracetamol
Other Trades: Apo-Acetaminophen, Panadol, Dymadon, Calpol
Uses: Analgesic
AAP: Maternal Medication Usually Compatible with Breastfeeding

Only small amounts are secreted into breastmilk and are considered too small to be hazardous. In a study of 11 mothers who received 650 mg of acetaminophen orally, the highest milk levels reported were from 10-15 mg/L.[1] The milk/plasma ratio was 1.08. In another study of three patients who received a single 500 mg oral dose, the reported milk and plasma concentrations of acetaminophen was 4.2 mg/L and 5.6 mg/L respectively.[2] The milk/plasma ratio was 0.76. The maximum observed concentration in milk was 4.4 mg/L. In another study of women who ingested 1000 mg acetaminophen, milk levels averaged 6.1 mg/L and provided an average dose of 0.92 mg/kg/d according to the authors. [3] There seems to be wide variation in the milk concentrations in these studies, but the relative infant dose is probably less than 6.4% of the maternal dose. This is significantly less than the pediatric therapeutic dose. Acetaminophen is compatible with breastfeeding.

Pregnancy Risk Category: B

Lactation Risk Category: L1

Adult Concerns: Few when taken in normal doses. Diarrhea, gastric upset sweating in overdose. Note: numerous cases of liver toxicity have been reported following 'chronic' abuse of acetaminophen at >200 mg/kg/day.

Pediatric Concerns: None reported via milk. Probably safe.

Drug Interactions: Rifampin can interact to reduce the analgesic effect of acetaminophen. Increased acetaminophen hepatotoxicity when used with barbiturates, carbamazepine, hydantoins, sulfinpyrazone, and chronic alcohol abuse.

Relative Infant Dose: 8.8% - 24.2%

Adult Dose: 325-650 mg every 4-6 hours PRN

Alternatives:

T ½	= 2 hours	M/P	= 0.91-1.42
PHL	= 1-3 hours	PB	= 25%
Tmax	= 0.5-2 hours	Oral	= >85%
MW	= 151	pKa	= 9.5
Vd	= 0.8-1.0		

References:
1. Berlin CM, Jr., Yaffe SJ, Ragni M. Disposition of acetaminophen in milk, saliva, and plasma of lactating women. Pediatr Pharmacol (New York) 1980; 1 (2):135-141.
2. Bitzen PO, Gustafsson B, Jostell KG, Melander A, Wahlin-Boll E. Excretion of paracetamol in human breast milk. Eur J Clin Pharmacol 1981; 20 (2):123-125.
3. Notarianni LJ, Oldham HG, Bennett PN. Passage of paracetamol into breast milk and its subsequent metabolism by the neonate. Br J Clin Pharmacol 1987; 24 (1):63-67.

ACETAZOLAMIDE   L2

Trade: Dazamide, Diamox
Other Trades: Acetazolam, Apo-Acetazolamide, Diamox
Uses: Diuretic
AAP: Maternal Medication Usually Compatible with Breastfeeding

Acetazolamide is a carbonic anhydrase inhibitor dissimilar to other thiazide diuretics. In general, diuretics have in the past been suggested to decrease the volume of breastmilk although this is totally undocumented. In a patient receiving 500 mg of acetazolamide twice daily, acetazolamide concentrations in milk were 1.3 to 2.1 mg/L while the maternal plasma levels ranged from 5.2-6.4 mg/L.[1] Plasma concentrations in exposed infants were 0.2 to 0.6 µg/mL two to 12 hours after breastfeeding. These amounts are unlikely to cause adverse effects in the infant.

Pregnancy Risk Category: C

Lactation Risk Category: L2

Adult Concerns: Anorexia, diarrhea, metallic taste, polyuria, muscular weakness, potassium loss. Malaise, fatigue, depression, renal failure have been reported.

Pediatric Concerns: None reported via milk.

Drug Interactions: Increases lithium excretion, reducing plasma levels. May increase toxicity of cyclosporine. Digitalis toxicity may occur if hypokalemia results from acetazolamide therapy.

Relative Infant Dose: 2.2%

Adult Dose: 500 mg BID

Alternatives:

T ½	= 2.4-5.8 hours	M/P	= 0.25
PHL	=	PB	= 70-95%
Tmax	= 1-3 hours	Oral	= Complete
MW	= 222	pKa	= 7.4
Vd	= 0.2		

References:
1. Soderman P, Hartvig P, Fagerlund C. Acetazolamide excretion into human breast milk. Br J Clin Pharmacol 1984; 17 (5):599-600.

ACETOHEXAMIDE   L3

Trade: Dymelor
Other Trades: Dimelor
Uses: Hypoglycemic agent
AAP: Not reviewed

Acetohexamide is an intermediate-acting hypoglycemic sulfonylurea antidiabetic agent.[1] Its structure is similar to tolbutamide, chlorpropamide, and tolazamide. No data are available on its transfer to human milk, but other sulfonylureas transfer to milk in minimal levels (see tolbutamide). The use of sulfonylureas in breastfeeding mothers is somewhat controversial due to limited studies but has not been noted in the literature to produce any problems.

Observe infant closely for hypoglycemia if used.

Pregnancy Risk Category: C

Lactation Risk Category: L3

Adult Concerns: The most common adverse effects include hypoglycemia, nausea, epigastric fullness, heartburn, and rashes.

Pediatric Concerns: None reported via milk, but observe for hypoglycemia.

Drug Interactions: Numerous drugs interact with sulfonylureas, please consult further references. Increased hypoglycemic effects occur when used with salicylates, beta blockers, MAO inhibitors, oral anticoagulants, NSAIDs, sulfonamides, insulin, etc. Reduced hypoglycemic effects may occur when used with cholestyramine, diazoxide, hydantoins, rifampin, and thiazides.

Relative Infant Dose:

Adult Dose: 250-1000 mg daily

Alternatives: Metformin

T ½	= 1.3-6 (metabolite) hours	M/P	=
PHL	=	PB	= 65-90%
Tmax	= 3 hours	Oral	= Good
MW	= 324	pKa	=
Vd	= 0.2		

References:
1.   Pharmaceutical Manufacturer Prescribing Information. 1999.

ACITRETIN   L5

Trade: Soriatane
Other Trades:
Uses: Retinoid-like compound
AAP: Maternal Medication Usually Compatible with
Breastfeeding

Acitretin is used in the treatment of severe psoriasis. It should only be used in non-pregnant patients who are unresponsive to other treatment options. Its exact mechanism of action is unknown, but it helps to normalize cell differentation and thin the cornified layer of the skin by reducing the rate of proliferation.[1] This product produces major human fetal abnormalities, and is retained in the body for long periods of time. Chronic use in breastfeeding mothers is probably not recommended. In the only study conducted on the transfer of acitretin into human milk, a 31 year old mother was taking 40 mg once daily and had milk concentrations of 30-40   µg/L. This indicated that an infant would receive only 1.8% of the maternal dose, however, due to the toxic potential of this medication, the authors concluded that acitretin should be avoided during breastfeeding.[2]

Pregnancy Risk Category: X

Lactation Risk Category: L5

Adult Concerns: Adverse effects include cheilitis, alopecia, skin peeling, hypercholesterolemia, hypertriglyceridemia, increased liver function tests, and rhinitis. It is significantly teratogenic and should never be used in pregnant or women who intend to become pregnant during therapy or anytime for at least three years after discontinuation of treatment. It must not be used by females who do not use reliable contraception.

Pediatric Concerns: No data are available.

Drug Interactions: Ethanol,   methotrexate,   progestins, sulfonylureas, tetracycline, and vitamin A.

Relative Infant Dose: 1.8%

Adult Dose: 25-50 mg/day

Alternatives:

T ½	= 49 hours	M/P	=
PHL	=	PB	= 99.9%
Tmax	= 2-5 hours	Oral	= 72%
MW	= 326	pKa	=
Vd	=		

References:
1. Pharmaceutical Manufacturer Prescribing Information. 2004.
2. Rollman O, Pihl-Lundin I. Acitretin Excretion into Human Breast Milk. Acta Derm Venereol 1990; 70:487-90.

ACYCLOVIR   L2

Trade: Zovirax
Other Trades: Apo-Acyclovir, Aviraz, Acyclo-V, Zyclir, Aciclover
Uses: Antiviral
AAP: Maternal Medication Usually Compatible with Breastfeeding

Acyclovir is converted by herpes simplex and varicella zoster virus to acyclovir triphosphate which interferes with viral HSV DNA polymerase. It is currently cleared for use in HSV infections, Varicella-Zoster, and under certain instances such as cytomegalovirus and Epstein-Barr infections. There is virtually no percutaneous absorption following topical application and plasma levels are undetectable. The pharmacokinetics in children are similar to adults. In neonates, the half-life is 3.8-4.1 hours, and in children one year and older it is 1.9-3.6 hours.

Acyclovir levels in breastmilk are reported to be 0.6 to 4.1 times the maternal plasma levels.[1] Maximum ingested dose was calculated to be 1500 μg/day assuming 750 mL milk intake. This level produced no overt side effects in one infant.

In a study by Meyer,[2] a patient receiving 200 mg five times daily produced breastmilk concentrations averaging 1.06 mg/L. Using this data an infant would ingest less than 1 mg acyclovir daily. In another study, doses of 800 mg five times daily produced milk levels that ranged from 4.16 to 5.81 mg/L (total estimated infant ingestion per day = 0.73 mg/kg/day).[3] Topical therapy on lesions other than nipple is probably safe. But mothers with lesions on or close to the nipple should not breastfeed. Toxicities associated with acyclovir are few and usually minor. Acyclovir therapy in neonatal units is common and produces few toxicities. Calculated intake by infant would be less than 0.87 mg/kg/d.

Pregnancy Risk Category: B

Lactation Risk Category: L2

Adult Concerns: Nausea, vomiting, diarrhea, sore throat, edema, and skin rashes.

Pediatric Concerns: None reported via milk in several studies.

Drug Interactions: Increased CNS side effects when used with zidovudine and probenecid.

Relative Infant Dose: 1.1% - 1.5%

Adult Dose: 200-800 mg every 4-6 hours

Alternatives:

T ½	= 2.4 hours	M/P	= 0.6-4.1
PHL	= 3.2 hours (neonates)	PB	= 9-33%
Tmax	= 1.5 - 2 hours	Oral	= 15-30%
MW	= 225	pKa	=
Vd	=		

References:
1. Lau RJ, Emery MG,GalinskyRE. Unexpected accumulation of acyclovir in breastmilk with estimation of infant exposure. Obstet Gynecol 1987;69 (3 Pt2):468-471.

2. Meyer LJ, de Miranda P, ShethN, Spruance S. Acyclovir in human breastmilk. Am J Obstet Gynecol1988;158:586-588.
3. Taddio A, Klein J, KorenG. Acyclovir excretion in human breastmilk. AnnPharmacother 1994;28 (5):585-587.

ADALIMUMAB   L3

Trade: Humira
Other Trades:
Uses: Anti-rheumatic, anti-tumor necrosis antibody
AAP: Not reviewed

Adalimumab is a recombinant humanized IgG1 monoclonal antibody specific for human tumor necrosis factor (TNF). TNF is implicated in the pain and destructive component of arthritis and other autoimmune syndromes. This product would be similar to others such as etanercept (Enbrel) and infliximab (Remicade). IgG transfer into human milk is significant the first 4 days postpartum, then is minimal afterwards. The primary immunoglobulin in mature human milk is IgA. Immunoglobulins are transferred into human milk by a very specific carrier protein which inhibits the transfer of IgG-like products. It is not known if these unusual immunoglobulins are transferred into milk, but it is unlikely. Specific data from my laboratories suggests that no infliximab transfers into human milk in mothers receiving IV doses.[1] It is not likely that adalimumab would transfer in clinically relevant amounts after the first week postpartum but no data are available at this time.

Pregnancy Risk Category: B

Lactation Risk Category: L3

Adult Concerns: May induce tuberculosis reactivations. May induce immunosuppression and reduce host defenses against infections. Serious infections, neurologic events, and malignancies have been reported.

Pediatric Concerns: None reported via milk. Unlikely to enter milk in clinically relevant amounts.

Drug Interactions: None reported.

Relative Infant Dose:

Adult Dose: 40 mg every other week subcutaneously.

Alternatives: Infliximab

T ½	= 2 weeks.	M/P	=
PHL	=	PB	= Nil
Tmax	=	Oral	= Low
MW	= 148,000	pKa	=
Vd	= 4.7		

References:
1. Hale TW, Fasanmade A. Unpublished data. 2002.

ADAPALENE   L3

Trade: Differin
Other Trades:
Uses: Topical acne remedy
AAP: Not reviewed

Adapalene is a retinoid-like compound (similar to Tretinoin) used topically for treatment of acne. No data are available on its transfer into human milk. However, adapalene is virtually unabsorbed when applied topically to the skin.[1] Plasma levels are almost undetectable (<0.25 ng/mL plasma), so milk levels would be infinitesimally low and probably undetectable.[2]

Pregnancy Risk Category: C

Lactation Risk Category: L3

Adult Concerns: Exacerbation of sunburn, irritation of skin, erythema, dryness, scaling, burning, itching.

Pediatric Concerns: None reported via milk. Very unlikely due to minimal maternal absorption.

Drug Interactions: Avoid sunlight.

Relative Infant Dose:

Adult Dose: Apply topical daily.

Alternatives: Tretinoin

References:
1. Pharmaceutical Manufacturer Prescribing Information. 2005.
2. Drug Facts and Comparisons 1999 ed. St. Louis: 1999.

ADEFOVIR DIPIVOXIL   L4

Trade: Hepsera
Other Trades:
Uses: Anti-Hepatitis B Virus agent
AAP: Not reviewed

Adefovir inhibits hepatitis B virus replication.[1] No data are available on the transfer of adefovir into in human milk, yet based on the kinetic profile (low protein binding and moderate oral bioavailability, it is possible that the drug would cross into the milk compartment to some degree. Because this drug is potentially toxic to a rapidly growing infant, and because it is used over long periods of time, it is not recommended for use in lactating mothers at this time.

Pregnancy Risk Category: C

Lactation Risk Category: L4

Adult Concerns: Adverse reactions include nephrotoxicity, or kidney dysfunction, lactic acidosis, severe hepatomegaly, feeling of weakness, headache, and abdominal pain.

Pediatric Concerns: No data are available. Milk levels are likely to be low.

Drug Interactions: Ibuprofen increases the oral bioavailability of adefovir. When used in combination with tenofovir, serum concentrations of both may be elevated.

Relative Infant Dose:

Adult Dose: 10 mg daily

Alternatives: Lamivudine, if not resistant

T ½	= 7.5 hours	M/P	=
PHL	=	PB	= 4%
Tmax	= 1.75 hours	Oral	= 59%
MW	= 501	pKa	=
Vd	= 0.4		

References:
1. Pharmaceutical Manufacturer Prescribing Information. 2006.

ALBENDAZOLE   L3

Trade: Albenza
Other Trades: Eskazole
Uses: Anthelminic for treatment of numerous varieties of worms
AAP: Not reviewed

Albendazole is a broad-spectrum anthelmintic used for treating intestinal parasite infections. It is virtually unabsorbed (<5%) orally and would be unlikely to harm an infant even if present in milk. It is often used to treat common parasitic infections in pediatric patients all over the world.

Pregnancy Risk Category: C

Lactation Risk Category: L3

Adult Concerns: Abdominal pain, nausea, vomiting, headache, dizziness, and fever have been reported.

Pediatric Concerns: No data are available in breastfeeding mothers. Milk levels are unlikely to be clinically relevant. Commonly used in infants and children.

Drug Interactions: Avoid use with corticosteroids including dexamethasone due to increased side effect profile. Avoid concomitant use with ginseng. Do not use with theophylline.

Relative Infant Dose:

Adult Dose: Highly variable and due to individual parasite. Check other source.

Alternatives: Mebendazole

T ½	= 8 hours	M/P	=
PHL	=	PB	= 70%
Tmax	= 2 hours	Oral	= <5%
MW	= 265	pKa	=
Vd	=		

References:
1. Pharmaceutical Manufacturer Prescribing Information. 2005.

ALBUTEROL

L1

Trade: Proventil, Ventolin

Other Trades: Novo-Salmol, Asmavent, Respax, Respolin, Ventolin, Asmol, Salbulin, Salbuvent, Salamol

Uses: Bronchodilator for asthma

AAP: Not reviewed

Albuterol is a very popular beta-2 adrenergic agonist that is typically used to dilate constricted bronchi in asthmatics.[1] It is active orally but is most commonly used via inhalation. When used orally, significant plasma levels are attained and transfer to breastmilk is possible. When used via inhalation, less than 10% is absorbed into maternal plasma. Small amounts are probably secreted into milk although no reports exist. It is very unlikely that pharmacologic doses will be transferred to the infant via milk following inhaler use. However, when used orally, breastmilk levels could be sufficient to produce tremors and agitation in infants. Commonly used via inhalation in treating pediatric asthma. This product is safe to use in breastfeeding mothers.

Pregnancy Risk Category: C

Lactation Risk Category: L1

Adult Concerns: Observe infant for tremors and excitement.

Pediatric Concerns: None reported via milk

Drug Interactions: Albuterol effects are reduced when used with beta blockers. Cardiovascular effects are potentiated when used with MAO inhibitors, tricyclic antidepressants, amphetamines, and inhaled anesthetics (enflurane).

Relative Infant Dose:

Adult Dose: 2-4 mg TID or QID

Alternatives:

T ½	= 3.8 hours	M/P	=
PHL	=	PB	=
Tmax	= 5-30 minutes	Oral	= 100%
MW	= 239	pKa	= 10.3
Vd	= 2.2		

References:
1. Pharmaceutical Manufacturer Prescribing Information. 1997.

ALBUTEROL AND IPRATROPIUM BROMIDE   L1

Trade: DuoNeb
Other Trades:
Uses: Bronchodilators
AAP: Not reviewed

Duo Neb is a combination product containing 0.103 mg albuterol and 0.018 mg of ipratropium bromide per metered-dose inhalation. See the individual monographs on this product.

Pregnancy Risk Category: C

Lactation Risk Category: L1

Adult Concerns:

Pediatric Concerns:

Drug Interactions:

Relative Infant Dose:

Adult Dose:

Alternatives:

References:

ALEFACEPT   L3

Trade: Amevive
Other Trades:
Uses: Immunosuppressant
AAP: Not reviewed

Alefacept is an immunosuppressant used in the treatment of chronic plaque psoriasis. It binds to the lymphocyte antigen CD2, thus inhibiting the LFA-3/CD2 interaction.[1] Although levels in milk have not been determined, its transfer into the milk compartment is highly unlikely due to its enormous molecular size (94 kilodaltons). Furthermore, due to low oral bioavailability, even if present in milk, it would be unabsorbed in an infant.

Pregnancy Risk Category: B

Lactation Risk Category: L3

Adult Concerns: Adverse reactions include lymphopenia, malignancies, infections and hypersensitivity.

Pediatric Concerns: No data are available, but it is unlikely to transfer into milk.

Drug Interactions: No data available.

Relative Infant Dose:

Adult Dose: 7.5 mg IV weekly

Alternatives:

T ½	= 270 hours	M/P	=
PHL	=	PB	=
Tmax	=	Oral	= Nil
MW	= 91,400	pKa	=
Vd	= 0.094		

References:
1. Pharmaceutical Manufacturer Prescribing Information. 2005.

ALEMTUZUMAB   L3

Trade: Campath
Other Trades:
Uses: Anti-leukemic agent
AAP: Not reviewed

Alemtuzumab is a recombinant DNA-derived humanized monoclonal antibody that is directed against specific cell receptors on leukemic cells. It is a large IgG1 antibody. No data are available on its transfer to human milk, but it is very unlikely to enter milk due to its large MW. However, the first 72 hours postpartum, IgG levels in milk are higher and this should be considered with this agent. While some IgG is still transferred into human milk, it is done so by a very specialized transporter. It is unlikely this transporter would transport this unusual monoclonal antibody.

Pregnancy Risk Category: C

Lactation Risk Category: L3
                               L4 during first week postpartum.

Adult Concerns: Adverse events include rigors post-infusion, fever, nausea, vomiting, hypotension, rash, fatigue, urticaria, dyspnea, pruritus, headache, and diarrhea. An elevated risk of infections is reported.

Pediatric Concerns: None reported via milk. Unlikely to penetrate milk after first week postpartum.

Drug Interactions:

Relative Infant Dose:

Adult Dose: Maintenance dose is 30 mg/day three times weekly on alternate days.

Alternatives:

T ½	= 12 days	M/P	=
PHL	=	PB	= Nil
Tmax	=	Oral	= Nil
MW	= 150,000	pKa	=
Vd	=		

References:
1. Pharmaceutical Manufacturers prescribing information. 2003.

ALENDRONATE SODIUM   L3

Trade: Fosamax
Other Trades:
Uses: Inhibits bone resorption
AAP: Not reviewed

Alendronate is a specific inhibitor of osteoclast-mediated bone resorption, thus reducing bone loss and bone turnover.[1] While incorporated in bone matrix, it is not pharmacologically active. Because concentrations in plasma are too low to be detected (<5 ng/mL), it is very unlikely that it would be secreted into human milk in clinically relevant concentrations. Concentrations in human milk have not been reported. Because this product has exceedingly poor oral bioavailability, particularly when ingested with milk, it is very unlikely that alendronate would be orally absorbed by a breastfeeding infant.

In one case of an unknown pregnancy, the mother was taking alendronate 0.12 mg/kg/day orally. Her baby was born with no physical abnormalities, and the baby's growth was normal.[2] No data were collected on the concentrations of alendronate in the mother's milk.

Pregnancy Risk Category: C

Lactation Risk Category: L3

Adult Concerns: Abdominal pain, nausea, dyspepsia, constipation, muscle cramps, headache, taste perversion. There are a number of case reports of esophagitis and esophageal ulceration in patients taking Fosamax.

Pediatric Concerns: None reported via milk.

Drug Interactions: Ranitidine will double the absorption of alendronate. Calcium, milk, and other multivalent cation containing foods reduce the bioavailability of alendronate.

Relative Infant Dose:

Adult Dose: 10 mg daily.

Alternatives:

T ½	= <3 hours (plasma)	M/P	=
PHL	=	PB	= 78%
Tmax	=	Oral	= <0.7%
MW	= 325	pKa	=
Vd	= 0.4		

References:
1. Pharmaceutical Manufacturer Prescribing Information. 1997.
2. Rutgers-Verhage AR, DeVries TW, Torringa MJL. No Effects of Bisphosphonates on the Human Fetus. Birth Defects Res., Part A 2003; 67:203-204.

ALFENTANIL   L2

Trade: Alfenta
Other Trades: Rapifen
Uses: Narcotic analgesic
AAP: Not reviewed

Alfentanil is secreted into breastmilk. Following a dose of 50 µg/kg IV (plus several additional 10 µg/kg doses), the mean levels of alfentanil in colostrum at 4 hours varied from 0.21 to 1.56 µg/L of colostrum, levels probably too small to produce overt toxicity in breastfeeding infants.[1] Mean levels 28 hours post-alfentanil were 0.05 µg/L.

Pregnancy Risk Category: C

Lactation Risk Category: L2

Adult Concerns: Observe for bradycardia, shivering, constipation and sedation. In neonates observe for severe hypotension.

Pediatric Concerns: None reported via milk.

Drug Interactions: Phenothiazines may antagonize the analgesic effects of opiates. Dextromethorphan may increase the analgesia of opiate agonists. Other CNS depressants such as benzodiazepines, barbiturates, tricyclic antidepressants, erythromycin, reserpine and beta blockers may increase the toxicity of this opiate.

Relative Infant Dose: 0.4%

Adult Dose: 8-40 µg/kg total

Alternatives: Remifentanil

T ½	= 1-2 hours	M/P	=
PHL	= 5-6 hours (neonates)	PB	= 92%
Tmax	= immediate	Oral	=
MW	= 417	pKa	= 6.5
Vd	= 0.3-1.0		

References:
1. Giesecke A, Rice I., Lipton J. Alfentaril in colostrum. Anesthesiology 63:A284 1985.
2. Spigset O. Anaesthetic agents and excretion in breast milk. Acta Anaesthesiol Scand 1994; 38 (2):94-103.

ALISKIREN   L3

Trade: Tekturna
Other Trades:
Uses: Renin inhibitor
AAP: Not reviewed

Aliskiren is a direct renin inhibitor, blocking the formation of angiotensin II and thus decreasing blood pressure. It works directly on renin, and therefore may be more clinically advantageous than a typical ACE inhibitor.[1] No data are available on its transfer into human milk. However, due to its high MW and low oral absorption (3%), it is unlikely that an infant would absorb enough to receive a therapeutic dose from breastmilk. Aliskiren should be avoided while breastfeeding premature infants, as the nephrons of the kidney are undeveloped. A risk versus benefit analysis should be conducted in each individual.

Pregnancy Risk Category: C in first trimester
D in second and third trimesters

Lactation Risk Category: L3
L5 in premature infants

Adult Concerns: Adverse reactions include dizziness, rash, diarrhea, increased serum creatinine and BUN.

Pediatric Concerns: No data are available.

Drug Interactions: Atorvastatin and ketoconazole may increase the effect of aliskerin, while furosemide may decrease the effect.

Relative Infant Dose:

Adult Dose: 150-300 mg/day

Alternatives: Methyldopa, metoprolol, hydrochlorothiazide, captopril, enalapril

T ½	= 24 hours	M/P	=
PHL	=	PB	=
Tmax	= 1-3 hours	Oral	= 3%
MW	= 609	pKa	=
Vd	=		

References:
1.   Pharmaceutical Manufacturer Prescribing Information. 2007.

ALLERGY INJECTIONS   L1

Trade:
Other Trades:
Uses: Desensitizing injections
AAP: Not reviewed

Allergy injections consist of protein and carbohydrate substances from plants, animals, and other species. There are no reported untoward effects. They are unlikely to enter milk.

Pregnancy Risk Category:

Lactation Risk Category: L1

Adult Concerns: Allergic pruritus, anaphylaxis, other immune reactions.
Pediatric Concerns: None reported in breastfeeding mothers.

Drug Interactions:

Relative Infant Dose:

Adult Dose: N/A

Alternatives:

References:

ALLOPURINOL   L2

Trade: Zyloprim, Lopurin
Other Trades: Alloprin, Apo-Allopurinol, Novo-Purol,
Zyloprim, Allorin, Capurate, Zygout, Zyloprim, Aluline,
Caplenal, Cosuric, Hamarin, Zyloric
Uses: Reduces uric acid levels
AAP: Maternal Medication Usually Compatible with
Breastfeeding

Allopurinol is a potent antagonist of xanthine oxidase, an enzyme
involved in the production of uric acid. It is used to reduce uric acid
levels in gouty individuals. In a nursing mother receiving 300mg/d
allopurinol, the breastmilk concentration at 2 and 4 hours was 0.9
and 1.4 µg/mL respectively.[1] The concentration of the metabolite,
oxypurinol, was 53.7 and 48.0 µg/mL at 2 and 4 hours respectively.
The milk/plasma ratio ranged from 0.9 to 1.4 for allopurinol and 3.9
for its metabolite, oxypurinol. The average daily dose that an infant
would receive from milk would be approximately 0.14-0.20 mg/kg of
allopurinol and 7.2-8.0 mg/kg of oxypurinol. No adverse effects were
noted in the infant after 6 weeks of therapy. Pediatric dosages for ages
6 and under is generally 10 mg/kg/24 hours.

Pregnancy Risk Category: C

Lactation Risk Category: L2

Adult Concerns: Itching skin rash. Fever, chills, nausea and
vomiting, diarrhea, gastritis,

Pediatric Concerns: No adverse effects were noted in one infant
after 6 weeks of therapy.

Drug Interactions: Alcohol decreases allopurinol efficacy. Inhibits
metabolism of azathioprine and mercaptopurine. Increased incidence
of skin rash when used with amoxicillin and ampicillin. Increased risk
of kidney stones when used with high doses of vitamin C. Allopurinol
prolongs half-life of oral anticoagulants, theophylline, chlorpropamide.

Relative Infant Dose: 4.9%

Adult Dose: 100-400 mg BID

Alternatives:

T ½	= 1-3 hours (allopurinol)	M/P	= 0.9-1.4
PHL	=	PB	= 0%
Tmax	= 2-6 hours	Oral	= 90%
MW	= 136	pKa	=
Vd	= 1.6		

References:
1. Kamilli I, Gresser U. Allopurinol and oxypurinol in human breast milk. Clin Investig 1993; 71 (2):161-164.

ALMOTRIPTAN   L3

Trade: Axert
Other Trades: Almogran
Uses: Acute migraine treatment
AAP: Not reviewed

Almotriptan is a selective serotonin receptor antagonist similar to sumatriptan although it is slightly more bioavailable orally. No data are available on its transfer to human milk. Clinically, it is not much better than oral sumatriptan[1], which has been well studied in breastfeeding women. See sumatriptan for alternative.

Pregnancy Risk Category: C

Lactation Risk Category: L3

Adult Concerns: Nausea, somnolence, headache, dry mouth, tachycardia, myocardial ischemia.

Pediatric Concerns: None reported.

Drug Interactions: Higher plasma level of almotriptan could result from use with ketoconazole, amiodarone, cimetidine, clarithromycin, erythromycin, nefazodone, and other inhibitors of CYP3A4. Do not use with ergot alkaloids, MAO inhibitors, verapamil, SSRIs such as fluoxetine, sertraline, etc.

Relative Infant Dose:

Adult Dose: 6.25-12.5 mg

Alternatives: Sumatriptan

T ½	= 3-4 hours	M/P	=
PHL	=	PB	= 35%
Tmax	= 2-4 hours	Oral	= 80%
MW	=	pKa	=
Vd	= 2.85		

References:
1. Spierings EL, Gomez-Mancilla B, Grosz DE, Rowland CR, Whaley FS, Jirgens KJ. Oral almotriptan vs. oral sumatriptan in the abortive treatment of migraine: a double-blind, randomized, parallel-group, optimum-dose comparison. Arch Neurol 2001; 58 (6):944-950.

ALOE VERA   L3

Trade: Aloe Vera, Cape, Zanzibar, Socotrine
Other Trades:
Uses: Extract from A. Vera
AAP: Not reviewed

There are over 500 species of aloes. The aloe plant yields two important products: Aloe latex derived from the outer skin and Aloe gel, a clear, gelatinous material derived from the inner tissue of the leaf. The aloe gel is the most commonly used product in cosmetic and health food products. The gel contains a polysaccharide glucomannan, similar to guar gum, which is responsible for its emollient effect. Aloe also contains tannins, polysaccharides, organic acids, enzymes, and other products. Bradykininase, a protease inhibitor, is believed to relieve pain and decrease swelling and pruritus. Other components such as an anti-prostaglandin compound is believed to reduce inflammation.[1] Aloe latex, a bitter yellow product derived from the outer skin, is a drastic cathartic and produces a strong purgative effect on the large intestine due to its anthraquinone barbaloin content. Do not use the latex orally in children.[1] The most common use of the aloe gel is in burn therapy for minor burns and skin irritation. Thus far, well controlled studies do not provide evidence of a clear advantage over aggressive wound care. Two FDA advisory panels failed to find sufficient evidence to show Aloe Vera is useful in treatment of minor burns, cuts, or vaginal irritation.

Recent evidence suggests that A. vera may accelerate wound healing such as in frostbite and in patients undergoing dermabrasion although another study suggests a delay in healing.[2,3] Numerous studies have suggested accelerated wound healing, reduction in arthritic inflammation, and other inflammatory diseases although these are, in many cases, poorly controlled.

The toxicity of A. vera gel when applied topically is minimal. Oral use of the latex derived from the outer skin of A. vera is strongly discouraged as they are drastic cathartics. Aloe emodin and other anthraquinones present in A. vera latex may cause severe gastric cramping and should never be used in pregnant women and children.

Pregnancy Risk Category:

Lactation Risk Category: L3

Adult Concerns: Severe gastric irritation, strong purgative effect and diarrhea when gel used orally.

Pediatric Concerns: No reports of untoward effects following maternal use or via milk ingestion.

Drug Interactions:

Relative Infant Dose:

Adult Dose: N/A

Alternatives:

References:
1. Review of Natural Products Ed: Facts and Comparisons 1997.
2. Leung AY. Encyclopedia of Common Natural Ingredients used in Food, Drugs and Cosmetics. J Wiley and Sons, 1980.
3. Fulton JE, Jr. The stimulation of postdermabrasion wound healing with stabilized aloe vera gel-polyethylene oxide dressing. J Dermatol Surg Oncol 1990; 16 (5):460-467.
4. Schmidt JM, Greenspoon JS. Aloe vera dermal wound gel is associated with a delay in wound healing. Obstet Gynecol 1991; 78 (1):115-117.

ALOSETRON   L3

Trade: Lotronex
Other Trades:
Uses: Treatment of Irritable Bowel Syndrome
AAP: Not reviewed

Alosetron (Lotronex) is a new 5-HT3 receptor antagonist which is used to control the symptoms of irritable bowel syndrome. No data are available on the transfer of this medication into human milk. While the manufacturer suggests it is present in animal milk, no data are provided.[1] The peak plasma levels (in young women) of this product are quite small, only averaging 9 nanogram/mL following a 1 mg dose.

Although the half-life of the parent alosetron is short (1.5 hours), its metabolites have much longer half-lives although their importance is unknown. Bioavailability is lessened (<25%) when mixed with food. With this data it is unlikely milk levels will be extraordinarily high, or that the levels transferred to the infant will be clinically relevant to the infant. However, its use in breastfeeding patients should be approached with caution until we have more clinical experience with this new product.

Pregnancy Risk Category: B

Lactation Risk Category: L3

Adult Concerns: Constipation is very common, hypertension, nausea less so.

Pediatric Concerns: None reported via milk, but no studies exist.

Drug Interactions: It is unlikely alosetron will inhibit the metabolism of drugs metabolized by the major CYP 450 enzymes.

Relative Infant Dose:

Adult Dose: 1 mg twice daily.

Alternatives:

T ½	= 1.5 hours	M/P	=
PHL	=	PB	= 82%
Tmax	= 1 hour	Oral	= 50-60%
MW	=	pKa	=
Vd	= 1.36		

References:
1.   Manufacturers package insert Glaxo-Wellcome 2000.

ALPRAZOLAM   L3

Trade: Xanax
Other Trades: Apo-Alpraz, Novo-Alprazol, Xanax, Kalma, Ralozam
Uses: Benzodiazepine antianxiety agent
AAP: Drugs whose effect on nursing infants is unknown but may be of concern

Alprazolam is a prototypic benzodiazepine drug similar to Valium but is now preferred in many instances because of its shorter half-life.

In a study of 8 women who received a single oral dose of 0.5 mg, the peak alprazolam level in milk was 3.7 µg/L which occurred at 1.1 hours; the observed milk/serum ratio (using AUC method) was 0.36.[1] The neonatal dose of alprazolam in breastmilk is low. The author estimates the average between 0.3 to 5 µg/kg per day. While the infants in this study did not breastfeed, these doses would probably be too low to induce a clinical effect.

In a brief letter, Anderson reports that the manufacturer is aware of withdrawal symptoms in infants following exposure in utero and via breastmilk.[2] In a mother who received 0.5 mg 2-3 times daily (PO) during pregnancy, a neonatal withdrawal syndrome was evident in the breastfed infant the first week postpartum. This data suggests that the amount of alprazolam in breastmilk is insufficient to prevent a withdrawal syndrome following prenatal exposure. In another case of infant exposure solely via breastmilk, the mother took alprazolam (dosage unspecified) for nine months while breastfeeding and withdrew herself from the medication over a 3 week period. The mother reported withdrawal symptoms in the infant including irritability, crying, and sleep disturbances. The benzodiazepine family, as a rule, are not ideal for breastfeeding mothers due to relatively long half-lives and the development of dependence. However, it is apparent that the shorter-acting benzodiazepines are safest during lactation provided their use is short-term or intermittent, low dose, and after the first week of life.[3]

Pregnancy Risk Category: D

Lactation Risk Category: L3

Adult Concerns: Drowsiness, fatigue, insomnia, confusion, dry mouth, constipation, nausea, vomiting.

Pediatric Concerns: Rarely, withdrawal syndrome reported in one breastfed infant. Observe for sedation, poor feeding, irritability, crying, insomnia on withdrawal. Use on an acute or short term basis is not contraindicated.

Drug Interactions: Decreased therapeutic effect when used with carbamazepine, disulfiram. Increased toxicity when used with oral contraceptives, CNS depressants, cimetidine and lithium.

Relative Infant Dose: 8.5%

Adult Dose: 0.5-1 mg TID

Alternatives: Lorazepam

T ½	= 12-15 hours	M/P	= 0.36
PHL	=	PB	= 80%
Tmax	= 1-2 hours	Oral	= Complete
MW	= 309	pKa	=
Vd	= 0.9-1.3		

References:

1. Oo CY, Kuhn RJ, Desai N, Wright CE, McNamara PJ. Pharmacokinetics in lactating women: prediction of alprazolam transfer into milk. Br J Clin Pharmacol 1995; 40 (3):231-236.
2. Anderson PO, McGuire GG. Neonatal alprazolam withdrawal--possible effects of breast feeding. DICP 1989; 23 (7-8):614.
3. Maitra R, Menkes DB. Psychotropic drugs and lactation. N Z Med J 1996; 109 (1024):217-218.

ALTEPLASE   L3

Trade: Activase
Other Trades: Actilyse
Uses: Thrombolytic agent
AAP: Not reviewed

Alteplase is a thrombolytic agent commonly known as tissue-type plasminogen activator (tPA). Alteplase is a large protein with 527 amino acids and with a large MW. It binds to fibrin in a thrombus and converts the plasminogen to plasmin which subsequently leads to a breakdown of the clot. Alteplase is rapidly cleared from the plasma, with an initial half-life of 5 minutes following rapid IV therapy and a somewhat longer half-life of 26-46 minutes following prolonged infusion.[1,2] Its transfer into mature milk would be negligible, but it could potentially pass in small amounts in colostrum. Whether it would be bioavailable in the gut of a newborn infant is questionable, but it would almost certainly not be bioavailable in an older infant. It is very unlikely it would produce adverse effects in breastfed infants.

Pregnancy Risk Category: C

Lactation Risk Category: L3

Adult Concerns: Hemorrhage, reperfusion arrhythmias, bradycardia and possibly seizures.

Pediatric Concerns: None reported.

Drug Interactions: May potentiate hemorrhage when used with other anticoagulants such as dicoumarol, warfarin, anisindione, acenocoumarol, phenindione, heparin and etc. Nitroglycerin may increase clearance of TPA.

Relative Infant Dose:

Adult Dose: 100 mg

Alternatives:

T ½	= 26-46 minutes	M/P	=
PHL	=	PB	=
Tmax	= 20-40 minutes	Oral	= Nil
MW	= Large	pKa	=
Vd	= 8.1		

References:

1. Pharmaceutical Manufacturer Prescribing Information, 2001.
2. Verstraete M, Su CA, Tanswell P, Feuerer W, Collen D. Pharmacokinetics and effects on fibrinolytic and coagulation parameters of two doses of recombinant tissue-type plasminogen activator in healthy volunteers. Thromb Haemost 1986; 56 (1):1-5.

ALVIMOPAN

Trade: Entereg
Other Trades:
Uses: Peripheral opiate receptor blocker for postoperative ileus.
AAP: Not reviewed

Alvimopan is a peripherally acting µ-opioid receptor antagonist indicated to accelerate the time to upper and lower gastrointestinal recovery following partial large or small bowel resection surgery with primary anastomosis. No data are available on its transfer into human milk. However, adult plasma levels are incredibly low, the oral bioavailability is low, and the MW is slightly high, so milk levels are estimated to be quite low.

Pregnancy Risk Category: B

Lactation Risk Category:

Adult Concerns: Side effects appear minimal but include: Anemia, constipation, dyspepsia, flatulence, hypokalemia, back pain and urinary retention.

Pediatric Concerns: None yet reported via milk.

Drug Interactions: No data yet.

Relative Infant Dose:

Adult Dose:

Alternatives:

T ½	= 10-17 hours	M/P	=
PHL	=	PB	= 80-94%
Tmax	~ 2 hours	Oral	= 6%
MW	= 460	pKa	=
Vd	= 0.42		

References:

AMANTADINE   L3

Trade: Symmetrel, Symadine
Other Trades: Endantanine, Gen-Amantadine, Mantadine
Uses: Anti-viral and antiparkinsonian
AAP: Not reviewed

Amantadine is a unique compound that has both antiviral activity against influenza A and is effective in treating Parkinsonian symptoms.[1] Pediatric indications for prevention of influenza for ages 1-10 are available. Only trace amounts are believed to be secreted in milk although no reports are found. Adult plasma levels following doses of 200 mg daily are 400-900 nanograms/mL.[2] Even assuming a theoretical milk/plasma ratio of 1.0, the average daily dose to a breastfeeding infant would be far less than 0.9 mg, a dose that would be clinically irrelevant compared to the 4-8 mg/kg dose used in 1 year old infants. However, amantadine is known to suppress prolactin production and should not be used in breastfeeding mothers or at least should be used with caution while observing for milk suppression.[3,4]

Pregnancy Risk Category: C

Lactation Risk Category: L3

Adult Concerns: Urinary retention, vomiting, skin rash in infants. Insomnia, depression, confusion, disorientation, nausea, anorexia, constipation, vomiting.

Pediatric Concerns: None reported via milk but a major reduction in prolactin levels has been reported. Avoid.

Drug Interactions: May increase anticholinergic effects when used with anticholinergic or CNS active drugs. Increased toxicity/levels when used with hydrochlorothiazide plus triamterene, or amiloride.

Relative Infant Dose:

Adult Dose: 100 mg BID

Alternatives:

T ½	= 1-28 hours	M/P	=
PHL	=	PB	= 67%
Tmax	= 1-4 hours	Oral	= 86-94%
MW	= 151	pKa	= 10.1
Vd	= 4.4		

References:

1. Pharmaceutical Manufacturer Prescribing Information. 1997.
2. Cedarbaum JM. Clinical pharmacokinetics of anti-parkinsonian drugs. Clin Pharmacokinet 1987; 13 (3):141-178.
3. Correa N, Opler LA, Kay SR, Birmaher B. Amantadine in the treatment of neuroendocrine side effects of neuroleptics. J Clin Psychopharmacol 1987; 7 (2):91-95.
4. Siever LJ. The effect of amantadine on prolactin levels and galactorrhea on neuroleptic-treated patients. J Clin Psychopharmacol 1981; 1 (1):2-7.

AMIKACIN   L2

Trade: Amikin
Other Trades:
Uses: Aminoglycoside antibiotic
AAP: Not reviewed

Amikacin is a typical aminoglycoside antibiotic used for gram negative infections. Other aminoglycoside antibiotics are poorly absorbed from GI tract in infants although they could produce changes in GI flora. Only very small amounts are secreted into breastmilk. Following 100 and 200 mg IM doses, only trace amounts have been found in breastmilk and then in only 2 of 4 patients studied.[1] In another study of 2-3 patients who received 100 mg IM, none to trace amounts were found in milk.[2]

Pregnancy Risk Category: D

Lactation Risk Category: L2

Adult Concerns: Diarrhea, changes in GI flora.

Pediatric Concerns: None reported via milk. Commonly used in neonates.

Drug Interactions: Increased aminoglycoside toxicity when used with indomethacin, amphotericin, loop diuretics, vancomycin, enflurane, methoxyflurane, depolarizing neuromuscular blocking agents.

Relative Infant Dose:

Adult Dose: 5-7.5 mg/kg/dose TID

Alternatives:

T ½	= 2.3 hours	M/P	=
PHL	= 4-5 hours	PB	= 4%
Tmax	= 0.75-2.0 hours	Oral	= Poor
MW	= 586	pKa	=
Vd	= 0.28		

References:
1. Matsuda C. A study of amikacin in the obstetrics field. Jpn J Antibiot 1974; 27:633-636.
2. Matsuda S. Transfer of antibiotics into maternal milk. Biol Res Pregnancy Perinatol 1984; 5 (2):57-60.

AMINOLEVULINIC ACID | L3

Trade: Levulan Kerastick
Other Trades:
Uses: Photosensitizing Agent
AAP: Not reviewed

Aminolevulinic acid is used to treat minimally to moderately thick keratoses. It is a metabolic precursor of the protoprophyrin IX, which is a photosensitizer. Upon stimulation with light, accumulated protoporphyrin forms free radicals that work to break down thick keratoses.[1] However, when applied topically the transcutaneous absorption of this product is minimal to nil. Milk levels, although unreported, are likely to be nil.

Pregnancy Risk Category: C

Lactation Risk Category: L3

Adult Concerns: Adverse reactions remain local and include burning, itching, redness and swelling.

Pediatric Concerns: No data are available, but milk levels are likely to be minimal to nil.

Drug Interactions: Other photosensitizing agents such as griseofulvin, thiazide diuretics, sulfonamides, sulfonylureas, phenothiazines, and tetracyclines may increase the photosensitizing potential.

Relative Infant Dose:

Adult Dose: Apply topically followed 14-18 hours later by blue light illumination

Alternatives:

T ½	= 0.7 hours	M/P	=
PHL	=	PB	=
Tmax	=	Oral	= 50-60% (oral)
MW	= 168	pKa	=
Vd	=		

References:
1.   Pharmaceutical Manufacturer Prescribing Information.

AMINOSALICYLIC ACID (PARA)   L3

Trade: Paser, PAS
Other Trades: Tubasal, Nemasol
Uses: Antitubercular
AAP: Drugs associated with significant side effects and should be given with caution

Paraminosalicylic acid inhibits folic acid synthesis and is selective only for tuberculosis bacteria. Following a maternal dose of 4.0 gm/day, the peak maternal plasma level was 70.1 mg/L and occurred at 2 hours. The breastmilk concentration of 5-ASA at 3 hours was 1.1 mg/L.[1] In another study, the concentration in milk ranged from 0.13 to 0.53 μmol/liter.[2] In a 29 year old mother who received 3 gm/day of 5- ASA for ulcerative colitis, the estimated intake for an infant receiving 120-200 mL of milk was 0.02 to 0.012 mg of 5-ASA.[3] The concentrations of 5-ASA and its metabolite Acetyl-5-ASA present in milk appear too low to produce overt toxicity in most infants. Only one report of slight diarrhea in one infant has been reported.

Pregnancy Risk Category: C

Lactation Risk Category: L3

Adult Concerns: Nausea, vomiting, diarrhea.

Pediatric Concerns: Only one report of slight diarrhea in one infant has been reported.

Drug Interactions: Reduces levels of digoxin and vitamin B-12.

Relative Infant Dose: 0.3%

Adult Dose: 150 mg/kg/day BID or TID

Alternatives:

T ½	= 1 hour	M/P	= 0.09-0.17
PHL	=	PB	= 50-73%
Tmax	= 2 hours	Oral	= >90%
MW	= 153	pKa	=
Vd	=		

References:
1. Holdiness MR. Antituberculosis drugs and breast-feeding. Arch Intern Med 1984; 144 (9):1888.
2. Christensen LA, Rasmussen SN, Hansen SH. Disposition of 5-aminosalicylic acid and N-acetyl-5-aminosalicylic acid in fetal and maternal body fluids during treatment with different 5-aminosalicylic acid preparations. Acta Obstet Gynecol Scand 1994; 73 (5):399-402.
3. Klotz U, Harings-Kaim A. Negligible excretion of 5-aminosalicylic acid in breast milk. Lancet 1993; 342 (8871):618-619.

AMIODARONE   L5

Trade: Cordarone
Other Trades: Aratac
Uses: Strong antiarrhythmic agent
AAP: Drugs whose effect on nursing infants is unknown but may be of concern

Amiodarone is a potent and sometimes dangerous antiarrhythmic drug and requires close supervision by clinicians. Although poorly absorbed by the mother (<50%), maximum serum levels are attained after 3- 7 hours. This drug has a very large volume of distribution, resulting in accumulation in adipose, liver, spleen, and lungs and has a high rate of fetal toxicity (10-17%). It should not be given to pregnant mothers unless critically required.

Significant amounts are secreted into breastmilk at levels higher than the plasma level. Breastmilk samples obtained at birth and at 2 and 3 weeks post-partum in 2 patients, contained levels of amiodarone and desethylamiodarone varying from 1.7 to 3.0 mg/L (mean= 2.3 mg/L) and 0.8 to 1.8 mg/L (mean= 1.1 mg/L), respectively.[1] Despite the concentrations of amiodarone in milk, the amounts were apparently not high enough to produce plasma levels of both drugs higher than about 0.1 µg/mL, which are minimal compared to the maternal plasma levels of 1.2 µg/mL or higher.

McKenna reported amiodarone milk levels in a mother treated with 400 mg daily.[2] In this study, at 6 weeks postpartum, breastmilk levels of amiodarone and desethylamiodarone varied during the day from 2.8-16.4 mg/L and 1.1-6.5 mg/L respectively. Reported infant plasma levels of amiodarone and desethylamiodarone were 0.4 and 0.25 respectively. The dose ingested by the infant was approximately 1.5 µg/kg/day. The authors suggest that the amount of amiodarone ingested was moderate and could expose the developing infant to a significant dose of the drug and should be avoided.

Because amiodarone inhibits extrathyroidal deiodinases, conversion of T4 to T3 is reduced. One reported case of hypothyroidism has been reported in an infant following therapy in the mother. Because of the long half-life and high concentrations in various organs, amiodarone could continuously build up to higher levels in the infant although it was not reported in the above studies. This product should be used only under the most extraordinary conditions, and the infant should be closely monitored for cardiovascular and thyroid function. Thus, breastfeeding should be avoided if this product is used chronically. Brief, 3-7 days use is probably not contraindicated if a 24-48 hour interruption is used before reinstating breastfeeding. One case reported a mother who took 200 mg amiodarone three times daily to treat fetal ascites and tachycardia. Upon delivery, the mother stopped taking amiodarone. Breastmilk was tested to determine the levels of amiodarone, which were found to be 0.6 mg/L, 2.1 mg/L, and undetectable on days 5, 11, and 25, respectively. The baby was monitored closely during this period. The authors suggest that in some instances, with close monitoring, breastfeeding can occur during amiodarone therapy.[3]

Pregnancy Risk Category: D

Lactation Risk Category: L5

Adult Concerns: Hypothyroidism, myocardial arrhythmias, pulmonary toxicity, serious liver injury, congestive heart failure.

Pediatric Concerns: Hypothyroidism has been reported. Extreme caution is urged.

Drug Interactions: Amiodarone interferes with the metabolism of a number of drugs including: oral anticoagulants, beta blockers, calcium channel blockers, digoxin, flecainide, phenytoin, procainamide, quinidine. Plasma levels of these drugs tend to be increased to hazardous levels.

Relative Infant Dose: 43.1%

Adult Dose: 200-800 mg BID

Alternatives: Disopyramide, Mexiletine

T ½	= 26-107 days	M/P	= 4.6-13
PHL	=	PB	= 99.98%
Tmax	= 3-7 hours	Oral	= 22-86%
MW	= 643	pKa	= 6.6
Vd	= 18-148		

References:
1. Plomp TA, Vulsma T, de Vijlder JJ. Use of amiodarone during pregnancy. Eur J Obstet Gynecol Reprod Biol 1992; 43 (3):201-207.
2. McKenna WJ, Harris L, Rowland E, Whitelaw A, Storcy G, Holt D. Amiodarone therapy during pregnancy. Am J Cardiol 1983; 51 (7):1231-1233.
3. Hall CM, McCormick KPB. Amiodarone and breast feeding. Arch Dis Child Fetal Neonatal Ed 2003 May; 88 (3):F255-F254.

AMITRIPTYLINE   L2

Trade: Elavil, Endep

Other Trades: Apo-Amitriptyline, Novo-Tryptin, Amitrol, Endep, Mutabon D, Tryptanol, Domical, Lentizol

Uses: Tricyclic antidepressant

AAP: Drugs whose effect on nursing infants is unknown but may be of concern

Amitriptyline and its active metabolite, nortriptyline, are secreted into breastmilk in small amounts. In one report of a mother taking 100 mg/day of amitriptyline, milk levels of amitriptyline and nortriptyline (active metabolite) averaged 143 µg/L and 55.5 µg/L respectively; maternal serum levels averaged 112 µg/L and 72.5 µg/L respectively.[1] No drug was detected in the infants serum. From this data, an infant would consume approximately 21.5 µg/kg/day, a dose that is unlikely to be clinically relevant.

In another study following a maternal dose of 25 mg/day, the amitriptyline and nortriptyline (active metabolite) levels in milk were

30 μg/L and <30 μg/L respectively.[2] In the same study when the dosage was 75 mg/day, milk levels of amitriptyline and nortriptyline averaged 88 μg/L and 69 μg/L respectively. Both drugs were essentially undetectable in the infant's serum. Therefore, the authors estimated that a nursing infant would receive less than 0.1 mg/day.

In another mother taking 175 mg/day, amitriptyline levels in the mother's milk were the same as in her serum on day one (24-27 μg/mL), but milk levels decreased to 54% of the serum concentration on days 2 to 26. Milk concentrations of nortriptyline were 74 percent of that in the mother's serum (87 ng/mL). Thus, the authors reported the absolute infant dose as 35 μg/kg, 80 times lower than the mother's dose. Neither compound could be detected in the infant's serum on day 26, nor were there any signs of sedation or other adverse effects.[4]

Pregnancy Risk Category: C

Lactation Risk Category: L2

Adult Concerns: Anticholinergic side effects, such as drying of secretions, dilated pupil, sedation.

Pediatric Concerns: No untoward effects have been noted in several studies. In studies of neurobehavioral development in at least 23 infants, no untoward effects or changes were noted from normal.[2,5,6,7]

Drug Interactions: Phenobarbital may reduce effect of amitriptyline. Amitriptyline blocks the hypotensive effect of guanethidine. May increase toxicity of amitriptyline when used with clonidine. Dangerous when used with MAO inhibitors, other CNS depressants. May increase anticoagulant effect of coumadin, warfarin. SSRIs (Prozac, Zoloft,etc) should not be used with or soon after amitriptyline or other TCAs due to serotonergic crisis.

Relative Infant Dose: 1.9% - 2.8%

Adult Dose: 15-150 mg BID

Alternatives: Amoxapine, Imipramine

T ½	= 31-46 hours	M/P	= 1.0
PHL	=	PB	= 94.8%
Tmax	= 2-4 hours	Oral	= Complete
MW	= 277	pKa	= 9.4
Vd	= 6-10		

References:
1.   Bader TF, Newman K. Amitriptyline in human breast milk and the nursing infant's serum. Am J Psychiatry 1980; 137 (7):855-856.

2. Brixen-Rasmussen L, Halgrener J, Jorgensen A. Amitriptyline and nortriptyline excretion in human breast milk. Psychopharmacology (Berl) 1982; 76 (1):94-95.
3. Matheson I, Skjaeraasen J. Milk concentrations of flupenthixol, nortriptyline and zuclopenthixol and between-breast differences in two patients. Eur J Clin Pharmacol 1988; 35 (2):217-220.
4. Breyer-Pfaff U, Nill K, Entenmann A, Gaertner HJ. Secretion of Amitriptyline and Metabolites Into Breast Milk. Am J Psychiatry 1995; 152 (5):812-813.
5. Misri S, Sivertz K. Tricyclic drugs in pregnancy and lactation: a preliminary report. Int J Psychiatry Med. 1991;21:157-71.
6. Yoshida K, Smith B, Kumar R. Psychotropic drugs in mothers' milk: a comprehensive review of assay methods, pharmacokinetics and safety of breast-feeding. J Psychopharmacol. 1999;13:64-80.
7. Nulman I, Rovet J, Stewart DE et al. Child development following exposure to tricyclic antidepressants or fluoxetine throughout fetal life: a prospective, controlled study. Am J Psychiatry. 2002;159:1889-95.

AMLODIPINE BESYLATE   L3

Trade: Norvasc
Other Trades: Istin
Uses: Antihypertensive, calcium channel blocker
AAP: Not reviewed

Amlodipine is a typical calcium channel blocker, antihypertensive agent which has greater bioavailability and a longer duration of action.[1] No data are currently available on transfer of amlodipine into breastmilk. Because most calcium channel blockers (CCB) readily transfer into milk, we should assume the same for this drug. Use caution if administering to lactating women.

Pregnancy Risk Category: C

Lactation Risk Category: L3

Adult Concerns: Hypotension, bradycardia, edema, headache, or nausea.

Pediatric Concerns: None reported but observe for bradycardia, hypotension upon prolonged use.

Drug Interactions: Cyclosporine levels may be increased when used with calcium channel blockers. Use with azole antifungals (fluconazole, itraconazole, ketoconazole, etc) may lead to enhanced amlodipine levels. Use with rifampin may significantly reduce plasma levels of calcium channel blockers.

Relative Infant Dose:

Adult Dose: 5-10 mg daily.

Alternatives: Nifedipine, Nimodipine

T ½	= 30-50 hours	M/P	=
PHL	=	PB	= 93%
Tmax	= 6-9 hours	Oral	= 64-65%
MW	= 408	pKa	=
Vd	= 21		

References:
1.   Pharmaceutical Manufacturer Prescribing Information, 2002.

AMOXAPINE   L2

Trade: Asendin
Other Trades: Asendis
Uses: Tricyclic antidepressant
AAP: Drugs whose effect on nursing infants is unknown but
        may be of concern

Amoxapine and its metabolite are both secreted into breastmilk at
relatively low levels. Following a dose of 250 mg/day, milk levels
of amoxapine were less than 20 µg/L and 113 µg/L of the active
metabolite.[1] Milk levels of the active metabolite varied from 113
to 168 µg/L in two other milk samples. Maternal serum levels of
amoxapine and metabolite at steady state were 97 µg/L and 375 µg/L
respectively.

Pregnancy Risk Category: C

Lactation Risk Category: L2

Adult Concerns: Dry mouth, constipation, urine retention, drowsiness
or sedation, anxiety, emotional disturbances, parkinsonism, tardive
dyskinesia, seizures.

Pediatric Concerns: None reported via milk.

Drug Interactions: Decreased effect of clonidine, guanethidine.
Amoxapine may increase effect of CNS depressants, adrenergic agents,
anticholinergic agents. Increased toxicity with MAO inhibitors.

Relative Infant Dose:

Adult Dose: 25 mg BID or TID

Alternatives:

T ½	= 8 hours (parent)	M/P	= 0.21
PHL	=	PB	= 15-25%
Tmax	= 2 hours	Oral	= 18-54%
MW	= 314	pKa	=
Vd	= 65.7		

References:
1. Gelenberg AJ. Single case study. Amoxapine, a new antidepressant, appears in human milk. J Nerv Ment Dis 1979; 167 (10):635-636.

AMOXICILLIN   L1

Trade: Larotid, Amoxil

Other Trades: Apo-Amoxi, Novamoxin, Alphamox, Moxacin, Cilamox, Betamox

Uses: Penicillin antibiotic

AAP: Maternal Medication Usually Compatible with Breastfeeding

Amoxicillin is a popular oral penicillin used for otitis media and many other pediatric/adult infections. In one group of 6 mothers who received 1 gm oral doses, the concentration of amoxicillin in breastmilk ranged from 0.68 to 1.3 mg/L of milk (average= 0.9 mg/L).[1] Peak levels occurred at 4- 5 hours. Milk/plasma ratios at 1, 2, and 3 hours were 0.014, 0.013, and 0.043. Less than 0.95% of the maternal dose is secreted into milk. his amounts to less than 0.5% of a typical infant dose of amoxicillin. No harmful effects have been reported.

Pregnancy Risk Category: B

Lactation Risk Category: L1

Adult Concerns: Diarrhea, rashes, and changes in GI flora. Pancytopenia, rarely pseudomembranous colitis.

Pediatric Concerns: None reported. Commonly used in neonates and children.

Drug Interactions: Efficacy of oral contraceptives may be reduced. Disulfiram and probenecid may increase plasma levels of amoxicillin. Allopurinol may increase the risk of amoxicillin skin rash.

Relative Infant Dose: 1%

Adult Dose: 500-875 mg BID

Alternatives:

T ½	= 1.7 hours	M/P	= 0.014-0.043
PHL	= 4 hours (neonate)	PB	= 18%
Tmax	= 1.5 hours	Oral	= 89%
MW	= 365	pKa	=
Vd	= 0.3		

References:
1. Kafetzis DA, Siafas CA, Georgakopoulos PA, Papadatos CJ. Passage of cephalosporins and amoxicillin into the breast milk. Acta Paediatr Scand 1981; 70 (3):285-288.

AMOXICILLIN + CLAVULANATE   L1

Trade: Augmentin
Other Trades: Clavulin
Uses: Penicillin antibiotic, extended spectrum
AAP: Not reviewed

Addition of clavulanate extends spectrum of amoxicillin by inhibiting beta lactamase enzymes. Small amounts of amoxicillin (0.9 mg/L milk) are secreted in breastmilk. No harmful effects were reported in one report.[1] In another study of 67 breastfeeding mothers, 27 mothers were treated with amoxicillin/ clavulanic acid and 40 mothers were treated with only amoxicillin. In the amoxicillin/ clavulanic acid group, 22.3% of the infants had mild adverse effects. Only 7.5% of the control group (amoxicillin-only) infants had adverse effects. However, the authors suggest that this difference in untoward effects is not clinically significant.[2] The reported side effects included constipation, rash, diarrhea, and irritability. This amounts to less than 0.5% of a typical infant dose of amoxicillin.

Pregnancy Risk Category: B

Lactation Risk Category: L1

Adult Concerns: Diarrhea, rash, thrush, irritability, or diarrhea.

Pediatric Concerns: None reported but observe for diarrhea, rash.

Drug Interactions: Efficacy of oral contraceptives may be reduced. Disulfiram and probenecid may increase plasma levels of amoxicillin. Allopurinol may increase the risk of amoxicillin skin rash.

Relative Infant Dose:

Adult Dose: 875 mg BID

Alternatives:

T ½	= 1.7 hours	M/P	= 0.014-0.043
PHL	= 4 hours (neonate)	PB	= 18%
Tmax	= 1.5 hours	Oral	= 89%
MW	= 365	pKa	=
Vd	= 0.3		

References:
1. Kafetzis DA, Siafas CA, Georgakopoulos PA, Papadatos CJ. Passage of cephalosporins and amoxicillin into the breast milk. Acta Paediatr Scand 1981; 70 (3):285-288.
2. Benyamini L et al. The Safety of Amoxicillin/Clavulanic Acid and Cefuroxime During Lactation. Ther Drug Monit 2005 Aug; 27 (4):499-502.

AMPHOTERICIN B   L3

Trade: Fungizone, Amphotec

Other Trades: Ambisome, Resteclin, Abelcet, Fungilin, Abelcet, Amphocel

Uses: Antifungal

AAP: Not reviewed

Amphotericin B is an intravenous antifungal effective for the treatment of a range of different organisms, including Candida albicans. Amphotericin is significantly toxic when given intravenously, and is reserved for life-threatening infections. No data are available on its transfer to human milk; however, it is virtually unabsorbed orally (<9%), has high protein binding, has a large MW, and is commonly used in pediatrics.[1,2] It is unlikely the amount in milk would be clinically relevant to a breastfeeding infant.

Pregnancy Risk Category: B

Lactation Risk Category: L3

Adult Concerns: Adverse effects include anemia, thrombocytopenia, congestive heart failure, thrombophlebitis, paresthesias, hypokalemia, hyperthermia, nephrotoxicity, hepatotoxicity, pulmonary toxicity, erythematous reactions, and anaphylaxis.

Pediatric Concerns: None reported. Unlikely to be absorbed orally.

Drug Interactions: Antagonism with azole antifungals. Enhanced renal toxicity with cyclosporin. Enhanced digitalis toxicity due to hypokalemia.

Relative Infant Dose:

Adult Dose: 0.25 to 1.0 mg/kg daily IV

Alternatives:

T ½	= 15 days	M/P	=
PHL	=	PB	= >90%
Tmax	= <1 hour	Oral	= <9%
MW	= 924	pKa	=
Vd	= 4		

References:
1. Pharmaceutical Manufacturer Prescribing Information, 2002.
2. Mactal-Haaf C, Hoffman M, Kuchta A. Use of anti-infective agents during lactation, Part 3: Antivirals, antifungals, and urinary antiseptics. J Hum Lact 2001 May; 17 (2):160-166.

AMPICILLIN   L1

Trade: Polycillin, Omnipen
Other Trades: Apo-Ampi, Novo-Ampicillin, NuAmpi, Penbriton, Ampicyn, Austrapen, Amfipen, Britcin, Vidopen
Uses: Penicillin antibiotic
AAP: Not reviewed

Low milk/plasma ratios of 0.2 have been reported.[1] In a study by Matsuda of 2-3 breastfeeding patients who received 500 mg of ampicillin orally, levels in milk peaked at 6 hours and averaged only 0.14 mg/L of milk.[2] The milk/plasma ratio was reported to be 0.03 at 2 hours.

In a group of 9 breastfeeding women sampled at various times and who received doses of 350 mg TID orally, milk concentrations ranged from 0.06 to 0.17 mg/L with peak milk levels at 3-4 hours after the dose.[3] Milk/plasma ratios varied between 0.01 and 0.58. The highest reported milk level (1.02 mg/L) was in a patient receiving 700 mg TID. Ampicillin was not detected in the plasma of any infant. Ampicillin is one of the most commonly used prophylactic antibiotics in pediatric neonatal nurseries. Neonatal half-life is 2.8 to 4 hours. Possible rash, sensitization, diarrhea, or candidiasis could occur, but unlikely. May alter GI flora.
Pregnancy Risk Category: B

Lactation Risk Category: L1

Adult Concerns: Diarrhea, rash, fungal overgrowth, agranulocytosis, pseudomembranous colitis, anaphylaxis.

Pediatric Concerns: None reported but observe for diarrhea.

Drug Interactions: Efficacy of oral contraceptives may be reduced. Disulfiram and probenecid may increase plasma levels of ampicillin. Allopurinol may increase the risk of ampicillin skin rash.

Relative Infant Dose: 0.2% - 1.5%

Adult Dose: 250-500 mg four times daily

Alternatives: Amoxicillin

T ½	= 1.3 hours	M/P	= 0.58
PHL	= 1.7 hours (neonate)	PB	= 8-20
Tmax	= 1-2 hours	Oral	= 50%
MW	= 349	pKa	=
Vd	= 0.38		

References:
1. Kafetzis DA, Siafas CA, Georgakopoulos PA, Papadatos CJ. Passage of cephalosporins and amoxicillin into the breast milk. Acta Paediatr Scand 1981; 70 (3):285-288.
2. Matsuda S. Transfer of antibiotics into maternal milk. Biol Res Pregnancy Perinatol 1984; 5 (2):57-60.
3. Branebjerg PE, Heisterberg L. Blood and milk concentrations of ampicillin in mothers treated with pivampicillin and in their infants. J Perinat Med 1987; 15 (6):555-558.

AMPICILLIN + SULBACTAM | L1

Trade: Unasyn
Other Trades: Dicapen
Uses: Penicillin antibiotic with extended spectrum.
AAP: Not reviewed

Small amounts of ampicillin may transfer (1 mg/L).[1] Possible rash, sensitization, diarrhea, or candidiasis could occur, but unlikely. This drug may alter GI flora. After a dose of 0.5 to 1 gram, sulbactam is secreted into milk at an average concentration of 0.52 μg/mL. This would lead to a maximal dose of 0.7 mg/kg/day in a breastfeeding infant, which equates to less than 1% of the maternal dose. Therefore, untoward effects are unlikely in a breastfeeding infant.[2]

Pregnancy Risk Category: B

Lactation Risk Category: L1

Adult Concerns: Diarrhea, rash, fungal overgrowth, agranulocytosis, pseudomembranous colitis, anaphylaxis.

Pediatric Concerns: None reported but observe for diarrhea.

Drug Interactions: Efficacy of oral contraceptives may be reduced. Disulfiram and probenecid may increase plasma levels of amoxicillin. Allopurinol may increase the risk of amoxicillin skin rash.

Relative Infant Dose: 0.6% - 1.5%

Adult Dose: 1.5-3 gm four times daily

Alternatives:

T ½	= 1.3 hours	M/P	= 0.01-0.5
PHL	= 1.7 hours (15-30 days old)	PB	= 28%
Tmax	= 1-2 hours	Oral	= 60%
MW	= 349	pKa	=
Vd	= 0.38		

References:
1. Kafetzis DA, Siafas CA, Georgakopoulos PA, Papadatos CJ. Passage of cephalosporins and amoxicillin into the breast milk. Acta Paediatr Scand 1981; 70 (3):285-288.
2. Foulds G, Miller RD, Knirsch AK, Thrupp LD. Sulbactam kinetics and excretion into breast milk in postpartum women. Clin Pharmacol Ther 1985; 38 (6):692-696.

ANAGRELIDE HCL   L4

Trade: Agrylin
Other Trades:
Uses: Platelet-reducing agent
AAP: Not reviewed

Anagrelide is used in the treatment of essential thrombocythemia and thrombocythemia associated with chronic myelogenous leukemia, polycythemia vera, and other myeloproliferative disorders. It inhibits the release of arachidonic acid from phospholipase, possibly by inhibiting phospholipase A2.[1] We do not have any data on its use in breastfeeding mothers, but some probably enters milk and would be orally absorbed by the infant. Since this drug is used for prolonged periods, untoward effects such as reduction of blood platelets (thrombocytopenia) and cardiovascular disorders in the infant are a possibility. While the risks of this drug are rather remote, chronic use in breastfeeding mothers should be discouraged or the infant closely monitored.

Pregnancy Risk Category: C

Lactation Risk Category: L4

Adult Concerns: Adverse reactions include palpitation, edema, headache, diarrhea, weakness, and dyspnea.

Pediatric Concerns: No data are available, but chronic use is discouraged.

Drug Interactions: May increase adverse effects of drotrecogin alfa, and adverse effects of anagrelide may be increased when taken with NSAIDs, salicylates, or treprostinil.

Relative Infant Dose:

Adult Dose:

Alternatives:

T ½	= 1.3 hours	M/P	=
PHL	=	PB	=
Tmax	= 1 hour	Oral	= 70%
MW	= 310	pKa	=
Vd	=		

References:
1. Pharmaceutical Manufacturer Prescribing Information. 1999.

ANAKINRA — L3

Trade: Kineret
Other Trades: Kineret
Uses: Anti-rheumatic
AAP: Not reviewed

Anakinra is a recombinant form of the human interleukin-1 receptor antagonist (IL-1RA) and is used to reduce the inflammatory stimuli that mediate various inflammatory and immunological responses common in rheumatoid arthritis. It is a large MW protein (17,300 daltons) administered subcutaneously. Due to its size, it is very unlikely to enter milk after the first week postpartum. In addition, it is not likely to be orally bioavailable in an infant. However, we do not have data on its transfer to human milk and if used the infant should be observed for increased risk of GI infections.

Pregnancy Risk Category: B

Lactation Risk Category: L3

Adult Concerns: Adverse events include a high risk of serious infections (2%), URI, headache, nausea, and diarrhea.

Pediatric Concerns: None reported via milk. This agent is too large to enter milk effectively after the first week postpartum.

Drug Interactions: None

Relative Infant Dose:

Adult Dose: 100 mg SC daily.

Alternatives:

T ½	= 4-6 hours	M/P	=
PHL	=	PB	= Nil
Tmax	=	Oral	= Nil
MW	= 17,300	pKa	=
Vd	=		

References:
1. Pharmaceutical Manufacturers prescribing information, 2003.

ANIDULAFUNGIN   L3

Trade: Eraxis
Other Trades:
Uses: Antifungal
AAP: Not reviewed

Anidulafungin is an injectable antifungal used in the treatment of Candida infections. It inhibits the formation of 1,3-beta-D-glucan, an essential polysaccharide in cell wall of Candida Albicans. This leads to cell lysis.[1] No data are available on levels in human milk, but due to the large MW, its high protein binding, and its large volume of distribution, it is highly unlikely that it will transfer into breastmilk. Lastly, it would not be orally bioavailable in the infant.

Pregnancy Risk Category: C

Lactation Risk Category: L3

Adult Concerns: Adverse reactions inlcude hypokalemia, diarrhea, and increased transaminase.

Pediatric Concerns: No data are available.

Drug Interactions:

Relative Infant Dose:

Adult Dose: 100 mg IV daily for 14 days

Alternatives: Fluconazole

T ½	= 27 hours	M/P	=
PHL	=	PB	= >99%
Tmax	=	Oral	= Nil
MW	= 1140.3	pKa	=
Vd	= 0.43-0.71		

References:
1.   Pharmaceutical Manufacturer Prescribing Information. 2007.

ANTHRALIN   L3

Trade: Anthra-Derm, Drithocreme, Dritho-Scalp, Micanol
Other Trades: Anthraforte, Anthranol, Anthrascalp, Dithranol, Alphodith
Uses: Anti-psoriatic
AAP: Not reviewed

Anthralin is a synthetic tar derivative used topically for suppression of psoriasis. Anthralin, when applied topically, induces burning and inflammation of the skin but is one of the most effective treatments for psoriasis. Purple-brown staining of skin and permanent staining of clothing and porcelain bathroom fixtures is frequent. Anthralin when applied topically is absorbed into the surface layers of the skin and only minimal amounts enter the systemic circulation. That absorbed is rapidly excreted via the kidneys almost instantly; plasma levels are very low to undetectable.[1] No data are available on its transfer into human milk. Most anthralin is eliminated by washing off and desquamation of dead surface cells.[2] For this reason, when placed directly on lesions on the areola or nipple, breastfeeding should be discouraged. Another similar anthraquinone is Senna (laxative), which even in high doses does not enter milk. While undergoing initial intense treatment, it would perhaps be advisable to interrupt breastfeeding temporarily, but this may be overly conservative. Observe the infant for diarrhea. It has been used in children over 2 years of age for psoriasis.

Pregnancy Risk Category: C

Lactation Risk Category: L3

Adult Concerns: Pruritus, skin irritation and inflammation. Purple-brown staining of skin and permanent staining of clothing and porcelain bathroom fixtures is frequent. Anthralin may have carcinogenic properties following high doses in mice. This may have no relevance to humans at all.

Pediatric Concerns: Diarrhea, nausea, vomiting via milk, but no reports have been published.

Drug Interactions:

Relative Infant Dose:

Adult Dose: Apply topical BID

Alternatives:

T ½	= Brief	M/P	=
PHL	=	PB	=
Tmax	=	Oral	= Complete
MW	= 226	pKa	=
Vd	=		

References:
1.   Goodfield MJ, Hull SM, Cunliffe WJ. The systemic effect of dithranol treatment in psoriasis. Acta Derm Venereol 1994; 74 (4):295-297.
2.   Shroot B. Mode of action of dithranol, pharmacokinetics/dynamics. Acta Derm Venereol Suppl (Stockh) 1992; 172:10-12.

ANTHRAX (BACILLUS ANTHRACIS)   L5

Trade: Anthrax Infection, Bacillus Anthracis
Other Trades:
Uses: Anthrax infection
AAP: Maternal Medication Usually Compatible with Breastfeeding

Anthrax is caused by the gram-positive, spore-forming bacterium bacillus anthracis. The spore may persist in nature for many years and infect grazing animals such as sheep, goats, and cattle. The most common forms of the disease are inhaled, oral, and cutaneous. The Center for Disease Control has recently published guidelines for treating or prophylaxing exposed breastfeeding mothers.[1]

Thus far, all of the anthrax strains released by bioterrorists have been sensitive to ciprofloxacin, doxycycline, and the penicillin family. In breastfeeding women, amoxicillin (80 mg/kg/d in 3 divided doses) is an option for antimicrobial prophylaxis when B. anthracis is known to be penicillin- susceptible and no contraindication to maternal amoxicillin use is indicated. The American Academy of Pediatrics also considers ciprofloxacin and tetracyclines (which include doxycycline) to be usually compatible with breastfeeding because the amount of either drug absorbed by infants is small, but little is known about the safety of long-term use.

Until culture sensitivity tests have been completed, the breastfeeding mother should be treated with ciprofloxacin (see ofloxacin or levofloxacin as alternates) or doxycycline (< 3 weeks). Once cultures show that the anthrax strain is sensitive to penicillins, then the mother can switch to amoxicillin for long term use up to 60 days or more. Due to possible dental staining following prolonged exposure, this author would not suggest long-term use (60 days) of doxycycline in a breastfeeding mother. The CDC offers several alternative antibiotics such as rifampin, vancomycin, imipenem, clindamycin, and clarithromycin in those patients with allergic conditions.[2] Check the CDC web sites for the most current recommendations.[3]

Pregnancy Risk Category:

Lactation Risk Category: L5 if infected

Adult Concerns:

Pediatric Concerns:

Drug Interactions:

Relative Infant Dose:

Adult Dose:

Alternatives:

References:
1. http://www.cdc.gov
2. Update: Investigation of bioterrorism-related anthrax and interim guidelines for exposure management and antimicrobial therapy, October 2001 MMWR Morb Mortal Wkly Rep 2001; 50 (42):909-919.
3. Center for Disease Control Web site: http://www.bt.cdc.gov/. 2004.

ANTHRAX VACCINE	L3

Trade: Anthrax Vaccine
Other Trades:
Uses: Vaccination
AAP: Not reviewed

The anthrax vaccine for humans licensed for use in the United States is a cell-free filtrate vaccine, which means it uses dead bacteria as opposed to live bacteria. The vaccine is reported to be 93% effective in protecting against cutaneous anthrax.[1] The vaccine should only be administered to healthy men and women from 18 to 65 years of age since investigations to date have been conducted exclusively in that population. Because it is not known whether the anthrax vaccine can cause fetal harm, pregnant women should not be vaccinated. There are no data or indications relative to its use in breastfeeding mothers. While it consists primarily of protein fragments of anthrax bacteria, it is very unlikely any would transfer into milk or even be bioavailable in the infant.

The CDC states that, "No data suggest increased risk for side effects or temporally related adverse events associated with receipt of anthrax vaccine by breast-feeding women or breast-fed children. Administration of nonliving vaccines (e.g., anthrax vaccine) during breast-feeding is not medically contraindicated."

Pregnancy Risk Category: C

Lactation Risk Category: L3

Adult Concerns: Mild local reactions occur in 30% of recipients and consist of slight tenderness and redness at the injection site. A moderate local reaction can occur if the vaccine is given to anyone with a past history of anthrax infection. Severe local reactions are very infrequent and consist of extensive swelling of the forearm in addition to the local reaction. Systemic reactions occur in fewer than 0.2% of recipients and are characterized by flu-like symptoms.

Pediatric Concerns: None reported via milk.

Drug Interactions:

Relative Infant Dose:

Adult Dose: 2-30 mg per day

Alternatives:

References:
1. Center for Disease Control Web site: http://www.bt.cdc.gov/. 2004.

ANTIHEMOPHILIC FACTOR-VON WILLEBRAND FACTOR COMPLEX   L3

Trade: Alphanate, Humate-P
Other Trades:
Uses: Antihemophilic agent
AAP: Not reviewed

This antihemophilic agent is used in hemophilia A and factor VIII deficiency to prevent and treat hemorrhagic episodes. It is also used to treat bleeding and as prophylaxis during procedures in patients with von Willebrand disease.[1] No data are available on the excretion of this antihemophilic agent into breast milk, however, it is highly unlikely due to the large MW. Further, it is minimally bioavailable when ingested orally.

Pregnancy Risk Category: C

Lactation Risk Category: L3

Adult Concerns: Adverse reactions include epistaxis, body pain, nausea, dyspnea, cardiorespiratory arrest, and chills.

Pediatric Concerns: No data available in infants.

Drug Interactions:

Relative Infant Dose:

Adult Dose: 15-80 IU/kg (individualize)

Alternatives:

T ½	= 10-12 hours	M/P	=
PHL	=	PB	=
Tmax	=	Oral	= Nil
MW	= 264,726	pKa	=
Vd	=		

References:
1. Pharmaceutical Manufacturer Prescribing Information. 2006.

ANTIPYRINE   L4

Trade: Antipyrine
Other Trades:
Uses: Analgesic, antipyretic
AAP: Not reviewed

In a group of 7 breastfeeding mothers who were receiving a single oral dose of 18 mg/kg of antipyrine in solution, peak levels in milk ranged from 10-30 mg/L. In five women peak concentrations were attained in milk and saliva by 1 hr and in the other two women by 3 hr.[1] Antipyrine half-life varied from 5.6 to 20.3 hours for saliva and from 5.7 to 21.7 hours for milk. The average amount of antipyrine available to the nursing infant was estimated at 6.4 mg/24 hours (range 3.0-11.1 mg).

According to the authors, this is approximately 0.25% to 1.07% of the maternal dose (not weigh-adjusted). The authors suggested that lactation may influence antipyrine drug metabolism. This product is no longer used in the USA due to high incidence of fatal bone marrow toxicity.

Pregnancy Risk Category: C

Lactation Risk Category: L4

Adult Concerns: Severe bone marrow toxicity.

Pediatric Concerns: None reported but due to better medications, this product should never be used.

Drug Interactions:

Relative Infant Dose: 8.3% - 25%

Adult Dose: 18 mg/kg/day

Alternatives: ibuprofen, acetaminophen

T ½	=	M/P	= 1.0
PHL	=	PB	= <1%
Tmax	= 1-2 hours	Oral	=
MW	= 188	pKa	= 1.4
Vd	= 0.56		

References:
1. Berlin CM, Jr., Vesell ES. Antipyrine disposition in milk and saliva of lactating women. Clin Pharmacol Ther 1982; 31 (1):38-44.

ARFORMOTEROL TARTRATE   L3

Trade: Brovana
Other Trades:
Uses: Beta-2 agonist
AAP: Not reviewed

Arformoterol tartrate is used for long-term treatment of bronchoconstriction in COPD. It is the (R,R)- enantiomer of the racemic formoterol, which relaxes bronchial smooth muscle by selective action on beta 2-receptors without affecting the cardiovascular system.[1] The average steady-state peak plasma concentration is 4.3 picograms/mL which means levels in milk would be incredibly low if even present. There have been no studies on the transfer of arformoterol tartrate into human breastmilk. However, due to the extremely low plasma levels, any transfer into milk would be minimal to nil. Just like all the other beta agonists used in asthma, it is unlikely that this product would pose a problem to a breastfeeding infant.

Pregnancy Risk Category: C

Lactation Risk Category: L3

Adult Concerns: Adverse reactions include chest pain, edema, rash, diarrhea, back pain, sinusitis, and dyspnea.

Pediatric Concerns: No data are available.

Drug Interactions: Alpha-/beta-blockers may decrease the bronchodilatory effect, atomoxetine may enhance the tachycardic effect. Betahistine may diminish the bronchodilator effect of beta agonists. Sympathomimetics may enhance the adverse effects of arformoterol.

Relative Infant Dose:

Adult Dose: 15 μg BID

Alternatives: Formoterol, albuterol

T ½	= 26 hours	M/P	=
PHL	=	PB	= 52-65%
Tmax	= 0.5-3 hours	Oral	=
MW	= 494.5	pKa	=
Vd	=		

References:
1. Pharmaceutical Manufacturer Prescribing Information. 2006.

ARGATROBAN   L4

Trade: Argatroban
Other Trades:
Uses: Synthetic direct thrombin inhibitor: anticoagulant
AAP: Not reviewed

Argatroban is a synthetic inhibitor of thrombin and is derived from L-arginine. It reversibly binds to the thrombin active site and exerts an anticoagulant effect by inhibiting thrombin-catalyzed reactions. It is primarily indicated as an anticoagulant for treatment of thrombosis in patients with heparin-induced thrombocytopenia. It is primarily in the extracellular fluid as evidenced by its low volume of distribution. No data are available on its transfer to human milk but it is reported present in rodent milk. It is not known if this product is orally bioavailable, but probably not. The presence of this product in milk could potentially induce GI hemorrhage in weak or susceptible infants including newborns, premature infants, infants with NEC, and other infants. Extreme caution is recommended until we know levels present in milk and more about its GI stability, absorption.

Pregnancy Risk Category: B

Lactation Risk Category: L4

Adult Concerns: Hemorrhage.

Pediatric Concerns: None reported via milk.

Drug Interactions: Prolongation of prothrombin times when co-administered with heparin, warfarin and potentially aspirin. Angelica, Bilberry, Arnica, Astragalus, and Anise may increase the risk of bleeding.

Relative Infant Dose:

Adult Dose: Initial: 25 µg/kg/min. Highly variable.

Alternatives:

T ½	= 39-51 minutes	M/P	=
PHL	=	PB	= 54%
Tmax	= 1-3 hours	Oral	= Unknown
MW	= 526	pKa	=
Vd	= 0.174		

References:
1. Pharmaceutical Manufacturers Prescribing Information, 2003.

ARGININE   L3

Trade: L-Arginine, Arginine
Other Trades:
Uses: Amino Acid; test for Growth Hormone release
AAP: Not reviewed

L-Arginine is a naturally occurring basic amino acid. It is classified as a semi essential amino acid and is a potent stimulant of pituitary growth hormone and insulin release. Found in most foods, it can also easily be synthesized by the human. L-Arginine participates in many biochemical reactions, but is most well known for its ability to stimulate endothelium-derived relaxing factor now known as nitric oxide (NO). NO plays critical roles in many diverse physiological processes including neurotransmission, vasorelaxation, and immune responses. Arginine plays an important role in wound healing removing ammonia from the body, immune function, and the release of hormones. There are unconfirmed reports that L- arginine may promote tumor growth in patients with malignancies who receive supplements. Numerous other studies do not show this effect at all.

L-Arginine is not overly toxic. Doses as high as 30 gm/day have been generally well tolerated in adults with the most common adverse effects of nausea and diarrhea being reported. No reports of its transfer into human milk are available. Most importantly, we do not know if high doses of oral L-Arginine subsequently increase Arginine levels in milk, although it would seem likely. As this product has limited usefulness in most patients, its use at high doses in breastfeeding mothers should be avoided until milk levels are reported.

Pregnancy Risk Category: B

Lactation Risk Category: L3

Adult Concerns: Allergic reactions have been reported upon the administration of L-Arginine. When infused intravenously, local irritation, nausea and vomiting are reported. Hyperkalemia has occurred. Use cautiously in patients with liver and/or renal disease.

Pediatric Concerns: None reported via milk.

Drug Interactions: Potentially fatal hyperkalemia when used with spironolactone.

Relative Infant Dose:

Adult Dose: 1-2 gm/day but highly variable. Doses as high as 30 gm/d have been used short-term.

Alternatives:

T ½	= <2 hours	M/P	=
PHL	=	PB	=
Tmax	= 1.5 hours	Oral	= 70%
MW	= 174	pKa	= 2.18 & 9.0
Vd	=		

References:
1.   Pharmaceutical Manufacturers Prescribing Information, 2003.

ARIPIPRAZOLE   L3

Trade: Abilify, Abilitat
Other Trades:
Uses: Antipsychotic
AAP: Not reviewed

Aripiprazole is a second-generation antipsychotic now first-line treatment for schizophrenia. In a small study of a single patient receiving 10 mg/day initially and then 15 mg subsequently, levels of aripiprazole in milk were reported to be 13 and 14 μg/L on two consecutive days (15 and 16 after initiation of therapy).[1] Maternal plasma levels at the same time were 71 and 71 μg/L. Levels were drawn in the morning before aripiprazole administration. Thus it appears from this brief report that they were drawn approximately 24 hours post dose. Several reports (personal communication) of somnolence have been reported to this author. The infant should be monitored for somnolence.

Pregnancy Risk Category: C

Lactation Risk Category: L3

Adult Concerns: Adverse reactions include headache, dizziness, akathisia, sedation, tremor, anxiety, insomnia and restlessness.

Pediatric Concerns: Several cases of somnolence in breastfed infants have been unofficially reported.

Drug Interactions: Carbamazepine may reduce levels of aripiprazole. Fluoxetine, itraconazole, ketoconazole, paroxetine, quinidine, and ranolazine have been reported to increase plasma levels of aripiprazole.

Relative Infant Dose: 0.9%

Adult Dose: 10-15 mg/day

Alternatives: Risperidone, olanzapine, quetiapine

T ½	= 75 hours	M/P	= 0.2
PHL	=	PB	= 99%
Tmax	= 3-5 hours	Oral	= 87%
MW	= 448	pKa	=
Vd	= 4.9		

References:
1. Schlotterbeck P, Leube D, Kircher T, Hiemke C, Grunder G. Aripiprazole in human milk . Int J Neuropsychopharmacol. 2007;10:433.

ARTICAINE + EPINEPHRINE   L3

Trade: Septocaine
Other Trades: Astracaine, Septanest
Uses: Local anesthetic
AAP: Not reviewed

Septocaine is a solution that contains the local anesthetic agent articaine, and the vasoconstrictor, epinephrine. Articaine is a local anesthetic with an intermediate-duration. It has a structure similar to lidocaine, etidocaine, and prilocaine. It has an ester bond mid-structure that permits it to be rapidly hydrolyzed by blood and tissue esterases. Although its potency is approximately equal to slightly more than that of lidocaine, it may be less toxic due to its more rapid metabolism. No data are available on its use in breastfeeding mothers. As with lidocaine, however, its transfer into human milk is probably minimal. If ingested, it would be rapidly hydrolyzed by gastric esterases.

Pregnancy Risk Category: C

Lactation Risk Category: L3

Adult Concerns: Side effects include: facial edema, headache, infection, pain, gingivitis, paresthesia, abdominal pain, migraine, tachycardia, constipation, nausea, myalgia and arthralgia.

Pediatric Concerns: None reported via milk. Unlikely to be orally absorbed.

Drug Interactions: Reported drug interactions are minimal. The use of St. John's Wort prior to surgery has been associated with severe hypotenison during anesthesia and delayed emergence from anesthesia. This seems unusual as SJW is known to 'stimulate' not suppress drug metabolism of many drugs.

Relative Infant Dose:

Adult Dose: Variable volumes of 1.5% solutions.

Alternatives: Lidocaine

T ½	= 1.8 hours	M/P	=
PHL	=	PB	= 60-80%
Tmax	= 25 minutes	Oral	= Poor
MW	= 320	pKa	= 7.8
Vd	=		

References:
1.   Pharmaceutical manufacturers prescribing information. 2005.

ASCORBIC ACID   L1

Trade: Ascorbicap, Cecon, Cevi-Bid, Ce-Vi-Sol, Vitamin C
Other Trades:
Uses: Vitamin C
AAP: Not reviewed

Ascorbic acid is an essential vitamin. Without supplementation, 75 mg/day is excreted in the urine of the average individual due to overabundance. Renal control of vitamin C is significant and maintains plasma levels at 0.4 to 1.5 mg/dL regardless of dose. Ascorbic acid is secreted into human milk in well-controlled sequence and mature milk. In a large number of studies, ascorbic acid levels in milk ranged from 35 to 200 mg/L depending on the oral intake of the mother.[1]

Excessive Vitamin C intake in the mother only modestly changes the controlled secretion into breastmilk. The recommended daily allowance for the mother is 100 mg/day. Maternal supplementation is only required in undernourished mothers. In a study of 25 lactating women given 90mg of ascorbic acid for 1 day, followed by 250, 500, or 1000 mg/day for 2 days, the levels in maternal milk did not significantly influence the vitamin C content in maternal milk.[2] Mean vitamin C intakes of infants ranged between 49 ± 9 and 86 ± 11 mg/d and were not statistically different among the five levels of maternal vitamin C intake. This lack of change in vitamin C content in milk suggests a regulatory mechanism for vitamin C levels. In cases where supplementation has reached 1000 to 1500 mg/day, reported milk levels were only slightly increased to 100 and 105 mg/L.[2,3]

Pregnant women should not use excessive ascorbic acid due to metabolic induction in the maternal or fetal liver, followed by a metabolic rebound scurvy early postpartum in the neonate. Ascorbic acid should not routinely be administered to breastfed infants unless to treat clinical scurvy.

Pregnancy Risk Category: A during first and second trimester
C during third trimester

Lactation Risk Category: L1

Adult Concerns: Renal calculi with large doses. Faintness, flushing, dizziness, nausea, vomiting, gastritis.

Pediatric Concerns: None reported via breastmilk, but excessive use prepartum is strongly discouraged.

Drug Interactions: Ascorbic acid decreases propranolol peak concentrations. Aspirin decreases ascorbate levels and increases aspirin levels. Reduced effect of warfarin when used with ascorbic acid. Urinary acidification results in decreased retention of many basic drugs, including tricyclic antidepressants, amoxapine, amphetamines. Do not use with aluminum antacids. Ascorbic acid reduces renal elimination of aluminum leading to encephalopathy, seizures, coma.

Relative Infant Dose:

Adult Dose: 45-60 mg daily.

Alternatives:

T ½	–	M/P	=
PHL	=	PB	–
Tmax	= 2-3 hours	Oral	= Complete
MW	= 176	pKa	–
Vd	=		

References:

1. Picciano MF. Handbook of milk composition. Jensen RG, ed. San Diego: Academic Press; 1995.
2. Byerley LO, Kirksey A. Effects of different levels of vitamin C intake on the vitamin C concentration in human milk and the vitamin C intakes of breast-fed infants. Am J Clin Nutr 1985 Apr;41 (4):665-71.
3. Kirksey A. and Rahmanifar A. Vitamin and mineral composition of preterm human milk: Implications for the nutritional management of the preterm infant. In "Vitamins and Minerals in Pregnancy and Lactation". H. Berger, ed. Pp 301-329, Raven Press.

ASPARTAME   L1

Trade: Nutrasweet
Other Trades:
Uses: Artificial sweetener
AAP: Not reviewed

Aspartame consists of two linked amino acids, aspartic acid and phenylalanine. Once in the GI tract, it is rapidly metabolized to phenylalanine and aspartic acid. Maternal ingestion of 50 mg/kg aspartame will approximately double (2.3 to 4.8 μmol/dL) aspartate milk levels. Phenylalanine milk levels similarly increased from 0.5 to 2.3 μmol/dL. This dose is 3-4 times the normal dose used. These milk levels are too low to produce significant side effects in normal infants.[1,2] Contraindicated in infants with proven phenylketonuria.

Pregnancy Risk Category: B

Lactation Risk Category: L1
                                          L5 if used in infants with PKU

Adult Concerns: Only contraindicated in infants with PKU.

Pediatric Concerns: None reported except contraindicated in infants with documented phenylketonuria.

Drug Interactions:

Relative Infant Dose:

Adult Dose:

Alternatives:

T ½	=	M/P	=
PHL	=	PB	=
Tmax	=	Oral	= Complete
MW	= 294	pKa	=
Vd	=		

References:
1. Levels of free amino acids in lactating women following ingestion of the sweetener aspartame Nutr Rev 1980; 38 (5):183-184.
2. Stegink LD, Filer LJ, Jr., Baker GL. Plasma, erythrocyte and human milk levels of free amino acids in lactating women administered aspartame or lactose. J Nutr 1979; 109 (12):2173-2181.

ASPIRIN   L3

Trade: Anacin, Aspergum, Empirin, Genprin, Arthritis
Foundation Pain Reliever, Ecotrin

Other Trades: Coryphen, Novasen, Entrophen, Disprin, Aspro,
Cartia

Uses: Salicylate analgesic

AAP: Drugs associated with significant side effects and should
be given with caution

Extremely small amounts are secreted into breastmilk. Few harmful effects have been reported. In one study, salicylic acid (active metabolite of Aspirin) penetrated poorly into milk (dose=454 mg ASA), with peak levels of only 1.12 to 1.60 µg/mL, whereas maternal peak plasma levels were 33 to 43.4 µg/mL.[1]

In another study of a rheumatoid arthritis patient who received 4 gm/day aspirin, none was detectable in her milk (<5mg/100cc).[2] Extremely high doses in the mother could potentially produce slight bleeding in the infant. Because aspirin is implicated in Reye Syndrome, it is a poor choice of analgesic to use in breastfeeding mothers. However, in rheumatic fever patients, it is still one of the anti-inflammatory drugs of choice and a risk-vs-benefit assessment must be done in this case.

In a study of a patient consuming aspirin chronically, salicylate concentrations in milk peaked at 3 hours at a concentration of 10 mg/L following a maternal dose of 975 mg.[3] Maternal plasma levels peaked at 2.25 hours at 108 mg/L. The milk/plasma ratio was reported to be 0.08.

In a study of 8 women following the use of 1 gram oral doses of aspirin, average milk levels of salicylic acid (active metabolite of aspirin) were 2.4 mg/L at 3 hours.[4] The metabolite salicyluric acid, reached a peak of 10.2 mg/L at 9 hours. Averaging total salicylates and salicyluric acid metabolites, the author suggests the relative infant dose would be 9.4% of the maternal dose.

While the direct use of aspirin in infants and children is definitely implicated in Reye syndrome, the use of the 82 mg/d dose in breastfeeding mothers is unlikely to increase the risk of this syndrome. Unfortunately we do not at present know of any dose-response relationship between aspirin and Reye syndrome other than in older children where even low plasma levels of aspirin were implicated in Reye syndrome during viral syndromes such as flu or chickenpox. Therefore, the use of aspirin in breastfeeding mothers is questionable, but the risk is probably low. See ibuprofen or acetaminophen as better choices. Never use these products if the infant has a viral syndrome.

Pregnancy Risk Category: C during first and second trimester
D during third trimester

Lactation Risk Category: L3
L5 in viral syndromes

Adult Concerns: GI ulceration, distress, esophagitis, nephropathy, hepatotoxicity, tinnitus, platelet dysfunction.

Pediatric Concerns: One 16 day old infant developed metabolic acidosis. Mother was consuming 3.9 grams/day of aspirin. Thrombocytopenia, petechaiae and anorexia were reported in an infant of 5 months following exposure to maternal/milk aspirin. Aspirin has definitively been associated with Reye syndrome in infants with viral fevers.

Drug Interactions: May decrease serum levels of other NSAIDs as well as GI distress. Aspirin may antagonize effect of probenecid. Aspirin may increase methotrexate serum levels, and increase free valproic acid plasma levels and valproate toxicity. May increase anticoagulant effect of warfarin.

Relative Infant Dose: 2.5% - 10.8%

Adult Dose: 325-900 mg QID

Alternatives: Ibuprofen, Acetaminophen

T ½	= 2.5-7 hours	M/P	= 0.03-0.08
PHL	=	PB	= 88-93%
Tmax	= 1-2 hours	Oral	= 80-100%
MW	= 180	pKa	=
Vd	= 0.15		

References:
1. Findlay JW, DeAngelis RL, Kearney MF, Welch RM, Findlay JM. Analgesic drugs in breast milk and plasma. Clin Pharmacol Ther 1981; 29 (5):625-633.
2. Erickson SH, Oppenheim GL. Aspirin in breast milk. J Fam Pract 1979; 8 (1):189-190.
3. Bailey DN, Welbert RT, Naylor A. A study of salicylate and caffeine excretion in the breast milk of two nursing mothers. J Anal Toxicol. 1982;6:64-8.
4. Putter J, Satravaha P, Stockhausen H. Quantitative analysis of the main metabolites of acetylsalicylic acid. Comparative analysis in the blood and milk of lactating women. Z Geburtshilfe Perinatol. 1974;178:135-8.

ATENOLOL   L3

Trade: Tenoretic, Tenormin

Other Trades: Apo-Atenolol, Anselol, Noten, Tenlol, Tensig, Antipress

Uses: Beta adrenergic blocker, antihypertensive

AAP: Drugs associated with significant side effects and should be given with caution

Atenolol is a potent cardio-selective beta-blocker. Data conflict on the secretion of atenolol into breastmilk. One author reports an incident of significant bradycardia, cyanosis, low body temperature, and low blood pressure in breastfeeding infant of mother consuming 100 mg atenolol daily while a number of others have failed to detect plasma levels in the neonate or untoward side effects.[1] Data seem to indicate that atenolol secretion into breastmilk is highly variable but may be as high as 10 times greater than for propranolol.

In one study, women taking 50-100 mg/day were found to have M/P ratios of 1.5-6.8. However, even with high M/P ratios, the calculated intake per day (at peak levels) for a breastfeeding infant would only be 0.13 mg.[2] In a study by White, breastmilk levels in one patient were 0.7, 1.2 and 1.8 mg/L of milk at doses of 25, 50 and 100 mg daily respectively.[3] In another study, the estimated daily intake for an infant receiving 500 mL milk per day, would be 0.3 mg.[4] In these five patients who received 100 mg daily, the mean milk concentration of atenolol was 630 µg/L. In a study by Kulas, the amount of atenolol transferred into milk varied from 0.66 mg/L with a maternal dose of 25 mg, 1.2 mg/L with a maternal dose of 50 mg, and 1.7 mg/L with a maternal dose of 100 mg per day.[5] Although atenolol is approved by the AAP, some caution is recommended due to the milk/plasma ratios and the reported problem with one infant.

Pregnancy Risk Category: D

Lactation Risk Category: L3

Adult Concerns: Persistent bradycardia, hypotension, heart failure, dizziness, fatigue, insomnia, lethargy, confusion, impotence, dyspnea, wheezing in asthmatics.

Pediatric Concerns: One report of bradycardia, cyanosis, low body temperature, and hypotension in a breastfeeding infant of mother consuming 100 mg atenolol daily, but other reports do not suggest clinical effects on breastfed infants.

Drug Interactions: Decreased effect when used with aluminum salts, barbiturates, calcium salts, cholestyramine, NSAIDs, ampicillin, rifampin, and salicylates. Beta blockers may reduce the effect of oral sulfonylureas (hypoglycemic agents). Increased toxicity/effect when used with other antihypertensives, contraceptives, MAO inhibitors, cimetidine, and numerous other products. See drug interaction reference for complete listing.

Relative Infant Dose: 6.6%

Adult Dose: 50-100 mg daily.

Alternatives: Propranolol, Metoprolol

T ½	= 6.1 hours	M/P	= 1.5-6.8
PHL	= 6.4 hours	PB	= 5%
Tmax	= 2-4 hours	Oral	= 50-60%
MW	= 266	pKa	= 9.6
Vd	= 1.3		

References:
1. Schimmel MS, Eidelman AI, Wilschanski MA, Shaw D, Jr., Ogilvie RJ, Koren G, Schmimmel MS, Eidelman AJ. Toxic effects of atenolol consumed during breast feeding. J Pediatr 1989; 114 (3):476-478.
2. Liedholm H, Melander A, Bitzen PO, Helm G, Lonnerholm G, Mattiasson I, Nilsson B, Wahlin-Boll E. Accumulation of atenolol and metoprolol in human breast milk. Eur J Clin Pharmacol 1981; 20 (3):229-231.
3. White WB, Andreoli JW, Wong SH, Cohn RD. Atenolol in human plasma and breast milk. Obstet Gynecol 1984; 63 (3 Suppl):42S-44S.

4. Thorley KJ, McAinsh J. Levels of the beta-blockers atenolol and propranolol in the breast milk of women treated for hypertension in pregnancy. Biopharm Drug Dispos 1983; 4 (3):299-301.

5. Kulas J, Lunell NO, Rosing U, Steen B, Rane A. Atenolol and metoprolol. A comparison of their excretion into human breast milk. Acta Obstet Gynecol Scand Suppl 1984; 118:65-69.

ATOMOXETINE   L4

Trade: Strattera
Other Trades:
Uses: Stimulant for treatment of ADHD
AAP: Not reviewed

Atomoxetine is a selective norepinephrine reuptake inhibitor that is presently indicated for the treatment of Attention-Deficit/Hyperactivity Disorder (ADHD). Atomoxetine metabolism is highly variable. One group of poor metabolizers (7%) may have extended half-lives (22 h) and higher plasma levels, while another group of normal metabolizers has a half-life of about 5 hours. No data are available on the transfer of Atomoxetine into human milk. Because this is a lipophilic, neuroactive drug, there is some potential risk coincident with its use in a breastfeeding mother, and mothers should probably be cautioned about its use while breastfeeding.

Pregnancy Risk Category: C

Lactation Risk Category: L4

Adult Concerns: Adverse events include abdominal pain, dyspepsia, vomiting, decreased appetite, dizziness, headache, and cough.

Pediatric Concerns: None reported via milk but no studies are available. If used, reduced weight gain, insomnia, and hyperactivity could occur in the infant.

Drug Interactions: Levels may be increased by inhibitors of CYP2D6 (paroxetine, fluoxetine, quinidine, etc). Albuterol may increase heart rate in patients treated with atomoxetine. Atomoxetine may increase plasma levels of midazolam. Do not use with or within two weeks of the use of a monoamine oxidase inhibitor (MAOI). Do not use in patients with narrow angle glaucoma.

Relative Infant Dose:

Adult Dose: 0.5-1.2 mg/kg/day

Alternatives: Methylphenidate

T ½	= 5.2 hours	M/P	=
PHL	=	PB	= 98%
Tmax	= 1-2 hours	Oral	= 63-94%
MW	= 291	pKa	=
Vd	= 0.85		

References:
1. Pharmaceutical Manufacturers prescribing information, 2003.

ATORVASTATIN CALCIUM   L3

Trade: Lipitor
Other Trades:
Uses: Cholesterol-lowering agent
AAP: Not reviewed

Atorvastatin is a typical HMG Co-A reductase inhibitor for lowering plasma cholesterol levels. It is known to transfer into animal milk, but human studies are not available.[1] Due to its poor oral absorption and high protein binding, it is unlikely that clinically relevant amounts would transfer into human milk. Nevertheless, atherosclerosis is a chronic process and discontinuation of lipid- lowering drugs during pregnancy and lactation should have little to no impact on the outcome of long- term therapy of primary hypercholesterolemia. Cholesterol and other products of cholesterol biosynthesis are essential components for fetal and neonatal development and the use of cholesterol- lowering drugs would not be advisable under most circumstances.

Pregnancy Risk Category: X

Lactation Risk Category: L3

Adult Concerns: Liver dysfunction, rhabdomyolysis with acute renal failure.

Pediatric Concerns: None reported, but the use of these products in lactating women is not recommended.

Drug Interactions: Increased risk of myopathy when used with cyclosporin, fibric acid derivatives, niacin, erythromycin, and azole antifungals (Diflucan, etc). Decreased plasma levels of atorvastatin when used with antacids, or colestipol.

Relative Infant Dose:

Adult Dose: 10-80 mg daily

Alternatives:

T ½	= 14 hours	M/P	=
PHL	=	PB	= 98%
Tmax	= 1-2 hours	Oral	= 12-30%
MW	= 1209	pKa	=
Vd	= 8		

References:
1. Pharmaceutical Manufacturer Prescribing Information. 1999.

ATOVAQUONE AND PROGUANIL   L3

Trade: Malarone
Other Trades:
Uses: Antimalarials
AAP: Not reviewed

Malarone is a fixed combination of atovaquone (250 mg) and proguanil (100 mg) (adult dose). The pediatric chewable tablet contains atovaquone (62.5) and proguanil (25 mg). Malarone is used both to prevent and treat malaria, particularly malaria resistant to certain other drugs. Both adult and pediatric formulations are available for treating pediatric patients down to 11 kg. Only trace quantities of proguanil were found in human milk. Further, while the pharmacokinetics of proguanil is similar in adults and pediatric patients, the elimination half-life of atovaquone is much shorter in pediatric patients (1-2 days) than in adult patients (2-3 days). Elimination half-life ranges from 32 to 84 hours for atovaquone and 12 to 21 hours for proguanil; the half-life of cycloguanil is approximately 14 hours.

For current information contact the CDC web site for information (www.cdc.gov). According to the CDC, breastfeeding mothers with infants less than 11 kg should use mefloquine instead of Malarone.[2]

	Atovaquone	Progaunil
T½	32-84 hours	12-21 hours
Oral bioavailability	23%	Complete
Protein Binding	> 99%	75%

Oral bio Atov=23% prog= complete PB = (atov) >99% PB (prog)= 75%

Pedi dose: One, two, or three MALARONE Pediatric Tablets (62.5 mg atovaquone and 25 mg proguanil HCl) once a day depending on your child's body weight. For children over 40 kg (88 pounds) in weight, one MALARONE tablet (adult dose) once a day.

Pregnancy Risk Category: C

Lactation Risk Category: L3

Adult Concerns: Headache, fever, myalgia, abdominal pain, cough, diarrhea, dyspepsia, back pain, gastritis have been reported.

Pediatric Concerns: None reported via milk.

Drug Interactions: Major reductions in plasma levels of atovaquone have been reported following the use of tetracycline (40%), metoclopramide, rifampin (50%), or rifabutin (34%).

Relative Infant Dose:

Adult Dose: Atovaquone (250 mg); Proguanil (100 mg) daily.

Alternatives: Mefloquine

References:
1. Pharmaceutical Manufacturer Prescribing Information, 2002.
2. http://www.cdc.gov/ncidod/dpd/parasites/malaria/default.htm. 2004.

ATROPINE   L3

Trade: Belladonna, Atropine
Other Trades: Atropine Minims, Atropisol, Isopto-Atropine, Atropt, Eyesule
Uses: Anticholinergic, drying agent
AAP: Maternal Medication Usually Compatible with Breastfeeding

Atropine is a powerful anticholinergic that is well distributed throughout the body.[1] Only small amounts are believed secreted in milk.[2] Effects may be highly variable. Slight absorption together with enhanced neonatal sensitivity creates hazardous potential. Use caution. Avoid if possible but not definitely contraindicated.

Pregnancy Risk Category: C

Lactation Risk Category: L3

Adult Concerns: Dry, hot skin. Decreased flow of breastmilk. Decreased bowel motility, drying of secretions, dilated pupil, and increased heart rate.

Pediatric Concerns: No reports are available, although caution is urged. Anticholinergics have been found in sheep to reduce prolactin production.

Drug Interactions: Phenothiazines, levodopa, antihistamines, may decrease anticholinergic effects of atropine. Increased toxicity when admixed with amantadine and thiazide diuretics.

Relative Infant Dose:

Adult Dose: 0.6 mg every 6 hours

Alternatives:

T ½	= 4.3 hours	M/P	=
PHL	=	PB	= 14-22%
Tmax	= 1 hour	Oral	= 90%
MW	= 289	pKa	= 9.8
Vd	= 2.3-3.6		

References:
1.   Drug Facts and Comparisons 1995 ed. ed. St. Louis: 1995.
2.   Wilson J. Drugs in Breast Milk. New York: ADIS Press 1981.

AZAPROPAZONE   L2

Trade:
Other Trades: Rheumox
Uses: Analgesic
AAP: Maternal Medication Usually Compatible with Breastfeeding

Azapropazone is a partial NSAID and anti-inflammatory. Unlike other NSAIDs its main effect is to stabilize the lysosomal membrane and only to a limited extent does it suppress prostaglandin synthetase. In a study of 4 patients each received 600 mg IV within 2 hours after giving birth and thereafter, they received 600 mg twice daily.[1] Milk levels of azapropazone were measured on days 4 and 6 postpartum. The amount of azapropazone excreted in the breast milk within 12 h ranged from 0.2 mg to 1.3 mg (mean 0.8 mg in 12 h) or an average milk concentration of 2.43 µg/mL. The volume of milk produced during this 12 hour period averaged 329 mL. The relative infant dose over 24 hours would be 2.1% of the maternal dose. The authors did not report side effects in the infants.

Pregnancy Risk Category:

Lactation Risk Category: L2

Adult Concerns: Adverse effects include diarrhea, vomiting, nausea, GI distress, GI bleeding, headache, edema, GI ulceration, and other typical side effects of NSAID drugs.

Pediatric Concerns: None reported via milk in one study.

Drug Interactions: Increased azapropazone levels when mixed with cimetidine. Enhanced anticoagulant effect when mixed with coumarins, and other anticoagulants. Reduced excretion of lithium, and methotrexate when admixed with azapropazone. May block antihypertensive effects of beta-blockers, calcium channel blockers and other antihypertensives.

Relative Infant Dose: 2.1%

Adult Dose: 600 mg twice daily.

Alternatives: Celecoxib

T ½	= 13-14 hours	M/P	=
PHL	=	PB	= 99%
Tmax	= 3-6 hours orally	Oral	= 83%
MW	=	pKa	=
Vd	= 0.17		

References:
1. Bald R, Bernbeck-Betthauser EM, Spahn H, Mutschler E. Excretion of azapropazone in human breast milk. Eur J Clin Pharmacol 1990; 39 (3):271-273.

AZATHIOPRINE   L3

Trade: Imuran
Other Trades: Thioprine
Uses: Immunosuppressive agent
AAP: Not reviewed

Azathioprine is a powerful immunosuppressive agent that is metabolized to 6-Mercaptopurine (6-MP). In two mothers receiving 75 mg azathioprine, the concentration of 6-Mercaptopurine in milk varied from 3.5-4.5 µg/L in one mother and 18 µg/L in the second mother.[1] Both levels were peak milk concentrations at 2 hours following the dose. The authors conclude that these levels would be too low to produce clinical effects in a breastfed infant. Using this data for 6-MP, an infant would absorb only 0.1 % of the weight-adjusted maternal dose, which is probably too low to produce adverse effects in a breastfeeding infant. Plasma levels in treated patients is maintained at 50 ng/mL or higher. One infant continued to breastfeed during therapy and displayed no immunosuppressive effects.

In another study of two infants who were breastfed by mothers receiving 75-100 mg/d azathioprine, milk levels of 6-MP were not measured. But both infants had normal blood counts, no increase in infections, and above-average growth rate.[2] However, caution is recommended.

Four mothers who were receiving 1.2-2.1 mg/kg/day of azathioprine throughout pregnancy and continued postpartum were studied while breastfeeding. Using high-performance liquid chromatography, the mothers' blood concentrations of 6-TGN and 6-MMPN (the metabolites of azathioprine) ranged from 234-291 and 284 to 1178 pmol/100 million RBC, respectively. Neither 6-TGN nor 6-MMPN could be detected in the exposed infants. The authors suggest that breastfeeding while taking azathioprine may be safe in mothers with 'normal' TPMT enzyme activity (the enzyme responsible for metabolizing 6-TGN).[3]

Four case reports were performed with mothers taking between 50 to 100 mg/day of azathioprine. No adverse events were reported in any of the infants, and milk concentrations in two mothers proved to be undetectable.[4]

Ten women at steady state on 75 to 150 mg/day azathioprine provided milk samples on days 3-4, days 7-10 and day 28 after delivery, between 3 and 18 hours after azathioprine administration. 6-MP was detected in only one case, at 1.2 and 7.6 ng/mL at 3 and 6 hours after azathioprine intake on day 28. However, 6-MP and 6-TGN were undetectable in the infants blood. There were no signs of immunosuppression, even in three preterm neonates. The authors suggest that azathioprine therapy should not deter mothers from breastfeeding.[5]

Another study of three mothers taking azathioprine while breastfeeding (doses of 100-175 mg) reported normal blood cell counts in all three infants, and only a low amount of 6-TGN in one infant on day 3. At age 3 weeks, this level decreased below the detectable range.[6]

In a group of 8 lactating women who received azathioprine (75-200 mg/day), levels in milk ranged from 2-50 µg/L.[7] After 6 h an average of 10% of the peak values were measured. The authors estimate the infants dose to be <0.008 mg/kg bodyweight/24 h. They suggest that breastfeeding during treatment with azathioprine seems safe and should be recommended.

In a 31 year old mother with Crohn's disease being treated with 100 mg/day azathioprine, peripheral blood levels of 6-MP and 6-TGN in the infant were undetectable at day 8 or after 3 months of therapy.[8] The infant was reported to be normal after 6 months.

Pregnancy Risk Category: D

Lactation Risk Category: L3

Adult Concerns: Bone marrow suppression, megaloblastic anemia, infections, skin cancers, lymphoma, nausea, vomiting, hepatoxicity, pulmonary dysfunction and pancreatitis.

Pediatric Concerns: None reported in several case reports, but caution is urged.

Drug Interactions: Increased toxicity when used with allopurinol. Reduce azathioprine dose to 1/3 to 1/4 of normal. Use with ACE inhibitors has produced severe leukopenia. It is best to avoid the following drugs when using mercaptopurine or azathioprine: Neuromuscular blocking agents (such as rocuronium, mivacurium, vercuronium, atracurium, tubocurarine), Warfarin, D-penicillamine, Cotrimoxazole, Captopril, Cimetidine, Indomethacin and live vaccines.

Relative Infant Dose: 0.1% - 0.3%

Adult Dose: 1-2.5 mg/kg/day

Alternatives:

T ½	= 0.6 hour	M/P	=
PHL	=	PB	= 30%
Tmax	= 1-2 hours	Oral	= 41-44%
MW	= 277	pKa	=
Vd	= 0.9		

References:

1. Coulam CB, Moyer TP, Jiang NS, Zincke H. Breast-feeding after renal transplantation. Transplant Proc 1982; 14 (3):605-609.
2. Grekas DM, Vasiliou SS, Lazarides AN. Immunosuppressive therapy and breast-feeding after renal transplantation. Nephron 1984; 37 (1):68.
3. Gardiner SJ, Gearry RB, Roberts RL, Zhang M, Barclay ML, Begg EJ. Exposure to thiopurine drugs through breast milk is low based on metabolite concentrations in mother-infant pairs. Br J Clin Pharmacol 2006; 62 (4):453-456.
4. Moretti ME, Verjee Z, Ito S, Koren G. Breast-Feeding During Maternal Use of Azathioprine. Ann Pharmacother 2006; 40:2269-2272.
5. Sau A, Clarke S, Bass J, Kaiser A, Marinaki A, Nelson-Piercy C. Azathioprine and breastfeeding- is it safe? BJOG 2007; 114:498-501.
6. Bernard N, Garayt C, Chol E, Vial T, Descotes J. Prospective clinical and biological follow-up of three breastfed babies from azathioprine-treated mothers. Fundam clin Pharmacol 2007; 21 (suppl.1):62-63. Abstract.
7. Christensen LA, Dahlerup JF, Nielsen MJ, Fallingborg JF, Schmiegelow K. Azathioprine treatment during lactation. Aliment Pharmacol Ther. 2008 Nov 15;28 (10):1209-13. Epub 2008 Aug 30.
8. Zelinkova Z, De Boer IP, Van Dijke MJ, Kuipers EJ, Van Der Woude CJ. Azathioprine treatment during lactation. Aliment Pharmacol Ther. 2009 Jul;30 (1):90-1;

AZELAIC ACID   L3

Trade: Azelex, Finevin
Other Trades: Skinoren
Uses: Topical treatment of acne
AAP: Not reviewed

Azelaic acid is a dicarboxylic acid derivative normally found in whole grains and animal products. Azelaic acid, when applied as a cream, produces a significant reduction of P. acnes and has an antikeratinizing effect as well. Small amounts of azelaic acid are normally present in human milk.[1] Azelaic acid is only modestly absorbed via skin (<4%), and it is rapidly metabolized. The amount absorbed does not change the levels normally found in plasma nor milk. Due to its poor penetration into plasma and rapid half-life (45 min), it is not likely to penetrate milk or produce untoward effects in a breastfed infant.

Pregnancy Risk Category: B

Lactation Risk Category: L3

Adult Concerns: Pruritus, burning, stinging, erythema, dryness, peeling and skin irritation.

Pediatric Concerns: None reported via milk. Normal constituent of milk.

Drug Interactions:

Relative Infant Dose:

Adult Dose: Apply topical BID

Alternatives:

T ½	= 45 minutes	M/P	=
PHL	=	PB	=
Tmax	=	Oral	=
MW	= 188	pKa	=
Vd	=		

References:
1. Pharmaceutical Manufacturer Prescribing Information. 1999.

AZELASTINE   L3

Trade: Astelin, Optivar
Other Trades: Azep, Rhinolast, Optilast
Uses: Antihistamine
AAP: Not reviewed

Azelastine (Astelin) is an antihistamine for oral, intranasal and ophthalmic administration. It is effective in treating seasonal and perennial rhinitis and nonallergic vasomotor rhinitis. Ophthalmically, it is effective for allergic conjunctivitis (itchy eyes). Oral bioavailability is 80%, and intranasal bioavailability is only 40%. No data are available on the transfer of azelastine into human milk. The doses used intranasally and ophthalmically are so low that it is extremely unlikely to produce clinically relevant levels in human milk. Oral administration could potentially lead to slightly higher levels but azelastine is relatively devoid of serious side effects and it is doubtful that any would occur in a breastfed infant. However, this is an extremely bitter product. It is possible that even miniscule amounts in milk could alter the taste of milk leading to rejection by the infant.

Pregnancy Risk Category: C

Lactation Risk Category: L3

Adult Concerns: Intranasal: nasal burning and bitter taste, headache, somnolence. Orally: drowsiness and bitter taste. Ophthalmic: transient eye burning/stinging, headache, and bitter taste.

Pediatric Concerns: None reported via milk. Levels in milk are unlikely to pose a problem. May impart bitter taste to milk, infant may reject milk.

Drug Interactions: Avoid use in asthmatics. Cimetidine significantly increases plasma levels of azelastine.

Relative Infant Dose:

Adult Dose: Variable: 1-2 sprays (137 μg/spray) per nostrile BID.

Alternatives: Loratadine, cetirizine

T ½	= 22 hours	M/P	=
PHL	=	PB	= 88%
Tmax	= 2-3 hours	Oral	= 80%
MW	– 418	pKa	=
Vd	= 14.5		

References:
1.   Pharmaceutical Manufacturers prescribing information, 2003.

AZITHROMYCIN   L2

Trade: Zithromax
Other Trades:
Uses: Antibiotic, macrolide
AAP: Not reviewed

Azithromycin belongs to the erythromycin family. It has an extremely long half-life, particularly in tissues.[1] Azithromycin is concentrated for long periods in phagocytes, which are known to be present in human milk. In one study of a patient who received 1 gm initially followed by 500 mg doses each at 24 hr intervals, the concentration of azithromycin in breastmilk varied from 0.64 mg/L (initially) to 2.8 mg/L on day three.[2] The predicted dose of azithromycin received by the infant would be approximately 0.4 mg/kg/day. This would suggest that the level of azithromycin ingested by a breastfeeding infant is not clinically relevant. New pediatric formulations of azithromycin have been recently introduced. Pediatric dosing is 10 mg/kg STAT followed by 5 mg/kg per day for up to 5 days.

Pregnancy Risk Category: B

Lactation Risk Category: L2

Adult Concerns: Diarrhea, loose stools, abdominal pain, vomiting, nausea.

Pediatric Concerns: None   reported   via   breastmilk.   Pediatric formulations are available.

Drug Interactions: Aluminum and magnesium-containing antacids may slow, but not reduce absorption of azithromycin. Increased effect/toxicity when used with tacrolimus, alfentanil, astemizole, terfenadine, loratadine, carbamazepine, cyclosporine, digoxin, disopyramide, triazolam.

Relative Infant Dose: 5.9%

Adult Dose: 250-500 mg daily.

Alternatives:

T ½	= 48-68 hours	M/P	=
PHL	=	PB	= 7-51%
Tmax	= 3-4 hours	Oral	= 37%
MW	= 749	pKa	=
Vd	= 23-31		

References:
1.   Pharmaceutical Manufacturer Prescribing Information. 1996.
2.   Kelsey JJ, Moser LR, Jennings JC, Munger MA. Presence of azithromycin breast milk concentrations: a case report. Am J Obstet Gynecol 1994; 170 (5 Pt 1):1375-1376.

AZTREONAM   L2

Trade: Azactam
Other Trades:
Uses: Antibiotic
AAP: Maternal Medication Usually Compatible with Breastfeeding

Aztreonam is a monobactam antibiotic whose structure is similar but different from the penicillins and is used for documented gram-negative sepsis. Following a single 1 g IV dose, breastmilk level was 0.18 mg/L at 2 hours and 0.22 mg/L at 4 hours.[1] An infant would ingest approximately 33.0 μg/kg/day or <0.03% of the maternal dose per day (not weight adjusted). The manufacturer reports that less than 1% of a maternal dose is transferred into milk.[2] Due to poor oral absorption (<1%), no untoward effects would be expected in nursing infants, aside from changes in GI flora. Aztreonam is commonly used in pediatric units. In another study of a patient early postpartum receiving a 1 gm intravenous injection, aztreonam levels in milk at 6 hours were 0.4 μg/mL to 1.0 μg/mL.[3]

Pregnancy Risk Category: B

Lactation Risk Category: L2

Adult Concerns: Changes in GI flora, diarrhea, rash, elevations of hepatic function tests.

Pediatric Concerns: None reported via milk in two cases.

Drug Interactions: Check hypersensitivity to penicillins and other beta-lactams. Requires dosage adjustment in renal failure.

Relative Infant Dose: 0.2% - 1%

Adult Dose: 1-2 g BID or QID

Alternatives:

T ½	= 1.7 hours	M/P	= 0.005
PHL	= 2.6 hours	PB	= 60%
Tmax	= 0.6-1.3 hours	Oral	= <1%
MW	= 435	pKa	=
Vd	= 0.26-0.36		

References:

1. Fleiss PM, Richwald GA, Gordon J, Stern M, Frantz M, Devlin RG. Aztreonam in human serum and breast milk. Br J Clin Pharmacol 1985; 19 (4):509-511.

2.   Pharmaceutical Manufacturer Prescribing Information. 1996.
3.   Ito K, Hirose R, Tamaya T, Yamada Y, Izumi K. Pharmacokinetic and clinical studies on aztreonam in the perinatal period. Jpn J Antibiot. 1990 Apr;43 (4):719-26.

BACLOFEN   L2

Trade: Lioresal, Atrofen
Other Trades: Novo-Baclofen, Apo-Baclofen, Clofen
Uses: Skeletal muscle relaxant
AAP: Maternal Medication Usually Compatible with Breastfeeding

Baclofen inhibits spinal reflexes and is used to reverse spasticity associated with multiple sclerosis or spinal cord lesions. Animal studies indicate baclofen inhibits prolactin release and may inhibit lactation. Small amounts of baclofen are secreted into milk. In one mother given a 20 mg oral dose, total consumption by infant over a 26 hour period is estimated to be 22 µg, about 0.1% of the maternal dose (authors estimate).[1] Milk levels ranged from 0.6 µmol/L (138 µg/L C_{max}) to 0.052 µmol/L at 26 hours. The maternal plasma and milk half-lives were 3.9 hours and 5.6 hours, respectively. It is quite unlikely that baclofen administered intrathecally would be secreted into milk in clinically relevant quantities.

Pregnancy Risk Category: C

Lactation Risk Category: L2

Adult Concerns: Drowsiness, excitement, dry mouth, urinary retention, tremor, rigidity, and wide pupils.
Pediatric Concerns: None reported.

Drug Interactions: Decreased effect when used with lithium. Increased effect of opiate analgesics, CNS depressants, alcohol (sedation), tricyclic antidepressants, clindamycin (neuromuscular blockade), guanabenz, MAO inhibitors.

Relative Infant Dose: 6.9%

Adult Dose: 5-25 mg TID

Alternatives:

T ½	= 3-4 hours	M/P	=
PHL	=	PB	= 30%
Tmax	= 2-3 hours	Oral	= Complete
MW	= 214	pKa	=
Vd	=		

References:
1. Eriksson G, Swahn CG. Concentrations of baclofen in serum and breast milk from a lactating woman. Scand J Clin Lab Invest 1981; 41 (2):185-187.

BALSALAZIDE DISODIUM   L3

Trade: Colazal
Other Trades:
Uses: Antiinflammatory drug for ulcerative colitis
AAP: Not reviewed

Balsalazide is a prodrug that is metabolized to mesalamine (5-aminosalicylic acid).[1] Balsalazide is delivered intact to the colon where it is cleaved by bacterial enzymes to release the active drug mesalamine. The oral absorption of balsalazide is very low. Less than 1% of the parent drug is recovered in the urine. Because it is metabolized to mesalamine, see mesalamine for breastmilk concentrations.

Pregnancy Risk Category: B

Lactation Risk Category: L3

Adult Concerns: Headache, abdominal pain, nausea, diarrhea, vomiting, respiratory infection, arthralgia have been reported.

Pediatric Concerns: Watery diarrhea with mesalamine in one breastfeeding infant. Close observation recommended but it can probably be used relatively safely in breastfeeding mothers.

Drug Interactions: May increase risk of myelosuppression when admixed with mercaptopurine, azathioprine. Tamarind may increase absorption of salicylates and cause salicylate toxicity.

Relative Infant Dose:

Adult Dose: 6.75 grams/day

Alternatives: Mesalamine, olsalazine

T ½	=	M/P	=
PHL	=	PB	= 99%
Tmax	= 1-2 hours	Oral	= <1%
MW	= 437	pKa	=
Vd	=		

References:
1.   Pharmaceutial Manufacturers Prescribing information, 2009.

BECLOMETHASONE   L2

Trade: Vanceril, Beclovent, Beconase, Becotide, Qvar
Other Trades: Propaderm, Becloforte, Aldecin,
Uses: Intranasal, intrapulmonary steroid
AAP: Not reviewed

Beclomethasone is a potent steroid that is generally used via inhalation in asthma or via intranasal administration for allergic rhinitis. Due to its potency, only very small doses are generally used and, therefore, minimal plasma levels are attained. Intranasal absorption is generally minimal.[1,2] Due to small doses administered, absorption into maternal plasma is extremely small. Therefore, it is unlikely that these doses would produce clinical significance in a breastfeeding infant. See corticosteroids.

Pregnancy Risk Category: C

Lactation Risk Category: L2

Adult Concerns: When administered intranasally or via inhalation, adrenal suppression is very unlikely. Complications include headaches, hoarseness, bronchial irritation, oral candidiasis, cough. When used orally, complications may include adrenal suppression.

Pediatric Concerns: None reported via milk and inhalation or intranasal use. Oral doses could suppress the adrenal cortex, and induce premature closure of the epiphysis, but would require high doses.

Drug Interactions: Corticosteroids have few drug interactions.

Relative Infant Dose:

Adult Dose: 504-840 μg daily.

Alternatives:

T ½	= 15 hours	M/P	=
PHL	=	PB	= 87%
Tmax	=	Oral	= 90% (oral)
MW	= 409	pKa	=
Vd	=		

References:
1. Pharmaceutical Manufacturer Prescribing Information. 2009.
2. McEvoy GE. AFHS Drug Information. New York, NY: 2008.

BENAZEPRIL HCL   L2

Trade: Lotensin, Lotrel
Other Trades:
Uses: Antihypertensive, ACE inhibitor
AAP: Not reviewed

Benazepril belongs to the ACE inhibitor family. Oral absorption is rather poor (37%). The active component (benazeprilat) reaches a peak at approximately 2 hours after ingestion.[1] In a patient receiving 20 mg daily for 3 days, milk levels averaged 0.15 ng/L.[2] Peak benazepril levels (C_{max}) were 0.92 ng/L. Thus, the levels in milk are almost unmeasurable. The manufacturer suggests a newborn infant ingesting only breastmilk would receive less than 0.1% of the mg/kg maternal dose of benazepril and benazeprilat. My calculations suggest much less, or a maximum of 0.00005% of the weight-adjusted maternal dose. Lotrel is a combination product containing benazepril and amlodipine, a calcium channel blocker.

Pregnancy Risk Category: D during second and third trimesters

Lactation Risk Category: L2

Adult Concerns: Significant fetal morbidity, hypotension. Contraindicated in 3rd trimester of pregnancy.

Pediatric Concerns: Levels in milk are reportedly exceedingly low. Unlikely to cause problems.

Drug Interactions: Decreased bioavailability with antacids. Reduced hypotensive effect with NSAIDS. Phenothiazines increase hypotensive effect. Allopurinol dramatically increase hypersensitivities (Steven-Johnson Syn.). ACE inhibitors dramatically increase digoxin levels. Lithium levels may be significantly increased with ACE use. Elevated potassium levels with oral potassium supplements.

Relative Infant Dose:

Adult Dose: 20-40 mg daily.

Alternatives: Enalapril, Captopril

T ½	= 10-11 hours	M/P	= 0.01
PHL	=	PB	= 96.7%
Tmax	= 0.5 - 1 hr.	Oral	= 37%
MW	= 424	pKa	=
Vd	=		

References:
1.   Pharmaceutical Manufacturer Prescribing Information. 2005.

BENDROFLUMETHIAZIDE   L4

Trade: Naturetin
Other Trades: Aprinox, Aprinox, Berkozide, Centyl, Urizid
Uses: Thiazide diuretic
AAP: Maternal Medication Usually Compatible with Breastfeeding

Bendroflumethiazide is a thiazide diuretic sometimes used to suppress lactation. In one study, the clinician found this thiazide to effectively inhibit lactation.[1] Use with caution. Not generally recommended in breastfeeding mothers.

Pregnancy Risk Category: C

Lactation Risk Category: L4

Adult Concerns: Diuresis, fluid loss, leukopenia, hypotension, dizziness, headache, vertigo, reduced milk production.

Pediatric Concerns: None reported, but may inhibit lactation.

Drug Interactions: Enhanced hyponatremia and hypotension when used with ACE inhibitors. May elevate lithium levels.

Relative Infant Dose:

Adult Dose: 2.5-10 mg daily.

Alternatives: Hydrochlorothiazide

T ½	= 3-3.9 hours	M/P	=
PHL	=	PB	= 94%
Tmax	= 2-4 hours	Oral	= Complete
MW	= 421	pKa	=
Vd	= 1,48		

References:
1. Healy M. Suppressing lactation with oral diuretics. The Lancet 1961;1353-1354.

BENZONATATE   L3

Trade: Tessalon Perles
Other Trades:
Uses: Antitussive
AAP: Advise not to breastfeed

Benzonatate is a non-narcotic cough suppressant similar to the local anesthetic tetracaine. It anesthetizes stretch receptors in respiratory passages, dampening their activity and reducing the cough reflex.[1] There are little pharmacokinetic data on this product and no data on transfer into human milk. Because codeine is almost equally effective as an antitussive, and because we know that codeine only marginally transfers into human milk, it is probably a preferred antitussive in breastfeeding mothers. While new data suggests that hypermetabolizers may increase the risks of using codeine in a breastfeeding mother,[2] used in small doses as an antitussive, codeine would still preferred over benzonatate in breastfeeding women. In addition, benzonatate in overdose (as little as 2 capsules in a child), is a very dangerous product, leading to seizures with cardiac arrest and death, particularly in children.

Pregnancy Risk Category: C

Lactation Risk Category: L3

Adult Concerns: Sedation, headache, dizziness, constipation, nausea, pruritus have been reported. Para-aminobenzoic acid is a metabolite of benzonatate. Severe allergic reactions have been reported in patients who are allergic to PABA. Severe sensitivity reactions to benzonatate have resulted in respiratory side effects such as bronchospasm, laryngospasm and cardiac arrest. Excessive absorption following chewing of capsules may result in the rapid numbness of mouth and throat and in extreme cases pulmonary aspiration may occur. Do not overdose and do not chew capsules.

Pediatric Concerns: None reported via milk. Dangerous in overdose. Use with great caution.

Drug Interactions:

Relative Infant Dose:

Adult Dose: 100 mg TID

Alternatives: Codeine

T ½	= <8 hours	M/P	=
PHL	=	PB	=
Tmax	= 20 minutes	Oral	= Good
MW	= 603	pKa	=
Vd	=		

References:

1.   Pharmaceutical manufacturer prescribing information. 2005.
2.   Koren G, Cairns J, Chitayat D, Gaedigk A, Leeder SJ. Pharmacogenetics of morphine poisoning in a breastfed neonate of a codeine-prescribed mother. Lancet 2006 Aug 19; 368 (9536):704.

BENZTROPINE MESYLATE   L3

Trade: Cogentin

Other Trades:

Uses: Anticholinergic for relief of antipsychotic agent-induced extrapyramidal reactions

AAP: Not reviewed

Benztropine is commonly used for the relief of parkinsonian signs (extrapyramidal reactions) commonly seen following the use of antipsychotic agents. Benztropine has about one-half the anticholinergic effects of atropine, and has antihistamine effects.

Its transfer into human milk has not been studied. Some caution is recommended if this product is used in breastfeeding mothers as some animal studies suggest anticholinergics reduce prolactin levels. The infant should be observed for drying symptoms, including dry mouth, reduced tearing, urinary retention, elevated body temperature, reduced sweating, tachycardia, and constipation.

Pregnancy Risk Category: C

Lactation Risk Category: L3

Adult Concerns: Side effects are typically those of anticholinergics and include : Confusion. drug-induced psychosis, hyperpyrexia, paralytic ileus, exaggeration of glaucoma and interocular pressure, reduced sweating and hyperpyrexia.

Pediatric Concerns: None reported but observe for anticholinergic symptoms including drying, constipation, reduced urine output.

Drug Interactions: Concomitant use with other products with anticholinergic symptoms may be hazardous.

Relative Infant Dose:

Adult Dose: 1-2 mg daily.

Alternatives:

T ½	= Long	M/P	=
PHL	=	PB	=
Tmax	= 1-2 hours	Oral	= Poor
MW	= 307	pKa	=
Vd	=		

References:
1.   Pharmaceutical manufacturers prescribing information. 2005.

BEPRIDIL HCL   L4

Trade: Vascor, Bepadin
Other Trades:
Uses: Antihypertensive, calcium channel blocker
AAP: Not reviewed

Bepridil is a calcium channel blocker that is known to have anti-anginal properties, but poorly characterized type 1 anti-arrhythmic and anti-hypertensive properties. It is not related chemically to other calcium channel blockers such as diltiazem HCl, nifedipine and verapamil HCl.

Following therapy with bepridil, milk levels were reported to approach 1/3 of serum levels.[1,2] As with some calcium channel blockers, this family has been found to produce embryotoxic effects and should be used cautiously in pregnant women. Long half-life, enhanced oral absorption, and potency of this compound would increase the danger in nursing infant. Caution is recommended if used in nursing mother. There are numerous other preferred CCBs.

Pregnancy Risk Category: C

Lactation Risk Category: L4

Adult Concerns: Bepridil is contraindicated in patients with history of serious ventricular arrhythmias, patients with sick sinus syndrome or patients with second- or third-degree AV block, patients with low blood pressure (less than 90 mm Hg systolic), patients with uncompensated cardiac insufficiency, patients with congenital QT interval prolongation and patients taking other drugs that prolong QT interval.

Pediatric Concerns: None reported, but other calcium channel blockers may be preferred. See nifedipine.

Drug Interactions: H2 blockers may enhance oral absorption of bepridil. Beta blockers may enhance hypotensive effect. Bepridil may increase carbamazepine, cyclosporin, digitalis, quinidine, theophylline levels when used with these products.

Relative Infant Dose:

Adult Dose: 300 mg daily.

Alternatives: Nifedipine, Nimodipine, Verapamil

T ½	= 42 hours	M/P	= 0.33
PHL	=	PB	= >99%
Tmax	= 2-3 hours	Oral	= 60%
MW	= 367	pKa	=
Vd	= 8		

References:
1. Pharmaceutical Manufacturer Prescribing Information. 2010.
2. Drug Facts and Comparisons St. Louis: 2010.

BETAMETHASONE   L3

Trade: Betameth, Celestone

Other Trades: Beben, Betadermetnesol, Diprolene, Dipr, Betnovate, Betnelan, Diprosone

Uses: Synthetic corticosteroid

AAP: Not reviewed

Betamethasone is a potent long-acting steroid. It generally produces less sodium and fluid retention than other steroids.[1] See prednisone.

Pregnancy Risk Category: C

Lactation Risk Category: L3

Adult Concerns: See prednisone.

Pediatric Concerns: None reported, used in pediatric patients.

Drug Interactions:

Relative Infant Dose:

Adult Dose: 2.4-4.8 mg BID or TID

Alternatives:

T ½	= 5.6 hours	M/P	=
PHL	=	PB	= 64%
Tmax	= 10-36 minutes	Oral	= Complete
MW	= 392	pKa	=
Vd	=		

References:
1. Drug Facts and Comparisons 1995 ed. ed. St. Louis: 1995.

BETAXOLOL   L3

Trade: Kerlone, Betoptic
Other Trades:
Uses: Beta blocker antihypertensive
AAP: Not reviewed

Betaxolol is a long-acting, cardioselective beta blocker primarily used for glaucoma but can be used orally for hypertension. One report by the manufacturer reports side effects which occurred in one nursing infant.[1] Many in this family readily transfer into human milk (see atenolol, acebutolol), others do so poorly (propranolol, metoprolol). Betaxolol when use ophthalmically, is apparently poorly absorbed systemically as no evidence of beta blockade can be found in patients following its use ophthalmically.

In a study of 28 women consuming 10 mg betaxolol during the perinatal period, the milk/plasma ratio in 3 patients was 3.0.[3] Note this was done early postnatally in colostrum and may not at all reflect postnatal levels in mature milk. In one case where the drug was administered 3 hours prior to delivery, colostrum levels were 48 µg/L at 24 h postpartum and 3 µg/L at 72 h postpartum. Nothing in this study should reflect levels in mature milk.

Pregnancy Risk Category: C

Lactation Risk Category: L3

Adult Concerns: Hypotension, bradycardia, fatigue.

Pediatric Concerns: No data is available on its transfer to milk. However, when use ophthalmically, no systemic beta blockade was noted, suggesting plasma levels are low to nil. Milk levels are likely low as well.

Drug Interactions: Decreased effect when used with aluminum salts, barbiturates, calcium salts, cholestyramine, NSAIDs, ampicillin, rifampin, and salicylates. Beta blockers may reduce the effect of oral sulfonylureas (hypoglycemic agents). Increased toxicity/effect when used with other antihypertensives, contraceptives, MAO inhibitors, cimetidine, and numerous other products. See drug interaction reference for complete listing.

Relative Infant Dose:

Adult Dose: 10 mg daily.

Alternatives: Propranolol, Metoprolol

T ½	= 14-22 hours	M/P	= 2.5-3.0
PHL	=	PB	= 50%
Tmax	= 3 hours	Oral	= 89%
MW	= 307	pKa	=
Vd	= 4.9		

References:

1. Pharmaceutical Manufacturer Prescribing Information. 1995.
2. Beresford R & Heel RC: Betaxolol: a review of its pharmacodynamic and pharmacokinetic properties, and therapeutic efficacy in hypertension. Drugs 1986; 31:6-28.
3. Morselli PL, Boutroy MJ, & Thenot JP: Pharmacokinetics of antihypertensive drugs in the neonatal period. Dev Pharmacol Ther 1989; 13:190-198.

BETHANECHOL CHLORIDE | L4

Trade: Urabeth, Urecholine

Other Trades: Duvoid, Urocarb, Myotonine

Uses: Cholinergic stimulant-agonist for urinary retention

AAP: Not reviewed

Bethanechol is a cholinergic stimulant useful for urinary retention. Although poorly absorbed from GI tract, no reports on entry into breastmilk are available. However, it could conceivably cause abdominal cramps, colicky pain, nausea, salivation, bronchial constriction, or diarrhea in infants. There are several reports of discomfort in nursing infants.[1] Use cautiously.

Pregnancy Risk Category: C

Lactation Risk Category: L4

Adult Concerns: Gastric distress such as colicky pain, cramping, nausea, salivation, breathing difficulties, diarrhea, hypotension, heart block, headache, urinary urgency. Contraindicated in patients with asthma, bradycardia, hypotension, epilepsy, etc.

Pediatric Concerns: GI distress, discomfort, diarrhea.

Drug Interactions: Bethanechol when used with ganglionic blockers may lead to significant hypotension. Bethanechol effects may be antagonized by procainamide and quinidine.

Relative Infant Dose:

Adult Dose: 10-50 mg BID-QID

Alternatives:

T ½	= 1-2 hours	M/P	=
PHL	=	PB	=
Tmax	= 60-90 minutes (oral)	Oral	= Poor
MW	= 197	pKa	=
Vd	=		

References:
1. Shore MF. Drugs can be dangerous during pregnancy and lactation. Can Pharmaceut J 1970; 103:358.

BEVACIZUMAB   L3

Trade: Avastin
Other Trades:
Uses: Immune modulator, VEGF inhibitor
AAP: Not reviewed

Bevacizumab is a recombinant humanized antibody that binds all forms of vascular endothelial growth factor (VEGF).[1] It has indications for the treatment of metastatic colorectal cancer, breast cancer, glioblastoma, and other forms of cancer. Recently, a number of reports have described the off-label use of intravitreally injected bevacizumab for the treatment of macular degeneration.

It has an approximate MW of 149 k Daltons. While we have no reports on its use in breastfeeding mothers, size alone would largely exclude it from the milk compartment. When used intravitreally, the dose (1.25 mg) is much lower than via systemic administration (5-10 mg/kg), and it is largely sequestered in the eye[2], thus plasma levels (and milk) would be be exceedingly low. The intravitreal use of this drug is probably compatible with breastfeeding. The systemic use of this drug would not be compatible with breastfeeding.

Pregnancy Risk Category: C

Lactation Risk Category: L3 intravitreal use
                                L5 sytemic use

Adult Concerns: Adverse reactions include: gastrointestinal perforations, surgery and wound healing complications, hemorrhage, venous thromboembolic events, neutropenia and infection, slight proteinuria, congestive heart failure, hypertension, diarrhea, leukopenia.

Pediatric Concerns: None reported via milk. Reduced growth in epiphyseal growth plates in monkey studies.

Drug Interactions: None yet reported.

Relative Infant Dose:

Adult Dose: 5-15 mg/kg every 2-3 weeks

Alternatives:

T ½	= 20 days	M/P	=
PHL	=	PB	=
Tmax	=	Oral	= Nil
MW	= 149,000	pKa	=
Vd	=		

References:
1. Pharmaceutical manufacturers prescribing information, 2009.
2. Julien S, Heiduschka P, Hofmeister S, Schraermeyer U. Immunohistochemical localisation of intravitreally injected bevacizumab at the posterior pole of the primate eye: implication for the treatment of retinal vein occlusion. Br J Ophthalmol. Oct 2008;92 (10):1424-1428.

BIMATOPROST L3

Trade: Lumigan
Other Trades:
Uses: Antiglaucoma agent
AAP: Not reviewed

Bimatoprost is used in open-angle glaucoma or ocular hypertension to reduce intraocular pressure. It is a synthetic structural analog of prostaglandin, and it mimics the effects of naturally occurring prostamides. Bimatoprost increases the outflow of aqueous humor through the trabecular meshwork and uveocleral routes.[1] No breastfeeding data are available. However, after intraocular administration, plasma levels peak at 10 minutes, then fall rapidly to undetectable levels within 1.5 hours. Combined with low plasma levels and high protein binding, it is unlikely this product would produce measurable levels in human milk.

Pregnancy Risk Category: C

Lactation Risk Category: L3

Adult Concerns: Adverse effects include conjunctival hyperemia, growth of eyelashes, and ocular pruritus.

Pediatric Concerns: No data are available.

Drug Interactions: Increase intraocular pressure is seen when used with latanoprost.

Relative Infant Dose:

Adult Dose: 1 drop every evening

Alternatives:

T ½	= 45 minutes	M/P	=
PHL	=	PB	= 88%
Tmax	= 10 minutes	Oral	=
MW	= 415	pKa	=
Vd	= 0.67		

References:
1.   Pharmaceutical Manufacturer Prescribing Information. 2004.

BIOTIN   L1

Trade:
Other Trades:
Uses: Vitamin B-7
AAP: Not reviewed

Biotin, also known as vitamin H or B7, is a coenzyme that assists in many metabolic chemical conversions, and assists in the metabolism of fatty acids, leucine and in gluconeogenesis. It is also required for normal neuronal and hematopoietic function. Symptoms of biotin deficiency include thinning of hair, skin rash, and depression. The recommended daily dose of biotin for a pregnant female is 30 μg/day, while that of a lactating female is 35 μg/day. An infant less than 6 months old needs 0.9 μg/kg/day, while an infant over 6 months should get 6 μg/day.[1] Levels of biotin in human milk range from 5 to 9 μg/L, indicating that there is active transport of biotin into milk.[2] No adverse effects have been found, nor has a toxic upper intake been established.

Pregnancy Risk Category:

Lactation Risk Category: L1

Adult Concerns: None.

Pediatric Concerns: None. Recommended dietary factor.

Drug Interactions:

Relative Infant Dose:

Adult Dose:

Alternatives:

T ½	=	M/P	=
PHL	=	PB	=
Tmax	=	Oral	= Complete
MW	= 244	pKa	=
Vd	=		

References:
1. Dietary Reference Intakes for Thiamin, Riboflavin, Niacin, Vitamin B6, Folate, Vitamin B12, Pantothenic Acid, Biotin, and Choline. Food and Nutrition Board. Institude of Medicine. Washington DC: National Academy Press; 1998.
2. Picciano MF. Handbook of milk composition. Jensen RG, ed. San Diego: Academic Press; 1995.

BISACODYL   L2

Trade: Bisacodyl, Dacodyl, Dulcolax, Fleet, Alophen, Correctol, Carter's Little Pills

Other Trades: Bisacolax, Laxit, Apo-Bisacodyl, Bisalax, Durolax, Paxolax

Uses: Laxative

AAP: Not reviewed

Bisacodyl is a stimulant laxative that selectively stimulates colon contractions and defecation. It has only limited secretion into breastmilk due to poor gastric absorption and subsequently minimal systemic levels.[1] Little or no known harmful effects on infants.

Pregnancy Risk Category: C

Lactation Risk Category: L2

Adult Concerns: Diarrhea, GI cramping, rectal irritation.

Pediatric Concerns: None reported via milk.

Drug Interactions: By speeding emptying of GI tract may reduce efficacy of warfarin, and other products by reducing absorption. Decreased effect of bisacodyl when coadministered with cimetidine, famotidine, ranitidine, or nizatidine. Numerous drug interactions, check other references.

Relative Infant Dose:

Adult Dose: 10-15 mg daily.

Alternatives:

T ½	= 16 hours	M/P	=
PHL	=	PB	=
Tmax	=	Oral	= < 5%
MW	= 361	pKa	=
Vd	=		

References:
1. Vorherr H. Drug excretion in breast milk. Postgrad Med 1974; 56 (4):97-104.

BISMUTH·SUBSALICYLATE | L3

Trade: Pepto-Bismol
Other Trades: Bismuth Liquid
Uses: Antisecretory, antimicrobial salt
AAP: Drugs whose effect on nursing infants is unknown but may be of concern

Bismuth subsalicylate is present in many diarrhea mixtures. Although bismuth salts are poorly absorbed from the maternal GI tract, significant levels of salicylate could be absorbed from these products.[1] While to date, bismuth subsalicylate and other nonacetylated salicylates have not been associated with Reye's syndrome, this drug should not be routinely used in breastfeeding women. Some forms (Parepectolin, Infantol Pink) may contain a tincture of opium (morphine).

Pregnancy Risk Category: C during first trimester
                                D during second and third trimester

Lactation Risk Category: L3

Adult Concerns: Constipation, salicylate poisoning (tinnitus). May enhance risk of Reye 's syndrome in children.

Pediatric Concerns: Risk of Reye syndrome in neonates, but has not been reported with this product in a breastfed infant.

Drug Interactions: May reduce effects of tetracyclines, and uricosurics. May increase toxicity of aspirin, warfarin, hypoglycemics.

Relative Infant Dose:

Adult Dose: 524-2096 mg daily.

Alternatives:

T ½	=	M/P	=
PHL	=	PB	=
Tmax	=	Oral	= Poor
MW	= 362	pKa	=
Vd	=		

References:
1. Findlay JW, DeAngelis RL, Kearney MF, Welch RM, Findlay JM. Analgesic drugs in breast milk and plasma. Clin Pharmacol Ther 1981; 29 (5):625-633.

BISOPROLOL   L3

Trade: Ziac, Zebeta
Other Trades: Amizide, Dichlotride, Emcor, Monocor
Uses: Beta-adrenergic antihypertensive
AAP: Not reviewed

Bisoprolol is a typical beta-blocker used to treat hypertension. The manufacturer states that small amounts (<2%) are secreted into milk of animals.[1] Others in this family are known to produce problems in lactating infants (see atenolol, acebutolol). Propranolol and metoprolol are ideal alternatives. Ziac is a combination of bisoprolol and hydrochlorothiazide.

Pregnancy Risk Category: C

Lactation Risk Category: L3

Adult Concerns: Bradycardia, hypotension, fatigue, excessive fluid loss.

Pediatric Concerns: None reported with this product, but other beta blockers have produced hypotension, hypoglycemia. See metoprolol as an alternative.

Drug Interactions: Decreased effect when used with aluminum salts, barbiturates, calcium salts, cholestyramine, NSAIDs, ampicillin, rifampin, and salicylates. Beta blockers may reduce the effect of oral sulfonylureas (hypoglycemic agents). Increased toxicity/effect when used with other antihypertensives, contraceptives, MAO inhibitors, cimetidine, and numerous other products. See drug interaction reference for complete listing.

Relative Infant Dose:

Adult Dose: 5-10 mg daily.

Alternatives: Propranolol, Metoprolol

T ½	= 9-12 hours	M/P	=
PHL	=	PB	= 30%
Tmax	= 2 - 3 hours	Oral	= 80%
MW	= 325	pKa	=
Vd	=		

References:
1. Pharmaceutical Manufacturer Prescribing Information. 1995.

BLACK COHOSH   L4

Trade: Bane berry, Black Snakeroot, Bugbane, Squaw root, Rattle root
Other Trades:
Uses: Herbal estrogenic compound
AAP: Not reviewed

The roots and rhizomes of this herb are used medicinally. Traditional uses include the treatment of dysmenorrhea, dyspepsia, rheumatism, and as an antitussive. It has also been used as an insect repellant. The standardized extract, called Remifemin, has been used in Germany for menopausal management.[1]

Black cohosh contains a number of alkaloids including N-methylcytosine, other tannins, and terpenoids. It is believed that the isoflavones or formononetin components may bind to estrogenic receptors.[2] Intraperitoneal injection of the extract selectively inhibits release of luteinizing hormone with no effect on the follicle-stimulating (FSH) hormone, or prolactin.[3] The data seems to suggest that this product interacts strongly at certain specific estrogen receptors and might be useful as estrogen replacement therapy in postmenopausal women although this has not been well studied. More studies are needed to address its usefulness in postmenopausal women and osteoporotic states.[1]

Other effects of black cohosh include: hypotension, hypocholesterolemic activity, and peripheral vasodilation in vasospastic conditions (due to acetin content).

Overdose may cause nausea, vomiting, dizziness, visual disturbances, bradycardia, and perspiration. Large doses may induce miscarriage. This product should not be used in pregnant women.[4] No data are available on the transfer of Black Cohosh into human milk, but due to its estrogenic activity, it could lower milk production although this is not known at this time. Caution is recommended in breastfeeding mothers. Use for more than 6 months is not recommended.[5]

Pregnancy Risk Category: X

Lactation Risk Category: L4

Adult Concerns: Large doses may induce miscarriage...this product should not be used in pregnant women. Other effects of black cohosh include: hypotension, hypocholesterolemic activity, and peripheral vasodilation in vasospastic conditions. Overdose may cause nausea, vomiting, dizziness, visual disturbances, bradycardia, and perspiration.

Pediatric Concerns: None reported via milk.

Drug Interactions:

Relative Infant Dose:

Adult Dose:

Alternatives:

References:
1. Murray M. Am.J.Nat.Med. 4[3], 3-5. 1997.
2. Jarry H. et al Planta Medica 1885; 4:316-319.
3. Jarry H. et al Planta Medica 1885; 1:46-49.
4. Newall C. Black Cohosh Herbal Medicines. Pharmaceutical Press 1996; 80:81.
5. The Complete German Commission E Monographs. Ed. M. Blumenthal Amer Botanical Council 1998.

BLESSED THISTLE   L3

Trade: Blessed Thistle
Other Trades:
Uses: Anorexic, antidiarrheal, febrifuge
AAP: Not reviewed

Blessed thistle contains an enormous array of chemicals, polyenes, steroids, terpenoids, and volatile oils. It is believed useful for diarrhea, hemorrhage, fevers, expectorant, bacteriostatic, loss of appetite, indigestion, promoting lactation, and other antiseptic properties. Traditionally it has been used for loss of appetite, flatulence, cough and congestion, gangrenous ulcers, and dyspepsia. It has been documented to be antibacterial against: *B. subtilis, Brucella abortus, B. bronchiseptica, E. coli, Proteus species, P. aeruginosa, Staph. aureus,* and *Strep. faecalis.*

The antibacterial and anti-inflammatory properties are due to its cnicin component.[1] While it is commonly use as a galactagogue, no data could be found supporting its use in this application in the German E commission, nor a number of other herbal references. It is virtually nontoxic (GRAS status), and there are only occasional suggestions that high doses may induce GI symptoms.[2]

Pregnancy Risk Category:

Lactation Risk Category: L3

Adult Concerns: Virtually nontoxic. In doses > 5 grams per cup, it has been associated with stomach irritation, nausea and vomiting. It also may induce allergies in individuals sensitive to ragweed, daisies, marigolds, and chrysanthemums.

Pediatric Concerns: None reported via milk but it lacks justification as a galactagogue.

Drug Interactions:

Relative Infant Dose:

Adult Dose: 1.5-3 grams as a tea up to three times daily

Alternatives:

References:
1. Vanhaelen-Fastre R. Cnicus benedictus: Seperation of antimicrobial constituents. Plant Med Phytother 1968; 2:294-299.
2. Newall C. Black Cohosh Herbal Medicines. Pharmaceutical Press 1996; 80:81.

BLUE COHOSH   L5

Trade: Blue ginseng, Squaw root, Papoose root, Yellow ginseng
Other Trades:
Uses: Uterine stimulant
AAP: Not reviewed

Blue Cohosh is also known as blue ginseng, squaw root, papoose root, or yellow ginseng. It is primarily used as a uterotonic drug to stimulate uterine contractions. In one recent paper, an infant born of a mother who ingested Blue Cohosh root for 3 weeks prior to delivery, suffered from severe cardiogenic shock and congestive heart failure.[1]

Subsequent studies have found it cardiotoxic in animals. Do not use in pregnant or breastfeeding mothers at any time.

Blue Cohosh root contains a number of chemicals, including the alkaloid methylcytosine and the glycosides caulosaponin and caulophyllosaponin. Methylcytosine is pharmacologically similar to nicotine and may result in elevated blood pressure, gastric stimulation, and hyperglycemia. Caulosaponin and caulophyllosaponin are uterine stimulants. They also, apparently, produce severe ischemia of the myocardium due to intense coronary vasoconstriction. This product should not be used in pregnant women. No data are available concerning its transfer into human milk. Do not use in pregnant or breastfeeding mothers at any time.

Pregnancy Risk Category: X

Lactation Risk Category: L5

Adult Concerns: The leaves and seeds contain alkaloids and glycosides that can cause severe stomach pain when ingested. Poisoning have been reported. Symptoms include irritation of mucous membranes, diarrhea, cramping, chest pain, and hyperglycemia. Due to these life-threatening side effects pregnant women should be advised not to ingest any blue cohosh product during pregnancy.

Pediatric Concerns: One case of severe neonatal acute myocardial infarction, congestive heart failure, and shock in a newborn one month prior to delivery. Do not use in breastfeeding mothers. In another case, seizures, renal failure and respiratory distress were reported in an infant whose mother took black and blue cohosh at 42 weeks gestation.

Drug Interactions:

Relative Infant Dose:

Adult Dose:

Alternatives:

References:
1. Jones TK, Lawson BM. Profound neonatal congestive heart failure caused by maternal consumption of blue cohosh herbal medication. J Pediatr 1998; 132 (3 Pt 1):550-552.

BORAGE   L5

Trade: Borage, Borage oil, Beebread, Bee plant, Burrage,
        Starflower, Ox
Other Trades:
Uses: Herbal expectorant, tonic, galactogogue
AAP: Not reviewed

Borage is also called Beebread, Bee Plant, Burrage, Starflower. Borage oil or other products may contain the powerful and dangerous pyrrolizidine-type alkaloids. Native Borage oil contains, amabiline, which is hepatotoxic pyrrolizidine alkaloid. The use of this product in pregnant or breastfeeding women is contraindicated unless it is certified to be free of amabiline. Ingestion of 1- 2 grams of borage oil per day could provide doses of unsaturated pyrrolizidine alkaloids equal = 10 µg, which is in excess of the 1 µg/day limit recommended by the German Federal Health Agency.

Pregnancy Risk Category: Contraindicated

Lactation Risk Category: L5

Adult Concerns: May contain amabiline, which is hepatotoxic pyrrolizidine alkaloid.

Pediatric Concerns: Caution, do not use in pregnant or breastfeeding women unless the oil is certified to be amabiline-free.

Drug Interactions:

Relative Infant Dose:

Adult Dose:

Alternatives:

References:
1. Newall C, Anderson LA, Phillipson JD. Borage. In. Herbal Medicine. A guide for the healthcare professionals. The Pharmaceutical Press, London; 1996.

BOSENTAN   L4

Trade: Tracleer
Other Trades:
Uses: Endothelin antagonist
AAP: Not reviewed

Bosentan is used in the treatment of pulmonary artery hypertension. It blocks endothelin receptors on vascular endothelium and smooth muscle, thus blocking vasoconstriction.[1] No data are available on the transfer into human milk, but bosentan is highly protein bound (98%), large MW product, and therefore only small amounts are likely to be found unbound in the plasma. As a result, the amount in the milk compartment would probably be very low. However, this product is highly teratogenic, is 50% bioavailable orally, and has a high incidence of liver toxicity in patients. Great caution is recommended with this product in breastfeeding mothers until we have published milk levels.

Pregnancy Risk Category: X

Lactation Risk Category: L4

Adult Concerns: Adverse effects include headache, nasopharyngitis, flushing, abnormal hepatic function, and edema. Potential Liver Injury: Elevations in ALT or AST by more than $3\times$ ULN were observed in 11% of bosentan-treated patients compared to 2% of placebo-treated patients. Three-fold increases were seen in 12% of 95 PAH patients on 125 mg b.i.d. and 14% of 70 PAH patients on 250 mg b.i.d. Eight-fold increases were seen in 2% of PAH patients on 125 mg b.i.d. and 7% of PAH patients on 250 mg b.i.d. Bilirubin increases to $\geq 3\times$ULN were associated with aminotransferase increases in 2 of 658 (0.3%) of patients treated with bosentan. The combination of hepatocellular injury (increases in aminotransferases of $> 3\times$ ULN) and increases in total bilirubin ($> 3\times$ ULN) is a marker for potential serious liver injury. Elevations of AST and/or ALT associated with bosentan are dose-dependent, occur both early and late in treatment, usually progress slowly, are typically asymptomatic, and usually have been reversible after treatment interruption or cessation.

Pediatric Concerns: No data are available. May be dosed down to children weighing at least 10 kg.

Drug Interactions: Bosentan induces CYP2C9 and 3A4. It also may decrease levels of hormonal contraceptives, and increase metabolism of oral anticoagulants and sildenafil. Rifampin may decrease levels of bosentan.

Relative Infant Dose:

Adult Dose: 125 mg BID

Alternatives:

T ½	= 5 hours	M/P	=
PHL	=	PB	= 98%
Tmax	= 3-5 hours	Oral	= 50%
MW	= 569	pKa	=
Vd	= 0.26		

References:
1. Pharmaceutical Manufacturer Prescribing Information. 2009.

BOTULINUM TOXIN   L3

Trade: Botox
Other Trades:
Uses: Botulism poisoning and cosmetic procedures
AAP: Not reviewed

Botulism is a syndrome produced by the deadly toxin secreted by the bacteria clostridium botulinum. Botulinum toxins are neuromuscular blocking agents that produce muscular paralysis. Although the bacteria is wide spread, its colonization in food or the intestine of infants produces a deadly toxin. The syndrome is characterized by GI distress, weakness, malaise, lightheadedness, sore throat, and nausea. Dry mouth is almost universal. In most adult poisoning, the bacteria is absent; only the toxin is present. In most pediatric poisoning, the stomach is colonized by the bacterium, often from contaminated honey.

In one published report, a breastfeeding woman severely poisoned by botulism toxin continued to breastfeed her infant throughout the illness.[1] Four hours after admission, her milk was tested and was free of botulinum toxin or C. botulinum bacteria, although she was still severely ill. The infant showed no symptoms of poisoning. It is apparent from this case that neither botulinum bacteria, nor the toxin is secreted in breastmilk.

Botox: The pharmaceutical product Botox contains a purified Botulinum A toxin.[2] It is commonly used for numerous cosmetic as well as other procedures such as for treatment of rectal tears, spasticity, cerebral palsy, strabismus, etc. When injected into the muscle, it produces a partial chemical denervation resulting in paralysis of the muscle. When injected properly, and directly into the muscle, the toxin does not enter the systemic circulation. Thus levels in maternal plasma, and milk are very unlikely. Waiting a few hours for dissipation of any toxin would all but eliminate any risk to the infant. Also, avoid use of generic or unknown sources of botulinum toxin, as some are known to produce significant plasma levels in humans.

Pregnancy Risk Category: C

Lactation Risk Category: L3

Adult Concerns: GI distress, weakness, malaise, lightheadedness, sore throat, nausea, dry mouth.

Pediatric Concerns: None reported in one case of poisoning. No data on its use in breastfeeding mothers.

Drug Interactions:

Relative Infant Dose:

Adult Dose: 1.25-5 units IM injection

Alternatives:

References:
1.   Middaugh J. Botulism and breast milk. N Engl J Med 1978; 298 (6):343.
2.   Pharmaceutical manufactures prescribing information. 2005.

BRIMONIDINE   L3

Trade: Alphagan
Other Trades: Enidin, Combigan, Dom-Brimonidine
Uses: Use to treat ocular hypertension
AAP: Not reviewed

Brimonidine is an alpha adrenergic receptor antagonist used to reduce intraocular pressure in open- angle glaucoma by reducing aqueous humor production and increasing uveocleral outflow. No data are available on its transfer into human milk. If used in breastfeeding mothers, observe the infant closely for alpha adrenergic blockage although this is unlikely. See side effects.

Pregnancy Risk Category: B

Lactation Risk Category: L3

Adult Concerns: Oral dryness, ocular hyperemia, burning and stinging, headache, blurring, fatigue/drowsiness, ocular allergies and pruritus.Brimonidine may produce mild hypotension, bradyarrhythmias, palpitations, and syncope.

Pediatric Concerns: No studies available. Use with caution.

Drug Interactions: Use cautiously with CNS depressants, tricyclic antidepressants, beta-blockers, antihypertensives, and/or digitalis. Do not use with MAO inhibitors.

Relative Infant Dose:

Adult Dose: One drop in eye three times daily.

Alternatives:

T ½	= 3 hours	M/P	=
PHL	=	PB	=
Tmax	= 1-4 hours	Oral	=
MW	= 442	pKa	=
Vd	=		

References:
1.   Pharmaceutical manufacturers prescribing information, 2005.

BROMIDES   L5

Trade:
Other Trades:
Uses: Sedatives
AAP: Maternal Medication Usually Compatible with Breastfeeding

Small amounts are known to be secreted in milk.[1] May cause persistent rash, drowsiness, or weakness in infants. Secretion in milk has been known for many years. Bromide preparations are no longer available in the US. They are poorly effective products and have no place in modern medicine. Contraindicated in nursing mothers.

Pregnancy Risk Category: D

Lactation Risk Category: L5

Adult Concerns: Rash, sedation.

Pediatric Concerns: Rash, drowsiness, weakness.

Drug Interactions:

Relative Infant Dose:

Adult Dose: 3-6 g daily.

Alternatives:

References:
1. Van der Bogert F. Bromine poisoning through mother's milk. Am J Dis Child 1921; 21:167.

BROMOCRIPTINE MESYLATE   L5

Trade:
Other Trades: Apo-Bromocriptine, Kripton, Bromolactin
Uses: Inhibits prolactin secretion
AAP: Drugs associated with significant side effects and should be given with caution

Bromocriptine is an anti-parkinsonian, synthetic ergot alkaloid which inhibits prolactin secretion and hence physiologic lactation. Most of the dose of bromocriptine is absorbed first-pass by the liver, leaving less than 6% to remain in the plasma. Maternal serum prolactin levels remain suppressed for up to 14 hours after a single dose. The FDA approved indication for lactation suppression has been withdrawn, and it is no longer approved for this purpose due to numerous maternal deaths, seizures, and strokes. Observe for transient hypotension or vomiting. It is sometimes used in hyperprolactinemic patients who have continued to breastfeed although the incidence of maternal side-effects is significant and newer products are preferred.[1,2] Several studies have shown the possibility of breastfeeding during bromocriptine therapy for pituitary tumors with no untoward effects in infants.[3,4] Caution is recommended as profound maternal postpartum hypotension has been reported. While bromocriptine is no longer recommended for suppression of lactation, a newer product cabergoline (Dostinex), is considered much safer for suppression of prolactin production.

Pregnancy Risk Category: B

Lactation Risk Category: L5 (milk suppression)

Adult Concerns: Most frequent side effects include nausea (49%), headache (19%), and dizziness (17%), peripheral vasoconstriction. Rarely, significant hypotension, shock, myocardial infarction. Transient hypotension and hair loss. A number of deaths have been associated with this product and it is no longer cleared for postpartum use to inhibit lactation.

Pediatric Concerns: No reports of direct toxicity to infant via milk but use with caution. Inhibits lactation. May be useful in patients with hyperprolactinemia who wish to continue breastfeeding, although cabergoline is probably preferred.

Drug Interactions: Amitriptyline, butyrophenones, imipramine, methyldopa, phenothiazines, reserpine, may decrease efficacy of bromocriptine at reducing serum prolactin. May increase toxicity of other ergot alkaloids.

Relative Infant Dose:

Adult Dose: 1.25-2.5 mg BID-TID

Alternatives: Cabergoline

T ½	= 50 hours	M/P	=
PHL	=	PB	= 90-96%
Tmax	= 1-3 hours	Oral	= <28%
MW	= 654	pKa	=
Vd	= 3.4		

References:
1. Meese MG. Reassessment of bromocriptine use for lactation suppression. P and T 1992; 17:1003-1004.
2. Spalding G. Bromocriptine (Parlodel) for suppression of lactation. Aust N Z J Obstet Gynaecol 1991; 31 (4):344-345.
3. Canales ES, Garcia IC, Ruiz JE, Zarate A. Bromocriptine as prophylactic therapy in prolactinoma during pregnancy. Fertil Steril 1981; 36 (4):524-526.
4. Verma S, Shah D, Faridi MMA. Breastfeeding a Baby with Mother on Bromocriptine. Indian J Pediatr 2006; 73 (5):435-436.

BROMPHENIRAMINE   L3

Trade: Dimetane, Brombay, Dimetapp, Bromfed
Other Trades:
Uses: Antihistamine
AAP: Not reviewed

Brompheniramine is a popular antihistamine sold as Dimetane or numerous other products, some that include pseudoephedrine. Although untoward effects appear limited, some reported side effects from Dimetapp preparations are known. Although only insignificant amounts of brompheniramine appear to be secreted into breastmilk, there are a number of reported cases of irritability, excessive crying, and sleep disturbances that have been reported in breastfeeding infants.[1] Note, many sinus products may contain pseudoephedrine, and should be avoided in breastfeeding mothers if possible.

Pregnancy Risk Category: C

Lactation Risk Category: L3

Adult Concerns: Drowsiness, dry mucosa, excessive crying, irritability, sleep disturbances.

Pediatric Concerns: Irritability, excessive crying, and sleep disturbances have been reported.

Drug Interactions: May enhance toxicity of other CNS depressants, MAO inhibitors, alcohol and tricyclic depressants.

Relative Infant Dose:

Adult Dose: 4 mg every 4-6 hours

Alternatives: Loratadine, Cetirizine

T ½	= 24.9 hours	M/P	=
PHL	=	PB	=
Tmax	= 3.1 hours	Oral	= Complete
MW	= 319	pKa	=
Vd	= 11.7		

References:

1. Paton DM, Webster DR. Clinical pharmacokinetics of H1-receptor antagonists (the antihistamines). Clin Pharmacokinet 1985; 10 (6):477-497.

BUDESONIDE INHALED   L1

Trade: Rhinocort, Pulmicort Respules, Symbicort
Other Trades:
Uses: Corticosteroid
AAP: Not reviewed

Budesonide is a potent corticosteroid used intranasally for allergic rhinitis, inhaled for asthma, and in capsule form for Crohn's disease. As such, the lung bioavailability is estimated to be 34% of the inhaled dose.[3] Once absorbed systemically, budesonide is a weak systemic steroid and should not be used to replace other steroids. In one 5 year study of children aged 2-7 years, no changes in linear growth, weight, and bone age were noted following inhalation.[2] Adrenal suppression at these doses is extremely remote. Using normal doses, it is unlikely that clinically relevant concentrations of budesonide would ever reach the milk nor be systemically bioavailable to a breastfed infant.

One study tested samples from 8 women before and after their first morning dose of 200 or 400 µg inhaled budesonide (Pulmicort Turbuhaler). Average milk level of budesonide (Cav) was 0.105-0.219 nmol/L with doses of 200 and 400 µg twice daily, respectively. Maternal plasma levels of budesonide reported (Cav) were 0.246--0.437 nmol/L at the doses above. Milk/plasma ratios were 0.428 and 0.502 at the doses above. Plasma samples from infants 1-1.5 hours after feeding showed levels below the limit of quantification. Therefore, the estimated daily infant dose is 0.3% of the mother's daily dose or approximately 0.0068-0.0142 µg/kg/day.[3]

Budesonide is also found in Symbicort, along with formoterol fumarate, as a long term therapy for asthma patients. It is available in 160/4.5 µg and 80/4.5 µg doses. See also formoterol fumarate.

Pregnancy Risk Category: C

Lactation Risk Category: L1

Adult Concerns: Adverse effects following intranasal use include irritation, pharyngitis, cough, bleeding, candidiasis, dry mouth. No adrenal suppression has been reported. Side effects following oral use include: headache, acne, bruising, and nausea.

Pediatric Concerns: None reported via milk. Pediatric use down to age 6 is permitted, but its used in infants routinely.

Drug Interactions: Ketoconazole (inhibitor of CYP3A4) causes an 8 fold increase of the systemic exposure to budesonide. Avoid using with ketoconazole, itraconazole, ritonavir, indinavir, erythromycin, and others that may inhibit this drug-metabolizing system.

Relative Infant Dose: 0.3%

Adult Dose: Intranasal: 200-400 µg BID; Oral: 9 mg daily.

Alternatives:

T ½	= 2.8 hours	M/P	= 0.50
PHL	=	PB	= 85-90% (oral)
Tmax	= 32-43 min (Inh)	Oral	= 10.7% (oral)
MW	= 430	pKa	=
Vd	= 4.3		

References:

1. Pharmaceutical Manufacturer Prescribing Information. 2007.
2. Volovitz B, Amir J, Malik H, Kauschansky A, Varsano I. Growth and pituitary-adrenal function in children with severe asthma treated with inhaled budesonide. N Engl J Med 1993; 329 (23):1703-1708.
3. Falt A, Bengtsson T, Gyllenberg A, Lindberg B, Strandgarden K. Negligible Exposure of Infants to Budesonide Via Breast Milk. J Allergy Clin Immunol 2007; 120 (4):798-802.

BUDESONIDE ORAL   L3

Trade: Entocort EC
Other Trades:
Uses: Corticosteroid
AAP: Not reviewed

Budesonide has a high topical corticosteroid activity and a substantial first pass elimination. Thus plasma levels are generally quite low.

The new oral formulation of budesonide (Entocort EC) is used for Crohn's disease and is placed in special granules that pass the stomach before releasing the drug in controlled-release manner in the duodenum. Plasma budesonide has a high clearance rate due to high uptake by the liver. Plasma levels are low and brief, and its ability to suppress normal cortisol levels is about half that of prednisone. Because of its high first-pass clearance, it is rather unlikely to produce high or even significant levels in milk, nor be orally bioavailable to a significant degree in breastfeeding infants.

Pregnancy Risk Category: C

Lactation Risk Category: L3

Adult Concerns: Use with caution in patient with tuberculosis, hypertension, diabetes mellitus, osteoporosis, peptic ulcer, glaucoma or cataracts, or with a family history of diabetes or glaucoma, or with any other condition where glucocorticosteroids may have unwanted effects. If use chronically, systemic glucocorticosteroid effects such as hypercorticism and adrenal suppression may occur.

Pediatric Concerns: None yet reported in breastfed infants. Unlikely.

Drug Interactions: Budesonide is metabolized via CYP3A4. Co-administration of ketoconazole results in an eight-fold increase in AUC of budesonide. Grapefruit juice, an inhibitor of gut mucosal CYP3A, approximately doubles the systemic exposure of oral budesonide. Conversely, induction of CYP3A4 can result in the lowering of budesonide plasma levels. Oral contraceptives containing ethinyl estradiol, which are also metabolized by CYP3A4, do not affect the pharmacokinetics of budesonide. Budesonide does not affect the plasma levels of oral contraceptives (ie, ethinyl estradiol).

Relative Infant Dose:

Adult Dose: 9 mg daily

Alternatives: Azathioprine, prednisone, methylprednisolone

T ½	= 2-3.6 hours	M/P	=
PHL	=	PB	= 85-90%
Tmax	= 30-600 minutes	Oral	= 9-21%
MW	= 430	pKa	=
Vd	= 3.9		

References:
1. Pharmaceutical manufacturers prescribing information, 2010.

BUMETANIDE   L3

Trade: Bumex
Other Trades: Burinex
Uses: Loop diuretic
AAP: Not reviewed

Bumetanide is a potent loop diuretic similar to Lasix.[1] As with all diuretics, some reduction in breastmilk production may result but it is rare. It is not known if bumetanide transfers into human milk. If needed furosemide may be a better choice, as the oral bioavailability of furosemide in neonates is minimal.

Pregnancy Risk Category: C

Lactation Risk Category: L3

Adult Concerns: Dehydration, hepatic cirrhosis, ototoxicity, potassium loss. See furosemide.

Pediatric Concerns: None reported via milk.

Drug Interactions: Numerous interactions exist, this is a partial list of the most important. NSAIDS may block diuretic effect. Lithium excretion may be reduced. Increased effect with other antihypertensives. May induce hypoglycemia when added to sulfonylurea users. Clofibrate may induce an exaggerated diuresis. Increased ototoxicity with aminoglycoside antibiotics. Increased anticoagulation with anticoagulants.

Relative Infant Dose:

Adult Dose: 0.5-2 mg daily.-TID

Alternatives: Furosemide

T ½	= 1-1.5	M/P	=
PHL	= 2.5 hours (neonate)	PB	= 95%
Tmax	= 1 hour (oral)	Oral	=
MW	= 364	pKa	=
Vd	=		

References:
1. Pharmaceutical Manufacturer Prescribing Information. 1999.

BUPIVACAINE   L2

Trade: Marcaine
Other Trades: Marcain
Uses: Epidural, local anesthetic
AAP: Not reviewed

Bupivacaine is the most commonly employed regional anesthetic used in delivery because its concentrations in the fetus are the least of the local anesthetics. In one study of five patients, levels of bupivacaine in breastmilk were below the limits of detection (<0.02 mg/L) at 2 to 48 hours postpartum.[1] These authors concluded that bupivacaine is a safe drug for perinatal use in mothers who plan to breastfeed.

In a study of 27 patients who received an average of 183.3 mg lidocaine and 82.1 mg bupivacaine via an epidural catheter, lidocaine plasma levels at 2, 6, and 12 hours post administration were 0.86, 0.46, and 0.22 mg/L respectively.[2] Levels of bupivacaine in milk at 2, 6, and 12 hours were 0.09, 0.06, 0.04 mg/L respectively. The milk/serum ratio bases upon area under the curve values (AUC) were 1.07 and 0.34 for lidocaine and bupivacaine respectively. Based on AUC data of lidocaine and bupivacaine milk levels, the average milk concentration of these agents over 12 hours was 0.5 and 0.07 mg/L. Most of the infants had a maximal APGAR score.

Pregnancy Risk Category: C

Lactation Risk Category: L2

Adult Concerns: Sedation, bradycardia, respiratory depression.

Pediatric Concerns: None reported via milk.

Drug Interactions: Increases effect of hyaluronidase, beta blockers, MAO inhibitors, tricyclic antidepressants, phenothiazines, and vasopressors.

Relative Infant Dose: 0.9%

Adult Dose: 25-100 mg once

Alternatives:

T ½	= 2.7 hours	M/P	=
PHL	= 8.1 hours	PB	= 95%
Tmax	= 30-45 minutes	Oral	=
MW	= 288	pKa	= 8.1
Vd	= 0.4-1.0		

References:
1. Naulty JS. Bupivacaine in breast milk following epidural anesthesia for vaginal delivery. Regional Anesthesia 1983; 8 (1):44-45.
2. Ortega D, Viviand X, Lorec AM, Gamerre M, Martin C, Bruguerolle B. Excretion of lidocaine and bupivacaine in breast milk following epidural anesthesia for cesarean delivery. Acta Anaesthesiol Scand 1999; 43 (4):394-397.

BUPRENORPHINE   L2

Trade: Buprenex, Subutex
Other Trades: Temgesic, Subutex
Uses: Narcotic analgesic
AAP: Not reviewed

Buprenorphine is a potent, long-acting narcotic agonist and antagonist and may be useful as a replacement for methadone treatment in addicts. It is also recently approved for the treatment of opiate dependence. Its elimination half-life varies from paper to paper, but new recent sublingual studies suggests it ranges from 23-30 hours.[1]

In one patient who received 4 mg/day to facilitate withdrawal from other opiates, the amount of buprenorphine transferred via milk was only 3.28 μg/day, an amount that was clinically insignificant.[2] No symptoms were noted in this breastfed infant.

In another study of continuous epidural bupivacaine and buprenorphine in post cesarean women for 3 days[3], it was suggested that buprenorphine may suppress the production of milk (and infant weight gain) although this was not absolutely clear.

In another study of one patient on buprenorphine maintenance for 7 months, and who received 8 mg daily sublingually over 4 days, milk levels of buprenorphine and norbuprenorphine ranged from 1.0 to 14.7 ng/mL and 0.6 to 6.3 ng/mL, respectively.[4] Plasma concentrations of both analytes ranged from 0.2 to 20.1 ng/mL (buprenorphine) and 1.2 to 4.4 ng/mL (norbuprenorphine) over 4 days of study. Using peak levels only, the concentration of buprenorphine and norbuprenorphine were 1.47 and 0.63 μg/100 mL of breast milk, respectively. Assuming an intake of 150 mL/kg/day, the authors estimated the daily dose would be less than 10 μg for a 4 kg infant, a dose that is probably far subclinical.

In a recent study of 7 women who were taking a median of 0.32 mg/kg/day buprenorphine, the median area under the curve estimates of milk levels were 0.12 mg.h/L for buprenorphine and 0.10 mg.h/L for norbuprenorphine. Levels of buprenorphine and norbuprenorphine in the infant plasma were approximately 4.5% and 11.7% of maternal levels.

Pregnancy Risk Category: C

Lactation Risk Category: L2

Adult Concerns: Typical opiate side effects include pruritus, sedation, analgesia, hallucinations, euphoria, dizziness, respiratory depression.

Pediatric Concerns: Low weight gain and reduced breast milk levels in one study, and no effects in two other studies.

Drug Interactions: May enhance effects of other opiates, benzodiazepines, and barbiturates.

Relative Infant Dose: 1.9%

Adult Dose: 0.3 mg every 6 hours PRN

Alternatives: Methadone

T ½	= 23-30 h sublingual	M/P	= 1.7 buprenorphine
PHL	=	PB	= 96%
Tmax	= 15-30 minutes	Oral	= 31%
MW	= 504	pKa	= 8.24, 9.92
Vd	= 97		

References:
1. McAleer SD, Mills RJ, Polack T et al. Pharmacokinetics of high-dose buprenorphine following single administration of sublingual tablet formulations in opioid naive healthy male volunteers under a naltrexone block. Drug Alcohol Depend. 2003;72:75-83.
2. Marquet P, Chevrel J, Lavignasse P, Merle L, Lachatre G. Buprenorphine withdrawal syndrome in a newborn. Clin Pharmacol Ther 1997; 62 (5):569-571.

3. Hirose M, Hosokawa T, Tanaka Y. Extradural buprenorphine suppresses breast feeding after caesarean section. Br J Anaesth 1997; 79 (1):120-121.
4. Grimm D, Pauly E, Poschl J et al. Buprenorphine and Norbuprenorphine Concentrations in Human Breast Milk Samples Determined by Liquid Chromatography-Tandem Mass Spectrometry. Ther Drug Monit. 2005;27:526-530.
5. Lindemalm S, Nydert P, Svensson JO, Stahle L, Sarman I. Transfer of buprenorphine into breast milk and calculation of infant drug dose. J Hum Lact. May 2009;25 (2):199-205.

BUPRENORPHINE + NALOXONE   L3

Trade: Suboxone

Other Trades:

Uses: Suppression of opiate withdrawal in drug addiction programs.

AAP: Not reviewed

Suboxone is a sublingual tablet that contains a partial opioid agonist (buprenorphine) and an opioid antagonist (naloxone) in a 4:1 (buprenorphine: naloxone) ratio. Buprenorphine reduces the patients' craving for opioids, and naloxone discourages the use of other opioids by blocking the opiate receptor. Naloxone is poorly absorbed orally and buprenorphine is only 31% absorbed. It is unlikely breast milk levels will be significant. See individual monographs on these two drugs.

Pregnancy Risk Category: C

Lactation Risk Category: L3

Adult Concerns: Side effects include headache, withdrawal syndrome, pain, nausea, insomnia, and sweating.

Pediatric Concerns: None reported but data is limited at these doses.

Drug Interactions:

Relative Infant Dose:

Adult Dose: 12-16 mg/day.

Alternatives:

References:
1.   Pharmaceutical Manufacturer Prescribing Information. 2006.

BUPROPION   L3

Trade: Wellbutrin, Zyban, Aplenzin
Other Trades:
Uses: Antidepressant, smoking deterrent
AAP: Drugs whose effect on nursing infants is unknown but may be of concern

Bupropion is an older antidepressant with a structure unrelated to tricyclics. One report in the literature indicates that bupropion probably accumulates in human milk although the absolute dose transferred appears minimal as in three infants studied, no bupropion was detected in the plasma compartment.

Following one 100 mg dose in a mother, the milk/plasma ratio ranged from 2.51 to 8.58, clearly suggesting a concentrating mechanism for this drug in human milk.[1] However, plasma levels of bupropion (or its metabolites) in the infant were undetectable, indicating that the dose transferred to the infant was low, and accumulation in infant plasma apparently did not occur under these conditions (infant was fed 7.5 to 9.5 hours after dosing). The peak milk bupropion level (0.189 mg/L) occurred two hours after a 100 mg dose. This milk level would provide 0.66% of the maternal dose, a dose that is likely to be clinically insignificant to a breastfed infant.

In a recent study of two breastfeeding patients consuming 75 mg twice daily and 150 mg (sustained release) daily respectively, no bupropion or metabolite were detected in either breastfed infant.[2] In the first patient at 17 weeks postpartum, plasma levels were drawn at 2 hours post-dose and bupropion or hydroxybupropion levels were undetectable. In the second patient at 29 weeks postpartum, bupropion and hydroxybupropion were undetectable as well. The limit of detection for bupropion was 5-10 ng/mL and for hydroxybupropion was 100-200 ng/mL.

Seizures in a 6 month old breastfed infant were reported four days following administration of 150 mg/day bupropion in the mother.[3] The mother discontinued bupropion and continued breastfeeding. No further seizures were reported. Due to persistent case reports to the author, bupropion may, in some women, suppress milk production. Some caution is recommended concerning changes to milk supply.

In a study of 10 breastfeeding patients who received 150 mg bupropion SR daily for 2 days and then 300 mg bupropion SR daily thereafter for 5 more days, milk concentrations of bupropion averaged 45 μg/L.[4]

The average infant dose via milk was 6.75 μg/kg/day. The reported relative infant dose was 0.14 % of the weight-normalized maternal dose. When the active metabolites present in milk were added, the RID would be 2% of the maternal dose. No side effects were noted in any of the infants.

In a study of 4 mothers consuming 150 to 300 mg/day of bupropion SR, peak and trough blood levels were highly variable, but averaged 64 ng/mL at peak and 9.2 ng/mL at trough.[5] Bupropion was detected in urine in only 1 of 4 infants (infant was 6 week premature). The average milk/serum ratio was 1.3.

Pregnancy Risk Category: C

Lactation Risk Category: L3

Adult Concerns: Seizures, restlessness, agitation, sleep disturbances. Probably contraindicated in patients with seizure disorders.

Pediatric Concerns: Thus far plasma levels in breastfed infants are undetectable. One case of seizure in a 6 month-old infant.

Drug Interactions: May increase clearance of diazepam, carbamazepine, phenytoin. May increase effects of MAO inhibitors.

Relative Infant Dose: 0.2% - 1.9%

Adult Dose: 100 mg TID

Alternatives: Sertraline, Paroxetine

T ½	= 8-24 hours	M/P	= 2.51-8.58
PHL	=	PB	= 75-88%
Tmax	= 2 hours	Oral	= 85%
MW	= 240	pKa	= 8.0
Vd	= 40		

References:
1. Briggs GG, Samson JH, Ambrose PJ, Schroeder DH. Excretion of bupropion in breast milk. Ann Pharmacother 1993; 27 (4):431-433.
2. Baab SW, Peindl KS, Piontek CM, Wisner KL. Serum bupropion levels in 2 breastfeeding mother-infant pairs. J Clin Psychiatry. 2002;63:910-911.
3. Chaudron LH and Schoenecker CJ. Bupropion and breastfeeding: a case of possible infant seizure. (Letter) J.Clin. Psychiatry 2004:64 (6):881-882
4. Haas JS, Kaplan CP, Barenboim D, Jacob P, III, Benowitz NL. Bupropion in breast milk: an exposure assessment for potential treatment to prevent post-partum tobacco use. Tob Control 2004 Mar; 13 (1):52-6.
5. Davis MF, Miller HS, Nolan PE, Jr. Bupropion levels in breast milk for 4 mother-infant pairs: more answers to lingering questions. J Clin Psychiatry. Feb 2009;70 (2):297-298.

BUSPIRONE   L3

Trade: BuSpar
Other Trades: Apo-Buspirone, Novo-Buspirone
Uses: Antianxiety medication
AAP: Not reviewed

No data exists on excretion into human milk. It is secreted into animal milk, so the same would be expected in human milk.[1] BuSpar is mg for mg equivalent to diazepam (Valium) in its anxiolytic properties but does not produce significant sedation or addiction as the benzodiazepine family. Its metabolite is partially active but has a brief half-life (4.8 hours) as well. Compared to the benzodiazepine family, this product would be a better choice for treatment of anxiety in breastfeeding women. Without accurate breastmilk levels, it is not known if the product is safe for breastfeeding women or the levels the infant would ingest daily. The rather brief half-life of this product and its metabolite would not likely lead to buildup in the infants plasma.

Pregnancy Risk Category: B

Lactation Risk Category: L3

Adult Concerns: Dizziness, nausea, drowsiness, fatigue, excitement, euphoria.

Pediatric Concerns: None reported.

Drug Interactions: Cimetidine may increase the effect of buspirone. Increased toxicity may occur when used with MAO inhibitors, phenothiazines, CNS depressants, digoxin and haloperidol.

Relative Infant Dose:

Adult Dose: 5 mg TID

Alternatives:

T ½	= 2-3 hours	M/P	=
PHL	=	PB	= 95%
Tmax	= 60-90 minutes	Oral	= 90%
MW	= 386	pKa	=
Vd	= 5.3		

References:
1. Pharmaceutical Manufacturer Prescribing Information. 1996.

BUSULFAN   L5

Trade: Myleran
Other Trades:
Uses: Antineoplastic, anticancer drug.
AAP: Not reviewed

Busulfan is a potent antineoplastic agent that can produce severe bone marrow suppression, anemia, loss of blood cells, and elevated risk of infection.[1] It is not known if busulfan is distributed to human milk. No data is available concerning breastmilk concentrations, but this agent would be extremely toxic to growing infants and continued breastfeeding would not be justified. Use of this drug during breastfeeding is definitely not recommended. Breastfeeding should be interrupted for a minimum of 24 hours following exposure to this agent.

Pregnancy Risk Category: D

Lactation Risk Category: L5

Adult Concerns: Severe bone marrow suppression, anemia, leukopenia, pulmonary fibrosis, cholestatic jaundice.

Pediatric Concerns: Extremely cytotoxic, use is not recommended in nursing women. Withhold breastfeeding for at least 24 hours following its use.

Drug Interactions:

Relative Infant Dose:

Adult Dose: 1 mg/kg/dose every 6 hours (16 doses total)

Alternatives:

T ½	= 2.6 hours	M/P	=
PHL	=	PB	= 14%
Tmax	= 0.5-2 hours	Oral	= Complete
MW	= 246	pKa	=
Vd	= 0.94		

References:
1. Pharmaceutical manufactures prescribing information. 2005.

BUTABARBITAL   L3

Trade: Butisol, Butalan, Ampyrox
Other Trades:
Uses: Sedative, hypnotic
AAP: Not reviewed

Butabarbital is an intermediate acting barbiturate similar to phenobarbital. Small amounts are secreted in breastmilk.[1] No harmful effects have been reported. Watch for drowsiness and sedation.

Pregnancy Risk Category: D

Lactation Risk Category: L3

Adult Concerns: Sedation, weakness.

Pediatric Concerns: None reported but observe for sedation.

Drug Interactions: May have a decreased effect when used with phenothiazines, haloperidol, cyclosporin, tricyclic antidepressants, doxycycline, beta-blockers. May increase effects of benzodiazepines, CNS depressants, valproic acid, methylphenidate, and chloramphenicol.

Relative Infant Dose:

Adult Dose: 15-30 mg TID or QID

Alternatives:

T ½	= 100 hours	M/P	=
PHL	=	PB	=
Tmax	= 3-4 hours	Oral	= Complete
MW	= 232	pKa	= 7.9
Vd	=		

References:
1. Tyson RM, Shrader EA, Perlman HH. Drugs transmitted through breast milk. II Barbiturates. J Pediatr 1938; 14:86-90.

BUTALBITAL COMPOUND   L3

Trade: Fioricet, Fiorinal, Bancap, Two-Dyne
Other Trades: Tecnal
Uses: Mild analgesic, sedative
AAP: Not reviewed

Mild analgesic with acetaminophen (325mg) or aspirin, caffeine (40mg), and butalbital (50mg). Butalbital is a mild, short-acting barbiturate that probably transfers into breastmilk to a limited degree although it is unreported.[1] No data is available on the transfer of butalbital to breastmilk, but it is likely minimal.

Pregnancy Risk Category: D

Lactation Risk Category: L3

Adult Concerns: Sedation.

Pediatric Concerns: Sedation.

Drug Interactions: Decreased effect when used with phenothiazines, haloperidol, cyclosporin, tricyclic antidepressants, and oral contraceptives. Increased effect when used with alcohol, benzodiazepines, CNS depressants, valproic acid, methylphenidate.

Relative Infant Dose:

Adult Dose: 50-100 mg every 4 hours

Alternatives:

T ½	= 40-140 hours	M/P	=
PHL	=	PB	= 26%
Tmax	= 40-60 minutes	Oral	= Complete
MW	= 224	pKa	=
Vd	= 0.8		

References:
1.   McEvoy GE. (ed):AFHS Drug Information. New York, NY: 2009.

BUTORPHANOL   L2

Trade: Stadol
Other Trades:
Uses: Potent narcotic analgesic
AAP: Maternal Medication Usually Compatible with Breastfeeding

Butorphanol is a potent narcotic analgesic. It is available as IV, IM, and a nasal spray. In one study of twelve breastfeeding women, six of whom received a single 2 mg IM dose, and 6 received a single 8 mg oral dose, the milk/serum ratio was constant over time and was 0.7 (intramuscular) and 1.9 (oral).[1] The average milk concentration following a 2 mg IM dose, were 1.5, 0.7, and 0.3 µg/L at 2, 4 and 8 hours respectively. Following an oral dose of 8 mg, milk levels were 3.6, 1.8, and 1.1 µg/L at 3,5, and 8 hours respectively. The elimination half-life in milk was approximately 2 hours. The estimated dose via milk is 0.1 µg/kg following an 8 mg oral dose, or 0.04 µg/kg following a 2 mg IM dose. The authors estimate that the infant would receive a maximum of only 4 micrograms butorphanol per day.

Levels received bu infants are considered very low to insignificant. Butorphanol undergoes first-pass extraction by the liver, thus only 17% of the oral dose reaches the plasma. Butorphanol has been frequently used in labor and delivery in women who subsequently nursed their infants, although, it has been noted to produce a sinusoidal fetal heart rate pattern and dysphoric or psychotomimetic responses in infants. Butorphanol use in breastfeeding mothers is however, of minimum risk to the normal term infant.

Pregnancy Risk Category: C during first and second trimester
                                         D during third trimester

Lactation Risk Category: L2

Adult Concerns: Sedation, respiratory depression. There have been rare reports of infant respiratory distress/apnea following the administration of butorphanol injection during labor. The reports of respiratory distress/apnea have been associated with administration of a dose within 2 hours of delivery, use of multiple doses, use with additional analgesic or sedative drugs, or use in preterm pregnancies. In a study of 119 patients, the administration of 1 mg of IV butorphanol injection during labor was associated with transient sinusoidal fetal heart rate patterns, but was not associated with adverse neonatal outcomes.

Pediatric Concerns: None reported via milk but sedation is possible in newborns.

Drug Interactions: May produce increase toxicity when used with CNS depressants, other opiates, phenothiazines, barbiturates, benzodiazepines, MAO inhibitors.

Relative Infant Dose: 0.1% - 0.5%

Adult Dose: 1-4 mg IM every 3-4 hours OR 0.5-2 mg IV every 3-4 hours

Alternatives: Ibuprofen, acetaminophen, hydrocodone

T ½	= 4.56 hours	M/P	= 0.7 (IM) - 1.9 (oral)
PHL	=	PB	= 80%
Tmax	= 1 hour	Oral	= 17 %
MW	= 327	pKa	= 8.6
Vd	= 6.9		

References:
1. Pittman KA, Smyth RD, Losada M, Zighelboim I, Maduska AL, Sunshine A. Human perinatal distribution of butorphanol. Am J Obstet Gynecol 1980; 138 (7 Pt 1):797-800.

CABERGOLINE   L4

Trade: Dostinex
Other Trades:
Uses: Inhibits prolactin secretion
AAP: Not reviewed

Cabergoline is a long-acting synthetic ergot alkaloid derivative which produces a dopamine agonist effect similar but much safer than bromocriptine (Parlodel). Cabergoline directly inhibits prolactin secretion by the pituitary.[1] It is primarily indicated for pathological hyperprolactinemia, but in several European studies, it has been used for inhibition of post-partum lactation.[2]

The dose regimen used for the inhibition of physiologic lactation is cabergoline 1 mg administered as a single dose on the first day post-partum. For the suppression of established lactation, cabergoline 0.25 mg is taken every 12 hours for 2 days for a total of 1 mg. Single doses of 1 mg have been found to completely inhibit postpartum lactation.[3] Transfer into human milk is not reported. In patients with hyperprolactinemia, it is possible to carefully administered doses to lower the prolactin to safe ranges, but high enough to retain lactation. In such cases, the infant should be observed for potential ergot side effects, if any. In addition, mothers treated with cabergoline early postpartum, may in some cases recover their milk supply following pumping and extensive breastfeeding.

Pregnancy Risk Category: B

Lactation Risk Category: L4 (suppress lactation)

Adult Concerns: Headache, dizziness, fatigue, orthostatic hypotension, nose bleed, inhibition of lactation.

Pediatric Concerns: Transfer via milk is unknown. Completely suppresses lactation and should not be used in mothers who are breastfeeding.

Drug Interactions: Do not use with other dopamine antagonists such as the phenothiazines (Thorazine,etc), butyrophenones (Haldol), thioxanthines, and metoclopramide (Reglan).

Relative Infant Dose:

Adult Dose: 0.25-1 mg twice a week

Alternatives:

T ½	= 63-69 hours	M/P	=
PHL	=	PB	=
Tmax	= 2-3 hours	Oral	= Complete
MW	= 451	pKa	=
Vd	=		

References:

1. Caballero-Gordo A, Lopez-Nazareno N, Calderay M, Caballero JL, Mancheno E, Sghedoni D. Oral cabergoline. Single-dose inhibition of puerperal lactation. J Reprod Med 1991; 36 (10):717-721.
2. Single dose cabergoline versus bromocriptine in inhibition of puerperal lactation: randomised, double blind, multicentre study. European Multicentre Study Group for Cabergoline in Lactation Inhibition BMJ 1991; 302 (6789):1367-1371.
3. Bravo-Topete EG, Mendoza-Hernandez F, Cejudo-Alvarez J, Briones-Garduno C. Cabergoline for inhibition of lactation. Cir Cir 2004; 72 (1):5-9.

CAFFEINE   L2

Trade: Vivarin, Nodoz, Coffee
Other Trades:
Uses: CNS stimulant
AAP: Maternal Medication Usually Compatible with Breastfeeding

Caffeine is a naturally occurring CNS stimulant present in many foods and drinks. While the half-life in adults is 4.9 hours, the half-life in neonates is as high as 97.5 hours. The half-life decreases with age to 14 hours at 3-5 months and 2.6 hours at 6 months and older. The average cup of coffee contains 100-150 mg of caffeine depending on preparation and country of origin.

Peak levels of caffeine are found in breast milk 60-120 minutes after ingestion. In a study of 5 patients following an ingestion of 150 mg caffeine, peak concentrations of caffeine in serum ranged from 2.39 to 4.05 μg/mL and peak concentrations in milk ranged from 1.4 to 2.41 mg/L with a milk/serum ratio of 0.52.[1] The average milk concentration at 30, 60, and 120 minute post dose was 1.58, 1.49, and 0.926 mg/L respectively.

In another study of 7 breastfeeding mothers who consumed 750 mg caffeine/day for 5 days, and were 11- 22 days postpartum, the average milk concentration was 4.3 mg/L.[2] Values ranged significantly from non detectable to 15.7 mg/L. The mean concentration of caffeine in sera of the infants on day 5 was 1.4 μg/mL (range non detectable to 2.8 μg/mL). In two patients whose milk levels were 13.4 and 28 mg/L the respective infant serum levels were 0.25 and 3.2 μg/mL.

In a study of 6 breastfeeding mothers who received one dose of 100 mg PO, peak levels (C_{max}) in maternal serum ranged from 0.5 to 1 hour and 0.75 to 2 hours in milk.[3] The maternal plasma C_{max} ranged from 3.6 to 6.15 μg/mL, while the C_{max} for their milk ranged from 1.98 to 4.3 mg/L. The average concentration of caffeine in milk was 2.45 mg/L at 1 hour. The average milk/plasma ratio (AUC) was 0.812 for both breasts. This elegant study shows that caffeine rapidly enters milk and that the decay of caffeine in milk is similar to that of plasma. In infants from 4 to 7 kg body weight, the estimated dose to the infant would be 1.77 to 3.10 mg/d following a 100 mg maternal dose. In a group of mothers who ingested from 35 to 336 mg of caffeine daily, the level of caffeine in milk ranged from 2.09 to 7.17 mg/L.[4] The author estimates the dose to infant at 0.01 to 1.64 mg/d or 0.06% to 1.5% of the maternal dose. An interesting review of the nutritional effects of caffeine ingestion on infants is provided by Nehlig.[5] There is some evidence that chronic coffee drinking may reduce the iron content of milk. Irritability and insomnia may occur and have been reported.[6] Occasional use of caffeine is not contraindicated, but persistent, chronic use may lead to high plasma levels in the infant particularly during the neonatal period.

Pregnancy Risk Category: C

Lactation Risk Category: L2

Adult Concerns: Agitation, irritability, poor sleeping patterns.

Pediatric Concerns: Rarely, irritability and insomnia.

Drug Interactions: Reduces vasodilation of adenosine. Reduces bioavailability of alendronate by 60%. Cimetidine reduces caffeine clearance by 50%. Fluoroquinolone antibiotics increases half-life of caffeine by 5 to 8 hours.

Relative Infant Dose: 6% - 25.9%

Adult Dose:

Alternatives:

T ½	= 4.9 hours	M/P	= 0.52 - 0.76
PHL	= 80-97.5 hours	PB	= 36%
Tmax	= 60 minutes	Oral	= 100%
MW	= 194	pKa	= 0.8
Vd	= 0.4-0.6		

References:
1. Tyrala EE, Dodson WE. Caffeine secretion into breast milk. Arch Dis Child 1979; 54 (10):787-800.
2. Ryu JE. Caffeine in human milk and in serum of breast-fed infants. Dev Pharmacol Ther 1985; 8 (6):329-337.
3. Stavchansky S, Combs A, Sagraves R, Delgado M, Joshi A. Pharmacokinetics of caffeine in breast milk and plasma after single oral administration of caffeine to lactating mothers. Biopharm Drug Dispos 1988; 9 (3):285-299.
4. Berlin CM, Jr., Denson HM, Daniel CH, Ward RM. Disposition of dietary caffeine in milk, saliva, and plasma of lactating women. Pediatrics 1984; 73 (1):59-63.
5. Nehlig A, Debry G. Consequences on the newborn of chronic maternal consumption of coffee during gestation and lactation: a review. J Am Coll Nutr 1994; 13 (1):6-21.
6. Munoz LM, Lonnerdal B, Keen CL, Dewey KG. Coffee consumption as a factor in iron deficiency anemia among pregnant women and their infants in Costa Rica. Am J Clin Nutr. 1988;48:645-51. PMID: 3414579

CALCIPOTRIENE   L3

Trade: Dovonex, Taclonex Scalp
Other Trades:
Uses: Synthetic Vitamin D3 used for treatment of psoriasis
AAP: Not reviewed

Calcipotriene is a synthetic vitamin D_3 derivative used topically for the treatment of plaque psoriasis. Only 5-6% is transcutaneously absorbed into the systemic circulation (via ointment). It is rapidly bound to plasma proteins, and excreted by the liver via bile. Less than 1% is absorbed from the scalp when the solution is used. It is unlikely plasma levels of calcipotriene would be elevated at all, and milk levels would be virtually nil because vitamin D transport to milk is normally quite low. Calcipotriene is active however, and used over wide areas of the body could (but unlikely) lead to some absorption. However, hypercalcemia in treated patients has been reported by only rarely.

Taclonex Scalp® Topical Suspension contains 52.18 µg of calcipotriene hydrate and 0.643 mg of betamethasone dipropionate.

Pregnancy Risk Category: C

Lactation Risk Category: L3

Adult Concerns: Adverse events include skin irritation, rare but reversible hypercalcemia, rash, pruritus, and worsening of psoriasis..

Pediatric Concerns: None reported via milk but no studies are available. Adverse effects in a breastfed infant are unlikely if the surface area treated is moderate to low.

Drug Interactions:

Relative Infant Dose:

Adult Dose: Apply to skin lesions twice daily.

Alternatives:

T ½	=	M/P	=
PHL	=	PB	=
Tmax	=	Oral	= Variable
MW	= 430	pKa	=
Vd	=		

References:
1.   Pharmaceutical Manufacturers Package Insert, 2009.

CALCITONIN   L3

Trade: Calcimar, Salmonine, Osteocalcin, Miacalcin
Other Trades: Caltine, Calcitare, Calsynar, Miacalcic
Uses: Calcium metabolism
AAP: Not reviewed

Calcitonin is a large polypeptide hormone (32 amino acids) secreted by the parafollicular cells of the thyroid that inhibits osteoclastic bone resorption, thus, maintaining calcium homeostasis in mammals.[1] It is used for control of postmenopausal osteoporosis and other calcium metabolic diseases. Calcitonins are destroyed by gastric acids, requiring parenteral (SC, IM) or intranasal dosing. Calcitonin is unlikely to penetrate human milk due to its large MW. Further, its oral bioavailability is nil due to destruction in the GI tract. It has been reported to inhibit lactation in animals although this has not been reported in humans.[2]

Pregnancy Risk Category: C

Lactation Risk Category: L3

Adult Concerns: Nausea, facial flushing, back pain, headache, arthalgia, shivering, edema, metallic taste, and increased urinary frequency.

Pediatric Concerns: None reported via milk. Unlikely to enter milk. Calcitonins have been reported to inhibit lactation in animals.

Drug Interactions: It is reported that ketoprofen inhibits the calciuric and uricosuric effect of porcine calcitonin. May have additive effect with plicamycin.

Relative Infant Dose:

Adult Dose: 50-100 units (salmon) three times weekly

Alternatives:

T ½	= 43 minutes	M/P	=
PHL	=	PB	=
Tmax	= 2 hours	Oral	= None
MW	=	pKa	=
Vd	=		

References:
1. Pharmaceutical Manufacturer Prescribing Information. 1997. 2. Fiore CE, Petralito A, Mazzarino MC, Liuzzo A, Malaponte G, Mangiafico RA,

Gibiino S. Effects of ketoprofen on the calciuric and uricosuric activities of calcitonin in man. J Endocrinol Invest 1981; 4 (1):81-84.

CALCITRIOL   L3

Trade: Rocaltrol
Other Trades:
Uses: Vitamin D analog
AAP: Not reviewed

Vitamin D typically undergoes a series of metabolic steps to become active. Calcitriol (1,25 dihydro cholecalciferol) is believed to be the active metabolite of vitamin D metabolism. Calcitriol is the most potent of the synthetic vitamin D analogs. It is indicated for treatment of hypocalcemia in patients undergoing chronic renal dialysis, and renal osteodystrophy. Calcitriol is also indicated in patients with severe liver dysfunction and who are unable to hydroxylate dihydrotachysterol to its active form. Because calcitriol works more quickly, it is useful in treatment of patients with severe hypocalcemia. Calcitriol is well absorbed from the GI tract with a peak at 3-6 hours.[1] It is 99.9% protein bound to a specific alpha-globulin vitamin D binding protein. The elimination half-life is about 5-8 hours in adults and 27 hours in pediatric age patients. However, plasma levels are quite low, averaging approximately 40 picograms/mL. Transfer of calcitriol into human milk is reported to be 2.2 picograms/mL.[2] It is not likely that normal doses of this vitamin D analog would lead to clinically relevant levels in human milk, particularly since vitamin D transfers only minimally into human milk anyway. While plasma levels of vitamin D are normally quite low in human milk (<20 IU/L), at least one study now suggests that supplementing a mother with extraordinarily high levels of vitamin D2 can elevate milk levels, and subsequently lead to hypercalcemia in a breastfed infant.[3] See Vitamin D for new data.

Pregnancy Risk Category: C

Lactation Risk Category: L3

Adult Concerns: Overdosage of any form of vitamin D is dangerous and could lead to severe hypercalcemia, hypercalciuria, and hyperphosphatemia. Hypercalcemia may subsequently lead to vascular calcification, nephrocalcinosis, and other soft-tissue calcification. Early symptoms include: Weakness, headache, somnolence, nausea, vomiting, dry mouth, constipation, muscle pain, bone pain and metallic taste. Late symptoms include:Polyuria, polydipsia, anorexia, weight loss, nocturia, conjunctivitis (calcific), pancreatitis, photophobia, rhinorrhea, pruritus, hyperthermia, decreased libido, elevated BUN, albuminuria, hypercholesterolemia, elevated SGOT and SGPT, ectopic calcification, hypertension, cardiac arrhythmias and, rarely, overt psychosis.

Pediatric Concerns: None reported via milk, but caution recommended at higher doses.

Drug Interactions: Cholestyramine, colestipol may reduce the oral absorption of calcitriol. Hypercalcemia may result from adding thiazide diuretics in patients receiving calcitriol. Ketoconazole, may reduce calcitriol concentrations in plasma. A functional antagonism can occur by adding corticosteroids to calcitriol. Avoid high-dose calcium supplements. Magnesium-containing antacid and calcitriol injection should not be used concomitantly, because such use may lead to the development of hypermagnesemia.

Relative Infant Dose:

Adult Dose: Variable, but 0.25-0.5 µg/day initially.

Alternatives: Vitamin D

T ½	= 5-8 hours	M/P	=
PHL	= 27 hour	PB	= 99.9%
Tmax	= 3-6 hours	Oral	= Complete
MW	= 416	pKa	=
Vd	=		

References:
1. Pharmaceutical Manufacturers prescribing information, 2003.
2. Teva Pharmaceuticals USA manufacturers prescribing information, 2008.
3. Greer FR, Hollis BW, Napoli JL. High concentrations of vitamin D2 in human milk associated with pharmacologic doses of vitamin D2. J Pediatr 1984; 105 (1):61-64.

CALENDULA   L3

Trade: Calendula, Marigold, Garden Marigold, Holligold, Gold Bloom, Marybud

Other Trades:

Uses: Herbal wound healing

AAP: Not reviewed

Calendula, grown worldwide, has been used topically to promote wound healing and to alleviate conjunctivitis and other ocular inflammations. It consists of a number of flavonol glycosides and saponins, but the active ingredients are unknown.[1] Despite these claims, there are almost no studies regarding its efficacy in any of these disorders. Further, there are no suggestions of overt toxicity, with exception of allergies. It should not be used in pregnant patients.[2] Although it may have some uses externally, its internal use as an antiphlogistic and spasmolytic is largely obsolete.

Pregnancy Risk Category: Contraindicated

Lactation Risk Category: L3

Adult Concerns: Allergies, anaphylactoid shock.

Pediatric Concerns: None reported via milk.

Drug Interactions: Caution when using calendula with sedative drugs. Calendula has been reported to increase hexobarbital sleep time in animal modes.

Relative Infant Dose:

Adult Dose: One cup of the tea (1-2 grams of the dried flowers) three times daily.

Alternatives:

References:
1. Bissett NG. In: Herbal Drugs and Phytopharmaceuticals. Medpharm Scientific Publishers, CRC Press, Boca Raton, 1994.2.   Natural Medicines Comprehensive Database, 2010.

CANDESARTAN   L3

Trade: Atacand, Amias
Other Trades:
Uses: Antihypertensive agent
AAP: Not reviewed

Candesartan is a specific blocker of the receptor site (AT1) for angiotensin II. It is typically used as an antihypertensive similar to the ACE inhibitor family.[1] Both the ACE inhibitor family and the specific AT1 inhibitors such as candesartan are contraindicated in the 2nd and 3rd trimesters of pregnancy due to severe hypotension, neonatal skull hypoplasia, irreversible renal failure, and death in the newborn infant. However, some of ACE inhibitors can be used in breastfeeding mothers postpartum without major risk in some cases with due caution. However, no data are available on candesartan in human milk although the manufacturer states that it is present in rodent milk and infants < 1 year of age should not be exposed to this drug. Some caution is recommended in the neonatal period and particularly when used in mothers with premature infants. Never use in pregnant women past the first trimester.

Pregnancy Risk Category: C in first trimester
D in second and third trimesters

Lactation Risk Category: L3

Adult Concerns: Headache, back pain, pharyngitis, and dizziness have been reported. The use of ACE inhibitors and angiotensin receptor blockers during pregnancy or the neonatal period is extremely dangerous and has resulted in hypotension, neonatal skull hypoplasia, anuria, renal failure and death. Other side effects include: asthenia, fever, paresthesia, vertigo, dyspepsia, gastroenteritis, tachycardia, palpitation, hyperglycemia, hypertriglyceridemia, hyperuricemia, myalgia, platelet/bleeding and clotting disorders, anxiety, depression, somnolence, dyspnea, rash, sweating increased and hematuria.

Pediatric Concerns: None reported via milk. Caution is recommended in the early postpartum period. Do not expose infants and children < 1 year of age to candesartan. The consequences of administering drugs that act directly on the renin-angiotensin system (RAS) can have effects on the development of immature kidneys.

Drug Interactions: Too numerous to mention. Consult drug interaction text.

Relative Infant Dose:

Adult Dose: 4-32 mg daily.

Alternatives: Captopril, Enalapril

T ½	= 9 hours	M/P	=
PHL	=	PB	= >99%
Tmax	= 3-4 hours	Oral	= 15%
MW	= 611	pKa	=
Vd	= 0.13		

References:
1. Pharmaceutical Manufacturer Prescribing Information. 2010.

CANNABIS   L5

Trade: Marijuana, Tetrahydrocannabinol
Other Trades:
Uses: Sedative, hallucinogen
AAP: Drugs of abuse for which adverse effects have been reported

Commonly called marijuana, the active component delta-9-THC (Tetrahydrocannabinol) is rapidly distributed to the brain and adipose tissue. It is stored in fat tissues for long periods (weeks to months). Small to moderate secretion into breastmilk has been documented.[1] In one mother who consumed marijuana once daily, milk levels were reportedly 105   µg/L. In another mother who consumed marijuana 7-8 time daily, milk levels of THC were 340   µg/L. Analysis of breastmilk in a chronic heavy user revealed an eight fold accumulation in breastmilk compared to plasma although the dose received is apparently insufficient to produce significant side effects in the infant. Studies have shown significant absorption and metabolism in infants although long term sequela are conflicting.

In one study of 27 women who smoked marijuana routinely during breastfeeding, no differences were noted in outcomes on growth, mental, and motor development.[2] In another study, marijuana in breastmilk was shown to be associated with a slight decrease in infant motor development at one year of age, especially when used during the first month of lactation.[3] This study's data was conflicted however, by the use of marijuana during the first trimester of pregnancy. Interestingly, in this study, maternal use of marijuana during pregnancy and lactation had no detectable effect on infant mental development at one year of age.[3] Another study of low-risk, predominantly middle-class infants found that the use of marijuana during lactation produced no effect.[4] Prenatal exposure to marijuana was not significantly related to any growth measures at birth, although a smaller head circumference observed at all ages reached statistical significance among the early adolescents born to the heavy marijuana users.

Studies in animals suggests that marijuana inhibits prolactin production and could inhibit lactation. This drug should not be used by nursing mothers. Infants exposed to marijuana via breastmilk will test positive in urine screens for long periods (2-3 weeks).

Pregnancy Risk Category: C

Lactation Risk Category: L5

Adult Concerns: Sedation, weakness, poor feeding patterns. Possible decreased milk production.

Pediatric Concerns: Sedation. Urine will be drug screen positive for weeks.

Drug Interactions:

Relative Infant Dose:

Adult Dose:

Alternatives:

T ½	= 25-57 hours	M/P	= 8
PHL	=	PB	= 99.9%
Tmax	=	Oral	= 6-20%
MW	= 314	pKa	=
Vd	= High		

References:
1. Perez-Reyes M, Wall ME. Presence of delta9-tetrahydrocannabinol in human milk. N Engl J Med 1982; 307 (13):819-820.
2. Tennes K, Avitable N, Blackard C, Boyles C, Hassoun B, Holmes L, Kreye M. Marijuana: prenatal and postnatal exposure in the human. NIDA Res Monogr 1985; 59:48-60.
3. Astley SJ, Little RE. Maternal Marijuana Use During Lactation and Infant Development at One Year. Neurotoxicol Teratol 1990; 12:161-168.
4. Fried PA, Watkinson B, Gray R. Growth from birth to early adolescence in offspring prenatally exposed to cigarettes and marijuana. Neurotoxicol Teratol. 1999 ;21:513-25.

CAPSAICIN   L3

Trade: Zostrix, Axsain, Capsin, Capzasin-P, No-Pain, Absorbine Jr. Arthritis, ArthriCare

Other Trades: Capsig, Natraflex

Uses: Analgesic, topical

AAP: Not reviewed

Capsaicin is an alkaloid derived from peppers from the Solanaceae family. After topical absorption it increases, depletes, and then suppresses substance P release from sensory neurons, thus preventing pain sensation. Substance P is the principal chemomediator of pain from the periphery to the CNS.[1,2] After repeated application (days to weeks), it depletes substance P and prevents reaccumulation in the neuron. Very little or nothing is known about the kinetics of this product. It is approved for use in children >2 years of age. No data is available on transfer into human milk. However, topical application to the nipple or areola should be avoided unless it is thoroughly removed prior to breastfeeding.

Pregnancy Risk Category: C

Lactation Risk Category: L3

Adult Concerns: Local irritation, burning, stinging, erythema. Cough and infrequently neurotoxicity. Avoid use near eyes, or on the nipple.

Pediatric Concerns: None reported. Avoid transfer to eye and other sensitive surfaces via hand contact.

Drug Interactions: May increase risk of cough with ACE inhibitors.

Relative Infant Dose:

Adult Dose:

Alternatives:

T ½	= Several hours	M/P	=
PHL	=	PB	=
Tmax	=	Oral	=
MW	= 305	pKa	=
Vd	=		

References:
1. Bernstein JE. Capsaicin in dermatologic disease. Semin Dermatol 1988; 7 (4):304-309.2.   Watson CP, Evans RJ, Watt VR. The post-mastectomy pain syndrome and the effect of topical capsaicin. Pain 1989; 38 (2):177-186.

CAPTOPRIL   L2

Trade: Capoten
Other Trades: Apo-Capto, Novo-Captopril, Acenorm, Enzace, Acepril
Uses: Antihypertensive drug (ACE inhibitor)
AAP: Maternal Medication Usually Compatible with Breastfeeding

Captopril is a typical angiotensin converting enzyme inhibitor (ACE) used to reduce hypertension. In one report of 12 women treated with 100 mg three times daily, maternal serum levels averaged 713 µg/L while breast milk levels averaged 4.7 µg/L at 3.8 hours after administration.[1]

Data from this study suggest that an infant would ingest approximately 0.002% of the free captopril consumed by its mother (300mg) on a daily basis. No adverse effects have been reported in this study. Use with care in mothers with premature infants.

Pregnancy Risk Category: C in first trimester
D in second and third trimesters

Lactation Risk Category: L2

Adult Concerns: Hypotension, bradycardia, decreased urine output and possible seizures. A decrease in taste acuity or metallic taste.

Pediatric Concerns: None reported but observe for hypotension.

Drug Interactions: Probenecid increases plasma levels of captopril. Captopril and diuretics have additive hypotensive effects. Antacids reduce bioavailability of ACE inhibitors. NSAIDS reduce hypotension of ACE inhibitors. Phenothiazines increase effects of ACEi. Allopurinol may increase risk of Steven-Johnson's syndrome with admixed with captopril. ACEi increase digoxin and lithium plasma levels. May elevate potassium levels when potassium supplementation is added.

Relative Infant Dose:

Adult Dose: 50 mg TID

Alternatives: Enalapril, benazepril

T ½	= 2.2 hours	M/P	= 0.012
PHL	=	PB	= 30%
Tmax	= 1 hr.	Oral	= 60-75%
MW	= 217	pKa	= 3.7, 9.8
Vd	= 0.7		

References:
1. Devlin R. Selective resistance to the passage of captopril into human milk. Clin Pharmacol Ther 27:250, 1980.

CARBAMAZEPINE   L2

Trade: Tegretol, Epitol, Carbatrol
Other Trades: Apo-Carbamazepine, Mazepine, Teril
Uses: Anticonvulsant
AAP: Maternal Medication Usually Compatible with Breastfeeding

Carbamazepine (CBZ) is a unique anticonvulsant commonly used for grand mal, clonic-tonic, simple and complex seizures. It is also used in manic depression and a number of other neurologic syndromes. It is one of the most commonly used anticonvulsants in pediatric patients.

In a brief study by Kaneko, with maternal plasma levels averaging 4.3 μg/mL, milk levels were 1.9 mg/L.[1] In a study of 3 patients who received from 5.8 to 7.3 mg/kg/day carbamazepine, milk levels were reported to vary from 1.3 to 1.8 mg/L while the epoxide metabolite varied from 0.5 to 1.1 mg/L. [2] No adverse effects were noted in any of the infants.

In another study by Niebyl, breast milk levels were 1.4 mg/L in the lipid fraction and 2.3 mg/L in the skim fraction in a mother receiving 1000 mg daily of carbamazepine.[3] This author estimated that the daily intake of 2 mg carbamazepine daily (0.5 mg/kg) in an infant ingesting 1 liter of milk per day.

In a study of CBZ and its epoxide metabolite (ECBZ) in milk, 16 patients received an average dose of 13.8 mg/kg/d.[4] The average maternal serum levels of CBZ and ECBZ were 7.1 and 2.6 μg/mL respectively. The average milk levels of CBZ and ECBZ were 2.5 and 1.5 mg/L respectively. The relative percent of CBZ and ECBZ in milk were 36.4% and 53% of the maternal serum levels. A total of 50 milk samples in 19 patients were analyzed. Of these, the lowest CBZ concentration in milk was 1.0 mg/L; the highest was 4.8 mg/L. The CBZ level was determined in 7 infants 4-7 days postpartum. All infants have CBZ levels below 1.5 μg/mL.

In a study of 7 women receiving 250-800 mg/d carbamazepine, the CBZ level ranged from 2.8-4.5 mg/L in milk to 3.2-15.0 mg/L in plasma.[5] The levels of ECBZ ranged from 0.5-1.7 mg/L in milk to 0.8-4.8 mg/L in plasma. The amount of CBZ transferred to the infant is apparently quite low. Although the half-life of CBZ in infants appears shorter than in adults, infants should still be monitored for sedative effects.

We have one report of a mother consuming 400 mg daily of carbamazepine, in which the infant at 9 days, had elevated liver function tests (GGT).[6] Serum carbamazepine levels in the infant at 2 days and 63 days of life, were 1.8 and 1.1 mg/L respectively. CBZ-induced hepatic dysfunction in neonates may be associated with exposure to CBZ via breast milk.

Infants of epileptic mothers treated with CBZ throughout pregnancy and breastfeeding should be carefully monitored for possible adverse effects.

Pregnancy Risk Category: D

Lactation Risk Category: L2

Adult Concerns: Sedation, nausea, respiratory depression, tachycardia, vomiting, diarrhea, blood dyscrasias. The US FDA warns that patients of Asian ancestry should be screened for the human leukocyte antigen (HLA) allele HLA-B*1502 before receiving carbamazepine therapy. The risk for Stevens Johnson syndrome (SJS) and toxic epidermal necrolysis (TEN) is higher among these patients.

Pediatric Concerns: None reported via milk.

Drug Interactions: Carbamazepine may induce the metabolism of warfarin, cyclosporin, doxycycline, oral contraceptives, phenytoin, theophylline, benzodiazepines, ethosuximide, valproic acid, corticosteroids, and thyroid hormones. Macrolide antibiotics, isoniazid, verapamil, danazol, diltiazem may inhibit metabolism of carbamazepine and increase plasma levels.

Relative Infant Dose: 3.8% - 5.9%

Adult Dose: 800-1200 mg daily. divided TID or QID

Alternatives:

T ½	= 18-54 hours	M/P	= 0.69
PHL	= 8-28 hours	PB	= 74%
Tmax	= 4-5 hours	Oral	= 100%
MW	= 236	pKa	= 7.0
Vd	= 0.8-1.8		

References:
1. Kaneko S, Sato T, Suzuki K. The levels of anticonvulsants in breast milk. Br J Clin Pharmacol 1979; 7 (6):624-627.
2. Pynnonen S, Kanto J, Sillanpaa M, Erkkola R. Carbamazepine: placental transport, tissue concentrations in foetus and newborn, and level in milk. Acta Pharmacol Toxicol (Copenh) 1977; 41 (3):244-253.
3. Niebyl JR, Blake DA, Freeman JM, Luff RD. Carbamazepine levels in pregnancy and lactation. Obstet Gynecol 1979; 53 (1):139-140.
4. Froescher W, Eichelbaum M, Niesen M, Dietrich K, Rausch P. Carbamazepine levels in breast milk. Ther Drug Monit 1984; 6 (3):266-271.

5. Shimoyama R, Ohkubo T, Sugawara K. Monitoring of carbamazepine and carbamazepine 10,11-epoxide in breast milk and plasma by high-performance liquid chromatography. Ann Clin Biochem 2000; 37 (Pt 2):210-215.
6. Merlob P, Mor N, Litwin A. Transient hepatic dysfunction in an infant of an epileptic mother treated with carbamazepine during pregnancy and breastfeeding. Ann Pharmacother. 1992 Dec;26 (12):1563-5.

CARBAMIDE PEROXIDE   L1

Trade: Gly-Oxide, Debrox, Auro Otic, Teeth whiteners, Peroxides, Debrox, Auro Ear Drops, Dewax

Other Trades: Exterol

Uses: Antibacterial, whitening agent

AAP: Not reviewed

Carbamide peroxide, also called urea peroxide, is stable while immersed in glycerin, but upon contact with moisture, releases hydrogen peroxide and nascent oxygen, both strong oxidizing agents. It is used to disinfect infected lesions, for the removal of earwax, and for whitening of teeth and dental appliances. Hydrogen peroxide is rapidly metabolized by hydroperoxidases, peroxidases, and catalase present in all tissues, plasma, and saliva. Its transfer to the plasma is minimal if at all. It would be all but impossible for any to reach breastmilk unless under extreme overdose.

Pregnancy Risk Category: C

Lactation Risk Category: L1

Adult Concerns: Dermal irritation, mucous membrane irritation, inflammation. Overgrowth of candida and other opportunistic infections.

Pediatric Concerns: Possibly toxic in major oral overdose. Exposure to small amounts may lead to inflamed membranes.

Drug Interactions:

Relative Infant Dose:

Adult Dose:

Alternatives:

T ½	=	M/P	=
PHL	=	PB	=
Tmax	=	Oral	=
MW	= 94	pKa	=
Vd	=		

References:

CARBENICILLIN   L1

Trade: Geopen, Geocillin, Carindacillin
Other Trades: Carbapen
Uses: Extended spectrum penicillin antibiotic
AAP: Not reviewed

Carbenicillin is an extended spectrum penicillin antibiotic. Only limited levels are secreted into breastmilk (0.26 mg/liter or about 0.001% of adult dose).[1] In a study of 2-3 women who received 1000 mg IM, the maximum milk level occurred at 4 hours and averaged 0.24 mg/L.[2] The average milk/plasma ratio reported was 0.045 at 4 hours. Due to its poor oral absorption (<10%) the amount absorbed by a nursing infant would be minimal.

Pregnancy Risk Category: B

Lactation Risk Category: L1

Adult Concerns: Rash, thrush, or diarrhea. Headache, rash, hyperthermia.

Pediatric Concerns: None reported via milk.

Drug Interactions: Coadministration of aminoglycosides (within 1 hrs) may inactivate both drugs. Increased half-life with probenecid.

Relative Infant Dose: 0.3%

Adult Dose: 382-764 mg every 6 hours

Alternatives:

T ½	= 1 hour	M/P	= 0.02
PHL	= 0.8-1.8 hours	PB	= 26-60%
Tmax	= 1-3 hours	Oral	= <10-30%
MW	= 378	pKa	=
Vd	=		

References:
1. Pharmaceutical Manufacturer Prescribing Information. 1996.
2. Matsuda S. Transfer of antibiotics into maternal milk. Biol Res Pregnancy Perinatol 1984; 5 (2):57-60.

CARBIDOPA   L3

Trade: Lodosyn
Other Trades: Sinemet, Kinson, Sinacarb
Uses: Inhibits levodopa metabolism
AAP: Not reviewed

Carbidopa inhibits the metabolism of levodopa in parkinsonian patients therefore extending the half- life of levodopa. Its effect on lactation is largely unknown, but skeletal malformations have occurred in pregnant rabbits.[1,2] Use discretion in administering to pregnant or lactating women. Warning: Carbidopa and levodopa are known to suppress prolactin production in normal, and breastfeeding mothers.[3,4,5,6]

Pregnancy Risk Category: C

Lactation Risk Category: L3

Adult Concerns: GI distress, nausea, vomiting, diarrhea.

Pediatric Concerns:

Drug Interactions: May interact with tricyclic antidepressants leading to hypertensive reactions.

Relative Infant Dose:

Adult Dose: 70-100 mg daily.

Alternatives:

T ½	= 1-2 hours	M/P	=
PHL	=	PB	= 36%
Tmax	=	Oral	= 40-70%
MW	= 244	pKa	=
Vd	=		

References:
1. Pharmaceutical Manufacturer Prescribing Information. 1996.
2. McEvoy GE. (ed):AFHS Drug Information. New York, NY: 1995.
3. Ayalon D, Peyser MR et al. Effect of L-dopa on galactopoiesis and gonadotropin levels in the inappropriate lactation syndrome. Obstet Gynecol. 1974;44:159-70.

4. Leblanc H, Yen SS. The effect of L-dopa and chlorpromazine on prolactin and growth hormone secretion in normal women. Am J Obstet Gynecol. 1976;126:162-4.
5. Board JA, Fierro RJ et al. Effects of alpha- and beta-adrenergic blocking agents on serum prolactin levels in women with hyperprolactinemia and galactorrhea. Am J Obstet Gynecol. 1977;127:285-7.
6. Rao R, Scommegna A, Frohman LA. Integrity of central dopaminergic system in women with postpartum hyperprolactinemia. Am J Obstet Gynecol. 1982;143:883-7.

CARBIMAZOLE   L3

Trade:
Other Trades: Neo-Mercazole
Uses: Thyroid inhibitor
AAP: Maternal Medication Usually Compatible with
             Breastfeeding

Carbimazole, a prodrug of methimazole, is rapidly and completely converted to the active methimazole in the plasma. Only methimazole is detected in plasma, urine and thyroid tissue. See breastfeeding specifics for methimazole.

In a study by Rylance suggests that subclinical levels of methimazole enter milk subsequent to a maternal dose of 30 mg/day carbimazole.[1] Free methimazole measured in milk on 10 occasions averaged 43 µg/L. Plasma methimazole in twins was 45 to 52 ng/mL. Thyroid suppression is believed to occur only when plasma levels exceed 50-100 ng/mL. No thyroid suppression was noted in these two twins. Peak transfer into milk occurred at 2-4 hours, and the lowest at 6 hours after the dose. The authors suggest that breastfeeding is permissible if the maternal dose is less than 30 mg/day.

In another study of 5 five lactating women receiving 40 mg/d, the mean concentration of methimazole in milk was 182 µg/L, with a mean milk/serum ratio of 0.98.[2] The mean total amount of methimazole excreted in milk over 8 h was 34 µg. The limited data above suggests that the transfer of carbimazole is too low to affect thyroid function in breastfeeding infants. However, close monitoring of infant thyroid function is probably advisable. See propylthiouracil as alternative. See propylthiouracil as alternative. However, close monitoring of infant thyroid function is probably advisable.

Pregnancy Risk Category: D

Lactation Risk Category: L3

Adult Concerns: Hypothyroidism, hepatic dysfunction, bleeding, drowsiness, skin rash, nausea, vomiting, fever.

Pediatric Concerns: None reported via milk, but propylthiouracil is generally preferred in breastfeeding women.

Drug Interactions: Use with iodinated glycerol, lithium, and potassium iodide may increase toxicity.

Relative Infant Dose: 2.3% - 5.3%

Adult Dose: < 30 mg daily

Alternatives: Propylthiouracil

T ½	= 6-13 hours	M/P	= 0.3-0.7
PHL	=	PB	= 0%
Tmax	= 4 hour	Oral	= Complete
MW	= 186	pKa	=
Vd	=		

References:
1. Rylance GW, Woods CG, Donnelly MC, Oliver JS, Alexander WD. Carbimazole and breastfeeding. Lancet 1987; 1 (8538):928.
2. Johansen K, Andersen AN, Kampmann JP, Molholm Hansen JM, Mortensen HB. Excretion of methimazole in human milk. Eur J Clin Pharmacol 1982; 23 (4):339-341.

CARBOPROST TROMETHAMINE   L3

Trade: Hemabate
Other Trades:
Uses: Oxytocic prostaglandin for postpartum hemorrhage
AAP: Not reviewed

Carboprost is a prostaglandin analogue (15-methyl prostaglandin F2-alpha) which stimulates the gravid uterus myometrial contractions similar to labor. It is a commonly used oxytocic agent used to prevent postpartum hemorrhage. No data are available on its transfer to human milk. Prostaglandins have brief half-lives and little distribution out of the plasma compartment. Even then, rather large intramuscular doses only produce picogram concentrations in the plasma of recipients. It is not likely it will penetrate milk in clinically relevant amounts.

Pregnancy Risk Category: C

Lactation Risk Category: L3

Adult Concerns: Adverse events include vomiting, diarrhea, leukocytosis, hypertension, headache, dystonic reactions, fever, uterine rupture, bronchoconstriction, and flushing of the skin.

Pediatric Concerns: None reported via milk. Commonly used in obstetrics without complication in breastfeeding mothers.

Drug Interactions: May augment other oxytocics.

Relative Infant Dose:

Adult Dose: 100-250 mg initially.

Alternatives:

T ½	= <1 hour	M/P	=
PHL	=	PB	=
Tmax	= 15-30 minutes	Oral	=
MW	= 489	pKa	=
Vd	=		

References:
1. Pharmaceutical Manufacturers prescribing information, 2003.

CARISOPRODOL   L3

Trade: Soma Compound, Solol
Other Trades: Soma, Carisoma
Uses: Muscle relaxant, CNS depressant
AAP: Not reviewed

Carisoprodol is a commonly used skeletal muscle relaxant that is a CNS depressant. It is metabolized to an active metabolite called meprobamate. As Soma Compound it also contains 325 mg of aspirin. In a study of one breastfeeding mother receiving 2100 mg/d, the average milk concentration of carisoprodol and meprobamate was 0.9 mg/L and 11.6 mg/L respectively.[1] No adverse effects on the infant were noted.

Pregnancy Risk Category: C

Lactation Risk Category: L3

Adult Concerns: Nausea, vomiting, hiccups, sedation, weakness, mild withdrawal symptoms after chronic use.

Pediatric Concerns: None reported, but observe for sedation.

Drug Interactions: Increased toxicity when added to alcohol, CNS depressants, MAO inhibitors.

Relative Infant Dose: 0.5% - 6.3%

Adult Dose: 350 mg TID-QID

Alternatives:

T ½	= 8 hours	M/P	= 2-4
PHL	=	PB	=
Tmax	=	Oral	= Complete
MW	= 260	pKa	=
Vd	=		

References:
1. Nordeng H, Zahlsen K, Spigset O. Transfer of carisoprodol to breast milk. Ther Drug Monit 2001; 23 (3):298-300.

CARTEOLOL   L3

Trade: Cartrol
Other Trades: Teoptic
Uses: Beta-adrenergic antihypertensive
AAP: Not reviewed

Carteolol is a typical beta-blocker used for hypertension. Carteolol is reported to be excreted in breastmilk of lactating animals.[1] No data are available on levels in human milk.

Pregnancy Risk Category: C

Lactation Risk Category: L3

Adult Concerns: Hypotension, bradycardia, lethargy, and sedation.

Pediatric Concerns: None reported but observe for hypoglycemia, hypotension, bradycardia, lethargy.

Drug Interactions: Decreased effect when used with aluminum salts, barbiturates, calcium salts, cholestyramine, NSAIDs, ampicillin, rifampin, and salicylates. Beta blockers may reduce the effect of oral sulfonylureas (hypoglycemic agents). Increased toxicity/effect when used with other antihypertensives, contraceptives, MAO inhibitors, cimetidine, and numerous other products. See drug interaction reference for complete listing.

Relative Infant Dose:

Adult Dose: 2.5-5 mg daily.

Alternatives: Propranolol, Metoprolol

T ½	= 6 hours	M/P	=
PHL	=	PB	– 23-30%
Tmax	=	Oral	= 80%
MW	– 292	pKa	=
Vd	=		

References:
1. Pharmaceutical Manufacturer Prescribing Information. 2010.

CARVEDILOL   L3

Trade: Coreg
Other Trades: Eucardio, Proreg, Dilatrend
Uses: Antihypertensive
AAP: Not reviewed

Carvedilol is a nonselective beta-adrenergic blocking agent (and partial alpha-1 blocking activity) with high lipid solubility and no intrinsic sympathomimetic activity.[1] There are no data available on the transfer of this drug into human milk. However, due to its high lipid solubility, some may transfer. As with any beta-blocker, some caution is recommended until milk levels are reported.

Pregnancy Risk Category: C

Lactation Risk Category: L3

Adult Concerns: Postural hypotension, fatigue, dizziness, lightheadedness, bradycardia, bronchospasm. Use with caution in asthmatics.

Pediatric Concerns: None reported via milk. Observe for hypotension, bradycardia, hypoglycemia.

Drug Interactions: Severe bradycardia may result when used with amiodarone. Digoxin may prolong AV conduction time. Severe hypotension when added with calcium channel blockers. Severe hypertension, bradycardia when used with epinephrine.

Relative Infant Dose:

Adult Dose: 6.25-12.5 mg BID

Alternatives: Propranolol, metoprolol

T ½	= 7-10 hours	M/P	=
PHL	=	PB	= 98%
Tmax	= 1-1.5 hours	Oral	= 25-35%
MW	=	pKa	=
Vd	= 1.88		

References:
1. Pharmaceutical Manufacturer Prescribing Information, 2010.

CASCARA SAGRADA   L3

Trade: Cascara Sagrada
Other Trades:
Uses: Laxative
AAP: Maternal Medication Usually Compatible with Breastfeeding

Cascara sagrada is a strong laxative. Trace amounts appear to be secreted into breastmilk.[1,2] No exact estimates have been published. May cause loose stools and diarrhea in neonates.

Pregnancy Risk Category: C

Lactation Risk Category: L3

Adult Concerns: Diarrhea, GI cramping.

Pediatric Concerns: May loosen stools in infants.

Drug Interactions: Decreased effect of oral anticoagulants.

Relative Infant Dose:

Adult Dose: 5 mL daily.

Alternatives:

References:
1. O'Brien TE. Excretion of drugs in human milk. Am J Hosp Pharm 1974; 31 (9):844-854.
2. Vorherr H. Drug excretion in breast milk. Postgrad Med 1974; 56 (4):97-104.

CASPOFUNGIN ACETATE | L3

Trade: Cancidas
Other Trades:
Uses: Antifungal
AAP: Not reviewed

Caspofungin is a unique semisynthetic lipopeptide that is active against *Aspergillus fumigatus*. It has a large polycyclic structure with a MW of 1213 daltons. The half-life of this product is unique with a polyphasic elimination curve with 3 distinct phases. The half-life varies from 11 hours in one phase to 40-50 hours in the last phase. This is a new product and limited data is available on its use, particularly in pediatrics. The pharmaceutical manufacture states that it was found in rodent milk; no data are available for human milk. Regardless, the oral bioavailability is reported as poor and it is unlikely an infant would absorb enough to be clinically relevant, but this is only speculative.

Pregnancy Risk Category: C

Lactation Risk Category: L3

Adult Concerns: Fever, nausea, vomiting, flushing, phlebitis, anemia, headache, etc.

Pediatric Concerns: None reported via milk. Not cleared for pediatric patients.

Drug Interactions: Cyclosporin increases AUC of Cancidas. Do not use with cyclosporin unless potential benefits outweigh risk. Cancidas reduces plasma levels of tacrolimus.

Relative Infant Dose:

Adult Dose: 70 mg STAT, 50 mg/d

Alternatives:

T ½	= >11 hours	M/P	=
PHL	=	PB	= 97%
Tmax	=	Oral	= Poor
MW	= 1213	pKa	= 5.1, 10.7
Vd	=		

References:
1. Pharmaceutical Manufacturer Prescribing Information, 2001.

CASTOR OIL   L3

Trade: Alphamul, Neoloid, Emulsoil
Other Trades: Castrol Oil, Seda-rash, Exzem Oil
Uses: Laxative
AAP: Not reviewed

Castor oil is converted to ricinoleic acid in the gut. Its transfer into milk is unknown. Caution should be used. Excess amounts could produce diarrhea, insomnia, and tremors in exposed infants.

Pregnancy Risk Category: X

Lactation Risk Category: L3

Adult Concerns: Insomnia, tremors, diarrhea.

Pediatric Concerns: Observe for diarrhea, insomnia, tremors in infants.

Drug Interactions:

Relative Infant Dose:

Adult Dose: N/A

Alternatives:

T ½	=	M/P	=
PHL	=	PB	=
Tmax	= 2-3 hours	Oral	= Unknown
MW	= 932	pKa	=
Vd	=		

References:

CEFACLOR   L1

Trade: Ceclor
Other Trades: Apo-Cefaclor, Keflor, Distaclor
Uses: Cephalosporin antibiotic
AAP: Not reviewed

Cefaclor is a commonly used pediatric cephalosporin antibiotic. Small amounts are known to be secreted into human milk. Following a single dose of 250 mg orally in 2 mothers, the levels in milk were undetectable in one, and ranged from 0.15 to 0.19 mg/L from 2 to 4 hours postdose. Following a 500 mg oral dose in 5 mothers, milk levels averaged 0.16 to 0.21 mg/L. Average levels were 0.18, 0.20, 0.21, and 0.16 μg/mL at 2, 3, 4, and 5 hours respectively.[1] Trace amounts were detected at 1 hour. Observe for changes in gut flora or diarrhea.

Pregnancy Risk Category: B

Lactation Risk Category: L1

Adult Concerns: Diarrhea, GI irritation, rash, penicillin allergy, delayed serum sickness at 14 days.

Pediatric Concerns: None reported via milk. Observe for changes in gut flora and diarrhea.

Drug Interactions: Probenecid may increase levels of cephalosporins by reducing renal clearance.

Relative Infant Dose: 0.4% - 0.8%

Adult Dose: 250-500 mg every 8 hours

Alternatives:

T ½	= 0.5-1 hr.	M/P	=
PHL	=	PB	⁻ 25%
Tmax	= 0.5-1 hr.	Oral	= 100%
MW	= 386	pKa	=
Vd	=		

References:
1. Takase Z. Clinical and laboratory studies of cefaclor in the field of obstetrics and gynecology. Chemotherapy 1979; 27. (Suppl)668.

CEFADROXIL   L1

Trade: Ultracef, Duricef
Other Trades: Baxan
Uses: Cephalosporin antibiotic
AAP: Maternal Medication Usually Compatible with Breastfeeding

Cefadroxil is a typical first-generation, cephalosporin antibiotic. Small amounts are known to be secreted into milk. Milk concentrations following a 1000 mg oral dose were 0.10 mg/L at 1 hour and 1.24 mg/L at 5 hours.[1] Milk/serum ratios were 0.009 at 1 hour and 0.019 at 3 hours. In a study of 2-3 patients who received an oral dose of 500 mg cefadroxil, milk levels peaked at 4 hours at an average of 0.4 mg/L which is only about 1.3% of the maternal dose.[2] The milk/plasma ratio was 0.085.

Pregnancy Risk Category: B

Lactation Risk Category: L1

Adult Concerns: Diarrhea, allergic rash.

Pediatric Concerns: None reported via milk. Observe for GI symptoms such as diarrhea.

Drug Interactions: Probenecid may decrease clearance. Furosemide, aminoglycosides may enhance renal toxicity.

Relative Infant Dose: 0.8% - 1.3%

Adult Dose: 0.5-1 g BID

Alternatives:

T ½	= 1.5 hours	M/P	= 0.009-0.019
PHL	=	PB	= 20%
Tmax	= 1-2 hours	Oral	= 100%
MW	= 381	pKa	=
Vd	=		

References:
1. Kafetzis DA, Siafas CA, Georgakopoulos PA, Papadatos CJ. Passage of cephalosporins and amoxicillin into the breast milk. Acta Paediatr Scand 1981; 70 (3):285-288.
2. Matsuda S. Transfer of antibiotics into maternal milk. Biol Res Pregnancy Perinatol 1984; 5 (2):57-60.

CEFAZOLIN   L1

Trade: Ancef, Kefzol
Other Trades: Cefamezin
Uses: Cephalosporin antibiotic
AAP: Maternal Medication Usually Compatible with Breastfeeding

Cefazolin is a typical first-generation, cephalosporin antibiotic that has adult and pediatric indications. It is only used IM or IV, never orally. In 20 patients who received a 2 gm STAT dose over 10 minutes, the average concentration of cefazolin in milk 2, 3, and 4 hours after the dose was 1.25, 1.51, and 1.16 mg/L respectively.[1] A very small milk/plasma ratio (0.023) indicates insignificant transfer into milk. Cefazolin is poorly absorbed orally; therefore, the infant would absorb a minimal amount. Plasma levels in infants are reported to be too small to be detected.

Pregnancy Risk Category: B

Lactation Risk Category: L1

Adult Concerns: Allergic rash, thrush, diarrhea.

Pediatric Concerns: None reported via milk. Observe for GI symptoms such as diarrhea.

Drug Interactions: Probenecid may decrease clearance. Furosemide, aminoglycosides may enhance renal toxicity.

Relative Infant Dose: 0.8%

Adult Dose: 250-2000 mg TID

Alternatives:

T ½	= 1.2-2.2 hours	M/P	= 0.023
PHL	=	PB	= 89%
Tmax	= 1-2 hours	Oral	= Poor
MW	= 455	pKa	=
Vd	=		

References:
1. Yoshioka H, Cho K, Takimoto M, Maruyama S, Shimizu T. Transfer of cefazolin into human milk. J Pediatr 1979; 94 (1):151-152.

CEFDINIR   L1

Trade: Omnicef
Other Trades:
Uses: Antibiotic
AAP: Not reviewed

Cefdinir is a broad-spectrum cephalosporin antibiotic. Following administration of a 600 mg oral dose, no cefdinir was detected in human milk.[1]

Pregnancy Risk Category: B

Lactation Risk Category: L1

Adult Concerns: Similar for other cephalosporins, and include diarrhea, vaginal moniliasis, nausea, and rash. Allergic reactions are possible.

Pediatric Concerns: None reported via milk. Milk levels virtually undetectable. Observe for diarrhea.

Drug Interactions: Reduced oral absorption following use of antacids. Probenecid will decrease renal excretion and a 54% increase in peak levels, and a 50% prolongation of clearance.

Relative Infant Dose:

Adult Dose: 14 mg/kg/day

Alternatives:

T ½	= 1.7 hours	M/P	=
PHL	=	PB	= 70%
Tmax	= 3 hours	Oral	= 21%
MW	= 395	pKa	=
Vd	= 0.35		

References:
1. Pharmaceutical Manufacturer Prescribing Information, 2010.

CEFDITOREN   L2

Trade: Spectracef
Other Trades:
Uses: Cephalosporin antibiotic
AAP: Not reviewed

Cefditoren is a new third generation cephalosporin antibiotic that is indicated in the treatment of acute bacterial exacerbations of chronic bronchitis, pharyngitis, tonsillitis, and uncomplicated skin infections. It is moderately active against resistant penicillin-resistant pneumococcus. It is cleared for use in children <12 years of age. No data are available on breastmilk levels.

Pregnancy Risk Category: B

Lactation Risk Category: L2

Adult Concerns: Diarrhea, nausea, headache, vaginal moniliasis.

Pediatric Concerns: No data reported in breastfed infants.

Drug Interactions:
Relative Infant Dose:

Adult Dose:

Alternatives: Cephalexin

T ½	= 1.3-2 hours	M/P	=
PHL	=	PB	= 88%
Tmax	= 1-3 hours	Oral	= 14%
MW	= 620	pKa	=
Vd	= 9.3		

References:
1. Pharmaceutical Manufacturer Prescribing Information, 2010.

CEFEPIME   L2

Trade: Maxipime
Other Trades:
Uses: Cephalosporin antibiotic
AAP: Not reviewed

Cefepime is a new 'fourth-generation' parenteral cephalosporin. Cefepime is secreted in human milk in small amounts averaging 0.5 mg/L.[1,2] In a mother consuming 2 gm/d, an infant would ingest approximately 75 µg/kg/d or only approximately 0.3% of the maternal dose. This amount is too small to produce any clinical symptoms other than possible changes in gut flora.

Pregnancy Risk Category: B

Lactation Risk Category: L2

Adult Concerns: Headache, blurred vision, dyspepsia, diarrhea, transient elevation of liver enzymes.

Pediatric Concerns: None reported via milk.

Drug Interactions: May produce additive nephrotoxic effects when used with aminoglycosides.

Relative Infant Dose: 0.3%

Adult Dose: 1-2 g BID

Alternatives:

T ½	= 2 hours	M/P	= 0.8
PHL	=	PB	= 16-19%
Tmax	= 0.5-1.5 hours	Oral	= Poor
MW	= 571	pKa	=
Vd	= 0.3		

References:
1. Pharmaceutical Manufacturer Prescribing Information. 1997.
2. Sanders CC. Cefepime: the next generation? Clin Infect Dis 1993; 17 (3):369-379.

CEFIXIME   L2

Trade: Suprax
Other Trades:
Uses: Cephalosporin antibiotic
AAP: Not reviewed

Cefixime is an oral, third-generation cephalosporin used in treating infections. It is poorly absorbed (30-50%) by the oral route. It is secreted to a limited degree in the milk although in one study of a mother receiving 100 mg, it was undetected in the milk from 1-6 hours after the dose.[1]

Pregnancy Risk Category: B

Lactation Risk Category: L2

Adult Concerns: Allergic rash, diarrhea, thrush.

Pediatric Concerns: None reported. Observe for GI symptoms such as diarrhea.

Drug Interactions: Probenecid may decrease clearance. Furosemide, aminoglycosides may enhance renal toxicity.

Relative Infant Dose:

Adult Dose: 200 mg BID

Alternatives:

T ½	= 7 hours	M/P	=
PHL	=	PB	= 70%
Tmax	= 2-6 hours	Oral	= 30-50%
MW	= 453	pKa	=
Vd	=		

References:
1. Pharmaceutical Manufacturer Prescribing Information. 2010.

CEFOPERAZONE SODIUM   L2

Trade: Cefobid
Other Trades: Dicapen
Uses: Cephalosporin antibiotic
AAP: Not reviewed

Cefoperazone is a broad-spectrum, third-generation cephalosporin antibiotic. It is poorly absorbed from GI tract and is only available via IV and IM injection. Cefoperazone is extremely labile in acid environments, which would account both for its destruction and its lack of absorption via the GI tract. Following an IV dose of 1000 mg, milk levels ranged from 0.4 to 0.9 mg/L.[1] In a study of 2-3 women who received 1000 mg IV, the maximum milk concentration was 0.4 mg/L at 6 hours.[2] The average milk/plasma ratio was 0.12 at 4 hours. Cefoperazone is extremely acid labile and would be destroyed in the GI tract of an infant. It is unlikely that significant absorption would occur.

Pregnancy Risk Category: B

Lactation Risk Category: L2

Adult Concerns: Diarrhea, allergic rash, thrush.

Pediatric Concerns: None reported. Observe for GI symptoms such as diarrhea.

Drug Interactions: Probenecid may decrease clearance. Furosemide, aminoglycosides may enhance renal toxicity.

Relative Infant Dose: 0.4% - 1%

Adult Dose: 1-2 g BID

Alternatives:

T ½	= 2 hours	M/P	= 0.12
PHL	= 6-10 hours (neonatal)	PB	= 82-93%
Tmax	= 73-153 minutes (IV)	Oral	= Poor
MW	= 645	pKa	=
Vd	=		

References:
1. Pfizer/Roerig Laboratories. Personal Communication. 1996.
2. Matsuda S. Transfer of antibiotics into maternal milk. Biol Res Pregnancy Perinatol 1984; 5 (2):57-60.

CEFOTAXIME   L2

Trade:	Claforan
Other Trades:	
Uses:	Cephalosporin antibiotic
AAP:	Maternal Medication Usually Compatible with Breastfeeding

Cefotaxime is poorly absorbed orally and is only used via IV or IM administration. Milk levels following a 1000 mg IV maternal dose were 0.26 mg/L at 1 hour, 0.32 mg/L at 2 hours, and 0.30 mg/L at 3 hours.[1] No effect on infant or lactation were noted. Milk/serum ratio at 3 hours was 0.160. In a group of 2-3 patients receiving 1000 mg IV, none to trace amounts were found in milk after 6 hours.[2]

Pregnancy Risk Category: B

Lactation Risk Category: L2

Adult Concerns: Diarrhea, allergic rash, thrush.

Pediatric Concerns: None reported. Observe for GI symptoms such as diarrhea.

Drug Interactions: Probenecid may decrease clearance. Furosemide, aminoglycosides may enhance renal toxicity.

Relative Infant Dose: 0.27% - 0.3%

Adult Dose: 1-2 g every BID

Alternatives:

T ½	= 1 hour	M/P	= 0.027 - 0.16
PHL	= 2-3.5 hours	PB	= 40%
Tmax	= 30 minutes	Oral	= Poor
MW	= 455	pKa	=
Vd	=		

References:

1. Kafetzis DA, Lazarides CV, Siafas CA, Georgakopoulos PA, Papadatos CJ. Transfer of cefotaxime in human milk and from mother to foetus. J Antimicrob Chemother 1980; 6 Suppl A:135-141.
2. Matsuda S. Transfer of antibiotics into maternal milk. Biol Res Pregnancy Perinatol 1984; 5 (2):57-60.

CEFOTETAN   L2

Trade: Cefotan
Other Trades: Apatef
Uses: Cephalosporin antibiotic
AAP: Not reviewed

Cefotetan is a third generation cephalosporin that is poorly absorbed orally and is only available via IM and IV injection. The drug is distributed into human milk in low concentrations. Following a maternal dose of 1000mg IM every 12 hours in 5 patients, breastmilk concentrations ranged from 0.29 to 0.59 mg/L.[1] Plasma concentrations were almost 100 times higher. In a group of 2-3 women who received 1000 mg IV, the maximum average milk level reported was 0.2 mg/L at 4 hours with a milk/plasma ratio of 0.02.[2]

In a study of 7 women who received a 1 gram dose IV, levels were undetectable in 2. In the remaining 5, milk levels ranged from 0.22-0.34 mg/L. The mean peak level was 0.34 mg/L at 4 hours.[3]

Pregnancy Risk Category: B

Lactation Risk Category: L2

Adult Concerns: Diarrhea, allergic rash, thrush.

Pediatric Concerns: None reported. Observe for GI symptoms such as diarrhea.

Drug Interactions: Probenecid may decrease clearance. Furosemide, aminoglycosides may enhance renal toxicity.

Relative Infant Dose: 0.2% - 0.3%

Adult Dose: 1-2 g BID

Alternatives:

T ½	= 3-4.6 hours	M/P	=
PHL	=	PB	= 76-91%
Tmax	= 1.5-3 hours	Oral	= Poor
MW	= 576	pKa	=
Vd	=		

References:
1. Novelli A. The penetration of intramuscular cefotetan disodium into human esta-vascular fluid and maternal milk secretion. Chemoterapia 1983; 11 (5):337-342.

2. Matsuda S. Transfer of antibiotics into maternal milk. Biol Res Pregnancy Perinatol 1984; 5 (2):57-60.
3. Cho N, Fukunaga K, Kuni K. Fundamental and clinical studies on cefotetan (YM09330) in the field of obstetrics and gynecology. Chemotherapy. 1982;30 (suppl 1):832-42.

CEFOXITIN   L1

Trade: Mefoxin
Other Trades:
Uses: Cephalosporin antibiotic
AAP: Maternal Medication Usually Compatible with Breastfeeding

Cefoxitin is a cephalosporin antibiotic with a spectrum similar to the second generation family. It is transferred into human milk in very low levels. In a study of 18 women receiving 2000-4000 mg doses, only one breast milk sample contained cefoxitin (0.9 mg/L), all the rest were too low to be detected.[1]

In another study of 2-3 women who received 1000 mg IV, only trace amounts were reported in milk over 6 hours.[2] In a group of 5 women who received an IM injection of 2000 mg, the highest milk levels were reported at 4 hours after dose.[3] The maternal plasma levels varied from 22.5 at 2 hours to 77.6 µg/mL at 4 hours. Maternal milk levels ranged from <0.25 to 0.65 mg/L. Observe for changes in gut flora.

In a group of 18 women, 25 milk samples were obtained following doses of 2-4 grams IV.[4] In only one case was cefoxitin found in milk (0.9 mg/L). In another group of 15 women receiving 1 gram IV one month postpartum, milk levels at 2 hours averaged 0.05 mg/L.[5]

Pregnancy Risk Category: B

Lactation Risk Category: L1

Adult Concerns: Diarrhea, allergic rash, thrush.

Pediatric Concerns: None reported. Observe for GI symptoms such as diarrhea.

Drug Interactions: Probenecid may decrease clearance. Furosemide, aminoglycosides may enhance renal toxicity.

Relative Infant Dose: 0.1% - 0.3%

Adult Dose: 1-2 g TID

Alternatives:

T ½	= 0.7-1.1 hour	M/P	=
PHL	=	PB	= 85-99%
Tmax	= 20-30 minutes (IM)	Oral	= Poor
MW	= 427	pKa	=
Vd	=		

References:
1. Roex AJ, van Loenen AC, Puyenbroek JI, Arts NF. Secretion of cefoxitin in breast milk following short-term prophylactic administration in caesarean section. Eur J Obstet Gynecol Reprod Biol 1987; 25 (4):299-302.
2. Matsuda S. Transfer of antibiotics into maternal milk. Biol Res Pregnancy Perinatol 1984; 5 (2):57-60.
3. Dresse A, Lambotte R, Dubois M, Delapierre D, Kramp R. Transmammary passage of cefoxitin: additional results. J Clin Pharmacol 1983; 23 (10):438-440.
4. Roex AJ, van Loenen AC, Puyenbroek JI, Arts NF. Secretion of cefoxitin in breast milk following short-term prophylactic administration in caesarean section. Eur J Obstet Gynecol Reprod Biol. 1987 Aug;25 (4):299-302.
5. Zhang Y, Zhang Q, Xu Z. [Tissue and body fluid distribution of antibacterial agents in pregnant and lactating women]. Zhonghua Fu Chan Ke Za Zhi. 1997 May;32 (5):288-92. Chinese.

CEFPODOXIME PROXETIL   L2

Trade: Vantin
Other Trades: Orelox
Uses: Cephalosporin antibiotic
AAP: Not reviewed

Cefpodoxime is a cephalosporin antibiotic that is subsequently metabolized to an active metabolite. Only 50% is orally absorbed. In a study of 3 lactating women, levels of cefpodoxime in human milk were 0%, 2%, and 6% of maternal serum levels at 4 hours following a 200 mg oral dose.[1] At 6 hours post-dosing, levels were 0%, 9%, and 16% of concomitant maternal serum levels. Pediatric indications down to 6 months of age are available.

Pregnancy Risk Category: B

Lactation Risk Category: L2

Adult Concerns: Diarrhea, allergic rash, thrush.

Pediatric Concerns: None reported. Observe for GI symptoms such as diarrhea.

Drug Interactions: Probenecid may decrease clearance. Furosemide, aminoglycosides may enhance renal toxicity. Antacids and H2 blockers reduce GI absorption of cefpodoxime.

Relative Infant Dose:

Adult Dose: 100-400 mg BID

Alternatives:

T ½	= 2.09-2.84 hours	M/P	= 0.16
PHL	=	PB	= 22-33%
Tmax	= 2-3 hours	Oral	= 50%
MW	= 558	pKa	=
Vd	=		

References:
1. Pharmaceutical Manufacturer Prescribing Information. 1996.

CEFPROZIL   L1

Trade: Cefzil
Other Trades:
Uses: Oral cephalosporin antibiotic
AAP: Maternal Medication Usually Compatible with Breastfeeding

Cefprozil is a typical second-generation, cephalosporin antibiotic. Following an oral dose of 1000 mg, the breastmilk concentrations were 0.7, 2.5, and 3.5 mg/L at 2, 4, and 6 hours post-dose respectively. The peak milk concentration occurred at 6 hours and was lower thereafter.[1] Milk/plasma ratios varied from 0.05 at 2 hours to 5.67 at 12 hours. However, the milk concentration at 12 hours was small (1.3 µg/mL). Using the highest concentration found in breastmilk (3.5 mg/L), an infant consuming 800 mL of milk daily would ingest about 2.8 mg of cefprozil daily. Because the dose used in this study is approximately twice that normally used, it is reasonable to assume that an infant would ingest less than 1.7 mg per day, an amount clinically insignificant. Pediatric indications for infants 6 months and older are available.

Pregnancy Risk Category: B

Lactation Risk Category: L1

Adult Concerns: Diarrhea, allergic rash, and thrush.

Pediatric Concerns: None reported. Observe for GI symptoms such as diarrhea.

Drug Interactions: Probenecid may decrease clearance. Furosemide, aminoglycosides may enhance renal toxicity.

Relative Infant Dose: 3.6% - 3.7%

Adult Dose: 250 mg BID

Alternatives:

T ½	= 78 minutes	M/P	= 0.05 - 5.67
PHL	=	PB	= 36%
Tmax	= 1.5 hours	Oral	= Complete
MW	=	pKa	=
Vd	=		

References:
1. Shyu WC, Shah VR, Campbell DA, Venitz J, Jaganathan V, Pittman KA, Wilber RB, Barbhaiya RH. Excretion of cefprozil into human breast milk. Antimicrob Agents Chemother 1992; 36 (5):938-941.

CEFTAZIDIME   L1

Trade: Ceftazidime, Fortaz, Tazidime, Ceptaz
Other Trades: Fortum
Uses: Cephalosporin antibiotic
AAP: Maternal Medication Usually Compatible with Breastfeeding

Ceftazidime is a broad-spectrum, third-generation, cephalosporin antibiotic. It has poor oral absorption (<10%). In a group of 11 lactating women who received 2000 mg (IV) every 8 hours for 5 days, concentrations of ceftazidime in milk averaged 3.8 mg/L before the dose and 5.2 mg/L at 1 hour after the dose and 4.5 mg/L 3 hours after the dose.[1] There is, however, no progressive accumulation of ceftazidime in breastmilk, as evidenced by the similar levels prior to and after seven doses. The therapeutic dose for neonates is 30-50 mg/kg every 12 hours.

Pregnancy Risk Category: B

Lactation Risk Category: L1

Adult Concerns: Diarrhea, allergic rash, thrush.

Pediatric Concerns: None reported. Observe for GI symptoms such as diarrhea.

Drug Interactions: Probenecid may decrease clearance. Furosemide, aminoglycosides may enhance renal toxicity.

Relative Infant Dose: 0.9%

Adult Dose: 500-2000 mg BID

Alternatives:

T ½	= 1.4-2 hours	M/P	=
PHL	= 2.2-4.7 hours (neonates)	PB	= 5-24%
Tmax	= 69-90 minutes	Oral	= <10%
MW	= 547	pKa	=
Vd	=		

References:
1. Blanco JD, Jorgensen JH, Castaneda YS, Crawford SA. Ceftazidime levels in human breast milk. Antimicrob Agents Chemother 1983; 23 (3):479-480.

CEFTIBUTEN   L2

Trade: Cedax
Other Trades:
Uses: Cephalosporin antibiotic
AAP: Not reviewed

Ceftibuten is a broad-spectrum, third generation oral cephalosporin antibiotic. No data yet available on penetration into human breastmilk.[1] Small to moderate amounts may penetrate into milk, but ceftibuten is cleared for pediatric use.[2] Its strength is in activity against gram negative species. Its weakness is in staphylococci and strep. pneumonia coverage (which causes many inner ear infections).

Pregnancy Risk Category: B

Lactation Risk Category: L2

Adult Concerns: Diarrhea, vomiting, loose stools, abdominal pain.

Pediatric Concerns: None reported. Observe for GI symptoms such as diarrhea.

Drug Interactions: Probenecid may decrease clearance. Furoscmide, aminoglycosides may enhance renal toxicity.

Relative Infant Dose:

Adult Dose: 400 mg daily.

Alternatives:

T ½	= 2.4 hours	M/P	=
PHL	= 2-3 hours	PB	= 65%
Tmax	= 2.6 hours	Oral	= High
MW	= 410	pKa	=
Vd	=		

References:
1. Pharmaceutical Manufacturer Prescribing Information. 1996.
2. Barr WH, Affrime M, Lin CC, Batra V. Pharmacokinetics of ceftibuten in children. Pediatr Infect Dis J 1995; 14 (7 Suppl):S93-101.

CEFTIZOXIME   L1

Trade: Cefizox, Baxam
Other Trades:
Uses: Cephalosporin antibiotic
AAP: Not reviewed

Ceftizoxime is a third generation cephalosporin used for many infections, similar to ceftriaxone and others. In a study of 18 patients who received 1 gm IV daily, milk levels of ceftizoxime averaged 0.52 mg/L. The maximum reported concentration was 2.38 mg/L.[1] In studies of 5 and 7 women (1 gm IV), milk levels averaged 0.43 and 0.54 mg/L.[2,3] In a study of 6 women who received 1 gm IV, milk levels of 0.25 mg/L were reported at 1 hour postdose.[4] In four good studies, Ceftizoxime produces only negligible levels in milk. Observe for changes in gut flora and diarrhea.

Pregnancy Risk Category: B

Lactation Risk Category: L1

Adult Concerns: Skin rash in allergic patients, nausea, vomiting, diarrhea.

Pediatric Concerns: None in three studies as milk levels are low. Some changes in gut flora could occur as with any antibiotic.

Drug Interactions: A decreased response to Typhoid vaccine. H2 antagonists (ranitidine, famotidine, etc) may reduce oral bioavailability of ceftizoxime.

Relative Infant Dose: 0.3% - 0.6%

Adult Dose: 1 gm IV daily

Alternatives: Ceftriaxone

T ½	= 2.3 hours	M/P	=
PHL	= 3-4 hours	PB	= 28-50%
Tmax	= <1 hour	Oral	= Minimal
MW	= 383	pKa	=
Vd	= 0.5		

References:
1. Matsuda S, Shimizu T, Ichinoe K, Cho N, Noda K, Ninomiya K, et al. [Pharmacokinetic and clinical studies of ceftizoxime in the perinatal period. The Chemotherapy Research Group for Mothers and Children]. Jpn J Antibiot 1988 Aug; 41 (8):1129-41.
2. Cho N, Fukunaga K, Kunii K, Tezuka K, Kobayashi I. [Studies of ceftizoxime in perinatal period]. Jpn J Antibiot 1988 Aug; 41 (8):1142-54.
3. Ito K, Izumi K, Takagi H, Yokoyama Y, Tamaya T, Baba Y, et al. [Pharmacokinetic and clinical studies of ceftizoxime in obstetrical and gynecological field (2)]. Jpn J Antibiot 1988 Aug; 41 (8):1155-63.
4. Gerding DN, Peterson LR. Comparative tissue and extravascular fluid concentrations of ceftizoxime. J Antimicrob Chemother 1982 Nov;10 Suppl C:105-16.:105-16.

CEFTRIAXONE   L1

Trade: Rocephin
Other Trades:
Uses: Cephalosporin antibiotic
AAP: Maternal Medication Usually Compatible with Breastfeeding

Ceftriaxone is a very popular third-generation broad-spectrum cephalosporin antibiotic. Small amounts are transferred into milk (3-4% of maternal serum level). Following a 1 gm IM dose, breastmilk levels were approximately 0.5-0.7 mg/L at between 4-8 hours.[1,2] The estimated mean milk levels at steady state were 3-4 mg/L. Another source indicates that following a 2 g/d dose and at steady state, approximately 4.4% of dose penetrates into milk.[3] In this study, the maximum breast milk concentration was 7.89 mg/L after prolonged therapy (7 days). Poor oral absorption of ceftriaxone would further limit systemic absorption by the infant. The half-life of ceftriaxone in human milk varies from 12.8 to 17.3 hours (longer than maternal serum). Even at this high dose, no adverse effects were noted in the infant. Ceftriaxone levels in breastmilk are probably too low to be clinically relevant, except for changes in GI flora. Ceftriaxone is commonly used in neonates.

Pregnancy Risk Category: B

Lactation Risk Category: L1

Adult Concerns: Diarrhea, allergic rash, pseudomembranous colitis, thrush.

Pediatric Concerns: None reported. Observe for GI symptoms such as diarrhea.

Drug Interactions: Probenecid   may   decrease   clearance. Furosemide, aminoglycosides may enhance renal toxicity.

Relative Infant Dose: 4.2%

Adult Dose: 1-2 g daily.-BID
Alternatives:

T ½	= 7.3 hours	M/P	= 0.03
PHL	=	PB	= 95%
Tmax	= 1 hour	Oral	= Poor
MW	= 555	pKa	=
Vd	= 0.192		

References:
1.   Kafetzis DA, Siafas CA, Georgakopoulos PA, Papadatos CJ. Passage of cephalosporins and amoxicillin into the breast milk. Acta Paediatr Scand 1981; 70 (3):285-288.
2.   Kafetzis DA, Brater DC, Fanourgakis JE, Voyatzis J, Georgakopoulos P. Ceftriaxone distribution between maternal blood and fetal blood and tissues at parturition and between blood and milk postpartum. Antimicrob Agents Chemother 1983; 23 (6):870-873.
3.   Bourget P, Quinquis-Desmaris V, Fernandez H. Ceftriaxone distribution and protein binding between maternal blood and milk postpartum. Ann Pharmacother 1993; 27 (3):294-297.

CEFUROXIME   L2

Trade: Ceftin, Zinacef, Kefurox
Other Trades: Zinnat
Uses: Cephalosporin antibiotic
AAP: Not reviewed

Cefuroxime is a broad-spectrum second-generation cephalosporin antibiotic that is available orally and IV The manufacturer states that it is secreted into human milk in small amounts, but the levels are not available.[1] In a study of 38 mothers who received cefuroxime, 2.6% reported mild side effects that were not significantly different from controls (9%).[2] Following a single dose of 750 mg in 5 women, the mean peak level reported in milk was 370 μg/L.[3] In another group of 8 women who received a single dose of 750 mg, milk levels at peak (8 hours) were 1.45 mg/L.[4] Cefuroxime has a very bitter taste. The IV salt form, cefuroxime sodium, is very poorly absorbed orally. Only the axetil salt form is orally bioavailable.

Pregnancy Risk Category: B

Lactation Risk Category: L2

Adult Concerns: Nausea, vomiting, diarrhea, GI distress, skin rash, allergies.

Pediatric Concerns: None reported. Observe for GI symptoms such as diarrhea, rash.

Drug Interactions: Probenecid may decrease clearance. Furosemide, aminoglycosides may enhance renal toxicity.

Relative Infant Dose: 0.6% - 2%

Adult Dose: 250-500 mg BID

Alternatives:

T ½	= 1.4 hours	M/P	=
PHL	=	PB	= 33-50%
Tmax	=	Oral	= 30-50%
MW	= 424	pKa	=
Vd	=		

References:
1. Pharmaceutical Manufacturer Prescribing Information. 1995.
2. Benyamini L et al. The Safety of Amoxicillin/Clavulanic Acid and Cefuroxime During Lactation. Ther Drug Monit 2005 Aug; 27 (4):499-502.

3. Takase Z, Shirofuji H, Uchida M. Fundamental and clinical studies of cefuroxime in the field of obstetrics and gynecology. Chemotherapy (Tokyo). 1979;27 (Suppl 6):600-2.
4. Voropaeva SD, Emelyanova AI, Ankirskaya AS et al. Cefuroxime efficacy in obstetrics and gynecology. Antibiotiki. 1981;27:697-701.

CELECOXIB	L2

Trade: Celebrex
Other Trades:
Uses: NSAID anti-inflammatory
AAP: Not reviewed

Celecoxib is an NSAID that specifically blocks the cycyclooxygenase-2 (COX-2) enzyme. It is primarily used for arthritic or inflammatory pain. In a case report of a patient receiving 100 mg twice daily, the authors report a milk level of 133 and 101 ng/mL in left and right breasts 4.75 hours after the dose.[1] They estimated (using the C_{max} levels) the M/P ratio to be 0.27 to 0.59 and that the infant's exposure would be approximately 20 µg/kg/day.

In data from our laboratories in 5 women receiving 200 mg once daily, the mean milk/plasma AUC ratio was 0.23.[2] The average concentration of celecoxib (AUC) in milk was 66 µg/L. The absolute infant dose averaged 9.8 µg/kg/day. Using this data, the relative infant dose was 0.30% of the maternal dose. Plasma levels of celecoxib in two infants studied were undetectable.

In another study, blood and milk were sampled for 48 hours after celecoxib 200 mg orally in six lactating volunteers. The median infant dose was 0.23% of the maternal dose after adjusting for weight. Therefore, the authors suggest that the relative dose that infants are exposed to via milk is very low and breastfeeding would probably not be a threat to the infant.[3]

Pregnancy Risk Category: C

Lactation Risk Category: L2

Adult Concerns: GI distress, diarrhea, dyspepsia, headache, aggravated hypertension and asthma.

Pediatric Concerns: None reported via milk. Plasma levels in 2 infants were undetectable. Milk levels are very low.

Drug Interactions: Celecoxib may significantly diminish antihypertensive effects of ACE inhibitors, and the natruretic effect of furosemide. Fluconazole may increase plasma levels of celecoxib two-fold. Celecoxib may increase lithium levels by 17%.

Relative Infant Dose: 0.3% - 0.7%

Adult Dose: 100-400 mg daily

Alternatives: Ibuprofen

T ½	− 11.2 hours	M/P	= 0.23
PHL	=	PB	= 97%
Tmax	= 2.8 hours	Oral	= 99%
MW	= 381	pKa	=
Vd	= 5.71		

References:
1. Knoppert DC, Stempak D, Baruchel S, Koren G. Celecoxib in human milk: a case report. Pharmacotherapy 2003; 23 (1):97-100.
2. Hale TW, McDonald R, Boger J. Transfer of celecoxib into human milk. J Hum Lact 2004 Nov; 20 (4):397-403.
3. Gardiner SJ, Doogue MP, Zhang M, Begg EJ. Quantification of infant exposure to celecoxib through breast milk. Br J Clin Pharmacol 2006; 61 (1):101-104.

CEPHALEXIN   L1

Trade: Keflex
Other Trades: Apo-Cephalex, Ceporex, Novo-Lexin
Uses: Cephalosporin antibiotic
AAP: Not reviewed

Cephalexin is a typical first-generation, cephalosporin antibiotic. Only minimal concentrations are secreted into human milk. Following a 1000 mg maternal oral dose, milk levels at 1, 2, 3, 4, and 5 hours ranged from 0.20, 0.28, 0.39, 0.50, and 0.47 mg/L respectively.[1] Milk/serum ratios varied from 0.008 at 1 hour to 0.140 at 3 hours. These levels are probably too low to be clinically relevant.

In a group of 2-3 patients who received 500 mg orally, milk levels averaged 0.7 mg/L at 4 hours although the average milk level was 0.36 mg/L over 6 hours.[2] The milk/plasma ratio was 0.25.

In another case report of a mother taking probenecid along with cephalexin to prolong the half-life of the cephalexin, the baby developed severe diarrhea. The average milk concentration of probenecid and cephalexin was 964 µg/L and 0.745 µg/L, respectively.

This corresponds to a relative infant dose of 0.7% for probenecid and 0.5% for cephalexin. The authors concluded that when using this combination of drugs in breast feeding women, clinicians should expect the possibility of adverse GI effects in the infant.[3]

Pregnancy Risk Category: B

Lactation Risk Category: L1

Adult Concerns: Diarrhea, allergic rash, thrush.

Pediatric Concerns: Diarrhea in the groups exposed to probenecid plus cephalexin.

Drug Interactions: Probenecid   may   decrease   clearance. Furosemide, aminoglycosides may enhance renal toxicity.

Relative Infant Dose: 0.2% - 1.5%

Adult Dose: 250-1000 mg every 6 hours

Alternatives:

T ½	= 50-80 minutes	M/P	= 0.008-0.14
PHL	=	PB	= 10%
Tmax	= 1 hour	Oral	= Complete
MW	= 347	pKa	=
Vd	=		

References:

1.   Kafetzis DA, Siafas CA, Georgakopoulos PA, Papadatos CJ. Passage of cephalosporins and amoxicillin into the breast milk. Acta Paediatr Scand 1981; 70 (3):285-288.
2.   Matsuda S. Transfer of antibiotics into maternal milk. Biol Res Pregnancy Perinatol 1984; 5 (2):57-60.
3.   Ilett K, Hackett P, Ingle B, Bretz PJ. Transfer of Probenecid and Cephalexin into Breast Milk. Ann Pharmacother 2006; 40:986-988.

CEPHALOTHIN   L1

Trade: Keflin
Other Trades: Ceporacin
Uses: Cephalosporin antibiotic
AAP: Not reviewed

Cephalothin is a first-generation, cephalosporin antibiotic for use by IM or IV administration. Following a 1000 mg IV maternal dose, milk levels varied from 0.27, 0.41, 0.47, 0.36, and 0.28 mg/L at 0.5, 1, 2, 3, and 4 hours respectively.[1] Milk/serum ratios varied from 0.06 at 1 hour to 0.51 at 3 hours.

Pregnancy Risk Category: B

Lactation Risk Category: L1

Adult Concerns: Diarrhea, allergic rash, thrush.

Pediatric Concerns: None reported. Observe for diarrhea.

Drug Interactions: Probenecid may decrease clearance. Furosemide, aminoglycosides may enhance renal toxicity.

Relative Infant Dose: 0.3% - 0.5%

Adult Dose: 500-2000 mg every 4-6 hours

Alternatives: Cephalexin, amoxicillin, dicloxacillin

T ½	= 30-50 minutes	M/P	= 0.06-0.5 1
PHL	=	PB	= 70%
Tmax	= 1-2 hours	Oral	= Poor
MW	= 396	pKa	=
Vd	=		

References:
1. Kafetzis DA, Siafas CA, Georgakopoulos PA, Papadatos CJ. Passage of cephalosporins and amoxicillin into the breast milk. Acta Paediatr Scand 1981; 70 (3):285-288.

CEPHAPIRIN   L1

Trade: Cefadyl
Other Trades: Cefadyl
Uses: Cephalosporin antibiotic
AAP: Not reviewed

Cephapirin is a typical first-generation, cephalosporin antibiotic for IM or IV administration. Following a 1000 mg IV maternal dose, milk levels varied from 0.26, 0.41, 0.43, 0.33, and 0.27 mg/L at 0.5, 1, 2, 3, and 4 hours respectively.[1] These are too low to be clinically relevant. Milk/serum ratios varied from 0.068 at 1 hour to 0.48 at 3 hours.

Pregnancy Risk Category: B

Lactation Risk Category: L1

Adult Concerns: Diarrhea, allergic rash, thrush.

Pediatric Concerns: None reported. Observe for GI symptoms such as diarrhea.

Drug Interactions: Probenecid may decrease clearance. Furosemide, aminoglycosides may enhance renal toxicity.

Relative Infant Dose: 0.3% - 0.4%

Adult Dose: 500-1000 mg every 6 hours

Alternatives:

T ½	= 24-36 minutes	M/P	= 0.068-0.48
PHL	=	PB	= 54%
Tmax	= 1-2 hours	Oral	= Poor
MW	= 445	pKa	=
Vd	=		

References:
1. Kafetzis DA, Siafas CA, Georgakopoulos PA, Papadatos CJ. Passage of cephalosporins and amoxicillin into the breast milk. Acta Paediatr Scand 1981; 70 (3):285-288.

CEPHRADINE   L1

Trade: Velosef, Anspor
Other Trades: Nicef
Uses: Cephalosporin antibiotic
AAP: Not reviewed

Cephradine is typical first-generation cephalosporin antibiotic. In a group of 6 lactating women receiving 500 mg orally every 6 hours for 2 days, milk levels averaged about 0.6 mg/L.[1] In another study group by this same author, the average milk level was 1.0 mg/L.[2] These levels are too low to be clinically relevant.

Pregnancy Risk Category: B

Lactation Risk Category: L1

Adult Concerns: Diarrhea, allergic rash, thrush, liver dysfunction.

Pediatric Concerns: None reported. Observe for GI symptoms such as diarrhea.

Drug Interactions: Probenecid may decrease clearance. Furosemide, aminoglycosides may enhance renal toxicity.

Relative Infant Dose: 0.3% - 0.5%

Adult Dose: 250-500 mg every 6-12 hours

Alternatives:

T ½	= 0.7-2 hours	M/P	= 0.2
PHL	=	PB	= 8-17%
Tmax	= 1 hour	Oral	= Complete
MW	= 349	pKa	=
Vd	=		

References:
1. Mischler TW, Corson SL, Larranaga A, Bolognese RJ, Neiss ES, Vukovich RA. Cephradine and epicillin in body fluids of lactating and pregnant women. J Reprod Med 1978; 21 (3):130-136.
2. Mischler TW. et.al. Presence of cephradine in body fluids of lactating and pregnant women. Clin Pharmacol Ther 1974; 15:214.

CETIRIZINE

L2

Trade: Zyrtec
Other Trades: Reactine, Zirtek
Uses: Antihistamine
AAP: Not reviewed

Cetirizine is a popular new antihistamine useful for seasonal allergic rhinitis. It is a metabolite of hydroxyzine and is one of the most potent of the antihistamines. It is rapidly and extensively absorbed orally and due to a rather long half-life is used only once daily. It penetrates the CNS poorly and therefore produces minimal sedation. Compared to other new antihistamines, cetirizine is not very toxic in overdose and produces few cardiovascular changes at higher doses.[1] Further, as with many other antihistamines, cetirizine has very few drug interactions, alcohol being the main one. Studies in dogs suggests that only 3% of the dose is transferred into milk.

Pregnancy Risk Category: B

Lactation Risk Category: L2

Adult Concerns: Sedation, fatigue, dry mouth.

Pediatric Concerns: None reported but observe for sedation.

Drug Interactions: Increased sedation with other CNS sedatives, alcohol.

Relative Infant Dose:

Adult Dose: 5-10 mg daily.

Alternatives:

T ½	= 8.3 hours	M/P	=
PHL	= 6.2 hours	PB	= 93%
Tmax	= 1.7 hour	Oral	= 70%
MW	= 389	pKa	=
Vd	=		

References:
1. Pharmaceutical Manufacturer Prescribing Information. 1996.

CEVIMELINE   L3

Trade: Evoxac
Other Trades:
Uses: Treatment of dry mouth; Alzheimer's disease
AAP: Not reviewed

Cevimeline is a cholinergic agonist agent, which binds to muscarinic receptors and can increase secretion of exocrine glands such as salivary and sweat glands, and increase tone in the GI and urinary tracts. It is indicated for the treatment of patients with Sjrogren's Syndrome. This drug has a large volume of distribution which suggests that most of the compound is stored in peripheral tissues, not the plasma compartment. Many such drugs produce lower milk levels. No data are available on its transfer into human milk. Due to its strong cholinergic effects, some caution is recommended in breastfeeding mothers. Observe closely for excess salivation, diarrhea, excess sweating, nausea, and urinary frequency and infection.

Pregnancy Risk Category: C

Lactation Risk Category: L3

Adult Concerns: Diaphoresis (excessive perspiration), nausea, rhinitis, urinary frequency, headache, diarrhea, and gastric cramping are reported.

Pediatric Concerns: No reports in breastfeeding mothers available.

Drug Interactions: None reported.

Relative Infant Dose:

Adult Dose: 30 mg TID

Alternatives: Oral pilocarpine

T ½	= 3-5 hours	M/P	=
PHL	=	PB	= <20%
Tmax	= 1-2 hours	Oral	= Complete
MW	= 244	pKa	=
Vd	= 6		

References:
1. Pharmaceutical Manufacturers Prescribing Information, 2010.

CHAMOMILE, GERMAN   L3

Trade: Hungarian Chamomile, Sweet False, Wild Chamomile
Other Trades:
Uses: Anti-inflammatory, carminative
AAP: Not reviewed

Chamomile has been used since Roman times and is primarily used for its anti-inflammatory, carminative, antispasmodic, mild sedative, and antiseptic properties. It has been used for flatulent dyspepsia, travel sickness, diarrhea, GI irritation.[1] It has been used topically for hemorrhoids and mastitis. Chamomile contains coumarins, flavonoids such as quercetin, rutin, and others. Anti-allergic and anti-inflammatory effects have been well documented and are due to the azulene components of the volatile oil which inhibit histamine release.[2] Matricin is reported to be a significant anti-inflammatory agent. In humans, German chamomile has been reported to exhibit anti-inflammatory, anti-peptic, and anti-spasmodic effects on the stomach.[2] Reports of allergic reactions to chamomile include two cases of anaphylaxis, although this is probably rare.[3,4,5] Asthmatics should probably avoid this product. German chamomile is reported to be uterotonic and teratogenic in rats, rabbits, and dogs although the dose of alpha-bisabolol used in these studies was excessively high.[6] Some authors suggest this product should be avoided in pregnant and breastfeeding mothers[7], but the German Commission E considers it safe.[8]

Pregnancy Risk Category:

Lactation Risk Category: L3

Adult Concerns: Reports of allergic reactions to chamomile are common, including two cases of anaphylaxis. Asthmatics should avoid this product. German chamomile is reported to be uterotonic and teratogenic in rats, rabbits, and dogs. This product should be avoided in pregnant and lactating patients.

Pediatric Concerns: None reported via milk, but hypersensitization is possible.

Drug Interactions: Do not use with benzodiazepines, CNS depressants, oral contraceptives, tamoxifen and warfarin.

Relative Infant Dose:

Adult Dose:

Alternatives:

References:

1. Berry M. The chamomiles. Pharm J 1995; 254:191-193.
2. Mann C, Staba EJ. The chemistry, pharmacology, and commercial formulations of chamomile. In: Herbs, spices, and medicinal plants: Recent advances in botany, horticulture, and pharmacology. Vol. 1. Arizona: Oryx Press, 1986.
3. Hausen BM. The sensitizing capacity of Compositae plants. Planta Med 1984; 50:229-234.
4. Casterline CL. Allergy to chamomile tea. JAMA 1980; 244 (4):330-331.
5. Benner MH, Lee HJ. Anaphylactic reaction to chamomile tea. J Allergy Clin Immunol 1973; 52 (5):307-308.
6. Habersang S, Leuschner F, Isaac O, Thiemer K. [Pharmacological studies with compounds of chamomile. IV. Studies on toxicity of (-)-alpha-bisabolol (author's transl)]. Planta Med 1979; 37 (2):115-123.
7. Newall C, Anderson LA, Phillipson JD. Chamomile, German. In. Herbal Medicine. A guide for the healthcare professionals. The Pharmaceutical Press, London, 1996.
8. The Complete German Commission E Monographs. Ed. M. Blumenthal Amer Botanical Council 1998.

CHLORAL HYDRATE   L3

Trade: Aquachloral, Noctec
Other Trades: Novo-Chlorhydrate, Dormel, Elix-Noctec
Uses: Sedative, hypnotic
AAP: Maternal Medication Usually Compatible with Breastfeeding

Chloral Hydrate is a sedative hypnotic. Small to moderate amounts are known to be secreted into milk. Mild drowsiness was reported in one infant following administration of dichloralphenazone (1300 mg/d), which is metabolized to the same active metabolite as chloral hydrate. Infant growth and development were reported to be normal. In a study of 50 postpartum women using a 1.3 gm rectal suppository, the average milk concentration of chloral hydrate at 1 hour was 3.2 mg/L.[1] The maximum milk level found in this study was 15 mg/L in one patient. The oral pediatric sedative dose of chloral hydrate is generally 5-15 mg/kg/dose every 8 hours.[2]

Pregnancy Risk Category: C

Lactation Risk Category: L3

Adult Concerns: Irritating to mucous membrane, laryngospasm, GI irritation, paradoxical excitement, delirium, hypotension, respiratory depression and sedation.

Pediatric Concerns: None reported via milk, but observe for sedation.

Drug Interactions: May potentiate effects of warfarin, CNS depressants such as alcohol, etc. Use with furosemide (IV) may induce flushing, hypotension.

Relative Infant Dose: 2.6%

Adult Dose: 250 mg TID

Alternatives: Alprazolam, Midazolam

T ½	= 7-10 hours	M/P	=
PHL	=	PB	= 35-41%
Tmax	= 30-60 minutes	Oral	= Complete
MW	= 165	pKa	= 10.0
Vd	= 0.6		

References:
1. Bernstine JB, Meyer AE, Bernstine RL. Maternal blood and breast milk estimation following the administration of chloral hydrate during the puerperium. J Obstet Gynaecol Br Emp 1956; 63 (2):228-231.
2. Johnson KB. ed. The Harriet Lane Handbook, Thirteenth Edition. Mosey, 1993.

CHLORAMPHENICOL   L4

Trade: Chloromycetin
Other Trades: Ak-Chlor, Chloroptic, Sopamycetin, Chlorsig, Biocetin
Uses: Antibiotic
AAP: Drugs whose effect on nursing infants is unknown but may be of concern

Chloramphenicol is a broad-spectrum antibiotic. In one study of 5 women receiving 250 mg PO four times daily, the concentration of chloramphenicol in milk ranged from 0.54 to 2.84 mg/L.[1] In the same study but in another group receiving 500 mg four times daily, the concentration of chloramphenicol in milk ranged from 1.75 to 6.10 mg/L. In a group of patients being treated for typhus, milk levels were lower than maternal plasma levels.[2] With maternal plasma levels of 49 and 26 mg/L in two patients, the milk levels were 26 and 16 mg/L respectively.

In a study of 2-3 patients who received a single 500 mg oral dose, the average milk concentration at 4 hours was 4.1 mg/L.[3] The milk/plasma ratio at 4 hours was 0.84. Safety in infants is highly controversial.

Milk levels are too low to produce overt toxicity in infants but could produce allergic sensitization to subsequent exposures. Generally, chloramphenicol is considered contraindicated in nursing mothers although it is occasionally used in infants. This antibiotic can be extremely toxic, particularly in newborns, and should not be used for trivial infections. Blood levels should be constantly monitored and kept below 20 µg/mL.

Pregnancy Risk Category: C

Lactation Risk Category: L4

Adult Concerns: Numerous blood dyscrasias, aplastic anemia, fever, skin rashes.

Pediatric Concerns: None reported via milk.

Drug Interactions: Phenobarbital and rifampin may reduce plasma levels of chloramphenicol. Chloramphenicol inhibits metabolism of chlorpropamide, phenytoin, and oral anticoagulants.

Relative Infant Dose: 3.2% - 8.5%

Adult Dose: 50-100 mg/kg daily. divided every 6 hours

Alternatives:

T ½	= 4 hours	M/P	= 0.5-0.6
PHL	= 22 hours (neonates)	PB	= 53%
Tmax	= 1 hour	Oral	= Complete
MW	= 323	pKa	= 5.5
Vd	= 0.57		

References:
1. Havelka J, Hejzlar M, Popov V, Viktorinova D, Prochazka J. Excretion of chloramphenicol in human milk. Chemotherapy 1968; 13 (4):204-211.
2. Smadel JE. et.al. Chloramphenicol in the treatment of tsutsugamushi disease. J Clin Invest 1949; 28:1196-1215.
3. Matsuda S. Transfer of antibiotics into maternal milk. Biol Res Pregnancy Perinatol 1984; 5 (2):57-60.

CHLORDIAZEPOXIDE   L3

Trade: Apo-Chlordiazepoxide, Librium, Libritabs, Solium
Other Trades: Medilium, Amitrol
Uses: Antianxiety, benzodiazepine sedative
AAP: Not reviewed

Chlordiazepoxide is an older benzodiazepine that belongs to Valium family. It is secreted in breastmilk in moderate but unreported levels.[1] See Diazepam.

Pregnancy Risk Category: D

Lactation Risk Category: L3

Adult Concerns: Sedation.

Pediatric Concerns: Observe for sedation.

Drug Interactions: Increased CNS sedation when used with other sedative-hypnotics. May increase risk when used with anticoagulants, alcohol, tricyclic antidepressants, MAO inhibitors.

Relative Infant Dose:

Adult Dose: 15-100 mg every 6-8 hours

Alternatives: Alprazolam

T ½	= 5-30 hours	M/P	=
PHL	=	PB	= 90-98%
Tmax	= 1-4 hours	Oral	= Complete
MW	= 300	pKa	= 4.8
Vd	= 0.3-0.5		

References:
1. Pharmaceutical Manufacturer Prescribing Information. 2010.

CHLORHEXIDINE | L4

Trade: Peridex, BactoShield, Betasept, Dyna-Hex, Hibiclens
Other Trades: Hibitane, Hexol, Savlon, Bactigras
Uses: Lozenge antimicrobial
AAP: Not reviewed

Chlorhexidine is a topical antimicrobial used in oral lozenges.[1] Pharmacokinetic studies with a 0.12% chlorhexidine gluconate oral rinse indicate approximately 30% of the active ingredient is retained in the oral cavity following rinsing. The drug retained in the oral cavity is slowly released into the oral fluids and swallowed. Studies conducted on human subjects and animals demonstrate chlorhexidine gluconate is poorly absorbed from the gastrointestinal tract.

In a study of 200 mothers in which 100 each received breast sprays containing water or 0.2% chlorhexidine in alcohol, the chlorhexidine/alcohol spray group showed greater compliance to breastfeeding and lower incidence of trauma and discomfort. No adverse effects occurred that could be attributed to the medications.[2]

In another case report, a mother used chlorhexidine spray (430 µg/spray) on her breasts to prevent mastitis starting with the third feed when the baby was 12 hours old. After 48 hours, the baby developed bradycardia. Some episodes over the next 2 days required atropine therapy, which subsequently increased the heart rate. An electrocardiogram confirmed sinus bradycardia. The chlorhexidine spray was discontinued and the bradycardia became less severe and less frequent. By day 6, bradycardia was no longer present. Each spray of chlorhexidine contains 430 µg and over 24 hours the baby could have ingested 2.5 mg.[3]

The differences between the two studies could be attributed to the difference in the amount of chlorhexidine available to the infants. Regardless, chlorhexidine should not be used on breastfeeding mother's nipples.

Pregnancy Risk Category: B

Lactation Risk Category: L4

Adult Concerns: Staining of teeth and dentures. Keep out of eyes. Changes in taste, increased plaque, staining of tongue.

Pediatric Concerns: Bradycardia in one infant exposed to chlorhexidine on the nipple.

Drug Interactions:

Relative Infant Dose:

Adult Dose: N/A

Alternatives:

T ½	= <4 hours	M/P	=
PHL	=	PB	=
Tmax	=	Oral	= Poor
MW	= 505	pKa	=
Vd	=		

References:

1. Lacy C. Drug information handbook. Lexi-Comp Inc. Cleveland, OH, 1996.
2. Herd B, Feeney JG. Two aerosol sprays in nipple trauma. Practicioner 1986; 230:31-38.
3. Quinn MW, Bini RM. Bradycardia associated with chlorhexidine spray. Arch Dis Child 1989; 64 (6):892-3.

CHLOROQUINE   L2

Trade: Aralen, Novo-Chloroquine

Other Trades: Chlorquin, Avloclor

Uses: Antimalarial

AAP: Maternal Medication Usually Compatible with Breastfeeding

Chloroquine is an antimalarial drug. In a group of 6 women who received 5 mg/kg IM during delivery, and then again at 17 days postpartum, milk levels averaged 0.227 mg/L and ranged from 0.192 to 0.319 mg/L.[1] The milk/blood ratio ranged from 0.268 to 0.462. Based on these levels, the infant would consume approximately 34 µg/kg/day, an amount considered safe. If an infant consumed 500 mL/day of milk, it would receive an average of 113.5 µg of chloroquine per day.

Other studies have shown absorption to vary from 2.2 to 4.2% of maternal dose.[2] The breastmilk concentration of chloroquine in this study averaged 0.58 mg/L following a single dose of 600 mg.

In a recent study of 16 women day 3 to 17-21 postpartum, the average concentration in milk (AUC) during the sampling time 167 µg/L for chloroquine and 54 µg/L for desethylchloroquine the possibly active metabolite.[3] Estimated absolute and absolute infant doses were 34 µg/kg/day and 15 µg/kg/day, and 2.3% and 1.0% for chloroquine and desethylchloroquine respectively. The authors suggested that chloroquine was compatible with breastfeeding.

The current recommended pediatric dose for patients exposed to malaria is 8.3 mg/kg per week which greatly exceeds that present in breastmilk. In a recent study, chloroquine was reported to reduce HIV transmission into human milk.[4] A recent study suggests that chloroquine may reduce levels of HIV RNA in breastmilk.[5]

Pregnancy Risk Category: C

Lactation Risk Category: L2

Adult Concerns: Ocular disturbances including blindness, skin lesions, headache, fatigue, nervousness, hypotension, neutropenia, aplastic anemia.

Pediatric Concerns: None reported but close observation is required. Observe for diarrhea, GI distress, hypotension.

Drug Interactions: Decreased oral absorption if used with kaolin and magnesium trisilicate. Increased toxicity if used with cimetidine.

Relative Infant Dose: 0.6% - 1.1%

Adult Dose: 300-600 mg every day

Alternatives:

T ½	= 72-120 hours	M/P	= 0.358
PHL	=	PB	= 61%
Tmax	= 1-2 hours	Oral	= Complete
MW	= 320	pKa	= 8.4, 10.8
Vd	= 116-285		

References:
1. Akintonwa A, Gbajumo SA, Mabadeje AF. Placental and milk transfer of chloroquine in humans. Ther Drug Monit 1988; 10 (2):147-149.
2. Edstein MD, Veenendaal JR, Newman K, Hyslop R. Excretion of chloroquine, dapsone and pyrimethamine in human milk. Br J Clin Pharmacol 1986; 22 (6):733-735.
3. Law I, Ilett KF, Hackett I.P, et.al. Transfer of chloroquine and desethylchloroquine across the placenta and into milk in Melanesian mothers. Br J Clin Pharmacol 2008, 65 (5):674-679.
4. Semrau K, Kuhn L, Kasonde P, et al. Impact of chloroquine on viral load in breast milk. Trop Med Int Health. Jun 2006;11 (6):800-803.
5. Semrau K, Kuhn L, Kasonde P, Sinkala M, Kankasa C, Shutes E, Vwalika C, Ghosh M, Aldrovandi G, Thea DM. Impact of chloroquine on viral load in breast milk. Trop Med Int Health. 2006 Jun;11 (6):800-3.

CHLOROTHIAZIDE   L3

Trade: HydroDIURIL
Other Trades: Chlotride, Saluric
Uses: Diuretic
AAP: Maternal Medication Usually Compatible with Breastfeeding

Chlorothiazide is a typical thiazide diuretic. In one study of 11 lactating women, each receiving 500 mg of chlorothiazide, the concentrations in milk samples taken one, two, and three hours after the dose were all less than 1 mg/L with a milk/plasma ratio of 0.05.[1] Although thiazide diuretics are reported to produce thrombocytopenia in nursing infants, it is remote and unsubstantiated. Most thiazide diuretics are considered compatible with breastfeeding if doses are kept low and milk production is unaffected.

Pregnancy Risk Category: C

Lactation Risk Category: L3

Adult Concerns: Fluid loss, dehydration, lethargy.

Pediatric Concerns: None reported but observe for reduced milk production.

Drug Interactions: NSAIDs may reduce hypotensive effect of chlorothiazide. Cholestyramine resins may reduce absorption of chlorothiazide. Diuretics reduce efficacy of oral hypoglycemics. May reduce lithium clearance leading to high levels. May elevate digoxin levels.

Relative Infant Dose: 2.1%

Adult Dose: 500-2000 mg every 12-24 hours

Alternatives:

T ½	= 1.5 hours	M/P	= 0.05
PHL	=	PB	= 95%
Tmax	= 1 hour	Oral	= 20%
MW	= 296	pKa	= 6.7, 9.5
Vd	=		

References:
1. Werthmann MW, Jr., Krees SV. Excretion of chlorothiazide in human breast milk. J Pediatr 1972; 81 (4):781-783.

CHLORPHENIRAMINE   L3

Trade: Aller Chlor, Chlor-Tripolon, Chlor-Trimeton
Other Trades: Demazin, Alunex, Piridon
Uses: Antihistamine
AAP: Not reviewed

Chlorpheniramine is a commonly used antihistamine. Although no data is available on secretion into breastmilk, it has not been reported to produce side effects. Sedation is the only likely side effect.[1]

Pregnancy Risk Category: B

Lactation Risk Category: L3

Adult Concerns: Sedation, dry mouth.

Pediatric Concerns: None reported but observe for sedation.

Drug Interactions: May increase sedation when used with other CNS depressants such as opiates, tricyclic antidepressants, MAO inhibitors.

Relative Infant Dose:

Adult Dose: 4 mg every 4-6 hours

Alternatives: Cetirizine, Loratadine

T ½	= 12-43 hours	M/P	=
PHL	= 9.5-13 hours	PB	= 70%
Tmax	= 2-6 hours	Oral	= 25-45%
MW	= 275	pKa	= 9.2
Vd	= 5.9		

References:
1. Paton DM, Webster DR. Clinical pharmacokinetics of H1-receptor antagonists (the antihistamines). Clin Pharmacokinet 1985; 10 (6):477-497.

CHLORPROMAZINE   L3

Trade: Thorazine, Ormazine
Other Trades: Chlorpromanyl, Largactil, Novo-
          Chlorpromazine, Chloractil
Uses: Tranquilizer
AAP: Drugs whose effect on nursing infants is unknown but
          may be of concern

Chlorpromazine is a powerful CNS tranquilizer. Small amounts are known to be secreted into milk. Following a 1200 mg oral dose, samples were taken at 60, 120, and 180 minutes.[1] Breastmilk concentrations were highest at 120 minutes and were 0.29 mg/L at that time. The milk/plasma ratio was less than 0.5. Ayd[2] suggests that in one group of 16 women who took chlorpromazine during, after pregnancy, and while breastfeeding, that the side effects were minimal and infant development was normal. In a group of 4 breastfeeding mothers receiving unspecified amounts of chlorpromazine, milk levels varied from 7 to 98 µg/L.[3] Maternal serum levels ranged from 16 to 52 µg/L. Only the infant who ingested milk with a chlorpromazine level of 92 µg/L showed drowsiness and lethargy.

Chlorpromazine has a long half-life and is particularly sedating. Long-term use of this product in a lactating mother may be risky to the breastfed infant. There are consistent reports of phenothiazine products increasing the risk of apnea and SIDS. Observer for sedation and lethargy and avoid if possible.

Pregnancy Risk Category: C

Lactation Risk Category: L3

Adult Concerns: Sedation, lethargy, extrapyramidal jerking motion. Apnea, SIDS.

Pediatric Concerns: One report of lethargy and sedation. Observe for apnea.

Drug Interactions: Additive effects when used with other CNS depressants. May increase valproic acid plasma levels.

Relative Infant Dose: 0.3%

Adult Dose: 200 mg daily.

Alternatives:

T ½	= 30 hours	M/P	= <0.5
PHL	=	PB	− 95%
Tmax	= 1-2 hours	Oral	= Complete
MW	= 319	pKa	= 9.3
Vd	= 10-35		

References:
1. Blacker KH, Weinstein BJ. et. al. Mothers milk and chlorpromazine. Am J Psychol 1962; 114:178-179.
2. Ayd FJ. Excretion of psychotropic drugs in breast milk. In: International Drug Therapy Newsletter.Ayd Medical Communications 8[November-December]. 1973.
3. Wiles DH, Orr MW, Kolakowska T. Chlorpromazine levels in plasma and milk of nursing mothers. Br J Clin Pharmacol 1978; 5 (3):272-273.

CHLORPROPAMIDE   L3

Trade: Diabinese
Other Trades: Apo-Chlorpropamide, Novopropamide, Melitase
Uses: Oral hypoglycemic
AAP: Not reviewed

Chlorpropamide stimulates the secretion of insulin in some patients. Following one 500 mg dose, the concentration of chlorpropamide in milk after 5 hours was approximately 5 mg/L of milk.[1] This study lacked details and may not be accurate. May cause hypoglycemia in infant although effects are largely unknown and unreported.

Pregnancy Risk Category: C

Lactation Risk Category: L3

Adult Concerns: Hypoglycemia, diarrhea, edema.

Pediatric Concerns: None actually reported, but observe for hypoglycemia although unlikely.

Drug Interactions: Thiazides and hydantoins reduce hypoglycemic effect of chlorpropamide. Chlorpropamide may increase disulfiram effects when used with alcohol. Increases anticoagulant effect when used with warfarin. Sulfonamides may decrease chlorpropamide clearance.

Relative Infant Dose: 10.5%

Adult Dose: 250-500 mg daily.

Alternatives: Metformin

T ½	= 33 hours	M/P	=
PHL	=	PB	= 96%
Tmax	= 3-6 hours	Oral	= Complete
MW	= 277	pKa	= 4.8
Vd	= 0.1-0.3		

References:
1. Pharmaceutical Manufacturer Prescribing Information, 2010.

CHLORPROTHIXENE   L3

Trade: Taractan
Other Trades: Tarasan
Uses: Sedative, tranquilizer.
AAP: Drugs whose effect on nursing infants is unknown but may be of concern

Sedative commonly used in psychotic or disturbed patients. Chlorprothixene is poorly absorbed orally (<40%) and has been found to increase serum prolactin levels in mothers. Although the milk/plasma ratios are relatively high, only modest levels of chlorprothixene are actually secreted into human milk. In one patient taking 200 mg/day, maximum milk concentrations of the parent and metabolite were 19 µg/L and 28.5 µg/L respectively.[1]

Pregnancy Risk Category: C

Lactation Risk Category: L3

Adult Concerns: Sedation, hypotension, pseudoparkinsonian jerking, constipation.

Pediatric Concerns: None reported, but observe for sedation.

Drug Interactions: May reduce effect of guanethidine. May increase effects of alcohol and other CNS sedatives.

Relative Infant Dose: 0.3%

Adult Dose: 25-50 mg three times daily

Alternatives:

T ½	= 8-12 hours	M/P	= 1.2-2.6
PHL	=	PB	=
Tmax	= 4.25 hours	Oral	= <40%
MW	= 316	pKa	= 8.8
Vd	= 11-23		

References:
1. Matheson I, Evang A, Overo KF, Syversen G. Presence of chlorprothixene and its metabolites in breast milk. Eur J Clin Pharmacol 1984; 27 (5):611-613.

CHOLERA VACCINE   L3

Trade: Cholera Vaccine, Dukoral
Other Trades:
Uses: Cholera vaccination.
AAP: Not reviewed

Cholera vaccine is available in an oral preparation and a sterile injectable solution containing equal parts of phenol inactivated Ogawa and Inaba serotypes of Vibrio cholerae bacteria.

Maternal immunization with cholera vaccine significantly increases levels of anti-cholera antibodies (IgA, IgG) in their milk.[1] It is not contraindicated in nursing mothers. Breastfed infants are generally protected from cholera transmission. Immunization is approved from the age of 6 months and older.

Pregnancy Risk Category: C

Lactation Risk Category: L3

Adult Concerns: Malaise, fever, headache, pain at injection site.

Pediatric Concerns: None reported.

Drug Interactions: Decreased effect when used with yellow fever vaccine. Wait at least 3 weeks between.

Relative Infant Dose:

Adult Dose: 2 0.5 mL injections (IM or SC) 1 week-month apart

Alternatives:

References:
1. Merson MH, Black RE, Sack DA, Svennerholm AM, Holmgren J. Maternal cholera immunisation and secretory IgA in breast milk. Lancet 1980; 1 (8174):931-932.

CHOLESTYRAMINE   L1

Trade: Questran, Cholybar
Other Trades: Novo-Cholamine
Uses: Cholesterol binding resin
AAP: Not reviewed

Cholestyramine is a bile salt chelating resin. Used orally in adults, it binds bile salts and prevents reabsorption of bile salts in the gut, thus reducing cholesterol plasma levels.[1] This resin is not absorbed from the maternal GI tract. Therefore, it is not secreted into breastmilk.

Pregnancy Risk Category: C

Lactation Risk Category: L1

Adult Concerns: Constipation, skin rash, nausea, vomiting, malabsorption, intestinal obstruction.

Pediatric Concerns: None reported via milk. Observe mother for vitamin deficiency states.

Drug Interactions: Decreases oral absorption of vitamins, digoxin, warfarin, thyroid hormones, thiazide diuretics, propranolol, phenobarbital, amiodarone, methotrexate, NSAIDs, and many other drugs.

Relative Infant Dose:

Adult Dose: 16-32 grams/day

Alternatives:

References:
1.   Pharmaceutical Manufacturer Prescribing Information. 2010.

CHONDROITIN SULFATE | L3

Trade: Viscoat
Other Trades:
Uses: Biologic polymer used for arthritis
AAP: Not reviewed

Chondroitin is a biological polymer that acts as a flexible connecting matrix between the protein filaments in cartilage. It is derived largely from natural sources such as shark or bovine cartilage and chemically is composed of a high-viscosity mucopolysaccharide (glycosaminoglycan) polymer found in most mammalian cartilaginous tissues.[1] Thus far, chondroitin has been found to be nontoxic. Its MW averages 50,000 daltons, which is far too large to permit its entry into human milk. Combined with a poor oral bioavailability and large MW, it is unlikely to pose a problem for a breastfed infant.

Pregnancy Risk Category:

Lactation Risk Category: L3

Adult Concerns: Virtually nontoxic and poorly absorbed orally.

Pediatric Concerns: None reported via milk.

Drug Interactions:

Relative Infant Dose:

Adult Dose:

Alternatives:

T ½	=	M/P	=
PHL	=	PB	=
Tmax	=	Oral	= 0-13%
MW	= 50,000	pKa	=
Vd	=		

References:
1. Review of Natural Products Facts and Comparisons, St Louis, MO 1996.

CHORIONIC GONADOTROPIN | L3

Trade: A.P.L., Chorex-5, Profasi, Gonic, Pregnyl, Novarel
Other Trades: Humegon Pregnyl, Profasi HP, Profasik, APL
Uses: Placental hormone
AAP: Not reviewed

Human chorionic gonadotropin (HCG) is a large polypeptide hormone produced by the human placenta with functions similar to luteinizing hormone (LH). Its function is to stimulate the corpus luteum of the ovary to produce progesterone, thus sustaining pregnancy.[1,2] During pregnancy, HCG secreted by the placenta maintains the corpus luteum, supporting estrogen and progesterone secretion and preventing menstruation. It is used for multiple purposes including pediatric cryptorchidism, male hypogonadism, and ovulatory failure. HCG has no known effect on fat mobilization, appetite, sense of hunger, or body fat distribution.

HCG has NOT been found to be effective in treatment of obesity.Due to the large MW (47,000) of HCG, it would be extremely unlikely to penetrate into human milk. Further, it would not be orally bioavailable due to destruction in the GI tract.

Choriogonadotropin alfa (Ovidrel) is a biosynthetic form of the human chorionic gonadotropin.

Pregnancy Risk Category: X

Lactation Risk Category: L3

Adult Concerns: Headache, irritability, restlessness, depression, fatigue, edema, gynecomastia, pain at injection site.

Pediatric Concerns: None reported via milk. Absorption unlikely due to gastric digestion and poor penetration into milk.

Drug Interactions:

Relative Infant Dose:

Adult Dose: 5000-10000 units X 1

Alternatives:

T ½	= 5.6 hours	M/P	=
PHL	=	PB	=
Tmax	= 6 hours	Oral	= 0%
MW	= 47,000	pKa	=
Vd	=		

References:
1. Drug Facts and Comparisons 1996 ed. ed. St. Louis: 1996.
2. Pharmaceutical Manufacturer Prescribing Information. 1997.

CHROMIUM   L3

Trade: Chromium Picrolinate
Other Trades:
Uses: Metal supplement
AAP: Not reviewed

Trace metal, required in glucose metabolism. Less than 1% is absorbed following oral administration. Chromium levels are depleted in multiparous women. Chromium levels in neonate are approximately 2.5 times that of mother due to concentrating mechanism during gestation. Because chromium is difficult to measure, levels reported vary widely.

One article reports that breastmilk levels are less than 2% of the estimated safe and adequate daily intake of 10 µg (which is probably excessive and needs review).[1] Most importantly, breastmilk levels are independent of dietary intake in mother and do not apparently increase with increased maternal intake. Chromium is apparently secreted into breastmilk by a well-controlled pumping mechanism. Hence, breastmilk levels of chromium are independent of maternal plasma levels. Increased maternal plasma levels may not alter milk chromium levels.

Pregnancy Risk Category: C

Lactation Risk Category: L3

Adult Concerns: Chromium poisoning if used in excess.

Pediatric Concerns: None reported.

Drug Interactions:

Relative Infant Dose:

Adult Dose: 200 µg/day

Alternatives:

T½	=	M/P	=
PHL	=	PB	=
Tmax	=	Oral	= <1%
MW	= 52	pKa	=
Vd	=		

References:
1. Anderson RA, Bryden NA, Patterson KY, Veillon C, Andon MB, Moser-Veillon PB. Breast milk chromium and its association with chromium intake, chromium excretion, and serum chromium. Am J Clin Nutr 1993; 57 (4):519-523.

CICLESONIDE   L3

Trade: Omnaris
Other Trades:
Uses: Corticosteroid
AAP: Not reviewed

Ciclesonide is a topical corticosteroid used presently for allergic rhinitis. Ciclesonide is a pro-drug that is enzymatically hydrolyzed to a pharmacologically active metabolite, C21-desisobutyryl-ciclesonide (des-ciclesonide or RM1). Ciclesonide and its metabolite, des-ciclesonide, has negligible oral bioavailability (< 1%) as it is poorly absorbed, and has a high first-pass absorption by the liver.[1] While we have no data on its use in breastfeeding mothers, as with the other nasal steroids, this product poses little risk.

Pregnancy Risk Category: C

Lactation Risk Category: L3

Adult Concerns: Headache, nose bleed, nasopharyngitis, ear pain.

Pediatric Concerns: None yet reported.

Drug Interactions: Ketoconazole may produce a 3.6-fold increase in des-ciclesonide AUC at steady state.

Relative Infant Dose:

Adult Dose: 100 µg/day in each nostril

Alternatives: Budesonide, fluticasone, mometasone

T ½	= 6-7 hours	M/P	=
PHL	=	PB	= 99%
Tmax	= 1.04 hours	Oral	= < 1%
MW	= 540	pKa	=
Vd	= 12.1		

References:
1. Pharmaceutical manufacturers prescribing information, 2009.

CICLOPIROX OLAMINE   L3

Trade: Loprox
Other Trades:
Uses: Antifungal
AAP: Not reviewed

Ciclopirox is a broad-spectrum antifungal and is active in numerous species including tinca, candida albicans, and trichophyton rubrum. An average of 1.3% ciclopirox is absorbed when applied topically although only 0.01% of the dose is found in the urine.[1] Topical application produces minimal systemic absorption; it is unlikely that topical use would expose the nursing infant to significant risks. The risk to a breastfeeding infant associated with application directly on the nipple is not known and it should not be used on the nipple. Ciclopirox and miconazole are comparable in treatment of vaginal candida.

Pregnancy Risk Category: B

Lactation Risk Category: L3

Adult Concerns: Pruritus and burning following topical therapy.

Pediatric Concerns: None via milk.

Drug Interactions:

Relative Infant Dose:

Adult Dose: apply topical BID

Alternatives: Fluconazole, Miconazole

T ½	− 1.7 hours	M/P	−
PHL	=	PB	= 98%
Tmax	= 6 hours	Oral	=
MW	= 268	pKa	=
Vd	=		

References:
1. Pharmaceutical Manufacturer Prescribing Information.

CIMETIDINE   L1

Trade: Tagamet
Other Trades: Apo-Cimetidine, Novo-Cimetine, Peptol,
        Magicul, Peptimax, Zita
Uses: Reduces gastric acid production
AAP: Maternal Medication Usually Compatible with
        Breastfeeding

Cimetidine is an antisecretory, histamine-2 antagonist that reduces
stomach acid secretion. Cimetidine is apparently actively transported
into human milk as evidenced by a higher milk/plasma ratio. In a study
of 12 women who received single oral doses of 100, 600, and 1200 mg
cimetidine, the observed milk/serum ratio was 5.65, 5.84, and 5.83
respectively.[1] The reported maximum concentration in milk were 2.5,
16.2, and 37.2 mg/L respectively.

In another study of one patient ingesting 600 mg daily, the reported
milk level was 5.6 mg/L.[2] The maximum potential dose from lactation
would be approximately 5.58 mg/kg/d, which is still quite small. The
pediatric dose administered IV for therapeutic treatment of pediatric
gastroesophageal reflux averages 8-20 mg/kg/24 hours. Other choices
for breastfeeding mothers should preclude the use of this drug
however. See famotidine, nizatidine. Short-term use (days) would not
be incompatible with breastfeeding.

Pregnancy Risk Category: B

Lactation Risk Category: L1

Adult Concerns: Headache, dizziness, somnolence.

Pediatric Concerns: None reported via milk. Frequently used in
pediatric patients.

Drug Interactions: Cimetidine inhibits the metabolism of
many drugs and may potentially increase their plasma levels. Such
drugs include: lidocaine, theophylline, phenytoin, metronidazole,
triamterene, procainamide, quinidine, propranolol, warfarin, tricyclic
antidepressants, diazepam, cyclosporin.

Relative Infant Dose: 9.8% - 32.6%

Adult Dose: 800 mg every HS

Alternatives: Famotidine, Nizatidine

T ½	= 2 hours	M/P	= 4.6-11.76
PHL	= 3.6 hours (neonate)	PB	= 19%
Tmax	= 0.75-1.5 hours	Oral	= 60-70%
MW	= 252	pKa	=
Vd	=		

References:
1. Oo CY, Kuhn RJ, Desai N, McNamara PJ. Active transport of cimetidine into human milk. Clin Pharmacol Ther 1995; 58 (5):548-555.
2. Somogyi A, Gugler R. Cimetidine excretion into breast milk. Br J Clin Pharmacol 1979; 7 (6):627-629.

CINNARIZINE   L3

Trade:
Other Trades: Arlevert
Uses: Antiemetic
AAP: Not reviewed

Cinnarizine is an antiemetic used for motion sickness, and is not available in the USA. It is an H1 histamine antagonist, and reduces the vascular response to epinephrine, norepinephrine, serotonin, angiotensin, dopamine, and other vasoactive hormones. It is primarily used for vestibular disorders of the inner ear and the vomiting center of the hypothalamus. No data are available on its use in breastfeeding mothers.

Pregnancy Risk Category:

Lactation Risk Category: L3

Adult Concerns: Adverse effects include drowsiness, headache, sweating, and weight gain.

Pediatric Concerns: Fatigue and slight hair loss have been reported from direct use of cinnarizine in children. No reports of complications via breastmilk.

Drug Interactions:

Relative Infant Dose:

Adult Dose: 25 mg

Alternatives:

T ½	= 3-6 hours	M/P	=
PHL	=	PB	= 91%
Tmax	= 1-3 hours	Oral	=
MW	= 368	pKa	=
Vd	=		

References:

CIPROFLOXACIN   L3

Trade: Cipro, Ciloxan
Other Trades: Ciproxin
Uses: Fluoroquinolone antibiotic
AAP: Maternal Medication Usually Compatible with Breastfeeding

Ciprofloxacin is a fluoroquinolone antibiotic primarily used for gram negative coverage and is presently the drug of choice for anthrax treatment and prophylaxis. Because it has been implicated in arthropathy in newborn animals, it is not normally used in pediatric patients. Levels secreted into breastmilk (2.26 to 3.79 mg/L) are somewhat conflicting. They vary from the low to moderate range to levels that are higher than maternal serum up to 12 hours after a dose. In one study of 10 women who received 750 mg every 12 hours, milk levels of ciprofloxacin ranged from 3.79 mg/L at 2 hours post-dose to 0.02 mg/L at 24 hours.[1] In another study of a single patient receiving one 500 mg tablet daily at bedtime, the concentrations in maternal serum and breast milk were 0.21 µg/mL and 0.98 µg/mL respectively.[2] Plasma levels were undetectable (<0.03 µg/mL) in the infant. The dose to the 4 month old infant was estimated to be 0.92 mg/day or 0.15 mg/kg/day. No adverse effects were noted in this infant.

There has been one reported case of severe pseudomembranous colitis in an infant of a mother who self-medicated with ciprofloxacin for 6 days (3). In a patient 17 days postpartum, who received 500 mg orally, ciprofloxacin levels in milk were 3.02, 3.02, 3.02 and 1.98 mg/L 4, 8, 12, and 16 hours post dose respectively.[4]

In another study of the direct application of ciprofloxacin to infants, 10 infants aged 4 days to 1 month old were given ciprofloxacin 10 to 40 mg/kg/day in 2 divided doses by slow IV infusion over 30 minutes for 10 to 20 days. Eight infants survived and 2 had greenish discoloration of the teeth at age 12-23 months. The discoloration requires further evaluation to determine the association with ciprofloxacin therapy.[5]

If used in lactating mothers, observe the infant closely for GI symptoms such as diarrhea. Current studies seem to suggest that the amount of ciprofloxacin present in milk is quite low. Ciprofloxacin was recently approved by the American Academy of Pediatrics for use in breastfeeding women and it is becoming increasingly popular for use in pediatric patients.[6] Ciprofloxacin is available in several ophthalmic preparations (Ciloxan), where the absorption and clinical dose is minimal. As the absolute dose presented to the nursing mother is minimal, ophthalmic formulations would not be contraindicated in breastfeeding mothers.

Pregnancy Risk Category: C

Lactation Risk Category: L3

Adult Concerns: Nausea, vomiting, diarrhea, abdominal cramps, GI bleeding. Several cases of tendon rupture have been noted.

Pediatric Concerns: Pseudomembranous colitis in one infant. Observe for diarrhea. Tooth discoloration in several infants reported.

Drug Interactions: Decreased absorption with antacids.
Quinolones cause increased levels of caffeine, warfarin, cyclosporine, theophylline. Cimetidine, probenecid, azlocillin increase ciprofloxacin levels. Increased risk of seizures when used with foscarnet.

Relative Infant Dose: 2.1% - 6.3%

Adult Dose: 500 mg BID

Alternatives: Norfloxacin, Ofloxacin

T ½	= 4.1 hours	M/P	– >1
PHL	= 2.5 hours	PB	= 40%
Tmax	= 0.5-2.3 hours	Oral	= 50-85%
MW	= 331	pKa	= 7.1
Vd	= 1.4		

References:

1. Giamarellou H, Kolokythas E, Petrikkos G, Gazis J, Aravantinos D, Sfikakis P. Pharmacokinetics of three newer quinolones in pregnant and lactating women. Am J Med 1989; 87 (5A):49S-51S.
2. Gardner DK, Gabbe SG, Harter C. Simultaneous concentrations of ciprofloxacin in breast milk and in serum in mother and breast-fed infant. Clin Pharm 1992; 11 (4):352-354.
3. Harmon T, Burkhart G, Applebaum H. Perforated pseudomembranous colitis in the breast-fed infant. J Pediatr Surg 1992; 27 (6):744-746.
4. Cover DL, Mueller BA. Ciprofloxacin penetration into human breast milk: a case report. DICP 1990; 24 (7-8):703-704.

5.   Lumbiganon P, Pengsaa K, Sookpranee T. Ciprofloxacin in Neonates and its Possible Adverse Effect on the Teeth. Pediatr Infect Dis J 1991; 10 (8):619-620.
6.   Ghaffar F, McCracken GH. Quinolones in Pediatrics. In: Hooper DC, Rubinstein E, editors. Quinolone Antimicrobial Agents. Washington, D.C.: ASM Press, 2003: 343-354.

CISAPRIDE   L2

Trade: Propulsid
Other Trades: Prepulsid
Uses: Gastrointestinal tract stimulant
AAP: Maternal Medication Usually Compatible with Breastfeeding

Cisapride is a gastrointestinal stimulant used to increase lower esophageal sphincter pressure and increase the rate of gastric emptying. It is frequently used in gastroesophageal reflux.[1] It is often preferred over metoclopramide (Reglan) due to the lack of CNS side effects. CNS concentrations are generally 2-3 fold less than the serum levels. It is frequently used in pediatric patients and neonates.

Breastmilk levels following a maternal dose of 60 mg/day for 4 days averaged 6.2 μg/L while maternal plasma levels averaged 137 μg/L.[2] The dose of cisapride absorbed in breastfeeding infants would be expected to be 600-800 times lower than the usual therapeutic dose. Manufacturers internal data suggest that breastmilk levels are less than 5% of maternal plasma levels (approximately 2.2 to 3.0 μg/L).[3]

Pregnancy Risk Category: C

Lactation Risk Category: L2

Adult Concerns: Diarrhea, abdominal pain, cramping. Note many drug-drug interactions.

Pediatric Concerns: None reported via milk.

Drug Interactions: Increased effect of atropine and digoxin. Increased toxicity when used with warfarin, diazepam levels may be increased, cimetidine, ranitidine, CNS depressants. Cisapride levels may rise when used with azole antifungals such as ketoconazole, fluconazole, erythromycins.

Relative Infant Dose: 0.1%

Adult Dose: 10 mg QID

Alternatives:

T ½	= 7-10 hours	M/P	= 0.045
PHL	=	PB	= 98%
Tmax	= 1-2 hours	Oral	= 35-40%
MW	= 466	pKa	=
Vd	=		

References:

1. McCallum RW, Prakash C, Campoli-Richards DM, Goa KL. Cisapride. A preliminary review of its pharmacodynamic and pharmacokinetic properties, and therapeutic use as a prokinetic agent in gastrointestinal motility disorders. Drugs 1988; 36 (6):652-681.
2. Hofmeyr GJ, Sonnendecker EW. Secretion of the gastrokinetic agent cisapride in human milk. Eur J Clin Pharmacol 1986; 30 (6):735-736.
3. Janssen Pharmaceuticals, personal communication. 1996.

CITALOPRAM   L2

Trade: Celexa
Other Trades: Cipramil, Talam, Talohexal
Uses: Antidepressant, SSRI
AAP: Not reviewed

Citalopram is an SSRI antidepressant. In one study of a 21 year old patient receiving 20 mg citalopram per day, citalopram levels in milk peaked at 3-9 hours following administration.[1] Peak milk levels varied during the day, but the mean daily concentration was 298 nM (range 270-311). The milk/serum ratio was approximately 3. The metabolite, desmethylcitalopram, was present in milk in low levels (23-28 nM). The concentration of metabolite in milk varied little during the day. Assuming a milk intake of 150 mL/kg baby, approximately 272 nM (88 µg or 16 ng/kg) of citalopram was passed to the baby each day. This amounts to only 0.4% of the dose administered to the mother. At three weeks, maternal serum levels of citalopram were 185 nM, compared to the infants plasma level of just 7 nM. No untoward effects were noted in this breastfed infant. In another study[2], a milk/serum ratio of 1.16 to 1.88 was reported. This study suggests the infant would ingest 4.3 µg/kg/day and a relative dose of 0.7 to 5.9% of the weight-adjusted maternal dose.

In another study of 7 women receiving an average of 0.41 mg/kg/d citalopram, the average peak level (C_{max}) of citalopram was 154 µg/L and 50 µg/L for desmethylcitalopram (metabolite is 8 times less potent than citalopram).[3] However, average milk concentrations

(AUC) were lower and averaged 97 μg/L for citalopram and 36 μg/L for desmethylcitalopram during the dosing interval. The mean peak milk/plasma AUC ratio was 1.8 for citalopram. Low concentrations of citalopram (around 2-2.3 μg/L) were detected in only three of the seven infant plasmas. No adverse effects were found in any of the infants. The authors estimate the daily intake to be approximately 3.7% of the maternal dose.

In a study of a single patient receiving 40 mg/day of citalopram, the concentration in milk and serum were 205 μg/L and 98.9 ng/mL respectively.[4] Infant serum levels were 12.7 ng/mL. This infant was noted to have 'uneasy' sleep patterns, which were reduced upon lowering the maternal dose.

In a recent study of women (n=31) who were consuming citalopram while breastfeeding, no significant difference was noted in infant side effect profiles as compared to depressed and non-depressed control patients who were not consuming citalopram.[5] In one infant, colic, decreased feeding and irritability/restlessness was reported. In another infant, irritability and restlessness was reported. The authors recommend continued breastfeeding while consuming citalopram.

Eleven mothers taking citalopram and their babies were monitored during pregnancy and lactation. Plasma and milk samples were taken that suggested citalopram and its metabolite concentrations in milk were 2-3 times higher than in maternal plasma, but infant plasma levels were very low or undetectable.[6]

One case reported an infant experiencing neonatal withdrawal syndrome after in utero exposure. The mother was taking 20-30 mg/day. The symptoms started upon delivery, and the child was discharged at day 7 with no medical treatment needed.[7]

Pregnancy Risk Category: C

Lactation Risk Category: L2

Adult Concerns: Diarrhea, headache, anxiety, dizziness, insomnia, constipation, nausea, vomiting, and tremor. Tachycardia, hypotension have been reported. Increased salivation, and flatulence. Amenorrhea, coughing, rash, pruritus, polyuria have been reported.

Pediatric Concerns: There have been two cases of excessive somnolence, decreased feeding, and weight loss in breastfed infants. However, the majority of studies show no or limited side effects in breastfed infants.

Drug Interactions: Increased citalopram levels when used with macrolide antibiotics (erythromycin), and azole antifungals such as fluconazole, itraconazole, ketoconazole, etc. Carbamazepine may reduce plasma levels of citalopram. Serious reactions may occur if citalopram is administered too soon after MAO use. Beta blocker (metoprolol) levels may increase by 2 fold when admixed with citalopram.

Relative Infant Dose: 3.6%

Adult Dose: 20-40 mg daily

Alternatives: Sertraline, escitalopram

T ½	= 36 hours	M/P	= 1.16 - 3
PHL	=	PB	= 80%
Tmax	= 2-4 hours	Oral	= 80%
MW	= 405	pKa	=
Vd	= 12		

References:

1. Jensen PN, Olesen OV, Bertelsen A, Linnet K. Citalopram and desmethylcitalopram concentrations in breast milk and in serum of mother and infant. Ther Drug Monit 1997; 19 (2):236-239.
2. Spigset O, Carieborg L, Ohman R, Norstrom A. Excretion of citalopram in breast milk. Br J Clin Pharmacol 1997; 44 (3):295-298.
3. Rampono J, Kristensen JH, Hackett LP, Paech M, Kohan R, Ilett KF. Citalopram and demethylcitalopram in human milk; distribution, excretion and effects in breast fed infants. Br J Clin Pharmacol 2000; 50 (3):263-268.
4. Schmidt K, Olesen OV, Jensen PN. Citalopram and breast-feeding: serum concentration and side effects in the infant. Biol Psychiatry 2000; 47 (2):164-165.
5. Lee A, Woo J, Ito S. Frequency of infant adverse events that are associated with citalopram use during breast-feeding. Am J Obstet Gynecol 2004 Jan; 190 (1):218-21.
6. Heikkinen T, Ekblad U, Kero P, Ekblad S, Laine K. Citalopram in pregnancy and lactation. Clin Pharmacol Ther 2002; 72 (2):184-191.
7. Nordeng H, Lindemann R, Perminov KV, Reikvam A. Neonatal withdrawl syndrome after in utero exposure to selective serotonin reuptake inhibitors. Acta Paediatr 2001; 90:288-91.

CLARITHROMYCIN   L1

Trade: Biaxin
Other Trades: Klacid, Klaricid
Uses: Antibiotic
AAP: Not reviewed

Antibiotic that belongs to erythromycin family. In a study of 12 mothers receiving 250 mg twice daily, the C_{max} occurred at 2.2 hours and was reported to be 0.85 mg/L.[1] The estimated average dose of clarithromycin via milk was reported to be 150 µg/kg/day, or 2% of the maternal dose. Clarithromycin is probably compatible with breastfeeding. Observe for diarrhea and thrush in the infant.

Pregnancy Risk Category: C

Lactation Risk Category: L1

Adult Concerns: Diarrhea, nausea, dyspepsia, abdominal pain, metallic taste.

Pediatric Concerns: None reported via milk. Pediatric indications are available.

Drug Interactions: Clarithromycin increases serum theophylline by as much as 20%. Increases plasma levels of carbamazepine, cyclosporin, digoxin, ergot alkaloids, tacrolimus, triazolam, zidovudine, terfenadine, astemizole, cisapride (serious arrhythmias). Fluconazole increases clarithromycin serum levels by 25%. Numerous other drug-drug interactions are unreported, but probably occur.

Relative Infant Dose: 2.1%

Adult Dose: 250 mg BID

Alternatives:

T ½	= 5-7 hours	M/P	= >1
PHL	=	PB	= 40-70%
Tmax	= 1.7 hours	Oral	= 50%
MW	= 748	pKa	=
Vd	=		

References:
1. Sedlmayr T, Peters F, Raasch W, Kees F. [Clarithromycin, a new macrolide antibiotic. Effectiveness in puerperal infections and pharmacokinetics in breast milk]. Geburtshilfe Frauenheilkd 1993 July; 53 (7):488-91.

CLEMASTINE   L4

Trade: Tavist
Other Trades: Tavegyl
Uses: Antihistamine
AAP: Drugs associated with significant side effects and should be given with caution

Clemastine is a long-acting antihistamine. Following a maternal dose of 1 mg twice daily a 10 week old breastfeeding infant developed drowsiness, irritability, refusal to feed, and neck stiffness.[1] Levels in milk and plasma (20 hours post dose) were 5-10 μg/L (milk) and 20 μg/L (plasma) respectively.

Pregnancy Risk Category: B

Lactation Risk Category: L4

Adult Concerns: Drowsiness, headache, fatigue, nervousness, appetite increase, depression.

Pediatric Concerns: Drowsiness, irritability, refusal to feed, and neck stiffness in one infant. Increased risk of seizures.

Drug Interactions: Increased toxicity when mixed with CNS depressants, anticholinergics, MAO inhibitors, tricyclic anti-depressants, phenothiazines.

Relative Infant Dose: 5.2%

Adult Dose: 1.34 to 2.68 mg BID or TID

Alternatives: Cetirazine, Loratadine

T ½	= 10-12 hours	M/P	= 0.25-0.5
PHL	=	PB	=
Tmax	= 2-5 hours	Oral	= 100%
MW	= 344	pKa	=
Vd	=		

References:
1. Kok TH, Taitz LS, Bennett MJ, Holt DW. Drowsiness due to clemastine transmitted in breast milk. Lancet 1982; 1 (8277):914-915.

CLINDAMYCIN   L2

Trade: Cleocin, Cleocin T
Other Trades: Dalacin, Clindatech
Uses: Antibiotic
AAP: Maternal Medication Usually Compatible with Breastfeeding

Clindamycin is a broad-spectrum antibiotic frequently used for anaerobic infections. In one study of two nursing mothers and following doses of 600 mg IV every 6 hours, the concentration of clindamycin in breastmilk was 3.1 to 3.8 mg/L at 0.2 to 0.5 hours after dosing.[1]

Following oral doses of 300 mg every 6 hours, the breastmilk levels averaged 1.0 to 1.7 mg/L at 1.5 to 7 hours after dosing.

In another study of 2-3 women who received a single oral dose of 150 mg, milk levels averaged 0.9 mg/L at 4 hours with a milk/plasma ratio of 0.47.[2] An alteration of GI flora is possible even though the dose is low.

One case of bloody stools (pseudomembranous colitis) has been associated with clindamycin and gentamicin therapy on day 5 postpartum, but this is considered rare.[3] In this case, the mother of a newborn infant was given 600 mg IV every 6 hours. In rare cases, pseudomembranous colitis can appear several weeks later.

In a study by Steen, in 5 breastfeeding patients who received 150 mg three times daily for 7 days, milk concentrations ranged from <0.5 to 3.1 mg/L with the majority of levels <0.5 mg/L.[4] There are a number of pediatric clinical uses of clindamycin (anaerobic infections, bacterial endocarditis, pelvic inflammatory disease, and bacterial vaginosis). The current pediatric dosage recommendation is 10-40 mg/kg/day divided every 6-8 hours.[5]

In a study of 15 women who received 600 mg clindamycin intravenously, levels of clindamycin in milk averaged 1.03 mg/L at two hours following the dose.[6]

Cleocin T topical solution or lotion contain clindamycin phosphate equivalent to 10 mg/mL. Transcutaneous absorption is minimal (<1-4%) and reported plasma levels are low to nil. Some does appear in urine of treated patients. Due to low maternal plasma levels, virtually none should be expected in breast milk. With the rise of resistant Staphlococcal infections, clindamycin use in infants has risen enormously. The amount in milk is unlikely to harm a breastfeeding infant.

Pregnancy Risk Category: B

Lactation Risk Category: L2

Adult Concerns: Diarrhea, rash, pseudomembranous colitis, nausea, vomiting, GI cramps.

Pediatric Concerns: One case of pseudomembranous colitis has been reported. But this is rare in infants. It is unlikely the levels in breastmilk would be clinically relevant. Commonly used in pediatric infections. Observe for diarrhea.

Drug Interactions: Increased duration of muscle blockade when administered with neuromuscular blockers such as tubocurarine and pancuronium. Antagonism has been demonstrated between clindamycin and erythromycin in vitro. Because of possible clinical significance, these two drugs should not be administered concurrently.

Relative Infant Dose: 1% - 7.3%

Adult Dose: 150-450 mg every 6 hours

Alternatives:

T ½	= 2.4 hours	M/P	= 0.47
PHL	= 3.6 hours (term)	PB	= 94%
Tmax	= 45-60 minutes	Oral	= 90%
MW	= 425	pKa	= 7.45
Vd	=		

References:

1. Smith JA. et.al. Clindamycin in human breast milk. Can Med Assn J 1975; 112:806.
2. Matsuda S. Transfer of antibiotics into maternal milk. Biol Res Pregnancy Perinatol 1984; 5 (2):57-60.
3. Mann CF. Clindamycin and breast-feeding. Pediatrics 1980; 66 (6):1030-1031.
4. Steen B, Rane A. Clindamycin passage into human milk. Br J Clin Pharmacol 1982; 13 (5):661-664.
5. Johnson KB. ed. The Harriet Lane Handbook. Thirteenth ed. Mosby Publishing, 1993.
6. Zhang Y, Zhang Q, Xu Z. Tissue and body fluid distribution of antibacterial agents in pregnant and lactating women. Zhonghua Fu Chan Ke Za Zhi. 1997;32:288-92.

CLINDAMYCIN VAGINAL   L2

Trade: Cleocin Vaginal
Other Trades: Dalacin Vaginal Cream, Dalacin T
Uses: Antibiotic
AAP: Maternal Medication Usually Compatible with Breastfeeding

Clindamycin when administered by IV has been found in breastmilk (see clindamycin). One case of bloody stools (pseudomembranous colitis) has been associated with oral clindamycin.

However, only about 5% of Clindamycin Vaginal (100 mg/dose) is absorbed into the maternal circulation, which would be approximately 5 mg clindamycin/day.[1] It is unlikely that clindamycin when administered via a vaginal gel would produce any significant danger to a breastfeeding infant.

Pregnancy Risk Category: B

Lactation Risk Category: L2

Adult Concerns: Diarrhea, rash, GI cramps, colitis, rarely bloody diarrhea. Transient neutropenia (leukopenia), eosinophilia, agranulocytosis, and thrombocytopenia have been reported. No direct etiologic relationship to concurrent clindamycin therapy could be made in any of these reports.

Pediatric Concerns: Unlikely to harm a breastfeeding infant.

Drug Interactions: Clindamycin has been shown to have neuromuscular blocking properties that may enhance the action of other neuromuscular blocking agents.

Relative Infant Dose:

Adult Dose: 100 mg intravaginally every HS

Alternatives:

T ½	= 2.9 hours	M/P	=
PHL	=	PB	= 94%
Tmax	=	Oral	= 90%
MW	= 425	pKa	=
Vd	=		

References:
1. Pharmaceutical Manufacturer Prescribing Information. 2010.

CLOBAZAM   L3

Trade: Frisium
Other Trades:
Uses: Benzodiazepine anxiolytic
AAP: Not reviewed

Clobazam (Frisium) is a typical benzodiazepine very similar to Valium.[1] It is primarily an anxiolytic, but it is sometimes used to treat refractory seizures. The median half-life for tolerance is only 3.5 months, so it would not be suitable for long-term therapy of seizures. It has a rather long half-life averaging 17-31 hours for the parent drug in young adults and 11-77 hours for the active metabolite desmethylclobazam. As with diazepam (Valium), it could possibly reach elevated levels in a breastfeeding infant over time. No data is available on breastmilk concentrations. See diazepam.

Pregnancy Risk Category: C

Lactation Risk Category: L3

Adult Concerns: Sedation, drowsiness, hangover, weakness, insomnia.

Pediatric Concerns: Typical benzodiazepine, use caution. See Diazepam.

Drug Interactions: May increase effects of opiates, CNS depressants. Macrolide (erythromycin) antibiotics may increase levels of clobazam. Clobazam may increase levels of carbamazepine.

Relative Infant Dose:

Adult Dose: 20-30 mg/day

Alternatives: Alprazolam

T ½	= 17-31 hours	M/P	=
PHL	=	PB	= 90%
Tmax	= 1-2 hours	Oral	= 87%
MW	= 301	pKa	=
Vd	= 0.87-1.8		

References:
1.   Pharmaceutical Manufacturer Prescribing Information. 2010.

CLOBETASOL PROPIONATE   L5

Trade: Clobevate, Clobex, Cormax, Olux-E, Olux, Temovate E, Temovate
Other Trades: Taro-Clobetasol, Dermovate, Gen-Clobetasol, Novo-Clobetasol
Uses: Topical Corticosteroid
AAP: Not reviewed

Clobetasol is a very high potency topical corticosteroid used for the short-term relief of inflammation of moderate to severe corticosteroid responsive dermatoses including psoriasis.[1] Because this is such a high potency steroid, oral absorption by an infant could be hazardous. Do not use this on the nipple or areola of a breastfeeding mother.

Pregnancy Risk Category: C

Lactation Risk Category: L5 on nipple or areola

Adult Concerns: Adverse reactions include adrenal suppression, application site burning, cracking, dryness, irritation, and glucosuria.

Pediatric Concerns: Use is not recommended in children under 12 years of age. Do not use on the nipple or areola of the breast of a breastfeeding mother.

Drug Interactions:

Relative Infant Dose:

Adult Dose: Apply bid

Alternatives: Hydrocortisone, mometasone ointments or creams

T ½	=	M/P	=
PHL	=	PB	=
Tmax	=	Oral	=
MW	= 467	pKa	=
Vd	=		

References:
1. Pharmaceutical Manufacturer Prescribing Information. 2002.

CLOFAZIMINE   L3

Trade: Lamprene
Other Trades:
Uses: Antimicrobial for leprosy
AAP: Drugs whose effect on nursing infants is unknown but may be of concern

Clofazimine exerts a slow bacteriocidal effect on M. Leprae. In a study of 8 female leprosy patients on clofazimine (50 mg/day or 100 mg on alternate days) for 1-18 months, blood samples were take at 4-6 hours after the dose.[1] Average plasma and milk levels were 0.9 mg/L and 1.33 mg/L (range= 0.8 to 1.7 mg/L), respectively. The milk/plasma ratio varied from 1.0 to 1.7 with a mean of 1.48. A red tint and pigmentation has been reported in breastfed infants.[2,3]

Pregnancy Risk Category: C

Lactation Risk Category: L3

Adult Concerns: Reversible red-brown discoloration of skin and eyes. Gastrointestinal effects include nausea, abdominal cramps and pain, nausea and vomiting. Splenic infarction, crystalline deposits of clofazimine in multiple organs and tissues.

Pediatric Concerns: Levels in milk are moderate to high. Reddish discoloration of milk and infant may occur. No toxicity in infants has been reported however.

Drug Interactions:

Relative Infant Dose: 14% - 28.2%

Adult Dose: 100-200 mg daily.

Alternatives:

T ½	= 70 days	M/P	= 1,7
PHL	=	PB	=
Tmax	=	Oral	= 45-70%
MW	= 473	pKa	=
Vd	=		

References:
1. Venkatesan K, Mathur A, Girdhar A, Girdhar BK. Excretion of clofazimine in human milk in leprosy patients. Lepr Rev 1997; 68 (3):242-246.
2. Farb H, West DP, Pedvis-Leftick A. Clofazimine in pregnancy complicated by leprosy. Obstet Gynecol 1982; 59 (1):122-123.

3.   Freerksen E, Seydel JK. Critical comments on the treatment of leprosy and other mycobacterial infections with clofazimine. Arzneimittelforschung 1992; 42 (10):1243-1245.

CLOMIPHENE   L3

Trade: Clomid, Serophene, Milophene
Other Trades:
Uses: Ovulation stimulator for ovulatory failure
AAP: Not reviewed

Clomiphene appears to stimulate the release of the pituitary gonadotropins, follicle-stimulating hormone (FSH), and luteinizing hormone (LH), which result in development and maturation of the ovarian follicle, ovulation, and subsequent development and function of the corpus luteum. It has both estrogenic and anti-estrogenic effects. LH and FSH peak at 5-9 days after completing clomiphene therapy.

In a study of 60 postpartum women (1-4 days postpartum), clomiphene was effective in totally inhibiting lactation early postnatally and in suppressing established lactation (day 4).[1] Only 7 of 40 women receiving clomiphene to inhibit lactation had signs of congestion or discomfort. In the 20 women who received clomiphene to suppress established lactation (on day 4), a rapid amelioration of breast engorgement and discomfort was produced. After 5 days of treatment, no signs of lactation were present. In another study of 177 postpartum women, clomiphene was very effective at inhibiting lactation.[2]

Bromocriptine, stilboestrol, clomiphene, testosterone and a placebo were given to 75 postpartum women for the suppression of puerperal lactation. An additional 15 women who breastfed their babies served as a control group.[3] Blood samples were taken for the determination of serum prolactin levels by a specific homologous double antibody radioimmunoassay. Concurrently, the clinical effectiveness of the various treatments was assessed. High levels of prolactin were found at the time of delivery. Bromocriptine effectively reduced serum prolactin and prevented lactation; stilboestrol increased serum prolactin and partially suppressed lactation; clomiphene citrate and testosterone propionate both lowered serum prolactin levels and partially suppressed lactation. The placebo showed almost no effect on serum prolactin.

Clomiphene appears to be very effective in suppressing lactation when used up to 4 days postpartum. However, its efficacy in reducing milk production in women, months after lactation is established, is unknown but believed to be minimal.[4]

Pregnancy Risk Category: X

Lactation Risk Category: L3 in late stage lactation
L4 early postpartum

Adult Concerns: Dizziness, insomnia, lightheadedness, hot flashes, ovarian enlargement, depression, headache, alopecia. May inhibit lactation early postpartum.

Pediatric Concerns: Transfer and effect on infant is unreported, but may suppress early lactation.

Drug Interactions:

Relative Infant Dose:

Adult Dose: 50 mg daily.

Alternatives:

T ½	= 5-7 days	M/P	=
PHL	=	PB	=
Tmax	–	Oral	= Complete
MW	= 406	pKa	=
Vd	=		

References:
1. Masala A, Delitala G, Alagna S, Devilla L, Stoppelli I, Lo DG. Clomiphene and puerperal lactation. Panminerva Med 1978; 20 (3):161-163.
2. Zuckerman H, Carmel S. The inhibition of lactation by clomiphene. J Obstet Gynaecol Br Commonw 1973; 80 (9):822-823.
3. Weinstein D, Ben-David M, Polishuk WZ. Serum prolactin and the suppression of lactation. Br J Obstet Gynaecol. 1976 Sep;83 (9):679-82.
4. J.N. Personal communication. 2001.

CLOMIPRAMINE   L2

Trade: Anafranil
Other Trades: Apo-Clomipramine, Placil
Uses: Anti-obsessional, antidepressant drug
AAP: Drugs whose effect on nursing infants is unknown but may be of concern

Clomipramine is a tricyclic antidepressant frequently used for obsessive-compulsive disorder.[1] In one patient taking 125 mg/day, on the 4th and 6th day postpartum, milk levels were 342.7 and 215.8 μg/L respectively.[2] Maternal plasma levels were 211 and 208.4 μg/L at day 4 and 6 respectively. Milk/plasma ratio varies from 1.62 to 1.04 on day 4 to 6 respectively. Neonatal plasma levels continued to drop from a high of 266.6 ng/mL at birth to 127.6 ng/mL at day 4, to 94.8 ng/mL at day 6, to 9.8 ng/mL at 35 days. In a study of four breastfeeding women who received doses of 75 to 125 mg/day, plasma levels of clomipramine in the breastfed infants were below the limit of detection, suggesting minimal transfer to the infant via milk.[3] No untoward effects were noted in any of the infants.

Pregnancy Risk Category: C

Lactation Risk Category: L2

Adult Concerns: Drowsiness, fatigue, dry mouth, seizures, constipation, sweating, reduced appetite.

Pediatric Concerns: None reported in several studies.

Drug Interactions: Decreased effect when used with barbiturates, carbamazepine and phenytoin. Increased sedation when used with alcohol, CNS depressants (hypnotics). Increased dangers when used with MAO inhibitors. Additive anticholinergic effects when used with other anticholinergics.

Relative Infant Dose: 2.8%

Adult Dose: 50 mg BID

Alternatives: Sertraline, Paroxetine, Fluoxetine

T ½	= 19-37 hours	M/P	= 0.84- 1.62
PHL	= 92.8 hours	PB	= 96%
Tmax	=	Oral	= Complete
MW	= 315	pKa	= 9.5
Vd	= 17		

References:
1.   Pharmaceutical Manufacturer Prescribing Information. 2010.
2.   Schimmell MS, Katz EZ, Shaag Y, Pastuszak A, Koren G. Toxic neonatal effects following maternal clomipramine therapy. J Toxicol Clin Toxicol 1991; 29 (4):479-484.
3.   Wisner KL, Perel JM, Foglia JP. Serum clomipramine and metabolite levels in four nursing mother-infant pairs. J Clin Psychiatry 1995; 56 (1):17-20.

CLONAZEPAM

L3

Trade: Klonopin

Other Trades: Rivotril, Apo-Clonazepam, PMS-Clonazepam, Paxam

Uses: Anticonvulsant, sedative

AAP: Not reviewed

Clonazepam is a typical benzodiazepine sedative, anticonvulsant. In one case report, milk levels varied between 11 and 13 µg/L (the maternal dose was omitted).[1] Milk/maternal serum ratio was approximately 0.33. In this report, the infant's serum level of clonazepam dropped from 4.4 µg/L at birth to 1.0 µg/L at 14 days while continuing to breastfeed, suggesting increasing clearance with time. In this case, excessive periodic breathing and apnea and cyanosis occurred in this infant (36 weeks gestation) at 6 hours until 10 days postpartum. The infant was exposed in utero as well as postpartum via breastmilk.

In another study of a mother treated with 2 mg clonazepam twice daily recorded peak milk concentrations of 10.7 µg/L at 4 hours post dose, and a maximum infant dose of 2.5% of the weight-adjusted maternal dose. The infant's serum level of clonazepam at days 2-4 was 4.7 µg/L.[2]

In a group of 11 mothers receiving 0.25 to 2 mg clonazepam daily, ten of 11 breastfed infants had no detectable (limit of detection: 5-14 µg/L) clonazepam or metabolites in their serum.[3] On infant (1.9 weeks old) had a serum concentration of 22 µg/L. Maternal dose was 0.5 mg daily.

These data suggest the low incidence of toxicity with this medication in breastfeeding infants.

Pregnancy Risk Category: D

Lactation Risk Category: L3

Adult Concerns: Apnea, sedation, ataxia, hypotonia. Behavioral disturbances (in children) include aggressiveness, irritability, agitation.

Pediatric Concerns: Apnea, cyanosis and hypotonia was reported in one infant at 6 hours postnatally to a woman consuming clonazepam throughout pregnancy. Maternal and cord serum levels of clonazepam were 32 ng/mL and 19 ng/mL respectively. The infant had prolonged apnea and hypotonia. The infant had repeated periodic breathing episodes up to 10 weeks of age.[1] In another group of 11 mothers consuming clonazepam, none of the infants had any reported side effects.[3]

Drug Interactions: Phenytoin and barbiturates may increase clearance of clonazepam. CNS depressants may increase sedation.

Relative Infant Dose: 2.8%

Adult Dose: 0.5-1 mg TID

Alternatives: Lorazepam

T ½	= 18-50 hours	M/P	= 0.33
PHL	=	PB	= 50-86%
Tmax	= 1-4 hours	Oral	= Complete
MW	= 316	pKa	= 1.5, 10.5
Vd	= 1.5-4.4		

References:
1. Fisher JB, Edgren BE, Mammel MC, Coleman JM. Neonatal apnea associated with maternal clonazepam therapy: a case report. Obstet Gynecol 1985; 66 (3 Suppl):34S-35S.
2. Soderman P, Matheson I. Clonazepam in breast milk. Eur J Pediatr 1988; 147 (2):212-213.
3. Birnbaum CS, Cohen LS, Bailey JW et al. Serum concentrations of antidepressants and benzodiazepines in nursing infants: a case series. Pediatrics. 1999;104:e11.

CLONIDINE   L3

Trade: Catapres
Other Trades: Dixarit, Apo-Clonidine, Novo-Clonidine
Uses: Antihypertensive
AAP: Not reviewed

Clonidine is an antihypertensive that reduces sympathetic nerve activity from the brain. Clonidine is excreted in human milk. In a study of 9 nursing women receiving between 241.7 and 391.7 µg/day of clonidine, milk levels varied from approximately 1.8 µg/L to as high as 2.8 µg/L on postpartum day 10-14.[1]

In another report following a maternal dose of 37.5 µg twice daily, maternal plasma was determined to be 0.33 ng/mL and milk level was 0.60 µg/L.[2] Clinical symptoms of neonatal toxicity are unreported and are unlikely in normal full term infants.

Clonidine may reduce prolactin secretion and could conceivably reduce milk production early postpartum. Transdermal patches produce maternal plasma levels of 0.39, 0.84, and 1.12 ng/mL using the 3.5, 7, and 10.5 cm square patches respectively. The 3.7 square cm patch would produce maternal plasma levels equivalent to the 37.5 µg oral dose and would likely produce milk levels equivalent to the above study.

Pregnancy Risk Category: C

Lactation Risk Category: L3

Adult Concerns: Drowsiness, dry mouth, hypotension, constipation, dizziness.

Pediatric Concerns: None reported, but may induce hypotension in infant. May reduce milk production by reducing prolactin secretion.

Drug Interactions: Tricyclic antidepressants inhibit hypotensive effect of clonidine. Beta blockers may potentiate slow heart rate when administered with clonidine. Discontinue beta blockers several days to week prior to using clonidine.

Relative Infant Dose: 0.01% - 7.1%

Adult Dose: 0.1-0.3 mg BID

Alternatives:

T ½	= 20-24 hours	M/P	= 2
PHL	–	PB	= 20-40%
Tmax	= 3-5 hours	Oral	= 75-100%
MW	= 230	pKa	= 8.3
Vd	= 3.2-5.6		

References:
1. Hartikainen-Sorri AL, Heikkinen JE, Koivisto M. Pharmacokinetics of clonidine during pregnancy and nursing. Obstet Gynecol 1987; 69 (4):598-600.
2. Bunjes R, Schaefer C, Holzinger D. Clonidine and breast-feeding. Clin Pharm 1993; 12 (3):178-179.

CLOPIDOGREL   L3

Trade: Plavix
Other Trades:
Uses: Platelet aggregation inhibitor
AAP: Not reviewed

Clopidogrel selectively inhibits platelet adenosine diphosphate-induced platelet aggregation. It is used to prevent ischemic events in patients at risk (e.g. cardiovascular disease, strokes, myocardial infarct). Aspirin is generally preferred as it is less expensive, quite tolerable, and very effective.

Clopidogrel is only used in those patients who are aspirin-intolerant. It is not known if it transfers into human milk, but it does enter rodent milk.[1] Although the plasma half-life is rather brief (8 hours), it's metabolite covalently bonds to platelet receptors with a half-life of 11 days. Because it produces an irreversible inhibition of platelet aggregation, any present in milk could inhibit an infant's platelet function for a prolonged period. Because aspirin affects platelet aggregation similarly, and its milk levels are quite low, it would appear to be an ideal alternative. However, aspirin also inhibits platelet aggregation for long periods as well and may increase the risk of Reye' s syndrome in infants. The choice between using clopidogrel and aspirin must be made on clinical grounds and following a risk vs. benefit assessment until we know more about the levels secreted into human milk.

Pregnancy Risk Category: B

Lactation Risk Category: L3

Adult Concerns: Contraindicated in individuals with bleeding phenomenon.

Pediatric Concerns: None reported via milk. The transfer of clinically relevant amounts to the infant is remote, but we do not have any data thus far suggesting milk levels and clinical dose transferred to the infant.

Drug Interactions: At high concentrations, clopidogrel inhibits Cytochrome P450 2C9, and may inhibit metabolism of phenytoin, tamoxifen, tolbutamide, warfarin, torsemide, fluvastatin, and many NSAIDs.

Relative Infant Dose:

Adult Dose: 75 mg daily

Alternatives:

T ½	= 8 hours	M/P	=
PHL	=	PB	= 9%
Tmax	= 1 hour	Oral	= 50%
MW	= 420	pKa	=
Vd	=		

References:
1. Pharmaceutical Manufacturer Prescribing Information. 2010.

CLORAZEPATE   L3

Trade: Tranxene, Tranxene-SD
Other Trades: Apo-Clorazepate, Novo-Clopate
Uses: Benzodiazepine sedative
AAP: Not reviewed

Clorazepate is a typical benzodiazepine. The primary metabolite, nordiazepam, is the same as from diazepam (Valium). Clorazepate has a brief half-life of less than 2 hours, and is rapidly converted to the active drug, nordiazepam, and oxazepam. The active metabolite has a prolonged half-life of 40-50 hours.

In 7 mothers who were breastfeeding early postnatally, and who received 20 mg IM clorazepate, levels of nordiazepam ranged from 7.5-15.5 µg/L 48 hours after the dose and 6-12 µg/L 4 days following the dose.

Pregnancy Risk Category: D

Lactation Risk Category: L3

Adult Concerns: Adverse reactions include drowsiness, dizziness, blurred vision, dry mouth, headache, fatigue, ataxia, slurred speech, and mental confusion.

Pediatric Concerns: Poor suckling, sedation, lethargy, constipation have been reported for diazepam.

Drug Interactions: This drug is additive for most all CNS sedatives. The may prolong the sleeping time after hexobarbital, ethyl alcohol, and other hypnotic sedatives including barbiturates, narcotics, phenothiazines, monoamine oxidase inhibitors, etc. Cimetidine may increase plasma levels of clorazepate.

Relative Infant Dose:

Adult Dose: 15-60 mg/day.

Alternatives: Lorazepam, midazolam

T ½	= 40-50 hours (metab)	M/P	=
PHL	=	PB	= 98%
Tmax	= 1 hour	Oral	= 97%
MW	= 408	pKa	= 3.5; 12.5
Vd	= 1.7		

References:
1. Pharmaceutical Manufacturers prescribing information, 2010.
2. Rey E, Giraux P, d'Athis P, Turquais JM, Chavinie J, Olive G. Pharmacokinetics of the placental transfer and distribution of clorazepate and its metabolite nordiazepam in the feto-placental unit and in the neonate. Eur J Clin Pharmacol. 1979 Apr 17;15 (3):181-5.

CLOTRIMAZOLE   L1

Trade: Gyne-Lotrimin, Mycelex, Lotrimin, FemCare, Trivagizole

Other Trades: Canesten, Clotrimaderm, Myclo, Hiderm, Clonea

Uses: Antifungal

AAP: Not reviewed

Clotrimazole is a broad-spectrum antifungal agent. It is generally used for candidiasis and various tinea species (athletes foot, ring worm). Clotrimazole is available in oral lozenges, topical creams, intravaginal tablets and creams. No data is available on penetration into breastmilk. However, after intravaginal administration, only 3-10% of the drug is absorbed (peak serum level= 0.01 to 0.03 µg/mL) and even less by oral lozenge.[1] Hence, following vaginal administration it seems unlikely that levels absorbed by a breastfeeding infant would be high enough to produce untoward effects. Safety of clotrimazole lozenges in children younger than 3 years of age has not been established. The risk of contact dermatitis with this agent may be higher.[2]

Pregnancy Risk Category: B for topical/vaginal preparations
                                C for oral preparations

Lactation Risk Category: L1

Adult Concerns: Nausea, vomiting from oral administration. Itching, burning and stinging following topical application. The following have been reported: erythema, stinging, blistering, peeling, edema, pruritus, urticaria, burning, and general irritation of the skin. Elevated liver enzymes in > 10% of treated. Contact dermatitis has been reported in breastfeeding women.

Pediatric Concerns: None reported via milk. Limited oral absorption probably limits clinical relevance in breastfed infants.

Drug Interactions: May inhibit amphotericin activity. Clotrimazole is reported to increase cyclosporin plasma levels. May enhance hypoglycemic effect of oral hypoglycemic agents. Clotrimazole inhibits cytochrome P450 IIIA and may inhibit metabolism of any number of other medications.

Relative Infant Dose:

Adult Dose: 500 mg intravaginally every HS

Alternatives: Fluconazole, Miconazole

T ½	= 3.5-5 hours	M/P	=
PHL	=	PB	=
Tmax	= 3 hours (oral)	Oral	= Poor
MW	= 345	pKa	=
Vd	=		

References:
1.   McEvoy GE. (ed):AFHS Drug Information. New York, NY: 2009.
2.   Newman J. Personal communication. 1999.

CLOXACILLIN   L2

Trade: Tegopen, Cloxapen
Other Trades: Apo-Cloxi, Novo-Cloxin, Orbenin, Alclox, Kloxerate-DC
Uses: Penicillin antibiotic
AAP: Not reviewed

Cloxacillin is an oral penicillinase-resistant penicillin frequently used for peripheral (non-CNS) Staphylococcus aureus and S. epidermidis infections, particularly mastitis. Following a single 500 mg oral dose of cloxacillin in lactating women, milk concentrations of the drug were zero to 0.2 mg/L one and two hours after the dose respectively and 0.2 to 0.4 mg/L after 6 hours.[1] Usual dose for adults is 250-500 mg four times daily for at least 10-14 days.[2] As with most penicillins, it is unlikely these levels would be clinically relevant.

Pregnancy Risk Category: B
Lactation Risk Category: L2

Adult Concerns: Rash, diarrhea, nephrotoxicity, fever, shaking, chills.

Pediatric Concerns: None reported but observe for GI symptoms such as diarrhea.

Drug Interactions: Efficacy of oral contraceptives may be reduced. Disulfiram, probenecid may increase cloxacillin levels. Increased effect of oral anticoagulants.

Relative Infant Dose: 0.4% - 0.8%

Adult Dose: 250-500 mg every 6 hours

Alternatives:

T ½	= 0.7-3 hours	M/P	=
PHL	= 0.8-1.5 hours	PB	= 90-96%
Tmax	= 0.5-2 hours	Oral	= 37-60%
MW	= 436	pKa	=
Vd	= 6.6-10.8		

References:
1.   Matsuda S. Transfer of antibiotics into maternal milk. Biol Res Pregnancy Perinatol 1984; 5 (2):57-60.
2.   McEvoy GE. (ed):AFHS Drug Information. New York, NY: 1995.

CLOZAPINE   L3

Trade: Clozaril
Other Trades:
Uses: Antipsychotic, sedative
AAP: Drugs whose effect on nursing infants is unknown but may be of concern

Clozapine is an atypical antipsychotic, sedative drug somewhat similar to the phenothiazine family. In a study of one patient receiving 50 mg/d clozapine at delivery, the maternal and fetal plasma were reported to be 14.1 ng/mL and 27 ng/mL respectively.

After 24 hours postpartum, the maternal plasma level was 14.7 ng/mL and maternal milk levels were 63.5 ng/mL. On day 7 postpartum and receiving a dose of 100 mg/d clozapine, the maternal plasma and milk levels were 41.1 ng/mL and 115.6 µg/L respectively. From this data it is apparent that clozapine concentrates in milk with a milk/plasma ratio of 4.3 at a dose of 50 mg/d and 2.8 at a dose of 100 mg/d.

The change from day one to seven suggests that clozapine entry into mature milk is less.

Pregnancy Risk Category: B

Lactation Risk Category: L3

Adult Concerns: Drowsiness, dizziness/vertigo, salivation, constipation, tachycardia, nausea, GI distress, extrapyramidal symptoms, tardive dyskinesia, agranulocytosis.

Pediatric Concerns: None reported but use with great caution.

Drug Interactions: Decreased effect of epinephrine, phenytoin. Increased sedation with CNS depressants. Increased effect with guanabenz, anticholinergics. Increased toxicity with cimetidine, MAO inhibitors, tricyclic antidepressants.

Relative Infant Dose: 1.4%

Adult Dose: 300-600 mg daily.

Alternatives:

T ½	= 8-12 hours	M/P	= 2.8-4.3
PHL	=	PB	= 95%
Tmax	= 2.5 hours	Oral	= 90%
MW	= 327	pKa	=
Vd	= 5		

References:
1. Barnas C, Bergant A, Hummer M, Saria A, Fleischhacker WW. Clozapine concentrations in maternal and fetal plasma, amniotic fluid, and breast milk. Am J Psychiatry 1994; 151 (6):945.

CO-TRIMOXAZOLE   L3

Trade: TMP-SMZ, Bactrim, Cotrim, Septra
Other Trades: Novo-Trimel, Septrin, Respax, Trimogal
Uses: Sulfonamide antibiotic
AAP: Maternal Medication Usually Compatible with Breastfeeding

Co-trimoxazole is the mixture of trimethoprim and sulfamethoxazole. See individual monographs for each of these products.

Pregnancy Risk Category: C
                             D at term

Lactation Risk Category: L3

Adult Concerns:

Pediatric Concerns: May increase the risk of hyperbilirubinemia in newborns. Caution recommended first 30 days postpartum.

Drug Interactions:

Relative Infant Dose:

Adult Dose: 160 mg BID

Alternatives:

References:

COAGULATION FACTOR VIIa   L2

Trade: NovoSeven
Other Trades:
Uses: Promotes coagulation in hemophilia
AAP: Not reviewed

Recombinant human coagulation Factor VIIa (rFVIIa) (NovoSeven) is intended to promote coagulation by activating the extrinsic pathway of the coagulation cascade. It is a vitamin K-dependent glycoprotein consisting of 406 amino acids and a MW of 50 K Dalton. NovoSeven is structurally similar to human plasma-derived Factor VIIa normally found in human plasma.

This is a large MW protein (50,000 daltons), which is very unlikely to enter milk. It is structurally similar to human plasma derived factor VIIa normally found in humans anyway.

Pregnancy Risk Category: C

Lactation Risk Category: L2

Adult Concerns: Adverse reactions include fever, allergic reaction, purpura, rash, hemorrhage hemarthrosis, and hypertension.

Pediatric Concerns: None reported via milk. It is unlikely to enter milk.

Drug Interactions: Do not use simultaneously with activated prothrombin complex.

Relative Infant Dose:

Adult Dose: 90 µg/kg/2 hours until hemostasis is achieved.

Alternatives:

T ½	= 1.7-2.7 hours	M/P	=
PHL	=	PB	=
Tmax	=	Oral	= Nil
MW	= 50,000	pKa	=
Vd	= 0.103		

References:
1. Pharmaceutical Manufacturers prescribing information, 2010.

COCAINE   L5

Trade: Crack
Other Trades:
Uses: Powerful CNS stimulant, local anesthetic
AAP: Drugs of abuse for which adverse effects have been reported

Cocaine is a local anesthetic and a powerful central nervous system stimulant. It is well absorbed from all locations including the stomach, nasal passages, intrapulmonary tissues via inhalation, and even via ophthalmic instillation. Adverse effects include agitation, nervousness, restlessness, euphoria, hallucinations, tremors, tonic-clonic seizures, and myocardial arrhythmias.

Although the pharmacologic effects of cocaine are relatively brief (20-30 min.) due to redistribution out of the brain, cocaine is slowly metabolized and excreted over a prolonged period. Urine samples can be positive for cocaine metabolites for up to 7 days or longer in adults. Breastfeeding infants will likewise become urine positive for cocaine for even longer periods. Even after the clinical effects of cocaine have subsided, the breastmilk will still probably contain significant quantities of benzoecgonine, the inactive metabolite of cocaine. The infant could still test positive for urine cocaine metabolites for long periods (days). The ingestion of small amounts of cocaine by infants via inhalation of smoke (environmental) is likely.

Studies of exact estimates of cocaine transmission to breastmilk have not been reported. Significant secretion into breastmilk is suspected with a probable high milk/plasma ratio. A mother of an 11 day-old infant applied cocaine powder to her nipples as an analgesic. Three hours following breastfeeding, she discovered the infant choking, blue and gasping for air. Upon arrival at he emergency room, the infant was hypertensive, tachycardic, ashen and cyanotic. The infant subsequently seized repeatedly.[1]

Another case report of a mother who used cocaine 3 days before delivery, reported a milk level 6 days later of 8 ng/mL. The authors propose that if this mother consumed 0.5 g of cocaine, then the infant would likely received 0.48 mg of cocaine, or 1.62% of the maternal dose per kilogram.[2]

In a study of 11 mothers who admitted prior use during pregnancy, cocaine was detected in six milk samples.[3] The highest cocaine concentration found was over 12 μg/mL. Topical application to nipples is EXTREMELY dangerous and is definitely contraindicated. Oral, intranasal, and smoking of crack cocaine is dangerous and definitely contraindicated.

Breastfeeding mothers should avoid cocaine absolutely. In those individuals who have ingested cocaine, a minimum pump and discard period of 24 hours is recommended for clearance. In addition, mothers who consume cocaine will continue to transfer the inactive metabolite of cocaine into their breast milk for many days, and the infant will become drug-screen-positive, even if not exposed to the parent, cocaine.

Pregnancy Risk Category: C during first and second trimester
X during third trimester

Lactation Risk Category: L5

Adult Concerns: Nausea, vomiting, CNS excitement, hypertension, tachycardia, arrhythmias.

Pediatric Concerns: Choking, vomiting, diarrhea, tremulousness, hyperactive startle reflex, gasping, agitation, irritability, hypertension, tachycardia. Extreme danger.

Drug Interactions: Increased toxicity when used with MAO inhibitors.

Relative Infant Dose:

Adult Dose: N/A

Alternatives:

T ½	= 0.8 hour	M/P	=
PHL	=	PB	= 91%
Tmax	= 15 minutes	Oral	= Complete
MW	= 303	pKa	= 8.6
Vd	= 1.6-2-7		

References:
1. Chaney NE, Franke J, Wadlington WB. Cocaine convulsions in a breast-feeding baby. J Pediatr 1988; 112 (1):134-135.
2. Sarkar M, Djulus J, Koren G. When a Cocaine-Using Mother Wishes to Breastfeed. Ther Drug Monit 2005; 27 (1):1-2.
3. Winecker RE, Goldberger BA, Tebbett IRet al. Detection of cocaine and its metabolites in breast milk. J Forensic Sci. 2001;46:12221-3.

CODEINE   L3

Trade: Empirin #3 # 4, Tylenol # 3 # 4
Other Trades: Paveral, Penntuss, Actacode, Codalgin, Codral, Panadeine, Veganin, Kaodene, Teropin
Uses: Analgesic
AAP: Maternal Medication Usually Compatible with Breastfeeding

Codeine is considered a mild opiate analgesic whose action is probably due to its metabolism to small amounts (about 7%) of morphine. The amount of codeine secreted into milk is low and dose dependent. Infant response is higher during neonatal period (first or second week).

Four cases of neonatal apnea have been reported following administration of 60 mg codeine every 4-6 hours to breastfeeding mothers although codeine was not detected in serum of the infants tested.[1] Apnea resolved after discontinuation of maternal codeine. Tylenol # 3 tablets contain 30 mg and Tylenol #4 tablets contain 60 mg of codeine in the USA.

In another study, following a dose of 60 mg, milk concentrations averaged 140 μg/L of milk with a peak of 455 μg/L at 1 hour.[2] Following 12 doses in 48 hours, the authors estimate the dose of codeine in milk (2000 mL milk) was 0.7 mg. There are few reported side effects following codeine doses of 30 mg, and it is believed to produce only minimal side effects in newborns.

In a study of 7 mothers, codeine and morphine levels were studied in breastmilk of 17 samples, and neonatal plasma of 24 samples from 11 healthy, term neonates. Milk codeine levels ranged from 33.8 to 314 μg/L 20 to 240 minutes after codeine; morphine levels ranged from 1.9 to 20.5 μg/L. Infant plasma samples one to four hours after feeding had codeine levels ranging from <0.8 to 4.5 μg/L; morphine ranged from <0.5 to 2.2 μg/L. The authors suggest that moderate codeine use during breastfeeding (< or = four 60 mg doses) is probably safe.[3]

In a recent report, an infant death was reported following the use of codeine (initially two tablets every 12 h, reduced to half that dose from day 2 to 2 weeks because of maternal somnolence and constipation) in a mother.[4] Codeine levels in milk were reported to be 87 μg/L while the average reported milk levels in most mothers range from 1.9 to 20.5 μg/L at doses of 60 mg every 6 hours. Genotype analysis of this specific mother indicated that his she was an ultra-rapid metabolizer of codeine. This genotype (which is very rare) leads to increased formation of morphine from codeine.

Ultimately, each infant's response to exposure to codeine should be independently determined. In the vast majority of mothers, codeine taken in moderation should be safe for their breastfed infant. However, any report of overt somnolence, apnea, poor feeding, grey skin, should be reported to the physician and could be associated with exposure to codeine.

Pregnancy Risk Category: C

Lactation Risk Category: L3
                                 L5 in rapid metabolizers

Adult Concerns: Sedation, respiratory depression, constipation.

Pediatric Concerns: Several rare cases of neonatal apnea have been reported, but at higher doses. Codeine analgesics are so commonly used postpartum, that side effect are extremely rare and seldom reported. Observe for sedation, apnea in premature or weakened infants.

Drug Interactions: Cigarette smoking increases effect of codeine. Increased toxicity/sedation when used with CNS depressants, phenothiazines, tricyclic antidepressants, other opiates, guanabenz, MAO inhibitors, neuromuscular blockers.

Relative Infant Dose: 8.1%

Adult Dose: 15-60 mg every 4-6 hours

Alternatives:

T ½	= 2.9 hours	M/P	= 1.3-2.5
PHL	=	PB	= 7%
Tmax	= 0.5-1 hour	Oral	= Complete
MW	= 299	pKa	= 8.2
Vd	= 3.5		

References:
1. Davis JM, Bhutari VK. Neonatal apnea and maternal codeine use. Pcd Res 1985; 19 (4):170A abstract.
2. Findlay JW, DeAngelis RL, Kearney MF, Welch RM, Findlay JM. Analgesic drugs in breast milk and plasma. Clin Pharmacol Ther 1981; 29 (5):625-633.
3. Meny RG, Naumburg EG, Alger LS, Brill-Miller JL, Brown S. Codeine and the breastfed neonate. J Hum Lact 1993 Dec; 9 (4):237-40.
4. Koren G, Cairns J, Chitayat D, Gaedigk A, Leeder SJ. Pharmacogenetics of morphine poisoning in a breastfed neonate of a codeine-prescribed mother. Lancet 2006 Aug 19; 368 (9536):704.

COENZYME Q10   L3

Trade: Ubiquinone, CoQ10, Ubidecarenone
Other Trades:
Uses: Cofactor in electron transport chain
AAP: Not reviewed

Coenzyme Q10, also known as ubiquinone and ubidecarenone, is a cofactor in the mitochondrial electron-transport chain in the synthesis of ATP within the cell. It may also possess antioxidant and membrane-stabilizing properties. Although it is a naturally occurring cofactor, it is generally synthesized within the cell. Those cells that have the highest metabolic activity such as the heart and the liver—have the highest CoQ10 concentrations.

The clinical uses of ubiquinone are quite interesting and include congestive heart disease, hypertension, periodontal disease, obesity, immune deficiencies, and angina.[1]

Ubiquinone is slowly absorbed requiring 5-10 hours to reach a peak. Following oral doses of 100 mg, peak blood levels of 1 µg/mL have been reported.[2] With doses of 300 mg/d, mean plasma levels were 5.4 µg/mL after 4 days. No data are available on ubiquinone levels in milk. However, ubiquinone is very lipid soluble and has a long plasma half-life; transfer to milk is likely. If one were to assume a milk/plasma ratio of 1.0 and a significant maternal dose of 300 mg/d, then the average daily intake via milk in an infant would be approximately 16% of the weight-adjusted maternal dose. Were these numbers correct, it is not likely that this dose would be overtly toxic to an infant. Although ubiquinone is relatively non-toxic in adults, there are no data on the relative toxicity of this substance in infants. Most references suggest that pregnant and lactating women should avoid supplementation with this cofactor.

Pregnancy Risk Category:

Lactation Risk Category: L3

Adult Concerns: Caution when using in patient with biliary obstruction. Caution when using with hypolipidemic agents, oral hypoglycemic agents, insulin, in patients with hepatic and renal insufficiency. Most common adverse effects include nausea, epigastric pain, diarrhea, heartburn, appetite suppression.

Pediatric Concerns: None reported but high dose supplementation should be avoided.

Drug Interactions: Do not use with oral hypoglycemics, hypolipidemic agents. May decrease INR in patients taking warfarin.

Relative Infant Dose:

Adult Dose:

Alternatives:

T ½	= 34 hours	M/P	=
PHL	=	PB	=
Tmax	= 5-10 hours	Oral	= Complete
MW	= 863	pKa	=
Vd	=		

References:

1. Gaby AR. Coenzyme Q10, in Pizzorno JE. Churchill Livingstone (eds): Textbook of Natural Medicine. 1999.
2. Greenberg S, Frishman WH. Co-enzyme Q10: a new drug for cardiovascular disease. J Clin Pharmacol 1990; 30 (7):596-608.

COLCHICINE   L4

Trade: Colchicine, Colcrys
Other Trades: Colgout
Uses: Analgesic in gouty arthritis
AAP: Maternal Medication Usually Compatible with Breastfeeding

Colchicine is an old product primarily used to reduce pain associated with inflammatory gout. Although it reduces the pain, it is not a true analgesic but simply reduces the inflammation associated with uric acid crystals by inhibiting leukocyte and other cellular migration into the region. However, it is quite toxic, and routine CBCs should be done while under treatment. Blood dyscrasias, hepatomegaly, and bone marrow depression are all possible, particularly in infants. Although the plasma half-life is only 20 minutes, it deposits in blood leukocytes and many other tissues thereby extending the elimination half-life to over 60 hours.

Little or no consistent data on breastmilk levels are available. In one study published, even the authors questioned the percent recovery in the breastmilk, so the data must be considered questionable. Nevertheless, the milk concentration varied from 1.2 to 2.5 μg/L (16-19 days postpartum) in one patient receiving 0.6 mg of colchicine twice daily.[1]

In an older study of a mother taking 1 mg once daily, average milk concentrations were 30 μg/L in the 8 hours following maternal drug ingestion, leading to a maximum of 10% of the weight-adjusted maternal dose in the infant. The authors suggest that if a mother chooses to breastfeed, she should wait 8 hours post dose before feeding, or pumping.[2] The use of colchicine in breastfeeding mothers is probably not advisable, as we have many other analgesics and anti-inflammatories that are superior for the treatment of gouty symptoms.

Pregnancy Risk Category: C

Lactation Risk Category: L4

Adult Concerns: Nausea, vomiting, diarrhea, myopathy, leukopenia, bone marrow suppression.

Pediatric Concerns: None reported in one case reviewed. Caution recommended and other alternative analgesics.

Drug Interactions: Colchicine is a P-gp and CYP3A4 substrate. Life-threatening and fatal drug interactions have been reported in patients treated with colchicine given with P-gp and strong CYP3A4 inhibitors. Cyclosporine, Amprenavir, Aprepitant, Diltiazem, Erythromycin, Fluconazole, Fosamprenavir, Grapefruit Juice, Verapamil, Atazanavir,

Clarithromycin, Indinavir, Itraconazole, Ketoconazole, Nefazodone, Nelfinavir, Ritonavir, Saquinavir, Telithromycin may significantly increase levels of colchicine. Colchichine reduces vitamin B-12 absorption. Avoid alcohol.

Relative Infant Dose: 4.7% - 31.5%

Adult Dose: 0.5-0.6 mg 1-4 times a week

Alternatives: Indomethacin

T ½	= 12-30 minutes	M/P	=
PHL	=	PB	= 10-31%
Tmax	= 1-2 hours	Oral	= Complete
MW	= 399	pKa	= 1.7, 12.4
Vd	= 10-12		

References:
1. Milunsky JM. Breast-feeding during colchicine therapy for familial Mediterranean fever. J Pediatr 1991; 119 (1 (Pt 1)):164.
2. Guillonneau M, Aigrain EJ, Galliot M, Binet M, Darbois Y. Colchicine is excreted at high concentrations in human breast milk. Eur J Obstet Gynaecol Reprod Biol 1995; 61:177-178.

COLESEVELAM HCL   L1

Trade: WelChol
Other Trades:
Uses: Cholesterol lower agent
AAP: Not reviewed

Colesevelam is a non-absorbed, polymeric, lipid-lowering agent that prevents the absorption of bile acids from the intestines. As bile acids are the precursors for cholesterol production, hepatic cholesterol production is lowered. Colesevelam is almost totally unabsorbed from the GI tract (only 0.05%) and is unlikely to enter milk at all (see cholestyramine). The only potential problem of using this product in breastfeeding mothers is the lowering of maternal plasma cholesterol levels, and the possible lowering of milk cholesterol levels. Milk cholesterol is particularly important in infant neurodevelopment.

Pregnancy Risk Category: B

Lactation Risk Category: L1

Adult Concerns: Constipation, dyspepsia and myalgia are the most commonly reported.

Pediatric Concerns: None reported via milk. It is totally unabsorbed so none would penetrate milk.

Drug Interactions: Apparently does not inhibit absorption of many drugs tested (as is seen with cholestyramine). May decrease absorption of verapamil.

Relative Infant Dose:

Adult Dose: Three to six 625 mg tablets daily.

Alternatives: Cholestyramine

T ½	=	M/P	=
PHL	=	PB	=
Tmax	=	Oral	= None
MW	=	pKa	=
Vd	=		

References:
1. Pharmaceutical Manufacturers prescribing information, 2010.

COMFREY — L5

Trade: Russian comfrey, Knitbone, Bruisewort, Blackwort, Slippery root

Other Trades:

Uses: Herbal poultice

AAP: Not reviewed

Comfrey has been claimed to heal gastric ulcers, hemorrhoids, and suppress bronchial congestion and inflammation.[1] The product contains allantoin, tannin, and a group of dangerous pyrrolizidine alkaloids. Ointments containing Comfrey have been found to be anti-inflammatory, probably due to the allantoin content. Some of the topically applied pyrrolizidine alkaloids are absorbed transcutaneously.

However, when administered orally to animals, most members of this family (Boraginaceae) have been noted to induce severe liver toxicity including elevated liver enzymes and liver tumors (hepatocellular adenomas).[2,3] Bladder tumors were noted at low concentrations. Russian Comfrey has been found to induce liver damage and pancreatic islet cell tumors.[4] A number of significant human toxicities have been reported including several deaths, all associated with the ingestion of Comfrey teas or yerba mate tea.[5] Even when applied to the skin, pyrrolizidine alkaloids were noted in the urine of rodents. Lactating rats excreted pyrrolizidine alkaloids into breastmilk.

Comfrey and members of this family are exceedingly dangerous and should not be used topically, ingested orally, or used in any form in breastfeeding or pregnant mothers.

Pregnancy Risk Category: X

Lactation Risk Category: L5

Adult Concerns: Liver toxicity, hepatic carcinoma, hepatocellular adenomas, hepatonecrosis.

Pediatric Concerns: Passes into animal milk. Absorbed topically. Too dangerous for breastfeeding mothers and infants in any form.

Drug Interactions:

Relative Infant Dose:

Adult Dose:

Alternatives:

T ½	=	M/P	=
PHL	=	PB	=
Tmax	=	Oral	= Complete
MW	=	pKa	=
Vd	=		

References:
1. Review of Natural Products Facts and Comparisons, St Louis, MO 1996.
2. Hirono I, Mori H, Haga M. Carcinogenic activity of Symphytum officinale. J Natl Cancer Inst 1978; 61 (3):865-869.
3. Yeong ML, Wakefield SJ, Ford HC. Hepatocyte membrane injury and bleb formation following low dose comfrey toxicity in rats. Int J Exp Pathol 1993; 74 (2):211-217.
4. Yeong ML, Clark SP, Waring JM, Wilson RD, Wakefield SJ. The effects of comfrey derived pyrrolizidine alkaloids on rat liver. Pathology 1991; 23 (1):35-38.
5. McGee J, Patrick RS, Wood CB, Blumgart LH. A case of veno-occlusive disease of the liver in Britain associated with herbal tea consumption. J Clin Pathol 1976; 29 (9):788-794.

CORTICOTROPIN   L3

Trade: ACT, Acthar, ACTH
Other Trades:
Uses: Stimulates cortisol release
AAP: Not reviewed

ACTH is secreted by the anterior pituitary in the brain and stimulates the adrenal cortex to produce and secrete adrenocortical hormones (cortisol, hydrocortisone). As a peptide product, ACTH is easily destroyed in the infants' GI tract. None would be absorbed by the infant. ACTH stimulates the endogenous production of cortisol, which theoretically can transfer to the breast fed infant. However, the use of ACTH in breastfeeding mothers largely depends on the dose and duration of exposure and the risks to the infant. Brief exposures are probably not contraindicated.

Pregnancy Risk Category: C

Lactation Risk Category: L3

Adult Concerns: Hypersensitivity reactions, increased risk of infection, embryocidal effects, other symptoms of hypercorticalism.

Pediatric Concerns: None reported via milk.

Drug Interactions:

Relative Infant Dose:

Adult Dose: 80 U injection (IM or SC)

Alternatives:

T ½	= 15 minutes	M/P	=
PHL	=	PB	=
Tmax	=	Oral	= 0%
MW	=	pKa	=
Vd	=		

References:

CROMOLYN SODIUM   L1

Trade: Nasalcrom, Gastrocrom, Intal

Other Trades: Nalcrom, Opticrom, Rhynacrom, Vistacrom, Cromese

Uses: Antiasthmatic, antiallergic

AAP: Not reviewed

Cromolyn is an extremely safe drug that is used clinically as an antiasthmatic, antiallergic, and to suppress mast cell degranulation and allergic symptoms. No data on penetration into human breastmilk are available, but it has an extremely low pKa, and minimal levels would be expected.[1] Less than 0.001% of a dose is distributed into milk of the monkey. No harmful effects have been reported on breastfeeding infants. Less than 1% of this drug is absorbed from the maternal (and probably the infant's) GI tract, so it is unlikely to produce untoward effects in nursing infants. This product is frequently used in pediatric patients and poses no risk for an infant when used in a breastfeeding mother.

Pregnancy Risk Category: B

Lactation Risk Category: L1

Adult Concerns: Headache, itching, nausea, diarrhea, allergic reactions, hoarseness, coughing.

Pediatric Concerns: None reported via milk. Probably quite safe.

Drug Interactions:

Relative Infant Dose:

Adult Dose: 20 mg QID via inhalation

Alternatives:

T ½	= 80-90 minutes	M/P	=
PHL	=	PB	=
Tmax	= <15 minutes	Oral	= <1%
MW	= 512	pKa	= Low
Vd	=		

References:
1. Pharmaceutical manufacturers prescribing information, 2010.

CYCLOBENZAPRINE   L3

Trade: Flexeril, Cycoflex
Other Trades: Flexeril, Novo-Cycloprine
Uses: Muscle relaxant, CNS depressant
AAP: Not reviewed

Cyclobenzaprine is a centrally acting skeletal muscle relaxant that is structurally and pharmacologically similar to the tricyclic antidepressants. Cyclobenzaprine is used as an adjunct to rest and physical therapy for the relief of acute, painful musculoskeletal conditions.[1] Studies have not conclusively shown whether the skeletal muscle relaxation properties are due to the sedation or placebo effects. At least one study has found it no more effective than placebo. It is not known if cyclobenzaprine is secreted in milk, but one must assume that its secretion would be similar to the tricyclics (see amitriptyline, desipramine). There are no pediatric indications for this product.

Pregnancy Risk Category: B

Lactation Risk Category: L3

Adult Concerns: Drowsiness, dry mouth, dizziness, nausea, vomiting, unpleasant taste sensation. Tachycardia, hypotension, arrhythmias.

Pediatric Concerns: None reported, but caution is urged.

Drug Interactions: Do not use with 14 days of MAO inhibitor. Additive effect with tricyclic antidepressants. Enhances effect of alcohol, barbiturates, and other CNS depressants.

Relative Infant Dose:

Adult Dose: 20-60 mg daily.

Alternatives: Metaxalone

T ½	= 24-72 hours	M/P	=
PHL	=	PB	= 93%
Tmax	= 3-8 hours	Oral	= Complete
MW	= 275	pKa	=
Vd	= High		

References:
1. Pharmaceutical manufacturers prescribing information, 2010.

CYCLOPENTOLATE   L3

Trade: AK-Pentolate, Cyclogyl, Cylate, Ocu-Pentolate,
           Pentolair
Other Trades: Diopentolate, Minims Cyclopentolate
Uses: Anticholinergic for the induction of mydriasis
AAP: Not reviewed

Cyclopentolate is use to dilate the pupils to facilitate refraction, eye examinations and other diagnostic purpose in the eye. Cyclopentolate is commonly used by ophthalmologists and optometrists because it works rapidly, and briefer than atropine. It is a potent anticholinergic and some is absorbed systemically. Children and particularly infants would be extremely susceptible to this agent. Several cases of pediatric seizures[1] and one case of necrotizing enterocolitis[2], have been reported following the ophthalmic use of this agent in children and an infant respectively. While no data are available on the transfer of this agent into human milk, it is rather unlikely that significant quantities would enter as plasma levels are so low, and milk levels would be even lower.

Plasma levels are approximately 3000 times lower than ophthalmic levels. Only 3-18% of muscarinic receptors were occupied after 55-124 minutes following administration. In healthy volunteers peak plasma concentration of cyclopentolate, 2.06 nM, occurred at 53 minute, maximum receptor occupancy being 5.9%.[3] After topical application plasma receptor occupancy was not high enough to cause any significant changes in heart rate and in PQ time. None of the subjects experienced subjectively or objectively adverse effects to be attributed to cyclopentolate. In another study, peak plasma drug concentrations of about 3 ng/mL occurred within 30 min after all formulations.[4] The mean elimination half-life of cyclopentolate was 111 min when all subjects and formulations were considered together.

Some caution is recommended with this product. A waiting period of perhaps 6 hours following its use would be sufficient to reduce risks.

Pregnancy Risk Category: C

Lactation Risk Category: L3 after 6 hours

Adult Concerns: While systemic side effects are rare, children, especially infants, are more susceptible than adults. Systemic effects are consistent with other anticholinergics and include: blurred vision, dry mouth, dry eye, urinary retention, seizures in infants and children, sedation, drowsiness, hyperpyrexia have all been reported.

Pediatric Concerns: None via milk, but caution is recommended. A brief interruption of breastfeeding is advised to reduce risk.

Drug Interactions: Additive with belladonna alkaloids and procainamide. May negate effects of cisapride on peristaltic contractions.

Relative Infant Dose:

Adult Dose: 1-2 drops in each eye.

Alternatives: Atropine

T ½	= 111 minutes	M/P	=
PHL	–	PB	=
Tmax	= 15 minutes	Oral	=
MW	=	pKa	=
Vd	=		

References:
1. Pharmaceutical Manufacturers prescribing information, 2010.

CYCLOPHOSPHAMIDE   L5

Trade: Neosar, Cytoxan
Other Trades: Procytox, Cycloblastin, Endoxan, Endoxana
Uses: Antineoplastic
AAP: Cytotoxic drug that may interfere with cellular metabolism of the nursing infant

Cyclophosphamide is a powerful and toxic antineoplastic drug. A number of reports in the literature indicate that cyclophosphamide can transfer into human milk as evidenced by the production of leukopenia and bone marrow suppression in at least 3 breastfed infants. In one case of a mother who received 800 mg/week of cyclophosphamide, her infant was significantly neutropenic following 6 weeks of exposure via breastmilk.[1] Major leukopenia was also reported in a second breastfed infant following only a brief exposure.[2] Thus far, no reports have provided quantitative estimates of cyclophosphamide in milk. See Appendix A for recommendations.

Pregnancy Risk Category: D

Lactation Risk Category: L5

Adult Concerns: Leukopenia, infections, anemia, GI distress, nausea, vomiting, diarrhea, hemorrhagic colitis.

Pediatric Concerns: Leukopenia and bone marrow suppression in at least 3 breastfed infants.

Drug Interactions: Cyclophosphamide may reduce digoxin serum levels. Increased bone marrow suppression when used with allopurinol, and cardiotoxicity when used with doxorubicin. May prolong effect of neuromuscular blocking agents. Chloramphenicol increases half-life of cyclophosphamide. Numerous others, see complete review.

Relative Infant Dose:

Adult Dose: 1-5 mg/kg daily.

Alternatives:

T ½	= 7.5 hours	M/P	=
PHL	=	PB	= 13%
Tmax	= 2-3 hours	Oral	= 75%
MW	= 261	pKa	=
Vd	=		

References:
1. Amato D, Niblett JS. Neutropenia from cyclophosphamide in breast milk. Med J Aust 1977; 1 (11):383-384.
2. Durodola JI. Administration of cyclophosphamide during late pregnancy and early lactation: a case report. J Natl Med Assoc 1979; 71 (2):165-166.
3. American Academy of Pediatrics, Committee on Drugs. Transfer of drugs and other chemicals into human milk. Pediatrics 2001; 108 (3):776-89.

CYCLOSERINE   L3

Trade: Seromycin
Other Trades: Closina, Cycloserine
Uses: Anti-tuberculosis drug
AAP: Maternal Medication Usually Compatible with Breastfeeding

Cycloserine is an antibiotic primarily used for treating tuberculosis. It is also effective against various staphylococcal infections. It is a small molecule with a structure similar to the amino acid, D-alanine. Following 250 mg oral dose given four times daily to mothers, milk levels ranged from 6 to 19 mg/L, an average of 13.4 mg/L.[1]

Pregnancy Risk Category: C

Lactation Risk Category: L3

Adult Concerns: Drowsiness, CNS confusion, dizziness, headache, lethargy, depression, seizures. Precautions urged in epilepsy, depression, severe anxiety.

Pediatric Concerns: None reported.

Drug Interactions: Increased toxicity with alcohol, isoniazid. Phenytoin levels may be elevated due to inhibition of metabolism.

Relative Infant Dose: 14.1%

Adult Dose: 250 mg BID

Alternatives:

T ½	= 12+ hours	M/P	= 0.72
PHL	=	PB	=
Tmax	= 3-4 hours	Oral	= 70-90%
MW	= 102	pKa	=
Vd	=		

References:
1. Charles E, McKenna MH, Morton RF. Studies on the absorption, diffusion, and excretion of cycloserine. Antibiot Annu 1955; 3:169-172.

CYCLOSPORINE   L3

Trade: Sandimmune, Neoral, Restasis
Other Trades:
Uses: Immunosuppressant
AAP: Cytotoxic drug that may interfere with cellular metabolism of the nursing infant

Cyclosporine is an immunosuppressant used to reduce organ rejection following transplant and in autoimmune syndromes such as arthritis, etc. In a recent report of 7 breastfeeding mothers treated with cyclosporine, the levels of cyclosporine in breastmilk ranged from 50 to 227 μg/L. Corresponding plasma levels in the breastfed infants were undetectable (<30 ng/mL) in all infants. In this study, the infants received less than 300 μg per day via breastmilk.[1] In another, following a dose of 320 mg/d, the milk level at 22 hours post dose was 16 μg/L and the milk/plasma ratio was 0.28.[2] In another report of a mother receiving 250 mg twice daily, the maternal plasma level of cyclosporine was measured at 187 μg/L, and the breastmilk level was 167 μg/L.[3] None was detected in the plasma of the infant.

In a study of a breastfeeding transplant patient who received 300 mg twice daily, maternal serum levels were 193, 273, and 123 ng/mL at 23 days, 6.5 and 9.7 weeks postpartum.[4] Corresponding milk cyclosporine levels were 160, 286, and 79 µg/L respectively. Using the higher milk level, an infant would receive less than 0.4% of the weight-adjusted maternal dose.

In another mother receiving cyclosporine (3 mg/kg/d), the concentration of cyclosporine in milk averaged 596 µg/L, or a dose of about <0.1 mg/kg to the infant.[5] The infant's trough blood level was always <3 µg/L while the mother's was 260 µg/L. No untoward effects were noted in the infant.

In a more recent study of 5 patients receiving 5.3, 4.0, 5, 4.11, and 5 mg/kg/day cyclosporine respectively, the average concentration of cyclosporine in the mothers was 403 µg/L, 465 µg/L, 97.6 µg/L, 117.7 µg/L, and 84-144 µg/L (range) respectively.[6] Hind milk levels were much higher in one case, probably due to the high lipid content. In mother one, the cyclosporine blood levels in the infant were 131 µg/L and 117 µg/L on two occasions which were near a therapeutic trough. In none of the other infants, were blood levels of cyclosporine determinable (<25 µg/L). This study clearly suggests that some infants could potentially attain near-therapeutic levels from ingesting breastmilk. From this data the relative infant dose would be approximately 0.78% of the weight-normalized maternal dose.

These studies together suggest cyclosporine transfer to milk is generally low, but the latter study suggests that some infants may receive more than has been expected from the prior studies. Therefore cyclosporine use in breastfeeding mothers should be followed by close observation of the infant to probably include monitoring of the infants plasma levels.

Pregnancy Risk Category: C

Lactation Risk Category: L3

Adult Concerns: Kidney toxicity, edema, tremor, seizures, elevated liver enzymes, hypertension, hirsutism. Use during pregnancy does not pose a major risk. Infections and possible lymphomas may result.

Pediatric Concerns: In 14 reported cases, milk levels were low and infant plasma levels low to undetectable. However one case of near-clinical levels in an infant have been reported.

Drug Interactions: Rifampin, phenytoin, phenobarbital decrease plasma concentrations of cyclosporine. Ketoconazole, fluconazole, and itraconazole increase plasma concentrations of cyclosporine. Do not use with St. John's wort.

Relative Infant Dose: 0.4% - 3%

Adult Dose: 5-15 mg/kg daily, but highly variable

Alternatives:

T ½	= 6-27 hours	M/P	= 0.28-0.4
PHL	=	PB	= 93%
Tmax	= 3.5 hours	Oral	= 28% pediatric
MW	=	pKa	=
Vd	= 3.1-4.3		

References:

1. Nyberg G, Haljamae U, Frisenette-Fich C, Wennergren M, Kjellmer I. Breast-feeding during treatment with cyclosporine. Transplantation 1998; 65 (2):253-255.
2. Flechner SM, Katz AR, Rogers AJ, Van Buren C, Kahan BD. The presence of cyclosporine in body tissues and fluids during pregnancy. Am J Kidney Dis 1985; 5 (1):60-63.
3. K.D.T. Personal communication. 1997.
4. Munoz-Flores-Thiagarajan KD, Easterling T, Davis C, Bond EF. Breast-feeding by a cyclosporine-treated mother. Obstet Gynecol 2001; 97 (5 Pt 2):816-818.
5. Thiru Y, Bateman DN, Coulthard MG. Successful breast feeding while mother was taking cyclosporin. BMJ 1997; 315 (7106):463.
6. Moretti ME, Sgro M, Johnson DW, Sauve RS, Woolgar MJ, Taddio A, Verjee Z, Giesbrecht E, Koren G, Ito S. Cyclosporine excretion into breast milk. Transplantation 2003; 75 (12):2144-2146.
7. American Academy of Pediatrics, Committee on Drugs. Transfer of drugs and other chemicals into human milk. Pediatrics 2001; 108 (3):776-89.

CYPROHEPTADINE   L3

Trade: Periactin
Other Trades: PMS-Cyproheptadine,
Uses: Antihistamine
AAP: Not reviewed

Cyproheptadine is a serotonin and histamine antagonist with anticholinergic and sedative effects. It has been used as an appetite stimulant in children and for rashes and pruritus (itching).[1] No data are available on its transfer to human milk.

Pregnancy Risk Category: B

Lactation Risk Category: L3

Adult Concerns: Sedation, nausea, vomiting, diarrhea, dizziness, blurred vision, constipation, dry mouth, throat, or nose, restlessness.

Pediatric Concerns: None reported. Observe for sedation.

Drug Interactions: Additive sedation when used with other antihistamines and CNS depressants. Increased toxicity (hallucinations) when used with MAO inhibitors.

Relative Infant Dose:

Adult Dose: 4 mg TID-QID

Alternatives: Hydroxyzine, cetirizine, loratadine

T ½	= 16 hours	M/P	=
PHL	=	PB	= 99%
Tmax	=	Oral	=
MW	= 287	pKa	= 9.3
Vd	=		

References:
1.   Pharmaceutical Manufacturers prescribing information, 2003.

CYTARABINE   L5

Trade: Cytosar
Other Trades: Alexan
Uses: Antineoplastic
AAP: Not reviewed

Cytarabine is an antimetabolite used to treat various leukemias and lymphomas. Cytarabine is converted intracellularly to a nucleotide that interrupts DNA synthesis. No data has been reported on transfer into breastmilk.[1] The compound is poorly absorbed orally and is therefore used IM or IV only. This drug would be extremely toxic to an infant and is generally contraindicated in breastfeeding mothers. See Cytosine arabinoside in Appendix A.

Pregnancy Risk Category: D

Lactation Risk Category: L5

Adult Concerns: Anemia, bone marrow suppression, nausea, vomiting, diarrhea, GI hemorrhage, elevated liver enzymes.

Pediatric Concerns: None reported via milk. But due to toxicity, this product should never be used in a breastfeeding mother.

Drug Interactions: Decreases effect of gentamycin flucytosine, digoxin. Increases toxicity of alkylating agents, radiation, purine analogs, methotrexate.

Relative Infant Dose:

Adult Dose: 100 mg/m (2) IV daily.

Alternatives:

T ½	= 1-3 hours	M/P	=
PHL	=	PB	= 13%
Tmax	=	Oral	~ <20%
MW	= 243	pKa	=
Vd	=		

References:
1. Pharmaceutical manufacturers prescribing information, 2010.

CYTOMEGALOVIRUS INFECTIONS

Trade: Human Cytomegalovirus, CMV
Other Trades:
Uses: Viral infection
AAP: Not reviewed

Cytomegalovirus is one of the family of herpes viruses that is rather ubiquitous. Many infants having been exposed in utero and later in day care centers.[1] Maternal cervical infection is very common. CMV is found in breastmilk of virtually all CMV positive women using the newer PCR techniques.[2] The timing of maternal infection is important. If the mother seroconverts early in gestation, the infant is likely to be affected in utero. Symptoms include: small for gestational age, jaundice, microcephaly, petechia, hepatosplenomegaly, hearing loss. If the mother seroconverts late in gestation, the infant is less likely to be severely affected. In most infants from seropositive mothers, the CMV found in breastmilk is not overtly dangerous, and these mothers can breastfeed successfully.[3]

However, a recent review of the risks of CMV acquisition in premature infants suggests a new look at this problem.[4] Depending on the population, approximately 74% of mothers delivering premature infants are already CMV-seropositive and that none of these infants had CMV isolated from their urine. From other studies, the relative risk of contracting CMV is about the same in infants fed milk from seropositive mothers (5.7%)[5] and those fed milk from seropositive mothers or formula ((0-11%).[6] This new data suggests that the relative risk of using milk from seropositive mothers, whether frozen or fresh, is low.

Pregnancy Risk Category:

Lactation Risk Category:

Adult Concerns: Asymptomatic to Hepatosplenomegaly. Fever, mild hepatitis.

Pediatric Concerns: CMV transfer into breastmilk is known but apparently of low risk to infants born of CMV positive mothers. Despite high CMV seropositivity rate in mothers of premature infants, the incidence of postnatal transmission of CMV is apparently low.

Drug Interactions:

Relative Infant Dose:

Adult Dose:

Alternatives:

References:
1. Dworsky M, Yow M, Stagno S, Pass RF, Alford C. Cytomegalovirus infection of breast milk and transmission in infancy. Pediatrics 1983; 72 (3):295-299.
2. Hotsubo T, Nagata N, Shimada M, Yoshida K, Fujinaga K, Chiba S. Detection of human cytomegalovirus DNA in breast milk by means of polymerase chain reaction. Microbiol Immunol 1994; 38 (10):809-811.
3. Lawrence RA. Breastfeeding: A guide for the medical profession. St. Louis: Mosby Publishers, 1994.
4. Schanler RJ. CMV acquisition in premature infants fed human milk: reason to worry? J Perinatol 2005 May; 25 (5):297-8.
5. Miron D, Brosilow S, Felszer K, Reich D, Halle D, Wachtel D, et al. Incidence and clinical manifestations of breast milk-acquired Cytomegalovirus infection in low birth weight infants. J Perinatol 2005 May; 25 (5):299-303.
6. Doctor S, Friedman S, Dunn MS, Asztalos EV, Wylie L, Mazzulli T, et al. Cytomegalovirus transmission to extremely low-birthweight infants through breast milk. Acta Paediatr 2005 Jan; 94 (1):53-8.

DALTEPARIN SODIUM | L2

Trade: Fragmin, Low MW Heparin
Other Trades:
Uses: Anticoagulant
AAP: Not reviewed

Dalteparin is a low MW polysaccharide fragment of heparin used clinically as an anticoagulant. In a study of two patients who received 5000-10,000 IU of dalteparin, none was found in human milk.[1]

In another study of 15 post-caesarian patients early postpartum (mean= 5.7 days), blood and milk levels of dalteparin were determined 3-4 hours post-treatment.[2] Following subcutaneous doses of 2500 IU, maternal plasma levels averaged 0.074 to 0.308 IU/mL. Breastmilk levels of dalteparin ranged from <0.005 to 0.037 IU/mL of milk. The milk/plasma ratio ranged from 0.025 to 0.224. Using this data, an infant ingesting 150 mL/kg/day would ingest approximately 5.5 IU/kg/day. Due to the polysaccharide nature of this production, oral absorption is unlikely. Further, because this study was done early postpartum, it is possible that the levels in 'mature' milk would be lower. The authors suggest that "it appears highly unlikely that puerperal thromboprophylaxis with LMWH has any clinically relevant effect on the nursing infant".

Pregnancy Risk Category: B

Lactation Risk Category: L2

Adult Concerns: Anticoagulant effects in adults when administered subcutaneously.

Pediatric Concerns: Transfer to milk is low. Oral bioavailability is minimal. Side effects remote. No adverse effects were reported.

Drug Interactions:

Relative Infant Dose:

Adult Dose: 2500 units daily

Alternatives: Enoxaparin.

T ½	= 2.3 hours	M/P	= 0.025-0.224
PHL	=	PB	=
Tmax	= 2-4 hours (SC)	Oral	= None
MW	= 4000	pKa	=
Vd	= 0.06		

References:

1. Harenberg J, Leber G, Zimmermann R, Schmidt W. [Prevention of thromboembolism with low-MW heparin in pregnancy]. Geburtshilfe Frauenheilkd 1987; 47 (1):15-18.
2. Richter C, Sitzmann J, Lang P, Weitzel H, Huch A, Huch R. Excretion of low MW heparin in human milk. Br J Clin Pharmacol 2001; 52 (6):708-710.

DANAZOL   L5

Trade: Danocrine
Other Trades: Cyclomen, Azol, Danocrine, Danol
Uses: Synthetic androgen, antigonadotropic agent
AAP: Not reviewed

Danazol suppresses the pituitary-ovarian axis by inhibiting ovarian steroidogenesis resulting in decreased secretion of estradiol and may increase androgens. Danazol is believed to reduce plasma prolactin levels in individuals.   The mechanisms through which Danazol treatment affects prolactin release has not been fully delineated, but it is probably due to the hypoestrogenic status resulting from the medication. Danazol is primarily used for treating endometriosis. Due to its effect on pituitary hormones and its androgenic effects, it may reduce the rate of breastmilk production although this has not been documented. No data on its transfer to human milk are available.

Pregnancy Risk Category: X

Lactation Risk Category: L5

Adult Concerns: Breast size reduction. Androgenic effects, hirsutism, acne, weight gain, edema, testicular atrophy, thrombocytopenia, thrombocytosis, hot flashes, breakthrough menstrual bleeding.

Pediatric Concerns: None reported, but caution is urged. May suppress prolactin production.

Drug Interactions: Decreased insulin requirements. May increase anticoagulation with warfarin therapy.

Relative Infant Dose:

Adult Dose: 50-200 mg BID

Alternatives:

T ½	= 4.5 hours	M/P	=
PHL	=	PB	=
Tmax	= 2 hours	Oral	= Complete
MW	= 337	pKa	=
Vd	=		

References:
1. Pharmaceutical Manufacturers prescribing information, 2010.

DANTROLENE   L4

Trade: Dantrium
Other Trades:
Uses: Skeletal muscle relaxant
AAP: Not reviewed

Dantrolene produces a direct skeletal muscle relaxation and is indicated for spasticity resulting from upper motor neuron disorders such as multiple sclerosis, cerebral palsy, etc.[1] It is not indicated for rheumatic disorders or musculoskeletal trauma.

In one study, a mother received IV dantrolene (160 mg) for symptoms of malignant hyperthermia, after the umbilical cord was clamped just after the delivery of her baby.[2] Concentrations of dantrolene in breastmilk ranged from 1.2 mg/L on day 2 to 0.05 mg/L on day 4. The relative infant dose is calculated at 7.9 % of the maternal dose. The highest concentration in breast milk was detected 36 hours after the first IV bolus of dantrolene. Based on the elimination half-life determined in this study (9.02 hours), the authors suggest that breastfeeding is safe 2 days after discontinuation of IV dantrolene administration in the mother. The infant should be monitored for nausea, vomiting, fatigue, and muscle weakness, which are all known side effects of therapeutic doses in adults.[2]

Pregnancy Risk Category: C

Lactation Risk Category: L4

Adult Concerns: Adverse effects are quite common and include weakness, dizziness, diarrhea, slurred speech, drooling, and nausea. Significant risk for hepatotoxicity. Visual and auditory hallucinations. Dantrolene should be used with caution in patients with impaired pulmonary function, particularly those with obstructive pulmonary disease, and in patients with severely impaired cardiac function due to myocardial disease. It should be used with caution in patients with a history of previous liver disease or dysfunction.

Pediatric Concerns: None reported, but caution is urged. A suitable waiting period for breastfeeding is recommended.

Drug Interactions: Increased toxicity with estrogens, CNS sedatives, MAO inhibitors, phenothiazines, calcium channel blockers, warfarin, and tolbutamide.

Relative Infant Dose: 7.9%

Adult Dose: 1-2 mg/kg TID-QID

Alternatives:

T ½	= 8.7 hours	M/P	=
PHL	= 7.3 hours	PB	=
Tmax	= 5 hours	Oral	= 35%
MW	= 314	pKa	=
Vd	=		

References:
1. Pharmaceutical Manufacturer Prescribing Information. 2010.
2. Fricker RM, Hoerauf KH, Drewe J, Kress HG. Secretion of Dantrolene into Breast Milk after Acute Therapy of a Suspected Malignant Hyperthermia Crisis during Cesarean Section. Anesthesiology 1998; 89 (4):1023-1025.

DAPSONE   L4

Trade: Dapsone, Aczone
Other Trades: Avlosulfon, Maloprim
Uses: Sulfone antibiotic
AAP: Maternal Medication Usually Compatible with Breastfeeding

Dapsone is a sulfone antibiotic useful for treating leprosy, tuberculoid leprosy, dermatitis herpetiformis, and Pneumocystis carinii pneumonia. In one case report of a mother consuming 50 mg daily while breastfeeding, both the mother and infant had symptoms of hemolytic anemia.[1] Plasma levels of dapsone in mother and infant were 1622 ng/mL and 439 ng/mL respectively. Breastmilk levels were reported to be 1092 µg/L. In another study of 3 patients receiving 100 mg/day, milk levels averaged 580 µg/L, but these were not steady state levels.[2] The authors estimated the dose via milk was 4.6 to 14.3% of the maternal dose.

Dapsone gel 5% (Aczone) has just been released for the treatment of acne. After application twice daily for 14 days, the dapsone AUC0-24 h was 415 ng-h/mL for Aczone Gel, 5%, whereas following a single 100 mg dose of oral dapsone the AUC was 52,641ng-h/mL. Apparently the transcutaneous absorption of dapsone is minimal.

Dapsone is one of those drugs which apparently has all the proper kinetic parameters to enter milk, high lipophilicity, low MW, high volume of distribution, high pKa, etc. While it is approved by the AAP, this is one exception that should be used very cautiously, if at all. Its topical use is probably of minimal risk to the infant.

Pregnancy Risk Category: C

Lactation Risk Category: L4

Adult Concerns: Adverse effects reported include hemolytic anemia (particularly in G6PD deficient persons), methemoglobinemia, aplastic anemia, psychotic episodes, peripheral neuropathy, acute renal failure, nephrotic syndrome, hepatotoxicity, exfoliative dermatitis, erythema multiforme, toxic epidermal necrolysis, and hypersensitivity reactions

Pediatric Concerns: Hemolytic anemia in one breastfeeding patient. Caution is recommended.

Drug Interactions: Increased dapsone levels when taken with Amprenavir, trimethoprim, delavirdine, and probenecid. Dapsone may increase chloramphenicol plasma levels. Rifampin may decrease plasma levels of dapsone. Concomitant administration of zidovudine with drugs like dapsone which are cytotoxic or suppress bone marrow function may increase the risk of hematologic toxicity

Relative Infant Dose: 6.3% - 22.5%

Adult Dose: 100 mg daily

Alternatives:

T ½	= 28 hours	M/P	=
PHL	=	PB	= 70-90%
Tmax	= 4-8 hours	Oral	= 86-100%
MW	= 248	pKa	=
Vd	= 1-2		

References:
1. Sanders SW, Zone JJ, Foltz RL, Tolman KG, Rollins DE. Hemolytic anemia induced by dapsone transmitted through breast milk. Ann Intern Med 1982; 96 (4):465-466.
2. Edstein MD, Veenendaal JR, Newman K, Hyslop R. Excretion of chloroquine, dapsone and pyrimethamine in human milk. Br J Clin Pharmacol 1986; 22 (6):733-735.

DAPTOMYCIN   L1

Trade: Cubicin
Other Trades:
Uses: Antibiotic for resistant staphylococcus infections.
AAP: Not reviewed

Daptomycin is used intravenously for the treatment of complicated skin and skin structure infections caused by susceptible strains of *Staphylococcus aureus* (including methicillin-resistant or MRSA strains), *Streptococcus pyogenes, S. agalactiae, S. dysgalactiae, Equisimilis, and Enterococcus faecalis.*[1]

In a mother 5 months postpartum who received 500 mg IV daily (6.7 mg/kg/d), the highest concentration measured in milk was 44.7 ng/mL at 8 hours following administration.[2] Reported levels in milk were 33.5, 44.7, 40.8, 39.3, and 29.2 ng/mL at 4, 8, 12, 16, and 20 hours respectively. The mother and infant received therapy for 4 weeks, and no adverse events were noted in mother or infant. In addition, the daptomycin present in milk is poorly absorbed orally.

Pregnancy Risk Category: B

Lactation Risk Category: L1

Adult Concerns: Elevations of creatinine kinase have been reported suggesting skeletal muscle toxicity and blood tests are required weekly during treatment. Gastrointestinal disorders, injection site reactions, fever, headache, insomnia, dizziness, and rash have been infrequently reported.

Pediatric Concerns: None reported via milk in one case exposed for 4 weeks.

Drug Interactions: When used with tobramycin, a small increase (12.7%) in plasma concentration of daptomycin was produced.

Relative Infant Dose: 0.09% - 0.1%

Adult Dose: 4 mg/kg infusions once every 24 hours for 7-14 days.

Alternatives: Nafcillin

T ½	= 9 hours	M/P	=
PHL	=	PB	= 92%
Tmax	= 0.5 hours	Oral	= Unlikely
MW	= 1620	pKa	=
Vd	= 0.9		

References:
1. Pharmaceutical Manufacturer Prescribing Information. 2003.
2. Buitrago MI, Crompton JA, Bertolami S, North DS, Nathan RA. Extremely low excretion of daptomycin into breast milk of a nursing mother with methicillin-resistant Staphylococcus aureus pelvic inflammatory disease. Pharmacotherapy. 2009 Mar;29 (3):347-51.

DARBEPOETIN ALFA   L3

Trade: Aranesp
Other Trades:
Uses: Colony stimulating factor
AAP: Not reviewed

Darbopoetin alfa is used to treat anemia in patients with chronic renal failure, and patients receiving chemotherapy. It stimulates erythropoiesis much the same way as endogenous erythropoietin. Administration can be either IV or subcutaneous, with peak serum levels following subcutaneous dosing occuring after 34 hours.[1] No data are available concerning levels in breast milk. However, this is a large MW protein that is unlikely to enter the milk compartment, or be orally bioavailable to an infant.

Pregnancy Risk Category: C

Lactation Risk Category: L3

Adult Concerns: Adverse effects include hypertension, hypotension, edema, fatigue, diarrhea, and infection.

Pediatric Concerns: No data are available. Because of its large MW, it is unlikely that this protein will enter breast milk.

Drug Interactions: No data available.

Relative Infant Dose:

Adult Dose: IV: 0.45 µg/kg once weekly; SQ: 2.25 µg/kg once weekly

Alternatives:

T ½	= 21 hours	M/P	=
PHL	=	PB	=
Tmax	=	Oral	= Nil
MW	= 37,000	pKa	=
Vd	= 0.06		

References:
1. Pharmaceutical Manufacturer Prescribing Information. 2010.

DARIFENACIN   L3

Trade: Enablex
Other Trades:
Uses: Anticholinergic agent used for overactive bladder
AAP: Not reviewed

Darifenacin (Enablex) is an anticholinergic agent used for the treatment of overactive bladder with symptoms of urgent urinary incontinence, urgency, and frequency.[1] It is not known if darifenacin is transfered into human milk, although its chemistry would probably limit its transfer into milk. However, some caution is recommended as this is a strong anticholinergic muscarinic agent and could cause urinary retention, dry mouth, mydriasis, constipation, and other GI symptoms in a breastfed infant.

Pregnancy Risk Category: C

Lactation Risk Category: L3

Adult Concerns: Observe for typical anticholinergic symptoms which include: dry mouth, blurred vision, dry eyes, dyspepsia, abdominal pain, urinary tract infection, constipation, urinary retention, and heat prostration due to decreased sweating. Do not use in patients with narrow angle glaucoma.

Pediatric Concerns: None reported in infants. No data available. Use with some caution and observe for anticholinergic symptoms.

Drug Interactions: Darifenacin is primarily metabolized by CYP2D6 and CYP3A4. Use with great caution with drugs that affect these enzyme systems such as: ketoconazole, itraconazole, fluconazole, ritonavir, nelfinavir, clarithromycin, nefazodone and many others. Check good drug-drug interaction reference.

Relative Infant Dose:

Adult Dose: 7.5 mg daily

Alternatives:

T ½	= 12.3 hours	M/P	=
PHL	=	PB	= 98%
Tmax	= 6.5 hours	Oral	= 15-19%
MW	= 507	pKa	=
Vd	= 2.3		

References:
1. Pharmaceutical manufacturers prescribing information. 2010.

DEET   L3

Trade: DEET, 6-12 Plus, Off!, Deep Woods Off!, Cutter
Insect Repellent, Muskol, Diethyl-m-Toluamide,
Diethyltoluamide
Other Trades:
Uses: Insect repellant
AAP: Not reviewed

N,N-diethyl-3-methylbenzamide is used worldwide as an insect repellant. The U.S. EPA estimates that 30% of the U.S. population applies DEET every year. In use for more than 45 years, the reports of adverse effects in humans have relatively rare, even though it has been used in billions of applications. Case reports of toxicity are invariably moderate to low, but some cases of death have been reported.

Skin absorption is significant and generally occurs within 2 hours of application. DEET is very lipophilic and has a large volume of distribution (2.7-6.21 L/kg) and remains in the skin and adipose tissue for long periods, slowly leaking into the plasma compartment and being eliminated. Between 5 and 17% of an applied dose is absorbed in 6 hours,[1] and most is eliminated from the plasma compartment within 4 hours via hepatic metabolism and excretion in urine. Animal data suggests highest concentrations in the lacrimal gland, liver, kidney, and nasal mucosa.

No data are available on the transfer of DEET into human milk, but due to its lipophilicity, some probably enters the milk compartment. Avoid the use of concentrated solutions (>25%) over large surface areas of the body if you are breastfeeding or pregnant. A brief waiting period of 4 hours or more may be useful in avoiding transfer of high levels into milk, but this is probably unnecessary under conditions of normal use. While there are numerous reports of DEET toxicity, most involve the use of concentrated solutions over large body areas, and repeated applications over many days.

The American Academy of Pediatrics recommends DEET concentrations of 10% or less for children and infants. Infants less than 2 months of age should not be exposed to this agent. Most commercial preparations for infants and children contain 5-7% DEET. DEET should be applied only to exposed skin. Avoid use on children's hands, so that the child does not ingest DEET directly. Mothers should avoid chronic use over large body areas, and should use lower concentrations.

Pregnancy Risk Category: Minimal

Lactation Risk Category: L3

Adult Concerns: Dyspnea, disorientation, seizures, tremors, ataxia and incoordination, depression, hypersalivation, have been reported. DEET has not be found to be a human teratogen, or induce malignancies.

Pediatric Concerns: Avoid use of solutions in children more than 10% DEET or of large surface areas.

Drug Interactions: Avoid use with other emollients, skin lotions, or alcohol which could increase the transcutaneous absorption of DEET.

Relative Infant Dose:

Adult Dose:

Alternatives:

T ½	= 2.5 hours	M/P	=
PHL	=	PB	=
Tmax	= 1-2 hours	Oral	= Complete; 9-56% cutaneous
MW	= 191	pKa	=
Vd	=		

References:
1. Robbins PJ, Cherniack MB. 1986. Review of the biodistribution and toxicity of the insect repellent N,N-diethyl-m-toluamide (DEET). J Toxicol Environ Health 18:502-525.
2. Selim S, Hartnagel R EJR, Osimitz TG, Gabriel KL, Schoenig GP. 1995. Absorption, metabolism, and excretion of N,N-diethyl-m-toluamide: Following dermal application to human volunteers. Fundam Appl Toxicol 25 (1):95-100.

DEFERASIROX   L3

Trade: Exjade
Other Trades:
Uses: Iron chelating agent
AAP: Not reviewed

Deferasirox is an orally bioavailable chelating agent that is selective for iron. It forms a complex with the iron that is unabsorbed and subsequently excreted in the feces. While deferasirox has a very low affinity for other metals such as zinc and copper, it still decreases serum concentrations of these metals. It is used in chronic iron overload due to blood transfusions.[1] No data are available on the concentrations in the breast milk compartment, however it is unlikely that high concentrations would be in breast milk due to high protein binding. Should the mother breastfeed, the infant's ferritin and iron levels should be monitored. Modest oral iron supplementation in the infant would block absorption of any deferasirox.

Pregnancy Risk Category: B

Lactation Risk Category: L3

Adult Concerns: Adverse reactions include diarrhea, vomiting, nausea, headache, abdominal pain, pyrexia, and cough.

Pediatric Concerns: No data available in infants. May test infant ferritin and iron levels and supplement with Fe drops if necessary.

Drug Interactions: Deferasirox should not be taken with aluminum-containing antacids or with other iron chelator therapies.

Relative Infant Dose:

Adult Dose: 20 mg/kg daily

Alternatives: Deferoxamine

T ½	= 8-16 hours	M/P	=
PHL	=	PB	= 99%
Tmax	= 2-4 hours	Oral	= 70%
MW	= 373	pKa	=
Vd	= 14.4		

References:
1. Pharmaceutical manufacturers prescribing information. 2010.

DEFEROXAMINE   L3

Trade: Desferal, Desferrioxamine
Other Trades:
Uses: Iron chelator
AAP: Not reviewed

Deferoxamine is an iron-chelating agent, commonly used to facilitate the increased clearance of iron from the plasma compartment. It is indicated for the treatment of acute iron intoxication and of chronic iron overload due to transfusion-dependent anemias.[1] No data are available on its transfer into human milk, but it is very unlikely. Further, oral bioavailability of this product is virtually nil and it is not likely to harm a breastfeeding infant.

Pregnancy Risk Category: C

Lactation Risk Category: L3

Adult Concerns: Adverse events include flushing, pain at injection site, erythema, urticaria, hypotension and shock. Other side effects which occur with chronic administration include allergy-type reactions, pruritus, rash, anaphylactoid reactions, ocular and otic effects, abdominal discomfort, leg cramps, etc. Ocular disturbances include: blurring of vision; cataracts after prolonged administration in chronic iron overload; decreased visual acuity including visual loss, visual defects, scotoma; impaired peripheral, color, and night vision; optic neuritis, cataracts, corneal opacities, and retinal pigmentary abnormalities. The auditory abnormalities reported have been tinnitus and hearing loss including high frequency sensorineural hearing loss. In most cases, both ocular and auditory disturbances were reversible upon immediate cessation of treatment

Pediatric Concerns: None reported via milk but no studies are available. Oral bioavailability is low to nil so it is not likely to be hazardous. However, observe for iron deficiency anemia.

Drug Interactions: Temporary loss of consciousness has been reported when used with prochlorperazine. Vitamin C is commonly added to deferoxamine therapy to enhance availability of iron for absorption.

Relative Infant Dose:

Adult Dose: 1 gm followed by 500 mg every 4 hours times two. Highly variable.

Alternatives:

T ½	= 3-6 hours	M/P	=
PHL	=	PB	=
Tmax	=	Oral	= Nil
MW	= 656	pKa	=
Vd	= 1.33		

References:
1. Pharmaceutical Manufacturer Prescribing Information. 2010.

DESIPRAMINE   L2

Trade: Pertofrane, Norpramin
Other Trades: Novo-Desipramine, Pertofran
Uses: Tricyclic antidepressant
AAP: Drugs whose effect on nursing infants is unknown but may be of concern

Desipramine is a prototypic tricyclic antidepressant. In one case report, a mother taking 200 mg of desipramine at bedtime had milk/plasma ratios of 0.4 to 0.9 with milk levels ranging between 17-35 µg/L.[1] Desipramine was not found in the infant's blood although these levels are probably too low to measure.

In another study of a mother consuming 300 mg of desipramine daily, the milk levels were 30% higher than the maternal serum.[2] The milk concentrations of desipramine were reported to be 316 to 328 µg/L with peak concentrations occurring at 4 hours post-dose. Assuming an average milk concentration of 280 µg/L an infant would receive approximately 42 µg/kg/day. No untoward effects have been reported.

Pregnancy Risk Category: C

Lactation Risk Category: L2

Adult Concerns: Anticholinergic side effects, such as drying of secretions, dilated pupil, sedation, constipation, fatigue, peculiar taste.

Pediatric Concerns: None reported in several studies.

Drug Interactions: Do not use with MAO inhibitors or within two weeks of therapy. Increased effects occur following use with stimulants, and benzodiazepines. Decreased effects occur with barbiturates, carbamazepine, and phenytoin use.

Relative Infant Dose: 0.3% - 0.9%

Adult Dose: 100-200 mg daily.

Alternatives: Amoxapine, Imipramine, Sertraline

T ½	= 7-60 hours	M/P	= 0.4-0.9
PHL	=	PB	= 82%
Tmax	= 4-6 hours	Oral	= 90%
MW	= 266	pKa	= 9.5
Vd	= 22-59		

References:
1. Sovner R, Orsulak PJ. Excretion of imipramine and desipramine in human breast milk. Am J Psychiatry 1979; 136 (4A):451-452.
2. Stancer HC, Reed KL. Desipramine and 2-hydroxydesipramine in human breast milk and the nursing infant's serum. Am J Psychiatry 1986; 143 (12):1597-1600.

DESLORATADINE   L2

Trade: Clarinex
Other Trades:
Uses: Antihistamine
AAP: Not reviewed

Desloratadine is the active metaboliteof loratadine (Claritin) and itshalf-life is longer than the parentcompound. While we do not have specificdata on desloratadine, we do have a goodreport on the prodrug loratadine.

During 48 hours following administration of 'loratadine', the amount of loratadine transferred via milk was 4.2 µg, which was 0.01% of the administered dose.[1] Through 48 hours, only 6.0 µg of desloratadine (active metabolite) (7.5 µg loratadine equivalents) were excreted into breast milk, or 0.029% of the administered dose of loratadine orits active metabolite were transferred via milk to the infant. A 4 kg infant would receive only 0.46% of the loratadine dose received by the mother on a mg/kg basis (2.9 µg/kg/day). It is very unlikely this dose would present a hazard to infants. Desloratadine does not transfer into the CNS of adults, so it is unlikely to induce sedation even in infants. The half-life in neonates is not known although it is likely quite long. Pediatric formulations are available.

Note, the AAP approves the use of loratadine in breastfeeding mothers. It has not yet reviewed desloratadine.

Pregnancy Risk Category: C

Lactation Risk Category: L2

Adult Concerns: Sedation, dry mouth, fatigue, nausea, tachycardia, palpitations.

Pediatric Concerns: None reported via milk. Levels of loratadine have been reported and are low. No adverse effects have been reported in breastfeeding infants with loratadine or desloratadine.

Drug Interactions: Clarithromycin,   erythromycin,   and ketoconazole may increase plasma levels of desloratadine but they do not appear to be hazardous.

Relative Infant Dose: 0.03%

Adult Dose: 5 mg daily

Alternatives: Loratadine, cetirizine

T ½	= 27 hours	M/P	=
PHL	=	PB	= 87%
Tmax	= 3 hours	Oral	= Good
MW	= 310	pKa	=
Vd	=		

References:
1. Pharmaceutical manufacturers prescribing information, 2010.

DESMOPRESSIN ACETATE | L2

Trade: DDAVP, Stimate
Other Trades: Rhinyle, Minirin, Desmospray
Uses: Synthetic antidiuretic hormone.
AAP: Not reviewed

Desmopressin (DDAVP) is a small synthetic octapeptide antidiuretic hormone.[1] Desmopressin increases reabsorption of water by the collecting ducts in the kidneys resulting in decreased urinary flow (ADH effect). Generally used in patients who lack pituitary vasopressin, it is primarily used intranasally or intravenous. Unlike natural vasopressin, desmopressin has no effect on growth hormone, prolactin, or leuteinizing hormone. Following intranasal administration, less than 10-20% is absorbed through the nasal mucosa. This peptide has been used in lactating women without effect on nursing infants.[2,3]

In a study of one breastfeeding mother receiving 10 μg twice daily of DDAVP (desmopressin), maternal plasma levels peaked at 40 minutes after the dose at approximately 7 ng/L, while milk levels were virtually unchanged at 1-1.5 ng/L.[4] Because DDAVP is easily destroyed in the gastrointestinal tract by trypsin, the oral absorption of these levels in milk would be nil.

Pregnancy Risk Category: B

Lactation Risk Category: L2

Adult Concerns: Reduced urine production, edema, fluid retention.

Pediatric Concerns: None reported. It is probably not absorbed orally.

Drug Interactions: Lithium, demeclocycline may decrease ADH effect. Chlorpropamide, fludrocortisone may increase ADH effect.

Relative Infant Dose: 0.1%

Adult Dose: 10-40 μg intranasally daily.

Alternatives:

T ½	= 75.5 minutes	M/P	= 0.2
PHL	=	PB	=
Tmax	= 40 minutes	Oral	= 0.16%
MW	= 1069	pKa	=
Vd	=		

References:
1. Pharmaceutical manufacturers prescribing information, 2010.
2. Hime MC, Richardson JA. Diabetes insipidus and pregnancy. Case report, incidence and review of literature. Obstet Gynecol Surv 1978; 33 (6):375-379.
3. Hadi HA, Mashini IS, Devoe LD. Diabetes insipidus during pregnancy complicated by preeclampsia. A case report. J Reprod Med 1985; 30 (3):206-208.
4. Burrow GN, Wassenaar W, Robertson GL, Sehl H. DDAVP treatment of diabetes insipidus during pregnancy and the post-partum period. Acta Endocrinol (Copenh) 1981; 97 (1):23-25.

DESOGESTREL + ETHINYL ESTRADIOL | L3

Trade: Mircette, Cyclessa
Other Trades:
Uses: Low dose oral contraceptive
AAP: Not reviewed

Mircette is a somewhat atypical lower-dose estrogen/progestin oral contraceptive. It contains a potent progestin desogestrel in combination with 10 or 20 micrograms/day of ethinyl estradiol (EE).[1] While most oral contraceptives contain 40 micrograms of EE or more, the reduced level estrogen in this product may be less inhibitory of milk production as is occasionally seen with the higher dose products. Small amounts of estrogens and progestins are known to pass into milk, but long-term follow-up of children whose mothers used combination hormonal contraceptives while breastfeeding has shown no deleterious effects on infants. Estrogen-containing contraceptives may interfere with milk production by decreasing the quantity and quality of milk production.

Cyclessa contains 100-150 µg desogestrel and 25 µg of ethinyl estradiol.

Pregnancy Risk Category: X

Lactation Risk Category: L3

Adult Concerns: Observe for reduced milk production. Breakthrough bleeding is more common with this product. Fluid retention has been reported. See typical oral contraceptive contraindications.

Pediatric Concerns: Reduced milk supply is possible. Do not use early postpartum.

Drug Interactions: Reduced efficacy when used with rifampin, barbiturates, phenytoin, carbamazepine, griseofulvin, ampicillin, and tetracyclines.

Relative Infant Dose:

Adult Dose: One daily.

Alternatives: Norethindrone

References:
1.   Pharmaceutical Manufacturer package insert, 2010.

DESVENLAFAXINE   L3

Trade: Pristiq
Other Trades:
Uses: Antidepressant, SSRI, SSNRI
AAP: Not reviewed

Desvenlafaxine (O-desmethylvenlafaxine) is an active metabolite of venlafaxine with similar antidepressant activity. While no data are available on the transmission of this product specifically into human milk, we do have excellent data on the transmission of desvenlafaxine into human milk following the use of its precursor, venlafaxine.[1,2]

In a study of 6 women receiving an average of 244 mg/day venlafaxine, the mean maximum concentration of desvenlafaxine in milk was 796 ng/mL. Desvenlafaxine was detected in the plasma of 4 of the infant ranging from 3 to 38 ng/mL.[1] All the infants were healthy and unaffected. The M/P ratio for venlafaxine and desvenlafaxine were 2.5 and 2.7 respectively.

In a group of 13 women who consumed from 37.5 to 300 mg/day (mean=194.3 mg/d) of venlafaxine, levels of desvenlafaxine in milk ranged from 318 to 1912.7 ng/mL with a mean of 919 ng/mL.[2] The RID for desvenlafaxine using the highest levels reported (C_{max}) ranged from 6.8% to 9.3%. This data clearly suggests that desvenlafaxine enters milk at a higher rate than the parent drug, venlafaxine. The highest desvenlafaxine levels occurred 8 hours after maternal ingestion.

Pregnancy Risk Category: C

Lactation Risk Category: L3

Adult Concerns: While these are a function of dose, the following are common side effects of desvenlafaxine: nausea, suicidal ideation, palpitations, dry mouth, diarrhea, constipation, fatigue, anorexia, dizziness, somnolence, headache, anorgasmia, erectile dysfunction, and ejaculation disorder.

Pediatric Concerns: None reported.

Drug Interactions: Do not use with monoamine oxidase inhibitors.

Relative Infant Dose: 6.8% - 9.3%

Adult Dose: 50-400 mg/day

Alternatives: Sertraline, Paroxetine, Venlafaxine, Fluoxetine

T ½	= 11 hours	M/P	= 2.7
PHL	=	PB	= 30%
Tmax	= 7.5 hours	Oral	= 80%
MW	= 263	pKa	=
Vd	= 3.4		

References:
1. Ilett KF, Hackett LP, Dusci LJ, et al. Distribution and excretion of venlafaxine and O-desmethylvenlafaxine in human milk. British Journal of Clinical Pharmacology. 1998;45 (5):459-462.
2. Newport DJ, Ritchie JC, Knight BT, Glover BA, Zach EB, Stowe ZN. Venlafaxine in human breast milk and nursing infant plasma: determination of exposure. J Clin Psychiatry. Sep 2009;70 (9):1304-1310.

DEXAMETHASONE   L3

Trade: Decadron, AK-Dex, Maxidex
Other Trades:
Uses: Corticosteroid anti-inflammatory
AAP: Not reviewed

Dexamethasone is a long-acting corticosteroid, similar in effect to prednisone, although more potent. Dexamethasone 0.75 mg is equivalent to a 5 mg dose of prednisone.[1] While the elimination half-life is brief, only 3-6 hours in adults, its metabolic effects last for up to 72 hours. No data are available on the transfer of dexamethasone into human milk. It is likely similar to that of prednisone which is extremely low. Doses of prednisone as high as 120 mg fail to produce clinically relevant milk levels. This product is commonly used in pediatrics for treating immune syndromes such as arthritis and, particularly, acute onset asthma or other bronchoconstrictive diseases. It is not likely that the amount in milk would produce clinical effects unless used in high doses over prolonged periods.

Pregnancy Risk Category: C

Lactation Risk Category: L3

Adult Concerns: In pediatrics: shortened stature, GI bleeding, GI ulceration, edema, osteoporosis, glaucoma, and other symptoms of hyperadrenalism.

Pediatric Concerns: None reported via milk. Avoid high doses over prolonged periods of time.

Drug Interactions: Barbiturates, phenytoin, rifampin may reduce the corticosteroid effect of dexamethasone. Dexamethasone may decrease effects of vaccines, salicylates, and toxoids.

Relative Infant Dose:

Adult Dose: 0.5-9 mg daily

Alternatives: Prednisone

T ½	= 3.3 hours	M/P	=
PHL	=	PB	=
Tmax	= 1-2 hours	Oral	= 78%
MW	= 392	pKa	=
Vd	= 2		

References:
1.   Pharmaceutical Manufacturer Prescribing Information. 1999.

DEXLANSOPRAZOLE   L2

Trade: Kapidex
Other Trades:
Uses: Suppresses gastric acid secretion
AAP: Not reviewed

Dexlansoprazole is a new proton pump inhibitor and is the active metabolite of lansoprazole (Prevacid). Due to poor stability at acid pH and short half-life, these products are encased in prolonged release formulations that open in the small intestine over a prolonged period of time. Structurally similar to omeprazole and lansoprazole, it is very unstable in stomach acid and to a large degree would be largely denatured by acidity of the infant's stomach.[1] A new study shows milk levels of omeprazole are minimal (see omeprazole) and it is likely milk levels of dexlansoprazole are small as well. Although there are no studies of dexlansoprazole in breastfeeding mothers, transfer to milk and its oral absorption (via milk) is likely to be minimal in a breastfed infant.

Pregnancy Risk Category: B

Lactation Risk Category: L2

Adult Concerns: Reduced stomach acidity. Diarrhea, nausea, elevated liver enzymes.

Pediatric Concerns: None reported via milk. It is unlikely to be absorbed while dissolved in milk due to instability in acid.

Drug Interactions: Decreased absorption of ketoconazole, itraconazole, and other drugs dependent on acid for absorption. Theophylline clearance is increased slightly. Reduced lansoprazole absorption when used with sucralfate (30%).

Relative Infant Dose:

Adult Dose: 30-60 mg daily

Alternatives: Omeprazole, lansoprazole, famotidine, ranitidine

T ½	= 1-2 hours	M/P	=
PHL	=	PB	= 98.8%
Tmax	= 1-2 hours	Oral	= Poor
MW	= 369	pKa	=
Vd	=		

References:
1.   Pharmaceutical manufacturers prescribing information, 2010.

DEXTROAMPHETAMINE | L3

Trade: Dexedrine, Amphetamine, Oxydess, Adderall, Vyvanse, Adderall XR
Other Trades: Dexamphetamine, Dexten
Uses: Powerful CNS stimulant
AAP: Drugs of abuse for which adverse effects have been reported

Dextroamphetamine is a potent and long-acting amphetamine. Following a 20 mg daily dose of racemic amphetamine administered at 1000, 1200, 1400, and 1600 hours each day (total= 80 mg/d) to a breastfeeding mother, amphetamine concentrations were determined in milk at 10 days and 42 days postpartum. Samples were taken at 20 min prior to the 1000 dose and immediately prior to the 1400 hour dose. Milk levels were 55 and 118 μg/L respectively.[1] Corresponding maternal plasma levels were 20 and 40 ng/mL at the same times. Milk/plasma ratios at these times were 2.8 and 3.0 respectively. At 42 days, breastmilk levels of amphetamine were 68 and 138 μg/L while maternal plasma levels were 9 and 21 ng/mL respectively. Milk/plasma ratios in the 42-day samples were 7.5 and 6.6 respectively. Although the milk/plasma ratios appear high, using a daily milk intake of 150 mL/kg/d, the relative infant dose would be only 1.8% of the weight-normalized maternal dose, which probably accounts for the fact that the infant in this study was unaffected.

In another study of 4 mothers who received 15-45 mg/day dextroamphetamine, the average absolute infant dose was 21 (11-39) µg/kg/day.[2] The authors suggest the relative infant dose was 5.7% (4-10.6). Plasma levels in the infants ranged from undetectable to 18 µg/L. No untoward effects were noted in any of the 4 infants.

Lisdexamfetamine dimesylate (Vyvanse) is a pro-drug of dextroamphetamine. After oral administration, lisdexamfetamine dimesylate is rapidly absorbed from the gastrointestinal tract and converted to dextroamphetamine.[3] The above data suggest that with normal therapeutic doses, the dose of dextroamphetamine in milk is probably subclinical. However, abusive use of this medication is common. Doses are unknown and sometimes extraordinarily high. Thus mothers should be strongly advised to withhold breastfeeding for 24 hours following the non-clinical use of dextroamphetamine.

Adderall XR is a continuous release formulation. Plasma levels are virtually identical to the twice daily dosing system. Thus if a patient is using XR 20 mg, plasma levels are identical to the 10 mg twice daily.

Pregnancy Risk Category: C

Lactation Risk Category: L3 in clinical doses
                                L5 if abused

Adult Concerns: Nervousness, insomnia, anorexia, hyperexcitability.

Pediatric Concerns: Possible   insomnia,   irritability,   anorexia, reduced weight gain, or poor sleeping patterns in infants. However in these studies, none of the infants were affected.

Drug Interactions: May precipitate hypertensive crisis in patients on MAO inhibitors and arrhythmias in patients receiving general anesthetics. Increased effect/toxicity with tricyclic antidepressants, phenytoin, phenobarbital, norepinephrine, meperidine.

Relative Infant Dose: 1.8% - 6.9%

Adult Dose: 5-60 mg daily

Alternatives: Methylphenidate

T ½	= 6-8 hours	M/P	= 2-5.2
PHL	=	PB	= 16-20%
Tmax	= 1-2 hours	Oral	= Complete
MW	= 368	pKa	= 9.9
Vd	= 3.2-5.6		

References:

1. Steiner E, Villen T, Hallberg M, Rane A. Amphetamine secretion in breast milk. Eur J Clin Pharmacol 1984; 27 (1):123-124.
2. Ilett KF, Hackett LP, Kristensen JH, Kohan R. Transfer of dexamphetamine into breast milk during treatment for attention deficit hyperactivity disorder. Br J Clin Pharmacol 2006; 63 (3): 371-375.
3. Pharmaceutical Manufacturer Prescribing Information. 2010.

DEXTROMETHORPHAN   L1

Trade: DM, Benylin, Delsym, Pertussin, Robitussin DM
Other Trades: Balminil-DM, Delsym, Benylin DM, Cosylan
Uses: Antitussive, Cough preparation
AAP: Not reviewed

Dextromethorphan is a weak antitussive commonly used in infants and adults. It is a congener of codeine and appears to elevate the cough threshold in the brain. It does not have addictive, analgesic, or sedative actions, and it does not produce respiratory depression at normal doses.[1] It is the safest of the antitussives and is routinely used in children and infants. No data on its transfer to human milk are available. It is very unlikely that enough would transfer via milk to provide clinically significant levels in a breastfed infant.

Pregnancy Risk Category: C

Lactation Risk Category: L1

Adult Concerns: Drowsiness, fatigue, dizziness, hyperpyrexia.

Pediatric Concerns: None reported.

Drug Interactions: May interact with MAO inhibitors producing hypotension, hyperpyrexia, nausea, coma.

Relative Infant Dose:

Adult Dose: 10-20 mg every 4 hours

Alternatives: Codeine

T ½	= <4 hours	M/P	=
PHL	=	PB	=
Tmax	= 1-2 hours	Oral	= Complete
MW	= 271	pKa	= 8.3
Vd	=		

References:
1. Pender ES, Parks BR. Toxicity with dextromethorphan-containing preparations: a literature review and report of two additional cases. Pediatr Emerg Care 1991; 7 (3):163-165.

DIAZEPAM   L3

Trade: Valium
Other Trades: Apo-Diazepam, Meval, Novo-Dipam, Vivol, Antenex, Ducene, Sedapam
Uses: Sedative, anxiolytic drug
AAP: Drugs whose effect on nursing infants is unknown but may be of concern

Diazepam is a powerful CNS depressant and anticonvulsant. Published data on milk and plasma levels are highly variable and many are poor studies. In 3 mothers receiving 10 mg three times daily for up to 6 days, the maternal plasma levels of diazepam averaged 491 ng/mL (day 4) and 601 ng/mL (day 6).[1] Corresponding milk levels were 51 ng/mL (day 4) and 78 ng/mL (day 6). The milk/plasma ratio was approximately 0.1.

In a case report of a patient taking 6-10 mg of diazepam daily, her milk levels varied from 7.5 to 87 µg/L.[2] In a study of 9 mothers receiving diazepam postpartum, milk levels of diazepam varied from approximately 0.01 to 0.08 mg/L.[3] Other reports suggest slightly higher values. Taken together, most results suggest that the dose of diazepam and its metabolite, desmethyldiazepam, to a suckling infant will be on average 0.78-9.1% of the weight-adjusted maternal dose of diazepam.[4] The active metabolite, desmethyldiazepam, in general has a much longer half-life in adults and pediatric patients and may tend to accumulate on longer therapy.

The excretion of diazepam, N-desmethyldiazepam, temazepam and oxazepam in breast milk was studied during withdrawal of a 22-year-old patient from combined high dose diazepam and oxazepam therapy.[5] Diazepam, N-desmethyldiazepam, temazepam and oxazepam were found in the maternal plasma and milk with mean milk: plasma ratios of 0.2, 0.13, 0.14 and 0.10 respectively. The infant received approximately 4.7% of the maternal dose. Diazepam could not be detected in the infant's plasma, but low levels of N-desmethyldiazepam (20 and 21 micrograms l-1), temazepam (7 micrograms l-1) and oxazepam (7.5 and 9.6 micrograms l-1) were present. The infant showed no overt physical or mental symptoms of benzodiazepine intoxication.

Some reports of lethargy, sedation, and poor suckling have been found. The acute use such as in surgical procedures is not likely to lead to significant accumulation. Long-term, sustained therapy may prove troublesome. The benzodiazepine family, as a rule, is not ideal for breastfeeding mothers due to relatively long half-lives and the development of dependence. However, it is apparent that the shorter-acting benzodiazepines (lorazepam, alprazolam) are safest during lactation provided their use is short-term or intermittent, low dose, and after the first week of life.[6]

Pregnancy Risk Category: D

Lactation Risk Category: L3
L4 if used chronically

Adult Concerns: Adverse reactions include drowsiness, dizziness, blurred vision, dry mouth, headache, fatigue, ataxia, slurred speech, and mental confusion.

Pediatric Concerns: Some reports of lethargy, sedation, poor suckling have been found.

Drug Interactions: May increase sedation when used with CNS depressants such as alcohol, barbiturates, opioids. Cimetidine may decrease metabolism and clearance of diazepam. Cisapride can dramatically increase plasma levels of diazepam. Valproic may displace diazepam from binding sites, thus increasing sedative effects. SSRIs (fluoxetine, sertraline, paroxetine) can dramatically increase diazepam levels by altering clearance, thus leading to sedation .

Relative Infant Dose: 2.7% - 7.1%

Adult Dose: 2-10 mg BID to QID

Alternatives: Lorazepam, Midazolam

T ½	= 43 hours	M/P	= 0.2-2.7
PHL	= 20-50 hours (full-term neo)	PB	= 99%
Tmax	= 1-2 hours	Oral	= Complete
MW	= 285	pKa	= 3.4
Vd	= 0.7-2.6		

References:
1. Erkkola R, Kanto J. Diazepam and breast-feeding. Lancet 1972; 1 (7762):1235-1236.
2. Wesson DR, Camber S, Harkey M, Smith DE. Diazepam and desmethyldiazepam in breast milk. J Psychoactive Drugs 1985; 17 (1):55-56.
3. Cole AP, Hailey DM. Diazepam and active metabolite in breast milk and their transfer to the neonate. Arch Dis Child 1975; 50 (9):741-742.
4. Spigset O. Anaesthetic agents and excretion in breast milk. Acta Anaesthesiol Scand 1994; 38 (2):94-103.
5. Dusci LJ, Good SM, Hall RW, Ilett KF. Excretion of diazepam and its metabolites in human milk during withdrawal from combination high dose diazepam and oxazepam. Br J Clin Pharmacol. 1990 Jan;29 (1):123-6.
6. Maitra R, Menkes DB. Psychotropic drugs and lactation. N Z Med J 1996; 109 (1024):217-218.

DIBUCAINE   L3

Trade: Nupercainal
Other Trades: Cinchocaine, Ultraproct, Dermacaine
Uses: Local anesthetic
AAP: Not reviewed

Dibucaine is a long-acting local anesthetic generally used topically. It is primarily used topically in creams and ointments, and due to toxicity, has been banned in the USA for IV or IM injections.[1] No data is available on transfer to breastmilk. Dibucaine is effective for sunburn, topical burns, rash, rectal hemorrhoids, and other skin irritations. Long-term use and use over large areas of the body are discouraged. Although somewhat minimal, some dibucaine can be absorbed from irritated skin.

Pregnancy Risk Category: C

Lactation Risk Category: L3

Adult Concerns: Rash or allergic symptoms.

Pediatric Concerns: None reported via milk.

Drug Interactions:

Relative Infant Dose:

Adult Dose: 10-30 g daily.

Alternatives:

T ½	=	M/P	=
PHL	=	PB	=
Tmax	=	Oral	=
MW	= 379	pKa	=
Vd	=		

References:
1. Pharmaceutical Manufacturer Prescribing Information. 1995.

DICLOFENAC   L2

Trade: Cataflam, Voltaren
Other Trades: Apo-Diclo, Novo-Difenac, Fenac, Voltarol
Uses: NSAID analgesic for arthritis
AAP: Not reviewed

Diclofenac is a typical nonsteroidal analgesic (NSAID). Voltaren is a sustained release product whereas Cataflam is an immediate release product. In one study of six postpartum mothers receiving three 50 mg doses on day 1, followed by two 50 mg doses on day 2, the levels of diclofenac in breastmilk were approximately 5 µg/L of milk, although the limit of detection was reported as <19 ng/mL.[1]

In another patient on long-term treatment with diclofenac, milk levels of 0.1 µg/mL milk were reported which would amount to 0.015 mg/kg/d ingested.[2] These amounts are probably far too low to affect an infant.

Pregnancy Risk Category: B topical
C oral
D third trimester

Lactation Risk Category: L2

Adult Concerns: GI distress, diarrhea, nausea, vomiting.

Pediatric Concerns: None reported via milk. Milk levels are extremely low.

Drug Interactions: May prolong prothrombin time when used with warfarin. Antihypertensive effects of ACEi family may be blunted or completely abolished by NSAIDs. Some NSAIDs may block antihypertensive effect of beta blockers, diuretics. Used with cyclosporin, may dramatically increase renal toxicity. May increase digoxin, phenytoin, lithium levels. May increase toxicity of methotrexate. May increase bioavailability of penicillamine. Probenecid may increase NSAID levels.

Relative Infant Dose:

Adult Dose: 75 mg BID

Alternatives: Ibuprofen

T ½	= 1.1 hours	M/P	=
PHL	=	PB	= 99.7%
Tmax	= 1 hour (Cataflam)	Oral	= Complete
MW	= 318	pKa	= 4.0
Vd	= 0.55		

References:
1. Sioufi A. et.al. Recent findings concerning clinically relevant pharmacokinetics of diclofenac sodium. In: Kass (ed), Voltaren-new findings. Hans Huber Publishers, Bern, 1982.
2. Pharmaceutical Manufacturer Prescribing Information.

DICLOXACILLIN   L1

Trade: Pathocil, Dycill, Dynapen
Other Trades: Diclocil, Dicloxsig
Uses: Penicillin antibiotic
AAP: Not reviewed

Dicloxacillin is an oral penicillinase-resistant penicillin frequently used for peripheral (non CNS) infections caused by *Staphlococcus aureus* and *Staphlococcus epidermidis* infections, particularly mastitis. Following oral administration of a 250 mg dose, milk concentrations of the drug were 0.1, and 0.3 mg/L at 2 and 4 hours after the dose respectively.[1] Levels were undetectable after 1-6 hours. Compatible with breastfeeding. Observe for diarrhea or candida diaper rash.

Pregnancy Risk Category: B

Lactation Risk Category: L1

Adult Concerns: Elimination is delayed in neonates. Rash, diarrhea.

Pediatric Concerns: None reported via milk. Observe for diarrhea and candida

Drug Interactions: May increase effect of oral anticoagulants. Disulfiram, probenecid may increase levels of penicillin. May reduce efficacy of oral contraceptives.

Relative Infant Dose: 0.6% - 1.4%

Adult Dose: 125-250 mg every 6 hours

Alternatives: Amoxicillin + clavulanate

T ½	= 0.6-0.8 hour	M/P	=
PHL	= 1.9 hours	PB	= 96%
Tmax	= 0.5-2 hours	Oral	= 35-76%
MW	= 470	pKa	=
Vd	=		

References:
1. Matsuda S. Transfer of antibiotics into maternal milk. Biol Res Pregnancy. 1984;5:57-60.

DICYCLOMINE — L4

Trade: Bentyl, Antispas, Spasmoject
Other Trades: Bentylol, Formulex, Lomine, Merbentyl
Uses: Anticholinergic, drying agent.
AAP: Not reviewed

Dicyclomine is a tertiary amine antispasmodic. It belongs to the family of anticholinergics such as atropine and the belladonna alkaloids. It was previously used for infant colic but due to overdoses and reported apnea, it is seldom recommended for this use. Infants are exceedingly sensitive to anticholinergics, particularly in the neonatal period. Following a dose of 20 mg in a lactating woman, a 12-day-old infant reported severe apnea. The manufacturer reports milk levels of 131 µg/L with corresponding maternal serum levels of 59 µg/L.[1] The reported milk/plasma level was 2.22.

Pregnancy Risk Category: B

Lactation Risk Category: L4

Adult Concerns: Apnea, dry secretions, urinary hesitancy, dilated pupils.

Pediatric Concerns: Severe apnea in one 12 day old infant. Observe for anticholinergic symptoms, drying, constipation, rapid heart rate.

Drug Interactions: Decreased effect with antacids, phenothiazines, haloperidol. Increased toxicity when used with other anticholinergics, amantadine, opiates, antiarrhythmics, antihistamines, tricyclic antidepressants.

Relative Infant Dose: 6.9%

Adult Dose: 20-40 mg QID

Alternatives:

T ½	= 9-10 hours	M/P	= 2.22
PHL	=	PB	=
Tmax	= 1-1.5 hours	Oral	= 67%
MW	= 345	pKa	=
Vd	=		

References:
1.   Pharmaceutical Manufacturer Prescribing Information. 2010.

DIETHYLPROPION   L5

Trade: Tepanil, Tenuate
Other Trades: Dospan
Uses: Anorexiant
AAP: Not reviewed

Diethylpropion belongs to the amphetamine family and is typically used to reduce food intake. No data available other than manufacturer states this medication is secreted into breastmilk.[1] Diethylpropion's structure is similar to amphetamines. Upon withdrawal, significant withdrawal symptoms have been reported in adults. Such symptoms could be observed in breastfeeding infants of mothers using this product. The use of this medication during lactation is simply unrealistic and not justified.

Pregnancy Risk Category: B

Lactation Risk Category: L5

Adult Concerns: Overstimulation, insomnia, anorexia, jitteriness, rapid heart rate, elevated blood pressure.

Pediatric Concerns: None reported, but observe for anorexia, agitation, insomnia.

Drug Interactions: Increased toxicity with MAO inhibitors, CNS depressants, general anesthetics (arrhythmias), other adrenergics.

Relative Infant Dose:

Adult Dose: 25 mg TID

Alternatives:

T ½	= 8 hours	M/P	=
PHL	=	PB	=
Tmax	= 2 hours	Oral	= 70%
MW	= 205	pKa	=
Vd	=		

References:
1. Pharmaceutical Manufacturer Prescribing Information. 2010.

DIETHYLSTILBESTROL   L5

Trade:
Other Trades: Honvol, Honvan, Fosfestrol, Apstil
Uses: Synthetic estrogen
AAP: Not reviewed

Diethylstilbestrol is a synthetic estrogen that is seldom used today. It is known to produce a high risk of cervical cancer in female infants exposed during pregnancy.[1,2] It has been shown to cause anatomical abnormalities in males and females, neoplasia, reduced fertility, and immunologic changes. Its effect in the breastfeeding infant is unknown but should be absolutely avoided. DES would probably inhibit milk production. Do not use this estrogen during breastfeeding. Contraindicated.

Pregnancy Risk Category: X

Lactation Risk Category: L5

Adult Concerns: Decreased breast milk production.

Pediatric Concerns: None reported via milk, but this product is too dangerous for use in breastfeeding mothers.

Drug Interactions:

Relative Infant Dose:

Adult Dose: 15 mg daily.

Alternatives:

T ½	=	M/P	=
PHL	=	PB	=
Tmax	=	Oral	= Complete
MW	= 268	pKa	=
Vd	=		

References:
1. O'Brien TE. Excretion of drugs in human milk. Am J Hosp Pharm 1974; 31 (9):844-854.
2. Shapiro S, Slone D. The effects of exogenous female hormones on the fetus. Epidemiol Rev 1979; 1:110-123.

DIFLUNISAL   L3

Trade: Dolobid
Other Trades: Apo-Diflunisal, Novo-Diflunisal
Uses: Nonsteroidal antiinflammatory analgesic
AAP: Not reviewed

Diflunisal is a derivative of salicylic acid. Diflunisal is excreted into human milk in concentrations 2-7% of the maternal plasma levels following 7 days of treatment with 125-250 mg twice daily.[1] No reports of side-effects have been located. This product is potentially a higher risk NSAID and other less toxic compounds should be used.

Pregnancy Risk Category: C in first and second trimester
                                D in third trimester

Lactation Risk Category: L3

Adult Concerns: Prolonged bleeding time, headache, GI distress, diarrhea, GI cramping, fluid retention. Ulcer complications. Worsening hypertension.

Pediatric Concerns: None reported but alternatives are suggested.

Drug Interactions: Antacids reduce effect. Increased toxicity of digoxin, methotrexate, anticoagulants, phenytoin, sulfonylureas, lithium acetaminophen.

Relative Infant Dose: 7.8% - 11.5%

Adult Dose: 500 mg BID or TID

Alternatives: Ibuprofen, celecoxib

T ½	= 8-12 hours	M/P	=
PHL	=	PB	− 99%
Tmax	= 2-3 hours	Oral	= Complete
MW	= 250	pKa	=
Vd	= 0.1-0.2		

References:
1. Pharmaceutical Manufacturer Prescribing Information. 2010.

DIGITOXIN   L3

Trade: Crystodigin
Other Trades: Digitaline
Uses: Cardiac stimulant
AAP: Not reviewed

No data available on digitoxin and its transfer to human milk.[1]
Digitoxin is occasionally given to infants. High lipid solubility and
good oral bioavailability would suggest some transfer into breastmilk.
See digoxin.

Pregnancy Risk Category: C

Lactation Risk Category: L3

Adult Concerns: Nausea, vomiting, anorexia, cardiac arrhythmias.

Pediatric Concerns: None reported thus far.

Drug Interactions: Reduced plasma levels when used with antacids,
penicillamine, bran fiber, sucralfate, cholestyramine, rifampin, etc.
Increased toxicity when used with diltiazem, ibuprofen, cimetidine,
omeprazole, etc.

Relative Infant Dose:

Adult Dose: 0.15 mg daily.

Alternatives:

T ½	= 6.7 days	M/P	=
PHL	=	PB	= 97%
Tmax	= 4 hours	Oral	= 90-100%
MW	= 765	pKa	=
Vd	= 7 (variable)		

References:

1.   Levy M, Granit L, Laufer N. Excretion of drugs in human milk. N Engl J Med 1977; 297 (14):789.

DIGOXIN   L2

Trade: Lanoxin, Lanoxicaps
Other Trades: Novo-Digoxin
Uses: Cardiac stimulant
AAP: Maternal Medication Usually Compatible with Breastfeeding

Digoxin is a cardiac stimulant used primarily to strengthen the contractile process. In one mother receiving 0.25 mg digoxin daily, the amount found in breast milk ranged from 0.96 to 0.61 µg/L at 4 and 6 hours post-dose respectively.[1] Mean peak breastmilk levels varied from 0.78 µg/L in one patient to 0.41 µg/L in another. Plasma levels in the infants were undetectable.

In another study of 5 women receiving digoxin therapy, the average breastmilk concentration was 0.64 µg/L.[2] From these studies, it is apparent that a breastfeeding infant would receive less than 1 µg/day of digoxin, too low to be clinically relevant. The small amounts secreted into breastmilk have not produced problems in nursing infants. Poor and erratic GI absorption could theoretically reduce absorption in nursing infant.

Digibind, or digoxin immune fab (ovine), is composed of antigen binding fragments made from antidigoxin antibodies. It is used for life-threatening digoxin toxicity or overdose. The dosage needed can be calculated using the ratio that one vial of Digibind (38 mg) will bind 0.5 mg of digoxin. The MW of these fragments are approximately 46.000 daltons, and thus would not be able to transfer into the milk compartment.[3]

Pregnancy Risk Category: C

Lactation Risk Category: L2

Adult Concerns: Nausea, vomiting, bradycardia, arrhythmias.

Pediatric Concerns: None reported in several studies.

Drug Interactions: Too numerous to list all. Decreased digoxin effect when used with antacids, bran fiber, sucralfate, sulfasalazine, diuretics, phenytoin, cholestyramine, aminoglutethimide. Increase digoxin effects may result when used with diltiazem, ibuprofen, cimetidine, omeprazole, bepridil, reserpine, amphotericin B, erythromycin, quinine, tetracycline, cyclosporine, etc.

Relative Infant Dose: 2.7% - 2.8%

Adult Dose: 0.125-0.5 mg daily.

Alternatives:

T ½	= 39 hours	M/P	= <0.9
PHL	= 20-180 hours	PB	= 25%
Tmax	= 1.5-3 hours	Oral	= 65-85%
MW	= 781	pKa	=
Vd	= 5.1-7.4		

References:
1. Loughnan PM. Digoxin excretion in human breast milk. J Pediatr 1978; 92 (6):1019-1020.
2. Levy M, Granit L, Laufer N. Excretion of drugs in human milk. N Engl J Med 1977; 297 (14):789.
3. Pharmaceutical Manufacturer Prescribing Information. 2006.

DILTIAZEM HCL | L3

Trade: Cardizem SR, Dilacor-XR, Cardizem CD, Cartia XT

Other Trades: Cardizem, Apo-Diltiazem, Apo-Diltiaz, Cardcal, Coras, Dilzem, Adizem, Britiazim, Tildiem

Uses: Antihypertensive, calcium channel blocker

AAP: Maternal Medication Usually Compatible with Breastfeeding

Diltiazem is an typical calcium channel blocker antihypertensive.[1] In a report of a single patient receiving 240 mg/d on day 14 postpartum, levels in milk were parallel those of serum (milk/plasma ratio is approximately 1.0).[2] Peak level in milk (and plasma) was slightly higher than 200 µg/L and occurred at 8 hours. While nifedipine is probably a preferred choice calcium channel blocker because of our experience with it, the relative infant dose with this agent is quite small and it is not likely to be problematic.

Pregnancy Risk Category: C

Lactation Risk Category: L3

Adult Concerns: Hypotension, bradycardia.

Pediatric Concerns: Hypotension, bradycardia is possible. See nifedipine.

Drug Interactions: H-2 blockers may increase bioavailability of diltiazem. Beta blockers may increase cardio depressant effect. May increase cyclosporine, and carbamazepine levels. Fentanyl may increase hypotension.

Relative Infant Dose:

Adult Dose: 30-90 mg QID

Alternatives: Nifedipine, Nimodipine, Verapamil

T ½	= 3.5-6 hours	M/P	= 1.0
PHL	=	PB	= 78%
Tmax	= 2-3 hours	Oral	= 40-60%
MW	= 433	pKa	=
Vd	= 1.7		

References:
1. Pharmaceutical Manufacturer Prescribing Information. 1995.
2. Okada M, Inoue H, Nakamura Y, Kishimoto M, Suzuki T. Excretion of diltiazem in human milk. N Engl J Med 1985; 312 (15):992-993.

DIMENHYDRINATE   L2

Trade: Marmine, Dramamine
Other Trades: Gravol, Traveltabs, Andrumin, Travacalm
Uses: Antihistamine for vertigo and motion sickness
AAP: Not reviewed

Consists of 55% diphenhydramine and 45% of 8-chlorotheophylline. Diphenhydramine (Benadryl) is considered to be the active ingredient. See Benadryl.

Pregnancy Risk Category: B

Lactation Risk Category: L2

Adult Concerns: Sedation, dry secretions.

Pediatric Concerns: None reported but observe for sedation. See diphenhydramine.

Drug Interactions: May enhance CNS depressants, anticholinergics, tricyclic antidepressants, and MAO exhibitors. Increased toxicity of antibiotics, especially aminoglycosides "ototoxicity".

Relative Infant Dose:

Adult Dose: 50-100 mg every 4-6 hours

Alternatives: Cetirizine, loratadine

T ½	= 8.5 hours	M/P	=
PHL	=	PB	= 78%
Tmax	= 1-2 hours	Oral	=
MW	= 470	pKa	=
Vd	=		

References:
1. Pharmaceutical Manufacturer Prescribing Information. 1995.

DIMETHYLSULFOXIDE | L3

Trade: DMSO, Rimso-50, DMSO2, MSM
Other Trades:
Uses: Solvent used for arthritis, etc.
AAP: Not reviewed

Dimethyl sulfoxide (DMSO) is a solvent that has been found useful for musculoskeletal inflammation and injury, and interstitial cystitis. It has been used topically, orally, and intravenously. DMSO is relatively nontoxic, requiring rather large intravenous doses to induce toxicity (20 gm). Following dermal application of 1 g/kg (640 mL/70 kg), reported serum concentrations were 560 mg/L within 4-8 hours. By 48 hours only traces were detectable.[1] Daily oral doses of 32 mL/70 kg for 14 days produced peak serum levels of 1850 mg/L. DMSO penetrates to many compartments and it would probably penetrate into milk in significant quantities. Due to the high plasma levels above, it is probable that milk levels would be quite high as well. Although the overall toxicity of this compound is quite minimal, exposing an infant to this agent, which is minimally efficacious, is probably not justified. DMSO is capable of transporting most substances across the skin. When contaminated with other solvents it can become quite dangerous. Only highly purified products should be used.

Methylsulfonylmethane (DMSO2, MSM, "Crystalline DMSO") is the normal oxidation product of DMSO. No data are available on this product, but it is probably distributed and eliminated the same as DMSO above.

Pregnancy Risk Category: C

Lactation Risk Category: L3

Adult Concerns: DMSO imparts a garlic-like breath, taste and body odor to all users. GI disturbances including vomiting and nausea, drowsiness, sedation, neuropathy, dizziness, headache and dermatologic rash have been reported. Hepatotoxicity, milk jaundice and hepatic precoma was reported in two elderly patients receiving IV infusions of 100 g of 20% DMSO.

Pediatric Concerns: None reported. This agent is not particularly effective, therefore the risks do not justify its use in breastfeeding mothers.

Drug Interactions:

Relative Infant Dose:

Adult Dose: Variable.

Alternatives:

T ½	= 11-14 hours (dermal)	M/P	=
PHL	=	PB	=
Tmax	= 4-8 hours (topically)	Oral	= Complete
MW	=	pKa	=
Vd	= 0.53		

References:
1. Baselt RC. Disposition of toxic drugs and chemicals in man. Foster City, CA: Chemical Toxicology Institute, 2000: 282-283.

DINOPROSTONE | L3

Trade: Prostin E2, Prepidil, Cervidil
Other Trades: Propress
Uses: Prostaglandin E-2
AAP: Not reviewed

Dinoprostone is a naturally occurring prostaglandin E2 that is primarily used for induction of labor, for cervical ripening, as an abortifacient, for postpartum bleeding, and for uterine atony.[1] Available as a vaginal gel or insert, it is slowly absorbed into the plasma where it is rapidly cleared and metabolized by most tissues and the lung. Its half-life is brief 2.5 to 5 minutes although absorption from the vaginal mucosa is slow. Neonatal effects from maternal dinoprostone include fetal heart rate abnormalities, and neonatal jaundice. The amount of dinoprostone entering milk is not known, but a brief wash out period would preclude any possible side effects.

However, dinoprostone has been used to suppress lactation. When used orally (Prostin E2, 2 mg orally/d on day 3 and 4; then 6 mg/d thereafter) it has been found to significantly suppress milk production.[2,3] However, the use of prostaglandin E2 products for cervical ripening (during delivery) is generally brief and probably does not clinically impact the production of breastmilk many hours or days later.

Pregnancy Risk Category: C during delivery
    X during first and second trimesters

Lactation Risk Category: L3

Adult Concerns: Side effects of vaginal dinoprostone are numerous and include, abortion, labor induction, blood loss, hypotension, syncope, tachycardia, dizziness, hyperthermia, nausea, vomiting, diarrhea, and taste disorders.

Pediatric Concerns: None reported via milk, but a washout period is suggested.

Drug Interactions:

Relative Infant Dose:

Adult Dose: 10-20 mg X 1-2

Alternatives:

T ½	= 2.5-5 minutes	M/P	=
PHL	=	PB	= High
Tmax	= 0.5-1 hour	Oral	=
MW	=	pKa	=
Vd	=		

References:
1. Pharmaceutical Manufacturer Prescribing Information. 2010.
2. Caminiti F, De Murtas M, Parodo G, Lecca U, Nasi A. Decrease in human plasma prolactin levels by oral prostaglandin E2 in early puerperium. J Endocrinol 1980; 87 (3):333-337.
3. Nasi A, De Murtas M, Parodo G, Caminiti F. Inhibition of lactation by prostaglandin E2. Obstet Gynecol Surv 1980; 35 (10):619-620.

DIPHENHYDRAMINE
L2

Trade: Benadryl, Cheracol
Other Trades: Allerdryl, Insomnal, Nytol, Delixir, Paedamin
Uses: Antihistamine, antitussive
AAP: Not reviewed

Small but unreported levels are thought to be secreted into breastmilk. In one study following an IM dose of 100 mg, drug levels in milk were undetectable in 2 individuals, and ranged from 42 to 100 µg/L in two subjects.[1] While these levels are low, the use of this sedating antihistamine in breastfeeding mothers is not ideal. Non-sedating antihistamines are generally preferred. There are anecdotal reports that diphenhydramine suppresses milk production. There are no data to support this theory.

Pregnancy Risk Category: B

Lactation Risk Category: L2

Adult Concerns: Sedation, drowsiness.

Pediatric Concerns: None reported, but observe for sedation. Some suggestions of reduced milk supply but these are unsubstantiated.

Drug Interactions: Increased sedation when used with other CNS depressants. MAO inhibitors may increase anticholinergic side effects.

Relative Infant Dose: 0.7% - 1.4%

Adult Dose: 25-50 mg TID or QID

Alternatives: Cetirizine, Loratadine

T ½	= 4.3 hours	M/P	=
PHL	=	PB	= 78%
Tmax	= 2-3 hours	Oral	= 43-61%
MW	= 255	pKa	= 8.3
Vd	= 3-4		

References:
1. Rindi V. La eliminazione degli antistaminici di sintesi con il latte e l'azione latto-goga de questi. Riv Ital Ginecol. 1951;34:147-57.

DIPHENOXYLATE | L3

Trade: Lomotil, Lofene
Other Trades: Lofenoxal, Tropergen
Uses: Antidiarrheal
AAP: Not reviewed

Lomotil is a combination product of diphenoxylate and atropine.[1] Diphenoxylate belongs to the opiate family (meperidine) and acts on the intestinal tract inhibiting GI motility and excessive GI propulsion. The drug has no analgesic activity. Although no reports on its transfer to human milk are available, it is probably secreted in breastmilk in very small quantities.[2] Some authors consider diphenoxylate to be contraindicated, but this is questionable.

Pregnancy Risk Category: C

Lactation Risk Category: L3

Adult Concerns: Anticholinergic effects, such as drying, constipation, and sedation.

Pediatric Concerns: None reported, but observe for dryness, constipation, sedation

Drug Interactions: Increased toxicity when used with MAO inhibitors, CNS depressants, anticholinergics.

Relative Infant Dose:

Adult Dose: 5 mg QID

Alternatives:

T ½	= 2.5 hours	M/P	=
PHL	=	PB	=
Tmax	= 2 hours	Oral	= 90%
MW	= 453	pKa	= 7.1
Vd	= 3.8		

References:
1. Drug Facts and Comparisons 2010 ed. ed. St. Louis: 2010.
2. Stewart JJ. Gastrointestinal drugs. In Wilson, J.T., ed. Drugs in Breast Milk. Balgowlah, Australia ADIS Press 1981;71.

DIPHTHERIA AND TETANUS TOXOID   L3

Trade: DT, Td
Other Trades: ADT, CDT, Triple Antigen
Uses: Vaccine
AAP: Not reviewed

Diphtheria and tetanus toxoid contains large MW protein toxoids. It is extremely unlikely proteins of this size would be secreted in breastmilk. No data are available on its transfer to human milk.

Pregnancy Risk Category: C

Lactation Risk Category: L3

Adult Concerns: Swelling, fretfulness, drowsiness, anorexia, vomiting.

Pediatric Concerns: None reported via breastmilk exposure.

Drug Interactions:

Relative Infant Dose:

Adult Dose: 0.5 ml injection (IM)

Alternatives:

References:

DIPHTHERIA-TETANUS-PERTUSSIS   L2

Trade: DTaP, Acel-Imune, Tripedia, Tetramune, DPT
Other Trades:
Uses: Vaccine
AAP: Not reviewed

DTP injections come in two forms: one including acellular pertussis (Acel-Imune, Tripedia), and one including whole-cell pertussis and Haemophilus influenzae Type B Conjugate (Tetramune).[1] Both are inactivated bacterial vaccines or toxoids.

The use of pertussis vaccinations in individuals over 7 years of age is generally contraindicated. Hence, there is no indication for administering this vaccine to adult mothers. Because this is an inactivated bacterial product, there is no specific contraindication in breastfeeding following injection with these vaccines.

Pregnancy Risk Category: B

Lactation Risk Category: L2

Adult Concerns: Pain, fever, swelling

Pediatric Concerns: None reported via breastmilk.

Drug Interactions: Immunosuppressive agents, high dose corticosteroids, may reduce immunogenicity.

Relative Infant Dose:

Adult Dose: N/A

Alternatives:

References:
1. Pharmaceutical Manufacturer Prescribing Information. 2010.

DIPIVEFRIN   L2

Trade: AK-Pro, Propine
Other Trades: PSM-Dipivefrin
Uses: Adrenergic for glaucoma
AAP: Not reviewed

Dipivefrin is a synthetic amine prodrug that is metabolized to epinephrine. Because of its structure, it is more lipophilic and better absorbed into the eye; hence, it is more potent.[1] Following absorption into the eye, dipivefrin reduces interocular pressure. It is not known if dipivefrin enters milk, but small amounts may be present. It is unlikely that any dipivefrin or epinephrine present in milk would be orally bioavailable to the infant.

Pregnancy Risk Category: B

Lactation Risk Category: L2

Adult Concerns: Infrequently, tachycardia, arrhythmias, hypertension have occurred with intraocular epinephrine. Burning, itching, tearing, hyperemia of eyes, redness of the eyes, burning and stinging have been reported.

Pediatric Concerns: None via milk.

Drug Interactions: When admixed with a pilocarpine Ocusert system, a transient increase in myopia was reported.

Relative Infant Dose:

Adult Dose: 1 drop affected eye every 12 hours to affected eye

Alternatives:

T ½	=		M/P	=
PHL	=		PB	=
Tmax	= 1 hour		Oral	= Minimal
MW	=		pKa	=
Vd	=			

References:
1. Pharmaceutical Manufacturer Prescribing Information. 2010.

DIPYRIDAMOLE   L3

Trade: Persantine
Other Trades: Apo-Dipyridamole, Novo-Dipiradol, Persantin
Uses: Vasodilator, antiplatelet agent
AAP: Not reviewed

Dipyridamole is most commonly used in addition to coumarin anticoagulants to prevent thromboembolic complications of cardiac valve replacement. According to the manufacturer, only small amounts are believed to be secreted in human milk.[1] No reported untoward effects have been reported.

Pregnancy Risk Category: B

Lactation Risk Category: L3

Adult Concerns: Headache, dizziness, GI distress, nausea, vomiting, diarrhea, flushing.

Pediatric Concerns: No untoward effects have been reported.

Drug Interactions: When used with Heparin, may increase anticoagulation. Theophylline may reduce the hypotensive effect of dipyridamole.

Relative Infant Dose:

Adult Dose: 75-100 mg QID

Alternatives:

T ½	= 10-12 hours	M/P	=
PHL	=	PB	= 91-99%
Tmax	= 45-150 minutes	Oral	= Poor
MW	= 505	pKa	=
Vd	= 2-3		

References:
1. Pharmaceutical Manufacturer Prescribing Information. 1995.

DIRITHROMYCIN　　　　　L3

Trade: Dynabac
Other Trades:
Uses: Macrolide antibiotic
AAP: Not reviewed

Dirithromycin is a macrolide antibiotic similar to the erythromycins but is characterized by low serum levels and high tissue levels.[1] Dirithromycin is metabolized to erythromycyclamine which is the active component. No data on the transfer of erythromycyclamine into human milk is available. Due to the kinetics of dirithromycin and its distribution largely to tissues, it is unlikely that major levels in milk will result. Suitable alternatives include erythromycin and azithromycin.

Pregnancy Risk Category: C

Lactation Risk Category: L3

Adult Concerns: GI distress, abdominal pain, diarrhea, nausea, vomiting, skin rash, headache and dizziness. Changes in liver function have been reported.

Pediatric Concerns: None reported via milk. Suitable alternatives are erythromycin and azithromycin.

Drug Interactions: Increased anticoagulant effect when used with warfarin, dicoumarol, phenindione, and anisindione. Dirithromycin may increase the level of astemizole significantly. May increase digoxin levels. Acute and dangerous toxicity have resulted following use of dirithromycin with ergot alkaloids. Increased serum levels of pimozide and triazolam may result.

Relative Infant Dose:

Adult Dose: 500 mg daily.

Alternatives: Azithromycin, erythromycin

T ½	= 20-50 hours	M/P	=
PHL	=	PB	= 15-30%
Tmax	= 3.9 hours	Oral	= 6-14%
MW	=	pKa	=
Vd	= 11		

References:
1. Pharmaceutical Manufacturer Prescribing Information.

DISOPYRAMIDE   L2

Trade: Norpace, Napamide
Other Trades: Rythmodan, Norpace, Isomide
Uses: Antiarrhythmic
AAP: Maternal Medication Usually Compatible with Breastfeeding

Disopyramide is used for treating cardiac arrhythmias similar to quinidine and procainamide. Small levels are secreted into milk. Following a maternal dose of 450 mg every 8 hours for two weeks, the milk/plasma ratio was approximately 1.06 for disopyramide and 6.24 for its active metabolite.[1] Although no disopyramide was measurable in the infant's plasma, the milk levels were 2.6-4.4 mg/L (disopyramide), and 9.6-12.3 mg/L (metabolite). Infant urine collected over an 8-hour period contained 3.3 mg/L of disopyramide. Such levels are probably too small to affect an infant. No side effects were reported.

In another study, in a woman receiving 100 mg five times daily, the maternal serum level was 10.3 μmol/L and the breast milk level was 4.0 μmol/L, giving a milk/serum ratio of 0.4.[2] From these levels, an infant ingesting 1 liter of milk would receive only 1.5 mg per day. Lowest milk levels are at 6-8 hours post-dose.

Pregnancy Risk Category: C

Lactation Risk Category: L2

Adult Concerns: Dry mouth, constipation, edema, hypotension, nausea, vomiting, diarrhea.

Pediatric Concerns: None reported.

Drug Interactions: Increased side effects with drugs such as phenytoin, phenobarbital, rifampin. Increased effects/toxicity with rifamycin. Increased plasma levels of digoxin.

Relative Infant Dose: 3.4%

Adult Dose: 150 mg every 6 hours

Alternatives:

T ½	= 8.3-11.65 hours	M/P	= 0.4-1.06
PHL	=	PB	= 50%
Tmax	= 2.3 hours	Oral	= 60-83%
MW	= 339	pKa	= 8.4
Vd	= 0.6-1.3		

References:
1. MacKintosh D, Buchanan N. Excretion of disopyramide in human breast milk. Br J Clin Pharmacol 1985; 19 (6):856-857.
2. Ellsworth AJ, Horn JR, Raisys VA, Miyagawa LA, Bell JL. Disopyramide and N-monodesalkyl disopyramide in serum and breast milk. DICP 1989; 23 (1):56-57.

DISULFIRAM   L5

Trade: Antabuse
Other Trades:
Uses: Inhibitor of alcohol metabolism
AAP: Not reviewed

Disulfiram is an old product that is occasionally used to prevent alcohol consumption in chronic alcoholics.[1,2] Disulfiram inhibits the enzyme, aldehyde dehydrogenase, (ADH) which is one of two enzymes responsible for the metabolism of alcohol. Patients receiving disulfiram, and who ingest alcohol, become extremely nauseated due to elevated plasma levels of acetaldehyde. This also results in flushing, thirst, palpitations, chest pain, vertigo, and hypotension. All sources of alcohol should be avoided including mouthwash, cough syrups, and after-shave. There are no data on the transfer of disulfiram into human milk, but due to its small MW, it likely penetrates milk to some degree. Because it produces an irreversible inhibition of aldehyde dehydrogenase, any absorbed via milk could potentially produce long-lasting inhibition of the infants' ADH. With the ingestion of any alcohol containing product, the infant could become seriously ill. Further, because the enzyme is permanently inhibited, the individual will be susceptible to alcohol toxicity for up to 2 weeks following discontinuing of the medication. Because so many products contain small amounts of alcohol (cough syrups, etc.), the use of this product in breastfeeding mothers is extremely risky and probably does not justify continued breastfeeding unless the mother is warned and compliant.

Pregnancy Risk Category: C

Lactation Risk Category: L5

Adult Concerns: Symptoms primarily occur following ingestion of alcohol, and include: ectopic heartbeats, tachycardia, chest pain, angina, palpitations, hypertension, headache, severe nausea and vomiting, leg and muscle cramps, dyspnea and shortness of breath.

Pediatric Concerns: None reported via milk, but with ingestion of alcohol could produce profound symptoms in infant.

Drug Interactions: Severe reactions may occur with any product containing alcohol. Concomitant therapy with amitriptyline or metronidazole has resulted in a confusional and psychotic mental state. When used with anisindione or dicumarol, an increased hypoprothrombinemic effect has been documented. Use with bacampicillin has resulted in an disulfiram-type reaction. Significantly increased plasma levels of chlordiazepoxide and diazepam, phenytoin and fosphenytoin when coadministered with disulfiram. An increased half-life and plasma level of desipramine.

Relative Infant Dose:

Adult Dose: 250 mg daily

Alternatives:

T ½	=	M/P	=
PHL	=	PB	= 96%
Tmax	= 1-2 hours	Oral	= 80-90%
MW	= 296	pKa	=
Vd	=		

References:
1.   Pharmaceutical Manufacturer Prescribing Information. 2010.
2.   McEvoy GE. (ed): AFHS Drug Information. New York, NY: 2009.

DOCOSANOL   L1

Trade: Abreva
Other Trades: Healip
Uses: Antiviral
AAP: Not reviewed

Docosanol is used to treat oral-facial herpes simplex only, it should not be used in the eyes or on the genitalia. It inhibits lipid-enveloped viruses from entering the cell by fusion between the plasma membrane and the viral envelope.[1] There have been no studies on docosanol in breastmilk, however it is not orally absorbed and therefore probably poses little threat to a nursing infant.

Pregnancy Risk Category:

Lactation Risk Category: L1

Adult Concerns: Adverse effects include headache, rash, and increased redness.

Pediatric Concerns: No data are available but it would be orally unabsorbable in an infant.

Drug Interactions:

Relative Infant Dose:

Adult Dose: Apply topically 5 times daily to lesions until healed

Alternatives:

T ½	=		M/P	=
PHL	=		PB	–
Tmax	=		Oral	= 0%
MW	= 327		pKa	=
Vd	=			

References:
1.   Pharmaceutical Manufacturer Prescribing Information. 2008.

DOCUSATE   L2

Trade: Colace, Docusate, Softgels, Dialose, Surfak

Other Trades: Albert Docusate, Colax-C, Coloxyl, Rectalad, Waxsol, Audinorm, Diocotyl-medo

Uses: Laxative, stool softener

AAP: Not reviewed

Docusate is a detergent commonly used as a stool softener. The degree of oral absorption is poor, but some is known to be absorbed and re-secreted in the bile. Although some drug is absorbed by mother via her GI tract, transfer into breastmilk is unknown but probably minimal. Watch for loose stools in infant. It is not likely this would be overly detrimental to a breastfed infant.

Pregnancy Risk Category: C

Lactation Risk Category: L2

Adult Concerns: Nausea, diarrhea.

Pediatric Concerns: None reported. Observe for loose stools.

Drug Interactions: Decreased effect of Coumadin with high doses of docusate. Increased toxicity with mineral oil, phenolphthalein.

Relative Infant Dose:

Adult Dose: 50-200 mg daily.

Alternatives:

T ½	=	M/P	=
PHL	=	PB	=
Tmax	=	Oral	= Poor
MW	= 444	pKa	=
Vd	=		

References:
1.   Pharmaceutical Manufacturer Prescribing Information, 2003.

DOLASETRON MESYLATE | L3

Trade: Anzemet
Other Trades:
Uses: Antinauseant and antiemetic
AAP: Not reviewed

Dolasetron and its active metabolite, hydrodolasetron, are selective serotonin 5-HT3 receptor antagonists, primarily in the chemoreceptor trigger zone responsible for control of nausea and vomiting. It is believed that chemotherapeutic agents release serotonin in the gastrointestinal tract that then activates the 5-HT3 receptors on the vagus nerve that initiates the vomiting reflex. This product is used prior to treatment cancer chemotherapeutic agents, or prior to surgery and general anesthesia.[1]

No data are available on its transfer to milk. The maximum concentration in maternal plasma would be 556 ng/mL, which is quite low. At this plasma level, an infant would likely receive far less than a milligram daily. It has been safely used in children 2 years of age at doses of 1.2 mg/kg.

Pregnancy Risk Category: B

Lactation Risk Category: L3

Adult Concerns: Changes in ECG intervals (PR, QT, JT prolongation, and QRS widening) have been reported but are dose related. Use cautiously in patients with hypokalemia or hypomagnesemia, patients on diuretics, or patients on other antiarrhythmics. Side effects include: headache, fatigue, diarrhea, bradycardia.

Pediatric Concerns: None reported via milk.

Drug Interactions: Drug-drug interactions are few, but include rifampin, and cimetidine.

Relative Infant Dose:

Adult Dose: 100 mg orally.

Alternatives:

T ½	= 8.1 hours	M/P	=
PHL	=	PB	= 77%
Tmax	~ 1 hour	Oral	= 75%
MW	= 438	pKa	=
Vd	= 5.8		

References:
1.   Pharmaceutical Manufacturer Prescribing Information.

DOMPERIDONE   L1

Trade:
Other Trades: Motilium, Motilidone
Uses: Gastrokinetic agent, galactagogue
AAP: Maternal Medication Usually Compatible with
    Breastfeeding

Domperidone (Motilium) is a peripheral dopamine antagonist (similar to Reglan) generally used for controlling nausea and vomiting, dyspepsia, and gastric reflux. It blocks peripheral dopamine receptors in the GI wall and in the CRTZ (nausea center) in the brain stem and is currently used in Canada as an antiemetic.[1] Unlike metoclopramide (Reglan), it does not enter the brain compartment and it has few CNS effects such as depression.

It is also known to produce significant increases in prolactin levels and has proven useful as a galactagogue. Serum prolactin levels have been found to increase from 8.1 ng/mL to 124.1 ng/mL in non-lactating women after one 20 mg dose.[2] Concentrations of domperidone reported in milk vary according to dose. But following a dose of 10 mg three times daily, the average concentration in milk was only 2.6 µg/L.[3]

In a study by da Silva, 16 mothers with premature infants and low milk production (mean= 112.8 mL/d in domperidone group; 48.2 mL/d in placebo group) were randomly chosen to receive placebo (n= 9) or domperidone (10 mg TID) (n= 7) for 7 days.[4] Milk volume increased from 112.8 to 162.2 mL/d in the domperidone group and 48.2 to 56.1 mL/d in the placebo group. Prolactin levels increased from 12.9 to 119.3 µg/L in the domperidone group and 15.6 to 18.1 µg/L in the placebo group. On day 5, the mean domperidone concentration was 6.6 ng/mL in plasma and 1.2 µg/L in breastmilk of the treated group (n= 6). No adverse effects were reported in infants or mothers.

In a new study just released, a group of 6 breastfeeding women were placed in a double blind randomized crossover trial to compare doses of domperidone.[5] In this trial, mothers were studied in a run-in phase (no drug treatment), 30 mg, or 60 mg domperidone daily doses (10 or 20 mg every 8 hours). Milk volume created per hour, and plasma prolactin levels were monitored. With milk production, two mothers did not respond to domperidone treatment. Four other mothers showed a significant increase from 8.7 gm/hour in the run-in phase to 23.6 gm/h for the 30 mg/d dose, to 29.4 gm/h for the 60 mg dose. While plasma prolactin levels were increased by domperidone treatment, there was no significant difference between levels at 30 mg and 60 mg doses. Median domperidone concentrations in milk were 0.28 µg/L and 0.49 µg/L for the 30 mg and 60 mg doses respectively. The mean Relative Infant Dose was 0.012% at 30 mg daily and 0.009% at the 60 mg/day dose. The authors suggest that, milk production increased at both doses and there was a small trend for a dose-response.

Forty-six mothers who had delivered infants at <31 weeks' gestation, and who experienced lactation failure, were randomly assigned to receive domperidone or placebo for 14 days.[6] Protein, energy, fat, carbohydrate, sodium, calcium, and phosphate levels in breast milk were measured on days 0, 4, 7, and 14, serum prolactin levels were measured on days 0, 4, and 14, and total milk production was recorded daily. By day 14, breast milk volumes has increased by 267% in the domperidone-treated group and by 18.5% in the placebo group. Serum prolactin increased by 97% in the domperidone group and by 17% in the placebo group. Mean breast milk protein declined by 9.6% in the domperidone group and increased by 3.6% in the placebo group. There were no changes in caloric content, fat, carbohydrate, sodium, or phosphate content. Significant increases in milk carbohydrate (2.7% vs -2.7%) and calcium (61.8% vs -4.4%) were noted in the domperidone-treated group. No adverse effects were observed in infants or mothers. The authors concluded that domperidone increases the volume of breast milk of preterm mothers experiencing lactation failure, without substantially altering the nutrient composition.

The usual oral dose for controlling GI distress is 10-20 mg three to four times daily although for nausea and vomiting the dose can be higher (up to 40 mg). The galactagogue dose is suggested to be 10-20 mg orally 3-4 times daily. The prior studies clearly suggest that doses of 10-20 mg three to four times daily elevate prolactin levels to levels more than adequate to produce milk. Doses higher than this should be avoided in breastfeeding mothers.

The US FDA has issued a warning on this product stating that it could induce arrhythmias in patients. These claims were derived from data many years old where domperidone was used intravenously as an antiemetic during cancer chemotherapy (20 mg stat followed by 10 mg/kg/24 h).[7] Many of these patients were undergoing extensive chemotherapy, were extremely ill, and hypokalemic to begin with. In addition, intravenous domperidone produces plasma levels many times higher than oral use. Thus far, we do not have any recent published data suggesting that domperidone used orally in breastfeeding mothers is arrhythmogenic, although its use in women who are already arrhythmic is not recommended.

Pregnancy Risk Category: C

Lactation Risk Category: L1

Adult Concerns: Dry mouth, skin rash, itching, headache, thirst, abdominal cramps, diarrhea, drowsiness. Seizures have occurred rarely. Could induce arrhythmias in hypokalemic patients, or patients subject to arrhythmias.

Pediatric Concerns: None reported in breastfed infants. Considered the ideal galactagogue.

Drug Interactions: Cimetidine, famotidine, nizatidine, ranitidine (H-2 blocker) plasma levels may be reduced by domperidone. Prior use of bicarbonate reduces absorption of domperidone.

Relative Infant Dose: 0.01% - 0.04%

Adult Dose: 10-20 mg 3-4 times daily

Alternatives: Metoclopramide

T ½	= 7-14 hours	M/P	= 0.25
PHL	=	PB	= 93%
Tmax	= 30 minutes	Oral	= 13-17%
MW	= 426	pKa	=
Vd	=		

References:

1. Hofmeyr GJ, van Iddekinge B. Domperidone and lactation. Lancet 1983; 1 (8325):647.
2. Brouwers JR, Assies J, Wiersinga WM, Huizing G, Tytgat GN. Plasma prolactin levels after acute and subchronic oral administration of domperidone and of metoclopramide: a cross-over study in healthy volunteers. Clin Endocrinol (Oxf) 1980; 12 (5):435-440.
3. Hofmeyr GJ, van Iddekinge B, Blott JA. Domperidone: secretion in breast milk and effect on puerperal prolactin levels. Br J Obstet Gynaecol 1985; 92 (2):141-144.
4. da Silva OP, Knoppert DC, Angelini MM, Forret PA. Effect of domperidone on milk production in mothers of premature newborns: a randomized, double-blind, placebo-controlled trial. CMAJ 2001; 164 (1):17-21.
5. Wan E W-X, Davey K, Page-Sharp M, Hartmann PE, Simmer K, Ilett KF. Dose-effect study of domperidone as a galactagogue in preterm mothers with insufficient milk supply, and its transfer into milk. British Journal of Clinical Pharmacology 2008 2008; 66 (2):283-9.6
6. Campbell-Yeo ML, Allen AC, Joseph KS, Ledwidge JM, Caddell K, Allen VM, Dooley KC. Effect of domperidone on the composition of preterm human breast milk. Pediatrics. 2010 Jan;125 (1):e107-14. Epub 2009 Dec 14.
7. Osborne RJ, Slevin ML, Hunter RW, Hamer J. Cardiac arrhythmias during cytotoxic chemotherapy: role of domperidone. Hum Toxicol 1985 Nov; 4 (6):617-26.

DONEPEZIL L3

Trade: Aricept
Other Trades:
Uses: Cholinesterase inhibitor in Alzheimer's disease
AAP: Not reviewed

Donepezil is a reversible inhibitor of acetylcholinesterase which ultimately increases synaptic levels of acetylcholine by inhibition of its breakdown. It is believed to improve mild to moderate dementia and cognitive function in patients with Alzheimer's disease. While this agent is only 'cleared' for treatment of patients with Alzheimer's disease, numerous other applications probably exist. No data are available on its transfer to human milk. Due to its long half-life, and its ability to affect cholinergic function in all mammals, some caution is recommended in breastfeeding women until data is available.

Pregnancy Risk Category: C

Lactation Risk Category: L3

Adult Concerns: May impede bladder emptying. Seizures, and convulsions have been reported. Increase gastric acid secretion. Patients at risk would be those subject to ulcers, using concurrent NSAIDs. Diarrhea, nausea, vomiting, muscle cramps, fatigue and loss of appetite have been reported. Should be used cautiously in patients with pulmonary diseases such as asthma.

Pediatric Concerns: None reported via milk.

Drug Interactions: Use cautiously with NSAIDs. Interfere with activity of anticholinergics such as atropine.

Relative Infant Dose:

Adult Dose: 5-10 mg daily.

Alternatives:

T ½	− 70 hours	M/P	=
PHL	=	PB	= 96%
Tmax	= 3-4 hours	Oral	= 100%
MW	= 415	pKa	=
Vd	− 12		

References:
1. Pharmaceutical Manufacturer Prescribing Information, 2003.

DOPAMINE-DOBUTAMINE   L2

Trade: Intropin
Other Trades: Revimine--Dobutrex
Uses: Adrenergic stimulants
AAP: Not reviewed

Dopamine and dobutamine are catecholamine pressor agents used in shock and severe hypotension.[1] They are rapidly destroyed in the GI tract and are only used IV. It is not known if they transfer into human milk, but the half-life is so short they would not last long. Dopamine, while in the plasma, significantly (>60%) inhibits prolactin secretion and would likely inhibit lactation while being used.

Pregnancy Risk Category: C

Lactation Risk Category: L2

Adult Concerns: Stimulation, agitation, tachycardia.

Pediatric Concerns: None reported. No GI absorption.

Drug Interactions: Increased effect when used with monoamine oxidase inhibitors MAO, alpha and beta adrenergic blockers, general anesthetics, and phenytoin.

Relative Infant Dose:

Adult Dose: 5-50 µg/kg/min IV

Alternatives:

T ½	= 2 minutes	M/P	=
PHL	= 7 minutes	PB	=
Tmax	= 5 minutes	Oral	= Poor
MW	= 153	pKa	=
Vd	=		

References:
1.   McEvoy GE. (ed):AFHS Drug Information. New York, NY: 2009.

DORIPENEM   L3

Trade: Doribax
Other Trades:
Uses: Antibiotic
AAP: Not reviewed

Doripenem is a new carbapenem antibiotic similar in structure to the penecillins. Doripenem is resistant to most beta-lactamases including penicillinases and cephalosporinases produced by gram-positive and gram-negative bacteria. It is cleared for treatment of various resistant bacteria. No data are available on its use in breastfeeding mothers, but levels in milk will likely be low, and the oral bioavailability in infants low as well. Observe for diarrhea and changes in gut flora.

Pregnancy Risk Category: B

Lactation Risk Category: L3

Adult Concerns: Diarrhea, headache.

Pediatric Concerns: None reported but observer for changes in gut flora, diarrhea.

Drug Interactions: Doripenem reduces the plasma levels of valproic acid. Probenecid reduces clearance of doripenem.

Relative Infant Dose:

Adult Dose: 500 mg every 8 hours IV

Alternatives: Piperacillin/tazobactam and imipenem, levofloxacin

T ½	= 1 hour	M/P	=
PHL	=	PB	= 8.1%
Tmax	= 1 hour	Oral	= Poor
MW	= 438	pKa	=
Vd	= 0.24		

References:
1. Pharmaceutical manufacturers prescribing information, 2010.

DORNASE   L2

Trade: Pulmozyme
Other Trades:
Uses: Mucolytic enzyme
AAP: Not reviewed

Dornase is a mucolytic enzyme used in the treatment of cystic fibrosis. It is a large MW peptide (260 amino acids, 37,000 daltons) that selectively digests DNA.[1] It is poorly absorbed by the pulmonary tissues. Serum levels are undetectable. Even if it were to reach the milk, it would not be orally bioavailable in the infant.

Pregnancy Risk Category: B

Lactation Risk Category: L2

Adult Concerns: In adults: hoarseness, sore throat, facial edema.

Pediatric Concerns: None reported.

Drug Interactions:

Relative Infant Dose:

Adult Dose: 2.5 mg via inhalation

Alternatives:

T ½	=	M/P	=
PHL	=	PB	=
Tmax	=	Oral	= None
MW	=	pKa	=
Vd	=		

References:
1. Pharmaceutical Manufacturer Prescribing Information. 1995.

DORZOLAMIDE   L3

Trade: Trusopt
Other Trades:
Uses: Carbonic anhydrase inhibitor for open-angle glaucoma
AAP: Not reviewed

Dorzolamide is a carbonic anhydrase inhibitor used to treat interocular hypertension, open-angle glaucoma, etc. It is a unique formulation that exerts its effects directly in the eye. No data are available on its transfer into human milk. However, this product would be only slightly absorbed by the mother. This agent is stored for long periods in the red blood cell, although plasma levels are exceedingly low.[1] Milk levels will probably be low to undetectable.

Pregnancy Risk Category: C

Lactation Risk Category: L3

Adult Concerns: Bitter or unusual taste, allergic reactions, contact dermatitis in the throat, vertigo, dizziness, This is a sulfonamide, so do not use in sulfa-allergic patients.

Pediatric Concerns: No breastfeeding studies thus far. Risks are probably minimal.

Drug Interactions: Do not use with topiramate.

Relative Infant Dose:

Adult Dose: One drop in eye three times daily.

Alternatives:

T ½	=	M/P	=
PHL	=	PB	= 33%
Tmax	= 2 hours	Oral	=
MW	= 361	pKa	=
Vd	=		

References:
1. Pharmaceutical Manufacturer Prescribing Information. 2005.

DOTHIEPIN
L2

Trade: Prothiaden
Other Trades: Dothep
Uses: Tricyclic antidepressant
AAP: Drugs whose effect on nursing infants is unknown but may be of concern

This is a new analog of the older tricyclic antidepressant amitriptyline. Dothiepin appears in breastmilk in a concentration of 11 µg/L following a dose of 75 mg/day while the maternal plasma level was 33 µg/L.[1] If the infant ingests 150 mL/kg/day of milk, the total daily dose of dothiepin ingested by the infant in this case would be approximately 1.7 µg/kg/day, approximately 1/650th of the adult dose. In an outcome study of 15 mother/infant pairs 3-5 years postpartum, no overall cognitive differences were noted in dothiepin treated mothers/infants, suggesting that this medication did not alter cognitive abilities in breastfed infants.[2]

In a study by Ilett[3], dothiepin concentrations in the milk of 8 mothers was determined (dose ranged from 25-225 mg/day). The mean post-feeding milk/plasma ratio was 1.59 and the mean post-feeding dothiepin concentration in milk ranged from 20-475 µg/L (median=52 µg/L). Mean daily infant doses on a weight basis (in dothiepin equivalents) was 4.4% for dothiepin and its metabolites. Blood levels in all 5 infants were low (>10 µg/L). No untoward effects were noted in any of the 8 infants following chronic maternal use.

Pregnancy Risk Category: D

Lactation Risk Category: L2

Adult Concerns: Anticholinergic side effects, such as drying of secretions, dilated pupil, sedation, dizziness, drowsiness, urinary retention.

Pediatric Concerns: None reported in numerous studies.

Drug Interactions: Phenobarbital may reduce effect of dothiepin. Dothiepin blocks the hypotensive effect of guanethidine. May increase toxicity of dothiepin when used with clonidine. Dangerous when used with MAO inhibitors, other CNS depressants. May increase anticoagulant effect of coumadin, warfarin. SSRIs (Prozac, Zoloft, etc) should not be used with or soon after dothiepin or other TCAs due to serotonergic crisis.

Relative Infant Dose: 0.2% - 2.2%

Adult Dose: 75-300 mg/day

Alternatives:

T ½	= 14.4-23.9 hours	M/P	= 0.3
PHL	=	PB	=
Tmax	= 3 hours	Oral	= 30%
MW	= 295	pKa	=
Vd	= 20-92		

References:
1. Rees JA. Serum and breast milk concentrations of dothcipin. Practitioner 1976; 217:686.
2. Buist A, Janson H. Effect of exposure to dothiepin and northiaden in breast milk on child development. Br J Psychiatry 1995; 167 (3):370-373.
3. Ilett KF, Lebedevs TH, Wojnar-Horton RE, Yapp P, Roberts MJ, Dusci LJ, Hackett LP. The excretion of dothiepin and its primary metabolites in breast milk. Br J Clin Pharmacol 1992; 33 (6):635-639.

DOXAZOSIN MESYLATE   L4

Trade: Cardura
Other Trades: Carduran
Uses: Antiadrenergic antihypertensive
AAP: Not reviewed

Studies in lactating animals indicate milk levels that are 20 times that of maternal plasma levels, suggesting a concentrating mechanism in breastmilk.[1] It is not known if this occurs in human milk. Extreme caution recommended.

Pregnancy Risk Category: C

Lactation Risk Category: L4

Adult Concerns: Low blood pressure, malaise, and edema.

Pediatric Concerns: None reported, but extreme caution is recommended.

Drug Interactions: Decreased antihypertensive effect with NSAIDs. Increased effect with other diuretics, antihypertensive medications particularly beta blockers.

Relative Infant Dose:

Adult Dose: 2-4 mg daily.

Alternatives: Propranolol, Metoprolol

T ½	= 9-22 hours	M/P	= 20
PHL	=	PB	= 98%
Tmax	= 2 hours	Oral	= 62-69%
MW	= 451	pKa	=
Vd	=		

References:
1. Pharmaceutical Manufacturer Prescribing Information. 2010.

DOXEPIN   L5

Trade: Adapin, Sinequan
Other Trades: Triadapin, Novo-Doxepin, Deptran
Uses: Antidepressant
AAP: Drugs whose effect on nursing infants is unknown but may be of concern

Small but significant amounts are secreted in milk. Two published reports indicate absorption by infant varying from significant to modest. One report of dangerous sedation and respiratory arrest in one infant.[1] Doxepin has an active metabolite with long half-life (37 hours). In one study, peak milk doxepin levels were 27 and 29 µg/L four-five hours after a dose of 25 mg, and the level of metabolite was 9 µg/L.[2] In this infant, the metabolite was believed responsible for the severe depression. Although the milk concentrations were low, the infant's plasma level of metabolite was similar to the maternal plasma level. It is apparent that the active metabolite of doxepin can concentrate in nursing infants and may be hazardous.

In another case report of a mother ingesting 35 mg/d, the infant was readmitted to the neonatal intensive care unit at day 9 postpartum because of poor sucking and swallowing, muscle hypotonia, vomiting, drowsiness, and jaundice.[3] Doxepin levels in the infant were found in small amounts. Breastmilk levels were reported at 60-100 µg/L with a milk/plasma ratio of 1.0-1.7. Upon withdrawal of breastfeeding the infant rapidly became lively and active. We have numerous other antidepressants that are much safer and are preferred in breastfeeding mothers.

Pregnancy Risk Category: C

Lactation Risk Category: L5

Adult Concerns: Respiratory arrest, sedation, dry mouth.

Pediatric Concerns: One report of dangerous sedation and respiratory arrest in an infant. Poor sucking and swallowing, muscle hypotonia, vomiting, drowsiness and jaundice reported in a second infant.

Drug Interactions: Decreased effect of Doxepin when use with bretylium, guanethidine, clonidine, levodopa, ascorbic acid and cholestyramine. Increased toxicity when used with carbamazepine, amphetamines, thyroid preparations. Increased toxicity with fluoxetine, thyroid preparations, MAO inhibitors, albuterol, CNS depressants such as benzodiazepines and opiate analgesics, anticholinergics, cimetidine.

Relative Infant Dose: 1.2% - 3%

Adult Dose: 75-300 mg daily.

Alternatives: Sertraline, Paroxetine

T ½	= 8-24 hours	M/P	= 1.08-1.66
PHL	=	PB	= 80-85%
Tmax	= 2 hours	Oral	= Complete
MW	= 279	pKa	= 8.0
Vd	= 9-33		

References:
1. Matheson I, Pande H, Alertsen AR. Respiratory depression caused by N-desmethyldoxepin in breast milk. Lancet 1985; 2 (8464):1124.
2. Kemp J, Ilett KF, Booth J, Hackett LP. Excretion of doxepin and N-desmethyldoxepin in human milk. Br J Clin Pharmacol 1985; 20 (5):497-499.
3. Frey OR, Scheidt P, von Brenndorff AI. Adverse effects in a newborn infant breast-fed by a mother treated with doxepin. Ann Pharmacother 1999; 33 (6):690-693.

DOXEPIN CREAM   L4

Trade: Zonalon cream
Other Trades: Zonalon
Uses: Antipruritic cream
AAP: Drugs whose effect on nursing infants is unknown but may be of concern

Doxepin cream is an antihistamine-like cream used to treat severe itching. In one study of 19 women, plasma levels ranged from zero to 47 µg/L following transcutaneous absorption.[1] Target therapeutic ranges in doxepin antidepressant therapy is 30-150 ng/mL. Small but significant amounts are secreted in milk. Two published reports indicate absorption by infant varying from significant to modest but only in mother consuming oral doses.[2,3] See doxepin.

Pregnancy Risk Category: B

Lactation Risk Category: L4

Adult Concerns: Respiratory arrest, sedation, dry mouth.

Pediatric Concerns: Sedation, respiratory arrest have been reported following oral administration.

Drug Interactions: Decreased effect of Doxepin when use with bretylium, guanethidine, clonidine, levodopa, ascorbic acid and cholestyramine. Increased toxicity when used with carbamazepine, amphetamines, thyroid preparations. Increased toxicity with fluoxetine, thyroid preparations, MAO inhibitors, albuterol, CNS depressants such as benzodiazepines and opiate analgesics, anticholinergics, cimetidine.

Relative Infant Dose:

Adult Dose: 150-300 mg daily.

Alternatives:

T ½	= 28-52 hours	M/P	= 1.08, 1.66
PHL	=	PB	= 80-85%
Tmax	= 2 hours	Oral	= Complete
MW	= 279	pKa	=
Vd	=		

References:
1. Drug Facts and Comparisons 1995 ed. ed. St. Louis: 1995.
2. Kemp J, Ilett KF, Booth J, Hackett LP. Excretion of doxepin and N-desmethyldoxepin in human milk. Br J Clin Pharmacol 1985; 20 (5):497-499.
3. Matheson I, Pande H, Alertsen AR. Respiratory depression caused by N-desmethyldoxepin in breast milk. Lancet 1985; 2 (8464):1124.

DOXERCALCIFEROL   L3

Trade: Hectorol
Other Trades:
Uses: Vitamin D analog
AAP: Not reviewed

Doxercalciferol is a vitamin D analog that following metabolic activation becomes 1,25-dihydroxyvitamin D2. Doxercalciferol is indicated for the treatment of hyperparathyroidism associated with patients with chronic renal failure undergoing hemodialysis. Excessive doses may lead to dangerously elevated plasma calcium levels. No data are available on its transfer into human milk. It is not likely that normal doses would lead to clinically relevant levels in human milk, particularly since vitamin D transfers only minimally into human milk. While plasma levels of vitamin D are normally quite low in human milk (<20 IU/L), at least one study now suggests that supplementing a mother with extremely high levels of vitamin D2 can significantly elevate milk levels, and subsequently lead to hypercalcemia in a breastfed infant.[1] Some caution with these highly active forms of vitamin D is recommended.

Pregnancy Risk Category: B

Lactation Risk Category: L3

Adult Concerns: Adverse events include hypercalcemia, hyperphosphatemia, and oversuppression of parathyroid hormone. Additional side effects include edema, headache, malaise, dizziness, pruritus, and constipation.

Pediatric Concerns: None reported via milk, but caution is recommended in breastfeeding mothers.

Drug Interactions: Do not use with magnesium antacids, as hypermagnesemia has been reported.

Relative Infant Dose:

Adult Dose: 4 µg three times weekly.

Alternatives: Vitamin D

T ½	= 32-37 hours	M/P	=
PHL	=	PB	= 99%
Tmax	= 8 hours	Oral	= Complete
MW	–	pKa	=
Vd	=		

References:
1. Greer FR, Hollis BW, Napoli JL. High concentrations of vitamin D2 in human milk associated with pharmacologic doses of vitamin D2. J Pediatr 1984; 105 (1):61-64.

DOXORUBICIN   L5

Trade: Adriamycin
Other Trades:
Uses: Anticancer drug
AAP: Cytotoxic drug that may interfere with cellular metabolism of the nursing infant

Doxorubicin and its metabolite are secreted in significant amounts in breastmilk. Following a dose of 70 mg/meter sq., peak milk levels of doxorubicin and metabolite occurred at 24 hours and were 128 and 111 µg/L respectively.[1] The highest milk/plasma ratio was 4.43 at 24 hours.

A classic anthracycline, doxorubicin is one of a number in this family. Doxorubicin when administered reaches a rapid C_{max} and disappears from the plasma compartment with a 3-exponential decay characterized by 3 differing half-lives, 3-5 minutes, 1-2 hours, and 24-36 hours.[2] A fourth curve has been identified with a half-life of 110 hours which accounts for approximately 30% of the total AUC. The last two elimination curves are probably due to this products high volume of distribution. In essence, it is distributed and stored in sites remote from the plasma compartment and leaks into the plasma over many days thereafter. However, the peak in milk occurred at 24 hours. Because this product is detectable in plasma (and milk) for long periods, a waiting period of approximately 7-10 days is recommended.

Pregnancy Risk Category: D

Lactation Risk Category: L5

Adult Concerns: Bone marrow suppression, cardiac toxicity, arrhythmias, nausea, vomiting, stomatitis, liver toxicity.

Pediatric Concerns: This product could be extremely toxic to a breastfeeding infant and is not recommended.

Drug Interactions: Doxorubicin may decrease digoxin plasma levels and renal excretion. Allopurinol and verapamil may increase cytotoxicity of doxorubicin.

Relative Infant Dose:

Adult Dose: 20-75 mg/sq. meter IV

Alternatives:

T ½	= 24-36 hours	M/P	= 4.43
PHL	=	PB	= 85%
Tmax	= 24 hours	Oral	= Poor
MW	= 544	pKa	=
Vd	= 25		

References:
1. Egan PC, Costanza ME, Dodion P, Egorin MJ, Bachur NR. Doxorubicin and cisplatin excretion into human milk. Cancer Treat Rep 1985; 69 (12):1387-1389.
2. Grochow LB, Ames MM. A clinician's guide to chemotherapy pharmacokinetics and pharamcodynamics. 1st ed. Baltimore, MD: Williams & Wilkins; 1998.
3. American Academy of Pediatrics, Committee on Drugs. Transfer of drugs and other chemicals into human milk. Pediatrics 2001; 108 (3):776-89.

DOXYCYCLINE   L3

Trade: Doxychel, Vibramycin, Periostat
Other Trades: Apo-Doxy, Doxycin, Vibra-Tabs, Doryx, Doxylin, Vibra-Tabs, Doxylar
Uses: Tetracycline antibiotic
AAP: Not reviewed

Doxycycline is a long half-life tetracycline antibiotic. In a study of 15 subjects, the average doxycycline level in milk was 0.77 mg/L following a 200 mg oral dose.[1] One oral dose of 100 mg was administered 24 hours later, and the breastmilk levels were 0.380 mg/L.

Following a dose of 100 mg daily in 10 mothers, doxycycline levels in milk on day 2 averaged 0.82 mg/L (range 0.37-1.24 mg/L) at 3 hours after the dose, and 0.46 mg/L (range 0.3-0.91 mg/L) 24 hours after the dose.[2] The relative infant dose in an infant would be < 6% of the maternal weight-adjusted dosage.

Following a single dose of 100 mg in 3 women or 200 mg in 3 women, peak milk levels occurred between 2 and 4 hours following the dose. The average peak milk levels were 0.96 mg/L (100 mg dose) or 1.8 mg/L (200 mg dose). After repeated dosing for 5 days, milk levels averaged 3.6 mg/L at doses of 100 mg twice daily.[3]

In a study of 13 women receiving 100-200 mg doses of doxycycline, peak levels in milk were 0.6 mg/L (n=3 @100 mg dose) and 1.1 mg/L (n=11 @ 200 mg dose).[4]

Tetracyclines administered orally to infants are known to bind in teeth, producing discoloration and inhibit bone growth, although doxycycline and oxytetracycline stain teeth the least severe. Although most tetracyclines secreted into milk are generally bound to calcium, thus inhibiting their absorption, doxycycline is the least bound (20%), and may be better absorbed in a breastfeeding infant than the older tetracyclines. While the absolute absorption of older tetracyclines may be dramatically reduced by calcium salts, the newer doxycycline and minocycline analogs bind less and their overall absorption while slowed, may be significantly higher than earlier versions. Prolonged use (months) could potentially alter GI flora, and induce dental staining although doxycycline produces the least dental staining. Short term use (three-four weeks) is not contraindicated. No harmful effects have yet been reported in breastfeeding infants but prolonged use is not advised. For prolonged administration such as for exposure to anthrax, check the CDC web site as they have published specific dosing guidelines.

Pregnancy Risk Category: D

Lactation Risk Category: L3
                                 L4 if used chronically

Adult Concerns: Nausea, vomiting, diarrhea, photosensitivity. Doxycycline decreased prothrombin activity.

Pediatric Concerns: None reported, but prolonged exposure may lead to dental staining, and decreased bone growth.

Drug Interactions: Reduced absorption with aluminum, calcium, or magnesium salts, iron or bismuth subsalicylate. Reduced doxycycline half-life when used with barbiturates, phenytoin, and carbamazepine. Concurrent use with methoxyflurane has resulted in fatal renal toxicity. May render oral contraceptives less effective.

Relative Infant Dose: 4.2% - 13.3%

Adult Dose: 100 mg daily

Alternatives:

T ½	= 15-25 hours	M/P	= 0.3-0.4
PHL	=	PB	= 90%
Tmax	= 1.5-4 hours	Oral	= 90-100%
MW	= 462	pKa	=
Vd	=		

References:

1. Morganti G, Ceccarelli G, Ciaffi G. [Comparative concentrations of a tetracycline antibiotic in serum and maternal milk]. Antibiotica 1968; 6 (3):216-223.
2. Lutziger H. Konzentrationsbestimmungen und klinisch wirksamkeit von doxycyclin (Vibramycin) in uterus, adnexen und muttermilch. Ther Umsch. 1969;26:476-80.
3   Tokuda G, Yuasa M, Mihara S et al. Clinical study of doxycycline in obstetrical and gynecological fields. Chemotherapy (Tokyo). 1969;17:339-44.
4. Borderon F, Soutoul JH et al. Excretion of antibiotics in human milk. Med Mal Infect. 1975; 5:373-6.

DOXYLAMINE   L3

Trade: Unisom Nighttime
Other Trades: Dozile, Mersyndol, Panalgesic, Syndol
Uses: Antihistamine, sedative.
AAP: Not reviewed

Doxylamine is an antihistamine similar in structure to Benadryl. Because it has strong sedative properties, it is primarily used in over-the-counter sleep aids. Like other such antihistamines, it should be used only cautiously in infants and particularly in premature or term neonates due to paradoxical effects such as CNS stimulation or even sedation.[1,2]

Levels in breastmilk are not known but caution is recommended particularly in infants with apnea or other respiratory syndromes.

Pregnancy Risk Category: A

Lactation Risk Category: L3

Adult Concerns: Sedation, paradoxical CNS stimulation, agitation.

Pediatric Concerns: None reported via milk, but observe for sedation and paradoxical CNS stimulation. Do not use in infants with apnea.

Drug Interactions: Increased CNS sedation when added to other antihistamines and CNS sedative-hypnotics.

Relative Infant Dose:

Adult Dose: 25-50 mg orally for insomnia

Alternatives: Diphenhydramine

T ½	= 10.1 hours	M/P	=
PHL	=	PB	=
Tmax	= 2.4 hours	Oral	= Complete
MW	= 270	pKa	= 9.2
Vd	= 2.7		

References:

1. Friedman H, Greenblatt DJ, Scavone JM, Burstein ES, Ochs HR, Harmatz JS, Shader RI. Clearance of the antihistamine doxylamine. Reduced in elderly men but not in elderly women. Clin Pharmacokinet 1989; 16 (5):312-316.
2. Friedman H, Greenblatt DJ. The pharmacokinetics of doxylamine: use of automated gas chromatography with nitrogen-phosphorus detection. J Clin Pharmacol 1985; 25 (6):448-451.

DROPERIDOL   L3

Trade: Inapsine
Other Trades: Droleptan
Uses: Tranquilizer, antiemetic
AAP: Not reviewed

Droperidol is a powerful tranquilizer. It is sometimes used as preanesthetic medication in labor and delivery because of fewer respiratory effects in neonates. In pediatric patients 2-12 years of age, it is sometimes used as an antiemetic (20-75 µg/kg IM, IV).[1,2] It apparently crosses the placenta only very slowly. There are no data available on secretion into breastmilk. Due to the potent sedative properties of this medication, caution is urged.

Pregnancy Risk Category: C

Lactation Risk Category: L3

Adult Concerns: Sedation, hypotension, dizziness, chills, shivering, unusual ocular movements.

Pediatric Concerns: None reported via milk, but observe for sedation, hypotension.

Drug Interactions: Can cause peripheral vasodilation and hypotension when used with certain anesthesia medications. Can potentiate effects of other CNS depressants and antidepressants such as barbiturates.

Relative Infant Dose:

Adult Dose: 2.5-10 mg injection (IM)

Alternatives: Haloperidol

T ½	= 2.2 hours	M/P	=
PHL	=	PB	= High
Tmax	= 10-30 minutes (IM)	Oral	=
MW	= 379	pKa	=
Vd	= 2.0		

References:
1.   McEvoy GE. (ed): AFHS Drug Information. 1992.
2.   Pharmaceutical Manufacturer Prescribing Information. 1995.

DROSPIRENONE   L3

Trade: Yasmin
Other Trades:
Uses: Synthetic progestin
AAP: Not reviewed

Drospirenone in combination with ethinyl estradiol (30 micrograms) is marketed at Yasmin. In a study of 6 women who received 3 mg drospirenone with ethinyl estradiol (Yasmin), the time to peak in plasma and milk was 2.5 and 2.8 hour respectively.[1]

Average concentrations at C_{max} were 30.8 and 13.5 ng/mL of serum or milk respectively. The mean milk/serum ratios increased from 0.16 to 0.57 at 2 hour following dosing and decreased to 0.16 at 24 hours although the AUC (0-48 h) ratio was only 0.23. The mean drospirenone concentration in breast milk over the 24 hour period was 3.7 ng/mL. Using this average, the relative infant dose would be approximately 1.2% of the maternal dose. The authors estimate in this group of 6 women, the average transfer of drospirenone was 635 ng/day. Although not clear in this study, the lower estimates could be due to lower milk production in this study.

This combination oral contraceptive also contains ethinyl estradiol. Estrogens are believed to strongly inhibit milk production in some women. Some caution is recommended.

Pregnancy Risk Category: X

Lactation Risk Category: L3

Adult Concerns: Reduced milk production in some mothers has been reported with combination birth control pills containing estrogens. Thrombophlebitis, pulmonary embolism, cerebral hemorrhage are possible but remote. Nausea, vomiting, abdominal cramping, spotting have been reported.

Pediatric Concerns: In the one study, transfer of drospirenone to milk was low. No untoward effects were noted in the infants.

Drug Interactions: Metabolism of ethinyl estradiol is increased by rifampin. St. John's Wort is believed to increase the metabolism of numerous drugs by induction of hepatic enzymes (Cy-450) and the p-glycoprotein transporter and may reduce the effectiveness of oral contraceptives as well as numerous other medications. Antibiotics have been reported to reduce effectiveness of oral contraceptives. Atorvastin may increase plasma levels significantly.

Relative Infant Dose: 1.4%

Adult Dose: 3 mg drosprenone/day

Alternatives: Micronor

T ½	= 31 hours	M/P	= 0.23
PHL	=	PB	= 97%
Tmax	= 1.7 hours	Oral	= 76%
MW	= 366	pKa	=
Vd	= 5		

References:
1.   Blode H, Foidart JM, Heithecker R. Transfer of drospirenone to breast milk after a single oral administration of 3 mg drospirenone + 30 µg ethinylestradiol to healthy lactating women. Eur J Contracept Reprod Health Care 2001; 6 (3):167-171.

DROTRECOGIN ALFA   L3

Trade: Xigris
Other Trades:
Uses: Activated Protein C
AAP: Not reviewed

Drotrecogin reduces the risk of mortality in severe sepsis. Protein C inhibits factors Va and VIIIa, thus interrupting the coagulation cascade.[1] There have been no studies performed to measure the amount of drotrecogin transferred into the breastmilk, however, the high MW indicates that the transfer to the milk compartment is improbable or nil.

Pregnancy Risk Category: C

Lactation Risk Category: L3

Adult Concerns: Adverse reactions include bruising and bleeding.

Pediatric Concerns: No data are available, but due to its high MW it is unlikely to enter milk.

Drug Interactions: Concurrent use of antiplatelets, heparins, NSAIDs, or warfarin can increase the risk of bleeding.

Relative Infant Dose:

Adult Dose: 24 μg/kg/hour for a total of 96 hours

Alternatives:

T ½	= 1.6	M/P	=
PHL	=	PB	=
Tmax	=	Oral	= Nil
MW	= 55,000	pKa	=
Vd	=		

References:
1. Pharmaceutical Manufacturer Prescribing Information. 2006.

DULOXETINE   L3

Trade: Cymbalta, Ariclaim, Duceten, Xeristar, Yentreve
Other Trades:
Uses: Antidepressant
AAP: Not reviewed

Duloxetine is a selective serotonin and norepinephrine reuptake inhibitor (SNRI) that is indicated for depression and for patient with neuropathic pain.[1] The primary role of SNRIs is as an alternative in patients with major depressive disorder who have responded poorly to other agents (e.g., tricyclics or SSRIs).

The transfer of duloxetine into breastmilk was studied in 6 women who were at least 12 weeks postpartum and taking 40 mg twice daily for 3.5 days.[2] Paired blood and breastmilk samples were taken at 0, 1,2,3,6,9, and 12 hours postdose. The milk/plasma ratio was reported to be about 0.267. The daily dose of duloxetine was estimated to be 7 µg/day (range=4-15 µg/day). According to the manufacturer, the weight-adjusted infant dose would be approximately 0.141% of the maternal dose. Further, even this is unlikely absorbed, as duloxetine is unstable under acid conditions of the infants stomach.

In a more recent study in a mother consuming duloxetine (60 mg daily), levels in milk were 31 µg/L and 64 µg/L at trough and peak respectively.[3] The milk/plasma ratios were 1.29 (trough) and 1.21 (peak). These authors suggest an RID of 0.14%.

Pregnancy Risk Category: C

Lactation Risk Category: L3

Adult Concerns: Common side effects include: nausea, dry mouth, constipation, diarrhea, vomiting, decreased appetite, fatigue, dizziness, somnolence, tremor, sweating, blurred vision, insomnia, erectile dysfunction, and others. Warnings of hepatic injury have been posted by the FDA and include abdominal pain, hepatomegaly, elevation of transaminase levels with our without jaundice.

Pediatric Concerns: Milk levels in one study (6 mothers) are low and the relative infant dose is low. Subsequent study suggests about same RID = 0.14%.

Drug Interactions: Numerous drug-drug interactions have been reported. Duloxetine is metabolized by CYP1A2 and CYP2D6. Drugs which inhibit duloxetine metabolism and may increase plasma levels in patients include: cimetidine, ciprofloxacin, enoxacin, and other fluoroquinolones, fluvoxamine. Consult a good drug reference for other interactions.

Relative Infant Dose: 0.1%

Adult Dose: 40-60 mg/day

Alternatives: Venlafaxine, sertraline, paroxetine

T ½	= 12 hours	M/P	= 0.267-1.29
PHL	=	PB	= >90%
Tmax	= 6 hours	Oral	= >70%
MW	= 333	pKa	=
Vd	= 23.4		

References:
1. Pharmaceutical manufacturers prescribing information.2005.
2. Lobo ED, Loghin C, Knadler MP et al. Pharmacokinetics of duloxetine in breast milk and plasma of healthy postpartum women. Clin Pharmacokinet. 2008;47:103-109.
3. Briggs GG, Ambrose PJ, Ilett KF, Hackett LP, Nageotte MP, Padilla G. Use of duloxetine in pregnancy and lactation. Ann Pharmacother. Nov 2009;43 (11):1898-1902.

DYPHYLLINE   L3

Trade: Dilor, Lufyllin, Dyphylline
Other Trades: Broncho-Grippol, Silbephylline, Noradran
Uses: Anti-asthmatic drug
AAP: Maternal Medication Usually Compatible with Breastfeeding

Dyphylline is a methylxanthine, bronchodilator similar to theophylline. It is apparently secreted into milk in small quantities. Following a 5 mg/kg dose IM, the milk/plasma ratio was 2.08. Using the kinetics provided, the average milk level at 2 hours would have been approximately 14.1 mg/L.[1] No reported untoward effects. Observe infant for irritability, insomnia, and elevated heart rate.

Pregnancy Risk Category: C

Lactation Risk Category: L3

Adult Concerns: Irritability, insomnia, tachycardia, arrhythmias, GI distress, headache, seizures, hyperglycemia.

Pediatric Concerns: None reported via milk, but observe for irritability, insomnia, tachycardia.

Drug Interactions: Probenecid significantly increases half-life of dyphylline and increases plasma levels.

Relative Infant Dose: 42.3%

Adult Dose: 15 mg/kg QID

Alternatives: Theophylline

T ½	= 3-12.8 hours	M/P	= 2.08
PHL	=	PB	= 56%
Tmax	= 1-2 hours (oral)	Oral	= Complete
MW	= 254	pKa	=
Vd	= 0.6-1.1		

References:
1. Jarboe CH, Cook LN, Malesic I, Fleischaker J. Dyphylline elimination kinetics in lactating women: blood to milk transfer. J Clin Pharmacol 1981; 21 (10):405-410.

ECHINACEA   L3

Trade: Echinacea angustifolia, Echinacea purpurea, American Cone Flower, Black Eyed Susan, Snakeroot

Other Trades: Antifect

Uses: Herbal immunostimulant

AAP: Not reviewed

Echinacea is a popular herbal remedy in the central US and has been traditionally used topically to stimulate wound healing and internally to stimulate the immune system. The plant contains a complex mixture of compounds and, thus far, no single component appears responsible for its immunostimulant properties. A number of in vitro and animal studies have documented the activation of immunologic properties although most of these are via intraperitoneal injections, not orally. The activity of orally administered extracts is unknown. Echinacea extracts appear to stimulate phagocytosis of macrophages, increase cellular respiration, and increase the mobility of phagocytic leukocytes.[1] Extracts of E. Purpurea are highly effective in stimulating macrophages (activation) to engulf tumor cells, to produce tumor necrosis factor, interleukin-1, and interferon beta. One study suggests a radioprotective effect (antioxidant) of Echinacea. Another study in humans suggests that while single doses may stimulate the immune system, repeated daily doses may actually suppress the immune response.[2] Thus far, little is known about the toxicity of this plant although its use has been widespread for many years. Apparently, purified Echinacea extract is relatively non-toxic even at high doses.[3,4]

No data are available on its transfer into human milk or its effect on lactation. It should not be used for more than 8 weeks.[5]

Pregnancy Risk Category:

Lactation Risk Category: L3

Adult Concerns: None reported.

Pediatric Concerns: None reported via milk.

Drug Interactions:

Relative Infant Dose:

Adult Dose:

Alternatives:

References:
1. Steinmuller C, Roesler J, Grottrup E, Franke G, Wagner H, Lohmann-Matthes ML. Polysaccharides isolated from plant cell cultures of Echinacea purpurea enhance the resistance of immunosuppressed mice against systemic infections with Candida albicans and Listeria monocytogenes. Int J Immunopharmacol 1993; 15 (5):605-614.
2. Coeugniet EG, Elek E. Immunomodulation with Viscum album and Echinacea purpurea extracts. Onkologie 1987; 10 (3 Suppl):27-33.
3. Review of Natural Products Facts and Comparisons, St Louis, MO 1996.
4. Bissett NG. In: Herbal Drugs and Phytopharmaceuticals. Medpharm Scientific Publishers, CRC Press, Boca Raton, 1994.
5. The Complete German Commission E Monographs. Ed. M. Blumenthal Amer Botanical Council 1998.

ECULIZUMAB   L3

Trade: Soliris
Other Trades:
Uses: Monoclonal Antibody
AAP: Not reviewed

Eculizumab is a large monoclonal antibody used in the treatment of paroxysmal nocturnal hemoglobinuria to reduce hemolysis, reducing the need for RBC transfusions. It is a monoclonal antibody with high affinity to complement protein C5. It is extremely unlikely that this antibody would be transported into human milk, and due to its size, it would be largely unable to penetrate the milk compartment after the first week postpartum. Oral bioavailability would be nil.

Pregnancy Risk Category: C

Lactation Risk Category: L3

Adult Concerns: Headache, nasopharyngitis, back pain, nausea and fatigue.

Pediatric Concerns: None reported via milk.

Drug Interactions:

Relative Infant Dose:

Adult Dose: Variable

Alternatives:

T ½	= 272 hours	M/P	=
PHL	=	PB	=
Tmax	=	Oral	= Nil
MW	= Large	pKa	=
Vd	= 7.7		

References:
1.   Pharmaceutical manufacturers prescribing information.2008.

EDROPHONIUM   L3

Trade: Enlon, Reversol
Other Trades: Tensilon
Uses: Cholinergic Agonist
AAP: Not reviewed

Edrophonium is used to diagnose myasthenia gravis, to differentiate cholinergic crises from myasthenia crises, and to reverse neuromuscular blockers. It inhibits acetylcholinesterase and thus prevents the metabolism of acetylcholine. This product is only used for acute episodes or for diagnosis, as its effects last only briefly (10 minutes) before it is rapidly redistributed to peripheral tissues. It also has a unique structure that would largely preclude its entry into human milk. A brief waiting period of a few hours would reduce any possible risk from this medication in breastfed infants.

Pregnancy Risk Category: C

Lactation Risk Category: L3 with brief withholding period

Adult Concerns: Adverse effects include arrhythmias, dizziness, headache, nausea, weakness, and bronchospasm.

Pediatric Concerns: Can be used in infants at a dose of 0.5 to 1 mg intramuscularly, and in children at a dose of 1 mg if under 34 kg, or 5 mg if over 34 kg. Unlikely to enter milk, or be orally absorbed.

Drug Interactions:

Relative Infant Dose:

Adult Dose: 10 mg IM, or 2 mg IV

Alternatives:

T ½	= 1.2-2.4 hours	M/P	=
PHL	=	PB	=
Tmax	=	Oral	= Nil
MW	= 166	pKa	=
Vd	= 1.1		

References:

EFALIZUMAB   L3

Trade: Raptiva
Other Trades:
Uses: Monoclonal antibody
AAP: Not reviewed

Efalizumab is an immunosuppressant used to treat moderate to severe plaque psoriasis. It binds to CD11a on surface of leukocytes, thus blocking multiple T cell mediated responses involved in the pathogencsis of psoriasis plaques.[1] No data are available on the transfer of efalizumab into human milk. Because this antibody is quite large (150 kilodaltons), its size alone would prohibit its transfer into human milk in clinically relevant amounts.

Pregnancy Risk Category: C

Lactation Risk Category: L3

Adult Concerns: Adverse effects include headache, chills, nausea, lymphocytosis, and leukocytosis.

Pediatric Concerns: No data available.

Drug Interactions: Other immunosuppressants may increase risk of infection.

Relative Infant Dose:

Adult Dose: 1 mg/kg SQ weekly

Alternatives:

T ½	=	M/P	=
PHL	=	PB	=
Tmax	=	Oral	= Nil
MW	= 150,000	pKa	=
Vd	=		

References:
1. Pharmaceutical Manufacturer Prescribing Information. 1997

EFLORNITHINE HCL   L3

Trade: Vaniqa
Other Trades:
Uses: Hair growth retardant
AAP: Not reviewed

Eflornithine HCl is used topically to remove unwanted facial hair in women. It is also available intravenously as an antiprotozoal agent for the treatment of sleeping sickness, although but it is not approved for this use. Eflornithine HCl is a suicide inhibitor of ornithine decarboxylase, the rate limiting enzyme in the biosynthesis of major polyamines in nucleated cells. The inhibition of this enzyme leads to a decreased rate of hair growth.[1] No data is available on the transfer of eflornithine, however, when used topically, this medication is less than 1% absorbed and produces steady state plasma levels of only 5-10 ng/mL, far too low to product clinically relevant milk levels. A risk-benefit assessment of this product does not necessarily suggest the benefits are worth the risk for a breastfed infant, even if the risks are quite low.

Pregnancy Risk Category: C

Lactation Risk Category: L3

Adult Concerns: Adverse effects include acne, pseudofolliculitis barbae, stinging skin, headache, itching, and tingling skin.

Pediatric Concerns: No data are available.

Drug Interactions: No data available.

Relative Infant Dose:

Adult Dose:

Alternatives:

T ½	= 8 hours	M/P	=
PHL	–	PB	=
Tmax	=	Oral	=
MW	= 218	pKa	=
Vd	=		

References:
1. Pharmaceutical Manufacturer Prescribing Information. 2004.

ELETRIPTAN   L2

Trade: Relpax
Other Trades:
Uses: Anti-migraine
AAP: Not reviewed

Eletriptan is a selective 5-hyroxytryptamine receptor agonist specifically use to treat migraine attacks. The bioavailability of eletriptan is greater than sumatriptan (Imitrex) and is faster acting.

The manufacturer reports that in one study of 8 women given a single dose of 80 mg eletriptan, the mean total amount of eletriptan in breast milk over 24 hours in this group was approximately 0.02% of the administered dose.[1] The milk/plasma ratio was 0.25 but there was great variability. The resulting eletriptan concentration-time profile in milk was similar to that seen in the plasma over 24 hours, with very low concentrations of drug (mean 1.7 ng/mL) still present in the milk 18-24 hours post dose. It is not likely the clinical dose delivered above would harm a breastfed infant.

Pregnancy Risk Category: C

Lactation Risk Category: L2

Adult Concerns: Nausea, asthenia, somnolence, dizziness, dry mouth, paresthesias, headache and abdominal cramps have been reported.

Pediatric Concerns: None reported via milk in one study.

Drug Interactions: Increased plasma levels of eletriptan could occur if given concomitantly with cyclosporine, erythromycin, amiodarone, amprenavir, aprepitant, clarithromycin, delavirdine, diltiazem, etc. Enhanced vasospastic reactions when given with ergot alkaloids such as dihydroergotamine, ergotamine, or methysergide.

Relative Infant Dose: 0.02%

Adult Dose: 20-40 mg initially for headache. One repeat dose after 2 hour if needed.

Alternatives: Sumatriptan

T ½	= 4 hours	M/P	= 0.25
PHL	=	PB	= 85%
Tmax	= 2 hours	Oral	= 50%
MW	= 463	pKa	=
Vd	= 1.97		

References:
1.   Pharmaceutical manufacturers presecribing information, 2003.

ENALAPRIL MALEATE   L2

Trade: Vasotec
Other Trades: Amprace, Renitec, Innovace
Uses: Antihypertensive, ACE inhibitor
AAP: Maternal Medication Usually Compatible with Breastfeeding

Enalapril maleate is an ACE inhibitor used as an antihypertensive. Upon absorption, it is rapidly metabolized by the adult liver to enalaprilat, the biologically active metabolite. In one study of 5 lactating mothers who received a single 20 mg dose, the mean maximum milk concentration of enalapril and enalaprilat was only 1.74 µg/L and 1.72 µg/L respectively.[1] The author suggests that an infant consuming 850 mL of milk daily would ingest less than 2 µg of enalaprilat daily. The milk/plasma ratios for enalapril and enalaprilat averaged 0.013 and 0.025 respectively. However, this was only a single dose study, and the levels transferred into milk at steady state may be slightly higher.

In a study by Rush of a patient receiving 10 mg/day, the total amount of enalapril and enalaprilat measured in milk during the 24 hour period was 81.9 ng and 36.1 ng respectively or 1.44 µg/L and 0.63 µg/L of milk respectively.[2] Some caution is recommended in using ACE inhibitors in mothers with premature infants due to possible renal toxicity.

Pregnancy Risk Category: C in first trimester
                                D in second and third trimesters

Lactation Risk Category: L2

Adult Concerns: Hypotension, bradycardia, headache, fatigue, diarrhea, rash, cough.

Pediatric Concerns: None reported via milk, but observe for hypotension.

Drug Interactions: Bioavailability of ACEIs may be decreased when used with antacids. Capsaicin may exacerbate coughing associated with ACE inhibitor treatment. Pharmacologic effects of ACE inhibitors may be increased. Increased plasma levels of digoxin may result. Increased serum lithium levels may result when used with ACE inhibitors.

Relative Infant Dose: 0.17%

Adult Dose: 10-40 mg daily.

Alternatives: Captopril, Benazepril

T ½	= 35 hours (metabolite)	M/P	=
PHL	=	PB	= 60%
Tmax	= 0.5-1.5 hours	Oral	= 60%
MW	= 492	pKa	=
Vd	=		

References:
1. Redman CW, Kelly JG, Cooper WD. The excretion of enalapril and enalaprilat in human breast milk. Eur J Clin Pharmacol 1990; 38 (1):99.
2. Rush JE, Snyder BA, Barrish A. et.al. Comment. Clin Nephrol 1991; 35:234.

ENCAINIDE   L3

Trade: Enkaid
Other Trades:
Uses: Antiarrhythmic agent
AAP: Not reviewed

Encainide is a local anesthetic-type antiarrhythmic agent. It was voluntarily removed from the market in 1999 but is available on a limited basis for certain patients with life-threatening arrhythmias. The plasma kinetics are highly variable depending on the metabolic capabilities of the maternal liver. The oral bioavailability is extremely variable and varies from 25-65% in extensive metabolizers to 80-90% in poor metabolizers. Half-lives are variable as well according to the metabolic capacity of the individual's liver.[1]

However, encainide and its 3 active metabolites are excreted into human milk. In one patient receiving 50 mg four times daily, milk concentrations of encainide and o-desmethyl encainide were 200-400 µg/L and 100-200 µg/L respectively.[2] These concentrations are similar to the maternal serum levels.

Pregnancy Risk Category: B

Lactation Risk Category: L3

Adult Concerns: Arrhythmias, chest pain, congestive heart failure, abdominal pain.

Pediatric Concerns: None reported, but extreme caution is recommended.

Drug Interactions: Use caution when encainide is used with any other drug that effects cardiac conduction. Cimetidine increases plasma concentrations of encainide.

Relative Infant Dose: 2.1%

Adult Dose: 50-200 mg daily in 3-4 divided doses.

Alternatives:

T ½	= 2-36 hours	M/P	= 1
PHL	=	PB	= 70.5-78%
Tmax	= 1.7 hours	Oral	= Variable
MW	= 352	pKa	=
Vd	= 2.7-4.3		

References:
1. Pharmaceutical Manufacturer Prescribing Information. 1992.
2. Briggs GG, Freeman RK, Yaffee SJ. Drugs in Pregnancy and Lactation. Philadelphia: Lippincott Williams & Wilkins, 1998.

ENOXACIN   L3

Trade: Penetrex
Other Trades: Enoxin, Comprecin
Uses: Antibiotic
AAP: Not reviewed

Enoxacin is a typical fluoroquinolone antibiotic similar to ciprofloxacin, norfloxacin, and others. No data are available on the transfer of enoxacin into human milk. See ofloxacin and norfloxacin as alternatives.

Pregnancy Risk Category: C

Lactation Risk Category: L3

Adult Concerns: Nausea, vomiting, diarrhea, abdominal cramps, GI bleeding, increased intracranial pressure, tremor, restlessness, other CNS reactions. Photosensitivity.

Pediatric Concerns: None reported via milk, but caution urged. See norfloxacin.

Drug Interactions: Decreased absorption with antacids. Quinolones cause increased levels of caffeine, warfarin, cyclosporine, theophylline. Cimetidine, probenecid, azlocillin increase ciprofloxacin levels. Increased risk of seizures when used with foscarnet.

Relative Infant Dose:

Adult Dose: 200-400 mg BID

Alternatives: Ofloxacin, norfloxacin, ciprofloxacin

T ½	= 3-6 hours	M/P	=
PHL	=	PB	= 40%
Tmax	=	Oral	= 90%
MW	=	pKa	=
Vd	= 2.5		

References:

ENOXAPARIN L3

Trade: Lovenox, Low MW Heparin
Other Trades: Clexane
Uses: Anticoagulant
AAP: Not reviewed

Enoxaparin is a low MW fraction of heparin used clinically as an anticoagulant. In a study of 12 women receiving 20-40 mg of enoxaparin daily for up to 5 days postpartum for venous pathology (n= 4) or caesarian section (n= 8), no change in anti-Xa activity was noted in the breastfed infants.[1] Because it is a peptide fragment of heparin, its MW is large (2000-8000 daltons). The size alone would largely preclude its entry into human milk at levels clinically relevant. Due to minimal oral bioavailability, any present in milk would not be orally absorbed by the infant. A similar compound, dalteparin, has been studied and milk levels are extremely low as well. See dalteparin.

Pregnancy Risk Category: B

Lactation Risk Category:　L3

Adult Concerns:　Anticoagulant effects in adults when administered subcutaneously.

Pediatric Concerns:　None reported via milk. MW is too large to produce clinically relevant milk levels.

Drug Interactions:　Anticoagulants and platelet inhibitors. NSAIDS may increase risk of bleeding.

Relative Infant Dose:

Adult Dose:　30 mg BID

Alternatives:　Dalteparin

T ½	= 4.5 hours	M/P	=
PHL	=	PB	=
Tmax	= 3-5 hours	Oral	= None
MW	= 8000	pKa	=
Vd	= 0.1		

References:

1. Guillonneau M, de Crepy A, Aufrant C, Hurtaud-Roux MF, Jacqz-Aigrain E. L'allaitement est possible en cas de traitement maternel par l'enoxaparien. Arch Pediatr 1996; 3 (5):513-514.

EPHEDRINE   L4

Trade:　Vatronol Nose Drops

Other Trades:　Amsec, Adalixin, Bethal, Anestan, Anodesyn, Cam

Uses:　Adrenergic stimulant, anti-asthmatic.

AAP:　Not reviewed

Ephedrine is a mild stimulant that belongs to the adrenergic family and functions similar to the amphetamines. Small amounts of d-isoephedrine, a close congener of ephedrine, is believed to be secreted into milk although no data is available on ephedrine itself.[1] This product is commonly used to support blood pressure of parturients during delivery. On an acute basis, it is not likely to harm a breastfeeding infant. However, it should not be used regularly by breastfeeding mothers.

Pregnancy Risk Category:　C

Lactation Risk Category:　L4

Adult Concerns: Anorexia, tachycardia, arrhythmias, agitation, insomnia, hyperstimulation.

Pediatric Concerns: None reported, but observe for anorexia, irritability, crying, disturbed sleeping patterns, excitement.

Drug Interactions: May increase toxicity and cardiac stimulation when used with theophylline. MAO inhibitors or atropine may increase blood pressure.

Relative Infant Dose:

Adult Dose: 25-50 mg injection

Alternatives:

T ½	= 3-5 hours	M/P	=
PHL	=	PB	=
Tmax	= 15-60 minutes	Oral	= 85%
MW	= 165	pKa	= 9.6
Vd	=		

References:
1. Mortimer EA, Jr. Drug toxicity from breast milk? Pediatrics 1977; 60 (5):780-781.

EPINEPHRINE   L1

Trade: Adrenalin, Sus-Phren, Medihaler, Primatene
Other Trades: Bronkaid, Epi-pen, Adrenutol, Eppy, Simplene
Uses: Stimulant
AAP: Not reviewed

Epinephrine is a powerful adrenergic stimulant. Although likely to be secreted in milk, it is rapidly destroyed in the GI tract.[1] It is unlikely that any would be absorbed by the infant unless in the early neonatal period or premature.

Pregnancy Risk Category: C

Lactation Risk Category: L1

Adult Concerns: Nervousness, tremors, agitation, tachycardia.

Pediatric Concerns: None reported, but observe for brief stimulation.

Drug Interactions: Increase cardiac irritability when used with halogenated inhaled anesthetics, alpha blocking agents. Do not use with MAO inhibitors.

Relative Infant Dose:

Adult Dose: 0.1-0.25 mg injection (IV)

Alternatives:

T ½	= 1 hour (inhalation)	M/P	=
PHL	=	PB	=
Tmax	= <1-10 minutes	Oral	= Poor
MW	= 183	pKa	=
Vd	=		

References:
1. Wilson J. Drugs in Breast Milk. New York: ADIS Press 1981.

EPLERENONE   L3

Trade: Inspra
Other Trades:
Uses: Aldosterone receptor antagonist
AAP: Not reviewed

Eplerenone blocks the binding of aldosterone by competitively inhibiting the aldosterone receptor and regulating blood pressure as a result. It is similar in structure to spironolactone, but has a lower affinity to steroid receptor, and thus has fewer adverse reactions.[1] It is indicated to improve survival of stable patients with left ventricular systolic dysfunction (ejection fraction <=40%) and clinical evidence of congestive heart failure after an acute myocardial infarction.

Pregnancy Risk Category: B

Lactation Risk Category: L3

Adult Concerns: Adverse reactions include angina, heart attack, diarrhea, hyperkalemia, headache, and coughing.   Observe for hyperkalemia.

Pediatric Concerns: No data are available.

Drug Interactions: Eplerenone is metabolized via the CYP3A4 pathway, and thus inhibitors of CYP3A4 will increase plasma levels. Concurrent use of potassium sparing diuretics or ACE inhibitors increase the chance of hyperkalemia when taken with eplerenone. No clinically significant drug-drug pharmacokinetic interactions were observed when eplerenone was administered with cisapride, cyclosporine, digoxin, glyburide, midazolam, oral contraceptives (norethindrone/ethinyl estradiol), simvastatin, or warfarin. St. John's Wort (a CYP3A4 inducer) caused a small (about 30%) decrease in eplerenone AUC.

Relative Infant Dose:

Adult Dose: 25-100 mg QD

Alternatives:

T ½	=	M/P	=
PHL	=	PB	= 50%
Tmax	= 1.5 hours	Oral	= 69%
MW	= 414	pKa	=
Vd	= 1.28		

References:
1. Pharmaceutical Manufacturer Prescribing Information. 2005.

EPOETIN ALFA   L3

Trade: Epogen
Other Trades:
Uses: Stimulates red blood cell production
AAP: Not reviewed

Epoetin alfa is a glycoprotein which stimulates red blood cell production. Structurally similar to the natural erythropoietin, it consists of 165 amino acids manufactured by recombinant DNA technology. It has a MW of 30,400 daltons. Large MW proteins in general are poorly transferred into human milk. Further, due to its protein nature, it would not likely be absorbed orally to any degree by the infant.

Pregnancy Risk Category: C

Lactation Risk Category: L3

Adult Concerns: Headache, hypertension, arthralgias, nausea, edema, vomiting and chest pain have been reported in adults.

Pediatric Concerns: None reported via milk.

Drug Interactions: None.

Relative Infant Dose:

Adult Dose: 50-100 Units three times weekly

Alternatives:

T ½	= 4-13 hours	M/P	=
PHL	= 4-13 hours	PB	=
Tmax	= 5-24 hours	Oral	= Nil
MW	= 30,400	pKa	=
Vd	=		

References:
1.   PM2001. Pharmaceutical Manufacturer Prescribing Information, 2003.

EPOPROSTENOL   L3

Trade: Flolan
Other Trades:
Uses: Vasodilator, platelet function inhibitor
AAP: Not reviewed

Epoprostenol (Prostacyclin; PGX; PGI-2) is a naturally occurring prostaglandin that is a potent inhibitor of platelet aggregation and a vasodilator. It is commonly used to treat primary pulmonary hypertension. It is rapidly metabolized in plasma to 6-keto-prostaglandin F1-alpha, which is biologically inactive, and has a half-life of only 3-5 minutes.[1] Prostaglandins are known to be transferred into human milk, but they are believed derived from mammary tissue and synthesis by the cellular components of breastmilk.[2] With the extraordinarily short half-life of this product, it is unlikely any would penetrate into milk, be retained for very long, or be stable in the infant's gut. Oral absorption by the infant is unlikely.

Pregnancy Risk Category: B

Lactation Risk Category: L3

Adult Concerns: Flushing, headache, nausea, vomiting, hypotension, anxiety, chest pain, dizziness, bradycardia, abdominal pain.

Pediatric Concerns: None reported, unlikely to be absorbed.

Drug Interactions: May decrease clearance of digoxin. Decreased oral clearance of furosemide.

Relative Infant Dose:

Adult Dose: 2 ng/kg per minute

Alternatives:

T ½	= 6 minutes	M/P	=
PHL	=	PB	=
Tmax	=	Oral	= Nil
MW	= 374	pKa	=
Vd	= 357 mL		

References:
1. Pharmaceutical Manufacturer Prescribing Information, 2010.
2. Friedman Z. Prostaglandins in breast milk. Endocrinol Exp 1986; 20 (2-3):285-291.

EPROSARTAN   L3

Trade: Teveten
Other Trades:
Uses: Antihypertensive, angiotensin receptor blocker
AAP: Not reviewed

Eprosartan is a angiotensin receptor blocker used in hypertension. No data are available on its use in breastfeeding mothers. Its use in mothers breastfeeding premature infants, or even infants less than 4 months should be avoided due to possible renal toxicity.

Pregnancy Risk Category: C
X during second and third trimester

Lactation Risk Category: L3 after 4 months
L4 early postpartum

Adult Concerns: Headache, dizziness, fatigue, facial edema, cough have been reported.

Pediatric Concerns: None yet via milk, however do not use in breastfeeding mothers with newborn or premature infants.

Drug Interactions: None yet reported.

Relative Infant Dose:

Adult Dose:

Alternatives: Captopril, enalapril, benazepril

T ½	= 20 hours	M/P	=
PHL	=	PB	= 98%
Tmax	= 1-2 hours	Oral	= 13%
MW	= 520	pKa	=
Vd	= 4.4		

References:
1. Pharmaceutical manufacturers prescribing information, 2010.

EPSTEIN-BARR VIRUS   L3

Trade: Mononucleosis, EBV
Other Trades:
Uses: Herpesvirus infection (EBV)
AAP: Not reviewed

The Epstein-Barr virus (EBV) is one of the causes of infectious mononucleosis. EBV belongs to the herpesvirus family. Symptoms include fever, exudative pharyngitis, lymphadenopathy, hepatosplenomegaly, and atypical lymphocytosis. Close personal contact is generally required for transmission and it is not known if EBV is secreted into human milk, although it is likely. Studies by Kusuhara[1] indicate that the seroprevalence of EBV at 12-23 months was the same in bottle-fed and in breastfed infants. This data suggests that breastmilk is not a significant source of early EBV infections.

Pregnancy Risk Category:

Lactation Risk Category: L3

Adult Concerns:

Pediatric Concerns:

Drug Interactions:

Relative Infant Dose:

Adult Dose:

Alternatives:

References:
1. Kusuhara K, Takabayashi A, Ueda K, Hidaka Y, Minamishima I, Take H, Fujioka K, Imai S, Osato T. Breast milk is not a significant source for early Epstein-Barr virus or human herpesvirus 6 infection in infants: a seroepidemiologic study in 2 endemic areas of human T-cell lymphotropic virus type I in Japan. Microbiol Immunol 1997; 41 (4):309-312.

EPTIFIBATIDE   L3

Trade: Integrilin
Other Trades:
Uses: Antiplatelet agent
AAP: Not reviewed

Eptifibatide is used in the treatment of acute coronary syndrome. It works by blocking the platelet glycoprotein IIb/IIIa receptor, and thus inhibits platelet aggregation.[1] It is a small peptide of approximately 831 daltons and is probably poorly absorbed orally if at all. No data are available on the transfer into human milk, however, due to the large MW of eptifibatide, it is unlikely that it would pass into the milk compartment.

Pregnancy Risk Category: B

Lactation Risk Category: L3

Adult Concerns: Adverse reactions include bleeding, hypotension, and thrombocytopenia.

Pediatric Concerns: No data are available. Unlikely to enter milk.

Drug Interactions: Cephalosporins, antiplatelet agents, heparin, aspirin, and warfarin can all increase the risk of bleeding.

Relative Infant Dose:

Adult Dose: 2 µg/kg/minute

Alternatives:

T ½	= 2.5 hours	M/P	=
PHL	=	PB	= 25%
Tmax	=	Oral	= Nil
MW	= 831	pKa	=
Vd	=		

References:
1. Pharmaceutical Manufacturer Prescribing Information. 1998.

ERGONOVINE MALEATE   L3

Trade: Ergotrate, Ergometrine
Other Trades: Syntometrine
Uses: Postpartum uterine bleeding
AAP: Not reviewed

Ergonovine and its close congener, methylergonovine maleate, directly stimulate uterine and vascula smooth muscle contractions. They are primarily used to prevent/treat postpartum hemorrhage. Although pharmacologically similar, many clinicians prefer methylergonovine because it produces less hypertension than ergonovine. In a study of 8 postpartum women receiving 0.125 mg three times daily until day 5 when a 0.25 mg tablet was introduced, measurable ergonovine was only found in 4 of 8 patients and averaged 0.8 µg/L.[1] These authors suggested that use of the drug during breastfeeding would not affect the infant.

In addition, the effect of ergonovine on prolactin levels is controversial. In one study methylergonovine did not alter postpartum maternal prolactin levels[2], while in another study[3] a significant reduction in prolactin production was produced by ergonovine. Ergonovine use in lactating women would presumably suppress lactation, whereas methylergonovine may not.

When used at doses of 0.2 mg up to 3-4 times daily, only small quantities of ergonovine are found in milk. Short-term (1 week) low-dose regimens of these agents do not apparently pose problems in nursing mothers or their infants. Methylergonovine is preferred because it does not inhibit lactation and levels in milk are minimal. The prolonged use of ergot alkaloids should be avoided and can lead to severe gangrenous manifestations.

Pregnancy Risk Category: X

Lactation Risk Category: L3

Adult Concerns: Hypertension, seizures, vomiting, diarrhea, cold extremities.

Pediatric Concerns: None reported, but long term exposure is not recommended. Methyl-ergonovine is commonly recommended early postpartum for breastfeeding mothers to reduce uterine bleeding.

Drug Interactions:

Relative Infant Dose: 1.9%

Adult Dose: 0.2 mg injection (IM) every 2-4 hours

Alternatives: Methylergonovine

T ½	= 0.5-2 hours	M/P	=
PHL	=	PB	=
Tmax	= 30- 180 minutes	Oral	= >60%
MW	= 441	pKa	=
Vd	=		

References:

1. Erkkola R, Kanto J, Allonen H, Kleimola T, Mantyla R. Excretion of methylergometrine (methylergonovine) into the human breast milk. Int J Clin Pharmacol Biopharm 1978; 16 (12):579-580.
2. Del Pozo E, Brun DR, Hinselmann M. Lack of effect of methyl-ergonovine on postpartum lactation. Am J Obstet Gynecol 1975; 123 (8):845-846.
3. Canales ES, Garrido JT, Zarate A, Mason M, Soria J. Effect of ergonovine on prolactin secretion and milk let-down. Obstet Gynecol 1976; 48 (2):228-229.

ERGOTAMINE TARTRATE   L4

Trade: Wigraine, Cafergot, Ergostat, Ergomar, DHE-45
Other Trades: Gynergen, Ergodryl, Migral, Lingraine
Uses: Anti-migraine, inhibits prolactin
AAP: Drugs associated with significant side effects and should be given with caution

Ergotamine is a potent vasoconstrictor generally used in acute phases of migraine headache. It is never used chronically for prophylaxis of migraine. Although early reports suggest ergotamine compounds are secreted in breastmilk[1] and cause symptoms of ergotism (vomiting, and diarrhea) in infants, other authors [2] suggest that the short term use of ergotamine (0.2 mg postpartum) generally presents no problem to a nursing infant. This is likely, due to the fact that less than 5% of ergotamine is orally absorbed in adults. However, excessive dosing and prolonged administration may inhibit prolactin secretion and hence lactation. Although the initial plasma half-life is only 2 hours, ergotamine is stored for long periods in various tissues producing long-lasting effects (terminal half-life= 21 hours). Use during lactation should be strongly discouraged.

Pregnancy Risk Category: X

Lactation Risk Category: L4

Adult Concerns: Ergotism, peripheral artery insufficiency, nausea, vomiting, paresthesia, cold skin temperatures, headache.

Pediatric Concerns: One case of ergotism reported and included symptoms such as vomiting and diarrhea. Long term exposure is contraindicated.

Drug Interactions: Rifamycin and other macrolide antibiotics may enhance ergot toxicity.

Relative Infant Dose:

Adult Dose: 2 mg every 30 minutes

Alternatives: Propranolol, Sumatriptan

T ½	= 21 hours (terminal)	M/P	=
PHL	=	PB	=
Tmax	= 0.5-3 hours	Oral	= <5%
MW	= 581	pKa	=
Vd	=		

References:
1. Fomina PL. Untersuchungen uber den ubergang des aktiven agens des Muttrkorns in die milch stillender Mutter. Arch Gynecol 1934; 157:275.
2. White G, White M. Breastfeeding and drugs in human milk. Vet and Human Tox 1984; 26:supplement 1.

ERTAPENEM   L2

Trade: Invanz
Other Trades:
Uses: Carbapenem antibiotic
AAP: Not reviewed

The manufacturer reports the concentration of ertapenem in breast milk from 5 lactating women with pelvic infections (5 to 14 days postpartum) was measured at random time points daily for 5 consecutive days following the last 1 gm dose of intravenous therapy (3-10 days of therapy). The concentration of ertapenem in breast milk within 24 hours of the last dose of therapy in all 5 women ranged from <0.13 (lower limit of quantitation) to 0.38 mg/L; peak concentrations were not assessed. By day 5 after discontinuation of therapy, the level of ertapenem was undetectable in the breast milk of 4 women and below the lower limit of quantitation (<0.13 µg/mL) in 1 woman.[1]

The above data does not report C_{max} concentrations in milk nor the time samples were collected, so it is virtually worthless for determining infant exposure to the medication during the day and following the administration.

Using the above data and an assumed average weight of 70 kg, the mothers received about 14.28 mg/kg/day. After 24 hours, the infant would ingest about 57 µg/kg/day. The relative infant dose would be 0.4% of the maternal dose at this time. Without good data it is not possible to estimate clinical dose to the infant, but it is likely small and its oral bioavailability is poor. Most all the penicillins and the carbapenems are safe to use in breastfeeding mothers.

Pregnancy Risk Category: B

Lactation Risk Category: L2

Adult Concerns: Diarrhea, infused vein complications, nausea, headache, vaginitis in females, thrombophlebitis, vomiting, fever, abdominal pain. Do not use if penicillin allergic. Seizures, altered mental status.

Pediatric Concerns: None reported via milk. However diarrhea, and perhaps less common pseudomembranous colitis could occur.

Drug Interactions: Increased levels when administered with probenecid.

Relative Infant Dose: 0.1% - 0.4%

Adult Dose: 1 g IV/IM daily.

Alternatives: Imipenem

T ½	= 4 hours	M/P	=
PHL	=	PB	= 95%
Tmax	= 2 hours	Oral	= Poor
MW	− 497	pKa	=
Vd	= 0.11		

References:
1. Pharmaceutical Manufacturer Prescribing Information, 2003.

ERYTHROMYCIN   L2

Trade: E-Mycin, Ery-Tab, Eryc, Ilosone
Other Trades: Erythromide, Novo-Rythro, PCE, Ilotyc,
      EMU-V, Ilosone, EES, Erythrocin, Ceplac, Erycen
Uses: Macrolide antibiotic
AAP: Maternal Medication Usually Compatible with
       Breastfeeding

Erythromycin is an older, narrow-spectrum antibiotic. In one study of patients receiving 400 mg three times daily, milk levels varied from 0.4 to 1.6 mg/L.[1] Doses as high as 2 gm per day produced milk levels of 1.6 to 3.2 mg/L. One case of hypertrophic pyloric stenosis apparently linked to erythromycin administration has been reported.[2] In a study of 2-3 patients who received a single 500 oral dose, milk levels at 4 hours ranged from 0.9 to 1.4 mg/L with a milk/plasma ratio of 0.92.[3] Newer macrolide-like antibiotics (azithromycin) may preclude the use of erythromycin. A recent and large study now suggests a strong positive correlation between the use of erythromycin in breastfeeding mothers and infantile hypertrophic pyloric stenosis in newborns.[4]

Pregnancy Risk Category: B

Lactation Risk Category: L2
                   L3 early postnatally (pyloric stenosis)

Adult Concerns: Abdominal cramping, nausea, vomiting, hepatitis, ototoxicity, and hypersensitivity.

Pediatric Concerns: Pyloric stenosis has been reported associated with the use of erythromycin early postpartum.

Drug Interactions: Erythromycin may decrease clearance of carbamazepine, cyclosporin, triazolam. Erythromycin may decrease theophylline clearance by as much as 60%. May increase terfenadine plasma levels and increase Q/T intervals. May potentiate anticoagulant effect of warfarin.

Relative Infant Dose: 1.4% - 1.7%

Adult Dose: 500-800 mg QID

Alternatives: Azithromycin, clarithromycin

T ½	= 1.5-2 hours	M/P	= 0.92
PHL	=	PB	= 84%
Tmax	= 2-4 hours	Oral	= Variable
MW	= 734	pKa	=
Vd	=		

References:
1. Knowles JA. Drugs in milk. Pediatr Currents 1972; 1:28-32.
2. Stang H. Pyloric stenosis associated with erythromycin ingested through breastmilk. Minn Med 1986; 69 (11):669-70, 682.
3. Matsuda S. Transfer of antibiotics into maternal milk. Biol Res Pregnancy Perinatol 1984; 5 (2):57-60.
4. Sorensen HT, Skriver MV, Pedersen L, Larsen H, Ebbesen F, Schonheyder HC. Risk of infantile hypertrophic pyloric stenosis after maternal postnatal use of macrolides. Scand J Infect Dis 2003; 35 (2):104-106.

ESCITALOPRAM   L2

Trade: Lexapro
Other Trades:
Uses: Antidepressant
AAP: Not reviewed

Escitalopram is a selective serotonin reuptake inhibitor (SSRI) used in the treatment of depression. It is the active S (+)-enantiomer of citalopram (Celexa). While this agent is very specific for the serotonin receptor site, it does apparently have a number of other side effects which may be related to activities at other receptors. Antagonism of muscarinic, histaminergic, and adrenergic receptors has been hypothesized to be associated with various anticholinergic, sedative and cardiovascular side effects.

In a case report of a 32 year old mother taking escitalopram (5 mg/day) while breastfeeding her newborn, the reported milk level was 24.9 ng/mL at one week postpartum. The infant's daily dose was estimated to be 3.74 µg/kg. At 7.5 weeks of age, the mother was taking 10 mg/day and the milk concentration level was 76.1 ng/mL. The infant daily dose was 11.4 µg/kg. There were no adverse events reported in the infant.[1]

In a recent study of eight breastfeeding women taking an average of 10 mg/day, the total relative infant dose of escitalopram and its metabolite was reported to be 5.3% of the mothers dose.[2] The mean M/P ratio (AUC) was 2.2 for escitalopram and 2.2 for demethylescitalopram.

Absolute infant doses were 7.6 µg/kg/day for escitalopram and 3.0 µg/kg/day for demethylescitalopram. The drug and its metabolite were undetectable in most of the infants tested. No adverse events in the infants were reported. Because the absolute infant dose of escitalopram is less than an equivalent antidepressant dose of racemic citalopram (Celexa), it's use is preferred over citalopram in treating depression in lactating women.

Pregnancy Risk Category: C

Lactation Risk Category: L2

Adult Concerns: Adverse events include nausea, sweating, dizziness, insomnia, somnolence, ejaculation disorder, diaphoresis, anorexia, and fatigue.

Pediatric Concerns: Recent data concerning the use of this product in breastfeeding mothers suggests the relative infant dose is low and levels in breastfed infant's plasma are largely undetectable.

Drug Interactions: Increased citalopram levels when used with macrolide antibiotics (erythromycin), cimetidine, and azole antifungals such as fluconazole, itraconazole, ketoconazole, etc. Carbamazepine may reduce plasma levels of citalopram. Serious reactions may occur if escitalopram is administered too soon after MAO use. Beta blocker (metoprolol) levels may increase by 2 fold when admixed with escitalopram. The combined used of escitalopram and sumatriptan (Imitrex) have been reported to produce weakness, hyperreflexia and incoordination. Escitalopram may increase levels of desipramine.

Relative Infant Dose: 5.2% - 7.9%

Adult Dose: 10-40 mg daily

Alternatives: Sertraline, fluoxetine

T ½	= 27-32 hours	M/P	= 2.2
PHL	=	PB	= 56%
Tmax	= 5 hours	Oral	= 80%
MW	= 414	pKa	=
Vd	= 12		

References:

1. Castberg I, Spigset O. Excretion of Escitalopram in Breast Milk. J Clin Psychopharm 2006; 26 (5):536-538.
2. Rampono J, Hackett LP, Kristensen JH, Kohan R, Page-Sharp M, Ilett KF. Transfer of escitalopram and its metabolite demethylescitalopram into breastmilk. Br J Clin Pharmacol 2006; 62 (3):316-322.

ESMOLOL
L3

Trade: Brevibloc
Other Trades:
Uses: Beta blocker antiarrhythmic
AAP: Not reviewed

Esmolol is an ultra short-acting beta blocker agent with low lipid solubility. It is of the same family as propranolol. It is primarily used for treatment of supraventricular tachycardia. It is only used IV and has an extremely short half-life. It is almost completely hydrolyzed in 30 minutes.[1,2] No data on breastmilk levels are available.

Pregnancy Risk Category: C

Lactation Risk Category: L3

Adult Concerns: Hypotension, bradycardia, dizziness, somnolence.

Pediatric Concerns: None reported.

Drug Interactions: Beta blockers may decrease the effect of sulfanurias. Increased effect with calcium channel blockers, contraceptives, ciprofloxacin, MAO inhibitors, thyroid hormones, haloperidol, and numerous other medications.

Relative Infant Dose:

Adult Dose: 100 µg/kg/minute

Alternatives: Propranolol, metoprolol

T ½	= 9 minutes	M/P	=
PHL	= 4.5 minutes	PB	= 55%
Tmax	= 15 minutes	Oral	= Poor
MW	= 295	pKa	=
Vd	=		

References:
1. McEvoy GE. (ed);AFHS Drug Information. New York, NY: 2009.
2. Lacy C. Drug information handbook. Lexi Comp Inc. Cleveland, OH, 1996.

ESOMEPRAZOLE   L2

Trade: Nexium
Other Trades:
Uses: Reduces gastric acid secretion
AAP: Not reviewed

Esomeprazole is just the L isomer of omeprazole (Prilosec) and is essentially identical to Prilosec. See omeprazole for breastfeeding recommendations.

Pregnancy Risk Category: C

Lactation Risk Category: L2

Adult Concerns:

Pediatric Concerns:

Drug Interactions:

Relative Infant Dose:

Adult Dose:

Alternatives:

T ½	= 1-1.5 hours	M/P	=
PHL	=	PB	= 97%
Tmax	= 1.5 hours	Oral	= 90%
MW	= 345.4	pKa	=
Vd	= 0.23		

References:
1. Pharmaceutical Manufacturer Prescribing Information, 2008.

ESTAZOLAM   L3

Trade: Prosom
Other Trades:
Uses: Benzodiazepine sedative
AAP: Not reviewed

Estazolam is a benzodiazepine sedative hypnotic that belongs to the Valium family. Estazolam, like other benzodiazepines, is secreted into rodent milk although the levels are unpublished.[1,2] No data are available on human milk levels. It is likely that some is secreted into human milk as well.

Pregnancy Risk Category: X

Lactation Risk Category: L3

Adult Concerns: Sedation.

Pediatric Concerns: None reported via milk, but observe for sedation, apnea.

Drug Interactions: Certain enzyme inducers such as barbiturates may increase the metabolism of estazolam. CNS depressants may increase adverse effects of estazolam. Cimetidine may decrease metabolism of estazolam.

Relative Infant Dose:

Adult Dose: 1-2 mg daily

Alternatives: Lorazepam, Midazolam, Alprazolam

T½	= 10-24 hours	M/P	=
PHL	=	PB	= 93%
Tmax	= 0.5-3 hours	Oral	= Complete
MW	= 295	pKa	=
Vd	=		

References:
1. Pharmaceutical Manufacturer Prescribing Information. 1995.
2. Drug Facts and Comparisons 1995 ed. ed. St. Louis: 1995.

ESTROGEN-ESTRADIOL   L3

Trade: Estratab, Premarin, Menext, Elestrin

Other Trades: Estrace, Estraderm, Delestrogen, Estinyl, Estring, Evorel

Uses: Estrogen hormone

AAP: Maternal Medication Usually Compatible with Breastfeeding

Although small amounts may pass into breastmilk, the effects of estrogens on the infant appear minimal. Early post-partum use of estrogens may reduce volume of milk produced and the protein content, but it is variable and depends on dose and the individual.[1,2,3,4] Breastfeeding mothers should attempt to wait until lactation is firmly established (6-8 weeks) prior to use of estrogen-containing oral contraceptives. In one study of six lactating women who received 50 or 100 mg vaginal suppositories of estradiol, the plasma levels peaked at 3 hours.[5] These doses are extremely large and are not used clinically. In another study of 11 women, the mean concentration of estradiol in breastmilk was found to be 113 picograms/mL.[6] This is very close to that seen when the woman begins ovulating during lactation. If oral contraceptives are used during lactation, the transfer of estradiol to human milk will be low and will not exceed the transfer during physiologic conditions when the mother has resumed ovulation. However, suppression of lactation is still the major concern with the use of these products in breastfeeding mothers. If at all possible, do not use in breastfeeding mothers. See oral contraceptives.

Pregnancy Risk Category: X

Lactation Risk Category: L3

Adult Concerns: Estrogen use has been associated with breast tenderness, increased risk of thromboembolic disorders, headache, nausea, vomiting, etc.

Pediatric Concerns: None reported. Infantile feminization is unlikely at normal dosages.

Drug Interactions: Rifampin reduces the serum levels of estrogen. Exogenous estrogens increase toxicity of hydrocortisone, and thromboembolic events with anticoagulants such as warfarin.

Relative Infant Dose:

Adult Dose: 10 mg TID

Alternatives: Norethindrone

T ½	= 60 minutes	M/P	= 0.08
PHL	=	PB	= 98%
Tmax	= Rapid	Oral	= Complete
MW	= 272	pKa	=
Vd	=		

References:

1. Booker DE, Pahl IR. Control of postpartum breast engorgement with oral contraceptives. Am J Obstet Gynecol 1967; 98 (8):1099-1101.
2. Kamal I, Hefnawi F, Ghoneim M, Abdallah M, Abdel RS. Clinical, biochemical, and experimental studies on lactation. V. Clinical effects of steroids on the initiation of lactation. Am J Obstet Gynecol 1970; 108 (4):655-658.
3. Kora SJ. Effect of oral contraceptives on lactation. Fertil Steril 1969; 20 (3):419-423.
4. Koetsawang S, Bhiraleus P, Chiemprajert T. Effects of oral contraceptives on lactation. Fertil Steril 1972; 23 (1):24-28.
5. Laukaran VH. The effects of contraceptive use on the initiation and duration of lactation. Int J Gynaecol Obstet 1987; 25 Suppl:129-142.
6. Nilsson S, Nygren KG, Johansson ED. Transfer of estradiol to human milk. Am J Obstet Gynecol 1978; 132 (6):653-657.

ESZOPICLONE   L3

Trade: Lunesta
Other Trades:
Uses: Hypnotic, sedative
AAP: Not reviewed

Eszopiclone is a non-benzodiazepine hypnotic-sedative drug, although they both interact at the same GABA receptor.[1] Used as a nighttime sedative, its transfer into human milk has not yet been reported. However, a derivative which is virtually identical, Zopiclone, has been studied (see zopiclone) and 1.5% of the maternal dose transferred into milk. Therefore, due to the structural similarly, one should expect about 1.5% of eszopiclone to transfer into human milk as well. The use of eszopiclone in mothers with premature infants or newborns, and particularly those with infants subject to apnea, should be avoided. Use in healthy older infants is probably less risky.

Pregnancy Risk Category: C

Lactation Risk Category: L3

Adult Concerns: Sedation. Rebound insomnia and other symptoms of withdrawal have been reported following discontinuation of eszopiclone. Headache, dry mouth, nausea, vomiting, unpleasant taste, brief memory loss, somnolence have been reported.

Pediatric Concerns: None reported. Observe closely for sedation in the infant.

Drug Interactions: Eszopiclone and lorazepam decrease each others C_{max} by 22%. Eszopiclone is metabolized by CYP3A4 and CYP2E1. Ketoconazole administration increased by 2.2 fold the exposure to eszopiclone. Additive effect with eszopiclone when mixed with alcohol. Levels of eszopiclone may be reduced by coadministration with rifampicin, a potent inducer of CYP3A4.

Relative Infant Dose:

Adult Dose: 2-3 mg at bedtime.

Alternatives: Zopiclone

T ½	= 6 hours	M/P	=
PHL	=	PB	= 59%
Tmax	= 1 hour	Oral	= >75%
MW	= 388	pKa	=
Vd	=		

References:
1. Pharmaceutical manufacturers package insert. 2005.

ETANERCEPT   L3

Trade: Enbrel
Other Trades:
Uses: Anti-arthritic
AAP: Not reviewed

Etanercept is a dimeric fusion protein consisting of the extracellular ligand-binding portion of tumor necrosis factor bound to human IgG1. Etanercept binds specifically to tumor necrosis factor (TNF) and blocks its inflammatory and immune activity in rheumatoid arthritis patients.[1] Elevated levels of TNF are found in the synovial fluid of arthritis patients.

In a recent study of a non-breastfeeding mother who received 25 mg twice weekly, etanercept was measured in the milk retained in the breast.[2] This mother was not breastfeeding but retained some milk in the breast after 30 days. The author reported milk levels of 75 ng/mL on the day after injection. While this data is interesting, measuring drug transfer in residual breast milk following involution of alveolar tissues is simply not clinically relevant. After involution, the alveolar system would be totally open to drug transfer due to the breakdown of the tight intercellular junctions between lactocytes.

Due to its enormous MW (150,000 daltons), I still believe it is extremely unlikely that clinically relevant amounts would transfer into milk in actively breastfeeding mothers. In addition, due to its protein structure, it would not be orally bioavailable in an infant. Infliximab is somewhat similar and is apparently not secreted into human milk (see infliximab).

Pregnancy Risk Category: B

Lactation Risk Category: L3

Adult Concerns: Etanercept may suppress the immune system and increase the risk of infections significantly. Incidence of infections is 38%. Headache, dizziness, cough, and rhinitis have been reported.

Pediatric Concerns: None reported via milk.

Drug Interactions: Do not administer live vaccines concurrent with etanercept.

Relative Infant Dose:

Adult Dose: 25 mg twice weekly

Alternatives: Infliximab

T ½	= 115 hours	M/P	=
PHL	=	PB	=
Tmax	= 72 hours	Oral	= Nil
MW	= 150000	pKa	=
Vd	= 0.24		

References:
1. Pharmaceutical Manufacturer Prescribing Information. 1999.
2. Ostensen M, Eigenmann GO. Etanercept in breast milk. J Rheumatol 2004 May; 31 (5):1017-8.

ETHACRYNIC ACID   L3

Trade: Edecrin
Other Trades:
Uses: Powerful loop diuretic
AAP: Not reviewed

Ethacrynic acid is a potent, short-acting loop diuretic similar to Lasix. It is listed by the manufacturer as contraindicated in nursing women. A significant decrease in maternal blood pressure or blood volume may reduce milk production. No data on transfer into human milk are available.[1,2]

Pregnancy Risk Category: B

Lactation Risk Category: L3

Adult Concerns: Diuresis, hypotension, diarrhea.

Pediatric Concerns: None reported.

Drug Interactions: Increased toxicity when used with antihypertensives, other diuretics, aminoglycosides. Increased risk of arrhythmias when used with digoxin. Probenecid reduces diuresis of this product.

Relative Infant Dose:

Adult Dose: 50-200 mg daily.

Alternatives: Furosemide

T ½	= 2-4 hours	M/P	=
PHL	=	PB	= 90%
Tmax	= 2 hours (oral)	Oral	= 100%
MW	= 303	pKa	=
Vd	=		

References:
1. Pharmaceutical Manufacturer Prescribing Information. 1996.
2. Lacy C. Drug information handbook. Lexi-Comp Inc. Cleveland, OH, 1996.

ETHAMBUTOL   L2

Trade: Ethambutol, Myambutol
Other Trades: Etibi
Uses: Antitubercular drug
AAP: Maternal Medication Usually Compatible with Breastfeeding

Ethambutol is an antimicrobial used for tuberculosis. Small amounts are secreted in milk although no studies are available which clearly document levels. In one unpublished study, the mother had an ethambutol plasma level of 1.5 mg/L three hours after a dose of 15 mg/kg daily. Following a similar dose, the concentration in milk was 1.4 mg/L.[1] In another patient, the plasma level was 4.62 mg/L and the corresponding milk concentration was 4.6 mg/L (no dose available).

Pregnancy Risk Category: B

Lactation Risk Category: L2

Adult Concerns: Optic neuritis, dizziness, confusion, nausea, vomiting, anorexia.

Pediatric Concerns: None reported, but caution is recommended.

Drug Interactions: Aluminum salts may decrease oral absorption.

Relative Infant Dose: 1.5%

Adult Dose: 15-25 mg/kg daily.

Alternatives:

T ½	= 3.1 hours	M/P	= 1.0
PHL	=	PB	= 8-22%
Tmax	= 2-4 hours	Oral	= 80%
MW	= 204	pKa	=
Vd	=		

References:
1. Snider DE, Jr., Powell KE. Should women taking antituberculosis drugs breast-feed? Arch Intern Med 1984; 144 (3):589-590.

ETHANOL   L3

Trade: Alcohol
Other Trades:
Uses: Depressant
AAP: Maternal Medication Usually Compatible with
Breastfeeding

Alcohol transfer into human milk readily, with an average milk/plasma ratio of about 1.0. This does not necessarily mean that the dose of alcohol in milk is high, only that the levels in plasma correspond closely with those in milk. The absolute amount (dose) of alcohol transferred into milk is generally low and is a function of the maternal level. Older studies, some in animals, suggested that beer (or more likely, barley) may stimulate prolactin levels.[1-4] While this may be true, we now know clearly that alcohol is a profound inhibitor of oxytocin release, and inevitably reduces milk letdown and the amount of milk delivered to the infant. Thus beer should not be considered a galactogogue.

In a study of twelve breastfeeding mothers who ingested 0.3 g/kg of ethanol in orange juice (equivalent to 1 can of beer for the average sized woman), the mean maximum concentration of ethanol in milk was 320 mg/L.[5] This report suggests a 23% reduction (156 to 120 mL) in breastmilk production following ingestion of beer and an increase in milk odor as a function of ethanol content.

In another group of 5 women, who consumed 0.4 grams/kg at one setting, milk and maternal plasma levels were similar. Levels of alcohol in milk averaged 0.44 g/L at peak and fell to 0.09 g/L at 180 minutes.[6]

In an interesting study of the effect of alcohol on milk ingestion by infants, the rate of milk consumption by infants during the 4 hours immediately after exposure to alcohol (0.3 g/kg) in 12 mothers was significantly less.[7] Compensatory increases in intake were then observed during the 8-16 hours after exposure when mothers refrained from drinking.

Excess levels may lead to drowsiness, deep sleep, weakness, and decreased linear growth in infant. Maternal blood alcohol levels must attain 300 mg/dL before significant side effects are reported in the infant. Reduction of letdown is apparently dose-dependent and requires alcohol consumption of 1.5 to 1.9 gm/kg body weight.[8] Other studies have suggested psychomotor delay in infants of moderate drinkers (2+ drinks daily). Avoid breastfeeding during and for at least 2-3 hours after drinking alcohol (moderate). Heavy drinkers should wait longer.

A new study suggests that the state of lactation metabolically changes the rate of alcohol bioavailability.[9] In this study, blood alcohol levels were significantly lower in lactating women as compared to non-lactating women. The reduced AUC levels for alcohol suggest that the metabolism of ethanol is higher in lactating women. However, the subject effects of alcohol were still similar.

Another study reported one infant that developed pseudo-Cushing syndrome as a result of exposure to alcohol in breast milk. The mother consumed at least 50- 12 ounce beers weekly in addition to other concentrated alcoholic beverages. She had stopped drinking while pregnant, and resumed postpartum. The infant showed signs of Cushing syndrome at age 8 weeks. When the mother stopped drinking while breastfeeding, the baby's appearance gradually returned to normal.[10] Adult metabolism of alcohol is approximately 1 oz in 3 hours, so mothers who ingest alcohol in moderate amounts can generally return to breastfeeding as soon as they feel neurologically normal. Chronic or heavy consumers of alcohol should not breastfeed. Readers are urged to consult Koren's excellent nomogram on counseling women concerning alcohol consumption.[11] Remember, this nomogram calculates, as a function of body weight and amount of alcohol consumed, the time to "zero" plasma levels in the mother.

Pregnancy Risk Category: D

Lactation Risk Category: L3

Adult Concerns: Sedation, decreased milk supply, altered milk taste.

Pediatric Concerns: One infant developed pseudo-Cushing syndrome as a result of exposure to alcohol in breast milk. The mother consumed at least 50- 12 ounce beers weekly in addition to other concentrated alcoholic beverages. She had stopped drinking while pregnant, and resumed postpartum. The infant showed signs of Cushing syndrome at age 8 weeks. When the mother stopped drinking while breastfeeding, the baby's appearance gradually returned to normal.[10] In another case report of a heavy user, the infant was restless and insomnic for several days then exhibited violent fits and tonic-clonic seizures.[12] After removal from this mothers breast, the infant calmed. Other studies suggest changes in behavioral state such as shorter periods of sleep, cried more often, and had heightened startling reflexes after exposure to alcohol.

Drug Interactions: Increased CNS depression when used with barbiturates, benzodiazepines, chloral hydrate, and other CNS depressants. A disulfiram-like reaction (flushing, weakness, sweating, tachycardia, etc.) may occur when used with cephalosporins, chlorpropamide, disulfiram, furazolidone, metronidazole, procarbazine. Increased hypoglycemia when used with sulfanurias and other hypoglycemic agents. Intolerance of bromocriptine.

Relative Infant Dose: 16%

Adult Dose:

Alternatives:

T ½	= 0.24 hours	M/P	= 1.0
PHL	=	PB	= 0%
Tmax	= 30-90 minutes (oral)	Oral	= 100%
MW	= 46	pKa	=
Vd	= 0.53		

References:
1. Marks V, Wright JW. Endocrinological and metabolic effects of alcohol. Proc R Soc Med 1977; 70 (5):337-344.
2. De Rosa G, Corsello SM, Ruffilli MP, Della CS, Pasargiklian E. Prolactin secretion after beer. Lancet 1981; 2 (8252):934.
3. Carlson HE, Wasser HL, Reidelberger RD. Beer-induced prolactin secretion: a clinical and laboratory study of the role of salsolinol. J Clin Endocrinol Metab 1985; 60 (4):673-677.
4. Koletzko B, Lehner F. Beer and breastfeeding. Adv Exp Med Biol 2000; 478:23-28.
5. Mennella JA, Beauchamp GK. The transfer of alcohol to human milk. Effects on flavor and the infant's behavior. N Engl J Med 1991; 325 (14):981-985.
6. da-Silva VA, Malheiros LR, Moraes-Santos AR, Barzano MA, McLean AE. Ethanol pharmacokinetics in lactating women. Braz J Med Biol Res. Oct 1993;26 (10):1097-1103.
7. Mennella JA. Regulation of milk intake after exposure to alcohol in mothers' milk. Alcohol Clin Exp Res 2001; 25 (4):590-593.
8. Cobo E. Effect of different doses of ethanol on the milk-ejecting reflex in lactating women. Am J Obstet Gynecol 1973; 115 (6):817-821.
9. Pepino MY, Steinmeyer AL, Mennella JA. Lactational state modifies alcohol pharmacokinetics in women. Alcohol Clin Exp Res. Jun 2007;31 (6):909-918.
10. Binkiewicz A, Robinson MJ, Senior B. Pseudo-Cushing syndrome caused by alcohol in breast milk. J Pediatr 1978 Dec; 93 (6):965-7.
11. Ho E, Collantes A, Kapur BM, Moretti M, Koren G. Alcohol and breast feeding: calculation of time to zero level in milk. Biol Neonate. 2001;80 (3):219-222.
12. Budin P. Lecture VI. In, The nursling: the feeding and hygiene of premature and full-term infants. London. Caxton Publishing Company. 1907;85-101.

ETHOSUXIMIDE   L4

Trade: Zarontin
Other Trades:
Uses: Anticonvulsant used in epilepsy
AAP: Maternal Medication Usually Compatible with Breastfeeding

Ethosuximide is an anticonvulsant used in epilepsy. Rane's data suggest that although significant levels of ethosuximide are transferred into human milk, the plasma level in the infant is quite low.[1] A peak milk concentration of approximately 55 mg/L was reported at 1 month postpartum. Milk/plasma ratios were reported to be 1.03 on day 3 postpartum and 0.8 during the first three months of therapy. The infant's plasma reached a peak (2.9 mg/dl) at approximately 1.5 months postpartum and then declined significantly over the next 3 months suggesting increased clearance by the infant. Although these levels are considered subtherapeutic, it is suggested that the infant's plasma levels be occasionally tested.

In another study of a women receiving 500 mg twice daily, her milk levels, as estimated from a graph, averaged 60-70 mg/L.[2] A total daily exposure to ethosuximide of 3.6-11 mg/kg as a result of nursing was predicted.

In a study by Kuhnz of 10 epileptic breastfeeding mothers (and 13 infants) receiving 3.5 to 23.6 mg/kg/day, the breastmilk concentrations were similar to those of the maternal plasma (milk/serum: 0.86) and the breastfed infants maintained serum levels between 15 and 40 μg/mL.[3] Maximum milk concentration reported was 77 mg/L although the average was 49.54 mg/L. Neonatal behavior complications such as poor suckling, sedation, and hyperexcitability occurred in 7 of the 12 infants. Interestingly, one infant who was not breastfed, exhibited severe withdrawal symptoms such as tremors, restlessness, insomnia, crying and vomiting which lasted for 8 weeks causing a slow weight gain. Thus the question remains, is it safer to breastfeed and avoid these severe withdrawal reactions?

These studies clearly indicate that the amount of ethosuximide transferred to the infant is significant. With milk/plasma ratios of approximately 0.86-1.0 and relatively high maternal plasma levels, the maternal plasma levels are a good indication of the dose transferred to the infant. Milk levels are generally high. Caution is recommended.

Pregnancy Risk Category: C

Lactation Risk Category: L4

Adult Concerns: Drowsiness, ataxia, nausea, vomiting, anorexia, rash.

Pediatric Concerns: Neonatal behavior complications such as poor suckling, sedation, and hyperexcitability occurred in 7 of 12 infants in one study. Milk levels are significant. Caution is recommended.

Drug Interactions: Decreased efficacy of ethosuximide when used with phenytoin, carbamazepine, primidone, phenobarbital (may reduce plasma levels). Elevated levels of ethosuximide may result when used with isoniazid.

Relative Infant Dose: 31.5%

Adult Dose: 250-750 mg BID

Alternatives:

T ½	= 30-60 hours	M/P	= 0.94
PHL	= 32-38 hours	PB	= 0%
Tmax	= 4 hours	Oral	= Complete
MW	= 141	pKa	= 9.3
Vd	= 0.72		

References:

1. Rane A, Tunell R. Ethosuximide in human milk and in plasma of a mother and her nursed infant. Br J Clin Pharmacol 1981; 12 (6):855-858.
2. Koup JR, Rose JQ, Cohen ME. Ethosuximide pharmacokinetics in a pregnant patient and her newborn. Epilepsia 1978; 19 (6):535-539.
3. Kuhnz W, Koch S, Jakob S, Hartmann A, Helge H, Nau H. Ethosuximide in epileptic women during pregnancy and lactation period. Placental transfer, serum concentrations in nursed infants and clinical status. Br J Clin Pharmacol 1984; 18 (5):671-677.

ETHOTOIN   L3

Trade: Peganone
Other Trades:
Uses: Anticonvulsant
AAP: Not reviewed

Ethotoin is a typical phenytoin-like anticonvulsant. Although no data is available on concentrations in breastmilk, its similarity to phenytoin would suggest that some is secreted via breastmilk.[1] No data is available in the literature. See phenytoin.

Pregnancy Risk Category: D

Lactation Risk Category: L3

Adult Concerns: Drowsiness, dizziness, insomnia, headache, blood dyscrasias.

Pediatric Concerns: None reported, but see phenytoin.

Drug Interactions: See phenytoin.

Relative Infant Dose:

Adult Dose:

Alternatives:

T ½	= 3-9 hours	M/P	=
PHL	=	PB	= Low- 41%
Tmax	= 1-2 hours	Oral	= Complete
MW	− 204	pKa	=
Vd	=		

References:
1. McEvoy GE. (ed):AFHS Drug Information. New York, NY: 2009.

ETIDRONATE   L3

Trade: Didronel
Other Trades:
Uses: Slows bone turnover
AAP: Not reviewed

Etidronate is a bisphosphonate that slows the dissolution of hydroxyapatite crystals in the bone, thus reducing bone calcium loss in certain syndromes such as Paget's syndrome.[1] Etidronate also reduces the remineralization of bone and can result in osteomalacia over time. It is not known how the administration of this product during active lactation would affect the maternal bone porosity. It is possible that milk calcium levels could be reduced although this has not been reported. Etidronate is poorly absorbed orally (1%) and must be administered in between meals on an empty stomach. Its penetration into milk is possible due to its small MW, but it has not yet been reported. However, due to the presence of fat and calcium in milk, its oral bioavailability in infants would be exceedingly low. Whereas the plasma half-life is approximately 6 hours, the terminal elimination half-life (from bone) is >90 days.

Pregnancy Risk Category: C

Lactation Risk Category: L3

Adult Concerns: Untoward effects include loss of taste, nephrotoxicity, risk of fractures, and focal osteomalacia after prolonged use. Fever, convulsions, bone pain.

Pediatric Concerns: None reported via milk. Although unreported, it could result in reduced milk calcium levels. Oral absorption in infant would be minimal.

Drug Interactions: IV Ranitidine doubles the oral absorption of alendronate (similar to etidronate). Oral products containing calcium or magnesium will significantly reduce oral bioavailability. Take on empty stomach.

Relative Infant Dose:

Adult Dose: 5-10 mg/kg daily

Alternatives:

T ½	= 6 hours (plasma)	M/P	=
PHL	=	PB	=
Tmax	= 2 hours	Oral	= 1-2.5%
MW	= 206	pKa	=
Vd	= 1.37		

References:
1. Drug Facts and Comparisons 1996 ed. ed. St. Louis: 1996.

ETODOLAC   L3

Trade: Etodolac, Lodine
Other Trades: Ultradol
Uses: Non-steroidal analgesic, antipyretic
AAP: Not reviewed

Etodolac is a prototypical nonsteroidal anti-inflammatory agent (NSAID) with analgesic, antipyretic, and anti-inflammatory properties.[1] Thus far no data are available regarding its secretion into human breastmilk. Shorter half-life varieties are preferred.

Pregnancy Risk Category: C in first and second trimesters
                                D in third trimester

Lactation Risk Category: L3

Adult Concerns: Dyspepsia, nausea, diarrhea, indigestion, heartburn, abdominal pain, and gastrointestinal bleeding.

Pediatric Concerns: None reported via milk, but observe for nausea, diarrhea, indigestion. Ibuprofen probably preferred at this time.

Drug Interactions: May prolong prothrombin time when used with warfarin. Antihypertensive effects of ACEi family may be blunted or completely abolished by NSAIDs. Some NSAIDs may block antihypertensive effect of beta blockers, diuretics. Used with cyclosporin, may dramatically increase renal toxicity. May increase digoxin, phenytoin, lithium levels. May increase toxicity of methotrexate. May increase bioavailability of penicillamine. Probenecid may increase NSAID levels.

Relative Infant Dose:

Adult Dose: 200-400 mg every 6-8 hours

Alternatives: Ibuprofen, Voltaren

T ½	= 7.3 hours	M/P	=
PHL	=	PB	= 95-99%
Tmax	= 1-2 hours	Oral	= 80-100%
MW	= 287	pKa	= 4.7
Vd	= 0.4		

References:
1. Pharmaceutical Manufacturer Prescribing Information. 1995.

ETONOGESTREL + ETHINYL ESTRADIOL   L3

Trade: NuvaRing
Other Trades:
Uses: Slow release vaginal ring contraceptive
AAP: Not reviewed

NuvaRing is a slow release vaginal ring which releases on average 0.120 mg/day of etonogestrel and 0.015 mg/day of ethinyl estradiol over a 3 week period of use. Etonogestrel is the biologically active metabolite of desogestrel and has both high progestational activity with low intrinsic androgenicity. The bioavailability of ethinyl estradiol when administered intravaginally is approximately 55.6%, which is comparable to that when it is administered orally. Small amounts of estrogens and progestins are known to pass into milk, but long-term follow-up of children whose mothers used combination hormonal contraceptives while breastfeeding has shown no deleterious effects on infants. Estrogen-containing contraceptives may interfere with milk production by decreasing the quantity and quality of milk production.

Pregnancy Risk Category: X

Lactation Risk Category: L3

Adult Concerns: Do not use in patients with: thrombophlebitis or thromboembolic disorders, cerebral vascular or coronary artery disease, severe hypertension. Numerous other contraindications exist, check the package insert.

Pediatric Concerns: This is an estrogen-containing contraceptive device. Estrogens in some patients may inhibit milk production significantly and change the quality of milk components. Caution patient to observe for suppression of milk production.

Drug Interactions: Check package insert

Relative Infant Dose:

Adult Dose:

Alternatives: Progestin-only oral contraceptives

T ½	= 29.3 hours	M/P	=
PHL	=	PB	= 96%
Tmax	= 200 hours	Oral	=
MW	= 324	pKa	=
Vd	=		

References:
1. Pharmaceutical Manufacturers Package Insert, 2003.

ETONOGESTREL IMPLANT | L2

Trade: Implanon
Other Trades:
Uses: Implantable progestin contraceptive.
AAP: Not reviewed

Implanon is a slow release single-rod contraceptive implant. It consists of a non-biodegradable rod measuring 40 mm in length and 2 mm in diameter which releases on average 40 μg/day of etonogestrel over a 3 year period of use. Etonogestrel is the biologically active metabolite of desogestrel and has both high progestational activity with low intrinsic androgenicity. Implanon does not contain estrogen, making it suitable for women who do not tolerate or are advised to not use estrogens. Small amounts of progestins are known to pass into milk, but long-term follow-up of children whose mothers used hormonal contraceptives while breastfeeding has shown no deleterious effects on infants.[2] Like other progestogen-only contraceptives, the use of Implanon is associated with irregular menstrual bleeding and sometimes absence of bleeding. Counseling is required to ensure women make informed choices.[1] Of the contraceptives, progestin-only contraceptives are generally preferred as they produce fewer changes in milk production compared to estrogen-containing products. This product is probably quite safe for use in breastfeeding mothers, although all mothers should be counseled to observe for changes in milk production.

Pregnancy Risk Category: X

Lactation Risk Category: L2

Adult Concerns: Adverse events include weight gain, acne, headaches.

Pediatric Concerns: Progestins generally have minimal effect on milk production, but some mothers have reported reduced milk production following the use of progestin oral contraceptives. Some caution is recommended although changes in milk supply are very unlikely. Transfer of progestins into milk and to the infant are remote.

Drug Interactions: Check package insert.

Relative Infant Dose:

Adult Dose: One implant every 3 years.

Alternatives: Norethindrone

T ½	= 29.3 hours	M/P	=
PHL	=	PB	=
Tmax	= 200 hours	Oral	=
MW	= 324	pKa	=
Vd	=		

References:
1. Pharmaceutical Manufacturers Package Insert, 2003.
2. Taneepanichskul S, Reinprayoon D, Thaithumyanon P, Praisuwanna P, Tosukhowong P, Dieben T. Effects of the etonogestrel-releasing implant Implanon and a nonmedicated intrauterine device on the growth of breast-fed infants. Contracept 2006; 73:368-371.

ETRETINATE   L5

Trade: Tegison
Other Trades: Tigason
Uses: Antipsoriatic
AAP: Not reviewed

Etretinate is an oral Vitamin A derivative primarily used for psoriasis and sometimes acne. It is teratogenic and should not be administered to pregnant women or women about to become pregnant. Etretinate is known to transfer into animal milk although no data are available in human milk.[1,2] Etretinate is still detectable in human serum up to 2.9 years after administration has ceased due to storage at high concentrations in adipose tissue. Mothers who wish to breastfeed following therapy with this compound should be informed of its long half-life in the human. The manufacturer considers this drug to be contraindicated in breastfeeding mothers due to the potential for serious adverse effects.

Pregnancy Risk Category: X

Lactation Risk Category: L5

Adult Concerns: Dry nose, chapped lips, nose bleeds, hair loss, peeling of skin on soles, palms, sunburns, and headaches. Elevated liver enzymes, lipids. Fatigue, headache, fever.

Pediatric Concerns: None reported but great caution is urged. Premature epiphyseal closure has been reported in children treated with this product.

Drug Interactions: Milk increases absorption of oral etretinate. Exogenous vitamin A increases toxicity.

Relative Infant Dose:

Adult Dose: 0.5-0.75 mg/kg BID

Alternatives:

T ½	= 120 days (terminal)	M/P	=
PHL	=	PB	= >99%
Tmax	= 2-6 hours	Oral	= Complete
MW	= 354	pKa	=
Vd	= High		

References:
1. Pharmaceutical Manufacturer Prescribing Information. 1995.
2. Lacy C. Drug information handbook. Lexi-Comp Inc. Cleveland, OH, 1996.

EVENING PRIMROSE OIL   L3

Trade: EPO
Other Trades: Efamol
Uses: Nutritional supplement
AAP: Not reviewed

Evening primrose oil is a rich source of essential polyunsaturated fatty acids (EFA) particularly gamma linoleic acid (GLA). Human milk is generally rich in 6-desaturated essential fatty acids including arachidonic, GLA, and dihomo-GLA (DGLA), which may play an important role in development of the infant brain. The brain contains about 20% of 6-desaturated EFAs. Supplementation in pregnant women has been found to significantly increase EFA content in human breastmilk.[1] Although there is some evidence that GLA may be beneficial in syndromes such as cardiovascular disease, rheumatoid arthritis, multiple sclerosis, and atopic dermatitis, many of these studies were sponsored by the manufacturer and need independent confirmation.[2,3] Overt toxicity of this product appears quite low. A number of studies in adults using GLA at rather high doses have not been found to produce significant toxicity.

Pregnancy Risk Category:

Lactation Risk Category: L3

Adult Concerns: Major untoward effects are largely unreported, although some patients have quit various studies for unspecified reasons.

Pediatric Concerns: None reported.

Drug Interactions:

Relative Infant Dose:

Adult Dose:

Alternatives:

References:
1. Cant A, Shay J, Horrobin DF. The effect of maternal supplementation with linoleic and gamma-linolenic acids on the fat composition and content of human milk: a placebo-controlled trial. J Nutr Sci Vitaminol (Tokyo) 1991; 37 (6):573-579.
2. Horrobin DF, Manku MS. How do polyunsaturated fatty acids lower plasma cholesterol levels? Lipids 1983; 18 (8):558-562.
3. Review of Natural Products Facts and Comparisons, St Louis, MO 1996.

EXENATIDE   L3

Trade: Byetta
Other Trades:
Uses: Improves glycemic control in diabetics
AAP: Not reviewed

Exenatide improves glycemic control in people with type 2 diabetes mellitus. It enhances glucose-dependent insulin secretion by the pancreatic beta-cell, suppresses glucagon secretion, and slows gastric emptying. Exenatide leads to an increase in both glucose-dependent synthesis of insulin, and in vivo secretion of insulin from pancreatic beta cells. Exenatide therefore promotes insulin release from beta cells in the presence of elevated glucose concentrations. Exenatide is a

39-amino acid peptide and has a MW of 4186 daltons which is far too large to enter milk in clinically relevant amounts. While it is reported to enter rodent milk at extremely low levels, we do not have human studies.

The plasma levels of this product are extraordinarily low (picograms), and I would imagine the transfer into human milk is much lower. It would be unlikely that this product would enter milk in clinically relevant amounts, nor would it be orally bioavailable in infants. But as yet, we have no data in breastfeeding mothers and caution is recommended if this product is used.

Pregnancy Risk Category: C

Lactation Risk Category: L3 during first week postpartum.
                                    L2 after first week postpartum.

Adult Concerns: Side effects include: nausea, vomiting, diarrhea, feeling jittery, dizziness, headache and dyspepsia.

Pediatric Concerns: None reported, but this product is all be unlikely to ever enter milk or be orally absorbed by an infant.

Drug Interactions: Exenatide reduced plasma levels (C_{max}) of digoxin by 17%. Levels of lovastatin were decreased by 40%. Levels of acetaminophen were reduced by 24%.

Relative Infant Dose:

Adult Dose: High variable, consult prescribing information.

Alternatives:

T ½	= 2.4 hours	M/P	=
PHL	=	PB	=
Tmax	= 2.1 hours	Oral	= Nil
MW	− 4186	pKa	= 0.4
Vd	= 0.4		

References:
1.   Pharmaceutical Manufacturers prescribing information. 2010.

EZETIMIBE

L3

Trade: Zetia
Other Trades:
Uses: Anti-cholesterol agent
AAP: Not reviewed

Ezetimibe reduces blood cholesterol by inhibiting the absorption of cholesterol from the small intesting.[1] It appears to act at the brush border of the small intestine and inhibits the absorption of cholesterol leading to a direct reduction in delivery of cholesterol to the liver. No data are available on the transfer of this agent to milk. This is a very lipophilic agent, but has reasonably poor oral bioavailability. It is not clear at all if it would be safe for use in a breastfed infant who needs high levels of cholesterol. Some caution is recommended until data are available but it is unlikely to produce significant levels in milk.

Pregnancy Risk Category: C

Lactation Risk Category: L3

Adult Concerns: Generally well tolerated but viral infection, headache, fatigue, and GI symptoms such as diarrhea and abdominal pain have been reported but these symptoms are rather low in incidence.

Pediatric Concerns: No data available on transfer to human milk. Some caution is recommended.

Drug Interactions: Additive when used with HMG CoA reductase inhibitors. Ezetimibe levels increased 12 fold in a renal transplant patient receiving cyclosporine and other agents. There is an increased risk of myopathy or rhabdomyolysis when used with fibric acid products (fenofibrate).

Relative Infant Dose:

Adult Dose: 10 mg daily.

Alternatives: Cholestyramine salts

T ½	= 22 hours	M/P	=
PHL	=	PB	= >90%
Tmax	= 4-12 hours	Oral	= 35-60%
MW	= 409	pKa	=
Vd	=		

References:
1. Pharmaceutical Manufacturers prescribing information, 2003.

FAMCICLOVIR | L2

Trade: Famvir
Other Trades:
Uses: Antiviral for Herpes Zoster
AAP: Not reviewed

Famciclovir is an antiviral use in the treatment of uncomplicated herpes zoster infection (shingles) and genital herpes. It is rapidly metabolized to the active metabolite, penciclovir. Although similar to Acyclovir, no data are available on levels in human milk. Oral bioavailability of famciclovir (77%) is much better than acyclovir (15-30%). Studies with rodents suggest that the milk/plasma ratio is greater than 1.0.[1,2] Because famciclovir provides few advantages over acyclovir, at this point acyclovir would probably be preferred in a nursing mother although the side-effect profile is still minimal with this product.

Pregnancy Risk Category: B

Lactation Risk Category: L2

Adult Concerns: Headache, dizziness, nausea, diarrhea, fever, anorexia.

Pediatric Concerns: None reported via milk.

Drug Interactions: Cimetidine increases plasma levels of the active metabolite penciclovir. Famciclovir increases digoxin plasma levels by 19%. Probenecid significantly increase penciclovir plasma levels.

Relative Infant Dose:

Adult Dose: 125 mg BID

Alternatives: Acyclovir

T ½	= 2-3 hours	M/P	= >1
PHL	=	PB	= <20%
Tmax	= 0.9 hours	Oral	= 77%
MW	=	pKa	=
Vd	= 1.13		

References:
1. Drug Facts and Comparisons 2010 ed. ed. St. Louis: 2010.
2. Pharmaceutical Manufacturer Prescribing Information. 1995.

FAMOTIDINE   L1

Trade: Pepcid, Axid-AR, Pepcid-AC

Other Trades: Apo-Famotidine, Novo-Famotidine, Amfamox, Pepcidine

Uses: Reduces gastric acid secretion

AAP: Not reviewed

Famotidine is a typical Histamine-2 antagonist that reduces stomach acid secretion. In one study of 8 lactating women receiving a 40 mg/day dose, the peak concentration in breastmilk was 72 µg/L and occurred at 6 hours post-dose.[1] The milk/plasma ratios were 0.41, 1.78, and 1.33 at 2, 6, and 24 hours respectively. These levels are apparently much lower than other histamine H-2 antagonists (ranitidine, cimetidine) and make it a preferred choice.

Pregnancy Risk Category: B

Lactation Risk Category: L1

Adult Concerns: Headache, constipation, increased liver enzymes.

Pediatric Concerns: None reported. Pediatric indications are available.

Drug Interactions: Famotidine reduces bioavailability of ketoconazole, itraconazole due to reduced oral absorption of these two products.

Relative Infant Dose: 1.9%

Adult Dose: 20-40 mg BID

Alternatives: Nizatidine

T ½	= 2.5-3.5 hours	M/P	= 0.41-1.78
PHL	=	PB	= 17%
Tmax	= 1-3.5 hours	Oral	= 50%
MW	= 337	pKa	=
Vd	=		

References:
1.   Courtney TP, Shaw RW. et.al. Excretion of famotidine in breast milk. Br J Clin Pharmacol 1988; 26:639.

FELBAMATE   L4

Trade: Felbatol
Other Trades:
Uses: Anticonvulsant
AAP: Not reviewed

Felbamate is an oral antiepileptic agent for partial seizures and Lennox-Gastaut syndrome. Due to serious side effects, the FDA recommends that felbamate be given only to patients with serious seizures refractory to all other medications. Felbamate is known to be secreted in rodent milk and was detrimental to their offspring.[1] No data is available on human milk. Due to the incidence of severe side effects, extreme caution is recommended with this medication in breastfeeding mothers.

Pregnancy Risk Category: C

Lactation Risk Category: L4

Adult Concerns: Aplastic anemia, weight gain, flu-like symptoms, tachycardia, nausea, vomiting, headache, insomnia.

Pediatric Concerns: None reported, but caution is urged.

Drug Interactions: Felbamate causes an increase in phenytoin plasma levels. Phenytoin produces a 45% decrease in felbamate levels. Carbamazepine levels may be decreased, whereas felbamate levels may drop by 40%. Valproic acid plasma levels may be increased.

Relative Infant Dose:

Adult Dose: 1200 mg/day in 3-4 divided doses

Alternatives:

T ½	= 20-23 hours	M/P	=
PHL	=	PB	= 25%
Tmax	= 1-4 hours	Oral	= 90%
MW	= 238	pKa	=
Vd	= 0.7-1.0		

References:
1. Pharmaceutical Manufacturer Prescribing Information. 1995.

FELODIPINE

L3

Trade: Plendil
Other Trades: Plendil, Renedil, Agon SR, Plendil ER
Uses: Calcium channel blocker, antihypertensive
AAP: Not reviewed

Felodipine is a calcium channel antagonist structurally related to nifedipine.[1] Because we have numerous studies on others in this family, it is advisable to use nifedipine or others that have breastfeeding studies available.

Pregnancy Risk Category: C

Lactation Risk Category: L3

Adult Concerns: Headache, dizziness, edema, flushing, hypotension, constipation, cardiac arrhythmias.

Pediatric Concerns: None reported via milk, but caution is recommended.

Drug Interactions: Barbiturates may reduce bioavailability of calcium channel blockers (CCB). Calcium salts may reduce hypotensive effect. Dantrolene may increase risk of hyperkalemia and myocardial depression. H2 blockers may increase bioavailability of certain CCBs. Hydantoins may reduce plasma levels. Quinidine increases risk of hypotension, bradycardia, tachycardia. Rifampin may reduce effects of CCBs. Vitamin D may reduce efficacy of CCBs. CCBs may increase carbamazepine, cyclosporin, encainide, prazosin levels.

Relative Infant Dose:

Adult Dose: 2.5-10 mg daily.

Alternatives: Nifedipine, Nimodipine, Verapamil

T ½	= 11-16 hours	M/P	=
PHL	=	PB	= >99%
Tmax	= 2.5-5 hours	Oral	= 20%
MW	= 384	pKa	=
Vd	=		

References:
1.   Pharmaceutical Manufacturer Prescribing Information. 1996.

FENDOLOPAM

L3

Trade: Corlopam
Other Trades:
Uses: Dopamine Agonist
AAP: Not reviewed

Fendolopam is a dopamine agonist used to treat severe hypertension in both adults and pediatrics. It is not known whether this drug transfers into the milk compartment. Further, dopamine agonists are known to suppress prolactin release, so some concern exists for the use of this product in breastfeeding mothers. However, its brief half-life would preclude large quantities from entering the milk compartment.

Pregnancy Risk Category: B

Lactation Risk Category: L3

Adult Concerns: Adverse effects include headache, nausea, hypotension, and dizziness.

Pediatric Concerns: In children, the most common adverse effects were hypotension and tachycardia. This medication is used in pediatrics aged <1 month to age 12 at doses of up to 0.8 µg/kg/minute for severe hypertension.

Drug Interactions: Acetaminophen use increases fendolopam levels, while beta-blockers increase the risk of hypotension.

Relative Infant Dose:

Adult Dose: max of 1.6 µg/kg/minute

Alternatives:

T ½	= 5 minutes	M/P	=
PHL	= 3-5 minutes	PB	=
Tmax	=	Oral	=
MW	= 305	pKa	=
Vd	= 0.6		

References:
1. Pharmaceutical Manufacturer Prescribing Information. 2006.

FENNEL   L4

Trade: Sweet Fennel, Bitter fennel, Carosella, Florence fennel,
Finocchio, Garden fennel, Wild fennel
Other Trades:
Uses: Estrogenic
AAP: Not reviewed

Fennel is an herb native to southern Europe and Asia Minor. The oils of sweet and bitter fennel contain up to 90% trans-anethole and up to 20% fenchone and numerous other lesser oils. An acetone extract of fennel has been shown to have estrogenic effects on the genital organs of male and female rats.[1] As an herbal medicine it is reputed to increase milk secretion, promote menstruation, facilitate birth, and increased libido. The estrogenic component is believed to be a polymer of the anethole such as dianethole or photoanethole.[2] Ingestion of the volatile oil may induce nausea, vomiting, seizures, pulmonary edema, and hallucinations.[3,4] An older survey of fennel samples in Italy found viable aerobic bacteria including coliforms, fecal streptococci, and salmonella species, suggesting the plant may serve as a vector for infectious gastrointestinal diseases.[5] Fennel is a popular herb that has been used since ancient times. It is primarily believed to be estrogenic. Because estrogens are known to suppress breastmilk production, its use in lactating women is questionable.

Pregnancy Risk Category:

Lactation Risk Category: L4

Adult Concerns: Allergic reactions, photodermatitis, contact dermatitis, and bacterial contamination.

Pediatric Concerns: None reported via milk. May potentially suppress milk production.

Drug Interactions:

Relative Infant Dose:

Adult Dose:

Alternatives:

References:

1. Malini T, Vanithakumari G, Megala N, Anusya S, Devi K, Elango V. Effect of Foeniculum vulgare Mill. seed extract on the genital organs of male and female rats. Indian J Physiol Pharmacol 1985; 29 (1):21-26.
2. Albert-Puleo M. Fennel and anise as estrogenic agents. J Ethnopharmacol 1980; 2 (4):337-344.
3. Marcus C, Lichtenstein EP. J. Agric Food Chem 1979; 27:1217.

4.   Duke JA. Handbook of Medicinal Herbs. Boca Raton, FL: CRC Press, 1985.
5.   Ercolani GL. Bacteriological quality assessment of fresh marketed lettuce and fennel. Appl Environ Microbiol 1976; 31 (6):847-852.

FENOFIBRATE   L3

Trade: Tricor
Other Trades:
Uses: Cholesterol lower agent
AAP: Not reviewed

Fenofibrate produces reduction in total cholesterol, LDL cholesterol, and triglycerides.[1] No data are available on its transfer into human milk however agents that reduce plasma cholesterol are not usually considered suitable for use in breastfeeding mothers. Milk levels of cholesterol are higher because of the newborns need for high levels of cholesterol for neurodevelopment. This and other hypocholesterolemic agents should probably not be used in breastfeeding mothers with exception of those with much older infants (>1 year).

Pregnancy Risk Category: C

Lactation Risk Category: L3

Adult Concerns: Adverse events include abdominal pain, back pain, headache, elevated liver function tests, chest pain, respiratory disorders.

Pediatric Concerns: None reported via milk, but this agent should not be used in breastfeeding mothers due to the infants need for cholesterol.

Drug Interactions: Potentiates coumarin anticoagulants.

Relative Infant Dose:

Adult Dose: 160 mg/day.

Alternatives:

T ½	= 20 hours	M/P	=
PHL	=	PB	= 99%
Tmax	=	Oral	= 85%
MW	= 361	pKa	=
Vd	=		

References:
1. Pharmaceutical Manufacturers prescribing information, 2003.

FENOPROFEN   L2

Trade: Nalfon
Other Trades: Fenopron, Progesic
Uses: NSAID, nonsteroidal analgesic
AAP: Not reviewed

Fenoprofen is a typical nonsteroidal antiinflammatory and analgesic. Following 600 mg four times daily for 4 days postpartum, the milk/plasma ratio was approximately 0.017 and fenoprofen levels in milk were too low to be accurately detected and was estimated to be approximately 1/60th of the maternal plasma level.[1] Fenoprofen was undetectable in cord blood, amniotic fluid, saliva, or washed red blood cells after multiple doses.

Pregnancy Risk Category: C during first and second trimesters
D during third trimester

Lactation Risk Category: L2

Adult Concerns: GI distress and bleeding, dyspepsia, nausea, constipation, ulcers, hepatotoxicity, rash, tinnitus.

Pediatric Concerns: None reported.

Drug Interactions: May prolong prothrombin time when used with warfarin. Antihypertensive effects of ACEi family may be blunted or completely abolished by NSAIDs. Some NSAIDs may block antihypertensive effect of beta blockers, diuretics. Used with cyclosporin, may dramatically increase renal toxicity. May increase digoxin, phenytoin, lithium levels. May increase toxicity of methotrexate. May increase bioavailability of penicillamine. Probenecid may increase NSAID levels.

Relative Infant Dose:

Adult Dose: 300-600 mg every 4-6 hours

Alternatives: Ibuprofen

T ½	= 2.5 hours	M/P	= 0.017
PHL	=	PB	= 99%
Tmax	= 1-2 hours	Oral	= 80%
MW	= 242	pKa	= 4.5
Vd	= 0.08-0.10		

References:

1.   Rubin A. et.al. A profile of the physiological disposition and gastrointestinal effects of fenoprofen in man. Curr Med Res Opin 1974; 2:529-544.

FENTANYL	L2

Trade: Sublimaze
Other Trades: Duragesic
Uses: Opiate analgesic
AAP: Maternal Medication Usually Compatible with Breastfeeding

Fentanyl is a potent narcotic analgesic used (IV, IM, transdermally) during labor and delivery. When used parenterally, its half-life is exceedingly short.[1]

The transfer of fentanyl into human milk has been documented but is low. In a group of ten women receiving a total dose of 50 to 400 μg fentanyl IV during labor, the concentration of fentanyl in milk was exceedingly low, generally below the level of detection (<0.05 ng/mL).[2] In a few samples, the levels were between 0.05 and 0.15 ng/mL. Using this data, an infant would ingest less than 3% of the weight-adjusted maternal dose per day.

In another study of 13 women who received 2 μg/kg IV after delivery and cord clamping, fentanyl concentration in colostrum was extremely low.[3] Peak colostrum concentrations occurred at 45 minutes follow intravenous administration and averaged 0.4 μg/L. Colostrum levels dropped rapidly and were undetectable after 10 hours. The authors conclude that with these small concentrations and fentanyl's low oral bioavailability, intravenous fentanyl analgesia may be used safely in breastfeeding women. The relatively low level of fentanyl found in human milk is presumably a result of the short maternal half-life, and the rather rapid redistribution out of the maternal plasma compartment. It is apparent that fentanyl transfer to milk under most clinical conditions is poor and is probably clinically unimportant.

In another study of chronic exposure to fentanyl for intractable pain, the mother was receiving by transdermal patch 100 μg/hour.[4] At approximately 27 days postpartum, the infants blood was negative for both fentanyl and its metabolite norfentanyl (sensitivity 0.1 ng/mL). The mother's milk contained 6.4 ng/mL fentanyl and 6.2 ng/mL norfentanyl. The authors calculated the dose via milk at 1.3 μg/kg/day. The infant was unaffected by exposure to fentanyl.

Pregnancy Risk Category: C

Lactation Risk Category: L2

Adult Concerns: Apnea, respiratory depression, muscle rigidity, hypotension, bradycardia.

Pediatric Concerns: No adverse effects reported via milk.

Drug Interactions: Increased toxicity when used with other CNS depressants, phenothiazines, tricyclic antidepressants.

Relative Infant Dose: 2.9% - 5%

Adult Dose: 2-20 µg/kg injection (IV)

Alternatives: Sufentanyl

T ½	= 2-4 hours	M/P	=
PHL	= 3-13 hours (neonates)	PB	= 80-86%
Tmax	= 7-8 minutes (IV)	Oral	= 25-75%
MW	= 336	pKa	= 8.4
Vd	= 3-8		

References:
1. Madej TH, Strunin L. Comparison of epidural fentanyl with sufentanil. Analgesia and side effects after a single bolus dose during elective caesarean section. Anaesthesia 1987; 42 (11):1156-1161.
2. Leuschen MP, Wolf LJ, Rayburn WF. Fentanyl excretion in breast milk. Clin Pharm 1990; 9 (5):336-337.
3. Steer PL, Biddle CJ, Marley WS, Lantz RK, Sulik PL. Concentration of fentanyl in colostrum after an analgesic dose. Can J Anaesth 1992 March; 39 (3):231-5.
4. Cohen RS. Fentanyl transdermal analgesia during pregnancy and lactation. J Hum Lact. Aug 2009;25 (3):359-361.

FENUGREEK   L3

Trade:
Other Trades:
Uses: Herbal spice
AAP: Not reviewed

Fenugreek is commonly sold as the dried, ripe seed and extracts are used as an artificial flavor for maple syrup.[1] The seeds contain from 0.1 to 0.9% diosgenin.[2] Several coumarin compounds have been noted in the seed as well as a number of alkaloids such as trigonelline, gentianin, and carpaine. The seeds also contain approximately 8% of a foul-smelling oil.

Fenugreek has been noted to reduce plasma cholesterol in animals when 50% of their diet contained fenugreek seeds.[3] The high fiber content may have accounted for this change although it may be due to the steroid saponins. A hypoglycemic effect has also been noted. When added to the diet of diabetic dogs, a decrease in insulin dose and hyperglycemia was noted.[4] It is not known if these changes are due to the fiber content of the seeds or a chemical component. Fenugreek has been reported to increase the anticoagulant effect of warfarin.[5] One case of GI bleeding in a premature infant (30 weeks) following introduction of fenugreek to the mother has been observed.[6] The implication of fenugreek in this hemorrhage is speculative.

In a group of 10 women (non-placebo controlled) with infants born between 24 to 38 weeks gestation (mean= 29 weeks) who ingested 3 fenugreek capsules 3 times daily (Nature's Way) for a week, the average milk production during the week increased significantly from a mean of 207 mL/day (range 57-1057 mL) to 464 mL/day (range 63-1140 mL).[8] No untoward effects were reported.

When dosed in moderation, fenugreek has limited toxicity and is listed in the US as a GRAS herbal (Generally Regarded As Safe). A maple syrup odor via urine and sweat is commonly reported. Higher doses may produce hypoglycemia. A stimulant effect on the isolated uterus (guinea pig) has been reported and its use in late pregnancy may not be advisable. Fenugreek's reputation as a galactagogue is widespread but undocumented. The dose commonly employed is variable but is approximately 2-3 capsules taken three times daily. The transfer of fenugreek into milk is unknown, but untoward effects have only rarely been reported.

Pregnancy Risk Category:

Lactation Risk Category: L3

Adult Concerns: Maple syrup odor in urine and sweat. Diarrhea, hypoglycemia, dyspnea (exaggeration of asthmatic symptoms). Once case of suspected GI bleeding in a premature infant has been reported.[6] Two cases of fenugreek allergy have been reported.[7]

Pediatric Concerns: One case of suspected GI bleeding in a premature infant has been reported.[6]

Drug Interactions:

Relative Infant Dose:

Adult Dose: 6 grams per day

Alternatives: Metoclopramide, domperidone

References:
1. Review of Natural Products Facts and Comparisons, St Louis, MO 1996.
2. Sauvaire Y, Baccou JC. Extraction of diosgenin, (25R)-spirost-5-ene-3beta-ol; problems of the hydrolysis of the saponins. Lloydia 1978; 41:247.
3. Valette G, Sauvaire Y, Baccou JC, Ribes G. Hypocholesterolaemic effect of fenugreek seeds in dogs. Atherosclerosis 1984; 50 (1):105-111.
4. Ribes G, Sauvaire Y, Baccou JC, Valette G, Chenon D, Trimble ER, Loubatieres-Mariani MM. Effects of fenugreek seeds on endocrine pancreatic secretions in dogs. Ann Nutr Metab 1984; 28 (1):37-43.
5. Lambert JP, Cormier A. Potential interaction between warfarin and boldo-fenugreek. Pharmacotherapy 2001; 21 (4):509-512.
6. DH. Personal communication. 2001.
7. Patil SP, Niphadkar PV, Bapat MM. Allergy to fenugreek (Trigonella foenum graecum). Ann Allergy Asthma Immunol 1997; 78 (3):297-300.
8. Swafford S, Berens P. Effect of fenugreek on breast milk production. Abstract. ABM News and Views 2000; 6 (3):2000.

FEXOFENADINE   L2

Trade: Allegra
Other Trades:
Uses: Antihistamine
AAP: Maternal Medication Usually Compatible with Breastfeeding

Fexofenadine is a non-sedating histamine-1 receptor antagonist and is the active metabolite of terfenadine (Seldane). It is indicated for symptoms of allergic rhinitis and other allergies. Unlike Seldane, no cardiotoxicity has been reported with this product.

In a study of 4 women receiving 60 mg/d terfenadine, no terfenadine was found in milk. However, the metabolite (fexofenadine) was present in small amounts. The average milk level of fexofenadine was 41 µg/L while the maternal plasma averaged 309 ng/mL. The time to peak for milk was 4.3 hours and the half-life in milk was 14.2 hours. The AUC (0-12) (ng.hr/mL) was 320 for milk and 1590 for plasma. The authors estimate that only 0.45% of the weight-adjusted maternal dose would be ingested by the infant.

Pregnancy Risk Category: C

Lactation Risk Category: L2

Adult Concerns: Drowsiness, fatigue, leukopenia, nausea, dyspepsia, dry mouth, headache and throat irritation have been reported. Thus far, no cardiotoxicity has been reported .

Pediatric Concerns: None reported.

Drug Interactions: Erythromycin and ketoconazole (and potentially other azole antifungals and macrolide antibiotics) may elevate the plasma level of fexofenadine (82%) significantly.

Relative Infant Dose: 0.7%

Adult Dose: 60 mg BID

Alternatives:

T ½	= 14.4 hours	M/P	= 0.21
PHL	=	PB	= 60-70%
Tmax	= 2.6 hours	Oral	= Complete
MW	= 538	pKa	=
Vd	=		

References:
1. Lucas BD, Jr., Purdy CY, Scarim SK, Benjamin S, Abel SR, Hilleman DE. Terfenadine pharmacokinetics in breast milk in lactating women. Clin Pharmacol Ther 1995; 57 (4):398-402.

FILGRASTIM   L2

Trade: Neupogen
Other Trades:
Uses: Synthetic hematopoietic agent
AAP: Not reviewed

Filgrastim is a large MW biosynthetic protein used to stimulate neutrophil production. It is more commonly called granulocyte colony stimulating factor (G-CSF).[1] There is no data on its entry into human milk, but due to its large MW (18,800 daltons) it is extremely remote that any would enter milk. Following use, the plasma levels in most individuals is often undetectable or in the picogram range. Further, due to its protein structure, it would not likely be orally bioavailable to the infant.

Pregnancy Risk Category: C

Lactation Risk Category: L2

Adult Concerns: Transient rash, nausea and vomiting, erythema and swelling at injection site, and splenomegaly.

Pediatric Concerns: None reported via milk.

Drug Interactions: Use caution with drugs such as lithium that induce release of neutrophils.

Relative Infant Dose:

Adult Dose: 5 μg/kg daily

Alternatives:

T ½	= 3.5 hours	M/P	=
PHL	=	PB	=
Tmax	= 2-8 hours	Oral	= None
MW	= 18,800	pKa	=
Vd	= 150		

References:

1. Pharmaceutical Manufacturer Prescribing Information. 1999.

FLAVOXATE   L3

Trade: Urispas
Other Trades:
Uses: Urinary tract antispasmodic
AAP: Not reviewed

Flavoxate is use as an antispasmodic to provide relief of painful urination, urgency, nocturia, urinary frequency, or incontinence.[1] It exerts a direct smooth muscle relaxation on the bladder wall and has been used in children for enuresis. No data are available on its transfer into human milk.

Pregnancy Risk Category: B

Lactation Risk Category: L3

Adult Concerns: Drowsiness, dry mouth and throat, nervousness, headache, confusion, nausea, vomiting, blurred vision. Do not use with pyloric or duodenal obstruction, GI hemorrhage, or obstructive uropathies.

Pediatric Concerns: None reported via milk.

Drug Interactions:

Relative Infant Dose:

Adult Dose: 100-200 mg TID-QID

Alternatives:

T ½	= <10 hours	M/P	=
PHL	=	PB	=
Tmax	= 2 hours	Oral	= Complete
MW	= 391	pKa	=
Vd	=		

References:
1.   Pharmaceutical Manufacturer Prescribing Information. 1997.

FLECAINIDE ACETATE   L3

Trade: Tambocor
Other Trades:
Uses: Antiarrhythmic agent
AAP: Maternal Medication Usually Compatible with Breastfeeding

Flecainide is a potent antiarrhythmic used to suppress dangerous ventricular arrhythmias.

In a group of 11 breastfeeding mothers receiving 100 mg oral flecainide (mean= 3.2 mg/kg/day) every 12 hours for 5.5 days beginning 1 day postpartum, apparent steady-state levels of flecainide in both milk and plasma were achieved in most cases by day 4 of the study.[1] Highest daily average concentration of flecainide in milk ranged from 270 to 1529 µg/L (mean= 953 µg/L) for the 11 subjects. Mean milk/plasma ratios were 3.7, 3.2, 3.5, and 2.6 on study days 2, 3, 4, and 5 respectively. After the last dose of flecainide, peak milk levels of the drug occurred at 3 to 6 hours and then declined monoexponentially. The half-life for elimination of flecainide from milk was 14.7 hours and is very similar to the plasma elimination half-life of flecainide in healthy human subjects. Based on the pharmacokinetics of flecainide in infants, the expected average steady-state plasma concentration of flecainide in a newborn infant consuming all of the milk production of its mother (approximately 700 mL/day at the highest flecainide level of 1529 µg/L), the average daily intake by the infant would be 1.07 mg. In a normal 4 kg infant, the average plasma concentration in a breastfed infant would not be expected to exceed about 62 ng/mL. The average plasma level in infants treated with therapeutic doses is 360 ng/mL.

In another study of one patient receiving 100 mg every 12 hours, milk levels of flecainide averaged 0.99 mg/L on day 4 and 5 postpartum.[2]

Pregnancy Risk Category: C

Lactation Risk Category: L3

Adult Concerns: Flecainide may induce arrhythmias in certain patients and congestive heart failure in approximately 2-5% of patients due to negative inotropy. Dizziness, nausea, blurred vision, dyspnea, and vomiting are reported. Flecainide should be reserved for patients with life-threatening arrhythmias. Withdrawal from flecainide therapy should be gradual due to the possibility of fatal cardiac arrest.

Pediatric Concerns: No adverse effects yet reported via milk, but observe for dizziness, faintness, dyspnea, headache, nausea, constipation.

Drug Interactions: Flecainide concentrations may be increased by digoxin and amiodarone. Arbutamine may exacerbate the arrhythmogenic effects of flecainide. Beta blockers, disopyramide, verapamil may enhance the negative inotropic effect of flecainide. Concurrent oral use of flecainide and cimetidine has been associated with a 46 to 65% increase in the elimination half-life, a 7 to 11% reduction in renal clearance, and a 15 to 32% reduction in the nonrenal clearance of flecainide.

Relative Infant Dose: 4.9% - 5.2%

Adult Dose: 50-100 mg BID

Alternatives:

T ½	= 7-22 hours	M/P	= 2.6-3.7
PHL	=	PB	= 50%
Tmax	= 4.5 hours	Oral	= 90%
MW	= 414	pKa	=
Vd	=		

References:
1. McQuinn RL, Pisani A, Wafa S, Chang SF, Miller AM, Frappell JM, Chamberlain GV, Camm AJ. Flecainide excretion in human breast milk. Clin Pharmacol Ther 1990; 48 (3):262-267.
2. Wagner X, Jouglard J, Moulin M, Miller AM, Petitjean J, Pisapia A. Coadministration of flecainide acetate and sotalol during pregnancy: lack of teratogenic effects, passage across the placenta, and excretion in human breast milk. Am Heart J 1990; 119 (3 Pt 1):700-702.

FLOXACILLIN   L1

Trade: Flucil
Other Trades: Fluclox, Flucloxacillin, Flopen, Floxapen, Staphylex, Flu-Amp, Flu-Clomix, Magnapen
Uses: Penicillin antibiotic
AAP: Not reviewed

Floxacillin, also called flucloxacillin, is a penicillinase-resistant penicillin frequently used for resistant staphylococcal infections. Only trace amounts are secreted into human milk.[1] Its congener, cloxacillin, is commonly used to treat mastitis in breastfeeding mothers and has been used in thousands of breastfeeding patients without problem. Changes in gut flora are possible but unlikely.

Pregnancy Risk Category: B

Lactation Risk Category: L1

Adult Concerns: Adverse effects of Floxacillin are similar to those of other penicillins, and include nausea, vomiting, diarrhea, constipation, and skin rashes; hemolytic anemia and interstitial nephritis have been reported rarely. Cases of acute hepatic cholestasis related to floxacillin therapy has been reported.

Pediatric Concerns: None reported via milk.

Drug Interactions: Concomitant penicillin and aminoglycoside therapy has been reported to result in inactivation of the aminoglycoside. Small changes in methotrexate plasma levels have been reported.

Relative Infant Dose:

Adult Dose: 250-500 mg four times daily

Alternatives: Cloxacillin, Dicloxacillin

T ½	= 1.5 hours	M/P	=
PHL	=	PB	= 94%
Tmax	= 1 hour	Oral	= 50%
MW	= 454	pKa	=
Vd	= 0.11		

References:
1. Pharmaceutical Manufacturer Prescribing Information, 2010.

FLUCONAZOLE   L2

Trade: Diflucan
Other Trades:
Uses: Antifungal, particularly candida infections
AAP: Maternal Medication Usually Compatible with Breastfeeding

Fluconazole is a synthetic triazole antifungal agent and is frequently used for vaginal, oropharyngeal, and esophageal candidiasis. Many of the triazole antifungals (itraconazole, terconazole) have similar mechanisms of action and are considered fungistatic in action. In vivo studies have found fluconazole to have fungistatic activity against a variety of fungal strains including C. albicans, C. tropicalis, T. glabrata, and C. neoformans.

The pharmacokinetics are similar following both oral and IV administration. The drug is almost completely absorbed orally (>90%). Peak plasma levels occur in 1-2 hours after oral administration. Unlike ketoconazole and itraconazole, fluconazole absorption is unaffected by gastric pH and does not require an acid pH to be absorbed. Steady state plasma levels are only attained after 5-10 days of therapy but can be achieved on day two with a loading dose (twice the daily dose) on the first day. Average plasma levels are 4.12 to 8.1 µg/mL. Fluconazole is widely and evenly distributed in most tissues and fluids and is distributed in total body water. Concentrations in skin and urine may be 10 fold higher than plasma levels. CSF concentrations are 50-94% of the plasma levels. Plasma protein binding is minimal at about 11%. Fluconazole is primarily excreted renally. Oral fluconazole is currently cleared for pediatric candidiasis for infants 6 months and older, and has an FDA Safety Profile for neonates 1 day and older. Clinical cure rate for oropharyngeal candidiasis in pediatric patients is reported at 86% with fluconazole (2-3 mg/kg/day) compared to 46% of nystatin treated patients. Fluconazole is transferred into human milk with a milk/plasma ratio of approximately 0.85.[1] Following a single 150 mg dose, milk levels at 2, 5, 24 and 48 hours were reported to be 2.93, 2.66, 1.76, and 0.98 µg/mL respectively. Plasma levels at 2, 5, 24, and 48 hours were 6.4, 2.79, 2.52, and 1.19 µg/mL respectively.[1]

Other Plasma Kinetics:

Plasma Half-Life= 35 hours
Breastmilk Half-life= 30 hours

From these data, and assuming an average milk level of 2.3 mg/L, an infant consuming 150 mL/kg/d of milk would receive an average of 0.34 mg/kg/d of fluconazole or 16% of the weight-adjusted maternal dose, and less than 5.8% of the pediatric dose (6 mg/kg/d).

In another study of one patient receiving 200 mg daily (1.5 times the above dose) for 18 days, the peak milk concentration was 4.1 mg/L at 2 hours following the dose.[2] However, the mean concentration of fluconazole in milk was not reported.

Pediatric Indications: While fluconazole is not cleared by the FDA for neonates, it is commonly used. It is however, cleared for infants 6 months and older. Due to the emergence of resistance to other antifungals, particularly nystatin, the use of fluconazole in pediatrics is increasing. Numerous reports now suggest that fluconazole is an effective and safe antifungal in low birth weight infants and neonates.[3,4,5,6,10] In one study of 40 low birth weight infants receiving fluconazole for up to 48 days, fluconazole produced few side effects.[7] Elevated liver enzymes were reported in only 2 of 40 serious ill LBW infants and due to other drugs; it is not known if this was associated with fluconazole therapy.

Dosage Recommendations:

Adult Vaginal Candidiasis: 150 mg PO-single dose.

Oropharyngeal Candidiasis: Varies, but 200 mg STAT followed by 100 mg daily for up to 14 days is recommended.

Systemic Candidiasis: For persistent or chronic infections, fluconazole has been used prophylactically in immunocompromised patients at a dose of 150 mg weekly to prevent recurrence[8,9].

Pediatric Dosing: The recommended pediatric dosing for oral candidiasis is 6 mg/kg STAT followed by 3 mg/kg/day. For systemic candidiasis, 6-12 mg/kg/day is generally recommended.[10] These current recommendations are for infants 6 months and older. The manufacturer states that a number of infants 1 day old and older have been safely treated. One study of premature infants suggests that the dose in very low birth weight infants should be 6 mg/kg every 2 to 3 days.[11]

Availability: 50, 100, 200 mg tablets. Oral suspensions= 10 mg/mL and 40 mg/mL

Fluconazole Dosage*

Indication	Day 1	Daily Therapy	Minimum Duration of Therapy
Oropharyngeal candidiasis	200 mg	100 mg	14 d
Esophageal candidiasis	200 mg	100 mg	21 d
Systemic candidiasis	400 mg	200 mg	28 d
Cryptococcal meningitis acute relapse	400 mg 200 mg	200 mg 200 mg	10-12 wk after CSF culture becomes negative

*Pharmaceutical Manufacturers Package Insert

Pregnancy Risk Category: C

Lactation Risk Category: L2

Adult Concerns: Adverse effects have only been reported in about 5-30% of patients, and in these, only 1-2.8% of patients have required discontinuation of the medication. Although adverse hepatic effects have been reported, they are very rare, and many occur coincident with the administration of other medications in AIDS patients. The most common complications include vomiting, diarrhea, abdominal pain, and skin rashes.

Pediatric Concerns: Pediatric complications from oral ingestion include GI symptoms such as vomiting, nausea, diarrhea, abdominal pain. Nephrotoxicity has not been reported. No complications from exposure to breastmilk have found.

Drug Interactions: Decreased hepatic clearance of fluconazole results from use with cyclosporin, zidovudine, rifabutin, theophylline, oral hypoglycemics (glipizide and tolbutamide), warfarin, phenytoin, and terfenadine. Decreased plasma levels of fluconazole have resulted following administration with rifampin, and cimetidine.

Relative Infant Dose: 16.4% - 21.5%

Adult Dose: 50-200 mg daily.

Alternatives:

T ½	= 30 hours	M/P	= 0.46-0.85
PHL	= 88.6 hours (neonate)	PB	= 15%.
Tmax	= 1-2 hours	Oral	= >90%
MW	= 306	pKa	=
Vd	=		

References:

1. Force RW. Fluconazole concentrations in breast milk. Pediatr Infect Dis J 1995; 14 (3):235-236.
2. Schilling CG. et.al. Excretion of fluconazole in human breast milk (abstract # 130). Pharmacotherapy 1993; 13:287.
3. Wainer S, Cooper PA, Gouws H, Akierman A. Prospective study of fluconazole therapy in systemic neonatal fungal infection. Pediatr Infect Dis J 1997; 16 (8):763-767.
4. Wiest DB, Fowler SL, Garner SS, Simons DR. Fluconazole in neonatal disseminated candidiasis. Arch Dis Child 1991; 66 (8):1002.
5. Gurses N, Kalayci AG. Fluconazole monotherapy for candidal meningitis in a premature infant. Clin Infect Dis 1996; 23 (3):645-646.
6. Driessen M, Ellis JB, Cooper PA, Wainer S, Muwazi F, Hahn D, Gous H, De Villiers FP. Fluconazole vs. amphotericin B for the treatment of neonatal fungal septicemia: a prospective randomized trial. Pediatr Infect Dis J 1996; 15 (12):1107-1112.
7. Huttova M, Hartmanova I, Kralinsky K, Filka J, Uher J, Kurak J, Krizan S, Kremery V, Jr. Candida fungemia in neonates treated with fluconazole: report of forty cases, including eight with meningitis. Pediatr Infect Dis J 1998; 17 (11):1012-1015.
8. Leen CL, Dunbar EM, Ellis ME, Mandal BK. Once-weekly fluconazole to prevent recurrence of oropharyngeal candidiasis in patients with AIDS and AIDS-related complex: a double-blind placebo-controlled study. J Infect 1990; 21 (1):55-60.
9. Winston DJ, Chandrasekar PH, Lazarus HM, Goodman JL, Silber JL, Horowitz H, Shadduck RK, Rosenfeld CS, Ho WG, Islam MZ, . Fluconazole prophylaxis of fungal infections in patients with acute leukemia. Results of a randomized placebo-controlled, double-blind, multicenter trial. Ann Intern Med 1993; 118 (7):495-503.
10. Viscoli C, Castagnola E, Corsini M, Gastaldi R, Soliani M, Terragna A. Fluconazole therapy in an underweight infant. Eur J Clin Microbiol Infect Dis 1989; 8 (10):925-926.
11. Saxen H, Hoppu K, Pohjavuori M. Pharmacokinetics of fluconazole in very low birth weight infants during the first two weeks of life. Clin Pharmacol Ther 1993; 54 (3):269-277.

FLUDEOXYGLUCOSE F 18   L3

Trade: Fludeoxyglucose F 18
Other Trades:
Uses: PET Scanning pharmaceutical
AAP: Not reviewed

Fludeoxyglucose F 18 is a positron-emitting radiopharmaceutical used in conjunction with positron emission tomography (PET Scanning) to detect alterations in tissue glucose metabolism and is useful in detecting brain tumors, certain malignancies, chronic coronary artery disease, partial epilepsy, and Alzheimer's disease.[1,2,3]

Fludeoxyglucose F 18 is rapidly distributed to all parts of the body that have significant glucose metabolism, including the breast. In a group of 6 lactating women, who received between 50-160 MBq FDG, amounts reported in milk were very low.[4] Decay-corrected activity measurable in breast milk ranged from 5.54 to 19.3 Bq/mL/MBq injected. Interestingly, the levels in breast tissue were quite high, but this product seems sequestered in breast tissue without penetrating into milk. The calculated maximum cumulative dose to the infant, 0.085 mSv with no interruption of breast-feeding, is well below the recommended limit of 1 mSv. Indeed, a higher radiation dose is received by the infant from close contact with the breast than from ingestion of radioactive milk. The authors suggest pumping of the milk and feeding in bottles by another individual to reduce direct exposure to radiation.

The half-life of the F-18 is short, only 110 minutes. Due to concentration in some tissues such as the bladder, radiation exposure could be a problem and emptying of the breast at routine intervals would reduce radiation exposure to breast tissue. The USPDI (1994) recommends interruption of breastfeeding for 12-24 hours. At 9 hours, 97% of the radioisotope would be decayed away.[5] It is likely that after 12 hours, almost all radioisotope would be decayed to almost background levels. Recommend pumping and dumping of breastmilk after the procedure for at least 12 hours to avoid all radiation.

Pregnancy Risk Category:

Lactation Risk Category: L3

Adult Concerns: No untoward effects have been reported for this product.

Pediatric Concerns: None reported, but possible radiation exposure if breastfed prior to 12-24 hours after dose.

Drug Interactions:

Relative Infant Dose:

Adult Dose:

Alternatives:

T ½	= 110 minutes	M/P	=
PHL	=	PB	= Minimal
Tmax	= 30 minutes	Oral	= Complete
MW	=	pKa	=
Vd	=		

References:

1. Jamieson D, Alavi A, Jolles P, Chawluk J, Reivich M. Positron emission tomography in the investigation of central nervous system disorders. Radiol Clin North Am 1988; 26 (5):1075-1088.

2. Jones SC, Alavi A, Christman D, Montanez I, Wolf AP, Reivich M. The radiation dosimetry of 2 [F-18]fluoro-2-deoxy-D-glucose in man. J Nucl Med 1982; 23 (7):613-617.

3. Som P, Atkins HL, Bandoypadhyay D, Fowler JS, MacGregor RR, Matsui K, Oster ZH, Sacker DF, Shiue CY, Turner H, Wan CN, Wolf AP, Zabinski SV. A fluorinated glucose analog, 2-fluoro-2-deoxy-D-glucose (F-18): nontoxic tracer for rapid tumor detection. J Nucl Med 1980; 21 (7):670-675.

4. Hicks RJ, Binns D, Stabin MG. Pattern of uptake and excretion of (18) F-FDG in the lactating breast. J Nucl Med. 2001 Aug;42 (8):1238-42. PubMed PMID: 11483686.

5. Jones SC, Alavi A, Christman D, Montanez I, Wolf AP, Reivich M. The radiation dosimetry of 2 [F-18]fluoro-2-deoxy-D-glucose in man. J Nucl Med 1982; 23 (7):613-617.

FLUDROCORTISONE   L3

Trade: Florinef, Myconef
Other Trades:
Uses: Mineralocorticoid
AAP: Not reviewed

Fludrocortisone is a halogenated derivative of hydrocortisone with very potent mineralocorticoid activity and is generally used to treat Addison's disease.[1,2] Although its glucocorticoid effect is 15 times more potent than hydrocortisone, it is primarily used for its powerful ability to retain sodium in the vascular compartment (mineralocorticoid activity). It is not known if fludrocortisone penetrates into milk but if it is similar to other corticosteroids, it is very unlikely the amounts in milk will be clinically relevant until extremely high doses are used, but caution is recommended.

Pregnancy Risk Category: C

Lactation Risk Category: L3

Adult Concerns: Hypertension, sodium retention, cardiac hypertrophy, congestive heart failure, and headache.

Pediatric Concerns: None via milk.

Drug Interactions: Excessive potassium levels may result from use with amphotericin B. Use with loop diuretics may dramatically increase potassium loss. Phenytoin, rifampin, phenobarbital, and fosphenytoin may increase hepatic metabolism of fludrocortisone and reduce its efficacy. Lithium may reduce efficacy of fludrocortisone. Tuberculin reactions may be suppressed for periods up to 6 weeks in patients receiving fludrocortisone.

Relative Infant Dose:

Adult Dose: 0.1-0.4 mg daily

Alternatives:

T ½	= 3.5 hours	M/P	=
PHL	=	PB	= 42%
Tmax	= 1.7 hours	Oral	= Complete
MW	= 380	pKa	=
Vd	=		

References:
1. Pharmaceutical Manufacturer Prescribing Information. 1999.
2. Drug Facts and Comparisons 1999 ed. ed. St. Louis: 1999.

FLUNARIZINE

L4

Trade: Sibelium
Other Trades: Novo-Flunarizine
Uses: Antihypertensive
AAP: Not reviewed

Flunarizine is a calcium channel blocker primarily indicated for use in migraine headache prophylaxis and peripheral vascular disease. It has a very long half-life and a huge volume of distribution, which contributes to the long half-life.[1] No data are available on the transfer of this product into human milk. However, due to its incredibly long half-life and high volume of distribution, it is possible that this product, over time, could build up and concentrate in a breastfed infant. Other calcium channel blockers may be preferred. Use with extreme caution.

Pregnancy Risk Category:

Lactation Risk Category: L4

Adult Concerns: Extrapyramidal symptoms in elderly patients, depression, porphyria, thrombophlebitis, drowsiness, headache, dizziness.

Pediatric Concerns: None reported via milk, but caution is advised.

Drug Interactions: Prolonged bradycardia with adenosine. Sinus arrest when used with amiodarone. Hypotension and bradycardia when used with beta blockers. Increase of carbamazepine and cyclosporin plasma levels when used with flunarizine.

Relative Infant Dose:

Adult Dose: 10 mg daily

Alternatives: Nifedipine, Nimodipine, Verapamil

T ½	= 19 days	M/P	=
PHL	= 23 days	PB	= 99%
Tmax	= 2-4 hours	Oral	= Complete
MW	=	pKa	–
Vd	= 43.2		

References:
1. Pharmaceutical Manufacturer Prescribing Information.

FLUNISOLIDE   L3

Trade: Nasalide, Aerobid
Other Trades: Bronalide, Rhinalar, PMS-Flunisolide, Syntaris
Uses: Inhaled and intranasal steroid.
AAP: Not reviewed

Flunisolide is a potent corticosteroid used to reduce airway hyperreactivity in asthmatics. It is also available as Nasalide for intranasal use for allergic rhinitis. Generally, only small levels of flunisolide are absorbed systemically (about 40%) thereby reducing systemic effects and presumably breastmilk levels as well.[1,2] After inhalation of 1 mg flunisolide, systemic availability was only 40% and plasma level was 0.4-1 nanogram/mL. Adrenal suppression in children has not been documented even after therapy of 2 months with 1600 µg/day. Once absorbed, flunisolide is rapidly removed from the plasma compartment by first-pass uptake in the liver. Although no data on breastmilk levels are yet available, it is unlikely that the level secreted in milk is clinically relevant.

Pregnancy Risk Category: C

Lactation Risk Category: L3

Adult Concerns: Most common side effect is irritation, due to vehicle not drug itself. Loss of taste, nasal irritation, flu-like symptoms, sore throat, headache.

Pediatric Concerns: None reported. Can be used in children down to age 6.

Drug Interactions:

Relative Infant Dose:

Adult Dose: 1 mg daily.

Alternatives:

T ½	= 1.8 hours	M/P	=
PHL	=	PB	=
Tmax	= 30 minutes	Oral	= 21% (oral)
MW	= 435	pKa	=
Vd	= 1.8		

References:
1. Pharmaceutical Manufacturer Prescribing Information. 1995.
2. Drug Facts and Comparisons 1995 ed. ed. St. Louis: 1995.

FLUNITRAZEPAM | L3

Trade: Rohypnol
Other Trades: Hypnodorm, Raohypnol
Uses: Benzodiazepine sedative
AAP: Not reviewed

Flunitrazepam is a prototypic benzodiazepine. Frequently called the "Date Rape Pill", it induces rapid sedation and significant amnesia, particularly when mixed with alcohol.[1,2] Effects last about 8 hours. It is recommended for adult insomnia and for pediatric preanesthetic sedation.

Pregnancy Risk Category: D

Lactation Risk Category: L3
L4 if used chronically

Adult Concerns: Drowsiness, amnesia, sedation, ataxia, headache, memory impairment, tremors.

Pediatric Concerns: None reported via milk, but observe for sedation.

Drug Interactions: Clarithromycin and other macrolide antibiotics may increase plasma levels for benzodiazepines by inhibiting metabolism. May have enhanced effect when added to fentanyl, ketamine, nitrous oxide. Addition of even small amounts of alcohol may produce profound sedation, psychomotor impairment, and amnesia. Theophylline may reduce the sedative effects of benzodiazepines.

Relative Infant Dose:

Adult Dose: 2 mg daily.

Alternatives: Lorazepam, Alprazolam

T ½	= 20-30 hours	M/P	=
PHL	=	PB	= 80%
Tmax	= 2 hours	Oral	= 80-90%
MW	– 313	pKa	=
Vd	= 3.6		

References:
1. Kanto J, Erkkola R, Kangas L, Pitkanen Y. Placental transfer of flunitrazepam following intramuscular administration during labour. Br J Clin Pharmacol 1987; 23 (4):491-494.
2. Kanto J, Kangas L, Leppanen T. A comparative study of the clinical effects of oral flunitrazepam, medazepam, and placebo. Int J Clin Pharmacol Ther Toxicol 1982; 20 (9):431-433.

FLUOCINOLONE + HYDROQUINONE + TRETINOIN   L3

Trade: Tri-Luma
Other Trades:
Uses: Treatment of melasma of the face.
AAP: Not reviewed

Tri-Luma cream is indicated for the short-term intermittent treatment of moderate to severe melasma of the face. It is a combination drug product containing corticosteroid (fluocinolone), retinoid (tretinoin), and bleaching agent (hydroquinone).See individual monographs for more data.

Percutaneous absorption of unchanged tretinoin, hydroquinone and fluocinolone acetonide into the systemic circulation of two groups of healthy volunteers (Total n= 59) was found to be minimal following 8 weeks of daily application of 1g (Group I, n= 45) or 6g (Group II, n= 14) of TRI-LUMA Cream. For tretinoin quantifiable plasma concentrations were obtained in 57.78% (26 out of 45) of Group I and 57.14% (8 out of 14) of Group II subjects. The exposure to tretinoin as reflected by the C_{max} values ranged from 2.01 to 5.34 ng/mL (Group I) and 2.0 to 4.99 ng/mL (Group II). Thus, daily application of TRI-LUMA Cream resulted in a minimal increase of normal endogenous levels of tretinoin. The circulating tretinoin levels represent only a portion of total tretinoin-associated retinoids, which would include metabolites of tretinoin and that sequestered into peripheral tissues.

For hydroquinone, quantifiable plasma concentrations were obtained in 18% (8 out of 44) Group I subjects. The exposure to hydroquinone as reflected by the C_{max} values ranged from 25.55 to 86.52 ng/mL. All Group II subjects (6g dose) had post-dose plasma hydroquinone concentrations below the quantitation limit. For fluocinolone acetonide, Groups I and II subjects had all post-dose plasma concentrations below quantitation limit.

We do not have specific data on this combination product, but levels of the individual products are not high and milk levels will be much lower. However, caution is still recommended and a risk:benefit analysis must justify its use in breastfeeding mothers.

Pregnancy Risk Category:

Lactation Risk Category: L3

Adult Concerns: See individual agents.

Pediatric Concerns: No reports in the literature. Risks are moderate to low.

Drug Interactions: See individual monographs on this product.

Relative Infant Dose:

Adult Dose:

Alternatives:

References:
1. Pharmaceutical manufacturers prescribing information. 2005.

FLUORESCEIN   L3

Trade: AK-Fluor, Fluorescite, Funduscein-10, Ophthifluor,
        Fluorescein sodium, Ful-Glo, Fluorets, Fluor-I-Strip
Other Trades:
Uses: Diagnostic dye in angiography
AAP: Maternal Medication Usually Compatible with
        Breastfeeding

Sodium fluorescein is a yellow, water-soluble dye. A 2% fluorescein ophthalmic solution or an impregnated fluorescein strip is used topically to detect corneal abrasions, for fitting of hard contact lenses, and intravenously for fluorescein angiography. Fluorescein is used in two ways. One, in which a small amount is added directly to the eye generally by ophthalmologists and optometrists, and secondly, when much larger quantities are administered intravenously (5 mL of 10% solution).

In a study of one patient who received an intravenous dose of fluorescein (5 mL of 10% fluorescein= 500 mg), breastmilk levels were monitored for over 76 hours.[1] Concentrations of 372 µg/L at 6 hours and 170 µg/L at 76 hours after the dose were reported. In this patient, the half-life of fluorescein in breastmilk appeared quite long, approximating 62 hours. While the authors conclude that this is a high dose via milk, in another patient who received slightly more (910 mg IV), the patient's plasma levels of fluorescein monoglucuronide were 37,000 µg/L.[2] Using this data, it would appear that an approximation of the milk/plasma ratio would be about 0.018, which suggests that very little of the absolute maternal dose enters milk. Nevertheless, fluorescein-induced phototoxicity remains a possibility in an infant fed breastmilk containing sodium fluorescein. One case of severe fluorescein phototoxicity has been reported in an infant receiving fluorescein intravenously.[3] If the infant is not undergoing phototherapy, it would appear that there is little risk to a breastfeeding infant.

Pregnancy Risk Category: C (topical)
                                X (parenteral)

Lactation Risk Category: L3

Adult Concerns: Fluorescein-induced phototoxicity. Nausea, vomiting, dizziness, syncope, pruritus, seizures, following IV therapy. Severe reactions are rare. Oral fluorescein appears to elicit very few adverse reaction.

Pediatric Concerns: None reported via milk, but avoid phototherapy if used.

Drug Interactions: Interferes with numerous laboratory tests.

Relative Infant Dose: 0.8%

Adult Dose: 500 mg intravenous

Alternatives:

T ½	= 4.4 hours (metabolite)	M/P	=
PHL	=	PB	= 70-85%
Tmax	= 1 hour	Oral	= 50%
MW	= 376	pKa	=
Vd	= 0.5		

References:
1. Maquire AM, Bennett J. Fluorescein elimination in human breast milk. Arch Ophthalmol 1988; 106 (6):718-719.
2. Kearns GL, Williams BJ, Timmons OD. Fluorescein phototoxicity in a premature infant. J Pediatr 1985; 107 (5):796-798.
3. Kearns GL, Williams BJ, Timmons OD. Fluorescein phototoxicity in a premature infant. J Pediatr 1985; 107 (5):796-798.

FLUORIDE   L2

Trade: Pediaflor, Flura
Other Trades: Fluor-A-Day, Fluotic, Fluorigard
Uses: Hardening enamel of teeth
AAP: Reported as having no effect on breastfeeding

Fluoride is an essential element required for bone and teeth development. It is available as salts of sodium and stannic (tin). Excessive levels are known to stain teeth irreversibly. One study shows breastmilk levels of 0.024-0.172 ppm in milk (mean= 0.077 ppm) of a population exposed to fluoridated water (0.7ppm).[1]

In another study of breastfeeding women from areas low and rich in fluoride, milk fluoride levels were similar.[2] The mean fluoride concentration was 0.36 µmol/L for colostrum and 0.37 µmol/L for mature milk in the region with 1 ppm fluoride enriched water. In the region with 0.2 ppm fluoride, the mean fluoride concentration of colostrum was 0.28 µmol/L. There was no statistical difference in any of these milk fluoride levels.

Fluoride probably forms calcium fluoride salts in milk which may limit the oral bioavailability of the fluoride provided by human milk. Maternal supplementation is unnecessary and not recommended in areas with high fluoride content (>0.7 ppm) in water.[3] Allergy to fluoride has been reported in one infant.[4] Younger children (2-6 years) should be instructed to use pea-sized quantities of toothpaste. Brushing should be limited to <= 2 times daily with fluridated toothpaste and to spit out excess toothpaste. The American Academy of Pediatrics no longer recommends supplementing of breastfed infants with oral fluoride for the first 6 months of life. From 6 months to 3 years of age, supplement fluoride drops only if drinking water levels are less than 0.3 ppm. Bottled water may or may not contain fluoride.

Fluoride Ion and Dosing Recommendations

Fluoride Content of Drinking Water	Daily Dose, Oral (mg) In Non-Breastfed Infants
<0.3 ppm	
Birth - 2 y	0.25
2-3 y	0.5
3-12 y	1
0.3-0.7 ppm	
Birth - 2 y	0
2-3 y	0.25
3-12 y	0.5

Pregnancy Risk Category: C

Lactation Risk Category: L2

Adult Concerns: Stained enamel, allergic rash.

Pediatric Concerns: Allergy to fluoride has been reported in one infant. Do not use maternal doses > 0.7 ppm.

Drug Interactions: Decreased absorption when used with magnesium, aluminum, and calcium containing products.

Relative Infant Dose:

Adult Dose: 1 mg daily.

Alternatives:

T ½	= 6 hours	**M/P**	=
PHL	=	**PB**	=
Tmax	=	**Oral**	= 90% (Na)
MW	= 19	**pKa**	=
Vd	= 0.5-0.7		

References:
1. Latifah R, Razak IA. Fluoride levels in mother's milk. J Pedod 1989; 13 (2):149-154.
2. Spak CJ, Hardell LI, De Chateau P. Fluoride in human milk. Acta Paediatr Scand 1983; 72 (5):699-701.
3. Fluoride supplementation of the breast-fed infant JAMA 1990; 263 (16):2179.
4. Shea J. et.al. Allergy to fluoride. Ann Allergy 1967; 25:388.

FLUOROURACIL   L5

Trade: 5FU, Adrucil, Efudex, Fluoroplex, Carac
Other Trades:
Uses: Anticancer drug, actinic keratosis
AAP: Not reviewed

Fluorouracil is a potent antineoplastic agent generally used topically for various skin cancers and IV for various carcinomas. No data is available on its transfer into breastmilk. 5FU is an extremely toxic and dangerous compound and is probably contraindicated in breastfeeding women following IV therapy.[1] It is rapidly cleared by the liver and two long-half-life metabolites (FdUMP, FUTP) are formed. The clinical effect and half-life of these metabolites is unknown.

5FU is commonly used topically as a cream for actinic or solar keratosis. The topical absorption of 5FU is minimal, reported to be less than 10%.[2] Although it is unlikely that significant quantities of 5FU would be transferred to a breastfed infant following topical application to small areas, caution is urged. If large body areas were exposed to this therapy, significant absorption could occur.

5FU is also sometimes used intraocularly following retinal surgery. Animal studies suggest that retention in the vitreous humor is long-lasting, thus the drug would be slowly released into the plasma compartment over several days. The doses here are small (5 mg) and are unlikely to produce significant plasma levels or milk levels of this drug. See Appendix A for more details.

Pregnancy Risk Category: D during first and second trimesters
                                 X during third trimester

Lactation Risk Category: L5

Adult Concerns: Nausea, vomiting, anorexia, blood dyscrasias, bone marrow suppression, myocardial toxicity, dyspnea, cardiogenic shock, rashes.

Pediatric Concerns: None reported but caution is recommended. A waiting period of 24 hours or more would largely reduce any risk.

Drug Interactions: Drug interactions are numerous and include allopurinol, cimetidine, methotrexate, leucovorin and others.

Relative Infant Dose:

Adult Dose: 6-12 mg/kg injection (IV) daily.

Alternatives:

T ½	= 8-22 minutes	M/P	=
PHL	=	PB	= 8-12%
Tmax	= Immediate (IV)	Oral	= 0-80%
MW	= 130	pKa	=
Vd	= 0.12		

References:
1. McEvoy GE. (ed):AFHS Drug Information. New York, NY: 2009.
2. Grochow LB, Ames MM. A clinician's guide to chemotherapy pharmacokinetics and pharamcodynamics. 1st ed. Baltimore, MD: Williams & Wilkins; 1998.

FLUOXETINE L2

Trade: Prozac
Other Trades: Apo-Fluoxetine, Novo-Fluoxetine, Lovan, Zactin
Uses: Antidepressant
AAP: Drugs whose effect on nursing infants is unknown but may be of concern

Fluoxetine is a very popular serotonin reuptake inhibitor (SSRI) currently used for depression and a host of other syndromes. Fluoxetine absorption is rapid and complete and the parent compound is rapidly metabolized to norfluoxetine, which is an active, long half-life metabolite (360 hours). Both fluoxetine and norfluoxetine appear to permeate breastmilk to levels approximately 1/5 to 1/4 of maternal plasma. In one patient at steady-state (dose=20mg/day), plasma levels of fluoxetine were 100.5 µg/L and levels of norfluoxetine were 194.5 µg/L.[1] Fluoxetine levels in milk were 28.8 µg/L and norfluoxetine levels were 41.6 µg/L. Milk/plasma ratios were 0.286 for fluoxetine, and 0.21 for norfluoxetine.

In another patient receiving 20 mg daily at bedtime, the milk concentration of fluoxetine was 67 µg/L and norfluoxetine 52 µg/L at four hours.[2] At 8 hours postdose, the concentration of fluoxetine was 17 µg/L and norfluoxetine was 13 µg/L. Using this data, the authors estimated that the total daily dose was only 15-20 µg/kg per day which represents a low exposure.

In another study of 10 breastfeeding women receiving 0.39 mg/kg/day of fluoxetine, the average breastmilk levels for fluoxetine and norfluoxetine ranged from 24.4-181.1 µg/L and 37.4-199.1 µg/L respectively.[3] Peak milk concentrations occurred within 6 hours. The milk/plasma ratios for fluoxetine and norfluoxetine were 0.88 and 0.72 respectively. Fluoxetine plasma levels in one infant were undetectable (<1 ng/mL). Using this data, an infant consuming 150 mL/kg/day would consume approximately 9.3-57 μg/kg/day total fluoxetine (and metabolite), which represents 5-9% of the maternal dose. No adverse effects were noted in the infants in this study.

Severe colic, fussiness, and crying have been reported in one case report.[4] The mother was receiving a dose of 20 mg fluoxetine per day. Concentrations of fluoxetine and norfluoxetine in breastmilk were 69 μg/L and 90 μg/L respectively. The plasma levels in the infant for fluoxetine and norfluoxetine were 340 ng/mL and 208 ng/mL respectively which is almost twice that of normal maternal ranges. The author does not report the maternal plasma levels but suggests they were similar to Isenberg's adult levels (100.5 ng/mL and 194.5 ng/mL for fluoxetine and norfluoxetine). In this infant, the plasma levels would approach those of a mother receiving twice the above 20 mg dose per day (40 mg/day). The symptoms resolved upon discontinuation of fluoxetine by the mother.

In a study by Brent [5], an infant exposed in utero and postpartum via milk, had moderate plasma fluoxetine levels that increased in the three weeks postpartum due to breastmilk ingestion. The infant's plasma levels of fluoxetine went from none detectable at day 13 to 61 ng/mL at day 21. The mean adult therapeutic range is 145 ng/mL. The infant in this study exhibited slight seizure activity at 3 weeks, 4 months, and 5 months.

Ilett reports that in a group of 14 women receiving 0.51 mg/kg/day fluoxetine, the mean M/P ratio was 0.67 (range 0.35 to 0.13) and 0.56 for norfluoxetine.[6] Mean total infant dose in fluoxetine equivalents was 6.81% of the weight-adjusted maternal dose. The reported infant fluoxetine and norfluoxetine plasma levels ranged from 20-252 μg/L and 17-187 μg/L respectively.

Neonatal withdrawl syndrome was reported in one infant exposed in utero. The mother was taking 20 mg/day, and delivered at 27 weeks. The baby was treated with nasal CPAP and phenobarbital at a dose of 5 mg/kg/day because the symptoms were interpreted as convulsions. The clinical picture was interpreted as neonatal withdrawl syndrome.[13]

It is not known if these reported side effects (seizures, colic, fussiness, crying) are common, although this author has received numerous other personal communications similar to this. Indeed in one case, the infant became comatose at 11 days postpartum with high plasma levels of norfluoxetine.[8] At present, fluoxetine is the only antidepressant cleared for use in pregnancy. This may pose an added problem in breastfed infants. Infants born of mothers receiving fluoxetine are born with full steady state plasma levels of the medication, and each time they are breastfed the level in the infant may rise further.

Several methods of reducing the risk to newborns is to reduce or eliminate the use of fluoxetine just prior to delivery, or to switch to an alternate antidepressant while breastfeeding (sertraline, paroxetine, etc.). While we do not know the real risk of side effects, they are apparently low for the population. If the patient cannot tolerate switching to another antidepressant, then fluoxetine should be continued.

Age at initiation of therapy is of importance. Use in older infants (4-6 months or older) is virtually without complications because they can metabolize and excrete the medication more rapidly. Data published in 1999 also suggest that weight gain in infants breastfed from mothers who were taking fluoxetine demonstrated a growth curve significantly below that of infants who were breastfed by mothers who did not take the drug. The average deficit in measurements taken between 2 and 6 months of age was 392 grams body weight. None of these infants were noted to have unusual behavior.[9] Another report suggests that fluoxetine may induce a state of anesthesia of the vagina and nipples, although the relevance of this to breastfeeding mothers is unknown.[10] The author has had another report of a paroxetine-induced reduction of milk ejection reflex. Whether or not a loss of MER is related to an anesthesia of the nipples is purely speculative.

One case reported toxicity in a preterm infant whose mother was taking 40 mg/day. At 4 hours of age, the infant was tachypneic with a respiratory rate of 100. The infant had an erythematous rash on both cheeks and petechiae on the abdomen, chest and extremeties, and scleral icterus. Plasma levels of fluoxetine and norfluoxetine at 96 hours of age were 92 and 34 ng/mL respectively, which is within the adult therapeutic range. This infant at 4 months of age had normal neurodevelopment.[11] This study suggests that seizure-like activity and toxicity can be expected in preterm infants.

Current data on Sertraline and escitalopram suggest these medications have difficulty entering milk, and more importantly, the infant. Therefore, they are preferred agents over fluoxetine for therapy of depression in breastfeeding mothers.[12] However, it is important to remember, that the risks of not breastfeeding far outweigh the risk of using fluoxetine and women who can only take fluoxetine should be advised to continue breastfeeding and observe the infant for side effects. Finally, fluoxetine therapy during breastfeeding is by no means contraindicated an has been used in many thousands of women.

GEMIFLOXACIN MESYLATE	L3

Trade: Factive
Other Trades:
Uses: Antibiotic
AAP: Not reviewed

A member of the fluoroquinolone family, gemifloxacin is used to treat a wide range of Gram-positive and Gram-negative microorganisms. It acts by inhibiting DNA gyrase and topoisomerase IV, thus inhibiting bacterial DNA synthesis. Gemifloxacin is effective against those organisms that have mutated and are unsusceptible to other fluoroquinolones.[1]

No data are available on the transfer of gemifloxacin into human milk. Other fluoroquinolones are suitable however, and it is unlikely this one will be that different. Some quinolones are excreted into breastmilk (ciprofloxacin) but are safe to use. This product has a high Vd, so milk levels will probably be lower than with ciprofloxacin. Observe for diarrhea.

Adult Concerns: Adverse reactions include headache, rash, hyperkalemia, diarrhea, nausea, and increased transaminases.

Pediatric Concerns: No data are available.

Drug Interactions: Concurrent use of corticosteroids may increase the risk of tendon rupture. Metal cations and antacids can decrease absorption of gemifloxacin. Gemifloxacin may increase the effect of glyburide and warfarin.

T ½	= 7 hours	M/P	=
PHL	=	PB	= 60-70%
Tmax	= 0.5-2 hours	Oral	= 71%
MW	= 485	pKa	=
Vd	= 4.2		

GENTAMICIN   L2

Trade: Garamycin

Other Trades: Alocomicin, Cidomycin, Garatec, Palacos, Septopal, Cidomycin

Uses: Aminoglycoside antibiotic

AAP: Maternal Medication Usually Compatible with Breastfeeding

Gentamicin is a narrow spectrum antibiotic generally used for gram negative infections. The oral absorption of gentamicin (<1%) is generally nil with the exception of premature neonates, where small amounts may be absorbed.[1] In one study of 10 women given 80 mg three times daily IM for 5 days postpartum, milk levels were measured on day 4.[2] Gentamicin levels in milk were 0.42, 0.48, 0.49, and 0.41 mg/L at 1, 3, 5, and 7 hours respectively. The milk/plasma ratios were 0.11 at one hour and 0.44 at 7 hours. Plasma gentamicin levels in neonates were small, were found in only 5 of the 10 neonates, and averaged 0.41 µg/mL. The authors estimate that daily ingestion via breastmilk would be 307 µg for a 3.6 Kg neonate (normal neonatal dose= 2.5 mg/kg every 12 hours). These amounts would be clinically irrelevant in most infants.

Pregnancy Risk Category: C

Lactation Risk Category: L2

Adult Concerns: Changes in GI flora, diarrhea, kidney damage, etc.

Pediatric Concerns: None reported.

Drug Interactions: Increased toxicity when used with certain penicillins, cephalosporins, amphotericin B, loop diuretics, and neuromuscular blocking agents.

Relative Infant Dose: 2%

Adult Dose: 1.5-2.5 mg/kg every 8 hours
Alternatives:

T ½	= 2-3 hours	M/P	= 0.11-0.44
PHL	= 3-5.5 hours (neonates)	PB	= <10-30%
Tmax	= 30-90 minutes (IM)	Oral	= <1%
MW	=	pKa	= 8.2
Vd	= 0.28 (adult)		

References:

1. Nelson JD, McCracken GH, Jr. The current status of gentamicin for tne neonate and young infant. Am J Dis Child 1972; 124 (1):13-14.

2.   Celiloglu M, Celiker S, Guven H, Tuncok Y, Demir N, Erten O. Gentamicin excretion and uptake from breast milk by nursing infants. Obstet Gynecol 1994; 84 (2):263-265.

GENTIAN VIOLET   L3

Trade: Crystal Violet, Methylrosaniline chloride, Gentian Violet
Other Trades:
Uses: Antifungal, antimicrobial
AAP: Not reviewed

Gentian violet is an older product that, when used topically and orally, is an exceptionally effective antifungal and antimicrobial.[1] It is a strong purple dye that is difficult to remove. Gentian violet has been found to be equivalent to ketoconazole and far superior to nystatin in treating oral (not esophageal) candidiasis in patients with advanced AIDS. It is also useful in treating purulent infections of the ear infected with methicillin-resistant Staphlococcus Aureus.[3]

Gentian violet (GV) solutions generally come as 1-2% Gentian violet dissolved in a 10% solution of alcohol. For use with infants, the solution should be diluted with distilled water to 0.25 to 0.5% Gentian violet. This reduces the irritant properties of GV and reduces the alcohol content as well. While the alcohol is irritating to the nipple, it is not detrimental to the infant.[2] Higher concentrations of GV are known to be very irritating, leading to oral ulceration and necrotic skin reactions in children. If used, a small swab should be soaked in the solution, and then swabbed in the infants gingivae. Apply it directly to the affected areas in the mouth no more than once or twice daily for no more than 3-7 days. Direct application to the nipple has been reported.

Pregnancy Risk Category: C

Lactation Risk Category: L3

Adult Concerns: Oral ulceration, stomatitis, staining of skin and clothing, nausea, vomiting, diarrhea.

Pediatric Concerns: Irritation leading to buccal ulcerations and necrotic skin reactions if used excessively and in higher concentrations. Nausea, vomiting, diarrhea.

Drug Interactions:

Relative Infant Dose:

Adult Dose: N/A

Alternatives:

T ½	=	M/P	=
PHL	=	PB	=
Tmax	=	Oral	=
MW	= 408	pKa	=
Vd	=		

References:
1. McEvoy GE. (ed):AFHS Drug Information. New York, NY: 2009.
2. Newman J. Personal communication. 1997.
3. Kayama C, Goto Y, Shimoya S, Hasegawa S, Murao S, Nakajo Y, Nibu K. Effects of Gentian Violet on Refractory Discharging Ears Infected with Methicillin-Resistant Staphylococcus aureus. J Otolaryngol 2006; 35 (6):384-386.

GINKGO BILOBA   L3

Trade: Ginkgo
Other Trades:
Uses: Herbal antioxidant
AAP: Not reviewed

Ginkgo Biloba is the world's oldest living tree. Extracts of the leaves (GBE) contain numerous chemical compounds including dimeric flavones and their glycosides, amino acids such as 6-hydroxyknurenic acid, and numerous other compounds. The seeds contain ginkgo toxin, which is particularly toxic, and should not be consumed. Numerous studies reviewing ginkgo have been reported, including treatments for cerebral insufficiency, asthma, dementia, and circulatory disorders. Ginkgo appears particularly efficient at increasing cerebral blood flow, with increases varying from 20-70%.[1,2] Older patients were more responsive. This supports the clinical use of GBE to treat cognitive impairment in the elderly. The anxiolytic properties of GBE have been reported to be due to MAO inhibition in animal studies. Ginkgolides inhibit platelet-activating factor and is believed responsible for the anti-allergic and anti-asthmatic properties of this extract. No data are available on the transfer of GBE into human milk. Thus far, with exception of the seeds, GBE appears relatively non-toxic.

Pregnancy Risk Category:

Lactation Risk Category: L3

Adult Concerns: Headache, dizziness, heart palpitations, GI symptoms, dermatologic reactions.

Pediatric Concerns: None reported via human milk.

Drug Interactions:

Relative Infant Dose:

Adult Dose:

Alternatives:

References:
1. Review of Natural Products Facts and Comparisons 1998.
2. Newall C, Anderson LA, Phillipson JD. Chamomile, German. In. Herbal Medicine. A guide for the healthcare professionals. The Pharmaceutical Press, London, 1996.

GINSENG   L3

Trade: Panax
Other Trades: Minomycin, Red Kooga
Uses: Herbal tonic
AAP: Not reviewed

Ginseng is perhaps the most popular and widely recognized product in the herbal remedy market. It is available in many forms, but the most common is the American root called Panax quinquefolium L. The root primarily contains steroid-like saponin glycosides (ginsenosides), of which there are at least two dozen and vary as a function of species, age, location, and season when harvested.[1]

Early claims have suggested that ginseng provided strengthening effects and included increased mental capacity for work. Animal studies have suggested that ginseng can increase swimming time, prevent stress-induced ulcers, stimulate certain immune cells, etc. A number of studies, mostly small and poorly controlled, have been reported and many suggest beneficial effects of ingesting ginseng with minimal side effects. Reported toxicities have included estrogen-like effects including diffuse mammary nodularity, vaginal bleeding, etc.[2] The most commonly reported event is nervousness, excitation, morning diarrhea, and inability to concentrate. In one case report, germanium, an ingredient in ginseng preparations, produced a significant diuretic resistance.[3] No data was found concerning transfer into human milk. It is recommended that it not be used for more than 6 weeks.[4]

Pregnancy Risk Category:

Lactation Risk Category: L3

Adult Concerns: Excitement, nervousness, inability to concentrate, diarrhea, skin eruptions, hypertension, hypoglycemia, mammary nodularity. Ginseng products sometimes contain germanium, which can induce a state of severe loop-diuretic resistance.

Pediatric Concerns: None reported, but caution is urged.

Drug Interactions:

Relative Infant Dose:

Adult Dose:

Alternatives:

References:
1.   Review of Natural Products Facts and Comparisons, St Louis, MO 1996.
2.   Bissett NG. In: Herbal Drugs and Phytopharmaceuticals. Medpharm Scientific Publishers, CRC Press, Boca Raton, 1994.
3.   Becker BN, Greene J, Evanson J, Chidsey G, Stone WJ. Ginseng-induced diuretic resistance. JAMA 1996; 276 (8):606-607.
4.   The Complete German Commission E Monographs. Ed. M. Blumenthal Amer Botanical Council 1998.

GLATIRAMER   L3

Trade: Copaxone
Other Trades:
Uses: Relapsing multiple sclerosis
AAP: Not reviewed

Glatiramer is a synthetic polypeptide indicated for the treatment of relapsing, remitting multiple sclerosis. It is primarily indicated for those who do not respond to interferons. Glatiramer is a mixture of random polymers of four amino acids: L-alanine, L-glutamic acid, L-lysine, and L-tyrosine. Its MW ranges from 4,700 to 13,000 daltons, which would reduce its ability to enter milk. It is antigenically similar to myelin basic protein, a natural component of the myelin sheath of neurons. No data are available on its transfer into human milk, but it is very unlikely. If ingested orally, it would likely be depolymerized into individual amino acids, so toxicity is unlikely.

Pregnancy Risk Category: B

Lactation Risk Category: L3

Adult Concerns: Dizziness, chest pain, palpitations, anxiety, hypertonia, sweating, nausea, weakness. Rash, hives, or severe pain where the shot is given.

Pediatric Concerns: None via milk.

Drug Interactions:

Relative Infant Dose:

Adult Dose: 20 mg subcutaneously once daily

Alternatives:

T ½	=	M/P	=
PHL	=	PB	=
Tmax	=	Oral	= Minimal
MW	= 4700+	pKa	=
Vd	=		

References:
1.   Pharmaceutical Manufacturer Prescribing Information.

GLIMEPIRIDE   L4

Trade: Amaryl
Other Trades:
Uses: Lowers plasma glucose
AAP: Not reviewed

Glimepiride is a second-generation sulfonylurea used to lower plasma glucose in patients with non-insulin dependent diabetes mellitus. No data are available on the transfer of this product into human milk. However, rodent studies demonstrated significant transfer and elevated plasma levels in pups.[1,2] Caution is urged if used in breastfeeding humans. Observe for hypoglycemia.

Pregnancy Risk Category: C

Lactation Risk Category: L4

Adult Concerns: Hypoglycemia, nausea, hyponatremia, dizziness, headache, elevated liver enzymes, blurred vision.

Pediatric Concerns: None   reported   via   milk.   Observe   for hypoglycemia.

Drug Interactions: The hypoglycemic effect of sulfonylureas may be increased by non-steroidal analgesics, salicylates, sulfonamides, coumarins, probenecid, and other drugs with high protein binding. Numerous other interactions exist, see product information.

Relative Infant Dose:

Adult Dose: 1-4 mg daily

Alternatives:

T ½	= 6-9 hours	M/P	=
PHL	=	PB	= >99.5%
Tmax	= 2-3 hours	Oral	= 100%
MW	= 490	pKa	=
Vd	= 0.113		

References:
1. Pharmaceutical Manufacturer Prescribing Information.
2. Bressler R, Johnson DG. Pharmacological regulation of blood glucose levels in non-insulin-dependent diabetes mellitus. Arch Intern Med 1997; 157 (8):836-848.

GLIPIZIDE   L3

Trade: Glucotrol XL, Glucotrol
Other Trades: Melizide, Minidiab, Glibenese
Uses: Prolonged release hypoglycemic agent
AAP: Not reviewed

Glipizide is a potent hypoglycemic agent that belongs to sulfonylurea family. It is formulated in regular and extended release formulations, and it is used only for non insulin-dependent (Type II) diabetes. Thus the half-life and time-to-peak depends on the formulation used. It reduces glucose levels by stimulating insulin secretion from the pancreas. In a group of 5 mothers who received daily doses of glyburide (non micronized 5 mg) or glipizide (immediate-release 5 mg) neither glyburide or glipizide were detectable in milk.[1] Detection limit for glipizide was 0.08 µg/mL. Infant plasma glucose levels were normal.

AHL= 2-5 hours (Glucotrol), 24 hours (Glucotrol-XL). The new product METAGLIP contains Glipizide and metformin.

Pregnancy Risk Category: C

Lactation Risk Category: L3

Adult Concerns: Hypoglycemia, jaundice, nausea, vomiting, diarrhea, constipation.

Pediatric Concerns: Milk levels were undetectable in one study.

Drug Interactions: The hypoglycemic effect may be enhanced by : anticoagulants, chloramphenicol, clofibrate, fenfluramine, fluconazole, H2 antagonists, magnesium salts, methyldopa, MAO inhibitors, probenecid, salicylates, TCAs, sulfonamides. The hypoglycemic effect may be reduced by: beta blockers, cholestyramine, diazoxide, phenytoin, rifampin, thiazide diuretics.

Relative Infant Dose:

Adult Dose: 15-40 mg daily.

Alternatives:

T ½	= 4-6 hours	M/P	=
PHL	=	PB	= 92-99 %
Tmax	= 6-12 hours (XL)	Oral	= 80-100%
MW	= 446	pKa	= 5.9
Vd	= 0.17-0.25		

References:
1. Feig DS, Briggs GG, Kraemer JM et al. Transfer of glyburide and glipizide into breast milk. Diabetes Care 2005; 28:1851-1855.

GLUCOSAMINE | L3

Trade: Glucosamine
Other Trades:
Uses: Antiarthritic
AAP: Not reviewed

Glucosamine is an endogenous amino monosaccharide that has been reported effective in resolving symptoms of osteoarthritis. It is one of the salt forms of the amino sugar glucosamine, which is a constituent of cartilage proteoglycans. Administered in large doses, most is sequestered in the liver with only minimal amounts reaching other tissues, thus oral bioavailability is low. Most of the oral dose is hepatically metabolized and subsequently incorporated into other plasma proteins.[1] No data are available on transfer into human milk. Because glucosamine is primarily sequestered and metabolized in the liver, and because the plasma levels are almost undetectable, it is unlikely that much would enter human milk. Further, the fact it is so poorly bioavailable, it is unlikely that an infant would receive clinically relevant amounts. Do not use with warfarin, as INR levels may double.

Pregnancy Risk Category:

Lactation Risk Category: L3

Adult Concerns: Minimal but include nausea, dyspepsia, vomiting, drowsiness, headache and skin rash. Peripheral edema and tachycardia have been reported. Some reports of exacerbation of asthma by glucosamine.

Pediatric Concerns: None reported via milk.

Drug Interactions: Do not use with warfarin as INR may increase significantly. S

Relative Infant Dose:

Adult Dose: 500 mg TID

Alternatives:

T ½	= 0.3 hours	M/P	=
PHL	=	PB	= 0%
Tmax	=	Oral	= <26%
MW	= 179	pKa	=
Vd	= 0.035		

References:
1. Setnikar I, Palumbo R, Canali S, Zanolo G. Pharmacokinetics of glucosamine in man. Arzneimittelforschung 1993; 43 (10):1109-1113.

GLYBURIDE   L2

Trade: Micronase, Diabeta, Glynase, Glucovance
Other Trades: Diabeta, Euglucon, Gen-Glybe, Diaformin,
            Daonil
Uses: Hypoglycemic, antidiabetic agent
AAP: Not reviewed

Glyburide is a second generation sulfonylurea agent useful in the treatment of non insulin-dependent (Type II) diabetes mellitus. It belongs to the sulfonylurea family (tolbutamide, glipizide) of hypoglycemic agents of which glyburide is one of the most potent. Glyburide apparently stimulates insulin secretion, thus reducing plasma glucose. In a study of 6 mothers who received a single dose (5 mg) and 2 mothers who received a single dose of 10 mg glyburide, all breast milk samples were below the limit of detection of 0.005 µg/mL.[1] In a group of 5 mothers who received daily doses of glyburide (non micronized 5 mg) or glipizide (immediate-release 5 mg) neither glyburide or glipizide were detectable in milk. Infant plasma glucose levels were normal.

The product Glucovance contains metformin and glyburide.

Pregnancy Risk Category: B

Lactation Risk Category: L2

Adult Concerns: In adults, hypoglycemia, headache, anorexia, nausea, heartburn, allergic skin rashes.

Pediatric Concerns: Milk levels undetectable. Transfer to infant of clinically relevant amounts is unlikely.

Drug Interactions: Thiazide diuretics and beta blockers may decrease efficacy of glyburide. Increased toxicity may result from use with phenylbutazone, oral anticoagulants, hydantoins, salicylates, NSAIDS, sulfonamides. Alcohol increases disulfiram effect.

Relative Infant Dose:

Adult Dose: 1.25-20 mg daily

Alternatives:

T ½	= 4-13.7 hours	M/P	=
PHL	=	PB	= 99%
Tmax	= 2 3 hours	Oral	= Complete
MW	= 494	pKa	= 5.3
Vd	= 0.73		

References:
1.   Feig DS, Briggs GG, Kraemer JM et al. Transfer of glyburide and glipizide into breast milk. Diabetes Care 2005; 28:1851-1855.

GLYCOPYRROLATE

L3

Trade: Robinul
Other Trades:
Uses: Anticholinergic
AAP: Not reviewed

Glycopyrrolate is a quaternary ammonium anticholinergic used prior to surgery to dry secretions. After administration, its plasma half-life is exceedingly short (<5 min.) with most of the product being distribution out of the plasma compartment rapidly.[1,2] No data are available on its transfer into human milk, but due to its short plasma half-life and its quaternary structure, it is very unlikely that significant quantities would penetrate milk. Further, along with the poor oral bioavailability of this product, it is very remote that glycopyrrolate would pose a significant risk to a breastfeeding infant.

Pregnancy Risk Category: B

Lactation Risk Category: L3

Adult Concerns: Blurred vision, dry mouth, tachycardia.

Pediatric Concerns: None reported via milk.

Drug Interactions: May reduce effect of levodopa. Increased toxicity when used with amantadine and cyclopropane.

Relative Infant Dose:

Adult Dose: 1-2 mg TID

Alternatives:

T ½	= 1.7 hours	M/P	=
PHL	=	PB	=
Tmax	= 5 hours (oral)	Oral	= 10-25%
MW	= 398	pKa	=
Vd	= 0.64		

References:
1. Lacy C. Drug information handbook. Lexi-Comp Inc. Cleveland, OH, 1996.
2. Drug Facts and Comparisons 1996 ed. ed. St. Louis: 1996.

GOLD COMPOUNDS   L5

Trade: Ridaura, Myochrysine, Solganal
Other Trades: Myocrisin
Uses: Antiarthritic
AAP: Maternal Medication Usually Compatible with Breastfeeding

Gold salts anti-inflammatory agents used to treat rheumatoid arthritis. Gold Salts are potent and toxic. Two injectable forms exist- gold sodium thiomalate (Myochrysine) and sodium aurothioglucose (Solganal). One oral form exists, auranofin (Ridaura). The plasma kinetics of the gold salts are highly variable and are difficult to report, but in general, their half-lives are very extended and increase as duration of treatment continues. Auranofin is the only orally available salt form and is approximately 20-25% bioavailable. They are all probably secreted into breastmilk in small quantities.

In a study by Blau [1], milk levels of gold (gold thioglucose) following a cumulative dose of 135 mg ranged from 0.86-0.99 mg/100 mL. These are quite high and exceed the data of others although this data was challenged on arithmetical grounds by others. The subsequent publication of several other studies (see below) seem to refute the transfer of high levels of gold in milk.

In one study of a patient receiving aurothiomalate (Myochrysine) 50 mg/week for 7 weeks, the concentration of gold sodium thiomalate varied from 0.022 to 0.04 mg/L at 66 hours and 7 days post-dose respectively.[2] Although the infant showed no signs or symptoms of toxicity during therapy, the authors noted that 3 months after treatment the infant developed transient facial edema of unexplained origin.

In two patients treated with 50 mg aurothiomalate IM, levels in milk varied from 27-153 µg/L and reached a peak at 17 hours following the injection.[3] The authors suggested approximately 10% or more of the concentration of gold measured in maternal serum appears in breastmilk.

In a study of a single patient receiving chronic aurothioglucose therapy (50 mg/week) (20 weeks), the mother's steady state plasma gold was 4.05 mg/l while it was 0.041 mg/l in breast milk.[4] The average amount of gold in breastmilk per 24 hours was only 0.0255 mg. The authors calculated that only 0.178 mg gold (0.71% of the weekly dose) would appear in the breast milk over a week. Gold was undetectable (<5 X 10 (-7) mg/l) in the infant's plasma or urine even following 20 weeks. The authors suggest that It is very unlikely that more than minute amounts of gold are absorbed from the mother's breast milk when breast feeding an infant.

In a study of a single patient receiving 10 mg/month aurothiomalate, Bennett found milk levels of gold ranged from 10-30 µg/liter.[5] Levels in the infant's plasma were 51 µg/liter.

The data published thus far varies widely. While small levels of gold may be found in milk, the oral absorption of gold is quite low, probably less than 20%. However, almost any gold absorbed would be retained in the infant for long periods (months) and some accumulation could occur following chronic therapy. For this reason prolonged exposure of a nursing infant to gold therapy is probably somewhat risky.

Pregnancy Risk Category: C

Lactation Risk Category: L5

Adult Concerns: GI distress, diarrhea, nausea, vomiting, exfoliative dermatitis, nephrotoxicity, proteinuria, and blood dyscrasias.

Pediatric Concerns: Possible facial edema 3 months after therapy. Relationship is questionable.

Drug Interactions: Decreased gold effects with penicillamine and acetylcysteine.

Relative Infant Dose: 0.6% - 2.8%

Adult Dose: 25-50 mg every week

Alternatives: NSAIDS

T ½	= 3-26 days	M/P	= 0.02-0.3
PHL	=	PB	= 95%
Tmax	= 3-6 hours (IM)	Oral	= 20-25% (auranofin)
MW	=	pKa	=
Vd	= 0.1		

References:
1. Blau SP. Letter: Metabolism of gold during lactation. Arthritis Rheum 1973; 16 (6):777-778.
2. Bell RA, Dale IM. Gold secretion in maternal milk. Arthritis Rheum 1976; 19 (6):1374.
3. Ostensen M, Skavdal K, Myklebust G, Tomassen Y, Aarbakke J. Excretion of gold into human breast milk. Eur J Clin Pharmacol 1986; 31 (2):251-252.
4. Rooney TW, Lorber A, Veng-Pedersen P, Herman RA, Meehan R, Hade J, et al. Gold pharmacokinetics in breast milk and serum of a lactating woman. J Rheumatol 1987 Dec; 14 (6):1120-2.
5. Bennett PN, Humphries SJ, Osborne JP, Clarke AK, Taylor A. Use of sodium aurothiomalate during lactation. Br J Clin Pharmacol 1990 Jun; 29 (6):777-9.

GONADORELIN ACETATE   L3

Trade: Lutrepulse
Other Trades: Wyerth-Ayerst HRF, Fertiral
Uses: Gonadotropin-releasing hormone
AAP: Not reviewed

Gonadorelin is used for the induction of ovulation in anovulatory women with primary hypothalamic amenorrhea. Gonadorelin is a small decapeptide identical to the physiologic GnRH secreted by the hypothalamus which stimulates the pituitary release of luteinizing hormone (LH) and to a lesser degree follicle stimulating hormone (FSH). LH and FSH subsequently stimulate the ovary to produce follicles. Gonadorelin plasma half-life is very brief (<2-4 minutes), and it is primarily distributed to the plasma only.[1] Gonadorelin has been detected in human breastmilk at concentrations of 0.1 to 3 nanograms/

mL (adult dose= 20-100 micrograms) although its oral bioavailability in the infant would be minimal to none.[2]

Pregnancy Risk Category: B

Lactation Risk Category: L3

Adult Concerns: Ovarian hyperstimulation, bronchospasm, tachycardia, flushing, urticaria, induration at injection site.

Pediatric Concerns: None reported via milk.

Drug Interactions:

Relative Infant Dose:

Adult Dose: 1-20 µg daily.

Alternatives:

T ½	= 2-4 minutes	M/P	=
PHL	=	PB	=
Tmax	=	Oral	= None
MW	=	pKa	=
Vd	= 0.14		

References:
1. Reynolds JEF. (Ed): Martindale: The Extra Pharmacopoeia (electronic version). Denver, CO: Micromedex, Inc., 1990.
2. Drug Facts and Comparisons 1996 ed. ed. St. Louis: 1996.

GOSERELIN ACETATE IMPLANT   L3

Trade: Zoladex
Other Trades:
Uses: Inhibitor of luteinizing hormone
AAP: Not reviewed

Goserelin is a synthetic decapeptide analogue of luteinizing hormone releasing factor and it acts as a potent inhibitor of pituitary gonadotropin secretion. Following initial administration in males, goserelin causes an initial increase in serum luteinizing hormone (LH) and follicle stimulating hormone (FSH) levels. Chronic administration of goserelin leads to sustained suppression of pituitary gonadotropins, and serum levels testosterone in males. In females, a down-regulation of the pituitary gland following chronic exposure leads to suppression of gonadotropin secretion, a decrease in serum estradiol to levels consistent with the menopausal state. Serum LH and FSH are suppressed to follicular phase levels within four weeks. No data are available on its transfer into human milk but due to its structure and MW it is very unlikely to enter milk, or to be orally bioavailable in the infant.

Pregnancy Risk Category: X

Lactation Risk Category: L3

Adult Concerns: Adverse events include hot flashes, sexual dysfunction, vaginitis, emotional lability, headache, abdominal pain, pelvic pain, depression, sweating, breast atrophy, edema, etc.

Pediatric Concerns: None reported via milk. While it is unlikely this peptide would enter milk, or be orally bioavailable to an infant, it is not known how it would affect milk production. Some caution is recommended concerning loss of milk supply.

Drug Interactions: None studied.

Relative Infant Dose:

Adult Dose: 3.6 mg subcutaneously every 28 days.

Alternatives:

T ½	= 2.3 hours	M/P	=
PHL	=	PB	= Low
Tmax	= 12-15 days	Oral	= Nil
MW	= 1269	pKa	=
Vd	= 0.28 (females)		

References:
1.   Pharmaceutical Manufacturers prescribing information, 2003.

GRANISETRON   L3

Trade: Kytril
Other Trades:
Uses: Antiemetic
AAP: Not reviewed

Granisetron is an antinauseant and antiemetic agent commonly used with chemotherapy. Following a 1 mg IV dose, the peak plasma concentration was only 3.63 ng/mL.[1] No data are available on its transfer into human milk but its levels are likely to be low. Further, this family of products (see ondansetron) are not highly toxic and are commonly used in children (2 years +). It is unlikely that this product will be overtly toxic to a breastfed infant. However, when used with chemotherapeutic agents, long waiting periods should be used for elimination of the chemotherapeutic agents anyway.

Pregnancy Risk Category: B

Lactation Risk Category: L3

Adult Concerns: Headache, asthenia, somnolence, diarrhea, dyspepsia, abdominal pain, constipation, and fever. Rarely elevations of liver enzymes been reported.

Pediatric Concerns: None reported via milk.

Drug Interactions: Ketoconazole may inhibit the metabolism of granisetron.

Relative Infant Dose:

Adult Dose: 2 mg Orally

Alternatives: Ondansetron

T ½	= 3-14 hours	M/P	=
PHL	=	PB	= 65%
Tmax	= 1 hour	Oral	= 60%
MW	= 349	pKa	=
Vd	= 2-4		

References:
1. Pharmaceutical Manufacturer Prescribing Information, 2002.

GREPAFLOXACIN   L4

Trade: Raxar
Other Trades:
Uses: Fluoroquinolone antibiotic
AAP: Not reviewed

Grepafloxacin is a typical fluoroquinolones antibiotic similar to Ciprofloxacin. The manufacturer suggests that grepafloxacin is detectable in human milk after a 400 mg dose but does not provide the exact levels.[1] Studies in rodents suggest a concentrating mechanism of about 16 times that of the plasma compartment. Because this fluoroquinolone has a rather long half-life, high volume of distribution, the ability to enter many body compartments, and is concentrated in rodent milk, it is probably advisable to use this product with extreme caution, if at all, in breastfeeding women.

Pregnancy Risk Category: C

Lactation Risk Category: L4

Adult Concerns: Nausea, taste perversion, dizziness, headache, diarrhea, abdominal pain.

Pediatric Concerns: None reported with this product, but diarrhea and pseudomembranous colitis has been reported with ciprofloxacin. Arthropathy has been reported following pediatric use of fluoroquinolones.

Drug Interactions: Decreased absorption with antacids. Quinolones cause increased levels of caffeine, warfarin, cyclosporine, theophylline. Cimetidine, probenecid, azlocillin increase ciprofloxacin levels. Increased risk of seizures when used with foscarnet.

Relative Infant Dose:

Adult Dose: 400-600 mg daily.

Alternatives: Norfloxacin, Ofloxacin, Levofloxacin, Ciprofloxacin

T ½	= 15.7 hours	M/P	=
PHL	=	PB	= 50%
Tmax	= 2-3 hours	Oral	= 72%
MW	= 422	pKa	=
Vd	= 5.07		

References:
1. Pharmaceutical Manufacturer Prescribing Information. 1999.

GRISEOFULVIN | L2

Trade: Fulvicin, Gris-PEG
Other Trades: Grisovin-FP, Fulcin, Griseostatin, Grisovin
Uses: Antifungal
AAP: Not reviewed

Griseofulvin is an older class antifungal. Much better safety profiles with the newer families of antifungals have reduced the use of griseofulvin. The drug is primarily effective against tinea species and not candida albicans.[1,2] There are no data available for humans. In one study in cows following a dose of 10 mg/kg/day for 5 days (human dose =5 mg/kg/day) milk concentrations were 0.16 mg/L. Although these data cannot be directly extrapolated to humans, they indicate transfer to milk in some species. Oral use in adults is associated with low risk of hepatic cancer. Griseofulvin is still commonly used in pediatric tinea capitis (ringworm), where it is a preferred medication.

Pregnancy Risk Category: C

Lactation Risk Category: L2

Adult Concerns: Headache, depression, hepatotoxicity, skin rashes, hallucinations. Symptoms of overdose include lethargy, vertigo, blurred vision, nausea, vomiting, and diarrhea.

Pediatric Concerns: None reported from breastmilk.

Drug Interactions: Barbiturates may reduce plasma levels. May inhibit warfarin activity. May reduce effectiveness of oral contraceptives. May produce increased toxicity and tachycardia when used with alcohol.

Relative Infant Dose:

Adult Dose: 500-1000 mg daily. (micro) or 330-375 mg daily (ultra)

Alternatives: Fluconazole

T ½	= 9-24 hours	M/P	=
PHL	=	PB	=
Tmax	= 4-8 hours	Oral	= Poor to 50%
MW	= 353	pKa	=
Vd	=		

References:
1.   McEvoy GE. (ed):AFHS Drug Information. New York, NY: 2009.

2.   Huddleston WA. Antifungal activity of Penicillium griseofulvin mycelium. Vet Rec 1970; 86 (3):75-76.

GUAIFENESIN   L2

Trade: GG, Robitussin, Mucinex
Other Trades: Balminil, Resyl, Benylin-E, Orthoxicol, Respenyl
Uses: Expectorant, loosens respiratory tract secretions
AAP: Not reviewed

Guaifenesin is an expectorant used to irritate the gastric mucosa and stimulate respiratory tract secretions in order to reduce phlegm viscosity. It does not suppress coughing and should not be used in persistent cough such as with smokers. No data are available on transfer into human breastmilk. In general, clinical studies documenting the efficacy of guaifenesin are lacking, and the usefulness of this product as an expectorant is highly questionable.[1] Poor efficacy of these drugs (expectorants in general) would suggest that they do not provide enough justification for use in lactating mothers. But untoward effects have not been reported.

Pediatric dose: <2 years= 12 mg/kg/day in 6 divided doses; 2-5 years= 50-100 mg every 4 hours; 6-11 years= 100-200 mg every 4 hours; Children >12 years and adults= 200-400 mg every 4 hours for a maximum of 2.4 gm/day. Always dose with large volumes of fluids.

Pregnancy Risk Category: C

Lactation Risk Category: L2

Adult Concerns: Vomiting, diarrhea, nausea, sedation, skin rash, GI dyspepsia.

Pediatric Concerns: None reported.

Drug Interactions:

Relative Infant Dose:

Adult Dose: 200-400 mg every 4 hours

Alternatives:

T ½	= <7 hours	M/P	=
PHL	=	PB	=
Tmax	=	Oral	= Complete
MW	= 198	pKa	=
Vd	= 1.0		

References:
1. Lacy C. Drug information handbook. Lexi-Comp Inc. Cleveland, OH, 1996.

GUANFACINE   L3

Trade: Tenex, Intuniv
Other Trades:
Uses: Antihypertensive
AAP: Not reviewed

Guanfacine is a centrally acting antihypertensive that stimulates alpha-2 adrenergic receptors (similar to Clonidine). Studies in animals indicate that guanfacine is secreted into milk (M/P ratio= 0.75), but human studies are lacking.[1,2] Because this product has a low MW (246), a high volume of distribution 6.3 L/kg), and penetrates the CNS at high levels, it is likely to penetrate milk at significant levels. Caution is urged.

Pregnancy Risk Category: B

Lactation Risk Category: L3

Adult Concerns: Bradycardia, hypotension, dry mouth, sedation, weakness, constipation.

Pediatric Concerns: None reported but observe for hypotension, sedation, weakness.

Drug Interactions: Decreased hypotensive effect when used with tricyclic antidepressants. Increased effect when used with other antihypertensive agents.

Relative Infant Dose:

Adult Dose: 1 mg daily.

Alternatives:

T ½	= 17 hours	M/P	=
PHL	=	PB	= 20-30%
Tmax	= 2.6 hours	Oral	= 81-100%
MW	= 246	pKa	=
Vd	= 6.3		

References:
1. Pharmaceutical Manufacturer Prescribing Information. 1995.
2. Lacy C. Drug information handbook. Lexi-Comp Inc. Cleveland, OH, 1996.

HAEMOPHILUS B CONJUGATE VACCINE.   L3

Trade: HibTITER, Haemophilus B Vaccine, ProHIBiT, OmniHIB

Other Trades: Act-HIB, PedvaxHIB, Hib Titer

Uses: H. influenza Vaccine

AAP: Not reviewed

Hib Vaccine is a purified capsular polysaccharide vaccine made from Haemophilus influenza bacteria. It is non-infective. It is currently recommended for initial immunizations in children at 2 months, and at 2 month intervals, for a total of 3 injections.[1] A booster is recommended at 12-15 months. Although there are no reasons for administering to adult mothers, it would not be contraindicated in breastfeeding mothers.

Pregnancy Risk Category: C

Lactation Risk Category: L3

Adult Concerns: Itching, skin rash, injection site reaction, vomiting, fever. Few anaphylactoid-type reaction.

Pediatric Concerns: Itching, skin rash, injection site reaction, vomiting, fever. Few anaphylactoid-type reaction.

Drug Interactions: Decreased immunogenicity when used with immunosuppressive agents. Immunoglobulins with 1 month may decrease antibody production.

Relative Infant Dose:

Adult Dose:

Alternatives:

References:
1. Pharmaceutical Manufacturer Prescribing Information. 1996.

HALAZEPAM   L3

Trade: Paxipam
Other Trades:
Uses: Benzodiazepine antianxiety drug
AAP: Not reviewed

Halazepam is a benzodiazepine (Valium family) used to treat anxiety disorders. Halazepam is metabolized to desmethyldiazepam, which has an elimination half-life of 50-100 hours.[1] Although no information is available on halazepam levels in human milk, it should be similar to diazepam. See diazepam.

Pregnancy Risk Category: D

Lactation Risk Category: L3

Adult Concerns: Sedation, bradycardia, euphoria, disorientation, confusion, nausea, constipation, hypotension.

Pediatric Concerns: None reported, but see diazepam.

Drug Interactions:

Relative Infant Dose:

Adult Dose: 20-40 mg TID-QID

Alternatives: Alprazolam, Lorazepam

T ½	= 14 hours	M/P	=
PHL	=	PB	= High
Tmax	= 1-3 hours	Oral	= Complete
MW	= 353	pKa	=
Vd	= 1.0		

References:
1. Pharmaceutical Manufacturer Prescribing Information. 1995.

HALOPERIDOL   L2

Trade: Haldol
Other Trades: Apo-Haloperidol, Novo-Peridol, Peridol,
        Serenace
Uses: Antipsychotic
AAP: Drugs whose effect on nursing infants is unknown but
        may be of concern

Haloperidol is a potent antipsychotic agent than is reported to increase prolactin levels in some patients. In one study of a woman treated for puerperal hypomania and receiving 5 mg twice daily, the concentration of haloperidol in milk was 0.0, 23.5, 18.0, and 3.25 µg/L on day 1, 6, 7, and 21 respectively.[1] The corresponding maternal plasma levels were 0, 40, 26, and 4 µg/L at day 1, 6, 7, and 21 respectively. The milk/plasma ratios were 0.58, 0.69, and 0.81 on days 6, 7, and 21 respectively. After 4 weeks of therapy the infant showed no symptoms of sedation and was feeding well.

In another study after a mean daily dose of 29.2 mg, the concentration of haloperidol in breastmilk was 5 µg/L at 11 hours post-dose.[2] In a study of 3 women on chronic haloperidol therapy receiving 3, 4, and 6 mg daily, milk levels were reported to be 32, 17, and 4.7 ng/mL.[3] The latter levels (4.7) were taken from a patient believed to be noncompliant.

Bennett calculates the relative infant dose to be 0.2-2.1% to 9.6% of the weight-adjusted maternal daily dose.[4]

Pregnancy Risk Category: C

Lactation Risk Category: L2

Adult Concerns: Extrapyramidal symptoms, sedation, anemia, tachycardia, hypotension.

Pediatric Concerns: None reported via milk. Observe for sedation, weakness.

Drug Interactions: Carbamazepine may increase metabolism and decrease effectiveness of haloperidol. CNS depressants may increase adverse effects. Epinephrine may cause hypotension. Concurrent use with lithium has caused acute encephalopathy syndromes.

Relative Infant Dose: 2.1% - 12%

Adult Dose: 0.5-5 mg BID-TID

Alternatives:

T ½	= 12-38 hours	M/P	= 0.58-0.81
PHL	=	PB	= 92%
Tmax	= 2-6 hours	Oral	= 60%
MW	= 376	pKa	= 8.3
Vd	= 18-30		

References:

1. Whalley LJ, Blain PG, Prime JK. Haloperidol secreted in breast milk. Br Med J (Clin Res Ed) 1981; 282 (6278):1746-1747.
2. Stewart RB, Karas B, Springer PK. Haloperidol excretion in human milk. Am J Psychiatry 1980; 137 (7):849-850.
3. Ohkubo T, Shimoyama R, Sugawara K. Measurement of haloperidol in human breast milk by high-performance liquid chromatography. J Pharm Sci 1992; 81 (9):947-949.
4. Bennett PN. Use of the monographs on drugs: In: Drugs and Human Lactation. Amsterdam, Elsevier, 1996.

HALOTHANE   L2

Trade: Fluothane
Other Trades:
Uses: Anesthetic gas
AAP: Maternal Medication Usually Compatible with Breastfeeding

Halothane is an anesthetic gas similar to enflurane, methoxyflurane, and isoflurane. Approximately 60-80% is rapidly eliminated by exhalation the first 24 hours postoperative, and only 15% is actually metabolized by the liver. Cote (1976) reviewed the secretion of halothane in breastmilk.[1] After a 3 hour surgery, only 2 ppm was detected in milk. At another exposure in one week, only 0.83 and 1.9 ppm were found. The authors assessed the exposure to the infant as negligible.

Halothane is probably stored in the adipose tissue and eliminated for several days. There is no available information on the oral bioavailability of halothane. Pumping and dumping milk the first 24 hours postoperatively is generally recommended but is probably unnecessary.

Pregnancy Risk Category: C

Lactation Risk Category: L2

Adult Concerns: Nausea, vomiting, sedation, transient hepatotoxicity.

Pediatric Concerns: None reported.

Drug Interactions: When used with rifampin, or phenytoin, may have increased risk of hepatotoxicity.

Relative Infant Dose:

Adult Dose:

Alternatives:

T ½	=	M/P	=
PHL	=	PB	=
Tmax	= 10-20 minutes	Oral	=
MW	= 197	pKa	=
Vd	= 1		

References:
1. Cote CJ, Kenepp NB, Reed SB, Strobel GE. Trace concentrations of halothane in human breast milk. Br J Anaesth 1976; 48 (6):541-543.

HCTZ + TRIAMTERENE   L3

Trade: Dyrenium, Maxzide
Other Trades: Dyazide, Novo-Triamzide, Hydrene
Uses: Diuretic
AAP: Not reviewed

Numerous diuretic products contain varying combinations of hydrochlorothiazide (HCTZ) and triamterene. For specifics on HCTZ, see the monograph on hydrochlorothiazide. Triamterene is a potassium sparing diuretic. Following a dose of 100-200 mg, it attains plasma levels in adults of 26-30 µg/L.[1] It is secreted in small amounts in cow's milk but no human data are available. Assuming a high milk/plasma ratio of one, an infant ingesting 125 mL/kg/day would theoretically ingest less than 4 µg/kg/day, an amount unlikely to provide clinical problems.

Pregnancy Risk Category: C

Lactation Risk Category: L3

Adult Concerns: Diarrhea, nausea, vomiting, hepatitis, leukopenia, hyperkalemia.

Pediatric Concerns: None reported. Hyperkalemia.

Drug Interactions: Increased risk of hyperkalemia when given with amiloride, spironolactone, and ACE inhibitors. Increased risk of toxicity with amantadine.

Relative Infant Dose: 0.2%

Adult Dose: 25-50 mg HCTZ (37.5-75 mg Triamterene) daily.

Alternatives:

T ½	= 1.5-2.5 hours	M/P	=
PHL	=	PB	= 55%
Tmax	= 1.5-3 hours	Oral	= 30-70%
MW	= 253	pKa	= 6.2
Vd	=		

References:
1.   Pharmaceutical Manufacturer Prescribing Information.

HEMIN   L3

Trade: Panhematin
Other Trades: Heminevrin, Normosang
Uses: Blood modifier
AAP: Not reviewed

Intravenous hemin is used to treat acute intermittent porphyria by inhibiting delta-aminolevulinic acid synthetase, the enzyme that regulates the heme/porphyrin synthesis pathway.[1] No data are available on the levels in breast milk. However, this is a large MW protein that is unlikely to enter the milk compartment, nor be orally bioavailable to an infant.

Pregnancy Risk Category: C

Lactation Risk Category: L3

Adult Concerns: Adverse effects include pyrexia, leukocytosis, and phlebitis.

Pediatric Concerns: No data are available. Probably unable to enter milk. Would not be orally bioavailable.

Drug Interactions:

Relative Infant Dose:

Adult Dose: 1-4 mg/kg/day administered over 10-15 minutes for 3-14 days

Alternatives:

T ½	=	M/P	=
PHL	=	PB	= High
Tmax	=	Oral	= Nil
MW	= 616	pKa	=
Vd	=		

References:
1. Pharmaceutical Manufacturer Prescribing Information. 2008.

HEPARIN   L1

Trade: Heparin
Other Trades: Hepalean, Canusal, Heplok, Pularin
Uses: Anticoagulant
AAP: Not reviewed

Heparin is a large protein molecule that is used subcutaneously, intramusculary, and intravenously. Due to its high MW (range= 12,000-15,000 daltons), it is unlikely any would transfer into breastmilk. Any present in milk would be rapidly destroyed in the gastric contents of the infant.

Pregnancy Risk Category: C

Lactation Risk Category: L1

Adult Concerns: Hemorrhage.

Pediatric Concerns: None reported via milk.

Drug Interactions: Increased toxicity with NSAIDS, aspirin, dipyridamole, hydroxychloroquine.

Relative Infant Dose:

Adult Dose: 4,000-5,000 units every 4 hours

Alternatives:

T ½	= 1-2 hours	M/P	=
PHL	=	PB	=
Tmax	= 20 minutes	Oral	= None
MW	= 12-15,000	pKa	=
Vd	=		

References:
1. McEvoy GE. (ed):AFHS Drug Information. New York, NY: 2009.

HEPATITIS A INFECTION   L3

Trade:
Other Trades:
Uses:
AAP: Not reviewed

Hepatitis A is an acute viral infection characterized by jaundice, fever, anorexia, and malaise. In infants, the syndrome is either asymptomatic or causes only mild nonspecific symptoms.[1] Current therapy recommended following exposure to Hepatitis A is an injection of gamma globulin. A majority of the population is immune to Hepatitis A due to prior exposure. Fulminant hepatitis A infection is rare in children and a carrier state is unknown. It is spread through fecal-oral contact and can be spread in day care centers. Viral shedding continues from onset up to 3 weeks. Unless the mother is jaundiced and acutely ill, breastfeeding can continue without interruption.[2] Proper hygiene should be stressed. Protect infant with IM gamma globulin.

Pregnancy Risk Category:

Lactation Risk Category: L3

Adult Concerns: Jaundice, fever, malaise.

Pediatric Concerns: None reported. Protect with gamma globulin injection.

Drug Interactions:

Relative Infant Dose:

Adult Dose:

Alternatives:

References:
1. American Academy of Pediatrics. Committee on Infectious Diseases. Red Book. 1997.
2. Gartner L. Personal communication. 1997.

HEPATITIS B IMMUNE GLOBULIN

L2

Trade: H-BIG, HEP-B-Gammagee, Hyperhep
Other Trades:
Uses: Anti-Hepatitis B Immune globulins
AAP: Not reviewed

HBIG is a sterile solution of immunoglobulin (10-18% protein) containing a high titer of antibody to hepatitis B surface antigen.[1] It is most commonly used as prophylaxis therapy for infants born to hepatitis B surface antigen positive mothers. The carrier state can be prevented in about 75% of such infections in newborns given HBIG immediately after birth. HBIG is generally administered to infants from HBsAg positive mothers who wish to breastfeed. The prophylactic dose for newborns is 0.5 mL IM (thigh) as soon after birth as possible, preferably within 1 hour.[2] The infant should also be immunized with Hepatitis B vaccine (0.5 mL IM) within 12 hours of birth (use separate site), and again at 1 and 6 months.

Pregnancy Risk Category: C

Lactation Risk Category: L2

Adult Concerns: Pain at injection site, erythema, rash, dizziness, malaise.

Pediatric Concerns: Pain at injection site, erythema, rash.

Drug Interactions:

Relative Infant Dose:

Adult Dose: 0.06 ml/kg post-exposure X 3 over 6 weeks

Alternatives:

T ½	=	M/P	=
PHL	=	PB	=
Tmax	= 1-6 days	Oral	= None
MW	=	pKa	=
Vd	=		

References:
1. Pharmaceutical Manufacturer Prescribing Information. 1995.
2. Lawrence RA. Breastfeeding: A guide for the medical profession. St. Louis: Mosby Publishers, 1994.

HEPATITIS B INFECTION

Trade: Hepatitis B Infection
Other Trades:
Uses: Hepatitis B exposure
AAP: Not reviewed

Hepatitis B virus (HBV) causes a wide spectrum of infections, ranging from a mild asymptomatic form to a fulminant fatal hepatitis. Mild asymptomatic illness is most common in pediatric patients although the chronic infectious state occurs in as many as 90% of infants who become infected by perinatal transmission. Chronically infected individuals are at increased risk for chronic liver diseases and liver cancer in later life. HBV is transmitted through blood or body fluids. Hepatitis B antigen has been detected in breastmilk.[1,2,3]

Infants of mothers who are HBV positive (HBsAg) should be given Hepatitis immune globulin (HBIG) (preferably within 1 hour of birth) and a Hepatitis B vaccination AT BIRTH, which is believed to effectively reduce the risk of post-natal transmission, particularly via breastmilk.[4] Inject in different sites. Thus far, several older studies have indicated that breastfeeding poses no additional risk of transmission if these immunizations are done, and thus far no cases of horizontal transmission of Hepatitis B via breastmilk have been reported following immunization.

Pregnancy Risk Category:

Lactation Risk Category:

Adult Concerns: Hepatitis, increased risk of liver cancer.

Pediatric Concerns: None reported if immunized with HBIG and HB vaccination.

Drug Interactions:

Relative Infant Dose:

Adult Dose:

Alternatives:

References:
1. Boxall EH, Flewett TH, Dane DS, Cameron CH, MacCallum FO, Lee TW. Letter: Hepatitis-B surface antigen in breast milk. Lancet 1974; 2 (7887):1007-1008.
2. Beasley RP, Stevens CE, Shiao IS, Meng HC. Evidence against breast-feeding as a mechanism for vertical transmission of hepatitis B. Lancet 1975; 2 (7938):740-741.

3. Woo D, Cummins M, Davies PA, Harvey DR, Hurley R, Waterson AP. Vertical transmission of hepatitis B surface antigen in carrier mothers in two west London hospitals. Arch Dis Child 1979; 54 (9):670-675.
4. American Academy of Pediatrics. Committee on Infectious Diseases. Red Book. 1994.

HEPATITIS B VACCINE   L2

Trade: Heptavax-B, Energix-B, Recombivax HB
Other Trades:
Uses: Hepatitis B vaccination
AAP: Not reviewed

Hepatitis B vaccine is an inactivated non-infectious hepatitis B surface antigen vaccine. It can be used in pediatric patients at birth. No data are available on its use in breastfeeding mothers, but it is unlikely to produce untoward effects on a breastfeeding infant. Hepatitis B vaccination is approximately 80-95% effective in preventing acute hepatitis B infections.[1,2] It requires at least 3 immunizations and the immunity lasts about 5-7 years. In infants born of HB surface antigen positive mothers, the American Academy of Pediatrics recommends hepatitis B vaccine (along with HBIG) should be administered to the infant within 1-12 hours of birth (0.5 mL IM) and again at 1 and 6 months. If so administered, breastfeeding poses no additional risk for acquisition of HBV by the infant.

Pregnancy Risk Category: C

Lactation Risk Category: L2

Adult Concerns: Pain at injection site, swelling, erythema, fever.

Pediatric Concerns: Fever, malaise, fatigue when directly injected. None reported via breastmilk.

Drug Interactions: Immunosuppressive agents would decrease effect.

Relative Infant Dose:

Adult Dose: 20 µg each for three injections over 7 months

Alternatives:

References:
1. Pharmaceutical Manufacturer Prescribing Information. 1996.
2. American Academy of Pediatrics. Committee on Infectious Diseases. Red Book. 1997.

HEPATITIS C INFECTION | L2

Trade: Hepatitis C Infection, HCV
Other Trades:
Uses: Hepatitis exposure
AAP: Not reviewed

Hepatitis C (HCV) is characterized by a mild or asymptomatic infection with jaundice and malaise. On average, 50% of patients develop chronic liver disease, including cirrhosis, and liver cancer in later life. HCV infection can be spread by blood-blood transmission although most are not associated with blood transfusions and may be transmitted by other unknown methods.

Although perinatal transmission can occur, its incidence is known to be very low.[2] The average incubation period is 7-9 weeks. Mothers infected with HCV should be advised that transmission of HCV by breastfeeding is possible but has not been documented. In one study, while transmission of HCV was significantly high (21%) in HIV infected individuals, perinatal transmission was not associated with breastfeeding.[1]

It is not known with certainty if the virus is shed in breastmilk although several studies so suggest. In one study of 17 HCV positive mothers, 11 of the 17 had HCV antibody present in milk, but zero of 17 had HCV-RNA in milk after birth, suggesting that the virus itself was not detected in milk.[3] Although it is possible that during episodes of direct exposure to blood such as from bleeding nipples or following initial infection and viremia that transmission could occur, this does not appear to be certain at this time.

Currently a number of other studies have yet to document horizontal transmission of HCV by breastmilk.[4,5] Available data seem to suggest an elevated risk of vertical transmission to the infant occurs in HIV infected women and women with elevated titers of HCV RNA. The risk of transmission of HCV via breastmilk is unknown at this time. HCV-infected women should be counseled that transmission of HCV by breastfeeding is theoretically possible but has not yet been documented.[6,7] The Center for Disease Control (CDC) does not consider chronic hepatitis C infection in the mother as a contraindication to breastfeeding. The decision to breastfeed should be based largely on informed discussion between the mother and her health care provider. It may be prudent however, for mothers who are seropositive for HCV to abstain from breastfeeding if their nipples are cracked and bleeding.[8]

Pregnancy Risk Category:

Lactation Risk Category: L2

Adult Concerns:

Pediatric Concerns:

Drug Interactions:

Relative Infant Dose:

Adult Dose:

Alternatives:

References:

1. Paccagnini S, Principi N, Massironi E, Tanzi E, Romano L, Muggiasca ML, Ragni MC, Salvaggio L. Perinatal transmission and manifestation of hepatitis C virus infection in a high risk population. Pediatr Infect Dis J 1995; 14 (3):195-199.
2. Nagata I, Shiraki K. et.al. Mother to infant transmission of hepatitis C virus. J Pediatrics 1992; 120:432-434.
3. Grayson ML, Braniff KM, Bowden DS, Turnidge JD. Breastfeeding and the risk of vertical transmission of hepatitis C virus. Med J Aust 1995; 163 (2):107.
4. Lin HH, Kao JH, Hsu HY, Ni YH, Chang MH, Huang SC, Hwang LH, Chen PJ, Chen DS. Absence of infection in breast-fed infants born to hepatitis C virus-infected mothers. J Pediatr 1995; 126 (4):589-591.
5. Zanetti. et.al. Mother to infant transmission of hepatitis C virus. Lancet 1995; 345 (8945):289-291.
6. American Academy of Pediatrics. Committee on Infectious Diseases. Red Book. 1997.
7. Lawrence RA. Breastfeeding: A guide for the medical profession. St. Louis: Mosby Publishers, 1994.
8. Mast EE. Mother-to-infant hepatitis C virus transmission and breastfeeding. Adv Exp Med Biol 2004; 554:211-6.:211-6.

HERBAL TEAS

Trade: Herbal Teas
Other Trades:
Uses: Herbal teas, tablets, powders, antioxidants.
AAP: Not reviewed

Herbal teas should be used with great caution, if at all. A number of reports in the literature indicate potential toxicity in pregnant women from some herbal teas which contain pyrrolizidine alkaloids (PA).[1,2] Such alkaloids have been associated with feticide, birth defects and liver toxicity.

Other reports of severe hepatotoxicity requiring liver transplant have occurred with an herbal antioxidant called Chaparral.[3] A Chinese herbal product called "Jin Bu Huan" has been implicated in clinically recognized hepatitis in 7 patients.[3] Other hepatotoxic remedies include gerrymander, comfrey, mistletoe and skullcap, margosa oil, mate tea, Gordolobo yerba tea, and pennyroyal (squawmint) oil.[4,5] A recent report of seven poisonings with anticholinergic symptoms following ingestion of "Paraguay Tea" was published and was an apparent adulteration.[6] A recent report on Blue Cohosh suggests it may be cardiotoxic when used late in pregnancy (see blue cohosh).[7,8]

Because exact ingredients are seldom listed on many teas, this author strongly suggests that lactating mothers limit exposure to these substances as much as possible. Never consume herbal remedies of unknown composition. Remember, breastfeeding infants are much more susceptible to such toxicants than are adults.

Pregnancy Risk Category:

Lactation Risk Category:

Adult Concerns: Severe toxicity including hepatotoxicity, anticholinergic poisoning, etc.

Pediatric Concerns: None reported via breastmilk, but caution is recommended. Agents listed above would be contraindicated.

Drug Interactions:

Relative Infant Dose:

Adult Dose:

Alternatives:

References:
1. Anonymous. Drug Therapy. J 1993; 16:64.
2. Ellenhorn MJ. Medical toxicology: a primer for the medicolegal age. Clin Toxicol 1978; 13 (4):439-462.

3. Gordon DW, Rosenthal G, Hart J, Sirota R, Baker AL. Chaparral ingestion. The broadening spectrum of liver injury caused by herbal medications. JAMA 1995; 273 (6):489-490.
4. Hsu CK, Leo P, Shastry D, Meggs W, Weisman R, Hoffman RS. Anticholinergic poisoning associated with herbal tea. Arch Intern Med 1995; 155 (20):2245-2248.
5. Siegel RK. Herbal Intoxication. JAMA 1976; 236:473-477.
6. Rosti L, Nardini A, Bettinelli ME, Rosti D. Toxic effects of a herbal tea mixture in two newborns. Acta Paediatr 1994; 83 (6):683.
7. Jones TK, Lawson BM. Profound neonatal congestive heart failure caused by maternal consumption of blue cohosh herbal medication. J Pediatr 1998; 132:550-2.
8. Gunn TR, Wright IMR. The use of blue and black cohosh in labour. NZ Med J 1996; 109:410-1.

HEROIN   L5

Trade: Heroin
Other Trades:
Uses: Narcotic analgesic
AAP: Drugs of abuse for which adverse effects have been reported

Heroin is diacetyl-morphine (diamorphine), a prodrug that is rapidly converted by plasma cholinesterases to 6-acetylmorphine and more slowly to morphine. With oral use, rapid and complete first-pass metabolism occurs in the liver. The half-life of diamorphine is only 3 minutes, with the large majority of the prodrug converted to morphine. Peak levels of morphine occur in about 30 minutes following oral doses. As an analgesic, morphine is generally considered to be an ideal choice for breastfeeding mothers when used postoperatively or for other forms of pain "in normal dosage ranges". Unfortunately, addicts and recreational users may use extraordinarily large doses of heroin, and at such doses, it is likely to be very dangerous for a breastfed infant. Heavily dependent users should probably be advised against breastfeeding and their infants converted to formula. While it could be argued that recreational users could continue to breastfeed if they avoid doing so while under the influence of the heroin or prior to its use, this still may not be advisable as it requires some understanding of the kinetics of morphine and its elimination. Heroin, as is morphine, is known to transfer into breastmilk.[1,2] See morphine for kinetics.

Pregnancy Risk Category: B
Lactation Risk Category: L5

Adult Concerns: Sedation, hypotension, euphoria, nausea, vomiting, dry mouth, respiratory depression, constipation.

Pediatric Concerns: Caution, observe for sedation. Tremors, restlessness, vomiting, poor feeding.

Drug Interactions:

Relative Infant Dose:

Adult Dose:

Alternatives:

T ½	= 1.5-2 hours	M/P	= 2.45
PHL	=	PB	= 35%
Tmax	= 0.5-1 hours	Oral	= Poor
MW	= 369	pKa	= 7.6
Vd	= 25		

References:
1. Feilberg VL, Rosenborg D, Broen CC, Mogensen JV. Excretion of morphine in human breast milk. Acta Anaesthesiol Scand 1989; 33 (5):426-428.
2. Wittels B, Scott DT, Sinatra RS. Exogenous opioids in human breast milk and acute neonatal neurobehavior: a preliminary study. Anesthesiology 1990; 73 (5):864-869.
3. American Academy of Pediatrics, Committee on Drugs. Transfer of drugs and other chemicals into human milk. Pediatrics 2001; 108 (3):776-89.

HERPES SIMPLEX INFECTIONS

Trade:

Other Trades:

Uses: Herpes simplex type I, II

AAP: Breastfeeding is acceptable if no lesions are on the breast or are adequately covered

HSV-1 and HSV-2 have been isolated from human milk, even in the absence of vesicular lesions or drainage.[1,2] Transmission after birth can occur and herpetic infections during the neonatal period are often severe and fatal.[3] Exposure to the virus from skin lesions of caregivers, including lesions of the breast, have been described. On average, however, perinatal infection is generally believed to occur during delivery rather than through breastmilk. Breastmilk does not appear to be a common mode of transmission although women with active lesions around the breast and nipple should refrain from breastfeeding until the lesions are adequately covered. Mothers with a lesion on one nipple, should breastfeed from the opposite side. A number of cases of herpes simplex transmission via breastmilk have been reported.[4,5] Women with active lesions should be extremely meticulous in hand washing to prevent spread of the disease from other active lesions.

Pregnancy Risk Category:

Lactation Risk Category:

Adult Concerns: Skin eruptions, CNS changes, gingivostomatitis, skin lesions, fever.

Pediatric Concerns: Transfer of virus to infants has been reported, but may be from exposure to lesions. Cover lesions on breast.

Drug Interactions:

Relative Infant Dose:

Adult Dose: N/A

Alternatives:

References:

1. Light IJ. Postnatal acquisition of herpes simplex virus by the newborn infant: a review of the literature. Pediatrics 1979; 63 (3):480-482.
2. Sullivan-Bolyai JZ, Fife KH, Jacobs RF, Miller Z, Corey L. Disseminated neonatal herpes simplex virus type 1 from a maternal breast lesion. Pediatrics 1983; 71 (3):455-457.
3. Whitley RJ, Nahmias AJ, Visintine AM, Fleming CL, Alford CA. The natural history of herpes simplex virus infection of mother and newborn. Pediatrics 1980; 66 (4):489-494.
4. Dunkle LM, Schmidt RR, O'Connor DM. Neonatal herpes simplex infection possibly acquired via maternal breast milk. Pediatrics 1979; 63 (2):250-251.
5. Quinn PT, Lofberg JV. Maternal herpetic breast infection: another hazard of neonatal herpes simplex. Med J Aust 1978; 2 (9):411-412.

HEXACHLOROPHENE | L4

Trade: Septisol, Phisohex, Septi-Soft
Other Trades: pHisoHex, Sapoderm, Dermalex
Uses: Antiseptic scrub
AAP: Not reviewed

Hexachlorophene is an antibacterial that is an effective inhibitor of gram positive organisms.[1] It is generally used topically as a surgical scrub and sometimes vaginally in mothers. Due to its lipophilic structure, it is well absorbed through intact and denuded skin producing significant levels in plasma, brain, fat, and other tissues in both adults and infants. It has been implicated in causing brain lesions (spongiform myelinopathy), blindness, and respiratory failure in both animals and humans.[2] Although there are no studies reporting concentrations of this compound in breastmilk, it is probably transferred to some degree. Transfer into breastmilk is known to occur in rodents. Topical use in infants is absolutely discouraged due to the high absorption of hexachlorophene through an infant's skin and proven toxicity.

Pregnancy Risk Category: C

Lactation Risk Category: L4

Adult Concerns: Seizures, respiratory failure, hypotension, brain lesions, blindness in overdose.

Pediatric Concerns: Following direct application, CNS injury, seizures, irritability have been reported in neonates. Toxicity via breastmilk has not been reported.

Drug Interactions:

Relative Infant Dose:

Adult Dose:

Alternatives:

T ½	=	M/P	=
PHL	= 6.1-44.2 hours	PB	=
Tmax	=	Oral	= Complete
MW	= 407	pKa	=
Vd	=		

References:
1. Pharmaceutical Manufacturer Prescribing Information. 1996.
2. Tyrala EE, Hillman LS, Hillman RE, Dodson WE. Clinical pharmacology of hexachlorophene in newborn infants. J Pediatr 1977; 91 (3):481-486.

HISTAMINE   L3

Trade: Histamine
Other Trades:
Uses: Diagnostic agent for asthma and gastric function
AAP: Not reviewed

Histamine is a normal substance found the mast cells and plays a major role in the allergic response, neurotransmission, gastric acid secretion and bronchial constriction. Physiologically, it interacts at any of three different cellular receptors - H1, H2, and H3. These receptors are in high concentrations in bronchi (H1) or gastric and other tissues (H2, H3). Histamine is primarily stored in the mast cell, which when destabilized by allergens, etc., releases histamine into the tissues and initiates the normal response to histamine. Histamine is primarily used pharmacologically as a diagnostic agent, to induce gastric acid release, or more often, stimulate bronchoconstriction in the diagnosis of asthma. Histamine is rapidly metabolized with a plasma half-life less than 3 minutes. No data are available on its transfer to human milk, but it is probably minimal. Waiting as little as 2 hours following exposure would largely eliminate all risks associated with the use of histamine in a breastfeeding mother.

Pregnancy Risk Category:

Lactation Risk Category: L3

Adult Concerns: Side effects include: flushing, vasodilation, hyper or hypotension, edema, tachycardia, headache, diarrhea, vomiting, hyperacidity, blurred vision, dizziness, bronchoconstriction, asthma symptoms,

Pediatric Concerns: None reported in breastfeeding infants. A 1-2 hour waiting period after the procedure is recommended.

Drug Interactions: Caution with use in asthmatics. Obviously, for diagnostic procedures, do not use with antihistamines.

Relative Infant Dose:

Adult Dose: Highly variable.

Alternatives:

T ½	= <3 minutes	M/P	=
PHL	=	PB	=
Tmax	=	Oral	= minimal
MW	= 307	pKa	=
Vd	=		

References:
1. Pharmaceutical manufacturers prescribing information. 2005.

HIV INFECTION   L5

Trade: AIDS
Other Trades:
Uses: Aids, HIV infections
AAP: Advise not to breastfeed

The AIDS (HIV) virus has been isolated from human milk. In addition, recent reports from throughout the world have documented the transmission of HIV through human milk.[1,2,3] At least 9 or more cases in the literature currently suggest that HIV-1 is secreted and can be transmitted horizontally to the infant via breastmilk. Although these studies clearly indicate a risk, currently no studies clearly show the exact risk associated with breastfeeding in HIV infected women. However, women who develop a primary HIV infection while breastfeeding may shed especially high concentrations of HIV viruses and pose a high risk of transmission to their infants. In some studies, the risk of transmission during primary infection was 29%. In various African populations, recent reports suggest the incremental risk of transmitting HIV via breastfeeding ranges from 3-12%.[6] Because the risk is now well documented, HIV infected mothers in the USA and others countries with safe alternative sources of feeding should be advised to not breastfeed their infants.[7] Mothers at-risk for HIV should be screened and counseled prior to initiating breastfeeding.

Pregnancy Risk Category:

Lactation Risk Category: L5 in developed countries

Adult Concerns:

Pediatric Concerns: HIV transmission has been documented. HIV infected women are advised not to breastfeed.

Drug Interactions:

Relative Infant Dose:

Adult Dose:

Alternatives:

References:

1.   Commitee on Pediatric AIDS. Human milk, breastfeeding, and transmission of human immunodeficiency virus in the United States. Pediatrics 1995; 96:977-979.
2.   Oxtoby MJ. Human immunodeficiency virus and other viruses in human milk: placing the issues in broader perspective. Pediatr Infect Dis J 1988; 7 (12):825-835.
3.   Goldfarb J. Breastfeeding. AIDS and other infectious diseases. Clin Perinatol 1993; 20 (1):225-243.
4.   Van de PP, Simonon A, Hitimana DG, Dabis F, Msellati P, Mukamabano B, Butera JB, Van Goethem C, Karita E, Lepage P. Infective and anti-infective properties of breastmilk from HIV-1-infected women. Lancet 1993; 341 (8850):914-918.
5.   Dunn DT, Newell ML, Ades AE, Peckham CS. Risk of human immunodeficiency virus type 1 transmission through breastfeeding. Lancet 1992; 340 (8819):585-588.
6.   St. Louis ME. et.al. The timing of HIV-1 transmission in an African setting. Presented at the First National Conference on Human Retroviruses and Related Infections. December 12-16; Washington DC. 1993.
7.   Report of the committee on Infectious Diseases. American Academy of Pediatrics. 1994.

HYALURONIC ACID   L3

Trade: Synvisc, Euflexxa, Healon, Hyalgan, Hylaform, Juvederm, Orthovisc, Provisc, Restylane

Other Trades: Cystistat, Durolane, Eyestil, Healon, OrthoVisc, Suplasyn

Uses: Viscoelastic agent, antirheumatic, anti-wrinkle

AAP: Not reviewed

Hyaluronic acid forms a viscoelastic solution in water, thus functioning as a joint lubricant, vitreous humor during opthalmic surgery, and even decreasing the depth of wrinkles when injected intradermally. Sodium hyaluronate is a polysaccharide found in the extracellular matrix of connective tissues.[1] There are no data available on the transfer of hyaluronic acid into breastmilk, but it would be minimal to nil. The repeating chains can be quite large, and therefore size would prohibit any drug that did get absorbed from transferring into the milk compartment.

A similar product is Hyalgan, which is sodium hyaluronate.

Pregnancy Risk Category:

Lactation Risk Category: L3

Adult Concerns: Pain at injection site. Arthralgia, bursitis, etc.

Pediatric Concerns: None reported in breastfed infants.

Drug Interactions:

Relative Infant Dose:

Adult Dose:

Alternatives:

T ½	=		M/P	=
PHL	=		PB	=
Tmax	=		Oral	= Nil
MW	= Large		pKa	=
Vd	=			

References:
1.   Pharmaceutical manufacturers prescribing information. 2005.

HYDRALAZINE   L2

Trade: Apresoline
Other Trades: Novo-Hylazin, Apo-Hydralazine, Alphapress
Uses: Antihypertensive
AAP: Maternal Medication Usually Compatible with
           Breastfeeding

Hydralazine is a popular antihypertensive used for severe pre-eclampsia and gestational and postpartum hypertension. In a study of one breastfeeding mother receiving 50 mg three times daily, the concentrations of hydralazine in breastmilk at 0.5 and 2 hours after administration was 762, and 792 nmol/L respectively.[1] The respective maternal serum levels were 1525, and 580 nmol/L at the aforementioned times. From these data, an infant consuming 1000 mL of milk would consume only 0.17 mg of hydralazine, an amount too small to be clinically relevant. The published pediatric dose for hydralazine is 0.75 to 1 mg/kg/day.

Pregnancy Risk Category: C

Lactation Risk Category: L2

Adult Concerns: Hypotension, tachycardia, renal failure, liver toxicity, paresthesias.

Pediatric Concerns: None reported but observe for hypotension, sedation, weakness.

Drug Interactions: Increased effect with other antihypertensives, MAO inhibitors. Decreased effect when used with indomethacin.

Relative Infant Dose: 1.2%

Adult Dose: 10-25 mg QID

Alternatives:

T ½	= 1.5-8 hours	M/P	= 0.49-1.36
PHL	=	PB	= 87%
Tmax	= 2 hours	Oral	= 30-50%
MW	= 160	pKa	= 7.1
Vd	= 1.6		

References:
1. Liedholm H, Wahlin-Boll E, Hanson A, Ingemarsson I, Melander A. Transplacental passage and breast milk concentrations of hydralazine. Eur J Clin Pharmacol 1982; 21 (5):417-419.

HYDROCHLOROTHIAZIDE | L2

Trade: HydroDIURIL, Esidrix, Oretic

Other Trades: Apo-Hydro, Diuchlor H, Hydrodiuril, Novo-Hydrazide, Amizide, Dyazide, Modizide, Direma, Esidrex

Uses: Thiazide diuretic

AAP: Maternal Medication Usually Compatible with Breastfeeding

Hydrochlorothiazide (HCTZ) is a typical thiazide diuretic. In one study of a mother receiving a 50 mg dose each morning, milk levels were almost 25% of maternal plasma levels.[1] The dose ingested (assuming milk intake of 600 mL) would be approximately 50 µg/day, a clinically insignificant amount. The concentration of HCTZ in the infant's serum was undetectable (<20 ng/mL). Some authors suggest that HCTZ can produce thrombocytopenia in nursing infant, although this is remote and unsubstantiated. Thiazide diuretics could potentially reduce milk production by depleting maternal blood volume although it is seldom observed. Most thiazide diuretics are considered compatible with breastfeeding if doses are kept low.

Pregnancy Risk Category: B

Lactation Risk Category: L2

Adult Concerns: Fluid loss, hypotension. May reduce milk supply.

Pediatric Concerns: None reported via milk, but may reduce milk supply in mother.

Drug Interactions: May increase hypoglycemia with antidiabetic drugs. May increase hypotension associated with other antihypertensives. May increase digoxin associated arrhythmias. May increase lithium levels.

Relative Infant Dose:

Adult Dose: 25-100 mg daily.

Alternatives:

T ½	= 5.6-14.8 hours	M/P	= 0.25
PHL	=	PB	= 58%
Tmax	= 2 hours	Oral	= 72%
MW	= 297	pKa	= 7.9, 9.2
Vd	= 3		

References:
1. Miller ME, Cohn RD, Burghart PH. Hydrochlorothiazide disposition in a mother and her breast-fed infant. J Pediatr 1982; 101 (5):789-791.

HYDROCODONE   L3

Trade: Lortab, Vicodin, Maxidone
Other Trades: Hycodan, Robidone, Hycomine, Actron
Uses: Analgesic for pain
AAP: Not reviewed

Hydrocodone is a narcotic analgesic and antitussive structurally related to codeine although somewhat more potent. It is commonly used in breastfeeding mothers throughout the USA. Most authors suggest that doses of 5 mg every 4 hours or more has a minimal effect on nursing infants, particularly older infants.[1,2,3] However, no data on hydrocodone levels in milk are available. To reduce exposure of the infant, attempt to feed infant prior to taking the medication. Neonates may be more sensitive to this product, observe for sedation or constipation. Lortab and Vicodin also contain acetaminophen.

Pregnancy Risk Category: B

Lactation Risk Category: L3

Adult Concerns: Sedation, dizziness, apnea, bradycardia, nausea, or constipation.

Pediatric Concerns: None reported via milk, but observe closely for sedation, apnea, constipation.

Drug Interactions: May reduce analgesia when used with phenothiazines. May increase toxicity associated with CNS depressants and tricyclic antidepressants.

Relative Infant Dose:

Adult Dose: 5-10 mg every 4-6 hours

Alternatives: Codeine

T ½	= 3.8 hours	M/P	=
PHL	=	PB	=
Tmax	= 1.3 hours	Oral	= Complete
MW	= 299	pKa	= 8.9
Vd	= 3.3-4.7		

References:

1. Horning MG. Identification and quantification of drugs and drug metabolites in human milk using GC-MS-COM methods. Mod Probl Pediatr 1975; 15:73-79.
2. Kwit NT, Hatcher RA. Excretion of drugs in milk. Am J Dis Child 1935; 49:900-904.
3. Anderson PO. Medication use while breast feeding a neonate. Neonatal Pharmacology Quarterly 1993; 2:3-12.

HYDROCORTISONE ENEMA   L3

Trade: Colocort, Cortenema, Hycort Enema, Rectoid
Other Trades:
Uses: Corticosteroid
AAP: Not reviewed

Hydrocortisone is a typical corticosteroid with weak glucocorticoid and mineralocorticoid activity.[1] The amount transferred into human milk has not been reported, but as with most steroids, is believed minimal. Hydrocortisone Rectal Suspension is absorbed from the colon, it acts both topically and systemically. Although rectal hydrocortisone has a low incidence of reported adverse reactions, prolonged use presumably may cause typical steroid systemic reactions.

In a study undertaken to determine changes in concentrations of cortisol in the mammary secretion of individual women during late pregnancy, lactogenesis, established lactation and after cessation of breast-feeding, the concentration of cortisol in colostrum averaged 7.5% of that found in serum during late pregnancy. Cortisol levels in colostrum during late pregnancy was 25.5 ng/mL and fell within 2 days postpartum to 10.2 ng/mL. At 10 days, levels were 1.8 ng/mL. During established lactation, cortisol levels ranged from 0.2 to 32 ng/mL but the mean was 7.2 ng/mL.[2]

Pregnancy Risk Category: C

Lactation Risk Category: L3

Adult Concerns: Rarely local pain or burning and rectal bleeding. Sodium retention; fluid retention; congestive heart failure in susceptible patients; potassium loss; hypokalemic alkalosis; hypertension. Muscle weakness, steroid myopathy, osteoporosis, peptic ulcer, pancreatitis, ulcerative esophagitis, impaired wound healing, glaucoma, cataracts, etc.

Pediatric Concerns: None via breastfeeding have been reported.

Drug Interactions: Over 600 hundred exist. Consult drug interactions textbook.

Relative Infant Dose:

Adult Dose: 100 mg nightly (60 ml) rectally

Alternatives:

T ½	= 1-2 hours	M/P	=
PHL	=	PB	= 90%
Tmax	=	Oral	= 96%
MW	= 362	pKa	=
Vd	= 0.48		

References:
1. Pharmaceutical manufacturers prescribing information, 2010.
2. Kulski JK, Hartmann PE. Changes in the concentration of cortisol in milk during different stages of human lactation. Aust J Exp Biol Med Sci. 1981 Dec;59 (Pt 6):769-78.

HYDROCORTISONE TOPICAL | L2

Trade: Westcort
Other Trades: Cortate, Cortone, Emo-Cort, Aquacort, Dermaid, Egocort, Hycor, Cortef, Dermacort
Uses: Corticosteroid
AAP: Not reviewed

Hydrocortisone is a typical corticosteroid with glucocorticoid and mineralocorticoid activity. When applied topically it suppresses inflammation and enhances healing. Initial onset of activity when applied topically is slow and may require several days for response. Absorption topically is dependent on placement; percutaneous absorption is 1% from the forearm, 2% from rectum, 4% from the scalp, 7% from the forehead, and 36% from the scrotal area.[1] The amount transferred into human milk has not been reported, but as with most steroids, is believed minimal. Topical application to the nipple is generally approved by most authorities if amounts applied and duration of use are minimized. Only small amounts should be applied and then only after feeding; larger quantities should be removed prior to breastfeeding. 0.5 to 1 % ointments, rather than creams, are generally preferred.

Pregnancy Risk Category: C

Lactation Risk Category: L2

Adult Concerns: Local irritation.

Pediatric Concerns: None reported via milk.

Drug Interactions:

Relative Infant Dose:

Adult Dose: Apply topical QID

Alternatives:

T ½	= 1-2 hours	M/P	=
PHL	=	PB	= 90%
Tmax	=	Oral	= 96%
MW	= 362	pKa	=
Vd	= 0.48		

References:
1. Derendorf H, Mollmann H, Barth J, Mollmann C, Tunn S, Krieg M. Pharmacokinetics and oral bioavailability of hydrocortisone. J Clin Pharmacol 1991; 31 (5):473-476.

HYDROMORPHONE   L3

Trade: Dilaudid
Other Trades: Hydromorph Contin, Palladone
Uses: Opiate analgesic
AAP: Not reviewed

Hydromorphone is a potent semisynthetic narcotic analgesic used to alleviate moderate to severe pain. It is approximately 7-10 times more potent that morphine, but is used in equivalently lower doses.[1] In a group of 8 women who received intranasal hydromorphone (2 mg), milk levels ranged from a high of about 6000 pg/mL at about 1 hour, to about 200 pg/mL at 24 hours, but averaged about 1.04 μg/L.[2] The observed milk/plasma ratio averaged 2.57. The half-life of hydromorphone in milk was estimated at 10.5 hours. The authors estimate a Relative Infant Dose of 0.67% of the maternal dose although I calculate it at 0.52%. Using this data an infant would consume (via milk) approximately 2.2 μg per day. This is significantly less than the clinical dose in infants and children of 15-30 μg/kg/dose every 4-6 hours.

Pregnancy Risk Category: C

Lactation Risk Category: L3

Adult Concerns: Hydromorphone is highly addictive. Adverse effects include dizziness, sedation, agitation, hypotension, respiratory depression, nausea, and vomiting.

Pediatric Concerns: Milk levels reported to be low. Caution recommended in weak or premature infants, or after prolonged use.

Drug Interactions: As with other opiates, barbiturates and benzodiazepines could potentiate the sedative/hypnotic properties of hydromorphone.

Relative Infant Dose: 0.52%

Adult Dose: 2-10 mg every 3-6 hours PRN

Alternatives: Codeine, Hydrocodone

T ½	= 11.1 hours	M/P	= 2.57
PHL	=	PB	=
Tmax	= 0.27 hours	Oral	= 51%
MW	= 285	pKa	=
Vd	= 2.9		

References:
1. Baselt RC. Disposition of toxic drugs and chemicals in man. Foster City, CA: Chemical Toxicology Institute, 2000: 426-427.
2   Edwards JE, Rudy AC, Wermeling DP, Desai N, McNamara PJ. Hydromorphone transfer into breast milk after intranasal administration. Pharmacotherapy 2003 February; 23 (2):153-8.

HYDROQUINONE   L3

Trade: Esoterica, Eldoquin, Melpaque, Melanex, Solaquin, Nuquin, Viquin

Other Trades:

Uses: Depigmenting agent for topical applications

AAP: Not reviewed

Hydroquinone is used for depigmentation of skin due to conditions such as freckles, melasma, senile lentigo, and inactive chloasma.[1] Hydroquinone is rapidly and extensively absorbed from the gut of animals. Absorption via the skin is slower but may be more rapid with vehicles such as alcohols. The transcutaneous absorption is reported to be about 35% which is relatively high for topical preparations. Hydroquinone distributes rapidly and widely and is metabolized to p-benzoquinone and other products. It is metabolized in the liver by conjugation to monoglucuronide, monosulfate, and mercapturic derivatives. The excretion of hydroquinone and its metabolites is rapid, and occurs primarily via the urine. No data are available on its transfer into human milk. Although it is quite polar and water soluble, it also has a rather high pKa (9.96) which could lead to some trapping in human milk. While it does not seem to be very toxic, its chronic use in breastfeeding mothers is probably not warranted for such benign syndromes that could wait until the mother has weaned.

Pregnancy Risk Category: C

Lactation Risk Category: L3

Adult Concerns: Adverse effects include mild skin irritation and sensitivity, dryness, and fissuring of paranasal and infraorbital areas. Cases of intoxication and death have been reported from the oral ingestion of photographic developing agents. Dermal applications of hydroquinone at concentration levels below 3% in different bases caused negligible effects in male volunteers. However, there are case reports suggesting that skin lightening creams containing 2% hydroquinone have produced leucoderma, as well as ochronosis.

Pediatric Concerns: No reports of its use in breastfeeding mothers. While not highly risky, its use in breastfeeding mothers may not be justified.

Drug Interactions: Combinations with corticosteroids may reduce skin irritation.

Relative Infant Dose:

Adult Dose: Apply 2-4% solutions twice daily. Limit areas treated.

Alternatives: Azelaic acid

T ½	=	M/P	=
PHL	=	PB	=
Tmax	=	Oral	=
MW	=	pKa	= 9.96
Vd	=		

References:
1.   Pharmaceutical Manufacturers Package Insert, 2003.

HYDROXYCHLOROQUINE   L2

Trade: Plaquenil
Other Trades:
Uses: Antimalarial, Antirheumatic
AAP: Maternal Medication Usually Compatible with Breastfeeding

Hydroxychloroquine (HCQ) is effective in the treatment of malaria but is also used in immune syndromes such as rheumatoid arthritis and Lupus erythematosus. HCQ is known to produce significant retinal damage and blindness if used over a prolonged period, and this could occur (theoretically but unlikely) in breastfed infants. Patients on this product should see an ophthalmologist routinely. It has a huge volume of distribution (Vd) which suggests milk levels will be quite low.

In one study of a mother receiving 400 mg HCQ daily, the concentrations of HCQ in breastmilk were 1.46, 1.09, and 1.09 mg/L at 2.0, 9.5, and 14 hours after the dose.[1] The average milk concentration was 1.1 mg/L. The milk/plasma ratio was approximately 5.5. On a body-weight basis, the infant's dose would be 2.9% of the maternal dose.

In another study of one mother receiving 200 mg twice daily milk levels were much lower than the previous study. Only a total of 3.2 micrograms of HCQ was detected in her milk over 48 hours.[2]

Two breastfeeding mothers taking hydroxychloroquine were tested to determine the concentration in their breastmilk one week after delivery. The concentrations were 344 and 1424 ng/mL, which corresponded to an infant dose of 0.06 and 0.2 mg/kg/d respectively.[3] HCQ is mostly metabolized to chloroquine and has an incredibly long half-life. The pediatric dose for malaria prophylaxis is 5 mg/kg/week, far larger than the dose received via milk. See chloroquine.

Pregnancy Risk Category: C

Lactation Risk Category: L2

Adult Concerns: Blood dyscrasias, nausea, vomiting, diarrhea, retinopathy, rash, aplastic anemia, psychosis, porphyries, psoriasis, corneal deposits.

Pediatric Concerns: None reported, but observe for retinal damage, blood dyscrasias.

Drug Interactions: Increased risk of blood dyscrasias when used with aurothioglucose. May increase serum digoxin levels.

Relative Infant Dose: 2.88%

Adult Dose: 400 mg every week for 10 weeks

Alternatives:

T ½	= >40 days	M/P	= 5.5
PHL	=	PB	= 63%
Tmax	= 1-2 hours	Oral	= 74%
MW	= 336	pKa	=
Vd	= 580-815		

References:

1. Nation RL, Hackett LP, Dusci LJ, Ilett KF. Excretion of hydroxychloroquine in human milk. Br J Clin Pharmacol 1984; 17 (3):368-369.
2. Ostensen M, Brown ND, Chiang PK, Aarbakke J. Hydroxychloroquine in human breast milk. Eur J Clin Pharmacol 1985; 28 (3):357.
3. Costedoat-Chalumeau N, Amoura Z, Aymard G et al. Evidence of transplacental passage of hydroxychloroquine in humans. Arthritis Rheum 2002; 46 (4):1123-1124.

HYDROXYUREA   L2

Trade: Hydrea
Other Trades:
Uses: Antineoplastic agent
AAP: Not reviewed

Hydroxyurea is an antineoplastic agent used to treat melanoma, leukemias, and other neoplasms. It is well absorbed orally and rapidly metabolized to urea by the liver. In one study following a dose of 500 mg three times daily for 7 days, milk samples were collected two hours after the last dose.[1] The concentration of hydroxyurea in breastmilk averaged 6.1 mg/L (range 3.8 to 8.4 mg/L). Hydroxyurea is rapidly cleared from the plasma compartment and appears to leave no residuals or metabolites. Approximately 80% of the dose is excreted renaly with 12 hours.

Pregnancy Risk Category: D

Lactation Risk Category: L2

Adult Concerns: Bone marrow suppression, drowsiness, convulsion, hallucinations, fever, nausea, vomiting, diarrhea, constipation.

Pediatric Concerns: None reported via milk, but extreme caution is recommended due to overt toxicity of this product.
Drug Interactions: May have increased toxicity and neurotoxicity when used with fluorouracil.

Relative Infant Dose: 4.3%

Adult Dose: 80 mg/kg every 3 days

Alternatives:

T ½	= 3-4 hours	M/P	=
PHL	=	PB	=
Tmax	= 2 hours	Oral	= Complete
MW	= 76	pKa	=
Vd	=		

References:
1. Sylvester RK, Lobell M, Teresi ME, Brundage D, Dubowy R. Excretion of hydroxyurea into milk. Cancer 1987; 60 (9):2177-2178.

HYDROXYZINE L1

Trade: Atarax, Vistaril
Other Trades: Apo-Hydroxyzine, Novo-Hydroxyzin
Uses: Antihistamine, antiemetic
AAP: Not reviewed

Hydroxyzine is an antihistamine structurally similar to cyclizine and meclizine. It produces significant CNS depression, anticholinergic side effects (drying), and antiemetic side effects.[1] Hydroxyzine is largely metabolized to cetirizine (Zyrtec). No data are available on secretion into breastmilk.

Pregnancy Risk Category: C

Lactation Risk Category: L1

Adult Concerns: Sedation, hypotension, dry mouth.

Pediatric Concerns: None reported via milk, but observe for sedation, tachycardia, dry mouth.

Drug Interactions: May reduce epinephrine vasopressor response. Increased sedation when used with CNS depressants. Increased anticholinergic side effects when admixed with other anticholinergics.

Relative Infant Dose:

Adult Dose: 50-100 mg QID

Alternatives: Cetirizine, Loratadine

T ½	= 3-7 hours	M/P	=
PHL	= 7.1 hrs	PB	=
Tmax	= 2 hours	Oral	= Complete
MW	= 375	pKa	= 2.1, 7.1
Vd	= 13-31		

References:
1. Paton DM, Webster DR. Clinical pharmacokinetics of H1-receptor antagonists (the antihistamines). Clin Pharmacokinet 1985; 10 (6):477-497.

HYLAN G-F 20 | L2

Trade: Synvisc
Other Trades:
Uses: Joint lubricant for arthritic pain
AAP: Not reviewed

Hylan G-F 20 (Synvisc) is an elastoviscous fluid containing hylan polymers produced from chicken combs. Hylans are a natural complex sugar of the glycosaminoglycan family.[1] Hylans are large MW polymers and would not be expected to enter milk. Average MW is 6 million daltons. This product would not pose a problem for a breastfeeding mother or infant.

Pregnancy Risk Category:

Lactation Risk Category: L2

Adult Concerns: Knee pain or swelling, rash, itching, nausea, vomiting.

Pediatric Concerns: None reported via milk. Probably too large to enter milk in clinically relevant amounts.

Drug Interactions:

Relative Infant Dose:

Adult Dose:

Alternatives:

T ½	=	M/P	=
PHL	=	PB	=
Tmax	=	Oral	= None
MW	= 6 mil	pKa	=
Vd	=		

References:
1. Pharmaceutical Manufacturer Prescribing Information. 1999.

HYOSCYAMINE   L3

Trade: Anaspaz, Levsin, NuLev
Other Trades: Buscopan, Levsin, Hyoscine
Uses: Anticholinergic, antisecretory agent
AAP: Not reviewed

Hyoscyamine is an anticholinergic, antisecretory agent that belongs to the belladonna alkaloid family. Its typical effects are to dry secretions, produce constipation, dilate pupils, blur vision, and may produce urinary retention.[1,2] Although no exact amounts are listed, hyoscyamine is known to be secreted into breastmilk in trace amounts.[3] Thus far, no untoward effects from breastfeeding while using hyoscyamine have been found. Levsin (hyoscyamine) drops have in the past been used directly in infants for colic although it is no longer recommended for this use. As with atropine, infants and children are especially sensitive to anticholinergics and their use is discouraged. Atropine is composed of two isomers of hyoscyamine. See atropine. Use with caution.

Pregnancy Risk Category: C

Lactation Risk Category: L3

Adult Concerns: Tachycardia, dry mouth, blurred vision, constipation, urinary retention.

Pediatric Concerns: Decreased heart rate, anticholinergic effects from direct use, but none reported from breastmilk ingestion. Never use directly in infants with projectile vomiting, or in infants with bilious (green) vomitus.

Drug Interactions: Decreased effect with antacids. Increased toxicity with amantadine, antimuscarinics, haloperidol, phenothiazines, tricyclic antidepressants, MAO inhibitors.

Relative Infant Dose:

Adult Dose: 0.125-0.25 mg QID
Alternatives:

T ½	= 3.5 hours	M/P	=
PHL	=	PB	= 50%
Tmax	= 40-90 minutes (oral)	Oral	= 81%
MW	= 289	pKa	=
Vd	=		

References:
1. Drug Facts and Comparisons 1995 ed. ed. St. Louis: 1995.
2. Pharmaceutical Manufacturer Prescribing Information. 1995.
3. Wilson J. Drugs in Breast Milk. New York: ADIS Press 1981.

I-125 I-131 I-123   L4

Trade: Radioactive Iodine, ^{125}Iodine, ^{131}Iodine, ^{123}Iodine, Iodotope, ^{125}I, ^{131}I, ^{123}I

Other Trades:

Uses: Radioactive iodine

AAP: Radioactive compound that requires temporary cessation of breastfeeding

The normal human body contains about 9-10 mg of iodine, 90% of which resides in the thyroid gland. The thyroid gland concentrates more than 100 times the recommended daily allowance. The thyroid gland, and the cells in the lactating breast, contain a transporter (symporter) that facilitates concentration of iodine in these tissues. The normal range of iodine in human milk is reported to be 20-150 µg/L, and is a function of geography. The daily dietary requirement for lactating women is about 30% higher than for the general public.

Radioactive iodine concentrates in the thyroid gland as well as in breastmilk, and if ingested by an infant, it may suppress its thyroid function or increase the risk of future thyroid carcinomas, and produce thyroid destruction in the infant. Radioactive iodine is clinically used to ablate or destroy the thyroid (dose= 355 MBq), or in much smaller doses (7.4 MBq), to scan the thyroid for malignancies. Following ingestion, radioactive iodine concentrates in the thyroid and lactating tissues, and it is estimated 27.9% of total radioactivity is secreted via breast milk.[1]

Two potential half-lives exist for radioactive iodine: one is the radioactive half-life which is solely dependent on radioactive decay of the molecule; and two, the biological half-life, which is often briefer and is the half-life of the iodine molecule itself in the human being. The latter half-life is influenced most by elimination via the kidneys and other routes.

Previously published data have suggested that ^{125}Iodine is present in milk for at least 12 days and ^{131}Iodine is present for 2-14 days, but these studies may be in error as they ignored the second component of the biexponential breastmilk disappearance curve.[2] The radioactive half-life of ^{131}I is 8.1 days. The half-life of ^{125}I is 60.2 days and the half-life of ^{123}I is 13.2 hours. The biological or effective half-life may be shorter due to excretion in urine, feces, and milk.

A well done study by Dydek reviewed the transfer of both tracer and ablation doses of ^{131}I into human milk.[3] If the tracer doses are kept minimal (0.1 µCi or 3.7 kBq), breastfeeding could resume as early as the eighth day. However, if larger tracer doses (8.6 µCi or 0.317 MBq) are used, nursing could not resume until 46 days following therapy. Doses used for ablation of the maternal thyroid (111 MBq) would require an interruption of breastfeeding for a minimum of 106 days or more. However, an acceptable dose to an infant, as a result of ingestion of radioiodine, is a matter for debate although an effective dose of <1 mSv has been suggested.

In another study of ^{131}I use in a mother, breastmilk levels were followed for 32 days. These authors recommend discontinuing breastfeeding for up to 50-52 days to ensure safety of the infant thyroid. Thyroid scans use either radioactive iodine or technetium-^{99m} pertechnetate. Technetium has a very short half-life and should be preferred in breastfeeding mothers for thyroid scanning.[3]

Due to the fact that significant concentrations of ^{131}I are concentrated in breastmilk, women should discontinue breastfeeding prior to treatment, as the cumulative exposure to breast tissues could be excessively high. It is sometimes recommended that women discontinue breastfeeding several days to weeks before undergoing therapy or that they pump and discard milk for several weeks after exposure to iodine to reduce the overall radioactive exposure to breast tissues. The estimated dose of radioactivity to the breasts would give a "theoretical" probability of induction of breast cancer of 0.32%.[1] In addition, holding the infant close to the breast or thyroid gland for long periods may expose the infant to gamma irradiation and is not recommended. Patients should consult with the radiologist concerning exposure of the infant.

One case of significant exposure was reported in a breastfed infant.[4] The mother received a 3.02 millicurie dose of ^{131}I and continued to breastfeed for the next 7 days before the mother admitted breastfeeding. During this 7 day period, the infant's thyroid contained 2.7 microcuries of ^{131}iodine which is an effective dose equivalent of 5.5 rads. Had the mother continued to breastfeed, the dose would have been much larger and potentially dangerous.

In another case report of a patient who received 14 microcuries of oral ^{131}Iodine, and then 5 millicuries of ^{99}Technetium, the mothers' milk was withdrawn and screened for radiation with a gamma counter.[5] On day 8 the measured radioactivity was 94 counts per minute (cpm).

On day 13, the measured radioactivity was 30 cpm, and by day 20, the radioactivity was measured at background levels (20 cpm). This data suggests that if the 131-I levels administered are equal to or less than 14 microcuries, then the mother could potentially return to breastfeeding after 20 days.

Another alternative is ^{123}I, a newer isotope that is increasing in popularity. [123]I has a short half-life of only 13.2 hours and is radiologically ideal for thyroid and other scans. If radioactive iodine compounds are mandatory for various "scanning" procedures, ^{123}I should be preferred, followed by pumping and dumping for 12-24 hours depending on the dose. However, the return to breastfeeding following ^{123}I therapy is dependent on the purity of this product. During manufacture of ^{123}I, [124]I and ^{125}I are created. If using ^{123}I, breastfeeding should be temporarily interrupted (see table in appendices). [123]I is not used for ablation of the thyroid.

In a study by Morita of the transfer of ^{123}I-sodium iodide, ^{123}I was excreted exponentially with an effective half-life of 5.5 hours.[6] A total of 2.5% of the total radioactivity administered was excreted in the breast milk over the 93 h, 95% of which was excreted within the first 24 h, and 98.2% within 36 h. The first milk sample collected at 7 hours after administration contained 48.5% of the total radioactivity excreted. The authors estimated the potential absorption of radioactivity to an infant's thyroid in uninterrupted breast-feeding to be 30.3 mGy. With a 24-hour interruption, the absorbed radioactivity would be 1.25 mGy; with a 36-hour interruption, it would be 0.24 mGy. They recommend that breastfeeding should be curtailed for 36 h to reduce the infant's exposure to ^{123}I radioactivity.

The Nuclear Regulatory Commission has released a table of instructions to mothers concerning the use of radioisotopes (see Appendix B). These instructions conclude that patients should not breastfeed following the use of [131]I. In a study by Hammami, radioactive ^{131}I was found to transfer into breasts weeks following cessation of lactation.[7] They suggest the breast is a "radioiodine reservoir".

Ultimately, the amount of radioiodine transferred into human milk depends on the clinical dose administered to the mother. Low scanning doses may present an opportunity to return to breastfeeding if the counts in milk are closely monitored in the coming weeks. Using extraordinarily high ablative doses may continue to be present in milk for many weeks. If one is able to measure the milk for radiation, then a return to baseline would allow a patient to reinitiate breastfeeding. See Appendix B for more recommendations and other radiopharmaceuticals. Mothers exposed to radioactive iodine released from nuclear power plant disasters, should be immediately treated with potassium iodide to prevent transmission of the radioactive iodine into human milk, and the infant's thyroid.

Pregnancy Risk Category:

Lactation Risk Category: L4
                                L5 with ablative doses

Adult Concerns: Ablation of thyroid function. Theoretical risk of breast cancer if used in lactating women.

Pediatric Concerns: None reported, but damage to thyroid is probable if the infant is breastfed while ^{131}I levels are high. See appendix B.

Drug Interactions:

Relative Infant Dose:

Adult Dose:

Alternatives: Technetium[99M]

T ½	=	M/P	=
PHL	=	PB	=
Tmax	=	Oral	= Complete
MW	=	pKa	=
Vd	=		

References:

1. Robinson PS, Barker P, Campbell A, Henson P, Surveyor I, Young PR. [131]Iodine in breast milk following therapy for thyroid carcinoma. J Nucl Med 1994; 35 (11):1797-1801.
2. Palmer KE. Excretion of 125I in breast milk following administration of labelled fibrinogen. Br J Radiol 1979; 52 (620):672-673.
3. Dydek GJ, Blue PW. Human breast milk excretion of [131]Iodine following diagnostic and therapeutic administration to a lactating patient with Graves' disease. J Nucl Med 1988; 29 (3):407-410.
4. [131]Iodine dose for whole body scan administered to a breast-feeding patient. Preliminary notification of event or unusual occurrence PNO-198-038. NRC. http://www.nrc.gov/OPA/pn/pn19838.htm. 2004.
5. Saenz RB. [131]Iodine elimination from breast milk: a case report. J Hum Lact 2000; 16 (1):44-46.
6. Morita S, Umezaki N, Ishibashi M, Kawamura S, Inada C, Hayabuchi N. Determining the breast-feeding interruption schedule after administration of 123I-iodide. Ann Nucl Med 1998; 12 (5):303-306.
7. Bakheet SM, Hammami MM. Patterns of radioiodine uptake by the lactating breast. Eur J Nucl Med 1994; 21 (7):604-608.

IBUPROFEN

L1

Trade: Advil, Nuprin, Motrin, Pediaprofen
Other Trades: Actiprofen, Amersol, ACT-3, Brufen, Nurofen, Rafen
Uses: Analgesic, antipyretic
AAP: Maternal Medication Usually Compatible with Breastfeeding

Ibuprofen is a nonsteroidal anti-inflammatory analgesic. It is frequently used for fever in infants. Ibuprofen enters milk only in very low levels (less than 0.6% of maternal dose). Even large doses produce very small milk levels. In one patient receiving 400 mg twice daily, milk levels were less than 0.5 mg/L.[1] In another study of twelve women who received 400 mg doses every 6 hours for a total of 5 doses, all breastmilk levels of ibuprofen were less than 1.0 mg/L, the lower limit of the assay.[2] Data in these studies document that no measurable concentrations of ibuprofen are detected in breastmilk following the above doses. Ibuprofen is presently popular for therapy of fever in infants. Current recommended dose in children is 5-10 mg/kg every 6 hours. Ibuprofen is an ideal analgesic for breastfeeding mothers.

Pregnancy Risk Category: B in first and second trimester
D in third trimester

Lactation Risk Category: L1

Adult Concerns: Nausea, epigastric pain, dizziness, edema, GI bleeding.

Pediatric Concerns: None reported from breastfeeding. Ideal analgesic.

Drug Interactions: Aspirin may decrease serum ibuprofen levels. May prolong prothrombin time when used with warfarin. Antihypertensive effects of ACEi family may be blunted or completely abolished by NSAIDs. Some NSAIDs may block antihypertensive effect of beta blockers, diuretics. Used with cyclosporin, may dramatically increase renal toxicity. May increase digoxin, phenytoin, lithium levels. May increase toxicity of methotrexate. May increase bioavailability of penicillamine. Probenecid may increase NSAID levels.

Relative Infant Dose: 0.7%

Adult Dose: 400 mg every 4-6 hours

Alternatives: Acetaminophen

T ½	= 1.8-2.5 hours	M/P	=
PHL	=	PB	= >99%
Tmax	= 1-2 hours	Oral	= 80%
MW	= 206	pKa	= 4.4
Vd	= 0.14		

References:
1. Weibert RT, Townsend RJ, Kaiser DG, Naylor AJ. Lack of ibuprofen secretion into human milk. Clin Pharm 1982; 1 (5):457-458.
2. Townsend RJ, Benedetti TJ, Erickson SH, Cengiz C, Gillespie WR, Gschwend J, Albert KS. Excretion of ibuprofen into breast milk. Am J Obstet Gynecol 1984; 149 (2):184-186.

ICARIDIN   L3

Trade: OFF Clean Feel, Cutter Advanced, Picaridin
Other Trades: Bayrepel
Uses: Insect repellant
AAP: Not reviewed

Icaridin, also know as Picaridin, is a newer and potentially safer alternative to the insect repellant DEET. It works by blocking the insect's ability to locate human skin. It does not cause irritation to the skin, and is odorless. Icaridin does not need to be washed off upon returning indoors. It is safe for use in children of all ages, and it will not affect plastics, synthetics, or plastic coatings. The WHO claims that icaridin is the best repellant against mosquitos carrying Malaria.[1] The EPA suggests that icaridin has a low acute oral, inhalation, or dermal toxicity.[2] At present, we were unable to determine transcutaneous absorption or potential plasma levels in users. Due to its lipid solubility, it is likely it would enter milk, but plasma levels are probably low. It is probably safer to use in breastfeeding mothers than DEET.

Pregnancy Risk Category:

Lactation Risk Category: L3

Adult Concerns: No adverse reactions noted.
Pediatric Concerns: No adverse reactions noted.

Drug Interactions:

Relative Infant Dose:

Adult Dose:

Alternatives:

T ½	=	M/P	=
PHL	=	PB	–
Tmax	=	Oral	=
MW	= 229	pKa	=
Vd	=		

References:
1. www.picaridin.com
2. www.http://www.epa.gov/opprd001/factsheets/picaridin.pdf

IMIPENEM-CILASTATIN — L2

Trade: Primaxin
Other Trades:
Uses: Antibiotic
AAP: Not reviewed

Imipenem is structurally similar to penicillins and acts similarly. Cilastatin is added to extend the half-life of imipenem. Both imipenem and cilastatin are poorly absorbed orally and must be administered IM or IV.[1,2] Imipenem is destroyed by gastric acidity. Transfer into breastmilk is probably minimal but no data are available. Changes in GI flora could occur but is probably remote.

Pregnancy Risk Category: C

Lactation Risk Category: L2

Adult Concerns: Nausea, diarrhea, vomiting, abdominal pain, decreased white blood cells, decreased hemoglobin, seizures.

Pediatric Concerns: No studies available. Probably similar to other penicillins.

Drug Interactions: May have increased toxicity when used with other beta lactam antibiotics. Probenecid may increase toxic potential.

Relative Infant Dose:

Adult Dose: 500-750 mg BID

Alternatives:

T ½	= 0.85-1.3 hours	M/P	=
PHL	= 1.5-2.6 hours (neonate)	PB	= 20-35%
Tmax	= Immediate (IV)	Oral	= Poor
MW	= 317	pKa	=
Vd	=		

References:
1. Pharmaceutical Manufacturer Prescribing Information. 1995.
2. McEvoy GE. (ed):AFHS Drug Information. New York, NY: 1995.

IMIPRAMINE   L2

Trade: Tofranil, Janimine
Other Trades: Apo-Imipramine, Impril, Novo-Pramine, Melipramine
Uses: Tricyclic antidepressant
AAP: Drugs whose effect on nursing infants is unknown but may be of concern

Imipramine is a classic tricyclic antidepressant. Imipramine is metabolized to desipramine, the active metabolite. Milk levels approximate those of maternal serum. In a patient receiving 200 mg daily at bedtime, the milk levels at 1, 9, 10, and 23 hours were 29, 24, 12, and 18 µg/L respectively.[1] However, in this study the mother was not in a therapeutic range. In another study of 4 women receiving 75-150 mg/day imipramine, levels of imipramine plus desipramine in fore milk ranged from 34-408 µg/L and in hind milk ranged from 48 to 622 µg/L.[2]

In several breastfed infants, levels of imipramine plus desipramine ranged from 0.6 µg/L in one individual (maternal dose= 75 mg/d) and to 5.5 µg/L (maternal dose = 100 mg/day).[3] Therapeutic plasma levels in older children 6-12 years are 200-225 µg/L.

Two good reviews of psychotropic drugs in breastfeeding patients are available.[4,5]

Pregnancy Risk Category: D

Lactation Risk Category: L2

Adult Concerns: Dry mouth, sedation, hypotension, arrhythmias, confusion, agitation, seizures.
Pediatric Concerns: None reported, but observe for sedation, dry mouth.

Drug Interactions: Barbiturates may lower serum levels of TCAs. Central and respiratory depressant effects may be additive. Cimetidine has increased serum TCA concentrations. Anticholinergic symptoms may be exacerbated. Use with clonidine may produce dangerous elevation in blood pressure and hypertensive crisis. Dicumarol anticoagulant capacity may be increased when used with TCAs. Co-use with fluoxetine may increase the toxic levels and effects of TCAs. Symptoms maypersist for several weeks after discontinuation of fluoxetine. Haloperidol may increase serum concentrations of TCAs. MAO inhibitors should never be given immediately after or with tricyclic antidepressants. Oral contraceptives may inhibit the metabolism of tricyclic antidepressants and may increase their plasma levels.

Relative Infant Dose: 0.1% - 4.4%

Adult Dose: 75-100 mg daily.

Alternatives: Amoxapine

T ½	= 8-16 hours	M/P	= 0.5-1.5
PHL	=	PB	= 90%
Tmax	= 1-2 hours	Oral	= 90%
MW	= 280	pKa	= 9.5
Vd	= 20-40		

References:

1. Sovner R, Orsulak PJ. Excretion of imipramine and desipramine in human breast milk. Am J Psychiatry 1979; 136 (4A):451-452.
2. Yoshida K, Smith B, Kumar R. Psychotropic drugs in mothers' milk: a comprehensive review of assay methods, pharmacokinetics and of safety of breast-feeding. J Psychopharmacol. 1999;13 (1):64-80. Review.
3. Yoshida K, Smith B, Craggs M et al. Investigation of pharmacokinetics and possible adverse effects in infants exposed to tricyclic antidepressants in breast-milk. J Affective Disord. 1997;43:225-37.
4. Buist A, Norman TR, Dennerstein L. Breastfeeding and the use of psychotropic medication: a review. J Affect Disord 1990; 19 (3):197-206.
5. Wisner KL, Perel JM, Findling RL. Antidepressant treatment during breast-feeding. Am J Psychiatry 1996; 153 (9):1132-1137.

INDAPAMIDE

L3

Trade: Lozol
Other Trades: Lozide, Gen-Indapamide, Apo-Indapamide,
        Dapa-Tabs, Nadide, Napamide, Natrilix
Uses: Antihypertensive diuretic
AAP: Not reviewed

Indapamide is the first of a new class of indoline diuretics used to treat hypertension. No data exists on transfer into human milk.[1] Some diuretics may reduce the production of breastmilk. See hydrochlorothiazide as alternative.

Pregnancy Risk Category: B

Lactation Risk Category: L3

Adult Concerns: Sodium and potassium loss, hypotension, dizziness, nausea, vomiting, constipation.

Pediatric Concerns: None reported, but observe for reduction in milk supply, and volume depletion.

Drug Interactions: May reduce effect of oral hypoglycemics. Cholestyramine may reduce absorption of indapamide. May increase the effect of furosemide and other diuretics. May increased toxicity and levels of lithium.

Relative Infant Dose:

Adult Dose: 2.5-5 mg daily.

Alternatives:

T ½	= 14 hours	M/P	=
PHL	=	PB	= 71%
Tmax	= 0.5-2 hours	Oral	= Complete
MW	= 366	pKa	=
Vd	=		

References:
1.   Pharmaceutical Manufacturer Prescribing Information. 1996.

¹¹¹ᴹINDIUM   L4

Trade: 111-Indium
Other Trades:
Uses: Radioactive diagnostic agent
AAP: Radioactive compound that requires temporary cessation of breastfeeding

¹¹¹ Indium is a radioactive material used for imaging neuroendocrine tumors. While the plasma half-life is extremely short (<10 minutes), with the majority of this product leaving the plasma compartment and distributing to tissue sites, the radioactive half-life is 2.8 days. In one patient receiving 12 MBq (0.32 mCi), the concentration in milk at 6 and 20 hours was 0.09 Bq/mL and 0.20 Bq/mL per MBq injected.[1] These data indicate that breastfeeding may be safe if this radiopharmaceutical is used. Assuming an ingestion of 500 cc daily, the infant would receive approximately 100 Bq per MBq given to the mother (approximately 0.1 μCi). The NRC recommends a waiting period of 1 week with doses of 20 MBq (0.5 mCi), however see appendix B for current recommendations.

Pregnancy Risk Category:

Lactation Risk Category: L4

Adult Concerns: Nausea, dizziness, headache, flushing, hypotension.

Pediatric Concerns: None reported, but slight risk of radiation exposure.

Drug Interactions:

Relative Infant Dose:

Adult Dose:

Alternatives:

T ½	= 2.8 days	M/P	=
PHL	=	PB	=
Tmax	= Immediate (IV)	Oral	=
MW	= 358	μKa	–
Vd	=		

References:
1. Pullar M, Hartkamp A. Excretion of radioactivity in breastmilk following administration of an ¹¹³Indium labeled chelate complex. Br J Radiol 1977; 50:846.

2.   American Academy of Pediatrics, Committee on Drugs. Transfer of drugs and other chemicals into human milk. Pediatrics 2001; 108 (3):776-89.

INDOMETHACIN   L3

Trade: Indocin

Other Trades: Apo-Indomethacin, Indocid, Novo-Methacin, Arthrexin, Hicin, Indoptol

Uses: Non-steroidal antiinflammatory

AAP: Maternal Medication Usually Compatible with Breastfeeding

Indomethacin is a potent, nonsteroidal antiinflammatory agent frequently used in arthritis. It is also used in newborns in neonatal units to close a patent ductus arteriosus. There is one reported case of convulsions in an infant of a breastfeeding mother early postpartum (day 7).[1]

In another report of 16 women who received 75 mg to 300 mg rectally daily, of 20 milk samples analyzed 12 were less than 20 µg/L (limit of detection) and the median milk/plasma ratio was 0.37.[2] The eight measurable samples ranged from 23 to 115 µg/L. The authors suggest the total infant dose, assuming daily milk intake of 150 mL/kg, would range from 0.07% to 0.98% of the weight adjusted maternal dose. Plasma samples derived from 6 of the 7 infants were below the sensitivity of the assay (<20 µg/L) and 47 µg/L in only one infant. Dose calculations for all 16 infants showed that absolute dose ranged from <0.003 to 0.017 mg/kg/day. In six of seven infants, indomethacin levels were below detection. In one infant the plasma level was 47 µg/L. No adverse affects were noted in this study.

Pregnancy Risk Category: B in first and second trimester
                               D in third trimester

Lactation Risk Category: L3

Adult Concerns: Renal dysfunction, GI distress, gastric bleeding, diarrhea, clotting dysfunction.

Pediatric Concerns: One case of seizures in neonate. Additional report suggests no untoward effects. Frequently used in neonatal nurseries for patent ductus.

Drug Interactions: May prolong prothrombin time when used with warfarin. Antihypertensive effects of ACEi family may be blunted or completely abolished by NSAIDs. Some NSAIDs may block antihypertensive effect of beta blockers, diuretics. Used with cyclosporin, may dramatically increase renal toxicity. May increase digoxin, phenytoin, lithium levels. May increase toxicity of methotrexate. May increase bioavailability of penicillamine. Probenecid may increase NSAID levels.

Relative Infant Dose: 1.2%

Adult Dose: 25-50 mg BID-TID

Alternatives: Ibuprofen

T ½	= 4.5 hours	M/P	= 0.37
PHL	= 30 hours (prematures)	PB	= >90%
Tmax	= 1-2 :2-4 (SR) hours	Oral	= 90%
MW	= 357	pKa	= 4.5
Vd	= 0.33-0.40		

References:
1. Eeg-Olofsson O, Malmros I, Elwin CE, Steen B. Convulsions in a breast-fed infant after maternal indomethacin. Lancet 1978; 2 (8082):215.
2. Lebedevs TH, Wojnar-Horton RE, Yapp P, Roberts MJ, Dusci LJ, Hackett LP, Ilett KF. Excretion of indomethacin in breast milk. Br J Clin Pharmacol 1991; 32 (6):751-754.

INFLIXIMAB   L2

Trade: Remicade
Other Trades:
Uses: Treatment of Crohn's, Rheumatoid arthritis
AAP: Not reviewed

Infliximab is a monoclonal antibody to tumor necrosis factor-alpha (TNF-alpha) used to treat Crohn's disease and rheumatoid arthritis. Infliximab is a very large MW antibody and is largely retained in the vascular system. In a study of one breastfeeding patient who received 5 mg/kg IV, infliximab levels were determined in milk at 0, 2, 4, 8, 24, 48, 72 hours, and 4, 5, and 7 days.[1] None was detected in milk at any time (detection limit <0.1 µg/mL).

In another study, a breastfeeding mother receiving 5 infusions of 10 mg/kg during pregnancy did not have a detectable amount of infliximab in her milk at any point. The baby's serum level after delivery was 39.5 µg/mL, likely due to placental transfer. The half-life of the drug appeared to be prolonged in the newborn.[2]

Another breastfeeding mother's milk was tested 24 hours and 1 week following her first infusion of a 5 mg/kg dose with milk levels below the limit of quantification in both cases.[3] Infliximab is probably too large to enter milk in clinically measurable amounts. It would not be orally bioavailable.

Pregnancy Risk Category: B

Lactation Risk Category: L2

Adult Concerns: Infusion-related reactions include fever, chills, pruritus, urticaria, chest pain, hypotension. A state of immunosuppression is induced thus serious infection including sepsis, disseminated tuberculosis and other infections have been reported.

Pediatric Concerns: None reported in three patients.

Drug Interactions:

Relative Infant Dose:

Adult Dose: 5 mg/kg (Crohn's)

Alternatives:

T ½	= 8-9.5 days	M/P	=
PHL	=	PB	=
Tmax	=	Oral	= Nil
MW	= 149,100	pKa	=
Vd	= 3		

References:

1. Hale TW, Fasanmade A. Personal communication. 2002.
2. Vasiliauskas EA, Church JA, Silverman N, Barry M, Targan SR, Dubinsky MC. Case Report: Evidence for Transplacental Trasfer of Maternally Administered Infliximab to the Newborn. Clin Gastroenterol Hepatol 2006; 4:1255-1258.
3. Peltier M, James D, Ford J, Wagner C, Davis H, Hanauer S. Infliximab levels in breast-milk of a nursing Crohn's patient. Am J Gastroenterol 2001; 96 (9):S312.

INFLUENZA VIRUS VACCINES | L1

Trade: Vaccine- Influenza, Flu-Imune, Fluogen, Fluzone,
         FluMist, Flu Vaccine
Other Trades: Fluviral
Uses: Vaccine
AAP: Not reviewed

Influenza virus vaccines come in two forms. One that is non-viable and requires injection, and the second, a live but attenuated vaccine for application in the nasal passages (FluMist).

Injectable (Flu-immune, Fluogen, Fluzone, etc.): This influenza vaccine is prepared from inactivated, non-viable influenza viruses and infection of the neonate via milk would not be expected. There are no reported side effects, nor published contraindications for using influenza virus vaccine during lactation.[1,2] Influenza vaccine is now indicated for breastfeeding mothers and their infants by the American Academy of Pediatrics.

Intranasal Live Influenza Virus Vaccine (FluMist): This vaccine consists of a live but attenuated and heat unstable form of influenza virus. Virus instilled in the nasal mucosa replicate thus producing immunity in the host. Virus that escape the nasal mucosa are unstable and die quickly. It is not known if this virus reaches the human milk compartment, but it is highly unlikely the virus could survive at this temperature in the plasma nor the milk compartment of the mother.

The CDC and the FDA recommend that all breastfeeding women be immunized. This will further protect the breastfed infant as these antibodies will pass into milk, and help protect the newborn breastfed infant from infection. Contents of influenza vaccines change from year to year. Presently, the multi-dose vials contain a small amount of mercury, but there is no evidence that this would even pass to a breastfeeding infant. Single dose vials do not contain mercury. The live attenuated vaccines, FluMist, are not recommended for breastfeeding women, although we know the risks are low. Despite misinformation, there is no squalene present in any of the influenza vaccines used in the USA.

For dosing regimens for antiviral drugs (Tamiflu), see Appendix E.

Pregnancy Risk Category: C

Lactation Risk Category: L1

Adult Concerns: Fever, myalgia.

Pediatric Concerns: None reported in breastfeeding mothers.

Drug Interactions: Decreased effect with immunosuppressants. Influenza vaccine may be administered simultaneously (but at a separate site and with a different syringe) with other routine immunizations in children.

Relative Infant Dose:

Adult Dose: 0.5 ml injection once. FluMist is a single unit dose.

Alternatives:

References:
1.   Kilbourne ED. Questions and answers. Artificial influenza immunization of nursing mothers not harmful. JAMA 1973; 226:87.
2.   Pharmaceutical Manufacturer Prescribing Information. 2005.

INSECT STINGS

Trade: Insect Stings, Spider Stings, Bee Stings
Other Trades:
Uses: Insect stings, envenomations
AAP: Not reviewed

Insect stings are primarily composed of small peptides, enzymes such as hyaluronidase, and other factors such as histamine. Because the total injectant is so small, most reactions are local. In cases of systemic reactions, the secondary release of maternal reactants produces the allergic response in the injected individual. Nevertheless, the amount of injection is exceedingly small. In the case of black widow spiders, the venom is so large in MW, it would not likely penetrate milk. In addition, most of the venoms and allergens would be destroyed in the acidic milieu of the infant's stomach. The sting of the Loxosceles spider (brown recluse, fiddleback) is primarily a local necrosis without systemic effects. No report of toxicity to nursing infants has been reported from insect stings.

Pregnancy Risk Category:

Lactation Risk Category:

Adult Concerns: Nausea, vomiting.

Pediatric Concerns: None reported via milk.

Drug Interactions:

Relative Infant Dose:

Adult Dose: N/A

Alternatives:

References:

INSULIN   L1

Trade: Humulin

Other Trades: Novolin, Humalog, Iletin, Mixtard, Protaphane, Monotard

Uses: Human insulin

AAP: Not reviewed

Insulin is a large peptide that is not secreted into milk. Even if secreted, it would be destroyed in the infant's GI tract leading to minimal or no absorption.

Pregnancy Risk Category: B

Lactation Risk Category: L1

Adult Concerns: Hypoglycemia.

Pediatric Concerns: None reported via milk.

Drug Interactions: A decreased hypoglycemic effect may result when used with oral contraceptives, corticosteroids, diltiazem, epinephrine, thiazide diuretics, thyroid hormones and niacin. Increased hypoglycemic effects may result when used with alcohol, beta blockers, fenfluramine, MAO inhibitors, salicylates, tetracyclines.

Relative Infant Dose:

Adult Dose: Highly Variable.

Alternatives:

T ½	=	M/P	=
PHL	=	PB	=
Tmax	=	Oral	= 0%
MW	= >6000	pKa	=
Vd	− 0.37		

References:
1. Pharmaceutical manufacturers prescribing information. 2005.

INSULIN GLARGINE

L1

Trade: Lantus
Other Trades:
Uses: Long-acting recombinant insulin
AAP: Not reviewed

Insulin glargine (rDNA origin) is a recombinant human insulin analog that is long-acting (up to 24 h). Insulin glargine differs from human insulin in that the amino acid asparagine at position A21 is replaced by glycine and two arginines are added to the C-terminus of the B-chain. This product when administered subcutaneously precipitates and forms crystals that are slow absorbing, thus producing a sustained release formulation with a half-life of about 198 minutes. While we have no studies on its transfer into human milk, we are certain that small levels of insulin are indeed present in human milk. However, most present in milk would likely be totally destroyed in the infant's GI tract prior to absorption. There are no contraindications to using insulin or its derivatives in breastfeeding mothers.

Pregnancy Risk Category: C

Lactation Risk Category: L1

Adult Concerns: Hypoglycemia.

Pediatric Concerns: None reported in breastfeeding infants.

Drug Interactions: A decreased hypoglycemic effect may result when used with oral contraceptives, corticosteroids, diltiazem, epinephrine, thiazide diuretics, thyroid hormones and niacin. Increased hypoglycemic effects may result when used with alcohol, beta blockers, fenfluramine, MAO inhibitors, salicylates, tetracyclines.

Relative Infant Dose:

Adult Dose: Highly variable.

Alternatives:

T ½	= 5-15 minutes	M/P	=
PHL	=	PB	= 5%
Tmax	= 6 hours	Oral	= None
MW	= 6063	pKa	=
Vd	= 0.15		

References:
1. Pharmaceutical manufacturers prescribing information. 2005.

INTERFERON ALPHA-N3 | L2

Trade: Alferon N, Interferon Alpha, PEG-Intron
Other Trades:
Uses: Immune modulator, antiviral.
AAP: Maternal Medication Usually Compatible with Breastfeeding

Interferon alpha is a pure clone of a single interferon subspecies with antiviral, antiproliferative, and immunomodulatory activity. The alpha-interferons are active against various malignancies and viral syndromes such as hairy cell leukemia, melanoma, AIDS-related Kaposi's sarcoma, condyloma acuminata, and chronic hepatitis B and C infection.[1] Other forms of interferons such as the Alfa-2b (Peg-Intron) are also available.

Very little is known about the secretion of interferons in human milk although some interferons are known to be secreted normally and may contribute to the antiviral properties of human milk. However, interferons are large in MW (16-28,000 daltons), which would limit their transfer into human milk. Following treatment with a massive dose of 30 million units IV in one breastfeeding patient, the amount of interferon alpha transferred into human milk was 894, 1004, 1551, 1507, 788, 721 units at 0 (baseline), 2, 4, 8, 12, and 24 hours respectively.[2] Hence, even following a massive dose, no change in breastmilk levels were noted from baseline. One thousand international units is roughly equivalent to 500 nanograms of interferon.

The oral absorption of interferons is controversial and is believed to be minimal. Interferons are relatively nontoxic unless extraordinarily large doses are administered parenterally. Interferons are sometimes used in infants and children to treat idiopathic thromboplastinemia (ITP) in huge doses.

Pregnancy Risk Category: C

Lactation Risk Category: L2

Adult Concerns: Thrombocytopenia and neutropenia. Flu-like syndrome which occurs 30 minutes after administration and persists for several hours. Fatigue, hyperglycemia, nausea and vomiting.

Pediatric Concerns: None reported via milk.

Drug Interactions: Hematologic abnormalities (granulocytopenia, thrombocytopenia) may occur when used with ACE inhibitors.

Relative Infant Dose:

Adult Dose: 0.05-0.5 mL per wart twice weekly

Alternatives:

T ½	= 5-7 hours	M/P	=
PHL	=	PB	=
Tmax	= Immediate	Oral	= Low
MW	= 28,000	pKa	=
Vd	= 0.44		

References:
1. Pharmaceutical Manufacturer Prescribing Information. 1997.
2. Kumar AR, Hale TW, Mock RE. Transfer of interferon alfa into human breast milk. J Hum Lact 2000; 16 (3):226-228.

INTERFERON BETA-1A   L2

Trade: Avonex, Rebif
Other Trades:
Uses: Immune modulator
AAP: Not reviewed

Interferon Beta-1A is a moderately large glycoprotein (166 amino acids) with antiviral, antiproliferative, and immunomodulator activity presently used for reducing the severity and frequency of exacerbations of relapsing-remitting multiple sclerosis.[1] Interferons are large in MW, generally containing 166 amino acids, which would limit their transfer into human milk. Their oral absorption is controversial but is believed to be minimal. In addition, most researchers find that plasma levels of interferons following IM injection are detectable for only a few hours, generally less than 15 hours following the dose. Thus the transfer of interferons into the plasma compartment are minimal and last only briefly. Generally they are low to undetectable.

In a group of 6 women receiving 30 µg (30,000,000 picograms) IM weekly, milk levels ranged from 33 picograms to 80 picograms/ mL milk.[2] Thus the transfer of interferon beta-1A into human milk is extraordinarly low (essentially nil) and would be of no risk to a breastfeeding infant.

Interferons are relatively nontoxic unless extraordinarily large doses are administered parenterally. Interferons are sometimes used in infants and children to treat idiopathic thromboplastinemia (ITP) in huge doses. See Interferon Alpha, Interferon 1B.

Pregnancy Risk Category: C

Lactation Risk Category: L2

Adult Concerns: Headache, myalgia, nausea, diarrhea, dyspepsia, fever, chills, malaise, sweating, depression, flu-like symptoms. These effects generally follow huge doses.

Pediatric Concerns: None reported via milk.

Drug Interactions: Do not use with live viral vaccines.

Relative Infant Dose:

Adult Dose: 30 μg weekly I.M.

Alternatives:

T ½	= 10 Hours	M/P	=
PHL	=	PB	=
Tmax	= 3-15 hours	Oral	= Minimal
MW	= 22,500	pKa	=
Vd	= 61.6 L		

References:
1. Chofflon M. Recombinant human interferon beta in relapsing-remitting multiple sclerosis: a review of the major clinical trials. Eur J Neurol 2000; 7 (4):369-380.
2. Hale TW. Transfer of interferon beta-1a into human milk. Unpublished results. 2010.

INTERFERON BETA-1B   L2

Trade: Betaseron, Extavia
Other Trades: Betaferon
Uses: Antiviral, immunomodulator
AAP: Not reviewed

Interferon Beta-1B is a glycoprotein with antiviral, antiproliferative, and immunomodulatory activity presently used for treatment of multiple sclerosis.[1,2] Very little is known about the secretion of interferons in human milk although some interferons are known to be secreted normally and may contribute to the antiviral properties of human milk. However, interferons are large in MW, generally containing 165 amino acids, which would limit their transfer into human milk.

Interferon Beta-1A: In a group of 6 women receiving 30 μg (30,000,000 picograms) IM weekly, milk levels ranged from 33 picograms to 80 picograms/mL milk.[3] Thus the transfer of interferon beta-1A into human milk is extraordinarly low (essentially nil) and would be of no risk to a breastfeeding infant. This obviously would apply for Interferon Beta-1B as well.

Interferons are relatively nontoxic unless extraordinarily large doses are administered parenterally. Interferons are sometimes used in infants and children to treat idiopathic thromboplastinemia (ITP) in huge doses. See Interferon Alpha, Interferon 1B.

The transfer of interferon Beta-1a (Avonex, Rebif) is essentially nil and it is likely the same for this product, interferon Beta-1b.

Pregnancy Risk Category: C

Lactation Risk Category: L2

Adult Concerns: Depression, headache, myalgia, nausea, diarrhea, dyspepsia, fever, chills, malaise, sweating, depression, flu-like symptoms. These effects generally follow huge doses. Injection site necrosis has been reported in 4% of users.

Pediatric Concerns: None reported via milk. However, interferon Beta1-a is virtually excluded from the milk compartment.

Drug Interactions: Hematologic abnormalities (granulocytopenia, thrombocytopenia) may occur when added to ACE inhibitors.

Relative Infant Dose:

Adult Dose: 0.25 mg every other day

Alternatives: Interferon Beta1-a

T ½	= 4.3 hours	M/P	=
PHL	=	PB	=
Tmax	= 3-15 hours (IM)	Oral	= Poor
MW	= 22,500	pKa	=
Vd	= 2.9		

References:
1. Chiang J, Gloff CA, Yoshizawa CN, Williams GJ. Pharmacokinetics of recombinant human interferon-beta ser in healthy volunteers and its effect on serum neopterin. Pharm Res 1993; 10 (4):567-572.
2. Wills RJ. Clinical pharmacokinetics of interferons. Clin Pharmacokinet 1990; 19 (5):390-399.
3. Hale TW. Transfer of interferon beta-1a into human milk. Unpublished results. 2010.

IODINATED GLYCEROL | L4

Trade: Organidin, Iophen, R-GEN
Other Trades:
Uses: Expectorant
AAP: Not reviewed

This product contains 50% organically bound iodine. High levels of iodine are known to be secreted in milk.[1] Milk/plasma ratios as high as 26 have been reported. Following absorption by the infant, high levels of iodine could lead to severe thyroid depression in infants. Normal iodine levels in breastmilk are already four times higher that RDA for infant. Expectorants, including iodine, work very poorly. Recently, many iodine containing products have been replaced with guaifenesin, which is considered safer. High levels of iodine-containing drugs should not be used in lactating mothers.

Pregnancy Risk Category: X

Lactation Risk Category: L4

Adult Concerns: Depressed thyroid function. Diarrhea, nausea, vomiting. Acne, dermatitis. Metallic taste.

Pediatric Concerns: Iodine concentrates in milk and should not be administered to breastfeeding mothers. Infantile thyroid suppression is likely.

Drug Interactions: Increased toxicity with disulfiram, metronidazole, procarbazine, MAO inhibitors, CNS depressants, lithium.

Relative Infant Dose:

Adult Dose:

Alternatives:

T ½	=	M/P	=
PHL	=	PB	=
Tmax	=	Oral	= Complete
MW	= 258	pKa	=
Vd	=		

References:
1. Postellon DC, Aronow R. Iodine in mother's milk. JAMA 1982; 247 (4):463.

IPRATROPIUM BROMIDE   L2

Trade: Atrovent
Other Trades: Apo-Ipravent
Uses: Bronchodilator in asthmatics
AAP: Not reviewed

Ipratropium is an anticholinergic drug that is used via inhalation for dilating the bronchi of asthmatics.[1] Ipratropium is a quaternary ammonium compound, and although no data exists, it probably penetrates into breastmilk in exceedingly small levels due to its structure. It is unlikely that the infant would absorb any, due to the poor tissue distribution and oral absorption of this family of drugs.

Pregnancy Risk Category: B

Lactation Risk Category: L2

Adult Concerns: Nervousness, dizziness, nausea, GI distress, drug mouth, bitter taste.

Pediatric Concerns: None reported. Commonly used in pediatric patients.

Drug Interactions: Albuterol may increase effect of ipratropium. May have increased toxicity when used with other anticholinergics.

Relative Infant Dose:

Adult Dose: 36 µg QID

Alternatives:

T ½	= 2 hours	M/P	=
PHL	=	PB	=
Tmax	= 1-2 hours	Oral	= 0-2%
MW	= 412	pKa	=
Vd	=		

References:
1. Pharmaceutical Manufacturer Prescribing Information. 1996.

IRBESARTAN   L3

Trade: Avapro
Other Trades: Avalide, Accuretic, Adizem, Amizide
Uses: Antihypertensive
AAP: Not reviewed

Irbesartan is an angiotensin-II receptor antagonist used as an antihypertensive. Low concentrations are known to be secreted into rodent milk, but human studies are lacking.[1] Both the ACE inhibitor family and the specific AT1 inhibitors such as irbesartan are contraindicated in the 2nd and 3rd trimesters of pregnancy due to severe hypotension, neonatal skull hypoplasia, irreversible renal failure, and death in the newborn infant. However, some of ACE inhibitors can be used in breastfeeding mothers postpartum. Some caution is recommended particularly with in mothers with premature infants.

Pregnancy Risk Category: C in first trimester
                               D in second or third trimesters

Lactation Risk Category: L3

Adult Concerns: Headache, back pain, pharyngitis, and dizziness have been reported. The use of ACE inhibitors and angiotensin receptor blockers during pregnancy or the neonatal period is extremely dangerous and has resulted in hypotension, neonatal skull hypoplasia, anuria, renal failure and death.

Pediatric Concerns: None reported via milk, but caution is recommended.

Drug Interactions: None reported thus far.

Relative Infant Dose:

Adult Dose: 150-300 mg daily.

Alternatives: Captopril, enalapril

T ½	− 11-15 hours	M/P	=
PHL	=	PB	= 90%
Tmax	= 1.5-2 hours	Oral	= 60-80%
MW	= 428	pKa	=
Vd	= 1.3		

References:
1. Pharmaceutical Manufacturer Prescribing Information. 1999.

IRON   L1

Trade: Fer-In-Sol
Other Trades: Infufer, Jectofer, Slow-Fe, Feospan
Uses: Metal supplement
AAP: Not reviewed

The secretion of iron salts into breastmilk appears to be very low although the bioavailability of that present in milk is high. One recent study suggests that supplementation is not generally required until the 4th month postpartum when some breastfed infants may become iron deficient although these assumptions are controversial.[1] Premature infants are more susceptible to iron deficiencies because they do not have the same hepatic stores available as full term infants. These authors recommend iron supplementation, particularly in exclusively breastfed infants, beginning at 4th month.[1] Supplementation in pre-term infants should probably be initiated earlier. However, oral supplemental iron may block some of the antibacterial properties of human milk. The use of relatively high doses in breastfeeding mothers is probably not contraindicated, due to the fact that iron transports very poorly to the milk compartment.

Pregnancy Risk Category:

Lactation Risk Category: L1

Adult Concerns: Constipation, GI distress.

Pediatric Concerns: None reported via milk. Iron transports poorly into milk.

Drug Interactions: Decreased iron absorption when used with antacids, cimetidine, levodopa, penicillamine, quinolones, tetracyclines. Slightly increased absorption with ascorbic acid.

Relative Infant Dose:

Adult Dose: 50-100 mg TID

Alternatives:

T ½	=	M/P	=
PHL	=	PB	=
Tmax	=	Oral	= <30%
MW	= 56	pKa	=
Vd	=		

References:
1. Calvo EB, Galindo AC, Aspres NB. Iron status in exclusively breast-fed infants. Pediatrics 1992; 90 (3):375-379.

IRON DEXTRAN   L2

Trade: INFeD
Other Trades:
Uses: Iron supplement
AAP: Not reviewed

Iron dextran is a colloidal solution of ferric hydroxide in a complex with partially hydrolyzed low MW dextran. It is used for severe iron deficiency anemia. Its MW is approximately 180,000 daltons. Approximately 99% of the iron in iron dextran is present as a stable ferric-dextran complex. Following IM injection, iron dextran is absorbed from the site principally through the lymphatic system and subsequently transferred to the reticuloendothelial system in the liver for metabolism. The initial phase of absorption lasts 3 days, which accounts for 60% of an IM dose. The other 40% requires up to 1-3 weeks to several months for complete absorption. While there are no data available on the transfer of iron dextran into human milk, it is extremely unlikely due to its massive MW. Further, iron is transferred into human milk by a tightly controlled pumping system that first chelates the iron to a high MW protein and then transfers it into the milk compartment. It is generally well known that dietary supplements of iron do not change milk levels of iron significantly.[1] Please note: while the pregnancy risk category is only C, it has been shown to be teratogenic in other species. Great care should be used in pregnant women. In breastfeeding mothers, supplementing with high doses is probably not contraindicated due to the poor passage of iron into milk. But some caution is still recommended.

Pregnancy Risk Category: C

Lactation Risk Category: L2

Adult Concerns: Local reactions at the site of injection. Abdominal pain, dyspepsia, nausea, vomiting and diarrhea. Headache, paresthesias, weakness, changes in taste perception, faintness, syncope, folic acid deficiency, and leukocytosis. Please note: while the pregnancy risk category is only C, it has been shown to be teratogenic in other species and great care should be used in pregnant women.

Pediatric Concerns: None via breast milk.

Drug Interactions:

Relative Infant Dose:

Adult Dose:

Alternatives:

References:
1. Lawrence RA. Breastfeeding: A guide for the medical profession. St. Louis: Mosby Publishers, 1994.

IRON SUCROSE   L3

Trade: Venofer
Other Trades:
Uses: Iron supplement
AAP: Not reviewed

Iron sucrose is used in the treatment of iron-deficiency anemia in chronic renal failure. Once dissociated, the iron is incorporated into hemoglobin.[1] There have been no studies of the secretion of iron sucrose in human milk. This product is a polymerized form of polynuclear iron (III)-hydroxide in sucrose. Used intravenously, it is sequestered in the liver where it is metabolized and free iron is released into the circulation. Due to its size, it is unlikely to enter mature milk.

Pregnancy Risk Category: B

Lactation Risk Category: L3

Adult Concerns: Adverse reactions include hypotension, headache, nausea, and muscle cramps.

Pediatric Concerns: No data available.

Drug Interactions: Iron sucrose injection may decrease the absorption of oral iron preparations.

Relative Infant Dose:

Adult Dose: total elemental dose of 1000 mg Intravenous

Alternatives:

T ½	= 6 hours	M/P	=
PHL	=	PB	=
Tmax	=	Oral	= Poor
MW	= 34,000-60,000	pKa	=
Vd	=		

References:
1. Pharmaceutical Manufacturer Prescribing Information. 2005.

ISOETHARINE   L2

Trade: Bronkosol, Bronkometer
Other Trades: Numotac
Uses: Bronchodilator
AAP: Not reviewed

Isoetharine is a selective beta-2 adrenergic bronchodilator for asthmatics. There are no reports on its secretion into human milk.[1] However, plasma levels following inhalation are exceedingly low, and breastmilk levels would similarly be low. Isoetharine is rapidly metabolized in the GI tract, so oral absorption by the infant would likely be minimal.

Pregnancy Risk Category: C

Lactation Risk Category: L2

Adult Concerns: Tremors and excitement, hypertension, anxiety, insomnia.

Pediatric Concerns: None reported via milk.

Drug Interactions: May have decreased effect with beta blockers and increased toxicity with other adrenergic stimulants such as epinephrine.

Relative Infant Dose:

Adult Dose:

Alternatives:

T ½	= 1-3 hours	M/P	=
PHL	=	PB	=
Tmax	= 5-15 minutes (inhaled)	Oral	=
MW	= 239	pKa	=
Vd	=		

References:
1. Pharmaceutical Manufacturer Prescribing Information. 1995.

ISOMETHEPTENE MUCATE   L3

Trade: Midrin
Other Trades:
Uses: For tension and migraine headache
AAP: Not reviewed

Isometheptene is a mild stimulate (sympathomimetic) that apparently acts by constricting dilated cranial and cerebral arterioles, thus reducing vascular headaches. It is listed as possibly effective by the FDA and is probably only marginally effective.[1] Midrin also contains acetaminophen and a mild sedative dichloralphenazone, of which little is known.

No data are available on transfer into human milk. Due to its size and molecular composition, it is likely to attain low to moderate levels in breastmilk. Because better drugs exist for migraine therapy, this product is probably not a good choice for breastfeeding mothers. See sumatriptan, amitriptyline, or propranolol as alternatives.

Pregnancy Risk Category:

Lactation Risk Category: L3

Adult Concerns: Dizziness, skin rash, hypertension, sedation.

Pediatric Concerns: None reported. Observe for stimulation.

Drug Interactions:

Relative Infant Dose:

Adult Dose:

Alternatives: Sumatriptan, amitriptyline, propranolol

References:
1. Pharmaceutical Manufacturer Prescribing Information. 1995.

ISONIAZID   L3

Trade: INH, Laniazid
Other Trades: Isotamine, PMS Isoniazid, Pycazide, Rimifon
Uses: Antituberculosis agent
AAP: Maternal Medication Usually Compatible with Breastfeeding

Isoniazid (INH) is an antimicrobial agent primarily used to treat tuberculosis. Following doses of 5 and 10 mg/kg, one report measured peak milk levels at 6 mg/L and 9 mg/L respectively.[1] Isoniazid was not measurable in the infant's serum but was detected in the urine of several infants.

In another study, following a maternal dose of 300 mg of isoniazid, the concentration of isoniazid in milk peaked at 3 hours at 16.6 mg/L while the acetyl derivative (AcINH) was 3.76 mg/L.[2] The 24 hour excretion of INH in milk was estimated at 7 mg. The authors felt this dose was potentially hazardous to a breastfed infant.

In a recent and well-done study in seven exclusively lactating women (at 33 days or steady state) who were receiving 300 mg isoniazid daily in a single dose (and rifampin and ethambutol) the mean (AUC) of isoniazid in plasma and milk was 18.4 µg/mL/24 hours and 14.4 µg/mL/24 hours respectively.[3] The mean Milk/Plasma ratio (AUC) was 0.89 and the calculated relative infant dose was 1.2%. In this nicely done study, peak levels are clearly evident at 1 hour and fall rapidly at 4 hours.

Caution and close monitoring of infant for liver toxicity and neuritis are suggested. Peripheral neuropathies, common in INH therapy, can be treated with 10-50 mg/day pyridoxine in adults. Suggest the mom breastfeed and then take isoniazid in an attempt to avoid the C_{max} (peak) at 1-2 hours.

Pregnancy Risk Category: C

Lactation Risk Category: L3

Adult Concerns: Mild hepatic dysfunction, peripheral neuritis, nausea, vomiting, dizziness.

Pediatric Concerns: None reported, but the infant should be closely monitored for toxicity including hepatitis, vision changes. Observe for fatigue, weakness, malaise, anorexia, nausea, vomiting.

Drug Interactions: Decreased effect/plasma levels of isoniazide with aluminum products. Increased toxicity/levels of oral anticoagulants, carbamazepine, cycloserine, phenytoin, certain benzodiazepines. Disulfiram reactions.

Relative Infant Dose: 1.2% - 18%

Adult Dose: 5 mg/kg daily.

Alternatives:

T ½	= 1.1 - 3.1 hours	M/P	=
PHL	= 8-20 hours (neonate)	PB	= 10-15%
Tmax	= 1-2 hours (oral)	Oral	= Complete
MW	= 137	pKa	= 1.9, 3.5
Vd	= 0.6		

References:
1. Snider DE, Jr., Powell KE. Should women taking antituberculosis drugs breast-feed? Arch Intern Med 1984; 144 (3):589-590.
2. Berlin CM, Lee C. Isoniazid and acetylisoniazid disposition in human milk, saliva and plasma. Fed Proc 1979; 38:426.
3. Singh N, Golani A, Patel Z, and Maitra A. Transfer of isoniazid from circulation to breast milk in lactating women on chronic therapy for tuberculosis. BJCP 2008;65 (3):418-422.

ISOPROTERENOL   L2

Trade: Medihaler-Iso, Isuprel
Other Trades: Isuprel, Medihaler-Iso, Isoprenaline, Isuprel, Saventrine
Uses: Bronchodilator
AAP: Not reviewed

Isoproterenol is an old adrenergic bronchodilator.[1] Currently it is seldom used for this purpose. There are no data available on breastmilk levels. It is probably secreted into milk in extremely small levels. Isoproterenol is rapidly metabolized in the gut, and it is unlikely a breastfeeding infant would absorb clinically significant levels.

Pregnancy Risk Category: C

Lactation Risk Category: L2

Adult Concerns: Insomnia, excitement, agitation, tachycardia.

Pediatric Concerns: None reported.

Drug Interactions: Increased toxicity when used with other adrenergic stimulants and elevation of blood pressure. When used with isoproterenol, general anesthetics may cause arrhythmias.

Relative Infant Dose:

Adult Dose: 10-30 mg QID

Alternatives: Albuterol

T ½	= 1-2 hours	M/P	=
PHL	=	PB	=
Tmax	= 10 minutes (Inhaled)	Oral	= Poor
MW	= 211	pKa	= 8.6
Vd	= 0.5		

References:
1.   Drug Facts and Comparisons 1995 ed. ed. St. Louis: 1995.

ISOSORBIDE DINITRATE   L3

Trade: Angidil, Angipec, Dilatate, Isordil
Other Trades: Apo-ISDN, Coronex, Coradur, Apo-ISDN,
           Carvasin, Angitak, Cedocard
Uses: Vasodilating agents
AAP: Not reviewed

Isosorbide dinitrate and its mononitrate cousin are vasodilating agents used in the treatment of angina and congestive heart failure, and many other syndromes. The treatment of anal fissures with isosorbide dinitrate early postpartum may impact breastfeeding with this medication. Absorption is highly variable but once absorbed it is metabolized to a 2-mononitrate and 5-mononitrate derivative. The 5-mononitrate has a half-life of approximately 5 hours. No data are available on the transfer of isosorbide dinitrate into human milk although small amounts may enter milk.

Pregnancy Risk Category: C

Lactation Risk Category: L3

Adult Concerns: Possible side effects include heart palpitations, headache, weakness, itching and rash, nervousness, low blood pressure, and dizziness.

Pediatric Concerns: No data are available on the transfer of isosorbide dinitrate into human milk. Methemoglobinemia has been reported in pure nitrite poisoning from drinking water, but this is highly unlikely to occur with the use of this drug. Use with some caution.

Drug Interactions: Drugs such as alcohol, aspirin and calcium channel blockers may increase the effect of isosorbes. Sildenafil may dramatically increase the effect of nitrates. Do not use with sildenafil (Viagra), tadalafil (Cialis), vardeanfil (Levitra).

Relative Infant Dose:

Adult Dose: 2.5-5 mg sublingually but highly variable. Check other resources.

Alternatives:

T ½	= 5 hours (metabolite)	M/P	=
PHL	=	PB	= low
Tmax	= 1 hour	Oral	= 10-90%
MW	=	pKa	=
Vd	= 6.3-8.9		

References:
1.   Manufacturers Prescribing information. 2005.

ISOSORBIDE MONONITRATE   L3

Trade: Imdur
Other Trades: Coronex, Duride, Corangin, Angeze, Dynamin, Imazin, Elantan
Uses: Vasodilating agent
AAP: Not reviewed

Isosorbide mononitrate and its dinitrate cousin are vasodilating agents used in the treatment of angina and congestive heart failure, and many other syndromes. While we have no data on the transfer of isosorbide mononitrate into human milk, we know that the transfer of nitrates into human milk in general is quite poor (see nitroglycerin).

Pregnancy Risk Category: C

Lactation Risk Category: L3

Adult Concerns: Cardiac dysrhythmias, edema, hypotension, dermal flushing, headache, methemoglobinemia, and other problems have been reported following the use of isosorbide mononitrate.

Pediatric Concerns: None reported. Use with some caution.

Drug Interactions: Drugs such as alcohol, aspirin and calcium channel blockers may increase the effect of isosorbes. Sildenafil may dramatically increase the effect of nitrates. Do not use with sildenafil (Viagra), tadalafil (Cialis), vardeanfil (Levitra).

Relative Infant Dose:

Adult Dose: 20 mg twice daily but highly variable. Check other resources.

Alternatives:

T ½	= 6.2 hours	M/P	=
PHL	=	PB	= <4%
Tmax	= 30-60 minutes	Oral	= 93%
MW	=	pKa	=
Vd	= 0.6		

References:
1. Pharmaceutical manufactures prescribing information, 2005.

ISOSULFAN BLUE — L4

Trade: Lymphazurin
Other Trades:
Uses: Contrast agent
AAP: Not reviewed

Isosulfan blue is a contrast agent used for visualization of the lymphatic system draining. Each mL of solution contains 10 mg isosulfan blue, 6.6 mg sodium monohydrogen phosphate, and 2.7 mg potassium dihydrogen phosphate.[1] Isosulfan blue has higher rate of success in detecting sentinel lymph nodes than does TSC.[2] Severe adverse reactions have been documented, such as a sudden drop in systolic arterial pressure during surgery only stabilized by continuous epinephrine infusions of 400 μg/hour.[3] Methylene blue dye has been shown to be equally effective without the chance of severe adverse side effects, and thus its use is increasing.[4]

No data has been reported on the transfer of isosulfan blue into breast milk, and therefore caution should be used in breastfeeding mothers.

Pregnancy Risk Category: C
Lactation Risk Category:

Adult Concerns: Adverse reactions include localized swelling and itching.

Pediatric Concerns: No data were available.

Drug Interactions:

Relative Infant Dose:

Adult Dose: 0.5 ml into 3 interdigital spaces

Alternatives:

T ½	=		M/P	=
PHL	=		PB	= 50%
Tmax	=		Oral	=
MW	= 566.7		pKa	=
Vd	=			

References:
1. Pharmaceutical Manufacturer Prescribing Information. 2006.
2. Saha S, Dan AG, Berman B et al. Lymphazurin 1% Versus ^{99m}Tc Sulfur Colloid for Lymphatic Mapping in Colorectal Tumors: A Comparative Analysis. Ann Surg Oncol 2003; 11 (1):21-26.
3. Stefanutto TB, Shapiro WA, Wright PMC. Anaphylactic reaction to isosulphan blue. Br J Anesth 2002; 89 (3):527-528.
4. Thevarajah S, Huston TL, Simmons RM. A comparison of the adverse reactions associated with isosulfan blue versus methylene blue dye in sentinel lymph node biopsy for breast cancer. Am J Surg 2005; 189 (2):236-239.

ISOTRETINOIN   L5

Trade: Accutane
Other Trades: Isotrex, Accure, Roaccutane
Uses: Vitamin A derivative used for acne
AAP: Not reviewed

Isotretinoin is a synthetic derivative of the Vitamin A family called retinoids. Isotretinoin is known to be incredibly teratogenic producing profound birth defects in exposed fetuses.[1] It is primarily used for cystic acne where it is extremely effective if used by skilled physicians. While only 25% reaches the plasma, the remaining is either metabolized in the GI tract or removed first-pass by the liver. It is distributed to the liver, adrenals, ovaries, and lacrimal glands. Unlike vitamin A, isotretinoin is not stored in the liver. Secretion into milk is unknown but is likely as with other retinoids. Isotretinoin is extremely lipid soluble, and concentrations in milk may be significant. The manufacturer strongly recommends against using isotretinoin in a breastfeeding mother.

Pregnancy Risk Category: X

Lactation Risk Category: L5

Adult Concerns: Cheilitis (inflammation of the lips), dry nose, pruritus, elevated serum triglycerides, arthralgia, altered CBC, fatigue, headache, anorexia, nausea, vomiting, abnormal liver function tests, birth defects.

Pediatric Concerns: None reported, but this product poses too many risks to use in a lactating woman.

Drug Interactions: May increased clearance of carbamazepine. Avoid use of other vitamin A products.

Relative Infant Dose:

Adult Dose: 0.5-2 mg/kg daily.

Alternatives:

T ½	= >20 hours	M/P	=
PHL	=	PB	= 99.9%
Tmax	= 3.2 hours	Oral	= 25%
MW	= 300	pKa	=
Vd	=		

References:
1. Zbinden G. Investigation on the toxicity of tretinoin administered systemically to animals. Acta Derm Verereol Suppl (Stockh) 1975; 74:36-40.

ISRADIPINE — L3

Trade: DynaCirc
Other Trades: Prescal
Uses: Calcium channel blocker, antihypertensive
AAP: Not reviewed

It is not known if isradipine is secreted into milk. However, other calcium channel blockers are transferred only minimally (see verapamil, nifedipine).[1] Observe for lethargy, low blood pressure, and headache. See verapamil or nifedipine as alternatives.

Pregnancy Risk Category: C

Lactation Risk Category: L3

Adult Concerns: Hypotension, headache, dizziness, fatigue, bradycardia, nausea, dyspnea.

Pediatric Concerns: None reported, but observe for hypotension, fatigue, bradycardia, apnea.

Drug Interactions: H2 blockers may increased oral absorption of isradipine. Carbamazepine levels may be increased. Cyclosporine levels may be increased. May increase hypotension associated with fentanyl use. Digitalis levels may be increased. May increase quinidine levels including bradycardia, arrhythmias, and hypotension.

Relative Infant Dose:

Adult Dose: 2.5-10 mg BID

Alternatives: Nifedipine, Verapamil, Nimodipine

T ½	= 8 hours	M/P	=
PHL	=	PB	= 95%
Tmax	= 1.5 hours	Oral	= 17%
MW	= 371	pKa	=
Vd	=		

References:
1.   Pharmaceutical Manufacturer Prescribing Information. 1996.

ITRACONAZOLE   L2

Trade: Sporanox
Other Trades:
Uses: Antifungal
AAP: Not reviewed

Itraconazole is an antifungal agent active against a variety of fungal strains. It is extensively metabolized to hydroxyitraconazole, an active metabolite.[1,2] Itraconazole has an enormous volume of distribution, and large quantities (20 fold compared to plasma) concentrate in fatty tissues, liver, kidney, and skin.

In a study of two women who received two oral doses of 200 mg itraconazole 12 hours apart, the average milk concentrations at 4, 24, and 48 hours after the second dose were 70, 28, and 16 µg/L respectively.[3] After 72 hours, itraconazole levels in one mother were

20 μg/L and undetectable in the other. Reported milk/plasma ratios at 4, 24, and 48 hours were 0.51, 1.61, and 1.77 respectively. However, itraconazole oral absorption in an infant is somewhat unlikely as it requires an acidic milieu for absorption, which may be unlikely in a diet high in milk.

Never use with terfenadine or astemizole. Itraconazole has also been reported to induce significant bone defects in newborn animals, and it is not cleared for pediatric use. Until further studies are done, fluconazole is probably a preferred choice in breastfeeding mothers.

Pregnancy Risk Category: C

Lactation Risk Category: L2

Adult Concerns: Nausea, vomiting, diarrhea, epigastric pain, dizziness, rash, hypertension, abnormal liver enzymes.

Pediatric Concerns: None reported via breastmilk. Absorption via milk is unlikely.

Drug Interactions: Decreased serum levels with isoniazid, rifampin and phenytoin. Decreased absorption under alkaline conditions. Agents which increase stomach pH such as H-2 blockers (cimetidine, famotidine, nizatidine, ranitidine), omeprazole, sucralfate, and milk significantly reduce absorption. Cyclosporin levels are significantly increased by 50%. May increase phenytoin levels, inhibit warfarin metabolism, and increase digoxin levels. Significantly increases terfenadine, astemizole plasma levels.

Relative Infant Dose: 0.18% - 0.2%

Adult Dose: 200-400 mg daily

Alternatives: Fluconazole

T ½	= 64 hours	M/P	= 0.51-1.77
PHL	=	PB	= 99.8%
Tmax	= 4 hours	Oral	= 55%
MW	= 706	pKa	=
Vd	= 10		

References:
1. Drug Facts and Comparisons 2010 ed. ed. St. Louis: 2010.
2. Pharmaceutical Manufacturer Prescribing Information. 1996.
3. Janssen Pharmaceuticals, personal communication. 1996.

IVERMECTIN   L3

Trade: Mectizan
Other Trades: Stromectol
Uses: Antiparasitic
AAP: Maternal Medication Usually Compatible with Breastfeeding

Ivermectin is now widely used to treat human onchocerciasis, lymphatic filariasis, and other worms and parasites such as head lice. In a study of 4 women given 150 µg/kg orally, the maximum breastmilk concentration averaged 14.13 µg/L.[1] Milk/plasma ratios ranged from 0.39 to 0.57 with a mean of 0.51. Highest breastmilk concentration was at 4-6 hours. Average daily ingestion of ivermectin was calculated at 2.1 µg/kg which is 10 fold less than the adult dose. No adverse effects were reported.

Pregnancy Risk Category: C

Lactation Risk Category: L3

Adult Concerns: Headaches, pruritus, transient hypotension.

Pediatric Concerns: None reported.

Drug Interactions:

Relative Infant Dose: 1.3%

Adult Dose: 150-200 µg/kg once

Alternatives:

T ½	= 28 hours	M/P	= 0.39-0.57
PHL	=	PB	=
Tmax	= 4 hours	Oral	= Variable
MW	=	pKa	=
Vd	=		

References:
1. Ogbuokiri JE, Ozumba BC, Okonkwo PO. Ivermectin levels in human breast milk. Eur J Clin Pharmacol 1994; 46 (1):89-90.

KANAMYCIN

L2

Trade: Kantrex
Other Trades: Kannasyn
Uses: Antibiotic
AAP: Maternal Medication Usually Compatible with Breastfeeding

Kanamycin is an aminoglycoside antibiotic primarily used for gram negative infections. In a study of 3 patients who received 1000 mg IV, milk levels at 1, 2, 4, and 6 hours were zero, 0.1 mg/L, 0.3 mg/L, 0.5 and 0.8 mg/L respectively.[1] The average milk level in this study was 0.25 mg/L although the highest milk level occurred at 1 hour following the IV infusion. The milk/plasma ratio at 6 hours was 0.045. It is probably advisable to refrain from breastfeeding for several hours following placement of the IV. This will drastically reduce the infant's exposure to kanamycin. However, poor oral absorption (only 1%) in the infant would limit amount absorbed although changes in GI flora are possible.

Pregnancy Risk Category: D

Lactation Risk Category: L2

Adult Concerns: Diarrhea, ototoxicity, nephrotoxicity.

Pediatric Concerns: None reported, but observe for diarrhea.

Drug Interactions: May have increased toxicity when used with penicillins, cephalosporins, amphotericin B, and diuretics. May increase neuromuscular blockade when used with neuromuscular blockingagents.

Relative Infant Dose: 0.3%

Adult Dose: 5-7.5 mg/kg every 8-12 hours

Alternatives:

T ½	= 2.4 hours	M/P	= 0.045
PHL	= 4-18 hours	PB	= 0%.
Tmax	= 1 hour	Oral	= 1%
MW	=	pKa	= 7.2
Vd	= 0.2-0.3		

References:
1. Matsuda S. Transfer of antibiotics into maternal milk. Biol Res Pregnancy Perinatol 1984; 5 (2):57-60.

KAOLIN - PECTIN   L1

Trade: Kaolin, Kaopectate
Other Trades: Donnagel-MB, Kao-Con
Uses: Antidiarrhea
AAP: Not reviewed

Kaolin and pectin (attapulgite) are used as antidiarrhea agents. Kaolin is a natural hydrated aluminum silicate. Pectin is a purified polymerized carbohydrate obtained from citrus fruits. Kaolin and pectin are not absorbed following oral use. Some preparations may contain opiate compounds and atropine-like substances. Observe bottle for ingredients. Never use in children less than 3 years of age.

Pregnancy Risk Category: C

Lactation Risk Category: L1

Adult Concerns: Constipation, fecal impaction, reduce drug absorption.

Pediatric Concerns: None reported via milk.

Drug Interactions: Decreases oral absorption of clindamycin, tetracyclines, penicillamine, digoxin.

Relative Infant Dose:

Adult Dose: 60-120 mL PRN

Alternatives:

References:

KAVA-KAVA   L5

Trade: Awa, Kew, Tonga
Other Trades:
Uses: Sedative and sleep enhancement
AAP: Not reviewed

Kava is the dried rhizome and roots of Piper methysticum. While more than 20 varieties are known, the black and white grades are most popular. Kava drink is prepared from the rhizome by steeping the pulverized root in hot water. It is then filtered and drunk. It is indigenous to the islands of the South Pacific where it is used similar to alcohol to induce relaxation.[1] The activity of kava appears related to several dihydropyrones that possess CNS activity, including methysticine, kawain, dihydromethysticin, and yangonin. Studies of these agents suggest that they may induce mephenesin-like muscle relaxation in animals, similar in effect to the local anesthetics. Masticated kava induces a local anesthetic effect in the mouth. It is not known with certainty how these agents work, but it is apparently not at the opiate receptors. However, they do induce sleep and reduce anxiety. The CNS activity of kava is due to the lipid components, not the more polar water soluble components. In humans, kava produces mild euphoria, happiness, fluent and lively speech. High doses may lead to muscle weakness, visual and auditory changes. Heavy users are underweight, have reduced plasma protein levels, facial edema, scaly rashes, elevated HDL cholesterol, blood in the urine, and abnormal CBS (elevated RBCs, reduced platelets, and lymphocytes). Discolored, flaky skin, and reddened eyes is common. Ethanol dramatically increases the toxicity of kava and should not be co-mixed. No data are available on its use in breastfeeding mothers, but care should be exercised. The German Commission E monographs state that it is contraindicated in pregnant and lactating women.[2]

Pregnancy Risk Category:

Lactation Risk Category: L5

Adult Concerns: High doses may lead to muscle weakness, visual and auditory changes. Heavy users are underweight, have reduced plasma protein levels, facial edema, scaly rashes, elevated HDL cholesterol, blood in the urine, and abnormal CBS (elevated RBCs, reduced platelets, and lymphocytes). Discolored, flaky skin, and reddened eyes is common. Ethanol dramatically increases the toxicity of kava, and should not be co-mixed.

Pediatric Concerns: None reported but caution is recommended.

Drug Interactions: Admixing with alcohol dramatically increases toxicity of kava.

Relative Infant Dose:

Adult Dose:

Alternatives:

References:
1.   Review of Natural Products Facts and Comparisons, St Louis, MO 1996.
2.   The Complete German Commission E Monographs. Ed. M. Blumenthal Amer Botanical Council 1998.

KETAMINE   L3

Trade: Ketanest, Ketaset, Ketalar, Ketanest S, Ketamax,
Calypsol, Brevinaze, Anesject
Other Trades:
Uses: Anesthetic agent
AAP: Not reviewed

Ketamine is a rapid acting general anesthetic agent with effects that include analgesia, anesthesia, and hallucinations. Often combined with midazolam, it is increasingly more popular, as it has fewer hemodynamic problems, and reduced postoperative depression. One interesting complication is the hallucinogenic effect commonly called a dissociative effect or emergence reaction.[1,2] Following the use of ketamine, patients may exhibit hallucinogenic effects upon withdrawal. This is often suppressed with the addition of midazolam or other benzodiazepines. The emergent reactions are apparently age-dependent, and appear to occur more frequently in adults (30-50%) and less frequently in children (5-15%).[1] One major benefit of ketamine is the production of excellent analgesia with minimal respiratory depression. No data are available on the transfer of ketamine into human milk. It has a short half-life of 2.5 hours but its redistribution half-life out of the plasma (to muscle and tissues) is much briefer (4.68 min.), thus milk levels are likely to be low.

Pregnancy Risk Category: B

Lactation Risk Category: L3

Adult Concerns: Sedationl, hallucinations, normal or slightly enhanced skeletal muscle tone, cardiovascular and respiratory stimulation, and occasionally a transient and minimal respiratory depression. Diplopia and nystagmus have been reported.

Pediatric Concerns: None reported via milk. Rapid redistribution from the plasma would probably reduce levels in milk.

Drug Interactions: Prolonged recovery times may occur if used with barbiturates or narcotics. Increased neuromuscular blockade when used with atracurium and tubocurarine. Increased risk of seizures with metrizamide, and theophylline. Increased risk of cardiovascular collapse with St. John's Wort. Increased risk of respiratory depression when used with tramadol.

Relative Infant Dose:

Adult Dose: Varies but 1-2 mg/kg IV may be used for induction in adults.

Alternatives: Propfol, sufentanil

T ½	= 2.5-3 hours	M/P	=
PHL	= 1-2	PB	= 47%
Tmax	= 0.4 hours epidural	Oral	= 16%
MW	= 237	pKa	= 7.5
Vd	= 2-3		

References:
1.   Bergman SA. Ketamine: review of its pharmacology and its use in pediatric anesthesia. Anesth Prog 1999;46 (1):10-20.
2.   White M, de GP, Renshof B, van KE, Dzoljic M. Pharmacokinetics of S (+) ketamine derived from target controlled infusion. Br J Anaesth 2006 March;96 (3):330-4.
3.   White PF, Ham J, Way WL, Trevor AJ. Pharmacology of ketamine isomers in surgical patients. Anesthesiology 1980 March;52 (3):231-9.

KETOCONAZOLE | L2

Trade: Nizoral Shampoo, Nizoral
Other Trades:
Uses: Antifungal, anti-dandruff
AAP: Maternal Medication Usually Compatible with Breastfeeding

Ketoconazole is an antifungal similar in structure to miconazole and clotrimazole. It is used orally, topically, and via shampoo.[1] Ketoconazole is not detected in plasma after chronic shampooing. In a study of one patient (82 kg) receiving 200 mg daily for 10 days, milk samples were taken at 1.75, 3.25, 6.0, 8.0, and 24 hours after the tenth dose.[2] The average concentration of ketoconazole over the 24 hours was 68 µg/L while the C_{max} at 3.25 hours was 0.22 mg/L. The absorption of ketoconazole is highly variable, and could be reduced in infants due to the alkaline condition induced by milk ingestion.[3] Ketoconazole requires acidic conditions to be absorbed, and its absorption and distribution in children is not known. Regardless, ketoconazole is probably safe in breastfeeding infants.L2;

Pregnancy Risk Category: C

Lactation Risk Category:

Adult Concerns: Nausea, vomiting, itching, dizziness, fever, chills, hypertension, hepatotoxicity.

Pediatric Concerns: None reported in one case.

Drug Interactions: Decreased ketoconazole levels occur with rifampin, isoniazid and phenytoin use. Theophylline levels may be reduced. Absorption requires acid pH, so anything increasing gastric pH will significantly reduce absorption. This includes cimetidine, ranitidine, famotidine, omeprazole, sucralfate, antacids, etc. Do not coadminister with cisapride or terfenadine (very dangerous). May increase cyclosporin levels by 50%, inhibits warfarin metabolism and prolongs coagulation.

Relative Infant Dose: 0.3%

Adult Dose: 200-400 mg daily.

Alternatives: Fluconazole

T ½	= 2-8 hours	M/P	=
PHL	=	PB	= 99%
Tmax	= 1-2 hours	Oral	= Variable (75%)
MW	= 531	pKa	=
Vd	=		

References:
1. Pharmaceutical Manufacturer Prescribing Information. 1996.
2. Moretti ME, Ito S, Koren G. Disposition of maternal ketoconazole in breast milk. Am J Obstet Gynecol 1995; 173 (5):1625-1626.
3. Force RW, Nahata MC. Salivary concentrations of ketoconazole and fluconazole: implications for drug efficacy in oropharyngeal and esophageal candidiasis. Ann Pharmacother 1995; 29 (1):10-15.

KETOPROFEN   L2

Trade: Orudis, Oruvail
Other Trades: Apo-Keto, Rhodis, Rhovail
Uses: NSAID analgesic
AAP: Not reviewed

Ketoprofen is a typical nonsteroidal analgesic. It is structurally similar to ibuprofen. Due to tablet formulation (Oruvail), maternal absorption is prolonged during the day, requiring 6-7 hours to peak levels.[1] In a recent study of 18 postnatal patients who received 100 mg every 12 hours IV for 3 doses, the average milk level was 57 µg/L and the highest level was 91 µg/L.[2] Assuming a milk volume of 150 mL/kg/day, the mean and maximum doses that a breastfed newborn would ingest during one day is 7.0 and 9.0 µg/kg/day or about 0.3% of the weight-adjusted maternal dose. The authors suggest that breastfeeding is permissible when ketoprofen is administered to the mother to treat postpartum pain.

Pregnancy Risk Category: B

Lactation Risk Category: L2

Adult Concerns: GI distress, diarrhea, vomiting, gastric bleeding.

Pediatric Concerns: None reported, but observe for GI symptoms including diarrhea, cramping.

Drug Interactions: May prolong prothrombin time when used with warfarin. Antihypertensive effects of ACEi family may be blunted or completely abolished by NSAIDs. Some NSAIDs may block antihypertensive effect of beta blockers, diuretics. Used with cyclosporin, may dramatically increase renal toxicity. May increase digoxin, phenytoin, lithium levels. May increase toxicity of methotrexate. May increase bioavailability of penicillamine. Probenecid may increase NSAID levels.

Relative Infant Dose: 0.29%
Adult Dose: 50-75 mg TID-QID

Alternatives: Ibuprofen

T ½	= 2-4 hours	M/P	=
PHL	=	PB	= >99%
Tmax	= 1.2	Oral	= 90%
MW	= 254	pKa	= 4.0
Vd	= 0.1-0.5		

References:
1.   Pharmaceutical Manufacturer Prescribing Information. 1996.
2.   Jacqz-Aigrain E, Serreau R, Boissinot C, Popon M, Sobel A, Michel J, Sibony O. Excretion of Ketoprofen and Nalbuphine in Human Milk During Treatment of Maternal Pain After Delivery. Ther Drug Monit. 2007 Dec;29 (6):815-818.

KETOROLAC
L2

Trade: Toradol, Acular
Other Trades: Acular, Toradol
Uses: Non-steroidal antiinflammatory, analgesic
AAP: Maternal Medication Usually Compatible with Breastfeeding

Ketorolac is a popular, nonsteroidal analgesic. Although previously used in labor and delivery, its use has subsequently been contraindicated because it is believed to adversely effect fetal circulation and inhibit uterine contractions, thus increasing the risk of hemorrhage.

In a study of 10 lactating women who received 10 mg orally four times daily, milk levels of ketorolac were not detectable in 4 of the subjects.[1] In the 6 remaining patients, the concentration of ketorolac in milk 2 hours after a dose ranged from 5.2 to 7.3 µg/L on day 1 and 5.9 to 7.9 µg/L on day 2. In most patients, the breastmilk level was never above 5 µg/L. The maximum daily dose an infant could absorb (maternal dose= 40 mg/day) would range from 3.16 to 7.9 µg/day assuming a milk volume of 400 mL or 1000 mL. An infant would therefore receive less than 0.2% of the daily maternal dose (Please note, the original paper contained a misprint on the daily intake of ketorolac (mg instead of µg).

Pregnancy Risk Category: C in first and second trimesters
D in third trimester

Lactation Risk Category: L2

Adult Concerns: GI irritability, dry mouth, nausea, vomiting, edema, or rash.

Pediatric Concerns: None reported in one study.

Drug Interactions: May prolong prothrombin time when used with warfarin. Antihypertensive effects of ACEi family may be blunted or completely abolished by NSAIDs. Some NSAIDs may block antihypertensive effect of beta blockers, diuretics. Used with cyclosporin, may dramatically increase renal toxicity. May increase digoxin, phenytoin, lithium levels. May increase toxicity of methotrexate. May increase bioavailability of penicillamine. Probenecid may increase NSAID levels.

Relative Infant Dose: 0.2%

Adult Dose: 30 mg every 6 hours

Alternatives: Ibuprofen

T ½	= 2.4-8.6 hours	M/P	= 0.015-0.037
PHL	=	PB	= 99%
Tmax	= 0.5 - 1 hour	Oral	= >81%
MW	= 255	pKa	= 3.5
Vd	= 0.15-0.33		

References:
1. Wischnik A, Manth SM, Lloyd J, Bullingham R, Thompson JS. The excretion of ketorolac tromethamine into breast milk after multiple oral dosing. Eur J Clin Pharmacol 1989; 36 (5):521-524.

KOMBUCHA TEA   L5

Trade:
Other Trades:
Uses: Herbal tea
AAP: Not reviewed

Kombucha tea is a popular health beverage made by incubating the Kombucha mushroom in sweet black tea.   During 1995, several reported cases of toxicity and one fatality were reported to the CDC.[1] Based on these reports, the Iowa Department of Health has recommended that persons refrain from drinking Kombucha tea until the role of the tea in these cases has been resolved

Pregnancy Risk Category:

Lactation Risk Category: L5

Adult Concerns: Shortness of breath, respiratory distress, fatigue, metabolic acidosis, disseminated intravascular coagulopathy.

Pediatric Concerns: Caution is recommended.

Drug Interactions:

Relative Infant Dose:

Adult Dose: N/A

Alternatives:

References:
1. Unexplained severe illness possibly associated with consumption of Kombucha tea--Iowa, 1995 MMWR Morb Mortal Wkly Rep 1995; 44 (48):892-900.

L-METHYLFOLATE   L3

Trade: Deplin, Metafolin
Other Trades:
Uses: Active folic acid metabolite
AAP: Not reviewed

L-Methylfolate, also called Metafolin, is the active biological isomer of folate and the form of circulating folate. Approximately 10% of the population lacks the enzymes necessary to metabolic folic acid to L-methylfolate. L-Methylfolate is the form transported across cell membranes, and is bioactive. No data are available on the transport of this form of folate into human milk. However, several studies of folic acid supplementation in breastfeeding mothers clearly suggest that folate is actively transported into human milk, but most importantly, supplementing of the mother only marginally if at all, increases milk folate levels.[1,2] This suggests that even following supplementation, milk levels would be unlikely to increase, unless the mother is deficient. Thus, this product is probably not hazardous to use in a breastfeeding mother.

Pregnancy Risk Category:

Lactation Risk Category: L3

Adult Concerns: First-generation anticonvulsants may cause decreased serum folate levels, and high doses of folates may actually reduce plasma levels of these anticonvulsants, thereby reducing their anticonvulsant effect.

Pediatric Concerns: None reported via milk.

Drug Interactions: Do not use with anticonvulsants. First-generation anticonvulsants (carbamazepine, phenytoin, fosphenytoin, phenobarbital, primidone, valproic acid) may not only reduce plasma folate levels, but high folate administration may also reduce plasma levels of these anticonvulsants. See prescribing information.

Relative Infant Dose:

Adult Dose: 7.5 mg daily

Alternatives: Folic acid

T ½	=	M/P	=
PHL	=	PB	=
Tmax	=	Oral	= Complete
MW	= 455	pKa	=
Vd	=		

References:
1. Tamura T, Yoshimura Y, Arakawa T. Human milk folate and folate status in lactating mothers and their infants. Am J Clin Nutr. 1980;33:193-197.
2. Smith AM, Picciano MF, Deering RH. Folate supplementation during lactation: maternal folate status, human milk folate content, and their relationship to infant folate status. J Pediatr Gastroenterol Nutr. 1983;2:622-628.

LABETALOL   L2

Trade: Trandate, Normodyne
Other Trades: Presolol, Labrocol
Uses: Antihypertensive, beta blocker
AAP: Maternal Medication Usually Compatible with Breastfeeding

Labetalol is a selective beta blocker with moderate lipid solubility that is used as an antihypertensive and for treating angina. In one study of 3 women receiving 600 mg, 600 mg, or 1200 mg/day, the peak concentration of labetalol in breastmilk was 129, 223, and 662 µg/L respectively.[1] In only one infant were measurable plasma levels found (18 µg/L) following a maternal dose of 600 mg. Therefore, only small amounts are secreted into human milk.

Pregnancy Risk Category: C

Lactation Risk Category: L2

Adult Concerns: Bradycardia, hypotension, dizziness, nausea, aggravation of asthma, lethargy.

Pediatric Concerns: None reported, but observe for hypotension, apnea.

Drug Interactions: Decreased effect when used with aluminum salts, barbiturates, calcium salts, cholestyramine, NSAIDs, ampicillin, rifampin, and salicylates. Beta blockers may reduce the effect of oral sulfonylureas (hypoglycemic agents). Increased toxicity/effect when used with other antihypertensives, contraceptives, MAO inhibitors, cimetidine, and numerous other products. See drug interaction reference for complete listing.

Relative Infant Dose: 0.2% - 0.6%

Adult Dose: 200-400 mg BID

Alternatives: Propranolol, Metoprolol

T ½	= 6-8 hours	M/P	= 0.8-2.6
PHL	=	PB	= 50%
Tmax	= 1-2 hours (oral)	Oral	= 30-40%
MW	= 328	pKa	= A7.4, B8.7
Vd	= 10		

References:
1.   Lunell NO, Kulas J, Rane A. Transfer of labetalol into amniotic fluid and breast milk in lactating women. Eur J Clin Pharmacol 1985; 28 (5):597-599.

LACOSAMIDE   L3

Trade: Vimpat
Other Trades:
Uses: Anticonvulsant
AAP: Not reviewed

Lacosamide is a new anticonvulsant used as adjunctive therapy in the treatment of partial-onset seizures in patients with epilepsy aged 17 years and older. It is functionalized amino acid that has activity in the maximal electroshock seizure test. Due to its structure, levels in milk may be significant.   No data are available on its transfer into human milk, but caution is recommended until we have more data.

Pregnancy Risk Category: C

Lactation Risk Category: L3

Adult Concerns: Lacosamide increases the risk of suicidal thoughts or behavior in patients taking these drugs for any indication. Patients treated with any AED for any indication should be monitored for the emergence or worsening of depression, suicidal thoughts or behavior, and/or any unusual changes in mood or behavior.   Vertigo, eye disorders, diplopia, vision blurred, gastrointestinal disorders, nausea, vomiting, diarrhea, fatigue, gait disturbance, asthenia, contusion, dizziness, headache, ataxia, somnolewnce, tremor, nystagmus, depresssion, pruritus, impaired memory have been reported.

Pediatric Concerns: None reported yet, but caution is recommended.

Drug Interactions: None yet reported.

Relative Infant Dose:

Adult Dose: 50-600 mg per day

Alternatives: Lamotrigine, carbamazepine

T ½	– 13 hours	M/P	=
PHL	=	PB	= 15%
Tmax	= 30-60 minutes	Oral	= Complete
MW	= 250	pKa	= 100%
Vd	= 0.6		

References:
1. Pharmaceutical manufacturers prescribing information, 2010.

LAMIVUDINE   L2

Trade: Epivir-HBV, 3TC
Other Trades:
Uses: Antiviral
AAP: Not reviewed

Lamivudine is a synthetic nucleoside analogue antiviral used for the treatment of Hepatitis B or HIV infections. It is presently in numerous other combination products (Combivir, Ziagen, etc.). In a study of 20 women receiving either 300 mg once daily or 150 mg twice daily one week postpartum, the mean breast milk concentration was 1.22 mg/L (range= 0.5-6.09) or 0.183 mg/kg/day. This is significantly less than the clinical dose normally administered to infants (4-8 mg/ kg/d). The authors suggested that the amount ingested via breast milk was negligible relative to therapeutic dosing and would not provide adequate antiretroviral drug concentrations for a neonate.

In another study of 18 women receiving antiretroviral treatment for HIV infections, median lamivudine concentrations in maternal serum, breast milk, and the infant's serum was 678 ng/mL, 1828 ng/mL and 28 ng/mL, respectively.[2] The median milk/serum ratio was 3.34 for lamivudine. The median infant concentration of lamivudine (28 ng/ mL) was 5% of the inhibitory concentration (50%) which is 550 ng/mL.

This data suggests that the serum levels of lamivudine attained in the infant are probably too low to produce side effects in the infant, and certainly too low to treat HIV effectively.

Pregnancy Risk Category: C

Lactation Risk Category: L2

Adult Concerns: Adverse events include lactic acidosis, severe hepatomegaly, pancreatitis, malaise, fatigue, upper respiratory infections, nausea, vomiting, headache and myalgia.

Pediatric Concerns: None reported in two study. Dose via milk is apparently too low to produce adverse effects.

Drug Interactions: Use with cotrimoxazole (trimethoprim and sulfamethoxazole) could potentially elevate levels of lamivudine. Plasma levels of loviride were reduced by lamivudine. Do not use with ribavirin due to risk of fatal lactic acidosis.

Relative Infant Dose: 4.3% - 6.3%

Adult Dose: 100 mg daily for hepatitis B infections.

Alternatives:

T ½	= 5-7 hours	M/P	=
PHL	= 13.95 hours	PB	= <36%
Tmax	= 1-1.5 hours	Oral	= 82%
MW	= 229	pKa	=
Vd	= 1.0		

References:
1. Moodley J, Moodley D, Pillay K, Coovadia H, Saba J, van Leeuwen R, Goodwin C, Harrigan PR, Moore KH, Stone C, Plumb R, Johnson MA. Pharmacokinetics and antiretroviral activity of lamivudine alone or when coadministered with zidovudine in human immunodeficiency virus type 1-infected pregnant women and their offspring. J Infect Dis 1998; 178 (5):1327-1333.
2. Shapiro RL, Holland DT, Capparelli E, Lockman S, Thior I, Wester C, et al. Antiretroviral concentrations in breast-feeding infants of women in Botswana receiving antiretroviral treatment. J Infect Dis 2005 Sep 1; 192 (5):720-7.

LAMOTRIGINE | L3

Trade: Lamictal
Other Trades:
Uses: Anticonvulsant
AAP: Drugs whose effect on nursing infants is unknown but may be of concern

Lamotrigine is a newer anticonvulsant primarily indicated for treatment of simple and complex partial seizures.

In a study of a 24 year old female receiving 300 mg/day lamotrigine during pregnancy, maternal serum levels and cord levels of lamotrigine at birth were 3.88 µg/mL in the mother and 3.26 µg/mL in the cord blood.[1] By day 22, the maternal serum levels were 9.61 µg/mL, the milk concentration was 6.51 mg/L, and the infant's serum level was 2.25 µg/mL. Following a reduction in dose, the prior levels decreased significantly over the next weeks. The milk/plasma ratio at the highest maternal serum level was 0.562. The estimated dose to infant would be approximately 2-5 mg per day assuming a maternal dose of 200-300mg per day. The infant developed normally in every way.

In another study of a single mother receiving 200 mg/day lamotrigine, milk levels of lamotrigine immediately prior to the next dose (trough) at steady state were 3.48 mg/L (13.6 µM).[2] The authors estimated the daily dose to infant to be 0.5 mg/kg/day. The above authors suggest that infants, while developing normally, should probably be monitored periodically for plasma levels of lamotrigine.

The manufacturer reports that in a group of 5 women (no dose listed), breastmilk concentrations of lamotrigine ranged from 0.07-5.03 mg/L.[3] Breastmilk levels averaged 40-45% of maternal plasma levels. No untoward effects were noted in the infants.

In a study by Ohman of 9 breastfeeding women at 3 weeks postpartum, the median milk/plasma ratio was 0.61, and the breastfed infants maintained lamotrigine concentrations of approximately 30% of the mother's plasma levels.[4] The authors estimated the dose to the infant to be 0.2-1 mg/kg/d. No adverse effects were noted in the infants.

One further study of 6 breastfeeding women consuming from 175-800 (mean −400) mg/day resulted in average infant doses of 0.45 mg/kg/day, and an average infant plasma concentration of 0.6 mg/L. No adverse effects in the infants were noted.[5]

In a study of four mothers with partial epilepsy on lamotrigine monotherapy, serum levels of lamotrigine in nursing newborns ranged from <1.0 to 2.0 µg/mL on day 10 of life.[6] Three babies had lamotrigine levels >1.0 µg/mL. Lamotrigine levels in newborns were on average 30% (range 20-43%) of the maternal drug level. Unfortunately, no decline was noted in two children with repeat levels at 2 months. The authors suggested significant genetic variability in the infants ability to metabolize this drug. Close monitoring of the infant plasma levels was recommended.[6]

In a recent and well-done study of thirty women under treatment with lamotrigine for seizure disorders, the average milk/plasma ratio was 0.413.[7] Infant plasma levels were 18.3% of maternal plasma levels. The theoretical daily infant dose was 0.51 mg/kg/day and the relative infant dose was 9.2% (range=3.1-21.1%). Most important, this study indicates that there is wide variability in milk levels that seem to be more related to the pharmacogenetic makeup of the individual than the dose.

It is important to remember, that the theoretic infant dose in these studies, that ranges from 0.51 mg/kg/day to perhaps as high as 1 mg/kg/day is still significantly less than the therapeutic dose (4.4 mg/k/day) administered to 17 day-old infants with neonatal seizures.[8]

However, one case of severe apnea has been recently reported in a 16 day old breastfed infant.[9] In this case, the mother was receiving 850 mg/day, had a plasma level of 14.93 µg/mL. The plasma level of the infant was 4.87 µg/mL. Interestingly, the milk/plasma ratio was higher, 0.79 to 0.96, suggesting higher transfer into milk than in the above studies.

The use of lamotrigine in breastfeeding mothers produces significant plasma levels in some breastfed infants, although they are apparently not high enough to produce side effects in most cases. Exposure in utero is considerably higher, and levels will probably drop in newborn breastfed infants who are breastfed. Nevertheless, it is advisable to monitor the infant's plasma levels closely to insure safety.

Pregnancy Risk Category: C

Lactation Risk Category: L3

Adult Concerns: Rash, fatigue, ataxia, dizziness, ataxia, somnolence, tremor, nausea, vomiting, and headache. Breast pain has been infrequently reported.

Pediatric Concerns: Breast milk levels are relatively high and RID is high as well. Reported infant plasma levels are about 30% of maternal plasma levels. One reported case of severe neonatal apnea in one infant. Closely monitor all infants exposed to lamotrigine via milk.

Drug Interactions: Acetaminophen reduces lamotrigine half-life by 15-20% and may require increased doses. Carbamazepine, phenytoin, phenobarbital, and other anticonvulsants may reduce plasma levels of lamotrigine by increasing clearance, but this is highly variable.

Relative Infant Dose: 9.2% - 22.8%

Adult Dose: 150-250 mg BID

Alternatives:

T ½	= 29 hours	M/P	= 0.562
PHL	=	PB	= 55%
Tmax	= 1-4 hours	Oral	= 98%
MW	= 256	pKa	= 5.7
Vd	= 0.9-1.3		

References:

1. Rambeck B, Kurlemann G, Stodieck SR, May TW, Jurgens U. Concentrations of lamotrigine in a mother on lamotrigine treatment and her newborn child. Eur J Clin Pharmacol 1997; 51 (6):481-484.
2. Tomson T, Ohman I, Vitols S. Lamotrigine in pregnancy and lactation: a case report. Epilepsia 1997; 38 (9):1039-1041.
3. Biddlecombe RA. Analysis of breast milk samples for lamotrigine. Internal document BDCR/93/0011. Glaxo-Wellcome 2004.
4. Ohman I, Vitols S, Tomson T. Lamotrigine in pregnancy: pharmacokinetics during delivery, in the neonate, and during lactation. Epilepsia 2000; 41 (6):709-713.
5. Page-Sharp M, Kristensen JH, Hackett LP, Beran RG, Rampono J, Hale TW, Kohan R, Ilett KF. Transfer of Lamotrigine Into Breast Milk. Ann Pharmacother 2006; 40:1470-1471.
6. Liporace J, Kao A, D'Abreu A. Concerns regarding lamotrigine and breast-feeding. Epilepsy Behav 2004; 5 (1):102-105.
7. Newport DJ, Pennell PB, Calamaras MR, et al. Lamotrigine in breast milk and nursing infants: determination of exposure. Pediatrics. 2008;122 (1):e223-e231.
8. Barr PA, Buettiker VE, Antony JH. Efficacy of lamotrigine in refractory neonatal seizures. Pediatr Neurol. Feb 1999;20 (2):161-163.
9. Nordmo E, Aronsen L, Wasland K, Smabrekke L, Vorren S. Severe apnea in an infant exposed to lamotrigine in breast milk. Ann Pharmacother. Nov 2009;43 (11):1893-1897.

LANSOPRAZOLE   L3

Trade: Prevacid, Prevpac, Prevacid NapraPak
Other Trades: Zoton
Uses: Reduces stomach acid secretion
AAP: Not reviewed

Lansoprazole is a new proton pump inhibitor that suppresses the release of acid protons from the parietal cells in the stomach, effectively raising the pH of the stomach. Structurally similar to omeprazole, it is very unstable in stomach acid and to a large degree is denatured by acidity of the infant's stomach.[1] A new study shows milk levels of omeprazole are minimal (see omeprazole) and it is likely milk levels of lansoprazole are small as well. Although there are no studies of lansoprazole in breastfeeding mothers, transfer to milk and its oral absorption (via milk) is likely to be minimal in a breastfed infant.

Lansoprazole is secreted in animal milk although no data are available on the amount secreted in human milk. The only likely untoward effects would be reduced stomach acidity. This product has no current pediatric indications although it is occasionally used in severe cases of erosive gastritis.

Prevpac contains Lansoprazole, Amoxicillin, and Clarithromycin. It is primarily indicated for treatment of H.Pylori infections which cause stomach ulcers.

Prevacid NapraPAC contains 15 mg lansoprazole and 500 mg naproxen for use in reducing the risk of NSAID-associated gastric ulcers in patients with a history of documented gastric ulcer that require the use of an NSAID for treatment of the signs and symptoms of rheumatoid arthritis, osteoarthritis, and ankylosing spondylitis.

Pregnancy Risk Category: B

Lactation Risk Category: L3

Adult Concerns: Reduced stomach acidity. Diarrhea, nausea, elevated liver enzymes.

Pediatric Concerns: None reported via milk. It is unlikely to be absorbed while dissolved in milk due to instability in acid.

Drug Interactions: Decreased absorption of ketoconazole, itraconazole, and other drugs dependent on acid for absorption. Theophylline clearance is increased slightly. Reduced lansoprazole absorption when used with sucralfate (30%).

Relative Infant Dose:

Adult Dose: 15-30 mg TID

Alternatives: Omeprazole, famotidine

T ½	= 1.5 hours	M/P	=
PHL	=	PB	= 97%
Tmax	= 1.7 hours	Oral	= 80% (Enteric only)
MW	= 369	pKa	=
Vd	=		

References:
1. Pharmaceutical Manufacturer Prescribing Information.

LATANOPROST   L3

Trade: Xalatan
Other Trades: Optimol, Betim
Uses: Prostaglandin for glaucoma
AAP: Not reviewed

Latanoprost is a prostaglandin F2-alpha analogue used for the treatment of ocular hypertension and glaucoma. One drop used daily is usually effective.[1] No data are available on the transfer of this product into human milk, but it is unlikely. Prostaglandins are by nature, rapidly metabolized. Plasma levels are barely detectable and then only for 1 hour after use. Combined with the short half-life, minimal plasma levels, and poor oral bioavailability, untoward effects via milk are unlikely.

Pregnancy Risk Category: C

Lactation Risk Category: L3

Adult Concerns: Ocular irritation, headache, rash, muscle aches, joint pain.

Pediatric Concerns: None reported via milk.

Drug Interactions:

Relative Infant Dose:

Adult Dose: 1 drop in affected eye daily.

Alternatives:

T ½	= <30 minutes	M/P	=
PHL	=	PB	=
Tmax	= <1 hour	Oral	= Nil
MW	=	pKa	=
Vd	= 0.16		

References:
1. Pharmaceutical Manufacturer Prescribing Information.

LEAD   L5

Trade:
Other Trades:
Uses: Environmental pollutant
AAP: Not reviewed

Lead is an environmental pollutant. It serves no useful purpose in the body and tends to accumulate in the body's bony structures based on their exposure. Due to the rapid development of the nervous system, children are particularly sensitive to elevated levels.

Lead apparently transfers into human milk at a rate proportional to maternal blood levels, but the absolute degree of transfer is controversial. Studies of milk lead levels vary enormously and probably reflect the enormous difficulty in accurately measuring lead in milk. In mothers who have previously been exposed to high lead environments, the greatest chance of lead toxicity will be with her first pregnancy. Her blood levels will be highest postpartum because blood lead levels increase during lactation, and her baby's greatest chance of toxicity will be prenatal, because intestinal absorption of lead from milk is low.[6]

One study evaluated lead transfer into human milk in population of women with an average blood lead of 45 μg/dL (considered very high).[1] The average lead level in milk was 2.47 μg/dL. Using these parameters, the average intake in an infant would be 8.1 μg/kg/d. The daily permissible level by WHO is 5.0 μg/kg/d. Using these parameters, mothers contaminated with lead should not breastfeed their infants.

However, in another study of two lactating women whose blood lead levels were 29 and 33 μg/dl, the breastmilk levels were <0.005 μg/mL and <0.010 μg/mL respectively.[2] Although both infants had high lead levels

(38 µg/dl and 44 µg/dl), it was probably derived from the environment or in-utero. Using this data, breastfeeding would appear to be safe. In a larger study of Shanghai mothers (n=165), the transfer of lead to the fetus was highly correlated with maternal blood lead levels (maternal blood vs. cord= 13.2 µg/dL and 6.9 µg/dL).[3] Lead levels in the cord blood and breastmilk increased with the lead level in the maternal blood, with coefficient of correlation of 0.714 and 0.353 respectively. The average concentration of lead in breastmilk for 12 occupationally exposed women (lead-exposed jobs) was 52.7 µg/L, which was almost 12 times higher than that for the occupationally non-exposed population (4.43 mg/dL). These results suggest that lead levels in milk could pose a potential health hazard to the breastfed infant but only in those moms with high plasma lead levels.

In another rather elegant study of milk lead levels, Gulson et.al. collected samples from 21 mothers and 24 infants over a 6 month period.[4] They reported lead concentrations in milk ranging from 0.09-3.1 µg Pb/kg or ppb (mean 0.73 µg/kg) while the blood lead levels were all less than 5 µg/dL with exception of one mother. The major source of lead to the infant during this period was from maternal bone and diet.

Nashashibi reports on the transfer of lead from the mother to fetus and into her breastmilk.[5] In a group of 47 women, the mean maternal blood lead concentration was 14.9 µg/dL, while in milk the mean lead level was 2.0 µg/dL. Mean lead level in cord blood was 13.1 µg/dL. These data suggest a close correlation between maternal blood and cord blood lead levels, and maternal blood and milk levels.

Lead exposure to military personnel on firing ranges has been questioned. Lead levels in frequent target shooters are known to be elevated as a result of exposure to lead from unjacketed bullets and lead in primers. Breastfeeding mothers should avoid confined, unventilated ranges, but brief exposure to military firing in well-ventilated areas with jacketed bullets is probably safe. Individuals should avoid dust in such areas, sweeping, or cleaning of fire ranges.[7]

In the last decade, the permissible blood level (according to CDC) in children has dropped from 25 to less than 10 µg/dL. Lead poisoning is known to significantly alter IQ and neuropsychologic development, particularly in infants. Therefore, infants receiving breastmilk from mothers with high lead levels should be closely

Pregnancy Risk Category:

Lactation Risk Category: L5

Adult Concerns: Constipation, abdominal pain, anemia, anorexia, vomiting, lethargy.

Pediatric Concerns: Pediatric lead poisoning, but appears unlikely via milk. More likely environmental.

Drug Interactions:

Relative Infant Dose:

Adult Dose:

Alternatives:

T ½	= 20-30 years (bone)	M/P	=
PHL	=	PB	=
Tmax	=	Oral	= 5-10%
MW	= 207	pKa	=
Vd	=		

References:

1. Namihira D, Saldivar L, Pustilnik N, Carreon GJ, Salinas ME. Lead in human blood and milk from nursing women living near a smelter in Mexico City. J Toxicol Environ Health 1993; 38 (3):225-232.
2. Baum C, Shannon M. Lead-Poisoned lactating women have insignificant lead in breast milk. J Clin Toxicol 1995; 33 (5):540-541.
3. Li PJ, Sheng YZ, Wang QY, Gu LY, Wang YL. Transfer of lead via placenta and breast milk in human. Biomed Environ Sci 2000; 13 (2):85-89.
4. Gulson BL, Jameson CW, Mahaffey KR, Mizon KJ, Patison N, Law AJ, Korsch MJ, Salter MA. Relationships of lead in breast milk to lead in blood, urine, and diet of the infant and mother. Environ Health Perspect 1998; 106 (10):667-674.
5. Nashashibi N, Cardamakis E, Bolbos G, Tzingounis V. Investigation of kinetic of lead during pregnancy and lactation. Gynecol Obstet Invest 1999; 48 (3):158-162.
6. Manton WI, Angle CR, Stanek KL, Kuntzelman D, Reese YR, Kuehnemann TJ. Release of lead from bone in pregnancy and lactation. Environ Res 2003; 92:139-151.
7. Gelberg KH, Depersis R. Lead exposure among target shooters. Arch Environ Occup Health. Summer 2009;64 (2):115-120.

LEFLUNOMIDE

L4

Trade: Arava
Other Trades:
Uses: Antimetabolite anti-inflammatory
AAP: Not reviewed

Leflunomide is a new anti-inflammatory agent used for arthritis. It is an immunosuppressant that reduces pyrimidine synthesis.[1] Leflunomide is metabolized to the active metabolite referred to as M1, which has a long half-life and slow elimination. This product is a potent immunosuppressant with a potential elevated risk of malignancy and teratogenicity in pregnant women. It is not known if it transfers into human milk, but use of this product while breastfeeding would be highly risky.

Pregnancy Risk Category: X

Lactation Risk Category: L4

Adult Concerns: Hypertension, diarrhea, respiratory infection, alopecia and rash are the most common adult side effects.

Pediatric Concerns: None via milk, but due to the danger of this product, breastfeeding is not recommended.

Drug Interactions: Cholestyramine produces a rapid reduction of plasma levels of the active metabolite. A significant increase in hepatotoxicity with admixed with other hepatotoxic drugs. Increased plasma drug levels (M1) when used with NSAIDs and rifampin May increase plasma free drug levels of tolbutamide.

Relative Infant Dose:

Adult Dose: 20 mg daily

Alternatives:

T ½	= >15-18 hours	M/P	=
PHL	=	PB	=
Tmax	= 6-12 hours	Oral	= 80%
MW	= 270	pKa	=
Vd	=		

References:

1. Pharmaceutical Manufacturer Prescribing Information. 1999.

LEPIRUDIN   L2

Trade: Refludan
Other Trades:
Uses: Thrombin inhibitor, anticoagulant
AAP: Not reviewed

Lepirudin is a large MW polypeptide that is a direct inhibitor of thrombin. It is a polypeptide that consists of 65 amino acids and has a MW of 6979 daltons. It is very unlikely this large peptide would be transported into human milk after 48 hours postnatally. Most risk would be the first 24-48 hours postnatally, when many proteins can be transported into human milk. However, it is still unlikely this agent would be stable or absorbed in the GI tract of an infant.

One study is available on the transfer of lepirudin into breastmilk. A mother experiencing a deep vein thrombosis seven weeks postpartum was given low MW heparins and developed heparin-induced thrombocytopenia. LMWH treatment was stopped and therapy with lepirudin 50 mg twice daily was started. Maternal plasma concentrations of hirudin were 0.5 to 1 mg/L 3 hours after injection. Milk samples 3 hours post-injection contained no detectable levels of hirudin. No untoward effects were noted in the infant who continued to breastfeed.[2] This product would not be orally bioavailable.

Pregnancy Risk Category: B

Lactation Risk Category: L2

Adult Concerns: Hemorrhagic events, bleeding. Bronchospasm, cough, stridor, dyspnea have been reported as common.

Pediatric Concerns: None reported via milk. Levels undetectable.

Drug Interactions: Additive with other anticoagulants such as coumarin, or antithrombotic agents, etc.

Relative Infant Dose:

Adult Dose: 0.15 mg/kg/hour administered continuously.

Alternatives:

T ½	= 1.3 hours	M/P	=
PHL	=	PB	=
Tmax	= 3-4 hours sc	Oral	= Nil
MW	= 6979	pKa	=
Vd	=		

References:
1. Pharmaceutical Manufacturers Prescribing Information, 2003.
2. Lindhoff-Last E, Willeke A, Thalhammer C, Nowak G, Bauersachs R. Hirudin treatment in a breastfeeding woman. Lancet 2000 Feb 5; 335:467-68.

LETROZOLE   L4

Trade: Femara
Other Trades:
Uses: Aromatase inhibitor of estrogen synthesis
AAP: Not reviewed

Letrozole is an aromatase inhibitor of estrogen synthesis and is used to treat estrogen-receptor positive breast cancer and other syndromes.[1] No data are available on its transfer to human milk but I would suspect the levels are low. However, it has a very long half-life which is concerning in a breastfed infant and could lead to higher plasma levels over time. Therefore, the transfer of small amounts of this agent to an infant could seriously impair bone growth or sexual development of an infant and for this reason it is probably somewhat hazardous to use in a breastfeeding mother.

Pregnancy Risk Category: D

Lactation Risk Category: L4

Adult Concerns: Adverse reactions include fatigue, chest pain, edema, hot flushes, hypertension, nausea, constipation, diarrhea, vomiting, bone pain, back pain, arthralgia, limb pain, dyspnea, cough, and chest wall pain.

Pediatric Concerns: None reported via milk, but this agent is probably too hazardous to use in a breastfeeding woman.

Drug Interactions: Tamoxifen may reduce letrozole plasma levels by 38%.

Relative Infant Dose:

Adult Dose: 2.5 mg/day.

Alternatives:

T ½	= 48 hours	M/P	=
PHL	=	PB	= Weak
Tmax	=	Oral	= 90%
MW	= 285	pKa	=
Vd	= 1.9		

References:
1. Pharmaceutical Manufacturers prescribing information, 2003.

LEUPROLIDE ACETATE   L5

Trade: Lupron, Viadur
Other Trades: Prostap
Uses: Gonadotropin-Releasing Hormone Analog
AAP: Not reviewed

Leuprolide is a synthetic nonapeptide analog of naturally occurring gonadotropin-releasing hormone with greater potency than the naturally occurring hormone. After initial stimulation, it inhibits gonadotropin release from the pituitary and after sustained use, suppresses ovarian and testicular hormone synthesis (2-4 weeks).[1] Almost complete suppression of estrogen, progesterone, and testosterone result.[2] Although Lupron is contraindicated in pregnant women, no reported birth defects have been reported in humans. It is commonly used prior to fertilization but should never be used during pregnancy.

It is not known whether leuprolide transfers into human milk, but due to its nonapeptide structure, it is not likely that its transfer would be extensive. In addition, animal studies have found that it has zero oral bioavailability; therefore, it is unlikely it would be orally bioavailable in the human infant if ingested via milk. Its effect on lactation is unknown, but it could suppress lactation particularly early postpartum.[3] Lupron would reduce estrogen and progestin levels to menopausal ranges, which may or may not suppress lactation, depending on the duration of lactation. Interestingly, several studies show no change in prolactin levels although these were not in lactating women. One study of a hyperprolactinemic patient showed significant suppression of prolactin which is the reason for my L5 risk categorization. It is of no risk to the breastfed infant, only to milk production.

Pregnancy Risk Category: X
Lactation Risk Category: L5

Adult Concerns: Vasomotor hot flashes, gynecomastia, edema, bone pain, thrombosis, and GI disturbances. Body odor, fever, headache.

Pediatric Concerns: May suppress lactation, particularly early in lactation.

Drug Interactions:

Relative Infant Dose:

Adult Dose: 3.75 mg every month

Alternatives:

T ½	= 3.6 hours	M/P	=
PHL	=	PB	= 43-49%
Tmax	= 4-6 hours	Oral	= None
MW	= 1400	pKa	=
Vd	= 0.52		

References:
1. Sennello LT, Finley RA, Chu SY, Jagst C, Max D, Rollins DE, Tolman KG. Single-dose pharmacokinetics of leuprolide in humans following intravenous and subcutaneous administration. J Pharm Sci 1986; 75 (2):158-160.
2. Chantilis SJ, Barnett-Hamm C, Byrd WE, Carr BR. The effect of gonadotropin-releasing hormone agonist on thyroid-stimulating hormone and prolactin secretion in adult premenopausal women. Fertil Steril 1995; 64 (4):698-702.
3. Frazier SH. Personnal communication. 1997.

LEVALBUTEROL   L2

Trade: Xopenex
Other Trades:
Uses: Bronchodilator
AAP: Not reviewed

Levalbuterol is the active (R)-enantiomer of the drug substance racemic albuterol. It is a popular and new bronchodilator used in asthmatics.[1] No data are available on breastmilk levels. After inhalation, plasma levels are incredibly low averaging 1.1 nanogram/mL. It is very unlikely that enough would enter milk to produce clinical effects in an infant. This product is commonly used in infancy for asthma and other bronchoconstrictive illnesses.

Pregnancy Risk Category: C

Lactation Risk Category: L2

Adult Concerns: Tachycardia, tremors, dizziness, dyspepsia.

Pediatric Concerns: None reported via milk.

Drug Interactions: Levalbuterol effects are reduce when used with beta blockers. Cardiovascular effects are potentiated when used with MAO inhibitors, tricyclic antidepressants, amphetamines, and inhaled anesthetics (enflurane).

Relative Infant Dose:

Adult Dose: 0.63 mg every 6-8 hours by nebulization

Alternatives:

T ½	= 3.3 hours	M/P	=
PHL	=	PB	=
Tmax	= 0.2 (inhalation)	Oral	= 100%
MW	= 275	pKa	=
Vd	=		

References:
1.   Pharmaceutical Manufacturer Prescribing Information.

LEVETIRACETAM | L3

Trade: Keppra
Other Trades:
Uses: Anticonvulsant
AAP: Not reviewed

Levetiracetam is a popular broad-spectrum antiepileptic agent. In a study of a single patient who received levetiracetam at 7 days postpartum (dose unreported), the breastmilk concentrations of levetiracetam were 99 μM three hours after administration. The corresponding plasma levels were 32 μM (milk/plasma ratio= 3.09). The mother was also ingesting phenytoin (3 x 100 mg/day) as well as valproic acid (4 x 500mg/d). The infant was preterm (36 weeks) and unstable at birth. After the addition of levetiracetam at day 7, the infant became increasingly hypotonic and drank poorly. The infant was removed from the breast and 96 hours later the infant's plasma levetiracetam levels were 6 μM. The authors strongly advise avoidance of levetiracetam, close monitoring of the infant in breastfeeding mothers.[1] In this case, the infant was exposed to three anticonvulsants, and it is difficult to suggest that levetiracetam was solely responsible for the hypnotic condition. This is further supported by the study below.

In a new study of 8 women receiving from 1500 to 3500 mg/day who were studied at birth (seven patients) and one at 10 months, the mean umbilical cord serum/maternal serum ratio was 1.14 (n= 4) at birth suggesting extensive transport of levetiracetam to the fetus.[2] The mean milk/maternal serum concentration ratio was 1.00 (range, 0.7-1.33) at 3 to 5 days after delivery (n= 7). Maternal milk levels ranged from 28 to 153 µM (4.8-26 µg/mL) but averaged 74 µM (12.6 mg/L). At 3 to 5 days after delivery, the infants had very low levetiracetam serum concentrations (<10-15 µM) (1.7-2.5 µg/mL), a finding that persisted during continued breastfeeding. One infant had a levetiracetam level of 77 µM (13 µg/mL) at day 1, but <10 µM at day 4, suggesting infants clear this product rapidly, and that breastfeeding contributes only a minimal dose. No malformations were detected at birth. No adverse effects were noted in any of the breastfeeding infants. The authors conclude that levetiracetam passes to the infant, but breast fed infants have very low serum concentrations, suggesting a rapid elimination of levetiracetam.

Another study of 14 women receiving 1,000 to 3,000 mg per day had a milk-to-plasma ratio of 1.05, with an infant dose of 2.4 mg/kg/day, or 7.9% of the maternal dose. Plasma concentrations in the infants were 13% of those in the mother's plasma, ranging from 4 to 20 µmol/L. There was no evidence of accumulation of levetiracetam in this study. The authors suggest that this study should be reassuring for breastfeeding mothers taking levetiracetam.[3]

Pregnancy Risk Category: C

Lactation Risk Category: L3

Adult Concerns: Somnolence, weakness, infection, headache, and dizziness.

Pediatric Concerns: None reported in one study of 8 patients.

Drug Interactions: Levetiracetam may significantly increase phenytoin plasma levels by as much as 52%.

Relative Infant Dose: 3.4% - 7.8%

Adult Dose: 1000 - 3000 mg daily.

Alternatives: Gabapentin, lamotrigine

T ½	= 6-8 hours	M/P	= 1.0
PHL	=	PB	= <10%
Tmax	= 1 hour	Oral	= 100%
MW	= 170	pKa	=
Vd	= 0.7		

References:
1. Kramer G, Hosli I, et.al. Levetiracetam accumulation in human breast milk. Epilepsia 2002; 43 (supplement 7):105.
2. Johannessen SI, Helde G, Brodtkorb E. Levetiracetam concentrations in serum and in breast milk at birth and during lactation. Epilepsia. 2005; 46:775-777.
3. Tomson T, Palm R, et.al. Pharmacokinetics of Levetiracetam during Pregnancy, Delivery, in the Neonatal Period, and Lactation. Epilepsia 2007; 48 (6):1111-1116.

LEVOBUNOLOL   L3

Trade: Bunolol
Other Trades: Betagan, Ophtho-Bunolol
Uses: Beta blocker for glaucoma
AAP: Not reviewed

Levobunolol is a typical beta blocker used ophthalmically for treatment of glaucoma.[1] Some absorption has been reported, with resultant bradycardia in patients. No data on transfer to human milk are available.

Pregnancy Risk Category: C

Lactation Risk Category: L3

Adult Concerns: Bradycardia, hypotension, headache, dizziness, fatigue, lethargy.

Pediatric Concerns: None reported via milk, but transfer of some beta blockers is reported. Observe for lethargy, hypotension, bradycardia, apnea.

Drug Interactions: May have increased toxicity when used with other systemic beta adrenergic blocking agents. May produce bradycardia following use with quinidine and verapamil.

Relative Infant Dose:

Adult Dose: 1-2 drops BID

Alternatives:

T ½	= 6.1 hours	M/P	=
PHL	=	PB	=
Tmax	= 3 hours	Oral	= Complete
MW	= 291	pKa	=
Vd	= 5.5		

References:
1. Pharmaceutical Manufacturer Prescribing Information. 1997.

LEVOCABASTINE   L2

Trade: Livostin
Other Trades:
Uses: Ophthalmic antihistamine for itching
AAP: Not reviewed

Levocabastine is an antihistamine primarily used via nasal spray and eye drops.[1] It is used for allergic rhinitis and ophthalmic allergies.[1] After application to eye or nose, very low levels are attained in the systemic circulation (<1 ng/mL). In one nursing mother, it was calculated that the daily dose of levocabastine in the infant was about 0.5 µg, far too low to be clinically relevant.

Pregnancy Risk Category: C

Lactation Risk Category: L2

Adult Concerns: Sedation, dry mouth, fatigue, eye and nasal irritation.

Pediatric Concerns: None reported via milk.

Drug Interactions:

Relative Infant Dose:

Adult Dose: 1 drop QID

Alternatives:

T ½	= 33-40 hours	M/P	=
PHL	=	PB	=
Tmax	= 1-2 hours	Oral	= 100%
MW	=	pKa	=
Vd	=		

References:
1. Pharmaceutical Manufacturer Prescribing Information. 1996.

LEVOCARNITINE   L3

Trade: Carnitor, Carnitor SF
Other Trades:
Uses: Dietary Supplement
AAP: Not reviewed

Levocarnitine supplements carnitine, a natural metabolic compound that facilitates the transfer of fatty acids into the mitochondria, thus ensuring energy production. A deficiency can be associated with excess acyl CoA esters and disruption of intermediary metabolism.[1] Supplementation has not been studied in nursing mothers but it not likely hazardous.

Pregnancy Risk Category: B

Lactation Risk Category: L3

Adult Concerns: Adverse effects include injection site pain, hypotension, diarrhea, hypervolemia, and pharyngitis.

Pediatric Concerns: No data available.

Drug Interactions:

Relative Infant Dose:

Adult Dose: 50 mg/kg every 3 hours

Alternatives:

T ½	= 17.4 hours	M/P	=
PHL	=	PB	= Low
Tmax	= 3.3 hours	Oral	= 10-20%
MW	= 161	pKa	=
Vd	=		

References:
1. Pharmaceutical Manufacturer Prescribing Information. 2005.

LEVOCETIRIZINE   L3

Trade: Xyzal
Other Trades:
Uses: Antihistamine
AAP: Not reviewed

Leveocetirizine is a third-generation non-sedating antihistamine. It is the active metabolite (L-enantiomer) of cetirizine. It has twice the binding affinity at the H1-receptor compared to cetirizine. No data on the transfer into human milk are available at this time. Just as with cetirizine, it is probably compatible with breastfeeding.

Pregnancy Risk Category: B

Lactation Risk Category: L3

Adult Concerns: Sedation, fatigue, dry mouth.

Pediatric Concerns: None reported via milk.

Drug Interactions: Increased sedation when administered with alcohol or other sedatives.

Relative Infant Dose:

Adult Dose: 5 mg daily.

Alternatives:

T ½	= 8 hours	M/P	=
PHL	=	PB	= 92%
Tmax	= 1 hour	Oral	= Complete
MW	= 389	pKa	=
Vd	= 0.4		

References:
1.   Pharmaceutical manufacturers prescribing information, 2010.

LEVODOPA   L4

Trade: Dopar, Larodopa
Other Trades: Sinemet, Prolopa, Endo Levodopa/Carbidopa,
          Kinson, Madopar, Brocadopa, Eldopa, Weldopa
Uses: Antiparkinsonian
AAP: Not reviewed

Levodopa is a prodrug of dopamine used primarily for parkinsonian symptoms. Its use during pregnancy is extremely dangerous. In one group of 30 patients, levodopa significantly reduced prolactin plasma levels.[1] It could under certain circumstances reduce milk production as well.

In a study of one mother with Parkinsonism, peak breast milk levodopa was measured to be 1.6 nmol/mL 3 hours after Sinemet CR 50/200 at steady state, and returned to baseline after 6 hours. Following administration of immediate release Sinemet, milk concentrations peaked at 3.47 nmol/mL after 3 hours, and returned to baseline in 6 hours. Based on milk concentrations, the infant would have ingested a maximum of 0.023 mg/kg, much less than the dose for a 6 month old with Parkinsonism. No adverse reactions were noted in the breastfed infant, as the ingested amount was subtherapeutic.[2]

Warning: Levodopa is known to suppress prolactin production in normal, and breastfeeding mothers.[3,4,5] In one group of 6 postpartum women (2-4 days), levodopa suppressed basal serum prolactin levels by as much as 78%.[6]

Pregnancy Risk Category: C

Lactation Risk Category: L4 (suppress lactation)

Adult Concerns: Nausea, vomiting, anorexia, orthostatic hypotension. Reduces prolactin levels and may reduce milk production. Do not use in glaucoma patients with MAO inhibitors, asthmatics, peptic ulcer disease, or parkinsonian disease.

Pediatric Concerns: None reported via milk, but reduce prolactin levels may reduce milk production.

Drug Interactions: MAO inhibitors may predispose to hypertensive reactions. Decreased effect when administered with phenytoin, pyridoxine, phenothiazines.

Relative Infant Dose: 1.7%

Adult Dose: 1-2 g TID

Alternatives:

T ½	= 1-3 hours	M/P	=
PHL	=	PB	= <36%
Tmax	= 1-2 hours	Oral	= 41%-70%
MW	= 197	pKa	=
Vd	=		

References:

1. Barbieri C, Ferrari C, Caldara R, Curtarelli G. Growth hormone secretion in hypertensive patients: evidence for a derangement in central adrenergic function. Clin Sci (Lond) 1980; 58 (2):135-138.
2. Thulin PC, Woodward WR, Carter JH, Nutt JG. Levodopa in human breast milk: Clinical implications. Neurology 1998; 50:1920-1921.
3. Ayalon D, Peyser MR et al. Effect of L-dopa on galactopoiesis and gonadotropin levels in the inappropriate lactation syndrome. Obstet Gynecol. 1974;44:159-70.
4. Leblanc H, Yen SS. The effect of L-dopa and chlorpromazine on prolactin and growth hormone secretion in normal women. Am J Obstet Gynecol. 1976;126:162-4.
5. Board JA, Fierro RJ et al. Effects of alpha- and beta-adrenergic blocking agents on serum prolactin levels in women with hyperprolactinemia and galactorrhea. Am J Obstet Gynecol. 1977;127:285-7.
6. Rao R, Scommegna A, Frohman LA. Integrity of central dopaminergic system in women with postpartum hyperprolactinemia. Am J Obstet Gynecol. 1982;143:883-7.

LEVOFLOXACIN   L3

Trade: Levaquin, Quixin
Other Trades:
Uses: Fluoroquinolone antibiotic
AAP: Not reviewed

Levofloxacin is a pure (S) enantiomer of the racemic fluoroquinolone Ofloxacin. Its kinetics, including milk levels, should be identical to Ofloxacin.[1,2] The use of fluoroquinolones is increasing in pediatrics due to minimal toxicity.[3]

In one case report of a mother receiving 500 mg/day, the 24 hour average milk level was reported to be approximately 5 µg/mL.[4] A peak level of 8.2 µg/mL was reported, and occurred at 5 hours after the dose. The half-life of levofloxacin in milk was estimated to be 7 hours, which would result in undetectable amounts in milk after 48 hours. The authors report the absolute infant dose would be 1.23 mg/kg/day, although this was calculated from the highest milk level of 8 samples.

While the peak levels were reported to be 8.2 μg/mL, the average milk level reported was 5 μg/mL. Using this data, the relative infant dose would range from 10.5% to 17%. However, the time-to-peak interval reported in this case was 5 hours, rather than 1-1.8 hours reported following both oral and IV doses in the prescribing information. Of the 10 reported levels in this study, only 1 was above 5 μg/mL. Thus the reported average level of 5 μg/mL is probably consistent with other data. This suggests a milk/plasma ratio of approximately 0.95 which is probably correct. Thus, levofloxacin concentrations in milk peak around 1-1.8 hours and at levels close to plasma levels. Observe the infant for changes in gut flora, candida overgrowth, or diarrhea.

Pregnancy Risk Category: C

Lactation Risk Category: L3

Adult Concerns: Nausea, vomiting, diarrhea, abdominal cramps, GI bleeding.

Pediatric Concerns: None reported in one case as milk levels are quite low. Observe for changes in gut flora.

Drug Interactions: Decreased absorption with antacids. Quinolones cause increased levels of caffeine, warfarin, cyclosporine, theophylline. Cimetidine, probenecid, azlocillin may increase ofloxacin levels. Increased risk of seizures when used with foscarnet.

Relative Infant Dose: 10.5% - 17.2%

Adult Dose: 500 mg daily

Alternatives: Norfloxacin, ofloxacin, ciprofloxacin

T ½	= 6-8 hours	M/P	= 0.95
PHL	=	PB	= 24-38%
Tmax	= 1-1.8 hours	Oral	= 99%
MW	= 370	pKa	=
Vd	= 1.27		

References:

1. Pharmaceutical Manufacturer Prescribing Information.
2. McEvoy GE. (ed): AFHS Drug Information. New York, NY: 1997.
3. Ghaffar F, McCracken GH. Quinolones in Pediatrics. In: Hooper DC, Rubinstein E, editors. Quinolone Antimicrobial Agents. Washington, D.C.: ASM Press, 2003: 343-354.
4. Cahill JB, Bailey EM, Chien S, Johnson GM. Levofloxacin Secretion in Breast Milk: A Case Report. Pharmacother 2005; 25 (1):116-118.

LEVONORGESTREL   L2

Trade: Norplant, Seasonale, Mirena IUD, Next Choice
Other Trades: Norplant, Triquilar, Levelen, Microlut, Microval,
          Norgeston, Levonelle, NorLevo
Uses: Implantable, oral, and intrauterine contraceptive
AAP: Maternal Medication Usually Compatible with
          Breastfeeding

Levonorgestrel (LNG) is the active progestin in Norplant and
Mirena. Norplant is a contraceptive method that involves placing
six match-size, flexible capsules under the skin of a woman's upper
arm. These release a low dose of synthetic progestin continuously
for up to five years. Mirena is a levonorgestrel-releasing intrauterine
(IUD) contraceptive that delivers 20   µg/day of levonorgestrel
directly into the uterus and protects against pregnancy for up
to 5 full years. The contraceptive effect of Mirena is mainly
based on the local effects of levonorgestrel in the uterine cavity.

From several studies, levonorgestrel appears to produce limited if
any effect on milk volume or quality.[1] One report of 120 women with
implants at 5-6 weeks postpartum showed no change in lactation.[2] The
level of progestin in the infant is approximately 10% that of maternal
circulation. In a study of 9 women who were taking levonorgestrel oral
minipills (30 µg daily) and 10 women who were using the subdermal
implants from 4-15 weeks postpartum, no significant differences
in infant follicle stimulating hormone (FSH), luteinizing hormone
(LH), or testosterone levels in urine were noted when compared
to controls.[3] These results suggest that the sexual development
of children exposed via milk to trace levels of LNG is normal.

The plasma concentration of levonorgestrel produced by Mirena
are even lower than those produced by LNG contraceptive implants
and with oral contraceptives. Because Mirena produces even lower
plasma levels of this progestin, it is probably less likely to affect
milk production than oral or implantable forms of progestins.

In a recent study of 163 and 157 women who received Mirena
intrauterine systems, or a Copper T380A intrauterine device
respectively, no change in breastfeeding rate, infant growth, or infant
development was noted over 12 months in either the LNG-containing
insert, or the copper insert.[4] Only approximately 0.1% of the serum
dose of LNG has been reported to transfer via milk to infants.[5]
Increased endometrial copper concentrations have been noted in a

study of 95 breastfeeding mothers with copper intrauterine devices, but no change was noted in serum or milk copper concentrations.[6]

The data from the levonorgestrel-only intrauterine devices suggests minimal to no effect on breastfeeding, but some caution is recommended as I've received three accounts of milk suppression following insertion of Mirena IUDs.

The new oral contraceptive Seasonale is extended-cycle oral contraceptive and contains both levonorgestrel and ethinyl estradiol. It is used continuously for a three month period followed by withdrawal and menstruation. Due to its estrogen content, caution is recommended in breastfeeding mothers due to potential reduced milk supply.

Plan B, Levonelle, or NorLevo: Nursing women at risk of pregnancy, may be candidates for the use of post-coital emergency contraception. These agents contain a high dose of levonorgestrel (1.5 mg). In a recent study, 12 exclusively breastfeeding mothers who received a single 1.5 mg dose, levonorgestrel concentrations peaked in plasma and in milk 1-4 h and 2-4 h after dosing, respectively.[7] Milk/plasma ratios averaged 0.28. The estimated infant dose of levonorgestrel was only 1.6 µg during the first 24 hours. If the mother interrupts breastfeeding for 8 hours, this dose was reduced to only 1 µg. The authors recommended that to limit exposure, the mother should not breastfeed for the first 8 hours, or at most 24 hours. The amount in milk after 24 hours was only 0.09% of the total dose.

Pregnancy Risk Category: X

Lactation Risk Category: L2
L3 for Seasonale

Adult Concerns: Interruption of the menstrual cycle and spotting, with headache, weight gain, and occasional depression.

Pediatric Concerns: None reported via milk. However, Seasonale should be used with caution due to estrogen content. Some mothers have reported reduced milk supply with some oral and injectable progestin-only contraceptives.

Drug Interactions: Reduced effect of carbamazepine and phenytoin.

Relative Infant Dose:

Adult Dose: Six 36 mg capsules subcutaneously

Alternatives:

T ½	= 24 hours	M/P	=
PHL	=	PB	= 97%
Tmax	= 1-2 hours	Oral	= Complete
MW	= 312	pKa	=
Vd	=		

References:

1. Shaaban MM, Salem HT, Abdullah KA. Influence of levonorgestrel contraceptive implants, NORPLANT, initiated early postpartum upon lactation and infant growth. Contracep 1985; 32 (6):623-635.
2. Shaaban MM. Contraception with progestogens and progesterone during lactation. J Steroid Biochem Mol Biol 1991; 40 (4-6):705-710.
3. Shikary ZK, Betrabet SS, Toddywala WS, Patel DM, Datey S, Saxena BN. Pharmacodynamic effects of levonorgestrel (LNG) administered either orally or subdermally to early postpartum lactating mothers on the urinary levels of follicle stimulating hormone (FSH), luteinizing hormone (LH) and testosterone (T) in their breast-fed male infants. Contracep 1986; 34 (4):403-412.
4. Shaamash AH, Sayed GH, Hussien MM, Shaaban MM. A comparative study of the levonorgestrel-releasing intrauterine system Mirena (R) versus the Copper T380A intrauterine device during lactation: breast-feeding performance, infant growth and infant development. Contracep 2005 Nov; 72 (5):346-51.
5. Haukkamaa M, Holma P. Five year clinical performance of the new formulation of the levonorgestrel releasing intrauterine system and serum levonorgestrel concentration with the new formulation compared to that with the original one. Leiras Clinical Study Report 1996.
6. Rodrigues da Cunha AC, Dorea JG, Cantuaria AA. Intrauterine device and maternal copper metabolism during lactation. Contracep 2001; 63 (1):37-39.
7. Gainer E, Massai R, Lillo S, Reyes V, Forcelledo ML, Caviedes R, Villarroel C, Bouyer J. Levonorgestrel pharmacokinetics in plasma and milk of lactating women who take 1.5 mg for emergency contraception. Hum Reprod. 2007 Jun;22 (6):1578-84.

LEVONORGESTREL (Plan B) | L2

Trade: Plan B
Other Trades:
Uses: Emergency contraceptive
AAP: Not reviewed

Levonorgestrel is a progestin that can be used as an emergency contraceptive. It is believed to act by preventing ovulation or fertilization by altering tubal transport of sperm and/or ova.[1] It may as well partially inhibit implantation by altering the endometrium. For more details on detailed monograph on levonorgestrel.

Plan B is an emergency contraceptive that can be used to prevent pregnancy following unprotected intercourse or a known or suspected contraceptive failure. It is not effective if the woman is already pregnant, or once the process of implantation has begun. To obtain maximal efficacy, the first tablet should be taken as soon as possible within 72 hours of intercourse. The second tablet should be taken 12 hour later.

A study of 12 breastfeeding mothers showed levonorgestrel peak concentrations in plasma at 1 to 4 hours post dose, and in milk 2 to 4 hours post dose after a 1.5 mg dose of levonorgestrel. Estimated infant exposure to the drug was 1.6 µg on the day of the dose, 0.3 µg the day after, and 0.2 µg on the third day. Therefore, nursing mothers who use relatively high doses of levonorgestrel are recommended to discontinue nursing for at least 8 hours post dose, and should resume feeding within 24 hours.[2]

Pregnancy Risk Category: X

Lactation Risk Category: L2

Adult Concerns: Adverse effects include nausea (23%), vomiting (6%), abdominal pain, fatigue, headache, heavier menstrual bleeding, dizziness, breast tenderness.

Pediatric Concerns: None reported via milk, but this progestin is unlikely to bother a breastfed infant or alter milk production in general.

Drug Interactions:

Relative Infant Dose:

Adult Dose: 0.75 mg (one tablet) initially following in 12 hours by second tablet.

Alternatives:

T ½	= 11-45	M/P	=
PHL	=	PB	=
Tmax	= 1.6 hours	Oral	= Complete
MW	= 312	pKa	=
Vd	=		

References:

1. Pharmaceutical Manufacturers prescribing information, 2003.
2. Gainer E, Massai R, Lillo S, Reyes V, Forcelledo ML, Caviedes R, Villarroel C, Bouyer J. Levonorgestrel pharmacokinetics in plasma and milk of lactating women who take 1.5 mg for emergency contraception. Hum Reprod 2007; 22 (6):1578-1584.

LEVONORGESTREL + ETHINYL ESTRADIOL — L3

Trade: Preven
Other Trades:
Uses: Emergency contraceptive
AAP: Not reviewed

Levonorgestrel and ethinyl estradiol (Preven) can be used as an emergency contraceptive.[1] It is believed to act by preventing ovulation or fertilization by altering tubal transport of sperm and/or ova. It may as well partially inhibit implantation by altering the endometrium. For more details on each ingredient see their individual monographs.

Preven is an emergency contraceptive that can be used to prevent pregnancy following unprotected intercourse or a known or suspected contraceptive failure. It is not effective if the woman is already pregnant, or once the process of implantation has begun. Each tablet contains 0.25 mg levonorgestrel and 0.05 mg ethinyl estradiol. They should not be used in known or suspected pregnancy, in patients with pulmonary edema, ischemic heart disease, deep vein thrombosis, etc. The initial treatment of 2 tablets should be administered as soon as possible but within 72 hours of unprotected intercourse. This is followed by the second dose of 2 tablets 12 hours later.

Pregnancy Risk Category:

Lactation Risk Category: L3

Adult Concerns: Adverse events include nausea, vomiting, menstrual cycle disturbances, breast tenderness, headaches, abdominal pain, and dizziness.

Pediatric Concerns: None reported in infants via milk. However estrogens and even progestins may in some patients suppress milk production. Caution is recommended.

Drug Interactions:

Relative Infant Dose:

Adult Dose: 2 tablets followed in 12 hours by 2 additional tablets.

Alternatives: Plan B

References:
1. Pharmaceutical Manufacturers prescribing information, 2003.

LEVOTHYROXINE   L1

Trade: Synthroid, Levothroid, Unithroid, Eltroxin, Levoxyl, Thyroid, Levoxyl

Other Trades: Eltroxin, Synthroid, Thyroxine, Oroxine

Uses: Thyroid supplements

AAP: Maternal Medication Usually Compatible with Breastfeeding

Levothyroxine is also called T4. Most studies indicate that minimal levels of maternal thyroid are transferred into human milk, and further, that the amount secreted is extremely low and insufficient to protect a hypothyroid infant even while nursing.[1,2,3] The amount secreted after supplementing a breastfeeding mother is highly controversial and numerous reports conflict. Anderson[4] indicates that levothyroxine is not detectable in breast milk although others using sophisticated assay methods have shown extremely low levels (4 ng/mL). It is generally recognized that some thyroxine will transfer but the amount will be extremely low. It is important to remember that supplementation with levothyroxine is designed to bring the mother into a euthyroid state, which is equivalent to the normal breastfeeding female. Hence, the risk of using exogenous thyroxine is no different than in a normal euthyroid mother. Liothyronine (T3) appears to transfer into milk in higher concentrations than levothyroxine (T4), but liothyronine is seldom used in clinical medicine due to its short half-life (<1 day).[4]

Pregnancy Risk Category: A

Lactation Risk Category: L1

Adult Concerns: Nervousness, tremor, agitation, weight loss.

Pediatric Concerns: None reported via milk.

Drug Interactions: Phenytoin may decrease levothyroxine levels. Cholestyramine may decreased absorption of levothyroxine. May increase oral hypoglycemic requirements and doses. May increase effects of oralanticoagulants. Use with tricyclic antidepressants may increase toxicity.

Relative Infant Dose:

Adult Dose: 75-125 μg daily

Alternatives:

T ½	= 6-7 days	M/P	=
PHL	=	PB	– 99%
Tmax	= 2-4 hours	Oral	= 50-80%
MW	= 798	pKa	=
Vd	=		

References:
1. Mizuta H, Amino N, Ichihara K, Harada T, Nose O, Tanizawa O, Miyai K. Thyroid hormones in human milk and their influence on thyroid function of breast-fed babies. Pediatr Res 1983; 17 (6):468-471.
2. Oberkotter LV. Thyroid function and human breast milk. Am J Dis Child 1983; 137 (11):1131.
3. Sack J, Amado O, Lunenfeld B. Thyroxine concentration in human milk. J Clin Endocrinol Metab 1977; 45 (1):171-173.
4. Anderson PO. Drugs and breast feeding. Semin Perinatol 1979; 3 (3):271-278.

LIDOCAINE   L2

Trade: Xylocaine
Other Trades: Xylocard, Lignocaine, EMLA
Uses: Local anesthetic
AAP: Maternal Medication Usually Compatible with Breastfeeding

Lidocaine is an antiarrhythmic and a local anesthetic. In one study of a breastfeeding mother who received IV lidocaine for ventricular arrhythmias, the mother received approximately 965 mg over 7 hours including the bolus starting doses.[1] At seven hours, breastmilk samples were drawn and the concentration of lidocaine was 0.8 mg/L or 40% of the maternal plasma level (2.0 mg/L). Assuming that the mothers' plasma was maintained at 5 µg/mL (therapeutic= 1.5-5 µg/mL), an infant consuming 1 L per day of milk would ingest approximately 2 mg/day. This amount is exceedingly low in view of the fact that the oral bioavailability of lidocaine is very poor (35%). The lidocaine dose recommended for pediatric arrhythmias is 1 mg/kg given as a bolus. Once absorbed by the liver, lidocaine is rapidly metabolized. These authors suggest that a mother could continue to breastfeed while on parenteral lidocaine.

Dryden and Lo have reported the transfer of lidocaine following tumescent liposuction in a 80 kg patient.[2] The areas undergoing liposuction were infiltrated with a 52.5 mg/kg dose of lidocaine dissolved in 8400 cc of solution (total= 4200 mg). Milk samples were drawn 17 hours, and plasma levels were drawn 18 hours following the procedure because other studies show lidocaine peaks in the plasma compartment at this time postoperatively. Milk levels of lidocaine were 0.55 mg/L while plasma levels were 1.2 mg/L. Breastmilk levels were 46% of the serum level. The authors conclude that it is unlikely toxic levels would be reached in a nursing infant.

In a study of 27 parturients who received an average of 82.1 mg bupivacaine and 183.3 mg lidocaine via an epidural catheter, lidocaine milk levels at 2, 6, and 12 hours post administration were 0.86, 0.46, and 0.22 mg/L respectively.[3] Levels of bupivacaine in milk at 2, 6, and 12 hours were 0.09, 0.06, 0.04 mg/L respectively. The milk/serum ratio bases upon area under the curve values (AUC) were 1.07 and 0.34 for lidocaine and bupivacaine respectively. Based on AUC data of lidocaine and bupivacaine milk levels, the average milk concentration of these agents over 12 hours was 0.5 and 0.07 mg/L. Most of the infants had a maximal APGAR score.

In a study of 7 nursing mothers who received 3.6-7.2 mL of 2% lidocaine without adrenaline, the concentration of lidocaine in milk 3 and 6 hours after injection averaged 97.5 µg/L and 52.7 µg/L respectively.[4] These authors suggest that mothers who receive local injections of lidocaine can safely breastfeed.

Recommended doses are as follows: Caudal blockade, <300 mg; Epidural blockade, <300 mg; Dental nerve block, <100 mg; tumescent liposuction, 4200 mg. When administered as a local anesthetic for dental and other surgical procedures, only small quantities are used, generally less than 40 mg. However, following liposuction, the amount used via instillation in the tissues is quite high. Nevertheless, maternal plasma and milk levels do not seem to approach high concentrations and the oral bioavailability in the infant would be quite low (<35%).

Pregnancy Risk Category: B

Lactation Risk Category: L2

Adult Concerns: Bradycardia, confusion, cardiac arrest, drowsiness, seizures, bronchospasm.

Pediatric Concerns: None reported via milk.

Drug Interactions: Use of local anesthetics with sulfonamides may reduce antibacterial efficacy.

Relative Infant Dose: 0.5% - 3.1%

Adult Dose: 50-100 mg PRN

Alternatives:

T ½	= 1.8 hours	M/P	= 0.4
PHL	= 3 hours (neonate)	PB	– 70%
Tmax	= Immediate (IM, IV)	Oral	= <35%
MW	= 234	pKa	= 7.9
Vd	= 1.3		

References:
1. Zeisler JA, Gaarder TD, De Mesquita SA. Lidocaine excretion in breast milk. Drug Intell Clin Pharm 1986; 20 (9):691-693.
2. Dryden RM, Lo MW. Breast milk lidocaine levels in tumescent liposuction. Plast Reconstr Surg 2000; 105 (6):2267-2268.
3. 2.Ortega D, Viviand X, Lorec AM, Gamerre M, Martin C, Bruguerolle B. Excretion of lidocaine and bupivacaine in breast milk following epidural anesthesia for cesarean delivery. Acta Anaesthesiol Scand 1999; 43 (4):394-397.
4. Giuliani M, Grossi GB, Pileri M, Lajolo C, Casparrini G. Could local anesthesia while breast-feeding be harmful to infants? J Pediatr Gastroenterol Nutr 2001; 32 (2):142-144.

LINCOMYCIN   L2

Trade: Lincocin
Other Trades:
Uses: Antibiotic
AAP: Not reviewed

Lincomycin is an effective antimicrobial used for gram positive and anacrobic infections. It is secreted into breastmilk in small but detectable levels. In a group of 9 mothers who received 500 mg every 6 hours 3 days, breastmilk concentrations ranged from 0.5 to 2.4 mg/L (mean= 1.28). In this same group, the maternal plasma levels averaged 1.37 mg/L.[1] Although effects on infant are unlikely, some modification of gut flora or diarrhea is possible.

Pregnancy Risk Category: C

Lactation Risk Category: L2

Adult Concerns: Diarrhea, changes in GI flora, colitis, blood dyscrasias, jaundice.

Pediatric Concerns: None reported via milk, but observe for GI symptoms such as diarrhea.

Drug Interactions: GI absorption of lincomycin is decreased when used with kaolin-pectin antidiarrheals. The actions of neuromuscular blockers may be enhanced when used with lincomycin.

Relative Infant Dose: 0.7%

Adult Dose: 500 mg every 6-8 hours

Alternatives: Clindamycin

T ½	= 4.4-6.4 hours	M/P	= 0.9
PHL	=	PB	= 72%
Tmax	= 2-4 hours	Oral	= <30%
MW	= 407	pKa	=
Vd	=		

References:
1. Medina A, Fiske N, Hjelt-Harvey I, Brown CD, Prigot A. Absorption, diffusion, and excretion of a new antibiotic lincomycin. Antimicrob Agents Chemother 1963; 161:189-196.

LINDANE   L4

Trade: Kwell, G-well, Scabene

Other Trades: Hexit, Kwellada, PMS-Lindane, Quellada, Desitan

Uses: Pediculicide, scabicide

AAP: Not reviewed

Lindane is an older pesticide also called gamma benzene hexachloride. It is primarily indicated for treatment of pediculus capitis (head lice) and less so for scabies (crab lice).[1,2] Because of its lipophilic nature, it is significantly absorbed through the skin of neonates (up to 13%) and has produced elevated liver enzymes, seizures disorders, and hypersensitivity. It is not recommended for use in neonates or young children. Lindane is transferred into human milk although the exact amounts are unpublished. Estimates by the manufacturer indicate a total daily dose of an infant ingesting 1 liter of milk daily (30 ng/mL) would be approximately 30 μg/day, an amount that would probably be clinically insignificant.

If used in children, lindane should not be left on the skin for more than 6 hours before being wash off as peak plasma levels occur in children at about 6 hours after application. Although there are reports of some resistance, head lice and scabies should generally be treated with permethrin products (NIX, Elimite), which are much safer in pediatric patients. See permethrin.

Pregnancy Risk Category: B

Lactation Risk Category: L4

Adult Concerns: Dermatitis, seizures (excess dose), nervousness, irritability, anxiety, insomnia, dizziness, aplastic anemia, thrombocytopenia, neutropenia.

Pediatric Concerns: Lindane is not recommended for children. Potential CNS toxicity includes lethargy, disorientation, restlessness, and tonic-clonic seizures.

Drug Interactions: Oil based hair dressings may enhance skin absorption.

Relative Infant Dose:

Adult Dose: Topical

Alternatives:

T ½	= 18-21 hours	M/P	=
PHL	= 17-22 hours	PB	=
Tmax	= 6 hours	Oral	=
MW	= 290	pKa	=
Vd	=		

References:
1. Pharmaceutical Manufacturer Prescribing Information. 1996.
2. Drug Facts and Comparisons 1996 ed. ed. St. Louis: 1996.

LINEZOLID   L3

Trade: Zyvox, Zyvoxam, Zyvoxid
Other Trades:
Uses: Antibiotic
AAP: Not reviewed

Linezolid is a new oxazolidinone family of antibiotics primarily used for gram positive infections but has some spectrum for gram negative and anaerobic bacteria. It is active against many strains, including resistant staph aureus (MRSA), streptococcus pneumonia, streptococcus pyogenes, and others. It is indicated for use in patients with vancomycin resistant enterococcus faecium infections, staph aureus pneumonias, resistant streptococcus pneumonia infections, etc.

Linezolid was found in the milk of lactating rats at concentrations similar to plasma levels although the dose was not indicated (rat milk levels are always higher than humans). Using this data, with an average maternal plasma concentration of 11.5 µg/mL and a theoretical milk/ plasma ratio of 1.0, an infant would ingest approximately 1.7 mg/kg/ day following a maternal dose of 1200 mg/day. This amount is likely a high estimate as doses given animals are extraordinarily high and rodent milk levels are generally many times higher than human milk. A number of recent studies in children have found linezolid safe. The half-life is shorter in children which requires dosing more often. Side effects in children are the same as adults. Observe for changes in gut flora and diarrhea.

Pregnancy Risk Category: C

Lactation Risk Category: L3

Adult Concerns: Thrombocytopenia has been reported in one patient. Observe for diarrhea, sometimes induced by overgrowth of C. Difficile (pseudomembranous colitis). Side effects include headache, nausea, tongue discoloration, taste perversion, and vomiting. Note numerous drug-drug interactions.

Pediatric Concerns: None via milk but observe for diarrhea.

Drug Interactions: Linezolid is a reversible, nonselective inhibitor of monoamine oxidase. Therefore it has the potential for interaction with adrenergic and serotonergic agents. This includes phenylephrine, phenylpropanolamine, pseudoephedrine, dopamine, and epinephrine. Thus far coadministration with SSRIs has not posed a problem, but caution is recommended.

Relative Infant Dose:

Adult Dose: 400-600 mg every 12 hours

Alternatives: Clindamycin

T ½	= 5.2 hours	M/P	=
PHL	= 3.0 hours	PB	= 31%
Tmax	= 1.5-2.2 hours	Oral	= 100%
MW	= 337	pKa	=
Vd	= 0.71		

References:
1. Pharmaceutical Manufacturer Prescribing Information.

LIOTHYRONINE   L2

Trade: Cytomel
Other Trades: Tertroxin
Uses: Thyroid supplement
AAP: Not reviewed

Liothyronine is also called T3. It is seldom used for thyroid replacement therapy due to its short half-life. It is generally recognized that only minimal levels of thyroid hormones are secreted in human milk although several studies have shown that hypothyroid conditions only became apparent when breastfeeding was discontinued.[1,2] Although some studies indicate that breastfeeding may briefly protect hypothyroid infants, it is apparent that the levels of T4 and T3 are too low to provide long-term protection from hypothyroid disease.[3,5,6] Levels of T3 reported in milk vary but, in general, are around 238 ng/dl and considerably higher than T4 levels. The maximum amount of T3 ingested daily by an infant would be 357 ng/kg/day, or approximately 1/10 the minimum requirement. From these studies, it is apparent that only exceedingly low levels of T3 are secreted into human milk and are insufficient to protect an infant from hypothyroidism.

Pregnancy Risk Category: A

Lactation Risk Category: L2

Adult Concerns: Tachycardia, tremor, agitation, hyperthyroidism.

Pediatric Concerns: None reported via milk.

Drug Interactions: Cholestyramine and colestipol may reduce absorption of thyroid hormones. Estrogens may decrease effectiveness of thyroid hormones. The anticoagulant effect of certain medications is increased. Serum digitalis levels are reduced in hyperthyroidism or when the hyperthyroid patient is converted to the euthyroid state. Therapeutic effects of digitalis glycosides may be reduced. A decrease in theophylline clearance can be expected.

Relative Infant Dose:

Adult Dose: 25-75 µg daily.

Alternatives:

T ½	= 25 hours	M/P	=
PHL	=	PB	= Low
Tmax	= 1-2 hours	Oral	= 95 %
MW	= 651	pKa	=
Vd	=		

References:

1. Bode HH, Vanjonack WJ, Crawford JD. Mitigation of cretinism by breast-feeding. Pediatrics 1978; 62 (1):13-16.
2. Rovet JF. Does breast-feeding protect the hypothyroid infant whose condition is diagnosed by newborn screening? Am J Dis Child 1990; 144 (3):319-323.
3. Varma SK, Collins M, Row A, Haller WS, Varma K. Thyroxine, tri-iodothyronine, and reverse tri-iodothyronine concentrations in human milk. J Pediatr 1978; 93 (5):803-806.
4. Hahn HB, Jr., Spiekerman AM, Otto WR, Hossalla DE. Thyroid function tests in neonates fed human milk. Am J Dis Child 1983; 137 (3):220-222.
5. Letarte J, Guyda H, Dussault JH, Glorieux J. Lack of protective effect of breast-feeding in congenital hypothyroidism: report of 12 cases. Pediatrics 1980; 65 (4):703-705.
6. Franklin R, O'Grady C, Carpenter L. Neonatal thyroid function: comparison between breast-fed and bottle-fed infants. J Pediatr 1985; 106 (1):124-126.

LISINOPRIL   L3

Trade: Prinivil, Zestril
Other Trades: Prinivil, Apo-Lisinopril, Prinvil, Carace
Uses: Antihypertensive, ACE inhibitor
AAP: Not reviewed

Lisinopril is a typical long-acting ACE inhibitor used as an antihypertensive.[1] No breastfeeding data are available on this product. See enalapril, benazepril, captopril as alternatives.

Pregnancy Risk Category: C in first trimester
                               D in second and third trimesters

Lactation Risk Category: L3

Adult Concerns: Hypotension, headache, cough, GI upset, diarrhea, nausea.

Pediatric Concerns: None reported, but observe for hypotension, weakness.

Drug Interactions: Probenecid increases plasma levels of ACEi. ACEi and diuretics have additive hypotensive effects. Antacids reduce bioavailability of ACE inhibitors. NSAIDS reduce hypotension of ACE inhibitors. Phenothiazines increase effects of ACEi. ACEi increase digoxin and lithium plasma levels. May elevate potassium levels when potassium supplementation is added.

Relative Infant Dose:

Adult Dose: 20-40 mg daily.

Alternatives: Captopril, Enalapril

T ½	= 12 hours	M/P	=
PHL	=	PB	= Low
Tmax	= 7 hours	Oral	= 29%
MW	= 442	pKa	=
Vd	=		

References:
1.   McEvoy GE. (ed):AFHS Drug Information. New York, NY: 2009.

LITHIUM CARBONATE   L3

Trade: Lithobid, Eskalith

Other Trades: Carbolith, Duralith, Lithane, Lithicarb, Camcolit, Liskonum, Phasal

Uses: Antimanic drug in bipolar disorders

AAP: Drugs associated with significant side effects and should be given with caution

Lithium is a potent antimanic drug used in bipolar disorder. Its use in the first trimester of pregnancy may be associated with a number of birth anomalies, particularly cardiovascular.[1] If used during pregnancy, the dose required is generally elevated due to the increased renal clearance during pregnancy. Soon after delivery, maternal lithium levels should be closely monitored as the mother's renal clearance drops to normal in the next several days. Several cases have been reported of lithium toxicity in newborns.

In a study of a 36 year old mother who received lithium during and after pregnancy, the infant's serum lithium level was similar to the mothers at birth (maternal dose= 400 mg) but dropped to 0.03 mmol/L by the sixth day.[2] While the mother's dose increased to 800 mg/day postpartum, the infant's serum level did not rise above 10% of the maternal serum levels. At 42 days postpartum, the maternal and infant serum levels were 1.1 and 0.1 mmol/L respectively.

Some toxic effects have been reported. In a mother receiving 600-1200 mg lithium daily during pregnancy, the concentration of lithium in breast milk at 3 days was 0.6 mEq/L.[3] The maternal and infant plasma levels were 1.5 mEq/L and 0.6 mEq/L respectively at 3 days. In this case the infant was floppy, unresponsive and exhibited inverted T waves which are indicative of lithium toxicity. In another study done 7 days postpartum, the milk and infant plasma levels were 0.3 mEq/L each, while the mother's plasma lithium levels were 0.9 mEq/L.[4] In a case report of a mother receiving 300 mg three times daily and breastfeeding her infant at two weeks postpartum, the mother and infant's lithium levels were 0.62 and 0.31 mmol/L respectively. The infant's neurobehavioral development and thyroid function were reported normal.[5]

In a group of 11 breastfeeding mothers who received from 600 to 1500 mg/day of lithium, the authors found wide interpatient variability in lithium dose offered to the infant through breast milk which ranged from 0% to 30% of maternal weight-adjusted dose.[6]

From these studies it is apparent that lithium can permeate milk and is absorbed by the breastfed infant. If the infant continues to breastfeed, it is strongly suggested that the infant be closely monitored for serum lithium levels, and BUN/Creatinine after 6 weeks or so. Levels drawn too early (7 days) may only reflect in utero exposure. Lithium does not reach steady state levels for approximately 10+ days. Clinicians may wish to wait at least this long prior to evaluating the infant's serum lithium level, or sooner if symptoms occur. In addition, lithium is known to reduce thyroxine production, and periodic thyroid evaluation should be considered. Because hydration status of the infant can alter lithium levels dramatically, the clinician should observe changes in hydration carefully. A number of studies of lithium suggest that lithium administration is not an absolute contraindication to breastfeeding, if the physician monitors the infant closely for elevated plasma lithium.[8] Current studies, as well as unpublished experience, suggest that the infant's plasma levels rise to about 30-40% of the maternal level, most often without untoward effects in the infant. Recent evidence suggests that certain anticonvulsants such as carbamazepine, valproic acid, lamotrigine, and others may be effective as lithium in treating some forms of mania. Because these medications are probably safer to use in breastfeeding mothers, the clinician may wish to explore the use of these medications in certain breastfeeding mothers suffering from bipolar symptoms.[7]

Pregnancy Risk Category: D

Lactation Risk Category: L3 with close observation

Adult Concerns: Nausea, vomiting, diarrhea, frequent urination, tremor, drowsiness.

Pediatric Concerns: In one study cyanosis, T-wave abnormalities, and decreased muscle tone were reported. Other studies report no side effects. Evaluate infant lithium levels along with mothers.

Drug Interactions: Decreased lithium effect with theophylline and caffeine. Increased toxicity with alfentanil. Thiazide diuretics reduce clearance and increase toxicity. NSAIDS, haloperidol, phenothiazines, fluoxetine and ACE inhibitors may increase toxicity.

Relative Infant Dose: 12% - 30.1%

Adult Dose: 600 mg TID

Alternatives: Valproic acid, carbamazepine

T ½	= 17-24 hours	M/P	= 0.24-0.66
PHL	= 17.9 hours	PB	= 0%
Tmax	= 2-4 hours	Oral	= Complete
MW	= 74	pKa	=
Vd	= 0.7-1.0		

References:
1. Schou M. Lithium treatment during pregnancy, delivery, and lactation: an update. J Clin Psychiatry 1990; 51 (10):410-413.
2. Sykes PA, Quarrie J, Alexander FW. Lithium carbonate and breast-feeding. Br Med J 1976; 2 (6047):1299.
3. Tunnessen WW, Jr., Hertz CG. Toxic effects of lithium in newborn infants: a commentary. J Pediatr 1972; 81 (4):804-807.
4. Fries H. Lithium in pregnancy. Lancet 1970; 1 (7658):1233.
5. Montgomery A. Use of lithium for treatment of bipolar disorder during pregnancy and lactation. Academy of breastfeeding Medicine News and Views 1997; 3 (1):4-5.
6. Moretti ME, Koren G, Verjee Z, Ito S. Monitoring lithium in breast milk: an individualized approach for breast-feeding mothers. Ther Drug Monit. 2003 Jun;25 (3):364-6. Review.
7. Llewellyn A, Stowe ZN, Strader JR, Jr. The use of lithium and management of women with bipolar disorder during pregnancy and lactation. J Clin Psychiatry 1998; 59 Suppl 6:57-64.
8. Viguera AC, Newport, DJ, Ritchie J, Stowe Z, Whitfield T, Mogielnicki J, Baldessarini RJ, Zurick A, Cohen LS. Lithium in breast milk and nursing infants: clinical implications. Am J Psychiatry 2007; 164 (2):342-345.

LOMEFLOXACIN   L3

Trade: Maxaquin
Other Trades: Okacyn
Uses: Fluoroquinolone antibiotic
AAP: Not reviewed

Lomefloxacin belongs the fluoroquinolone family of antimicrobials.[1] The fluoroquinolones in general are becoming more popular in pediatric-aged patients due to the introduction of recent studies.[2] In addition, the FDA is reviewing several pediatric indications for this group. At least one case of bloody colitis (pseudomembranous colitis) has been reported in a breastfeeding infant whose mother ingested ciprofloxacin. It is reported that lomefloxacin is excreted in the milk of lactating animals although levels are low.

Pregnancy Risk Category: C

Lactation Risk Category: L3

Adult Concerns: GI distress, diarrhea, colitis, headaches, phototoxicity.

Pediatric Concerns: None   reported   with   this   drug. Pseudomembranous colitis has been reported with another member of this family. Observe closely for bloody diarrhea.

Drug Interactions: Antacids, iron salts, sucralfate, and zinc salts may interfere with the GI absorption of the fluoroquinolones resulting in decreased serum levels. Cimetidine may interfere with the elimination of the fluoroquinolones. Nitrofurantoin may interfere with the antibacterial properties of the fluoroquinolone family. Probenecid may reduce renal clearance as much as 50%. Nephrotoxic side effects of cyclosporine may be significantly increased when used with fluoroquinolones. Phenytoin serum levels may be reduced producing a decrease in therapeutic effects. Anticoagulant effects may be increased when used with fluoroquinolones. Decreased clearance and increased plasma levels and toxicity of theophylline have been reported with the use of the fluoroquinolones.

Relative Infant Dose:

Adult Dose: 400 mg daily.

Alternatives: Norfloxacin, Ofloxacin, Trovafloxacin

T ½	= 8 hours	M/P	=
PHL	=	PB	= 20.6 %
Tmax	= 0.7-2.0 hours	Oral	= 92%
MW	= 351	pKa	=
Vd	= 2		

References:
1. Pharmaceutical Manufacturer Prescribing Information. 1996.
2. Ghaffar F, McCracken GH. Quinolones in Pediatrics. In: Hooper DC, Rubinstein E, editors. Quinolone Antimicrobial Agents. Washington, D.C.: ASM Press, 2003: 343-354.

LOPERAMIDE   L2

Trade: Imodium, Pepto Diarrhea Control, Maalox Anti-Diarrheal Caplets, Kaopectate II Caplets, Imodium Advanced

Other Trades: Novo-Loperamide, Gastro-Stop

Uses: Antidiarrheal drug

AAP: Maternal Medication Usually Compatible with Breastfeeding

Loperamide is an antidiarrheal drug.Because it is only minimally absorbedorally (0.3%), only extremely smallamounts are secreted into breast milk.Following a 4 mg oral dose twice dailyin 6 women (early postpartum), milklevels at 12 hours after the followingdose averaged 0.18 µg/L, and 6 hoursafter the second dose were 0.27 µg/L.[1]A breastfeeding infant consuming 165mL/kg/day of milk would ingest 2000times less than the recommended dailydose. It is very unlikely these reportedlevels in milk (Relative infant dose=0.03%) would ever produce clinicaleffects in a breastfed infant.

Pregnancy Risk Category: B

Lactation Risk Category: L2

Adult Concerns: Fatigue, dry mouth, respiratory depression, dry mouth, and constipation.

Pediatric Concerns: One case of mild delirium has been reported in a 4 year old infant.

Drug Interactions: CNS depressants, phenothiazines, and TCA antidepressants may potentiate adverse effects.

Relative Infant Dose: 0.03%

Adult Dose: 4 mg PRN

Alternatives:

T ½	= 10.8 hours	M/P	= 0.5-0.36
PHL	=	PB	=
Tmax	= 4-5 hours (capsules)	Oral	= 0.3%
MW	= 477	pKa	=
Vd	=		

References:
1. Nikodem VC, Hofmeyr GJ. Secretion of the antidiarrhoeal agent loperamide oxide in breast milk. Eur J Clin Pharmacol 1992; 42 (6):695-696.

LORACARBEF   L2

Trade: Lorabid
Other Trades:
Uses: Synthetic penicillin-like antibiotic
AAP: Not reviewed

Loracarbef is a synthetic beta-lactam antibiotic. It is structurally similar to the cephalosporin family.[1] It is used for gram negative and gram positive infections. Pediatric indications are available for infants 6 months and children to 12 years of age. No data are available on levels in breastmilk.

Pregnancy Risk Category: B

Lactation Risk Category: L2

Adult Concerns: Nausea, vomiting, diarrhea, allergic rashes.

Pediatric Concerns: None reported. Observe for GI changes such as diarrhea.

Drug Interactions: Probenecid may increase levels of cephalosporins by reducing renal clearance.

Relative Infant Dose:

Adult Dose: 200-400 mg BID

Alternatives:

T ½	= 1 hour	M/P	=
PHL	=	PB	- 25%
Tmax	= 1.2 hours	Oral	= 90%
MW	=	pKa	=
Vd	=		

References:
1. Pharmaceutical Manufacturer Prescribing Information. 1995.

LORATADINE

L1

Trade: Claritin
Other Trades: Claratyne, Clarityn
Uses: Long-acting antihistamine
AAP: Maternal Medication Usually Compatible with Breastfeeding

Loratadine is a long-acting antihistamine with minimal sedative properties. During 48 hours following administration, the amount of loratadine transferred via milk was 4.2 µg, which was 0.01% of the administered dose.[1] Through 48 hours, only 6.0 µg of descarboethoxyloratadine (metabolite) (7.5 µg loratadine equivalents) were excreted into breast milk, or 0.029% of the administered dose of loratadine or its active metabolite were transferred via milk to the infant. A 4 kg infant would receive only 0.46% of the loratadine dose received by the mother on a mg/kg basis (2.9 µg/kg/day). It is very unlikely this dose would present a hazard to infants. Loratadine does not transfer into the CNS of adults, so it is unlikely to induce sedation even in infants. The half-life in neonates is not known although it is likely quite long. Pediatric formulations are available.

Pregnancy Risk Category: B

Lactation Risk Category: L1

Adult Concerns: Sedation, dry mouth, fatigue, nausea, tachycardia, palpitations.

Pediatric Concerns: None reported, but observe for sedation, dry mouth, tachycardia.

Drug Interactions: Increased plasma levels of loratadine may result when used with ketoconazole, the macrolide antibiotics, and other products.

Relative Infant Dose: 0.3% - 0.5%

Adult Dose: 10 mg daily.

Alternatives: Cetirizine

T ½	= 8.4-28 hours	M/P	= 1.17
PHL	=	PB	= 97%
Tmax	= 1.5 hours	Oral	= Complete
MW	= 383	pKa	=
Vd	=		

References:
1. Hilbert J, Radwanski E, Affrime MB, Perentesis G, Symchowicz S, Zampaglione N. Excretion of loratadine in human breast milk. J Clin Pharmacol 1988; 28 (3):234-239.

LORAZEPAM   L3

Trade: Ativan
Other Trades: Apo-Lorazepam, Novo-Lorazepam, Almazine
Uses: Antianxiety, sedative drug
AAP: Drugs whose effect on nursing infants is unknown but may be of concern

Lorazepam is a typical benzodiazepine from the Valium family of drugs. It is frequently used prenatally and presurgically as a sedative agent. In one prenatal study, it has been found to produce a high rate of depressed respiration, hypothermia, and feeding problems in newborns.[1] Newborns were found to secrete lorazepam for up to 11 days postpartum. In McBrides's study[2], the infants were unaffected following the prenatal use of 2.5 mg IV prior to delivery. Plasma levels of lorazepam in infants were equivalent to those of the mothers. The rate of metabolism in mother and infant appears slow but equal following delivery. In this study there were no untoward effects noted in any of the infants.

In one patient receiving 2.5 mg twice daily for 5 days postpartum, the breastmilk levels were 12 µg/L.[3] In another patient four hours after an oral dose of 3.5 mg, milk levels averaged 8.5 µg/L.[4] Summerfield reports an average concentration in milk of 9 µg/L and an average milk/plasma ratio of 0.22.[4] It would appear from these studies that the amount of lorazepam secreted into milk would be clinically insignificant under most conditions.

The benzodiazepine family, as a rule, is not ideal for breastfeeding mothers due to relatively long half-lives and the development of dependence. However, it is apparent that the shorter-acting benzodiazepines are safer during lactation provided their use is short-term or intermittent, low dose, and after the first week of life.[5]

Pregnancy Risk Category: D

Lactation Risk Category: L3

Adult Concerns: Sedation, agitation, respiratory depression, withdrawal syndrome.

Pediatric Concerns: None reported via milk, but observe for sedation.

Drug Interactions: Increased sedation when used with morphine, alcohol, CNS depressants, MAO inhibitors, loxapine, and tricyclic antidepressants.

Relative Infant Dose: 2.9%

Adult Dose: 1-3 mg BID-TID

Alternatives: Midazolam

T ½	= 12 hours	M/P	= 0.15-0.26
PHL	=	PB	= 85%
Tmax	= 2 hours	Oral	= 90%
MW	= 321	pKa	= 1.3, 11.5
Vd	= 0.9-1.3		

References:
1. Johnstone M. Effect of maternal lorazepam on the neonate. Br Med J (Clin Res Ed) 1981; 282 (6280):1973-1974.
2. McBride RJ, Dundee JW, Moore J, Toner W, Howard PJ. A study of the plasma concentrations of lorazepam in mother and neonate. Br J Anaesth 1979; 51 (10):971-978.
3. Whitelaw AG, Cummings AJ, McFadyen IR. Effect of maternal lorazepam on the neonate. Br Med J (Clin Res Ed) 1981; 282 (6270):1106-1108.
4. Summerfield RJ, Nielsen MS. Excretion of lorazepam into breast milk. Br J Anaesth 1985; 57 (10):1042-1043.
5. Maitra R, Menkes DB. Psychotropic drugs and lactation. N Z Med J 1996; 109 (1024):217-218.

LORMETAZEPAM   L3

Trade:
Other Trades: Lormetazepam, Noctamid
Uses: Hypntic sedative
AAP: Not reviewed

Lormetazepam is a benzodiazepine available in the UK. It binds to the benzodiazepine receptor and enhances the GABAa receptor. Lormetazepam alters electrical activity in the brain, and thus EEG can be used to measure the sedative effects of lormetazepam.

In one study of 5 breastfeeding women taking 2 mg every evening for 10 days, levels of lormetazepam were below the limits of detection, except in a few milk samples. The milk to plasma ratio was estimated to be no more than 0.06. Lormetazepam transfer to milk is lower than diazepam, N-desmethyldiazepam, and flunitrazepam. The maximum dose that these infants would have received is 100 ng/kg, or about 0.35% of the mothers' dose. No free lormetazepam was found in the infants' plasma, nor were any adverse side effects noted in these infants.[1]

Pregnancy Risk Category: D

Lactation Risk Category: L3

Adult Concerns: Side effects are similar to other benzodiazepams and include drowsiness and sedation.

Pediatric Concerns: Milk levels are extremely low. No untoward side effects were reported in this study.

Drug Interactions:

Relative Infant Dose:

Adult Dose: 1mg every evening

Alternatives: Midazolam, alprazolam

T ½	= 10-12 hours	M/P	=
PHL	=	PB	=
Tmax	=	Oral	= 80%
MW	= 335.2	pKa	=
Vd	=		

References:
1. Humpel M, Stoppelli I, Milia S, Rainer E. Pharmacokinetics and Biotransformation of the New Benzodiazepine, Lormetazepam, in Man. Eur J Clin Pharmacol 1982; 21:421-425.

LOSARTAN   L3

Trade: Cozaar, Hyzaar
Other Trades:
Uses: ACE-like antihypertensive
AAP: Not reviewed

Losartan is a new ACE-like antihypertensive. Rather than inhibiting the enzyme that makes angiotensin such as the ACE inhibitor family, this medication selectively blocks the ACE receptor site preventing attachment of angiotensin II.[1,2] No data are available on its transfer to human milk. Although it penetrates the CNS significantly, its high protein binding would probably reduce its ability to enter milk. This product is only intended for those few individuals who cannot take ACE inhibitors. No data on transfer into human milk are available. The trade name Hyzaar contains losartan plus hydrochlorothiazide.

Pregnancy Risk Category: C in first trimester
                                     D in 2 nd and 3 rd trimesters

Lactation Risk Category: L3

Adult Concerns: Dizziness, insomnia, hypotension, anxiety, ataxia, confusion, depression. Cough, nor angioedema, commonly associated with ACE inhibitors does not apparently occur with losartan.

Pediatric Concerns: None reported.

Drug Interactions: Decreased effect when used with phenobarbital, ketoconazole, troleandomycin, sulfaphenazole. Increased effect when used with cimetidine, moxonidine.

Relative Infant Dose:

Adult Dose: 25-50 mg daily.-BID

Alternatives: Captopril, Enalapril

T ½	= 4-9 hours (metabolite)	M/P	=
PHL	=	PB	= 99.8%
Tmax	= 1 hour	Oral	– 25-33%
MW	=	pKa	=
Vd	= 12		

References:
1. Lacy C. Drug information handbook. Lexi-Comp Inc. Cleveland, OH, 1996.
2. Pharmaceutical Manufacturer Prescribing Information. 1997.

LOVASTATIN	L3

Trade: Mevacor
Other Trades: Apo-Lovastatin
Uses: Hypocholesterolemic
AAP: Not reviewed

Lovastatin is an effective inhibitor of hepatic cholesterol synthesis. It is primarily used for hypercholesterolemia. Pregnancy normally elevates maternal cholesterol and triglyceride levels. Following delivery, lipid levels gradually decline to pre-pregnancy levels within about 9 months.

Small but unpublished levels are known to be secreted into human breastmilk.[1] Less then 5% of a dose reaches the maternal circulation due to extensive first-pass removal by the liver. The effect on the infant is unknown, but it could reduce hepatic cholesterol synthesis. There is little justification for using such a drug during lactation, but due to the extremely small maternal plasma levels, it is unlikely that the amount in breastmilk would be clinically active. Others in this same family of drugs include simvastatin, pravachol, atorvastatin, and fluvastatin. Atherosclerosis is a chronic process, and discontinuation of lipid-lowering drugs during pregnancy and lactation should have little to no impact on the outcome of long-term therapy of primary hypercholesterolemia. Cholesterol and other products of cholesterol biosynthesis are essential components for fetal and neonatal development, and the use of cholesterol-lowering drugs would not be advisable under most circumstances in breastfeeding mothers.

Pregnancy Risk Category: X

Lactation Risk Category: L3

Adult Concerns: Diarrhea, dyspepsia, flatulence, constipation, headache.

Pediatric Concerns: None reported but its use is not recommended.

Drug Interactions: Increased toxicity when added to gemfibrozil (myopathy, myalgia, etc), clofibrate, niacin (myopathy), erythromycin, cyclosporine, oral anticoagulants (elevated bleeding time).

Relative Infant Dose:

Adult Dose: 20-80 mg daily.

Alternatives:

T ½	= 1.1-1.7	M/P	=
PHL	=	PB	= >95%
Tmax	= 2-4 hours	Oral	= 5-30%
MW	= 405	pKa	=
Vd	=		

References:
1. Pharmaceutical Manufacturer Prescribing Information. 1999.

LOXAPINE   L4

Trade: Loxitane
Other Trades: Loxapac, PMS-Loxapine, Loxapac
Uses: CNS tranquilizer
AAP: Not reviewed

Loxapine produces pharmacologic effects similar to the phenothiazines and haloperidol family.[1] The drug does not appear to have antidepressant effects and may lower the seizure threshold. It is a powerful tranquilizer and has been found to be secreted into the milk of animals, but no data are available for human milk. This is a potent tranquilizer than could produce significant sequelae in breastfeeding infants. Caution is urged.

Pregnancy Risk Category: C

Lactation Risk Category: L4

Adult Concerns: Drowsiness, tremor, rigidity, extrapyramidal symptoms.

Pediatric Concerns: None reported, but extreme caution is recommended.

Drug Interactions: Increased toxicity when used with CNS depressants, metrizamide, and MAO inhibitors.

Relative Infant Dose:

Adult Dose: 10-50 mg BID-QID

Alternatives: Haloperidol

T ½	= 19 hours	M/P	=
PHL	=	PB	=
Tmax	= 1-2 hours	Oral	= 33%
MW	= 328	pKa	= 6.6
Vd	=		

References:
1. McEvoy GE. (ed):AFHS Drug Information. New York, NY: 2009.

LSD   L5

Trade:
Other Trades:
Uses: Hallucinogen
AAP: Not reviewed

LSD is a power hallucinogenic drug.[1] No data are available on transfer into breastmilk. However, due to its extreme potency and its ability to pass the blood-brain-barrier, LSD is likely to penetrate milk and produce hallucinogenic effects in the infant. This drug is definitely CONTRAINDICATED. Maternal urine may be positive for LSD for 34-120 hours post ingestion.

Pregnancy Risk Category:

Lactation Risk Category: L5

Adult Concerns: Hallucinations, dilated pupil, salivation, nausea.

Pediatric Concerns: None reported via milk, but due to potency, hallucinations are likely. Contraindicated.

Drug Interactions:

Relative Infant Dose:

Adult Dose:

Alternatives:

T ½	= 3 hours	M/P	=
PHL	=	PB	=
Tmax	= 30-60 minutes (oral)	Oral	= Complete
MW	= 268	pKa	=
Vd	=		

References:
1. Ellenhorn MJ, Barceloux DG. In: Medical Toxicology. New York, NY: Elsevier, 1988.

LUBIPROSTONE   L3

Trade: Amitiza
Other Trades:
Uses: Gastrointestinal Agent
AAP: Not reviewed

Lubiprostone is used for treating chronic idiopathic constipation. It is a local-acting chloride channel activator, which in turn increases chloride-rich intestinal fluid secretion without altering other serum electrolyte concentrations. Increasing the intestinal fluid secretion results in an increased motility in the intestine, and increased passage of stool.[1] No data on the concentration in human milk are available, but given that the oral absorption is nil, plasma levels in the adult are undetectable, and lubiprostone is 94% protein bound, the amount delivered to a breastfeeding infant through milk would likely be nil. Monitor baby for signs of diarrhea but this is unlikely.

Pregnancy Risk Category: C

Lactation Risk Category: L3

Adult Concerns: Adverse effects include headache, nausea, and diarrhea.

Pediatric Concerns: No data are available.

Drug Interactions:

Relative Infant Dose:

Adult Dose: 24 µg bid

Alternatives:

T ½	= 0.9-1.4 hours	M/P	=
PHL	=	PB	= 94%
Tmax	= 1.14 hours	Oral	= Nil
MW	= 390.46	pKa	=
Vd	=		

References:
1. Pharmaceutical Manufacturer Prescribing Information. 2006.

LYME DISEASE

Trade: Lyme Disease, Borrelia
Other Trades:
Uses: Borrelia Burgdorferi infections
AAP: Not reviewed

Lyme disease is caused by infection with the spirochete, borrelia burgdorferi. This spirochete is transferred in-utero to the fetus and is secreted into human milk[1] and can cause infection in breastfed infants.[2] If diagnosed postpartum or in a breastfeeding mother, the mother and infant should be treated immediately. In children (>7 years) and adults, preferred therapy is doxycycline (100 mg PO twice daily for 14-21 days), or amoxicillin (500 mg three times daily for 21 days). In breastfeeding patients, amoxicillin therapy is probably preferred but doxycycline can safely be used. In the infant, use amoxicillin (40 mg/kg/day (max 3 gm) with probenecid (25 mg/kg/day) divided in three doses/day for a duration of 21 days.[3]

Alternative therapy for adults includes clarithromycin (500 mg PO twice daily for 21 days), azithromycin (500 mg PO daily for 14-21 days), or cefuroxime axetil (500 mg PO twice daily for 21 days.[4] Although doxycycline therapy is not definitely contraindicated in breastfeeding mothers, alternates such as amoxicillin, cefuroxime, clarithromycin, or azithromycin should be preferred.

Pregnancy Risk Category:

Lactation Risk Category:

Adult Concerns:

Pediatric Concerns:

Drug Interactions:

Relative Infant Dose:

Adult Dose:

Alternatives:

References:
1. Schmidt BL, Aberer E, Stockenhuber C, Klade H, Breier F, Luger A. Detection of Borrelia burgdorferi DNA by polymerase chain reaction in the urine and breast milk of patients with Lyme borreliosis. Diagn Microbiol Infect Dis 1995; 21 (3):121-128.
2. Stiernstedt G. Lyme borreliosis during pregnancy. Scand J Infect Dis Suppl 1990; 71:99-100.
3. Bartlett JG. In: Pocket Book of Infectious Disease Therapy. Baltimore, USA: Williams and Wilkins, 1996.

4. Nelson JD. In: Pocket Book of Pediatric Antimicrobial Therapy. Baltimore, USA: Williams and Wilkins, 1995.

LYME DISEASE VACCINE | L2

Trade: LYMErix
Other Trades:
Uses: Lyme Disease Vaccine
AAP: Not reviewed

LYMErix is a noninfectious recombinant vaccine containing a lipoprotein from the outer surface of Borrelia burgdorferi. The lipoprotein from this causative agent is a single polypeptide chain of 257 amino acids with lipids covalently bonded to the N terminus.[1] No substance of animal origin is used in the manufacturing process. It is primarily indicated for individuals 15-70 years of age. It is very unlikely to enter milk. Officials from the CDC suggest that it is not contraindicated for use in breastfeeding patients.[2]

Pregnancy Risk Category: C

Lactation Risk Category: L2

Adult Concerns: Pain at injection site, headache, fatigue, arthralgia, myalgia.

Pediatric Concerns: None reported via milk. Unlikely to enter milk compartment.

Drug Interactions: No known interactions have been published. Avoid use in patients taking anticoagulants.

Relative Infant Dose:

Adult Dose:

Alternatives:

References:
1. Pharmaceutical Manufacturer Prescribing Information.
2. Hayes N. Center for Disease Control, Personal communication. 2000.

LYSINE   L2

Trade: Lysine, L-Lysine
Other Trades:
Uses: Amino acid food supplement
AAP: Not reviewed

Lysine is a naturally occurring amino acid; the average American ingests from 6-10 grams daily. Aside from its use as a supplement in patients with poor nutrition, it is most often used for the treatment of recurrent herpes simplex infections. The clinical efficacy of lysine in herpes infections is highly controversial with some advocates[1,2] and many detractors.[3] Upon absorption, most is sequestered in the liver, but blood levels do rise transiently. However, the risk of toxicity is considered quite low in both adults and infants. Rather high doses have been studied in infants as young as 4 months, with doses from 60 to 1080 mg L-lysine per 8 ounces of milk.[4] At the higher level, 5.18 grams of L-lysine was consumed. Plasma lysine levels varied only with normal limits, while urinary lysine levels were roughly proportional to the amount of supplementation.

Thomas et al. has reported an elegant study of the transfer of radiolabeled L-lysine into numerous compartments, including milk.[5,6] In a group of 5 lactating women who received L-lysine (15N-lysine and 13C-lysine (5 mg/kg/each)), milk levels of labeled lysine reached a peak at approximately 150 minutes. Labeled lysine levels in milk were slightly higher with M/P ratios ranging from 1.29 to 1.43. However, the total amount of radiolabeled lysine present in milk was low. Only 0.54% of the administered dose of lysine was secreted into milk proteins. Further, the lysine present in milk was present as protein, not free amino acid.

Therefore supplementation of breastfeeding mothers with L-lysine will probably not result in significantly elevated levels of free lysine in milk.

Pregnancy Risk Category:

Lactation Risk Category: L2

Adult Concerns: GI distress. Lysine may cause cholesterol and triglyceride levels in the blood to rise.

Pediatric Concerns: None reported.

Drug Interactions:

Relative Infant Dose:

Adult Dose:

Alternatives:

T ½	= 3.66 hours	M/P	=
PHL	=	PB	=
Tmax	=	Oral	= 83%
MW	= 146	pKa	=
Vd	=		

References:
1. Griffith RS, Walsh DE, Myrmel KH, Thompson RW, Behforooz A. Success of L-lysine therapy in frequently recurrent herpes simplex infection. Treatment and prophylaxis. Dermatologica 1987; 175 (4):183-190.
2. Walsh DE, Griffith RS, Behforooz A. Subjective response to lysine in the therapy of herpes simplex. J Antimicrob Chemother 1983; 12 (5):489-496.
3. DiGiovanna JJ, Blank H. Failure of lysine in frequently recurrent herpes simplex infection. Treatment and prophylaxis. Arch Dermatol 1984; 120 (1):48-51.
4. Anderson SA, Raiten DJ. (eds): "Safety of Amino Acids in Dietary Supplements." Life Sciences Research Office, Bethesda, MD: FASEB Special Publications Office, 1999.
5. Thomas MR, Irving CS, Reeds PJ, Malphus EW, Wong WW, Boutton TW, Klein PD. Lysine and protein metabolism in the young lactating woman. Eur J Clin Nutr 1991; 45 (5):227-242.
6. Irving CS, Malphus EW, Thomas MR, Marks L, Klein PD. Infused and ingested labeled lysines: appearance in human-milk proteins. Am J Clin Nutr 1988; 47 (1):49-52.

MAGNESIUM HYDROXIDE | L1

Trade: Milk of Magnesia

Other Trades: Citro-Mag, Phillips Milk of Magnesia, Mylanta, Gastrobrom

Uses: Laxative, antacid

AAP: Not reviewed

Poorly absorbed from maternal GI tract. Only about 15-30 % of an orally ingested magnesium product is absorbed. Magnesium rapidly deposits in bone (>50%) and is significantly distributed to tissue sites. See magnesium sulfate.

Pregnancy Risk Category: B

Lactation Risk Category: L1

Adult Concerns: Hypotension, diarrhea, nausea.

Pediatric Concerns: None reported.

Drug Interactions: Decreased absorption of tetracyclines, digoxin, indomethacin, and iron salts.

Relative Infant Dose:

Adult Dose: 5-30 mL PRN

Alternatives:

T ½	=	M/P	=
PHL	=	PB	= 33%
Tmax	=	Oral	= 15-30%
MW	= 58	pKa	=
Vd	=		

References:

MAGNESIUM SULFATE   L1

Trade: Epsom salt
Other Trades: Magnoplasm, Salvital, Zinvit, Epsom Salts
Uses: Saline laxative and anticonvulsant (IV,IM)
AAP: Maternal Medication Usually Compatible with Breastfeeding

Magnesium is a normal plasma electrolyte. It is used pre and postnatally as an effective anticonvulsant in preeclamptic patients. In one study of 10 preeclamptic patients who received a 4 gm IV loading dose followed by 1 gm per hour IV for more than 24 hours, the average milk magnesium levels in treated subjects were 6.4 mg/dl, only slightly higher than controls (untreated) which were 4.77 mg/dl.[1] On day 2, the average milk magnesium levels in treated groups were 3.83 mg/dl, which was not significantly different from untreated controls, 3.19 mg/dl. By day 3, the treated and control groups breastmilk levels were identical (3.54 vs. 3.52 mg/dl). The mean maternal serum magnesium level on day 1 in treated groups was 3.55 mg/dL, which was significantly higher than control untreated, 1.82 mg/dl. In both treated and control subjects, levels of milk magnesium were approximately twice those of maternal serum magnesium levels, with the milk-to-serum ratio being 1.9 in treated subjects and 2.1 in control subjects.

This study clearly indicates a normal concentrating mechanism for magnesium in human milk. It is well known that oral magnesium absorption is very poor, averaging only 4%.[2] Further, this study indicates that in treated groups, infants would only receive about 1.5 mg of oral magnesium more than the untreated controls. It is very unlikely that the amount of magnesium in breastmilk would be clinically relevant.

Pregnancy Risk Category: B

Lactation Risk Category: L1

Adult Concerns: IV-hypotension, sedation, muscle weakness.

Pediatric Concerns: None reported via milk. Sedation, hypotonia following in-utero exposure.

Drug Interactions: May decrease the hypertensive effect of nifedipine. May increase the depression associated with other CNS depressants, neuromuscular blocking agents, and the cardiotoxicity associated with ritodrine.

Relative Infant Dose: 0.2%

Adult Dose: 1-2 g every 4-6 hours PRN

Alternatives:

T ½	= <3 hours	M/P	= 1.9
PHL	=	PB	= 0%
Tmax	= Immediate (IV)	Oral	= 4%
MW	= 120	pKa	=
Vd	=		

References:
1. Cruikshank DP, Varner MW, Pitkin RM. Breast milk magnesium and calcium concentrations following magnesium sulfate treatment. Am J Obstet Gynecol 1982; 143 (6):685-688.
2. Morris ME, LeRoy S, Sutton SC. Absorption of magnesium from orally administered magnesium sulfate in man. J Toxicol Clin Toxicol 1987; 25:371-82.

MANNITOL   L3

Trade: Osmitrol
Other Trades:
Uses: Osmotic diuretic
AAP: Not reviewed

Mannitol is a hexahydroxy alcohol chemically related to mannose and is used as an osmotic diuretic.[1] As such, it does not readily enter the cellular compartment and remains in the extracellular compartment. Hepatic metabolism is minimal and the drug is primarily excreted unchanged in the urine by glomerular filtration. The elimination half-life is 71-100 minutes. Mannitol does not normally enter the CNS or the eye. It is freely filtered by the kidneys with less than 10% tubular reabsorption which is the basis for its use as a diuretic. It is not known if it enters the milk compartment, but it is likely only during the first few days postpartum when the tight-junctions in the alveolar system are immature. After 48-72 hours the entry of mannitol into human milk is probably minimal. Oral absorption in infants would be minimal except early postpartum when their GI tract is relative porous.

Pregnancy Risk Category: C

Lactation Risk Category: L3

Adult Concerns: Hypernatremia, hyponatremia, elevated potassium, diarrhea, kidney failure, pulmonary edema, and congestive heart failure.

Pediatric Concerns: None reported via milk, but watery diarrhea is remotely possible. Due to its osmotic diuresis, it is possible that it could briefly reduce the production of milk.

Drug Interactions: May enhance diuresis with added with loop and other diuretics. May increase elimination of lithium.

Relative Infant Dose:

Adult Dose: High variable, check other references.

Alternatives:

T ½	= 71-100 minutes	M/P	=
PHL	=	PB	= 0%
Tmax	=	Oral	= 17%
MW	= 182	pKa	=
Vd	= Low		

References:

1. Pharmaceutical Manufacturers prescribing information, 2003.

MAPROTILINE   L3

Trade: Ludiomil
Other Trades: Novo-Maprotilene, Ludiomil
Uses: Antidepressant
AAP: Not reviewed

Maprotiline is a unique structured (tetracyclic) antidepressant dissimilar to others but has clinical effects similar to the tricyclic antidepressants. While it has fewer anticholinergic side effects than the tricyclics, it is more sedating and has similar toxicities in overdose. In one study following an oral dose of 50 mg three times daily, milk and maternal blood levels were greater than 200 µg/L.[1] Milk/plasma ratios varied from 1.3 to 1.5. While these levels are quite low, it is not known if they are hazardous to a breastfed infant, but caution is recommended.

Pregnancy Risk Category: B

Lactation Risk Category: L3

Adult Concerns: Side effects include drowsiness, sedation, vertigo, blurred vision, dry mouth, and urinary retention. Skin rashes, seizures, myoclonus, mania and hallucinations have been reported.

Pediatric Concerns: None reported via milk, but caution is recommended.

Drug Interactions: Maprotiline levels may be decreased by barbiturates, phenytoin, and carbamazepine. Increased toxicity may result when used with CNS depressants, quinidine, MAO inhibitors, anticholinergics, sympathomimetics, phenothiazines (seizures), benzodiazepines. Due to hazard of increased QT intervals, do not admix with cisapride.

Relative Infant Dose: 1.4%

Adult Dose: 25-75 mg daily

Alternatives: Sertraline, venlafaxine, paroxetine

T ½	= 27-58 hours	M/P	= 1.5
PHL	=	PB	= 88%
Tmax	= 12 hours	Oral	= 100%
MW	= 277	pKa	=
Vd	= 22.6		

References:

1. Riess W. The relevance of blood level determinations during the evaluation of maprotiline in man. In:Murphy (ed): Research and Clinical Investigations in Depression. Northhampton: Cambridge Medical Publications 1976: 19-37.

Measles Virus Vaccine, Live

Trade:
Other Trades:
Uses: Vaccination for Measles
AAP: Not reviewed

MMR vaccine is a mixture of live, attenuated viruses from measles, mumps, and rubella strains. It is usually administered to children at 12-15 months of age. NEVER administer to a pregnant woman. Rubella, and perhaps measles and mumps virus, are undoubtedly transferred via breastmilk and have been detected in throat swabs of 56% of breastfeeding infants. [1-4] Infants exposed to the attenuated viruses via breastmilk had only mild symptoms. If medically required, MMR vaccine can be administered early postpartum.[5]

Pregnancy Risk Category:

Lactation Risk Category:

Adult Concerns:

Pediatric Concerns:

Drug Interactions:

Relative Infant Dose:

Adult Dose:

Alternatives:

References:

MEBENDAZOLE   L3

Trade: Vermox
Other Trades: Sqworm
Uses: Anthelmintic
AAP: Not reviewed

Mebendazole is an anthelmintic used primarily for pin worms although it is active against round worms, hookworms, and a number of other nematodes. Mebendazole is poorly absorbed orally. In one patient who received 100 mg twice daily for three days, milk production was drastically reduced.[1] However in another report of four postpartum breastfeeding mothers who received 100 mg twice daily for 3 days, milk levels of mebendazole were undetectable in one patient sample. No change in milk production was noted in the latter study.[2] Considering the poor oral absorption and high protein binding, it is unlikely that mebendazole would be transmitted to the infant in clinically relevant concentrations.

Pregnancy Risk Category: C

Lactation Risk Category: L3

Adult Concerns: Diarrhea, abdominal pain, nausea, vomiting, headache. Observe mother for reduced production of breast milk.

Pediatric Concerns: None reported via milk. May inhibit milk production.

Drug Interactions: Carbamazepine and phenytoin may increase metabolism of mebendazole.

Relative Infant Dose:

Adult Dose: 100 mg BID

Alternatives: Pyrantel

T ½	= 2.8-9 hours	M/P	=
PHL	=	PB	= High
Tmax	= 0.5-7.0 hours	Oral	= 2-10%
MW	= 295	pKa	–
Vd	=		

References:
1. Rao TS. Does mebendazole inhibit lactation? N Z Med J 1983; 96 (736):589-590.
2. Kurzel RB, Toot PJ, Lambert LV, Mihelcic AS. Mebendazole and postpartum lactation. N Z Med J 1994; 107 (988):439.

MECLIZINE   L3

Trade: Antivert, Bonine
Other Trades: Bonamine, Ancolan, Sea-legs
Uses: Antiemetic, antivertigo, motion sickness
AAP: Not reviewed

Meclizine is an antihistamine frequently used for nausea, vertigo, and motion sickness although it is inferior to scopolamine. Meclizine was previously used for nausea and vomiting of pregnancy.[1] No data are available on its secretion into breastmilk. There are no pediatric indications for this product.

Pregnancy Risk Category: B

Lactation Risk Category: L3

Adult Concerns: Drowsiness, sedation, dry mouth, blurred vision.

Pediatric Concerns: None reported.

Drug Interactions: May have increased sedation when used with CNS depressants and other neuroleptics and anticholinergics.

Relative Infant Dose:

Adult Dose: 25-100 mg daily.

Alternatives: Hydroxyzine, Cetirizine

T ½	= 6 hours	M/P	=
PHL	=	PB	=
Tmax	= 1-2 hours	Oral	= Complete
MW	= 391	pKa	=
Vd	=		

References:
1. Vorherr H. Drug excretion in breast milk. Postgrad Med 1974; 56 (4):97-104.

MEDROXYPROGESTERONE | L1

Trade: Provera, Depo-Provera, Cycrin
Other Trades: Depo-Provera, Alti-MPA, Gen-Medroxy,
   Farlutal, Provelle, Divina, Ralovera
Uses: Injectable progestational agent
AAP: Maternal Medication Usually Compatible with
   Breastfeeding

Depo Medroxyprogesterone (DMPA) is a synthetic progestin compound. It is used orally for amenorrhea, dysmenorrhea, uterine bleeding, and infertility. It is used intramuscularly for contraception. Due to its poor oral bioavailability, it is seldom used orally.

Saxena has reported that the average concentration in milk is 1.03 µg/L.[1] Koetswang reported average milk levels of 0.97 µg/L.[2] In a series of huge studies, the World Health Organization reviewed the developmental skills of children and their weight gain following exposure to progestin-only contraceptives during lactation.[3,4] These studies documented that no adverse effects on overall development, or rate of growth, were notable. Further, they suggested there is no apparent reason to deny lactating women the use of progestin-only contraceptives, preferably after 6 weeks postpartum.

There have been consistent and controversial studies suggesting that males exposed to early postnatal progestins have higher feminine scores. However, Ehrhardt's studies have provided convincing data that males exposed to early progestins were no different than controls.[5] A number of other short and long-term studies available on development of children have found no differences with control groups.[6,7]

Interestingly, an excellent study of the transfer of DMPA into breastfed infants has been published.[8] In this study of 13 breastfeeding women who received 150 mg injections of DMPA on day 43 and again on day 127 postpartum, urine and plasma collections in infants (n= 22) from day 38 to day 137 were collected. Urinary follicle stimulating hormone (FSH), luteinizing hormone (LH), unconjugated testosterone, unconjugated cortisol, medroxyprogesterone and metabolites were measured. No differences (from untreated controls) were found in LH, FSH, or unconjugated testosterone urine levels in the infants. Urine cortisol levels were not altered from those of control infants. Medroxyprogesterone or its metabolites were at no time detected in any of the infant urine samples. This data concludes that only small trace amounts of MPA are transferred to breastfeeding infants and that these amounts are not expected to have any influence on breastfeeding infants. In support of this, using calculations based on MPA levels in the blood of DMPA users and a plasma to milk MPA ratio, Benagiano and Fraser suggest that the actual amounts of MPA in the infant's system is probably at or below trace levels.[9] Koetsewant states that the small amount of MPA present in milk is unlikely to have any significant clinical adverse effects on the infant.[2] A long-term follow-up study by Jimenez found no changes in growth, development and health status in 128 breast-fed infants at 4.5 years of age.[10] DMPA mothers lactated significantly longer than controls in this study.

The use of Depo-Provera in breastfeeding women is common but will probably always be somewhat controversial. Depo Provera has been documented to significantly elevate prolactin levels in breastfeeding mothers[11] and increase milk production in some mothers.[12]

It is well known that estrogens suppress milk production. With progestins, it has been suggested that some women may experience a decline in milk production or arrested early production, following an injection of DMPA, particularly when the progestin is used early postpartum (12-48 hours).[13] At present there are no published data to support this, nor is the relative incidence of this untoward effect known. Therefore, in some instances, it might be advisable to recommend treatment with oral progestin-only contraceptives postpartum rather than DMPA, so that women who experience reduced milk supply could easily withdraw from the medication without significant loss of breast milk supply. Progestins should be avoided early postnatally, and perhaps longer.[13]

Pregnancy Risk Category: X

Lactation Risk Category: L1
                                          L4 if used first 3 days postpartum

Adult Concerns: Fluid retention, GI distress, menstrual disorders, breakthrough bleeding, weight gain.

Pediatric Concerns: None   reported   via   milk,   although unsubstantiated reports of reduced milk supply have been made.

Drug Interactions: Aminoglutethimide may increase the hepatic clearance of medroxyprogesterone, reducing its efficacy.

Relative Infant Dose:

Adult Dose: 5-10 mg daily

Alternatives:

T ½	= 14.5 hours	M/P	=
PHL	=	PB	=
Tmax	=	Oral	= 0.6-10%
MW	= 344	pKa	=
Vd	=		

References:

1. Saxena NB. et.al. Level of contraceptive steroids in breast milk and plasma of lactating women. Contracept 1977; 16:605-613.

2. Koetsawang S, Nukulkarn P, Fotherby K, Shrimanker K, Mangalam M, Towobola K. Transfer of contraceptive steroids in milk of women using long-acting gestagens. Contracept 1982; 25 (4):321-331.

3. Progestogen-only contraceptives during lactation: I. Infant growth. World Health Organization Task force for Epidemiological Research on Reproductive Health; Special Programme of Research, Development and Research Training in Human Reproduction. Contracept 1994; 50 (1):35-53.

4. Progestogen-only contraceptives during lactation: II. Infant development. World Health Organization, Task Force for Epidemiological Research on Reproductive Health; Special Programme of Research, Development, and Research Training in Human Reproduction. Contracep 1994; 50 (1):55-68.

5. Ehrhardt AA, Grisanti GC, Meyer-Bahlburg HF. Prenatal exposure to medroxyprogesterone acetate (MPA) in girls. Psychoneuroendocrinology 1977; 2 (4):391-398.

6. Schwallie PC. The effect of depot-medroxyprogesterone acetate on the fetus and nursing infant: a review. Contracep 1981; 23 (4):375-386.

7. Pardthaisong T, Yenchit C, Gray R. The long-term growth and development of children exposed to Depo-Provera during pregnancy or lactation. Contracep 1992; 45 (4):313-324.3.

8. Virutamasen P, Leepipatpaiboon S, Kriengsinyot R, Vichaidith P, Muia PN, Sekadde-Kigondu CB, Mati JK, Forest MG, Dikkeschei LD, Wolthers BG, d'Arcangues C. Pharmacodynamic effects of depot-medroxyprogesterone acetate (DMPA) administered to lactating women on their male infants. Contracep 1996; 54 (3):153-157.

9. Benagiano G, Fraser I. The Depo-Provera debate. Commentary on the article "Depo-Provera, a critical analysis". Contracep 1981; 24 (5):493-528.

10. Jimenez J, Ochoa M, Soler MP, Portales P. Long-term follow up of children breast-fed by mothers receiving depot-medroxyprogesterone acetate. Contracep 1984; 30 (6):523-533.

11. Ratchanon S, Taneepanichskul S. Depot medroxyprogesterone acetate and basal serum prolactin levels in lactating women. Obstet Gynecol 2000; 96 (6):926-928.

12. Fraser IS. Long acting injectable hormonal contraceptives. Clin Reprod Fertil 1982; 1 (1):67-88.

13. Kennedy KI, Short RV, Tully MR. Premature introduction of progestin-only contraceptive methods during lactation. Contracep 1997; 55 (6):347-350.

MEDROXYPROGESTERONE AND ESTRADIOL CYPIONATE

L3

Trade: Lunelle

Other Trades:

Uses: Once-a-month birth control injection

AAP: Not reviewed

Lunelle is a new, once-a-month injectable birth control product. It contains medroxyprogesterone acetate (25 mg), which is the active ingredient in Depo-Provera, and also contains 5 mg estradiol cypionate, which is a repository form of estrogen that is slowly released from the injection site over 30 days.

The amount of medroxyprogesterone for this one month injection is 25 mg. The amount of Depo-Provera providing 3 month's coverage is 150 mg. Because this injection contains estrogen, it may potentially reduce the production of milk and caution is recommended.[1] Although small amounts of estrogens and progestins may pass into breastmilk, the effects of these hormones on an infant appear minimal. Use of estrogen containing products, particularly early postpartum, may dramatically reduce the volume of milk produced. Mothers should attempt to delay use of these products for as long as possible postpartum (at least 6-8 weeks), if at all. Because of the estrogen content and the prolonged release formula, caution is recommended in breastfeeding mothers.

Pregnancy Risk Category: X

Lactation Risk Category: L3

Adult Concerns: Side effects are typical of oral contraceptives and include thromboembolism, cerebral hemorrhage, hypertension, infarction, cerebral ischemia, gallbladder disease, pulmonary embolism, thrombophlebitis. Abdominal pain, acne, etc. See package insert for numerous others.

Pediatric Concerns: Possibility of reduce milk supply. Long term followup of infants has shown no untoward effects.

Drug Interactions: Aminoglutethimide may decrease effectiveness and serum concentration of MPA. Rifampin may increase metabolism of estrogens/progestins. Anticonvulsants such as phenobarbital, phenytoin, and carbamazepine have been shown to increase metabolism of some estrogens and progestins and could reduce contraceptive effectiveness. Some antibiotics (ampicillin, tetracycline and griseofulvin) may reduce contraceptive effectiveness. St. Johns wort may also reduce contraceptive effectiveness by enhancing metabolism of numerous drugs.

Relative Infant Dose:

Adult Dose: 25 mg MPA, 5 mg estradiol cypionate monthly

Alternatives: Micronor, Ovrette

References:
1. Booker DE, Pahl IR. Control of postpartum breast engorgement with oral contraceptives. Am J Obstet Gynecol 1967; 98 (8):1099-1101.

MEFLOQUINE   L2

Trade: Lariam
Other Trades: Lariam
Uses: Antimalarial
AAP: Not reviewed

Mefloquine is an antimalarial and a structural analog of quinine. It is concentrated in red cells and therefore has a long half-life.[1] Following a single 250 mg dose in two women, the milk/plasma ratio was only 0.13 to 0.16 the first 4 days of therapy.[2] The concentration of mefloquine in milk ranged from 32 to 53 µg/L. Unfortunately, these studies were not carried out after steady state conditions, which would probably increase to some degree the amount transferred to the infant. According to the manufacturer, mefloquine is secreted in small concentrations approximating 3% of the maternal dose. Assuming a milk level of 53 µg/L and a daily milk intake of 150 mL/kg/day, an infant would ingest approximately 8 µg/kg/day of mefloquine, which is not sufficient to protect the infant from malaria. The therapeutic dose for malaria prophylaxis is 62 mg in a 15-19 kg infant. Thus far, no untoward effects have been reported.

Pregnancy Risk Category: C

Lactation Risk Category: L2

Adult Concerns: GI upset, dizziness, elevated liver enzymes, possible retinopathy.

Pediatric Concerns: None reported but discontinue lactation if neuropsychiatric disturbances occur.

Drug Interactions: Decreases effect of valproic acid. Increased toxicity of beta blockers, chloroquine, quinine, quinidine.

Relative Infant Dose: 0.1% - 0.2%

Adult Dose: 1.25 g once OR 250 mg every week

Alternatives:

T ½	= 10-21 days	M/P	= 0.13-0.27
PHL	=	PB	= 98%
Tmax	= 1-2 hours	Oral	= 85%
MW	= 414	pKa	=
Vd	= 19		

References:
1. Pharmaceutical Manufacturer Prescribing Information. 1995.
2. Edstein MD, Veenendaal JR, Hyslop R. Excretion of mefloquine in human breast milk. Chemotherapy 1988; 34 (3):165-169.

MELATONIN   L3

Trade:
Other Trades:
Uses: Hormone
AAP: Not reviewed

Melatonin (N-acetyl-5-methoxytryptamine) is a normal hormone secreted by the pineal gland in the human brain. It is circadian in rhythm, with nighttime values considerably higher than daytime levels. It is postulated to induce a sleep-like pattern in humans. It is known to be passed into human milk and is believed responsible for entraining the newborn brain to phase shift its circadian clock to that of the mother by communicating the time of day information to the newborn.

On the average, the amount of melatonin in human milk is about 35% of the maternal plasma level but can range to as high as 80%.[1] Post feeding milk levels appear to more closely reflect the maternal plasma level than pre-feeding values, suggesting that melatonin may be transported into milk at night, during the feeding, rather than being stored in foremilk. In neonates, melatonin levels are low and progressively increase up to the age of 3 months when the characteristic diurnal rhythm is detectible.[2] Night-time melatonin levels reach a maximum at the age of 1-3 years and thereafter decline to adult values.[3,4,5] While night-time maternal serum levels average 280 pmol/L, milk levels averaged 99 pmol/L in a group of ten breastfeeding mothers.[1] The effect of orally administered melatonin on newborns is unknown, but melatonin has thus far not been associated with significant untoward effects.

Pregnancy Risk Category:

Lactation Risk Category: L3

Adult Concerns: Headache and confusion, drowsiness, fatigue, hypothermia, and dysphoria in depressed patients.

Pediatric Concerns: None reported.

Drug Interactions:

Relative Infant Dose:

Adult Dose:

Alternatives:

T ½	= 30-50 minutes	M/P	= 0.35-0.8
PHL	=	PB	=
Tmax	= 0.5-2 hours	Oral	= Complete
MW	= 232	pKa	=
Vd	=		

References:

1. Illnerova H, Buresova M, Presl J. Melatonin rhythm in human milk. J Clin Endocrinol Metab 1993; 77 (3):838-841.
2. Hartmann L, Roger M, Lemaitre BJ, Massias JF, Chaussain JL. Plasma and urinary melatonin in male infants during the first 12 months of life. Clin Chim Acta 1982; 121 (1):37-42.
3. Aldhous M, Franey C, Wright J, Arendt J. Plasma concentrations of melatonin in man following oral absorption of different preparations. Br J Clin Pharmacol 1985; 19 (4):517-521.
4. Attanasio A, Rager K, Gupta D. Ontogeny of circadian rhythmicity for melatonin, serotonin, and N-acetylserotonin in humans. J Pineal Res 1986; 3 (3):251-256.
5. Dollins AB, Lynch HJ, Wurtman RJ, Deng MH, Kischka KU, Gleason RE, Lieberman HR. Effect of pharmacological daytime doses of melatonin on human mood and performance. Psychopharmacology (Berl) 1993; 112 (4):490-496.

MELOXICAM   L3

Trade: Mobic
Other Trades:
Uses: Nonsteroidal anti-inflammatory agent
AAP: Not reviewed

Meloxicam is a nonsteroidal anti-inflammatory drug that appears more selective for the COX-2 receptor.[1] No data are available for transfer into human milk although it does transfer into rodent milk. Due to its long half-life and good bioavailability, another NSAID would probably be preferred.

Pregnancy Risk Category: C

Lactation Risk Category: L3

Adult Concerns: Leukopenia, elevated liver enzymes, headache, abdominal pain, constipation, diarrhea, angina, anaphylaxis in aspirin sensitive patients.

Pediatric Concerns: None reported via milk.

Drug Interactions: May reduce coagulation in patients using anticoagulants and other platelet inhibitory drugs. NSAIDs may decrease the antihypertensive effect of ACE inhibitors. May increase blood pressure in hypertensive patients using beta blockers and other antihypertensives. May increase risk of gastric hemorrhage with calcium channel blockers. Numerous other drug-drug interactions listed, consult another text.

Relative Infant Dose:

Adult Dose: 7.5 mg/d

Alternatives: Ibuprofen, celecoxib

T ½	= 20.1 hours	M/P	=
PHL	=	PB	= 99.4
Tmax	= 4.9 hours	Oral	= 89%
MW	= 351	pKa	= 4.2
Vd	= 0.14		

References:
1. Pharmaceutical Manufacturer Prescribing Information, 2002.

MEMANTINE   L3

Trade: Namenda
Other Trades: Ebixa
Uses: NMDA Receptor Antagonist
AAP: Not reviewed

Memantine is used to treat moderate to severe dementia associated with Alzheimer's disease. It blocks NMDA receptors, blocking glutamate from exciting the neuronal cells. The over-excitation of NMDA receptors is postulated to contribute to the disease. It binds to the magnesium binding site for longer periods of time than magnesium, causing receptor blockade under excessive stimulation. There are not data available one the transfer of memantine into human milk, but due to the large volume of distribution, it is unlikely that it would transfer to any measurable extent.

Pregnancy Risk Category: B

Lactation Risk Category: L3

Adult Concerns: Adverse reactions seen include hypertension, dizziness, confusion, headache, constipation, vomiting, and cough.

Pediatric Concerns: No data are available.

Drug Interactions:

Relative Infant Dose:

Adult Dose: 20 mg/day

Alternatives:

T ½	= 60-80 hours	M/P	=
PHL	=	PB	= 45%
Tmax	= 3-7 hours	Oral	= Complete
MW	= 216	pKa	=
Vd	= 9-11		

References:
1.   Pharmaceutical Manufacturer Prescribing Information. 2007.

MENINGOCOCCAL VACCINE | L1

Trade: Menomune
Other Trades:
Uses: Vaccine
AAP: Not reviewed

Meningococcal polysaccharide vaccine is a freeze-dried preparation of group-specific antigens from Neisseria meningitidis. This vaccine is not infectious. This vaccine is useful to prevent endemic and epidemic meningitis and meningococcemia in children and young adults. There are no contraindications for using this in breastfeeding mothers other than allergic hypersensitivity to some of the ingredients.

Pregnancy Risk Category: C

Lactation Risk Category: L1

Adult Concerns: Pain erythema, induration at injection site. Headaches, malaise, chills and elevated temperature have been reported.

Pediatric Concerns: None via milk.

Drug Interactions:

Relative Infant Dose:

Adult Dose: 0.5 mL subcutaneously

Alternatives:

References:
1.   Pharmaceutical Manufacturers Prescribing Information, 2003.

MENOTROPINS   L3

Trade: Pergonal, Humegon, Repronex
Other Trades:
Uses: Produces follicle growth
AAP: Not reviewed

Menotropins is a purified preparation of gonadotropins hormones extracted from the urine of postmenopausal women. It is a biologically standardized form containing equal activity of follicle stimulating hormone (FSH) and luteinizing hormone (LH).[1-3] Menotropins and human chorionic gonadotropins (see chorionic gonadotropins) are given sequentially to induce ovulation in the anovulatory female. FSH and LH are large MW peptides and would not likely penetrate into human milk. Further, they are unstable in the GI tract and their oral bioavailability would be minimal to zero even in an infant.

Pregnancy Risk Category: X

Lactation Risk Category: L3

Adult Concerns: Ovarian enlargement, cysts, hemoperitoneum, fever, chills, aches, join pains, nausea, vomiting, abdominal pain, diarrhea, bloating, rash, dizziness.

Pediatric Concerns: None reported via milk.   These agents are very unlikely to enter milk. But observe closely for changes in milk production which could occur.

Drug Interactions:

Relative Infant Dose:

Adult Dose: 75-150 units each FSH & LH daily

Alternatives:

T ½	= 3.9 and 70.4 hours	M/P	=
PHL	=	PB	=
Tmax	= 6 hours	Oral	= 0%
MW	= 34,000	pKa	=
Vd	= 1.08		

References:

1. Sharma V, Riddle A, Mason B, Whitehead M, Collins W. Studies on folliculogenesis and in vitro fertilization outcome after the administration of follicle-stimulating hormone at different times during the menstrual cycle. Fertil Steril 1989; 51 (2):298-303.
2. Kjeld JM, Harsoulis P, Kuku SF, Marshall JC, Kaufman B, Fraser TR. Infusions of hFSH and hLH in normal men. I. Kinetics of human follicle stimulating hormone. Acta Endocrinol (Copenh) 1976; 81 (2):225-233.
3. Yen SC, Llerena LA, Pearson OH, Littell AS. Disappearance rates of endogenous follicle-stimulating hormone in serum following surgical hypophysectomy in man. J Clin Endocrinol Metab 1970; 30 (3):325-329.

MEPERIDINE   L2

Trade: Demerol
Other Trades: Pethidine
Uses: Narcotic analgesic
AAP: Maternal Medication Usually Compatible with Breastfeeding

Meperidine is a potent opiate analgesic. It is rapidly and completely metabolized by the adult and neonatal liver to an active form, normeperidine. Significant but small amounts of meperidine are secreted into breast milk. In a study of 9 nursing mothers two hours after a 50 mg IM injection, the average concentration of meperidine in milk was 82 µg/L and a milk/plasma ratio of 1.12.[1] The highest concentration of meperidine in breastmilk at 2 hours after dose was 0.13 mg/L.

In another study, the maximum concentration of meperidine in milk ranged from 134 to 244 µg/L in 5 patients at 1-2 hours after administration and 76 to 318 µg/L at 2-4 hours after administration of 25 mg intravenously (in 3 patients).[2] According to these authors, the maximum dose to an infant would be approximately 9.5 µg/kg or 1.2% to 3.5% of the weight-adjusted maternal dose.

In a study of two nursing mothers who received varying amounts of meperidine following delivery (up to 1275 mg within 72 hours), the levels in milk of meperidine ranged from 36.2 to 314 µg/L with an average of 225 µg/L. Breastmilk levels of normeperidine ranged from zero to 333 µg/L with an average of 142 µg/L.[3] This study clearly shows a much longer half-life for the active metabolite, normeperidine. Normeperidine levels were detected after 56 hours post-administration in human milk (8.1 ng/mL) following a single 50 mg dose. The milk/plasma ratios varied from 0.82 to 1.59 depending on dose and timing of sampling.

Published half-lives for meperidine in neonates (13 hours) and normeperidine (63 hours) are long and with time could concentrate in the plasma of a neonate. Wittels studies clearly indicate that infants from mothers treated with meperidine (PCA post-cesarean) were neurobehaviorally depressed after three days. Infants from similar groups treated with morphine were not affected.

Pregnancy Risk Category: C

Lactation Risk Category: L2
                                L3 if used early postpartum

Adult Concerns: Sedation, respiratory depression.

Pediatric Concerns: Sedation, poor suckling reflex, neurobehavioral delay.

Drug Interactions: Phenytoin may decrease analgesic effect. Meperidine may aggravate adverse effects of isoniazid. MAO inhibitors, Fluoxetine and other SSRIs, and tricyclic antidepressants may greatly potentiate the effects of meperidine.

Relative Infant Dose: 1.4% - 13.9%

Adult Dose: 50-100 mg every 3-4 hours PRN

Alternatives: Morphine, Fentanyl, Hydrocodone

T ½	= 3.2 hours	M/P	= 0.84-1.59
PHL	= 6-32 hours	PB	= 65-80%
Tmax	= 30-50 minutes (IM)	Oral	= <50%
MW	= 247	pKa	= 8.6
Vd	= 3.7-4.2		

References:
1. Peiker G, Muller B, Ihn W, Noschel H. [Excretion of pethidine in mother's milk (author's transl)]. Zentralbl Gynakol 1980; 102 (10):537-541.
2. Borgatta L, Jenny RW, Gruss L, Ong C, Barad D. Clinical significance of methohexital, meperidine, and diazepam in breast milk. J Clin Pharmacol 1997; 37 (3):186-192.

3. Quinn PG, Kuhnert BR, Kaine CJ, Syracuse CD. Measurement of meperidine and normeperidine in human breast milk by selected ion monitoring. Biomed Environ Mass Spectrom 1986; 13 (3):133-135.
4. Wittels B, Scott DT, Sinatra RS. Exogenous opioids in human breast milk and acute neonatal neurobehavior: a preliminary study. Anesthesiology 1990; 73 (5):864-869.

MEPINDOLOL SULFATE | L2

Trade:
Other Trades: Corindolan
Uses: Non-specific beta blocker
AAP: Not reviewed

Mepindolol is a non-selective beta receptor blocking agent. In a study of 5 women (day 3 postpartum) who received 20 mg daily for 5 days, the concentrations of mepindolol in plasma and milk of five breastfeeding mothers were determined one day one and after 5 daily doses of mepindolol sulphate 20 mg.[1] In the newborns plasma levels were measured once on the first and fifth days of the study. The mean maternal plasma concentration of mepindolol 2 hours after administration was 52 µg/L both after 1 and 5 doses. Average milk concentrations of mepindolol were 18 µg/L after one dose, and 22 µg/L after 5 daily doses. The average milk/plasma ratio was 0.4. Plasma levels in the newborn were below the detection limit of 1 µg/L, except for one baby in whom 2 and 5 µg/L were measured. The relative infant dose would be 1.1% of the maternal dose. No drug-related side effects were noted in these 5 infants.

Pregnancy Risk Category: C in first trimester
D in second and third trimesters

Lactation Risk Category: L2

Adult Concerns: Bradycardia, asthmatic symptoms, hypotension, sedation, weakness, hypoglycemia.

Pediatric Concerns: None reported in one study of 5 breastfed infants.

Drug Interactions: Beta blockers may reduce the effect of oral sulfonylureas (hypoglycemic agents). Increased toxicity/effect when used with other antihypertensives, contraceptives, MAO inhibitors, cimetidine, and numerous other products. See drug interaction reference for complete listing.

Relative Infant Dose: 1%

Adult Dose: 20 mg daily.

Alternatives: Propranolol, metoprolol

T ½	= 3-4 hours	M/P	= <0.4
PHL	=	PB	= 50%
Tmax	= 1-3 hours	Oral	= >95%
MW	=	pKa	=
Vd	= 5.7		

References:
1. Krause W, Stoppelli I, Milia S, Rainer E. Transfer of mepindolol to newborns by breast-feeding mothers after single and repeated daily doses. Eur J Clin Pharmacol 1982; 22 (1):53-55.

MEPIVACAINE   L3

Trade: Carbocaine, Polocaine
Other Trades: Carbocaine, Polocaine
Uses: Local anesthetic
AAP: Not reviewed

Mepivacaine is a long acting local anesthetic similar to bupivacaine.[1-3] Mepivacaine is used for infiltration, peripheral nerve blocks, and central nerve blocks (epidural or caudal anesthesia). No data are available on the transfer of mepivacaine into human milk; however, its structure is practically identical to bupivacaine and one would expect its entry into human milk is similar and low. Bupivacaine enters milk in exceedingly low levels (see bupivacaine). Due to higher fetal levels and reported toxicities, mepivacaine is never used antenatally. For use in breastfeeding patients, bupivacaine is preferred.

Pregnancy Risk Category: C

Lactation Risk Category: L3

Adult Concerns: Sedation, bradycardia, respiratory sedation, transient burning, anaphylaxis.

Pediatric Concerns: None reported via milk. Neonatal depression and convulsive seizures occurred in 7 neonates 6 hours after delivery.

Drug Interactions: Increases effect of hyaluronidase, beta blockers, MAO inhibitors, tricyclic antidepressants, phenothiazines, and vasopressors.

Relative Infant Dose:

Adult Dose: 50-300 mg X 1

Alternatives:

T ½	= 1.9-3.2 hours	M/P	=
PHL	= 8.7-9 hours	PB	= 60-85%
Tmax	= 30 minutes	Oral	=
MW	=	pKa	= 7.6
Vd	=		

References:
1. Pharmaceutical Manufacturer Prescribing Information. 1997.
2. Hillman LS, Hillman RE, Dodson WE. Diagnosis, treatment, and follow-up of neonatal mepivacaine intoxication secondary to paracervical and pudendal blocks during labor. J Pediatr 1979; 95 (3):472-477.
3. Teramo K, Rajamaki A. Foetal and maternal plasma levels of mepivacaine and foetal acid-base balance and heart rate after paracervical block during labour. Br J Anaesth 1971; 43 (4):300-312.

MEPROBAMATE   L3

Trade: Equanil, Miltown
Other Trades: Novo-Mepro, Apo-Meprobamate, Meprate
Uses: Antianxiety drug
AAP: Not reviewed

Meprobamate is an older antianxiety drug.[1] It is secreted into milk at levels 2-4 times that of the maternal plasma level.[2] It could produce some sedation in a breastfeeding infant.

Pregnancy Risk Category: D

Lactation Risk Category: L3

Adult Concerns: Blood dyscrasias, sedation, hypotension, withdrawal reactions.

Pediatric Concerns: None reported, but observe for sedation.

Drug Interactions: May have increased CNS depression when used with other neuroleptic depressants.

Relative Infant Dose:

Adult Dose: 300-400 mg TID-QID

Alternatives: Lorazepam, Alprazolam

T ½	= 6-17 hours	M/P	= 2-4
PHL	=	PB	= 15%
Tmax	= 1-3 hours	Oral	= Complete
MW	= 218	pKa	=
Vd	= 0.7		

References:
1. Pharmaceutical Manufacturer Prescribing Information. 1993.
2. Wilson JT, Brown RD, Cherek DR, Dailey JW, Hilman B, Jobe PC, Manno BR, Manno JE, Redetzki HM, Stewart JJ. Drug excretion in human breast milk: principles, pharmacokinetics and projected consequences. Clin Pharmacokinet 1980; 5 (1):1-66.

MERCAPTOPURINE   L3

Trade: Purinethol, 6-MP
Other Trades: Puri-Nethol
Uses: Antimetabolite, immunosuppressant
AAP: Not reviewed

Mercaptopurine is an anticancer drug that acts intracellularly as an purine antagonist, ultimately inhibiting DNA and RNA synthesis.[1] It is the active metabolite of the drug azathioprine. See azathioprine and Appendix A.

Pregnancy Risk Category: D

Lactation Risk Category: L3

Adult Concerns: Bone marrow suppression, liver toxicity, nausea, vomiting, diarrhea.

Pediatric Concerns: No data are available on 6-MP, but data on azathioprine has been published. See azathioprine.

Drug Interactions: When used with allopurinol, reduced mercaptopurine to 1/3 to 1/4 the usual dose. When used with trimethoprim sulfamethoxazole, may enhance bone marrow suppression. It is best to avoid the following drugs when using mercaptopurine or azathioprine: Neuromuscular blocking agents (such as rocuronium, mivacurium, vercuronium, atracurium, tubocurarine), Warfarin, D-penicillamine, Cotrimoxazole, Captopril, Cimetidine, Indomethacin and live vaccines.

Relative Infant Dose:

Adult Dose: 1.5-2.5 mg/kg daily

Alternatives: Infliximab

T ½	= 21-90 minutes	M/P	=
PHL	=	PB	= 19%
Tmax	= 2 hours	Oral	= 50%
MW	= 170	pKa	= 7.6
Vd	=		

References:
1. Pharmaceutical Manufacturer Prescribing Information. 1995.

MERCURY   L5

Trade: Mercury
Other Trades:
Uses: Environmental contaminate
AAP: Not reviewed

Mercury is an environmental contaminate that is available in multiple salt forms. Elemental mercury, the form found in thermometers, is poorly absorbed orally (0.01%) but completely absorbed via inhalation (>80%).[1] Inorganic mercury causes most forms of mercury poisoning and is available in mercury disk batteries (7-15% orally bioavailable). Organic mercury (methyl mercury fungicides, phenyl mercury) is readily absorbed (90% orally). Mercury poisoning produces encephalopathy, acute renal failure, severe GI necrosis, and numerous other systemic toxicities. Mercury transfers into human milk with a milk/plasma ratio that varies according to the mercury form. Pitkin reports that in the USA that 100 unexposed women had 0.9 µg/L total mercury in their milk.[2] Concentrations of mercury in human milk are generally much higher in populations that ingest large quantities of fish. Mothers known to be contaminated with mercury should not breastfeed.

The transfer of mercury from dental amalgams has been studied to some degree. In mothers with mercury-containing amalgams, the transfer of mercury during gestation to the fetus is generally much higher than from human milk.[3,4] Mercury levels in milk are highest immediately after birth, and these are significantly correlated with the number and size of amalgam fillings present in the mother[5,6], although others disagree.[7] In this study breast milk levels of mercury dropped significantly after 2 months and are more positively associated with the amount of fish ingested, rather than the number of amalgam fillings. At birth mercury levels in milk averaged 0.9 µg/L

(0.25 to 20.3 µg/L) and after two months mercury levels averaged 0.25 µg/L (0.25-11.7 µg/L). The authors suggest that the exposure to mercury of breastfed infants from maternal amalgam fillings is of minor importance compared to maternal fish consumption.

Oskarsson suggests in a study of Swedish women, that the exposure of the infant to mercury from breast milk was less than 0.3 µg/kg/d. This exposure is only approximately one-half the tolerable daily intake for adults recommended by the World Health Organization.[6]

These studies generally conclude that while mercury fillings may increase the transfer of mercury to the infant, most occurs in utero. Secondly, the transfer of mercury into human milk is transiently high at birth and then drops significantly at 2 months. Apparently the diet provides the greatest source of maternal mercury to human milk, much less is provided by older amalgam fillings. Further, the replacement of amalgam fillings should if possible be postponed until after pregnancy, and breastfeeding as the removal of amalgam fillings while breastfeeding could potentially increase the transfer of mercury to the breastfed infant and largely (this largely depends on the precautions taken by the dentist).

There are several routine precautions that the dentist could use when removing the old amalgam. Because heat during the grinding process can vaporize the mercury and enhance absorption by the mother, suggest that the dentist use copious amounts of cold water irrigation to minimize heat, use a rubber dam to isolate her mouth from the particles, and use an alternate source of air (oxygen) to minimize mercury vapor inhalation during removal of the amalgam.

While the USA has removed methylmercury from virtually all pediatric immunizations, other countries have not. In infants receiving three doses of hepatitis B vaccine and three DTP vaccines during the first 6 months of life, the exposure to ethylmercury was 25 µg Hg for each vaccine. Infant hair-Hg increased 446% during these six months, while maternal hair-Hg decreased 57%. This provides evidence that the extra mercury exposure is due to the vaccinations rather than maternal milk.[8]

Pregnancy Risk Category:

Lactation Risk Category: L5

Adult Concerns: Brain damage, acute renal failure, severe GI necrosis, and numerous other systemic toxicities.

Pediatric Concerns: Mercury transfer into milk is significant. Transfer to the infant is a function of levels in the mother. Dental amalgams provide some but not significant levels of transfer. Most mercury transfers in utero, not in milk. Mercury levels in milk drop significantly after 2 months. Caution is recommended in removing amalgams while pregnant or breastfeeding.

Drug Interactions:

Relative Infant Dose:

Adult Dose:

Alternatives:

T ½	= 70 days	M/P	= 0.27 -1.0
PHL	-	PB	=
Tmax	=	Oral	= Variable
MW	= 201	pKa	=
Vd	=		

References:

1. Wofff MS. Occupationally derived chemicals in breast milk. Amer J Indust Med 1983; 4:359-281.

2. Pickin RM, Bahns JA, Filer LJ, Reynolds WA. Mercury in human maternal and cord blood, placenta, and milk. Proc Soc Exp Med 1976; 151:65-567.

3. Ramirez GB, Cruz MC, Pagulayan O, Ostrea E, Dalisay C. The Tagum study I: analysis and clinical correlates of mercury in maternal and cord blood, breast milk, meconium, and infants' hair. Pediatrics 2000; 106 (4):774-781.

4. Yang J, Jiang Z, Wang Y, Qureshi IA, Wu XD. Maternal-fetal transfer of metallic mercury via the placenta and milk. Ann Clin Lab Sci 1997; 27 (2):135-141

5. Drexler H, Schaller KH. The mercury concentration in breast milk resulting from amalgam fillings and dietary habits. Environ Res 1998; 77 (2):124-129.

6. Oskarsson A, Schultz A, Skerfving S, Hallen IP, Ohlin B, Lagerkvist BJ. Total and inorganic mercury in breast milk in relation to fish consumption and amalgam in lactating women. Arch Environ Health 1996; 51 (3):234-241.

7. Klemann D, Weinhold J, Strubelt O, Pentz R, Jungblut JR, Klink F. [Effects of amalgam fillings on the mercury concentrations in amniotic fluid and breast milk]. Dtsch Zahnarztl Z 1990; 45 (3):142-145.

8. Marques, RC, Dorea JG, Fonseca MF, Bastos WR, Malm O. Hair mercury in breast-fed infants exposed to thimerosal-preserved vaccines. Eur J Pediatr 2007; [Epub ahead of print]

MEROPENEM   L3

Trade: Merrem
Other Trades: Meronem
Uses: Semisynthetic carbapenem antibiotic
AAP: Not reviewed

Meropenem is a new antibiotic similar to the older imipenem although it has greater activity against gram-negative species, but has slightly less activity against gram-positive species.[1] No data are available on its transfer into human milk but like others in this family, it is likely low. Further this agent is not orally bioavailable to any degree. Changes in gut flora could be expected in breastfed infants.

Pregnancy Risk Category: B

Lactation Risk Category: L3

Adult Concerns: Headache, seizures (0.5%), nausea, abdominal pain, diarrhea, and elevated liver function tests have been reported.

Pediatric Concerns: None reported via milk. Unlikely to enter milk significantly. Changes in gut flora could occur.

Drug Interactions: Increased plasma levels with probenecid.

Relative Infant Dose:

Adult Dose: 1 gm IV every 8 hours.

Alternatives: Imipenem-Cilistatin

T ½	= 1 hour	M/P	=
PHL	= 1.5 hours	PB	= 2%
Tmax	= Immediate	Oral	= Nil
MW	= 437	pKa	=
Vd	= 0.28		

References:
1. Pharmaceutical Manufacturers prescribing information, 2003.

MESALAMINE   L3

Trade: Asacol, Pentasa, Rowasa, Canasa, Colazal, Lialda
Other Trades: Salofalk, Mesasal, Quintasa, Mesalazine
Uses: Antiinflammatory in ulcerative colitis
AAP: Should be given to nursing mothers with caution

Mesalamine or Mesalazine (UK) is an anti-inflammatory agent used in ulcerative colitis. Although it contains 5-aminosalicylic acid (5-ASA), the mechanism of action is unknown. Some 5-aminosalicylic acid can be converted into salicylic acid and absorbed, but the amount is very small. Acetyl-5-aminosalicyclic (Acetyl-5-ASA) acid is the common metabolite and has been found in breastmilk. The effect of mesalamine is primarily local on the mucosa of the colon itself. Mesalamine is poorly absorbed from the GI tract. Only 20-30% of a dose is absorbed orally and plasma levels are exceedingly low (< 2 μg/mL). Oral tablets are enteric coated for delayed absorption.

In one patient receiving 500 mg mesalamine orally three times daily, the concentration of 5-ASA in breastmilk was 0.11 mg/L, and the Acetyl-5-ASA metabolite was 12.4 mg/L of milk. The milk/plasma ratio for 5-ASA was 0.27 and for Acetyl-5-ASA was 5.1.[1] Using this data, the weight-adjusted relative infant dose of metabolite and active ingredient would be 8.7%.

In another patient receiving 1000 mg PO three times daily, milk levels of 5 aminosalicylic acid following 7 and 11 days of treatment and 5 hours following the dose were both 0.1 mg/L, and the milk/plasma ratios were 0.07 and 0.09.[2]

Mesalamine is useful in patients allergic to sulfasalazine or salicylazosulfapyridine. At least one report of a watery diarrhea in an infant whose mother was using rectal 5-ASA has been reported.[3] Each time treatment was reinstated diarrhea recurred.

In a more recent study of four breastfeeding mothers ingesting mesalazine (dosage unreported), milk levels of 5 aminosalicylic acid ranged from 1-40 μg/L while those its inactive metabolite, N-Ac-5-ASA, were 5-14.9 mg/L. The authors did not report any complications in these breastfeeding mothers/infants.[4]

A new product, Colazal (Balsalazide), is a prodrug of mesalamine (5-aminosalicylic acid; 5-ASA). Lialda is just a prolonged release formulation of mesalamine. However, its upper dosage range is 4.5 gm/

day. At these newer and higher doses, some caution is recommended. Observe for GI changes such as watery diarrhea in breastfed infants.

Mesalamine administered rectally (Rowasa) is poorly absorbed systemically. About 10-30% of the administered dose can be recovered in the urine in 24 hours. However, plasma levels are exceedingly low (about 2 µg/mL or less). Breastmilk levels would be quite low as well.

Pregnancy Risk Category: B

Lactation Risk Category: L3

Adult Concerns: Watery diarrhea, abdominal pain, cramps, flatulence, nausea, headache.

Pediatric Concerns: Watery diarrhea in one breastfed patient, although this appears rare.

Drug Interactions: May significantly reduce bioavailability of digoxin. Coadministration of mesalamine and azathioprine may result in an increased risk of blood disorders. Use with glyburide may increase the risk of hypoglycemia. Many more drug-drug interactions. Please check drug interaction textbook.

Relative Infant Dose: 0.1% - 8.8%

Adult Dose: 800 mg TID

Alternatives:

T ½	= 5-10 hours (metabolite)	M/P	= 0.27, 5.1
PHL	=	PB	= 55%
Tmax	= 4-12 hours	Oral	= 20-30%
MW	= 153	pKa	=
Vd	=		

References:
1. Jenss H, Weber P, Hartmann F. 5-Aminosalicylic acid and its metabolite in breast milk during lactation. Am J Gastroenterol 1990; 85 (3):331.
2. Klotz U, Harings-Kaim A. Negligible excretion of 5-aminosalicylic acid in breast milk. Lancet 1993; 342 (8871):618-619.
3. Nelis GF. Diarrhoea due to 5-aminosalicylic acid in breast milk. Lancet 1989; 1 (8634):383.
4. Silverman DA, Ford J, Shaw I, Probert CS. Is mesalazine really safe for use in breastfeeding mothers? Gut 2005 Jan; 54 (1):170-1.

MESORIDAZINE   L4

Trade: Serentil
Other Trades:
Uses: Phenothiazine antipsychotic
AAP: Drugs whose effect on nursing infants is unknown but may be of concern

Mesoridazine is a typical phenothiazine antipsychotic used for treatment of schizophrenia. No data on transfer into human milk are available.[1] However, the use of the phenothiazine family in breastfeeding mothers is risky and may increase the risk of SIDS.

Pregnancy Risk Category: C

Lactation Risk Category: L4

Adult Concerns: Adverse effects include leukopenia, eosinophilia, thrombocytopenia, anemia, aplastic anemia, hypotension, drowsiness, agitation, dystonic reactions, seizures, galactorrhea, gynecomastia, dry mouth, nausea, vomiting, constipation, priapism, incontinence, and phototoxicity.

Pediatric Concerns: None reported via milk, but use in breastfeeding mothers is discouraged due to possible sedation in infant and elevated risk of SIDS.

Drug Interactions: Decreased effect with anticonvulsants, anticholinergics. Increased toxicity when used with CNS depressants, metrizamide (increased seizures) and propranolol.

Relative Infant Dose:

Adult Dose: 25-50 mg TID

Alternatives:

T ½	= 24-48 hours	M/P	=
PHL	=	PB	= 91%
Tmax	= 4 hours	Oral	= Erratic
MW	=	pKa	=
Vd	=		

References:
1. Ayd FJ. Excretion of psychotropic drugs in breast milk. In: International Drug Therapy Newsletter.Ayd Medical Communications 8[November-December]. 1973.

METAMIZOLE

L3

Trade: Dipyrone, Algosfar, Algozone, Analagin, Novalgin
Melubrin, Novalgina
Other Trades:
Uses: Analgesic, antipyretic
AAP: Not reviewed

Dipyrone was removed from the U.S. market due to serious adverse effects including agranulocytosis, aplastic anemia, thrombocytopenic purpura, and hemolytic anemia. However, it is still commonly used in many other countries. Recent analysis suggest that the risk is rather low compared to other commonly used drugs. Recent estimates suggest that the incidence rate of metamizole-induced agranulocytosis is between 0.2 and 2 cases per million person days of use. This is lower than many commonly used drugs in the US.

In one patient who took 3 doses of 500 mg orally over a 16 hour period, dipyrone concentrations in mother's serum and milk and in infant's serum and urine were 3.3, 4.3 and 3.2, 3.74 µg/mL respectively.[1] Dipyrone was detected in one breastfed infant's serum and urine after his mother took 1500 mg of dipyrone over a 16-hour period. The infant's dipyrone serum concentration was 3.2 mg/L and urine concentration was 3.74 mg/L.

In a group of 8 women, 3-5 days postpartum, who received 1 gram doses of dipyrone, milk levels of dipyrone metabolites were determined between 2.5 and 5.5 hours.[2] Four metabolites were measure were: 4-methylaminoantipyrine (MAA), 4-aminoantipyrine (AA), 4-formylaminoantipyrine (FAA) and 4-acetylaminoantipyrine (AAA). The sum of the mean concentrations of all four metabolites in milk was 20.37 mg/L. The mean concentration of MAA, the only active metabolite, was 11.2 µg/mL. Using the MAA data, the RID would be 1.2%. All metabolites were undetectable by 48 hours.

Dipyrone is an effective analgesic and antipyretic. But because of its known complications, such as agranulocytosis and other blood dyscrasias, it is no longer recommended as an analgesic in many countries. Other safer alternatives are available. However, in severe life-threatening and refractory fever, it is a suitable antipyretic.

Pregnancy Risk Category:

Lactation Risk Category:　　L3
L4 at doses > 1000 mg

Adult Concerns: Dipyrone was removed from the U.S. market due to serious adverse effects including agranulocytosis, aplastic anemia, thrombocytopenic purpura, and hemolytic anemia. Hypotension, skin rash, urticaria, toxic epidermal necrolysis have been reported.

Pediatric Concerns: Two cyanotic episodes were noted in a 42 day-old infant approximately 30 minutes following the maternal dose of 1500 mg.[1]

Drug Interactions: Numerous drug-drug interactions. Reduced antihypertensive effect of beta blockers, atenolol, acebutolol, etc. Consult drug interactions text.

Relative Infant Dose: 1.2%

Adult Dose: 0.5 - 1 gram

Alternatives: Ibuprofen, acetaminophen, ketorolac

T ½	= 2-3 hours (4-MAA)	M/P	= 1.37 (MAA)
PHL	=	PB	= 58%
Tmax	= 1 hour	Oral	= Complete
MW	= 311	pKa	=
Vd	= 0.57		

References:
1. Rizzoni G, Furlanut M. Cyanotic crisis in a breast-fed infant from mother taking dipyrone. Hum Toxicol. 1984;3:505-7.
2. Zylber-Katz E Linder N, Granit L, Levy M. Excretion of dipyrone metabolites in human breast milk. Eur J Clin Pharmacol. 1986;30:359-61.

METAXALONE   L3

Trade: Skelaxin
Other Trades:
Uses: Sedative, skeletal muscle relaxant
AAP: Not reviewed

Metaxalone is a centrally acting sedative used primarily as a muscle relaxant.[1] Its ability to relax skeletal muscle is weak and is probably due to its sedative properties. Hypersensitivity reactions in adults (allergic) have occurred as well as liver toxicity. No data are available on its transfer into breastmilk.

Pregnancy Risk Category:

Lactation Risk Category: L3

Adult Concerns: Sedation, nausea, vomiting, GI upset, hemolytic anemia, abnormal liver function.

Pediatric Concerns: None reported. No data available.

Drug Interactions:

Relative Infant Dose:

Adult Dose: 800 mg TID-QID

Alternatives:

T ½	= 2-3 hours	M/P	=
PHL	=	PB	=
Tmax	= 2 hours	Oral	=
MW	= 221	pKa	=
Vd	=		

References:
1.   Pharmaceutical Manufacturer Prescribing Information. 1995.

METFORMIN   L1

Trade: Glucophage, Glucovance
Other Trades: Glucophage, Gen-Metformin, Glycon, Diabex,
          Diaformin, Diguanil
Uses: Oral hypoglycemic agent for diabetes
AAP: Not reviewed

Metformin belongs to the biguanide family and is used to reduce glucose levels in non-insulin dependent diabetics. Oral bioavailability is only 50%. In a study of 7 women taking metformin (median dose 1500 mg/d), the mean milk-to-plasma ratio (AUC) for metformin was 0.35.[1] The mean average concentration in milk over the dose interval was 0.27 mg/L. The absolute infant dose averaged 0.04 mg/kg/d and the mean relative infant dose was 0.28%. Metformin was present in very low or undetectable concentrations in the plasma of four of the infants who were studied. No health problems were found in the six infants who were evaluated.

In another study of five subjects the median milk/plasma ratio (AUC) for metformin was 0.47.[2] The median calculated infant dose was 0.2% of the weight-adjusted maternal dose. None of the infants exposed to their mothers' milk had detectable levels of metformin in their plasma, nor were any side effects noted.

In a recent study of 5 women consuming an average dose of 500 mg twice daily, the mean peak and trough metformin concentrations in breast milk were 0.42 mg/L (range 0.38-0.46 mg/L) and 0.39 mg/L (range 0.31-0.52 mg/L), respectively.[3] The average milk/serum ratio was 0.63 (range 0.36-1.00) and the estimated relative infant dose was 0.65% (range 0.43-1.08%). Blood glucose concentrations in 3 infants were normal, ranging from 47-77 mg/dL. The mothers reported no side effects were noted in the breastfed infants.

Metformin is also used to treat polycystic ovary syndrome. In one study of 61 nursing infants whose mothers were taking a median of 2.55 g/day throughout pregnancy and lactation, the growth, motor, and social development of the infants was recorded to be normal. The authors concluded that metformin was safe and effective during lactation in the first 6 months of an infant's life.[4]

The new product Glucovance contains metformin and glyburide. The new product METAGLIP contains Glipizide and metformin.

Pregnancy Risk Category: B

Lactation Risk Category: L1

Adult Concerns: Diarrhea, nausea, vomiting, bloating, lactic acidosis, hypoglycemia.

Pediatric Concerns: No side effects noted in three studies. Plasma levels undetectable.

Drug Interactions: Alcohol potentiates the effect of metformin on lactic metabolism. Cimetidine produces a 60% increase in peak metformin plasma levels. Furosemide may increase metformin plasma levels by 22%. Use of iodinated contrast material in patients receiving metformin has produced acute renal failure and been associated with lactic acidosis. Use of nifedipine increases oral bioavailability of metformin by 20%.

Relative Infant Dose:

Adult Dose: 500 mg BID

Alternatives:

T ½	= 6.2 hours (plasma)	M/P	= 0.35-0.63
PHL	=	PB	= Minimal
Tmax	= 2.75 hours	Oral	= 50%
MW	= 129	pKa	= 11.5
Vd	= 3.7		

References:
1. Hale TW, Kristensen JH, Hackett LP, Kohan R, Ilett KF. Transfer of metformin into human milk. Diabetologia 2002; 45 (11):1509-1514.
2. Gardiner SJ, Kirkpatrick CM, Begg EJ, Zhang M, Moore MP, Saville DJ. Transfer of metformin into human milk. Clin Pharmacol Ther 2003; 73 (1):71-77.
3. Briggs GG, Ambrose PJ, Nageotte MP, Padilla G, Wan S. Excretion of metformin into breast milk and the effect on nursing infants. Obstet Gynecol 2005 Jun; 105 (6):1437-41.
4. Glueck CJ, Salehi M, Sieve L, Wang P. Growth, motor, and social developemnt in breast- and formula- fed infants of metformin-treated women with polycyctic ovary syndrome. J Pediatr 2006; 148:628-632.

METHACHOLINE CHLORIDE | L3

Trade: Arthralgen, Mecholyl, Provocholine
Other Trades:
Uses: Bronchoconstrictor used for diagnosis of asthma
AAP: Not reviewed

Methacholine is an analog of acetylcholine and is used via inhalation to diagnose asthma. When inhaled in patients with symptoms of asthma, acute bronchoconstriction occurs, confirming the diagnosis of asthma. Although it is unlikely this product would enter milk in clinically relevant amounts, it is also unlikely to survive the GI tract. Because this is a one-time test, a brief interruption of breastfeeding for a few hours (4) would all but eliminate any risk.

Pregnancy Risk Category: C

Lactation Risk Category: L3

Adult Concerns: Methacholine induces clinically apparent dyspnea, asthma and wheezing.

Pediatric Concerns: None reported via milk.

Drug Interactions: Methacholine interacts with numerous medications. Most important however are the beta blockers. Methacholine by inhalation should be avoided in patients who are receiving beta blocking agents. The use of methacholine in patients receiving beta blockers may produce exaggerated or prolonged responses that will not respond adequately to bronchodilator therapy.

Relative Infant Dose:

Adult Dose: Highly variable. Consult product information.

Alternatives:

T ½	= Brief	M/P	=
PHL	=	PB	=
Tmax	= 1-4 minutes	Oral	= Low to nil
MW	= 195	pKa	=
Vd	=		

References:
1. Pharmaceutical Manufacturers Prescribing Information, 2005.

METHADONE   L3

Trade: Dolophine, Metadon
Other Trades: Physeptone, Biodone forte, Physeptone, Methex
Uses: Narcotic analgesic
AAP: Maternal Medication Usually Compatible with Breastfeeding

Methadone is a potent and very long-acting opiate analgesic. It is primarily used to prevent withdrawal in opiate addiction. In one study of 10 women receiving methadone 10-80 mg/day, the average milk/plasma ratio was 0.83.[1] Due to the variable doses used, the milk concentrations ranged from 0.05 mg/L in one patient receiving 10 mg/day, to 0.57 mg/L in a patient receiving 80 mg/day. One infant death has been reported in a breastfeeding mother receiving maintenance methadone therapy [2], although it is not clear that the only source of methadone to this infant was from breastmilk.

In a more recent study of 12 breastfeeding women on methadone maintenance doses ranging from 20-80 mg/day, the mean concentration of methadone in plasma and milk was 311 (207-416) µg/L and 116 (72-160) µg/L respectively yielding a mean M/P ratio of 0.44 (0.24-0.64).[3] The mean absolute oral dose to infant was 17.4 (10.8-24) µg/kg/day. This equates to a mean of 2.79% of the maternal dose per day. In this study, 64% of the infants exhibited neonatal abstinence syndrome requiring treatment.

In two women receiving 30 mg twice daily and another who received 73 mg of methadone once daily, the average breast milk methadone concentrations was 0.169 mg/L and 0.132 mg/L respectively.[4] The milk/plasma ratios were 1.215 and 0.661 respectively. While the infant of the second mother died at 3 1/2 months of SIDS, it was apparently not due to methadone, as none was present in the infant's plasma and the infant was significantly supplemented with formula.

In an excellent study 8 mother/infant pairs ingesting from 40 to 105 mg/day methadone, the average (AUC) concentration of R-methadone and S-methadone enantiomers varied from 42-259 μg/L and 26-126 μg/L respectively.[5] The relative infant dose was estimated to be 2.8% of the maternal dose. Interestingly, there was little difference in methadone milk levels in immature and mature milk.

Most studies thus far show that only small amounts of methadone pass into breastmilk despite doses as high as 105 mg/day. In fact, neonatal abstinence syndromes are well known to occur in breastfeeding infants following delivery. In one study, 58% of infants developed neonatal abstinence syndrome while still breastfeeding.[3] However, some methadone is undoubtedly transferred via milk, and abrupt cessation of breastfeeding during high dose therapy has resulted in neonatal abstinence in some infants.[6]

In a recent study of eight methadone-maintained lactating women (dose= 50-105 mg/day), the concentration of methadone in milk was low (range: 2-462 ng/mL) and interestingly, were not related to maternal dose.[7] Maternal plasma levels rose over a 4 week period postpartum to reach a high at 30 days. Median milk/plasma ratios ranged from 0.22 to 0.92. The average amount of methadone ingestible by the infant was estimated to be < 0.2mg/day at day 30 postpartum. Infant plasma levels of methadone ranged from 2.2 to 8.1 ng/mL. Again, there was not correlation between maternal dose and infant plasma level. There were no significant neurobehavioral changes noted.

In a recent study of 4 methadone consuming mothers whose doses ranged from 60-110 mg/day, milk levels ranged from as low as 27 ng/ml to as high as 407 ng/mL. While the dose and sampling method was high variable, the authors estimated that the average daily dose to an infant was about 330 μg/day.[8]

In summary, the dose of R plus S methadone transferred via milk is largely dose dependent but generally averages less than 2.8% of the maternal dose.[5] This is significantly less than the conventional cut-off value of 10% of the maternal dose corrected for weight. However, the amount in milk is insufficient to prevent neonatal withdrawal syndrome, although another new study suggests that it actually reduces the incidence of neonatal abstinence syndrome when infants are breastfed (OR=0.55).[9] The Academy of Pediatrics has placed methadone in the "approved" category for breastfeeding women.

Pregnancy Risk Category: C

Lactation Risk Category: L3

Adult Concerns: Nausea, vomiting, constipation, respiratory depression, sedation, withdrawal syndrome.

Pediatric Concerns: Observe for sedation, respiratory depression, addiction, withdrawal syndrome. Neonatal abstinence syndrome.

Drug Interactions: Phenytoin, pentazocine, and rifampin may increase metabolism of methadone and produce withdrawal syndrome. CNS depressants, phenothiazines, tricyclic antidepressants, and MAO inhibitors may increase adverse effects of methadone.

Relative Infant Dose: 1.9% - 6.5%

Adult Dose: 2.5-10 mg every 3-4 hours PRN

Alternatives:

T ½	= 13-55 hours	M/P	= 0.68 (R)
PHL	=	PB	= 89%
Tmax	= 0.5-1 hours	Oral	= 50%
MW	= 309	pKa	= 8.6
Vd	= 4-5		

References:

1. Blinick G, Inturrisi CE, Jerez E, Wallach RC. Methadone assays in pregnant women and progeny. Am J Obstet Gynecol 1975; 121 (5):617-621.
2. Smialek JE, Monforte JR, Aronow R, Spitz WU. Methadone deaths in children. A continuing problem. JAMA 1977; 238 (23):2516-2517.
3. Wojnar-Horton RE, Kristensen JH, Yapp P, Ilett KF, Dusci LJ, Hackett LP. Methadone distribution and excretion into breast milk of clients in a methadone maintenance programme. Br J Clin Pharmacol 1997; 44 (6):543-547.
4. Geraghty B, Graham EA, Logan B, Weiss EL. Methadone levels in breast milk. J Hum Lact 1997; 13 (3):227-230.
5. Begg EJ, Malpas TJ, Hackett LP, Ilett KF. Distribution of R- and S-methadone into human milk during multiple, medium to high oral dosing. Br J Clin Pharmacol 2001; 52 (6):681-685.
6. Malpas TJ, Darlow BA. Neonatal abstinence syndrome following abrupt cessation of breastfeeding. N Z Med J 1999; 112 (1080):12-13.
7. Jansson LM, Choo R, Velez ML et al. Methadone maintenance and breastfeeding in the neonatal period. Pediatrics. 2008;121:106-114.
8. Jansson LM, Choo R, Velez ML, Lowe R, Huestis MA. Methadone maintenance and long-term lactation. Breastfeed Med. Mar 2008;3 (1):34-37.
9. Dryden C, Young D, Hepburn M, Mactier H. Maternal methadone use in pregnancy· factors associated with the development of neonatal abstinence syndrome and implications for healthcare resources. BJOG. Apr 2009;116 (5):665-671.

METHAMPHETAMINE | L5

Trade: Desoxyephedrine, Desoxyn, Pervitin, Anadrex, Methedrine
Other Trades:
Uses: CNS Stimulant
AAP: Advise not to breastfeed

Methamphetamine is a potent CNS stimulant commonly used as a drug of abuse with a prolonged half-life. In a study of two women who were occasional recreational users of intravenous amphetamines, replicate milk samples were drawn over 24 hours.[1] The IV dose was unknown.

In the 24 h after dose, average concentrations in milk were 111 ng/mL and 281 ng/mL for methamphetamine and 4 ng/mL and 15 ng/mL for amphetamine in the two subjects. Methamphetamine is partially metabolized by N-demethylation to amphetamine. Absolute infant doses for methamphetamine plus amphetamine (as methamphetamine equivalents) were 17.5 µg/kg/day and 44.7 µg/kg/day, respectively, for subjects 1 and 2.

Methamphetamine is a potent neurotoxin, known to cause dopaminergic degeneration, with loss of brain dopamine and serotonin neurons. Methamphetamine is a strong CNS stimulant that is strongly addictive. After prolonged use it is known to induce paranoid symptoms.

Breastfeeding mothers should avoid using this drug, or pump and discard milk for at least 48 hours.

Pregnancy Risk Category:

Lactation Risk Category: L5

Adult Concerns: Physical effects may include anorexia, hyperactivity, mydriasis, dry mouth, headache, tachycardia, elevated blood pressure, hyperthermia, diarrhea, arrhythmia, insomnia, stroke and even death.

Severe dental decay and acne are common in frequent abusers. Psychological effects include euphoria, increased libido, anxiety, grandiosity, sociability, aggressive behavior, paranoid schizophrenic symptoms, and psychosis.

Pediatric Concerns: One reported case of infant death following exposure to breast milk.[2] However, the plasma levels in the infant were reportedly too low to induce such symptoms, so the etiology of this death is in question.

Drug Interactions: Numerous. Do not use with antidepressants such as tricyclics, SSRIs, monoamine oxidase inhibitors and numerous other CNS active medications. Consult drug interaction text.

Relative Infant Dose:

Adult Dose: 5 mg

Alternatives:

T ½	= 4-13.6 hours	M/P	=
PHL	=	PB	=
Tmax	=	Oral	= 63%
MW	− 185.7	pKa	= 3-7
Vd	=		

References:
1. Bartu A, Dusci LJ, Ilett KF. Transfer of methylamphetamine and amphetamine into breast milk following recreational use of methylamphetamine. Br J Clin Pharmacol. Apr 2009;67 (4):455-459.
2. Ariagno R, Karch SB, Middleberg R, Stephens BG, Valdes-Dapena M. Methamphetamine ingestion by a breast-feeding mother and her infant's death: People v Henderson. JAMA. Jul 19 1995;274 (3):215.

METHICILLIN   L3

Trade: Staphcillin, Celbenin
Other Trades: Metin,
Uses: Penicillin antibiotic
AAP: Not reviewed

Methicillin is a penicillin antibiotic only available by IM and IV formulations.[1] It is extremely unstable at acid pH (stomach); hence, it would have only limited oral absorption. No data available on transfer into breastmilk although it would appear to be similar to other penicillins.

Pregnancy Risk Category: B

Lactation Risk Category: L3

Adult Concerns: Allergic rash, thrush, diarrhea, drug fever, changes in GI flora, renal toxicity, pseudomembranous colitis.

Pediatric Concerns: None reported via milk.

Drug Interactions: The effect of oral contraceptives may be reduced. Disulfiram and probenecid may significantly increase penicillin levels. Methicillin may increase the effect of anticoagulants.

Relative Infant Dose:

Adult Dose: 1 g every 6 hours

Alternatives:

T ½	= 1-2 hours	M/P	=
PHL	= 1.4-2.4 hours	PB	= 40%
Tmax	= 30-60 minutes	Oral	= Poor
MW	= 402	pKa	=
Vd	=		

References:

1.   Drug Facts and Comparisons 2010 ed. ed. St. Louis: 2010.

METHIMAZOLE   L3

Trade: Tapazole

Other Trades:

Uses: Antithyroid agent

AAP: Maternal Medication Usually Compatible with Breastfeeding

Methimazole, carbimazole, and propylthiouracil are used to inhibit the secretion of thyroxine. Carbimazole is a prodrug of methimazole and is rapidly converted to methimazole.

Milk levels of methimazole depend on maternal dose but appear too low to produce clinical effect. In one study of a patient receiving 2.5 mg methimazole every 12 hours, the milk/serum ratio was 1.16, and the dose per day was calculated at 16-39 µg methimazole.[1] This was equivalent to 7-16% of the maternal dose. In a study of 35 lactating women receiving 5 to 20 mg/day of methimazole, no changes in the infant thyroid function were noted in any infant, even those at higher doses.[2]

Further, studies by Lamberg in 11 women, who were treated with the methimazole derivative carbimazole (5-15 mg daily, equal to 3.3 -10 mg methimazole), found all 11 infants had normal thyroid function following maternal treatments.[3] Thus, in small maternal doses, methimazole may also be safe for the nursing mother. In a study of a woman with twins who was receiving up to 30 mg carbimazole daily, the average methimazole concentration in milk was 43 µg/L.[4] The average plasma concentrations in the twin infants were 45 and 52 ng/mL, which is below therapeutic range. Methimazole milk concentrations peaked at 2-4 hours after a carbimazole dose. No changes in thyroid function in these infants were noted.

In a large study of over 139 thyrotoxic lactating mothers and their infants, even at methimazole doses of 20 mg/day, no changes in infant TSH, T4 or T3 were noted in over 12 months of study.[5] The authors conclude that both PTU and methimazole can safely be administered during lactation. However, during the first few months of therapy, monitoring of infant thyroid functioning is recommended.

Pregnancy Risk Category: D

Lactation Risk Category: L3

Adult Concerns: Hypothyroidism, hepatic dysfunction, bleeding, drowsiness, skin rash, nausea, vomiting, fever.

Pediatric Concerns: None reported in several studies, but propylthiouracil may be a preferred choice in breastfeeding women.

Drug Interactions: Use with iodinated glycerol, lithium, and potassium iodide may increase toxicity.

Relative Infant Dose: 2.3%

Adult Dose: 5-30 mg daily.

Alternatives: Propylthiouracil

T ½	= 6-13 hours	M/P	= 1.0
PHL	=	PB	= 0%
Tmax	= 1 hour	Oral	= 80-95%
MW	= 114	pKa	=
Vd	=		

References:
1. Tegler L, Lindstrom B. Antithyroid drugs in milk. Lancet 1980; 2 (8194):591.
2. Azizi F. Effect of methimazole treatment of maternal thyrotoxicosis on thyroid function in breast-feeding infants. J Pediatr 1996; 128 (6):855-858.
3. Lamberg BA, Ikonen E, Osterlund K, Teramo K, Pekonen F, Peltola J, Valimaki M. Antithyroid treatment of maternal hyperthyroidism during lactation. Clin Endocrinol (Oxf) 1984; 21 (1):81-87.
4. Rylance GW, Woods CG, Donnelly MC, Oliver JS, Alexander WD. Carbimazole and breastfeeding. Lancet 1987; 1 (8538):928.
5. Azizi F, Khoshniat M, Bahrainian M, Hedayati M. Thyroid function and intellectual development of infants nursed by mothers taking methimazole. J Clin Endocrinol Metab 2000; 85 (9):3233-3238.

METHOCARBAMOL   L3

Trade: Robaxisal, Robaxin
Other Trades:
Uses: Muscle relaxant
AAP: Not reviewed

Methocarbamol is a centrally acting sedative and skeletal muscle relaxant. Only minimal amounts have been found in milk.[1] Observe for sedation.

Pregnancy Risk Category: C

Lactation Risk Category: L3

Adult Concerns: Drowsiness, nausea, metallic taste, vertigo, blurred vision, fever, headache.

Pediatric Concerns: None reported, but studies are limited.

Drug Interactions: May see increased toxicity when used with CNS depressants.

Relative Infant Dose:

Adult Dose: 4-4.5 g every 4-6 hours

Alternatives:

T ½	= 0.9-1.8 hours	M/P	=
PHL	=	PB	=
Tmax	= 1-2 hours	Oral	= Complete
MW	= 241	pKa	=
Vd	=		

References:
1. Pharmaceutical Manufacturer Prescribing Information. 1995.

METHOHEXITAL   L3

Trade: Brevital
Other Trades: Brietal
Uses: Anesthetic agent
AAP: Maternal Medication Usually Compatible with Breastfeeding

Methohexital is an ultra short-acting barbiturate used for induction in anesthesia. The duration of action is approximately 1/2 that of thiopental sodium or less than 8 minutes depending on dose. Although the elimination half-life is 3.9 hours, within 30 minutes there is complete redistribution of methohexital to tissues other than the brain, primarily the liver.[1,2] Methohexital levels in the breast milk were found to decline rapidly within the first hour and are undetectable after 24 hours.[3] The maximum milk level occured at 63 minutes after administration of anesthesia and was found to be 407 µg/L via breastmilk.

Pregnancy Risk Category: B

Lactation Risk Category: L3

Adult Concerns: Hypotension, lethargy, restlessness, confusion, headache, delirium and excitation

Pediatric Concerns: None reported via milk. Levels would be too low.

Drug Interactions: CNS depressants such as barbiturates, benzodiazepines, etc, may potentiate sedation with methohexital.

Relative Infant Dose: 2.8%

Adult Dose: 20-40 mg every 4-7 minutes during surgery

Alternatives:

T ½	= 3.9 hours	M/P	= 1.1 (blood)
PHL	=	PB	= 73%
Tmax	= Instant	Oral	=
MW	= 262	pKa	=
Vd	–		

References:
1. Drug Facts and Comparisons 1999 ed. ed. St. Louis: 1999.
2. McEvoy GE. (ed): AFHS Drug Information. New York, NY: 2009.3. Borgatta L, Jenny RW, Gruss L, Ong C, Barad D. Clinical Significance of Methohexital, Meperidine, and Diazepam in Breast Milk. J Clin Pharmacol 1997; 37:186-192.

METHOTREXATE   L3

Trade: Folex, Rheumatrex
Other Trades: Ledertrexate, Methoblastin, Arthitrex
Uses: Antimetabolite, anticancer, antirheumatic
AAP: Cytotoxic drug that may interfere with cellular metabolism of the nursing infant

Methotrexate is a potent and potentiallydangerous folic acid antimetabolite usedin arthritic and other immunologicsyndromes. It is also used as anabortifacient in tubal pregnancies.Methotrexate is secreted into breastmilkin small levels.

Following a dose of 22.5 mg to onepatient two hours post-dose, themethotrexate concentration in breastmilkwas 2.6 µg/L of milk with a milk/plasmaratio of 0.08.[1] The cumulativeexcretion of methotrexate in the first12 hours after oral administration wasonly 0.32 µg in milk. These authorsconclude that methotrexate therapy inbreastfeeding mothers would not pose acontraindication to breastfeeding.However, methotrexate is believed to beretained in human tissues (particularlyneonatal GI cells and ovarian cells) forlong periods (months).[2] One study hasindicated a higher risk of fetalmalformation in mothers who receivedmethotrexate months prior to becomingpregnant.[3] Therefore, pregnancy shouldbe delayed if either partner isreceiving methotrexate for at least 3months following therapy. Elimination ofmethotrexate is by a two-compartmentmodel with a terminal eliminationhalf-life of 8-15 hours.[4] Patientswith poor renal function have prolongedmethotrexate half-lives. It is apparentthat the concentration of methotrexatein human milk is minimal, although dueto the toxicity of this agent, it isprobably wise to pump and discard themother's milk for a minimum of 4 days.This may require extending if the doseused is quite high.

Pregnancy Risk Category: X

Lactation Risk Category: L3 for acute use
                               L5 for chronic use

Adult Concerns: Bone marrow suppression, anemia, vasculitis, vomiting, diarrhea, GI bleeding, stomatitis, bloody diarrhea, kidney damage, seizures, etc.

Pediatric Concerns: None reported via milk, but caution is recommended.

Drug Interactions: Aminoglycosides may significantly decrease absorption of methotrexate. Etretinate has produced hepatotoxicity in several patients receiving methotrexate. The use of folic acid or its derivatives may reduce the response to MTX. The use of NSAIDs with methotrexate is contraindicated, several deaths have occurred due to elevated MTX levels. Phenytoin serum levels may be decreased. Procarbazine may increase nephrotoxicity of MTX.

Relative Infant Dose: 0.1%

Adult Dose: 10-30 mg

Alternatives:

T ½	= 8-15 hours	M/P	= >0.08
PHL	= 1.7 hours	PB	= 34-50%
Tmax	= 1-2 hours	Oral	= 33-90%
MW	= 454	pKa	= 4.3, 5.5
Vd	= 2.6		

References:

1. Johns DG, Rutherford LD, Leighton PC, Vogel CL. Secretion of methotrexate into human milk. Am J Obstet Gynecol 1972; 112 (7):978-980.
2. Fountain JR, Hutchison DJ, Waring GB, Burchenal JH. Persistence of amethopterin in normal mouse tissues. Proc Soc Exp Biol Med 1953; 83 (2):369-373.
3. Walden PA, Bagshawe KD. Pregnancies after chemotherapy for gestational trophoblastic tumours. Lancet 1979; 2 (8154):1241.
4. Grochow LB, Ames MM. A clinician's guide to chemotherapy pharmacokinetics and pharmacodynamics. 1st ed. Baltimore, MD: Williams & Wilkins; 1998.
5. American Academy of Pediatrics, Committee on Drugs. Transfer of drugs and other chemicals into human milk. Pediatrics 2001; 108 (3):776-89.

METHSCOPOLAMINE   L3

Trade: Pamine, Aerohist, AlleRx, Amdry-D
Other Trades:
Uses: Anticholinergic, antispasmotic
AAP: Not reviewed

Methscopolamine is an anticholinergic commonly used for stomach/intestinal spasms, antiemetic, antivertigo, urinary antispasmodic, to decrease salivation, to reduce stomach acid secretion and motility, and may be used for other purposes. No data are available on its transfer to milk, but it is probably minimal due to its quaternary ammonium structure. Little is known about its kinetics but its effect persists for about 4-6 hours. It is commonly reported that anticholinergics suppress milk production but this data is anecdotal and has not been confirmed by this author. It is rather unlikely that this product would produce clinical levels in infants following ingestion of milk. But infants should be monitored for classic 'anticholinergic' symptoms such as drying of oral and ophthalmic secretions, constipation, and urinary retention.

Pregnancy Risk Category: C

Lactation Risk Category: L3

Adult Concerns: Constipation, dry mouth, trouble urinating, nausea or dizziness, increased pulse and other anticholinergic symptoms may occur.

Pediatric Concerns: None reported via milk. Rather unlikely due to the structure of this compound.

Drug Interactions: Tell your doctor of all nonprescription and prescription medication you use, especially of: antidepressants (tricyclic type), MAO inhibitors (e.g., phenelzine, linezolid, tranylcypromine, isocarboxazid, selegiline, furazolidone), quinidine, amantadine, antihistamines (e.g., diphenhydramine), other anticholinergics, potassium chloride supplements, antacids, absorbent-type anti-diarrhea medicines (e.g., kaolin-pectin), phenothiazines (e.g., chlorpromazine, promethazine

Relative Infant Dose:

Adult Dose: 2.5 mg four times a day in adults.

Alternatives: Atropine

T ½	= <4 hours	M/P	=
PHL	=	PB	=
Tmax	=	Oral	= 10-25%
MW	= 398	pKa	=
Vd	=		

References:
1. Pharmaceutical manufacturers prescribing information, 2005.

METHYLDOPA | L2

Trade: Aldomet
Other Trades: Apo-Methyldopa, Dopamet, Nova-Medopa, Aldopren, Hydopa, Nudopa
Uses: Antihypertensive
AAP: Maternal Medication Usually Compatible with Breastfeeding

Alpha-methyldopa is a centrally acting antihypertensive. It is frequently used to treat hypertension during pregnancy. In a study of 2 lactating women who received a dose of 500 mg, the maximum breastmilk concentration of methyldopa ranged from 0.2 to 0.66 mg/L.[1] In another patient who received 1000 mg dose, the maximum concentration in milk was 1.14 mg/L.[1] The milk/plasma ratios varied from 0.19 to 0.34. The authors indicated that if the infant were to ingest 750 mL of milk daily (with a maternal dose= 1000mg), the maximum daily ingestion would be less than 855 µg or approximately 0.02 % of the maternal dose.

In another study of 7 women who received 0.750-2.0 gm/day of methyldopa, the free methyldopa concentrations in breastmilk ranged from zero to 0.2 mg/L while the conjugated metabolite had concentrations of 0.1 to 0.9 mg/L.[2] These studies generally indicate that the levels of methyldopa transferred to a breastfeeding infant would be too low to be clinically relevant.

However, gynecomastia and galactorrhea has been reported in one full-term two week old female neonate following seven days of maternal therapy with methyldopa, 250 mg three times daily.[3]

Pregnancy Risk Category: B

Lactation Risk Category: L2

Adult Concerns: Hemolytic anemia, hepatitis, fever, rashes, dizziness, hypotension, sleep disturbances, dry mouth, depression, colitis.

Pediatric Concerns: None reported in several studies. Gynecomastia and galactorrhea in one personal communication.

Drug Interactions: Iron supplements can interact and cause a significant increase in blood pressure. Increased toxicity with lithium has been reported.

Relative Infant Dose: 0.1% - 0.3%

Adult Dose: 250-500 mg BID-QID

Alternatives:

T ½	= 105 minutes	M/P	= 0.19-0.34
PHL	=	PB	= Low
Tmax	= 3-6 hours	Oral	= 25-50%
MW	= 211	pKa	=
Vd	= 0.3		

References:
1. White WB, Andreoli JW, Cohn RD. Alpha-methyldopa disposition in mothers with hypertension and in their breast-fed infants. Clin Pharmacol Ther 1985; 37 (4):387-390.
2. Jones HM, Cummings AJ. A study of the transfer of alpha-methyldopa to the human foetus and newborn infant. Br J Clin Pharmacol 1978; 6 (5):432-434.
3. E.D.M. Personal Communication. 1997.

METHYLENE BLUE   L4

Trade: Dolsed, Atrosept, Prosed, Urimar-T
Other Trades:
Uses: Diagnostic Agent
AAP: Not reviewed

Methylene blue is a blue dye that is used in diagnostic procedures, to treat drug-induced methemoglobinemia, and to prevent ifosfamide-induced encephalopathy in oncology. No data are available on its transfer into human milk, but some should be expected. Oral absorption is considered poor. The apparent half-life in humans is approximately 5.25 hours, thus interruption of breastfeeding for 24 hours is probably advisable.

Pregnancy Risk Category: C

Lactation Risk Category: L4

Adult Concerns: Cardiac dysrhythmias and hypertension. Sweating, discoloration of skin, malignant hyperthermia, diarrhea, burning in mouth and oropharynx, nausea and vomiting,

Pediatric Concerns: None reported via milk. Oral absorption is poor.

Drug Interactions: Do not use with MAO inhibitors. Use cautiously in patients taking SSRIs.

Relative Infant Dose:

Adult Dose: 0.1 - 1 mg/Kg

Alternatives:

T ½	= 5.25	M/P	=
PHL	=	PB	=
Tmax	=	Oral	=
MW	= 319	pKa	=
Vd	–		

References:
1. Peter C, Hongwan D, Küpfer A, Lauterburg BH. Pharmacokinetics and organ distribution of intravenous and oral methylene blue. Eur J Clin Pharmacol. 2000 Jun;56 (3):247-50.

METHYLERGONOVINE | L2

Trade: Methergine
Other Trades: Ergometrine, Methylerometrine
Uses: Vasoconstrictor, uterine stimulant
AAP: Not reviewed

Methylergonovine is an amine ergot alkaloid used to control postpartum uterine bleeding. The ergot alkaloids are powerful vasoconstrictors. In a group of 8 postpartum women receiving 0.125 mg three times daily for 5 days, the concentration of methylergonovine ranged from <0.5 in 4 patients to 1.3 µg/L in one patient at one hour postdose.[1] In this study, only 5 of 16 milk samples had detectable methylergonovine levels.

Using a dose of 1.3 µg/L of milk, an infant would only consume approximately 0.2 µg/kg/day, which is incredibly low compared to the usual 0.375 mg daily dose. The milk/plasma ratio averaged about 0.3. Short-term (1 week), low-dose regimens of these agents do not apparently pose problems in nursing infants/mothers.[2]

Many studies have been performed showing no diffence in prolactin levels between mothers treated with methylergonovine and those receiving placebo, while some show a suppression in prolactin and thus milk production. One study suggested a 50% decrease in prolactin levels 30 to 75 minutes after a 0.2 mg intramuscular injection of methylergonovine.[3] In 30 lactating women receiving 0.6 mg orally from day 1 to day 7 postpartum, prolactin levels were significantly lower at day 7, while milk production was significantly reduced at days 3 and 7.[4] In a study of 14 postpartum women who received 0.2 mg intramuscularly, plasma prolactin concentrations were lower

(141 ng/mL) as compared to the control group (266.4 ng/mL).[5]

In those situations with longer therapy, a benefit to risk assessment is required, but it is not likely to be overly hazardous to the infant. Methylergonovine is preferred over ergonovine because it does not inhibit lactation to the same degree, and levels in milk are minimal.

Pregnancy Risk Category: C

Lactation Risk Category: L2
                               L4 for chronic use

Adult Concerns: Nausea, vomiting, diarrhea, dizziness, rapid pulse.

Pediatric Concerns: None reported, but long term exposure is not recommended. Methylergonovine is commonly recommended early postpartum for breastfeeding mothers with bleeding.

Drug Interactions: Use caution when using with other vasoconstrictors or pressor agents.

Relative Infant Dose: 2%

Adult Dose: 0.2-0.4 mg every 6-12 hours as needed

Alternatives:

T ½	= 20-30 minutes	M/P	= 0.3
PHL	=	PB	= 36%
Tmax	= 0.5-3 hours	Oral	= 60%
MW	= 339	pKa	=
Vd	=		

References:
1. Erkkola R, Kanto J, Allonen H, Kleimola T, Mantyla R. Excretion of methylergometrine (methylergonovine) into the human breast milk. Int J Clin Pharmacol Biopharm 1978; 16 (12):579-580.
2. Del Pozo E, Brun DR, Hinselmann M. Lack of effect of methyl-ergonovine on postpartum lactation. Am J Obstet Gynecol 1975; 123 (8):845-846.
3. Perez-Lopez FR, Delvoye P, Denayer P, L'Hermite M, Roncero MC, Robyn C. Effectof methylergobasine maleate on serum gonadotrophin and prolactin in humans. Acta Endocrinol (Copenh) 1975; 79 (4):644-657.
4. Peters F, Lummerich M, Breckwoldt M. Inhibition of prolactin and lactation by methylergometrine hydrogenmaleate. Acta Endocrinol (Copenh) 1979; 91 (2):213-216.
5. Weiss G, Klein S, Shenkman L, Kataoka K, Hollander CS. Effect of methylergonovine on puerperal prolactin secretion. Obstet Gynecol 1975; 46 (2):209-210.

METHYLPHENIDATE | L3

Trade: Ritalin, Concerta, Metadate CD, Metadate ER, Methylin, Daytrana, Focalin XR
Other Trades: PMS-Methylphenidate, Riphenidate
Uses: CNS stimulant, treatment of ADHD
AAP: Not reviewed

The pharmacologic effects of methylphenidate are similar to those of amphetamines and include CNS stimulation.[1] It is presently used for narcolepsy and attention deficit hyperactivity syndrome. In a study of 3 women receiving an average of 52 (35-80) mg/day of methylphenidate, the average drug in milk was 19 (13-28) μg/L.[2] The milk/plasma ratio averaged 2.8 (2-3.6). The absolute infant dose averaged 2.9 (2-4.25) μg/kg/d. The average relative infant dose was 0.9% (0.7-1.1). In the one infant studied, plasma levels were <1 μg/L. These levels are probably too low to clinically relevant.

Another case reported a mother taking 15 mg/day with breast milk concentrations averaging 2.5 ng/mL. The daily infant dose was estimated at 0.38 μg/kg, which corresponds to 0.16% of the maternal dose.[3] No drug was detected in breast milk 20-21 hours after the maternal dose.

A mother taking 80 mg/day was determined to have a milk-to-plasma ratio of 2.7, giving an absolute infant dose of 2.3 μg/kg/day, or 0.2% of the maternal dose. Methylphenidate was not detected in the infant's plasma.[4] No adverse effects were noted in any of the infants. These levels are significantly less than for dextroamphetamine. Infants should be observed for agitation, and reduced weight gain although these are quite unlikely at these levels.

The trade name Focalin XR, or dexmethylphenidate HCl, is simply the active dextro-rotary enantiomer of methylphenidate, and therefore kinetic and breastmilk data should be similar to that of methylphenidate.

Pregnancy Risk Category: C

Lactation Risk Category: L3

Adult Concerns: Nervousness, hyperactivity, insomnia, agitation, and lack of appetite.

Pediatric Concerns: None reported in 3 infants, but observe for stimulation, insomnia, anorexia, reduced weight gain.

Drug Interactions: Methylphenidate may reduce the effects of guanethidine and bretylium. May increased serum levels of tricyclic antidepressants, phenytoin, warfarin, phenobarbital, and primidone. Use with MAOI may produce significant increased effects of methylphenidate.

Relative Infant Dose: 0.2% - 0.4%

Adult Dose: 10 mg BID-TID. Higly variable.

Alternatives:

T ½	= 1.4-4.2 hours	M/P	= 2.8
PHL	=	PB	=
Tmax	= 1 - 3 hours	Oral	= 95%
MW	= 233	pKa	= 8.8
Vd	= 11-33		

References:

1. Pharmaceutical Manufacturer Prescribing Information. 1996.
2. Hackett LP, Ilett KF, Kristensen JH, Kohan R, Hale TW. Infant dose and safety of breastfeeding for dexamphetamine and methylphenidate in mothers with attention deficit hyperactivity disorder. Proceedings of the 9th International Congress of Therapeutic Drug Monitoring and Clinical Toxicology, Louisville, USA, April 23-28, 2005, Therapeutic Drug Monitoring 2005; 27:220. (Abstract # 40).
3. Spigset O, Brede WR, Zahlsen K. Excretion of methylphenidate in Breast Milk. Am J Psychiatry 2007; 164 (2):348.
4. Hackett LP, Kristensen JH, Hale TW, Paterson R, Ilett, KF. Methylphenidate and Breast-Feeding. Ann Pharmacother 2006; 40 (10):1890-1891.

METHYLPREDNISOLONE   L2

Trade: Solu-Medrol, Depo-Medrol, Medrol

Other Trades: Medrol, Depo-Medrol, Solu-Medrol, Neo-Medrol, Advantan

Uses: Corticosteroid

AAP: Maternal Medication Usually Compatible with Breastfeeding

Methylprednisolone (MP) is the methyl derivative of prednisolone. Four milligrams of methylprednisolone is roughly equivalent to 5 mg of prednisone. Multiple dosage forms exist and include the succinate salt which is rapidly active, the methylprednisolone base which is the tablet formulation for oral use, and the methylprednisolone acetate suspension (Depo-Medrol) which is slowly absorbed over many days to weeks. Depo-Medrol is generally used intrasynovially, IM, or epidurally and is slowly absorbed from these sites. They would be very unlikely to affect a breastfed infant, but this depends on dose and duration of exposure. For a complete description of corticosteroid use in breastfeeding mothers see the prednisone monograph. In general, the amount of methylprednisolone and other steroids transferred into human milk is minimal as long as the dose does not exceed 80 mg per day.[1] However, relating side effects of steroids administered via breastmilk and their maternal doses is rather difficult and each situation should be evaluated individually. Extended use of high doses could predispose the infant to steroid side effects including decreased linear growth rate, but these require rather high doses. Low to moderate doses are believed to have minimal effect on breastfed infants. See prednisone.

High dose pulsed intravenous or oral administrations of methylprednisolone (MP) have become increasingly important as a treatment for acute relapses or progressively worsening of multiple sclerosis (MS).[2-6] Even though prednisolone is approved by the American Academy of Pediatrics for use in breastfeeding women, when MP is used in such high doses in patients with MS, questions concerning when mothers can return to breastfeeding have arisen. While there are extensive kinetic data on the plasma levels, metabolism and clearance of methylprednisolone from normal and MS patients [8], no data are available on the transfer of MP into human milk subsequent to using such high pulse IV doses in breastfeeding mothers. Simulation of MP elimination curves by the author shows a rapid and complete elimination from the maternal plasma compartment.[9] From this simulation, it would appear a brief pumping and discarding of milk for a period of 8-24 hours following the IV administration of MP (at doses up to 1 gm) would significantly reduce an infant's exposure to this corticosteroid. This simulation estimates the infant dose at 12 hours post-administration of MP to be approximately 1.24 µg/kg/day. These are only theoretical predictions as no one yet has published milk levels following IV administration of 1 gram doses.

Pregnancy Risk Category: C

Lactation Risk Category: L2

Adult Concerns: In pediatrics: shortened stature, GI bleeding, GI ulceration, edema, osteoporosis.

Pediatric Concerns: None reported via breastmilk. Limit dose and length of exposure if possible. High doses and prolonged durations may inhibit epiphyseal bone growth, induce gastric ulcerations, glaucoma, etc.

Drug Interactions: Barbiturates may significantly reduce the effects of corticosteroids. Cholestyramine may reduce absorption of methylprednisone. Oral contraceptives may reduce half-life and concentration of steroids. Ephedrine may reduce the half-life and increase clearance of certain steroids. Phenytoin may increase clearance. Corticosteroid clearance may be decreased by ketoconazole. Certain macrolide antibiotics may significantly decrease clearance of steroids. Isoniazid serum concentrations may be decreased.

Relative Infant Dose:

Adult Dose: 2-60 mg daily

Alternatives: Prednisone

T ½	= 2.8 hours	M/P	=
PHL	=	PB	=
Tmax	=	Oral	= Complete
MW	= 374	pKa	=
Vd	= 1.5		

References:

1. Anderson PO. Corticosteroid use by breast-feeding mothers. Clin Pharm 1987; 6 (6):445.

2. Miller DM, Weinstock-Guttman B, Bethoux F, Lee JC, Beck G, Block V, Durelli L, LaMantia L, Barnes D, Sellebjerg F, Rudick RA. A meta-analysis of methylprednisolone in recovery from multiple sclerosis exacerbations. Mult Scler 2000; 6 (4):267-273.

3. Hommes OR, Barkhof F, Jongen PJ, Frequin ST. Methylprednisolone treatment in multiple sclerosis: effect of treatment, pharmacokinetics, future. Mult Scler 1996; 1 (6):327-328.

4. Goas JY, Marion JL, Missoum A. High dose intravenous methyl prednisolone in acute exacerbations of multiple sclerosis. J Neurol Neurosurg Psychiatry 1983; 46 (1):99.

5. Sellebjerg F, Frederiksen JL, Nielsen PM, Olesen J. Double-blind, randomized, placebo-controlled study of oral, high-dose methylprednisolone in attacks of MS. Neurology 1998; 51 (2):529-534.

6. Barnes D, Hughes RA, Morris RW, Wade-Jones O, Brown P, Britton T, Francis DA, Perkin GD, Rudge P, Swash M, Katifi H, Farmer S, Frankel J. Randomised trial of oral and intravenous methylprednisolone in acute relapses of multiple sclerosis. Lancet 1997; 349 (9056):902-906.

7. Vree TB, Verwey-van Wissen CP, Lagerwerf AJ, Swolfs A, Maes RA, van Ooijen RD, Eikema Hommes OR, Jongen PJ. Isolation and identification of the C6-hydroxy and C20-hydroxy metabolites and glucuronide conjugate of methylprednisolone by preparative high-performance liquid chromatography from urine of patients receiving high-dose pulse therapy. J Chromatogr B Biomed Sci Appl 1999; 726 (1-2):157-168.

8. Vree TB, Lagerwerf AJ, Verwey-van Wissen CP, Jongen PJ. High-performance liquid chromatography analysis, preliminary pharmacokinetics, metabolism and renal excretion of methylprednisolone with its C6 and C20 hydroxy metabolites in multiple sclerosis patients receiving high-dose pulse therapy. J Chromatogr B Biomed Sci Appl 1999; 732 (2):337-348.

9. Hale TW, Ilett K. Unpublished data. 2000.

METOCLOPRAMIDE   L2

Trade: Reglan
Other Trades: Apo-Metoclop, Emex, Maxeran, Reglan, Maxolon, Pramin, Gastromax, Paramid
Uses: GI stimulant, prolactin stimulant
AAP: Drugs whose effect on nursing infants is unknown but may be of concern

Metoclopramide has multiple functions but is primarily used for increasing the lower esophageal sphincter tone in gastroesophageal reflux in patients with reduced gastric tone. In breastfeeding, it is sometimes used in lactating women to stimulate prolactin release from the pituitary and enhance breastmilk production. Since 1981, a number of publications have documented major increases in breastmilk production following the use of metoclopramide, domperidone, or sulpiride. With metoclopramide, the increase in serum prolactin and breastmilk production appears dose-related up to a dose of 15 mg three times daily.[1] Many studies show 66 to 100 % increases in milk production depending on the degree of breastmilk supply in the mother prior to therapy and maybe her initial prolactin levels. Doses of 15 mg/day were found ineffective, whereas doses of 30-45 mg/day were most effective. In most studies, major increases in prolactin were observed such as from 12.5 ng/mL to 172 ng/mL in one patient.[2]

In Kauppila's study[3], the concentration of metoclopramide in milk was consistently higher than the maternal serum levels. The peak occurred at 2-3 hours after administration of the medication. During the late puerperium, the concentration of metoclopramide in the milk varied from 20 to 125 μg/L, which was less than the 28 to 157 μg/L noted during the early puerperium. The authors estimated the daily dose to infant to vary from 6 to 24 μg/kg/day during the early puerperium and from 1 to 13 μg/kg/day during the late phase. These doses are minimal compared to those used for therapy of reflux in pediatric patients (0.1 to 0.5 mg/kg/day). In these studies, only 1 of 5 infants studied had detectable blood levels of metoclopramide; hence, no accumulation or side effects were observed. While plasma prolactin levels in the newborns were comparable to those in the mothers prior to treatment, Kauppila found slight increases in prolactin levels in 4 of 7 newborns following treatment with metoclopramide although a more recent study did not find such changes. However, prolactin levels are highly variable and subject to diurnal rhythm, thus timing is essential in measuring prolactin levels and could account for this inconsistency.

In another study of 23 women with premature infants, milk production increased from 93 mL/day to 197 mL/day between the first and 7th day of therapy with 30 mg/day.[4] Prolactin levels, although varied, increased from 18.1 to 121.8 ng/mL. While basal prolactin levels were elevated significantly, metoclopramide seems to blunt the rapid rise of prolactin when milk was expressed. Nevertheless, milk production was still elevated.

Gupta studied 32 mothers with inadequate milk supply.[5] Following a dose of 10 mg three times daily, a 66-100% increase in milk supply was noted. Of twelve cases of complete lactation failure, 8 responded to treatment in an average of 3-4 days after starting therapy. In this study, 87.5% of the total 32 cases responded to metoclopramide therapy with greater milk production. No untoward effects were noted in the infants.

In a study of 5 breastfeeding women who were receiving 30 mg/day, daily milk production increased significantly from 150.9 mL/day to 276.4 mL/day in this group.[6] Infant plasma prolactin levels in breastfed infants were determined as well on the 5th postnatal day and no changes were noted; thus, the amount of metoclopramide transferred in milk was not enough to change the infants' prolactin levels.

In a study by Lewis in ten patients who received a single oral dose of 10 mg, the mean maternal plasma and milk levels at 2 hours was 68.5 ng/mL and 125.7 µg/L respectively.[7]

Hansen's study showed that 28 women receiving 30 mg/day had no significant increase in milk production as compared to the placebo group.[9] However, this study was initiated with 96 hours of delivery, a time when virtually all mothers would have had exceedingly high plasma prolactin levels anyway. Metoclopramide should not be expected to work as a galactagogue when plasma prolactin levels are high.

It is well recognized that metoclopramide increases a mother's milk supply, but it is exceedingly dose dependent, and yet some mothers simply do not respond. In those mothers who do not respond, Kauppila's work suggests that such patients may already have elevated prolactin levels. In his study, 3 of the 5 mothers who did not respond with increased milk production, had the highest basal prolactin levels (300-400 ng/mL).[3] Thus it may be advisable to do plasma prolactin levels on under-producing mothers prior to instituting metoclopramide therapy to assess the response prior to treating.

Side effects such as gastric cramping and diarrhea limit the compliance of some patients but are rare. Further, it is often found that upon rapid discontinuation of the medication, the supply of milk may in some instances reduce significantly. Tapering of the dose is generally recommended and one possible regimen is to decrease the dose by 10 mg per week. Long-term use of this medication (>4 weeks) may be accompanied by increased side effects such as depression in the mother although some patients have used it successfully for months. Another dopamine antagonist, Domperidone, due to minimal side effects, is a preferred choice but is unfortunately not available in the USA other than in compounding pharmacies.

Two recent cases of serotonin-like reactions (agitation, dysarthria, diaphoresis and extrapyramidal movement disorder) have been reported when metoclopramide was used in patients receiving sertraline or venlafaxine.[8] The FDA has recently warned of symptoms of tardive dyskinesia after 3 months of exposure.

Pregnancy Risk Category: B

Lactation Risk Category: L2

Adult Concerns: Diarrhea, sedation, gastric upset, nausea, extrapyramidal symptoms, severe depression.

Pediatric Concerns: None reported in infants via milk. Commonly used in pediatrics.

Drug Interactions: Anticholinergic drugs may reduce the effects of metoclopramide. Opiate analgesics may increase CNS depression. Two cases of serotonin-like syndrome have been reported when used with the metoclopramide (Reglan). Two recent cases of serotonin-like reactions (agitation, dysarthria, diaphoresis and extrapyramidal movement disorder) have been reported when metoclopramide was used in patients receiving sertraline or venlafaxine.[8]

Relative Infant Dose: 4.7% - 14.3%

Adult Dose: 10-15 mg TID

Alternatives: Domperidone

T ½	= 5-6 hours	M/P	= 0.5-4.06
PHL	=	PB	= 30%
Tmax	= 1-2 hours (oral)	Oral	– 30-100%
MW	= 300	pKa	=
Vd	=		

References:

1. Kauppila A, Kivinen S, Ylikorkala O. A dose response relation between improved lactation and metoclopramide. Lancet 1981; 1 (8231):1175-1177.
2. Budd SC, Erdman SH, Long DM, Trombley SK, Udall JN, Jr. Improved lactation with metoclopramide. A case report. Clin Pediatr (Phila) 1993; 32 (1):53-57.
3. Kauppila A, Arvela P, Koivisto M, Kivinen S, Ylikorkala O, Pelkonen O. Metoclopramide and breast feeding: transfer into milk and the newborn. Eur J Clin Pharmacol 1983; 25 (6):819-823.

4. Ehrenkranz RA, Ackerman BA. Metoclopramide effect on faltering milk production by mothers of premature infants. Pediatrics 1986; 78 (4):614-620.

5. Gupta AP, Gupta PK. Metoclopramide as a lactogogue. Clin Pediatr (Phila) 1985; 24 (5):269-272.

6. Ertl T, Sulyok E, Ezer E, Sarkany I, Thurzo V, Csaba IF. The influence of metoclopramide on the composition of human breast milk. Acta Paediatr Hung 1991; 31 (4):415-422.

7. Lewis PJ, Devenish C, Kahn C. Controlled trial of metoclopramide in the initiation of breast feeding. Br J Clin Pharmacol 1980; 9 (2):217-219.

8   Fisher AA, Davis MW. Serotonin syndrome caused by selective serotonin reuptake-inhibitors-metoclopramide interaction. Ann Pharmacother 2002; 36:67-71.

9. Hansen WF, McAndrew S, Harris K, Zimmerman MB. Metoclopramide Effect on Breastfeeding the Preterm Infant: A Randomized Trial. Obstet Gynecol 2005; 105 (2):383-389.

METOPROLOL	L3

Trade: Toprol-XL, Lopressor

Other Trades: Apo-Metoprolol, Betaloc, Novo-Metoprol, Minax

Uses: Antihypertensive, beta blocker

AAP: Maternal Medication Usually Compatible with Breastfeeding

At low doses, metoprolol is a very cardioselective Beta-1 blocker, and it is used for hypertension, angina, and tachyarrhythmias. In a study of 3 women 4-6 months postpartum who received 100 mg twice daily for 4 days, the peak concentration of metoprolol ranged from 0.38 to 2.58 μmol/L, whereas the maternal plasma levels ranged from 0.1 to 0.97 μmol/L.[1] The mean milk/plasma ratio was 3.0. Assuming ingestion of 75 mL of milk at each feeding, and the maximum concentration of 2.58 μmol/L, an infant would ingest approximately 0.05 mg metoprolol at the first feeding and considerably less at subsequent feedings.

In another study of 9 women receiving 50-100 mg twice daily, the maternal plasma and milk concentrations ranged from 4-556 nmol/L and 19-1690 nmol/L respectively.[2] Using this data, the authors calculated an average milk concentration throughout the day as 280 μg/L of milk. This dose is 20-40 times less than a typical clinical dose. The milk/plasma ratio in these studies averaged 3.72.

Although the milk/plasma ratios for this drug are in general high, the maternal plasma levels are quite small so the absolute amount transferred to the infant are quite small. Although these levels are probably too low to be clinically relevant, clinicians should use metoprolol under close supervision.

Pregnancy Risk Category: C

Lactation Risk Category: L3

Adult Concerns: Hypotension, weakness, depression, bradycardia.

Pediatric Concerns: None reported in several studies, but close observation for hypotension, weakness, bradycardia is advised.

Drug Interactions: Decreased effect when used with aluminum salts, barbiturates, calcium salts, cholestyramine, NSAIDs, ampicillin, rifampin, and salicylates. Beta blockers may reduce the effect of oral sulfonylureas (hypoglycemic agents). Increased toxicity/effect when used with other antihypertensives, contraceptives, MAO inhibitors, cimetidine, and numerous other products. See drug interaction reference for complete listing.

Relative Infant Dose: 1.4%

Adult Dose: 100-450 mg daily.

Alternatives: Propranolol

T ½	= 3-7 hours	M/P	= 3-3.72
PHL	=	PB	= 12%
Tmax	= 2.5-3 hours	Oral	= 40-50%
MW	= 267	pKa	= 9.7
Vd	= 2.5-5.6		

References:
1. Liedholm H, Melander A, Bitzen PO, Helm G, Lonnerholm G, Mattiasson I, Nilsson B, Wahlin-Boll E. Accumulation of atenolol and metoprolol in human breast milk. Eur J Clin Pharmacol 1981; 20 (3):229-231.
2. Sandstrom B, Regardh CG. Metoprolol excretion into breast milk. Br J Clin Pharmacol 1980; 9 (5):518-519.
3. Kulas J, Lunell NO, Rosing U, Steen B, Ranc A. Atenolol and metoprolol. A comparison of their excretion into human breast milk. Acta Obstet Gynecol Scand Suppl 1984; 118:65-69.

METRONIDAZOLE   L2

Trade: Flagyl, Metizol, Trikacide, Protostat, Noritate
Other Trades: Apo-Metronidazole, Flagyl, NeoMetric, Novo-Nidazol, Metrozine, Rozex
Uses: Antibiotic, amebicide
AAP: Drugs whose effect on nursing infants is unknown but may be of concern

Metronidazole is indicated in the treatment of vaginitis due to Trichomonas Vaginalis and various anaerobic bacterial infections including Giardiasis, H. Pylori, B. Fragilis, and Gardnerella vaginalis. Metronidazole has become the treatment of choice for pediatric giardiasis (AAP).

Metronidazole absorption is time and dose dependent and also depends on the route of administration (oral vs. vaginal). Following a 2 gm oral dose milk levels were reported to peak at 50-57 mg/L at 2 hours. Milk levels after 12 hours were approximately 19 mg/L and at 24 hours were approximately 10 mg/L.[1] The average drug concentration reported in milk at 2, 8, 12, and 12-24 hours was 45.8, 27.9, 19.1, and 12.6 mg/L respectively. If breastfeeding were to continue uninterrupted, an infant would consume 21.8 mg via breastmilk. With a 12 hour discontinuation, an infant would consume only 9.8 mg.

In a group of 12 nursing mothers receiving 400 mg three times daily, the mean milk/plasma ratio was 0.91.[2] The mean milk metronidazole concentration was 15.5 mg/L. Infant plasma metronidazole levels ranged from 1.27 to 2.41 µg/mL. No adverse effects were attributable to metronidazole therapy in these infants.

In another study in patients receiving 600 and 1200 mg daily, the average milk metronidazole concentration was 5.7 and 14.4 mg/L respectively.[3] The plasma levels of metronidazole (2 hours) at the 600 mg/d dose were 5 µg/mL (mother) and 0.8 µg/mL (infant). At the 1200 mg/d dose (2 hours), plasma levels were 12.5 µg/mL (mother) and 2.4 µg/mL (infant). The authors estimated the daily metronidazole dose received by the infant at 3.0 mg/kg with 500 mL milk intake per day, which is well below the advocated 10-20 mg/kg recommended therapeutic dose for infants.

For treating trichomoniasis, many physicians now recommend 2 gm single oral dose with an interruption of breastfeeding for 12-24 hours, then reinstitute breastfeeding. Thus far, no reports of untoward effects in breastfed infants have been published for the 2 gm STAT dose or the 250 mg three times daily for 10 day dosage regimen.

In a study of 6 women receiving 400 mg TID for 3 days, the average milk concentration was 13.5 mg/L with a milk/plasma ratio of 0.9.[4]

For intravaginal use see MetroGel. MetroGel vaginal jell produces only 2% of the mean peak serum level concentration of a 500 mg oral metronidazole tablet. The maternal plasma level following use of each dose of vaginal gel averaged only 237 µg/L, far less than orally administered tablet formulations. Milk levels following intravaginal use would probably be exceedingly low Milk/plasma ratios, although published for oral metronidazole, may be different for this route of administration.

It is true that the relative infant dose via milk is moderately high depending on the dose and timing. Infants whose mothers ingest 1.2 gm/d will receive approximately 13.5% or less of the maternal dose or approximately 2.3 mg/kg/day. Bennett has calculated the relative infant dose from 11.7% to as high as 24% of the maternal dose.[8] Heisterberg found metronidazole levels in infant plasma to be 16% and 19% of the maternal plasma levels following doses of 600 mg/d and 1200 mg/d.[1] While these levels seem significant, it is still pertinent to remember that metronidazole is a commonly used drug in premature neonates, infants, and children, and 2.3 mg/kg/d is still much less than the therapeutic dose used in infants/children (7.5-30 mg/kg/d). Thus far, virtually no adverse effects have been reported.

INTRAVENOUS STUDIES

Metronidazole is approximately 98% bioavailable orally and it is rapidly absorbed. In one study of intravenous kinetics, the authors found peak plasma levels of 28.9 µg/mL in adults following a 500 mg TID dose.[5] In another study of oral and intravenous kinetics, the authors used 400 mg orally, and 500 mg intravenously.[6] Following 400 mg orally, the C_{max} at 90 minutes was 17.4 µg/mL. Following 500 mg IV, the C_{max} at 90 minutes was 23.6 µg/mL. Reducing the IV dose to 400 mg would have given a plasma level of approximately 18.8

Pregnancy Risk Category: B

Lactation Risk Category: L2

Adult Concerns: Nausea, dry mouth, vomiting, diarrhea, abdominal discomfort. Drug may turn urine brown.

Pediatric Concerns: Numerous studies show no untoward effects. One letter to the editor suggests an infant developed diarrhea, and a case of lactose intolerance. The link to metronidazole is tenuous.

Drug Interactions: Phenytoin and phenobarbital may decrease half-life of metronidazole. Alcohol may induce disulfiram-like reactions. May increase prothrombin times when used with warfarin.

Relative Infant Dose: 12.6% - 13.5%

Adult Dose: 250-500 mg BID

Alternatives:

T ½	= 8.5 hours	M/P	= 1.15
PHL	= 25-75 hours	PB	= 10%
Tmax	= 2-4 hours	Oral	= 100%
MW	= 171	pKa	=
Vd	=		

References:
1. Erickson SH, Oppenheim GL, Smith GH. Metronidazole in breast milk. Obstet Gynecol 1981; 57 (1):48-50.
2. Passmore CM, McElnay JC, Rainey EA, D'Arcy PF. Metronidazole excretion in human milk and its effect on the suckling neonate. Br J Clin Pharmacol 1988; 26 (1):45-51.
3. Heisterberg L, Branebjerg PE. Blood and milk concentrations of metronidazole in mothers and infants. J Perinat Med 1983; 11 (2):114-120.
4. Amon I, Amon K. Wirkstoffkonzentrationen von metronidazol bie schwangeren und postpartal. Fortschritte der antimikrobiellen und antineoplastischen. Chemotherapie 2004; Band 2-4:605-612.
5. Ti TY, Lee HS, Khoo YM. Disposition of intravenous metronidazole in Asian surgical patients. Antimicrob Agents Chemother 1996; 40 (10):2248-2251.
6. Earl P, Sisson PR, Ingham HR. Twelve-hourly dosage schedule for oral and intravenous metronidazole. J Antimicrob Chemother 1989; 23 (4):619-621.
7. Loft S, Dossing M, Poulsen HE, Sonne J, Olesen KL, Simonsen K, Andreasen PB. Influence of dose and route of administration on disposition of metronidazole and its major metabolites. Eur J Clin Pharmacol 1986; 30 (4):467-473.
8. Bennett PN. Use of the monographs on drugs: In: Drugs and Human Lactation. Amsterdam, Elsevier, 1996.
9. Falagas ME, Walker AM, Jick H, Ruthazer R, Griffith J, Snydman DR. Late incidence of cancer after metronidazole use: a matched metronidazole user/nonuser study. Clin Infect Dis 1998; 26 (2):384-388.
10. Fahrig R, Engelke M. Reinvestigation of in vivo genotoxicity studies in man. I. No induction of DNA strand breaks in peripheral lymphocytes after metronidazole therapy. Mutat Res 1997; 395 (2-3):215-221.
11. Roe FJ. Toxicologic evaluation of metronidazole with particular reference to carcinogenic, mutagenic, and teratogenic potential. Surgery 1983; 93 (1 Pt 2):158-164.
12. Bergan T, Leinebo O, Blom-Hagen T, Salvesen B. Pharmacokinetics and bioavailability of metronidazole after tablets, suppositories and intravenous administration. Scand J Gastroenterol Suppl 1984; 91:45-60.

METRONIDAZOLE TOPICAL GEL   L3

Trade: MetroGel Topical
Other Trades: Metro-Gel, Metrogyl, Metrogel
Uses: Topical antibacterial
AAP: Not reviewed

Metronidazole topical gel is primarily indicated for acne and is a gel formulation containing 0.75% metronidazole. For metronidazole kinetics and entry into human milk see metronidazole. Following topical application of 1 gm of metronidazole gel to the face (equivalent to 7.5 mg metronidazole base), the maximum serum concentration was only 66 nanograms/mL in only one of 10 patients (In three of the ten patients, levels were undetectible).[1,2] This concentration is 100 times less than the serum concentration achieved following the oral ingestion of just one 250 mg tablet. Therefore, the topical application of metronidazole gel provides only exceedingly low plasma levels in the mother and minimal to no levels in milk.

Pregnancy Risk Category: B

Lactation Risk Category: L3

Adult Concerns: Watery eyes if the gel is applied too close to eyes. Minor skin irritation, redness, milk dryness, burning.

Pediatric Concerns: None reported via milk. Milk levels would be exceedingly low to nil.

Drug Interactions: Although many known interactions with oral metronidazole are documented, due to minimal plasma levels of this preparation, they would be extremely remote.

Relative Infant Dose:

Adult Dose: apply topical BID

Alternatives:

T ½	= 8.5 hours	M/P	= 0.4-1.8
PHL	=	PB	= 10%
Tmax	=	Oral	= Complete
MW	= 171	pKa	=
Vd	=		

References:
1.Drug Facts and Comparisons 1996 ed. ed. St. Louis: 1996.
2.Pharmaceutical Manufacturer Prescribing Information. 1997.

METRONIDAZOLE VAGINAL GEL   L2

Trade: MetroGel Vaginal
Other Trades: Metrogel
Uses: Antibiotic
AAP: Drugs whose effect on nursing infants is unknown but may be of concern

Both topical and vaginal preparations of metronidazole contain only 0.75% metronidazole. Plasma levels following administration are exceedingly low.[1] This metronidazole vaginal product produces only 2% of the mean peak serum level concentration of a 500 mg oral metronidazole tablet. The maternal plasma level following use of each dose of vaginal gel averaged 237 µg/L compared to 12,785 µg/L following an oral 500 mg tablet. Milk levels following intravaginal use would probably be exceeding low.

Milk/plasma ratios, although published for oral metronidazole, may be different for this route of administration, primarily due to the low plasma levels attained with this product. Topical and intravaginal metronidazole gels are indicated for bacterial vaginosis.

Pregnancy Risk Category: B

Lactation Risk Category: L2

Adult Concerns: Mild irritation to vaginal wall.

Pediatric Concerns: None reported.

Drug Interactions: Phenytoin and phenobarbital may decrease half-life of metronidazole. Alcohol may induce disulfiram-like reactions. May increase prothrombin times when used with warfarin.

Relative Infant Dose:

Adult Dose: 37.5 mg BID

Alternatives:

T ½	= 8.5 hours	M/P	=
PHL	=	PB	= 10%
Tmax	= 6-12 hours	Oral	= Complete
MW	= 171	pKa	=
Vd	=		

References:
1. Pharmaceutical Manufacturer Prescribing Information. 1996.

METYRAPONE   L2

Trade: Metopyrone
Other Trades:
Uses: Diagnostic Agent, Radiopharmaceutical Imaging
AAP: Not reviewed

Metopirone is an inhibitor of endogenous adrenal corticosteroid synthesis and is a diagnostic drug for diagnosis and treatment of adrenocortical hyperfunction.

In a case report of a single patient who received 250 mg four times daily for almost 9 weeks, and who was 1 week postpartum, breastmilk samples were analyzed for metopirone and metabolite. At steady state, the average concentrations in milk and absolute and relative infant doses were 11 µg/L, 1.7 µg/kg/d, and 0.02%, respectively, for metyrapone, and 48.5 µg/L, 7.3 µg/kg/d, and 0.08%, respectively, for rac-metyrapol. The authors suggest that maternal metyrapone use during breastfeeding is unlikely to be a significant risk to an infant.

Pregnancy Risk Category:

Lactation Risk Category: L2

Adult Concerns: Hypertension, alopecia and hirsutism, bone marrow depression, adrenal insufficiency have been reported.

Pediatric Concerns: None yet. Levels probably too low.

Drug Interactions: Increased risk of acetaminophen toxicity.

Relative Infant Dose: 0.06% - 0.1%

Adult Dose: 30 mg/kg

Alternatives:

T ½	=	M/P	=
PHL	=	PB	=
Tmax	= 1 hour	Oral	= Complete
MW	= 226	pKa	=
Vd	=		

References:
1. Hotham NJ, Ilett KF, Hackett LP, Morton MR, Muller P, Hague WM. Transfer ofmetyrapone and its metabolite, rac-metyrapol, into breast milk. J Hum Lact. 2009 Nov;25 (4):451-4.

MEXILETINE HCL   L2

Trade: Mexitil
Other Trades: Mexitil, Novo-Mexiletine
Uses: Antiarrhythmic
AAP: Maternal Medication Usually Compatible with Breastfeeding

Mexiletine is an antiarrhythmic agent with activity similar to lidocaine. In a study on one patient who was receiving 600 mg/day in divided doses, the milk level at steady state was 0.8 mg/L, which represented at milk/plasma ratio of 1.1.[1] Mexiletine was not detected in the infant nor were untoward effects noted. In another study on day 2 to 5 postpartum and in a patient receiving 200 mg three times daily, the mean peak concentration of mexiletine in breastmilk was 959 µg/L, and the maternal serum was 724 µg/L.[2] In this study the milk plasma ratio varied from 0.78 to 1.89 with an average of 1.45. It is unlikely this exposure would lead to untoward side effects in a breastfeeding infant.

Pregnancy Risk Category: C

Lactation Risk Category: L2

Adult Concerns: Arrhythmias, bradycardia, hypotension, tremors, dizziness.

Pediatric Concerns: None reported in two studies.

Drug Interactions: Aluminum, magnesium hydroxide, atropine, and narcotics may reduce the oral absorption of mexiletine. Cimetidine may increase or decreased mexiletine plasma levels. Hydantoins such as phenytoin may increase mexiletine clearance and reduce plasma levels. Rifampin may increase mexiletine clearance leading to lower levels. Mexiletine may reduce the clearance of caffeine by 50%. Serum theophylline levels may be increased significantly to toxic levels.

Relative Infant Dose: 1.4% - 1.6%

Adult Dose: 200 mg every 8 hours

Alternatives:

T ½	= 9.2 hours	M/P	= 1.45
PHL	=	PB	= 63%
Tmax	= 2-3 hours (oral)	Oral	= 90%
MW	= 179	pKa	= 8.4
Vd	= 6-12		

References:

1. Lewis AM, Patel L, Johnston A, Turner P. Mexiletine in human blood and breast milk. Postgrad Med J 1981; 57 (671):546-547.
2. Timmis AD, Jackson G, Holt DW. Mexiletine for control of ventricular dysrhythmias in pregnancy. Lancet 1980; 2 (8195 pt 1):647-648.

MICONAZOLE   L2

Trade: Monistat IV, Monistat 3, 7
Other Trades: Micatin, Monistat, Daktarin, Daktozin, Fungo
Uses: Antifungal for candidiasis
AAP: Not reviewed

Miconazole is an effective antifungal that is commonly used IV, topically, and intravaginally. After intravaginal application, approximately 1% of the dose is absorbed systemically.[1,2] After topical application, there is little or no absorption (0.1%). It is unlikely that the limited absorption of miconazole from vaginal application would produce significant milk levels. Milk concentrations following oral and IV miconazole have not been reported. Oral absorption of miconazole is poor, only 25-30%. Miconazole is commonly used in pediatric patients less than 1 year of age.

Pregnancy Risk Category: C

Lactation Risk Category: L2

Adult Concerns: Nausea, vomiting, diarrhea, anorexia, itching, rash, local irritation.

Pediatric Concerns: None reported via milk.

Drug Interactions: May increase warfarin anticoagulant effect. May increase hypoglycemia of oral sulfonylureas. Phenytoin levels may be increased.

Relative Infant Dose:

Adult Dose: 200-1200 mg TID

Alternatives:

T ½	= 20-25 hours	M/P	=
PHL	=	PB	= 91-93%
Tmax	= Immediate (IV)	Oral	= 25-30%
MW	= 416	pKa	=
Vd	=		

References:
1.   Drug Facts and Comparisons 1995 ed. ed. St. Louis: 1995.
2.   McEvoy GE. (ed):AFHS Drug Information. New York, NY: 1995.

MIDAZOLAM   L2

Trade: Versed
Other Trades: Versed, Hypnovel
Uses: Short acting benzodiazepine sedative, hypnotic
AAP: Drugs whose effect on nursing infants is unknown but may be of concern

Midazolam is a very short acting benzodiazepine primarily used as an induction or preanesthetic medication. The onset of action of midazolam is extremely rapid, its potency is greater than diazepam, and its metabolic elimination is more rapid. With a plasma half-life of only 1.9 hours, it is preferred for rapid induction and maintenance of anesthesia. After oral administration of 15 mg for up to 6 days postnatally in 22 women, the mean milk/plasma ratio was 0.15 and the maximum level of midazolam in breastmilk was 9 µg/L and occurred 1-2 hours after administration.[1] Midazolam and its hydroxy-metabolite were undetectable 4 hours after administration. Therefore, the amount of midazolam transferred to an infant via early milk is minimal, particularly if the baby is breastfed more than 4 hours after administration.

In another study of five lactating women who received a single 2 mg IV dose, milk levels of midazolam were exceedingly low after 7 hours. The median amount of midazolam recovered within 24 hours was only 26 µg which was only 0.004% of the maternal dose of 2 mg.[2] Midazolam is so rapidly redistributed to other tissues from the plasma compartment, milk levels will invariably be exceedingly low.

Pregnancy Risk Category: D

Lactation Risk Category: L2

Adult Concerns: Sedation, respiratory depression.

Pediatric Concerns: None reported in several studies. Milk levels exceedingly low after brief wait.

Drug Interactions: Theophylline may reduce the sedative effects of midazolam. Other CNS depressants may potentiate the depressant effects of midazolam. Cimetidine may increase plasma levels of midazolam.

Relative Infant Dose: 0.6%

Adult Dose: 1-2.5 mg once or twice

Alternatives: Lorazepam

T ½	= 2-5 hours	M/P	= 0.15
PHL	= 6.5-23 hours	PB	= 97%
Tmax	= 20-50 minutes (oral)	Oral	= 27-44%
MW	= 326	pKa	= 6.2
Vd	= 1.0-2.5		

References:
1. Matheson I, Lunde PK, Bredesen JE. Midazolam and nitrazepam in the maternity ward: milk concentrations and clinical effects. Br J Clin Pharmacol 1990; 30 (6):787-793.
2. Nitsun M, Szokol JW, Saleh HJ, Murphy GS, Vender JS, Luong L, Raikoff K, Avram MJ. Pharmacokinetics of midazolam, propofol, and fentanyl transfer to human breast milk. Clin Pharmacol Ther 2006; 79 (6):549-557.

MIDODRINE   L3

Trade: ProAmatine
Other Trades: Amatine,Gutron, Midon
Uses: Vasopressor / Antihypotensive agent
AAP: Not reviewed

Midodrine is a vasopressor used to increase blood pressure. Midodrine is a prodrug that is metabolized to desglymidodrine. This metabolite is a long-acting alpha-1 agonist. It produces an increase in vascular tone and elevation of blood pressure. Desglymidodrine does not stimulate cardiac beta-1 receptors, nor does it pass the blood-brain barrier. No data are available on its transfer to human milk, but some should be expected. This product is small in MW, belongs to the phenylethylamine family, is lipophilic, and is likely to penetrate milk as do the other members of this family. Some caution is recommended.

Pregnancy Risk Category: C

Lactation Risk Category: L3

Adult Concerns: Supine hypertension, pruritus, pilomotor reactions, chills, painful urination retention, and GI symptoms have been reported. CNS reactions include headache, insomnia, stimulation, restlessness, dizziness. A vagal reflex may occur following use and produce a reflex bradycardia.

Pediatric Concerns: None reported via milk, but some caution is recommended. Observer for hypertension, insomnia, and excitement.

Drug Interactions: Additive with other adrenergic stimulants such as pseudoephedrine, ephedrine, phenylephrine or phenylpropanolamine. Digoxin may enhance or precipitate reflex bradycardia. The concurrent use of prazosin or other alpha blockers may inhibit the effects of midodrine. Use with tricyclic antidepressants may precipitate arrhythmias and tachycardia.

Relative Infant Dose:

Adult Dose: 10 mg 3 times daily at 4-hour intervals for orthostatic hypotension

Alternatives:

T ½	= 3-4 hours (metabolite)	M/P	=
PHL	=	PB	=
Tmax	= 1-2 hours	Oral	= 93%
MW	= 290	pKa	=
Vd	=		

References:
1. Pharmaceutical Manufacturers Prescribing Information, 2003.

MIFEPRISTONE   L3

Trade: Mifeprex
Other Trades: Mifegyn, Pencroftonum
Uses: Antiprogestational agent.
AAP: Not reviewed

Mifepristone is an antiprogestational agent which competitively binds with the progesterone receptor. Based on studies with various oral doses in several animal species (mouse, rat, rabbit and monkey), the compound inhibits the activity of endogenous or exogenous progesterone.[1] Among it uses is to terminate pregnancies. Mifepristone binds to plasma protein receptors and has a biphasic elimination phase with a terminal elimination half-life of 18 hours. No data are available on its transfer into milk, but steroids transfer into human milk poorly. Interestingly, studies in monkeys found increased production of colostrum and increased weight gain in infant monkeys. This correlates with the effect of progesterone receptor activation in inhibiting milk production early postnatally such as with retained placenta.

Pregnancy Risk Category: X

Lactation Risk Category: L3 in nonpregnant patient
L5 in pregnant patient

Adult Concerns: Bleeding and cramping, abdominal pain, including uterine cramping. Other commonly reported side effects are nausea, vomiting and diarrhea. Pelvic pain, fainting, headache, dizziness, and asthenia occurred rarely.

Pediatric Concerns: No studies in humans. Studies in monkeys suggest it increases milk production early postnatally.

Drug Interactions:

Relative Infant Dose:

Adult Dose: 600 mg STAT

Alternatives:

T ½	= 18 hours	M/P	=
PHL	=	PB	= 98%
Tmax	⁻ 1-3 hours	Oral	= 69%
MW	= 426	pKa	=
Vd	= 1.5		

References:
1. Pharmaceutical manufacturers prescribing information, 2005.
2. Wolf JP, Sinosich M, Anderson TL, Ulmann A, Baulieu EE, Hodgen GD. Progesterone antagonist (RU 486) for cervical dilation, labor induction, and delivery in monkeys: effectiveness in combination with oxytocin. Am J Obstet Gynecol 1989 Jan; 160 (1):45-7.

MIGLITOL L2

Trade: Glyset, Diastabol
Other Trades: Glyset
Uses: Anti diabetic agent
AAP: Not reviewed

Miglitol is an oral alpha-glycosidase inhibitor for use in non-insulin depended diabetes mellitus. Miglitol delays the digestion of ingested carbohydrates thereby resulting in a small rise in blood glucose concentration following meals. Miglitol does not stimulate insulin release nor does it inhibit lactase, nor does it induce hypoglycemia. The oral absorption of miglitol is saturable in adults in doses higher than 25 mg. A dose of 100 mg is only 50-70% absorbed orally.

The manufacturer reports that milk levels are very small. Total excretion into milk accounted for 0.02% of a 100 mg maternal dose. The estimated exposure to a nursing infant is approximately 0.4% of the maternal dose.

Pregnancy Risk Category: B

Lactation Risk Category: L2

Adult Concerns: Flatulence, soft stools, diarrhea, abdominal discomfort are the most commonly reported side effects.

Pediatric Concerns: No reports of use in breastfeeding mothers.

Drug Interactions: Glyburide may reduce plasma levels (17-25%) of miglitol. Only small but insignificant changes were noted when coadministered with metformin.

Relative Infant Dose: 0.4%

Adult Dose: 50 mg three times daily

Alternatives: Metformin

T ½	= 2 hours	M/P	=
PHL	=	PB	= <4%
Tmax	= 2-3 hours	Oral	= Variable
MW	= 207	pKa	= 5.9
Vd	= 0.18		

References:
1.   Pharmaceutical Manufacturers Prescribing Information, 2003.

MILK THISTLE   L3

Trade: Holy Thistle, Lady Thistle, Marian Thistle, Silybum, Silymarin

Other Trades:

Uses: Hepatoprotectant

AAP: Not reviewed

Milk Thistle has been used since 23 AD as a liver protectant.[1] Silymarin, a mixture of three isomeric flavonolignans, consists of Silybin, silychristin, and silidianin.[2] Silybin is the most biologically active and is believed to be a potent antioxidant and hepatoprotective agent. Silymarin is poorly soluble in water so aqueous preparations such as teas are ineffective. The oral bioavailability is likewise poor, only 23-47% is absorbed orally. Oral forms are generally concentrated. Silymarin effects are almost exclusively on the liver and kidney and concentrates in liver cells. It is believed to inhibit oxidative damage to cells by increasing glutathione synthesis. It is believed to also stimulate the regenerative capacity of liver cells. While it has been advocated for the stimulation of milk synthesis, little evidence of efficacy exists. No data are available concerning Silymarin transfer to human milk but some probably transfers. However, it is rather devoid of reported toxicity with only brief GI intolerance and mild allergic reactions.[3,4]

Pregnancy Risk Category:

Lactation Risk Category: L3

Adult Concerns: Mild GI intolerance and allergic reactions.

Pediatric Concerns: None reported via milk.

Drug Interactions:

Relative Infant Dose:

Adult Dose: 200-400 mg daily via extracts

Alternatives:

T ½	=		M/P	=
PHL	=		PB	=
Tmax	=		Oral	= 23-47%
MW	= 482		pKa	=
Vd	=			

References:
1. Foster S. Milk thistle-Silybum marianum. Botanical Series No. 305. American Botanical Council, Austin, TX 1991; 3-7.
2. Leung AY. Encyclopedia of Common Natural Ingredients used in Food, Drugs and Cosmetics. J Wiley and Sons, 1980.
3. Review of Natural Products Facts and Comparisons 1999.
4. Awang D. Can Pharm J Oct 1993; 403-404.

MINOCYCLINE   L2

Trade: Minocin, Dynacin, Arestin
Other Trades: Minocin, Novo-Minocycline, Akamin,
Minomycin, Minocin, Blemix
Uses: Tetracycline antibiotic
AAP: Not reviewed

Minocycline is a broad-spectrum tetracycline antibiotic with significant side effects in pediatric patients, including dental staining and reduced bone growth.[1,2] It is probably secreted into breastmilk in small but clinically insignificant levels. Because tetracyclines, in general, bind to milk calcium they would have reduced absorption in the infant, but minocycline may be absorbed to a greater degree than the older tetracyclines. Although most tetracyclines secreted into milk are generally bound to calcium, thus inhibiting their absorption, minocycline is poorly bound and may be better absorbed in a breastfeeding infant than the older tetracyclines. While the absolute absorption of older tetracyclines may be dramatically reduced by calcium salts, the newer doxycycline and minocycline analogs bind less and their overall absorption, while slowed, may be significantly higher than earlier versions. A dosage of tetracycline 2 gm/day for 3 days has achieved a milk/plasma ratio of 0.6 to 0.8. In another study of 5 lactating women receiving tetracycline 500 mg PO four times daily, the breastmilk concentrations ranged from 0.43 mg/L to 2.58 mg/L. Levels in infants were below the limit of detection. Because we have many other antimicrobials with similar spectrums, the use of tetracyclines in breastfeeding women is not generally recommended but not necessarily contraindicated. Short-term use (<3 weeks) is probably safe, longer therapy should be avoided. There is little risk of permanent dental staining with only a brief exposure (several weeks).

Pregnancy Risk Category: D

Lactation Risk Category: L2 for acute use
L4 for chronic use

Adult Concerns: Adverse effects include GI distress, dizziness, thyroid pigmentation, vomiting, diarrhea, nephrotoxicity, photosensitivity.

Pediatric Concerns: None via breastmilk, but pediatric side effects include decreased linear bone growth and dental staining after prolonged exposure.

Drug Interactions: Absorption may be reduced or delayed when used with dairy products, calcium, magnesium, or aluminum containing antacids, oral contraceptives, iron, zinc, sodium bicarbonate, penicillins, cimetidine. Increased toxicity may result when used with methoxyflurane anesthesia. Use with warfarin anticoagulants may increase anticoagulation.

Relative Infant Dose: 0.2% - 1.4%

Adult Dose: 100 mg BID

Alternatives: Doxycycline

T ½	= 15-20 hours	M/P	=
PHL	=	PB	= 76%
Tmax	= 3 hours	Oral	= 90-100%
MW	= 457	pKa	=
Vd	=		

References:
1. Drug Facts and Comparisons 1996 ed. ed. St. Louis: 1996.
2. McEvoy GE. (ed):AFHS Drug Information. New York, NY: 1995.

MINOXIDIL — L2

Trade: Loniten, Minodyl, Rogaine
Other Trades: Loniten, Rogaine, Apo-Gain, Minox
Uses: Antihypertensive
AAP: Maternal Medication Usually Compatible with Breastfeeding

Minoxidil is a potent vasodilator and antihypertensive. It is also used for hair loss and baldness. When applied topically, only 1.4% of the dose is absorbed systemically. Following a dose of 7.5 mg, minoxidil was secreted into human milk in concentrations ranging from trough levels of 0.3 µg/L at 12 hours to peak levels of 41.7-55 µg/L at 1 hour following an oral dose of 7.5 mg.[1] Long-term exposure of breastfeeding infants in women ingesting oral minoxidil may not be advisable. However, in those using topical minoxidil, the limited absorption via skin would minimize systemic levels and significantly reduce risk of transfer to infant via breastmilk. It is unlikely that the amount absorbed via topical application would produce clinically relevant concentrations in breastmilk.

Pregnancy Risk Category: C

Lactation Risk Category: L2 topically
L3 orally

Adult Concerns: Hypotension, tachycardia, headache, weight gain, skin pigmentation, rash, renal toxicity, leukopenia.

Pediatric Concerns: None reported.

Drug Interactions: Profound orthostatic hypotension when used with guanethidine. May potentiate hypotensive effect of other antihypertensives.

Relative Infant Dose: 9.1%

Adult Dose: 10-40 mg daily.

Alternatives:

T ½	= 3.5-4.2 hours	M/P	= 0.75-1.0
PHL	=	PB	= Low
Tmax	= 2-8 hours	Oral	= 90-95%
MW	= 209	pKa	=
Vd	=		

References:
1. Valdivieso A, Valdes G, Spiro TE, Westerman RL. Minoxidil in breast milk. Ann Intern Med 1985; 102 (1):135.

MIRTAZAPINE   L3

Trade: Remeron
Other Trades: Avanza, Zispin
Uses: Antidepressant
AAP: Not reviewed

Mirtazapine is a unique antidepressant structurally dissimilar to the SSRIs, tricyclics, or the monoamine oxidase inhibitors. Mirtazapine has little or no serotonergic-like side effects, fewer anticholinergic side effects than amitriptyline, it produces less sexual dysfunction, and has not demonstrated cardiotoxic or seizure potential in a limited number of overdose cases.[1]

In a study of 3 women who received 45, 60, and 45 mg/day mirtazapine, the average concentration (AUC) in milk was 77, 75, and 47 µg/L, respectively.[2] The absolute infant dose was 10, 11.3, and 7.1 µg/kg/d, respectively. The relative infant dose was 1.9%, 1.1%, and 1.5% of the weight-normalized maternal dose, respectively. Mirtazapine was below the limit of quantitation in two of the infants and only 1.5 ng/mL in the second infant. The infants were meeting all developmental milestones and were without side effects.

Another study of 8 women taking an average of 38 mg/day showed average milk concentrations of 53 µg/L and 13 µg/L of mirtazapine and its metabolite, respectively. The average absolute infant dose was 495 µg/kg/day, indicating a relative infant dose of 1.9%. The authors of this study suggest that breastfeeding is safe during mirtazapine therapy.[3]

In another mother who took 22.5 mg/day, milk levels were 130 µg/L 4 hours after dosing and 61 µg/L 10 hours after the dose (foremilk). This suggests the relative infant dose was 3.9-4.4% and 1.8-2.7% respectively of the weight-adjusted maternal dose at these two times. At 12.5 hours postdose, infant plasma levels were undetectable.[4]

Pregnancy Risk Category: C

Lactation Risk Category: L3

Adult Concerns: Drowsiness (54%), dizziness, dry mouth, constipation, increased appetite (17%), and weight gain (12%) have been reported.

Pediatric Concerns: None reported via milk but observe for sedation.

Drug Interactions: Enhanced impairment of cognitive function when administered with alcohol. Mirtazapine is a weak inhibitor of cytochrome P450 2D6 and others. Drugs metabolized by this enzyme system may have enhanced activity. Coadministration with benzodiazepines may reduce cognitive function.

Relative Infant Dose: 1.6% - 6.3%

Adult Dose: 15-45 mg daily

Alternatives: Sertraline, venlafaxine, paroxetine

T ½	= 20-40 hours	M/P	= 0.76
PHL	=	PB	= 85%
Tmax	= 2 hours	Oral	= 50%
MW	= 265	pKa	=
Vd	=		

References:
1. Pharmaceutical Manufacturer Prescribing Information. 1999.
2. Ilett KF, Hackett LP, Kristensen JH, Rampono J. Distribution and excretion of the novel antidepressant mirtazapine in human milk. International Lactation Consultants Meeting, Sydney, July 31- August 3, 2003.
3. Kristensen JH, Ilett KF, Rampono J, Kohan R, Hackett LP. Transfer of the antidepressant mirtazapine into breast milk. Br J Clin Pharmacol 2006; 63 (3):322-327.
4. Klier CM, Mossaheb N, Lee A, Zernig G. Mirtazapine and Breastfeeding: Maternal and Infant Plasma Levels. Am J Psychiatry 2007; 164 (2):348-349.

MISOPROSTOL   L3

Trade: Cytotec
Other Trades: Cytotec
Uses: Prostaglandin hormone, gastric protectant
AAP: Not reviewed

Misoprostol is a prostaglandin E1 compound that is useful in treating nonsteroidal-induced gastric ulceration. Misoprostol is absorbed orally and rapidly metabolized. Intact misoprostol is not detectable in plasma and is rapidly metabolized to misoprostol acid which is biologically active.[1]

In a study of 5 mothers receiving 200 µg, misoprostol acid levels in milk rose rapidly and peaked at an average of 7.6 pg/mL at 1.1 hours, followed by a rapid decline to 0.2 pg/mL at 5 hours. The milk-to-plasma ratio was 0.05 on average. The authors suggest that misoprostol be taken immediately after a feed and the next feed be given 4 hours later, when milk levels are below 1 pg/mL.[2] Infants should be monitored for signs of diarrhea.

Pregnancy Risk Category: X

Lactation Risk Category: L3

Adult Concerns: Diarrhea, abdominal cramps and pain, uterine bleeding and abortion.

Pediatric Concerns: None reported, but observe for diarrhea, abdominal cramps.

Drug Interactions: Levels are diminished when administered with food. Antacids reduce total bioavailability but this does not appear clinically significant.

Relative Infant Dose:

Adult Dose: 100-200 µg QID

Alternatives:

T ½	= 20-40 minutes	M/P	= 0.05
PHL	=	PB	= 80-90%
Tmax	= 14-20 minutes (oral)	Oral	= Complete
MW	= 383	pKa	=
Vd	=		

References:
1. Pharmaceutical Manufacturer Prescribing Information. 1995.

2. Vogel D, Burkhardt T, Rentsch K et al. Misoprostol versus methylergometrine: Pharmacokinetics in human milk. Am J Obstet Gynecol 2004; 191:2168-2173.

MITOXANTRONE   L5

Trade: Novantrone
Other Trades: Onkotrone, Novantrone
Uses: Immunosuppressant for MS
AAP: Not reviewed

Mitoxantrone is an antineoplastic agent used in the treatment of relapsing multiple sclerosis. It is a DNA-reactive agent that intercalates into DNA via hydrogen bonding, causing crosslinks. It inhibits B cell, T cell, and macrophage proliferation. In a study of a patient who received 3 treatments of mitoxantrone (6 mg/m2) on days 1 to 5. Mitoxantrone levels in milk measured 120 ng/mL just after treatment (on the third day of treatment), and dropped to a stable level of 18 ng/mL for the next 28 days.[1] This agent has an enormous volume of distribution and is sequestered in at least 7 organs including the liver and bone marrow and in another study, 15% of the dose remained 35 days after exposure.[2] Assuming a mother were breastfeeding, these levels would provide about 18 µg/L of milk consumed after the first few days following exposure to the drug. In addition, it would be sequestered for long periods in the infant as well. As this is a DNA-reactive agent, and it has a huge volume of distribution leading to prolonged tissue, plasma, and milk levels, mothers should be strongly advised to not breastfeed following its use.

Pregnancy Risk Category: D

Lactation Risk Category: L5

Adult Concerns: Leukopenia and thrombocytopenia are the most common adverse effects. Cardiotoxicity, nausea, vomiting, diarrhea, mucositis, hepatotoxicity, alopecia, pruritus, phlebitis have been reported. Neuropathy and paralysis of the bowel and bladder are reported.

Pediatric Concerns: None reported but extreme caution is recommended. Probably contraindicated.

Drug Interactions: Avoid vaccinations with live or attenuated vaccines (Smallpox, Rotavirus, etc). The half-life of mitoxantrone is increased (1.8 fold) by use with valspodar.

Relative Infant Dose:

Adult Dose: 12 mg/meter^2*

Alternatives:

T ½	= 23-215 hours	M/P	=
PHL	=	PB	= 78%
Tmax	=	Oral	= Poor
MW	= 517	pKa	=
Vd	= 14-54		

References:
1. Azuno Y, Kaku K, Fujita N, Okubo M, Kaneko T, Matsumoto N. Mitoxantrone and etoposide in breast milk. Am J Hematol 1995 Feb; 48 (2):131-2.
2. Alberts DS, Peng YM, Leigh S, Davis TP, Woodward DL. Disposition of mitoxantrone in cancer patients. Cancer Res 1985 Apr; 45 (4):1879-84.

MIVACURIUM   L2

Trade: Mivacron
Other Trades: Mivacrom
Uses: Neuromuscular blocking agent
AAP: Not reviewed

Mivacurium is a short-acting neuromuscular blocking agent used to relax skeletal muscles during surgery. Its duration is very short and complete recovery generally occurs in 15-30 minutes.[1,2] No data are available on its transfer to breastmilk. However, it has an exceedingly short plasma half-life and probably poor to no oral absorption. It is very unlikely that it would be absorbed by a breastfeeding infant.

Pregnancy Risk Category: C

Lactation Risk Category: L2

Adult Concerns: Flushing, hypotension, weakness.

Pediatric Concerns: None reported.

Drug Interactions: Inhaled anesthetics, local anesthetics, calcium channel blockers, antiarrhythmic such as quinidine, and certain antibiotics such as amino glycosides, tetracyclines, vancomycin, and clindamycin may significantly prolong neuromuscular blockade with mivacurium.

Relative Infant Dose:

Adult Dose: 0.1-0.15 mg/kg every 15 minutes PRN

Alternatives:

T ½	= <30 minutes	M/P	=
PHL	=	PB	=
Tmax	=	Oral	= Poor
MW	=	pKa	=
Vd	=		

References:
1. McEvoy GE. (ed):AFHS Drug Information. New York, NY: 2009.
2. Pharmaceutical Manufacturer Prescribing Information. 1995.

MMR VACCINE   L2

Trade: MMR Vaccine, Measles - Mumps - Rubella
Other Trades:
Uses: Live attenuated triple virus vaccine
AAP: Not reviewed

MMR vaccine is a mixture of live, attenuated viruses from measles, mumps, and rubella strains. It is usually administered to children at 12-15 months of age. NEVER administer to a pregnant woman. Rubella, and perhaps measles and mumps virus, are undoubtedly transferred via breastmilk and have been detected in throat swabs of 56% of breastfeeding infants.[1-4] Infants exposed to the attenuated viruses via breastmilk had only mild symptoms. If medically required, MMR vaccine can be administered early postpartum.[5] See rubella.

Pregnancy Risk Category:

Lactation Risk Category: L2

Adult Concerns: Mild symptoms, fever, flu-like symptoms.

Pediatric Concerns: Mild symptoms of rubella have been reported in one newborn infant.

Drug Interactions:

Relative Infant Dose:

Adult Dose: 0.5 mL once

Alternatives:

References:
1. Buimovici-Klein E, Hite RL, Byrne T, Cooper LZ. Isolation of rubella virus in milk after postpartum immunization. J Pediatr 1977; 91 (6):939-941.

2. Losonsky GA, Fishaut JM, Strussenberg J, Ogra PL. Effect of immunization against rubella on lactation products. I. Development and characterization of specific immunologic reactivity in breast milk. J Infect Dis 1982; 145 (5):654-660.
3. Losonsky GA, Fishaut JM, Strussenberg J, Ogra PL. Effect of immunization against rubella on lactation products. II. Maternal-neonatal interactions. J Infect Dis 1982; 145 (5):661-666.
4. Landes RD, Bass JW, Millunchick EW, Oetgen WJ. Neonatal rubella following postpartum maternal immunization. J Pediatr 1980; 97 (3):465-467.
5. Lawrence RA. Breastfeeding: A guide for the medical profession. St. Louis: Mosby Publishers, 1994.

MOCLOBEMIDE   L3

Trade:

Other Trades: Apo-Moclobemide, Manerix, Arima, Aurorix

Uses: MAO inhibitor, antidepressant.

AAP: Not reviewed

Unlike older MAO inhibitors, moclobemide is a selective and reversible inhibitor of MAO-A isozyme and thus is not plagued with the dangerous side effects of the older MAO inhibitor families. It is an effective treatment for depression.[1] In a study by Pons in 6 lactating women, who received a single oral dose of 300 mg, the concentration of moclobemide (C_{max}) was highest at 3 hours after the dose and averaged 2.7 mg/L.[2] The average (AUC) milk concentration throughout the 12 hour period was 0.97 mg/L hour. The minimal levels of moclobemide found in milk are unlikely to produce untoward effects according to the authors.

Pregnancy Risk Category:

Lactation Risk Category: L3

Adult Concerns: Dry mouth, headache, dizziness, tremor, sweating, insomnia, and constipation.

Pediatric Concerns: None reported via milk.

Drug Interactions: Serotonergic syndrome is unlikely, but possible when admixed with SSRI antidepressants, clomipramine, fluoxetine, etc. Do not coadminister with SSRIs and tricyclic antidepressants. Do not administer with meperidine (pethidine) or dextromethorphan. Sympathomimetic hyperactivity (hypertension, headache, hyperpyrexia, arrhythmias, cerebral hemorrhage) may occur when admixed with tyramine, ephedrine, pseudoephedrine, phenylephrine, epinephrine, norepinephrine and other sympathomimetics.

Relative Infant Dose: 3.4%

Adult Dose: 450 mg/day

Alternatives:

T ½	= 1-2.2 hours	M/P	= 0.72
PHL	=	PB	= 50%
Tmax	= 2 hours	Oral	= 80%
MW	= 269	pKa	= 6.3
Vd	= 1-2		

References:
1. Fulton B, Benfield P. Moclobemide. An update of its pharmacological properties and therapeutic use. Drugs 1996; 52 (3):450-474.
2. Pons G, Schoerlin MP, Tam YK, Moran C, Pfefen JP, Francoual C, Pedarriosse AM, Chavinie J, Olive G. Moclobemide excretion in human breast milk. Br J Clin Pharmacol 1990; 29 (1):27-31.

MODAFINIL   L4

Trade: Provigil
Other Trades: Alertec, Provigil
Uses: Wakefulness-promoting agent
AAP: Not reviewed

Modafinil is a wakefulness-promoting agent used for the treatment of narcolepsy. Although its pharmacologic results are similar to amphetamines and methylphenidate (Ritalin), its method of action is unknown. No data are available on its transfer into human milk. Some caution is recommended as it is small in MW and very lipid soluble, both characteristics which may ultimately lead to higher milk levels. In addition, it apparently stimulates dopamine levels. Compounds that stimulate dopamine levels in brain often reduce prolactin secretion. Milk production may suffer, but this is only supposition.

Pregnancy Risk Category: C

Lactation Risk Category: L4

Adult Concerns: May increase incidence of headache, chest pain, palpitations, dyspnea, and transient T-wave changes on ECG. CNS changes include delusions, auditory hallucinations and sleep deprivation. Diarrhea, dry mouth, nausea, and rhinitis have been reported.

Pediatric Concerns: None reported. Observe for reduced milk supply.

Drug Interactions: May increase plasma levels of diazepam, phenytoin and propranolol. Caution when used with tricyclic and SSRI antidepressants. May induce hepatic enzymes, thus reducing circulating levels of cyclosporine, theophylline, and steroidal contraceptives.

Relative Infant Dose:

Adult Dose: 200-400 up to twice daily

Alternatives:

T ½	= 15 hours	M/P	=
PHL	=	PB	= 60%
Tmax	= 2-4 hours	Oral	= Complete
MW	= 273	pKa	=
Vd	= 0.9		

References:
1. Pharmaceutical Manufacturer Prescribing Information, 2001.

MOMETASONE   L3

Trade: Elocon, Nasonex
Other Trades:
Uses: Corticosteroid
AAP: Not reviewed

Mometasone is a corticosteroid primarily intended for intranasal and topical use. It is considered a medium-potency steroid, similar to betamethasone and triamcinolone. Following topical application to the skin, less than 0.7% is systemically absorbed over an 8 hour period.[1,2] It is extremely unlikely mometasone would be excreted into human milk in clinically relevant levels following topical or intranasal administration.

Pregnancy Risk Category: C

Lactation Risk Category: L3

Adult Concerns: Topically only minimal side effects have been reported and include irritation, burning, stinging, and dermal atrophy. After nasal administration, common adverse effects include headache, pharyngitis, epistaxis, and cough.

Pediatric Concerns: None reported via milk.

Drug Interactions:

Relative Infant Dose:

Adult Dose: Apply topically 2-3 times daily

Alternatives:

References:
1.   Pharmaceutical Manufacturer Prescribing Information. 1999.
2.   Drug Facts and Comparisons 1999 ed. ed. St. Louis: 1999.

MONTELUKAST SODIUM   L3

Trade: Singulair
Other Trades:
Uses: Antiasthmatic agent
AAP: Advise not to breastfeed

Montelukast is a leukotriene receptor inhibitor similar to Accolate and is used as an adjunct in the treatment of asthma. The manufacturer reports that montelukast is secreted into animal milk, but no data on human milk is available.[1] This product is cleared for use in children aged 6 and above. This product does not enter the CNS nor many other tissues. Although the milk levels in humans are unreported, they are probably quite low.

Pregnancy Risk Category: B

Lactation Risk Category: L3

Adult Concerns: Abdominal pain, fever, dyspepsia, dental pain, dizziness, headache, cough and nasal congestion, some changes in liver enzymes.

Pediatric Concerns: None reported via milk.

Drug Interactions: Phenobarbital may reduce plasma levels by 40%. Although unreported, other inhibitors of Cytochrome P450 may affect plasma levels.

Relative Infant Dose:

Adult Dose: 10 mg daily

Alternatives: Zafirlukast

T ½	= 2.7-5.5 hours	M/P	=
PHL	=	PB	= 99%
Tmax	= 2-4 hours	Oral	= 64%
MW	= 608	pKa	=
Vd	= 0.15		

References:
1. Pharmaceutical Manufacturer Prescribing Information.

MORPHINE	L3

Trade: Duramorph, Infumorph

Other Trades: Epimorph, Morphitec, M.O.S. MS Contin, Statex, Morphalgin, Ordine, Anamorph, Kapanol, Oramorph, Sevredol

Uses: Narcotic analgesic

AAP: Maternal Medication Usually Compatible with Breastfeeding

Morphine is a potent narcotic analgesic. In a group of 5 lactating women, the highest morphine concentration in breastmilk following two epidural doses was only 82 µg/L at 30 minutes.[1] The highest breastmilk level following 15 mg IV/IM was only 0.5 mg/L although it dropped to almost 0.01 mg/L in 4 hours. In this study and following two 4 mg epidural doses, the peak milk level was 82 µg/L or a relative infant dose of 19.1%.

In another study of women receiving morphine via PCA pumps for 12-48 hours postpartum, the concentration of morphine in breastmilk ranged from 50-60 µg/L (estimated from graph).[2] None of the infants in this study were neurobehaviorally delayed at 3 days. Because of the poor oral bioavailability of morphine (26%) it is unlikely these levels would be clinically relevant in a stable breastfeeding infant.

However, data from Robieux suggests the levels transferred to the infant are higher.[3] In this study of a single patient, plasma levels in the breastfed infant were within therapeutic range (4 ng/mL) although the infant showed no untoward signs or symptoms. However, this case was somewhat unique in that the mother received daily morphine (50 mg PO every 6 hours) during the third trimester for severe back pain. One week postpartum, the morphine was discontinued and then 5 days later reinstated due to withdrawal effects in the mother. The reported concentration in foremilk and hind milk was 100 ng/mL and 10 ng/mL respectively and the authors suggested that the dose to the infant would be 0.8 to 12% of the maternal oral dose (0.15 to 2.41 mg/day). Although this study suggests that the amount of morphine transferred in milk can be clinically relevant, the authors calculated the infant dose from the highest milk concentration and a milk intake of 150 mL/kg/day, thus the dose of morphine to the infant would have been substantially lower (53 µg/day). This study seems flawed because the plasma levels and the doses via milk just don't correlate. That this infant showed no untoward effects, can be explained by the fact that it may have exhibited tolerance after long exposure, that the reported analgesic-therapeutic level required in neonates is actually slightly higher than in adults, or the plasma levels assayed in this infant were in error.

Infants under 1 month of age have a prolonged elimination half-life and decreased clearance of morphine relative to older infants. The clearance of morphine and its elimination begins to approach adult values by 2 months of age. In summary, morphine is probably the preferred opiate in breastfeeding mothers primarily due to its poor oral bioavailability. It is unfortunate that the clinical studies above do not necessarily suggest this. However, high doses over prolonged periods could lead to sedation and respiratory problems in newborn infants.

Pregnancy Risk Category: C

Lactation Risk Category: L3

Adult Concerns: Sedation, flushing, CNS depression, respiratory depression, bradycardia.

Pediatric Concerns: None reported via milk but sedation is possible with higher doses.

Drug Interactions: Barbiturates may significantly increase respiratory and CNS depressant effects of morphine. The admixture of cimetidine has produced CNS toxicity such as confusion, disorientation, respiratory depression, apnea, and seizures when used with narcotic analgesics. Diazepam may produce cardiovascular depression when used with opiates. Phenothiazines may antagonize the analgesic effect of morphine.

Relative Infant Dose: 9.1% - 34.9%

Adult Dose: 10-30 mg every 4 hours PRN

Alternatives: Codeine

T ½	= 1.5-2 hours	M/P	= 1.1-3.6
PHL	= 13.9 hours (neonates)	PB	= 35%
Tmax	= 0.5-1 hours	Oral	= 26%
MW	= 285	pKa	= 8.1
Vd	= 2-5		

References:
1. Feilberg VL, Rosenborg D, Broen CC, Mogensen JV. Excretion of morphine in human breast milk. Acta Anaesthesiol Scand 1989; 33 (5):426-428.
2. Wittels B, Scott DT, Sinatra RS. Exogenous opioids in human breast milk and acute neonatal neurobehavior: a preliminary study. Anesthesiology 1990; 73 (5):864-869.

3.   Robieux I, Koren G, Vandenbergh H, Schneiderman J. Morphine excretion in breast milk and resultant exposure of a nursing infant. J Toxicol Clin Toxicol 1990; 28 (3):365-370.

MOXIFLOXACIN   L2

Trade: Avelox, Vigamox
Other Trades: Avelox
Uses: Fluoroquinolone antibiotic
AAP: Not reviewed

Moxifloxacin is a quinolone antibiotic for use orally, intravenously, and in the eye. It is a new-generation fluoroquinolone which exhibits improved activity against S. pneumonia and other species. No data are available on its transfer into human milk so until we have data, one should opt for using ofloxacin or levofloxacin for which published data is available.

Pregnancy Risk Category: C

Lactation Risk Category: L2 Ophthalmically
                                L3 Orally, IV

Adult Concerns: Nausea and diarrhea are the most common complications following oral use in adults. It should be avoided in patients with prolonged QT intervals.

Pediatric Concerns: No reports available, but changes in gut flora, and diarrhea are possible. Complications following ophthalmic use are extremely remote as the plasma levels are very low.

Drug Interactions: Moxifloxacin can be administered concurrently with food. Do not take with antacids containing magnesium, aluminum, sucralfate, metal cations such as iron or zinc. Wait a minimum of 4 hours after using these products.

Relative Infant Dose:

Adult Dose: Oral = 400 mg daily

Alternatives: Ofloxacin, Levofloxacin, Ciprofloxacin

T ½	= 9-16 hours	M/P	=
PHL	=	PB	= 50%
Tmax	= 1-3 hours	Oral	= 90%
MW	= 437	pKa	=
Vd	= 1.7-3		

References:
1. Pharmaceutical Manufacturer Prescribing Information, 2003.

Mumps Virus Vaccine, Live

Trade:
Other Trades:
Uses: Vaccination for Mumps
AAP: Not reviewed

MMR vaccine is a mixture of live, attenuated viruses from measles, mumps, and rubella strains. It is usually administered to children at 12-15 months of age. NEVER administer to a pregnant woman. Rubella, and perhaps measles and mumps virus, are undoubtedly transferred via breastmilk and have been detected in throat swabs of 56% of breastfeeding infants.[1-4] Infants exposed to the attenuated viruses via breastmilk had only mild symptoms. If medically required, MMR vaccine can be administered early postpartum.[5]

Pregnancy Risk Category:

Lactation Risk Category:

Adult Concerns:

Pediatric Concerns:

Drug Interactions:

Relative Infant Dose:

Adult Dose:

Alternatives:

References:

MUPIROCIN OINTMENT   L1

Trade: Bactroban
Other Trades: Bactroban
Uses: Antibacterial ointment
AAP: Not reviewed

Mupirocin is a topical antibiotic used for impetigo, Group A beta-hemolytic strep, and strep. Pyogenes. Mupirocin is only minimally absorbed following topical application. In one study, less than 0.3% of a topical dose was absorbed after 24 hours. Most remained adsorbed to the corneum layer of the skin. The drug is absorbed orally, but it is so rapidly metabolized that systemic levels are not sustained. It is quite safe for breastfeeding mothers.

Pregnancy Risk Category: B

Lactation Risk Category: L1

Adult Concerns: Rash, irritation.

Pediatric Concerns: None reported. Commonly used in pediatric patients.

Drug Interactions:

Relative Infant Dose:

Adult Dose: Apply sparingly.

Alternatives:

T ½	= 17-36 minutes	M/P	=
PHL	=	PB	=
Tmax	=	Oral	= Complete
MW	= 501	pKa	=
Vd	=		

References:

MYCOPHENOLATE   L4

Trade: CellCept
Other Trades: CellCept
Uses: Immunosuppressive agent
AAP: Not reviewed

Mycophenolate is an immunosuppressive agent used to prevent rejection of allogenic transplants (kidney, heart, liver, intestine, limb, small bowel, etc.). It is well absorbed and rapidly metabolized to MPA, the active metabolite. MPA glucuronide then subsequently enters the small intestine and is reabsorbed by enterohepatic recirculation. No data are available on its transfer into human milk. The average blood level is about 63.9 µg/mL (AUC) which is relatively high. Until we have data on human breast milk levels this agent should be considered relatively hazardous.

Pregnancy Risk Category: C

Lactation Risk Category: L4

Adult Concerns: Increased risk for diarrhea, leukopenia, sepsis, vomiting, headache, tremor, insomnia, high risk of infections, lymphoma and other malignancies, bone marrow suppression.

Pediatric Concerns: This product is a high risk product for breastfeeding mothers. Great caution is recommended. See cyclosporin and others as alternatives.

Drug Interactions: Comcomitant use with azathioprine is not recommended, use cautiously with drugs that affect enterohepatic recirculation, such as cholestyramine. Avoid use of live attenuated vaccines. Numerous other drug-drug reactions occur, consult other references.

Relative Infant Dose:

Adult Dose: 1-1.5 gm orally twice daily

Alternatives: Cyclosporine

T ½	= 17.9 hours	M/P	=
PHL	=	PB	= 97%
Tmax	= 1 hour	Oral	= 94% (parent)
MW	= 433	pKa	=
Vd	= 4		

References:
1. Pharmaceutical Manufacturers prescribing information, 2003.

NABUMETONE   L3

Trade: Relafen
Other Trades: Relafen, Relifex
Uses: Antiinflammatory agent for arthritic pain
AAP: Not reviewed

Nabumetone is a non-steroidal antiinflammatory agent for arthritic pain.[1] Immediately upon absorption, nabumetone is metabolized to the active metabolite. The parent drug is not detectable in plasma. It is not known if the nabumetone metabolite (6MNA) is secreted in human milk. It is known to be secreted into animal milk and has a very long half-life. NSAIDS are not generally recommended in nursing mothers, with the exception of ibuprofen. See ibuprofen as alternative.

Pregnancy Risk Category: C in first and second trimesters
                               D in third trimester

Lactation Risk Category: L3

Adult Concerns: GI distress, nausea, vomiting, diarrhea.

Pediatric Concerns: None reported via milk. Observe for GI distress.

Drug Interactions: May prolong prothrombin time when used with warfarin. Antihypertensive effects of ACEi family may be blunted or completely abolished by NSAIDs. Some NSAIDs may block antihypertensive effect of beta blockers, diuretics. Used with cyclosporin, may dramatically increase renal toxicity. May increase digoxin, phenytoin, lithium levels. May increase toxicity of methotrexate. May increase bioavailability of penicillamine. Probenecid may increase NSAID levels.

Relative Infant Dose:

Adult Dose: 500-1000 mg daily.-BID

Alternatives: Ibuprofen

T ½	= 22-30 hours	M/P	=
PHL	=	PB	= 99%
Tmax	= 2.5-4 hours	Oral	= 38%
MW	= 228	pKa	=
Vd	=		

References:
1. Pharmaceutical Manufacturer Prescribing Information.

NADOLOL   L4

Trade: Corgard
Other Trades: Corgard, Syn-Nadolol, Novo-Nadolol
Uses: Antihypertensive, antianginal, beta blocker
AAP: Maternal Medication Usually Compatible with Breastfeeding

Nadolol is a long-acting beta adrenergic blocker used as an antihypertensive. It is secreted into breastmilk in moderately high concentrations. Following a maternal dose of 20 mg/day, breast milk levels at 38 hours postpartum were 146 µg/L.[1] In another study of 12 women receiving 80 mg daily the mean steady-state concentrations in milk were 357 µg/L.[2] The time to maximum concentration was 6 hours. The milk/serum ratio was reported to average 4.6. A five kg infant would receive from 4-7% of the maternal dose. The authors recommended caution with the use of this beta blocker in breastfeeding patients. Due to its long half-life and high milk/plasma ratio, this would not be a preferred beta blocker.

Pregnancy Risk Category: C

Lactation Risk Category: L4

Adult Concerns: Hypotension, nausea, diarrhea, bradycardia, apnea, depression.

Pediatric Concerns: None reported, but due to the high M/P ratio of 4.6, this product is not recommended.

Drug Interactions: Decreased effect when used with aluminum salts, barbiturates, calcium salts, cholestyramine, NSAIDs, ampicillin, rifampin, and salicylates. Beta blockers may reduce the effect of oral sulfonylureas (hypoglycemic agents). Increased toxicity/effect when used with other antihypertensives, contraceptives, MAO inhibitors, cimetidine, and numerous other products. See drug interaction reference for complete listing.

Relative Infant Dose: 4.4% - 6.9%

Adult Dose: 40-80 mg daily.

Alternatives: Propranolol, Metoprolol

T ½	= 20-24 hours	M/P	= 4.6
PHL	=	PB	= 30%
Tmax	= 2-4 hours	Oral	= 20-40%
MW	= 309	pKa	= 9.7
Vd	= 1.5-3.6		

References:
1. Fox RE, Marx C, Stark AR. Neonatal effects of maternal nadolol therapy. Am J Obstet Gynecol 1985; 152 (8):1045-1046.
2. Devlin RG, Duchin KL, Fleiss PM. Nadolol in human serum and breast milk. Br J Clin Pharmacol 1981; 12 (3):393-396.

NAFCILLIN   L1

Trade: Unipen, Nafcil
Other Trades: Unipen
Uses: Penicillin antibiotic
AAP: Not reviewed

Nafcillin is a penicillin antibiotic that is poorly and erratically absorbed orally.[1] The only formulations are IV and IM No data are available on concentration in milk, but it is likely small. Oral absorption in the infant would be minimal. See other penicillins.

Pregnancy Risk Category: B

Lactation Risk Category: L1

Adult Concerns: Neutropenia, hypokalemia, pseudomembranous colitis, allergic rash.

Pediatric Concerns: None reported. Observe for GI symptoms such as diarrhea. Nafcillin is frequently used in infants.

Drug Interactions: Chloramphenicol may decreased nafcillin levels. Nafcillin may inhibit efficacy of oral contraceptives. Probenecid may increase nafcillin levels. May increase anticoagulant effect of warfarin and heparin.

Relative Infant Dose:

Adult Dose: 250-1000 mg every 4-6 hours

Alternatives:

T ½	= 0.5-1.5 hours	M/P	=
PHL	= 2.2-5.5 hours (neonates).	PB	= 70-90%
Tmax	= 30-60 minutes (IM).	Oral	= 50%
MW	= 436	pKa	=
Vd	=		

References:
1. McEvoy GE. (ed):AFHS Drug Information. New York, NY: 2009.

NALBUPHINE   L2

Trade: Nubain
Other Trades: Nubain
Uses: Analgesic
AAP: Not reviewed

Nalbuphine is a potent narcotic analgesic similar in potency to morphine. Nalbuphine is both an antagonist and agonist of opiate receptors and should not be mixed with other opiates due to interference with analgesia.

In a group of 20 postpartum mothers who received a single 20 mg IM nalbuphine dose, the total amount of nalbuphine excreted into human milk during a 24 hour period averaged 2.3 micrograms, which is equivalent to 0.012% of the maternal dosage.[1] The mean milk/plasma ratio using the AUC was 1.2. According to the authors, an oral intake of 2.3 micrograms nalbuphine per day by an infant would not show any measurable plasma concentrations in the neonate.

In another study of 18 mothers who received 0.2 mg/kg every 4 hours over 2-3 days, the average concentration in breast milk was 42 µg/L, with a maximum of 61 µg/L. The reported infant dose was an average of 7 µg/kg/day, with a maximum of 9 µg/kg/day.[2] The authors estimate the RID = 0.59% of the weight-adjusted maternal daily dose and suggest breastfeeding is permissible.

Pregnancy Risk Category: B

Lactation Risk Category: L2

Adult Concerns: Hypotension, sedation, withdrawal syndrome, respiratory depression.

Pediatric Concerns: Levels in milk are low. No complications reported.

Drug Interactions: May reduce efficacy of other opioid analgesics. Barbiturates may increase CNS sedation.

Relative Infant Dose: 0.6%

Adult Dose: 10-20 mg every 3-6 hours PRN

Alternatives:

T ½	= 5 hours	M/P	= 1,2
PHL	= 0.86 hours	PB	=
Tmax	= 2-15 minutes (IV,IM)	Oral	= 16%
MW	= 357	pKa	=
Vd	= 2.4-7.3		

References:

1. Wischnik A, Wetzelsberger N, Lucker PW. Elimination of nalbuphine in human milk. Arzneimittelforschung 1988; 38 (10):1496-1498.
2. Jacqz-Aigrain E, Serreau R, Boissinot C, Popon M, Sobel A, Michel J, Sibony O. Excretion of Ketoprofen and Nalbuphine in Human Milk During Treatment of Maternal Pain After Delivery. Ther Drug Monit. 2007 Dec;29 (6):815-818.

NALIDIXIC ACID   L3

Trade: NegGram
Other Trades: NegGram
Uses: Urinary anti-infective
AAP: Maternal Medication Usually Compatible with Breastfeeding

Nalidixic is an old urinary antiseptic and belongs to the fluoroquinolone family. In a group of 4 women receiving 1000 mg orally/day the concentration in breast milk was approximately 5 mg/L.[1] Hemolytic anemia has been reported in one infant whose mother received 1 gm nalidixic acid 4 times daily. Use with extreme caution. A number of new and less toxic choices (ofloxacin) should preclude the use of this compound.[2]

A more recent study of 13 lactating women taking 2 grams of nalidixic acid, milk levels after 4 hours were 0.64 µg/mL. Levels at 10.5 hours after administration averaged 0.20 µg/mL. The maximum possible dose for a breastfeeding infant with these milk levels was 0.1 mg/kg/day, far less than the recommended dosage for children. The authors suggested that breastfeeding is not contraindicated during nalidixic acid therapy.[3] This is an old product and newer products such as ofloxacin, ciprofloxacin, or levofloxacin are preferred.

Pregnancy Risk Category: B

Lactation Risk Category: L3

Adult Concerns: Hemolytic anemia, headache, drowsiness, blurred vision, nausea, vomiting.

Pediatric Concerns: Hemolytic anemia in one infant. This is an old product that should not be used currently.

Drug Interactions: Decreased efficacy/oral bioavailability when used with antacids. Increased anticoagulation with warfarin.

Relative Infant Dose: 0.4% - 5.2%

Adult Dose: 1 g QID

Alternatives: Norfloxacin, ofloxacin, levofloxacin

T ½	= 1-2.5 hours	M/P	= 0.08-0.13
PHL	=	PB	= 93%
Tmax	= 1-2 hours	Oral	= 60%
MW	= 232	pKa	=
Vd	=		

References:
1. Belton EM, Jones RV. Haemolytic anaemia due to nalidixic acid. Lancet 1965; 2 (7414):691.
2. Drug Facts and Comparisons 2010 ed. ed. St. Louis: 2010.
3. Traeger A, Peiker G. Excretion of Nalidixic Acid via Mother's Milk. Arch Toxicol Suppl 1980; 4:388-390.

NALOXONE   L3

Trade: Narcan
Other Trades: Narcan, Nalone
Uses: Narcotic antagonist.
AAP: Not reviewed

Naloxone is a narcotic antagonist that when administered occupies the opiate receptor site, or when opiates are present, displaces them from the active site. It is commonly used for the treatment of opiate overdose, and now to prevent opiate abuse in patients undergoing withdrawal treatment. Naloxone is poorly absorbed orally and plasma levels in adults are undetectable (<0.05ng/mL) two hours after oral doses. Following intravenous use (0.4 mg), plasma naloxone levels averaged <0.084 µg/mL. Side effects are minimal except in narcotic-addicted patients. The AAP has advised that naloxone should not be administered (directly) to infants of narcotic-dependent mothers. Its use in breastfeeding mothers would be unlikely to cause problems as its milk levels would likely be low and its oral absorption is minimal to nil.

Pregnancy Risk Category: C

Lactation Risk Category: L3

Adult Concerns: Withdrawal effects in narcotic-addicted patients. Avoid direct use in infants of narcotic-addicted women. Ventricular tachycardia and fibrillation, hypertension, headache, and rarely seizures have been reported.

Pediatric Concerns: No breastfeeding studies are available. However, levels of naloxone in milk are likely to be quite low. In addition it is virtually unabsorbed orally. This product poses minimal risks to infants of women not addicted to opiates. However, even small amounts present in milk could accelerate slight withdrawal symptoms in infants of narcotic-addicted women.

Drug Interactions: Rapidly blocks the effect of most opiates precipitating withdrawal in addicts, or pain in other individuals. When used with clonidine, may reduce the hypotensive effects of this drug.

Relative Infant Dose:

Adult Dose: Highly variable but an initial dose of 0.4 to 2 mg intravenously is used for opiate withdrawal.

Alternatives:

T ½	= 64 minutes	M/P	=
PHL	= 2.5-3.5 hours	PB	= 45%
Tmax	=	Oral	= Nil
MW	= 399	pKa	= 7.9
Vd	= 2.6-2.8		

References:
1.   Pharmaceutical Manufacturer Prescribing Information. 2005.

NALTREXONE   L1

Trade: ReVia
Other Trades: ReVia, Nalorex
Uses: Narcotic antagonist
AAP: Not reviewed

Naltrexone is a long acting narcotic antagonist similar in structure to Naloxone. Orally absorbed, it has been clinically used in addicts to prevent the action of injected heroin. It occupies and competes with all opioid medications for the opiate receptor. When used in addicts, it can induce rapid and long lasting withdrawal symptoms. Although the half-life appears brief, the duration of antagonism is long lasting (24-72 hours).[1-5] Naltrexone is quite lipid soluble, has a high pKa, and transfers into the brain easily (brain/plasma ratio= 0.81). It is readily metabolized to 6-beta-naltrexol (active) and two minor metabolites. The activity of naltrexone is believed to be mainly due to parent and 6-beta-naltrexol.

In a study of one patient (60 kg) receiving 50 mg/day, the average concentration of naltrexone and 6-beta-naltrexol in milk were 1.7 and 46 µg/L.[6] The milk/plasma ratios of naltrexone and 6-beta-naltrexol were 1.9 and 3.4 respectively. The absolute infant dose was 0.26 and 6.86 µg/kg/day, respectively. The relative infant dose was 0.06 and 1.0% (range= 0.86-1.06%). The infant was reported to have achieved all expected milestones and showed no drug-related side effects. Naltrexone was undetectable in the infants' plasma and levels of 6-beta-naltrexol were only marginally detectable, at 1.1 µg/L.

Pregnancy Risk Category: C

Lactation Risk Category: L1

Adult Concerns: Rapid opiate withdrawal symptoms. Dizziness, anorexia, rash, nausea, vomiting, and hepatocellular toxicity. Liver toxicity is common at doses approximately 5 times normal or less. A Narcan challenge test should be initiated in patients prior to therapy with naltrexone.

Pediatric Concerns: None reported in one case. Plasma levels of 6-beta-naltrexol were only marginally detectable, at 1.1 µg/L.

Drug Interactions: Suppresses narcotic analgesia and sedation.

Relative Infant Dose: 1.4%

Adult Dose: 50-150 mg daily.

Alternatives:

T ½	= 4-13 hours	M/P	= 1.9 (3.4 metabolite)
PHL	=	PB	= 21%
Tmax	= 1 hour	Oral	= 96%
MW	= 341	pKa	= 7.9
Vd	= 19		

References:

1. Bullingham RE, McQuay HJ, Moore RA. Clinical pharmacokinetics of narcotic agonist-antagonist drugs. Clin Pharmacokinet 1983; 8 (4):332-343.
2. Crabtree BL. Review of naltrexone, a long-acting opiate antagonist. Clin Pharm 1984; 3 (3):273-280.
3. Ludden TM, Malspeis L, Baggot JD, Sokoloski TD, Frank SG, Reuning RH. Tritiated naltrexone binding in plasma from several species and tissue distribution in mice. J Pharm Sci 1976; 65 (5):712-716.
4. Verebey K, Volavka J, Mule SJ, Resnick RB. Naltrexone: disposition, metabolism, and effects after acute and chronic dosing. Clin Pharmacol Ther 1976; 20 (3):315-328.
5. Wall ME, Brine DR, Perez-Reyes M. Metabolism and disposition of naltrexone in man after oral and intravenous administration. Drug Metab Dispos 1981; 9 (4):369-375.
6. Chan CF, Page-Sharp M, Kristensen JH, O'Neil G, Ilett KF. Transfer of naltrexone and its metabolite 6,beta naltrexol into human milk. J Hum Lac 2004; 20 (3):322-326

NAPROXEN   L3

Trade: Anaprox, Naprosyn, Aleve

Other Trades: Anaprox, Apo-Naproxen, Naprosyn, Naxen, Inza, Proxen SR, Synflex

Uses: NSAID, analgesic for arthritis

AAP: Maternal Medication Usually Compatible with Breastfeeding

Naproxen is a popular NSAID analgesic. In a study done at steady state in one mother consuming 375 mg twice daily, milk levels ranged from 1.76-2.37 mg/L at 4 hours.[1,2] Total naproxen excretion in the infant's urine was only 0.26% of the maternal dose. Although the amount of naproxen transferred via milk is minimal, one should use with caution in nursing mothers because of its long half-life and its effect on infant cardiovascular system, kidneys, and GI tract. However, its short term use postpartum or infrequent or occasional use would not necessarily be incompatible with breastfeeding. One case of prolonged bleeding, hemorrhage, and acute anemia has been reported in a seven-day-old infant.[3] The relative infant dose on a weight-adjusted maternal daily dose would probably be less than 3.3%.

Pregnancy Risk Category: C

Lactation Risk Category: L3
L4 for chronic use

Adult Concerns: GI distress, gastric bleeding, hemorrhage.

Pediatric Concerns: One reported case of prolonged bleeding, hemorrhage, and acute anemia in a seven-day-old infant.

Drug Interactions: May prolong prothrombin time when used with warfarin. Antihypertensive effects of ACEi family may be blunted or completely abolished by NSAIDs. Some NSAIDs may block antihypertensive effect of beta blockers, diuretics. Used with cyclosporin, may dramatically increase renal toxicity. May increase digoxin, phenytoin, lithium levels. May increase toxicity of methotrexate. May increase bioavailability of penicillamine. Probenecid may increase NSAID levels.

Relative Infant Dose: 3.32%

Adult Dose: 250-500 mg BID

Alternatives: Ibuprofen

T ½	= 12-15 hours	M/P	= 0.01
PHL	= 12-15 hours	PB	= 99.7%
Tmax	= 2-4 hours	Oral	= 74-99%
MW	= 230	pKa	= 5.0
Vd	= 0.09		

References:

1. Jamali F, Stevens DR. Naproxen excretion in milk and its uptake by the infant. Drug Intell Clin Pharm 1983; 17 (12):910-911.
2. Jamali F. et.al. Naproxen excretion in breast milk and its uptake by sucking infant. Drug Intell Clin Pharm 1982; 16:475 (Abstr).
3. Figalgo I. et.al. Anemia aguda, rectaorragia y hematuria asociadas a la ingestion de naproxen. Anales Espanoles de Pediatrica 1989; 30:317-319.

NARATRIPTAN   L3

Trade: Amerge
Other Trades: Naramig
Uses: Migraine headaches
AAP: Not reviewed

Naratriptan is a 5-HT1D and 5-HT1B receptor stimulant and is used for treatment of acute migraine headache. No data are currently available on its transfer into human milk although the manufacturer suggests it penetrates the milk of rodents.[1] Naratriptan is a close congener of sumatriptan, only slightly better absorbed orally, and may produce few side effects in sumatriptan-sensitive patients. Some studies suggest that sumatriptan is equal to if not more effective than naratriptan.[2] Sumatriptan has been studied in breastfeeding mothers and produces minimal milk levels. See sumatriptan.

Pregnancy Risk Category: C

Lactation Risk Category: L3

Adult Concerns: Chest discomfort including pain, pressure, heaviness, tightness has been reported. Nausea, dizziness, paresthesias are infrequently reported. Cardiovascular events are rare but include hypertension, and tachyarrhythmias.

Pediatric Concerns: None reported via milk.

Drug Interactions: MAOIs can markedly increase naratriptan systemic effect and elimination including elevated plasma levels. Ergot containing drugs have caused prolonged vasospastic reactions, do not use within 24 hours after using an ergot-containing product. There have been rare reports of weakness, hyperreflexia, and incoordination with combined use with SSRIs such as fluoxetine, paroxetine, sertraline and fluvoxamine.

Relative Infant Dose:

Adult Dose: 1-2.5 mg every 4 hours X 2-3

Alternatives: Sumatriptan

T ½	= 6 hours	M/P	=
PHL	=	PB	= 31%
Tmax	= 2-3 hours	Oral	= 70%
MW	= 372	pKa	=
Vd	= 2.42		

References:
1. Pharmaceutical Manufacturer Prescribing Information. 1999.
2. Dahlof C, Winter P. et. al. Randomized, double-blind, placebo-controlled comparison of oral naratriptan and oral sumatriptan in the acute treatment of migraine (abstract). Neurology 1997; 48 (suppl):A85-A86.

NATALIZUMAB | L3

Trade: Tysabri
Other Trades:
Uses: Treatment of multiple sclerosis
AAP: Not reviewed

Natalizumab is a recombinant humanized IgG4k monoclonal antibody used to suppress immunity in patients with multiple sclerosis. Because it is a large molecular IgG, its transfer into milk is probably negligible, but as yet, we do not have data on its transfer to human milk. The transfer of native IgG into human milk is low. When small amounts of this product are added to vast quantities of IgG in the plasma, only a small percentage of natalizumab would ever be available for transport into milk. It is rather unlikely this product would be detrimental to a breastfeeding infant, but we do not know this for sure at this time.

Pregnancy Risk Category: C

Lactation Risk Category: L3

Adult Concerns: Hypersensitivity reactions have been reported which include urticaria, dizziness, fever, rash, pruritus, nausea, flushing, hypotension, dyspnea and chest pain.

Pediatric Concerns: No data are available at this time.

Drug Interactions: Interferon (Avonex) reduces clearance of natalizumab by approximately 30%.

Relative Infant Dose:

Adult Dose: 300 mg IV monthly

Alternatives:

T ½	= 11 days	M/P	=
PHL	–	PB	=
Tmax	=	Oral	= Nil
MW	= 149,000	pKa	=
Vd	= 0.08		

References:
1. Pharmaceutical Manufacturer Prescribing Information. 2005.

NEBIVOLOL   L3

Trade: Bystolic
Other Trades: Nebilet, Nebicard, Nubeta, Nodon
Uses: Beta-blocker
AAP: Not reviewed

Nebivolol is a beta-1 selective antagonist used for the treatment of hypertension. No data are available on the transfer of this drug into human milk. Due to the high protein binding and very large volume of distribution, it is unlikely that nebivolol would transfer to milk in clinically relevant amounts.

Pregnancy Risk Category: C in first trimester
                                                    D in second and third trimesters

Lactation Risk Category: L3

Adult Concerns: Adverse reactions include edema, headache, fatigue, dizziness, insomnia, diarrhea, and nausea.

Pediatric Concerns: Neonatal hypoglycemia have been reported in breastfeeding infants during maternal use of beta blockers.

Drug Interactions:

Relative Infant Dose:

Adult Dose: 5 mg daily

Alternatives: Metoprolol

T ½	= 10-12 hours	M/P	=
PHL	=	PB	= 98%
Tmax	= 0.5-4 hours	Oral	= 12-96%
MW	= 442	pKa	=
Vd	= 8-12		

References:
1. Pharmaceutical Manufacturer Prescribing Information. 2007.

NEDOCROMIL SODIUM | L2

Trade: Tilade
Other Trades: Tilade, Mireze
Uses: Inhaled anti-inflammatory for asthmatics
AAP: Not reviewed

Nedocromil is believed to stabilize mast cells and prevent release of bronchoconstrictors in the lung following exposure to allergens. The systemic effects are minimal due to reduced plasma levels. Systemic absorption averages less than 8-17% of the total dose even after continued dosing, which is quite low.[1,2] The poor oral bioavailability of this product and the reduced side effect profile of this family of drugs suggest that it is unlikely to produce untoward effects in a nursing infant. See cromolyn as comparison.

Pregnancy Risk Category: B

Lactation Risk Category: L2

Adult Concerns: Poor taste. Dizziness, headache, nausea and vomiting, sore throat, and cough.

Pediatric Concerns: None reported via milk.

Drug Interactions:

Relative Infant Dose:

Adult Dose: 3.5-4 mg QID

Alternatives:

T ½	= 3.3 hours	M/P	–
PHL	=	PB	= 89%
Tmax	= 28 minutes	Oral	= 8-17%
MW	= 371	pKa	–
Vd	=		

References:
1. Pharmaceutical Manufacturer Prescribing Information. 1996.
2. Drug Facts and Comparisons 1995 ed. ed. St. Louis: 1995.

NEFAZODONE HCL   L4

Trade: Serzone
Other Trades: Serzone, Dutonin
Uses: Antidepressant
AAP: Not reviewed

Nefazodone is an antidepressant similar to trazodone but structurally dissimilar from the other serotonin reuptake inhibitors. It is rapidly metabolized to three partially active metabolites that have significantly longer half-lives (1.5 to 18 hours).[1]

In a study of one patient receiving 200 mg in the morning and 100 mg at night, the infant at 9 weeks of age (2.1 kg), was admitted for drowsiness, lethargy, failure to thrive, and poor temperature control.[2] The infant was born premature at 27 weeks. The maximum milk concentration of nefazodone was 358 µg/L while the maternal plasma C_{max} was 1270 µg/L. The concentration of the metabolites was reported to be 83 µg/L for triazoledione, 32 µg/L for HO-Nefazodone, and 18 µg/L for m-Chlorophenylpiperazine. The relative infant dose was calculated to be 0.45 % of the weight-adjusted maternal dose. The AUC milk/plasma ratio ranged from 0.02 to 0.27. Unfortunately, no infant plasma samples were taken for analysis.

Dodd et.al.[3] recently reported a M/P ratio of only 0.1 for nefazodone in a patient receiving 200 mg twice daily. This is approximately one-third of the M/P ratio (0.27) reported by Yapp. However, the Yapp study used AUC data over many points and is probably a more accurate reflection of nefazodone transfer into milk during the day.

This medication should probably not be used in breastfeeding mothers with young infants, premature infants, infants subject to apnea, or other weakened infants.

Pregnancy Risk Category: C

Lactation Risk Category: L4

Adult Concerns: Weakness, hypotension, somnolence, dizziness, dry mouth, constipation, nausea, headache.

Pediatric Concerns: Drowsiness, lethargy, failure to thrive, and poor temperature control in one infant.

Drug Interactions: Sometimes fatal reactions may occur with MAOI. Plasma levels of astemizole and terfenadine may be increased. Clinically important increases in plasma concentrations of alprazolam and triazolam have been reported. Serum concentrations of digoxin have been increased by nefazodone by 29%. Haloperidol clearance decreased by 35%. Nefazodone may decrease propranolol plasma levels by as much as 30%.

Relative Infant Dose: 1.2%

Adult Dose: 150-300 mg BID

Alternatives: Sertraline, Paroxetine, Trazodone

T ½	= 1-4 hours	M/P	= 0.1-0.27
PHL	=	PB	= >99%
Tmax	= 1 hour	Oral	= 20%
MW	= 507	pKa	= 6.6
Vd	= 0.9		

References:

1. Pharmaceutical Manufacturer Prescribing Information. 1996.
2. Yapp P, Ilett KF, Kristensen JH, Hackett LP, Paech MJ, Rampono J. Drowsiness and poor feeding in a breast-fed infant: association with nefazodone and its metabolites. Ann Pharmacother 2000; 34 (11):1269-1272.
3. Dodd S, Buist A, Burrows GD, Maguire KP, Norman TR. Determination of nefazodone and its pharmacologically active metabolites in human blood plasma and breast milk by high-performance liquid chromatography. J Chromatogr B Biomed Sci Appl 1999; 730 (2):249-255.

NESIRITIDE   L3

Trade: Natrecor
Other Trades:
Uses: B-type naturetic peptide
AAP: Not reviewed

Nesiritide is a recombinanat form of human B-type natriure. It is used to treat acutely decompensated congestive heart failure. BNP binds to guanylate cyclase receptors on smooth muscle cells, increasing intracellular cGMP and causing relaxation of the vasculature.[1] No studies have been performed on the concentrations of nesiritide in human milk. However, due to the large MW of this peptide, it is unlikely that it would pass into the milk compartment nor be orally bioavailble to a breastfeeding infant.

Pregnancy Risk Category: C

Lactation Risk Category: L3

Adult Concerns: Adverse reactions include hypotension, incrased serum creatinine, ventricular tachycardia, nausea, and headache.

Pediatric Concerns: No data are available. It is unlikely to enter milk.

Drug Interactions: Increased hypotension can be seen when taken with ACE inhibitors, diuretics, and/or hypotensive agents.

Relative Infant Dose:

Adult Dose: 0.01 µg/kg/minute

Alternatives:

T ½	= 18 minutes	M/P	=
PHL	=	PB	=
Tmax	= 1 hour	Oral	= Nil
MW	= 3464	pKa	=
Vd	= 0.19		

References:
1.   Pharmaceutical Manufacturer Prescribing Information. 2004.

NETILMICIN   L3

Trade: Netromycin
Other Trades: Netromycin, Nettilin
Uses: Aminoglycoside antibiotic
AAP: Not reviewed

Netilmicin is a typical aminoglycoside antibiotic (see gentamicin). Poor oral absorption limits its use to IM and IV administration although some studies suggest significant oral absorption in infancy.[1,2] Only small levels are believed to be secreted into human milk although no reports exist. See gentamicin.

Pregnancy Risk Category: D

Lactation Risk Category: L3

Adult Concerns: Kidney damage, hearing loss, changes in GI flora.

Pediatric Concerns: None reported, but observe for GI symptoms such as diarrhea.

Drug Interactions: Risk of nephrotoxicity may be increased when used with cephalosporins, enflurane, methoxyflurane, and vancomycin. Auditory toxicity may increase when used with loop diuretics. The neuromuscular blocking effects of neuromuscular blocking agents may be increased when used with aminoglycosides.

Relative Infant Dose:

Adult Dose: 1.3-2.2 mg/kg every 8 hours

Alternatives:

T ½	= 2-2.5 hours	M/P	=
PHL	= 4.5-8 hours (neonates)	PB	= <10%
Tmax	= 30-60 minutes (IM)	Oral	= Negligable
MW	= 476	pKa	=
Vd	=		

References:
1. Pharmaceutical Manufacturer Prescribing Information. 1995.
2. McEvoy GE. (ed):AFHS Drug Information. New York, NY: 1995.

NEUROMUSCULAR BLOCKING AGENTS — L3

Trade: Anectine, Mivacron, Tracrium, Nuromax, Pavulon, Arduan, Raplon, Zemuron, Norcuron

Other Trades:

Uses: Muscle Relaxants for surgery

AAP: Not reviewed

Neuromuscular blocking agents are similar to curare and are primarily used to relax skeletal muscle during surgery.[1,2] They typically have a three phase elimination curve. The first phase elimination is rapid, averaging about <5 minutes. The second phase half-life ranges from 7-40 minutes, and a third phase half-life is 2-3 hours. It is not known if any of these agents penetrate into human milk, but it is very unlikely. First they are large in MW, have highly polar structures, and they are virtually excluded from most cells. Oral bioavailability is not reported, but it is likely small to nil. A brief waiting period (few hours) after surgery will eliminate most risks associated with the use of these products. See table in appendix.

Pregnancy Risk Category: C

Lactation Risk Category: L3

Adult Concerns: Adverse effects include prolonged apnea, residual muscle weakness, and allergic reactions. Other side effects include hypotension, bronchospasms, cardiac arrhythmias. Histamine-related events include flushing, erythema, pruritus, urticaria, wheezing and bronchospasm.

Pediatric Concerns: None reported via milk. They are unlikely to penetrate into milk in significant levels.

Drug Interactions: There are literally dozens of drug-drug interactions with the neuromuscular blocking agents. Consult a more thorough text.

Relative Infant Dose:

Adult Dose: Variable depending on individual agent.

Alternatives:

T ½	= Variable	M/P	=
PHL	=	PB	= 50%
Tmax	=	Oral	= Nil
MW	= Large	pKa	=
Vd	=		

References:
1. Pharmaceutical Manufacturers Package Insert, 2004.
2. Baselt RC. Disposition of toxic drugs and chemicals in man. Foster City, CA: Chemical Toxicology Institute, 2000.

NEVIRAPINE   L3

Trade: Viramune
Other Trades: Viramune
Uses: Antiretroviral agent used in HIV infections.
            Antiretroviral drug
AAP: Not reviewed

Nevirapine selectively inhibits reverse transcriptase activity and replication of HIV-1. It is commonly used in mixtures with other antiretroviral drugs to treat HIV.[1] Its transport into human milk was recently published. In a study of 20 women receiving 200 mg twice daily at steady state, median nevirapine levels at 4 hours postdose in maternal serum, breast milk, and infant serum were 9534 ng/mL, 6795 ng/mL and 971 ng/mL, respectively.[2] The milk/serum ratio was 0.67.

The median infant serum concentration of nevirapine (971 ng/mL) was at least 40 times the 50% inhibitory concentration and similar to peak concentrations after a single 2-mg/kg dose of nevirapine. The authors concluded that HIV-1 inhibitory concentrations of nevirapine are achieved in breast-feeding infants of mothers receiving nevirapine, exposing infants to the potential for beneficial and adverse effects of nevirapine ingestion.

Pregnancy Risk Category: B

Lactation Risk Category: L3

Adult Concerns: Reported side effects in adults are numerous and include: Rash, nausea, granulocytopenia, headache, fatigue, diarrhea, abdominal pain, myalgia. Observe for liver function, CBC, routine blood chemistry.

Pediatric Concerns: None reported in several papers. Levels in milk are moderate and levels in infant plasma are supratherapeutic.

Drug Interactions: Numerous drug-drug interactions have been reported and include: didanosine, efavirenz, Indinavir, lopinavir, nelfinavir, ritonavir, sawuinavir, stavudine, zalcitabine, clarithromycin, ethinyl estradiol, norethindrone, fluconazole, ketoconazole, rifabutin, rifampin, St. John's Wort. Check a drug interaction reference for more.

Relative Infant Dose: 17.8%

Adult Dose: 200 mg twice daily but highly variable.

Alternatives:

T ½	= 25-30 hours	M/P	= 0.67
PHL	=	PB	= 60%
Tmax	= 4 hours	Oral	= 90%
MW	= 266	pKa	=
Vd	= 1.4		

References:
1.   Pharmaceutical manufacturers prescribing information.
2.   Shapiro RL, Holland DT, Capparelli E, Lockman S, Thior I, Wester C, et al. Antiretroviral concentrations in breast-feeding infants of women in Botswana receiving antiretroviral treatment. J Infect Dis 2005 Sep 1; 192 (5):720-7.

NICARDIPINE   L2

Trade: Cardene
Other Trades: Cardene
Uses: Antihypertensive, calcium channel blocker
AAP: Not reviewed

Nicardipine is a typical calcium channel blocker structurally related to nifedipine. In a study of 11 mothers consuming 20-120 mg nicardipine daily in various dosage forms, the milk/plasma ratio at 3 hours postdose averaged 0.25 (range 0.08-0.75), and the peak milk concentration (C_{max}) was 7.3 µg/L (range 1.9-18.8).[1] The mean milk concentration was 4.4 µg/L (range 1.3-13.8). The authors estimate the relative infant dose to be 0.07% (range: 0.3-0.14) of the weight-adjusted maternal dose.

Another study of 7 lactating women receiving a dose of 1 to 6.5 mg/hr found 82% of 34 milk samples to have undetectable levels. Six samples contained between 5.1 to 18.5 µg/L. The maximum infant exposure was calculated to be less than 300 ng/day, a level much lower than the dose used in neonates.[2]

Pregnancy Risk Category: C

Lactation Risk Category: L2

Adult Concerns: Headache, peripheral edema, flushing, hypotension, bradycardia, gingival hyperplasia.

Pediatric Concerns: None reported in one study. Levels in milk are very low.

Drug Interactions: Barbiturates may reduce bioavailability of calcium channel blockers (CCB). Calcium salts may reduce hypotensive effect. Dantrolene may increase risk of hyperkalemia and myocardial depression. H2 blockers may increase bioavailability of certain CCBs. Hydantoins may reduce plasma levels. Quinidine increases risk of hypotension, bradycardia, tachycardia. Rifampin may reduce effects of CCBs. Vitamin D may reduce efficacy of CCBs. CCBs may increase carbamazepine, cyclosporin, encainide, prazosin levels.

Relative Infant Dose: 0.1%

Adult Dose: 20-50 twice daily.

Alternatives: Nifedipine, Nimodipine

T ½	= 6-10 hours	M/P	= 0.25
PHL	=	PB	= >95%
Tmax	= 0.5-2 hours	Oral	= 35%
MW	= 480	pKa	=
Vd	= 0.6-2.0		

References:
1. Jarreau P, Beller CL, Guillonneau M, Jacqz-Aigrain E. Excretion of nicardipine in human milk. 2000; 4 (1):28-30.
2. Bartels P, Hanff L, mathot R, Steegers E, Vulto A, Visser W. Nicardipine in pre-eclamptic patients: placental transfer and disposition in breast milk. BJOG 2007 Feb;114 (2):230-3.

NICOTINE PATCHES, GUM, INHALER   L2

Trade: Habitrol, NicoDerm, Nicotrol, ProStep

Other Trades: Habitrol, Nicoderm, Nicorette, Prostep Nicabate, Nicotinell TTS

Uses: Nicotine withdrawal systems

AAP: Not reviewed

Nicotine and its metabolite cotinine are both present in milk. Fifteen lactating women (mean age, 32 years; mean weight, 72 kg) who were smokers (mean of 17 cigarettes per day) participated in a trial of the nicotine patch to assist in smoking cessation.[1] Serial milk samples were collected from the women over sequential 24-hour periods when they were smoking and when they were stabilized on the 21-mg/d, 14-mg/d, and 7-mg/d nicotine patches. Nicotine and cotinine concentrations in milk were not significantly different between smoking (mean of 17 cigarettes per day) and the 21-mg/d patch, but concentrations were significantly lower when patients were using the 14-mg/d and 7-mg/d patches than when smoking. There was also a downward trend in absolute infant dose (nicotine equivalents) from smoking or the 21-mg patch through to the 14-mg and 7-mg patches. Milk intake by the breast-fed infants was similar while their mothers were smoking (585 mL/d) and subsequently when their mothers were using the 21-mg (717 mL/d), 14-mg (731 mL/d), and 7-mg (619 mL/d) patches. The authors conclude that the absolute infant dose of nicotine and its metabolite cotinine decreases by about 70% from when subjects were smoking or using the 21-mg patch to when they were using the 7-mg patch. In addition, use of the nicotine patch had no significant influence on the milk intake by the breastfed infant. Undertaking maternal smoking cessation with the nicotine patch is, therefore, a safer option than continued smoking.

With nicotine gum, maternal serum nicotine levels average 30-60% of those found in cigarette smokers. While patches (transdermal systems) produce a sustained and lower nicotine plasma level, nicotine gum may produce large variations in peak levels when the gum is chewed rapidly, fluctuations similar to smoking itself. Mothers who choose to use nicotine gum and breastfeed should be counseled to refrain from breastfeeding for 2-3 hours after using the gum product.

The nicotine inhaler (Nicotrol) only dispenses about 4 mg of nicotine following 80 inhalations, of which, only 2 mg is actually absorbed. Plasma levels slowly reach levels of about 6 ng/mL in contrast to those of a cigarette, which reach a C_{max} of approximately 49 ng/mL in only 5 minutes. These levels (6 ng/mL) are probably too low to affect a breastfeeding infant.

Nicotine has been suggested to decrease in basal prolactin production.[2,3] One study clearly suggests that cigarette smoking significantly reduces breastmilk production at two weeks postpartum from 514 mL/day in non-smokers to 406 mL/day in smoking mothers.[4] However, Ilett's well-done study above did not detect any change in milk production at all, although the methods of these two studies were not identical. Therefore, the risk of using nicotine patches while breastfeeding is much less than the risk of formula feeding. Mothers should be advised to limit smoking as much as possible and to smoke only after they have fed their infant, or to switch to the use of nicotine patches.

Pregnancy Risk Category: X if used in overdose
                                                D if used in third trimester

Lactation Risk Category: L2

Adult Concerns: Tachycardia, GI distress, vomiting, diarrhea, rapid heart beat, and restlessness. Smoking during pregnancy has been associated with preterm births, decreased birth weight, and an increased risk of abortion and stillbirth . The use of nicotine during the last trimester has been associated with a decrease in fetal breathing movements, possibly resulting from decreased placental perfusion induced by nicotine. However, the use of nicotine patches instead of smoking is still preferred .

Pediatric Concerns: No untoward effects were noted from nicotine patch study.

Drug Interactions: Cessation of smoking may alter response to a number of medications in ex-smokers. Including are acetaminophen, caffeine, imipramine, oxazepam, pentazocine, propranolol, and theophylline. Smoking may reduce diuretic effect of furosemide.

Smoking while continuing to use patches may dramatically elevate nicotine plasma levels.

Relative Infant Dose:

Adult Dose: 7-21 mg daily

Alternatives:

T ½	= 2.0 hours (non-patch)	M/P	= 2.9
PHL	=	PB	= 4.9%
Tmax	= 2-4 hours	Oral	= 30%
MW	= 162	pKa	=
Vd	=		

References:
1. Ilett KF, Hale TW, Page-Sharp M, Kristensen JH, Kohan R, Hackett LP. Use of nicotine patches in breast-feeding mothers: transfer of nicotine and cotinine into human milk. Clin Pharmacol Ther 2003; 74 (6):516-524.
2. Benowitz NL. Nicotine replacement therapy during pregnancy. JAMA 1991; 266 (22).3174-3177.
3. Matheson I, Rivrud GN. The effect of smoking on lactation and infantile colic. JAMA 1989; 261 (1):42-43.
4. Hopkinson JM, Schanler RJ, Fraley JK, Garza C. Milk production by mothers of premature infants: influence of cigarette smoking. Pediatrics 1992; 90 (6):934-938.

NICOTINIC ACID   L3

Trade: Nicobid, Nicolar, Niacels, Niacin, Nicotinamide, Niaspan
Other Trades:
Uses: Vitamin B-3
AAP: Not reviewed

Nicotinic acid, commonly called niacin, is a component of two coenzymes which function in oxidation-reduction reactions essential for tissue respiration. It is converted to nicotinamide in vivo. Although considered a vitamin, large doses (2-6 gm/day) are effective in reducing serum LDL cholesterol and triglyceride and increasing serum HDL. From numerous studies, niacin content (even when supplemented with moderately low amounts) seems to vary from about 1.1 to 3.9 mg/L under normal circumstances.[1] Supplementation apparently does increase milk niacin levels. The concentration transferred into milk as a function of dose or following high maternal doses has not been reported, but it is presumed that elevated maternal plasma levels may significantly elevate milk levels of niacin as well. Because niacin is known to be hepatotoxic in higher doses, breastfeeding mothers should not significantly exceed the RDA such as with the 2 gm/day doses used to treat hypercholesterolemia.

Pregnancy Risk Category: A during first and second trimesters
                                 C during third trimester

Lactation Risk Category: L3

Adult Concerns: Flushing, peripheral dilation, itching, nausea, bloating, flatulence, vomiting. In high doses, some abnormal liver function tests.

Pediatric Concerns: None reported via milk, but do not exceed RDA.

Drug Interactions: Niacin may produce fluctuations in blood glucose levels and interfere with oral hypoglycemics. May inhibit uricosuric effects of sulfinpyrazone and probenecid. Increased toxicity (myopathy) when used with lovastatin and other cholesterol-lowering drugs.

Relative Infant Dose:

Adult Dose: 10-20 mg daily

Alternatives:

T ½	= 45 minutes	M/P	=
PHL	=	PB	=
Tmax	= 45 minutes	Oral	= Complete
MW	= 123	pKa	= 4.85
Vd	=		

References:
1. Pratt jp, Hamil BM, Moyer EZ, et.al. Metabolism of women during the reproductive cycle. XVIII. The effect of multivitamin supplements on the secretion of B vitamins in human milk. J Nutr 1951; 44 (1):141-157.

NIFEDIPINE | L2

Trade: Adalat, Procardia
Other Trades: Adalat, Apo-Nifed, Novo-Nifedin, Nu-Nifed, Nifecard, Nyefax, Nefensar XL
Uses: Antihypertensive calcium channel blocker
AAP: Maternal Medication Usually Compatible with Breastfeeding

Nifedipine is an effective antihypertensive. It belongs to the calcium channel blocker family of drugs. Two studies indicate that nifedipine is transferred to breastmilk in varying but generally low levels. In one study in which the dose was varied from 10-30 mg three times daily, the highest concentration (53.35 μg/L) was measured at 1 hour after a 30 mg dose.[1] Other levels reported were 16.35 μg/L 60 minutes after a 20 mg dose and 12.89 μg/L 30 minutes after a 10 mg dose. The milk levels fell linearly with the milk half-lives estimated to be 1.4 hours for the 10 mg dose, 3.1 hours for the 20 dose, and 2.4 hours for the 30 mg dose. The milk concentration measured 8 hours following a 30 mg dose was 4.93 μg/L. In this study, using the highest concentration found and a daily intake of 150 mL/kg of human milk, the amount of nifedipine intake would only be 8 μg/kg/day (less than 1.8% of the therapeutic pediatric dose). The authors conclude that the amount ingested via breast milk poses little risk to an infant.

In another study, concentrations of nifedipine in human milk 1 to 8 hours after 10 mg doses varied from <1 to 10.3 μg/L (median 3.5 μg/L) in six of eleven patients.[2] In this study, milk levels three days after discontinuing medication ranged from <1 to 9.4 μg/L. The authors concluded the exposure to nifedipine through breastmilk is not significant. In a study by Penny and Lewis, following a maternal dose of 20 mg nifedipine daily for 10 days, peak breastmilk levels at 1 hour were 46 μg/L.[3] The corresponding maternal serum level was 43 μg/L. From this data the authors suggest a daily intake for an infant would be approximately 6.45 μg/kg/day.

Nifedipine has been found clinically useful for nipple vasospasm. Because of the similarity to Raynaud's Phenomenon, sustained release formulations providing 30-60 mg per day are suggested.

Pregnancy Risk Category: C

Lactation Risk Category: L2

Adult Concerns: Headache, peripheral edema, gingival hyperplasia, hypotension. Distortion of smell and taste.

Pediatric Concerns: None reported via milk.

Drug Interactions: Barbiturates may reduce bioavailability of calcium channel blockers (CCB). Calcium salts may reduce hypotensive effect. Dantrolene may increase risk of hyperkalemia and myocardial depression. H2 blockers may increase bioavailability of certain CCBs. Hydantoins may reduce plasma levels. Quinidine increases risk of hypotension, bradycardia, tachycardia. Rifampin may reduce effects of CCBs. Vitamin D may reduce efficacy of CCBs. CCBs may increase carbamazepine, cyclosporin, encainide, prazosin levels.

Relative Infant Dose: 2.3% - 3.4%

Adult Dose: 10-20 mg TID

Alternatives: Nimodipine

T ½	= 1.8-7 hours	M/P	= 1.0
PHL	= 26.5 (neonatal)	PB	= 92-98%
Tmax	= 45 min-4 hours	Oral	= 50%
MW	= 346	pKa	=
Vd	=		

References:
1. Ehrenkranz RA, Ackerman BA, Hulse JD. Nifedipine transfer into human milk. J Pediatr 1989; 114 (3):478-480.
2. Manninen AK, Juhakoski A. Nifedipine concentrations in maternal and umbilical serum, amniotic fluid, breast milk and urine of mothers and offspring. Int J Clin Pharmacol Res 1991; 11 (5):231-236.
3. Penny WJ, Lewis MJ. Nifedipine is excreted in human milk. Eur J Clin Pharmacol 1989; 36 (4):427-428.

NIMODIPINE   L2

Trade: Nimotop
Other Trades: Nimotop
Uses: Antihypertensive, calcium channel
AAP: Not reviewed

Nimodipine is a calcium channel blocker although it is primarily used in preventing cerebral artery spasm and improving cerebral blood flow. Nimodipine is effective in reducing neurologic deficits following subarachnoid hemorrhage, acute stroke, and severe head trauma. It is also useful in prophylaxis of migraine.

In one study of a patient 3 days postpartum who received 60 mg every 4 hours for one week, breastmilk levels paralleled maternal serum levels with a milk/plasma ratio of approximately 0.33.[1] The highest milk concentration reported was approximately 3.5 µg/L while the maternal plasma was approximately 16 µg/L.

In another study (2), a 36 year old mother received a total dose of 46 mg IV over 24 hours. Nimodipine concentration in milk was much lower than in maternal serum, with a milk/serum ratio of 0.06 to 0.15. During IV infusion, nimodipine concentrations in milk raised initially to 2.2 µg/L and stabilized at concentrations between 0.87 and 1.6 µg/L of milk. Assuming a daily milk intake of 150 mg/kg, an infant would ingest approximately 0.063 to 0.705 µg/kg/day or 0.008 to 0.092% of the weight-adjusted dose administered to the mother.

Pregnancy Risk Category: C

Lactation Risk Category: L2

Adult Concerns: Hypotension, diarrhea, nausea, cramps.

Pediatric Concerns: None reported via milk in two studies.

Drug Interactions: When used with adenosine, prolonged bradycardia may result. Use with amiodarone may lead to sinus arrest and AV block. H2 blockers may increase bioavailability of nimodipine. Beta blockers may increase cardiac depression. May increase carbamazepine levels with admixed. May increase cyclosporine, digoxin, quinidine plasma levels. May increase theophylline effects. Used with fentanyl, it may increase hypotension.

Relative Infant Dose: 0.04%

Adult Dose: 60 mg every 4 hours

Alternatives: Verapamil, Nifedipine

T ½	= 9 hours	M/P	= 0.06 to 0.33
PHL	=	PB	= 95%
Tmax	= 1 hour	Oral	= 13%
MW	= 418	pKa	=
Vd	= 0.94		

References:
1. Tonks AM. Nimodipine levels in breast milk. Aust N Z J Surg 1995; 65 (9):693-694.
2. Carcas AJ, Abad-Santos F, de Rosendo JM, Frias J. Nimodipine transfer into human breast milk and cerebrospinal fluid. Ann Pharmacother 1996; 30 (2):148-150.

NISOLDIPINE   L3

Trade: Sular
Other Trades: Syscor
Uses: Antihypertensive
AAP: Not reviewed

Nisoldipine is a typical calcium channel blocker antihypertensive.[1] No data are available on its transfer into human milk. For alternatives see nifedipine and verapamil. Due to its poor oral bioavailability, presence of lipids which reduce its absorption, and high protein binding, it is unlikely to penetrate milk and be absorbed by the infant (undocumented).

Pregnancy Risk Category: C

Lactation Risk Category: L3

Adult Concerns: Hypotension, bradycardia, peripheral edema.

Pediatric Concerns: None reported via milk. Observe for hypotension, sedation although unlikely.

Drug Interactions: Barbiturates may reduce bioavailability of calcium channel blockers (CCB). Calcium salts may reduce hypotensive effect. Dantrolene may increase risk of hyperkalemia and myocardial depression. H2 blockers may increase bioavailability of certain CCBs. Hydantoins may reduce plasma levels. Quinidine increases risk of hypotension, bradycardia, tachycardia. Rifampin may reduce effects of CCBs. Vitamin D may reduce efficacy of CCBs. CCBs may increase carbamazepine, cyclosporin, encainide, prazosin levels.

Relative Infant Dose:

Adult Dose: 20-40 mg daily.

Alternatives: Nifedipine, Verapamil, Nimodipine

T ½	= 7-12 hours	M/P	=
PHL	=	PB	= 99%
Tmax	= 6-12 hours	Oral	= 5%
MW	= 388	pKa	=
Vd	= 4		

References:
1. Pharmaceutical Manufacturer Prescribing Information.

NITAZOXANIDE — L3

Trade: Alinia
Other Trades:
Uses: Antibiotic for parasitic infections
AAP: Not reviewed

Nitazoxanide is a new thiazolide antiprotozoan agent that shows excellent in vitro activity against a wide variety of protozoa and helminth. It is a suitable alternative for metronidazole in many infections including Giardia lamblia and Cryptosporidium parvum. Once absorbed it is rapidly converted to the active metabolite tizoxanide.[1] No data are available on its transfer to human milk.

Pregnancy Risk Category: B

Lactation Risk Category: L3

Adult Concerns: Abdominal pain, diarrhea, headache and nausea have been reported in clinical trials.

Pediatric Concerns: None reported, but no data are available.

Drug Interactions: None reported.

Relative Infant Dose:

Adult Dose: 500 mg every 12 hours with food.

Alternatives: Metronidazole

T ½	= 1-1.6 hours	M/P	=
PHL	=	PB	= 99%
Tmax	= 4 hours	Oral	= Good
MW	= 307	pKa	=
Vd	=		

References:
1. Pharmaceutical manufacturers package insert. 2005

NITRAZEPAM   L2

Trade: Mogadon
Other Trades: Mogadon, Nitrazadon, Alodorm, Atempol,
        Nitrodos
Uses: Sedative, hypnotic
AAP: Not reviewed

Nitrazepam is a typical benzodiazepine (Valium family) used as a sedative. In a study of 9 women who received 5 mg nitrazepam at night, the concentration in milk increased over a period of 5 days from 30 nmol/L to 48 nmol/L over 5 days.[1] The mean milk/plasma ratio after 7 hours was 0.27 in 32 paired samples and did not vary from day 1 to day 5. The mean concentration of nitrazepam in milk was 13 µg/L and the C_{max} was 0.20 µg/L. Nitrazepam levels in a 6 day old infant were below the limits of detection. No adverse effects were noted in the infants breastfed for 5 days.

Pregnancy Risk Category:

Lactation Risk Category: L2 (short term)

Adult Concerns: Sedation, disorientation.

Pediatric Concerns: None reported, but observe for sedation.

Drug Interactions:

Relative Infant Dose: 2.9%

Adult Dose: 5-10 mg daily.

Alternatives: Alprazolam, Lorazepam

T ½	= 30 hours	M/P	= 0.27
PHL	=	PB	= 90%
Tmax	= 0.5 - 5 hours	Oral	= 53-94%
MW	= 281	pKa	= 3.2,10.8
Vd	= 2-5		

References:
1. Matheson I, Lunde PK, Bredesen JE. Midazolam and nitrazepam in
   the maternity ward: milk concentrations and clinical effects. Br J Clin
   Pharmacol 1990; 30 (6):787-793.

NITRENDIPINE   L2

Trade: Baypress
Other Trades:
Uses: Calcium channel blocker, antihypertensive
AAP: Not reviewed

Nitrendipine is a typical calcium channel antihypertensive. In a group of 3 breastfeeding mothers who received 20 mg/d for 5 days, nitrendipine was excreted in breast milk at peak concentrations ranging from 4.3 to 6.5 µg/L 1-2 h after acute dosing while its inactive pyridine metabolite ranged from 6.9 to 11.9 µg/L.[1] After 5 days of dosing, the C_{max} remained in the same range and the breast milk/plasma ratio for nitrendipine was 0.2 to 0.5. On the fourth day of continuous dosing, average concentrations of nitrendipine from 24-h collections of the milk were 1.1 to 3.8 µg/L. Thus, nitrendipine and its metabolite are excreted in very low concentrations in human breast milk. Based on a maternal dose of 20 mg daily, a newborn infant would ingest an average of 1.7 µg/d of nitrendipine, or a relative dose of 0.095%.

Pregnancy Risk Category:

Lactation Risk Category: L2

Adult Concerns: Headache, hypotension, peripheral edema, cardiac arrhythmias, fatigue.

Pediatric Concerns: None reported via milk.

Drug Interactions: Barbiturates may reduce bioavailability of calcium channel blockers (CCB). Calcium salts may reduce hypotensive effect. Dantrolene may increase risk of hyperkalemia and myocardial depression. H2 blockers may increase bioavailability of certain CCBs. Hydantoins may reduce plasma levels. Quinidine increases risk of hypotension, bradycardia, tachycardia. Rifampin may reduce effects of CCBs. Vitamin D may reduce efficacy of CCBs. CCBs may increase carbamazepine, cyclosporin, encainide, prazosin levels.

Relative Infant Dose: 0.1%

Adult Dose: 10-80 mg/day

Alternatives: Nifedipine, Nimodipine

T ½	= 8-11 hours	M/P	= 0.2-0.5
PHL	=	PB	= 98%
Tmax	= 1-2 hours	Oral	= 16-20%
MW	= 360	pKa	=
Vd	=		

References:
1. White WB, Yeh SC, Krol GJ. Nitrendipine in human plasma and breast milk. Eur J Clin Pharmacol 1989; 36 (5):531-534.

NITROFURANTOIN | L2

Trade: Furadantin, Macrodantin, Furan, Macrobid

Other Trades: Apo-Nitrofurantoin, Macrodantin, Nephronex, Furadantin

Uses: Urinary antibiotic

AAP: Maternal Medication Usually Compatible with Breastfeeding

Nitrofurantoin is an old urinary tract antimicrobial. It is secreted in breastmilk but in very small amounts. In one study of 20 women receiving 100 mg four times daily, none was detected in milk.[1] In another group of nine nursing women who received 100-200 mg every 6 hours, nitrofurantoin was undetectable in the milk of those treated with 100 mg and only trace amounts were found in those treated with 200 mg (0.3-0.5 mg/L milk).[2] In these two patients the milk/plasma ratio ranged from 0.27 to 0.31.

In a well-done study of 4 breastfeeding mothers who ingested 100 mg nitrofurantoin with a meal, the milk/serum ratio averaged 6.21 suggesting an active transfer into milk.[3] Regardless of an active transfer, the average milk concentration throughout the day (AUC) was only 1.3 mg/L. According to the authors, the estimated dose an infant would ingest was 0.2 mg/kg/day or 6.8% of the weight-adjusted maternal dose if they consumed 200 mg/d nitrofurantoin. The therapeutic dose administered to infants is 5-7 mg/kg/day.

Use with caution in infants with G6PD or in infants less than 1 month of age with hyperbilirubinemia, due to displacement of bilirubin from albumin binding sites.

Pregnancy Risk Category: B

Lactation Risk Category: L2

Adult Concerns: Nausea, vomiting, brown urine, hemolytic anemia, hepatotoxicity.

Pediatric Concerns: None reported via milk, however, do not use in infants with G6PD or in infants less than 1 month of age.

Drug Interactions: Anticholinergics increase nitrofurantoin bioavailability by delaying gastric emptying and increasing absorption. Magnesium salts may delay or decrease absorption. Uricosurics may increase nitrofurantoin levels by decreasing renal clearance.

Relative Infant Dose: 6.83%

Adult Dose: 50-100 mg QID

Alternatives:

T ½	= 20-58 minutes	M/P	= 0.27-6.2
PHL	=	PB	= 20-60%
Tmax	= 4.9 hours	Oral	= 94%
MW	= 238	pKa	= 7.2
Vd	=		

References:
1. Hosbach RH, Foster RB. Absence of nitrofurantoin from human milk. JAMA 1967; 202 (11):1057.
2. Varsano I, Fischl J, Shochet SB. The excretion of orally ingested nitrofurantoin in human milk. J Pediatr 1973; 82 (5):886-887.
3. Gerk PM, Kuhn RJ, Desai NS, McNamara PJ. Active transport of nitrofurantoin into human milk. Pharmacotherapy 2001; 21 (6):669-675.

NITROGLYCERIN, NITRATES, NITRITES | L4

Trade: Nitrostat, Nitrolingual, Nitrogard, Amyl Nitrite, Nitrong, Nitro-Bid, Nitroglyn, Minitran, Nitro-Dur

Other Trades: Nitrong SR, Nitrol, Transderm-Nitro, Nitro-Dur, Anginine, Nitrolingual Spray, Nitradisc, Deponit

Uses: Vasodilator

AAP: Not reviewed

Nitroglycerin is a rapid and short acting vasodilator used in angina and other cardiovascular problems including congestive heart failure. Nitroglycerin, as well as numerous other formulations (amyl nitrate, isosorbide dinitrate, etc.) all work by release of the nitrite and nitrate molecule. Nitrates come in numerous formulations, some for acute use (sublingual), others are more sustained (Nitro-Dur). Nitrates and Nitrites are derived from multiple sources, including medications in the form of nitroglycerin, or isosorbide dinitrate, or from food and water sources. Elevated nitrate levels in drinking water in the USA are common in rural areas. Numerous cases of nitrate-induced methemoglobinemia have been reported in infants exposed to well water with high levels of nitrates when they were fed foods/formulas prepared with contaminated water. Only one case of a breastfed infant has been reported and it is questionable.[1] Thus far, it is less certain that the oral ingestion of nitrates can penetrate into human milk in clinically relevant amounts.

Two studies suggest that while nitrates/nitrites are well absorbed orally in the mother (approx. 50%), little seems to be transported to human milk. In a study by Dusdieker[2], following a mean total nitrate intake from diet and water of 46.6, 168.1, and 272 mg/day, milk levels only averaged 4.4, 5.1, and 5.2 mg/L respectively. Thus higher maternal intake did not necessarily correlate with higher milk levels. The authors conclude that mothers who ingest nitrate of 100 mg/day or less do not produce milk with elevated nitrate levels.

In a study by Green[3], milk levels were not different from maternal plasma levels. Thus it is apparent that even at relatively high rates of ingestion, nitrate levels do not concentrate in milk and may not be high enough to harm an infant. However, these studies were done using nitrates in water and may not correlate with the ingestion of high and prolonged concentrations of nitrates from medications administered orally, buccally, or transcutaneously. No studies have been found comparing milk nitrates with oral nitroglycerin or isosorbide dinitrate.

While it is apparent that milk levels are not high following the ingestion of oral nitrates, infants younger than 6 months are most at risk from nitrate intoxication because of their susceptibility to methemoglobinemia.[4]

In another study of 59 women living in regions with high nitrate levels, breastmilk levels of nitrates and nitrites were 2.83 mg/L and 0.46 mg/L respectively, while those living in low nitrate regions were 2.75 mg/L and 0.32 mg/L respectively.[5] They were not significantly different. Breastfeed with caution at higher doses and with prolonged exposure. Observe the infant for methemoglobinemia.

Pregnancy Risk Category: C

Lactation Risk Category: L4

Adult Concerns: Postural hypotension, flushing, headache, weakness, drug rash, exfoliative dermatitis, bradycardia, nausea, vomiting, methemoglobinemia (overdose), sweating.

Pediatric Concerns: None are reported via milk. Observe for methemoglobinemia.

Drug Interactions: IV nitroglycerin may counteract the effects of heparin. Increased toxicity when used with alcohol, beta-blockers. Calcium channel blockers may increase hypotensive effect of nitrates.

Relative Infant Dose:

Adult Dose: 1.3-6.5 mg BID

Alternatives:

T ½	= 1-4 minutes	M/P	–
PHL	=	PB	= 60%
Tmax	= 2-20 minutes	Oral	= Complete
MW	= 227	pKa	=
Vd	=		

References:
1. Donahoe WE. Cyanosis in infants with nitrates in drinking water as a cause. Pediatrics 1949; 3:308.
2. Dusdieker LB, Stumbo PJ, Kross BC, Dungy CI. Does increased nitrate ingestion elevate nitrate levels in human milk? Arch Pediatr Adolesc Med 1996; 150 (3):311-314.
3. Green LC, Tannenbaum SR, Fox JG. Nitrate in human and canine milk. N Engl J Med 1982; 306 (22):1367-1368.
4. Johnson CJ, Kross BC. Continuing importance of nitrate contamination of groundwater and wells in rural areas. Am J Ind Med 1990; 18 (4):449-456.
5. Paszkowski T, Sikorski R, Kozak A, Kowalski B, Jakubik J. [Contamination of human milk with nitrates and nitrites]. Pol Tyg Lek 1989; 44 (46-48):961-963.

NITROPRUSSIDE | L4

Trade: Nitropress
Other Trades: Nipride
Uses: Hypotensive agent
AAP: Not reviewed

Nitroprusside is a rapid acting hypotensive agent of short duration (1-10 minutes). Besides rapid hypotension, nitroprusside is converted metabolically to cyanogen (cyanide radical) which is potentially toxic. Although rare, significant thiocyanate toxicity can occur at higher doses (>2 µg/kg/min.) and longer durations of exposure (>1-2 days).[1] When administered orally, nitroprusside is reported to not be active although one report suggests a modest hypotensive effect. No data are available on transfer of nitroprusside nor thiocyanate into human milk. The half-life of the thiocyanate metabolite is approximately 3 days. Because the thiocyanate metabolite is orally bioavailable, some caution is advised if the mother has received nitroprusside for more than 24 hours.[2]

Pregnancy Risk Category: C

Lactation Risk Category: L4

Adult Concerns: Hypotension, methemoglobinemia, headache, drowsiness, cyanide toxicity, hypothyroidism, nausea, vomiting.

Pediatric Concerns: None reported but caution is urged due to thiocyanate metabolite.

Drug Interactions: Clonidine may potentiate the hypotensive effect of nitroprusside. May reduce [131]Iodine uptake and induce hypothyroidism.

Relative Infant Dose:

Adult Dose: 0.3-10 µg/kg/minute X 10 minutes

Alternatives:

T ½	= 3-4 minutes	M/P	=
PHL	=	PB	=
Tmax	= 1-2 minutes	Oral	= Poor
MW	=	pKa	=
Vd	=		

References:
1. Page IH, Corcoran AC, Dustan HP, Koppanyi T. Cardiovascular actions of sodium nitroprusside in animals and hypertensive patients. Circulation 1955; 11 (2):188-198.
2. Benitz WE, Malachowski N, Cohen RS, Stevenson DK, Ariagno RL, Sunshine P. Use of sodium nitroprusside in neonates: efficacy and safety. J Pediatr 1985; 106 (1):102-110.

NITROUS OXIDE | L3

Trade:
Other Trades: Entonox
Uses: Anesthetic gas
AAP: Not reviewed

Nitrous oxide is a weak anesthetic gas. It provides good analgesia and a weak anesthesia. It is rapidly eliminated from the body due to rapid exchange with nitrogen via the pulmonary alveoli (within minutes).[1] A rapid recovery generally occurs in 3-5 minutes. Due to poor lipid solubility, uptake by adipose tissue is relatively poor, and only insignificant traces of nitrous oxide circulate in blood after discontinuing inhalation of the gas. No data exists on the entry of nitrous oxide into human milk. Ingestion of nitrous oxide orally via milk is unlikely. Chronic exposure may lead to elevated risks of fetal malformations, abortions, and bone marrow toxicity (particular in dental care workers).[2]

Pregnancy Risk Category:

Lactation Risk Category: L3

Adult Concerns: Chronic exposure can produce bone marrow suppression, headaches, hypotension and bradycardia.

Pediatric Concerns: None reported via milk.

Drug Interactions:

Relative Infant Dose:

Adult Dose: Inhalation 30% with 70% oxygen

Alternatives:

T ½	= <3 minutes	M/P	=
PHL	=	PB	=
Tmax	= 15 minutes	Oral	= Poor
MW	= 44	pKa	=
Vd	=		

References:

1. General Anesthetics. In: Drug Evaluations Annual 1995 American Medical Association, 1995.
2. Adriani J. General Anesthetics. In: Clinical Management of Poisoning and Drug Overdose. W.B. Saunders & Co., 1983.

NIZATIDINE   L2

Trade: Axid
Other Trades: Axid, Apo-Nizatidine, Tazac
Uses: Reduces gastric acid secretion
AAP: Not reviewed

Nizatidine is an antisecretory, histamine-2 antagonist that reduces stomach acid secretion. In one study of 5 lactating women using a dose of 150 mg, milk levels of nizatidine were directly proportional to circulating maternal serum levels, yet were very low.[1] Over a 12 hour period 96 µg (less than 0.5% of dose) was secreted into the milk. No effects on infant have been reported.

Pregnancy Risk Category: B

Lactation Risk Category: L2

Adult Concerns: Headache, GI distress.

Pediatric Concerns: None reported.

Drug Interactions: Elevated salicylate levels may occur when nizatidine is used with high doses of salicylates.

Relative Infant Dose: 0.5%

Adult Dose: 150-300 mg daily.

Alternatives: Famotidine

T ½	= 1.5 hours	M/P	=
PHL	=	PB	= 35%
Tmax	= 0.5-3 hours	Oral	= 94%
MW	= 331	pKa	=
Vd	=		

References:
1. Obermeyer BD, Bergstrom RF, Callaghan JT, Knadler MP, Golichowski A, Rubin A. Secretion of nizatidine into human breast milk after single and multiple doses. Clin Pharmacol Ther 1990; 47 (6):724-730.

NORELGESTROMIN + ETHINYL ESTRADIOL   L3

Trade: Ortho Evra
Other Trades:
Uses: Patch combination contraceptive
AAP: Not reviewed

Ortho Evra is a new combination progestin and estrogen-containing patch. It delivers approximately 150 µg/day norelgestromin and 20 µg/d ethinyl estradiol to the plasma compartment of the female. Small amounts of estrogens and progestins are known to pass into milk, but long-term follow-up of children whose mothers used combination hormonal contraceptives while breastfeeding has shown no deleterious effects on infants. Estrogen-containing contraceptives may interfere with milk production by decreasing the quantity and quality of milk production.

Pregnancy Risk Category:

Lactation Risk Category: L3

Adult Concerns: Side effects include: breast tenderness and enlargement headache, nausea menstrual changes, abdominal cramps and bloating, vaginal discharge and irritation at the site of application.

Pediatric Concerns: Potential reduction of daily milk production due to estrogen content.

Drug Interactions: Same   as   with   all   combination   oral contraceptives. Effectiveness may be reduced if co-administered with certain antibiotics, antifungals, anticonvulsants, protease inhibitors, or other drugs that affect hepatic metabolism. Other drugs include: St. John's Wort, barbiturates, griseofulvin, rifampin, phenytoin, and carbamazepine.

Relative Infant Dose:

Adult Dose: Applied for 7 days times 3 per month.

Alternatives: Norethindrone

References:
1.   Pharmaceutical Manufacturer Prescribing Information, 2003.

NORETHINDRONE   L1

Trade: Aygestin, Norlutate, Micronor, NOR-Q.D.
Other Trades: Micronor, Norlutate, Norethisterone, Brevinor
Uses: Progestin for oral contraceptives
AAP: Not reviewed

Norethindrone is a typical synthetic progestational agent that is used for oral contraception and other endocrine functions. It is believed to be secreted into breastmilk in small amounts. It produces a dose-dependent suppression of lactation at higher doses, although somewhat minimal at lower doses. It may reduce lactose content and reduce overall milk volume and nitrogen/protein content, resulting in lower infant weight gain although these effects are unlikely if doses are kept low.[1-5] Progestin-only mini pills are preferred oral contraceptives in breastfeeding mothers.

However, recent reports claim that Micronor can be associated with decreased breastmilk production. In a report of 13 women taking Micronor who presented with poor milk production, 10 women experienced an increase in lactation upon withdrawl of Micronor.[6] While norethindrone birth control pill are considered ideal for most breastsfeeding mothers, some women retain sensitivity to these products and may suffer from reduced milk production. Each and every breastfeeding mother should be individually counselled about the possible reduction in milk synthesis following the use of this product.

Pregnancy Risk Category: X

Lactation Risk Category: L1

Adult Concerns: Changes in menstruation, breakthrough bleeding, nausea, abdominal pain, edema, breast tenderness.

Pediatric Concerns: None reported via milk. Observe for reduced milk production.

Drug Interactions: Rifampin may reduce the plasma level of norethindrone possibly decreasing its effect.

Relative Infant Dose:

Adult Dose: 0.35-5 mg daily.

Alternatives:

T ½	= 4-13 hours	M/P	=
PHL	=	PB	= 97%
Tmax	= 1-2 hours	Oral	= 60%
MW	= 298	pKa	=
Vd	=		

References:
1. Kora SJ. Effect of oral contraceptives on lactation. Fertil Steril 1969, 20 (3):419-423.
2. Miller GH, Hughes LR. Lactation and genital involution effects of a new low-dose oral contraceptive on breast-feeding mothers and their infants. Obstet Gynecol 1970; 35 (1):44-50.
3. Karim M, Ammar R, el Mahgoub S, el Ganzoury B, Fikri F, Abdou I. Injected progestogen and lactation. Br Med J 1971; 1 (742):200-203.
4. Lonnerdal B, Forsum E, Hambraeus L. Effect of oral contraceptives on composition and volume of breast milk. Am J Clin Nutr 1980; 33 (4):816-824.
5. Laukaran VH. The effects of contraceptive use on the initiation and duration of lactation. Int J Gynaecol Obstet 1987; 25 Suppl:129-142.
6. Norethindrone (Micronor): suspected association with decreased breast milk production. CARN 2007 July; 17 (3):4.

Norethindrone and Ethinyl estradiol   L3

Trade: femhrt
Other Trades:
Uses: Estrogen/progestin for treatment of menopausal symptoms
AAP: Not reviewed

Combination of the progestin norethindrone acetate (1 mg) and ethinyl estradiol (5 µg). It is indicated for postmenopausal vasomotor symptoms (hot flash) and osteoporosis. While the dose of estradiol is low, it still may be low enough to suppress milk production.

Pregnancy Risk Category:

Lactation Risk Category: L3

Adult Concerns: Observe for reduced milk production. See other indications under each monograph in this book.

Pediatric Concerns: None reported. Observe for suppression of milk production.

Drug Interactions:

Relative Infant Dose:

Adult Dose:

Alternatives:

References:

NORETHYNODREL   L2

Trade: Enovid
Other Trades:
Uses: Progestational agent
AAP: Maternal Medication Usually Compatible with Breastfeeding

Norethynodrel is a synthetic progestational agent used in oral contraceptives. Limited or no effects on infant. May decrease volume of breastmilk to some degree in some mothers if therapy initiated too soon after birth and if dose is too high.[1-3] See norethindrone, medroxyprogesterone.

Pregnancy Risk Category: X

Lactation Risk Category: L2

Adult Concerns: Changes in menstruation, breakthrough bleeding, nausea, abdominal pain, edema, breast tenderness.

Pediatric Concerns: None reported. May suppress lactation.

Drug Interactions:

Relative Infant Dose:

Adult Dose:

Alternatives:

T ½	=	M/P	=
PHL	=	PB	=
Tmax	=	Oral	=
MW	= 298	pKa	=
Vd	=		

References:
1.   Booker DE, Pahl IR. Control of postpartum breast engorgement with oral contraceptives. Am J Obstet Gynecol 1967; 98 (8):1099-1101.
2.   Laukaran VH. The effects of contraceptive use on the initiation and duration of lactation. Int J Gynaecol Obstet 1987; 25 Suppl:129-142.

3. Kora SJ. Effect of oral contraceptives on lactation. Fertil Steril 1969; 20 (3):419-423.

NORFLOXACIN   L3

Trade: Noroxin
Other Trades: Noroxin
Uses: Fluoroquinolone antibiotic
AAP: Not reviewed

Although other members in the fluoroquinolone family are secreted into breastmilk (see ciprofloxacin, ofloxacin), only limited data is available on this drug.[1] Wise has suggested that norfloxacin is not present in breastmilk. [2] The manufacturer's product information states that doses of 200 mg do not produce detectable concentrations in milk although this was a single dose.[3] Of the fluoroquinolone family, norfloxacin, levofloxacin, or perhaps ofloxacin may be preferred over others for use in a breastfeeding mother.

Pregnancy Risk Category: C

Lactation Risk Category: L3

Adult Concerns: Nausea, vomiting, GI dyspepsia, depression, dizziness, pseudomembranous colitis in pediatric patients.

Pediatric Concerns: None reported via milk. Observe for diarrhea.

Drug Interactions: Decreased absorption with antacids. Quinolones cause increased levels of caffeine, warfarin, cyclosporine, theophylline. Cimetidine, probenecid, azlocillin increase norfloxacin levels. Increased risk of seizures when used with foscarnet.

Relative Infant Dose:

Adult Dose: 400 mg BID

Alternatives: Ofloxacin, levofloxacin

T ½	= 3.3 hours	M/P	=
PHL	=	PB	= 20%
Tmax	= 1-2 hours	Oral	= 30-40%
MW	= 319	pKa	=
Vd	=		

References:
1. Harmon T, Burkhart G, Applebaum H. Perforated pseudomembranous colitis in the breast-fed infant. J Pediatr Surg 1992; 27 (6):744-746.

2.   Wise R. Norfloxacin--a review of pharmacology and tissue penetration. J Antimicrob Chemother 1984; 13 Suppl B:59-64.
3.   Pharmaceutical Manufacturer Prescribing Information. 1999.

NORTRIPTYLINE   L2

Trade: Aventyl, Pamelor
Other Trades: Aventyl, Norventyl, Apo-Nortriptyline, Allegron
Uses: Tricyclic antidepressant
AAP: Drugs whose effect on nursing infants is unknown but may be of concern

Nortriptyline (NT) is a tricyclic antidepressant and is the active metabolite of amitriptyline (Elavil). In one patient receiving 125 mg of nortriptyline at bedtime, milk concentrations of NT averaged 180 µg/L after 6-7 days of administration.[1] Based on these concentrations, the authors estimate the average daily infant exposure would be 27 µg/kg/d. The relative dose in milk would be 1.5% of the maternal dose. Several other authors have been unable to detect NT in maternal milk nor the serum of infants after prolonged exposure.[2,3] So far no untoward effects have been noted.

A pooled analysis of 35 studies with an average dose of 78 mg/day reported a detectable level of nortriptyline in breast milk in only one patient, with a concentration of 230 ng/mL. The authors suggest that breastfeeding infants exposed to nortriptyline are unlikely to develop detectable concentrations in plasma, and therefore breastfeeding during nortriptyline therapy is not contraindicated.[4]

Pregnancy Risk Category: D

Lactation Risk Category: L2

Adult Concerns: Sedation, dry mouth, constipation, urinary retention, blurred vision.

Pediatric Concerns: None reported in several studies.

Drug Interactions: Phenobarbital may reduce effect of nortriptyline. Nortriptyline blocks the hypotensive effect of guanethidine. May increase toxicity of nortriptyline when used with clonidine. Dangerous when used with MAO inhibitors, other CNS depressants. May increase anticoagulant effect of coumadin, warfarin. SSRIs (Prozac, Zoloft,etc) should not be used with or soon after nortriptyline or other TCAs due to serotonergic crisis.

Relative Infant Dose: 1.7% - 3.1%

Adult Dose: 25 mg TID-QID

Alternatives: Imipramine

T ½	= 16-90 hours	M/P	= 0.87-3.71
PHL	=	PB	= 92%
Tmax	= 7-8.5 hours	Oral	= 51%
MW	= 263	pKa	= 9.7
Vd	= 20-57		

References:
1. Matheson I, Skjaeraasen J. Milk concentrations of flupenthixol, nortriptyline and zuclopenthixol and between-breast differences in two patients. Eur J Clin Pharmacol 1988; 35 (2):217-220.
2. Wisner KL, Perel JM. Serum nortriptyline levels in nursing mothers and their infants. Am J Psychiatry 1991; 148 (9):1234-1236.
3. Brixen-Rasmussen L, Halgrener J, Jorgensen A. Amitriptyline and nortriptyline excretion in human breast milk. Psychopharmacology (Berl) 1982; 76 (1):94-95.
4. Weissman AM, Levy BT, Hartz AJ, et.al. Pooled Analysis of Antidepressant Levels in Lactating Mothers, Breast Milk, and Nursing Infants. Am J Psychiatry 2004 June; 161 (6):1066-1078.

NYSTATIN   L1

Trade: Mycostatin, Nilstat
Other Trades: Mycostatin, Nadostine, Nilstat, Candistatin, Nystan
Uses: Antifungal
AAP: Not reviewed

Nystatin is an antifungal primarily used for candidiasis topically and orally. The oral absorption of nystatin is extremely poor, and plasma levels are undetectable after oral administration.[1] The likelihood of secretion into milk is remote due to poor maternal absorption. It is frequently administered directly to neonates in neonatal units for candidiasis. In addition, absorption into infant circulation equally unlikely. Dose: neonates= 100,000 units; children=200,000 units, 400,000-600,000 units in older children, administered four times daily. Current studies suggest that resistance to nystatin is growing.

Pregnancy Risk Category: B

Lactation Risk Category: L1

Adult Concerns: Bad taste, diarrhea, nausea, vomiting.

Pediatric Concerns: None reported. Nystatin is commonly used in infants.

Drug Interactions:

Relative Infant Dose:

Adult Dose: 500,000-1 million units TID

Alternatives: Fluconazole

T ½	=		M/P	=
PHL	=		PB	=
Tmax	=		Oral	= Poor
MW	=		pKa	=
Vd	=			

References:
1. Rothermel P, Faber M. Drugs in breast milk: a consumer's guide. Birth and Family J 1975; 2:76-78.

OCTREOTIDE ACETATE AND ^{111}INDIUM OCTREOTIDE   L3

Trade: Sandostatin LAR, OctreoScan, ^{111}Indium Octreotide, Octreotide Acetate

Other Trades:

Uses: Somatostatin analog

AAP: Not reviewed

Octreotide (Sandostatin LAR) is a long acting form consisting of microspheres containing octreotide. Octreotide is a close analog of and provides activity similar to the natural hormone somatostatin. Like somatostatin, it also suppresses LH response to GnRH, decreases splanchnic blood flow, and inhibits release of serotonin, gastrin, vasoactive intestinal peptide, secretin, motilin, and pancreatic polypeptide. It is used to treat acromegaly and carcinoid tumors. This product, if present in milk, would not likely be absorbed to any degree. Radioactivity leaves the plasma rapidly; one third of the radioactive injected dose remains in the blood pool at 10 minutes after administration. Plasma levels continue to decline so that by 20 hours post-injection, about 1% of the radioactive dose is found in the blood pool. The "biological" half-life of indium ^{111}In pentetreotide is only 6 hours while the radioactive half-life is 2.8 days. Half of the injected dose is recoverable in urine within six hours after injection,

85% is recovered in the first 24 hours, and over 90% is recovered in urine by two days. Hepatobiliary excretion represents a minor route of elimination, and less than 2% of the injected dose is recovered in feces within three days after injection. The return to breastfeeding is largely dependent on the dose, but 3 days would largely eliminate any risks at the lower dose, but this is largely dependent on the dose.

Radioactive [111]Indium Octreotide (OctreoScan): OctreoScan is an imaging agent that can help find primary and metastatic neuroendocrine tumors. The concentration of radioactive octreotide in breastmilk in a 10 weeks postpartum woman was measured at daily intervals for three days after injection of 5.3 mCi (196 MBq) of [111]Indium-octreotide (OctreoScan).[1] The disappearance of radiolabeled octreotide from the breastmilk exhibited a bi-exponential pattern with a maximum concentration of 14.2 nCi (0.54 kBq) per 125 mL feeding at 4 hours. The maximum reading was 8.3 mrem x h (-1) (0.83 mSv x h (-1)) immediately after administration. This decreased rapidly (85%) due to rapid urinary clearance by 24 h.

Breastmilk content of radio-active octreotide and external surveys at the breast surface were determined at 3 h intervals for up to 10 days. Assuming an infant is breastfed for the first 10 days following therapy, the internal and external dose equivalents would be 22.97 mrem (0.23 mSv) and 27.86 mrem (0.28 mSv) respectively, for a total of 50.83 mrem (0.5 mSv). In this paper, the patient resumed breastfeeding on day 10, when the newborn received a total dose equivalent of 1.55 mrem (0.016 mSv). The 10 day waiting period used in this study was based on very conservative assumptions and assumed 100% of the ingested ^{111}In is orally bioavailable. However, oral indium has been shown to be poorly absorbed from the gastrointestinal tract (approximately 0.15%), which suggests the infant's dose could be considerably less. The authors suggest that a briefer interruption deserves attention although they provide no numbers.

Pregnancy Risk Category: B

Lactation Risk Category: L3 for nonradioactive octreotide
L4 for radioactive product

Adult Concerns: May inhibit gallbladder contractility and decrease bile secretion. Hypoglycemia or hyperglycemia, hypothyroidism may result. Bradycardia, arrhythmias in acromegalic patients. Numerous other adverse effects, consult package insert.

Pediatric Concerns: None reported via milk.

Drug Interactions: May reduce absorption of cyclosporin and other drugs by altering oral absorption. Patients receiving insulin, oral hypoglycemic agents, beta blockers, and other drugs may require dosage adjustment of these therapeutic agents.

Relative Infant Dose:

Adult Dose: Non-radioactive: 50 mg TID (non-depo form) - Radioactive: 3-6 mCi (111-222 MBq)

Alternatives:

T ½	= 1.7 hours	M/P	=
PHL	=	PB	= 65%
Tmax	= 0.4 hours	Oral	= 0.15
MW	= 1019	pKa	=
Vd	= 13.6		

References:
1. Castronovo FP, Jr., Stone H, Ulanski J. Radioactivity in breast milk following 111In-octreotide. Nucl Med Commun 2000; 21 (7):695-699.

OFLOXACIN   L2

Trade: Floxin
Other Trades: Floxin, Ocuflox, Tarivid
Uses: Fluoroquinolone antibiotic
AAP: Maternal Medication Usually Compatible with Breastfeeding

Ofloxacin is a typical fluoroquinolone antimicrobial. Breastmilk concentrations are reported equal to maternal plasma levels. In one study in lactating women who received 400 mg oral doses twice daily, drug concentrations in breastmilk averaged 0.05-2.41 mg/L in milk (24 hours and 2 hours post-dose respectively).[1] The drug was still detectable in milk 24 hours after a dose. The fluoroquinolones are becoming more popular in pediatrics due to recent studies and reviews showing their safe use.[2] It is very unlikely that arthropathy would ensue following the dose received via milk. The only probably risk is a change in gut flora, diarrhea, and a remote risk of overgrowth of C. Difficile. Ofloxacin levels in breastmilk are consistently lower (37%) than ciprofloxacin. If a fluoroquinolone is required, ofloxacin, levofloxacin, or norfloxacin are probably the better choices for breastfeeding mothers.

Pregnancy Risk Category: C

Lactation Risk Category: L2

Adult Concerns: Nausea, vomiting, diarrhea, abdominal cramps, GI bleeding.

Pediatric Concerns: None reported, but caution recommended. Observe for diarrhea.

Drug Interactions: Decreased absorption with antacids. Quinolones cause increased levels of caffeine, warfarin, cyclosporine, theophylline. Cimetidine, probenecid, azlocillin may increase ofloxacin levels. Increased risk of seizures when used with foscarnet.

Relative Infant Dose: 3.1%

Adult Dose: 200-400 mg BID

Alternatives: Norfloxacin, Trovafloxacin

T ½	= 5-7 hours	M/P	= 0.98-1.66
PHL	=	PB	= 32%
Tmax	= 0.5-2 hours	Oral	= 98 %
MW	= 361	pKa	=
Vd	= 1.4		

References:

1. Giamarellou H, Kolokythas E, Petrikkos G, Gazis J, Aravantinos D, Sfikakis P. Pharmacokinetics of three newer quinolones in pregnant and lactating women. Am J Med 1989; 87 (5A):49S-51S.
2. Ghaffar F, McCracken GH. Quinolones in Pediatrics. In: Hooper DC, Rubinstein E, editors. Quinolone Antimicrobial Agents. Washington, D.C.: ASM Press, 2003: 343-354.

OLANZAPINE   L2

Trade: Zyprexa, Symbyax
Other Trades: Zyprexa
Uses: Antipsychotic
AAP: Not reviewed

Olanzapine is a typical antipsychotic agent structurally similar to clozapine and may be used for treating schizophrenia.[1] It is rather unusual in that it blocks serotonin receptors rather than dopamine receptors.

In a recent and excellent study of seven mother-infant nursing pairs receiving a median dose of olanzapine of 7.5 mg/day (range = 5-20 mg/day), the median infant dose ingested via milk was approximately 1.02% of the maternal dose.[2] The median milk/plasma AUC ratio was 0.38. Olanzapine was undetected in the plasma of six infants tested. All infants were healthy and experienced no observable side effects. The maximum relative infant dose was approximately 1.2%.

In a case report of a mother taking 20 mg/day, the milk/plasma ratio was 0.35, giving a relative infant dose of about 4% at steady state. This milk was not fed to the infant, so infant plasma levels were not performed.[3]

A study of 5 mothers receiving olanzapine at a dose of 2.5-20 mg/day reported milk/plasma ratios of 0.2 to 0.84, with an average relative infant dose of 1.6%. The authors reported no untoward effects on the infants attributable to olanzapine.[4]

The new product Symbyax contains both fluoxetine and olanzapine for treatment of Bipolar Depression.

Pregnancy Risk Category: C

Lactation Risk Category: L2

Adult Concerns: Agitation, dizziness, somnolence, constipation, weight gain, elevated liver enzymes.

Pediatric Concerns: None reported in one excellent study. Probably safe.

Drug Interactions: Ethanol may potentiate the effects of olanzapine. Fluvoxamine may inhibit olanzapine metabolism. Carbamazepine may increase clearance of olanzapine by 50%. Levodopa may antagonize the effect of olanzapine.

Relative Infant Dose: 1.2%

Adult Dose: 5-10 mg daily.

Alternatives: Risperidone, Haloperidol, Quetiapine

T ½	= 21-54 hours	M/P	= 0.38
PHL	=	PB	= 93%
Tmax	= 5-8 hours	Oral	= >57%
MW	= 312	pKa	= 5.0, 7.4
Vd	= 14.3		

References:
1.   Pharmaceutical Manufacturer Prescribing Information. 1997.
2.   Gardiner SJ, Kristensen JH, Begg EJ, Hackett LP,Wilson DA,Ilett KF, Kohan R and Rampono J, Transfer of olanzapine into breast milk, calculation of infant drug dose, and effect on breast-fed infants. Am J Psychiatry 2003; 160:1428-1431.
3.   Ambresin G, Berney P, Schulz P, Bryois C. Olanzapine Excretion Into Breast Milk: A Case Report. J Clin Psychopharmacol 2004; 24 (1):93-95.
4.   Croke S, Buist A, Hackett LP, Ilett KF, Norman TR, Burrows GD. Olanzapine exretion in human breast milk: estimation of infant exposure. Int J Neuropsychoph 2002; 5:243-247.

OLMESARTAN MEDOXOMIL | L3

Trade: Benicar, Benicar HCT
Other Trades:
Uses: Antihypertensive
AAP: Not reviewed

Olmesartan (Benicar) and Olmesartan plus Hydrochlorothiazide (Benicar HCT) are antihypertensives. Olmesartan is an angiotensin II receptor antagonist and hydrochlorothiazide is a diuretic. Olmesartan medoxomil is a prodrug and is rapidly metabolized in the GI tract to the active Olmesartan antihypertensive. It affectively blocks the angiotensin II receptor site. While it is different from the ACE inhibitors, it effectively produces the same end result, hypotension. Use in pregnancy is contraindicated. No data are available on its transfer to human milk, but its use in newborn infants could be risky.

Pregnancy Risk Category: C in first trimester
                                                        D in second and third trimesters

Lactation Risk Category: L3 in older infants

Adult Concerns: Adverse effects include dizziness and low blood pressure.

Pediatric Concerns: None via milk. No data are available.

Drug Interactions: No major drug-drug interaction are noted with exception of its use with adrenergics.

Relative Infant Dose:

Adult Dose: 20-40 mg daily.

Alternatives: Captopril, enalapril

T ½	= 13 hours	M/P	=
PHL	=	PB	=
Tmax	= 1-2 hours	Oral	= 26%
MW	= 558	pKa	=
Vd	= 0.24		

References:
1.   Pharmaceutical Manufacturers prescribing information, 2003.

OLOPATADINE OPHTHALMIC | L2

Trade: Patanol
Other Trades: Opatanol
Uses: Ophthalmic antihistamine
AAP: Not reviewed

Olopatadine is a selective H1-receptor antagonist and inhibitor of histamine release from mast cells. It is used topically in the eye. Kinetic studies by the manufacturer suggest that absorption is low in adults and that plasma levels are undetectable in most cases (<0.5 ng/mL).[1] Samples in which olopatadine was found in the plasma compartment were at 2 hours and were <1.3 ng/mL. Because adult plasma levels are so low, it is extremely unlikely any would be detectable in human milk. No data are available reporting levels in human milk but the risk is probably quite low.

Pregnancy Risk Category: C

Lactation Risk Category: L2

Adult Concerns: Headache have been reported in 7% of patients. Asthenia, blurred vision, burning, dry eye, redness, lid edema, pruritus and rhinitis have been reported.

Pediatric Concerns: None reported via milk.

Drug Interactions:

Relative Infant Dose:

Adult Dose: One drop in affected eye twice daily.

Alternatives:

T ½	= 3 hours	M/P	=
PHL	=	PB	=
Tmax	= 2 hours	Oral	=
MW	= 373	pKa	=
Vd	=		

References:
1. Pharmaceutical Manufacturers Prescribing Information, 2003.

OLSALAZINE   L3

Trade: Dipentum
Other Trades: Dipentum
Uses: Antiinflammatory
AAP: Not reviewed

Olsalazine is converted to 5-aminosalicylic acid (mesalamine:5-ASA) in the gut which has antiinflammatory activity in ulcerative colitis.[1] After oral administration, only 2.4% is systemically absorbed while the majority is metabolized in the GI tract to 5-ASA. 5-ASA is slowly and poorly absorbed. Plasma levels are exceedingly small (1.6-6.2 mmol/L), the half-life very short, and protein binding is very high. In rodents fed up to 20 times the normal dose, olsalazine produced growth retardation in pups. In one study of a mother who received a single 500 mg dose of olsalazine, acetylated-5-ASA achieved concentrations of 0.6, 0.86, and 1.24 μmol/L in breastmilk at 10, 14, and 24 hours respectively.[2] Olsalazine, olsalazine-S, and 5-ASA were undetectable in breastmilk. While clinically significant levels in milk are remote, infants should be closely monitored for gastric changes such as diarrhea.

Pregnancy Risk Category: C

Lactation Risk Category: L3

Adult Concerns: Watery diarrhea, dyspepsia, diarrhea, nausea, pain/cramping, headache

Pediatric Concerns: None specifically reported with this product, but observe for diarrhea and cramping if used for longer periods.

Drug Interactions:

Relative Infant Dose:

Adult Dose: 500 mg BID

Alternatives:

T ½	= 0.9 hours	M/P	=
PHL	—	PB	= >99%
Tmax	= 1-2 hours	Oral	= 2.4% (olsalazine)
MW	= 346	pKa	=
Vd	=		

References:
1. Drug Facts and Comparisons 1995 ed. ed. St. Louis: 1995.

2. Miller LG, Hopkinson JM, Motil KJ, Corboy JE, Andersson S. Disposition of olsalazine and metabolites in breast milk. J Clin Pharmacol 1993; 33 (8):703-706.

OMALIZUMAB   L3

Trade: Xolair
Other Trades: Xolair
Uses: Monoclonal antibody
AAP: Not reviewed

Omalizumab (Xolair) is used to treat persistent allergic asthma that cannot be controlled using inhaled corticosteroids. It works by inhibiting IgE binding to the receptor on mast cells and basophils, in turn decreasing the release of mediators in the allergic response.[1]

The manufacturer suggests that omalizumab may be secreted into human breastmilk based on monkey studies where milk levels were only 1.5% of maternal blood levels, which would be exceedingly low. However, no studies have been performed in humans. This product would not be orally bioavailable in an infant.

Pregnancy Risk Category: B

Lactation Risk Category: L3

Adult Concerns: Adverse reactions include headache, injection site reaction, upper respiratory tract infection, and viral infection.

Pediatric Concerns: No data are available.

Drug Interactions: No drug interactions have been noted.

Relative Infant Dose:

Adult Dose: 150-300 mg every 2-4 weeks

Alternatives:

T ½	= 26 days	M/P	=
PHL	=	PB	=
Tmax	= 7-8 days	Oral	= 62%
MW	= 149,000	pKa	=
Vd	=		

References:
1. Pharmaceutical Manufacturer Prescribing Information. 2007.

OMEPRAZOLE   L2

Trade: Prilosec
Other Trades: Prilosec, Losec
Uses: Reduces gastric acid secretion
AAP: Not reviewed

Omeprazole is a potent inhibitor of gastric acid secretion. In a study of one patient receiving 20 mg omeprazole daily, the maternal serum concentration was negligible until 90 minutes after ingestion and then reached 950 nM at 240 min.[1] The breastmilk concentration of omeprazole began to rise minimally at 90 minutes after ingestion and peaked after 180 minutes at only 58 nM, or less than 7% of the highest serum level. This would indicate a maximum dose of 3 µg/kg/day in a breastfed infant. Omeprazole milk levels were essentially flat over 4 hours of observation. Omeprazole is extremely acid labile with a half-life of 10 minutes at pH values below 4.[2] Virtually all omeprazole ingested via milk would probably be destroyed in the stomach of the infant prior to absorption.

Pregnancy Risk Category: C

Lactation Risk Category: L2

Adult Concerns: Headache, diarrhea, elevated liver enzymes.

Pediatric Concerns: None reported via milk in one case.

Drug Interactions: Administration of Omeprazole and clarithromycin may result in increased plasma levels of omeprazole. Omeprazole produced a 130% increase in the half-life of diazepam, reduced the plasma clearance of phenytoin by 15%, and increased phenytoin half-life by 27%. May prolong the elimination of warfarin.

Relative Infant Dose: 1.1%

Adult Dose: 20 mg BID

Alternatives: Famotidine, Nizatidine

T ½	= 1 hr.	M/P	=
PHL	=	PB	= 95%
Tmax	= 0.5-3.5 hours	Oral	= 30-40%
MW	= 345	pKa	=
Vd	=		

References:
1. Marshall JK, Thompson AB, Armstrong D. Omeprazole for refractory gastroesophageal reflux disease during pregnancy and lactation. Can J Gastroenterol 1998; 12 (3):225-227.
2. Pilbrant A, Cederberg C. Development of an oral formulation of omeprazole. Scand J Gastroenterol Suppl 1985; 108:113-120.

ONDANSETRON | L2

Trade: Zofran
Other Trades: Zofran
Uses: Antiemetic
AAP: Not reviewed

Ondansetron is used clinically for reducing the nausea and vomiting associated with chemotherapy. It has occasionally been used during pregnancy without effect on the fetus.[1,2] It is available for oral and IV administration. Ondansetron is secreted in animal milk, but no data on humans is available. Four studies of ondansetron use in pediatric patients 4-18 years of age are available.

Pregnancy Risk Category: B

Lactation Risk Category: L2

Adult Concerns: Headache, drowsiness, malaise, clonic-tonic seizures, and constipation.

Pediatric Concerns: None reported via milk.

Drug Interactions: The clearance and half-life of ondansetron may be changed when used with barbiturates, carbamazepine, rifampin, phenytoin.

Relative Infant Dose:

Adult Dose: 8 mg BID

Alternatives:

T ½	= 3.6 hours	M/P	=
PHL	= 2.7 hours	PB	= 70-76%
Tmax	= 1.73.1 (IV,PO)	Oral	= 56-66%
MW	= 293	pKa	=
Vd	=		

References:
1. Pharmaceutical Manufacturer Prescribing Information. 1996.

2. Spratto GR. In: Nurse's Drug Reference. Albany, NY: Delmar Publishers Inc., 1995.

ORAL CONTRACEPTIVES   L3

Trade: Norinyl, Norlestrin, Ovral, Ortho-Novum
Other Trades: Nornyl, Cilest, Brevinor
Uses: Contraceptive
AAP: Maternal Medication Usually Compatible with Breastfeeding

Oral contraceptives, particularly those containing estrogens, tend to the volume of milk produced.[1] Quality (fat content) may similarly be reduced, although one recent study of the fat, energy, protein, and lactose concentration in milk of mothers using oral contraceptives showed no effect of contraceptives.[4] The earlier oral contraceptives are started, the greater the negative effect on lactation.[2,3] Suppression of breastmilk production with estrogen-progestin contraceptives is well known, is more prevalent early postpartum, and is common. Although it was previously believed that waiting for 6 weeks would preclude breastfeeding problems, this is apparently not accurate. Numerous examples of supply problems have occurred months postpartum in some patients.

Breastfeeding women should be strongly advised to avoid using combination (estrogen-containing) oral contraceptives while breastfeeding because combination oral contraceptives have been shown to interfere with the production of milk and will reduce the duration of breastfeeding.[4-9]

Clinicians should suggest that the mother establish a good flow (60-90 days) prior to beginning oral contraceptives. Avoid combination (estrogen-progestin) contraceptives it at all possible. Use oral progestin-only preparations initially preferably after 6 weeks postpartum. Warn mothers that even progestin-only preparations may rarely suppress milk production and to discontinue them at the first sign of low milk supply.

Use Depo-Provera (medroxyprogesterone) only in those patients who have used it previously and have not experienced breastmilk supply problems, or in those who have used progestin-only mini pills without problems. Attempt to wait for 6 weeks postpartum prior to using Depo-Provera. The transfer of progestins and estrogens into breast milk is exceedingly low, and numerous studies confirm that they have minimal or no effect on sexual development in infants.

Pregnancy Risk Category: X

Lactation Risk Category: L3

Adult Concerns: Reduced milk production, particularly with estrogen containing preparations, but also rarely with progestin only products.

Pediatric Concerns: None reported via milk. May suppress lactation, reducing weight gain of infant.

Drug Interactions: Barbiturates, hydantoins, and rifampin, may increase the clearance of oral contraceptives resulting in decreased effectiveness of the oral contraceptives. Co-administration of griseofulvin, penicillin, or tetracyclines with oral contraceptives may decrease the efficacy of oral contraceptives possibly due to altered gut metabolism. May increase or decrease anticoagulant efficacy. Co-administration with cyclosporine, or carbamazepine may result in decreased oral contraceptive efficacy.

Relative Infant Dose:

Adult Dose:

Alternatives: Norethindrone

References:
1. Booker DE, Pahl IR. Control of postpartum breast engorgement with oral contraceptives. Am J Obstet Gynecol 1967; 98 (8):1099-1101.
2. Laukaran VH. The effects of contraceptive use on the initiation and duration of lactation. Int J Gynaecol Obstet 1987; 25 Suppl:129-142.
3. Kora SJ. Effect of oral contraceptives on lactation. Fertil Steril 1969; 20 (3):419-423.
4. Costa TH, Dorea JG. Concentration of fat, protein, lactose and energy in milk of mothers using hormonal contraceptives. Ann Trop Paediatr 1992; 12 (2):203-209.
5. McCann MF, Potter LS. Progestin-only oral contraception: a comprehensive review. Contraception. 1994 Dec;50 (6 Suppl 1):S1-195. Review.
6. Peralta O, Díaz S, Juez G, Herreros C, Casado ME, Salvatierra AM, Miranda P, Durán E, Croxatto HB. Fertility regulation in nursing women: V. Long-term influence of a low-dose combined oral contraceptive initiated at day 90 postpartum upon lactation and infant growth. Contraception. 1983 Jan;27 (1):27-38.
7. Croxatto HB, Díaz S, Peralta O, Juez G, Herreros C, Casado ME, Salvatierra AM, Miranda P, Durán E. Fertility regulation in nursing women: IV. Long-term influence of a low-dose combined oral contraceptive initiated at day 30 postpartum upon lactation and infant growth. Contraception. 1983 Jan;27 (1):13-25.
8. Díaz S, Peralta O, Juez G, Herreros C, Casado ME, Salvatierra AM, Miranda P, Durán E, Croxatto HB. Fertility regulation in nursing women: III. Short-term influence of a low-dose combined oral contraceptive upon lactation and infant growth. Contraception. 1983 Jan;27 (1):1-11.
9. Effects of hormonal contraceptives on breast milk composition and infant growth. World Health Organization (WHO) Task Force on Oral Contraceptives. Stud Fam Plann. 1988 Nov-Dec;19 (6 Pt 1):361-9.

ORLISTAT
L3

Trade: Xenical, Alli
Other Trades: Xenical
Uses: Lipase inhibitor
AAP: Not reviewed

Orlistat, now available over the counter as well as prescription, is used in the management of obesity. It is a reversible inhibitor of gastric and pancreatic lipases, thus it inhibits absorption of dietary fats by 30%.[1] No studies have been performed on the transmission of orlistat into the breastmilk. With high protein binding, moderately high MW, and poor oral absorption, it is unlikely that orlistat would enter breastmilk in clinically relevant amounts, or affect a breastfeeding infant. However, due to orlistat's effect on the absorption of fat soluble vitamins and other fats, nutritional status of a breastfeeding mother should be closely monitored.

Pregnancy Risk Category: B

Lactation Risk Category: L3

Adult Concerns: Adverse effects include headache, oily spotting, abdominal pain, flatus with discharge, fecal urgency, fatty/oily stool, back pain, and upper respiratory infection.

Pediatric Concerns: Children aged 12-16 years experienced similar adverse effects as did the adult population.

Drug Interactions: Orlistat may decrease amiodarone and cyclosporine. Also, vitamin K absorption may be decreased leading to a change in warfarin effects. Absorption of fat soluble vitamins may be decreased with orlistat use, and thus patients should take a multivitamin containing vitamins A, D, E, and K once daily, at least 2 hours before or after orlistat.

Relative Infant Dose:

Adult Dose: 60-120 mg TID

Alternatives:

T ½	= 1-2 hours	M/P	–
PHL	=	PB	= >99%
Tmax	= 8 hours	Oral	= minimal
MW	= 495	pKa	=
Vd	=		

References:
1. Pharmaceutical Manufacturer Prescribing Information. 2007.

ORPHENADRINE CITRATE   L3

Trade: Norflex, Banflex, Norgesic, Flexon
Other Trades: Disipal, Norflex, Orfenace, Norgesic
Uses: Muscle relaxant
AAP: Not reviewed

Orphenadrine is an analog of Benadryl.[1] It is primarily used as a muscle relaxant although its primary effects are anticholinergic. No data is available on its secretion into breastmilk.

Pregnancy Risk Category: C

Lactation Risk Category: L3

Adult Concerns: Agitation, aplastic anemia, dizziness, tremor, dry mouth, nausea, constipation.

Pediatric Concerns: None reported due to limited studies.

Drug Interactions: Increased anticholinergic side effects may be noted when used with amantadine. Orphenadrine may reduce therapeutic efficacy of phenothiazine family.

Relative Infant Dose:

Adult Dose: 100 mg BID

Alternatives:

T ½	= 14 hours	M/P	=
PHL	=	PB	=
Tmax	= 2-4 hours	Oral	= 95%
MW	= 269	pKa	=
Vd	=		

References:
1. McEvoy GE. (ed):AFHS Drug Information. New York, NY: 2009.

OSELTAMIVIR PHOSPHATE   L2

Trade: Tamiflu
Other Trades: Tamiflu
Uses: Anti-viral for influenza A and B
AAP: Not reviewed

Oseltamivir (Tamiflu) is indicated for the treatment of uncomplicated acute illness due to influenza A and B infection in adults who have been symptomatic for no more than 2 days. Oseltamivir is an oral viral neuraminidase inhibitor, which blocks or prevents viral seeding or release from infected cells and prevents viral aggregation.

In a recent study of one patient who was receiving 75 mg twice daily, for 5 days, the active carboxylate metabolite reached stated-state levels after 3 days and was reported to be 37-39 ng/mL.[1] Based on this data, the authors estimated the relative infant dose to be 0.5% of the maternal weigh-adjusted dose. Thus, this dose is unlikely to produce clinical levels in a breastfed infant. It has recently been recommended for use in breastfeeding mothers by the CDC.

Pregnancy Risk Category: C

Lactation Risk Category: L2

Adult Concerns: Nausea and vomiting are most common. Diarrhea, bronchitis, abdominal pain are less common.

Pediatric Concerns: None reported via milk.

Drug Interactions: None yet reported.

Relative Infant Dose: 0.5%

Adult Dose: 75 mg twice daily for 5 days.

Alternatives:

T ½	= 6-10 hours	M/P	=
PHL	=	PB	= 42%
Tmax	=	Oral	= 75%
MW	− 312	pKa	=
Vd	= 0.37		

References:
1. Wentges-van HN, van EM, van der Laan JW. Oseltamivir and breastfeeding. Int J Infect Dis. 2008;.

OSMOTIC LAXATIVES   L1

Trade: Milk of Magnesia, Fleet Phospho-Soda, Citrate of
Magnesia, Epsom Salt

Other Trades: Acilac, Citromag, Fleet Phosph-Soda, Sorbilax,
Duphalac

Uses: Laxatives

AAP: Not reviewed

Osmotic or Saline laxatives comprise a large number of magnesium
and phosphate compounds, but all work similarly in that they
osmotically pull and retain water in the GI tract, thus functioning as
laxatives. Because they are poorly absorbed, they largely stay in the
GI tract and are eliminated without significant systemic absorption.[1,2]
The small amount of magnesium and phosphate salts absorbed are
rapidly cleared by the kidneys. Products considered osmotic laxatives
include: Milk of Magnesia, Epsom Salts, Citrate of Magnesia,
Fleets Phospho-soda, and other sodium phosphate compounds.

Because milk electrolytes and ion concentrations are tightly controlled
by the maternal alveolar cell, the secretion of higher than normal levels
into milk is rare and unlikely. It is not known for certainty if these
products enter milk in higher levels than are normally present, but it
is very unlikely.

Pregnancy Risk Category: C

Lactation Risk Category: L1

Adult Concerns: Diarrhea, nausea, vomiting, hypocalcemia,
hypermagnesemia.

Pediatric Concerns: None reported via milk.

Drug Interactions: May reduce absorption of anticoagulants such
as coumarin, and dicoumarol.

Relative Infant Dose:

Adult Dose:

Alternatives:

References:
1. Drug Facts and Comparisons 1997 ed. ed. St. Louis: 1997.
2. Pharmaceutical Manufacturer Prescribing Information. 1997.

OXAPROZIN   L3

Trade: Daypro
Other Trades: Daypro
Uses: Nonsteroidal analgesic
AAP: Not reviewed

Oxaprozin belongs to the NSAID family of analgesics and is reputed to have lesser GI side effects than certain others.[1] Although its long half-life could prove troublesome in breastfed infants, it is probably poorly transferred to human milk. No data on transfer into human milk are available although it is known to transfer into animal milk.

Pregnancy Risk Category: C

Lactation Risk Category: L3

Adult Concerns: Headache, nausea, abdominal pain, gastric bleeding, diarrhea, vomiting, bleeding, constipation.

Pediatric Concerns: None reported, but ibuprofen preferred in absence of data.

Drug Interactions: May prolong prothrombin time when used with warfarin. Antihypertensive effects of ACEi family may be blunted or completely abolished by NSAIDs. Some NSAIDs may block antihypertensive effect of beta blockers, diuretics. Used with cyclosporin, may dramatically increase renal toxicity. May increase digoxin, phenytoin, lithium levels. May increase toxicity of methotrexate. May increase bioavailability of penicillamine. Probenecid may increase NSAID levels.

Relative Infant Dose:

Adult Dose: 600-1200 mg daily.

Alternatives: Ibuprofen, celecoxib

T ½	= 42-50 hours	M/P	=
PHL	=	PB	= 99%
Tmax	= 3-5 hours	Oral	= 95%
MW	= 293	pKa	–
Vd	=		

References:
1. Pharmaceutical Manufacturer Prescribing Information.

OXAZEPAM   L3

Trade: Serax
Other Trades: Apo-Oxazepam, Novoxapam, Serax, Zapex,
       Alepam, Murelax, Serepax, Oxanid
Uses: Benzodiazepine antianxiety drug
AAP: Not reviewed

Oxazepam is a typical benzodiazepine (See Valium) and is used in anxiety disorders. Of the benzodiazepines, oxazepam is the least lipid soluble, which accounts for its low levels in milk. In one study of a patient receiving 10 mg three times daily for 3 days, the concentration of oxazepam in breastmilk was relatively constant between 24 and 30 µg/L from the evening of the first day.[1] The milk/plasma ratio ranged from 0.1 to 0.33.

Pregnancy Risk Category: D

Lactation Risk Category: L3

Adult Concerns: Sedation.

Pediatric Concerns: None reported in one study.

Drug Interactions: May increase sedation when used with CNS depressants such as alcohol, barbiturates, opioids. Cimetidine may decrease metabolism and clearance of oxazepam. Cisapride can dramatically increase plasma levels of diazepam. SSRIs (fluoxetine, sertraline, paroxetine) can dramatically increase benzodiazepine levels by altering clearance, thus leading to sedation . Digoxin plasma levels may be increased.

Relative Infant Dose: 1%

Adult Dose: 10-30 mg TID-QID

Alternatives:

T ½	= 12 hours	M/P	= 0.1-0.33
PHL	= 22 hours	PB	= 97%
Tmax	= 1-2 hours	Oral	= 97%
MW	= 287	pKa	= 1.7,11.6
Vd	= 0.7-1.6		

References:
1. Wretlind M. Excretion of oxazepam in breast milk. Eur J Clin Pharmacol 1987; 33 (2):209-210.

OXCARBAZEPINE   L3

Trade: Trileptal
Other Trades: Trileptal
Uses: Anticonvulsant
AAP: Not reviewed

Oxcarbazepine is a derivative of carbamazepine and is used in the treatment of partial seizures in adults and as adjunctive therapy in the treatment of partial seizures in children. It is rapidly metabolized to a longer half-life active metabolite 10-hydroxy-carbazepine (MHD). In a brief and somewhat incomplete study of a pregnant patient who received 300 mg three times daily while pregnant, plasma levels were studied in her infant for the first 5 days postpartum while the infant was breastfeeding.[1] While no breastmilk levels were reported, plasma levels of MHD were essentially the same as the mothers immediately after delivery, suggesting complete transfer transplacentally of the drug. However, while breastfeeding for the next 5 days, plasma levels of MHD in the infant declined significantly from approximately 7 µg/mL to 0.2 µg/mL on the fifth day. The decay of MHD concentrations in neonatal plasma during the first 4 days postpartum indicated first order elimination. The plasma MHD levels on day 5 amounted to 7% of those one day postpartum (93% drop in 5 days). The authors estimated the milk/plasma ratio to be 0.5. No neonatal side effects were reported by the authors.

Pregnancy Risk Category: C

Lactation Risk Category: L3

Adult Concerns: Cognitive symptoms include psychomotor slowing, difficulty with concentration, speech or language problems, somnolence or fatigue, ataxia and gait disturbances. Hyponatremia has been reported.

Pediatric Concerns: None reported in one study.

Drug Interactions: Slight increases in other anticonvulsant plasma levels have been reported and include phenobarbital, phenytoin. A reduction in plasma levels of oxcarbazepine have been reported with admixed with phenobarbital, carbamazepine, phenytoin, etc. Major reductions in plasma levels of estrogens and other hormonal contraceptives has been reported and may render oral contraceptives less effective.

Relative Infant Dose:

Adult Dose: 300-600 mg BID

Alternatives: Carbamazepine

T ½	= 9 hours MHD	M/P	= 0.5
PHL	=	PB	= 40%
Tmax	= 4.5 hours	Oral	= Complete
MW	= 252	pKa	=
Vd	= 0.7		

References:
1. Bulau P, Paar WD, von Unruh GE. Pharmacokinetics of oxcarbazepine and 10-hydroxy-carbazepine in the newborn child of an oxcarbazepine-treated mother. Eur J Clin Pharmacol 1988; 34 (3):311-313.

OXYBUTYNIN   L3

Trade: Ditropan
Other Trades: Ditropan, Apo-Oxybutynin, Oxybutyn
Uses: Anticholinergic, antispasmodic
AAP: Not reviewed

Oxybutynin is an anticholinergic agent used to provide antispasmodic effects for conditions characterized by involuntary bladder spasms and reduces urinary urgency and frequency. It has been used in children down to 5 years of age at doses of 15 mg daily.[1] No data on transfer of this product into human milk is available. But oxybutynin is a tertiary amine which is poorly absorbed orally (only 6%). Further, the maximum plasma levels (C_{max}) generally attained are less than 31.7 nanogram/mL.[2] If one were to assume a theoretical M/P ratio of 1.0 (which is probably unreasonably high) and a daily ingestion of 1 Liter of milk, then the theoretical dose to the infant would be <2 micrograms/day, a dose that would be clinically irrelevant to even a neonate.

Pregnancy Risk Category: B

Lactation Risk Category: L3

Adult Concerns: Nausea, dry mouth, constipation, esophagitis, urinary hesitancy, flushing and urticaria. Palpitations, somnolence, hallucinations infrequently occur.

Pediatric Concerns: Suppression of lactation has been reported by the manufacturer.

Drug Interactions: May potentiate the anticholinergic effect of biperiden and other anticholinergics such as the tricyclic antidepressants. May counteract the effects of cisapride and metoclopramide.

Relative Infant Dose:

Adult Dose: 5 mg BID-QID

Alternatives:

T ½	= 1-2 hours	M/P	=
PHL	=	PB	=
Tmax	= 3-6 hours	Oral	= 6%
MW	= 393	pKa	= 6.96
Vd	=		

References:
1. Pharmaceutical Manufacturer Prescribing Information. 1997.
2. Douchamps J, Derenne F, Stockis A, Gangji D, Juvent M, Herchuelz A. The pharmacokinetics of oxybutynin in man. Eur J Clin Pharmacol 1988; 35 (5):515-520.

OXYCODONE   L3

Trade: Tylox, Percodan, OxyContin, Roxicet, Endocet, Roxiprin, Percocet

Other Trades: Supeudol, Endone, Proladone

Uses: Narcotic analgesic

AAP: Not reviewed

Oxycodone is similar to hydrocodone and is a mild analgesic somewhat stronger than codeine. Small amounts are secreted in breastmilk. Following a dose of 5-10 mg every 4-7 hours, maternal levels peaked at 1-2 hours, and analgesia persisted for up to 4 hours.[1] Reported milk levels range from <5 to 226 µg/L. Maternal plasma levels were 14-35 µg/L. The authors suggest a milk/plasma ratio of approximately 3.4. Although active metabolites were not measured, the authors suggest that an exclusively breastfed infant would receive a maximum 8% of the maternal dosage of oxycodone. No reports of untoward effects in infants have been found although sedation is a possibility in some infants.

In another study, 50 post-cesarean women received 30 mg oxycodone rectally, and 10 mg orally up to every 2 hours as needed. The average maternal plasma levels at 0-24 hours and 24-48 hours were 18 (range 0-42) ng/mL and 12 (range 0-40) ng/mL, respectively. Average milk concentrations in samples taken during 0-24 hours and 24-48 hours were 58 (range 7-130) ng/mL and 49 (range 0-168) ng/mL, respectively. Milk/Plasma ratios were therefore calculated to be 3.2-3.4. Only one infant had a detectable level of oxycodone in their plasma, with a concentration of 6.6-7.4 ng/mL.[2] These plasma and milk levels suggest that oxycodone concentrates in the milk compartment, however, the authors suggest that at doses less than 90 mg/day for up to 3 days, maternal use of oxycodone poses only a minimal threat to breastfeeding infants. This study did not measure plasma or milk concentrations at steady state or during peak plasma concentrations, therefore,levels may have been higher at times.

Endocet, Percocet, Roxicet and Roxiprin are all just formulations of oxycodone and acetaminophen.

Pregnancy Risk Category: B

Lactation Risk Category: L3

Adult Concerns: Drowsiness, sedation, nausea, vomiting, constipation.

Pediatric Concerns: None reported via milk but observe for sedation.

Drug Interactions: Cigarette smoking increases effect of codeines. Increased toxicity/sedation when used with CNS depressants, phenothiazines, tricyclic antidepressants, other opiates, guanabenz, MAO inhibitors, neuromuscular blockers.

Relative Infant Dose: 3.5%

Adult Dose: 5 mg every 6 hours

Alternatives: Codeine

T ½	= 3-6 hours	M/P	= 3.4
PHL	=	PB	=
Tmax	= 1-2 hours	Oral	= 50%
MW	= 315	pKa	= 8.5
Vd	= 1.8-3.7		

References:
1. Marx CM, Pucin F, Carlson JD. et.al. Oxycodone excretion in human milk in the puerperium. Drug Intel Clin 1986; 20:474.
2. Seaton S, Reeves M, McLean S. Oxycodone as a component of multimodal analgesia for lactating mothers after Caesarean section: Relationships between maternal plasma, breast milk and neonatal plasma levels. Aust NZ J Obstet Gyn 2007; 47:181-85.

OXYMORPHONE   L3

Trade: Numorphane, Opana
Other Trades:
Uses: Opiate analgesic
AAP: Not reviewed

Oxymorphone is a potent opioid analgesic used to treat moderate to severe pain. On a weight basis, it is 8-10 times more potent than morphine, and it may produce more nausea and vomiting, but less constipation than morphine. It differs from morphine in its effects in that it generates less euphoria, sedation, itching and other histamine effects and it has no antitussive properties. It is poorly absorbed orally. Milk levels are as yet unreported. However, some caution is recommended with the prolonged use of this opioid analgesic.

Pregnancy Risk Category: C

Lactation Risk Category: L3

Adult Concerns: Nausea, pyrexia, somnolence, vomiting, pruritus, headache and dizziness have been reported. Tachycardia, hypotension, vomiting, constipation, dry mouth, abdominal distention, flatulence, sweating, dizziness, somnolence, headache, anxiety, sedation have been reported.

Pediatric Concerns: None yet, but observed for apnea, constipation, and sedation.

Drug Interactions: Extensive. Avoid use with other opiates, barbiturates, codeine, hydrocodone, sedatives including benzodiazepines such as diazepan, alprazolam, etc.

Relative Infant Dose:

Adult Dose: 10-20 every 4-6 hours

Alternatives: Morphine, hydrocodone, oxycodone

T ½	= 7.8 hours (oral)	M/P	=
PHL	=	PB	= 12%
Tmax	= 1.9 hours	Oral	= 10%
MW	= 337	pKa	=
Vd	=		

References:
1. Pharmaceutical manufacturers prescribing information, 2010.

OXYTOCIN   L2

Trade: Pitocin
Other Trades: Toesen, Syntocinon, Syntometrine
Uses: Labor induction
AAP: Not reviewed

Oxytocin is an endogenous nonapeptide hormone produced by the posterior pituitary and has uterine and myoepithelial muscle cell stimulant properties, as well as vasopressive and antidiuretic effects. Prepared synthetically, it is bioavailable via IV and intranasal applications. It is destroyed orally by chymotrypsin in the stomach of adults and systemically by the liver. It is known to be secreted in small amounts into human milk. Takeda reported that mean oxytocin concentrations in human milk at postpartum day 1 to 5 were 4.5, 4.7, 4.0, 3.2, and 3.3 microunits/mL respectively.[1] The oral absorption in neonates is unknown but probably minimal.

Intranasal sprays (Syntocinon) contained 40 IU/mL with a recommended typical dose being one spray (3 drops) in each nostril to induce letdown. This is roughly equivalent to 2 IU per drop or a total dose of approximately 12 IU per letdown dose.

Oxytocin has been used to help mothers express milk for premature infants. The efficacy was tested in a randomized trial, where 27 mothers received intranasal oxytocin and 24 received placebo. There was no difference in total milk production between the two groups, indicating that oxytocin did not improve breast milk expression.[2] Thus this study suggests that oxytocin may not be effective in mothers 'who already have oxytocin mediated letdowns'. But it still may have some usefulness in mother who apparently do not have letdowns.

Although oxytocin is secreted in small amounts in breastmilk, no untoward effects have been noted. However, chronic use of intranasal oxytocin may lead to dependence and should be limited to the first week postpartum. See index for intranasal formulation.

Pregnancy Risk Category:

Lactation Risk Category: L2

Adult Concerns: Hypotension, hypertension, water intoxication and excessive uterine contractions, uterine hypertonicity, spasm, etc. May induce bradycardia, arrhythmias, intracranial hemorrhage, neonatal jaundice.

Pediatric Concerns: None via breast milk.

Drug Interactions: When used within 3-4 hours of cyclopropane, hypotension may result.

Relative Infant Dose:

Adult Dose: 40-80 units daily.

Alternatives:

T ½	= 3-5 minutes	M/P	=
PHL	=	PB	=
Tmax	=	Oral	= Minimal
MW	= >1000	pKa	=
Vd	=		

References:
1. Takeda S, Kuwabara Y, Mizuno M. Concentrations and origin of oxytocin in breast milk. Endocrinol Jpn 1986; 33 (6):821-826.
2. Fewtrell MS, Loh KL, Blake A, Ridout DA, Hawdon J. Randomised, double blind trial of oxytocin nasal spray in mothers expressing breast milk for preterm infants. Arch Dis Child Fetal Neonatal Ed 2006; 91 (3):F169-174.

PACLITAXEL | L5

Trade: Taxol
Other Trades: Paxene, Taxol, Anzatax
Uses: Antineoplastic agent
AAP: Not reviewed

Paclitaxel is a diterpene plant product with antineoplastic activity that is derived from the bark of the western yew tree. It is an antimicrotubule agent that promotes assembly of dimeric tubulin, which is stable to depolymerization.[1] It is a large MW, highly lipophilic agent with only minimal kinetic data available. It is not known if paclitaxel enters milk, but due to the extraordinary toxicity and lipophilicity of this compound, it would be inadvisable to breastfeed while under therapy with this drug.

Pregnancy Risk Category: D

Lactation Risk Category: L5

Adult Concerns: Anaphylaxis and severe hypersensitivity reactions including fatal dyspnea and hypotension, and angioedema have been reported. Neutropenia, leukopenia, abnormal ECG, myalgia, arthralgia, nausea, vomiting, and diarrhea.

Pediatric Concerns: None reported via milk, but extreme caution is recommended.

Drug Interactions: Increased myelosuppression when admixed with cisplatin. Increased levels of doxorubicin when admixed with paclitaxel.

Relative Infant Dose:

Adult Dose: 135-175 mg/m (2) every 3 weeks

Alternatives:

T ½	= 13-52 hours	M/P	=
PHL	=	PB	= 89-98%
Tmax	=	Oral	=
MW	= 853	pKa	=
Vd	= 688 L/sq meter		

References:
1.   Pharmaceutical Manufacturer Prescribing Information. 1999.

PALONOSETRON HCL   L3

Trade: Aloxi
Other Trades:
Uses: Antiemetic
AAP: Not reviewed

Palonosetron is a selective 5HT3 receptor antagonist, blocking serotonin binding and reducing the vomiting reflex. It is used to reduce chemotherapy induced nausea and vomiting.[1] It works similarly to ondansetron. No data are available on its transfer into human milk. Fortunately, this family of drugs is largely devoid of major side effects.

Pregnancy Risk Category: B

Lactation Risk Category: L3

Adult Concerns: Adverse reactions include headache, constipation, diarrhea, and dizziness.

Pediatric Concerns: No data are available.

Drug Interactions: Profound   hypotension   when   used   with apomorphine.

Relative Infant Dose:

Adult Dose: 0.25 mg 30 minutes befroe chemotherapy

Alternatives: Ondansetron

T ½	= 40 hours	M/P	=
PHL	=	PB	= 62%
Tmax	=	Oral	=
MW	= 333	pKa	=
Vd	= 8.3		

References:
1. Pharmaceutical Manufacturer Prescribing Information. 2004.

PAMIDRONATE   L2

Trade: Aredia

Other Trades:

Uses: Bisphosphonate bone-resorption inhibitor.

AAP: Not reviewed

Pamidronate is an inhibitor of bone-resorption. Although its mechanism of action is obscure, it possibly absorbs to the calcium phosphate crystal in bone and blocks dissolution (reabsorption) of this mineral component in bone, thus reducing turnover of bone calcium. A 39 year-old patient presented in the first month of pregnancy with reflex sympathetic dystrophy. Because she wished to continue breastfeeding, she was treated with monthly IV doses of pamidronate (30 mg). Following the first dose, breastmilk was assayed for pamidronate content. After infusion, breastmilk was pumped and collected into two portions: 0-24 h and 25-48 h. None was detected (limit of detection, 0.4 micromol/L). The authors suggested that pamidronate could be considered safe for use in lactating women. Pamidronate is poorly absorbed (0.3% to 3% of a dose) after oral administration and thus any present in milk would not likely be absorbed by the infant.

Pregnancy Risk Category: D

Lactation Risk Category: L2

Adult Concerns: Adverse effects include fever and malaise, anemia (6%), leukopenia, thrombocytopenia, hypertension, hypocalcemia, abdominal pain, anorexia, constipation, nausea and vomiting. Numerous other side effects, consult package insert.

Pediatric Concerns: None reported via milk.

Drug Interactions: None reported.

Relative Infant Dose:

Adult Dose: 60 to 90 milligrams as a single intravenous infusion.

Alternatives:

T ½	= 28 hours	M/P	=
PHL	=	PB	=
Tmax	=	Oral	= 0.3% to 3%
MW	= 369	pKa	=
Vd	=		

References:
1. Siminoski K, Fitzgerald AA, Flesch G, Gross MS. Intravenous pamidronate for treatment of reflex sympathetic dystrophy during breast feeding. J Bone Miner Res 2000; 15 (10):2052-2055.

PANTOPRAZOLE   L1

Trade: Protonix
Other Trades: Pantoloc
Uses: Suppresses gastric acid production
AAP: Not reviewed

Pantoprazole is a proton-pump inhibitor similar to omeprazole (Prilosec). It is used primarily to suppress acid production in the stomach for treatment of gastroesophageal reflux or peptic ulcer disease. The pharmaceutical manufacturer reports 0.02% of an administered dose is excreted into milk.[1] In a 61.6 Kg patient who received a single 40 mg tablet, pantoprazole levels in milk were undetectable except at 2 hours (0.036 mg/L and 4 hours (0.024 mg/L after administration.[2] The pantoprazole levels in milk were estimated to be only 2.8% of the maternal plasma levels (AUC) so the M/P ratio is extraordinarily low. Using the highest concentration achieved, the relative infant dose would only be 0.95%. The daily dose would be many times lower than this as the milk levels were undetectable at 5 hours.

As with all the proton-pump inhibitors, pantoprazole is completely unstable in an acid milieu and when presented in milk, it would be largely destroyed before absorption.

Pregnancy Risk Category: B

Lactation Risk Category: L1

Adult Concerns: Headache, diarrhea, flatulence, and rash.

Pediatric Concerns: None reported via milk.

Drug Interactions: None reported.

Relative Infant Dose: 0.9%

Adult Dose: 40-80 mg daily

Alternatives: Omeprazole

T ½	= 1.5 hour	M/P	= 0.028
PHL	=	PB	= 98%
Tmax	− 2.4 hours	Oral	= 77% Enteric coated
MW	= 383	pKa	=
Vd	= 0.32		

References:
1.   Pharmaceutical Manufacturer Prescribing Information. 2003.
2.   Plante L, Ferron GM, Unruh M, Mayer PR. Excretion of pantoprazole in human breast. J Reprod Med 2004 Oct; 49 (10):825-7.

PANTOTHENIC ACID

L1

Trade:

Other Trades:

Uses: Vitamin B-5

AAP: Not reviewed

Pantothenic acid, or vitamin B-5, is needed to form coenzyme-A, which is a carrier carbon within the cell. Pantothenic acid is often used in high doses in excess of 10 g/day for the treatment of acne.[1] The recommended daily allowance for pregnant women is 6 mg/day, while breastfeeding women need 7 mg/day. The recommended dose for infants less than 6 months is 1.7 mg/day, while infants over 6 months are to receive 2 mg/day. No adverse effects from oral administration of higher oral dosages of pantothenic acid were found.[3] Concentrations found in milk are between 2 and 2.5 mg/L, with a weak correlation between maternal intake and milk levels.[2] This would correspond to a daily dose of around 0.33-0.375 mg/kg/day for breastfeeding infants.

Pregnancy Risk Category: A
                                  C if dose exceeds RDA

Lactation Risk Category: L1

Adult Concerns: Diarrhea at large doses. Skin rash.

Pediatric Concerns: Possible skin rash, or GI symptoms including diarrhea if large doses are used by the mother.

Drug Interactions:

Relative Infant Dose:

Adult Dose:

Alternatives:

T ½	=	M/P	=
PHL	=	PB	=
Tmax	=	Oral	=
MW	= 219	pKa	=
Vd	=		

References:
1. Leung LH. Pantothenic acid deficiency as the pathogenesis of acne vulgaris. Med Hypotheses 1995 Jun; 44 (6):490-492.
2. Picciano MF. Handbook of milk composition. Jensen RG, ed. San Diego: Academic Press; 1995.
3. Dietary Reference Intakes for Thiamin, Riboflavin, Niacin, Vitamin B6, Folate, Vitamin B12, Pantothenic Acid, Biotin, and Choline. Food and Nutrition Board. Institude of Medicine. Washington DC: National Academy Press; 1998.

PAREGORIC   L3

Trade:

Other Trades:

Uses: Opiate analgesic used for diarrhea.

AAP: Not reviewed

Paregoric is camphorated tincture of opium, and contains approximately 2 mg morphine per 5cc (teaspoonful) in 45% alcohol.[1] It is frequently used for diarrhea and in the past for withdrawal symptoms in neonates (Tincture of Opium is now preferred). Because the active ingredient is morphine, see morphine for breastfeeding indications. Due to its camphor content, the pediatric use of paregoric is discouraged.

Pregnancy Risk Category: B

Lactation Risk Category: L3

Adult Concerns: Sedation, constipation, apnea, nausea, vomiting.

Pediatric Concerns: None reported. See morphine.

Drug Interactions: See morphine.

Relative Infant Dose:

Adult Dose: 5-10 mL (2-4 mg morphine) BID-QID

Alternatives:

T ½	= 1.5-2 hours	M/P	= 1.1-3.6
PHL	= 13.9 hours (neonatal)	PB	= 35%
Tmax	= 0.5-1 hours	Oral	= 26%
MW	=	pKa	=
Vd	=		

References:
1.   Drug Facts and Comparisons 1995 ed. ed. St. Louis: 1995.

PAROMOMYCIN | L3

Trade: Paromomycin
Other Trades: Humatin
Uses: Amebicide
AAP: Not reviewed

Paromomycin is used to treat acute and chronic intestinal amebiasis. It interferes with bacterial protein synthesis by binding to the 30S ribosomal subunits.[1] Paromomycin is not systemically absorbed after oral ingestion and therefore poses little risk to a breastfeeding infant.

Pregnancy Risk Category: C

Lactation Risk Category: L3

Adult Concerns: Adverse reactions include diarrhea, abdominal cramps, nausea, vomiting, and heartburn.

Pediatric Concerns: No data available.

Drug Interactions: Paromomycin decreases the effects of digoxin, vitamin A, and methotrexate. It increases the effects of anticoagulants, neuromuscular blockers, and polypeptide antibiotics.

Relative Infant Dose:

Adult Dose: 25-35 mg/kg/day in 3 divided doses for 5-10 days

Alternatives:

T ½	=	M/P	=
PHL	=	PB	=
Tmax	=	Oral	= None
MW	= 615	pKa	=
Vd	=		

References:
1. Pharmaceutical Manufacturer Prescribing Information. 2001.

PAROXETINE   L2

Trade: Paxil
Other Trades: Paxil, Aropax 20, Seroxat
Uses: Antidepressant, serotonin reuptake inhibitor
AAP: Drugs whose effect on nursing infants is unknown but may be of concern

Paroxetine is a typical serotonin reuptake inhibitor. Although it undergoes hepatic metabolism, the metabolites are not active. Paroxetine is exceedingly lipophilic and distributes throughout the body with only 1% remaining in plasma. In one case report of a mother receiving 20 mg/day paroxetine at steady state[1], the breastmilk level at peak (4 hours) was 7.6 µg/L. While the maternal paroxetine dose was 333 µg/kg, the maximum daily dose to the infant was estimated at 1.14 µg/kg or 0.34% of the maternal dose.

In two studies of 6 and 4 nursing mothers respectively[2], the mean dose of paroxetine received by the infants in the first study was 1.13% (range 0.5-1.7) of the weight adjusted maternal dose. The mean M/P (AUC) was 0.39 (range 0.32-0.51) while the predicted M/P was 0.22.

In the second study, the mean dose of paroxetine received by the infants was 1.25% (range 0.38-2.24%) of the weight adjusted maternal dose with a mean M/P of 0.96 (range 0.31-3.33). The drug was not detected in the plasma of 7 of the 8 infants studied and was detected (<4 mg/L) in only one infant. No adverse effects were observed in any of the infants.

In a recent study of 16 mothers by Stowe, paroxetine levels in milk were low and varied according to maternal dose.[3] Milk/plasma ratios varied from 0.056 to 1.3. Milk levels ranged from approximately 17 µg/L, 45 µg/L, 70 µg/L, 92 µg/L, and 101 µg/L in mothers receiving a dose of 10, 20, 30, 40, and 50 mg/day respectively. Levels of paroxetine were below the limit of detection (<2 ng/mL) in all 16 infants.

In a study of 6 women receiving 20-40 mg/day, the milk/plasma ratio ranged from 0.39 to 1.11 but averaged 0.69.[4] The average estimated dose to the infants ranged from 0.7 to 2.9% of the weight-adjusted maternal dose. In a seventh patient, and based on area-under-the-curve data, the milk/plasma ratio was 0.69 at a dose of 20 mg and 0.72 at a dose of 40 mg/day. The estimated dose to the infant was 1.0% and 2.0% of the weight-adjusted maternal dose at 20 and 40 mg respectively. Paroxetine levels in milk averaged 44.3 and 78.5 μg/L over 6 hours following 20 and 40 mg doses respectively. No adverse reactions or unusual behaviors were noted in any of the infants.

In another study of 24 breastfeeding mothers who received an average dose of 17.6 mg/d (range 10-40 mg/d) the average level of paroxetine in maternal serum and milk was 45.2 ng/mL and 19.2 ng/mL respectively.[5] The average milk/plasma ratio was 0.53. The authors estimated the average infant dose to be 2.88 μg/kg/d or 2.88% of the weight-adjusted maternal dose. All infant serum levels were below the limit of detection.

Yet another study of 16 mothers taking an average of 18.75 mg/day showed that paroxetine was undetectable in any of the breastfeeding infants exposed to paroxetine.[8]

A pooled analysis of 68 breastfeeding mothers taking between 10-50 mg/day reported breastmilk levels between 0-153 μg/mL, with an average of 28 μg/mL. No untoward effects were noted in any of these infants exposed to paroxetine through breastmilk. One infant did experience lethargy and poor weight gain, but this infant had prenatal exposure.[9] These studies generally conclude that paroxetine can be considered relatively 'safe' for breastfeeding infants as the absolute dose transferred is quite low. Plasma levels in the infant were generally undetectable. Recent data suggests that a neonatal withdrawal syndrome may occur in newborns exposed in utero to paroxetine[6,10] although there is significant difficulty in differentiating between withdrawal and toxicity.[7] Symptoms include jitteriness, vomiting, irritability, hypoglycemia, and necrotizing enterocolitis. Suicide ideation and withdrawal sympmtoms seem worse with this product and it should not be used in adolescent patients due to the risk of suicide. In addition, the Swedish birth registries have found that pregnant women who consumed Paroxetine were 1.5-2.0 times more likley to give birth to a baby with severe heart defects. Paroxetine is no longer recommended by some for use in pregnancy. While all of these complications may arise in pregnancy and in adolescents, paroxetine is still a suitable SSRI for breastfeeding women simply because the clinical dose consumed by the infant via breastmilk is exceedingly low. This said, it is still probably smart to use sertraline or another SSRI at this time.

Pregnancy Risk Category: D

Lactation Risk Category: L2

Adult Concerns: Sedation, headache, dry mouth, dizziness, nausea, insomnia, constipation, seizures. Use in children and adolescents suggests increased risk of suicide. New data may suggest an increased risk of congenital malformations if this product is used during the first trimester. Some caution is recommended.

Pediatric Concerns: Numerous studies suggest minimal to no effect on breastfed infants. A neonatal withdrawal effect (early postnatally) may following in utero exposure. Most studies show minimal to no plasma levels in breastfed infants. Severe heart defects have been reported in infants exposed in utero to paroxetine.

Drug Interactions: Decreased effect with phenobarbital and phenytoin. Increased toxicity with alcohol, cimetidine, MAO inhibitors (serotonergic syndrome). Increased effect with fluoxetine, tricyclic antidepressants, sertraline, phenothiazines, warfarin.

Relative Infant Dose: 1.2% - 2.8%

Adult Dose: 20-50 mg daily.

Alternatives: Sertraline

T ½	= 21 hours	M/P	= 0.056-1.3
PHL	=	PB	= 95%
Tmax	= 5-8 hours	Oral	= Complete
MW	= 329	pKa	=
Vd	= 3-28		

References:
1. Spigset O, Carleborg L, Norstrom A, Sandlund M. Paroxetine level in breast milk. J Clin Psychiatry 1996; 57 (1):39.
2. Begg EJ, Duffull SB, Saunders DA, Buttimore RC, Ilett KF, Hackett LP, Yapp P, Wilson DA. Paroxetine in human milk. Br J Clin Pharmacol 1999; 48 (2):142-147.
3. Stowe ZN, Cohen LS, Hostetter A, Ritchie JC, Owens MJ, Nemeroff CB. Paroxetine in human breast milk and nursing infants. Am J Psychiatry 2000; 157 (2):185-189.
4. Ohman R, Hagg S, Carleborg L, Spigset O. Excretion of paroxetine into breast milk. J Clin Psychiatry 1999; 60 (8):519-523.
5. Misri S, Kim J, Riggs KW, Kostaras X. Paroxetine levels in postpartum depressed women, breast milk, and infant serum. J Clin Psychiatry 2000; 61 (11):828-832.

6. Stiskal JA, Kulin N, Koren G, Ho T, Ito S. Neonatal paroxetine withdrawal syndrome. Arch Dis Child Fetal Neonatal Ed 2001; 84 (2):F134-F135.
7. Isbister GK, Dawson A, Whyte IM, Prior FH, Clancy C, Smith AJ. Neonatal paroxetine withdrawal syndrome or actually serotonin syndrome? Arch Dis Child Fetal Neonatal Ed 2001; 85 (2):F147-F148.
8. Hendrick V, Fukuchi A, Altshuler L, Widawski M, Wertheimer A, Brunhuber MV. Use of sertraline, paroxetine and fluvoxamine by nursing women. Br J Psychiatry 2001; 179:163-166.
9. Weissman AM, Levy BT, Hartz AJ, et.al. Pooled Analysis of Antidepressant Levels in Lactating Mothers, Breast Milk, and Nursing Infants. Am J Psychiatry 2004 June; 161 (6):1066-1078.
10. Nordeng H, Lindemann R, Perminov KV, Reikvam A. Neonatal withdrawl syndrome after in utero exposure to selective serotonin reuptake inhibitors. Acta Paediatr 2001; 90:288-91.

PEGAPTANIB SODIUM   L3

Trade: Macugen
Other Trades: Macugen
Uses: Angiogenesis inhibitor
AAP: Not reviewed

Pegaptanib is used in the treatment of neovascular age-related macular degeneration. Pegaptanib can bind to vascular endothelial growth factor inhibiting its binding with receptors and thus blocking neovascularization (inhibits intravitreal antivascular endothelial growth factor (VEGF)) and slows vision loss.[1] There have been no studies performed to measure the levels in human milk. It would be exceedingly unlikely this large polymer would ever enter the milk compartment, or be orally bioavailable.

Pregnancy Risk Category: B

Lactation Risk Category: L3

Adult Concerns: Adverse effects include hypertension, blurred vision, corneal edema,

Pediatric Concerns: No data are available.

Drug Interactions:

Relative Infant Dose:

Adult Dose: 0.3 mg every 6 weeks

Alternatives:

T ½	= 10 days	M/P	=
PHL	=	PB	=
Tmax	=	Oral	= Nil
MW	= 50,000	pKa	=
Vd	=		

References:
1. Pharmaceutical Manufacturer Prescribing Information. 2005.

PEGFILGRASTIM   L3

Trade: Neulasta
Other Trades:
Uses: Colony stimulating factor
AAP: Not reviewed

Pegfilgrastim, the pegylated form of filgrastim, acts on hematopoietic cells stimulating production and maturation of neutrophil precursors. It is used to enhance neutrophil recovery following chemotherapy as well as to decrease infection in patients receiving myelosuppressive anti-cancer drugs.[1] There are no reported levels in human milk. Due to large MW of this drug, milk levels and oral bioavailability are likely to be low. Lactation studies in rodents did not show any untoward effects on growth and development of breastfed rodents.

Pregnancy Risk Category: C

Lactation Risk Category: L3

Adult Concerns: Adverse reactions include bone pain, alopecia, diarrhea, pyrexia, myalgia and headache. Rare cases of splenic rupture have been reported.

Pediatric Concerns: No data are available. Due to its large MW, it is unlikely to enter milk in clinically relevant concentrations. No problems were noted in rodent lactation study.

Drug Interactions: Lithium may increase the expected levels of white blood cells.

Relative Infant Dose:

Adult Dose: 6 mg once per chemotherapy cycle

Alternatives:

T ½	= 15-80 hours	M/P	=
PHL	=	PB	=
Tmax	=	Oral	= Nil
MW	= 39,000	pKa	=
Vd	=		

References:
1. Pharmaceutical Manufacturer Prescribing Information. 2007.

PENCICLOVIR   L3

Trade: Denavir
Other Trades: Vectavir
Uses: Antiviral agent
AAP: Not reviewed

Penciclovir is an antiviral agent for the treatment of cold sores (herpes simplex labialis) of the lips and face and occasionally for herpes zoster (Shingles).[1] Following topical administration, plasma levels are undetectable.[2] Because oral bioavailability is nil and maternal plasma levels are undetectable following topical therapy, it is extremely unlikely that detectable amounts would transfer into human milk or be absorbable by an infant.

Pregnancy Risk Category: B

Lactation Risk Category: L3

Adult Concerns: Following topical application only mild erythema was occasionally observed.

Pediatric Concerns: None reported.

Drug Interactions: None reported.

Relative Infant Dose:

Adult Dose: Topical application every 2 hours

Alternatives:

T ½	= 2.3 hours	M/P	=
PHL	=	PB	= <20%
Tmax	=	Oral	= 1.5%
MW	=	pKa	=
Vd	=		

References:
1. Hodge RA, Perkins RM. Mode of action of 9- (4-hydroxy-3-hydroxymethylbut-1-yl)guanine (BRL 39123) against herpes simplex virus in MRC-5 cells. Antimicrob Agents Chemother 1989; 33 (2):223-229.
2. Pharmaceutical Manufacturer Prescribing Information.

PENICILLAMINE   L4

Trade: Cuprimine, Depen

Other Trades: Cuprimine, Depen, D-Penamine, Distamine, Pendramine

Uses: Used in arthritis, autoimmune syndromes

AAP: Not reviewed

Penicillamine is a potent chelating agent used to chelate copper, iron, mercury, lead, and other metals. It is also used to suppress the immune response in rheumatoid arthritis and other immunologic syndromes. It is extremely dangerous during pregnancy. Safety has not been established during lactation. Penicillamine is a potent drug that requires constant observation and care by attending physicians. Recommend discontinuing lactation if this drug is mandatory.[1]

Pregnancy Risk Category: D

Lactation Risk Category: L4

Adult Concerns: Anorexia, nausea, vomiting, diarrhea, alteration of taste, elevated liver enzymes, kidney damage.

Pediatric Concerns: None reported, but caution is recommended.

Drug Interactions: An increased risk of serious hematologic and renal reactions may occur if used with gold therapy, antimalarial, or other cytotoxic drugs. The absorption of penicillamine is decreased by 35% when used with iron salts. The absorption of penicillamine is decreased by 66% when used with antacids. Digoxin plasma levels may be reduced.

Relative Infant Dose:

Adult Dose: 250-500 mg QID

Alternatives:

T ½	= 1.7-3.2 hours	M/P	=
PHL	=	PB	=
Tmax	= 1 hour	Oral	= Complete
MW	= 149	pKa	=
Vd	=		

References:

1. Ostensen M, Husby G. Antirheumatic drug treatment during pregnancy and lactation. Scand J Rheumatol 1985; 14 (1):1-7.

PENICILLIN G   L1

Trade: Pfizerpen

Other Trades: Crystapen, Megacillin, Bicillin L-A, Ayercillin

Uses: Antibiotic

AAP: Maternal Medication Usually Compatible with Breastfeeding

Penicillins generally penetrate into breastmilk in small concentrations which is largely determined by class. Following IM doses of 100,000 units, the milk/plasma ratios varied between 0.03 - 0.13.[1,2] Milk levels varied from 7 units to 60 units/L. Possible side effects in infants would include alterations in GI flora or allergic responses in a hypersensitive infant. Compatible with breastfeeding in non-hypersensitive infants.

Pregnancy Risk Category: B

Lactation Risk Category: L1

Adult Concerns: Changes in GI flora, allergic rashes.

Pediatric Concerns: None reported via milk, but observe for changes in GI flora, diarrhea.

Drug Interactions: Probenecid may increase penicillin levels. Tetracyclines may decrease penicillin effectiveness.

Relative Infant Dose:

Adult Dose: 1.2-2.4 million units daily.

Alternatives:

T ½	= <1.5 hours	M/P	= 0.03-0.13
PHL	=	PB	= 60-80%
Tmax	= 1-2 hours	Oral	= 15-30%
MW	= 372	pKa	=
Vd	=		

References:
1. Matsuda S. Transfer of antibiotics into maternal milk. Biol Res Pregnancy Perinatol 1984; 5 (2):57-60.
2. Greene H, Burkhart B, Hobby G. Excretion of penicillin human milk following partiturition. Am J Obstet Gynecol 1946; 51:732.

PENTAZOCINE   L3

Trade: Talwin, Talacen
Other Trades: Talwin, Fortral
Uses: Analgesic
AAP: Not reviewed

Pentazocine is a synthetic opiate and is also an opiate antagonist. Once absorbed it undergoes extensive hepatic metabolism and only small amounts achieve plasma levels.[1] It is primarily used as a mild analgesic. No data are available on transfer into breastmilk.

Pregnancy Risk Category: C

Lactation Risk Category: L3

Adult Concerns: Sedation, respiratory depression, nausea, vomiting, dry mouth, taste alteration.

Pediatric Concerns: None reported due to limited studies.

Drug Interactions: May reduce the analgesic effect of other opiate agonists such as morphine. Increased toxicity when used with tripelennamine can be lethal. Increased toxicity when used with CNS depressants such as phenothiazines, sedatives, hypnotics, or alcohol.

Relative Infant Dose:

Adult Dose: 50-100 mg every 3-4 hours PRN

Alternatives:

T ½	= 2-3 hours	M/P	=
PHL	=	PB	= 60%
Tmax	= 1-3 hours	Oral	= 18%
MW	= 285	pKa	= 9.0
Vd	= 4.4-7.8		

References:
1. McEvoy GE. (ed):AFHS Drug Information. New York, NY: 2009.

PENTOBARBITAL   L3

Trade: Nembutol
Other Trades: Nembutal, Nova-Rectal, Novo-Pentobarb,
Barbopen, Carbrital, Lethobarb
Uses: Sedative, hypnotic
AAP: Not reviewed

Pentobarbital is a short acting barbiturate primarily used at a
sedative. Following a dose of 100 mg for 3 days, the concentration of
pentobarbital 19 hours after the last dose was 0.17 mg/L.[1] The effect
of short acting barbiturates on the breastfed infant is unknown, but
significant tolerance and addiction can occur.[2-4] Use caution if used in
large amounts. No reported harmful effects breastfeeding infants.

Pregnancy Risk Category: D

Lactation Risk Category: L3

Adult Concerns: Sedation, respiratory arrest, tachycardia, physical
dependence.

Pediatric Concerns: None reported, but observe for sedation,
dependence.

Drug Interactions: Barbiturates may decrease the antimicrobial
activity of metronidazole. Phenobarbital may significantly reduce
the serum levels and half-life of quinidine. Barbiturates decrease
theophylline levels. The clearance of verapamil may be increased and
its bioavailability decreased.

Relative Infant Dose: 1.8%

Adult Dose: 20-40 mg BID-QID

Alternatives:

T ½	= 15-50 hours	M/P	=
PHL	=	PB	= 35-45%
Tmax	= 30-60 minutes (oral)	Oral	= 95%
MW	= 248	pKa	= 7.9
Vd	= 0.5-1.0		

References:
1. Wilson JT, Brown RD, Cherek DR, Dailey JW, Hilman B, Jobe PC, Manno BR, Manno JE, Redetzki HM, Stewart JJ. Drug excretion in human breast milk: principles, pharmacokinetics and projected consequences. Clin Pharmacokinet 1980; 5 (1):1-66.
2. Tyson RM, Shrader EA, Perlman HH. Drugs transmitted through breast milk. II Barbiturates. J Pediatr 1938; 14:86-90.
3. Kaneko S, Sato T, Suzuki K. The levels of anticonvulsants in breast milk. Br J Clin Pharmacol 1979; 7 (6):624-627.
4. Horning MG. Identification and quantification of drugs and drug metabolites in human milk using GC-MS-COM methods. Mod Probl Pediatr 1975; 15:73-79.

PENTOSAN POLYSULFATE   L2

Trade: Elmiron
Other Trades: Elmiron
Uses: Urinary tract analgesic
AAP: Not reviewed

Pentosan polysulfate is a negatively-charged synthetic sulfated polysaccharide with Heparin-like properties although it is used as a urinary tract analgesic for interstitial cystitis. It is structurally related to dextran sulfate with a MW of 4000-6000 daltons. Oral bioavailability is low, only 6% is absorbed systemically. Pentosan adheres to the bladder wall mucosa and may act as a buffer to control cell permeability preventing irritating solutes in the urine from reaching the cell membrane.[1,2] Although no data are available on its transfer into human milk, its large MW and its poor oral bioavailability would largely preclude the transfer and absorption of clinically relevant amounts in breastfed infants.

Pregnancy Risk Category: B

Lactation Risk Category: L2

Adult Concerns: Alopecia areata. Weak anticoagulant (1/15th activity of heparin). Mildly hepatotoxic. Headache, depression, insomnia, pruritus, urticaria, diarrhea, nausea, vomiting, etc. have been reported.

Pediatric Concerns: None reported via milk. Unlikely to enter milk.

Drug Interactions: May increase bleeding time when used with cisapride.

Relative Infant Dose:

Adult Dose: 100 mg TID

Alternatives:

T ½	= <5 hours	M/P	=
PHL	=	PB	≈
Tmax	= 3 hours	Oral	= 3%
MW	= 6000	pKa	–
Vd	=		

References:
1. Wagner WH. Hoe/Bay 946--a new compound with activity against the AIDS virus. Arzneimittelforschung 1989; 39 (1):112-113.
2. Asmal AC, Leary WP, Carboni J, Lockett CJ. The effects of sodium pentosan polysulphate on peripheral metabolism. S Afr Med J 1975; 49 (27):1091-1094.

PENTOXIFYLLINE   L2

Trade: Trental
Other Trades: Trental, Apo-Pentoxifylline
Uses: Reduces blood viscosity
AAP: Not reviewed

Pentoxifylline and its metabolites improve the flow properties of blood by decreasing its viscosity. It is a methylxanthine derivative similar in structure to caffeine and is extensively metabolized although the metabolites do not have long half-lives. In a group of 5 breastfeeding women who received a single 400 mg dose, the mean milk/plasma ratio was 0.87 for the parent compound.[1] The milk/plasma ratios for the metabolites were lower: 0.54, 0.76, and 1.13. Average milk concentration at 2 hours following the dose was 73.9 µg/L.

Pregnancy Risk Category: C

Lactation Risk Category: L2

Adult Concerns: Bleeding. Dyspepsia, bloating, diarrhea, nausea, vomiting, bad taste, dyspnea.

Pediatric Concerns: None reported.

Drug Interactions: Bleeding, and prolonged prothrombin times when used with coumarins. Use with other theophylline containing products leads to increased theophylline plasma levels.

Relative Infant Dose: 0.2%

Adult Dose: 400 mg TID

Alternatives:

T ½	= 0.4-1.6 hours	M/P	=
PHL	=	PB	=
Tmax	= 1 hour	Oral	= Complete
MW	= 278	pKa	=
Vd	=		

References:
1. Witter FR, Smith RV. The excretion of pentoxifylline and its metabolites into human breast milk. Am J Obstet Gynecol 1985; 151 (8):1094-1097.

PERFLUTREN PROTEIN TYPE A   L3

Trade: Optison
Other Trades:
Uses: Diagnostic agent
AAP: Not reviewed

Perflutren protein type A is a unique contrast agent used in patients with suboptimal echocardiograms to make the left ventricular chamber opaque.[1] this product releases perflutren gas molecules that are completely eliminated in the human lung in 10 minutes. Perflutren gas is not metabolized but passes rapidly from the body. Although there are no data on levels in human milk, this product is so rapidly dissipated, that the risk to the infant would be nil.

Perflutren lipid microsphere (Definity) is a new formulation of the same gas above. Again, half-life of about 1.3 minutes.

Pregnancy Risk Category: C

Lactation Risk Category: L3

Adult Concerns: Adverse reactions include flushing, headache, dizziness, nausea, vomiting, and altered taste.

Pediatric Concerns: No data are available.

Drug Interactions:

Relative Infant Dose:

Adult Dose: 0.5 mL IV

Alternatives:

T ½	= 1.3 minutes	M/P	=
PHL	=	PB	=
Tmax	=	Oral	= Nil
MW	=	pKa	=
Vd	=		

References:
1. Pharmaceutical Manufacturer Prescribing Information. 2003.

PERMETHRIN   L2

Trade: Nix, Elimite, A-200, Pyrinex, Pyrinyl, Acticin
Other Trades: Nix, Pyrifoam, Quellada, Lyclear
Uses: Insecticide, scabicide
AAP: Not reviewed

Permethrin is a synthetic pyrethroid structure of the natural ester pyrethrum, a natural insecticide, and used to treat lice, mites, and fleas. Permethrin absorption through the skin following application of a 5% cream is reported to be less than 2%.[1] Permethrin is rapidly metabolized by serum and tissue enzymes to inactive metabolites and rapidly excreted in the urine. Overt toxicity is very low. It is not known if permethrin is secreted in human milk although it has been found in animal milk after injection of significant quantities intravenously. In spite of its rapid metabolism, some residuals are sequestered in fat tissue.

To use, recommend that the hair be washed with detergent, and then saturated with permethrin liquid for 10 minutes before rinsing with water. One treatment is all that is required. At 14 days, a second treatment may be required if viable lice are seen. Elimite cream is generally recommended for scabies infestations and should be applied head to toe for 8-12 hours in infants, and body (not head) only in adults. Reapplication may be needed in 7 days if live mites appear.

Pregnancy Risk Category: B

Lactation Risk Category: L2

Adult Concerns: Itching, rash, skin irritation. Dyspnea has been reported in one patient.

Pediatric Concerns: None via milk.

Drug Interactions:

Relative Infant Dose:

Adult Dose:

Alternatives:

T ½	=		M/P	=
PHL	=		PB	=
Tmax	=		Oral	=
MW	= 391		pKa	=
Vd	=			

References:
1. Pharmaceutical Manufacturer Prescribing Information.

PERPHENAZINE AND AMITRIPTYLINE   L3

Trade: Triavil, Etrafon

Other Trades:

Uses: Phenothiazine antipsychotic and antidepressant

AAP: Drugs whose effect on nursing infants is unknown but may be of concern

Commonly combined in the USA with amitriptyline it is called Etrafon or Triavil. For information on amitriptyline see individual monograph.

Perphenazine is a phenothiazine derivative used as an antipsychotic or sedative. In a study of one patient receiving either 16 or 24 mg/day of perphenazine divided in two doses at 12 hour intervals, milk levels were 2.1 µg/L and 3.2 µg/L respectively.[1] The authors estimated the dose to the infant at 1.06 µg (0.3 µg/kg) or 1.59 µg (0.45 µg/kg) respective of dose. Serum perphenazine levels in the mother drawn 12 hours after doses of 16 or 24 mg/d were 2.0 and 4.9 ng/mL respectively. Hence milk/plasma ratios were approximately 1.1 and 0.7 respective of the dose. The authors estimate the dose to be approximately 0.1% of the weight-adjusted maternal dose. The authors report that during a 3 month exposure, the infant thrived and had no adverse response to the medication.

Pregnancy Risk Category: C

Lactation Risk Category: L3

Adult Concerns: Sedation, extrapyramidal symptoms, tardive dyskinesia, anticholinergic symptoms, postural hypotension, obstructive jaundice.

Pedlatric Concerns: None reported via milk. Observe for sedation. Rate of SIDS may be increased in infants exposed to phenothiazines.

Drug Interactions: Anticholinergics used to control extrapyramidal side effects may reduce oral absorption of perphenazine, and antagonize the behavioral and antipsychotic effects of the drug. They may also enhance the anticholinergic side effects.Enhanced cardiotoxicity with cisapride. Check drug reference for numerous others.

Relative Infant Dose: 0.1%

Adult Dose: 12-64 mg daily

Alternatives:

T ½	= 8-12 hours	M/P	= 1.1
PHL	=	PB	=
Tmax	= 3 hours	Oral	= Complete
MW	= 403	pKa	= 7.8
Vd	= 10-35		

References:
1.   Olesen OV, Bartels U, Poulsen JH. Perphenazine in breast milk and serum. Am J Psychiatry 1990; 147 (10):1378-1379.

PHENAZOPYRIDINE HCL   L3

Trade: Pyridium, Eridium, Azo-Standard
Other Trades: Phenazo, Pyridium, Pyronium, Uromide
Uses: Urinary tract analgesic
AAP: Not reviewed

Phenazopyridine is an azo dye that is rapidly excreted in the urine, where it exerts a topical analgesic effect on urinary tract mucosa.[1] Pyridium is only moderately effective and produces a reddish-orange discoloration of the urine. It may also ruin contact lenses. It is not known if Pyridium transfers into breastmilk, but it probably does to a limited degree. This product, due to limited efficacy, should probably not be used in lactating women although it is doubtful that it would be harmful to an infant. This product is highly colored and can stain clothing. Stains can be removed by soaking in a solution of 0.25% sodium dithionite.

Pregnancy Risk Category: B

Lactation Risk Category: L3

Adult Concerns: Anemia, nausea, vomiting, diarrhea, colored urine, methemoglobinemia, hepatitis, GI distress,

Pediatric Concerns: None reported via lactation.

Drug Interactions:

Relative Infant Dose:

Adult Dose: 100-200 mg TID

Alternatives:

T ½	=		M/P	=
PHL	=		PB	=
Tmax	=		Oral	= Complete
MW	= 250		pKa	=
Vd	=			

References:
1.   Drug Facts and Comparisons 2010 ed. ed. St. Louis: 2010.

PHENCYCLIDINE   L5

Trade: PCP, Angel Dust
Other Trades:
Uses: Hallucinogen
AAP: Drugs of abuse for which adverse effects have been reported

Phencyclidine, also called Angel Dust, is a potent and extremely dangerous hallucinogen. High concentrations are secreted into breastmilk (>10 times plasma level) of mice.[1] Continued secretion into milk occurs over long periods of time (perhaps months). One patient who consumed PCP 41 days prior to lactating had a milk level of 3.90 µg/L.[2]

EXTREMELY DANGEROUS TO NURSING INFANT. PCP is stored for long periods in adipose tissue. Urine samples are positive for 14-30 days in adults and probably longer in infants. The infant could test positive for PCP long after maternal exposure, particularly if breastfeeding. Definitely contraindicated.

Pregnancy Risk Category: X

Lactation Risk Category: L5

Adult Concerns: Hallucinations, psychosis.

Pedlatric Concerns: Significant concentrations would likely transfer to infant. Extremely dangerous.

Drug Interactions:

Relative Infant Dose:

Adult Dose:

Alternatives:

T ½	= 24-51 hours	M/P	= >10
PHL	=	PB	= 65%
Tmax	= Immediate	Oral	= Complete
MW	= 243	pKa	= 8.5
Vd	= 5.3-7.5		

References:
1. Nicholas JM, Lipshitz J, Schreiber EC. Phencyclidine: its transfer across the placenta as well as into breast milk. Am J Obstet Gynecol 1982; 143 (2):143-146.
2. Kaufman KR, Petrucha RA, Pitts FN, Jr., Weekes ME. PCP in amniotic fluid and breast milk: case report. J Clin Psychiatry 1983; 44 (7):269-270.
3. American Academy of Pediatrics, Committee on Drugs. Transfer of drugs and other chemicals into human milk. Pediatrics 2001; 108 (3):776-89.

PHENOBARBITAL   L3

Trade: Luminal
Other Trades: Barbilixir, Phenobarbitone, Gardenal
Uses: Long acting barbiturate sedative, anticonvulsant
AAP: Drugs associated with significant side effects and should be given with caution

Phenobarbital is a long half-life barbiturate frequently used as an anticonvulsant in adults and during the neonatal period. Its long half-life in infants may lead to significant accumulation and blood levels higher than mother although this is infrequent. During the first 3-4 weeks of life, phenobarbital is poorly absorbed by the neonatal GI tract.

However, protein binding by neonatal albumin is poor, 36-43%, as compared to the adult, 51%. Thus, the volume of distribution is higher in neonates and the tissue concentrations of phenobarbital may be significantly higher. The half-life in premature infants can be extremely long (100-500 hours) and plasma levels must be closely monitored. Although varied, milk/plasma ratios vary from 0.46 to 0.6.[1,2,3]

In one study, following a dose of 30 mg four times daily, the milk concentration of phenobarbital averaged 2.74 mg/L 16 hours after the last dose.[3] The dose an infant would receive was estimated at 2-4 mg/day.[4]

Phenobarbital should be administered with caution and close observation of infant is required, including plasma drug levels. One should generally expect the infant's plasma level to be approximately 30-40% of the maternal level. In some reported cases, the infant plasma levels have reached twice what the maternal plasma levels were, 2.5 hours after the maternal dose.[5]

Pregnancy Risk Category: D

Lactation Risk Category: L3

Adult Concerns: Drowsiness, sedation, ataxia, respiratory depression, withdrawal symptoms.

Pediatric Concerns: Phenobarbital sedation has been reported, but is infrequent. Expect infant plasma levels to approximate one-third (or lower) of maternal plasma level. Withdrawal symptoms have been reported.

Drug Interactions: Barbiturates may decrease the antimicrobial activity of metronidazole. Phenobarbital may significantly reduce the serum levels and half-life of quinidine. Barbiturates decrease theophylline levels. The clearance of verapamil may be increased and its bioavailability decreased.

Relative Infant Dose: 23.97%

Adult Dose: 100-200 mg daily.

Alternatives:

T ½	= 53-140 hours	M/P	= 0.4-0.6
PHL	= 36-144 hours	PB	= 51%
Tmax	= 8-12 hours	Oral	= 80% (Adult)
MW	= 232	pKa	= 7.2
Vd	= 0.5-0.6		

References:
1.   Tyson RM, Shrader EA, Perlman HH. Drugs transmitted through breast milk. II Barbiturates. J Pediatr 1938; 14:86-90.

2. Kaneko S, Sato T, Suzuki K. The levels of anticonvulsants in breast milk. Br J Clin Pharmacol 1979; 7 (6):624-627.
3. Nau H, Kuhnz W, Egger HJ, Rating D, Helge H. Anticonvulsants during pregnancy and lactation. Transplacental, maternal and neonatal pharmacokinetics. Clin Pharmacokinet 1982; 7 (6):508-543.
4. Horning MG. Identification and quantification of drugs and drug metabolites in human milk using GC-MS-COM methods. Mod Probl Pediatr 1975; 15:73-79.
5. Pote M, Kulkarni R, Agarwal M. Phenobarbital Toxic Levels in a Nursing Neonate. Indian Pediatr 2004; 41:963-964.

PHENTERMINE   L4

Trade: Fastin, Zantryl, Ionamin, Adipex-P
Other Trades: Ionamin, Duromine, Ponderax caps
Uses: Appetite suppressant
AAP: Not reviewed

Phentermine is an appetite suppressant structurally similar to the amphetamine family. As such it frequently produces CNS stimulation.[1] No data is available on transfer to human milk. This product has a very small MW (149) and would probably transfer into human milk in significant quantities and could product stimulation, anorexia, tremors, and other CNS side effects in the newborn. The use of this product in breastfeeding mothers would be difficult to justify and is not advised.

Pregnancy Risk Category: C

Lactation Risk Category: L4

Adult Concerns: Hypertension, tachycardia, palpitations, nervousness, tremulousness, insomnia, dizziness, depression, headache, cerebral infarct, paranoid psychosis, heat stroke, nausea, vomiting, physical dependence as evidenced by withdrawal syndrome.

Pediatric Concerns: Growth impairment has been reported from direct use of phentermine in children age 3-15 years.

Drug Interactions: Decreased effect of guanethidine, CNS depressants. Increased toxicity of MAO inhibitors, other stimulants.

Relative Infant Dose:

Adult Dose: 8 mg TID

Alternatives:

T ½	= 7-20 hours	M/P	=
PHL	=	PB	=
Tmax	= 8 hours	Oral	= Complete
MW	= 149	pKa	=
Vd	=		

References:
1. Silverstone T. Appetite suppressants. A review. Drugs 1992; 43 (6):820-836.

PHENYLEPHRINE   L3

Trade: Neo-Synephrine, AK-Dilate, Vicks Sinex Nasal, Neofrin
Other Trades: Mydfrin, Dionephrine, Albalone, Fenox
Uses: Decongestant
AAP: Not reviewed

Phenylephrine is a sympathomimetic most commonly used as a nasal decongestant due to its vasoconstrictive properties but also for treatment of ocular uveitis, inflammation, and glaucoma as a mydriatic agent to dilate the pupil during examinations, and for cardiogenic shock.[1] Phenylephrine is a potent adrenergic stimulant and systemic effects (tachycardia, hypertension, arrhythmias), although rare, have occurred following ocular administration in some sensitive individuals. Phenylephrine is most commonly added to cold mixtures and nasal sprays for use in respiratory colds, flu, and congestion. Numerous pediatric formulations are in use and it is generally considered safe in pediatric patients.

Used ophthalmically in eye exams, the maternal dose of the medication would be very low and it is not likely to pose a problem for a breastfeeding infant.

Although no data are available on its secretion into human milk, it is probable that very small amounts will be transferred into milk, but due to its poor oral bioavailability (<38%), it is not likely that it would produce clinical effects in a breastfed infant unless the maternal doses were quite high. Because of pseudoephedrine's effect on milk production, concerns that phenylephrine may suppress milk production, have not been confirmed as yet. There is no evidence that this occurs at all.

Pregnancy Risk Category: C

Lactation Risk Category: L3

Adult Concerns: Local ocular irritation, transient tachycardia, hypertension, and sympathetic stimulation.

Pediatric Concerns: None reported via milk.

Drug Interactions: Concomitant use with other sympathomimetics may exacerbate cardiovascular effects of phenylephrine. This includes albuterol, amitriptyline, other tricyclic antidepressants, MAO inhibitors, furazolidone, guanethidine, and others. Increased effect when used with oxytocic drugs.

Relative Infant Dose:

Adult Dose: 1-10 mg IM

Alternatives: Pseudoephedrine

T ½	= 2-3 hours	M/P	=
PHL	=	PB	=
Tmax	= 10-60 minutes	Oral	= 38%
MW	= 203	pKa	=
Vd	= 0.57		

References:
1. Pharmaceutical Manufacturer Prescribing Information.

PHENYLPROPANOLAMINE | L2

Trade: Dexatrim, Acutrim
Other Trades: Caldomine-DH, Dimetapp, Eskornade
Uses: Adrenergic, nasal decongestant, anorexiant.
AAP: Not reviewed

Phenylpropanolamine is an adrenergic compound frequently used in nasal decongestants and also diet pills. It produces significant constriction of nasal mucosa and is a common ingredient in cold preparations. No data are available on its secretion into human milk, but due to its low MW and its rapid entry past the blood-brain-barrier, it should be expected. It has recently been withdrawn from the US market.

Pregnancy Risk Category: C

Lactation Risk Category: L2

Adult Concerns: Hypertension, bradycardia, AV block, arrhythmias, paranoia, seizures, psychosis, tremor, excitement, insomnia, seizures, anorexia and physical dependence.

Pediatric Concerns: None reported via milk but observe for excitement, loss of appetite, insomnia.

Drug Interactions: Hypertensive crisis when admixed with MAO inhibitors. Increased toxicity (pressor effects) with beta blockers. Decreased effect of antihypertensives.

Relative Infant Dose:

Adult Dose: 12.5-25 mg every 4-6 hours

Alternatives:

T ½	= 5.6 hours	M/P	=
PHL	=	PB	= Low
Tmax	= 1 hour	Oral	= 100%
MW	= 188	pKa	= 9.1
Vd	= 4.5		

References:

PHENYTOIN   L2

Trade: Dilantin
Other Trades: Dilantin, Novo-Phenytoin, Epanutin
Uses: Anticonvulsant
AAP: Maternal Medication Usually Compatible with Breastfeeding

Phenytoin is an old and efficient anticonvulsant. It is secreted in small amounts into breastmilk. The effect on infant is generally considered minimal if the levels in the maternal circulation are kept in low-normal range (10 µg/mL). Phenytoin levels peak in milk at 3.5 hours.

In one study of 6 women receiving 200-400 mg/day, plasma concentrations varied from 12.8 to 78.5 µmol/L, while their milk levels ranged from 1.61 to 2.95 mg/L.[1] The milk/plasma ratios were low, ranging from 0.06 to 0.18. In only two of these infants were plasma concentrations of phenytoin detectible (0.46 and 0.72 µmol/L). No untoward effects were noted in any of these infants.

Others have reported milk levels of 6 μg/mL[2], or 0.8 μg/mL.[3] Although the actual concentration in milk varies significantly between studies, the milk/plasma ratio appears relatively similar at 0.13 to 0.45. Breastmilk concentrations varied from 0.26 to 1.5 mg/L depending on the maternal dose

.

In a mother receiving 250 mg twice daily, milk levels were 0.26 and the milk/plasma ratio was 0.45.[4] The maternal plasma level was phenytoin was 0.58. In another study of two patients receiving 300-600 mg/d, the average milk level was 1.9 mg/L.[5] The maximum observed milk level was 2.6 mg/L

The neonatal half-life of phenytoin is highly variable for the first week of life. Monitoring of the infants' plasma may be useful although it is not definitely required. All of the current studies indicate rather low levels of phenytoin in breastmilk and minimal plasma levels in breastfeeding infants.

Pregnancy Risk Category: D

Lactation Risk Category: L2

Adult Concerns: Sedation, hypertrophied gums, ataxia, liver toxicity.

Pediatric Concerns: Only one case of methemoglobinemia, drowsiness, and poor sucking has been reported. Most other studies suggest no problems.

Drug Interactions: Increased effects of phenytoin may occur when used with: amiodarone, benzodiazepines, chloramphenicol, cimetidine, disulfiram, ethanol, fluconazole (azoles), isoniazid, metronidazole, omeprazole, sulfonamides, valproic acid, TCAs, ibuprofen. Decreased effects of phenytoin may occur when used with: barbiturates, carbamazepine, rifampin, antacids, charcoal, sucralfate, folic acid, laxapine, nitrofurantoin, pyridoxine. May others have been reported, please consult more complete reference.

Relative Infant Dose: 0.6% - 7.7%

Adult Dose: 300 mg daily.

Alternatives:

T ½	= 6-24 hours	M/P	= 0.18-0.45
PHL	= 20-160 hours (premature)	PB	= 89%
Tmax	= 4-12 hours	Oral	= 70-100%
MW	= 252	pKa	= 8.3
Vd	= 0.5-0.8		

References:
1. Steen B, Rane A, Lonnerholm G, Falk O, Elwin CE, Sjoqvist F. Phenytoin excretion in human breast milk and plasma levels in nursed infants. Ther Drug Monit 1982; 4 (4):331-334.
2. Svensmark O, Schiller PJ, Buchthal F. 5, 5-Diphenylhydantoin (dilantin) blood levels after oral or intravenous dosage in man. Acta Pharmacol Toxicol (Copenh) 1960; 16:331-346.
3. Kaneko S, Sato T, Suzuki K. The levels of anticonvulsants in breast milk. Br J Clin Pharmacol 1979; 7 (6):624-627.
4. Rane A, Garle M, Borga O, Sjoqvist F. Plasma disappearance of transplacentally transferred diphenylhydantoin in the newborn studied by mass fragmentography. Clin Pharmacol Ther 1974; 15 (1):39-45.
5. Mirkin BL. Diphenylhydantoin: placental transport, fetal localization, neonatal metabolism, and possible teratogenic effects. J Pediatr 1971; 78 (2):329-337.

PHYTONADIONE   L1

Trade: Phytonadione, AquaMEPHYTON, Konakion, Mephyton, Vitamin K1
Other Trades: Konakion
Uses: Vitamin K1
AAP: Maternal Medication Usually Compatible with Breastfeeding

Vitamin K1 is often used to reverse the effects of oral anticoagulants and to prevent hemorrhagic disease of the newborn (HDN).[1,2,3] The use of vitamin K has long been accepted primarily because it reduces the decline of the vitamin K dependent coagulation factors II, VII, IX, and X. A single IM injection of 0.5 to 1 mg or an oral dose of 1-2 mg during the neonatal period is recommended by the AAP. Although controversial, it is generally recognized that exclusive breastfeeding may not provide sufficient vitamin K1 to provide normal clotting factors, particularly in the premature infant or those with malabsorptive disorders. Vitamin K concentration in breastmilk is normally low (<5-20 ng/mL), and most infants are born with low coagulation factors (30-60%) of normal. Although vitamin K is transferred to human milk, the amount may not be sufficient to prevent hemorrhagic disease of the newborn. Vitamin K requires the presence of bile and other factors for absorption, and neonatal absorption may be slow or delayed due to the lack of requisite gut factors.

Pregnancy Risk Category: C

Lactation Risk Category: L1

Adult Concerns: Adverse effects include hemolytic anemia, thrombocytopenia, thrombosis, hypotension, prothrombin abnormalities, pruritus, and cutaneous reactions. Anaphylaxis.

Pediatric Concerns: Vitamin K transfer to milk is low.

Drug Interactions: Decreased effect when used with coumarin/warfarin anticoagulants.

Relative Infant Dose:

Adult Dose: 65 µg daily

Alternatives:

T ½	=	M/P	–
PHL	= 26-193 hours	PB	=
Tmax	= 12 hours	Oral	= Complete
MW	= 450	pKa	=
Vd	=		

References:
1. Olson JA. Recommended dietary intakes (RDI) of vitamin K in humans. Am J Clin Nutr 1987; 45 (4):687-692.
2. Lane PA, Hathaway WE. Vitamin K in infancy. J Pediatr 1985; 106 (3):351-359.
3. Vitamin and mineral supplement needs in normal children in the United States Pediatrics 1980; 66 (6):1015-1021.

PILOCARPINE   L3

Trade: Isopto Carpine, Pilocar, Akarpine, Ocusert Pilo
Other Trades: Minims Pilocarpine, Ocusert-Pilo
Uses: Intraocular hypotensive
AAP: Not reviewed

Pilocarpine is a direct acting cholinergic agent used primarily in the eyes for treatment of open-angle glaucoma. The ophthalmic dose is approximately 1 mg or less per day, while the oral adult dose is approximately 15-30 mg daily.[1,2] It is not known if pilocarpine enters milk, but it probably does in low levels due to its minimal plasma level. It is not likely that an infant would receive a clinical dose via milk, but this is presently unknown. Side effects would largely include diarrhea, gastric upset, excessive salivation, and other typical cholinergic symptoms.

Pregnancy Risk Category: C

Lactation Risk Category: L3

Adult Concerns: Common side effects from ophthalmic use include burning or itching, blurred vision, poor night vision, headaches. Following oral use, excessive sweating may occur.

Pediatric Concerns: None reported via milk but observe for vomiting, epigastric distress, abdominal cramping and diarrhea.

Drug Interactions: A decreased response when added with anticholinergic agents. Diprivan and pilocarpine may increase myopia and increase blurred vision. Sulfacetamide ophthalmic solutions may precipitate pilocarpine prior to absorption and should not be used together.

Relative Infant Dose:

Adult Dose: 5-10 mg TID

Alternatives:

T ½	= 0.76-1.55 hours	M/P	=
PHL	=	PB	= 0%
Tmax	= 1.25 hours	Oral	= Good
MW	= 208	pKa	= 7.15
Vd	=		

References:
1. Drug Facts and Comparisons 1999 ed. ed. St. Louis: 1999.
2. Pharmaceutical Manufacturer Prescribing Information. 1999.

PIMECROLIMUS   L2

Trade: Elidel
Other Trades: Elidel
Uses: Cytokine inhibitor used for atopic dermatitis
AAP: Not reviewed

Pimecrolimus is a topical agent used as a cytokine inhibitor for atopic dermatitis. While its mechanism of action is unknown, it inhibits the release of various inflammatory cytokines for T cells and many others. Systemic absorption following topical application is minimal with reported blood concentrations consistently below 0.5 ng/milliliter following twice-daily application of the 1% cream.[1] Oral absorption is unreported but probably low to moderate as plasma levels of 54 ng/mL have been reported following twice daily oral doses of 30 mg.[2] Pimecrolimus is cleared for use in pediatric patients 2 years and older.

No data are available on its transfer to human milk, but because the maternal plasma levels are so low, it is extremely remote that this agent would penetrate milk in clinically relevant amounts. However, its use on or around the nipples should be avoided as the clinical dose absorbed orally in the infant could be significant.

Pregnancy Risk Category: C

Lactation Risk Category: L2
                                L4 on nipple.

Adult Concerns: Adverse reactions include excessive skin warmth and burning. Elevated risk of skin infection (varicella zoster virus infection, herpes simplex virus infection, or eczema herpeticum) and skin cancer is possible. Hives or itching, swelling of the face, tightness in the chest, and fever have been reported. The US FDA has issued a warning concerning elevated risks of skin cancers and lymphomas in patients exposed to this product. This warning is highly controversial and is not supported by many dermatologic organizations.

Pediatric Concerns: None reported via milk. It is commonly used in children 2 years old and greater. It is unlikely to penetrate milk in clinically relevant amounts. Should not be used directly on the nipple, or areola. The US FDA has issued a warning concerning elevated risks of skin cancers and lymphomas in patients exposed to this product. This warning is highly controversial and is not supported by many dermatologic organizations.

Drug Interactions:

Relative Infant Dose:

Adult Dose: Apply twice daily to skin.

Alternatives:

T ½	=	M/P	=
PHL	=	PB	= 87%
Tmax	=	Oral	= Moderate
MW	= 810	pKa	=
Vd	=		

References:
1. Pharmaceutical Manufacturers prescribing information, 2003.
2. Harper J, Green A, Scott G, Gruendl E, Dorobek B, Cardno M, Burtin P. First experience of topical SDZ ASM 981 in children with atopic dermatitis. Br J Dermatol 2001; 144 (4):781-787.

PIMOZIDE   L4

Trade: Orap
Other Trades: Orap
Uses: Potent tranquilizer
AAP: Not reviewed

Pimozide is a potent neuroleptic agent primarily used for Tourette's syndrome and chronic schizophrenia which induces a low degree of sedation.[1,2] No data are available on the secretion of pimozide into breastmilk. This is a highly risky product and numerous other antipsychotics are available. So this product is probably not worth the risk to the infant.

Pregnancy Risk Category: C

Lactation Risk Category: L4

Adult Concerns: Extrapyramidal symptoms, anorexia, weight loss, GI distress, seizures.

Pediatric Concerns: None reported but caution is urged. No pediatric studies are found.

Drug Interactions: Increases toxicity of alfentanil, CNS depressants, guanabenz, and MAO inhibitors. Do not use with macrolide antibiotics such as clarithromycin, erythromycin, azithromycin and dirithromycin, due to two reported deaths.

Relative Infant Dose:

Adult Dose: 7-16 mg daily.

Alternatives:

T ½	= 55 hours	M/P	=
PHL	= 66 hours	PB	=
Tmax	= 6-8 hours	Oral	= >50%
MW	= 462	pKa	=
Vd	=		

References:
1. Pharmaceutical Manufacturer Prescribing Information. 1996.
2. Drug Facts and Comparisons 1996 ed. ed. St. Louis: 1996.

PIOGLITAZONE | L3

Trade: Actos
Other Trades:
Uses: Oral antidiabetic agent
AAP: Not reviewed

Pioglitazone is a thiazolidinediones family oral antidiabetic agent similar to troglitazone and rosiglitazone. It acts primarily by increasing insulin receptor sensitivity. In essence, the insulin receptor is activated reducing insulin resistance. This family also decreases hepatic gluconeogenesis and increases insulin-dependent muscle glucose uptake. They do not increase the release or secretion of insulin. No data are available on its entry into human milk.

Pregnancy Risk Category: C

Lactation Risk Category: L3

Adult Concerns: Hypoglycemia, upper respiratory tract infection, headache, sinusitis, myalgia, elevated liver enzymes. Elevated CPK. Edema, anemia, and pharyngitis have been reported but are rare.

Pediatric Concerns: None reported via milk, but no data are available.

Drug Interactions: May reduce plasma levels of oral contraceptives, estrogens and progestins, by 30% which could lead to loss of contraception.

Relative Infant Dose:

Adult Dose: 15-30 mg once daily.

Alternatives: Metformin

T ½	= 16-24 hours	M/P	=
PHL	=	PB	= >99%
Tmax	= 2 hours	Oral	=
MW	= 392	pKa	=
Vd	= 0.63		

References:
1. Pharmaceutical Manufacturer Prescribing Information.

PIPERACILLIN

L2

Trade: Zosyn, Pipracil
Other Trades: Pipracil, Pipril, Tazocin
Uses: Penicillin antibiotic
AAP: Not reviewed

Piperacillin is an extended-spectrum penicillin. It is not absorbed orally and must be given IM or IV. Piperacillin when combined with tazobactam sodium is called Zosyn.[1] Tazobactam is a penicillin-like inhibitor of the enzyme beta lactamase and has few clinical effects. Concentrations of piperacillin secreted into milk are believed to be extremely low.[2] Its poor oral absorption would limit its absorption. I've had one report that it turned the milk blue.

Pregnancy Risk Category: B

Lactation Risk Category: L2

Adult Concerns: Allergic skin rash, blood dyscrasias, diarrhea, nausea, vomiting, kidney toxicity, changes in GI flora.

Pediatric Concerns: None reported via milk.

Drug Interactions: Tetracyclines may reduce penicillin effectiveness. Probenecid may increase penicillin levels.

Relative Infant Dose:

Adult Dose: 4-5 g BID-TID

Alternatives:

T ½	= 0.6-1.3 hours	M/P	=
PHL	= 3.6 hours (neonate)	PB	= 30 %
Tmax	= 30 - 50 minutes	Oral	= Poor
MW	= 518	pKa	=
Vd	=		

References:
1. Pharmaceutical Manufacturer Prescribing Information. 1996.
2. Chaplin S, Sanders GL, Smith JM. Drug excretion in human breast milk. Adv Drug React Ac Pois Rev 1982; 1:255-287.

PIRBUTEROL ACETATE | L2

Trade: Maxair
Other Trades: Maxair, Evirel
Uses: Bronchodilator for asthmatics
AAP: Not reviewed

Pirbuterol is a classic beta-2 drug (similar to albuterol) for dilating pulmonary bronchi in asthmatic patients. It is administered by inhalation and, occasionally, orally.[1] Plasma levels are all but undetectable with normal inhaled doses. No data exists on levels in milk, but they would probably be minimal if administered via inhalation. Oral preparations would provide much higher plasma levels and would be associated with a higher risk for breastfeeding infants.

Pregnancy Risk Category: C

Lactation Risk Category: L2

Adult Concerns: Irritability, tremors, dry mouth, excitement, palpitations, and tachycardia.

Pediatric Concerns: None reported via milk, but observe for irritability, tremors.

Drug Interactions: Decreased effect when used with beta blockers. Increased toxicity with other beta agonists, MAOi, and TCAs.

Relative Infant Dose:

Adult Dose: 0.2-0.4 mg every 4-6 hours

Alternatives:

T ½	= 2-3 hours	M/P	=
PIIL	=	PB	=
Tmax	= 5 minutes (Aerosol)	Oral	= Complete
MW	= 240	pKa	=
Vd	=		

References:
1. Pharmaceutical Manufacturer Prescribing Information. 1993, 1994.

PIROXICAM   L2

Trade: Feldene
Other Trades: Apo-Piroxicam, Feldene, Novo-Pirocam, Candyl, Mobilis, Pirox
Uses: Non-steroidal analgesic for arthritis
AAP: Maternal Medication Usually Compatible with Breastfeeding

Piroxicam is a typical nonsteroidal antiinflammatory commonly used in arthritics. In one patient taking 40 mg/day, breastmilk levels were 0.22 mg/L at 2.5 hours after dose.[1] In another study of long-term therapy in four lactating women receiving 20 mg/day, the mean piroxicam concentration in breastmilk was 78 μg/L which is approximately 1-3% of the maternal plasma concentration.[2] The daily dose ingested by the infant was calculated to average 3.4% of the weight-adjusted maternal dose of piroxicam. Even though piroxicam has a very long half-life, this report suggests its use to be safe in breastfeeding mothers.

Pregnancy Risk Category: C

Lactation Risk Category: L2

Adult Concerns: Gastric distress, GI bleeding, constipation, vomiting, edema, dizziness, liver toxicity.

Pediatric Concerns: None reported via milk in several studies.

Drug Interactions: May prolong prothrombin time when used with warfarin. Antihypertensive effects of ACEi family may be blunted or completely abolished by NSAIDs. Some NSAIDs may block antihypertensive effect of beta blockers, diuretics. Used with cyclosporin, may dramatically increase renal toxicity. May increase digoxin, phenytoin, lithium levels. May increase toxicity of methotrexate. May increase bioavailability of penicillamine. Probenecid may increase NSAID levels.

Relative Infant Dose: 3.4% - 5.8%

Adult Dose: 20 mg daily.

Alternatives: Ibuprofen

T ½	= 30-86 hours	M/P	= 0.008-0.013
PHL	=	PB	= 99.3%
Tmax	= 3-5 hours	Oral	= Complete
MW	= 331	pKa	= 5.1
Vd	= 0.31		

References:
1. Ostensen M. Piroxicam in human breast milk. Eur J Clin Pharmacol 1983; 25 (6):829-830.
2. Ostensen M, Matheson I, Laufen H. Piroxicam in breast milk after long-term treatment. Eur J Clin Pharmacol 1988; 35 (5):567-569.

PNEUMOCOCCAL VACCINE | L1

Trade: Prevnar, Pneumovax 23
Other Trades: Pneuno 23, Pneumovax 23
Uses: Vaccine
AAP: Not reviewed

The pneumococcal vaccine is an inactivated product that consists of a mixture of polysaccharides from the 23 most prevalent types of Streptococcus pneumonia. It is non-infectious. It is available as a formulation containing 7 strains (7-valent) conjugate, and a 23 strain (valent) conjugate vaccine. The 7-valent vaccine is for use in children less than 2 years of age, and is recommended at ages 2, 4, 6 and 12-15 months. The 23-valent vaccine is for use in adults age 65 years or older (one dose), anyone age two years or older that is immunocompromized, or anyone who has or is getting a cochlear implant.[1] Although technically not approved for use in breastfeeding mothers, Prevnar 7 is recommended by the AAP for use in infants 2 months of age and older. The CDC also suggests Pneumovax is of minimal risk to a breastfeeding infant. Therefore it is unlikely to produce an untoward effect in a breastfed infant.

Pregnancy Risk Category: C

Lactation Risk Category: L1

Adult Concerns: Adverse reactions with the 23 valent conjugate vaccine include malaise, headache, nausea, vomiting, scrum sickness, and fever.

Pediatric Concerns: Adverse reactions with the 7-valent pneumococcal conjugate vaccine include fever, irritability, drowsiness, erythema, decreased appetite, vomiting, diarreha, and local tenderness

Drug Interactions: Immunosupressants may decrease the efficacy of the vaccine.

Relative Infant Dose:

Adult Dose: 0.5 mL IM

Alternatives:

T ½	=	M/P	=
PHL	=	PB	=
Tmax	=	Oral	= Nil
MW	=	pKa	=
Vd	=		

References:
1.   Pharmaceutical Manufacturer Prescribing Information. 2007.

PODOFILOX   L3

Trade: Condylox, Podophyllotoxin
Other Trades:
Uses: Antimitotic agent use topically for treatment of genital
warts.
AAP: Not reviewed

Podofilox (also called Podophyllotoxin) is an antimitotic agent used
to treat genital warts and Condyloma acuminatum. Its transcutaneous
absorption is minimal, plasma levels in 52 patients following use
of 0.05 mL of 0.5% podofilox solution to external genitalia did not
result in detectable serum levels. However, applications of 0.1 to 1.5
mL resulted in plasma levels of 1-17 ng/mL one to two hours post
treatment. The drug does not accumulate after multiple treatments. No
data on its transfer to human milk are available. It would be advisable
to limit the dosage used in breastfeeding women, and to wait for a
minimum of 4 hours following application before breastfeeding. The
infant should be closely monitored for GI distress. The use of this
product in breastfeeding women should be avoided if possible.

Pregnancy Risk Category: C

Lactation Risk Category: L3

Adult Concerns: Burning, pain, inflammation, erosion and itching
at site of injection. Insomnia, bleeding, tenderness, malodor, dizziness,
scaring have been reported.

Pediatric Concerns: No data are available, but extreme caution
is recommended if used. A brief waiting period of 4 hours or more
following application is recommended.

Drug Interactions:

Relative Infant Dose:

Adult Dose: Variable, but 0.5% Solution applied topically every 12
hours is indicated for genital warts.

Alternatives:

T ½	= 1-4.5 hours	M/P	=
PHL	=	PB	=
Tmax	= 1-2 hours	Oral	=
MW	= 414	pKa	=
Vd	=		

References:
1. Pharmaceutical manufacturers prescribing information. 2005.

POLIO VACCINE, ORAL   L2

Trade: Vaccine-Live Oral Trivalent Polio
Other Trades:
Uses: Vaccine
AAP: Not reviewed

Oral polio vaccine is a mixture of three, live, attenuated oral polio viruses.[1] Human milk contains oral polio antibodies consistent with that of the maternal circulation.[2] Early exposure of the infant may reduce production of antibodies in the infant later on but this is not a major problem. Immunization of infant prior to 6 weeks of age is not recommended due to reduced antibody production. At this age, the effect of breastmilk antibodies on the infant's development of antibodies is believed minimal. Wait until infant is 6 weeks of age before immunizing mother.

Pregnancy Risk Category: C

Lactation Risk Category: L2

Adult Concerns: Rash, fever.

Pediatric Concerns: None reported via milk.

Drug Interactions: May have inadequate response when used with immunosuppressants. Cholera vaccine may reduce seroconversion rate when coadministered, wait at least 30 days.

Relative Infant Dose:

Adult Dose:

Alternatives:

References:
1. Pharmaceutical Manufacturer Prescribing Information. 1996.
2. Adcock E, Greene H. Poliovirus antibodies in breast-fed infants. Lancet 1971; 2 (7725):662-663.

POLYETHYLENE GLYCOL-ELECTROLYTE SOLUTIONS | L3

Trade: GoLYTELY, Col-Lav, Colovage, Colyte, OCL
Other Trades: PegLyte
Uses: Bowel evacuant
AAP: Not reviewed

PEG-ES is a polyethylene glycol-3350 saline laxative.[1] It is a non-absorbable solution used as an osmotic agent to cleanse the bowel. It is completely non-absorbed from the adult GI tract and would not likely penetrate human milk. This product is often used in children and infants prior to GI surgery. Although no data are available on transfer into human milk, it is highly unlikely that enough maternal absorption would occur to produce milk levels.

Pregnancy Risk Category: C

Lactation Risk Category: L3

Adult Concerns: Diarrhea, bad taste, intestinal fullness. Do not use in GI obstruction, gastric retention, bowel preformation, toxic colitis, megacolon or ileus.

Pediatric Concerns: None reported via milk.

Drug Interactions: Due to intense diarrhea produced, it would dramatically reduce oral absorption of any other orally administered medicine.

Relative Infant Dose:

Adult Dose: 240 mL every 10 minutes up to 4 L

Alternatives:

T ½	=	M/P	=
PHL	=	PB	=
Tmax	=	Oral	= None
MW	=	pKa	=
Vd	=		

References:

1. Pharmaceutical Manufacturer Prescribing Information. 1996.

POLYMYXIN B SULFATE   L2

Trade: Polysporin, Bacitracin, Ak-Spore, Akorn, Aerosporin, Neosporin, Cortisporin

Other Trades: Aerosporin, Aerocortin

Uses: Antibacterial

AAP: Not reviewed

Polymyxin B is a commonly used topical, ophthalmic, and rarely injectable antibiotic. Most commonly used with other antibiotics, including neomycin and corticosteroids (hydrocortisone), it is commonly used to treat conjunctivitis, blepharitis, keratitis, and other topical infections. It primarily covers most gram negative bacteria and some gram positive. It has been used in infants via injection (40,000 units/kg/d) but this is extremely rare. When applied ophthalmically, it is almost completely unabsorbed into surrounding tissues.

No data are available on its transfer to human milk. However, when used topically it is very unlikely enough would be absorbed transcutaneously to produce plasma or milk levels. Orally, it would be largely destroyed by the gastric acid in the infant as it is very unstable in acidic milieu. When applied topically to nipples in small amounts it is unlikely to produce problems in a breastfed infant.

Pregnancy Risk Category: B

Lactation Risk Category: L2

Adult Concerns: Plasma concentrations exceeding 5 µg/mL in adults may produce paresthesias, dizziness, weakness, drowsiness, ataxia, etc. But these are only seen following IM, IV, or intrathecal injections, not via topical application.

Pediatric Concerns: The adult observations are rarely seen in children.

Drug Interactions: Additive effects when polymyxin is added to neuromuscular blockers. Incompatible with acids, alkali solutions, amphotericin B solutions.

Relative Infant Dose:

Adult Dose: Topical: 10,000-25,000 units/mL

Alternatives:

T ½	= 6 hours	M/P	=
PHL	=	PB	= Low
Tmax	= 2 hours	Oral	= Minimal
MW	= Large	pKa	=
Vd	=		

References:

POTASSIUM IODIDE   L4

Trade: SSKI
Other Trades:
Uses: Antithyroid agent, Expectorant
AAP: Not reviewed

Potassium iodide is frequently used to suppress thyroxine secretion in hyperthyroid patients (thyroid storm). About 30% of the oral dose administered is taken up by the thyroid gland, 20% goes to faecal excretion, the rest is cleared renally. Thus the biological half-lives are: blood, 6 hours; thyroid gland, 80 days; rest of the body, 12 days.[1]

Most of a dose administered is rapidly cleared from the body via feces and urine. Part (30%) is sequestered for long periods in the thyroid gland. Because plasma iodine is the only source of iodine uptake in breastmilk, and it is cleared rapidly with a 6 hour half-life, mothers could theoretically return to breastfeeding after exposure to potassium iodide within approximately 24-48 hours.

Iodide salts are known to be secreted into milk in high concentrations.[2,3] Milk/plasma ratios as high at 23 have been reported. Iodides are sequestered in the thyroid gland at high levels and can potentially cause severe thyroid depression in a breastfed infant.[1] Use with extreme caution if at all. Combined with the fact that it is a poor expectorant and that it is concentrated in breastmilk, it is not recommended in breastfeeding mothers. However, following treatment of thyroid storm, mothers should pump and discard milk for at least 24-48 hours.

Pregnancy Risk Category: D

Lactation Risk Category: L4

Adult Concerns: Thyroid depression, goiter, GI distress, rash, GI bleeding, fever, weakness.

Pediatric Concerns: Thyroid suppression may occur. Do not use doses higher than RDA.

Drug Interactions:

Relative Infant Dose:

Adult Dose: 5-10 mg daily.

Alternatives:

T ½	= 6 hours (blood)	M/P	= 23
PHL	=	PB	–
Tmax	=	Oral	= Complete
MW	= 166	pKa	=
Vd	=		

References:

1. KKramer GH, Hauck BM, Chamberlain MJ. Biological half-life of iodine in adults with intact thyroid function and in athyreotic persons. Radiat Prot Dosimetry.2002;102 (2):129-35. PubMed PMID: 12408489
2. Delange F, Chanoine JP, Abrassart C, Bourdoux P. Topical iodine, breastfeeding, and neonatal hypothyroidism. Arch Dis Child 1988; 63 (1):106-107.
3. Postellon DC, Aronow R. Iodine in mother's milk. JAMA 1982; 247 (4):463.

POVIDONE IODIDE   L4

Trade: Betadine, Iodex, Operand, Pharmadine
Other Trades: Betadine, Proviodine, Isodine, Viodine, Minidine
Uses: Special chelated iodine antiseptic
AAP: Maternal Medication Usually Compatible with Breastfeeding

Povidone iodide is a chelated form of iodine. It is primarily used as an antiseptic and antimicrobial. When placed on the adult skin, very little is absorbed. When used intravaginally, significant and increased plasma levels of iodine have been documented. In a study of 62 pregnant women who used povidone-iodine douches, significant increases in plasma iodine were noted, and a seven fold increase in fetal thyroid iodine content was reported.[1] Topical application to infants has resulted in significant absorption through the skin. Once plasma levels are attained in the mother, iodide rapidly sequester in human milk at high milk/plasma ratios.[2,3] See potassium iodide. High oral iodine intake in mothers is documented to produce thyroid suppression in breastfed infants.[2] Use with extreme caution or not at all. Repeated use of povidone iodide is not recommended in nursing mothers or their infants.

Pregnancy Risk Category: D

Lactation Risk Category: L4

Adult Concerns: Iodine toxicity, hypothyroidism, goiter, neutropenia.

Pediatric Concerns: Transfer of absorbed iodine could occur leading to neonatal thyroid suppression. Avoid if possible.

Drug Interactions:

Relative Infant Dose:

Adult Dose:

Alternatives:

T ½	=	M/P	= >23
PHL	=	PB	=
Tmax	=	Oral	= Complete
MW	=	pKa	=
Vd	=		

References:
1. Mahillon I, Peers W, Bourdoux P, Ermans AM, Delange F. Effect of vaginal douching with povidone-iodine during early pregnancy on the iodine supply to mother and fetus. Biol Neonate 1989; 56 (4):210-217.
2. Delange F, Chanoine JP, Abrassart C, Bourdoux P. Topical iodine, breastfeeding, and neonatal hypothyroidism. Arch Dis Child 1988; 63 (1):106-107.
3. Postellon DC, Aronow R. Iodine in mother's milk. JAMA 1982; 247 (4):463.

PRAMIPEXOLE   L4

Trade: Mirapex
Other Trades: Mirepexin
Uses: Dopamine agonist for Parkinson's disease
AAP: Not reviewed

Pramipexole is a nonergot dopamine agonist for use in treating the symptoms of Parkinson's disease and restless leg syndrome.[1] While rodent studies showed rather high levels in milk, rats studies simply don't correlate with humans. No human studies are available concerning levels in milk. Regardless, pramipexole is known to reduce the secretion of prolactin, and it is possible that it could significantly reduce milk synthesis. This product should probably not be used in breastfeeding mothers.

Pregnancy Risk Category: C

Lactation Risk Category: L4

Adult Concerns: Adverse events include falling asleep during the day. Such events may occur without warning. Other adverse effects include dizziness, insomnia, extrapyramidal symptoms, headache, nausea, vomiting, constipation, dry mouth, postural hypotension and confusion.

Pediatric Concerns: None reported via milk, but inhibition of prolactin secretion could severely reduce milk production.

Drug Interactions: Cimetidine produced a 50% increase in pramipexole levels. Dopamine antagonists such as metoclopramide, domperidone, and others, may significantly interfere with the activity of pramipexole.

Relative Infant Dose:

Adult Dose: 1.5-4.5 mg/day

Alternatives:

T ½	= 8 hours	M/P	=
PHL	=	PB	= 15%
Tmax	= 2 hours	Oral	= >90%
MW	= 302	pKa	=
Vd	= 7.14		

References:
1. Pharmaceutical Manufacturers prescribing information, 2003.

PRAMLINTIDE ACETATE   L3

Trade: Symlin
Other Trades:
Uses: Antihyperglycemic agent for diabetics
AAP: Not reviewed

Symlin (pramlintide acetate) is an antihyperglycemic agent used in diabetics. Pramlintide is a synthetic analog of human amylin, a naturally occurring peptide created by the pancreatic beta cells that contributes to glucose control during the postprandial period. Amylin is co-located in beta cells and is co-secreted with insulin in response to food intake. Amylin has a number of biologic functions including: slowing gastric emptying, and suppressing glucagon secretion, which reduces glucose output by the liver. It also reduces appetite by action in the CNS. In diabetics both insulin and amylin secretion are reduced in response to food. Pramlintide is a small peptide with a MW of 3949 daltons and is administered subcutaneously. Although we do not have data on its transfer to milk, this product is probably far too large to enter milk in clinically relevant amounts after the first 3-7 days postpartum. Being a small peptide, it is also unlikely to be absorbed orally in infants. Even when injected subcutaneously it is only 30-40% bioavailable. I do not think it would be contraindicated in breastfeeding infants, but we have no data yet and some caution is certainly recommended.

Pregnancy Risk Category: C

Lactation Risk Category: L3 during first week postpartum.
                                L2 after first week postpartum.

Adult Concerns: Pramlintide in combination with insulin may lead to hypoglycemia. Nausea, headache, anorexia, vomiting, dizziness have been reported.

Pediatric Concerns: None reported via milk. Unlikely to enter milk or be orally bioavailable in the infant.

Drug Interactions: May affect the absorption of many drugs due to its affect on gastric emptying.

Relative Infant Dose:

Adult Dose: Highly variable, consult prescribing information.

Alternatives:

T ½	= 48 minutes	M/P	=
PHL	=	PB	=
Tmax	= 20 minutes	Oral	= 40% SC
MW	= 3949	pKa	=
Vd	=		

References:
1.   Pharmaceutical Manufacturers Prescribing Information. 2005.

PRAVASTATIN | L3

Trade: Pravachol
Other Trades: Pravachol, Lipostat
Uses: Lowers blood cholesterol
AAP: Not reviewed

Pravastatin belongs to the HMG-CoA reductase family of cholesterol lowering drugs.[1] Small amounts are believed to be secreted into human milk but the levels were unreported. The effect on an infant is unknown, but it could reduce cholesterol synthesis. Atherosclerosis is a chronic process and discontinuation of lipid-lowering drugs during pregnancy and lactation should have little to no impact on the outcome of long-term therapy of primary hypercholesterolemia. Cholesterol and other products of cholesterol biosynthesis are essential components for fetal and neonatal development and the use of cholesterol-lowering drugs would not be advisable under any circumstances.

Pregnancy Risk Category: X

Lactation Risk Category: L3

Adult Concerns: Leukopenia, elevated liver enzymes, depression, neuropathy, etc.

Pediatric Concerns: None reported via milk but studies are limited.

Drug Interactions: The anticoagulant effect of warfarin may be increased. Use with bile acid sequestrants may reduce pravastatin bioavailability by 50%. May increased toxicities of cyclosporine. Concurrent use of niacin may increase risk of severe myopathy.

Relative Infant Dose:

Adult Dose: 10-20 mg daily.

Alternatives:

T ½	= 77 hours	M/P	=
PHL	=	PB	= 50%
Tmax	= 1-1.5 hours	Oral	= 17%
MW	= 446	pKa	=
Vd	=		

References:
1. Pharmaceutical Manufacturer Prescribing Information.

PRAZEPAM   L3

Trade: Centrax
Other Trades: Centrax
Uses: Antianxiety agent
AAP: Drugs whose effect on nursing infants is unknown but may be of concern

Prazepam is a typical benzodiazepine that belongs to Valium family. It has a long half-life in adults. Peak plasma level occurs 6 hours post-dose.[1] An active metabolite with a longer half-life is produced. No data is available on transfer into human milk. Most benzodiazepines have high milk/plasma ratios and transfer into milk readily. Observe infant closely for sedation. See diazepam.

Pregnancy Risk Category: D

Lactation Risk Category: L3

Adult Concerns: Sedation, hypotension, depression.

Pediatric Concerns: None reported via milk, but benzodiazepines may induce sedation in breastfed infants.

Drug Interactions: May decrease effect of levodopa. May produce increased toxicity when used with other CNS depressants, disulfiram, cimetidine, anticoagulants, and digoxin.

Relative Infant Dose:

Adult Dose: 10 mg TID

Alternatives: Lorazepam, Alprazolam

T ½	= 30-100 hours	M/P	=
PHL	=	PB	= >70%
Tmax	= 6 hours	Oral	= Complete
MW	= 325	pKa	= 2.7
Vd	= 12-14		

References:
1. Drug Facts and Comparisons 1995 ed. ed. St. Louis: 1995.

PRAZIQUANTEL   L2

Trade: Biltricide
Other Trades: Biltricide
Uses: Anthelmintic
AAP: Not reviewed

Praziquantel is a trematodicide used for treatment of schistosome infections and infestations of liver flukes. In a study of 10 women who received 1) a single dose of 50 mg/kg; or 2) 20 mg/kg three times daily, milk and plasma levels were determined at multiple time intervals over the next 32 hours.[1] In group one the average milk concentration was 0.190mg/L. In group 2 the average milk concentration was 0.198 mg/L. Throughout the duration of this study, the infants in group 1 ingested 27.4 µg and those in group 2 ingested 25.6 µg of praziquantel. On average, the plasma concentrations were four times higher than milk concentrations. Using this data, the relative infant dose would be approximately 0.05% of the maternal dose in both groups. These values are probably too low to harm an infant.

Pregnancy Risk Category: B

Lactation Risk Category: L2

Adult Concerns: Fever, dizziness, headache, abdominal pain, drowsiness and malaise.

Pediatric Concerns: None reported via milk.

Drug Interactions: May increase levels of albendazole with admixed. Carbamazine, dexamethasone, and phenytoin may decrease praziquantel AUC significantly. Cimetidine may increase plasma levels by 300%.

Relative Infant Dose: 0.1%

Adult Dose: 10-25 mg/kg BID-TID X 1 day

Alternatives:

T ½	= 0.8-3 hours	M/P	= 0.25%
PHL	=	PB	= 80%
Tmax	= 1-3 hours	Oral	= 80%
MW	= 312	pKa	=
Vd	=		

References:
1. Leopold G, Ungethum W, Groll E, Diekmann HW, Nowak H, Wegner DH. Clinical pharmacology in normal volunteers of praziquantel, a new

drug against schistosomes and cestodes. An example of a complex study covering both tolerance and pharmacokinetics. Eur J Clin Pharmacol 1978; 14 (4):281-291.

PRAZOSIN   L4

Trade: Minipress
Other Trades: Minipress, Apo-Prazo, Novo-Prazin, Pressin, Hypovasl
Uses: Strong antihypertensive
AAP: Not reviewed

Prazosin is a selective alpha-1-adrenergic antagonist used to control hypertension. It is structurally similar to doxazosin and terazosin.[1,2] Antihypertensives may reduce breastmilk production and prazosin may do likewise. Others in this family (doxazosin) are known to concentrate in milk. Exercise extreme caution when administering to nursing mothers.

Pregnancy Risk Category: C

Lactation Risk Category: L4

Adult Concerns: Leukopenia, tachycardia, hypotension, dizziness, fainting, headache, edema, diarrhea, urinary frequency.

Pediatric Concerns: None reported via milk, but some in this family are concentrated in milk. Observe extreme caution.

Drug Interactions: Beta blockers may enhance acute postural hypotensive reaction. The antihypertensive action of prazosin may be decreased by NSAIDs. Verapamil appears to increase serum prazosin levels. The antihypertensive effect of clonidine may be decreased when used with Prazosin.

Relative Infant Dose:

Adult Dose: 3-7.5 mg BID

Alternatives:

T ½	= 2-3 hours	M/P	=
PHL	=	PB	= 97%
Tmax	= 2-3 hours	Oral	=
MW	= 383	pKa	= 6.5
Vd	= 0.6		

References:
1. Drug Facts and Comparisons 2010 ed. ed. St. Louis: 2010.
2. Pharmaceutical Manufacturer Prescribing Information. 1993, 1994.

PREDNICARBATE   L3

Trade: Dermatop
Other Trades:
Uses: High potency steroid ointment
AAP: Not reviewed

Prednicarbate is a high potency steroid ointment. Its absorption via skin surfaces is exceedingly low, even in infants. Its oral absorption is not reported but would probably be equivalent to prednisolone, or high. If recommended for topical application on the nipple, other less potent steroids should be suggested, including hydrocortisone or triamcinolone. If applied to the nipple, only extremely small amounts should be applied. See appendix C for other steroid ointment choices.

Pregnancy Risk Category: C

Lactation Risk Category: L3

Adult Concerns: Symptoms of adrenal steroid suppression, fluid retention, gastric erosions.

Pediatric Concerns: None reported via milk.

Drug Interactions:

Relative Infant Dose:

Adult Dose:

Alternatives:

T ½	=	M/P	=
PHL	=	PB	=
Tmax	=	Oral	=
MW	= 488	pKa	=
Vd	=		

References:

PREDNISONE-PREDNISOLONE | L2

Trade: Prednisone, Prednisolone
Other Trades:
Uses: Steroid, corticosteroid
AAP: Maternal Medication Usually Compatible with Breastfeeding

Small amounts of most corticosteroids are secreted into breastmilk. Following a 10 mg oral dose of prednisone, peak milk levels of prednisolone and prednisone were 1.6 µg/L and 2.67 µg/L, respectively.[1] In a group of 10 women who received 10-80 mg/d prednisolone, the milk levels were only 5-25% of the maternal serum levels.[2]

In one patient who received 80 mg/day prednisolone, the C_{max} at 1 hour was 317 µg/L. The AUC average milk concentration in this mother was 156 µg/L over 6 hours.[2] This is significantly less than 2% of the weight-normalized maternal dose. Because this last estimate was only determined over 6 hours and this dose was administered once each 24 hours, the total daily estimate would be much less than the 2% estimate.

In another study of a single patient who received 120 mg prednisone/day, the total combined steroid levels (prednisone + prednisolone) peaked at 2 hours.[3] The peak level of combined steroid was 627 µg/L. Assuming the infant received 120 mL of milk every 4 hours, the total possible ingestion would only be 47 µg/day.

In a group of 7 women who received radioactive labeled prednisolone 5 mg, the total recovery per liter of milk during the 48 hours after the dose was 0.14%.[4]

In small doses, most steroids are certainly not contraindicated in nursing mothers. Whenever possible use low-dose alternatives such as aerosols or inhalers. Following administration, wait at least 4 hours if possible prior to feeding infant to reduce exposure. With high doses (>40 mg/day), particularly for long periods, steroids could potentially produce problems in infant growth and development, although we have absolutely no data in this area, or which doses would pose problems. Brief applications of high dose steroids are probably not contraindicated as the overall exposure is low. With prolonged high dose therapy, the infant should be closely monitored for growth and development.

Pregnancy Risk Category: C

Lactation Risk Category: L2

Adult Concerns: Gastric distress, gastric ulceration, glaucoma, thinning skin.

Pediatric Concerns: None reported via milk. Limit degree and duration of exposure if possible. Use inhaled or intranasal steroids to reduce exposure. Short-term use is safe.

Drug Interactions: Decreased effect when used with barbiturates, phenytoin, rifampin.

Relative Infant Dose: 1.8% - 5.3%

Adult Dose: 5-120 mg/day

Alternatives:

T ½	= 24+ hours	M/P	= 0.25
PHL	=	PB	= 75%
Tmax	= 1 hour (milk)	Oral	= Complete
MW	= 346	pKa	=
Vd	=		

References:
1. Katz FH, Duncan BR. Letter: Entry of prednisone into human milk. N Engl J Med 1975; 293 (22):1154.
2. Ost L, Wettrell G, Bjorkhem I, Rane A. Prednisolone excretion in human milk. J Pediatr 1985; 106 (6):1008-1011.
3. Berlin CM, Kaiser DG, Demmers L. Excretion of prednisone and prednisolone in human milk. Pharmacologist 1979; 21:264.
4. McKenzie SA, Selley JA, Agnew JE. Secretion of prednisolone into breast milk. Arch Dis Child 1975; 50 (11):894-896.

PREGABALIN   L3

Trade: Lyrica
Other Trades: Lyrica
Uses: Analgesic
AAP: Not reviewed

Pregabalin binds to a subunit of voltage gated calcium channels in central nervous system tissues reducing the calcium-dependant release of several neurotransmitters. It is used in the management of neuropathic pain associated with diabetic peripheral neuropathy, and postherpetic neuralgia.[1] There are no data available on the transfer of pregabalin into human milk. However, due to the kinetics of the drug, its passage into the milk compartment is probable, and its oral bioavailability to the infant would be high. Therefore, nursing mothers should use caution taking pregabalin while nursing.

Pregnancy Risk Category: C

Lactation Risk Category: L3

Adult Concerns: Adverse reactions include asthenia, dry mouth, edema, dizziness, somnolence, and constipation.

Pediatric Concerns: No data available in infants.

Drug Interactions: Pregabalin should not be used with CNS depressants or thiazolidinediones.

Relative Infant Dose:

Adult Dose: 150-600 mg/day in divided doses

Alternatives:

T ½	= 6 hours	M/P	=
PHL	=	PB	=
Tmax	= 1.5 hours	Oral	= 90%
MW	= 159	pKa	= 10.6
Vd	= 0.5		

References:
1.   Pharmaceutical Manufacturer Prescribing Information.

PRIMAQUINE PHOSPHATE   L3

Trade:
Other Trades: Primacin, Primaquine phosphate,
Uses: Antimalarial
AAP: Not reviewed

Primaquine is a typical antimalarial medication that is primarily used as chemoprophylaxis after the patient has returned from the region of exposure with the intention of preventing relapses of plasmodium vivax and or ovale. It is used in pediatric patients at a dose of 0.3 mg/kg/day for 14 days.[1-3] No data are available on its transfer into human milk. Maternal plasma levels are rather low, only 53-107 nanogram/mL, suggesting that milk levels might be rather low as well.

Pregnancy Risk Category: C

Lactation Risk Category: L3

Adult Concerns: Blood dyscrasias including granulocytopenia, anemia, leukocytosis, methemoglobinemia. Arrhythmia, hypertension, abdominal pain, cramps, visual (ocular) disturbances.

Pediatric Concerns: None reported from milk.

Drug Interactions: Elevated risk of blood dyscrasias with aurothioglucose. May reduce plasma levels of oral contraceptives.

Relative Infant Dose:

Adult Dose: 15 mg daily

Alternatives:

T ½	= 4-7 hours	M/P	=
PHL	=	PB	=
Tmax	= 1-2 hours	Oral	= 96%
MW	= 259	pKa	=
Vd	=		

References:
1. Mihaly GW, Ward SA, Edwards G, Orme ML, Breckenridge AM. Pharmacokinetics of primaquine in man: identification of the carboxylic acid derivative as a major plasma metabolite. Br J Clin Pharmacol 1984; 17 (4):441-446.
2. Mihaly GW, Ward SA, Edwards G, Nicholl DD, Orme ML, Breckenridge AM. Pharmacokinetics of primaquine in man. I. Studies of the absolute bioavailability and effects of dose size. Br J Clin Pharmacol 1985; 19 (6):745-750.
3. Bhatia SC, Saraph YS, Revankar SN, Doshi KJ, Bharucha ED, Desai ND, Vaidya AB, Subrahmanyam D, Gupta KC, Satoskar RS. Pharmacokinetics of primaquine in patients with P. vivax malaria. Eur J Clin Pharmacol 1986; 31 (2):205-210.

PRIMIDONE   L3

Trade: Mysoline
Other Trades: Apo-Primidone, Mysoline, Sertan, Misolyne
Uses: Anticonvulsant
AAP: Drugs associated with significant side effects and should be given with caution

Primidone is metabolized in adults to several derivatives including phenobarbital. After chronic therapy, levels of phenobarbital rise to a therapeutic range. Primidone is metabolized in adults to several derivatives including phenobarbital. After chronic therapy, levels of phenobarbital rise to a therapeutic range. Hence, problems for the infant would not only include primidone but, subsequently, phenobarbital.

In one study of 2 women receiving primidone, the steady-state concentrations of primidone in neonatal serum via ingestion of breastmilk were 0.7 and 2.5 µg/mL.[1] The steady-state phenobarbital levels in neonatal serum were between 2.0 to 13.0 µg/mL. The calculated dose of phenobarbital per day received by each infant ranged from 1.8 to 8.9 mg/day. Some sedation has been reported, particularly during the neonatal period.

In another group of 4 women receiving 7.3 mg/kg/d primidone, levels in milk averaged 4.2 mg/L.[2] In another patient receiving 750 mg/d and valproic acid 2.4 g/d, breastmilk levels of primidone averaged 6 mg/L.[3]

Pregnancy Risk Category: D

Lactation Risk Category: L3

Adult Concerns: Sedation, apnea, reduced suckling.

Pediatric Concerns: Some sedation, during neonatal period.

Drug Interactions: Acetazolamide may decrease primidone plasma levels. Co-administration of carbamazepine may lower primidone and phenobarbital concentrations and elevate carbamazepine concentrations. Use of phenytoin may reduce primidone concentrations. Primidone concentrations may be increased when used with isoniazid. The clearance of primidone may be decreased with nicotinamide.

Relative Infant Dose: 8.4% - 8.6%

Adult Dose: 250 mg TID

Alternatives:

T ½	= 10-21 hours (primidone)	M/P	= 0.72
PHL	=	PB	= <20%
Tmax	= 0.5-5 hours	Oral	= 90%
MW	= 218	pKa	=
Vd	= 0.5-1.0		

References:
1. Kuhnz W, Koch S, Helge H, Nau H. Primidone and phenobarbital during lactation period in epileptic women: total and free drug serum levels in the nursed infants and their effects on neonatal behavior. Dev Pharmacol Ther 1988; 11 (3):147-154.
2. Nau H, Rating D, Hauser I et al. Placental transfer and pharmacokinetics of primidone and its metabolites phenobarbital, PEMA, and hydroxyphenobarbital in neonates and infants of epileptic mothers. Eur J Clin Pharmacol. 1980;18:31-42.

3. Espir MLE, Benton P, Will E et al. Sodium valproate - some clinical and pharmacological aspects. In: Legg NJ, ed. Clinical and pharmacological aspects of sodium valproate in the treatment of epilepsy: proceedings of a symposium. 1976;145-51.

PROBENECID   L2

Trade: Benemid, Benecid, Probanalan, Probenecid, Proben,
            Apurina, Uricosid
Other Trades:
Uses: Used in treatment of gout
AAP: Not reviewed

Probenecid is a uricosuric agent which accelerates the urinary excretion of uric acid by inhibiting the reabsorption of uric acid in the proximal convoluted tubule in the kidney. Hence it dramatically reduces plasma uric acid. It is also used to prevent the elimination of various penicillins and cephalosporins and is used to prolong their elimination half-lives.

In a study of a single patient consuming 500 mg four times daily, milk levels of probenecid averaged 964 µg/L corresponding to an absolute dose of 145 µg/kg/day and a relative infant dose of 0.7%.[1] In this case of a mother receiving both probenecid and cephalexin, the infant suffered adverse effects (diarrhea). This complication was probably due to prolonged and increased exposure to cephalexin induced by small levels of probenecid.

Pregnancy Risk Category:

Lactation Risk Category: L2

Adult Concerns: Adverse reactions include, headache, dizziness, hepatic necrosis, vomiting, nausea, anorexia and sore gums. Nephrotic syndrome may occur with presence of uric acid stones, renal colic and urinary frequency. Anaphylaxis, fever, urticaria, pruritus, aplastic anemia, leukopenia, neutropenia, and thrombocytopenia have been reported.

Pediatric Concerns: Although milk levels are quite low, the renal excretion of many drugs is significantly impeded by probenecid. Thus when used in combination with other medications, the infant may have complications from altered half-lives of other medications. Observe closely for drug-drug interactions.

Drug Interactions: Profound increases in plasma levels and prolonged half-lives of penicillin and cephalosporin products when probenecid administered. Salicylates antagonized the uricosuric effect of probenecid. Probenecid produces an modest increase in free sulfonamide plasma concentrations but a significant increase in total sulfonamide plasma levels. Probenecid may prolong or enhance the action of oral sulfonylureas and thereby increase the risk of hypoglycemia. Probenecid has been shown to more than double the plasma levels of oseltamivir.

It has been reported that patients receiving probenecid require significantly less thiopental for induction of anesthesia. In addition, ketamine and thiopental anesthesia may be prolonged.

The concomitant use of probenecid increases the mean plasma half-life of a number of drugs, including: indomethacin, acetaminophen, naproxen, ketoprofen, meclofenamate, lorazepan, and rifampin.

In animals, probenecid may dramatically increase plasma concentrations of methotrexate.

Relative Infant Dose: 0.7%

Adult Dose: 500 mg four times daily or less.

Alternatives:

T ½	= 6-12 hours	M/P	= 0.03
PHL	=	PB	= 75-95%
Tmax	=	Oral	= Complete
MW	= 285	pKa	=
Vd	=		

References:
1.   Ilett KF, Hackett LP, Ingle B, Bretz PJ. Transfer of probenecid and cephalexin into breast milk. Ann Pharmacother 2006 May;40 (5):986-9.

PROCAINAMIDE   L3

Trade: Pronestyl, Procan
Other Trades: Pronestyl, Procan SR, Apo-Procainamide
Uses: Antiarrhythmic
AAP: Maternal Medication Usually Compatible with Breastfeeding

Procainamide is an antiarrhythmic agent. Procainamide and its active metabolite are secreted into breastmilk in moderate concentrations. In one patient receiving 500 mg four times daily, the breast milk levels of procainamide at 0, 3, 6, 9, and 12 hours were 5.3, 3.9, 10.2, 4.8, and 2.6 mg/L respectively.[1] The milk/serum ratio varied from 1.0 at 12 hours to 7.3 at 6 hours post-dose (mean= 4.3). The milk levels averaged 5.4 mg/L for parent drug and 3.5 mg/L for metabolite. Although levels in milk are still too small to provide significant blood levels in an infant, use with caution.

Pregnancy Risk Category: C

Lactation Risk Category: L3

Adult Concerns: Nausea, vomiting, liver toxicity, blood dyscrasias, hypotension,

Pediatric Concerns: None reported via milk. Observe for liver toxicity, hypotension, but very unlikely.

Drug Interactions: Propranolol may increase procainamide serum levels. Cimetidine and ranitidine appear to increase bioavailability of procainamide. Use with lidocaine may increase cardio depressant action of procainamide.

Relative Infant Dose: 5.4%

Adult Dose: 500-1000 mg every 4-6 hours

Alternatives:

T ½	= 3.0 hours	M/P	= 1-7.3
PHL	= 13.5 hours (neonate)	PB	= 16%
Tmax	= 0.75-2.5 hours	Oral	= 75-90%
MW	= 271	pKa	= 9.2
Vd	= 3.3-4.8		

References:
1. Pittard WB, III, Glazier H. Procainamide excretion in human milk. J Pediatr 1983; 102 (4):631-633.

PROCAINE HCL

L3

Trade: Novocain
Other Trades:
Uses: Local anesthetic
AAP: Not reviewed

Procaine is an ester-type local anesthetic with low potential for systemic toxicity and short duration of action.[1] Procaine is generally used for infiltration or local anesthesia, peripheral nerve block, or rarely, spinal anesthesia. Procaine is rapidly metabolized by plasma pseudocholinesterase to p-aminobenzoic acid.[2] No data are available on its transfer to human milk, but it is unlikely. Most other local anesthetics (see bupivacaine, lidocaine) penetrate milk only poorly and it is likely that procaine, due to its brief plasma half-life, would produce even lower milk levels. Due to its ester bond, it would be poorly bioavailable.

Pregnancy Risk Category: C

Lactation Risk Category: L3

Adult Concerns: High plasma concentrations of PROCAINE due to excessive dosage, orinadvertent intravascular injection may result in systemic adverse effects involving the cardiovascular and central nervous systems including nervousness, drowsiness, or blurred vision. Allergic reactions due to the p-aminobenzoic acid metabolite have been reported and may produce urticaria and edema.

Pediatric Concerns: None reported via milk.

Drug Interactions:

Relative Infant Dose:

Adult Dose: 350-600 mg X 1

Alternatives:

T ½	= 7.7 minutes	M/P	=
PHL	=	PB	= 5.8%
Tmax	=	Oral	= Poor
MW	= 236	pKa	= 9.1
Vd	=		

References:
1.   Drug Facts and Comparisons 1999 ed. ed. St. Louis: 1999.
2.   McEvoy GE. (ed): AFHS Drug Information. New York, NY: 2009.

PROCHLORPERAZINE | L3

Trade: Compazine
Other Trades: Prorazin, Stemetil, Nu-Prochlor, Buccastem
Uses: Antiemetic, tranquilizer-sedative
AAP: Not reviewed

Prochlorperazine is a phenothiazine primarily used as an antiemetic in adults and pediatric patients.[1] There are no data yet concerning breastmilk levels but other phenothiazine derivatives enter milk in small amounts. Because infants are extremely hypersensitive to these compounds, I suggest caution in younger infants. This product may also increase prolactin levels.[2] See promethazine as a safer alternative, although neonatal apnea is a consistent problem with this family of drugs. Use with extreme caution in infants subject to apnea.

Pregnancy Risk Category: C

Lactation Risk Category: L3

Adult Concerns: Sedation, extrapyramidal effects, seizures, weight gain, liver toxicity.

Pediatric Concerns: None reported via milk, but caution is recommended.

Drug Interactions: May have increased toxicity when used with other CNS depressants, anticonvulsants. Epinephrine may cause hypotension.

Relative Infant Dose:

Adult Dose: 5-10 mg TID-QID

Alternatives: Promethazine

T ½	= 10-20 hours	M/P	=
PHL	=	PB	= 90%
Tmax	= 3.4-9.9 (oral)	Oral	= Complete
MW	= 374	pKa	=
Vd	=		

References:
1. Drug Facts and Comparisons 1995 ed. ed. St. Louis: 1995.
2. McEvoy GE. (ed):AFHS Drug Information. New York, NY: 1995.

PROGESTERONE   L3

Trade: Crinone, Prometrium, Progesterone Vaginal Ring
Other Trades: Crinone, Gesterol, Cyclogest, Gestone
Uses: Progestational agent
AAP: Maternal Medication Usually Compatible with Breastfeeding

Progesterone is a naturally occurring steroid (progestin) that is secreted by the ovary, placenta, and adrenal gland. Oral administration is hampered by rapid and extensive intestinal and liver metabolism leading to poorly sustained serum concentrations and poor bioavailability.[1] As progesterone is virtually unabsorbed orally, the vaginal route has become the most established way to deliver natural progesterone because it is easily administered, avoids liver first-pass metabolism, and has no systemic side-effects. Absorption through the vagina produces higher uterine levels and is called the 'uterine first-pass effect'. A study by Levine[2] suggests the area under the curve is about 38 times less with oral administration as with progesterone vaginal gel (Crinone). Thus fewer systemic effects are noted.

With the use of progesterone in breastfeeding mothers, two principles are of paramount interest. What effect does it have on milk production and the components of milk? Does it transfer into milk in high enough levels to affect the infant directly? In general, there is significant confusion in the literature as to the effect of progestins on milk composition, but the compositional changes do not appear major, volume is normal or higher, and some authors report minor changes in lipid and protein content.[3-5] However, the majority of the studies are with other progestins (e.g. medroxyprogesterone). Shaaban studied the effect of an intravaginal progesterone ring (10 mg/d) in 120 women and found no changes in growth and development of the infant or breastfeeding performance of the study participants.[6] The author suggests the ring adds a measure of safety because the amount of steroid present in milk would be effectively absorbed from the infant's gut. Another new study also suggests no impact on breastfeeding from the intravaginal progesterone ring.[7]

The effect of progestins on milk production is poorly studied. Early postpartum, while progestin receptors are still present in the breast, administering progestins may actually suppress milk production just as it does in the pregnant women. This has been seen occasionally in patients early postpartum. Several days to a week later, most progestin receptors disappear from the lactocyte and breast tissues become relatively immune to the effects of progestins. Thus it is advisable to wait as long as possible postpartum prior to instituting therapy with progesterone to avoid reducing the milk supply.

The direct effect of progesterone therapy on the nursing infant is generally unknown, but it is believed minimal to none as natural progesterone is poorly bioavailable to the infant via milk. Several cases of gynecomastia in infants have been reported but are extremely rare.

Pregnancy Risk Category:

Lactation Risk Category: L3

Adult Concerns: Bloating, cramps, pain, dizziness, headache, nausea, breast pain, constipation, diarrhea, nausea, somnolence, breast enlargement.

Pediatric Concerns: None reported, not bioavailable.

Drug Interactions: May increase estrogen levels when co-administered with estrogen-containing tablets. Increased doxorubicin-induced neutropenia when co-administered. Ketoconazole may increase levels of progesterone.

Relative Infant Dose:

Adult Dose: 90 mg daily

Alternatives:

T ½	= 13-18 hours	M/P	=
PHL	=	PB	= 99%
Tmax	= 6 hours	Oral	= Low
MW	= 314	pKa	=
Vd	=		

References:

1. Levy T, Gurevitch S, Bar-Hava I, Ashkenazi J, Magazanik A, Homburg R, Orvieto R, Ben Rafael Z. Pharmacokinetics of natural progesterone administered in the form of a vaginal tablet. Hum Reprod 1999; 14 (3):606-610.
2. Naqvi HM, Baseer A. Milk composition changes--a simple and non-invasive method of detecting ovulation in lactating women. J Pak Med Assoc 2001; 51 (3):112-115.
3. Rodriguez-Palmero M, Koletzko B, Kunz C, Jensen R. Nutritional and biochemical properties of human milk: II. Lipids, micronutrients, and bioactive factors. Clin Perinatol 1999; 26 (2):335-359.
4. Costa TH, Dorea JG. Concentration of fat, protein, lactose and energy in milk of mothers using hormonal contraceptives. Ann Trop Paediatr 1992; 12 (2):203-209.
5. Sas M, Gellen JJ, Dusitsin N, Tunkeyoon M, Chalapati S, Crawford MA, Drury PJ, Lenihan T, Ayeni O, Pinol A. An investigation on the influence of steroidal contraceptives on milk lipid and fatty acids in Hungary

and Thailand. WHO Special Programme of Research, Development and Research Training in Human Reproduction. Task Force on oral contraceptives. Contracep 1986; 33 (2):159-178.

6.   Shaaban MM. Contraception with progestogens and progesterone during lactation. J Steroid Biochem Mol Biol 1991; 40 (4-6):705-710.

7.   Massai R, Quinteros E, Reyes MV, Caviedes R, Zepeda A, Montero JC, et al. Extended use of a progesterone-releasing vaginal ring in nursing women: a phase II clinical trial. Contracep 2005 Nov;72 (5):352-7.

PROMETHAZINE   L2

Trade: Phenergan, Promethegan

Other Trades: Histanil, Phenergan, PMS Promethazine, Avomine

Uses: Phenothiazine used as antihistamine

AAP: Not reviewed

Promethazine is a phenothiazine that is primarily used for nausea, vomiting, and motion sickness. It has been used safely for many years in adult and pediatric patients for vomiting, particularly associated with pregnancy. No data are available on the transfer of promethazine into milk, but small amounts probably do transfer. However, this product has been safely used in many pediatric conditions, and it is unlikely to product untoward effects in older infants and children. Observe for sedation and apnea, particularly in younger infants. There are numerous suggestions that his product may increase the risk of SIDS. Do not use in infants subject to apnea. Long term followup (6 years) has found no untoward effects on development.[1]

Pregnancy Risk Category: C

Lactation Risk Category: L2

Adult Concerns: Sedation, apnea, extrapyramidal symptoms.

Pediatric Concerns: None reported via breastmilk, but promethazine has been implicated in SIDS. Some caution is recommended.

Drug Interactions: Epinephrine may cause significant decrease in blood pressure.

Relative Infant Dose:

Adult Dose: 12.5-25 mg every 4-6 hours

Alternatives:

T ½	= 12.7 hours	M/P	=
PHL	=	PB	= 76-80%
Tmax	= 2.7	Oral	= 25%
MW	= 284	pKa	= 9.1
Vd	= 9-19		

References:

1. Kris EB. Children born to mothers maintained on pharmacotherapy during pregnancy and postpartum. Recent Adv Biol Psychiatry 1961; 4:180-187.

PROPAFENONE   L2

Trade: Rythmol
Other Trades: Arythmol
Uses: Antiarrhythmic agent
AAP: Not reviewed

Propafenone is a class 1C antiarrhythmic agent with structural similarities to propranolol. In a mother receiving 300 mg three times daily and at 3 days postpartum, maternal serum levels of propafenone and 5-OH-propafenone (active metabolite) were 219 µg/L and 86 µg/L respectively. The breastmilk level of propafenone and 5-OH-propafenone was 32 µg/L and 47 µg/L respectively. The milk/plasma ratios for drug and metabolite were 0.15 and 0.54 respectively. The authors estimate that the daily intake of drug and active metabolite in their infant (3.3 kg) would have been 16 µg and 24 µg per day respectively.

Pregnancy Risk Category: C

Lactation Risk Category: L2

Adult Concerns: Adverse effects include dizziness, unusual taste, first degree AV block, intraventricular conduction delay, nausea and/or vomiting, and constipation. In addition, dyspnea, CHF and proarrhythmia has been reported. Less frequently hepatotoxicity, agranulocytosis, leukopenia, and positive ANA have been reported. Other side effects include sexual dysfunction.

Pediatric Concerns: None reported via milk. Levels are quite low.

Drug Interactions: Increased levels with cimetidine, beta blockers, quinidine, warfarin, cyclosporin and other drugs metabolized by this enzyme.Rifampin may reduce levels of propafenone.

Relative Infant Dose: 0.1%

Adult Dose: 150-225 mg TID

Alternatives:

T ½	= 2-10 hours	M/P	= 0.15
PHL	=	PB	= 85-97%
Tmax	= 2-3 hours	Oral	= 12%
MW	=	pKa	=
Vd	= 4		

References:
1. Libardoni M, Piovan D, Busato E, Padrini R. Transfer of propafenone and 5-OH-propafenone to foetal plasma and maternal milk. Br J Clin Pharmacol 1991; 32 (4):527-528.

PROPOFOL   L2

Trade: Diprivan
Other Trades: Diprivan
Uses: Preanesthetic sedative
AAP: Not reviewed

Propofol is an IV sedative hypnotic agent for induction and maintenance of anesthesia. It is particularly popular in various pediatric procedures. Although the terminal half-life is long, it is rapidly distributed out of the plasma compartment to other peripheral compartments (adipose) so that anesthesia is short (3-10 minutes). Propofol is incredibly lipid soluble. However, only very low concentrations of propofol have been found in breastmilk.

In one study of 4 women who received propofol 2.5 mg/kg IV followed by a continuous infusion, the breastmilk levels at 4 hours ranged from 0.04 to 0.24 mg/L during the induction phase only.[1] Following continued infusion of propofol in some patients at 5 mg/kg/h, milk samples at 4 hours ranged from 0.04 to 0.74 mg/L. The second breastmilk level, obtained 24 hours after delivery, contained only 6% of the 4-hour sample. Similar levels (0.12-0.97 mg/L) were noted by Schmitt in colostrum samples obtained 4-8 hours after induction with propofol.[2] From these data it is apparent that only minimal amounts of propofol are transferred to human milk. No data are available on the oral absorption of propofol. Propofol is rapidly cleared from the neonatal circulation.[1]

Pregnancy Risk Category: B

Lactation Risk Category: L2

Adult Concerns: Sedation, apnea.

Pediatric Concerns: None reported in several studies.

Drug Interactions: Anaphylactoid reactions when used with atracurium. May potentiate the neuromuscular blockade of vecuronium. May be additive with other CNS depressants. Theophylline may antagonize the effect of propofol.

Relative Infant Dose: 4.4%

Adult Dose: 6-12 mg/kg/hour

Alternatives: Midazolam

T ½	= 1-3 days	M/P	=
PHL	=	PB	= 99%
Tmax	= Instant (IV)	Oral	=
MW	= 178	pKa	= 11.0
Vd	= 60		

References:

1. Dailland P, Cockshott ID, Lirzin JD, Jacquinot P, Jorrot JC, Devery J, Harmey JL, Conseiller C. Intravenous propofol during cesarean section: placental transfer, concentrations in breast milk, and neonatal effects. A preliminary study. Anesthesiology 1989; 71 (6):827-834.
2. Schmitt JP, Schwoerer D, Diemunsch P, Gauthier-Lafaye J. [Passage of propofol in the colostrum. Preliminary data]. Ann Fr Anesth Reanim 1987; 6 (4):267-268.

PROPOXYPHENE   L2

Trade: Darvocet N, Propacet, Darvon

Other Trades: Darvon-N, Novo-Propoxyn, Dextropropoxyphene, Capadex, Paradex, Di-Gesic, Doloxene, Progesic

Uses: Mild narcotic analgesic

AAP: Maternal Medication Usually Compatible with Breastfeeding

Propoxyphene is a mild narcotic analgesic similar in efficacy to aspirin. The amount secreted into milk is extremely low and is generally too low to produce effects in infant (<1 mg/day).[1] Maternal plasma levels peak at 2 hours. Propoxyphene is metabolized to norpropoxyphene (which has weaker CNS effects). Adult half-life= 6-12 hours (propoxyphene),

30-36 hours (norpropoxyphene). The milk to plasma ratio averages 0.417 for propoxyphene, and 0.382 for norpropoxyphene.[2] Thus far, no reports of untoward effects in infants have been reported.

Pregnancy Risk Category: C

Lactation Risk Category: L2

Adult Concerns: Nausea, respiratory depression, sedation, agitation, seizures, anemia, liver toxicity, withdrawal symptoms.

Pediatric Concerns: None reported but observe for sedation.

Drug Interactions: Additive sedation may occur when used with CNS depressants such as barbiturates. Carbamazepine levels may be increased. Use with cimetidine may produce CNS toxicity such as confusion, disorientation, apnea, seizures.

Relative Infant Dose:

Adult Dose: 65 mg every 4 hours as needed

Alternatives: Ibuprofen, Acetaminophen

T ½	= 6-12 hours (propoxyphene)	M/P	= 0.41
PHL	=	PB	= 78%
Tmax	= 2 hours	Oral	= Complete
MW	= 339	pKa	= 6.3
Vd	= 12-26		

References:
1. Catz CS, Giacoia GP. Drugs and breast milk. Pediatr Clin North Am 1972; 19 (1):151-166.
2. Kunka RL, Venkataramanan R, Stern RM, Ladick CF. Excretion of propoxyphene and norpropoxyphene in breast milk. Clin Pharmacl Ther 1984; 35 (5):675-680.

PROPRANOLOL   L2

Trade: Inderal
Other Trades: Detensol, Inderal, Novo-Pranol, Deralin,
     Cardinol
Uses: Beta-blocker, antihypertensive
AAP: Maternal Medication Usually Compatible with
     Breastfeeding

Propranolol is a popular beta blocker used in treating hypertension,
cardiac arrhythmia, migraine headache, and numerous other syndromes.
In general, the maternal plasma levels are exceedingly low, hence the
milk levels are low as well. Milk/plasma ratios are generally less than
one. In one study of 3 patients, the average milk concentration was
only 35.4 µg/L after multiple dosing intervals. The milk/plasma ratio
varied from 0.33 to 1.65.[1] Using this data, the authors suggest that an
infant would receive only 70 µg/Liter of milk per day, which is <0.1%
of the maternal dose.

In another study of a patient receiving 20 mg twice daily, milk levels
varied from 4 to 20 µg/L with an estimated average dose to infant of 3
µg/day.[2] In another patient receiving 40 mg four times daily, the peak
concentration occurred at 3 hours after dosing.[3] Milk levels varied
from zero to 9 µg/L.

After a 30 day regimen of 240 mg/day propranolol, the pre-dose and
post dose concentration in breastmilk was 26 and 64 µg/L respectively.[3]
No symptoms or signs of beta blockade were noted in this infant. The
above amounts in milk would likely be clinically insignificant. Long
term exposure has not been studied, and caution is urged. Of the beta
blocker family, propranolol is probably preferred in lactating women.
Use with great caution, if at all, in mothers or infants with asthma.

Pregnancy Risk Category: C

Lactation Risk Category: L2

Adult Concerns: Bradycardia, asthmatic symptoms, hypotension,
sedation, weakness, hypoglycemia. Do not use in asthmatics.

Pediatric Concerns: None reported via breastmilk in numerous
studies. Do not use in mothers breastfeeding infants subject to reactive
airway disease (asthma).

Drug Interactions: Decreased effect when used with aluminum
salts, barbiturates, calcium salts, cholestyramine, NSAIDs, ampicillin,
rifampin, and salicylates. Beta blockers may reduce the effect of oral
sulfonylureas (hypoglycemic agents). Increased toxicity/effect when

used with other antihypertensives, contraceptives, MAO inhibitors, cimetidine, and numerous other products. See drug interaction reference for complete listing.

Relative Infant Dose: 0.3% - 0.5%

Adult Dose: 160-240 mg daily.

Alternatives: Metoprolol

T ½	= 3-5 hours	M/P	= 0.5
PHL	=	PB	= 90%
Tmax	= 60-90 minutes	Oral	= 30%
MW	= 259	pKa	= 9.5
Vd	= 3-5		

References:
1. Smith MT, Livingstone I, Hooper WD, Eadie MJ, Triggs EJ. Propranolol, propranolol glucuronide, and naphthoxylactic acid in breast milk and plasma. Ther Drug Monit 1983; 5 (1):87-93.
2. Taylor EA, Turner P. Anti-hypertensive therapy with propranolol during pregnancy and lactation. Postgrad Med J 1981; 57 (669):427-430.
3. Bauer JH, Pape B, Zajicek J, Groshong T. Propranolol in human plasma and breast milk. Am J Cardiol 1979; 43 (4):860-862.

PROPYLTHIOURACIL   L2

Trade: PTU
Other Trades: Propyl-Thyracil
Uses: Antithyroid
AAP: Maternal Medication Usually Compatible with Breastfeeding

Propylthiouracil reduces the production and secretion of thyroxine by the thyroid gland. Only small amounts are secreted into breastmilk. Reports thus far suggest that levels absorbed by infant are too low to produce side effects.[1] In one study of nine patients given 400 mg doses, mean serum and milk levels were 7.7 mg/L and 0.7 mg/L respectively.[2] No changes in infant thyroid have been reported. PTU is the best of antithyroid medications for use in lactating mothers. Monitor infant thyroid function (T4, TSH) carefully during therapy.

Pregnancy Risk Category: D

Lactation Risk Category: L2

Adult Concerns: Hypothyroidism, liver toxicity, aplastic anemia, anemia.

Pediatric Concerns: None reported, but observed closely for thyroid function.

Drug Interactions: Activity of oral anticoagulants may be potentiated by PTU associated anti-vitamin K activity.

Relative Infant Dose: 1.837% - 1.84%

Adult Dose: 100 mg TID

Alternatives:

T ½	= 1-2 hours	M/P	= 0.1
PHL	=	PB	= 80%
Tmax	= 1-1.5 hours	Oral	= 50-95%
MW	= 170	pKa	=
Vd	=		

References:
1. Cooper DS. Antithyroid drugs: to breast-feed or not to breast-feed. Am J Obstet Gynecol 1987; 157 (2):234-235.
2. Kampmann JP, Johansen K, Hansen JM, Helweg J. Propylthiouracil in human milk. Revision of a dogma. Lancet 1980; 1 (8171):736-737.

PSEUDOEPHEDRINE   L3

Trade: Sudafed, Halofed, Novafed
Other Trades: Eltor, Pseudofrin, Sudafed, Balminil, Contac
Uses: Decongestant
AAP: Maternal Medication Usually Compatible with
Breastfeeding

Pseudoephedrine is an adrenergic compound primarily used as a nasal decongestant. It is secreted into breast milk but in low levels. In a study of 3 lactating mothers who received 60 mg of pseudoephedrine, the milk/plasma ratio was as high as 2.6-3.9.[1] The average pseudoephedrine milk level over 24 hours was 264 µg/L. The calculated dose that would be absorbed by the infant was still very low (0.4 to 0.6% of the maternal dose).

In a study of eight lactating women who received a single 60 mg dose of pseudoephedrine, the 24 hour milk production was reduced by 24% from 784 mL/d in the placebo period to 623 mL/d in the pseudoephedrine period. While this study was done with a single 60 mg dose, if the normal dosing rate of 60 mg four times daily was used, the estimated infant dose of pseudoephedrine would have been 4.3% of the weight-adjusted maternal dose. While these results are preliminary, it is apparent that mothers in late-stage lactation may be more sensitive to pseudoephedrine and have greater loss in milk production. Therefore breastfeeding mothers with poor or marginal milk production should be exceedingly cautious in using pseudoephedrine. While there are anecdotal reports of its use in mothers with engorgement, we do not know if it is effective, or recommend its use for this purpose at this time.

Pregnancy Risk Category: C

Lactation Risk Category: L3 for acute use
                                L4 for chronic use

Adult Concerns: Irritability, agitation, anorexia, stimulation, insomnia, hypertension, tachycardia.

Pediatric Concerns: One case of irritability via milk. Reduced milk production has been reported in late stage lactation. Mothers with marginal production should avoid this medication.

Drug Interactions: May have increased toxicity when used with MAOI.

Relative Infant Dose: 4.7%

Adult Dose: 60 mg every 4-6 hours

Alternatives:

T ½	= <4 hours	M/P	= 2.6-3.3
PHL	=	PB	=
Tmax	= 0.5-1 hours	Oral	= 90%
MW	= 165	pKa	= 9.7
Vd	=		

References:
1. Findlay JW, Butz RF, Sailstad JM, Warren JT, Welch RM. Pseudoephedrine and triprolidine in plasma and breast milk of nursing mothers. Br J Clin Pharmacol 1984; 18 (6):901-906.
2. Aljazaf K, Hale TW, Ilett KF, Hartmann PE, Mitoulas LR, Kristensen JH, Hackett LP. Pseudoephedrine: effects on milk production in women and estimation of infant exposure via breastmilk. Br J Clin Pharmacol 2003; 56 (1):18-24.

PYRANTEL   L3

Trade: Pin-Rid, Reeses Pinworm, Antiminth, Pin-X
Other Trades: Combantrin, Early Bird
Uses: Anthelmintic
AAP: Not reviewed

Pyrantel is an anthelmintic used to treat pinworm, hookworm, and round worm infestations. It is only minimally absorbed orally, with the majority being eliminated in feces. Peak plasma levels are generally less than 0.05 to 0.13 µg/mL and occur prior to 3 hours. Reported side effects are few and minimal. No data on transfer of pyrantel in human milk are available, but due to minimal oral absorption, and low plasma levels, it is unlikely that breastmilk levels would be clinically relevant. Generally it is administered as a single dose.

Pregnancy Risk Category: C

Lactation Risk Category: L3

Adult Concerns: Side effects are generally minimal and include headache, dizziness, somnolence, insomnia, nausea, vomiting, abdominal cramps, diarrhea and pain. Only moderate changes in liver enzymes have been noted, without serious hepatotoxicity.

Pediatric Concerns: None reported via milk.

Drug Interactions: Pyrantel and piperazine should not be mixed because they are antagonistic. Pyrantel increases theophylline plasma levels.

Relative Infant Dose:

Adult Dose: 11 mg/kg X 2 over two weeks

Alternatives:

T ½	=	M/P	=
PHL	=	PB	=
Tmax	= <3 hours	Oral	= <50%
MW	= 206	pKa	=
Vd	=		

References:
1. Pharmaceutical Manufacturers Prescribing Information, 2008.

PYRAZINAMIDE   L3

Trade: Pyrazinamide, D-50, MK-56
Other Trades: PMS-pyrazinamide, Tebrazid, Zinamide
Uses: Antitubercular antibiotic
AAP: Not reviewed

Pyrazinamide is a typical antituberculosis antibiotic used as first-line therapy in tuberculosis infections. In one patient three hours following an oral dose of 1000 mg, peak milk levels were 1.5 mg/Liter of milk.[1] Peak maternal plasma levels at 2 hours were 42 µg/mL.

Pregnancy Risk Category: C

Lactation Risk Category: L3

Adult Concerns: The most common side effect is hepatotoxicity, nausea and vomiting. Transient increases in liver enzymes, including fever, anorexia, malaise, jaundice, and liver tenderness have been reported. Hyperuricemia including gout has been reported. Maculopapular rashes, arthralgia, acne and numerous other side effects have been noted.

Pediatric Concerns: None reported via milk.

Drug Interactions:

Relative Infant Dose: 1.5%

Adult Dose: 15-30 mg/kg daily

Alternatives:

T ½	= 9-10 hours	M/P	=
PHL	=	PB	= 17%
Tmax	= 2 hours	Oral	= Complete
MW	= 123	pKa	=
Vd	=		

References:
1. Holdiness MR. Antituberculosis drugs and breast-feeding. Arch Intern Med 1984; 144 (9):1888.

PYRIDOSTIGMINE   L2

Trade: Mestinon, Regonol
Other Trades: Mestinon, Regonol
Uses: Anticholinesterase muscle stimulant
AAP: Maternal Medication Usually Compatible with Breastfeeding

Pyridostigmine is a potent cholinesterase inhibitor used in myasthenia gravis to stimulate muscle strength. In a group of 2 mothers receiving from 120-300 mg/day, breastmilk concentrations varied from 5 to 25 µg/Liter.[1] The calculated milk/plasma ratios varied from 0.36 to 1.13. No cholinergic side effects were noted and no pyridostigmine was found in the infants' plasma.

Because the oral bioavailability is so poor (10-20%), the actual dose received by the breastfed infant would be significantly less than the above concentrations. Please note the dosage is highly variable and may be as high as 600 mg/day in divided doses. The authors estimated total daily intake at 0.1% or less of the maternal dose.

Pregnancy Risk Category: C

Lactation Risk Category: L2

Adult Concerns: Nausea, vomiting, salivation, sweating, weakness, asthmatic symptoms, muscle cramps, fasciculations, constricted pupils.

Pediatric Concerns: None reported in one study of two infants.

Drug Interactions: Increased effect of neuromuscular blockers such as succinylcholine. Increased toxicity with edrophonium.

Relative Infant Dose: 0.1%

Adult Dose: 60-180 mg BID-QID

Alternatives:

T ½	= 3.3 hours	M/P	= 0.36-1.13
PHL	=	PB	= 0%
Tmax	= 1-2 hours	Oral	= 10-20%
MW	= 261	pKa	=
Vd	=		

References:
1. Hardell LI, Lindstrom B, Lonnerholm G, Osterman PO. Pyridostigmine in human breast milk. Br J Clin Pharmacol 1982; 14 (4):565-567.

PYRIDOXINE   L2

Trade: Vitamin B-6, Hexa-Betalin
Other Trades: Hexa-Betalin, Pyroxin, Comploment continus
Uses: Vitamin B-6
AAP: Maternal Medication Usually Compatible with Breastfeeding

Pyridoxine is vitamin B-6. The recommended daily allowance for non-pregnant women is 1.6 mg/day. Pyridoxine is secreted in milk in direct proportion to the maternal intake and concentrations in milk vary from 123 to 314 ng/mL depending on the study. Pyridoxine is required in slight excess during pregnancy and lactation and most prenatal vitamin supplements contain from 12-25 mg/day. Very high doses (600 mg/day) were reported to suppress prolactin secretion and therefore production of breastmilk.[1,2] However, this data has been refuted in two studies where high doses of pyridoxine failed to suppress prolactin levels or lactation.[3,4]

It is not advisable to use in excess of 40 mg/day. One study clearly indicates that pyridoxine readily transfers into breastmilk and that B-6 levels in milk correlate closely with maternal intake, thus the reason for not using excessive doses.[5] Breastfeeding mothers who are deficient in pyridoxine should be supplemented with modest amounts (<=40 mg/day).

Pregnancy Risk Category: A

Lactation Risk Category: L2
                              L4 in high doses

Adult Concerns: Reduced milk production, sensory neuropathy, GI distress, sedation.

Pediatric Concerns: Excessive oral doses have been reported to produce sedation, hypotonia and respiratory distress in infants, although none have been reported via breastmilk.

Drug Interactions: Decreased serum levels with levodopa, phenobarbital, and phenytoin.

Relative Infant Dose:

Adult Dose: 40 mg/day or less.

Alternatives:

T ½	= 15-20 days	M/P	=
PHL	=	PB	=
Tmax	= 1-2 hours	Oral	= Complete
MW	= 205	pKa	=
Vd	=		

References:

1. Marcus RG. Suppression of lactation with high doses of pyridoxine. S Afr Med J 1975; 49 (52):2155-2156.
2. Foukas MD. An antilactogenic effect of pyridoxine. J Obstet Gynaecol Br Commonw 1973; 80 (8):718-720.
3. de Waal JM, Steyn AF, Harms JH, Slabber CF, Pannall PR. Failure of pyridoxine to suppress raised serum prolactin levels. S Afr Med J 1978; 53 (8):293-294.
4. Canales ES, Soria J, Zarate A, Mason M, Molina M. The influence of pyridoxine on prolactin secretion and milk production in women. Br J Obstet Gynaecol 1976; 83 (5):387-388.
5. Kang-Yoon SA, Kirksey A, Giacoia G, West K. Vitamin B-6 status of breast-fed neonates: influence of pyridoxine supplementation on mothers and neonates. Am J Clin Nutr 1992; 56 (3):548-558.

PYRIMETHAMINE   L3

Trade: Daraprim
Other Trades: Daraprim, Fansidar, Maloprim
Uses: Antimalarial, folic acid antagonist
AAP: Maternal Medication Usually Compatible with Breastfeeding

Pyrimethamine is a folic acid antagonist that has been used for prophylaxis of malaria. Maternal peak plasma levels occur 2-6 hours post-dose.[1] Pyrimethamine is secreted into human milk. In a group of mothers receiving 25, 50, and 75 mg/day of pyrimethamine for 10 days, milk levels ranged from 0.125 to 0.155 µg/L twenty four hours following the dose. The peak concentration was 3.3 mg/L.[2] An infant would receive an estimated dose of 3-4 mg in a 48 hour period (following 75 mg maternal dose).

In another study, three women received a dose of 12.5 mg orally 2-5 days postpartum. The infants were reported to receive about 0.14, 0.21, and 0.34 mg pyrimethamine over 5 days.[3] The authors estimate the RID to be 46%.

No adverse effects were reported in any of the infants.

Pregnancy Risk Category: C

Lactation Risk Category: L3

Adult Concerns: Anemia, blood dyscrasias, folate deficiency states, carcinogenesis, insomnia, headache, anorexia, vomiting, megaloblastic anemia, leukopenia.

Pediatric Concerns: None reported, but possible carcinogenesis may preclude its use in breastfed infants.

Drug Interactions: Use of pyrimethamine with other antifolate drugs (methotrexate, sulfonamides, TMP-SMZ) may increase the risk of bone marrow suppression and folate deficiency states.

Relative Infant Dose: 45.8%

Adult Dose: 25 mg every week

Alternatives:

T ½	= 96 hours	M/P	= 0.2-0.43
PHL	=	PB	= 87%
Tmax	= 2-6 hours	Oral	= Complete
MW	= 249	pKa	=
Vd	=		

References:
1. Pharmaceutical Manufacturer Prescribing Information. 1996.
2. Clyde DF, Press J, Shute GT. Transfer of pyrimethamine in human milk. J Trop Med Hyg 1956; 59 (12):277-284.
3. Edstein MD, Veenendaal JR, Newman K et al. Excretion of chloroquine, dapsone and pyrimethamine in human milk. Br J Clin Pharmacol. 1986; 22:733-5.

QUADRIVALENT HUMAN PAPILLMOAVIRUS VACCINE

L3

Trade: Gardasil
Other Trades:
Uses: HPV vaccine
AAP: Not reviewed

This is a non-infectious recombinant vaccine prepared from the purified virus like particles from the major capsid protein of four different virus types (6,11,16, and 18). Current recommendations are to begin the series in 11-26 year old females, with 4 weeks between the first and second doses, and 12 weeks between the second and third doses.[1] It is not known whether vaccine antigens or antibodies are excreted in human milk. One study showed an increase risk of serious adverse event, but was judged by the investigator to be non-vaccine related.[1] Also, a higher number of infants whose mothers received the vaccine had acute respiratory illnesses within 30 days after the vaccination.

Pregnancy Risk Category: B

Lactation Risk Category: L3

Adult Concerns: Adverse effects included fever and injection site pain, swelling, and redness.

Pediatric Concerns: No data available.

Drug Interactions:

Relative Infant Dose:

Adult Dose: 0.5 mL IM

Alternatives:

References:
1. Pharmaceutical Manufacturer Prescribing Information. 2006.

QUAZEPAM   L2

Trade: Doral, Dormalin
Other Trades:
Uses: Sedative, hypnotic
AAP: Drugs whose effect on nursing infants is unknown but may be of concern

Quazepam is a long half-life benzodiazepine (Valium-like) medication used as a sedative and hypnotic. It is selectively metabolized to several metabolites that have even longer half-lives. In a study of four breastfeeding mothers who received a single 15 mg dose of quazepam, the average milk/plasma ratio (AUC) was 4.18.[1] The C_{max} of quazepam in milk occurred at 3 hours and was 95.8 µg/L and over the 48 hours, only 11.59 µg quazepam was recovered. The average concentration (AUC) of quazepam equivalents over 48 hours was 19.6 µg/L. However, including metabolites, the authors suggest that 17.1 µg of quazepam equivalents or 0.11% of the administered dose was recovered in milk. The authors estimated that 28.7 µg quazepam equivalents, or 0.19% of the quazepam dose would be excreted in breast milk every 24 hours. These estimates were not weight-adjusted.

Pregnancy Risk Category: X

Lactation Risk Category: L2

Adult Concerns: Drowsiness, sedation.

Pediatric Concerns: None reported via breastmilk. Observe for sedation.

Drug Interactions: May increase sedation when used with CNS depressants such as alcohol, barbiturates, opioids. Cimetidine may decrease metabolism and clearance of benzodiazepines. Valproic may displace BZs from binding sites, thus increasing sedative effects. SSRIs (fluoxetine, sertraline, paroxetine) can dramatically increase BZs levels by altering clearance, thus leading to sedation .

Relative Infant Dose: 1.4%

Adult Dose: 15 mg daily

Alternatives: Lorazepam, Alprazolam

T ½	= 39 hours	M/P	= 4.18
PHL	=	PB	= >95%
Tmax	= 2 hours	Oral	= Complete
MW	= 387	pKa	=
Vd	=		

References:

1. Hilbert JM, Gural RP, Symchowicz S, Zampaglione N. Excretion of quazepam into human breast milk. J Clin Pharmacol 1984; 24 (10):457-462.

QUETIAPINE FUMARATE   L2

Trade: Seroquel
Other Trades:
Uses: Antipsychotic drug
AAP: Not reviewed

Quetiapine (Seroquel) is indicated for the treatment of psychotic disorders.[1] It has some affinity for histamine receptors, which may account for its sedative properties. It has been shown to increase the incidence of seizures, prolactin levels, and to lower thyroid levels in adults.

In a patient (92 kg) receiving 200 mg/day of quetiapine throughout pregnancy, samples were expressed just before dosing, and at 1,2,4, and 6 hours postdose.[2] The average milk concentration (AUC) of quetiapine over the 6 hours was 13 µg/liter, with a maximum concentration of 62 µg/liter at 1 hour. Levels of quetiapine rapidly fell to almost predose levels by 2 hours. The authors report that an exclusively breastfed infant would ingest only 0.09% of the weight-adjusted maternal dose. At maximum, the infant would ingest 0.43% of the weight-adjusted maternal dose. Although only one patient was studied, the data suggests levels in milk are minimal at this maternal dose.

One study of 6 mothers taking a combination of quetiapine, paroxetine, clonazepam, trazodone, and/or venlafaxine showed that no medication was detectable in 3 of the mothers' milk. In two of the other cases, quetiapine levels were below 0.01 mg/kg/day infant dose, while the final mother expressed an infant dose of less than 0.10 mg/kg/day. The mothers' doses of quetiapine ranged from 25-400 mg. The authors reported that no correlation was noted between drug exposure and developmental outcomes.[3]

In another study of one mother receiving 400 mg quetiapine per day 3 months postpartum, expressed milk contained with an average drug concentration of 41 µg/L, and a milk-to-plasma ratio of 0.29. The relative infant dose reported was 0.09% of the mother's dose. The infant's plasma concentration was 1.4 µg/L, or 6% of the mother's plasma concentration. No adverse effects were reported in the infant, but the authors suggest monitoring the infant's progress and quetiapine serum concentration.[4]

Pregnancy Risk Category: C

Lactation Risk Category: L2

Adult Concerns: The side effects of quetiapine are similar to other anti-psychotic drugs and include sedation, tardive dyskinesia, seizures, priapism, hypothermia, dysphagia, hyperprolactinemia, orthostatic hypotension, cataracts, and hypothyroidism.

Pediatric Concerns: None reported via milk in one small study.

Drug Interactions: Phenytoin increases clearance of quetiapine significantly (5X). Other drugs which increase clearance include: cimetidine, thioridazine, and other P450 3a inhibitors. Lorazepam levels may be reduced by 20% when used with quetiapine.

Relative Infant Dose: 0.07% - 0.1%

Adult Dose: 300-400 mg daily

Alternatives: Risperidone, olanzapine

T ½	= 6 hours	M/P	= 0.29
PHL	=	PB	= 83%
Tmax	= 1.5 hours	Oral	= 100%
MW	= 883	pKa	=
Vd	= 10		

References:
1. Pharmaceutical Manufacturer Prescribing Information. 1999.
2. Lee A, Giesbrecht B, Dunn E, Ito S. Excretion of Quetiapine in Breast Milk. Am J Psychiatry 2004; 161 (9):1715-6.
3. Misri S, Corral M, Wardrop AA, Kendrick K. Quetiapine Augmentation in Lactation: A Series of Case Reports. J Clin Psychopharmacol 2006; 26 (5):508-511.
4. Rampono J, Kristensen JH, Ilett KF, Hackett P, Kohan R. Quetiapine and Breast Feeding. Ann Pharmacother 2007; 41:711-714.

QUINACRINE | L4

Trade: Atabrine
Other Trades:
Uses: Antimalarial, giardiasis
AAP: Not reviewed

Quinacrine was once used for malaria but has been replaced by other preparations. It is primarily used for giardiasis.[1,2] Small to trace amounts are secreted into milk. No known harmful effects except in infants with G6PD deficiencies. However, quinacrine is eliminated from the body very slowly, requiring up to 2 months for complete elimination. Quinacrine levels in liver are extremely high. Accumulation in infant is likely due to slow rate of excretion. Caution is urged.

Pregnancy Risk Category: C

Lactation Risk Category: L4

Adult Concerns: GI distress, liver toxicity, seizures, aplastic anemia, retinopathy.

Pediatric Concerns: None reported via milk, but accumulation may occur after prolonged exposure. Use with caution.

Drug Interactions: Primaquine toxicity is increased by quinacrine. Concomitant use is contraindicated.

Relative Infant Dose:

Adult Dose: 100 mg TID

Alternatives:

T ½	= >5 days	M/P	=
PHL	=	PB	= High
Tmax	= 1-3 hours	Oral	= Complete
MW	= 400	pKa	=
Vd	=		

References:
1. Drug Facts and Comparisons 2010 ed. ed. St. Louis: 2010.
2. McEvoy GE. (ed): AFHS Drug Information. 1992.

QUINAPRIL   L2

Trade: Accupril, Accuretic
Other Trades: Accupril, Accupril, Asig, Accupro
Uses: ACE inhibitor, antihypertensive
AAP: Not reviewed

Quinapril is an angiotensin converting enzyme inhibitor (ACE) used as an antihypertensive. Accuretic products also contain the diuretic hydrochlorothiazide. Once in the plasma compartment, quinapril is rapidly converted to quinaprilat, the active metabolite. In a study of 6 women who received 20 mg/d the milk/plasma ratio for quinapril was 0.12.[1] Quinapril was not detected in milk after 4 h. No quinaprilat (metabolite) was detected in any of the milk samples. The estimated 'dose' of quinapril that would be received by the infant was 1.6% of the maternal dose, adjusted for respective weights. The authors suggest that quinapril appears to be 'safe' during breastfeeding although, as always, the risk:benefit ratio should be considered when it is to be given to a nursing mother. ACE inhibitors are generally contraindicated during pregnancy due to increased fetal morbidity.

Pregnancy Risk Category: C in first trimester
D in second and third trimesters

Lactation Risk Category: L2
L4 if used early postpartum

Adult Concerns: Cough, hypotension, nausea, vomiting.

Pediatric Concerns: None reported in one study. Levels are so low this agent is probably quite safe in most instances.

Drug Interactions: Probenecid increases plasma levels of ACEi. ACEi and diuretics have additive hypotensive effects. Antacids reduce bioavailability of ACE inhibitors. NSAIDS reduce hypotension of ACE inhibitors. Phenothiazines increase effects of ACEi. ACEi increase digoxin and lithium plasma levels. May elevate potassium levels when potassium supplementation is added.

Relative Infant Dose: 1.6%

Adult Dose: 20-80 mg daily.

Alternatives: Captopril, Enalapril

T ½	= 2 hours	M/P	= 0.12
PHL	=	PB	= 97%
Tmax	= 2 hour	Oral	= Complete
MW	= 474	pKa	=
Vd	=		

References:

1. Begg EJ, Robson RA, Gardiner SJ, Hudson LJ, Reece PA, Olson SC, Posvar EL, Sedman AJ. Quinapril and its metabolite quinaprilat in human milk. Br J Clin Pharmacol 2001; 51 (5):478-481.

QUINIDINE   L2

Trade: Quinaglute, Quinidex

Other Trades: Apo-Quinidine, Cardioquin, Novo-Quinidin, Kinidin Durules, Kiditard

Uses: Antiarrhythmic agent

AAP: Maternal Medication Usually Compatible with Breastfeeding

Quinidine is used to treat cardiac arrhythmias. Three hours following a dose of 600 mg, the level of quinidine in the maternal serum was 9.0 mg/L and the concentration in her breast milk was 6.4 mg/L.[1] Subsequently, a level of 8.2 mg/L was noted in breastmilk. Quinidine is selectively stored in the liver. Long-term use could expose an infant to liver toxicity. Monitor liver enzymes.

Pregnancy Risk Category: C

Lactation Risk Category: L2

Adult Concerns: Blood dyscrasias, hypotension, thrombocytopenia, depression, fever.

Pediatric Concerns: None reported, but observe for changes in liver function.

Drug Interactions: Quinidine levels may be elevated with amiodarone, certain antacids, cimetidine, verapamil. Digoxin plasma levels may be increased with quinidine. Quinidine may increase anticoagulant levels with used with warfarin. Quinidine levels or effect may be reduced when used with barbiturates, nifedipine, rifampin, sucralfate, or phenytoin. Effects of procainamide may be dangerously increased when used with quinidine. Clearance of TCAs may be decreased by quinidine.

Relative Infant Dose: 14.4%

Adult Dose: 200-400 mg TID-QID

Alternatives:

T ½	= 6-8 hours	M/P	= 0.71
PHL	=	PB	= 87%
Tmax	= 1-2 hours	Oral	= 80%
MW	= 324	pKa	= 4.2,8.3
Vd	= 1.8-3.0		

References:
1. Hill LM, Malkasian GD, Jr. The use of quinidine sulfate throughout pregnancy. Obstet Gynecol 1979; 54 (3):366-368.

QUININE   L2

Trade: Quinamm

Other Trades: Novo-Quinine, Biquinate, Myoquin, Quinbisul, Quinate

Uses: Antimalarial

AAP: Maternal Medication Usually Compatible with Breastfeeding

Quinine is a cinchona alkaloid primarily used in malaria prophylaxis and treatment. Small to trace amounts are secreted into milk. No reported harmful effects have been reported except in infants with G6PD deficiencies. In a study of 6 women receiving 600-1300 mg/day, the concentration of quinine in breastmilk ranged from 0.4 to 1.6 mg/L at 1.5 to 6 hours postdose.[1] The authors suggest these levels are clinically insignificant. In another study, with maternal plasma concentrations of 0.5 to 8 mg/L, the milk/plasma ratio ranged from 0.11 to 0.53.[2] The total daily consumption by a breastfed infant was estimated to be 1-3 mg/day.

Pregnancy Risk Category: D

Lactation Risk Category: L2

Adult Concerns: Blood dyscrasias, thrombocytopenia, retinal toxicity, tongue discoloration, kidney damage.

Pediatric Concerns: None reported via breastmilk in several studies.

Drug Interactions: Aluminum containing antacid may delay or decrease absorption. Quinine may depress vitamin K dependent clotting factors. Therefore increasing warfarin effects. Cimetidine may reduce quinine clearance. Digoxin serum levels may be increased. Do not use with mefloquine.

Relative Infant Dose: 0.7% - 1.3%

Adult Dose: 650 mg every 8 hours

Alternatives:

T ½	= 11 hours	M/P	= 0.11-0.53
PHL	=	PB	= 93%
Tmax	= 1-3 hours	Oral	= 76%
MW	= 324	pKa	= 4.3,8.4
Vd	= 1.8-3.0		

References:
1. Terwillinger WG, Hatcher RA. The elimination of morphine and quinine in human milk. Surg Gynecol Obstet 1934; 58:823.
2. Phillips RE, Looareesuwan S, White NJ, Silamut K, Kietinun S, Warrell DA. Quinine pharmacokinetics and toxicity in pregnant and lactating women with falciparum malaria. Br J Clin Pharmacol 1986; 21 (6):677-683.

QUINUPRISTIN AND DALFOPRISTIN   L3

Trade: Synercid
Other Trades:
Uses: Antimicrobial
AAP: Not reviewed

Synercid is a streptogramin antibacterial agent for intravenous use only. It is indicated for the treatment of vancomycin-resistant enterococcus faecium as well as for treatment of susceptible staph aureus. It has some use against methicillin-resistant organisms. No data are available on its transfer to human milk. However, due to its acidity and large MW, milk levels will probably be low.

Pregnancy Risk Category: B

Lactation Risk Category: L3

Adult Concerns: This product is well-tolerated. Infusion site problems such as pain and erythema have been reported. Headache, GI disturbances, and elevated liver enzymes report. Arthralgia, myalgia have been reported.

Pediatric Concerns: None reported via milk.

Drug Interactions: Synercid inhibits cytochrome P450 3A4. Thus numerous interactions with other drugs metabolized by this enzyme. A partial list includes: cyclosporin, midazolam, nifedipine, and terfenadine. Check numerous other drug interactions with alternate drug source.

Relative Infant Dose:

Adult Dose: 7.5 mg/kg every 8 h

Alternatives:

T ½	= 1-3 hours	M/P	=
PHL	=	PB	= 32%q + 56%d
Tmax	= 1 hour	Oral	= Nil
MW	= 1022	pKa	=
Vd	= 0.45q and 0.24d		

References:
1. Pharmaceutical Manufacturer Prescribing Information, 2002.

RABEPRAZOLE   L3

Trade: Aciphex
Other Trades:
Uses: Antisecretory, antacid
AAP: Not reviewed

Rabeprazole is an antisecretory proton pump inhibitor similar to omeprazole (Prilosec). Rodent studies suggest a high milk/plasma ratio, but as we know, these do not correlate well with humans. No data are available in humans. Further, rabeprazole is only 52% bioavailable in adults when enteric coated due to its instability in gastric acids. As presented in milk, it would be virtually destroyed in the infants stomach prior to absorption.

Pregnancy Risk Category: B

Lactation Risk Category: L3

Adult Concerns: Asthenia, fever, allergies, malaise, chest pain, photosensitivity. Myalgia, arthritis, leg cramps and bone pain have been reported.

Pediatric Concerns: None reported via milk.

Drug Interactions: None are reported.

Relative Infant Dose:

Adult Dose: 20 mg daily

Alternatives: Omeprazole

T ½	= 1-2 hours	M/P	=
PHL	=	PB	= 96.3
Tmax	= 2-5 hours	Oral	= 52% (enteric)
MW	= 381	pKa	=
Vd	=		

References:
1.   Pharmaceutical Manufacturer Prescribing Information, 2002.

RABIES INFECTION   L3

Trade: Rabies Infection
Other Trades:
Uses: Viral infection
AAP: Not reviewed

Rabies is an acute rapidly progressing illness caused by an RNA-containing virus that is usually fatal. Infection is via other warm-blooded mammals. Incubation is prolonged and can be up to 4-6 weeks.[1] The virus multiplies locally, passes into local neurons and progressively ascends to the central nervous system. The virus is seldom found in the plasma compartment. The issue of breastfeeding following exposure to an animal bite is contentious and somewhat obscure. Person to person transmission has not been documented, nor has there been documentation of transmission of the rabies virus into human milk.[2,3] If a breastfeeding women is exposed to the rabies virus, she should receive the human rabies immune globulin and begin the vaccination series.[4] Most sources agree that once immunization has begun, the mother can continue breastfeeding. For a thorough review, see reference 4.

Pregnancy Risk Category:

Lactation Risk Category: L3 upon immunization

Adult Concerns:

Pediatric Concerns: None reported.

Drug Interactions:

Relative Infant Dose:

Adult Dose:

Alternatives:

References:

1. American Academy of Pediatrics. In: Pickering LK, ed. 2000 Red Book: Report of the Committee on Infectious Diseases. 25th ed. ed. Elk Grove Village, IL: 2000.
2. Lawrence RA. Breastfeeding: A guide for the medical profession. St. Louis: Mosby Publishers, 1994.
3. Hall TG. Diseases Transmitted from Animal to Man. Springfield, IL: Thomas, 1963.
4. Meerwood A, Philipp B. Breastfeeding: Conditions and Diseases. 1st ed. Amarillo, TX: Pharmasoft Publishing L.P., 2001.

RABIES VACCINE   L3

Trade: Imovax Rabies Vaccine
Other Trades:
Uses: Vaccination for rabies.
AAP: Not reviewed

Rabies vaccine is prepared from inactivated rabies virus. No data are available on transmission to breastmilk. Even if transferred to breastmilk, it is unlikely to produce untoward effects.[1]

Pregnancy Risk Category:

Lactation Risk Category: L3

Adult Concerns: Rash, anaphylactoid reactions, nausea, vomiting, diarrhea, etc.

Pediatric Concerns: No untoward effect reported.

Drug Interactions:

Relative Infant Dose:

Adult Dose: 1 mL X 3 over 21-28 days

Alternatives:

References:

1. Pharmaceutical Manufacturer Prescribing Information. 1995.

RADIOPAQUE AGENTS | L2

Trade: Omnipaque, Conray, Cholebrine, Telepaque, Oragrafin, Bilivist, Hypaque, Optiray

Other Trades:

Uses: Radio-contrast agents

AAP: Some approved by the American Academy of Pediatrics for use in breastfeeding mothers

Radiocontrast or radiopaque agents are opaque to X-rays and are used to visualize blood vessels in various tissues. Barium sulfate was one of the original agents used, while organic iodinated compounds are used primarily in CAT scans and for various X-ray procedures. While iodinated products in general are contraindicated in breastfeeding mothers due to the high milk transfer of iodine, in these products the iodine is covalently bound to the organic molecule and is metabolically stable and essentially not bioavailable. For the most part, these organic radiocontrast agents are rapidly excreted without significant metabolism, and the amount of elemental iodine released is minimal.[1] Virtually all of these agents have very short plasma half-lives (<1 h), and for those studied, milk concentrations are extremely low (see table below).[2,3,4,5,6] Of the minimal amount in milk, virtually none is bioavailable to the infant as these agents are largely unabsorbed orally. According to several manufacturers, less than 0.005% of the iodine is free. These contrast agents are in essence pharmacologically inert, not metabolized, unabsorbed, and are rapidly excreted by the kidney (80-90% with 24 hours). See Appendices for other information on these agents.

Pregnancy Risk Category:

Lactation Risk Category: L2

Adult Concerns: GI distress, rash, anaphylaxis.

Pediatric Concerns: None reported via milk. Commonly used in pediatric patients for diagnostic purposes.

Drug Interactions:

Relative Infant Dose:

Adult Dose:

Alternatives:

T ½	= 20-90 minutes	M/P	=
PHL	=	PB	= 0-10%
Tmax	= <1 hr	Oral	= Minimal
MW	=	pKa	=
Vd	=		

References:

1. Pharmaceutical Manufacturer Prescribing Information. 1993.
2. Nielsen ST, Matheson I, Rasmussen JN, Skinnemoen K, Andrew E, Hafsahl G. Excretion of iohexol and metrizoate in human breast milk. Acta Radiol 1987; 28 (5):523-526.
3. Holmdahl KH. Cholecystography during lactation. Acta Radiol 1956; 45 (4):305-307.
4. Ilett KF, Hackett LP, Paterson JW, McCormick CC. Excretion of metrizamide in milk. Br J Radiol 1981; 54 (642):537-538.
5. Rofsky NM, Weinreb JC, Litt AW. Quantitative analysis of gadopentetate dimeglumine excreted in breast milk. J Magn Reson Imaging 1993; 3 (1):131-132.
6. FitzJohn TP, Williams DG, Laker MF, Owen JP. Intravenous urography during lactation. Br J Radiol 1982; 55 (656):603-605.

RALOXIFENE HCL   L3

Trade: Evista
Other Trades: Evista
Uses: Selective estrogen receptor modulator
AAP: Not reviewed

Raloxifene is a selective estrogen receptor modulator. It blocks such estrogen effects as those that lead to breast cancer and uterine cancer. In addition, it also prevents bone loss and improved lipid profiles. It is used to prevent osteoporosis in postmenopausal women.[1] It is poorly absorbed orally (2%).

Pregnancy Risk Category: X

Lactation Risk Category: L3

Adult Concerns: Adverse reactions include hot flashes, arthralgia, flu syndrome, infection, and headache.

Pediatric Concerns: No data are available.

Drug Interactions: Cholestyramine may decrease the absorption of raloxifene, and raloxifene may decrease levothyroxine absorption.

Relative Infant Dose:

Adult Dose: 60 mg/day

Alternatives:

T ½	= 27-32 hours	M/P	=
PHL	=	PB	= >95%
Tmax	=	Oral	= 2%
MW	= 510	pKa	=
Vd	= 2348		

References:
1. Pharmaceutical Manufacturer Prescribing Information. 2003.

RAMELTEON   L3

Trade: Rozerem
Other Trades:
Uses: Nonbenzodiazepine hypnotic
AAP: Not reviewed

Used for insomnia, Ramelteon is a melatonin receptor agonist, and assists in the synchronization of the circadian rhythm and induces sleep.[1] Unlike the benzodiazepines, ramelteon does not bind to the GABA receptors. There have been no studies of levels of ramelteon in human milk. However, probable small amount in milk would only be 1.8% bioavailable. It is unlikely to sedate an infant.

Pregnancy Risk Category: C

Lactation Risk Category: L3

Adult Concerns: Adverse reactions include headache, fatigue, somnolence, dizziness, and nausea.

Pediatric Concerns: No data are available.

Drug Interactions: CNS depressants may have an additive effect on the depressant effect of ramelteon. CYP1A2 inhibitors will increase concentrations of ramelteon, as will fluconazole, fluvoxamine, and ketoconazole. Rifampin will decrease serum concentrations of ramelteon. Do not take with fluvoxamine (luvox) or if you have liver problems.

Relative Infant Dose:

Adult Dose: 8 mg nightly

Alternatives:

T ½	= 1-2.6 hours	M/P	=
PHL	=	PB	= 82%
Tmax	= 0.5-1.5 hours	Oral	= 1.8%
MW	= 259	pKa	=
Vd	= 1.06		

References:
1. Pharmaceutical Manufacturers prescribing information, 2006.

RAMIPRIL   L3

Trade: Altace
Other Trades: Altace, Ramace, Tritace
Uses: ACE inhibitor, antihypertensive
AAP: Not reviewed

Ramipril is rapidly metabolized to ramiprilat which is a potent ACE inhibitor with a long half-life. It is used in hypertension. ACE inhibitors can cause increased fetal and neonatal morbidity and should not be used in pregnant women. Ingestion of a single 10 mg oral dose produced an undetectable level in breastmilk.[1,2] However, animal studies have indicated that ramiprilat is transferred into milk in concentrations about one-third of those found in serum, but animal studies (lactation) are always high and do not at all correlate with humans. Only 0.25% of the total dose is estimated to penetrate into milk.

Pregnancy Risk Category: C in first trimester
                              D in second and third trimesters

Lactation Risk Category: L3

Adult Concerns: Hypotension, cough, nausea, vomiting, dizziness.

Pediatric Concerns: None reported via milk. Observe for hypotension.

Drug Interactions: Probenecid increases plasma levels of ACEi. ACEi and diuretics have additive hypotensive effects. Antacids reduce bioavailability of ACE inhibitors. NSAIDS reduce hypotension of ACE inhibitors. Phenothiazines increase effects of ACEi. ACEi increase digoxin and lithium plasma levels. May elevate potassium levels when potassium supplementation is added.

Relative Infant Dose: 0.3%

Adult Dose: 2.5-20 mg daily.

Alternatives: Captopril, Enalapril

T ½	= 13-17 hours	M/P	=
PHL	=	PB	= 56%
Tmax	= 2-4 hours	Oral	= 60%
MW	= 417	pKa	=
Vd	=		

References:
1. Pharmaceutical Manufacturer Prescribing Information. 1996.
2. Ball SG, Robertson JI. Clinical pharmacology of ramipril. Am J Cardiol 1987; 59 (10):23D-27D.

RANIBIZUMAB   L3

Trade: Lucentis
Other Trades:
Uses: Angiogenesis inhibitor
AAP: Not reviewed

Ranibizumab binds to and inhibits human vascular endothelial growth factor A, inhibiting it from binding to its receptor and suppressing neovascularization and slowing vision loss.[1] No data are available on the transfer of ranibizumab into the milk compartment, however, due to the large MW, it is unlikely that this drug would pose a threat to a breastfeeding infant after the first week postpartum.

Pregnancy Risk Category: C

Lactation Risk Category: L3

Adult Concerns: Adverse reactions include headache, arthralgia, conjunctival hemorrhage, eye pain, increased intraocular pressure, nasopharyngitis and upper respiratory tract infection.

Pediatric Concerns: No data are available.

Drug Interactions:

Relative Infant Dose:

Adult Dose: 0.5 mg every month

Alternatives: Pegaptanib

T ½	= 9 days	M/P	=
PHL	=	PB	=
Tmax	=	Oral	= Nil
MW	= 48,000	pKa	=
Vd	=		

References:
1. Pharmaceutical Manufacturer Prescribing Information. 2007.

RANITIDINE   L2

Trade: Zantac

Other Trades: Apo-Ranitidine, Novo-Ranidine, Zantac, Nu-Ranit

Uses: Reduces gastric acid secretion

AAP: Not reviewed

Ranitidine is a prototypic histamine-2 blocker used to reduce acid secretion in the stomach. It has been widely used in pediatrics without significant side effects primarily for gastroesophageal reflux (GER). Following a dose of 150 mg for four doses, concentrations in breastmilk were 0.72, 2.6, and 1.5 mg/L at 1.5, 5.5 and 12 hours respectively.[1] The milk/serum ratios varied from 6.81, 8.44 to 23.77 at 1.5, 5.5 and 12 hours respectively. Although the milk/plasma ratios are quite high, using this data, an infant would ingest at most 0.4 mg/kg/d. This amount is quite small considering the pediatric dose currently recommended is 2-4 mg/kg/24 hours. See nizatidine or famotidine for alternatives.

Pregnancy Risk Category: B

Lactation Risk Category: L2

Adult Concerns: Side effects are generally minimal and include headache, GI distress, dizziness.

Pediatric Concerns: None reported via milk. Although ranitidine is concentrated in milk, the overall dose is less than therapeutic.

Drug Interactions: Ranitidine may decrease the renal clearance of procainamide. May decrease oral absorption of diazepam. Ranitidine may increase the hypoglycemic effect of glipizide or glyburide. Ranitidine may reduce warfarin clearance, thus increasing anticoagulation.

Relative Infant Dose: 1.3% - 4.6%

Adult Dose: 150 mg BID

Alternatives: Famotidine, Nizatidine

T ½	= 2-3 hours	M/P	= 1.9-6.7
PHL	=	PB	= 15%
Tmax	= 1-3 hours	Oral	= 50%
MW	= 314	pKa	= 2.3,8.2
Vd	= 1.6-2.4		

References:
1. Kearns GL, McConnell RF, Jr., Trang JM, Kluza RB. Appearance of ranitidine in breast milk following multiple dosing. Clin Pharm 1985; 4 (3):322-324.

REMIFENTANIL   L3

Trade: Ultiva
Other Trades: Ultiva
Uses: Opioid analgesic
AAP: Not reviewed

Remifentanil is a new opioid analgesic similar in potency and use as fentanyl. It is primarily metabolized by plasma and tissue esterases (in adults and neonates) and has an incredibly short elimination half-life of only 10-20 minutes, with an effective biological half-life of only 3 to 10 minutes.[1] Unlike other fentanyl analogs, the half-life of remifentanil does not increase with prolonged administration. Although remifentanil has been found in rodent milk, no data are available on its transfer into human milk. It is cleared for use in children >2 years of age. As an analog of fentanyl, breastmilk levels should be similar and probably exceedingly low. In addition, remifentanil metabolism is not dependent on liver function and should be exceedingly short even in neonates. Due to its kinetics and brief half-life and its poor oral bioavailability, it is unlikely this product will produce clinically relevant levels in human breastmilk.

Pregnancy Risk Category: C

Lactation Risk Category: L3

Adult Concerns: Nausea, hypotension, sedation, vomiting, bradycardia.

Pediatric Concerns: None reported via milk. Not orally bioavailable.

Drug Interactions: May potentiate the effects of other opioids.

Relative Infant Dose:

Adult Dose: 0.25-0.4 µg/kg/minute

Alternatives:

T ½	= 10-20 minutes	M/P	=
PHL	=	PB	= 70%
Tmax	=	Oral	= Poor
MW	= 412	pKa	= 7.07
Vd	= 0.1		

References:
1. Pharmaceutical Manufacturer Prescribing Information. 1997.

REPAGLINIDE   L4

Trade: Prandin
Other Trades: Gluconorm, Novonorm
Uses: Antidiabetic agent
AAP: Not reviewed

Repaglinide is a non-sulfonylurea hypoglycemic agent that lowers blood glucose levels in Type 2 non-insulin dependent diabetics by stimulating the release of insulin from functional beta cells. No data are available on its transfer to human milk, but rodent studies suggest that it may transfer into milk and induce hypoglycemic and skeletal changes in young animals via milk. Unfortunately, no dosing regimens were mentioned in these studies, so it is not known if normal therapeutic doses would produce such changes in humans. Dosing of repaglinide is rather unique, with doses taken prior to each meal due to its short half-life and according to the need of each patient. At this point, we do not know if it is safe for use in breastfeeding patients. But if it is used, the infant should be closely monitored for hypoglycemia and should not be fed until at least several hours after the dose to reduce exposure.

Pregnancy Risk Category: C

Lactation Risk Category: L4

Adult Concerns: In adults, hypoglycemia and headache were the most common side effects.

Pediatric Concerns: Hypoglycemia in animal studies via milk, but doses were not mentioned.

Drug Interactions: Metabolism and increased effect may occur when used with azole antifungals such as ketoconazole, itraconazole and other drugs which inhibit liver enzymes such as erythromycin. Decreased effect may result following use of rifampin, troglitazone, barbiturates and carbamazepine. Reduced protein binding and increased effect may result when repaglinide is used with NSAIDs, salicylates, sulfonamides, etc. Numerous other drugs may interfere with the hypoglycemic effect"check a drug interaction reference for a complete listing. Use with gemfibrozil (Lopid) may cause a significant reduction in blood glucose levels.

Relative Infant Dose:

Adult Dose: 0.5-4 mg BID-QID

Alternatives:

T ½	= 1 hour	M/P	=
PHL	=	PB	= 98%
Tmax	= 1 hour	Oral	= 56%
MW	=	pKa	=
Vd	= 31		

References:
1. Pharmaceutical Manufacturer Prescribing Information. 1999.
2. Drug Facts and Comparisons 1999 ed. ed. St. Louis: 1999.

RESERPINE   L4

Trade: Raudixin, Serpasil
Other Trades: Serpasil, Adelphane, Abicol
Uses: Antihypertensive
AAP: Not reviewed

Reserpine is an old and seldom used antihypertensive. Reserpine is known to be secreted into human milk although the levels are unreported.[1,2,3] Increased respiratory tract secretions, severe nasal congestion, cyanosis, and loss of appetite can occur. Some reports suggest no observable effect but should use with extreme caution if at all. Because safer, more effective products are available, reserpine should be avoided in lactating patients.

Pregnancy Risk Category: C

Lactation Risk Category: L4

Adult Concerns: Hypotonia, sedation, hypotension, nasal congestion, diarrhea, nausea, vomiting.

Pediatric Concerns: None reported via milk, but observe for nasal stuffiness, sedation, hypotonia. Use with caution.

Drug Interactions: Reserpine may decrease the effect of other sympathomimetics. May increased effect of MAOI and tricyclic antidepressants.

Relative Infant Dose:

Adult Dose: 125-250 µg daily.-BID

Alternatives:

T ½	= 50-100 hours	M/P	=
PHL	=	PB	= 96%
Tmax	= 2 hours	Oral	= 40%
MW	= 609	pKa	=
Vd	=		

References:
1. O'Brien TE. Excretion of drugs in human milk. Am J Hosp Pharm 1974; 31 (9):844-854.
2. Vorherr H. Drug excretion in breast milk. Postgrad Med 1974; 56 (4):97-104.
3. Anderson PO. Drugs and breast feeding. Semin Perinatol 1979; 3 (3):271-278.

RETAPAMULIN   L3

Trade: Altabax
Other Trades:
Uses: Antibacterial
AAP: Not reviewed

Retapamulin is a topical antibacterial used to treat impetigo caused by S. aureus (not MRSA) in both children and adults. It is only minimally absorbed systemically when applied topically.[1] No data are available on the transfer of retapamulin into human milk, however since systemic absorption is quite low, and this medication is used in children, retapamulin would probably be safe for use in breastfeeding mothers.

Pregnancy Risk Category: B

Lactation Risk Category: L3

Adult Concerns: Adverse reactions include headache, application site irritation, and nasopharyngitis.

Pediatric Concerns: Adverse effects seen in pediatric patients over 9 months of age include itching, eczema, and diarrhea. No data on transfer into milk.

Drug Interactions: Ketoconazole increases retapamulin concentrations.

Relative Infant Dose:

Adult Dose: Apply to affected area BID

Alternatives: Mupirocin

T ½	=	M/P	=
PHL	=	PB	= 94%
Tmax	=	Oral	=
MW	= 517.8	pKa	=
Vd	=		

References:
1. Pharmaceutical Manufacturer Prescribing Information. 2007.

RHO (D) IMMUNE GLOBULIN | L2

Trade: Rhogam, Gamulin RH, Hyprho-D, Mini-Gamulin RH
Other Trades:
Uses: Immune globulin
AAP: Not reviewed

RHO (D) immune globulin is an immune globulin prepared from human plasma containing high concentrations of Rh antibodies. Only trace amounts of anti-Rh are present in colostrum and none in mature milk in women receiving large doses of Rh immune globulin. No untoward effects have been reported. Most immunoglobulins are destroyed in the gastric acidity of the newborn infant. Rh immune globulins are not contraindicated in breastfeeding mothers.[1]

Pregnancy Risk Category:

Lactation Risk Category: L2

Adult Concerns: Infrequent allergies, discomfort at injection site.

Pediatric Concerns: None reported via milk.

Drug Interactions:

Relative Infant Dose:

Adult Dose: 300 μg X 1-2

Alternatives:

T ½	= 24 days	M/P	=
PHL	=	PB	=
Tmax	=	Oral	= None
MW	=	pKa	=
Vd	=		

References:
1. Lawrence RA. Breastfeeding: A guide for the medical profession. St. Louis: Mosby Publishers, 1994.

RIBAVIRIN   L4

Trade: Virazole, Rebetol
Other Trades: Virazole, Virazide
Uses: Antiviral agent
AAP: Not reviewed

Ribavirin is a synthetic nucleoside used as an antiviral agent and is effective in a wide variety of viral infections.[1] It has heretofore been used acutely in respiratory syncytial virus infections in infants without major complications. However, its current use in breastfeeding patients for treatment of Hepatitis C infections when combined with interferon alfa (Rebetron) for periods up to one year may be more problematic as high concentrations of ribavirin could accumulate in the breastfed infant. No data are available on its transfer to human milk, but it is probably low and its oral bioavailability is low as well. However, ribavirin concentrates in peripheral tissues and in the red blood cells in high concentrations over time (Vd= 802).[2] Its elimination half-life at steady state averages 298 hours, which reflects slow elimination from non-plasma compartments. Red cell concentrations on average are 60 fold higher than plasma levels and may account for the occasional hemolytic anemia. It is likely the acute exposure of a breastfed infant would produce minimal side effects. However, chronic exposure over 6-12 months may be more risky, so caution is recommended.

Pregnancy Risk Category: X

Lactation Risk Category: L4

Adult Concerns: Rash, conjunctivitis, hemolytic anemia, congestive heart failure, seizures, asthenia, hypotension, bradycardia, reticulocytosis, bronchospasm, pulmonary edema, etc. Ribavirin may be a potent teratogen. Nursing personnel exposed to inhaled ribavirin should avoid environmental exposure.

Pediatric Concerns: None yet reported via breast milk.

Drug Interactions:

Relative Infant Dose:

Adult Dose: 12.5 L mist/minute (190 µg/L) 12-18 hours daily.

Alternatives:

T ½	= 298 hours (SS)	M/P	=
PHL	=	PB	= 0%
Tmax	= 1.5 hours	Oral	= 44%
MW	~ 244	pKa	=
Vd	= 40.4		

References:
1. Pharmaceutical Manufacturer Prescribing Information. 1999.
2. Lertora JJ, Rege AB, Lacour JT, Ferencz N, George WJ, VanDyke RB, Agrawal KC, Hyslop NE, Jr. Pharmacokinetics and long-term tolerance to ribavirin in asymptomatic patients infected with human immunodeficiency virus. Clin Pharmacol Ther 1991; 50 (4):442-449.

RIBAVIRIN + INTERFERON ALFA-2B   L4

Trade: Rebetron
Other Trades:
Uses: Antivirals for Hepatitis C treatment
AAP: Not reviewed

Rebetron is a combination product containing the antiviral Ribavirin and the immunomodulator drug called interferon alfa-2b. This new combination product is indicated for the long-term treatment of hepatitis C. The typical dose for an individual <75 kg consists of 1000 mg ribavirin daily in divided doses and 3 million units of interferon three times weekly.

Ribavirin is a synthetic nucleoside used as an antiviral agent and is effective in a wide variety of viral infections. It has heretofore been used acutely in respiratory syncytial virus infections in infants without major complications. However, its current use in breastfeeding patients, for treatment of Hepatitis C infections, when combined with interferon alfa (Rebetron) for periods up to one year may be more problematic as high concentrations of ribavirin could accumulate in the breast fed infant over time. No data are available on its transfer to human milk, but it is probably low and its oral bioavailability is low as well. However, ribavirin concentrates in peripheral tissues and in the red blood cells in high concentrations over time (Vd= 802).[1] Its elimination half-life at steady state averages 298 hours, which reflects slow elimination from non-plasma compartments. Red cell concentrations on average are 60 fold higher than plasma levels and may account for the occasional hemolytic anemia. It is likely the acute exposure of a breastfed infant would produce minimal side effects. However, chronic exposure over 12 months may be more risky, so caution is recommended.

Very little is known about the secretion of interferons in human milk although some interferons are known to be secreted normally and may contribute to the antiviral properties of human milk. However, interferons are large in MW (16-28,000 daltons) which would limit their transfer into human milk. Following treatment with a massive dose of 30 million units IV of interferon alpha in a breastfeeding patient, the amount of interferon alpha transferred into human milk was 894, 1004, 1551, 1507, 788, 721 IU at 0 (baseline), 2, 4, 8, 12, and 24 hours respectively.[2] Hence, even following a massive dose, no change in breastmilk levels were noted. One thousand international units is roughly equivalent to 500 nanograms of interferon. So it is unlikely that the interferon in Rebetron would transfer to milk or the infant in amounts clinically relevant.

Rebetron is extremely dangerous to a fetus and is extremely teratogenic at doses even 1/20th of the above therapeutic doses. Pregnancy must be strictly avoided if this product is used in either the male or female partner. Due to the long half-life of this product, pregnancy should be avoided for at least 6 months following use.

Pregnancy Risk Category: X

Lactation Risk Category: L4

Adult Concerns: Anemia, insomnia, depression and irritability are common. Headache, fatigue, rigors, fever, flu-like symptoms, dizziness, nausea, myalgia, insomnia and numerous other symptoms are typical.

Pediatric Concerns: None reported via breast milk, but caution is recommended.

Drug Interactions:

Relative Infant Dose:

Adult Dose:

Alternatives:

T ½	= 298 hours	M/P	=
PHL	=	PB	=
Tmax	=	Oral	=
MW	=	pKa	=
Vd	=		

References:
1. Lertora JJ, Rege AB, Lacour JT, Ferencz N, George WJ, VanDyke RB, Agrawal KC, Hyslop NE, Jr. Pharmacokinetics and long-term tolerance to ribavirin in asymptomatic patients infected with human immunodeficiency virus. Clin Pharmacol Ther 1991; 50 (4):442-449.
2. Kumar AR, Hale TW, Mock RE. Transfer of interferon alfa into human breast milk. J Hum Lact 2000; 16 (3):226-228.

RIBOFLAVIN   L1

Trade: Vitamin B-2
Other Trades: Abdec, Accomin
Uses: Vitamin B2
AAP: Maternal Medication Usually Compatible with Breastfeeding

Riboflavin is a B complex vitamin, also called Vitamin B-2. Riboflavin is absorbed by the small intestine by a well established transport mechanism. It is easily saturable, so excessive levels are not absorbed. Riboflavin is transported into human milk in concentrations proportional to dietary intake but generally averaged 400 ng/mL.[1] Maternal supplementation is permitted if dose is not excessive. No untoward effects have been reported.

Pregnancy Risk Category: A

Lactation Risk Category: L1

Adult Concerns: Yellow colored urine.

Pediatric Concerns: None reported via milk.

Drug Interactions:

Relative Infant Dose:

Adult Dose: 1-4 mg daily.

Alternatives:

T ½	= 14 hours	M/P	=
PHL	=	PB	=
Tmax	= Rapid	Oral	= Complete
MW	= 376	pKa	=
Vd	=		

References:
1. Deodhar AD, Hajalakshmi R, Ramakrishnan CV. Studies on human lactation. III. Effect of dietary vitamin supplementation on vitamin contents of breastfmilk. Acta Paediatr 1964; 53:42-48.

RIFAMPIN   L2

Trade: Rifadin, Rimactane

Other Trades: Rifadin, Rimactane, Rofact, Rifampicin, Rimycin

Uses: Antitubercular drug

AAP: Maternal Medication Usually Compatible with Breastfeeding

Rifampin is a broad-spectrum antibiotic with particular activity against tuberculosis. It is secreted into breastmilk in very small levels. One report indicates that following a single 450 mg oral dose, maternal plasma levels averaged 21.3 mg/L and milk levels averaged 3.4 - 4.9 mg/L.[1] Vorherr reported that after a 600 mg dose of rifampin, peak plasma levels were 50 mg/L while milk levels were 10-30 mg/L.[2]

Pregnancy Risk Category: C

Lactation Risk Category: L2

Adult Concerns: Hepatitis, anemia, headache, diarrhea, pseudomembranous colitis.

Pediatric Concerns: None reported via milk.

Drug Interactions: Rifampin is known to reduce the plasma level of a large number of drugs including: acetaminophen, anticoagulants, barbiturates, benzodiazepines, beta blockers, contraceptives, corticosteroids, cyclosporine, digitoxin, phenytoin, methadone, quinidine, sulfonylureas, theophylline, verapamil, and a large number of others.

Relative Infant Dose: 5.3% - 11.5%

Adult Dose: 600 mg daily.

Alternatives:

T ½	= 3.5 hours	M/P	– 0.16-0.23
PHL	= 2.9 hours	PB	= 80%
Tmax	= 2-4 hours	Oral	= 90-95%
MW	= 823	pKa	=
Vd	=		

References:
1. Lenzi F, Santuari S. Preliminary observations on the use of a new semi-synthetic rifamycin derivative in gynecology and obstetrics. Atti Accad Lancisiana Roma 1969; 13 (suppl 1):87-94.
2. Vorherr H. Drug excretion in breast milk. Postgrad Med 1974; 56 (4):97-104.

RIFAXIMIN   L3

Trade: Xifaxan
Other Trades:
Uses: Non-systemic antibiotic for diarrhea.
AAP: Not reviewed

Rifaximin is a new antibiotic used for the treatment of traveller's diarrhea. It is poorly absorbed orally (<0.4%) and plasma levels are extremely low.[1] While we do not have data in breastfeeding mothers, it is unlikely enough would enter the maternal plasma compartment to produce clinically relevant levels in milk.

Pregnancy Risk Category: C

Lactation Risk Category: L3

Adult Concerns: Flatulence, headache, nausea, increased sweating, abdominal pain have been reported in adults.

Pediatric Concerns: Maternal plasma levels are extremely low. It is unlikely enough would enter the plasma compartment to produce clinically relevant levels in milk.

Drug Interactions:

Relative Infant Dose:

Adult Dose: 200 mg three times daily for 3 days for diarrhea.

Alternatives:

T ½	= 5.85 hours	M/P	=
PHL	=	PB	=
Tmax	= 1.25 hours	Oral	= <0.4%
MW	= 785	pKa	=
Vd	=		

References:
1.   Pharmaceutical manufacturers prescribing information. 2005.

RIMANTADINE HCL   L3

Trade: Flumadine
Other Trades:
Uses: Antiviral, anti-influenza A
AAP: Not reviewed

Rimantadine is an antiviral agent primarily used for influenza A infections. It is concentrated in rodent milk.[1] Levels in animal milk 2-3 hours after administration were approximately twice those of the maternal serum, suggesting a milk/plasma ratio of about 2. The manufacturer alludes to toxic side effects but fails to state them. No side effects yet reported in breastfeeding infants. Rimantadine is, however, indicated for prophylaxis of influenza A in pediatric patients >1 year of age.

Pregnancy Risk Category: C

Lactation Risk Category: L3

Adult Concerns: Gastrointestinal distress, nervousness, fatigue, and sleep disturbances.

Pediatric Concerns: None reported via milk.

Drug Interactions: The use of acetaminophen significantly reduces rimantadine plasma levels by 11%. Peak plasma levels of rimantadine were reduce 10% by aspirin. Rimantadine clearance was reduced by 16% when used with cimetidine.

Relative Infant Dose:

Adult Dose: 100 mg BID

Alternatives:

T ½	= 25.4 hours	M/P	= 2
PHL	=	PB	= 40%
Tmax	= 6 hours	Oral	= 92%
MW	= 179	pKa	=
Vd	=		

References:
1. Pharmaceutical Manufacturer Prescribing Information. 1996.

RISEDRONATE   L3

Trade: Actonel
Other Trades: Actonel
Uses: Prevents bone resorption
AAP: Not reviewed

Risedronate is a bisphosphonate that slows the dissolution of hydroxyapatite crystals in the bone, thus reducing bone calcium loss in certain syndromes such as Paget's syndrome. Its penetration into milk is possible due to its small MW, but it has not yet been reported except in rats. However, due to the presence of fat and calcium in milk, its oral bioavailability in infants would be exceedingly low. However, the presence of this product in an infant's growing bones is concerning, and due caution is recommended.

Pregnancy Risk Category: C

Lactation Risk Category: L3

Adult Concerns: Nausea, diarrhea, flatulence, gastritis, arthralgia have been reported.

Pediatric Concerns: None via milk.

Drug Interactions: Oral products containing calcium or magnesium will significantly reduce oral bioavailability. Take on empty stomach.

Relative Infant Dose:

Adult Dose: 30 mg/d for 2 months

Alternatives:

T ½	= 480 hours	M/P	=
PHL	=	PB	= 24%
Tmax	= 1 hour	Oral	= 0.63%
MW	= 305	pKa	=
Vd	= 6.3		

References:
1. Pharmaceutical Manufacturer Prescribing Information, 2002.

RISPERIDONE   L3

Trade: Risperdal, Invega
Other Trades: Risperdal
Uses: Antipsychotic
AAP: Not reviewed

Risperidone is a potent antipsychotic agent belonging to a new chemical class and is a dopamine and serotonin antagonist. Risperidone is metabolized to an active metabolite, 9-hyrdoxyrisperidone. In a study of one patient receiving 6 mg/day of risperidone at steady state, the peak plasma level of approximately 130 µg/L occurred 4 hours after an oral dose.[1] Peak milk levels of risperidone and 9-hydroxyrisperidone were approximately 12 µg/L and 40 µg/L respectively. The estimated daily dose of risperidone and metabolite (risperidone equivalents) was 4.3% of the weight-adjusted maternal dose. The milk/plasma ratios calculated from areas under the curve over 24 hours were 0.42 and 0.24 respectively for risperidone and 6-hydroxyrisperidone.

In another study, the transfer of risperidone and 9-hydroxyrisperidone into milk was studied in 2 breastfeeding women and one woman with risperidone-induced galactorrhea.[2] In case two (risperidone dose= 42.1 µg/kg/d), the average concentration of risperidone and 9-hydroxyrisperidone in milk (Cav) was 2.1 and 6 µg/L respectively. The relative infant dose was 2.8% of the maternal dose.

In case 3 (risperidone dose= 23.1 µg/kg/d), the average concentration of risperidone and 9-hydroxyrisperidone in milk (Cav) was 0.39 and 7.06 µg/L respectively. The milk/plasma ratio determined in 2 women was <0.5 for both risperidone compounds. The relative infant doses were 2.3%, 2.8%, and 4.7% (as risperidone equivalents) of the maternal weight-adjusted doses in these three cases. Risperidone and 9-hydroxyrisperidone were not detected in the plasma of the 2 breastfed infants studied, and no adverse effects were noted.

Paliperidone (Invega), the active metabolite of risperidone, is available in extended release tablets. This formulation has a volume of distribution of 6.95 L/kg, 74% protein binding, and a bioavailability of 28%.[3]

Pregnancy Risk Category: C

Lactation Risk Category: L3

Adult Concerns: Risks include neuroleptic malignant syndrome, tardive dyskinesia, myocardial arrhythmias, orthostatic hypotension, seizures, hyperprolactinemia, somnolence. Galactorrhea has been reported.

Pediatric Concerns: None reported via milk.

Drug Interactions: Do not use with alcohol. May enhance the hypotensive response of other antihypertensives. May antagonize the effect of levodopa. Carbamazepine or clozapine may increase clearance of risperidone.

Relative Infant Dose: 2.8% - 9.1%

Adult Dose: 3 mg BID

Alternatives: Quetiapine

T ½	= 3-20 hours	M/P	= 0.42
PHL	=	PB	= 90%
Tmax	= 3-17 hours	Oral	= 70-94%
MW	= 410	pKa	=
Vd	=		

References:
1. Hill RC, McIvor RJ, Wojnar-Horton RE, Hackett LP, Ilett KF. Risperidone distribution and excretion into human milk: case report and estimated infant exposure during breast-feeding. J Clin Psychopharmacol 2000; 20 (2):285-286.
2. Ilett KF, Hackett LP, Kristensen JH, Vaddadi KS, Gardiner SJ, Begg EJ. Transfer of risperidone and 9-hydroxyrisperidone into human milk. Ann Pharmacother 2004; 38 (2):273-276.
3. Pharmaceutical Manufacturer Prescribing Information. 2007.

RITODRINE   L3

Trade: Pre-Par, Yutopar
Other Trades: Yutopar
Uses: Adrenergic agent
AAP: Not reviewed

Ritodrine is primarily used to reduce uterine contractions in premature labor due to its beta-2 adrenergic effect on uterine receptors.[1] No data are available on its transfer to human milk.

Pregnancy Risk Category: B

Lactation Risk Category: L3

Adult Concerns: Fetal and maternal tachycardia, hypertension, lethargy, sleepiness, ketoacidosis, pulmonary edema.

Pediatric Concerns: None reported via milk.

Drug Interactions: Use cautiously with steroids due to pulmonary edema. Acebutolol and other beta blockers would block efficacy of ritodrine. Use with atropine may lead to systemic exaggerated. hypertension. Use with bupivacaine has lead to extreme hypotension. Numerous other interactions are listed, please review.

Relative Infant Dose:

Adult Dose: 10-20 mg every 4-6 hours

Alternatives:

T ½	= 15 hours	M/P	=
PHL	=	PB	= 32%
Tmax	= 40-60 minutes	Oral	= 30%
MW	= 287	pKa	= 9
Vd	= 0.7		

References:
1. Gandar R, de Zoeten LW, van der Schoot JB. Serum level of ritodrine in man. Eur J Clin Pharmacol 1980; 17 (2):117-122.

RITUXIMAB   L3

Trade: Rituxan
Other Trades:
Uses: Antineoplastic agent, monoclonal antibody
AAP: Not reviewed

Rituximab, an IgG antibody, binds to the CD20 antigen found on the surface of B lymphocytes.[1] It is used in the treatment of non-Hodgkin's lymphoma, rheumatoid arthritis, and lymphoid leukemia. There are no reported levels in human milk. Levels of IgG antibodies in human milk are generally low. In addition, oral bioavailability of this protein is likely to be nil.

Pregnancy Risk Category: C

Lactation Risk Category: L3

Adult Concerns: Common adverse effects include fever and chills, nausea, pruritus, angioedema, asthenia, hypotension, headache, bronchospasm.

Pediatric Concerns: No data are available. Due to its large MW, it is unlikely to enter milk in clinically relevant concentrations.

Drug Interactions: Rituximab interacts with live vaccines, increasing the risk of infection by the vaccines. Cisplatin used concurrently increases the risk of renal failure.

Relative Infant Dose:

Adult Dose: non-Hodgkin's lymphoma: 375 mg/square meter IV

Alternatives:

T ½	= 206 hours	M/P	=
PHL	=	PB	=
Tmax	=	Oral	= Nil
MW	= 145,000	pKa	=
Vd	= 4.3		

References:
1. Pharmaceutical Manufacturer Prescribing Information. 2007.

RIZATRIPTAN   L3

Trade: Maxalt
Other Trades: Maxalt
Uses: Antimigraine
AAP: Not reviewed

Rizatriptan is a selective serotonin receptor agonist, similar in effect to sumatriptan.[1] It is primarily indicated for acute migraine headache treatment. No data are available on its transfer into human milk, but it is concentrated in rodent milk (M/P=5). Until we have clear data on breastmilk levels, the kinetics of this drug may predispose to higher milk levels and sumatriptan should be preferred.

Pregnancy Risk Category: C

Lactation Risk Category: L3

Adult Concerns: Do not use in patients with ischemic heart disease, coronary artery vasospasm, or significant underlying cardiac disease. Rizatriptan should not be used within 24 hours of an ergot alkaloid, dihydroergotamine, or methysergide. Side effects include chest pain, paresthesia, dry mouth, nausea, dizziness, and somnolence.

Pediatric Concerns: None reported via milk, but caution is recommended.

Drug Interactions: Plasma levels may be increased when used with a MAO inhibitor, or shortly thereafter. Concurrent use of propranolol produced a 70% increase in plasma level of rizatriptan. No interactions were noted with nadolol or metoprolol.

Relative Infant Dose:

Adult Dose: 5-10 mg orally, repeat only after 2 hours

Alternatives: Sumatriptan

T ½	= 2-3 hours	M/P	=
PHL	=	PB	= 14%
Tmax	= 1-1.5 hours	Oral	= 45%
MW	= 269	pKa	=
Vd	= 2		

References:
1. Pharmaceutical Manufacturer Prescribing Information. 1999.

ROFECOXIB

L2

Trade: Vioxx
Other Trades: Vioxx
Uses: NSAID analgesic
AAP: Not reviewed

Rofecoxib is one of the newer Cyclooxigenase-2 (COX-2) inhibitors. It was recently removed from the market in this country for increasing the risk of cardiovascular events following long-term use.

In a new study of six breastfeeding mothers at steady state who received 25 mg/day the absolute infant dose in milk was about 0.008 mg/kg per day.[1] The relative infant dose ranged from 1.8 to 3.2% of the maternal dose. The Tmax for milk ranged from 1 to 4 hours. The authors suggest that rofecoxib is compatible with breastfeeding.

Pregnancy Risk Category: C

Lactation Risk Category: L2

Adult Concerns: Abdominal pain, fatigue, dizziness, diarrhea, headache,

Pediatric Concerns: None reported via milk but observe for GI cramping, distress, diarrhea. Probably quite safe for breastfeeding infants.

Drug Interactions: May reduce efficacy of ACE inhibitors with elevation of blood pressure. Increased plasma concentrations of rofecoxib result when coadministered with cimetidine. May increase lithium levels, and reduce the efficacy of diuretics. May increase plasma concentrations of methotrexate by 23%. Rifampin may increase rofecoxib plasma levels by 50%. When added to warfarin therapy, may increase INR by 8%.

Relative Infant Dose: 1.8-3.2%

Adult Dose: 12.5 to 25 mg once daily.

Alternatives: Ibuprofen, celecoxib

T ½	= 17 hours	M/P	= 0.16-0.32
PHL	=	PB	= 87%
Tmax	= 2-3 hours	Oral	= 93%
MW	= 314	pKa	=
Vd	= 1.3		

References:
1. Gardiner SJ, Begg EJ, Zhang M, Hughes RC. Transfer of rofecoxib into human milk. Eur J Clin Pharmacol 2005; 61:405-408.

ROPINIROLE   L4

Trade: Requip
Other Trades:
Uses: Dopamine stimulating agent used for Restless Legs and Parkinson's syn.
AAP: Not reviewed

Ropinirole is a non-ergoline dopamine agonist. It is used to treat Parkinson's and Restless leg syndromes. While it has not been studied in breastfeeding mothers, it should not be used. Ropinirole is known to reduce prolactin levels, even in men and would likely reduce milk production in breastfeeding mothers.

Pregnancy Risk Category: C (hazardous)

Lactation Risk Category: L4

Adult Concerns: Ropinirole may potentiate the dopaminergic side effects of L-dopa and may cause and/or exacerbate preexisting dyskinesia in patients treated with L-dopa. Cases of retroperitoneal fibrosis, pulmonary infiltrates, pleural effusion, pleural thickening, pericarditis, and cardiac valvulopathy have been reported. Patients should be advised that they may develop postural (orthostatic) hypotension with or without symptoms such as dizziness, nausea, fainting, and sometimes sweating. Daytime sleepiness or episodes of falling asleep have been reported and are of some concern for active individuals.

Pediatric Concerns: None reported, but a reduction of prolactin could severely reduce milk supply.

Drug Interactions: Co-administration of ciprofloxacin with ropinirole increased ropinirole AUC by 84% on average and C_{max} by 60% in 12 patients. Estrogens may reduced the oral clearance of ropinirole by 36%. Dopamine antagonists (metoclopramide, domperidone, etc.) may diminish the effectiveness of ropinirole.

Relative Infant Dose:

Adult Dose: 0.25-1.0 mg three times daily

Alternatives:

T ½	= 6 hours	M/P	=
PHL	=	PB	= 40%
Tmax	= 1-2 hours	Oral	= 55%
MW	= 297	pKa	=
Vd	= 7.5		

References:
1. Pharmaceutical Manufacturers Prescribing information. 2005.

ROPIVACAINE   L2

Trade: Naropin
Other Trades: Naropin
Uses: Local anesthetic
AAP: Not reviewed

Ropivacaine is a newer local anesthetic commonly used as a regional anesthetic and for epidural infusions. It is believed to produce less hypotension when compared to bupivacaine. No data are available on its transfer into human milk, but the manufacture suggests it is probably much lower than the infant receives in utero. This agent is commonly used in obstetrics and probably poses few if any problems to a breastfeeding infant.

Pregnancy Risk Category: B

Lactation Risk Category: L2

Adult Concerns: Adverse effects following epidural administration include hypotension, tachycardia, shivering, urinary retention, vomiting, nausea, headache, and back pain.

Pediatric Concerns: None reported in breastmilk. This agent is commonly used in obstetrics and is unlikely to affect and infant via milk.

Drug Interactions: Fluvoxamine and other CYP1A2 inhibitors may reduce plasma clearance of ropivacaine metabolites by 70%. CYP2A4 inhibitors such as ketoconazole may reduce clearance of ropivacaine as well.

Relative Infant Dose:

Adult Dose: Epidural = 75-150 mg

Alternatives: Bupivacaine

T ½	= 4.2 hours (epidural)	M/P	=
PHL	=	PB	= 94%
Tmax	= 43 minutes (epidural)	Oral	=
MW	= 328	pKa	= 8.07
Vd	= 0.58		

References:
1. Pharmaceutical Manufacturers prescribing information, 2003.

ROSIGLITAZONE   L3

Trade: Avandia
Other Trades:
Uses: Oral antidiabetic agent
AAP: Not reviewed

Rosiglitazone is an oral antidiabetic agent which acts primarily by increasing insulin sensitivity. In essence, the insulin receptor is activated reducing insulin resistance. It also decreases hepatic gluconeogenesis and increases insulin-dependent muscle glucose uptake. It does not increase the release of or secretion of insulin. No data are available on its entry into human milk. The maximum plasma concentration following a 2 mg dose is only 156 nanograms/mL.[1] Assuming a dose of 2 mg every 12 hours and a theoretical milk/plasma ratio of 1.0 (which is probably high), an infant would likely ingest about 23.4 μg/kg/day via milk. In a 5 kg infant, this would be approximately 2.8% of the maternal dose. But these data are only theoretical.

Pregnancy Risk Category: C

Lactation Risk Category: L3

Adult Concerns: Elevated liver enzymes in small percentage of patients. Hypoglycemia, increased body weight gain, edema, anemia.

Pediatric Concerns: None via milk, but it has not been studied.

Drug Interactions: Metformin may enhance hypoglycemic effect. Rosiglitazone may reduce effectiveness of oral contraceptives containing estrogen and progestins by reducing plasma levels of these hormones. These changes could result in loss of contraception. Consider a higher dose contraceptive. Rosiglitazone may reduce cyclosporine levels.

Relative Infant Dose:

Adult Dose: 2-8 mg daily

Alternatives:

T ½	= 3-4 hours	M/P	=
PHL	=	PB	= 99.8%
Tmax	= 1 hour	Oral	= 99%
MW	= 357	pKa	= 6.8
Vd	= 0.25		

References:
1.   Pharmaceutical Manufacturer Prescribing Information.

ROSUVASTATIN CALCIUM | L3

Trade: Crestor
Other Trades: Crestor
Uses: HMG-CoA reductase inhibitor
AAP: Not reviewed

Rosuvastatin, like other statins, is used to reduce cholesterol synthesis in patients with hypercholesterolemia. It works by blocking HMG-CoA reductase, the rate limiting enzyme in cholesterol synthesis.[1] No data are available on the excretion of this product into human milk, however due to the large MW and high protein binding, it would be unlikely that a therapeutic concentration would be passed to a breastfeeding infant. Nevertheless, atherosclerosis is a chronic process and the discontinuation of lipid-lowering medications while breastfeeding would have little to no effect on the overall treatment of hypercholesterolemia. Therefore, since cholesterol and other products of cholesterol biosynthesis are so vital to proper infant development, the potential harm to an infant would outweigh the benefit a mother would receive from continued therapy. The use of anti-hyperlipidemia medications would not be advisable under most circumstances in breastfeeding mothers.

Pregnancy Risk Category: X

Lactation Risk Category: L3

Adult Concerns: Adverse reactions include chest pain, hypertension, headache, anxiety, depression, rash, pharyngitis, bruising, myalgia, and cough.

Pediatric Concerns: No data are available.

Drug Interactions: Antacids and cholestyramine reduce plasma concentrations of rosuvastatin. Niacin, clofibrate, and colchicine can increase the risk of myopathy. Cyclosporine and gemfibrozil can increase serum concentrations of rosuvastatin. Rosuvastatin may increase serum plasma concentrations of ethinyl estradiol and norgestrel.

Relative Infant Dose:

Adult Dose: 5-40 mg/day

Alternatives:

T ½	= 19 hours	M/P	=
PHL	=	PB	= 90%
Tmax	= 3-5 hours	Oral	= 20%
MW	= 1001	pKa	=
Vd	= 1.9		

References:
1. Pharmaceutical Manufacturer Prescribing Information. 2007.

ROTIGOTINE   L4

Trade: Neupro
Other Trades:
Uses: Dopamine agonist
AAP: Not reviewed

Rotigotine is a dopamine agonist used to treat the signs and symptoms of Parkinson's disease. It is thought to stimulate postsynaptic dopamine D2-type auto receptors in the brain, leading to improved dopaminergic transmission in the motor areas of the basal ganglia.[1] No data are available on the transfer of rotigotine into human milk. According to the manufacturer, rotigotine stimulates dopamine and thus reduces prolactin secretion from the pituitary. It is possible that this medication could significantly decrease prolactin release and in turn, decrease milk production. Therefore, milk production should be monitored carefully if this medication is used in a lactating mother.

Pregnancy Risk Category: C

Lactation Risk Category: L4

Adult Concerns: Adverse reactions include somnolence, dizziness, headache, nausea, vomiting, and application site reactions.

Pediatric Concerns: No data are available.

Drug Interactions: Typical antipsychotics and metoclopramide may decrease the efficacy of rotigotine, while CNS depressants may enhance the adverse effects.

Relative Infant Dose:

Adult Dose: 1-2 mg/24 hour patch daily

Alternatives:

T ½	= 5-7 hours	M/P	=
PHL	=	PB	= 90%
Tmax	= 15-18 hours	Oral	=
MW	= 315.48	pKa	=
Vd	= 84		

References:
1. Pharmaceutical Manufacturer Prescribing Information. 2004.

RUBELLA VIRUS VACCINE, LIVE   L2

Trade: Meruvax, Rubella Vaccine, Measles Vaccine
Other Trades:
Uses: Live attenuated (measles) vaccine
AAP: Not reviewed

Rubella virus vaccine contains a live attenuated virus. The American College of Obstetricians and Gynecologists and the CDC currently recommends the early postpartum immunization of women who show no or low antibody titers to rubella. At least four studies have found rubella virus to be transferred via milk although presence of clinical symptoms was not evident.[1-3] Rubella virus has been cultured from the throat of one infant while another infant was clinically ill with minor symptoms and serologic evidence of rubella infection.[4] In general, the use of rubella virus vaccine in breastfeeding mothers of full-term, normal infants has not been associated with untoward effects and is generally recommended.[5]

Pregnancy Risk Category: X

Lactation Risk Category: L2

Adult Concerns: Burning, stinging, lymphadenopathy, rash, malaise, sore throat, etc.

Pediatric Concerns: One case report of rash, vomiting, and mild rubella infection.

Drug Interactions: Immunosuppressants and immune globulins may reduce immunogenicity. Concurrent use of interferon may reduce antibody response.

Relative Infant Dose:

Adult Dose: 0.5 mL X 1

Alternatives:

References:
1. Buimovici-Klein E, Hite RL, Byrne T, Cooper LZ. Isolation of rubella virus in milk after postpartum immunization. J Pediatr 1977; 91 (6):939-941.
2. Losonsky GA, Fishaut JM, Strussenberg J, Ogra PL. Effect of immunization against rubella on lactation products. I. Development and characterization of specific immunologic reactivity in breast milk. J Infect Dis 1982; 145 (5):654-660.
3. Losonsky GA, Fishaut JM, Strussenberg J, Ogra PL. Effect of immunization against rubella on lactation products. II. Maternal-neonatal interactions. J Infect Dis 1982; 145 (5):661-666.
4. Landes RD, Bass JW, Millunchick EW, Oetgen WJ. Neonatal rubella following postpartum maternal immunization. J Pediatr 1980; 97 (3):465-467.
5. Lawrence RA. Breastfeeding: A guide for the medical profession. St. Louis: Mosby Publishers, 1994.

SACCHARIN   L3

Trade: Saccharin
Other Trades:
Uses: Sweetener
AAP: Not reviewed

In one group of 6 women who received 126 mg (per 12 oz drink) every 6 hours for 9 doses, milk levels varied greatly from <200 µg/L after one dose to 1.765 mg/L after 9 doses.[1] Under these dosing conditions, saccharin levels appear to accumulate over time. Half-life in serum and milk were 4.84 hours and 17.9 hours respectively after 3 days. Even after such doses, these milk levels are considered minimal. Moderate intake should be compatible with nursing.

Pregnancy Risk Category: C

Lactation Risk Category: L3

Adult Concerns:

Pediatric Concerns: None reported via milk.

Drug Interactions:

Relative Infant Dose: 3.6%

Adult Dose:

Alternatives:

T ½	= 4.84 hours	M/P	=
PHL	=	PB	=
Tmax	=	Oral	= Complete
MW	= 183	pKa	=
Vd	=		

References:
1.   Egan PC, Marx CM. et.al. Saccharin excretion in mature human milk. Drug Intell Clin Pharm 1984; 18:511.

SAGE   L4

Trade: Sage, Dalmatian Sage, Spanish Sage
Other Trades:
Uses: Herbal product
AAP: Not reviewed

Salvia officinalis L. (Dalmatian sage) and Salvia lavandulaefolia Vahl (Spanish sage) are most common of the species. Extracts and teas have been used to treat digestive disorders (antispasmodic), as an antiseptic and astringent, for treating diarrhea, gastritis, sore throat, and other maladies.[1] The dried and smoked leaves have been used for treating asthma symptoms. These uses are largely unsubstantiated in the literature.

Sage extracts have been found to be strong antioxidants and with some antimicrobial properties (staph. aureus) due to the phenolic acid salvin content. Sage oil has antispasmodic effects in animals and this may account for its moderating effects on the GI tract. For the most part, sage is relatively nontoxic and nonirritating. Ingestion of significant quantities may lead to cheilitis, stomatitis, dry mouth, or local irritation.[2]

Due to drying properties and pediatric hypersensitivity to anticholinergics, sage should be used with some caution in breastfeeding mothers.

Pregnancy Risk Category:

Lactation Risk Category: L4

Adult Concerns: Observe for typical anticholinergic effects such as cheilitis, stomatitis, dry mouth or local irritation.

Pediatric Concerns: None reported but observe for dry mouth, stomatitis, cheilitis.

Drug Interactions:

Relative Infant Dose:

Adult Dose:

Alternatives:

References:
1. Leung AY. Encyclopedia of Common Natural Ingredients used in Food, Drugs and Cosmetics. J Wiley and Sons, 1980.
2. Bissett NG. In: Herbal Drugs and Phytopharmaceuticals. Medpharm Scientific Publishers, CRC Press, Boca Raton, 1994.

SALICYLIC ACID, TOPICAL   L3

Trade: Occlusal-HP
Other Trades:
Uses: Keratolytic, Antiacne
AAP: Not reviewed

Salicylic acid is often used in anti-acne preparations, as well as in many wart and corn removal products. Salicylic acid concentrations vary, ranging from 0.5% to 60%, in gels, shampoos, ointments and creams. Salicylic acid acts as a keratolytic at concentrations of 3-6%, and above 6% becomes destructive. Systemic absorption depends on the concentration of the product used, the amount applied, and duration of use. Absorption increases with the duration of use. The systemic absorption relative to the dose has been found to range from 9.3 to 25.1%.

Due to systemic absorption, topical salicylic acid should not be used while breastfeeding. It is known that salicylates are excreted in mothers' milk, and have been attributed to certain conditions such as Reye's syndrome in children.

Pregnancy Risk Category:

Lactation Risk Category: L3

Adult Concerns: Adverse reactions include burning and stinging, as well as redness around the application area.

Pediatric Concerns: No data are available.

Drug Interactions:

Relative Infant Dose:

Adult Dose:

Alternatives:

T ½	=	M/P	=
PHL	=	PB	= 50-80%
Tmax	=	Oral	=
MW	= 138.12	pKa	=
Vd	= 0.17		

References:

SALINE LAXATIVES   L2

Trade: Phillips Milk of Magnesia, Fleet, Visicol, Tridate, X-Prep
Other Trades:
Uses: Laxative
AAP: Maternal Medication Usually Compatible with Breastfeeding

Saline laxatives work by retaining water content in the GI tract. Saline laxatives come in two forms, magnesium salts and phosphate-containing salt forms. Neither are substantially absorbed in normal individuals, but instead most is retained in the gut. Magnesium and phosphate salts absorbed systemically would be rapidly eliminated by the kidneys in normal individuals. Caution is recommended in individuals with cardiovascular or renal anomalies.

Magnesium Forms (Milk of Magnesia, Citrate of Magnesia, Phillips Milk of Magnesia, etc.): Magnesium citrate, magnesium hydroxide, and magnesium sulfate compose the usual forms of magnesium laxatives. Only 15-30% of magnesium salts may be absorbed from the GI tract, the remaining is retained in the intestinal lumen and keeps water in the intestinal lumen thus producing a laxative effect.

Phosphate Forms (Fleet, Visicol): Sodium phosphate solutions containing both dibasic sodium phosphate and monobasic sodium phosphate are used to empty the bowel prior to colonoscopy and other procedures. Approximately 1-20% of the sodium and phosphate in such preparations is absorbed.

It is very unlikely that the use of these saline laxatives would increase maternal plasma levels high enough to induce changes in electrolyte content of human milk. While we do not have specific data on the use of higher doses of oral magnesium salts or of the phosphates, the lactocyte controls the microelectrolyte concentrations of milk closely. Minute changes in maternal levels which could potentially occur following the use of these laxatives, would not likely alter milk content of these electrolytes.

Pregnancy Risk Category:

Lactation Risk Category: L2

Adult Concerns: Diarrhea, gut cramping, hyperphosphatemia and serious electrolyte disturbances have been reported in some patients at increased risk for electrolyte disturbances. With magnesium salts, especially in renally impaired patients, hypotension, cardiac arrhythmias or arrest, loss of deep tendon reflexes, and confusion may occur.

Pediatric Concerns: None reported via milk.

Drug Interactions: May reduce oral bioavailability of many drugs.

Relative Infant Dose:

Adult Dose: Highly variable.

Alternatives:

T ½	=		M/P	=	
PHL	=		PB	=	
Tmax	=		Oral	= 33%	
MW	=		pKa	=	
Vd	=				

References:
1. AHFS Drug Information. Bethesda, Md; American Society of Health System Pharmacists, 2003.

SALMETEROL XINAFOATE | L2

Trade: Serevent
Other Trades: Serevent
Uses: Long acting beta adrenergic bronchodilator
AAP: Not reviewed

Salmeterol is a long acting beta-2 adrenergic stimulant used as a bronchodilator in asthmatics. Maternal plasma levels of salmeterol after inhaled administration are very low (85-200 pg/mL), or undetectable.[1] Studies in animals have shown that plasma and breastmilk levels are very similar. Oral absorption of both salmeterol and the xinafoate moiety are good. The terminal half-life of salmeterol is 5.5 hours, xinafoate is 11 days. No reports of use in lactating women are available.

Pregnancy Risk Category: C

Lactation Risk Category: L2

Adult Concerns: Tremor, dizziness, hypertension.

Pediatric Concerns: None reported via milk, but studies are limited.

Drug Interactions: Use with MAOI may result in severe hypertension, severe headache, and hypertensive crisis. Tricyclic antidepressants may potentiate the pressure response. The pressor response of salmeterol may be reduced by lithium.

Relative Infant Dose:

Adult Dose: 50 µg BID

Alternatives:

T ½	= 5.5 hours	M/P	= 1.0
PHL	–	PB	= 98%
Tmax	= 10-45 minutes	Oral	= Complete
MW	=	pKa	=
Vd	=		

References:
1. Pharmaceutical Manufacturer Prescribing Information. 1996.

SALSALATE

L4

Trade: Amigesic
Other Trades: Amigesic, Salflex, Disalcid
Uses: NSAID
AAP: Drugs associated with significant side effects and should be given with caution

Salsalate is a non-steroidal anti-inflammatory drug used to treat minor pain or fever and arthritis. Salsalate is a dimer of salicylic acid, that when ingested releases pure salicylic acid.[1] Absorption of salicylic acid (SA) is complete. SA inhibits prostaglandin synthesis and acts on the hypothalamus heat-regulating center to reduce fever. Salicylic acid is excreted in breast milk (see aspirin) and chronic use of salicylates should be avoided. Therefore, salsalate should not be used while breastfeeding.

Pregnancy Risk Category: C in first and second trimesters
D in third trimester

Lactation Risk Category: L4

Adult Concerns: Adverse effects include nausea, heartburn, stomach pain, and dyspepsia.

Pediatric Concerns: Avoid use in breastfeeding mothers due to the risk of Reye Syndrome in infants. One case of neonatal metabolic acidosis has been reported in a mother consuming aspirin.[2]

Drug Interactions: A decreased effect is seen with urinary alkalinizers, antacids, and corticosteroids. Salsalate can decrease the effect of uricosurics and spironolactone. Also, ACE inhibitor effects may be decreased with NSAID use.

Relative Infant Dose:

Adult Dose: 3000 mg/day in 2-3 divided doses

Alternatives: Acetaminophen, ibuprofen

T ½	= 7-8 hours	M/P	=
PHL	=	PB	= 80-90%
Tmax	=	Oral	= Complete
MW	= 258	pKa	=
Vd	=		

References:
1.   Pharmaceutical Manufacturer Prescribing Information. 1997.

2. Clark JH, Wilson WG. A 16-day-old breast-fed infant with metabolic acidosis caused by salicylate. Clin Pediatr. 1981;20:53-4.

SCOPOLAMINE   L3

Trade: Transderm Scope
Other Trades: Transderm-V, Buscopan, Benacine, Scopoderm TTS
Uses: Anticholinergic
AAP: Maternal Medication Usually Compatible with Breastfeeding

Scopolamine is a typical anticholinergic used primarily for motion sickness and preoperatively to produce amnesia and decrease salivation.[1-3] Scopolamine is structurally similar to atropine but is known for its prominent CNS effects, including reducing motion sickness. There are no reports on its transfer into human milk, but due to its poor oral bioavailability it is generally believed to be minimal. However, following prolonged exposure in a newborn, some anticholinergic symptoms could appear, and include drying, constipation, and urinary retention.

Pregnancy Risk Category: C

Lactation Risk Category: L3

Adult Concerns: Blurred vision, dry mouth, drowsiness, constipation, confusion, drowsiness, bradycardia, hypotension, dermatitis.

Pediatric Concerns: None via milk. Observe for anticholinergic symptoms such as drowsiness, dry mouth.

Drug Interactions: Decreased effect of acetaminophen, levodopa, ketoconazole, digoxin. GI absorption of the following drugs may be altered: ketoconazole, digoxin, potassium supplements, acetaminophen, levodopa.

Relative Infant Dose:

Adult Dose: 0.3-0.6 mg once

Alternatives:

T ½	= 2.9 hours	M/P	=
PHL	=	PB	=
Tmax	= 1 hour	Oral	= 27%
MW	= 303	pKa	= 7.55
Vd	= 1.4		

References:
1. Lacy C. Drug information handbook. Lexi-Comp Inc. Cleveland, OH, 1996.
2. Drug Facts and Comparisons 1996 ed. ed. St. Louis: 1996.
3. Pharmaceutical Manufacturer Prescribing Information. 1997.

SECOBARBITAL   L3

Trade: Seconal

Other Trades: Novo-Secobarb, Seconal

Uses: Short acting barbiturate sedative

AAP: Maternal Medication Usually Compatible with Breastfeeding

Secobarbital is a sedative, hypnotic barbiturate. It is probably secreted into breastmilk, although levels are unknown, and may be detectable in milk for 24 hours or longer.[1,2,3] Recommend mothers delay breastfeeding for 3-4 hours to reduce possible transfer to infant if exposure to this barbiturate is required.

Pregnancy Risk Category: D

Lactation Risk Category: L3

Adult Concerns: Respiratory depression, sedation, addiction.

Pediatric Concerns: None reported via milk, but observer for sedation.

Drug Interactions:

Relative Infant Dose:

Adult Dose: 100 mg daily.

Alternatives:

T ½	= 15-40 hours	M/P	=
PHL	=	PB	= 30-45%
Tmax	= 2-4 hours	Oral	= 90%
MW	= 260	pKa	= 7.9
Vd	= 1.6-1.9		

References:
1. Tyson RM, Shrader EA, Perlman HH. Drugs transmitted through breast milk. II Barbiturates. J Pediatr 1938; 14:86-90.
2. Kaneko S, Sato T, Suzuki K. The levels of anticonvulsants in breast milk. Br J Clin Pharmacol 1979; 7 (6):624-627.

3. Wilson JT, Brown RD, Cherek DR, Dailey JW, Hilman B, Jobe PC, Manno BR, Manno JE, Redetzki HM, Stewart JJ. Drug excretion in human breast milk: principles, pharmacokinetics and projected consequences. Clin Pharmacokinet 1980; 5 (1):1-66.

SELEGILINE   L4

Trade: Eldepryl, Emsam, Zelapar
Other Trades:
Uses: Monoamine Oxidase Inhibitor
AAP: Not reviewed

Selegiline is a selective irreversible inhibitor of monoamine oxidase, which in turn increases dopaminergic activity. It is used to treat parkinsonian patients, major depressive disorder, and ADHD. It is available in a capsule form, an orally disintegrating tablet (Zelapar), as well as a transdermal system (Emsam). The transdermal application has a half-life of 18-25 hours, and an absorption of 25-30% over 24 hours. The orally disintegrating tablet concentration peaks at 10-15 minutes, and has a half-life of 10 hours. No data are available on the transfer of selegiline into human milk. However, MAO inhibitors require extraordinarily careful use and have many food-drug and drug-drug interactions that could be dangerous. These products should not be used in breastfeeding mothers.

Pregnancy Risk Category: C

Lactation Risk Category: L4

Adult Concerns: Adverse effects include headache, insomnia, nausea, and dizziness. As with most antidepressant therapies, caution should be taken toward suicidal ideations.

Pediatric Concerns: Do not use in breasfeeding mothers.

Drug Interactions: There are many drug interactions, particularly with amphetamines, anorexiants, atomoxetine, barbiturates, and SSRIs. See product information for a complete list of drug interactions.

Relative Infant Dose:

Adult Dose: 10 mg daily (capsule)

Alternatives:

T ½	= 10 hours	M/P	=
PHL	=	PB	= 99.5%
Tmax	=	Oral	= 5.5%
MW	= 187	pKa	=
Vd	=		

References:
1.   Pharmaceutical Manufacturer Prescribing Information. 2007.

SELENIUM SULFIDE   L3

Trade: Selsun, Exsel, Head and Shoulders, Selsun Blue
Other Trades:
Uses: Topical antimicrobial
AAP: Not reviewed

Selenium sulfide is an anti-infective compound with mild antibacterial and antifungal activity. It is commonly used for Tinea Versicolor and seborrheic dermatitis such as dandruff. Selenium is not apparently absorbed significantly through intact skin but is absorbed by damaged skin or open lesions.[1] There are no data on its transfer into human milk. If used properly on undamaged skin, it is very unlikely that enough would be absorbed systemically to produce untoward effects in a breastfed infant. Do not apply directly to nipple as enhanced absorption by the infant could occur.

Pregnancy Risk Category:

Lactation Risk Category: L3

Adult Concerns: Changes in hair color and loss of hair have been reported. Extensive washing of hair reduces the incidence of these problems. Extensive systemic absorption can occur with application to broken skin. Nausea, vomiting, diarrhea.

Pediatric Concerns: None reported via milk. Do not apply directly to nipple.

Drug Interactions:

Relative Infant Dose:

Adult Dose: Apply topic twice weekly

Alternatives: Topical Clotrimazole, itraconazole

References:
1.   McEvoy GE. (ed): AFHS Drug Information. New York, NY: 2009.

SENNA LAXATIVES | L3

Trade: Senokot, Senexon, Ex Lax, Senna-Gen, Black-Draught,
  Fletcher, Castoria, Agoral
Other Trades:
Uses: Laxative
AAP: Maternal Medication Usually Compatible with
  Breastfeeding

Senna is a potent, proven laxative. Anthraquinones, its key ingredient, are believed to increase bowel activity due to secretion of anthraquinones into the colon. Side effects such as abdominal cramping and colic are unpredictable with homemade varieties of this plant. Most sources recommend taking a standardized formulation commonly available. This product is only recommended for short use, such as 10 days. Do not use for intestinal obstruction, or appendicitis, or abdominal pain of unknown origin. Senna laxatives are occasionally used in postpartum women to alleviate constipation. In one study of 23 women who received Senokot (100 mg containing 8.602 mg of Sennosides A and B), no sennoside A or B was detectable in their milk.[1] Of 15 mothers reporting loose stools, two infants had loose stools.

Pregnancy Risk Category:

Lactation Risk Category: L3

Adult Concerns: Diarrhea, abdominal cramps, dark colored urine, chronic diarrhea, fluid loss.

Pediatric Concerns: Several infants had loose stools although no drug was detected in milk.

Drug Interactions:

Relative Infant Dose:

Adult Dose: 100 mg daily.

Alternatives:

References:
1. Werthmann MW, Jr., Krees SV. Quantitative excretion of Senokot in human breast milk. Med Ann Dist Columbia 1973; 42 (1):4-5.

SERTRALINE   L2

Trade: Zoloft
Other Trades: Zoloft, Lustral
Uses: Antidepressant
AAP: Drugs whose effect on nursing infants is unknown but may be of concern

Sertraline is a typical serotonin reuptake inhibitor similar to Prozac and Paxil, but unlike Prozac, the longer half-life metabolite of sertraline is only marginally active. In one study of a single patient taking 100 mg of sertraline daily for 3 weeks postpartum, the concentration of sertraline in milk was 24, 43, 40, and 19 µg/Liter of milk at 1, 5, 9, and 23 hours respectively following the dose.[1] The maternal plasma levels of sertraline after 12 hours was 48 ng/mL. Sertraline plasma levels in the infant at three weeks were below the limit of detection (<0.5 ng/mL) at 12 hours post-dose. Routine pediatric evaluation after 3 months revealed a neonate of normal weight who had achieved the appropriate developmental milestones.

In another study of 3 breastfeeding patients who received 50-100 mg sertraline daily, the maternal plasma levels ranged from 18.4 to 95.8 ng/mL, whereas the plasma levels of sertraline and its metabolite, desmethylsertraline, in the three breastfed infants was below the limit of detection (<2 ng/mL).[2] Milk levels were not measured. Desmethylsertraline is poorly active, less than 10% of the parent sertraline.

Another recent publication reviewed the changes in platelet serotonin levels in breastfeeding mothers and their infants who received up to 100 mg of sertraline daily.[3] Mothers treated with sertraline had significant decreases in their platelet serotonin levels, which is expected. However, there was no change in platelet serotonin levels in breastfed infants of mothers consuming sertraline, suggesting that only minimal amounts of sertraline are actually transferred to the infant. This confirms other studies.

Studies by Stowe of eleven mother/infant pairs (maternal dose= 25-150 mg/day) further suggest minimal transfer of sertraline into human milk.[4] From this superb study, the concentration of sertraline peaked in the milk at 7-8 hours and the metabolite (desmethylsertraline) at 5-11 hours. The reported concentrations of sertraline and desmethylsertraline in breastmilk were 17-173 µg/L and 22-294 µg/L respectively. The reported dose of sertraline to the infant via milk varied from undetectable (5 of 11) to 0.124 mg/day in one infant. The infant's serum concentration of sertraline varied from undetectable to 3.0 ng/mL but was undetectable in 7 of 11patients. No developmental abnormalities were noted in any of the infants studied.

In a study of eight women taking sertraline (1.05 mg/kg/d) the mean milk/plasma ratio was 1.93 and 1.64 for sertraline and N-desmethylsertraline.[5] Infant exposure estimated from actual milk produced was 0.2% and 0.3% of the weight-adjusted maternal dose for sertraline and N-desmethylsertraline (sertraline equivalents) respectively. Assuming a 150 mL/kg/d intake, infant exposure was significantly greater at 0.90% and 1.32% for sertraline and N-desmethylsertraline respectively. Neither sertraline nor its N-desmethyl metabolite could be detected in plasma samples from the four infants tested. No adverse effects were observed in any of the eight infants and all had achieved normal developmental milestones.

Sertraline is a potent inhibitor of 5-HT transporter function both in the CNS and platelets. One recent study assessed the effect of sertraline on platelet 5-HT transporter function in 14 breastfeeding mothers (dose= 25-200 mg/d) and their infants to determine if even low levels of sertraline exposure could perhaps lead to changes in the infant's blood platelet 5-HT levels and, therefore, CNS serotonin levels.[6] While a significant reduction in platelet levels of 5-HT were noted in the mothers, no changes in 5-HT levels were noted in the 14 infants. Thus, it appears that at typical clinical doses, maternal sertraline has a minimal effect on platelet 5-HT transport in breastfeeding infants.

These studies generally confirm that the transfer of sertraline and its metabolite to the infant is minimal, and that attaining clinically relevant plasma levels in infants is remote at maternal doses less than 150 mg/day. Thorough reviews of antidepressant use in breastfeeding mothers are available.[7-9]

Pregnancy Risk Category: C

Lactation Risk Category: L2

Adult Concerns: Diarrhea, nausea, tremor, and increased sweating.

Pediatric Concerns: Of the cases reported in the literature, only one infant developed benign neonatal sleep at age 4 months which spontaneous resolved at 6 months. Its relationship, if any, to sertraline is unknown.

Drug Interactions: All SSRIs inhibit Cytochrome P450 enzymes and may inhibit metabolism of desipramine, dextromethorphan, encainide, haloperidol, metoprolol, etc. May induce serotonergic hyperstimulation when added too soon after MAO inhibitors, tricyclic antidepressants, and lithium. May displace warfarin from binding sites increasing anticoagulation. Two recent cases of serotonin-like reactions (agitation, dysarthria, diaphoresis and extrapyramidal movement disorder) have been reported when metoclopramide was used in patients receiving sertraline or venlafaxine.[7]

Relative Infant Dose: 0.4% - 2.2%

Adult Dose: 50-200 mg daily.

Alternatives: Escitalopram, Paroxetine, Fluoxetine

T ½	= 26 hours	M/P	= 0.89
PHL	=	PB	= 98%
Tmax	= 7-8 hours	Oral	= Complete
MW	= 306	pKa	=
Vd	= 20		

References:
1. Altshuler LL, Burt VK, McMullen M, Hendrick V. Breastfeeding and sertraline: a 24-hour analysis. J Clin Psychiatry 1995; 56 (6):243-245.
2. Mammen OK, Perel JM, Rudolph G, Foglia JP, Wheeler SB. Sertraline and norsertraline levels in three breastfed infants. J Clin Psychiatry 1997; 58 (3):100-103.
3. Epperson CN. et.al. Sertraine and Breastfeeding. NEJM 1997; 336 (16):1189-1190.
4. Stowe ZN, Owens MJ, Landry JC, Kilts CD, Ely T, Llewellyn A, Nemeroff CB. Sertraline and desmethylsertraline in human breast milk and nursing infants. Am J Psychiatry 1997; 154 (9):1255-1260.
5. Kristensen JH, Ilett KF, Dusci LJ, Hackett LP, Yapp P, Wojnar-Horton RE, Roberts MJ, Paech M. Distribution and excretion of sertraline and N-desmethylsertraline in human milk. Br J Clin Pharmacol 1998; 45 (5):453-457.
6. Epperson N, Czarkowski KA, Ward-O'Brien D, Weiss E, Gueorguieva R, Jatlow P, Anderson GM. Maternal sertraline treatment and serotonin transport in breast-feeding mother-infant pairs. Am J Psychiatry 2001; 158 (10):1631-1637.
7. Wisner KL, Perel JM, Findling RL. Antidepressant treatment during breast-feeding. Am J Psychiatry 1996; 153 (9):1132-1137.
8. Stowe ZN, Hostetter AL, Owens MJ, Ritchie JC, Sternberg K, Cohen LS, Nemeroff CB. The pharmacokinetics of sertraline excretion into human brest milk: determinants of infant serum concentrations. J Clin Psychiatry 2003; 64 (1):73-80.
9. Weissman AM, Levy BT, Hartz AJ, et.al. Pooled Analysis of Antidepressant Levels in Lactating Mothers, Breast Milk, and Nursing Infants. Am J Psychiatry 2004 June; 161 (6):1066-1078.

SEVOFLURANE   L3

Trade: Ultane
Other Trades:
Uses: Anesthetic gas
AAP: Not reviewed

Sevoflurane is a gaseous halogenated general anesthetic drug that is particularly popular because of its rapid wash-out. Average patient time to emergence is approximately 8.2 minutes. It is commonly used in adult and pediatric patients, and is used in cesarean sections. The manufacturer states that while the concentration of sevoflurane have not been measured in breastmilk, they are probably of no clinical importance 24 hours after anesthesia. Because of its rapid wash-out, sevoflurane concentrations in milk are predicted to be below those found with many other volatile anesthatics.[1] Sevoflurane follows a three term exponential decay with half-lives of 11min (18% of the dose in plasma compartment), 1.8 hours (15% from muscle compartment), and 20 hours (6% from fat compartment).[2] Small (3%) amounts of sevoflurane are metabolized and result in plasma levels that average 36 µM/liter. Levels reported are temporary and completely dissipate by 6 days. The fluoride ion released is not high enough to be a contraindication to breastfeeding. Further, the oral absorption of fluoride in infants is believed poor as it is chelated with calcium ions orally in milk.

While no data on levels of sevoflurane in breast milk are available, this product, due to its rapid clearance from the body (100 fold drop in 120 minutes), should not pose a problem for continued breastfeeding soon after exposure.

Pregnancy Risk Category: B

Lactation Risk Category: L3

Adult Concerns: Malignant hyperthermia, bradycardia, agitation, laryngospasm, shivering, hypotension, etc. Check anesthesia text for more.

Pediatric Concerns: None reported via milk. Milk levels are likely insignificant, and oral bioavailability is unlikely.

Drug Interactions: Sevoflurane increases intensity and duration of neuromuscular blockade by nondepolarizing muscle relaxants.

Relative Infant Dose:

Adult Dose: Variable.

Alternatives:

T ½	= 1.8-3.8 hours	M/P	=
PHL	=	PB	= 0%
Tmax	=	Oral	=
MW	= 200	pKa	=
Vd	= 0.5		

References:
1. Pharmaceutical Manufacturer Prescribing Information, 2003.
2. Holaday DA, Smith FR. Clinical characteristics and biotransformation of sevoflurane in healthy volunteers. Anesthesiology 1981; 54:100-106.

SIBUTRAMINE   L4

Trade: Meridia
Other Trades: Meridia
Uses: Appetite suppressant
AAP: Not reviewed

Sibutramine is a nonamphetamine appetite suppressant. Due to its effect on serotonin and norepinephrine reuptake, it is considered an antidepressant as well. Sibutramine is rather small in MW, active in the CNS, extremely lipid soluble, and has two 'active' metabolites with long half-lives (14-16 hours).[1-3] Although no data are available on its transfer into human milk, the pharmacokinetics of this drug theoretically suggest that it might have a rather high milk/plasma ratio and could enter milk in significant levels. Until we know more, a risk assessment may not support the use of this product in breastfeeding mothers.

Pregnancy Risk Category: C

Lactation Risk Category: L4

Adult Concerns: Adult side effects include headache, insomnia, back pain, flu-like syndrome, abdominal pain, seizures (rarely), and elevated liver enzymes. Cardiovascular events include tachycardia, hypertension.

Pediatric Concerns: None reported via milk. Caution is recommended.

Drug Interactions: Use of Sibutramine with drugs that may increase blood pressure (decongestants, cough and cold remedies) could be hazardous. Do not use with MAO inhibitors. Do not admix with drugs that inhibit cytochrome P450 enzymes in the liver (ketoconazole, cimetidine, erythromycin (minor effect).

Relative Infant Dose:

Adult Dose: 5-15 mg daily

Alternatives:

T ½	= 12.5-21.8 hours	M/P	=
PHL	=	PB	= 94%
Tmax	= 3-4 hours	Oral	= 77%
MW	= 334	pKa	=
Vd	=		

References:
1.   Lean ME. Sibutramine--a review of clinical efficacy. Int J Obes Relat Metab Disord 1997; 21 Suppl 1:S30-S36.
2.   Stock MJ. Sibutramine: a review of the pharmacology of a novel anti-obesity agent. Int J Obes Relat Metab Disord 1997; 21 Suppl 1:S25-S29.
3.   Pharmaceutical Manufacturer Prescribing Information.

SILDENAFIL   L3

Trade: Viagra, Revatio
Other Trades: Viagra
Uses: For erectile dysfunction and pulmonary hypertension
AAP: Not reviewed

Sildenafil is an inhibitor of nitrous oxide metabolism, thus increasing levels of nitrous oxide, smooth muscle relaxation, and an increased flow of blood in the corpus cavernosum of the penis.[1] While not currently indicated for women, illicit use is increasing. No data are available on the transfer of sildenafil into human milk, but it is unlikely that significant transfer will occur due to its larger MW and short half-life. However, caution is recommended in breastfeeding mothers. While not reported, persistent abnormal erections (priapism) could potentially occur in male infants.

Pregnancy Risk Category: B

Lactation Risk Category: L3

Adult Concerns: Changes in visual color perception is common. Other side effects include headache, flushing, dyspepsia, nasal congestion, and hypotension.

Pediatric Concerns: None reported via milk. If used, observe for priapism in male infants.

Drug Interactions: Do not admix with any form of nitrate, including nitroglycerine. Because it is metabolized by cytochrome P450 CYP3A4 and 2C9, increased plasma levels may result when admixed with azole antifungals, erythromycins, cimetidine and other such enzyme inhibitors. Serious prolonged erections have been reported with the co-administration of dihydrocodeine.

Relative Infant Dose:

Adult Dose: 50 mg daily

Alternatives:

T ½	= 4 hours	M/P	=
PHL	=	PB	= 96%
Tmax	= 60 minutes	Oral	= 40%
MW	= 666	pKa	=
Vd	= 1.5		

References:
1.   Pharmaceutical Manufacturer Prescribing Information. 1999.

SILICONE BREAST IMPLANTS   L3

Trade:
Other Trades:
Uses: Silicone mammoplasty
AAP: Not reviewed

Augmentation mammoplasty with silicone implants has only recently been available in the USA.   Millions of women have silicone implants for various esthetic reasons.   In general, placement of the

implant behind the breast seldom produces interruption of vital ducts, nerve supply, or blood supply. Periareolar incisions should be avoided, as   they might interrupt nerves vital to prolactin production. Most women have been able to breastfeed. Breast reduction surgery, on the other hand, has been found to produce significant interruption of the nervous supply (particularly the ductile tissue), leading to a reduced ability to lactate.

Other reports suggesting autoimmune diseases such as schleroderma with esophageal dysfunction in breastfed infants[1,2] have failed to be confirmed. Silicone transfer to breastmilk has been studied in one group of 15 lactating mothers with bilateral silicone breast implants.[3] Silicon levels were measured in breastmilk, whole blood, cow's milk, and 26 brands of infant formula. Comparing implanted women to controls, mean silicon levels were not significantly different in breastmilk (55.45 +/- 35 and 51.05 +/- 31 ng/mL respectively) or in blood (79.29 +/- 87 and 103.76 +/- 112 ng/mL respectively. Mean silicon level measured in store-bought cow's milk was 708.94 ng/mL and that for 26 brands of commercially available infant formula was 4402.5 ng/mL (ng/mL= parts per billion). The authors concluded that lactating women with silicone implants are similar to control women with respect to levels of silicon in their breastmilk and blood. From these studies, silicon levels are 10 times higher in cow's milk and even higher in infant formulas.

It is not known for certain if ingestion of leaking silicone by a nursing infant is dangerous. Although one article has been published showing esophageal strictures, it has subsequently been recalled by the author. Silicone by nature is extremely inert and is unlikely to be absorbed in the GI tract by a nursing infant although good studies are lacking. Silicone is a ubiquitous substance, found in all foods, liquids, etc.

Pregnancy Risk Category:

Lactation Risk Category: L3

Adult Concerns:

Pediatric Concerns: None reported via milk.

Drug Interactions:

Relative Infant Dose:

Adult Dose: N/A

Alternatives:

References:

1. Spiera RF, Gibofsky A, Spiera H. Scleroderma in women with silicone breast implants: comment on the article by Sanchez-Guerrero et al. Arthritis Rheum. May 1995;38 (5):719, 721.
2. Spiera H, Kerr LD. Scleroderma following silicone implantation: a cumulative experience of 11 cases. J Rheumatol. Jun 1993;20 (6):958-961.
3. Semple JL, Lugowski SJ, Baines CJ, Smith DC, McHugh A. Breast milk contamination and silicone implants: preliminary results using silicon as a proxy measurement for silicone. Plast Reconstr Surg 1998; 102 (2):528-533.

SILVER SULFADIAZINE   L3

Trade: Silvadene, SSD Cream, Thermazene
Other Trades: Flamazine, Dermazin, SSD, Silvazine, Flamazine
Uses: Topical antimicrobial cream
AAP: Not reviewed

Silver sulfadiazine is a topical antimicrobial cream primarily used for reducing sepsis in burn patients. The silver component is not absorbed from the skin.[1] Sulfadiazine is partially absorbed. After prolonged therapy of large areas, sulfadiazine levels in plasma may approach therapeutic levels. Although sulfonamides are known to be secreted into human milk, they are not particularly problematic except in the newborn period when they may produce kernicterus.

Pregnancy Risk Category: B

Lactation Risk Category: L3

Adult Concerns: Allergic rash, renal failure, crystalluria.

Pediatric Concerns: None reported, but studies are limited. Observe caution during the neonatal period.

Drug Interactions:

Relative Infant Dose:

Adult Dose:

Alternatives:

T ½	= 10 hours (sulfa)	M/P	=
PHL	=	PB	=
Tmax	=	Oral	= Complete
MW	=	pKa	=
Vd	=		

References:
1. McEvoy GE. (ed):AFHS Drug Information. New York, NY: 2009.

SIMVASTATIN   L3

Trade: Zocor
Other Trades: Zocor, Lipex
Uses: Reduces cholesterol
AAP: Not reviewed

Simvastatin is an HMG-CoA reductase inhibitor that reduces the production of cholesterol in the liver. Like lovastatin, simvastatin reduces blood cholesterol levels. Others in this family are known to be secreted into human and rodent milk, but no data are available on simvastatin.[1] It is likely that milk levels will be low because less than 5% of simvastatin reaches the plasma, most being removed first-pass by the liver.

Atherosclerosis is a chronic process and discontinuation of lipid-lowering drugs during pregnancy and lactation should have little to no impact on the outcome of long-term therapy of primary hypercholesterolemia. Cholesterol and other products of cholesterol biosynthesis are essential components for fetal and neonatal development, and the use of cholesterol-lowering drugs would not be advisable under any circumstances.

Pregnancy Risk Category: X

Lactation Risk Category: L3

Adult Concerns: GI distress, headache, hypotension, elevated liver enzymes.

Pediatric Concerns: None reported.

Drug Interactions: Increased toxicity when added to gemfibrozil (myopathy, myalgia, etc), clofibrate, niacin (myopathy), erythromycin, cyclosporine, oral anticoagulants (elevated bleeding time).

Relative Infant Dose:

Adult Dose: 5-10 mg daily.

Alternatives:

T ½	= Long	M/P	=
PHL	=	PB	= 95%
Tmax	= 1.3-2.4 hours	Oral	= Poor
MW	= 419	pKa	=
Vd	=		

References:
1. Drug Facts and Comparisons 1995 ed. ed. St. Louis: 1995.

SINCALIDE   L3

Trade: Kinevac
Other Trades:
Uses: Diagnostic agent for cholecystography
AAP: Not reviewed

Kinevac is a synthetic, C-terminal octapeptide fragment of cholecystokinin, a cystopancreatic-gastrointestinal hormone peptide which when injected produces a substantial contracture of the gall bladder. Sincalide is therefore used to assess biliary and gall bladder function. No data are available on the transfer of this peptide into human milk, but due to its MW it is extremely unlikely significant quantities would ever reach the milk compartment. It has a brief but unreported half-life.

Pregnancy Risk Category: B

Lactation Risk Category: L3

Adult Concerns: Adverse effects include GI and abdominal pain, nausea, the urge to defecate, flushing, dizziness, and cramping.

Pediatric Concerns: None reported via milk. While it is unlikely to enter milk, a brief interruption of breastfeeding (1-2 hours) would preclude any possible side effects.

Drug Interactions:

Relative Infant Dose:

Adult Dose: 0.02 µg/kg over 30 seconds.

Alternatives:

T ½	= Brief	M/P	=
PHL	=	PB	=
Tmax	=	Oral	= Nil
MW	= 1143	pKa	=
Vd	=		

References:
1. Pharmaceutical Manufacturers Package Insert, 2003.

SIROLIMUS   L4

Trade: Rapamune, Rapamycin, NSC-226080
Other Trades: Rapamune
Uses: Immunosuppressant
AAP: Not reviewed

Sirolimus is an immunosuppressant sometimes used in combination with cyclosporin in renal transplants. No data are available on its transfer to human milk. Average plasma levels are quite low (264 ng x hr/mL) and the drug is strongly attached to cellular components and plasma levels are low. It is not likely it will penetrate milk in levels that are significant. However, it is a potent inhibitor of the enzyme 70 K S6 kinase, which is stimulated in breast tissue by prolactin. This agent, in rodent mammary tissue, strongly inhibits milk component production.[1] It could potentially suppress milk production in lactating mothers and caution is recommended.

Pregnancy Risk Category: C

Lactation Risk Category: L4

Adult Concerns: Anemia, thrombocytopenia, leukopenia, hypertension, headache, hyperlipidemia, hypophosphatemia, urinary tract infection, interstitial pneumonitis.

Pediatric Concerns: None via milk, but reduced milk production could occur.

Drug Interactions: Drugs which inhibit cytochrome P450 3A4 may significantly increase levels of sirolimus. These include: bromocriptine, carbamazepine, cimetidine, cisapride, clarithromycin, clotrimazole, danazol, diltiazem, erythromycin, fluconazole, fosphenytoin, metoclopramide, etc. Co-administration with cyclosporine may increase levels of sirolimus. Numerous other drug-drug contraindications may exist, consult drug interaction reference.

Relative Infant Dose:

Adult Dose: 2 mg/d

Alternatives:

T ½	= 57-63 hours	M/P	=
PHL	=	PB	=
Tmax	= 1-3 hours	Oral	= 15%
MW	= 914	pKa	=
Vd	= 12		

References:
1. Hang J, Rillema JA. Effect of rapamycin on prolactin-stimulated S6 kinase activity and milk product formation in mouse mammary explants. Biochim Biophys Acta 1997; 1358 (2):209-214.

SITAGLIPTIN PHOSPHATE   L3

Trade: Januvia
Other Trades:
Uses: Antidiabetic agent in Type 2 diabetics
AAP: Not reviewed

Sitagliptin phosphate is a dipeptidyl peptidase IV inhibitor resulting in prolonged active incretin levels, thus increasing insulin release from pancreatic beta cells in Type 2 diabetics and decreasing glucagon secretion from pancreatic alpha cells, and ultimately decreasing blood glucose levels.[1] It does not lower blood glucose or cause hypoglycemia in healthy subjects. There are no data available on the transfer of sitagliptin into human milk. Levels will probably be quite low due to its size and kinetics. Some caution is recommended until we have data.

Pregnancy Risk Category: B

Lactation Risk Category: L3

Adult Concerns: Adverse reactions include headache, diarrhea, upper respiratory tract infection, and nasopharyngitis.

Pediatric Concerns: No data are available.

Drug Interactions: Sitagliptin is a minor substrate of CYP2C8 and CYP3A4, but has not shown any significant drug interactions.

Relative Infant Dose:

Adult Dose: 100 mg QD

Alternatives: Metformin

T ½	= 12 hours	M/P	=
PHL	=	PB	= 38%
Tmax	= 1-4 hours	Oral	= 87%
MW	= 523	pKa	=
Vd	= 2.8		

References:
1. Pharmaceutical Manufacturer Prescribing Information. 2008.

SMALLPOX VACCINE   L4

Trade: Smallpox Vaccine, Dryvax
Other Trades:
Uses: Vaccine for vaccinia virus
AAP: Not reviewed

Smallpox is a viral syndrome caused by infection with the vaccinia virus. The smallpox vaccine contains a live but attenuated (weakened) preparation of vaccinia virus. The reconstituted vaccine contains approximately 100 million infectious vaccinia viruses per mL. Introduction of potent smallpox vaccine into the superficial layers of the skin results in viral multiplication, immunity, and cellular hypersensitivity. With the primary vaccination, a papule appears at the site of vaccination on the 2nd to 5th day. It then becomes a pustule surrounded by erythema and induration. The erythema and swelling then subside after about 10 days and the crust forms. Secretions from the lesions are capable of inoculating other individuals and care should be exercised around pregnant women, infants, and particularly premature infants. No data are available suggesting the degree of transmission into human milk, but it is likely to enter milk to some degree. Infants are at increased risk from vaccinia infections and the use of smallpox vaccine in infants is contraindicated unless it is an emergency situation. Although the use of the smallpox vaccine in children is not recommended in non-emergent situations, it was safely used in the past. The product information suggests that pregnant and breastfeeding mothers should not receive the vaccination under non-emergent conditions. However, there are no absolute contraindications regarding vaccination of a person with a high-risk exposure to smallpox. In breastfeeding mothers who are not at high risk, the use of smallpox vaccinations is not justified (Center of Disease Control).

Pregnancy Risk Category: C

Lactation Risk Category: L4

Adult Concerns: Adverse effects include fever, lymphedema, urticaria, secondary pyogenic infections, vesicular rash.

Pediatric Concerns: No data are available on its use in breastfeeding mothers or its transfer into human milk. However, vaccinia virus is likely transmitted via milk and is probably infectious. Its use in breastfeeding mothers is not recommended in non-emergent situations.

Drug Interactions:

Relative Infant Dose:

Adult Dose:

Alternatives:

References:
1. Pharmaceutical Manufacturers prescribing information, 2003.

SODIUM OXYBATE   L4

Trade: Xyrem
Other Trades: Xyrem
Uses: CNS depressant
AAP: Not reviewed

Sodium oxybate is a central nervous system depressant used to treat excessive daytime sleepiness and cataplexy in patients with narcolepsy. Its mechanism of action is unknown, but it may work by inhibiting GABA receptors.[1] No data are available on the transfer of oxybate into human breastmilk, but due to the low MW and low protein binding, it is likely this medication will be secreted in human milk and be passed to a breastfeeding infant. Due to the sedative properties of this drug, this product should be used very cautiously in breastfeeding mothers, if at all.

Pregnancy Risk Category: B

Lactation Risk Category: L4

Adult Concerns: Adverse reactions include dizziness, headache, nausea, vomiting, confusion, and pain.

Pediatric Concerns: No data are available.

Drug Interactions: Use with other central nervous system depressants is contraindicated.

Relative Infant Dose:

Adult Dose: 6-9 g/day

Alternatives:

T ½	= 0.5-1 hour	M/P	=
PHL	=	PB	= <1%
Tmax	= 0.5-1.25 hours	Oral	= 25%
MW	= 126	pKa	=
Vd	= 0.19-0.384		

References:
1. Pharmaceutical Manufacturer Prescribing Information. 2005.

SODIUM PHOSPHATE DIBASIC - DIBASIC ANHYDROUS   L3

Trade: Visicol, OsmoPrep
Other Trades:
Uses: Laxative
AAP: Not reviewed

This is a saline laxative used to evacuate the bowels for colonoscopy exams. It exerts its osmotic effect in the small intestine by drawing water into the lumen of the gut, producing distention and causing peristalsis and emptying of the bowel.[1] However, some phosphorus is absorbed and can produce elevated levels in the plasma (hyperphosphatemia). While it is not known if this would change breastmilk phosphate levels, it is very unlikely. However, some caution is recommended in mothers who consume this product. A brief interruption of breastfeeding may be warranted for perhaps 12 hours following use.

Pregnancy Risk Category: C

Lactation Risk Category: L3

Adult Concerns: Adverse effects include bloating, nausea, abdominal pain, and electrolyte abnormalities.

Pediatric Concerns: No data available but a brief interruption is warranted.

Drug Interactions: Medications taken in close proximity may not be absorbed by the intestinal tract. ACE inhibitors and diuretics may increase the risk of electrolyte abnormalities. Antacids and sucralfate both bind phosphate. Bisphosphonates may increase the risk of hypoglycemia.

Relative Infant Dose:

Adult Dose:

Alternatives:

T ½	=	M/P	=
PHL	=	PB	=
Tmax	= 3 hours	Oral	= 1-20%
MW	= 142	pKa	=
Vd	=		

References:
1.   Pharmaceutical Manufacturer Prescribing Information. 2005.

SOLIFENACIN SUCCINATE   L4

Trade: VESIcare
Other Trades:
Uses: Muscarinic agonist for bladder hyperactivity
AAP: Not reviewed

Solifenacin is a muscarinic agonist drug that reduces the symptoms of overactive bladder disorder (OAB) and has a high affinity for the M3 muscarinic receptor. OAB is a medical condition that causes the bladder muscle (known as the detrusor muscle) to contract while the bladder is filling with urine, rather than when the bladder is full. Patients with OAB feel the urge to urinate more often (urgency), without advance warning, and when the bladder isn"t completely full.

Solifenacin is an unusual anticholinergic, structurally different but similar in effect to atropine. We do not have data on its use in breastfeeding mothers. However, the potency of this product, its affect on numerous important organs, the sensitivity of infants to anticholinergic agents, and its long-half life make this product problematic for breastfeeding infants. While I predict that milk levels will ultimately be low (due to its structure), we do not have that data at present, and caution is recommended.

The manufacturer reports some side effects (reduced body weight, etc.) in lactating mice at doses 3.6 times the normal dose. The relevance of rodent studies to humans is usually minimal. This product should be used with significant caution in breastfeeding mothers, if at all. Infants should be closely watched for urinary retention, dry mouth, constipation, UTI, and other antimuscarinic symptoms.

Pregnancy Risk Category: C

Lactation Risk Category: L4

Adult Concerns: Dry mouth, constipation, nausea, dyspepsia, blurred vision, tachycardia, and drowsiness. Do not use in patients with glaucoma.

Pediatric Concerns: None reported but caution is recommended due to the anticholinergic effects and long half-life of this product.

Drug Interactions: Do not exceed doses of 5 mg/day when used with ketoconazole or other azole antifungals.

Relative Infant Dose:

Adult Dose: 5-10 mg daily.

Alternatives: Tolterodine

T ½	= 45-68 hours	M/P	=
PHL	=	PB	= 98%
Tmax	= 3-8 hours	Oral	= 90%
MW	= 480	pKa	=
Vd	= 8.57		

References:
1. Pharmaceutical Manufacturers Prescribing Information. 2005.

SOMATREM, SOMATROPIN | L3

Trade: Human Growth Hormone, Nutropin, Humatrope, Growth
Hormone, Saizen

Other Trades: Protropin, Humatrope, Genotropin, Norditropin,
Somatropin

Uses: Human growth hormone

AAP: Not reviewed

Somatrem and somatropin are purified polypeptide hormones of
recombinant DNA origin. It is a large protein. They are structurally
similar or identical to human growth hormone (hGH). One study
in 16 women indicates that hGH treatment for 7 days stimulated
breastmilk production by 18.5% (verses 11.6% in controls) in a group
of normal lactating women.[1] No adverse effects were noted. Leukemia
has occurred in a small number of children receiving hGH, but the
relationship is uncertain. Because it is a peptide of 191 amino acids
and its MW is so large, its transfer into milk is very unlikely. Further,
its oral absorption would be minimal to nil.

Pregnancy Risk Category: C

Lactation Risk Category: L3

Adult Concerns: Some fatalities have been reported in pediatric
patients with Prader-Willi syndrome. Hypothyroidism and
hypoglycemia have been reported.

Pediatric Concerns: None reported via milk. Absorption is very
unlikely.

Drug Interactions:

Relative Infant Dose:

Adult Dose: 0.1-0.3 mg/kg every week

Alternatives:

T ½	=	M/P	=
PHL	=	PB	=
Tmax	= 7.5 hours	Oral	= Poor
MW	= 22,124	pKa	=
Vd	=		

References:
1. Milsom SR, Breier BH, Gallaher BW, Cox VA, Gunn AJ, Gluckman PD. Growth hormone stimulates galactopoiesis in healthy lactating women. Acta Endocrinol (Copenh) 1992; 127 (4):337-343.

SOTALOL   L3

Trade: Betapace
Other Trades: Sotacor, Apo-Sotalol, Rylosol, Cardol
Uses: Antihypertensive, beta-blocker
AAP: Maternal Medication Usually Compatible with Breastfeeding

Sotalol is a typical beta blocker antihypertensive with low lipid solubility. It is secreted into milk in high levels. Sotalol concentrations in milk ranged from 4.8 to 20.2 mg/L (mean= 10.5 mg/L) in 5 mothers.[1] The mean maternal dose was 433 mg/day. Although these milk levels appear high, no evidence of toxicity was noted in 12 infants.

Another study of a 22 year old mother taking 120 to 240 mg daily reported an infant dose of 20-23% of the weight adjusted maternal dose in milk. This would relate to an infant dose of 0.41 to 0.58 mg/kg. However, there were no untoward effects noted in the infant.[2] It is suggested that if a mother decides to breastfeed while taking sotalol, the baby should receive close monitoring for side effects.

Pregnancy Risk Category: B

Lactation Risk Category: L3

Adult Concerns: Bradycardia, hypotension, sedation, poor sucking.

Pediatric Concerns: None reported via milk, but observe for sedation, bradycardia, hypotension, weakness.

Drug Interactions: Decreased effect when used with aluminum salts, barbiturates, calcium salts, cholestyramine, NSAIDs, ampicillin, rifampin, and salicylates. Beta blockers may reduce the effect of oral sulfonylureas (hypoglycemic agents). Increased toxicity/effect when used with other antihypertensives, contraceptives, MAO inhibitors, cimetidine, and numerous other products. See drug interaction reference for complete listing.

Relative Infant Dose: 25.5%

Adult Dose: 80-160 mg BID

Alternatives: Propranolol, Metoprolol

T ½	= 12 hours	M/P	= 5.4
PHL	=	PB	= 0%
Tmax	= 2.5 - 4 hours	Oral	= 90-100%
MW	= 272	pKa	= 8.3,9.8
Vd	= 1.6-2.4		

References:
1. O'Hare MF, Murnaghan GA, Russell CJ, Leahey WJ, Varma MP, McDevitt DG. Sotalol as a hypotensive agent in pregnancy. Br J Obstet Gynaecol 1980; 87 (9):814-820.
2. Hackett LP, Wojnar-Horton RE, Dusci LJ, Ilett KF, Roberts MJ. Excretion of sotalol in breast milk. Br J Clin Pharmac 1990; 29:277-279.

SPIRONOLACTONE   L2

Trade: Aldactone
Other Trades: Aldactone, Novospiroton, Spiractin
Uses: Potassium sparing diuretic
AAP: Maternal Medication Usually Compatible with Breastfeeding

Spironolactone is metabolized to canrenone, which is known to be secreted into breastmilk. In one mother receiving 25 mg of spironolactone at 2 hours postdose the maternal serum and milk concentrations of canrenone were 144 and 104 µg/L respectively.[1] At 14.5 hours, the corresponding values for serum and milk were 92 and 47 µg/L respectively. Milk/plasma ratios varied from 0.51 at 14.5 hours, to 0.72 at 2 hours.

Pregnancy Risk Category: D

Lactation Risk Category: L2

Adult Concerns: Nausea, vomiting, elevated serum potassium, hepatitis.

Pediatric Concerns: None reported via milk, but suppression of milk supply is possible but unlikely.

Drug Interactions: Use with anticoagulants may reduce the anticoagulant effect. Use with potassium preparations may increase potassium levels in plasma. Use with ACE inhibitors may elevate serum potassium levels. The diuretic effect of spironolactone may be decreased by use with salicylates.

Relative Infant Dose: 4.3%

Adult Dose: 50-100 mg daily.

Alternatives:

T ½	= 10-35 hours	M/P	= 0.51-0.72
PHL	=	PB	= >90%
Tmax	= 1-2 hours	Oral	= 70%
MW	= 417	pKa	=
Vd	=		

References:
1. Phelps DL, Karim Z. Spironolactone: relationship between concentrations of dethioacetylated metabolite in human serum and milk. J Pharm Sci 1977; 66 (8):1203.

ST. JOHN'S WORT   L2

Trade: St. John's Wort, Saint John's Wort, SJW
Other Trades:
Uses: Antidepressant
AAP: Not reviewed

St. John's Wort (hypericum perforatum L.) consists of the whole fresh or dried plant or its components containing not less than 0.04% naphthodianthrones of the hypericin group.   Hypericum contains many biologically active compounds and most researchers consider its effect due to a combination of constituents rather than any single component.[1]   However, the naphthodianthrones hypericin and pseudohypericin and numerous flavonoids have stimulated the most interest as antidepressants and antivirals.   Following doses of (3 x 300 mg/day), peak steady state concentrations of hypericin and pseudohypericin were 8.5 ng/mL and 5.8 ng/mL respectively.[2] Concentrations in brain appear to be the least of all compartments.

Hypericum has become increasingly popular for the treatment of depression following results from numerous studies showing efficacy and good data suggesting that it is associated with fewer and less severe side effects. Many studies have been flawed due to the use of poor extracts or questionable preparations. However the German extract WS5570 has grown in popularity and is now often used as the standard preparation for clinical studies. Two recent studies using this SJW extract WS5570 showed this preparation to be very effective at treating depression,[3-4] and just as effective as the SSRI paroxetine.[4] The latter study was double blinded and well done. These newer studies suggest that SJW may indeed be an active and clinically effective product for treating depression when good preparations are used. Several other studies show that St. John's Wort may significantly stimulate Cytochrome P450 3A4, which is a major drug metabolizing enzyme in the liver.[5-9] Following such induction, major reductions (50% or more) in plasma levels of a number of important drugs have been reported and include: cyclosporin, midazolam, indinavir, and possibly numerous other drugs. Patients taking anticonvulsants and other critically important drugs should be advised about the possible interaction with these medications leading to major reductions in plasma levels. Patients should always advise their physicians of their use of St. John's Wort.

In a recent prospective, observational, cohort study of the safety of SJW in 33 breastfeeding mothers, along with matched controls, no significant differences were found in maternal or infant demographics or maternal adverse effects following treatment with SJW.[10] In another study of a single patient receiving 3 daily doses of Jarsin 300, hypericin levels in milk were undetectable (<0.2 ng/mL).[11] Hyperforin levels in milk ranged from 0.58 to 18.2 ng/mL. Maternal plasma levels of hypericin and hyperforin were 10.71 and 154 ng/mL respectively. Both components were undetectable in the plasma of the infant. No side effects of any kind were noted in the infant and the Denver Developmental Screen was normal.

Please be aware that many products produced and sold in the USA and Canada may be of poor quality and contain little or no SJW. Users should only purchase standardized or assayed products from reputable sources.

Pregnancy Risk Category:

Lactation Risk Category: L2

Adult Concerns: Caution, because of uterotonic effects, hypericum should not be used in pregnant patients. Dry mouth, dizziness, constipation, and confusion have been infrequently reported. Overt toxicity is generally considered quite low. Photosensitization in fair-skinned people has been noted. No teratogenic effects has been documented.

Pediatric Concerns: None reported in two studies. Probably safe.

Drug Interactions: May prolong narcotic-induced sedation and sleeping times. May reduce barbiturate-induced sleeping times.   A recent report in Lancet suggests St. John's wort may induce the cytochrome P-450 enzyme system.   The data indicates a major interaction between St. John's wort and the HIV-1 protease inhibitor, Indinavir, where indinavir AUC was reduced by a mean of 57%. In addition, trough concentrations of indinavir at 8 hours were reduced by 81%.   Another   report indicates acute rejection episodes in two heart transplant patients who had initiated St. John's wort for depression. Although each patient recovered after the St. John's wort was discontinued, this again implicates P-450 induction activity of St. John's wort.   SJW may decrease digoxin plasma levels (AUC) by 25%, and theophylline levels significantly.

Relative Infant Dose:

Adult Dose: 300mg TID dry-powdered (0.3% hypericin)

Alternatives: Sertraline, Paroxetine

T ½	= 26.5 hours	M/P	=
PHL	=	PB	=
Tmax	= 5.9 hours	Oral	=
MW	= 504	pKa	=
Vd	=		

References:
1. Upton R. St. John's Wort. American Herbal Pharmacopoeia and Therapeutic Compendium 1997.
2. Stock S, Holzl J. Pharmacokinetic tests of (14C)-labeled hypericin and pseudohypericin from Hypericum perforatum and serum kinetics of hyperich in man. Planta Medica 1991; 57 (suppl 2):A61.
3. Lecrubier Y, Clerc G, Didi R, Kieser M. Efficacy of St. John's wort extract WS 5570 in major depression: a double-blind, placebo-controlled trial. Am J Psychiatry 2002 Aug; 159 (8):1361-6.
4. Szegedi A, Kohnen R, Dienel A, Kieser M. Acute treatment of moderate to severe depression with hypericum extract WS 5570 (St John's wort): randomised controlled double blind non-inferiority trial versus paroxetine. BMJ 2005 Mar 5; 330 (7490):503.
5. Durr D, Stieger B, Kullak-Ublick GA, Rentsch KM, Steinert HC, Meier PJ, Fattinger K. St John's Wort induces intestinal P-glycoprotein/MDR1 and intestinal and hepatic CYP3A4. Clin Pharmacol Ther 2000; 68 (6):598-604.
6. Barone GW, Gurley BJ, Ketel BL, Lightfoot ML, Abul-Ezz SR. Drug interaction between St. John's wort and cyclosporine. Ann Pharmacother 2000; 34 (9):1013-1016.
7. Obach RS. Inhibition of human cytochrome P450 enzymes by constituents of St. John's Wort, an herbal preparation used in the treatment of depression. J Pharmacol Exp Ther 2000; 294 (1):88-95.

8. Roby CA, Anderson GD, Kantor E, Dryer DA, Burstein AH. St John's Wort: effect on CYP3A4 activity. Clin Pharmacol Ther 2000; 67 (5):451-457.
9. De Smet PA, Touw DJ. Safety of St John's wort (Hypericum perforatum). Lancet 2000; 355 (9203):575-576.
10. Lee A, Minhas R, Matsuda N et al. The safety of St. John's wort (Hypericum perforatum) during breastfeeding. J Clin Psychiatry. 2003; 64:966-968.
11. Klier CM, Schafer MR, Schmid-Siegel B et al. St. John's wort (Hypericum perforatum)--is it safe during breastfeeding? Pharmacopsychiatry 2002; 35:29-30.

STREPTOMYCIN   L3

Trade:
Other Trades: Streptobretin, Streptotriad
Uses: Antibiotic
AAP: Maternal Medication Usually Compatible with Breastfeeding

Streptomycin is an aminoglycoside antibiotic from the same family as gentamicin. It is primarily administered IM or IV although it is seldom used today with exception of the treatment of tuberculosis. One report suggests that following a 1 g dose (IM), levels in breastmilk were 0.3 to 0.6 mg/L (2-3% of plasma level).[1] Another report suggests that only 0.5% of a 1 gm IM dose is excreted in breastmilk within 24 hours.[2] Because the oral absorption of streptomycin is very poor, absorption by infant is probably minimal (unless premature or early neonate).

Pregnancy Risk Category: D

Lactation Risk Category: L3

Adult Concerns: Deafness, anemia, kidney toxicity.

Pediatric Concerns: None reported via milk, but observe for changes in GI flora.

Drug Interactions: Increased toxicity when used with certain penicillins, cephalosporins, amphotericin B, loop diuretics, and neuromuscular blocking agents.

Relative Infant Dose: 0.3% - 0.6%

Adult Dose: 1-2 g daily.

Alternatives:

T ½	= 2.6 hours	M/P	= 0.12-1.0
PHL	= 4-10 hours (neonates)	PB	= 34%
Tmax	= 1-2 hours (IM)	Oral	= Poor
MW	= 582	pKa	=
Vd	=		

References:
1. Wilson J. Drugs in Breast Milk. New York: ADIS Press 1981.
2. Snider DE, Jr., Powell KE. Should women taking antituberculosis drugs breast-feed? Arch Intern Med 1984; 144 (3):589-590.

STRONTIUM-89 CHLORIDE   L5

Trade: Metastron
Other Trades:
Uses: Radioactive product for bone pain
AAP: Not reviewed

Metastron behaves similarly to calcium. It is rapidly cleared from plasma and sequestered into bone where its radioactive emissions relieve metastatic bone pain.[1] Radioactive half-life is 50.5 days. Transfer into milk is unreported but likely. This radioactive product is too dangerous to use in lactating mothers. See Appendix B.

Pregnancy Risk Category: D

Lactation Risk Category: L5

Adult Concerns: Severe bone marrow suppression, septicemia.

Pediatric Concerns: None reported via milk. But this product is probably too dangerous to use with breastfed infants.

Drug Interactions:

Relative Infant Dose:

Adult Dose: 4 mCi every 90 days

Alternatives:

T ½	= 50.5 days	M/P	=
PHL	=	PB	=
Tmax	= Immediate (IV)	Oral	=
MW	= 159	pKa	=
Vd	=		

References:
1.   Drug Facts and Comparisons 1995 ed. ed. St. Louis: 1995.

SUCCIMER   L3

Trade: Chemet
Other Trades:
Uses: Lead Chelator for lead poisoning
AAP: Not reviewed

Succimer is a chelating agent containing dimercaptosuccinic acid. It is commonly used to chelate and increase the urinary excretion of lead.[1] While removing lead is important, some chelators (EDTA) are noted for increasing the plasma levels of lead and promoting its migration to neural and other tissues. In the instance of a breastfeeding woman, this could theoretically increase milk lead levels. However, succimer as studied in rodents has been found to increase the urinary elimination of lead without redistribution of lead to other compartments (this would theoretically include milk).[2] While we do not have studies of succimer transfer into human milk, due to its low pKa of succimer, it is unlikely that lead, chelated to succimer, would transfer into human milk. But this is not known for sure. Clinical studies in succimer-treated patients indicate that lead levels reach their lowest point after 4-5 days of therapy with succimer.[3] If breastfeeding patients were to pump and discard milk for 5 days while under therapy with succimer, it would significantly remove the risk of lead transfer into milk (if this occurs?). However, more data are required before breastfeeding can be recommended following the use of succimer.

Pregnancy Risk Category: C

Lactation Risk Category: L3

Adult Concerns: Nausea, vomiting, diarrhea, appetite loss, thrombocytosis, intermittent eosinophilia, arrhythmias, neutropenia, drowsiness, dizziness, neuropathies, headache, rash, and paresthesias.

Pediatric Concerns: None reported.

Drug Interactions:

Relative Infant Dose:

Adult Dose: 30 milligrams/kg/day for 5 days

Alternatives:

T ½	= 2 -48 hours	M/P	=
PHL	=	PB	=
Tmax	= 1-2 hours	Oral	= Complete
MW	= 182	pKa	= 3.0
Vd	=		

References:
1. Pharmaceutical Manufacturer Prescribing Information, 2001.
2. Graziano JH, Lolacono NJ, Moulton T, Mitchell ME, Slavkovich V, Zarate C. Controlled study of meso-2,3-dimercaptosuccinic acid for the management of childhood lead intoxication. J Pediatr 1992; 120 (1):133-139.
3. Graziano JH, Lolacono NJ, Meyer P. Dose-response study of oral 2,3-dimercaptosuccinic acid in children with elevated blood lead concentrations. J Pediatr 1988; 113 (4):751-757.

SUCRALFATE   L2

Trade: Carafate
Other Trades: Sulcrate, Novo-Sucralfate, Nu-Sucralfate, Carafate, SCF, Ulcyte, Antepsin
Uses: For peptic ulcers
AAP: Not reviewed

Sucralfate is a sucrose aluminum complex used for stomach ulcers. When administered orally sucralfate forms a complex that physically covers stomach ulcers.[1] Less than 5% is absorbed orally. At these plasma levels it is very unlikely to penetrate into breastmilk.

Pregnancy Risk Category: B

Lactation Risk Category: L2

Adult Concerns: Constipation.

Pediatric Concerns: None reported via milk. Absorption is very unlikely.

Drug Interactions: The use of aluminum containing antacids and sucralfate may increase the total body burden of aluminum. Sucralfate may reduce the anticoagulant effect of warfarin. Serum digoxin levels may be reduced. Phenytoin absorption may be decreased. Ketoconazole bioavailability may be decreased. Serum quinidine levels may be reduced. Bioavailability of the fluoroquinolone family may be decreased.

Relative Infant Dose:

Adult Dose: 1 g QID

Alternatives:

T ½	=	M/P	=
PHL	=	PB	=
Tmax	=	Oral	= <5%
MW	= 2087	pKa	=
Vd	=		

References:
1. Drug Facts and Comparisons 1995 ed. ed. St. Louis: 1995.

SULCONAZOLE NITRATE | L3

Trade: Exelderm
Other Trades: Exelderm
Uses: Antifungal cream
AAP: Not reviewed

Exelderm is a broad-spectrum antifungal topical cream.[1] Although no data exist on transfer into human milk, it is unlikely that the degree of transdermal absorption would be high enough to produce significant milk levels. Only 8.7% of the topically administered dose is transcutaneously absorbed.

Pregnancy Risk Category: C

Lactation Risk Category: L3

Adult Concerns: Rash, skin irritation, burning, stinging.

Pediatric Concerns: None reported via milk.

Drug Interactions:

Relative Infant Dose:

Adult Dose: Topical

Alternatives:

References:
1. Pharmaceutical Manufacturer Prescribing Information. 1996.

SULFAMETHOXAZOLE   L3

Trade: Gantanol

Other Trades: Apo-Methoxazole, Gantanol, Bactrim, Resprim, Septrin

Uses: Sulfonamide antibiotic

AAP: Not reviewed

Sulfamethoxazole is a common and popular sulfonamide antimicrobial. It is secreted in breastmilk in small amounts.[1] It has a longer half-life than other sulfonamides. Use with caution in weakened infants and premature infants or neonates with hyperbilirubinemia. Gantrisin (Sulfisoxazole) is considered the best choice of sulfonamides due to reduced transfer to infant. Compatible but exercise caution. PHL= 14.7-36.5 hours (neonate), 8-9 hours (older infants).

Pregnancy Risk Category: C

Lactation Risk Category: L3

Adult Concerns: Anemia, blood dyscrasias, allergies.

Pediatric Concerns: None reported via milk, but use with caution in hyperbilirubinemic neonates and in infants with G6PD.

Drug Interactions: Decreased effect with paraaminobenzoic acid or PABA metabolites of drugs such as procaine and tetracaine. Increased effect of oral anticoagulants, oral hypoglycemic agents, and methotrexate.

Relative Infant Dose:

Adult Dose: 1-2 g BID

Alternatives:

T ½	= 10.1 hours	M/P	= 0.06
PHL	= 14.7-36.5 hours (neonate)	PB	= 62%
Tmax	= 1-4 hours	Oral	= Complete
MW	= 253	pKa	=
Vd	=		

References:
1. Rasmussen F. Mammary excretion of sulphonamides. Acta Pharmacol Toxicol 1958; 15:138-148.

SULFASALAZINE | L3

Trade: Azulfidine
Other Trades: PMS Sulfasalazine, Salazopyrin, SAS-500
Uses: Anti-inflammatory for ulcerative colitis
AAP: Drugs associated with significant side effects and should be given with caution

Sulfasalazine is a conjugate of sulfapyridine and 5-Aminosalicylic acid and is used as an anti-inflammatory for ulcerative colitis. Only one-third of the dose is absorbed by the mother. Most stays in the GI tract. Secretion of 5-aminosalicylic acid (active compound) and its inactive metabolite (acetyl -5-ASA) into human milk is very low.

In one study of 12 women receiving 1 to 2 grams/day of sulfasalazine, the amount of sulfasalazine in milk in patients receiving 1 gm/day was far less than 1 mg/L and approximately 0.5 to 2 mg/L in those receiving 2 gm/day.[1] In this study, small milk levels were found in only 2 women. It was estimated by the authors that breastfed infants would receive approximately 0.3 mg/kg/day of sulfapyridine. This very small amount may be regarded as negligible in considering kernicterus because sulfapyridine and sulfadiazine are known to have a poor bilirubin-displacing capacity.

Berlin reported a single case treated with salicylazosulfapyridine (Azulfidine).[2] No 5-amino salicylate compound was found in milk. The sulfapyridine levels were approximately 3 to 6 mg/L. The study by Jarnerot suggests that while sulfasalazine levels in milk were negligible, sulfapyridine levels were approximately 45% of the maternal serum levels and the infant was likely to receive about 3-4 mg/kg of body weight.[1]

In a study of a patient receiving 1 gm of 5-aminosalicylic acid three times daily, the milk level for 5-ASA and its acetyl derivative (acetyl 5-aminosalicylic acid) was 0.1 µg/mL and 12.3 µg/mL respectively at 5 days postpartum. These results suggest that even with high doses (3 gm/d) the amount of 5-ASA transferred is minimal.[3]

In another study of 3 mothers receiving a dose of 0.5 g four times per day, the average maternal serum concentration of sulphasalazine and 5-ASA was 8.8 and 0.6 µg/mL, respectively. The milk concentrations were 2.7 and 0.8 µg/mL, respectively. The authors reported sulfasalazine levels in breastmilk are approximately 30% of maternal serum levels. No adverse reactions were noted in any infant.[5]

Few if any adverse effects have been observed in most nursing infants. However, one reported case of toxicity which may have been an idiosyncratic allergic response.[4] Use with caution.

Pregnancy Risk Category: B

Lactation Risk Category: L3

Adult Concerns: Watery diarrhea, GI distress, nausea, vomiting, rapid breathing.

Pediatric Concerns: Only one reported case of hypersensitivity. Most studies show minimal effects via milk. Observe for diarrhea, GI discomfort.

Drug Interactions: Decreased effect when used with iron, digoxin, and paraaminobenzoic acid containing drugs. Decreased effect of oral anticoagulants, methotrexate, and oral hypoglycemic agents.

Relative Infant Dose: 0.3% - 1.1%

Adult Dose: 500 mg every 6 hours

Alternatives:

T ½	= 7.6 hours	M/P	= 0.09-0.17
PHL	=	PB	=
Tmax	=	Oral	= Poor
MW	= 398	pKa	=
Vd	=		

References:
1. Jarnerot G, Into-Malmberg MB. Sulphasalazine treatment during breast feeding. Scand J Gastroenterol 1979; 14 (7):869-871.
2. Berlin CM, Jr., Yaffe SJ. Disposition of salicylazosulfapyridine (Azulfidine) and metabolites in human breast milk. Dev Pharmacol Ther 1980; 1 (1):31-39.
3. Klotz U, Harings-Kaim A. Negligible excretion of 5-aminosalicylic acid in breast milk. Lancet 1993; 342 (8871):618-619.
4. Branski D, Kerem E, Gross-Kieselstein E, Hurvitz H, Litt R, Abrahamov A. Bloody diarrhea--a possible complication of sulfasalazine transferred through human breast milk. J Pediatr Gastroenterol Nutr 1986; 5 (2):316-317.
5. Khan AK, Truelove SC. Placental and mammary transfer of sulphasalazine. Br Med J 1979; 2 (6204):1553.

SULFISOXAZOLE   L2

Trade: Gantrisin, AZO-Gantrisin
Other Trades: Novo-Soxazole, Sulfizole
Uses: Sulfonamide antibiotic
AAP: Maternal Medication Usually Compatible with Breastfeeding

Sulfisoxazole is a popular, sulfonamide antimicrobial. It is secreted in breastmilk in small amounts although the actual levels are somewhat controversial.[1] Kauffman (1980) reports the total amount of sulfisoxazole recovered over 48 hours following a dose of 1 gm every 6 hours (total=4gm) was 0.45% of the total dose.[2] The milk/plasma ratio was quite low for sulfisoxazole, only 0.06, and for n-acetyl sulfisoxazole, 0.22. The infant secreted 1,104 μg total sulfisoxazole in his urine over 24 hours, compared to the 1,142 μg secreted in milk. Less than 1% of the maternal dose is secreted into human milk. This is probably insufficient to produce problems in a normal newborn. Sulfisoxazole appears to be best choice with lowest milk/plasma ratio. Use with caution in weakened infants or those with hyperbilirubinemia.

Pregnancy Risk Category: C

Lactation Risk Category: L2

Adult Concerns: Elevated bilirubin, rash.

Pediatric Concerns: None reported via milk. Use with caution in hyperbilirubinemia neonates and in infants with G6PD.

Drug Interactions: The anesthetic effects of thiopental may be enhanced with sulfisoxazole. Cyclosporine concentrations may be decreased by sulfonamides. Serum phenytoin levels may be increased. The risk of methotrexate induced bone marrow suppression may be enhanced. Increased sulfonylurea half-lives and hypoglycemia when used with sulfonamides.

Relative Infant Dose:

Adult Dose: 1-4 g every 4-6 hours

Alternatives:

T ½	= 4.6-7.8 hours	M/P	= 0.06
PHL	=	PB	= 91%
Tmax	= 2-4 hours	Oral	= 100%
MW	= 267	pKa	=
Vd	=		

References:
1. Rasmussen F. Mammary excretion of sulphonamides. Acta Pharmacol Toxicol 1958; 15:138-148.
2. Kauffman RE, O'Brien C, Gilford P. Sulfisoxazole secretion into human milk. J Pediatr 1980; 97 (5):839-841.

SULPIRIDE   L2

Trade:
Other Trades: Dolmatil, Sulparex, Sulpitil
Uses: Antidepressant, antipsychotic
AAP: Not reviewed

Sulpiride is a selective dopamine antagonist used as an antidepressant and antipsychotic. Sulpiride is a strong neuroleptic antipsychotic drug; however, several studies using smaller doses have found it to significantly increase prolactin levels and breastmilk production in smaller doses that do not produce overt neuroleptic effects on the mother.[1] In a study with 14 women who received sulpiride (50 mg three times daily), and in a subsequent study with 36 breastfeeding women, Ylikorkala found major increases in prolactin levels and significant but only moderate increases in breastmilk production.[2,3] In a group of 20 women who received 50 mg twice daily, breastmilk samples were drawn 2 hours after the dose.[4] The concentration of sulpiride in breastmilk ranged from 0.26 to 1.97 mg/L. No effects on breastfed infants were noted. The authors concluded that sulpiride, when administered early in the postpartum period, is useful in promoting initiation of lactation.

In a study by McMurdo, sulpiride was found to be a potent stimulant of maternal plasma prolactin levels.[5] Interestingly, it appears that the prolactin response to sulpiride is not dose-related and reached a maximum at 3-10 mg and thereafter, further increased doses did not further increase prolactin levels. Sulpiride is not available in the USA.

Pregnancy Risk Category:

Lactation Risk Category: L2

Adult Concerns: Tardive dyskinesia, extrapyramidal symptoms, sedation, neuroleptic malignant syndrome, cholestatic jaundice.

Pediatric Concerns: None reported via milk.

Drug Interactions: Antacids and sucralfate may reduce absorption of sulpiride. Increased risk of seizure may result from use of tramadol or zotepine with sulpiride.

Relative Infant Dose: 2.7% - 20.7%

Adult Dose: 50 mg BID

Alternatives: Metoclopramide, domperidone

T ½	= 6-8 hours	M/P	=
PHL	=	PB	=
Tmax	= 2-6 hours	Oral	= 27-34%
MW	= 341	pKa	=
Vd	= 2.7		

References:

1. Wiesel FA, Alfredsson G, Ehrnebo M, Sedvall G. The pharmacokinetics of intravenous and oral sulpiride in healthy human subjects. Eur J Clin Pharmacol 1980; 17 (5):385-391.
2. Ylikorkala O, Kauppila A, Kivinen S, Viinikka L. Sulpiride improves inadequate lactation. Br Med J (Clin Res Ed) 1982; 285 (6337):249-251.
3. Ylikorkala O, Kauppila A, Kivinen S, Viinikka L. Treatment of inadequate lactation with oral sulpiride and buccal oxytocin. Obstet Gynecol 1984; 63 (1):57-60.
4. Aono T, Shioji T, Aki T, Hirota K, Nomura A, Kurachi K. Augmentation of puerperal lactation by oral administration of sulpiride. J Clin Endocrinol Metab 1979; 48 (3):478-482.
5. McMurdo ME, Howie PW, Lewis M, Marnie M, McEwen J, McNeilly AS. Prolactin response to low dose sulpiride. Br J Clin Pharmacol 1987; 24 (2):133-137.

SUMATRIPTAN SUCCINATE   L3

Trade: Imitrex, Treximet
Other Trades: Imitrex, Imigran
Uses: Anti-migraine medication.
AAP: Maternal Medication Usually Compatible with Breastfeeding

Sumatriptan is a 5-HT (Serotonin) receptor agonist and a highly effective new drug for the treatment of migraine headache. It is not an analgesic, rather, it produces a rapid vasoconstriction in various regions of the brain, thus temporarily reducing the cause of migraines.

In one study using 5 lactating women, each were given 6 mg subcutaneous injections and samples drawn for analysis over 8 hours.[1] The highest breastmilk levels were 87.2 µg/L at 2.6 hours post-dose and rapidly disappeared over the next 6 hours. The mean total recovery of sumatriptan in milk over the 8 hour duration was only 14.4 µg. On a weight-adjusted basis this concentration in milk corresponded to a mean infant exposure of only 3.5% of the maternal dose. Further, assuming an oral bioavailability of only 14%, the weight-adjusted dose an infant would absorb would be approximately 0.49% of the maternal dose. The authors suggest that continued breastfeeding following sumatriptan use would not pose a significant risk to the sucking infant.

The maternal plasma half-life is 1.3 hours; the milk half-life is 2.2 hours. Although the milk/plasma ratio was 4.9 (indicating significant concentrating mechanisms in milk), the absolute maternal plasma levels were small; hence, the absolute milk concentrations were low.

Treximet is a combination product containing sumatriptan (85 mg) and naproxen (500 mg).

Pregnancy Risk Category: C

Lactation Risk Category: L3

Adult Concerns: Flushing, hot tingling sensations.

Pediatric Concerns: None reported via milk.

Drug Interactions: MAOIs can markedly increase sumatriptan systemic effect and elimination including elevated sumatriptan plasma levels. Ergot containing drugs have caused prolonged vasospastic reactions. There have been rare reports of weakness, hyperreflexia, and incoordination with combined use with SSRIs such as fluoxetine, paroxetine, sertraline and fluvoxamine.

Relative Infant Dose: 3.5% - 15.3%

Adult Dose: 25-100 mg BID-TID

Alternatives: Zolmitriptan

T ½	= 1.3 hours	M/P	= 4.9
PHL	=	PB	= 14-21%
Tmax	= 12 minutes (IM)	Oral	= 10-15%
MW	= 413	pKa	=
Vd	=		

References:
1.   Wojnar-Horton RE, Hackett LP, Yapp P, Dusci LJ, Paech M, Ilett KF. Distribution and excretion of sumatriptan in human milk. Br J Clin Pharmacol 1996; 41 (3):217-221.

TACROLIMUS   L3

Trade: Prograf, Protopic
Other Trades: Protopic
Uses: Immunosuppressant
AAP: Not reviewed

Tacrolimus is an immunosuppressant formerly known as SK506. It is used to reduce rejection of transplanted organs including liver and kidney.[1] In one report of 21 mothers who received tacrolimus while pregnant, milk concentrations in colostrum averaged 0.79 ng/mL and varied from 0.3 to 1.9 nanograms/mL.[2] Maternal doses (PO) ranged from 9.8 to 10.3 mg/day. Milk/blood ratio averaged 0.54. Using this data and an average daily milk intake of 150 mL/kg, the average dose to the infant per day via milk would be <0.1 µg/kg/day. Because the oral bioavailability is poor (<32%), an infant would likely ingest less than 100 ng/kg/day. The usual pediatric dose (PO) for preventing rejection varies from 0.15 to 0.20 mg/kg/day (equivalent to 150,000-200,000 nanograms/kg/day). In a 32-year-old woman who had taken tacrolimus 0.1 mg/kg/d throughout pregnancy, samples were manually expressed at 0 (trough), 1, 6, 9, 11, and 12 hours after the morning dose.[3]

The C_{max} occurred at 1 hour and was 0.57 µg/L. Using AUC data, the mean milk concentration was calculated to be 0.429 ng/mL. From these measurements, the exclusively breast-fed infant would ingest, on average, 0.06 µg/kg/d, which corresponds to 0.06% of the mother's weight-normalized dose. Given the low oral bioavailability of tacrolimus, the maximum amount the baby would receive is 0.02% of the mother's weight-adjusted dose. The milk/blood ratios of tacrolimus at pre-dosing and 1-hour post-dosing concentrations were calculated to be 0.08 and 0.09, respectively. At 2.5 months of age, the infant was developing well both physically and neurologically. The authors suggest that maternal therapy with tacrolimus for liver transplant may be compatible with breastfeeding.

In a more recent study, a 29 year old woman with a 3 month old breastfed infant, was receiving 2 mg tacrolimus twice daily, azathioprine 100 mg, prednisone 5 mg, diltiazem 180 mg, atenolol 100 mg, and furosemide 20 mg daily.[4] The milk-to-blood ratio was 0.23, and the average tacrolimus concentration in milk was 1.8 µg/L. The authors estimated the daily intake in the infant to be 0.5% of the maternal weight-adjusted dose (RID) or 0.27 µg/kg/day. This is less than 0.2% of the recommended pediatric dose for renal or liver transplant. The concentration-time profile of tacrolimus in milk was essentially flat. The highest concentration of tacrolimus in milk was at 4 and 8.5 hours postdose.

Recently the FDA has approved a topical form of tacrolimus (Protopic) for use in moderate to severe eczema, in those for whom standard eczema therapies are deemed inadvisable because of potential risks, or who are not adequately treated by, or who are intolerant of standard eczema therapies. Absorption via skin is minimal. In a study of 46 adult patients after multiple doses, plasma levels ranged from undetectable to 20 ng/mL, with 45 of the patients having peak blood concentrations less than 5 ng/mL.[1] In another study, the peak blood levels averaged 1.6 ng/mL, which is significantly less than the therapeutic range in kidney transplantation (7-20 ng/mL). While the absolute transcutaneous bioavailability is unknown, it is apparently very low. Combined with the poor oral bioavailability of this product, it is not likely a breastfed infant will receive enough following topical use (maternal) to produce adverse effects.

Pregnancy Risk Category: C

Lactation Risk Category: L3

Adult Concerns: Edema, renal shutdown. The US FDA has issued a warning concerning elevated risks of skin cancers and lymphomas in patients exposed to this product. This warning is highly controversial and is not supported by many dermatologic organizations.

Pediatric Concerns: None reported. The US FDA has issued a warning concerning elevated risks of skin cancers and lymphomas in patients exposed to this product. This warning is highly controversial and is not supported by many dermatologic organizations.

Drug Interactions: Drugs that may increase tacrolimus levels include: calcium channel blockers, azole antifungals, macrolide antibiotics (erythromycin, clarithromycin), cisapride, metoclopramide, bromocriptine, cimetidine, cyclosporine, danazol, methylprednisolone, protease inhibitors. Drugs that may decrease tacrolimus blood levels include: carbamazepine, phenobarbital, phenytoin, rifabutin, rifampin.

Relative Infant Dose: 0.1% - 0.5%

Adult Dose: 0.15-0.3 mg/kg daily.

Alternatives:

T ½	= 34.2 hours	M/P	= 0.54
PHL	= 11.5 hours	PB	= 99%
Tmax	= 1.6 hours	Oral	= 14-32%
MW	= 822	pKa	=
Vd	= 2.6		

References:
1.   Pharmaceutical Manufacturer Prescribing Information, 2001.

2. Jain A, Venkataramanan R, Fung JJ, Gartner JC, Lever J, Balan V, Warty V, Starzl TE. Pregnancy after liver transplantation under tacrolimus. Transplantation 1997; 64 (4):559-565.
3. French AE, Soldin SJ, Soldin OP, Koren G. Milk transfer and neonatal safety of tacrolimus. Ann Pharmacother 2003; 37 (6):815-818.
4. Gardiner SJ, Begg EJ. Breastfeeding during tacrolimus therapy. Obstet Gynecol 2006; 107:453-5.

TAMOXIFEN   L5

Trade: Nolvadex
Other Trades: Apo-Tamox, Nolvadex, Tamofen, Tamone, Tamoxen, Genox, Eblon, Noltam
Uses: Anti-estrogen, anticancer
AAP: Not reviewed

Tamoxifen is a nonsteroidal antiestrogen. It attaches to the estrogen receptor and produces only minimal stimulation, thus it prevents estrogen from stimulating the receptor. Aside from this, it also produces a number of other effects within the cytoplasm of the cell and some of its anticancer effects may be mediated by its effects at sites other than the estrogen receptor.

Tamoxifen is metabolized by the liver and has an elimination half-life of greater than 7 days (range 3-21 days).[1] It is well absorbed orally, and the highest tissue concentrations are in the liver (60 fold). It is 99% protein bound and normally reduces plasma prolactin levels significantly (66% after 3 months). At present, there are no data on its transfer into breastmilk; however, it has been shown to inhibit lactation early postpartum in several studies. In one study, doses of 10-30 mg twice daily early postpartum, completely inhibited postpartum engorgement and lactation.[2] In a second study, tamoxifen doses of 10 mg four times daily significantly reduced serum prolactin and inhibited milk production as well.[3] We do not know the effect of tamoxifen on established milk production.

Tamoxifen is potentially teratogenic (category D) and should never be used in pregnant women (Note: it is useful in conjunction with clomiphene to stimulate ovulation...short term use only). It has a pKa of 8.85 which may suggest some trapping in milk compared to the maternal plasma levels.

This product has a very long half-life, and the active metabolite is concentrated in the plasma (2 fold). This drug has all the characteristics that would suggest a concentrating mechanism in breastfed infants over time. Its prominent effect on reducing prolactin levels will inhibit early lactation and may ultimately inhibit established lactation. In this instance, the significant risks to the infant from exposure to tamoxifen probably outweigh the benefits of breastfeeding. Mothers receiving tamoxifen should not breastfeed until we know more about the levels transferred into milk and the plasma/tissue levels found in breastfed infants. See Appendix A.

Pregnancy Risk Category: D

Lactation Risk Category: L5

Adult Concerns: Hot flashes, nausea, vomiting, vaginal bleeding/discharge, menstrual irregularities, amenorrhea.

Pediatric Concerns: None reported but caution is urged.

Drug Interactions: Increased anticoagulant effect when used with coumarin-type anticoagulants. Tamoxifen is a potent inhibitor of drug metabolizing enzymes in the liver, observe for elevated levels of many drugs.

Relative Infant Dose:

Adult Dose: 10-20 mg BID

Alternatives:

T ½	= >7 days	M/P	=
PHL	=	PB	= 99%
Tmax	= 2-3 hours	Oral	= Complete
MW	= 371	pKa	= 8.85
Vd	=		

References:
1. Pharmaceutical Manufacturer Prescribing Information. 1997.
2. Shaaban MM. Suppression of lactation by an antiestrogen, tamoxifen. Eur J Obstet Gynecol Reprod Biol 1975; 4 (5):167-169.
3. Masala A, Delitala G, Lo DG, Stoppelli I, Alagna S, Devilla L. Inhibition of lactation and inhibition of prolactin release after mechanical breast stimulation in puerperal women given tamoxifen or placebo. Br J Obstet Gynaecol 1978; 85 (2):134-137.

TAMSULOSIN HCL | L3

Trade: Flomax
Other Trades: Flomax, Flomax CR
Uses: Alpha1 adrenergic antagonist
AAP: Not reviewed

Tamsulosin is not approved for use in women, but is used in men for benign prostatic hyperplasia. It is occasionally used in women to assist in the passage of a kidney stone or for bladder motility problems. It works by blocking the alpha1A adrenoreceptors, thus reducing ureter contractility.[1] Due to its high protein binding, and larger MW, it is unlikely that tamsulosin would be excreted in human milk. But no breastfeeding data are presently available.

Pregnancy Risk Category: B

Lactation Risk Category: L3

Adult Concerns: Adverse reactions include orthostatic hypotension, headache, dizziness, rhinitis, and infection.

Pediatric Concerns: No data are available.

Drug Interactions: Calcuim channel blockers and beta blockers may both increase the risk of hypotension when used with tamulosin. Cimetidine decreases tamsulosin clearance. CYP3A4 and CYP2D6 inhibitors may increase the levels of tamulosin.

Relative Infant Dose:

Adult Dose: 0.4 mg QD

Alternatives:

T ½	= 13 hours	M/P	=
PHL	=	PB	= 94-99%
Tmax	= 4-7 hours	Oral	= 90%
MW	= 445	pKa	=
Vd	= 0.23		

References:
1. Pharmaceutical Manufacturer Prescribing Information, 2008.

TAZAROTENE

L3

Trade: Tazorac
Other Trades: Zorac
Uses: Anti-psoriatic
AAP: Not reviewed

Tazarotene is a specialized retinoid for topical use and is used for the topical treatment of stable plaque psoriasis and acne. Following topical application, tazarotene is converted to an active metabolite; transcutaneous absorption is minimal (<1%).[1] Applied daily, it is indicated for treatment of stable plaque psoriasis of up to 20% of the body surface area. Only 2-3% of the topically applied drug is absorbed transcutaneously. Tazarotene is metabolized to the active ingredient, tazarotenic acid. Following topical application, tazarotene is converted to an active metabolite; transcutaneous absorption is minimal (<1%). Little compound could be detected in the plasma. At steady state, plasma levels were only 0.09 ng/mL although this value is largely a function of surface area treated. When applied to large surface areas, systemic absorption is increased. Data on transmission to breastmilk are not available. The manufacturer reports some is transferred to rodent milk, but it has not been tested in humans.

Pregnancy Risk Category: X

Lactation Risk Category: L3

Adult Concerns: Hypertriglyceridemia, peripheral edema, pruritus, erythema, burning, contact dermatitis have been reported. This drug is potentially a significant teratogen and should not ever be used in pregnant patients or those not protected with a suitable birth-control measure.

Pediatric Concerns: None via milk. Some caution is recommended if used over large surface areas (20-30%)..

Drug Interactions: Do not use concomitantly with drying agents.

Relative Infant Dose:

Adult Dose: Apply daily.

Alternatives:

T ½	= 18 hours (met)	M/P	=
PHL	=	PB	= 99%
Tmax	= 8 hours	Oral	= Complete
MW	= 351	pKa	=
Vd	=		

References:
1. Pharmaceutical Manufacturer Prescribing Information, 2002.

TEA TREE OIL
L3

Trade: Tea Tree Oil
Other Trades:
Uses: Antibacterial, antifungal
AAP: Not reviewed

Tea tree oil, as derived from Melaleuca alternifolia, has recently gained popularity for its antiseptic properties. The essential oil, derived by steam distillation of the leaves, contains terpin-4-ol in concentrations of 40% or more.[1] TTO is primarily noted for its antimicrobial effects without irritating sensitive tissues. It is antimicrobial when tested against Candida albicans, E. coli, S. Aureus, Staph. epidermidis, and pseudomonas aeruginosa. In several reports it is suggested to have antifungal properties equivalent to tolnaftate and clotrimazole. Although the use of TTO in adults is mostly nontoxic, the safe use in infants is unknown. Use directly on the nipple should be minimized.

Pregnancy Risk Category:

Lactation Risk Category: L3

Adult Concerns: Toxic effects include allergic eczema. Petechial body rash and leukocytosis in one individual who ingested 1/2 teaspoonful orally. Ataxia and drowsiness following oral ingestion of < 10 cc by a 17 month old infant.

Pediatric Concerns: None reported via milk.

Drug Interactions:

Relative Infant Dose:

Adult Dose:

Alternatives:

References:
1. Review of Natural Products Ed: Facts and Comparisons 1997.

^{99M}TECHNETIUM   L4

Trade: ^{99m}Technetium
Other Trades:
Uses: Radioactive imaging
AAP: Radioactive compound that requires temporary cessation of breastfeeding

Radioactive ^{99M}technetium (^{99m}Tc) is present in milk for at least 15 hours to 3 days, and significant quantities have been reported in the thyroid and gastric mucosa of infants ingesting milk from treated mothers. Technetium is one of the halide elements and is handled, biologically, much like iodine. Like iodine, it concentrates in thyroid tissues, the stomach, and breastmilk of nursing mothers. It has a radioactive half-life of 6.02 hours. Following a dose of 15 mCi of ^{99m}Tc for a brain scan, the concentration of ^{99m}Tc in breastmilk at 4, 8.5, 20, and 60 hours was 0.5 µCi, 0.1 µCi, 0.02 µCi, and 0.006 µCi respectively.[1] In another study, following a dose of 10 mCi of NaTcO4, breastmilk levels were 5.7, 1.5, 0.015 µCi/mL at 3.25, 7.5, and 24 hours respectively.[2] The estimated dose to infant was 1,036, 284, and 2.7 µCi/180 mL milk. These authors recommended pumping and discarding of milk for 48 hours. ^{99m}Technetium is used in many salt and chemical forms, but the radioactivity and decay are the same although the concentration in milk may be influenced by the salt form.

In another study using Technetium MAG3 in two mothers receiving 150 MBq of radioactivity, the total percent of ingested radioactivity ranged from 0.7 to 1.6% of the total.[3] These authors suggested that the DTPA salt of technetium would produce the least breastmilk levels and would be preferred in breastfeeding mothers. The NRC table in the Appendix B suggests duration of interruption of breastfeeding of 12 to 24 hours for 12 and 30 mCi respectively, but this depends on the salt form used. See Appendix B for numerous other preparations and recommendations.

Pregnancy Risk Category: C

Lactation Risk Category: L4

Adult Concerns:

Pediatric Concerns: None reported, but may be transferred to infant thyroid. Pump and dump for a minimum of 48 hours.

Drug Interactions:

Relative Infant Dose:

Adult Dose: 15-20 mCi X 1

Alternatives:

T ½	= <6 hours	M/P	–
PHL	=	PB	=
Tmax	=	Oral	= Complete
MW	=	pKa	=
Vd	=		

References:
1. Rumble WF, Aamodt RL, Jones AE, Henkin RI, Johnston GS. Accidental ingestion of Tc-99m in breast milk by a 10-week-old child. J Nucl Med 1978; 19 (8):913-915.
2. Maisels MJ, Gilcher RO. Excretion of technetium in human milk. Pediatrics 1983; 71 (5):841-842.
3. Evans JL, Mountford AN, Herring AN, Richardson MA. Secretion of radioactivity in breast milk following administration of 99Tcm-MAG3. Nuc Med Comm 1993; 14:108-111.
4. American Academy of Pediatrics, Committee on Drugs. Transfer of drugs and other chemicals into human milk. Pediatrics 2001; 108 (3):776-89.

TEGASEROD MALEATE   L3

Trade: Zelnorm
Other Trades: Zelnorm
Uses: Treatment of irritable bowel syndrome
AAP: Not reviewed

Tegaserod is a serotonin agonist (stimulant) used to treat the symptoms of irritable bowel syndrome. Oral absorption is only 10 % (fasting) and is reduced 40-65% by food. In patients receiving oral doses of 2, 6, and 12 mg, mean peak plasma concentrations were 0.9, 2.9, and 6.3 µg/L respectively.[1] Studies in rats suggest it transfers with a higher milk/plasma ratio, but this is common for rodent studies and the dose was 320 times that given humans.[2] No data are available on its transfer to human milk. Tegaserod is a lipophilic drug which would assist its transfer into human milk, however, its low plasma levels, poor oral bioavailability (particularly with food), and large volume of distribution suggests that the actual amount transferred into human milk is probably quite low. Recently this drug was restricted for use by the FDA due to reported higher chances of heart attack, stroke and unstable angina.

Pregnancy Risk Category: B

Lactation Risk Category: L3

Adult Concerns: Adverse events may include abdominal pain, diarrhea, nausea, flatulence, headache, pain, flushing, hypotension, and vertigo. Use of Zelnorm was previously restricted at the request of FDA in 2007 following a safety analysis that found a higher chance of heart attack, stroke, and unstable angina (heart/chest pain) in patients treated with Zelnorm compared with those treated with an inactive substance (placebo).

Pediatric Concerns: None reported via milk, but rat milk levels have been detected. Note new warnings on this drug.

Drug Interactions: None reported.

Relative Infant Dose:

Adult Dose: 6 mg twice daily.

Alternatives:

T ½	= 11 hours	M/P	=
PHL	=	PB	= 98%
Tmax	= 1 hour	Oral	= 10%
MW	= 417	pKa	=
Vd	= 368		

References:
1. Pharmaceutical Manufacturers prescribing information, 2003.
2. Appel-Dingemanse S. Clinical pharmacokinetics of tegaserod, a serotonin 5-HT (4) receptor partial agonist with promotile activity. Clin Pharmacokinet 2002; 41 (13):1021-1042.

TELBIVUDINE   L4

Trade: Tyzeka
Other Trades:
Uses: Hepatitis B antiviral
AAP: Not reviewed

Telbivudine is a thymidine nucleoside analog that inhibits reverse transcriptase and DNA polymerase in hepatitis B virus infections. It does not inhibit human cellular polymerase. Telbivudine is used in adults with chronic hepatitis B that have evidence of either increased liver function tests or an active infection.[1] It is considered safe in pregnancy, but is very lipid soluble, therefore its transfer into milk may be likely, but probably not clinically relevant. However, this product is intended for chronic use, and exposing an infant to a potential hepatotoxin such as this over a prolonged period is not justified.

Pregnancy Risk Category: B

Lactation Risk Category: L4

Adult Concerns: Adverse reactions are include fatigue, muscle pain, headache, lactic acidosis, hepatomegaly, steatosis and abdominal pain.

Pediatric Concerns: No data are available.

Drug Interactions: Telebivudine is renally excreted, therefore medications that altar renal function may alter plasma concentrations.

Relative Infant Dose:

Adult Dose: 600 mg daily

Alternatives:

T ½	= 40-49 hours	M/P	=
PHL	=	PB	= 3.3%
Tmax	= 1-4 hours	Oral	=
MW	= 242	pKa	=
Vd	=		

References:
1. Pharmaceutical Manufacturer Prescribing Information. 2006.

TELITHROMYCIN   L3

Trade: Ketek
Other Trades:
Uses: Erythromycin-like antibiotic
AAP: Not reviewed

Telithromycin is an erythromycin-like antibiotic. No data are available on its transfer into human milk. Due to its large MW, the amount in milk is likely low. About 1-2% of the maternal dose of erythromycin passes into milk. Please be advised that telithromycin is an erythromycin-like antibiotic and perhaps hundreds of drug-drug interactions are possible.

Pregnancy Risk Category: C

Lactation Risk Category: L3

Adult Concerns: Side effects include: diarrhea (10.8%), nausea (7.9%), headache (5.5%), dizziness, vomiting, loose stools, Visual disturbances have been reported. May produce changes in QTc prolongation. Do not use in patients with myasthenia gravis.

Pediatric Concerns: No data are available on the transfer of telithromycin into human milk. Probably similar to azithromycin.

Drug Interactions: Numerous drug-drug interactions exist, including the azole antifungals. Others include: Acecainide, Ajmaline, Amiodarone, Amisulpride, Amitriptyline, Amoxapine, Aprindine, Astemizole, Atorvastatin, Bretylium, Carbamazepine, and dozens more. Please check other authoritative sources or your pharmacist.

Relative Infant Dose:

Adult Dose: 800 mg every 24 hours.

Alternatives: Azithromycin, clarithromycin

T ½	= 9.8 hours	M/P	=
PHL	=	PB	= 60-70%
Tmax	= 1 hour	Oral	= 57%
MW	= 812	pKa	=
Vd	= 2.9		

References:
1. Pharmaceutical manufacturers prescribing information. 2005.

TELMISARTAN   L3

Trade: Micardis, Micardis HCT
Other Trades: Micardis
Uses: Angiotensin II receptor antagonist
AAP: Not reviewed

Telmisartan is a potent antihypertensive that blocks the angiotensin II receptor site. Micardis HCT also contains hydrochlorothiazide 12.5 mg. This agent should never be used in pregnant patients, as fetal demise has been reported with similar agents in this class. No data are available on its use in lactating mothers. However, its use early postpartum in lactating mothers should be approached with caution, particularly in mothers with premature infants.

Pregnancy Risk Category: C in first trimester
                                 D in second and third trimesters

Lactation Risk Category: L3
                                 L4 if used in neonatal period

Adult Concerns: UTI infection, back pain, sinusitis and diarrhea have been reported. Flu-like symptoms, myalgia, coughing, hypotension have been reported.

Pediatric Concerns: None reported, but use caution early postpartum.

Drug Interactions: When coadministered with digoxin, a 50% increase in digoxin peak plasma levels occurred, and a 13-20% increase in trough levels.

Relative Infant Dose:

Adult Dose: 40 mg daily

Alternatives:

T ½	= 24 hours	M/P	=
PHL	–	PB	= 99.5%
Tmax	= 1 hour	Oral	= 42-58%
MW	= 514	pKa	=
Vd	= 7.14		

References:
1. Pharmaceutical Manufacturer Prescribing Information, 2002.

TEMAZEPAM   L3

Trade: Restoril

Other Trades: Restoril, PMS-Temazepam, Euhypnos, Noctume, Temaze, Temtabs, Normison

Uses: Short acting benzodiazepine (Valium-like) hypnotic

AAP: Drugs whose effect on nursing infants is unknown but may be of concern

Temazepam is a short acting benzodiazepine that belongs to the Valium family primarily used as a nighttime sedative. In one study the milk/plasma ratio varied from <0.09 to <0.63 (mean= 0.18).[1] Temazepam is relatively water soluble and therefore partitions poorly into breastmilk. Levels of temazepam were undetectable in the infants studied although these studies were carried out 15 hours post-dose. Although the study shows low neonatal exposure to temazepam via breastmilk, the infant should be monitored carefully for sleepiness and poor feeding.

Pregnancy Risk Category: X

Lactation Risk Category: L3

Adult Concerns: Sedation.

Pediatric Concerns: None reported via milk, but observe for sedation, poor feeding.

Drug Interactions: Increased effect when used with other CNS depressants.

Relative Infant Dose:

Adult Dose: 7.5-30 mg daily.

Alternatives: Lorazepam, Alprazolam

T ½	= 9.5-12.4 hours	M/P	= 0.18
PHL	=	PB	= 96%
Tmax	= 2-4 hours	Oral	= 90%
MW	= 301	pKa	= 1.3
Vd	= 0.8-1.0		

References:
1. Lebedevs TH, Wojnar-Horton RE, Yapp P, Roberts MJ, Dusci LJ, Hackett LP, Ilett KF. Excretion of temazepam in breast milk. Br J Clin Pharmacol 1992; 33 (2):204-206.

TENOFOVIR DISOPROXIL FUMARATE   L3

Trade: Viread
Other Trades: Viread
Uses: Antiretroviral agent
AAP: Not reviewed

Tenofovir is used in the management of HIV and hepatitis B infections. It interferes with the viral RNA dependent DNA polymerase, inhibiting viral replication.[1]

In a recent study in two Rhesus macaques monkeys, and following a subcutaneous dose of 30 mg/kg tenofovir, peak plasma levels were reported to be 18.3 and 30.3 µg/mL.[2] Peak levels in milk were reported to be 0.808 and 0.610 µg/mL. The AUC levels were 68.9 and 12.8 ug.h/mL for plasma and milk in one animal and 56.2 and 12.1 ug.h/mL for plasma and milk in the second animal. Using this peak data, the relative infant dose would only be 0.4% of the maternal dose. In addition, the oral bioavailability of tenofovir (non salt form) is negligible (5%). Thus the overall risk to a breastfeeding infant would probably be low.

Pregnancy Risk Category: B

Lactation Risk Category: L3

Adult Concerns: Adverse reactions include pain, nausea, diarrhea, and weakness.

Pediatric Concerns: Data on humans is not available, but milk levels in monkeys are quite low.

Drug Interactions: Antiviral agents may increase the serum concentrations of tenofovir. Concurrent use of didanosine will increase serum concentrations of didanosine. Nephrotoxic agents will decrease the elimination of tenofovir. Tenofovir will decrease the serum concentrations of protease inhibitors.

Relative Infant Dose: 0.4%

Adult Dose: 300 mg daily

Alternatives:

T ½	= 17 hours	M/P	=
PHL	=	PB	= 7%
Tmax	= 36-144 minutes	Oral	= 25-40%
MW	= 636	pKa	=
Vd	= 1.2-1.3		

References:
1. Pharmaceutical Manufacturer Prescribing Information. 2005.
2. K. Van Rompay, M. Hamilton, B. Kearney and N. Bischofberger, Pharmacokinetics of tenofovir in breast milk of lactating rhesus macaques Antimicrob Agents Chemother 49, 2093-2094 (2005).

TERAZOSIN HCL   L4

Trade: Hytrin
Other Trades: Hytrin
Uses: Antihypertensive
AAP: Not reviewed

Terazosin is an antihypertensive that belongs to the alpha-1 blocking family. This family is generally very powerful, produces significant orthostatic hypotension and other side effects.[1] Terazosin has rather powerful effects on the prostate and testes producing testicular atrophy in some animal studies (particularly newborn) and is therefore not preferred in pregnant or in lactating women. No data are available on transfer into human milk.

Pregnancy Risk Category: C

Lactation Risk Category: L4

Adult Concerns: Hypotension, bradycardia, sedation.

Pediatric Concerns: None   reported,   but   extreme   caution   is recommended.

Drug Interactions: Decreased antihypertensive effect when used with NSAIDs. Increased hypotensive effects when used with diuretics and other antihypertensive beta blockers.

Relative Infant Dose:

Adult Dose: 1-10 mg daily.

Alternatives:

T ½	= 9-12 hours	M/P	=
PHL	=	PB	= 94%
Tmax	= 1-2 hours	Oral	= 90%
MW	= 423	pKa	=
Vd	=		

References:
1.   Pharmaceutical Manufacturer Prescribing Information. 1995.

TERBINAFINE   L2

Trade: Lamisil
Other Trades: Lamisil
Uses: Antifungal
AAP: Not reviewed

Terbinafine is an antifungal agent primarily used for tinea species such as athletes foot and ringworm. Systemic absorption following topical therapy is minimal.[1] Following an oral dose of 500 mg in two volunteers, the total dose of terbinafine secreted in breastmilk during the 72 hour post-dosing period was 0.65 mg in one mother and 0.15 mg in another.[2] The total excretion of terbinafine in breastmilk ranged from 0.13% to 0.03% of the total maternal dose respectively. Topical absorption through the skin is minimal.[3]

Pregnancy Risk Category: B

Lactation Risk Category: L2

Adult Concerns: Topical: burning, pruritus. Oral: fatigue, headache, GI distress, elevated liver enzymes, alopecia.

Pediatric Concerns: None reported via milk.

Drug Interactions: Terbinafine clearance is decreased 33% by cimetidine, and 16% by terfenadine. Terbinafine increases clearance of cyclosporin (15%). Rifampin increases terbinafine clearance by 100%.

Relative Infant Dose:

Adult Dose: 250 mg daily.

Alternatives: Fluconazole

T ½	= 26 hours	M/P	=
PHL	=	PB	= 99%
Tmax	= 1-2 hours	Oral	= 80%
MW	= 291	pKa	=
Vd	= >28		

References:
1. Pharmaceutical Manufacturer Prescribing Information. 1996.
2. Drug Facts and Comparisons 1996 ed. St. Louis: 1996.
3. Birnbaum JE. Pharmacology of the allylamines. J Am Acad Dermatol 1990; 23 (4 Pt 2):782-785.

TERBUTALINE   L2

Trade: Bricanyl, Brethine
Other Trades: Bricanyl
Uses: Bronchodilator for asthma
AAP: Maternal Medication Usually Compatible with Breastfeeding

Terbutaline is a popular Beta-2 adrenergic used for bronchodilation in asthmatics. It is secreted into breastmilk but in low quantities. Following doses of 7.5 to 15 mg/day of terbutaline, milk levels averaged 3.37 µg/L.[1] Assuming a daily milk intake of 165 mL/kg, these levels would suggest a daily intake of less than 0.5 µg/kg/day which corresponds to 0.2 to 0.7% of maternal dose.

In another study of a patient receiving 5 mg three times daily, the mean milk concentrations ranged from 3.2 to 3.7 µg/L.[2] The author calculated the daily dose to infant at 0.4-0.5 µg/kg body weight. Terbutaline was not detectable in the infant's serum. No untoward effects have been reported in breastfeeding infants.

Pregnancy Risk Category: B

Lactation Risk Category: L2

Adult Concerns: Tremors, nervousness, tachycardia.

Pediatric Concerns: None reported via milk.

Drug Interactions: Decreased effect when used with beta blockers. May increase toxicity when used with MAOI and TCAs.

Relative Infant Dose: 0.2% - 0.3%

Adult Dose: 5 mg TID

Alternatives:

T ½	= 14 hours	M/P	= <2.9
PHL	=	PB	= 20%
Tmax	= 5-30 minutes	Oral	= 33-50%
MW	= 225	pKa	=
Vd	= 1-2		

References:
1. Lindberg C, Boreus LO, De Chateau P, Lindstrom B, Lonnerholm G, Nyberg L. Transfer of terbutaline into breast milk. Eur J Respir Dis Suppl 1984; 134:87-91.
2. Lonnerholm G, Lindstrom B. Terbutaline excretion into breast milk. Br J Clin Pharmacol 1982; 13 (5):729-730.

TERCONAZOLE   L3

Trade: Terazol 3, Terazol 7
Other Trades: Terazol
Uses: Antifungal, vaginal.
AAP: Not reviewed

Terconazole is an antifungal primarily used for vaginal candidiasis. It is similar to fluconazole and itraconazole. When administered intravaginally, only a limited amount (5-16%) is absorbed systemically (mean peak plasma level= 6 ng/mL).[1,2] It is well absorbed orally. Even at high doses, the drug is not mutagenic, nor fetotoxic. At high doses, terconazole is known to enter breastmilk in rodents although no data are available on human milk. The milk levels are probably too small to be clinically relevant.

Pregnancy Risk Category: C

Lactation Risk Category: L3

Adult Concerns: Vaginal burning, itching, flu-like symptoms.

Pediatric Concerns: None reported due to minimal studies.

Drug Interactions:

Relative Infant Dose:

Adult Dose: 5 g daily.

Alternatives: Fluconazole

T ½	= 4-11.3 hours	M/P	=
PHL	=	PB	=
Tmax	=	Oral	= Complete
MW	= 532	pKa	=
Vd	=		

References:
1. Pharmaceutical Manufacturer Prescribing Information. 1996.
2. McEvoy GE. (ed):AFHS Drug Information. New York, NY: 1995.

TERIPARATIDE   L3

Trade: Forteo
Other Trades:
Uses: Human parathyroid hormone
AAP: Not reviewed

Teriparatide is the identical peptide hormone secreted by the parathyroid gland in humans. This leads to an increase in skeletal mass, markers of bone formation and resorption, and bone strength. Teriparatide is used to treat osteoporosis.[1] No studies are available on the levels in breast milk, however, due to the high MW and poor oral bioavailabiltiy, it is unlikely that teriparatide will cross into the milk or be absorbed by an infant.

Pregnancy Risk Category: C

Lactation Risk Category: L3

Adult Concerns: Adverse reactions include dizziness, nausea, dyspepsia, arthralgia, weakness, rhinitis, and pharyngitis.

Pediatric Concerns: No data are available, but this is the normal human parathyroid hormone.

Drug Interactions: Hypercalcemia may increase the risk of digitalis toxicity.

Relative Infant Dose:

Adult Dose: 20 μg SQ daily

Alternatives:

T ½	= 1 hour	M/P	=
PHL	=	PB	=
Tmax	=	Oral	= Nil
MW	= 4118	pKa	=
Vd	= 0.12		

References:
1. Pharmaceutical Manufacturer Prescribing Information. 2004.

TETRACYCLINE   L2

Trade: Achromycin, Sumycin, Terramycin

Other Trades: Achromycin, Aureomycin, Tetracyn, Mysteclin, Tetrex, Tetrachel

Uses: Antibiotic

AAP: Maternal Medication Usually Compatible with Breastfeeding

Tetracycline is a broad-spectrum antibiotic with significant side effects in pediatric patients, including dental staining and reduced bone growth. It is secreted into breastmilk in extremely small levels. Because tetracyclines bind to milk calcium they would have reduced oral absorption in the infant.

Posner reports that in a patient receiving 500 mg four times daily, the average concentration of tetracycline in milk was 1.14 mg/L.[1] The maternal plasma level was 1.92 mg/L and the milk/plasma ratio was 0.59. The absolute dose to the infant ranged from 0.17 to 0.39 mg/kg/day. None was detected in the plasma compartment of the infant (limit of detection 0.05 mg/L).

In a mother receiving 275 mg/d, milk levels averaged 1.25 mg/L with a maximum of 2.51 mg/L.[2] None was detected in the infants plasma. In another study of 2-3 patients receiving a single 150 mg/d dose, milk levels ranged from 0.3 to 1.2 mg/L at 4 hours (C_{max}). The maximum reported milk level was 1.2 mg/L.[3] A milk/plasma ratio of 0.58 was reported.

From the above studies, the relative infant dose is 0.6%, 4.77% and 8.44%. Thus a high degree of variability exists in these studies. Invariably mixture of tetracyclines in milk would greatly limit their oral bioavailability.

The short-term exposure of infants to tetracyclines (via milk) is not contraindicated (<3 weeks). However, the long-term exposure of breastfeeding infants to tetracyclines, such as when used daily for acne, could cause problems. The absorption of even small amounts over a prolonged period could result in dental staining.

Pregnancy Risk Category: D

Lactation Risk Category: L2

Adult Concerns: Pediatric: dental staining, decreased bone growth, altered GI flora.

Pediatric Concerns: None reported via milk. Poor oral absorption of tetracyclines generally limits effects. Avoid long-term exposure.

Drug Interactions: Absorption may be reduced or delayed when used with dairy products, calcium, magnesium, or aluminum containing antacids, oral contraceptives, iron, zinc, sodium bicarbonate, penicillins, cimetidine. Increased toxicity may result when used with methoxyflurane anesthesia. Use with warfarin anticoagulants may increase anticoagulation.

Relative Infant Dose: 0.6%

Adult Dose: 500 mg QID

Alternatives:

T ½	= 6-12 hours	M/P	= 0.58-1.28
PHL	=	PB	= 25%
Tmax	= 1.5-4 hours	Oral	= 75%
MW	= 444	pKa	=
Vd	=		

References:
1. Posner AC, Prigot A, Konicoff NG. Further observations on the use of tetracycline HCl in prophylaxis and treatment of obstetric infections. New York: Antibiotics Annual 1954-1955. In: Medical Encyclopedia, 1955.
2. Graf von H, Riemann S. Untersuchungen uber die konzentration von pyrrolidino-methyl-tetracyclin in der muttermilch. Dtsch med wochenschr 1959; 84:1694-1696.
3. Matsuda S. Transfer of antibiotics into maternal milk. Biol Res Pregnancy Perinatol 1984; 5 (2):57-60.

^{201}THALLIUM

L3

Trade: ^{201}Thallium
Other Trades:
Uses: Radioactive tracer
AAP: Not reviewed

^{201}Thallium in the form of thallous chloride is used extensively for myocardial perfusion imaging to delineate ischemic myocardium. Following infusion, almost 85% of the administered dose is extracted into the heart on the first pass. Less than 5% of the dose remains free in the plasma in as little as 5 minutes after administration. Whereas ^{201}Thallium has a radioactive half-life of only 73 hours, the terminal elimination half-life of the Thallium ion from the body is about 10 days. Most all radiation will be decayed in 5-6 half-lives (15 days). In a study of one breastfeeding patient who received 111MBq (3 mCi) for a brain scan, the amount of ^{201}Thallium in breastmilk at 4 hours was 326 Bq/mL and subsequently dropped to 87 Bq/mL after 72 hours.[1] Even without interrupting breastfeeding, the infant would have received less than the NCRP radiation safety guideline dose for infrequent exposure for a 1 year old infant. However, a brief interruption of breastfeeding was nevertheless recommended. The length of interrupted breastfeeding is dependent on age of infant and dose of Thallium. With an interruption time varying from 2, 24, 48, to 96 hours, the respective Thallium dose to the infant would be 0.442, 0.283, 0.197, and 0.101 MBq compared to the maternal dose of 111 MBq.

In another study of a breastfeeding mother who received 111 MBq (3 mCi), the calculated dose an infant (without any interruption of breastfeeding and assuming the consumption of 1000 mL of milk daily) would receive is approximately 0.81 MBq, which is presently less than the maximal allowed radiation dose (NCRP) for an infant.[2] The authors therefore recommend that breastfeeding be discontinued for at least 24-48 hours following the administration of 111 MBq of ^{201}Thallium. The amount of infant exposure from close contact with the mother was also measured and found to be very small in comparison to the orally ingested dose via milk.

Thus the interruption of breastfeeding largely depends on the dose and the volume of milk consumed by the infant. Most authors recommend interruption for 24 up to 96 hours[1,2,3], although the NRC commission (see Appendix) recommends interruption for 2 weeks. See Appendix B for more recommendations.

Pregnancy Risk Category:

Lactation Risk Category: L3 with interruption

Adult Concerns:

Pediatric Concerns: None reported in one case, but a brief interruption for 24-48 hours (depending on dose) is advised.

Drug Interactions:

Relative Infant Dose:

Adult Dose:

Alternatives:

T ½	− 73 hours	M/P	=
PHL	=	PB	=
Tmax	= <60 minutes	Oral	=
MW	=	pKa	=
Vd	=		

References:

1. Johnston RE, Mukherji SK, Perry RJ, Stabin MG. Radiation dose from breastfeeding following administration of thallium-201. J Nucl Med 1996; 37 (12):2079-2082.

2. Murphy PH, Beasley CW, Moore WH, Stabin MG. [201]Thallium in human milk: observations and radiological consequences. Health Phys 1989; 56 (4):539-541.

3. Stabin MG, Breitz HB. Breast milk excretion of radiopharmaceuticals: mechanisms, findings, and radiation dosimetry. J Nucl Med 2000 May; 41 (5):863-73.

THEOPHYLLINE   L3

Trade: Aminophylline, Quibron, Theo-Dur

Other Trades: Theo-Dur, Pulmophylline, Quibron-T/SR, Austyn, Nuelin

Uses: Bronchodilator

AAP: Maternal Medication Usually Compatible with Breastfeeding

Theophylline is a methylxanthine bronchodilator. It has a prolonged half-life in neonates which may cause retention. Milk concentrations are approximately equal to the maternal plasma levels. If a mother is maintained at 10-20 µg/mL, the milk concentrations are closely equivalent. Estimates generally indicate that less than 1% of dose is absorbed by infant. Assuming maternal plasma levels of 10-20 μg/mL, the theophylline levels in a neonate would range from 0.9 to 3.6 μg/mL.[1]

In another study of 12 patients receiving 300 mg theophylline, followed 5 hours later by 200 mg, the reported milk concentration was 2.8 mg/L and the milk/plasma ratio ranged from 0.6 to 0.89.[2] The reported maximum concentration was 6.0 mg/L. The relative infant dose would be approximately 5.8% of the weight normalized maternal dose.

One reported case of irritability and fretful sleeping was reported in an infant exposed to breastmilk only on days when the mother reported taking theophylline. The average milk concentration of theophylline in this case was 0.7 mg/L.

Pregnancy Risk Category: C

Lactation Risk Category: L3

Adult Concerns: Irritability, nausea, vomiting, tachycardia, seizures.

Pediatric Concerns: None reported via milk. One case of irritability and fretful sleeping.

Drug Interactions: Numerous drug interactions exist. Agents that decrease theophylline levels include barbiturates, phenytoin, ketoconazole, rifampin, cigarette smoking, carbamazepine, isoniazid, loop diuretics, and others. Agents that increase theophylline levels include allopurinol, beta blockers, calcium channel blockers, cimetidine, oral contraceptives, corticosteroids, disulfiram, ephedrine, influenza virus vaccine, interferon, macrolides, mexiletine, quinolones, thiabendazole, thyroid hormones, carbamazepine, isoniazid, and loop diuretics.

Relative Infant Dose: 5.9%

Adult Dose: 3 mg/kg every 8 hours

Alternatives:

T ½	= 3-12.8 hours	M/P	= 0.67
PHL	= 30 hours	PB	= 56%
Tmax	= 1-2 hours (oral)	Oral	= 76%
MW	= 180	pKa	= 8.6
Vd	= 0.3-0.7		

References:
1. Stec GP, Greenberger P, Ruo TI, Henthorn T, Morita Y, Atkinson AJ, Jr., Patterson R. Kinetics of theophylline transfer to breast milk. Clin Pharmacol Ther 1980; 28 (3):404-408.

2. Reinhardt D, Richter O, Brandenburg G. [Pharmacokinetics of drugs from the breast-feeding mother passing into the body of the infant, using theophylline as an example]. Monatsschr Kinderheilkd 1983; 131 (2):66-70.

3. Yurchak AM, Jusko WJ. Theophylline secretion into breast milk. Pediatrics 1976; 57 (4):518-520.

THIABENDAZOLE   L3

Trade: Mintezol
Other Trades: Mintezol
Uses: Anthelmintic, antiparasitic
AAP: Not reviewed

Thiabendazole is an antiparasitic agent for the treatment of roundworm, pinworm, hookworm, whipworm, and other parasitic infections. After absorption it is completely eliminated from the plasma by 48 hours although most is excreted by 24 hours. Can be used in children. Although it is effective in pinworms, other agents with less side effects are preferred. No reports on its transfer to breastmilk have been found.

Pregnancy Risk Category: C

Lactation Risk Category: L3

Adult Concerns: Hypotension, nausea, vomiting, psychotic reactions (seizures, hallucinations, delirium), rash, pruritus, intrahepatic cholestasis.

Pediatric Concerns: None reported.

Drug Interactions: May increase theophylline and other xanthines levels by 50%.

Relative Infant Dose:

Adult Dose: 1.5 g BID

Alternatives: Pyrantel

T ½	=	M/P	=
PHL	=	PB	=
Tmax	= 1-2 hours	Oral	= Complete
MW	= 201	pKa	=
Vd	=		

References:

THIAMINE   L1

Trade: Vitamin B1
Other Trades: Betaxin
Uses: Vitamin
AAP: Maternal Medication Usually Compatible with Breastfeeding

Thiamine, also known as Vitamin B-1, is used to treat thiamine deficiency. It is an essential coenzyme in carbohydrate metabolism, combining with adenosine triphosphate to form thiamine pyrophosphate. Thiamine has been shown to cross into human milk, with average concentrations in milk of 200 µg/L under normal circumstances. Thiamine deficiency causes beriberi, which presents with weight loss, mental changes, muscle weakness, or cardiovascular effects. The recommended daily allowance for infants 0 to 12 months is 0.03 mg/kg/day. The recommended daily intake for pregnant and lactating females is 1.2 mg/day. The concentration of thiamine in human milk increases with the progression of lactation, with an average milk level of 200 µg/L.[2] We do not know what milk levels would be following the use of extraordinarily large oral doses, although it appears that it would be a linear increase in milk levels. Supra-therapeutic doses should be avoided in breastfeeding mothers. Long term high doses (3 gm/day) have been associated with adult toxicity.

Pregnancy Risk Category:

Lactation Risk Category: L1

Adult Concerns: Adverse reactions include cyanosis, restlessness, nausea, edema, and weakness.

Pediatric Concerns: No data are available.

Drug Interactions:

Relative Infant Dose:

Adult Dose: 1.4 mg daily

Alternatives:

T ½	=	M/P	=
PHL	=	PB	=
Tmax	=	Oral	= Adequate
MW	= 265	pKa	=
Vd	=		

References:

1. Dietary Reference Intakes for Thiamin, Riboflavin, Niacin, Vitamin B6, Folate, Vitamin B12, Pantothenic Acid, Biotin, and Choline. Food and Nutrition Board. Institude of Medicine. Washington DC: National Academy Press; 1998.
2. Picciano MF. Handbook of milk composition. Jensen RG, ed. San Diego: Academic Press; 1995.

THIOPENTAL SODIUM   L3

Trade: Pentothal
Other Trades: Pentothal, Intraval
Uses: Barbiturate anesthetic agent
AAP: Maternal Medication Usually Compatible with Breastfeeding

Thiopental is an ultra short-acting, barbiturate sedative. Used in the induction phase of anesthesia, it rapidly redistributes from the brain to adipose and muscle tissue; hence, the plasma levels are small, and the sedative effects are virtually gone in 20 minutes. Thiopental sodium is secreted into milk in low levels. In a study of two groups of 8 women who received from 5.0 to 5.4 mg/kg thiopental sodium, the maximum concentration in breastmilk was 0.9 mg/L in mature milk and in colostrum was 0.34 mg/L.[1] The milk/plasma ratio was 0.3 for colostrum and 0.4 for mature milk. The maximum daily dose to infant would be 0.135 mg/kg or approximately 2.5% of the adult dose.

Pregnancy Risk Category: C

Lactation Risk Category: L3

Adult Concerns: Hemolytic anemia has been reported. Respiratory depression, renal failure, delirium, nausea, vomiting, pruritus.

Pediatric Concerns: None reported in a study of 16 women receiving induction doses.

Drug Interactions: Increased depression when used with CNS depressants (especially opiates and phenothiazines), and with salicylates or sulfisoxazole.

Relative Infant Dose: 2.6%

Adult Dose: 50-100 mg X 2

Alternatives:

T ½	= 3-8 hours	M/P	= 0.3-0.4
PHL	= 15 hours	PB	= 60-96%
Tmax	= 1-2 minutes	Oral	= Variable
MW	= 264	pKa	=
Vd	= 1.4		

References:

1. Andersen LW, Qvist T, Hertz J, Mogensen F. Concentrations of thiopentone in mature breast milk and colostrum following an induction dose. Acta Anaesthesiol Scand 1987; 31 (1):30-32.

THIORIDAZINE   L4

Trade: Mellaril

Other Trades: Apo-Thioridazine, Mellaril, Novo-Ridazine, Aldazine

Uses: Antipsychotic

AAP: Not reviewed

Thioridazine is a potent phenothiazine tranquilizer. It has a high volume of distribution and long half-life. No data are available on its secretion into human milk, but it should be expected.[1] Pediatric indications (2-12 years of age) are available although neonatal apnea is associated with this family of drugs.

Pregnancy Risk Category: C

Lactation Risk Category: L4

Adult Concerns: Blood dyscrasias, arrhythmias, sedation, gynecomastia, nausea, vomiting, constipation, dry mouth, retinopathy.

Pediatric Concerns: None reported due to limited studies. Neonatal apnea is common in this family of drugs.

Drug Interactions: Alcohol may enhance CNS depression. Aluminum salts may reduce GI absorption. Other anticholinergics may reduce the therapeutic actions the phenothiazines. Barbiturates may reduce phenothiazine plasma levels. Bromocriptine effectiveness may be inhibited by phenothiazines. Propranolol and phenothiazines may result in increased plasma levels of both drugs. Tricyclic antidepressant concentrations, serum concentrations may be increased the phenothiazines. Valproic acid clearance may be decreased.

Relative Infant Dose:

Adult Dose: 100-400 mg daily.

Alternatives:

T ½	= 21-24 hours	M/P	=
PHL	=	PB	=
Tmax	=	Oral	= Complete
MW	= 371	pKa	= 9.5
Vd	= 18		

References:
1. O'Brien TE. Excretion of drugs in human milk. Am J Hosp Pharm 1974; 31 (9):844-854.

THIOTHIXENE   L4

Trade: Navane
Other Trades: Navane
Uses: Antipsychotic agent
AAP: Not reviewed

Thiothixene is an antipsychotic agent similar in action to the phenothiazines, butyrophenones (Haldol), and chlorprothixene. There are no data on its transfer into human milk. Of this family, thiothixene has a rather higher risk of extrapyramidal symptoms and lowered seizure threshold.[1,2] Only two agents in these families have been studied with respect to milk levels: haloperidol and chlorpromazine. Both produced rather low milk levels. However these agents generally have long half-lives and some concern exists for long-term exposure. Observe infant for sedation, seizures, or jerks.

Pregnancy Risk Category: C

Lactation Risk Category: L4

Adult Concerns: Decreases seizure threshold. Sedation, lethargy, extrapyramidal jerking motion.

Pediatric Concerns: None via milk.

Drug Interactions: Thiothixene may be additive when coadministered with other sedative drugs, alcohol, anticholinergics, and hypotensive agents. Aluminum salts may reduce oral absorption of phenothiazines. Anticholinergics may reduce efficacy of thiothixene. Thiothixene may increase tricyclic antidepressant plasma levels.

Relative Infant Dose:

Adult Dose: 5-15 mg TID-QID

Alternatives: Haloperidol

T ½	= 34 hours	M/P	=
PHL	=	PB	=
Tmax	= 1-2 hours	Oral	= Complete
MW	= 443	pKa	=
Vd	=		

References:
1. Drug Facts and Comparisons 1999 ed. ed. St. Louis: 1999.
2. McEvoy GE. (ed): AFHS Drug Information. New York, NY: 2009.

THYROID SCAN   L4

Trade: Thyroid Scan
Other Trades:
Uses: Radiographic scan of thyroid gland
AAP: Not reviewed

Thyroid scanning with radioiodine (^{131}I) or ^{99m} technetium is useful in delineating structural abnormalities of the thyroid, e.g., to distinguish Grave's disease from multinodular goiter and a single toxic adenoma or to determine the functional state of a single nodule ("hot" vs. "cold").

In one procedure, the radiologist uses radioactive ^{99m}Technetium pertechnetate, which has a short half-life of 6.7 hours. At least 97% of the radioactivity would be decayed in 5 half-lives (33.5 hours), after which it would be presumably safe to breastfeed.

In the second procedure (an uptake scan) radioactive Iodine^{131} is used. The radioactive half-life of ^{131}I is 8.1 days. Five half-lives in this situation is 40.5 days. Although the biologic half-life of iodine would be less than the 40.5 days, it is not known with certainty how long is required before breastmilk samples are at background levels. For safety in this case, breast milk samples should be counted by a gamma counter prior to reinstituting breastfeeding. ^{131}I is sequestered in high concentrations in breastmilk, and breastmilk levels could be exceedingly high. Excessive exposure of the infants thyroid to ^{131}I is exceedingly dangerous.[1-6] See Appendix B for more information.

Pregnancy Risk Category:

Lactation Risk Category: L4

Adult Concerns: High milk radioactive levels.

Pediatric Concerns: Possible thyroid suppression is possible if high levels of ^{131}I are used. Count breastmilk samples to determine radiation levels.

Drug Interactions:

Relative Infant Dose:

Adult Dose:

References:
1. American Academy of Pediatrics, Committee on Drugs. Transfer of drugs and other chemicals into human milk. Pediatrics 2001; 108 (3):776-89.
2. Palmer KE. Excretion of 125I in breast milk following administration of labelled fibrinogen. Br J Radiol 1979; 52 (620):672-673.
3. Karjalainen P, Penttila IM, Pystynen P. The amount and form of radioactivity in human milk after lung scanning, renography and placental localization by 131 I labelled tracers. Acta Obstet Gynecol Scand 1971; 50 (4):357-361.
4. Hedrick WR, Di Simone RN, Keen RL. Radiation dosimetry from breast milk excretion of radioiodine and pertechnetate. J Nucl Med 1986; 27 (10):1569-1571.
5. Romney B, Nickoloff EL, Esser PD. Excretion of radioiodine in breast milk. J Nucl Med 1989; 30 (1):124-126.
6. Robinson PS, Barker P, Campbell A, Henson P, Surveyor I, Young PR. [131]Iodine in breast milk following therapy for thyroid carcinoma. J Nucl Med 1994; 35 (11):1797-1801.

THYROTROPIN   L1

Trade: Thyrotropin, TSH, Thyrogen
Other Trades: Thytropar
Uses: Thyroid-stimulating hormone
AAP: Not reviewed

Thyrotropin (TSH) is known to be secreted into breastmilk, but in low levels. Because TSH is significantly elevated in hypothyroid mothers, if present in milk at high levels, it could theoretically cause a hyperthyroid condition in the breastfeeding infant. In a 34 year old breastfeeding mother with severe hypothyroidism, maternal plasma levels of TSH were measured at 110 mU/L. Milk levels of TSH were 1.4 mU/L.[1] The author suggests that breastmilk TSH was too low too affect thyroid function in a breastfeeding infant, even with milk from a severe hypothyroid mother.

Pregnancy Risk Category: C

Lactation Risk Category: L1

Adult Concerns: Elevated thyroxine levels in breastfeeding infant.

Pediatric Concerns: None reported via milk. Breastfeeding by hypothyroid mother is permissible.

Drug Interactions:

Relative Infant Dose:

Adult Dose: 10 units daily

Alternatives:

T ½	=		M/P	=
PHL	=		PB	=
Tmax	=		Oral	= Poor
MW	= 359		pKa	=
Vd	=			

References:
1. Robinson P, Hoad K. Thyrotropin in human breast milk. Aust N Z J Med 1994; 24 (1):68.

TIAGABINE   L3

Trade: Gabitril
Other Trades: Gabitril
Uses: Anticonvulsant
AAP: Not reviewed

Tiagabine is a GABA inhibitor useful for the treatment of partial epilepsy. It works by enhancing the activity of gamma aminobutyric acid (GABA), the major inhibitory neurotransmitter in the central nervous system.[1] No data are available on its transfer to human milk. It has been used in pediatric patients 3-10 years of age. Use in women who are breastfeeding only if the benefits clearly outweigh the risks.

Pregnancy Risk Category: C

Lactation Risk Category: L3

Adult Concerns: Asthenia, sedation, dizziness, headache, mild memory impairment, and abdominal pain and nausea have been reported.

Pediatric Concerns: None reported via milk. Observe for somnolence.

Drug Interactions: Enhanced clearance of tiagabine has been reported when coadministered with carbamazepine, fosphenytoin,

phenytoin, primidone, and phenobarbital. Clearance was 60% or more greater when admixed with other enzyme-inducing AEDs (phenobarbital, phenytoin, etc). Valproic acid produces a 10% drop in tiagabine plasma levels but with a significant drop in plasma protein binding (may enhance the effect).

Relative Infant Dose:

Adult Dose: 32-56 mg daily

Alternatives: Gabapentin, lamotrigine

T ½	= 7-9 hours	M/P	=
PHL	= 3.2-5.7 hours	PB	= 96%
Tmax	= 45 minutes	Oral	= 90%
MW	= 412	pKa	=
Vd	=		

References:
1. Pharmaceutical Manufacturer Prescribing Information. 2005

TICARCILLIN   L1

Trade: Ticar, Timentin
Other Trades: Ticar, Tarcil, Ticillin
Uses: Penicillin antibiotic
AAP: Maternal Medication Usually Compatible with Breastfeeding

Ticarcillin is an extended-spectrum penicillin, used only IM or IV, and is not appreciably absorbed via oral ingestion.[1,2] In a study of 2-3 patients who received 1000 mg IV, only trace amounts were detected in milk and were too low to measure.[3] In a study of 10 patients who received 5 g TID IV, the amount of ticarcillin in milk ranged from 2- 2.5 mg/L.[4] Twelve hours after discontinuing ticarcillin, it was undetectable in milk. As with many penicillins, only minimal levels are secreted into milk. Poor oral absorption would limit exposure of breastfeeding infant. May cause changes in GI flora and possibly fungal overgrowth. Timentin is ticarcillin with clavulanate added.

Pregnancy Risk Category: B

Lactation Risk Category: L1

Adult Concerns: Neutropenia, anemia, kidney toxicity. Changes in GI flora, diarrhea, candida overgrowth.

Pediatric Concerns: None reported via milk. Observe for changes in GI flora, diarrhea.

Drug Interactions: Probenecid may increase penicillin levels. Tetracyclines may decrease penicillin effectiveness.

Relative Infant Dose: 0.2%

Adult Dose: 150-300 mg daily.

Alternatives:

T ½	= 0.9-1.3 hours	M/P	=
PHL	= 3.5 - 5.6 hours (neonate)	PB	= 54%
Tmax	= 0.5 - 1.25 hours (IM)	Oral	= Poor
MW	= 384	pKa	=
Vd	=		

References:
1. Drug Facts and Comparisons 1995 ed. ed. St. Louis: 1995.
2. Pharmaceutical Manufacturer Prescribing Information. 1995.
3. Matsuda S. Transfer of antibiotics into maternal milk. Biol Res Pregnancy Perinatol 1984; 5 (2):57-60.
4. von Kobyletzki D, Dalhoff A, Lindemeyer H, Primavesi CA. Ticarcillin serum and tissue concentrations in gynecology and obstetrics. Infection 1983; 11 (3):144-149.

TICLOPIDINE   L4

Trade: Ticlid
Other Trades: Ticlid, Apo-Ticlopidine, Tilodene
Uses: Inhibits platelet aggregation
AAP: Not reviewed

Ticlopidine is useful in preventing thromboembolic disorders, increased cardiovascular mortality, stroke, infarcts, and other clotting disorders. Ticlopidine is reported to be excreted into rodent milk.[1] No data are available on penetration into human breastmilk. However it is highly protein bound, and the levels of ticlopidine in plasma are quite low.

Pregnancy Risk Category: B

Lactation Risk Category: L4

Adult Concerns: Bleeding, neutropenia, maculopapular rash.

Pediatric Concerns: None reported via milk, but caution is recommended.

Drug Interactions: Antacids may reduce absorption of ticlopidine. Chronic cimetidine administration has reduced the clearance of ticlopidine by 50%. Use of aspirin may alter platelet aggregation. Digoxin plasma levels may be slightly decreased by 15%. Theophylline elimination half-life was significantly increased from 8-10 hours.

Relative Infant Dose:

Adult Dose: 250 mg BID

Alternatives:

T ½	= 12.6 hours	M/P	=
PHL	=	PB	= 98%
Tmax	= 2 hours	Oral	– 80%
MW	= 264	pKa	=
Vd	=		

References:
1.   Pharmaceutical Manufacturer Prescribing Information. 1996.

TIGECYCLINE   L3

Trade: Tygacil
Other Trades:
Uses: Antibiotic
AAP: Not reviewed

Tigecycline is a glycylcycline antibiotic similary to related tetracyclines. Tigecycline is not affected by the major mechanisms of resistance, and thus is effective against a broad-spectrum of bacterial pathogens.[1] Tigecycline may cause fetal harm when administered to a pregnant woman, as well as tooth discoloration when used during tooth development. There have been no studies performed on the transmission of tigecycline into a mother's breastmilk, however, due to the limited oral bioavailability, it would be unlikely that the infant would absorb clinically relevant levels over a brief exposure. However, prolonged exposure (> 3 weeks) is not recommended.

Pregnancy Risk Category: D

Lactation Risk Category: L3

Adult Concerns: Adverse effects include nausea, vomiting, diarrhea, fever, and abdominal pain.

Pediatric Concerns: Use of tigecycline during tooth development (fetus-age 8) has resulted in tooth discoloration.

Drug Interactions: Decreased effectiveness of oral contraceptives, increased warfarin exposure, and increased risk of pseudotumor cerebri with retinoic acid derivatives have been observed with concurrent use of tygecycline.

Relative Infant Dose:

Adult Dose: 50mg IV every 12 hours for 5-14 days

Alternatives:

T ½	= 27-42 hours	M/P	=
PHL	=	PB	= 71-89%
Tmax	=	Oral	= Nil
MW	= 586	pKa	=
Vd	= 7-9		

References:
1.   Pharmaceutical Manufacturer Prescribing Information. 2007.

TIMOLOL   L2

Trade: Blocadren

Other Trades: Apo-Timol, Blocadren, Timoptic, Novo-Timol, Tenopt, Timpilo, Betim, Timoptol

Uses: Beta blocker for hypertension and glaucoma

AAP: Maternal Medication Usually Compatible with Breastfeeding

Timolol is a beta blocker used for treating hypertension and glaucoma. It is secreted into milk. Following a dose of 5 mg three times daily, milk levels averaged 15.9 µg/L.[1] Both oral and ophthalmic drops produce modest levels in milk. Breastmilk levels following ophthalmic use of 0.5% timolol drops was 5.6 µg/L at 1.5 hours after the dose.[2] Untoward effects on infant have not been reported. These levels are probably too small to be clinically relevant.

Pregnancy Risk Category: C

Lactation Risk Category: L2

Adult Concerns: Hypotension, bradycardia, depression, sedation.

Pediatric Concerns: None reported via milk, but observe for hypotension, weakness, hypoglycemia, sedation, depression.

Drug Interactions: Decreased effect when used with aluminum salts, barbiturates, calcium salts, cholestyramine, NSAIDs, ampicillin, rifampin, and salicylates. Beta blockers may reduce the effect of oral sulfonylureas (hypoglycemic agents). Increased toxicity/effect when used with other antihypertensives, contraceptives, MAO inhibitors, cimetidine, and numerous other products. See drug interaction reference for complete listing.

Relative Infant Dose: 1.1%

Adult Dose: 10 20 mg BID

Alternatives: Propranolol, Metoprolol

T ½	= 4 hours	M/P	= 0.8
PHL	=	PB	= 10%
Tmax	= 1-2 hours	Oral	= 50%
MW	= 316	pKa	= 8.8
Vd	= 1-3		

References:
1. Fidler J, Smith V, De Swiet M. Excretion of oxprenolol and timolol in breast milk. Br J Obstet Gynaecol 1983; 90 (10):961-965.
2. Lustgarten JS, Podos SM. Topical timolol and the nursing mother. Arch Ophthalmol 1983; 101 (9):1381-1382.

TINIDAZOLE

L2

Trade: Tindamax
Other Trades: Fasigyn
Uses: Antimicrobial agent for protozoal and anaerobic bacterial infections.
AAP: Drugs whose effect on nursing infants is unknown but may be of concern

Tinidazole is an antimicrobial agent that is sometimes used for the treatment of anaerobic infections and protozoal infections such as intestinal amebiasis, Giardia and trichomoniasis. It is similar to metronidazole. Tinidazole is highly lipophilic and passes membranes easily attaining high concentrations in virtually all body tissues. Concentrations in saliva and bile are equivalent to that of the plasma compartment.

In a study of 24 women, who received a single IV infusion immediately postpartum of 500 mg, aliquots of milk and serum were collected at 12, 24, 48, 72, and 96 hours after the injection.[1] At 48 and 72 hours, fore and hind milk samples were also taken, whereas at 12 and 24 hours only mixed milk samples were collected. Milk levels at 12 and 24 hours were 5.8 and 3.5 mg/L respectively. Serum levels at 12 and 24 hours averaged 6.1 and 3.7 mg/L respectively. The milk/serum ratios at 12 and 24 hours were 0.94 and 0.95 respectively, further suggesting the high lipid solubility of this product.

At 48 and 72 hours, the fore milk levels were 1.28 and 0.32 mg/L respectively. Hind milk levels at these same times were 1.2 and 0.3 respectively. At 96 hours only trace amounts were present in milk and none in serum.

As this study was done early postpartum, when milk levels are low and lipid content is low, as well, it should be presumed that milk levels in mature, more lipid rich milk, might actually be higher than reported in this study. The maximum relative infant dose (12 hours) would be 12.1%, but this is assuming milk intake of 150 mL/kg/d.

One other study of 5 women taking a dose of 1600 mg IV reported milk-to-plasma ratios of between 0.62 and 1.39. After 72 hours, the majority of the milk samples were below 0.5 μg/mL. The authors therefore concluded that breastfeeding should be withheld for 72 hours after a 1600 mg IV dose of tinidazole.[2]

Pregnancy Risk Category: C

Lactation Risk Category: L2

Adult Concerns: Headaches, confusion, dizziness, fatigue, malaise and weakness occur in 2% or less of patients. Agitation, tingling, numbness, and drowsiness have been reported. Dark-colored urine is common. A metallic or bitter taste has been reported, as well as nausea and anorexia. A disulfiram-like reaction when taken with alcohol.

Pediatric Concerns: Levels in milk were low in 24 women studied, no untoward effects were reported in breastfed infants.

Drug Interactions: None reported.

Relative Infant Dose: 12.2%

Adult Dose: 2 grams daily for 1 to 3 days

Alternatives: Metronidazole

T ½	= 11-14.7 hours	M/P	= 1.28
PHL	=	PB	= 12%
Tmax	= 2 hours	Oral	= 100%
MW	=	pKa	=
Vd	= 0.8		

References:
1. Mannisto PT, Karhunen M, Koskela O et al. Concentrations of tinidazole in breast milk. Acta Pharmacol Toxicol (Copenh) 1983; 53:254-256.
2. Evaldson GR, Lindgren S, Nord CE, Rane AT. Tinidazole milk excretion and pharmacokinetics in lactating women. Br J Clin Pharmac 1985; 19:503-507.

TINZAPARIN SODIUM   L3

Trade: Innohep
Other Trades: Innohep, Logiparin
Uses: Anticoagulant low MW heparin
AAP: Not reviewed

Tinzaparin is a depolymerized heparin (low MW heparin) similar to several others such as dalteparin, enoxaparin, nadroparin or parnaparin. The average MW range of tinzaparin is approximately one-half that of regular (unfractionated) heparin (5500-7500 vs 12,000 daltons). No data are available on the transfer of this anticoagulant into human milk but it is likely low. In studies with dalteparin none was found in milk in one study, and only small amounts in another (see dalteparin). In studies with enoxaparin, no changes in anti-Xa activity were noted in breastfed infants. It is very unlikely any would be orally bioavailable.

Other typical low MW heparins: Dalteparin (Fragmin), enoxaparin (Lovenox), nadroparin (Fraxiparin), parnaparin (Fluxum)

Pregnancy Risk Category: B

Lactation Risk Category: L3

Adult Concerns: Hemorrhage, thrombocytopenia, hematoma a site of injection, allergic reaction, and vaginal bleeding.

Pediatric Concerns: None reported via milk. Milk levels in other LMWHs are reportedly low, it is likely similar for tinzaparin as well.

Drug Interactions: Do not use with other anticoagulants with includes many NSAIDs, aspirin, herbal remedies, and other agents which inhibit thrombus formation. Check other sources for complete lists.

Relative Infant Dose:

Adult Dose: 175 IU/Kg/day (highly variable)

Alternatives: Dalteparin, enoxaparin

T ½	= 3-4 hours	M/P	=
PHL	=	PB	= 0%
Tmax	= 4-5 hours (SC)	Oral	= Nil
MW	= <7500	pKa	=
Vd	= 3.1-5.0		

References:
1. Pharmaceutical Manufacturer Prescribing Information, 2002.

TIZANIDINE   L4

Trade: Zanaflex
Other Trades:
Uses: Muscle relaxant
AAP: Not reviewed

Tizanidine is a centrally acting muscle relaxant. It has demonstrated efficacy in the treatment of tension headache and spasticity associate with multiple sclerosis. It is not known if it is transferred into human milk although the manufacturer states that due to its lipid solubility, it likely penetrates milk.[1] This product has a long half-life, high lipid solubility, and significant CNS penetration, all factors that would increase milk penetration. While the half-life of the conventional formulation is only 4-8 hours, the half-life of the sustained release formulation is 13-22 hours.[2] Further, 48% of patients complain of sedation. Use caution if used in a breastfeeding mother.

Pregnancy Risk Category: C

Lactation Risk Category: L4

Adult Concerns: Hypotension (49%), sedation (48%), dry mouth, asthenia, dizziness, and other symptoms have been reported. Nausea and vomiting have been reported. A high risk of elevated liver enzymes (5%).

Pediatric Concerns: None reported via milk, but caution is recommended.

Drug Interactions: Alcohol may increase plasma levels of tizanidine by 20%. Oral contraceptives may significantly (50%) reduce clearance of tizanidine.

Relative Infant Dose:

Adult Dose: 8 mg every 6 hours PRN

Alternatives:

T ½	= 13-22 hours	M/P	=
PHL	=	PB	= 30%
Tmax	= 1.5 hours	Oral	= 40%
MW	=	pKa	=
Vd	– 2.4		

References:
1. Pharmaceutical Manufacturer Prescribing Information. 1999.
2. Wagstaff AJ, Bryson HM. Tizanidine. A review of its pharmacology, clinical efficacy and tolerability in the management of spasticity associated with cerebral and spinal disorders. Drugs 1997; 53 (3):435-452.

TOBRAMYCIN   L3

Trade: Nebcin, Tobrex, Tobi
Other Trades: Nebcin, Tobrex, Tobi, Tobralex
Uses: Antibiotic
AAP: Not reviewed

Tobramycin is an aminoglycoside antibiotic similar to gentamicin.[1] Although small levels of tobramycin are known to transfer into milk, they probably pose few problems.

In one study of 5 patients, following an 80 mg IM dose, tobramycin levels in milk ranged from undetectable to 0.5 mg/L in only one patient.[2] In a case report of a mother receiving 150 mg three times daily for 14 days (IV), milk concentrations were determined on day four, before administration, and 60, 120, 180, 240, and 300 minutes after dosing. Tobramycin was undetectable in all samples. The limit of detection was >0.18 mg/L. No untoward effects were noted in the infant.[3] In another study of one mother who received 80 mg every 8 hours (IM), milk levels ranged from 0.6 mg/L at 1 hour to 0.58 mg/L at 8 hours postdose.[4]

Levels in milk are generally low, but could produce minor changes in gut flora. As oral tobramycin is not absorbed orally, systemic levels in infant would be unexpected.

Pregnancy Risk Category: D

Lactation Risk Category: L3

Adult Concerns: Changes in GI flora.

Pediatric Concerns: Observe for changes in GI flora.

Drug Interactions: Increased toxicity when used with certain penicillins, cephalosporins, amphotericin B, loop diuretics, and neuromuscular blocking agents.

Relative Infant Dose: 2.6% - 7.9%

Adult Dose: 1 mg/kg every 8 hours

Alternatives:

T ½	= 2-3 hours	M/P	=
PHL	= 4.6 hours (neonates)	PB	= <5%
Tmax	= 30-90 minutes (IM)	Oral	= Nil
MW	= 468	pKa	=
Vd	= 0.22-0.31		

References:
1.   Pharmaceutical Manufacturer Prescribing Information. 1996.
2.   Takase Z. Laboratory and clinical studies on tobramycin in the field of obstetrics and gynecology. Chemotherapy (Tokyo) 1975; 23:1402.
3.   Festini F, Ciuti R, Taccetti G, Repetto T, Campana S, Martino M. Breast feeding in a woman with cystic fibrosis undergoing antibiotic intravenous treatment. J Matern Fetal Neonatal Med 2006; 19 (6):375-376.
4.   Uwaydah M, Bibi S. and Salman S, Therapeutic efficacy of tobramycin--a clinical and laboratory evaluation. J Antimicrob Chemother 1975; 1:429-437.

TOCAINIDE   L4

Trade: Tonocard
Other Trades: Xylotocan
Uses: Antiarrhythmic
AAP: Not reviewed

Tocainide is an antiarrhythmic reserved for the treatment of ventricular arrhythmias. It is an oral analogue of and similar in structure and pharmacology to lidocaine. In a study of a single patient who received 400 mg every 8 hours, milk and serum levels were drawn 0.5 hours before administration and 2 hours after administration of a 400 mg dose.[1] The reported level in plasma and milk were 5.6 and 12 µg/mL respectively, 0.5 hours before the dose. Levels at 2 hours following the dose were 9.2 and 28 µg/mL respectively. The relative infant dose via milk would then be approximately 24.5% of the weight-normalized maternal dose. Caution is recommended as these levels are quite high and this product is well absorbed.

Pregnancy Risk Category: C

Lactation Risk Category: L4

Adult Concerns: Prolonged QRS complex. Severe vomiting followed by nodal bradycardia. Heart failure, hypotension, pericarditis has been reported.

Pediatric Concerns: None reported via milk.

Drug Interactions: Cimetidine, rifampin, and rifapentine may reduce its effectiveness. Coadministration of lidocaine may increase their combined toxicity.

Relative Infant Dose: 24.5%

Adult Dose: 400 mg three times daily.

Alternatives: Lidocaine

T ½	= 11-22 hours	M/P	= 1.6-2.3
PHL	=	PB	= 22%
Tmax	= 0.5-2 hours	Oral	= 100%
MW	= 192	pKa	=
Vd	= 1.4-32		

References:
1. Wilson JH. Breast milk tocainide levels. J Cardiovasc Pharmacol 1988 Oct; 12 (4):497.

TOLBUTAMIDE   L3

Trade: Oramide, Orinase

Other Trades: Apo-Tolbutamide, Mobenol, Novo-Butamide, Orinase, Glyconon, Rastinon

Uses: Antidiabetic

AAP: Maternal Medication Usually Compatible with Breastfeeding

Tolbutamide is a short-acting sulfonylurea used to stimulate insulin secretion in type II diabetics. Only low levels are secreted into breastmilk. Following a dose of 500 mg twice daily, milk levels in two patients were 3 and 18 µg/L respectively.[1] Maternal serum levels averaged 35 and 45 µg/L. Observe infant closely for jaundice and hypoglycemia.

Pregnancy Risk Category: C

Lactation Risk Category: L3

Adult Concerns: Hypoglycemia, nausea, dyspepsia.

Pediatric Concerns: None reported via milk.

Drug Interactions: The hypoglycemic effect may be enhanced by : anticoagulants, chloramphenicol, clofibrate, fenfluramine, fluconazole, H2 antagonists, magnesium salts, methyldopa, MAO inhibitors, probenecid, salicylates, TCAs, sulfonamides. The hypoglycemic effect may be reduced by: beta blockers, cholestyramine, diazoxide, phenytoin, rifampin, thiazide diuretics.

Relative Infant Dose: 0.02%

Adult Dose: 250-2000 mg daily.

Alternatives:

T ½	= 4.5-6.5 hours	M/P	= 0.09-0.4
PHL	=	PB	= 93%
Tmax	= 3.5 hours	Oral	= Complete
MW	= 270	pKa	= 5.3
Vd	= 0.10-0.15		

References:
1.   Moiel RH, Ryan JR. Tolbutamide orinase in human breast milk. Clin Pediatr (Phila) 1967; 6 (8):480.

TOLMETIN SODIUM   L3

Trade: Tolectin
Other Trades: Tolectin
Uses: Non-steroidal analgesic, used for arthritis, etc.
AAP: Maternal Medication Usually Compatible with Breastfeeding

Tolmetin is a standard non-steroidal analgesic. Tolmetin is known to be distributed into milk but in small amounts. In one patient given 400 mg, the milk level at 0.67 hours was 0.18 mg/L.[1] The estimate of dose per day an infant would receive is 115 µg/Liter of milk. Tolmetin is sometimes used in pediatric rheumatoid patients (>2 years).

Pregnancy Risk Category: C in first and second trimesters
                               D in third trimester

Lactation Risk Category: L3

Adult Concerns: GI distress, bleeding, vomiting, nausea, edema.

Pediatric Concerns: None reported via milk.

Drug Interactions: May prolong prothrombin time when used with warfarin. Antihypertensive effects of ACEi family may be blunted or completely abolished by NSAIDs. Some NSAIDs may block antihypertensive effect of beta blockers, diuretics. Used with cyclosporin, may dramatically increase renal toxicity. May increase digoxin, phenytoin, lithium levels. May increase toxicity of methotrexate. May increase bioavailability of penicillamine. Probenecid may increase NSAID levels.

Relative Infant Dose: 0.5%

Adult Dose: 200-600 mg TID

Alternatives: Ibuprofen

T ½	= 1-1.5 hours	M/P	= 0.0055
PHL	=	PB	= 99%
Tmax	= 0.5-1 hour	Oral	= Complete
MW	= 257	pKa	= 3.5
Vd	=		

References:
1. Sagraves R, Waller ES, Goehrs HR. Tolmetin in breast milk. Drug Intell Clin Pharm 1985; 19 (1):55-56.

TOLTERODINE L3

Trade: Detrol
Other Trades: Detrol, Detrusitol
Uses: Urinary incontinence
AAP: Not reviewed

Tolterodine is a muscarinic anticholinergic agent similar in effect to atropine but is more selective for the urinary bladder.[1] Tolterodine levels in milk have been reported in mice, where offspring exposed to extremely high levels had slightly reduced body weight gain, but no other untoward effects. While it is more selective for the urinary bladder, preclinical trials still showed adverse effects including blurred vision, constipation, and dry mouth in adults. While we have no data on human milk, it is unlikely concentrations will be high enough to produce untoward effects in infants. However, the infant should be monitored for classic anticholinergic symptoms including dry mouth, constipation, poor tearing, etc.

Pregnancy Risk Category: C

Lactation Risk Category: L3

Adult Concerns: Blurred vision, constipation, and dry mouth in adults.

Pediatric Concerns: None by milk, but observe for anticholinergic symptoms such as dry mouth, constipation, poor tearing, poor urinary output.

Drug Interactions: Fluoxetine reduces metabolism of tolterodine significantly and may increase plasma levels by 4.8 fold.

Relative Infant Dose:

Adult Dose: 2 mg BID

Alternatives:

T ½	= 1.9-3.7 hours	M/P	=
PHL	=	PB	= 96%
Tmax	= 1-2 hours	Oral	= 77%
MW	=	pKa	=
Vd	= 1.6		

References:
1.   Pharmaceutical Manufacturer Prescribing Information.

TOPIRAMATE   L3

Trade: Topamax
Other Trades: Topamax
Uses: Anticonvulsant
AAP: Not reviewed

Topiramate is an anticonvulsant used in controlling refractory partial seizures. In a group of 2 women receiving topiramate (150-200 mg/day) at three weeks postpartum the mean milk/plasma ratio was 0.86 (range=0.67-1.1).[1] The concentration of topiramate in milk averaged 7.9 µM (range= 1.6 to 13.7). The weight normalized relative infant dose (RID), assuming a milk intake of 150 mL/kg/d, was 3-23% of the maternal dose/day. The absolute infant dose was 0.1 to 0.7 mg/kg/day. The plasma concentrations of topiramate in two infants were 1.4 and 1.6 µM, respectively. The plasma level in another infant was undetectable. The plasma concentrations in the two infants were 10-20% of the maternal plasma level. At 4 weeks, the milk/plasma ratio had dropped to 0.69 and plasma levels in the infant were <0.9 µM and 2.1 µM, respectively.

Topiramate has become increasingly popular due to its fewer adverse side effects.[2-5] Due to the fact that the plasma levels found in breastfeeding infants were significantly less than in maternal plasma, the risk of using this product in breastfeeding mothers is probably acceptable. Close observation for sedation is advised.

Pregnancy Risk Category: C

Lactation Risk Category: L3

Adult Concerns: Topiramate induces a significant Cognitive dysfunction, particularly in older patients. Paresthesias, sedation, weight loss (7%), diarrhea.

Pediatric Concerns: None reported in two cases. Milk levels were moderate and infant plasma levels were 10-20% of maternal levels.

Drug Interactions: A 40 % decrease in topiramate concentration has been reported when carbamazepine was added to topiramate therapy. Do not use topiramate with dichlorphenamide due to increased risk of nephrolithiasis. Serum digoxin levels (AUC) are decreased by 12% in patients receiving digoxin and topiramate. Efficacy of combination birth control pills may be reduced when adding topiramate. A 25% decrease in phenytoin levels have been reported when topirmate was added. Phenobarbital may reduce half-life of topirmate by 11%.

Relative Infant Dose: 24.5%

Adult Dose: 200 mg BID

Alternatives:

T ½	= 18-24 hours	M/P	= 0.86
PHL	=	PB	= 15%
Tmax	= 1.5-4 hours	Oral	= 75%
MW	= 339	pKa	=
Vd	= 0.7		

References:

1. Ohman I, Vitols S, Luef G, Soderfeldt B, Tomson T. Topiramate kinetics during delivery, lactation, and in the neonate: preliminary observations. Epilepsia 2002; 43 (10):1157-1160.
2. Patsalos PN, Sander JW. Newer antiepileptic drugs. Towards an improved risk-benefit ratio. Drug Saf 1994; 11 (1):37-67.
3. Bialer M. Comparative pharmacokinetics of the newer antiepileptic drugs. Clin Pharmacokinet 1993; 24 (6):441-452.
4. Britton JW, So EL. New antiepileptic drugs: prospects for the future. J Epilepsy 1995; 8:267-281.
5. Pharmacokinetics of topiramate in pregnancy and lactation-transplacental transfer and excretion in breast-milk. Fifth Eilat Conference on Antiepileptic Drugs, Eilat, Israel. 00 Jun; 2000.

TORSEMIDE   L3

Trade: Demadex
Other Trades: Demadex, Torem
Uses: Potent Loop diuretic
AAP: Not reviewed

Torsemide is a potent loop diuretic generally used in congestive heart failure and other conditions which require a strong diuretic.[1] There are no reports of its transfer into human milk. Its extraordinary high protein binding would likely limit its transfer into human milk. As with many diuretics, reduction of plasma volume and hypotension may adversely reduce milk production although this is rare. See furosemide.

Pregnancy Risk Category: B

Lactation Risk Category: L3

Adult Concerns: Hypotension, hypokalemia, volume depletion, headache, excessive urination, dizziness.

Pediatric Concerns: None reported. Renal calcification have been reported with other loop diuretics in premature infants, but not via milk supply.

Drug Interactions: When used with salicylates, elevated plasma salicylate levels may occur. Coadministration with other NSAIDS may increase the risk of renal dysfunction. Cholestyramine administration reduces bioavailability of torsemide. Use caution in using with lithium.

Relative Infant Dose:

Adult Dose: 5-10 mg daily.

Alternatives: Furosemide

T ½	= 3.5 hours	M/P	=
PHL	=	PB	= >99%
Tmax	= 1 hour	Oral	= 80%
MW	= 348	pKa	=
Vd	= 0.21		

References:
1.   Pharmaceutical Manufacturer Prescribing Information. 1997.

TRAMADOL   L2

Trade: Ultram, Ultracet
Other Trades: Tramal, Nycodol, Tramake, Zydol, Zamadol, Dromadol
Uses: Analgesic
AAP: Not reviewed

Tramadol is a new class analgesic that most closely resembles the opiates although it is not a controlled substance and appears to have reduced addictive potential. It appears to be slightly more potent than codeine. After oral use, its onset of analgesia is within 1 hour and reaches a peak in 2-3 hours. Following a single IV 100 mg dose of tramadol, the cumulative excretion in breastmilk within 16 hours was 100 µg of tramadol (0.1% of the maternal dose) and 27 µg of the M1 metabolite.[1]

In a recent study of 75 mothers who received 100 mg every 6 hours after Cesesarian section, milk samples were taken on days 2-4 postpartum in transitional milk.[2] At steady state, the Milk/Plasma ratio averaged 2.4 for rac-tramadol and 2.8 for rac-O-desmethyltramadol. The estimated absolute and relative infant doses were 112 µg/kg/day and 30 µg/kg/day for rac-tramadol and its desmethyl metabolite. The relative infant dose was 2.24% and 0.64% for rac-tramadol and its desmethyl metabolite, respectively. No significant neurobehavioral adverse effects were noted between controls and exposed infants.

Pregnancy Risk Category: C

Lactation Risk Category: L2

Adult Concerns: Sedation, respiratory depression, nausea, vomiting, constipation.

Pediatric Concerns: None reported via milk. Observe for sedation.

Drug Interactions: Use with carbamazepine dramatically increases tramadol metabolism and reduces plasma levels. Use with MAOI may increase toxicity.

Relative Infant Dose: 2.9%

Adult Dose: 50-100 mg every 4-6 hours PRN

Alternatives: Hydrocodone

T ½	= 7 hours	M/P	= 2.4
PHL	=	PB	= 20%
Tmax	= 2 hours	Oral	= 60%
MW	= 263	pKa	=
Vd	=		

References:
1. Pharmaceutical Manufacturer Prescribing Information. 1996.
2. Ilett KF, Paech MJ, Page-Sharp M, et.al. Use of a sparse sampling study design to assess transfer of tramadol and its O-desmethyl metabolite into transitional breast milk. Br J Clin Pharmacol 65 (5):661-666, 2008

TRAMADOL AND ACETAMINOPHEN   L2

Trade: Ultracet
Other Trades:
Uses: Analgesic
AAP: Not reviewed

Ultracet is the combination of 37.5 mg of tramadol (Ultram) and 325 mg acetaminophen. See individual monographs.

Pregnancy Risk Category:

Lactation Risk Category: L2

Adult Concerns:

Pediatric Concerns:

Drug Interactions:

Relative Infant Dose:

Adult Dose:

Alternatives:

References:

TRASTUZUMAB   L4

Trade: Herceptin
Other Trades:
Uses: Anticancer antibody
AAP: Not reviewed

Trastuzumab is recombinant DNA-derived humanized monoclonal antibody that selectively binds to receptors common on certain breast cancers. It is indicated in the treatment of patients with metastatic breast cancer whose tumors over express the HER2 protein. It is an IgG1 kappa that contains human framework regions that bind to the HER2 receptors on cancer cells. While IgG transfer minimally into human milk, we do not have data on the transfer of this recombinant product into human milk. Studies on cynomolgus monkeys at doses 25 times the weekly human dose demonstrated that trastuzumab is secreted in milk (levels were not reported). However, it was not associated with any adverse effects on the growth or development of these infant monkeys. It is not likely that this agent at doses used in humans would cause appreciable problems in a breastfeeding human. However, it is not clear that mothers with breast cancer should breastfeed, as we do not yet understand how lactation would affect the mother's response to anticancer agents. See Appendix A for more information.

Pregnancy Risk Category: B

Lactation Risk Category: L4

Adult Concerns: Adverse events include pain, asthenia, fever, chills, back and abdominal pain, headache, nausea, diarrhea, vomiting, insomnia, cough, dyspnea, rhinitis, and rash.

Pediatric Concerns: None reported via milk. Studies in monkeys at 25 X doses did not produce toxicity in breastfed offspring.

Drug Interactions: Increased risk of cardiac toxicity when admixed with anthracyclines, and cyclophosphamide. Paclitaxel may increase the plasma levels of trastuzumab by 1.5 times.

Relative Infant Dose:

Adult Dose: 2 mg/kg/week

Alternatives:

T ½	= 1.7-12 days	M/P	=
PHL	=	PB	=
Tmax	=	Oral	= Nil
MW	= 185,000	pKa	=
Vd	= 0.044		

References:
1.   Pharmaceutical Manufacturer Prescribing Information. 2003.

TRAZODONE   L2

Trade: Desyrel

Other Trades: Desyrel, Trazorel, Apo-Trazodone, Novo-Trazodone, Molipaxin

Uses: Antidepressant, serotonin reuptake inhibitor

AAP: Drugs whose effect on nursing infants is unknown but may be of concern

Trazodone is an antidepressant whose structure is dissimilar to the tricyclics and to the other antidepressants. In six mothers who received a single 50 mg dose, the milk/plasma ratio averaged 0.14.[1] Peak milk concentrations occurred at 2 hours and were approximately 110 µg/L (taken from graph) and declined rapidly thereafter. On a weight basis, an adult would receive 0.77 mg/kg whereas a breastfeeding infant, using this data, would consume only 0.005 mg/kg. The authors estimate that about 0.6% of the maternal dose was ingested by the infant over 24 hours.

Pregnancy Risk Category: C

Lactation Risk Category: L2

Adult Concerns: Dry mouth, sedation, hypotension, blurred vision.

Pediatric Concerns: None reported via milk.

Drug Interactions: May enhance the CNS depressant effect of alcohol, barbiturates, and other CNS depressants. Digoxin serum levels may be increased. Use caution when administering with MAOI. Phenytoin serum levels may be increased. Use with warfarin may increase anticoagulant effect.

Relative Infant Dose: 2.8%

Adult Dose: 150-400 mg daily.

Alternatives:

T ½	= 4-9 hours	M/P	= 0.142
PHL	=	PB	= 85-95%
Tmax	= 1-2 hours	Oral	= 65%
MW	= 372	pKa	=
Vd	= 0.9-1.5		

References:
1. Verbeeck RK, Ross SG, McKenna EA. Excretion of trazodone in breast milk. Br J Clin Pharmacol 1986; 22 (3):367-370.

TRETINOIN   L3

Trade: Retin - A, Renova
Other Trades: Retin-A, Stieva-A, Vitamin A Acid, Renova, Vesanoid
Uses: Treatment of acne
AAP: Not reviewed

Tretinoin is a retinoid derivative similar to Vitamin A. It is primarily used topically for acne and wrinkling and sometimes administered orally for leukemias and psoriasis. Used topically, tretinoin stimulates epithelial turnover and reduces cell cohesiveness.[1] Blood concentrations measured 2-48 hours following application are essentially zero. Absorption of Retin-A via topical sources is reported to be minimal, and breastmilk would likely be minimal to none.[2] However, if it is used orally, transfer into milk is likely and should be used with great caution in a breastfeeding mother.

Pregnancy Risk Category: C for topical
                               D for oral

Lactation Risk Category: L3 if used topically
                               L4 if used orally

Adult Concerns: Leukocytosis, dry skin, skin irritation, blistering, scaling, pigmentary changes, nausea, vomiting. Side effects of oral use are similar to hypervitaminosis A, and include headache, increased CSF pressure, anorexia, nausea, scaling of skin, fatigue, hepatosplenomegaly.

Pediatric Concerns: None reported via milk. Do not breastfeed if used orally.

Drug Interactions: Use other topical medications such as sulfur, resorcinol, benzoyl peroxide or salicylic acid with caution due to accelerated skin irritation.

Relative Infant Dose:

Adult Dose: Variable

Alternatives:

T ½	= 2 hours	M/P	=
PHL	=	PB	=
Tmax	=	Oral	= 70%
MW	= 300	pKa	=
Vd	= 0.44		

References:

1. Zbinden G. Investigation on the toxicity of tretinoin administered systemically to animals. Acta Derm Verereol Suppl (Stockh) 1975; 74:36-40.
2. Lucek RW, Colburn WA. Clinical pharmacokinetics of the retinoids. Clin Pharmacokinet 1985; 10 (1):38-62.

TRIAMCINOLONE ACETONIDE — L3

Trade: Nasacort, Azmacort, Tri-Nasal

Other Trades: Aristocort, Azmacort, Kenalog, Triaderm, Nasacort, Kenalone, Adcortyl

Uses: Corticosteroid

AAP: Not reviewed

Triamcinolone is a typical corticosteroid (see prednisone) that is available for topical, intranasal, injection, inhalation, and oral use. When applied topically to the nose (Nasacort) or to the lungs (Azmacort), only minimal doses are used and plasma levels are exceedingly low to undetectable.[1] Although no data are available on triamcinolone secretion into human milk, it is likely that the milk levels would be exceedingly low and not clinically relevant when administered via inhalation or intranasally. While the oral adult dose is 4-48 mg/day, the inhaled dose is 200 µg three times daily, and the intranasal dose is 220 µg/day. There is virtually no risk to the infant following use of the intranasal products in breastfeeding mothers.

Pregnancy Risk Category: C

Lactation Risk Category: L3

Adult Concerns: Intranasal and inhaled: nasal irritation, dry mucous membranes, sneezing, throat irritation, hoarseness, candida overgrowth.

Pediatric Concerns: None reported via milk. Observe growth rate.

Drug Interactions:

Relative Infant Dose:

Adult Dose: 200 µg TID-QID

Alternatives:

T ½	= 88 minutes	M/P	=
PHL	=	PB	=
Tmax	=	Oral	= Complete
MW	= 434	pKa	=
Vd	=		

References:
1. Pharmaceutical Manufacturer Prescribing Information. 1996.

TRIAMTERENE   L3

Trade: Dyrenium
Other Trades: Dyrenium, Dyazide, Hydrene
Uses: Diuretic
AAP: Not reviewed

Triamterene is a potassium-sparing diuretic, commonly used in combination with thiazide diuretics such as hydrochlorothiazide (Dyazide). Plasma levels average 26-30 nanograms/mL.[1] No data are available on the transfer of triamterene into human milk, but it is known to transfer into animal milk. Because of the availability of other less dangerous diuretics, triamterene should be used as a last resort in breastfeeding mothers.

Pregnancy Risk Category: C

Lactation Risk Category: L3

Adult Concerns: Leukopenia, hyperkalemia, diarrhea, nausea, vomiting, hepatitis.

Pediatric Concerns: None reported via milk.

Drug Interactions: Hyperkalemia when administered with potassium supplements. Triamterene may reduce clearance of amantadine. May increase plasma potassium levels when administered with amiloride, or ACE inhibitors, cyclosporine. May reduce clearance of lithium. Enhanced bone marrow suppression when administered with methotrexate. Use with spironolactone may result in hyperkalemia.

Relative Infant Dose:

Adult Dose: 25-100 mg daily

Alternatives: Hydrochlorothiazide

T ½	= 1.5-2.5 hours	M/P	=
PHL	= 4.3 hours	PB	= 55%
Tmax	= 1.5-3 hours	Oral	= 30-70%
MW	= 253	pKa	=
Vd	=		

References:
1. Mutschler E, Gilfrich HJ, Knauf H, Mohrke W, Volger KD. Pharmacokinetics of triamterene. Clin Exp Hypertens A 1983; 5 (2):249-269.

TRIAZOLAM   L3

Trade: Halcion
Other Trades: Apo-Triazo, Halcion, Novo-Triolam
Uses: Benzodiazepine (Valium-like) hypnotic
AAP: Not reviewed

Triazolam is a typical benzodiazepine used as a nighttime sedative. Animal studies indicate that triazolam is secreted into milk although levels in human milk have not been reported.[1] As with all the benzodiazepines, some penetration into breastmilk is likely.

Pregnancy Risk Category: X

Lactation Risk Category: L3

Adult Concerns: Sedation, addiction.

Pediatric Concerns: None reported for triazolam, but side effects for benzodiazepines include sedation, depression.

Drug Interactions: See diazepam.

Relative Infant Dose:

Adult Dose: 0.125-0.25 mg daily.

Alternatives: Lorazepam, Alprazolam

T ½	= 1.5-5.5 hours	M/P	=
PHL	=	PB	= 89%
Tmax	= 0.5-2 hours	Oral	= 85%
MW	= 343	pKa	=
Vd	= 1.1-2.7		

References:
1. Drug Facts and Comparisons 1995 ed. ed. St. Louis: 1995.

TRIMEBUTINE MALEATE | L3

Trade:
Other Trades: Apo-Trimebutine, Modulon
Uses: 5HT3 receptor antagonist
AAP: Not reviewed

Trimebutine is used to treat irritable bowel syndrome and to accelerate intestinal transit following abdominal surgery.[1] Trimebutine maleate is not available in the U.S. No data are available on the use of this product in breastfeeding mothers.

Pregnancy Risk Category:

Lactation Risk Category: L3

Adult Concerns: Adverse reactions include dry mouth, diarrhea, foul taste, epigastric pain, nausea, drowsiness, and headache.

Pediatric Concerns: Not recommended for patients under 12 years of age.

Drug Interactions: Neuromuscular blocking agents may have prolonged effects.

Relative Infant Dose:

Adult Dose: 20 mg TID

Alternatives:

T ½	= 10-12 hours	M/P	= 78-82
PHL	=	PB	= <5%
Tmax	= 1 hour	Oral	=
MW	= 387	pKa	=
Vd	=		

References:
1. Pharmaceutical Manufacturer Prescribing Information. 2002.

TRIMEPRAZINE — L3

Trade: Temaril
Other Trades: Panectyl, Vallergan
Uses: Antihistamine, antipruritic.
AAP: Not reviewed

Trimeprazine is an antihistamine from the phenothiazine family used for itching. It is secreted into human milk but in very low levels.[1] Exact data is not available.

Pregnancy Risk Category: C

Lactation Risk Category: L3

Adult Concerns: Sedation, hypotension, bradycardia.

Pediatric Concerns: None reported, but as with other antihistamines, observe for sedation.

Drug Interactions:

Relative Infant Dose:

Adult Dose: 5 mg BID

Alternatives:

T ½	= 5 hours	M/P	=
PHL	=	PB	=
Tmax	= 3.5 hours	Oral	= 70%
MW	= 298	pKa	=
Vd	=		

References:
1. O'Brien TE. Excretion of drugs in human milk. Am J Hosp Pharm 1974; 31 (9):844-854.

TRIMETHOBENZAMIDE | L4

Trade: Tigan, Trimazide, Tebamide, T-Gen, Arrestin, Ticon
Other Trades:
Uses: Antiemetic, antivertigo
AAP: Not reviewed

Trimethobenzamide is an older generation antiemetics whose use has been supplanted by newer more effective agents. It is most commonly used in suppository form in adults and rarely in infants. Maternal plasma levels following a 500 mg oral dose are 1-2 µg/mL. No data are available on breastmilk levels. But if one were to assume a milk plasma ratio of 1.0 (which is probably high), then the theoretical infant dose would only be about 0.3 mg/kg/day, which is far less than the oral dose of 300-400 mg/day used in 15 kg infants. It is unlikely the amount of trimethobenzamide present in breastmilk would produce a clinical effect in an infant.

Pregnancy Risk Category: C

Lactation Risk Category: L4

Adult Concerns: Extrapyramidal symptoms, drowsiness, depression, dizziness, headache, vertigo, blood dyscrasias have been reported following higher oral/IM/rectal doses.

Pediatric Concerns: None reported via milk.

Drug Interactions:

Relative Infant Dose:

Adult Dose: 250 mg TID-QID

Alternatives: Ondansetron

T ½	= Short	M/P	=
PHL	=	PB	=
Tmax	=	Oral	= Good
MW	=	pKa	=
Vd	=		

References:
1. Drug Facts and Comparisons 1999 ed. ed. St. Louis: 1999.

TRIMETHOPRIM   L2

Trade: Proloprim, Trimpex
Other Trades: Proloprim, Alprim, Triprim, Ipral, Monotrim, Tiempe
Uses: Antibiotic
AAP: Maternal Medication Usually Compatible with Breastfeeding

Trimethoprim is an inhibitor of folic acid production in bacteria. In one study of 50 patients, average milk levels were 2.0 mg/L.[1] Milk/plasma ratio was 1.25. In another group of mothers receiving 160 mg 2-4 times daily, concentrations of 1.2 to 5.5 mg/L were reported in milk. Because it may interfere with folate metabolism, its long-term use should be avoided in breastfeeding mothers, or the infant should be supplemented with folic acid. However, trimethoprim apparently poses few problems in full term or older infants where it is commonly used clinically.[2]

Pregnancy Risk Category: C

Lactation Risk Category: L2

Adult Concerns: Rash, pruritus nausea, vomiting, anorexia, altered taste sensation.

Pediatric Concerns: None reported via milk.

Drug Interactions: May increase phenytoin plasma levels.

Relative Infant Dose: 9.02%

Adult Dose: 200 mg daily.

Alternatives:

T ½	= 8-10 hours	M/P	= 1.25
PHL	= 14.7-40 hours (neonate)	PB	= 44%
Tmax	= 1-4 hours	Oral	= Complete
MW	= 290	pKa	=
Vd	=		

References:
1.   Miller RD, Salter AJ. The passage of trimethoprim/sulphamethoxazole into breast milk and its significance. In Daikos GK, ed. Progress in Chemotherapy, Proceedings of the Eight International Congress of Chemotherapy, Athens, 1973. Athens: Hellenic Society for Chemotherapy, 1974.

2. Pagliaro, Levin. Problems in Pediatric Drug Therapy. Hamilton, IL: Drug Intelligence Publications, 1979.
3. Arnauld R. Etude du passage de la trimethoprime dans le lait maternel. Ouest Med. 1972;25:959.
4. American Academy of Pediatrics, Committee on Drugs. Transfer of drugs and other chemicals into human milk. Pediatrics 2001;108 (3):776-89.

TRIPELENNAMINE L4

Trade: PBZ, Colrex, Tromide
Other Trades: Pyrabenzamine
Uses: Antihistamine
AAP: Not reviewed

Tripelennamine is an older class of antihistamine. This product is generally not recommended in pediatric patients, particularly neonates due to increased sleep apnea.[1] The drug has been shown to be secreted into milk of animals.[2] No human data exist.

Pregnancy Risk Category: B

Lactation Risk Category: L4

Adult Concerns: Sleep apnea in children, peptic ulcer, sedation, dry mouth, GI distress.

Pediatric Concerns: None reported, but observe for sedation, sleep apnea.

Drug Interactions: Increased sedation when used with CNS depressants, other antihistamines, alcohol, MAO inhibitors.

Relative Infant Dose:

Adult Dose: 25-50 mg every 4-6 hours

Alternatives:

T ½	= 2-3 hours	M/P	=
PHL	=	PB	=
Tmax	= 2 - 3 hours	Oral	= Complete
MW	= 255	pKa	= 4.2,8.7
Vd	= 9-12		

References:
1. O'Brien TE. Excretion of drugs in human milk. Am J Hosp Pharm 1974; 31 (9):844-854.
2. Pharmaceutical Manufacturer Prescribing Information. 1996.

TRIPROLIDINE   L1

Trade: Actidil, Actacin
Other Trades: Actifed, Codral, Pro-Actidil
Uses: Antihistamine
AAP: Maternal Medication Usually Compatible with Breastfeeding

Triprolidine is an antihistamine. It is secreted into milk but in very small levels and is marketed with pseudoephedrine as Actifed. In a study of three patients who received 2.5 mg triprolidine, the average concentration in milk ranged from 1.2 to 4.4 µg/L over 24 hours.[1] The relative infant dose is less than 1.8% of the weight-normalized maternal dose. This dose is far too low to be clinically relevant.

Pregnancy Risk Category: C

Lactation Risk Category: L1

Adult Concerns: Sedation, dry mouth, anticholinergic side effects.

Pediatric Concerns: None reported. Observe for sedation.

Drug Interactions: Increased sedation when used with CNS depressants, other antihistamines, alcohol, MAO inhibitors.

Relative Infant Dose: 1.8%

Adult Dose: 2.5 mg every 4-6 hours

Alternatives:

T ½	= 5 hours	M/P	= 0.5-1.2
PHL	=	PB	=
Tmax	= 2 hours	Oral	= Complete
MW	= 278	pKa	=
Vd	=		

References:
1. Findlay JW, Butz RF, Sailstad JM, Warren JT, Welch RM. Pseudoephedrine and triprolidine in plasma and breast milk of nursing mothers. Br J Clin Pharmacol 1984; 18 (6):901-906.

TRIPTORELIN PAMOATE   L3

Trade: Trelstar LA, Trelstar Depo
Other Trades:
Uses: Analog of luteinizing hormone releasing hormone
AAP: Not reviewed

Triptorelin is a potent inhibitor of gonadotropin secretion when given continuously. After chronic administration, a sustained decrease of luteinizing hormone (LH) and follicle stimulating hormone (FSII) secretion and marked reduction of testicular and ovarian steroidogenesis occurs. Continuous use in breastfeeding mothers would ultimately lead to reduced levels of ovulation and sex steroids. In a study in males, prolactin levels were actually increased.[1] Thus it is difficult to discern what if any effect this agent would have on milk production in breastfeeding mothers. Some caution is recommended until more is known about this drugs effect on milk production. It is extremely unlikely this agent would penetrate milk due to its high MW. Also, it is not orally bioavailable, so it is very unlikely to harm a breastfeeding infant.

Pregnancy Risk Category: X

Lactation Risk Category: L3

Adult Concerns: Side effects include vaginal dryness, hot flashes, leg pain, headache, breakthrough bleeding, skeletal pain, edema in legs, decreased libido, and dizziness.

Pediatric Concerns: None reported. Unlikely to penetrate milk, or be orally bioavailable.

Drug Interactions:

Relative Infant Dose:

Adult Dose: 11.25 mg every 84 days IM

Alternatives:

T ½	= 3 hour IV	M/P	=
PHL	=	PB	= 0%
Tmax	= 1 week	Oral	= Nil
MW	= 1699	pKa	=
Vd	= 33		

References:

1. Stoffel-Wagner B, Sommer L, Bidlingmaier F, Klingmuller D. Effects of the gonadotropin-releasing-hormone agonist, D-Trp-6-GnRH, on prolactin secretion in healthy young men. Horm Res 1995;43:266-272.

TROPICAMIDE	L3

Trade: Mydral, Mydriacyl, Tropicacyl

Other Trades: Diotrope, Mydriacyl

Uses: Mydriatic ophthalmic agent

AAP: Not reviewed

Tropicamide is used as a short-acting pupil dilator used in diagnostic procedures. It is an antimuscarinic agent which produces competitive antagonism of the actions of acetylcholine, thus preventing the sphincter muscle of the iris and the muscle of the ciliary body from responding to cholinergic stimulation.[1] It is unlikely that systemic levels in adults will be sufficient to produce clinically relevant levels in milk. Infants, however should be observed for anticholinergic effects (dry mouth, mydriasis, sedation, tachycardia). A brief waiting period of 3-4 hours would eliminate most risks.

Pregnancy Risk Category: C

Lactation Risk Category: L3

Adult Concerns: Adverse reactions include cardiorespiratory collapse, tachycardia, sedation, dry mouth, blurred vision, corneal irritation, and increased intraocular pressure.

Pediatric Concerns: Pediatric patients may require smaller doses to avoid systemic effects. Levels in milk are probably too low to affect an infant.

Drug Interactions: Cisapride may lose effectiveness when administered with troicamide.

Relative Infant Dose:

Adult Dose: 1-2 drops 15-20 minutes before exam

Alternatives:

T ½	=	M/P	=
PHL	=	PB	= 45%
Tmax	=	Oral	=
MW	= 284	pKa	=
Vd	=		

References:
1. Pharmaceutical Manufacturer Prescribing Information. 2000.

TROPISETRON   L3

Trade:
Other Trades: Navoban
Uses: Antiemetic for chemotherapy
AAP: Not reviewed

Tropisetron is a serotonergic (5-HT3) receptor antagonist with antiemetic activity similar to ondansetron and many others. No data are available on its transfer to human milk. See ondansetron as alternative in USA.

Pregnancy Risk Category: B3 (Australian)

Lactation Risk Category: L3

Adult Concerns: Adverse effects include occasional extrapyramidal reactions, headache, rash, fever, constipation, fatigue, sedation, dizziness, diarrhea, and hypotension or hypertension.

Pediatric Concerns: None reported via milk.

Drug Interactions: None reported.

Relative Infant Dose:

Adult Dose: 5 mg orally every 6-24 hours.

Alternatives: Ondansetron

T ½	= 5.6-8.6	M/P	=
PHL	=	PB	= 71%
Tmax	= 2 hours	Oral	= 60%
MW	=	pKa	=
Vd	= 7.14		

References:
1. Pharmaceutical Manufacturers prescribing information, 2003.

TROVAFLOXACIN MESYLATE   L4

Trade: Trovan, Alatrofloxacin
Other Trades:
Uses: Antibiotic
AAP: Not reviewed

Trovafloxacin mesylate is a synthetic broad-spectrum antibiotic for oral use. The IV formula is called alatrofloxacin mesylate which is metabolized to trovafloxacin in vivo. Trovafloxacin is a fluoroquinolone antibiotic similar to ciprofloxacin, norfloxacin, and others. Trovafloxacin was found in measurable but low concentrations in breastmilk of three breastfeeding mothers.[1] Following an IV dose of 300 mg trovafloxacin equivalent and repeated oral 200 mg doses of trovafloxacin mg daily, breastmilk levels averaged 0.8 mg/L and ranged from 0.3 to 2.1 mg per liter of milk. This would average less than 4% of the weight-normalized maternal dose. New data on this antibiotic documents a higher risk of hepatotoxicity and its use is restricted. This agent has been withdrawn from the US market due to risk of acute liver failure.

Pregnancy Risk Category: C

Lactation Risk Category: L4

Adult Concerns: Dizziness, nausea, headache, vomiting, diarrhea have been reported.

Pediatric Concerns: None reported via milk. Only small amounts are secreted in milk.

Drug Interactions: Antacids, Morphine, Sucralfate, and iron significantly reduce oral absorption.

Relative Infant Dose: 4.2%

Adult Dose: 200-300 mg daily

Alternatives: Norfloxacin, Ofloxacin

T ½	= 12,2 hours	M/P	=
PHL	=	PB	= 76%
Tmax	= 1,2 hours	Oral	= 88%
MW	= 512	pKa	=
Vd	= 1.3		

References:
1. Pharmaceutical Manufacturer Prescribing Information.

TUBERCULIN PURIFIED PROTEIN DERIVATIVE   L2

Trade: Tubersol, Aplisol, Sclavo, PPD, Mantoux
Other Trades:
Uses: Tuberculin skin test
AAP: Not reviewed

Tuberculin (also called Mantoux, PPD, Tine test) is a skin-test antigen derived from the concentrated, sterile, soluble products of growth of M. Tuberculosis or M. bovis. Small amounts of this purified product when placed intradermally, produce a hypersensitivity reaction at the place of injection in those individuals with antibodies to M. tuberculosis.[1,2] Preliminary studies also indicate that breast-fed infants may passively acquire sensitivity to mycobacterial antigens from mothers who are sensitized. There are no contraindications to using PPD tests in breastfeeding mothers as the proteins are sterilized and unlikely to penetrate milk.

Pregnancy Risk Category: C

Lactation Risk Category: L2

Adult Concerns: Local vesiculation, irritation, bruising, and rarely hypersensitivity.

Pediatric Concerns: None via milk.

Drug Interactions:

Relative Infant Dose:

Adult Dose: 5 units X 1

Alternatives:

References:
1. Drug Facts and Comparisons 1999 ed. cd. St. Louis: 1999.
2. McEvoy GE. (ed): AFHS Drug Information. New York, NY: 2009.

TYPHOID VACCINE   L3

Trade: Vivotif Berna, Typhim Vi
Other Trades: Vivotif Berna
Uses: Vaccination
AAP: Not reviewed

Typhoid vaccine promotes active immunity to typhoid fever. It is available in an oral form (Ty21a) which is a live attenuated vaccine for oral administration.[1] The parenteral (injectable) form is derived from acetone-treated killed and dried bacteria, phenol-inactive bacteria, or a special capsular polysaccharide vaccine extracted from killed S. typhi Ty21a strains. Due to a limited lipopolysaccharide coating, the Ty21a strains are limited in their ability to produce infection.

No data are available on its transfer into human milk. If immunization is required, a killed species would be preferred, as infection of the neonate would be unlikely.

Pregnancy Risk Category: C

Lactation Risk Category: L3 (injectable)

Adult Concerns: Following oral administration, nausea, abdominal cramps, vomiting, urticaria. IM preparations may produce soreness at injection site, tenderness, malaise, headache, myalgia, fever.

Pediatric Concerns: None reported, but killed species suggested.

Drug Interactions: Use cautiously in patients receiving anticoagulants. Do not coadminister with plague vaccine. Do not administer the live-attenuated varieties to immunocompromised patients. Phenytoin may reduce antibody response to this product. Do not use with sulfonamides.

Relative Infant Dose:

Adult Dose: 0.5 mL X 2 over 4 weeks

Alternatives:

References:
1. Pharmaceutical Manufacturer Prescribing Information, 2008.

URSODIOL   L3

Trade: Actigall
Other Trades: Urso, Combidol, Destolit, Lithofalk, Urdox,
    Ursogal
Uses: Bile acid for dissolving gall stones
AAP: Not reviewed

Ursodiol (ursodeoxycholic acid) is a bile salt found in small amounts
in humans that is used to dissolve cholesterol gallstones. It is almost
completely absorbed orally via the portal circulation and is extracted
almost completely by the liver. Ursodiol suppresses hepatic synthesis
and excretion of cholesterol. Following extraction by the liver, it is
conjugated with glycine or taurine and is re-secreted into the hepatic
bile duct. Only trace amounts are found in the plasma and it is not likely
significant amounts would be present in milk.[1] While no breastfeeding
data are available, only small amounts of bile salts are known to be
present in milk.[2] It is not likely with the low levels of ursodiol in the
maternal plasma, that clinically relevant amounts would enter milk.

Pregnancy Risk Category: B

Lactation Risk Category: L3

Adult Concerns: Insomnia, headache, abdominal pain, flatulence,
cholecystitis, constipation, diarrhea (rare), nausea, vomiting.

Pediatric Concerns: None via breast milk.

Drug Interactions: Cholestyramine,   antacids,   charcoal   and
colestipol may interfere with GI absorption.

Relative Infant Dose:

Adult Dose: 8-10 mg/kg/day in 3 divided doses

Alternatives:

T ½	=	M/P	=
PHL	=	PB	=
Tmax	=	Oral	= 90%
MW	= 392	pKa	=
Vd	=		

References:
1. Bachrach WH, Hofmann AF. Ursodeoxycholic acid in the treatment of
   cholesterol cholelithiasis. part I. Dig Dis Sci 1982; 27 (8):737-761.
2. Forsyth JS, Ross PE, Bouchier IA. Bile salts in breast milk. Eur J Pediatr
   1983; 140 (2):126-127.

VALACYCLOVIR   L1

Trade: Valtrex
Other Trades: Valtrex, Valaciclovir
Uses: Antiviral, for herpes simplex
AAP: Not reviewed

Valacyclovir is a prodrug that is rapidly metabolized in the plasma to acyclovir. In a study of 5 women who received 500 mg twice daily for 7 days after delivery, the median peak acyclovir concentration in breast milk was 4.2 mg/L at 4 hours while the average concentration (AUC) was 2.24 mg/L if 12 hour dosing intervals were used.[1] Thus the relative infant dose would be 4.7% of the weight-normalized maternal dose. The ratio of milk/serum ratio was highest 4 hours after the initial dose at 3.4 and reached steady state ratio at 1.85. Valacyclovir is rapidly converted to acyclovir which transfers into breast milk. However, the amount of acyclovir in breast milk after valacyclovir administration is considerably less than that used in therapeutic dosing of neonates.

Pregnancy Risk Category: B

Lactation Risk Category: L1

Adult Concerns: Nausea, vomiting, diarrhea, sore throat, edema, and skin rashes.

Pediatric Concerns: None reported via milk.

Drug Interactions:

Relative Infant Dose: 4.7%

Adult Dose: 500-1000 mg BID-TID

Alternatives: Acyclovir

T ½	= 2.5-3 hours	M/P	= 0.6-4.1
PHL	= 3.2 hours (neonates)	PB	= 9-33%
Tmax	= 1.5 hours	Oral	= 54%
MW	=	pKa	=
Vd	=		

References:
1.   Sheffield JS, Fish DN, Hollier LM, Cadematori S, Nobles BJ, Wendel GD, Jr. Acyclovir concentrations in human breast milk after valaciclovir administration. Am J Obstet Gynecol 2002; 186 (1):100-102.

VALERIAN OFFICINALIS   L3

Trade: Valerian Root
Other Trades:
Uses: Herbal sedative
AAP: Not reviewed

Valerian root is most commonly used as a sedative/hypnotic. Of the numerous chemicals present in the root, the most important chemical group appears to be the valepotriates. This family consists of at least a dozen or more related compounds and is believed responsible for the sedative potential of this plant although it is controversial. The combination of numerous components may inevitability account for the sedative response. Controlled studies in man have indicated a sedative/hypnotic effect with fewer night awakenings and significant somnolence.[1-3] The toxicity of valerian root appears to be low, with only minor side effects reported. However, the valepotriates have been found to be cytotoxic, with alkylating activity similar to other nitrogen mustard-like anticancer agents. Should this prove to be so in vivo, it may preclude the use of this product in humans. No data are available on the transfer of valerian root compounds into human milk. However, the use of sedatives in breastfeeding mothers is generally discouraged, due to a possible increased risk of SIDS.

Pregnancy Risk Category:

Lactation Risk Category: L3

Adult Concerns: Ataxia, hypothermia, muscle relaxation. Headaches, excitability, cardiac disturbances.

Pediatric Concerns: None reported via human milk.

Drug Interactions:

Relative Infant Dose:

Adult Dose:

Alternatives:

References:
1. Leathwood PD, Chauffard F, Heck E, Munoz-Box R. Aqueous extract of valerian root (Valeriana officinalis L.) improves sleep quality in man. Pharmacol Biochem Behav 1982; 17 (1):65-71.
2. von Eickstedt KW, Rahman S. [Psychopharmacologic effect of valepotriates]. Arzneimittelforschung 1969; 19 (3):316-319.
3. Leathwood PD, Chauffard F. Aqueous extract of valerian reduces latency to fall asleep in man. Planta Med 1985; 51 (2):144-148.

VALGANCICLOVIR   L3

Trade: Valcyte, Cytovene
Other Trades: Valcyte
Uses: Antiviral
AAP: Not reviewed

Valganciclovir is a prodrug that is rapidly metabolized to the active antiviral drug ganciclovir. It is used for cytomegalovirus infections particularly in HIV infected patients. The oral bioavailability of valganciclovir is 60% while only 6% with its active metabolite ganciclovir. Further it is very water soluble and lipophobic, which would suggest milk levels will be low. No data are available on its use in breastfeeding mothers but its oral absorption in the infant is likely low.

Pregnancy Risk Category: C

Lactation Risk Category: L3

Adult Concerns: Adverse events include diarrhea, neutropenia, nausea, headache, insomnia, abdominal pain, anemia, and catheter-related infections.

Pediatric Concerns: None reported via milk. No studies thus far. Due to its use in HIV infected patients, it is unlikely this agent will be used in breastfeeding mothers. Poor oral bioavailability would limit absorption in an infant.

Drug Interactions: Minimal but check other references.

Relative Infant Dose:

Adult Dose: 450-900 mg daily.

Alternatives:

T ½	= 4 hours	M/P	=
PHL	=	PB	= 1-2%
Tmax	= 1-3 hours	Oral	= 61%
MW	= 390	pKa	= 7.6
Vd	= 0.7		

References:
1. Pharmaceutical Manufacturers package insert, 2000.

VALPROIC ACID   L2

Trade: Depakene, Depakote, Stavzor
Other Trades: Depakene, Novo-Valproic, Deproic, Epilim,
    Valpro, Convulex, Epilim
Uses: Anticonvulsant
AAP: Maternal Medication Usually Compatible with
    Breastfeeding

Valproic acid is a popular anticonvulsant used in grand mal, petit mal, myoclonic, and temporal lobe seizures. In a study of 16 patients receiving 300-2400 mg/d, valproic acid concentrations ranged from 0.4 to 3.9 mg/L (mean=1.9 mg/L).[1] The milk/plasma ratio averaged 0.05.

In a study of one patient receiving 250 mg twice daily, milk levels ranged from 0.18 to 0.47 mg/L. The milk/plasma ratio ranged from 0.01 to 0.02.[2] Alexander reports milk levels of 5.1 mg/L following a larger dose of up to 1600 mg/d.[3]

In a study of 6 women receiving 9.5 to 31 mg/kg/d valproic acid, milk levels averaged 1.4 mg/L while serum levels averaged 45.1 mg/L.[4] The average milk/serum ratio was 0.027.

Most authors agree that the amount of valproic acid transferring to the infant via milk is low. Breastfeeding would appear safe. However, the infant may need monitoring for liver and platelet changes.

Pregnancy Risk Category: D

Lactation Risk Category: L2

Adult Concerns: Sedation, thrombocytopenia, tremor, nausea, diarrhea, liver toxicity.

Pediatric Concerns: None reported via milk. Observe infant for changes in liver enzymes, clinical status, and platelet levels.

Drug Interactions: Valproic acid levels may be reduced by charcoal, rifampin, carbamazepine, clonazepam, lamotrigine, phenytoin. Valproic acid levels may be increased when used with chlorpromazine, cimetidine, felbamate, salicylates, alcohol. Valproic acid use may increase levels or the effect of barbiturates, warfarin, benzodiazepines, clozapine.

Relative Infant Dose: 1.4% - 1.7%

Adult Dose: 10-30 mg/kg daily.

Alternatives:

T ½	= 14 hours	M/P	= 0.42
PHL	= 10-67 hours (neonate)	PB	= 94%
Tmax	= 1-4 hours	Oral	= Complete
MW	= 144	pKa	= 4.8
Vd	= 0.1-0.4		

References:
1. von Unruh GE, Froescher W, Hoffmann F, Niesen M. Valproic acid in breast milk: how much is really there? Ther Drug Monit 1984; 6 (3):272-276.
2. Dickinson RG, Harland RC, Lynn RK, Smith WB, Gerber N. Transmission of valproic acid (Depakene) across the placenta: half-life of the drug in mother and baby. J Pediatr 1979; 94 (5):832-835.
3. Alexander FW. Sodium valproate and pregnancy. Arch Dis Child 1979; 54 (3):240.
4. Nau H, Rating D, Koch S, Hauser I, Helge H. Valproic acid and its metabolites: placental transfer, neonatal pharmacokinetics, transfer via mother's milk and clinical status in neonates of epileptic mothers. J Pharmacol Exp Ther 1981; 219 (3):768-777.

VALSARTAN   L3

Trade: Diovan
Other Trades: Diovan
Uses: Antihypertensive
AAP: Not reviewed

Valsartan is a new angiotensin II receptor antagonist used to treat hypertension. While it is believed to enter the milk of rodents, no human data are available.[1,2] Use with caution in breastfeeding mothers.

Pregnancy Risk Category: C in first trimester
                               D in second and third trimesters

Lactation Risk Category: L3

Adult Concerns: Occasional increase in liver enzymes. Small decreases in hemoglobin have been reported. Significant increases (> 20%) in serum potassium levels have been reported. Dizziness, insomnia, viral infection, cough, diarrhea, etc. have been reported.

Pediatric Concerns: None via milk, but caution is recommended.

Drug Interactions: May significantly increase digoxin levels by 49%.

Relative Infant Dose:

Adult Dose: 80-320 mg daily.

Alternatives:

T ½	= 9 hours	M/P	=
PHL	=	PB	= 97%
Tmax	= 2-4 hours	Oral	= 23%
MW	=	pKa	=
Vd	= 0.24		

References:
1. Pharmaceutical Manufacturer Prescribing Information. 1999.
2. McEvoy GE. (ed): AFHS Drug Information. New York, NY: 2009.

VANCOMYCIN   L1

Trade: Vancocin
Other Trades: Vancocin, Vancoled
Uses: Antibiotic
AAP: Not reviewed

Vancomycin is an antimicrobial agent. Only low levels are secreted into human milk. Milk levels were 12.7 mg/L four hours after infusion in one woman receiving 1 gm every 12 hours for 7 days.[1] Its poor absorption from the infants GI tract would limit its systemic absorption. Low levels in infant could provide alterations of GI flora.

Pregnancy Risk Category: C

Lactation Risk Category: L1

Adult Concerns: Alteration of GI flora, neutropenia, hypotension, kidney and hearing damage.

Pediatric Concerns: None reported via milk.

Drug Interactions: When used with aminoglycosides, risk of nephrotoxicity may be increased. Use with anesthetics may produce erythema and histamine-like flushing in children. May increase risk of neuromuscular blockade when used with neuromuscular blocking agents.

Relative Infant Dose: 6.7%

Adult Dose: 125-500 mg every 6 hours

Alternatives:

T ½	= 5.6 hours	M/P	=
PHL	= 5.9-9.8 hours (neonates)	PB	= 10-30%
Tmax	=	Oral	= Minimal
MW	= 1449	pKa	=
Vd	= 0.3-0.7		

References:
1. Reyes MP, Ostrea EM, Jr., Cabinian AE, Schmitt C, Rintelmann W. Vancomycin during pregnancy: does it cause hearing loss or nephrotoxicity in the infant? Am J Obstet Gynecol 1989; 161 (4):977-981.

VARENICLINE   L4

Trade: Chantix
Other Trades: Champix
Uses: Smoking cessation
AAP: Not reviewed

Varenicline is used to assist smoking cessation. It is a partial alpha-4-beta-2-nicotinic receptor partial agonist that binds to nicotine receptors in the brain, thus preventing nicotine stimulation. It stimulates dopamine activity, but to a lesser extent than does nicotine, thus reducing craving and withdrawal symptoms.[1] There have been no studies performed on the transfer of varenicline into human milk, but transfer is possible as it easily passes into the CNS and it has an intermediate MW. Caution should be used in breastfeeding mothers.

Pregnancy Risk Category: C

Lactation Risk Category: L4

Adult Concerns: Adverse effects include nausea, sleep disturbance, neuropsychiatric changes, constipation, flatulence, and vomiting. Dose adjustments must be made in severe renal failure.

Pediatric Concerns: No data are available on levels in milk, but due to long half-life and kinetics, some caution should be exercised in using this in breastfeeding mothers.

Drug Interactions: Cimetidine increases varenicline concentrations by as much as 29% due to decreased varenicline clearance. Coadministration of transdermal nicotine with varenicline increases incidence of dyspepsia, nausea, vomiting, headache, dizziness, and fatigue.

Relative Infant Dose:

Adult Dose: 1mg BID

Alternatives:

T ½	= 24 hours	M/P	=
PHL	=	PB	= 20%
Tmax	= 3-4 hours	Oral	= High
MW	= 361	pKa	=
Vd	=		

References:
1. Pharmaceutical Manufacturer Prescribing Information. 2006.

VARICELLA VIRUS VACCINE   L2

Trade: Varivax
Other Trades:
Uses: Vaccination for Varicella (Chickenpox)
AAP: Not reviewed

A live attenuated varicella vaccine (Varivax - Merck) was recently approved for marketing by the US Food and Drug Administration. Although effective, it does not apparently provide the immunity attained from infection with the parent virus and may not provide life-long immunity. The Oka/Merck strain used in the vaccine is attenuated by passage in human and embryonic guinea pig cell cultures. It is not known if the vaccine-acquired VZV is secreted in human milk, nor its infectiousness to infants. Interestingly, in two women with varicella-zoster infections, the virus was not culturable from milk.[1] Mothers of immunodeficient infants should not breastfeed following use of this vaccine. Recommendations for Use: Varicella vaccine is only recommended for children >1 year of age up to 12 years of age with no history of varicella infection. Both the AAP[2] and the Center for Disease Control approve the use of varicella-zoster vaccines in breastfeeding mothers, if the risk of infection is high.

Pregnancy Risk Category: C

Lactation Risk Category: L2

Adult Concerns: Tenderness and erythema at the injection site in about 25% of vaccinees and a sparse generalized maculopapular rash occurring within one month after immunization in about 5%. Spread of the vaccine virus to others has been reported. Susceptible, immunodeficient individuals should be protected from exposure.

Pediatric Concerns: None reported via milk, but no studies are available. Immunocompromised infants should not be exposed to this product.

Drug Interactions:

Relative Infant Dose:

Adult Dose: 0.5 mL X 2 over 4-8 weeks

Alternatives:

References:
1. Frederick IB, White RJ, Braddock SW. Excretion of varicella-herpes zoster virus in breast milk. Am J Obstet Gynecol 1986; 154 (5):1116-1117.
2. American Academy of Pediatrics. Committee on Infectious Diseases. Red Book. 1997.

VARICELLA-ZOSTER VIRUS   L4

Trade: Chickenpox
Other Trades:
Uses: Chickenpox
AAP: Not reviewed

Chickenpox virus has been reported to be transferred via breastmilk in one 27 year old mother who developed chickenpox postpartum.[1] Her 2 month old son also developed the disease 16 days after mother. Chickenpox virus was detected in the mother's milk and may suggest that transmission can occur via breastmilk. However, in a study of 2 breastfeeding patients who developed varicella-herpes zoster infections, in neither case was the virus isolated and cultured from their milk.[2] According to the American Academy of Pediatrics, neonates born to mothers with active varicella should be placed in isolation at birth and, if still hospitalized, until 21 or 28 days of age, depending on whether they received VZIG (Varicella Zoster Immune Globulin).[3] Candidates for VZIG include: immunocompromised children, pregnant women, and a newborn infant whose mother has onset of VZV within 5 days before or 48 hours after delivery. For an excellent review of VZV and breastfeeding see Merewood and Philipp.[4]

Pregnancy Risk Category:

Lactation Risk Category: L4

Adult Concerns:

Pediatric Concerns: Varicella-zoster virus transfers into human milk.   Infants should not breastfeed unless protected with VZIG.

Drug Interactions:

Relative Infant Dose:

Adult Dose:

Alternatives:

References:
1. Yoshida M, Yamagami N, Tezuka T, Hondo R. Case report: detection of varicella-zoster virus DNA in maternal breast milk. J Med Virol 1992; 38 (2):108-110.
2. Frederick IB, White RJ, Braddock SW. Excretion of varicella-herpes zoster virus in breast milk. Am J Obstet Gynecol 1986; 154 (5):1116-1117.
3. Report of the committee on Infectious Diseases. American Academy of Pediatrics. 1994.
4. Meerwood A, Philipp B. Breastfeeding: Conditions and Diseases. 1st ed. ed. Amarillo, TX: Pharmasoft Publishing L.P., 2001.

VASOPRESSIN — L3

Trade: Pitressin
Other Trades: Pitressin, Pressyn, Pitresin
Uses: Antidiuretic hormone
AAP: Not reviewed

Vasopressin, also know as the antidiuretic hormone, is a small peptide (8 amino acids) that is normally secreted by the posterior pituitary.[1] It reduces urine production by the kidney. Although it probably passes to some degree into human milk, it is rapidly destroyed in the GI tract by trypsin and must be administered by injection or intranasally. Hence, oral absorption by a nursing infant is very unlikely. Desmopressin is virtually identical and milk levels have been reported to be very low. See desmopressin.

Pregnancy Risk Category: C

Lactation Risk Category: L3

Adult Concerns: Increased blood pressure, water retention and edema, sweating, tremor, and bradycardia.

Pediatric Concerns: None reported via milk.

Drug Interactions:

Relative Infant Dose:

Adult Dose: 5-10 units BID-QID PRN

Alternatives:

T ½	= 10-20 minutes	M/P	=
PHL	=	PB	=
Tmax	= 1 hour	Oral	= None
MW	=	pKa	=
Vd	=		

References:
1. McEvoy GE. (ed):AFHS Drug Information. New York, NY: 2009.

VENLAFAXINE   L3

Trade: Effexor
Other Trades: Efexor
Uses: Antidepressant
AAP: Not reviewed

Venlafaxine is a new serotonin reuptake inhibitor antidepressant. It inhibits both serotonin reuptake and norepinephrine reuptake. It is somewhat similar in mechanism to other antidepressants such as Prozac, but has fewer anticholinergic side-effects.

In an excellent study of three mothers (mean age = 34.5 years, 84.5 kg) receiving venlafaxine (225-300 mg/d), the mean milk/plasma ratios for venlafaxine (V) and O-desmethylvenlafaxine (ODV) were 2.5 and 2.7 respectively.[1] The mean maximum concentrations of V and ODV in milk were 1.16 mg/L and 0.796 mg/L. The C_{max} for milk was 2.25 hours. The mean infant exposure was 3.2% for V and 3.2% for ODV of the weight-adjusted maternal dose. Venlafaxine was detected in the plasma of one of seven infants while ODV was detected in four of the seven infants. The infants were healthy and showed no acute adverse effects.

In a study of 11 women consuming an average of 194.3 mg/day of venlafaxine, the theoretical infant dose of venlafaxine and desvenlafaxine was 0.208 mg/kg/d, or a relative infant dose of 8.1% of the maternal dose. The maximum level in milk occurred at 8 hours after maternal ingestion. Infant plasma levels for V + D were 37.1% of maternal levels. No adverse effects were noted in any of the infants.[3]

However, recent data (MedWatch, FDA) has suggested that infants exposed in utero to various SNRIs such as venlafaxine, may have profound adverse effects immediately upon delivery. These include: respiratory distress, cyanosis, apnea, seizures, temperature instability, etc. It is not known if these adverse events are due to a direct toxic effect of venlafaxine on the fetus, or due to a discontinuation (withdrawal) syndrome. Studies have shown that these adverse effects may be partially relieved with venlafaxine received through breast milk.[4]

The new product Pristiq (desvenlafaxine) consists of the active component from venlafaxine (ODV).

Pregnancy Risk Category: C

Lactation Risk Category: L3

Adult Concerns: Nausea/vomiting, somnolence, dry mouth, dizziness, headache, weakness.

Pediatric Concerns: None reported via milk, but no studies are available. Recent data has suggested that infants exposed during pregnancy to venlafaxine and other SNRIs have developed complications requiring prolonged hospitalization, respiratory support, and tube feeding. Such complications arise immediately upon delivery. The implication for breastfeeding is not known.

Drug Interactions: Serious, sometimes fatal reactions when used with MAO inhibitors, or if used within 7-14 days of their use. Serious organic psychosis has been reported with the co-administration of propafenone (Rythmol). Two recent cases of serotonin-like reactions (agitation, dysarthria, diapyhoresis and extrapyramidal movement disorder) have been reported when metoclopramide was used in patients receiving sertraline or venlafaxine.[2]

Relative Infant Dose: 6.8% - 8.1%

Adult Dose: 75 mg TID

Alternatives: Sertraline, fluoxetine

T ½	= 5 hours (venlafaxine)	M/P	= 2.75
PHL	=	PB	= 27%
Tmax	= 2.25	Oral	= 92%
MW	= 313	pKa	= 9.4
Vd	= 4-12		

References:
1. Ilett KF, Kristensen JH, Hackett LP, Paech M, Kohan R, Rampono J. Distribution of venlafaxine and its O-desmethyl metabolite in human milk and their effects in breastfed infants. Br J Clin Pharmacol 2002; 53 (1):17-22.
2. Fisher AA, Davis MW. Serotonin syndrome caused by selective serotonin reuptake-inhibitors-metoclopramide interaction. Ann Pharmacother 2002;36 (1):67-71.

3. Newport DJ, Ritchie JC, Knight BT, Glover BA, Zach EB, Stowe ZN. Venlafaxine in human breast milk and nursing infant plasma: determination of exposure. J Clin Psychiatry. Sep 2009;70 (9):1304-1310.
4. Koren G, Moretti, Kapur B. Can Venlafaxine in Breast Milk Attenuate the Norepinephrine and Serotonin Reuptake Neonatal Withdrawal Syndrome? JOGC 2006 April; 28 (4):299-302.

VERAPAMIL   L2

Trade: Calan, Isoptin, Covera-HS
Other Trades: Apo-Verap, Isoptin, Novo-Veramil, Anpec, Coridlox, Veracaps SR, Berkatens, Univer
Uses: Calcium channel blocker for hypertension
AAP: Maternal Medication Usually Compatible with Breastfeeding

Verapamil is a typical calcium channel blocker used as an antihypertensive. It is secreted into milk but in very low levels, which are highly controversial. Anderson reports that in one patient receiving 80 mg three times daily, the average steady-state concentrations of verapamil and norverapamil in milk were 25.8 and 8.8 µg/L respectively.[1] The respective maternal plasma level was 42.9 µg/L. The milk/plasma ratio for verapamil was 0.60. No verapamil was detected in the infant's plasma. Inoue reports that in one patient receiving 80 mg four times daily, the milk level peaked at 300 µg/L at approximately 14 hours.[2] These levels are considerably higher than the aforementioned. In another study of a mother receiving 240 mg daily, the concentrations in milk were never higher than 40 µg/L.[3]

From these three studies, the relative infant dose would vary from 0.15%, 0.98%, and 0.18% respectively. Regardless of the variability, the relative amount transferred to the infant is still quite small.

Pregnancy Risk Category: C

Lactation Risk Category: L2

Adult Concerns: Hypotension, bradycardia, peripheral edema.

Pediatric Concerns: None reported via milk. Observe for hypotension, bradycardia, weakness.

Drug Interactions: Barbiturates may reduce bioavailability of calcium channel blockers (CCB). Calcium salts may reduce hypotensive effect. Dantrolene may increase risk of hyperkalemia and myocardial depression. H2 blockers may increase bioavailability of certain CCBs. Hydantoins may reduce plasma levels. Quinidine increases risk of hypotension, bradycardia, tachycardia. Rifampin may reduce effects of CCBs. Vitamin D may reduce efficacy of CCBs. CCBs may increase carbamazepine, cyclosporin, encainide, prazosin levels.

Relative Infant Dose: 0.15% - 0.2%

Adult Dose: 80-100 mg TID

Alternatives: Bepridil, Nifedipine, Nimodipine

T ½	= 3-7 hours	M/P	= 0.94
PHL	=	PB	= 83-92%
Tmax	= 1-2.2	Oral	= 90%
MW	= 455	pKa	=
Vd	= 2.5-6.5		

References:

1. Anderson P, Bondesson U, Mattiasson I, Johansson BW. Verapamil and norverapamil in plasma and breast milk during breast feeding. Eur J Clin Pharmacol 1987; 31 (5):625-627.
2. Inoue H, Unno N, Ou MC, Iwama Y, Sugimoto T. Level of verapamil in human milk. Eur J Clin Pharmacol 1984; 26 (5):657-658.
3. Andersen HJ. Excretion of verapamil in human milk. Eur J Clin Pharmacol 1983; 25 (2):279-280.

VERTEPORFIN

L3

Trade: Visudyne
Other Trades: Visudyne
Uses: Photosensitizing agent to treat macular degeneration
AAP: Not reviewed

Verteporfin is a photosensitizing agent used in the treatment of neovascularization associated with macular degeneration. When administered, verteporfin is transported to the neovascular endothelium, where it needs to be activated by nonthermal red light, resulting in local damage to the endothelium. This leads to temporary choroidal vessel occlusion.[1]

The manufacturer reports verteporfin and its metabolites have been found in the breast milk of one women after a 6 mg/m2 infusion.[1] Milk levels were up to 66% of the corresponding plasma levels. Verteporfin was undetectable after 12 hours but its metabolites were present for up to 48 hours. A waiting period of 24 hours is recommended.

Pregnancy Risk Category: C

Lactation Risk Category: L3

Adult Concerns: Adverse reactions include headache, blurred vision, decreased visual acuity, and visual disturbances.

Pediatric Concerns: Milk levels are significant but brief. Breastfeeding should be interruped for 24 hours.

Drug Interactions: Calcium channel blockers, polymyxin B,and radiation therapy could enhance the rate of uptake of verteporfin. Drugs that decrease clotting, beta-carotene, dimethyl sulfoxide, ethanol, formate, mannitol, or other drugs that decrease oxygen radicals can decrease the efficacy of verteporfin. Also, increased photosensitivity is seen when taken with drugs such as griseofluvin, sulfonamides, sulfonylureas, tetracyclines, or thiazide diuretics.

Relative Infant Dose:

Adult Dose: 6 mg/m2

Alternatives:

T ½	= 5-6 hours	M/P	=
PHL	=	PB	=
Tmax	=	Oral	= Nil
MW	= 718	pKa	=
Vd	=		

References:
1. Pharmaceutical Manufacturer Prescribing Information. 2005.

VIGABATRIN   L3

Trade: Sabril
Other Trades:
Uses: Anticonvulsant
AAP: Not reviewed

Vigabatrin is a newer anticonvulsant and a synthetic derivative of gamma-aminobutyric acid. It is an effective adjunctive anticonvulsant for the treatment of multi-drug resistant complex partial seizures. It has also shown efficacy in controlling seizures and spasm in infants 3 months and older. No data are available on its transfer into human milk. However, the plasma levels of this drug (dose=1.5 gm) are quite low, 93 µmol/L, which would suggest that the amount in milk would probably be low even if the drug had a milk/plasma ratio of 1 or greater, but this is not known for sure.[1] However, regardless of the kinetics of this drug, it irreversibly inactivates gamma-aminobutyric acid.[2] The effect of this property on neonatal brains is not known. Some caution is recommended in breastfeeding mothers.

Pregnancy Risk Category: Contraindicated

Lactation Risk Category: L3

Adult Concerns: Changes in visual field defects have been noted. Drowsiness, fatigue, and acute psychosis (7%) have been described particularly in patients with a history of psychiatric disorders. Psychosis and an increased frequency of seizures have been reported upon abrupt withdrawal of vigabatrin therapy.

Pediatric Concerns: None reported via milk.

Drug Interactions: May decrease phenytoin levels by 30%. Few other interactions are noted which is a plus for this drug.

Relative Infant Dose:

Adult Dose: 1-4 gm daily

Alternatives:

T ½	= 7 hours	M/P	=
PHL	=	PB	= 0%
Tmax	= 0.5-2 hours	Oral	= 50%
MW	= 129	pKa	=
Vd	= 0.8		

References:
1.   Grant SM, Heel RC. Vigabatrin. A review of its pharmacodynamic and pharmacokinetic properties, and therapeutic potential in epilepsy and disorders of motor control. Drugs 1991; 41 (6):889-926.
2.   Dichter MA, Brodie MJ. New antiepileptic drugs. N Engl J Med 1996; 334 (24):1583-1590.

VITAMIN A   L3

Trade: Aquasol A, Del-VI-A, Vitamin A, Retinol
Other Trades: Aquasol A, Avoleum
Uses: Vitamin supplement
AAP: Not reviewed

Vitamin A (retinol) is a typical retinoid. It is a fat soluble vitamin that is secreted into human milk and primarily sequestered in high concentrations in the liver (90%).[1] Retinol is absorbed in the small intestine by a selective carrier-mediated uptake process. Levels in infants are generally unknown. The overdose of Vitamin A is extremely dangerous and is characterized by nausea, vomiting, headache, vertigo, and muscular incoordination. Acute toxicity generally occurs at doses of 25,000 IU/kg. Chronic exposure to levels of 4,000 IU/kg daily for 6 or more months is hazardous. Liver damage can occur at doses as low as 15,000 IU per day. In infants, a bulging fontanel is also indicative of Vitamin A toxicity.

The suggested adult female dose is listed at 700 µg or 2300 IU. Upper limit is normally 3000 µg or 10,000 IU. Adults should never exceed 5000 units/day unless under the direct supervision of a physician and for specific diseases. Use normal doses in breastfeeding mothers if at all possible. Mature human milk is rich in retinol and contains 750 µg/ Liter (2800 units). At this point we do not know if vitamin A levels in milk correlate with maternal plasma levels, but they probably are. Caution is recommended in supratherapeutic dosing in breastfeeding mothers.

Pregnancy Risk Category: A

Lactation Risk Category: L3

Adult Concerns: Liver toxicity in overdose. Numerous other symptoms are possible including drying of mucous membranes, alopecia, fever, fatigue, weight loss, etc.

Pediatric Concerns: None reported via milk, but do not use vitamin A in excess of 5000 IU/day.

Drug Interactions:

Relative Infant Dose:

Adult Dose: < 5000 IU daily

Alternatives:

T ½	=	M/P	=
PHL	=	PB	=
Tmax	=	Oral	= Complete
MW	= 286	pKa	=
Vd	=		

References:
1. McEvoy GE. (ed):AFHS Drug Information. New York, NY: 2005,

VITAMIN B-12   L1

Trade: Cyanocobalamin
Other Trades: Rubramin, Anacobin, Cytacon
Uses: Vitamin supplement
AAP: Maternal Medication Usually Compatible with Breastfeeding

Vitamin B-12 is also called cyanocobalamin and is used for the treatment of pernicious anemia. It is an essential vitamin that is secreted in human milk at concentrations of 0.1 µg/100 mL. B-12 deficiency is very dangerous (severe brain damage) to an infant. Vegan mothers and certain other vegetarians should be supplemented during pregnancy. Milk levels vary in proportion to maternal serum levels.[1] Vegetarian mothers may have low levels unless supplemented. Supplementation of nursing mothers is generally recommended.

Following the maternal administration of radiolabeled cyanocobalamin during a Schilling test, peak concentrations occur 24 hours. However, the amount absorbed by an infant is less than the current regulatory limit at any time. Therefore, discarding the first feed at four hours after administration (as advised by the Administration of Radioactive Substances Advisory Committee) is not warranted.[2] B-12 is now available in many forms, including injections, oral tablets, and intranasal gels, all of which are safe in breastfeeding mothers and infants.

Pregnancy Risk Category: A

Lactation Risk Category: L1

Adult Concerns: Itching, skin rash, mild diarrhea, megaloblastic anemia in vegetarian mothers.

Pediatric Concerns: None reported with exception of B-12 deficiency states.

Drug Interactions:

Relative Infant Dose:

Adult Dose: 25 µg daily

Alternatives:

T ½	=	M/P	=
PHL	=	PB	=
Tmax	= 2 hours	Oral	= Variable
MW	= 1355	pKa	=
Vd	=		

References:
1. Lawrence RA. Breastfeeding: A guide for the medical profession. St. Louis: Mosby Publishers, 1994.
2. Pomeroy KM, Sawyer LJ, Evans MJ. Estimated radiation dose to breast feeding infant following maternal administration of 57Co labelled to vitamin B12. Nucl Med Commun 2005 Sept; 26 (9):839-41.

VITAMIN D   L2

Trade: Calciferol, Delta-D, Vitamin D

Other Trades: Calciferol, Calcijex, Drisdol, Hytakerol, Radiostol

Uses: Vitamin D supplement

AAP: Maternal Medication Usually Compatible with Breastfeeding

Vitamin D is secreted into milk in limited concentrations and is somewhat proportional to maternal serum levels.[1] Excessive doses can produce elevated calcium levels in the infant[2]; therefore, doses lower than 10,000 IU/day are suggested in undernourished mothers. There has been some concern that mothers deficient in vitamin D may not provide sufficient vitamin D to the infant and hence impede bone mineralization in their infants. In a study by Greer[3], breastfed infants who received oral vitamin D supplementation had greater bone mineralization than those who were not supplemented. However, a more recent study of Korean women in winter who were not supplemented with vitamin D, and whose infants were either fed with human milk or artificial cow's formula (with vitamin D added), suggested that even though the breastfed groups plasma 25-hydroxyvitamin D concentration was lower, bone mineralization was equivalent in both breastfed and formula-fed infants.[4] The authors speculated that adequate bone mineralization occurs during the breastfeeding period from a predominantly vitamin D independent passive transport mechanism.

Human milk is known to have rather minimal concentrations of vitamin D. On average, breast milk contains approximately 26 IU/L (range= 5-136). Supplementing a mother with even moderate doses of vitamin D does not substantially increase milk levels.

In 2003 the Academy of Pediatrics, responding to the increased reports of rickets in breastfeeding infants, published a recommendation that all US infants should consume at least 200 IU of vitamin D per day by supplementation if needed. These recommendations are somewhat controversial for at least two reasons. One, we do not know with certainty the minimal but adequate dose of vitamin D required by breastfed infants, and two, they suggest that a mother's milk may in some cases be nutritionally inadequate. Regardless of these concerns, mothers who have limited vitamin D intake due to poor nutrition, or whose bodies have limited exposure to sunlight, probably need supplementation as their milk is likely deficient in vitamin D. In addition, infants of these mothers (who have limited or no exposure to sunlight or inadequate intake) may need supplementation, as these infants (particularly dark skinned) are most at risk for developing rickets.

The most recent study to evaluate the use of higher maternal doses of vitamin D and its transmission into human milk suggests that relatively higher maternal doses may actually increase milk levels of vitamin D significantly. In two groups of exclusively lactating women (n= 18) who were consuming 1600 IU vitamin D2 and 400 IU vitamin D3 (prenatal vitamin), or 3600 IU vitamin D2 and 400 IU vitamin D3, supplementation at these higher levels increased circulating 25-hydroxyvitamin D [25 (OH)D] concentrations for both groups.[5] The vitamin D activity of milk from mothers receiving 2000 IU/d vitamin D increased by 34.2 IU/L, on average, whereas the activity in the 4000 IU/d group increased by 94.2 IU/L. Infants of mothers receiving 4000 IU/d exhibited increases in circulating 25 (OH)D3 and 25 (OH)D2 concentrations from 12.7 to 18.8 ng/mL and from 0.8 to 12.0 ng/mL, respectively. Total circulating 25 (OH)D concentrations increased from 13.4 to 30.8 ng/mL.

This latter study clearly shows that increasing the maternal intake of vitamin D significantly increases milk vitamin D content. Further using the typical 400 IU dose (RDA) in adults is all but worthless in increasing maternal or the infants plasma 25 (OH)D concentrations. Maternal doses of 4000 IU/day may be required to facilitate increased transfer of 25 (OH)D to the infant. For a review of this issue read Greer.[6]

Pregnancy Risk Category: A

Lactation Risk Category: L2

Adult Concerns: Elevated calcium levels in the plasma following chronic high doses (>10,000 IU/day).

Pediatric Concerns: None reported via milk. The AAP recommends an infant dose of 200 IU/day.

Drug Interactions:

Relative Infant Dose:

Adult Dose: RDA = 400 IU/day.

Alternatives:

T ½	=	M/P	=
PHL	=	PB	=
Tmax	=	Oral	= Variable
MW	= 396	pKa	=
Vd	=		

References:

1. Rothberg AD, Pettifor JM, Cohen DF, Sonnendecker EW, Ross FP. Maternal-infant vitamin D relationships during breast-feeding. J Pediatr 1982; 101 (4):500-503.
2. Goldberg LD. Transmission of a vitamin-D metabolite in breast milk. Lancet 1972; 2 (7789):1258-1259.
3. Greer FR, Searcy JE, Levin RS, Steichen JJ, Asch PS, Tsang RC. Bone mineral content and serum 25-hydroxyvitamin D concentration in breast-fed infants with and without supplemental vitamin D. J Pediatr 1981; 98 (5):696-701.
4. Park MJ, Namgung R, Kim DH, Tsang RC. Bone mineral content is not reduced despite low vitamin D status in breast milk-fed infants versus cow's milk based formula-fed infants. J Pediatr 1998; 132 (4):641-645.
5. Hollis BW, Wagner CL. Vitamin D requirements during lactation: high-dose maternal supplementation as therapy to prevent hypovitaminosis D for both the mother and the nursing infant. Am J Clin Nutr 2004 Dec; 80 (6 Suppl):1752S-8S.
6. Greer FR. Issues in establishing vitamin D recommendations for infants and children. Am J Clin Nutr 2004 Dec; 80 (6 Suppl):1759S-62S.

VITAMIN E   L2

Trade: Alpha Tocopherol, Aquasol E
Other Trades: Aquasol E, Bio E
Uses: Vitamin E supplement
AAP: Not reviewed

Vitamin E (alpha tocopherol) is secreted in milk in higher concentrations than in the maternal serum. Vitamin E is particularly important biologically to infants and premature infants may require supplementation with oral vitamin E as they are relatively deficient at birth, and the amount in milk may not be sufficient due to their more rapid growth rate, and their poor absorption via the gut. Vitamin E has been repeatedly found to reduce the risk of intraventricular hemorrhage and retinopathy of prematurity to slight degrees.

Following topical administration to nipples (400 IU/feeding), Vitamin E plasma levels in breastfeeding infants were 40% higher than controls in just 6 days.[1] In numerous studies, the concentration of alpha tocopherol varies enormously from as little as 0.1 mg/dL to as much as 0.86 mg/dL.[2,3] Further, vitamin E levels also change with stage of lactation. In one study, the mean value for vitamin E at 2 weeks postpartum was 0.67 mg/dL and subsequently dropped to 0.4, 0.37, and 0.37 at 6, 12, and 16 weeks postpartum.[4]

The effect of maternal supplementation with vitamin E is obscure. In one study, supplementing with as little as 50 mg/day did not increase vitamin E content in human milk.[4] However a later study suggests that supplementing with large quantities may indeed increase milk levels to a minimal degree. In a study of a mother who supplemented with an average of 1090 mg/day, milk levels averaged 1.1 mg/dL.[5]

Do not overdose. Do not apply concentrated products to nipples unless concentrations are low (<50-100 IU) and then, only infrequently. The application of pure vitamin E oil (1000 IU/gm) to nipples could be hazardous to the infant. For an excellent review see Jensen.[6]

Pregnancy Risk Category: A

Lactation Risk Category: L2

Adult Concerns:

Pediatric Concerns: None reported via milk, but caution is recommended. Do not use highly concentrated vitamin E oils directly on nipple.

Drug Interactions:

Relative Infant Dose:

Adult Dose: 16-18 IU (1 mg d-Alpha-tocopherol) daily

Alternatives:

T ½	= 282 hours (IV)	M/P	=
PHL	=	PB	=
Tmax	=	Oral	= Variable
MW	= 431	pKa	=
Vd	=		

References:

1. Marx CM, Izquierdo A, Driscoll JW, Murray MA, Epstein MF. Vitamin E concentrations in serum of newborn infants after topical use of vitamin E by nursing mothers. Am J Obstet Gynecol 1985; 152 (6 Pt 1):668-670.
2. Kobayashi H, Kanno C, Yamauchi K, Tsugo T. Identification of alpha-, beta-, gamma-, and delta-tocopherols and their contents in human milk. Biochim Biophys Acta 1975 Feb 20; 380 (2):282-90.
3. Haug M, Laubach C, Burke M, Harzer G. Vitamin E in human milk from mothers of preterm and term infants. J Pediatr Gastroenterol Nutr 1987 Jul; 6 (4):605-9.
4. Lammi-Keefe CJ. Tocopherols in human milk: analytical method using high-performance liquid chromatography. J Pediatr Gastroenterol Nutr 1986 Nov; 5 (6):934-7.
5. Anderson DM, Pittard WB, III. Vitamin E and C concentrations in human milk with maternal megadosing: a case report. J Am Diet Assoc 1985 Jun; 85 (6):715-7.
6. Lammi-Keefe, CJ. Vitamins D and E in Human Milk. In: Handbook of milk composition. San Diego: Academic Press; 1995.

WARFARIN   L2

Trade: Coumadin, Panwarfin

Other Trades: Coumadin, Warfilone, Marevan

Uses: Anticoagulant

AAP: Maternal Medication Usually Compatible with Breastfeeding

Warfarin is a potent anticoagulant. Warfarin is highly protein bound in the maternal circulation and therefore very little is secreted into human milk. Very small and insignificant amounts are secreted into milk but it depends to some degree on the dose administered. In one study of two patients who were anticoagulated with warfarin, no warfarin was detected in the infant's serum, nor were changes in coagulation detectable.[1] In another study of

13 mothers, less than 0.08 μmol per liter (25 ng/mL) was detected in milk, and no warfarin was detected in the infants' plasma.[2]

According to these authors, maternal warfarin apparently poses little risk to a nursing infant and thus far has not produced bleeding anomalies in breastfed infants. Other anticoagulants, such as phenindione, should be avoided. Observe infant for bleeding such as excessive bruising or reddish petechia (spots). While the risks in breastfeeding premature infants (which are more susceptible to intracranial bleeding) is still low, oral supplementation with vitamin K1 will preclude any chance of hemorrhage. Even modest doses of Vitamin K1 counteract high doses of warfarin.

Pregnancy Risk Category: X

Lactation Risk Category: L2

Adult Concerns: Bleeding, bruising.

Pediatric Concerns: None reported via milk, but observe for bleeding, bruising.

Drug Interactions: The drug interactions of warfarin are numerous. Agents that may increase the anticoagulant effect and the risk of bleeding include: acetaminophen, androgens, beta blockers, clofibrate, corticosteroids, disulfiram, erythromycin, fluconazole, hydantoins, ketoconazole, miconazole, sulfonamides, thyroid hormones, and numerous others. Agents that may decrease the anticoagulant effect of warfarin include: ascorbic acid, dicloxacillin, ethanol, griseofulvin, nafcillin, sucralfate, trazodone, amino glutethimide, barbiturates, carbamazepine, ctretinate, rifampin. Due to numerous drug interactions, please consult additional references.

Relative Infant Dose:

Adult Dose: 2-10 mg daily.

Alternatives:

T ½	= 1-2.5 days	M/P	=
PHL	=	PB	= 99%
Tmax	= 0.5-3 days	Oral	= Complete
MW	= 308	pKa	= 5.1
Vd	= 0.1-0.2		

References:
1. McKenna R, Cole ER, Vasan U. Is warfarin sodium contraindicated in the lactating mother? J Pediatr 1983; 103 (2):325-327.
2. Orme ML, Lewis PJ, De Swiet M, Serlin MJ, Sibeon R, Baty JD, Breckenridge AM. May mothers given warfarin breast-feed their infants? Br Med J 1977; 1 (6076):1564-1565.

WEST NILE FEVER   L4

Trade:
Other Trades:
Uses: Viral febrile infection
AAP: Not reviewed

West Nile fever in humans usually is a febrile, influenza-like illness characterized by an abrupt onset (incubation period is 3 to 6 days) of moderate to high fever (3 to 5 days, infrequently biphasic, sometimes with chills), headache (often frontal), sore throat, backache, myalgia, arthralgia, fatigue, conjunctivitis, retrobulbar pain, maculopapular or roseolar rash, lymphadenopathy, anorexia, nausea, abdominal pain, diarrhea, and respiratory symptoms. It is not known whether the virus transfers into human milk, nor if it is communicable if present in milk although its transmission is believed unlikely. Thus far, there has been no documented occurrence of a mother passing the West Nile virus via maternal milk. Infected mosquitoes are the primary vector for West Nile virus although both hard and soft ticks have been found infected with West Nile virus in nature, but their role in the transmission and maintenance of the virus is uncertain. Mosquitoes, largely bird-feeding species, are the principal vectors of West Nile virus. The virus has been isolated from 43 mosquito species, predominantly of the genus Culex.[1,2,3]

For answers to questions about West Nile virus, please see the CDC web site http://www.cdc.gov/ncidod/dvbid/westnile/q&a.htm

Pregnancy Risk Category:

Lactation Risk Category: L4

Adult Concerns: Febrile influenza-like illness, characterized by an abrupt onset of moderate to high fever, headache (often frontal), sore throat, backache, myalgia, arthralgia, fatigue, conjunctivitis, retrobulbar pain, maculopapular or roseolar rash, lymphadenopathy, anorexia, nausea, abdominal pain, diarrhea, and respiratory symptoms.

Pediatric Concerns: No transmission reported via milk but it has not been studied.

Drug Interactions:

Relative Infant Dose:

Adult Dose:

Alternatives:

References:
1. Hayes C. West Nile Fever. In: Monath TP (ed). The arboviruses: epidemiology and ecology, Vol 5. Boca Raton, FL: CRC Press, 1989.

2. Shope RE. Other Flavivirus Infections. In: Guerrant RL, Walker DH, and Weller PF (eds). Tropical Infectious Diseases: Principals, Pathogens, and Practice. Philadelphia, PA: Churchill Livingstone, 2004.
3. Hubalek Z, Halouzka J. West Nile fever--a reemerging mosquito-borne viral disease in Europe. Emerg Infect Dis 1999; 5 (5):643-650.

XENON-133 — L3

Trade: Xenon-133
Other Trades:
Uses: Evaluation of pulmonary obstruction
AAP: Not reviewed

Xenon-133 (T1/2 = 5.3 days) and Xenon-127 (T1/2=36.4 days) are noble gases.[1] As such they are chemically inert and are used often for ventilation and for cerebral blood flow studies. The patient is asked to inhale a gas mixed with either of these isotopes, followed by a brief 5 min wash out period. Obstructions in the lung appear as hot spots. Because these gases are inert, they would not be stored or any length of time in the human and would be rapidly exhaled within minutes. This is a typical case were the biological half-life (time stored in body, minutes in this case) is incredibly short compared to the radioactive half life (5.3 days). Xenon-133 would not likely be hazardous to a breastfeeding infant as long as a brief wash out period of an hour or more is used. See Appendix B.

Pregnancy Risk Category:

Lactation Risk Category: L3

Adult Concerns: None.

Pediatric Concerns: None if brief wash out period is used.

Drug Interactions:

Relative Infant Dose:

Adult Dose:

Alternatives:

T ½	= 5.3 days	M/P	=
PHL	=	PB	=
Tmax	=	Oral	= None
MW	=	pKa	=
Vd	=		

References:
1. Gopal B, Saha. Fundamentals of Nuclear Pharmacy. 3rd ed. ed. Springer-Verlag Publishers, 1992.

YELLOW FEVER VACCINE | L4

Trade: YF-Vax
Other Trades: Arilvax, Stamaril
Uses: Vaccine
AAP: Not reviewed

Yellow fever is an acute viral illness caused by a mosquito-borne flavivirus. The clinical spectrum of yellow fever is highly variable, from subclinical infection to overwhelming pansystemic disease. Yellow fever has an abrupt onset after an incubation period of 3 to 6 days, and usually includes fever, prostration, headache, photophobia, lumbosacral pain, extremity pain (especially the knee joints), epigastric pain, anorexia, and vomiting. The illness may progress to liver and renal failure, and hemorrhagic symptoms and signs caused by thrombocytopenia and abnormal clotting and coagulation may occur. The case-fatality rate of yellow fever varies widely in different studies and may be different for Africa compared to South America, but is typically 20% or higher. Jaundice or other gross evidence of severe liver disease is associated with higher mortality rates.[1] Yellow fever occurs only in Africa and South America. The World Health Organization (WHO) estimates that a total of 200,000 cases of yellow fever occur each year.

Yellow fever vaccine is a live, attenuated virus preparation made from the 17D yellow fever virus strain. Historically, the 17D vaccine has been considered to be one of the safest and most effective live virus vaccines ever developed. The virus is grown in chick embryos. Persons aged >9 months who are traveling to or living in areas of South America and Africa where yellow fever infection is officially reported should be vaccinated.

The CDC recommends that due to certain risks that breastfeeding mothers not be immunized unless they are entering regions of high risk.[2] This vaccine is a live attenuated vaccine, so there is significant risk the infant will at least ingest some virus. A recent report strongly suggests that the yellow fever virus (17DD) may be transmitted via milk.[3] A 22 year old breastfeeding mother received a yellow fever vaccination at 15 days postpartum. At 22 days of age, the infant developed fever, irritability and refused to feed. The next day the infant began seizing and was hospitalized. The infant's CSF tested positive for yellow fever vaccine virus (17DD). Unfortunately, the mother's milk was not tested. The presumption is that the virus was transmitted via milk.

The WHO recognizes that situations occur in which vaccination of an infant aged <9 months might be considered such as the mothers entry into high endemic areas. Another such situation is the unavoidable exposure of children aged 6-8 months to an environment where an increased likelihood of becoming infected with the yellow fever virus exists (e.g., a setting of endemic or epidemic yellow fever). Because of the risk for viral encephalitis, in no instance should infants aged <6 months receive yellow fever vaccine. Therefore, if the infant is between 1 and 5 months, the mother should NOT be immunized. If the infant is >6 months, and the mother is entering a region of high risk for the infection, then at least the mother, and perhaps the infant should be immunized directly. Based on a theoretic risk of transmission via milk, the CDC now strongly recommends against the use of yellow fever vaccines in breastfeeding mothers, except in situations where the risk of contracting the disease is unavoidable. Check the CDC for current recommendations.

Pregnancy Risk Category: C

Lactation Risk Category: L4

Adult Concerns: Adverse effects are numerous and include: mild headaches, myalgia, low-grade fevers. Local reactions include edema, hypersensitivity, and pain at the injection site.

Pediatric Concerns: One reported case of severe seizures and vaccine encephalitis in an infant who's mother received yellow fever vaccination eight days prior. While not adequately documented that the infection was via milk, the CDC strongly suggests that this infant probably received the virus via its mother's breastmilk. Risks in infants and children can be severe and include: vaccine induced encephalitis, most of which have occurred in infants < 4 months of age (n=14), and in children > 3 years (n=7).

Drug Interactions:

Relative Infant Dose:

Adult Dose:

Alternatives:

References:
1. Pharmaceutical manufacturers prescribing information. 2005.
2. http://www.cdc.gov/mmwr/preview/mmwrhtml/rr5117a1.htm
3. MMWR Morbidity and Mortality Weekly Report, February 12, 2010, volume 59, no. 5.

ZAFIRLUKAST   L3

Trade: Accolate
Other Trades: Accolate
Uses: Leukotriene inhibitor for Asthma
AAP: Not reviewed

Zafirlukast is a new competitive receptor antagonist of leukotriene D4 and other components of slow-reacting substance of anaphylaxis which are mediators of bronchoconstriction in asthmatic patients. Zafirlukast is not a bronchodilator and should not be used for acute asthma attacks.

Zafirlukast is excreted into milk in low concentrations. Following repeated 40 mg doses twice daily (please note: average adult dose is 20 mg twice daily), the average steady-state concentration in breastmilk was 50 µg/L compared to 255 ng/mL in maternal plasma.[1] Zafirlukast is poorly absorbed when administered with food. It is likely the oral absorption via ingestion of breastmilk would be low. The manufacturer recommends against using in breastfeeding mothers.

Pregnancy Risk Category: B

Lactation Risk Category: L3

Adult Concerns: Pharyngitis, aggravation reaction, headache, nausea, diarrhea have been reported.

Pediatric Concerns: None reported.

Drug Interactions: Erythromycin reduces oral bioavailability of zafirlukast by 40%. Aspirin increase zafirlukast plasma levels by 45%. Theophylline reduces zafirlukast plasma levels by 30%. Zafirlukast increase warfarin anticoagulation by 35%. Terfenadine reduces zafirlukast plasma levels by 54%.

Relative Infant Dose:

Adult Dose: 20 mg BID

Alternatives:

T ½	= 10-13 hours	M/P	= 0.15
PHL	=	PB	= >99%
Tmax	= 3 hours	Oral	= Poor
MW	= 575	pKa	=
Vd	=		

References:
1. Pharmaceutical Manufacturer Prescribing Information. 1997.

ZALEPLON   L2

Trade: Sonata
Other Trades: Starnoc, Sonata
Uses: Hypnotic agent used for insomnia
AAP: Not reviewed

Zaleplon is a nonbenzodiazepine hypnotic sedative that interacts at the GABA receptor. In a study of 5 lactating mothers who received doses of 10 mg orally, the peak milk level occurred at 1.2 hours and averaged 14 µg/L.[1] Milk levels decreased rapidly following a peak at 1.2 hours to less than 3 µg/L four hours following administration. The authors suggest that these levels would be subclinical to the infant.

Pregnancy Risk Category: C

Lactation Risk Category: L2

Adult Concerns: Headache, drowsiness, peripheral edema, dizziness have been reported. Avoid alcohol and other depressants.

Pediatric Concerns: None reported via milk. Milk levels were reported to be subclinical.

Drug Interactions: Zaleplon potentiates the CNS effects of alcohol, imipramine, thioridazine. Rifampin decreases the plasma levels of zaleplon. Cimetidine produces a significant increase in plasma levels of zaleplon.

Relative Infant Dose: 1.5%

Adult Dose: 10 mg nightly

Alternatives:

T ½	= 1.2 hours	M/P	= 0.5
PHL	–	PB	=
Tmax	= 1.2 hours	Oral	= Complete
MW	=	pKa	=
Vd	=		

References:
1. Darwish M, Martin PT, Cevallos WH, Tse S, Wheeler S, Troy SM. Rapid disappearance of zaleplon from breast milk after oral administration to lactating women. J Clin Pharmacol 1999; 39 (7):670-674.

ZANAMIVIR   L3

Trade: Relenza
Other Trades: Relenza
Uses: Treatment of Influenza viral infections
AAP: Not reviewed

Zanamivir is a viral neuraminidase inhibitor that blocks or prevents viral seeding or release from infected cells and prevents viral aggregation. It is only moderately effective and is believed to reduce symptoms by only 30% or several days, and only if treatment is instituted within 2 days of infection.

It is administered via inhalation using a Diskhaler device. Only 4-17% of the inhaled drug is systemically absorbed. Peak plasma concentrations are only 17-142 ng/mL within 2 hours of administration and then rapidly decline. The manufacturer reports that it is present in the milk of rodents although no human data are available. Due to the poor oral or inhaled absorption and the incredibly low plasma levels, it is unlikely to produce untoward effects in breastfed infants. However, due to its limited efficacy (reduces length of illness by 1 to 1.5 days), its use in breastfeeding mothers is probably not warranted, unless in high-risk patients with other severe medical conditions.

Pregnancy Risk Category: C

Lactation Risk Category: L3

Adult Concerns: Bronchospasm may occur in patients with asthma or obstructive pulmonary disease.

Pediatric Concerns: None reported via milk but not studies exist.

Drug Interactions: None yet reported.

Relative Infant Dose:

Adult Dose: 10 mg twice daily.

Alternatives:

T ½	= 2.5-5.1 hours	M/P	=
PHL	=	PB	= <10%
Tmax	= 1-2 hours	Oral	= 4-17%
MW	= 332	pKa	=
Vd	=		

References:
1. Drug Facts and Comparisons 1999 ed. ed. St. Louis: 1999.
2. Pharmaceutical Manufacturer Prescribing Information.

ZIDOVUDINE	L3

Trade: Retrovir, Combivir
Other Trades: Novo-Azt, Combivir
Uses: Antiretroviral agent used in HIV
AAP: Not reviewed

Zidovudine in an antiretroviral agent used in the treatment of HIV.

In a study of 18 women receiving 300 mg twice daily at steady state, median zidovudine levels at 5.4 hours postdose in maternal serum, breast milk, and infant serum were 58 ng/mL, 207 ng/mL and 123 ng/mL, respectively.[1] The milk/serum ratio was 3.21. The median infant serum concentration of zidovudine (123 ng/mL) was at least 25 times the 50% inhibitory concentration for HIV. Infant serum concentrations of zidovudine were a median of 2.5 times higher than the respective maternal concentration of zidovudine. The elevated infant serum levels are somewhat inexplicable since the relative infant dose is so low, and the plasma half-life is quite short as well. Some caution should probably be observed with this product until we have more data confirming these high infant serum levels.

Combivir contains both lamivudine and zidovudine.

Pregnancy Risk Category: C

Lactation Risk Category: L3

Adult Concerns: Side effects include: cardiomyopathy, congestive heart failure, skin and nail discoloration, gynecomastia, lactic acidosis, anorexia, nausea, vomiting, esophageal ulcer, dyspnea, cough, headache. Many other side effects have been reported. Consult the prescribing information.

Pediatric Concerns: None reported but milk levels are moderately high, and serum levels in infants are 3.2 times higher than maternal serum levels.

Drug Interactions: Drug interactions are numerous. Nelfinavir, trimethoprim/sulfa, atovaquone, fluconazole, methadone, nelfinavir, probenecid, ritonavir, valproic acid are a few that have been reported to alter the plasma levels of zidovudine. Consult other texts for full list of drug-drug interactions.

Relative Infant Dose: 0.4%

Adult Dose: 300 mg twice daily.

Alternatives: Nevirapine, Lamivudine

T ½	= <3 hours	M/P	= 3.21
PHL	= 1.9 hours	PB	= <38%
Tmax	= 1.5 hours	Oral	= 61%
MW	= 267	pKa	=
Vd	= 1.6		

References:
1.   Shapiro RL, Holland DT, Capparelli E, Lockman S, Thior I, Wester C, et al. Antiretroviral concentrations in breast-feeding infants of women in Botswana receiving antiretroviral treatment. J Infect Dis 2005 Sep 1; 192 (5):720-7.

ZILEUTON   L3

Trade: Zyflo
Other Trades:
Uses: Lipoxygenase inhibitor
AAP: Not reviewed

Zileuton is used for chronic treatment of asthma. It inhibits leukotriene formation, which in turn inhibits neutrophil and eosinophil migration, neutrophil and monocyte aggregation, and leukocyte adhesion, minimizing inflammation and bronchoconstriction in the airways.[1] No data are available on its transfer into human milk. It is not significantly toxic nor does it have severe side effects.

Pregnancy Risk Category: C

Lactation Risk Category: L3

Adult Concerns: Adverse reactions include headache, pain, dyspepsia, nausea, asthenia, and abdominal pain.

Pediatric Concerns: No data are available.

Drug Interactions: Zileuton may increase the levels of aminophylline, fluvoxamine, mexiletine, mirtazapine, ropinirole, theophylline, propranolol and trifluoperazine. Concomitant use with warfarin can increase prothrombin time.

Relative Infant Dose:

Adult Dose: 600 mg QID

Alternatives:

T ½	= 2.5 hours	M/P	=
PHL	=	PB	= 93%
Tmax	= 1.7 hours	Oral	=
MW	− 236	pKa	=
Vd	= 1.2		

References:
1. Pharmaceutical Manufacturer Prescribing Information. 2005.

ZINC SALTS	L2

Trade: Zinc
Other Trades:
Uses: Zinc supplements
AAP: Not reviewed

Zinc is an essential element that is required for enzymatic function within the cell. Zinc deficiencies have been documented in newborns and premature infants with symptoms such as anorexia nervosa, arthritis, diarrheas, eczema, recurrent infections, and recalcitrant skin problems.

The Recommended Daily Allowance for adults is 12-15 mg/day. The average oral dose of supplements is 25-50 mg/day; higher doses may lead to gastritis. Doses used for treatment of cold symptoms averaged 13.3 mg (lozenges) every 2 hours while awake for the duration of cold symptoms. The acetate or gluconate salts are preferred due to reduced gastric irritation and higher absorption. Zinc sulfate should not be used. Excessive intake is detrimental. Eleven healthy males who ingested 150 mg twice daily for 6 weeks showed significant impairment of lymphocyte and polymorphonuclear leukocyte function and a significant reduction of HDL cholesterol.

Interestingly, absorption of dietary zinc is nearly twice as high during lactation as before conception. In 13 women studied, zinc absorption at preconception averaged 14% and during lactation, 25%.[1] There was no difference in serum zinc values between women who took iron supplements and those who did not although iron supplementation may reduce oral zinc absorption. Zinc absorption by the infant from human milk is high, averaging 41%, which is significantly higher than from soy or cow formulas (14% and 31% respectively). Minimum daily requirements of zinc in full term infants vary from 0.3 to 0.5 mg/kg/day.[2] Daily ingestion of zinc from breastmilk has been estimated to be 0.35 mg/kg/day and declines over the first 17 weeks of life as older neonates require less zinc due to slower growth rate. Supplementation with 25-50 mg/day is probably safe, but excessive doses are discouraged. Another author has shown that zinc levels in breastmilk are independent of maternal plasma zinc concentrations or dietary zinc intake.[3] Other body pools of zinc (i.e., liver and bone) are perhaps the source of zinc in breastmilk. Therefore, higher levels of oral zinc intake probably have minimal effect on zinc concentrations in milk but excessive doses are not recommended.

Pregnancy Risk Category:

Lactation Risk Category: L2

Adult Concerns: Oral Zinc salts may cause gastritis, GI upset. Gluconate salts, and lower doses are preferred.

Pediatric Concerns: None reported via milk.

Drug Interactions: Zinc may reduce absorption of ciprofloxacin, tetracyclines, norfloxacin, ofloxacin. Iron salts may reduce absorption of zinc. Foods containing high concentrations of phosphorus, calcium (diary foods), or phytates (bran, brown bread) may reduce oral zinc absorption. Coffee reduces zinc absorption by 50%.

Relative Infant Dose:

Adult Dose: 15 mg daily

Alternatives:

T ½	=	M/P	=
PHL	=	PB	=
Tmax	=	Oral	= 41%
MW	=	pKa	=
Vd	=		

References:
1. Fung EB, Ritchie LD, Woodhouse LR, Roehl R, King JC. Zinc absorption in women during pregnancy and lactation: a longitudinal study. Am J Clin Nutr 1997; 66 (1):80-88.
2. Drug Facts and Comparisons 1997 ed. ed. St. Louis: 1997.
3. Krebs NF, Reidinger CJ, Hartley S, Robertson AD, Hambidge KM. Zinc supplementation during lactation: effects on maternal status and milk zinc concentrations. Am J Clin Nutr 1995; 61 (5):1030-1036.

ZIPRASIDONE   L2

Trade: Geodon
Other Trades:
Uses: Antipsychotic
AAP: Not reviewed

Ziprasidone is an atypical antipsychotic agent chemically unrelated to phenothiazines or butyrophenones.[1] In a brief case report of 1 patient receiving a dose of 160 mg/day with a plasma level of 177 ng/mL, milk levels were undetectable until day 10 of therapy which was 11 ng/mL and 170 ng in maternal plasma.[2] Milk/plasma ratio was 0.06. The authors estimate the RID = 1.2%. No untoward effects were noted in the infant.

In another case report of an infant exposed throughout pregnancy and subsequently breastfed for 6 months, the infant (2.64 kg) was delivered at 39 weeks, and did not exhibit discontinuation symptoms or any other drug-related symptoms. While milk levels were not determined, no symptoms of ziprasidone were noted. The infant developed normally over the following 6 months.

Pregnancy Risk Category: C

Lactation Risk Category: L2

Adult Concerns: Side effects include somnolence, prolonged QT/QTc intervals, nausea, dyspepsia, headache, skin rash, elevated liver enzymes. Relative incidence of extrapyramidal symptoms is low. Elevation of serum prolactin levels is common with this family and should be expected, although it appears minimal with this agent. Prolonged QT intervals are potentially quite hazardous so should be used with caution in individuals with bradycardia, hypokalemia, and/or hypomagnesemia.

Pediatric Concerns: None reported in one case report.

Drug Interactions: Too numerous to list. The manufacturer states that concomitant use of ziprasidone and Class III antiarrhythmic agents is contraindicated. An increased risk of cardiotoxicity is reported for many drugs (QT prolongation, torsades de pointes, cardiac arrest).

Relative Infant Dose: 0.1% - 1.2%

Adult Dose: 20 - 80 mg BID

Alternatives: Risperidone, Olanzapine

T ½	= 7 hours	M/P	= 0.06
PHL	=	PB	= 99%
Tmax	= 4-5 hours	Oral	= 60%
MW	= 419	pKa	=
Vd	= 1.5		

References:

1. Pharmaceutical Manufacturers prescribing information, 2003.
2. Schlotterbeck P, Saur R, Hiemke C, et al. Low concentration of ziprasidone in human milk: a case report. Int J Neuropsychopharmacol. Apr 2009;12 (3):437-438.
3. Werremeyer A. Ziprasidone and citalopram use in pregnancy and lactation in a woman with psychotic depression. Am J Psychiatry. Nov 2009;166 (11):1298.

ZOLMITRIPTAN   L3

Trade: Zomig, Zomig-ZMT
Other Trades: Zomig, Rapimelt
Uses: Migraine analgesic
AAP: Not reviewed

Zolmitriptan is a selective serotonin-1D receptor antagonist that is specifically indicated for treating acute migraine headaches. Peak plasma levels of zolmitriptan during migraine attacks are generally 8-14 ng/mL and occur before 4 hours.[1,2] Zolmitriptan is structurally similar to sumatriptan but has better oral bioavailability, higher penetration into the CNS, and may have dual mechanisms of action. No data are available on its penetration into human milk. See sumatriptan as preferred alternate.

Pregnancy Risk Category: C

Lactation Risk Category: L3

Adult Concerns: Asthenia, dizziness, paresthesias, drowsiness, nausea, throat tightness, tight chest. Tachycardia and palpitations have been reported.

Pediatric Concerns: None reported via milk. See sumatriptan as alternative.

Drug Interactions:

Relative Infant Dose:

Adult Dose: 2.5 mg every 2 hours PRN

Alternatives: Sumatriptan

T ½	= 3 hours	M/P	=
PHL	=	PB	=
Tmax	= 2-4 hours	Oral	= 48%
MW	=	pKa	=
Vd	=		

References:
1. Seaber E, On N, Dixon RM, Gibbens M, Leavens WJ, Liptrot J, Chittick G, Posner J, Rolan PE, Pack RW. The absolute bioavailability and metabolic disposition of the novel antimigraine compound zolmitriptan (311C90). Br J Clin Pharmacol 1997; 43 (6):579-587.
2. Palmer KJ, Spencer CM. Zolmitriptan (Adis new drug profile). CNS Drugs Jun 1997; 7 (6):468-478.

ZOLPIDEM TARTRATE   L3

Trade: Ambien, Ambien CR, Edluar
Other Trades:
Uses: Sedative, sleep aid
AAP: Maternal Medication Usually Compatible with Breastfeeding

Zolpidem, although not a benzodiazepine, interacts with the same GABA-BZ receptor site and shares some of the same pharmacologic effects of the benzodiazepine (Valium) family.[1] In a study of 5 lactating mothers receiving 20 mg daily, the maximum plasma concentration occurred between 1.75 and 3.75 hours and ranged from 90 to 364 µg/L.[2] The authors suggest that the amount of zolpidem recovered in breastmilk 3 hours after administration ranged between 0.76 and 3.88 µg or 0.004 to 0.019% of the total dose administered. Breastmilk clearance of zolpidem is very rapid and none was detectable (below 0.5 ng/mL) by 4-5 hours postdose.

One case of infant sedation and poor appetite related to zolpidem use has been reported following the nightly use of sertraline (100mg) and 10 mg Zolpidem.[3] Upon discontinuation of zolpidem, the infant regained appetite and became more alert.

Pregnancy Risk Category: C

Lactation Risk Category: L3

Adult Concerns: Sedation, anxiety, fatigue, irritability. Sweating, tachycardia, tachypnea, tremors, and severe anxiety have been reported upon discontinuation of zolpidem.

Pediatric Concerns: One case of infant drowsiness and poor feeding. Discontinuation symptoms are known in adults and may be present in infants following long exposure.

Drug Interactions: Use with food may significantly decrease plasma levels by 25%.

Relative Infant Dose: 4.7 - 19.1%

Adult Dose: 5-10 mg daily.

Alternatives:

T ½	= 2.5-5 hours	M/P	= 0.13-0.18
PHL	=	PB	= 92.5%
Tmax	= 1.6 hours	Oral	= 70%
MW	= 307	pKa	=
Vd	=		

References:
1. Pharmaceutical Manufacturer Prescribing Information. 1996.
2. Pons G, Francoual C, Guillet P, Moran C, Hermann P, Bianchetti G, Thiercelin JF, Thenot JP, Olive G. Zolpidem excretion in breast milk. Eur J Clin Pharmacol 1989; 37 (3):245-248.
3. A.K. Personnal communication. 1999.

ZONISAMIDE   L5

Trade: Zonegran
Other Trades:
Uses: Anti-convulsant
AAP: Not reviewed

Zonisamide is a broad-spectrum anticonvulsant medication chemically classified as a sulfonamide. It has a long half-life and high pKa which from the data below leads to high maternal milk and plasma concentrations. In a study of one patient receiving 100 mg three times daily of zonisamide on postpartum day 0, 3, 6, 14, and 30, the reported milk levels were drawn at 1.5 to 2.5 hours following administration of the medication. The reported milk levels ranged from 8.25 to 10.5 mg/L (mean= 9.5) while the maternal plasma levels ranged from 9.52 to 10.6 mg/L (mean= 10.13). The milk/plasma ratio averaged 0.93.

Using the highest reported milk level, the relative infant dose would be 33% of the maternal dose. This is quite high. Significant caution is recommended with this medication as a number of pediatric adverse effects have been noted in older children.

Pregnancy Risk Category: C

Lactation Risk Category: L5

Adult Concerns: Adverse reactions include somnolence, dizziness, headache, nausea, anorexia, agitation, irritability, speech abnormalities, diplopia, chest pain, paresthesias, psychosis, leukopenia, weight loss, SJ syndrome, oligohidrosis and hyperthermia in pediatric patients. Seizures on withdrawal have been reported. Nephrolithiasis is reported in 4% of patients.

Pediatric Concerns: None via breastmilk, but levels are extremely high.

Drug Interactions: Carbamazepine may increase the plasma clearance of zonisamide. Do not use with Evening primrose oil or Ginko as seizure thresholds may be lowered. Phenobarbital reduces plasma half-life of zonisamide signficantly.

Relative Infant Dose: 33.2%

Adult Dose: 100-200 mg/day

Alternatives:

T ½	= 63 hours	M/P	= 0.93
PHL	=	PB	= 40%
Tmax	= 2-6 hours	Oral	=
MW	= 212	pKa	= 10.2
Vd	= 1.45		

References:
1. Shimoyama R, Ohkubo T, Sugawara K. Monitoring of zonisamide in human breast milk and maternal plasma by solid-phase extraction HPLC method. Biomed Chromatogr 1999; 13 (5):370-372.

ZOPICLONE   L2

Trade:

Other Trades: Apo-Zopiclone, Dom-Zopiclone, PMS-
Zopiclone, Rhovan, Alti-Zopiclone, Ratio-Zopiclone,
Imovane, Zileze

Uses: Hypnotic sedative

AAP: Not reviewed

Zopiclone is a sedative/hypnotic which, although structurally dissimilar to the benzodiazepines, shares their pharmacologic profile.[1] In a group of 12 women who received 7.5 mg of Zopiclone, the average peak milk concentration at 2.4 hours was 34 µg/L[2], but the average milk concentration was 10.92 µg/L. The milk half-life was 5.3 hours compared to the maternal plasma half-life of 4.9 hours. The milk/plasma AUC ratio was 0.51 and ranged from 0.4 to 0.7. The authors report that the average infant dose of Zopiclone via milk would be 1.4% of the weight adjusted dose ingested by the mother.

Pregnancy Risk Category:

Lactation Risk Category: L2

Adult Concerns: Sedation.

Pediatric Concerns: None reported via milk.

Drug Interactions:

Relative Infant Dose: 1.5%

Adult Dose: 7.5 mg orally

Alternatives:

T ½	= 4-5 hours	M/P	= 0.51
PHL	=	PB	= 45%
Tmax	= 1.6 hours	Oral	= 75%
MW	= 388	pKa	=
Vd	= 1.51		

References:
1. Gaillot J, Heusse D, Hougton GW, Marc AJ, Dreyfus JF. Pharmacokinetics and metabolism of zopiclone. Pharmacology 1983; 27 Suppl 2:76-91.
2. Matheson I, Sande HA, Gaillot J. The excretion of zopiclone into breast milk. Br J Clin Pharmacol 1990; 30 (2):267-271.

ZUCLOPENTHIXOL   L3

Trade:
Other Trades: Clopixol-Acuphase, Clopixol Depot, Clopixol
Uses: Antipsychotic agent
AAP: Not reviewed

Zuclopenthixol is a typical antipsychotic agent used in the management of schizophrenia. It is not available in the USA. It works by blocking the postsynaptic dopaminergic receptors.[1]

In a study of a single patient who initially received 24 mg zuclopenthixol for 4 days and then 14 mg/day thereafter, levels in milk averaged 20 µg/L following the 24 mg dose, and 5 µg/L at the 14 mg dose. Based on these concentrations, the authors estimated the absolute infant dose at 0.8 to 3.0 µg/kg and the relative infant dose at 0.3 to 0.8% of the maternal dose.[2]

In a group of six patients ranging from 3 days to 10 months postpartum, the dose ranged from 4 mg/day to 72 mg/2 weeks (IM).[3] In all instances, milk levels were much lower than plasma. Zuclopenthixol levels in milk averaged 29% of the maternal plasma levels. The daily dose to an infant was estimated to be approximately 0.5- 5 µg/day which roughly corresponds to a relative infant dose of 0.03 to 0.38% of the weight-adjusted maternal dose.

The plasma levels of zuclopenthixol in infants were low in both studies. No untoward effects were noted in the infants although some caution is recommended with prolonged exposure to this medication.

Pregnancy Risk Category: C

Lactation Risk Category: L3

Adult Concerns: Adverse reactions include drowsiness, anxiety, insomnia, xerostomia, hypertonia, tremor, and weakness.

Pediatric Concerns: No untoward effects were noted in 7 infants studied thus far.

Drug Interactions: Zuclopenthixol is a major substrate of CYP2D6, and thus drug interactions are numerous. Some reported are aluminum salts, anticholinergics, antihypertensives, bromocriptine, CNS depressants, epinepherine, levodopa, lithium, phenytoin, propranolol, tricyclic antidepressants, trazodone, and valproic acid. Consult other texts for a full list of drug-drug interactions.

Relative Infant Dose: 0.4% - 0.9%

Adult Dose: Oral = 10-150 mg/day: IM=50-150 mg every 48-72 hours.

Alternatives: Risperidone, Olanzapine

T ½	= 20 hours	M/P	= 0.29
PHL	=	PB	= 98
Tmax	= 4 hours	Oral	= 49%
MW	= 443-555	pKa	=
Vd	= 15-20		

References:
1. Pharmaceutical Manufacturer Prescribing Information. 2006.
2. Matheson I, Skjaeraasen J. Milk concentrations of flupenthixol, nortriptyline and zuclopenthixol and between-breast differences in two patients. Eur J Clin Pharmacol 1988; 35 (2):217-220.
3. Aaes-Jorgensen T, Bjorndal F, Bartels U. Zuclopenthixol levels in serum and breast milk. Psychopharmacology (Berl) 1986; 90 (3):417-418.

Appendix A

Cancer Chemotherapeutic Agents

The use of anticancer drugs in breastfeeding mothers is highly risky. We have almost no data on the transfer of these agents into human milk. However, with many of these products, mothers could conceivably return to breastfeeding after a suitable period of pumping and discarding of the milk. But two major questions still remain unanswered: 1) in mothers with various kinds of cancer, will the tumor respond appropriately, while it is under the hormonal influence present during lactation; and 2) just how long must a mother interrupt breastfeeding to make sure all the medications used are cleared from the body. No one seems to know the answer to the first question, as I have asked it repeatedly to cancer experts. But as to clearance of the medication, we do have a body of literature that lends itself toward estimating rather accurately the clearance of these agents from the human body. This section is derived from that literature.

Therefore in this section, I have provided my recommendations for interrupting breastfeeding based entirely on the published rate of clearance of the agent from the human body. **Clearance may vary from one individual to another, so the clinician involved may have to alter these recommendations depending on the liver and renal function in the individual case.**

Drugs are cleared from the body by numerous mechanisms. Some drugs are metabolized to both active and inactive metabolites, and some are stored in remote body tissues. Therefore, I carefully evaluated the longest elimination half-life of the parent drug or its 'active' metabolite, and made my recommendations using this data. Many drugs have several half-lives. Often the first half-life (alpha) is just 'redistribution' from the plasma compartment to other compartments (e.g. liver). Some drugs subsequently distribute to more remote compartments (e.g. heart, fat, bone, etc) and slowly leak from these deep compartments overtime. This is especially true of platinum and doxorubicin, and the elimination of these agents requires many weeks. Thus, I used the longest half-life reported for the product (generally beta or gamma) to be certain that no remaining drug is present to enter the milk compartment. Often, this was between five and ten elimination (gamma or beta) half-lives.

Because chemotherapy often consists of numerous medications used simultaneously, you should always choose to discontinue breastfeeding relative to the agent with the longest half-life. I cannot assure you that in your particular case, these recommendations are actually safe, but they are the best estimate that pharmacokinetics can provide us. If you have poor renal output, or decreased liver function, you should extend the periods recommended below.

I cannot completely assure you that these recommendations are safe in your particular case, but if followed closely by your physician, many infants could return safely to the breast without complications. As always, this is a discussion you should have with your attending physician.

◆ ◆ ◆

Alemtuzumab

Trade: Campath

Alemtuzumab is a recombinant DNA-derived humanized monoclonal antibody that is directed against specific cell receptors on leukemic cells. It is a large IgG1 antibody.[1] No data are available on its transfer to human milk, but it is very unlikely to enter milk, due to its large molecular weight. However, the first 72 hours postpartum, IgG levels in milk are higher, and this should be considered with this agent. While some IgG is still transferred into human milk, it is done so by a very specialized transporter. It is unlikely this transporter would transport this unusual monoclonal antibody.

Kinetics: T½ = 12 days

Recommendations: Mothers should avoid breastfeeding, if this product is used with 2 weeks of delivery. Otherwise, the amount present in milk is likely quite low. This is a large molecular weight antibody that is unlikely to enter milk in significant quantities.

References:
1.   Pharmaceutical Manufacturers prescribing information. 2003.

Altretamine

Trade: Hexalen

Used to treat ovarian, breast, cervix, pancreatic, and other cancers, altretamine requires metabolism to the cytotoxic derivative. While it is well absorbed orally, its oral bioavailability is low, due to first pass metabolism and uptake by the liver. Its usefulness is limited by its toxicity. Following oral administration of radiolabeled altretamine, urinary recovery of radioactivity was 61% at 24 hours and 90% at 72 hours.[1] Human urinary metabolites were N-demethylated homologues of altretamine with <1% unmetabolized altretamine excreted at 24 hours. No data on entry into human milk are available.

Kinetics: T½ (beta) = 4.7-10.5 hours
                 Peak 0.5 to 3 hours.
Recommendations: Withhold breastfeeding for at least 72 hours.

References:
1.   Pharmaceutical manufacturers prescribing information. 2005.

Anastrozole

Trade: Arimidex

Anastrozole is a potent and selective non-steroidal aromatase inhibitor. It significantly lowers serum estradiol concentrations and has no detectable effect on formation of adrenal corticosteroids or aldosterone. Orally administered anastrozole is well absorbed into the systemic circulation with 83 to 85% of the drug recovered in urine and feces. Anastrozole has a mean terminal elimination half-life of approximately 50 hours in postmenopausal women.[1] The major circulating metabolite of anastrozole, triazole, lacks pharmacologic activity. As with other aromatase inhibitors, this product, even in low concentrations in milk, could permanently bind to specific receptors, and potentially suppress estrogen formation completely in a breastfed infant. Mothers should discontinue breastfeeding for at least 15 days after consuming this medication

Kinetics: T½ = 50 hours

Recommendations: Mothers should discontinue breastfeeding for at least 15 days after consuming this medication.

References:
1.   Pharmaceutical manufacturers prescribing nformation. 2005.

Asparaginase

Trade: Kidrolase, L-asparaginase, Colaspase, L-ASP, Crasnitin, Elspar

Asparaginase is used for a number of different cancers. Asparaginase contains the enzyme L-asparagine amidohydrolase derived from E. Coli.   Asparaginase removes asparagine from leukemic cells, thus requiring that these cells obtain it from an exogenous source for survival, which cancer cells are unable to do normal cells. Fortunately, normal cells are able to synthesize asparagine.[1] It does not have active metabolites and does not pass the blood brain barrier (<1%). No data are available on its transfer to human milk. But due to its long half-life and large Vd, some Asparaginases may be present in milk.

Kinetics: T½ = 27-32 hours.
                        Vd = 245 L/kg

Recommendations: Withhold breastfeeding for a minimum of 7 days.

References:
1.   Pharmaceutical manufacturers prescribing information. 2005.

Bevacizumab

Trade: Avastin

Bevacizumab is a monoclonal IgG antibody that binds to vascular endothelial growth factor, preventing it from binding to endothelial receptors, thus blocking angiogenesis. This slows the growth of all tissues, including metastatic tissues. It is used in colorectal, lung, breast, prostate, and ovarian cancers, as well as for age-related macular degeneration.[1] There have been no studies reporting the concentration of bevacizumab in human milk; however, due to the large molecular weight, it is very unlikely that it would pass into the milk compartment. Nonetheless, caution should be used in a rapidly growing breastfeeding infant.

Kinetics: $T\frac{1}{2}$ = 20 days
            Vd = 0.046 L/kg

Recommendations: This product should be avoided in breastfeeding mothers, if possible. Even if small amounts were to penetrate milk, the gastric complications of this product in the infant could be significant. Mothers should be advised to discontinue breastfeeding following the use of this product.

References:
1.   Pharmaceutical Manufacturers prescribing information, 2006.

Bleomycin Sulfate

Trade: Blenoxane, Bleocin, Bleo-cell, Bleo-S

Bleomycin is used for a number of different cancers including: testicular, head and neck cancer, Hodgkin's and non-Hodgkin's lymphomas, and cervical cancer. Seventy percent of the dose is recovered in urine 24 hours after dosing.[1] The elimination of bleomycin is described by two bioexponential curves with a terminal $T\frac{1}{2}$(beta) of 134-238 minutes. In patients with severely reduced kidney function, the $T\frac{1}{2}$(beta) increases to 13.5 hours. No data are available on its transfer to milk, but its transfer to milk in clinically relevant levels is remote as its molecular weight is 1415 daltons. Secondly, its oral bioavailability is probably low to nil.

Kinetics: T½(beta) = 134-238 minutes
Vd = 0.35-0.45 L/kg

Recommendations: Withhold breastfeeding for at least 24 hours. Extend this recommendation in mothers with poor renal function.

References:
1.   Grochow LB, Ames MM. A clinician's guide to chemotherapy pharmacokinetics and pharmacodynamics. 1st ed. Baltimore, MD: Williams & Wilkins; 1998.

Busulfan

Trade: Myleran, Busilvex

Busulfan is an alkylating agent used in chronic myeloid leukemia, and bone marrow transplant. See monograph in this book for more data. Oral absorption varies enormously but is probably 100%. Its elimination is described by a monoexponential curve with a plasma elimination half-life of approximately 2.6 hours. Volume of distribution varies but is reported to be two to three fold higher in young children.[1] No data are available on the transfer of busulfan into human milk. However, approximately 20% enters the CNS, which suggest similar amounts could enter the milk compartment.

Kinetics: T½ = 2.6 hours
Vd = 0.94 L/kg

Recommendations: Withhold breastfeeding for at least 24 hours.

References:
1.   Pharmaceutical manufacturers prescribing information. 2005.

Capecitabine

Trade: Xeloda

Capecitabine is an antineoplastic agent commonly used in the treatment of colon cancer. It is converted enzymatically to the active drug 5-Fluorouracil.[1] Capecitabine is readily absorbed orally and rapidly metabolized in most tissues to 5-FU in about two hours following administration. Review the kinetics of fluorouracil for breastfeeding recommendations, as they will be the same for this product and fluorouracil.

Kinetics: T½ (capecitabine) = 38-45 minutes

Recommendations: See fluorouracil.

References:
1.   Pharmaceutical manufacturers prescribing information. 2005.

Carboplatin

Trade: Carboplat, Carbosin, Emorzim, Novoplat, Paraplatin

Carboplatin is a platinum derivative anticancer agent similar to cisplatin. Platinum agents have high affinity for plasma proteins.[1] Approximately 90% of carboplatin is covalently bound to plasma proteins after 24 hours. Estimates of plasma half-life are as high as 49 hours. Once bound and distributed, it has a large volume of distribution of 20-30 liters. However, carboplatin is apparently more rapidly cleared when compared to cisplatin. After 24 hours, only 23-35% of the platinum is still present, which is much less than with cisplatin. However, the T½(beta) is still long, about five days.[2] About 65% is eliminated renally in the first 24 hours, and the remaining 35% is retained for long periods in other tissues. See cisplatin for levels present in human milk.

Kinetics: T½ (alpha) = 49 hours
                T½ (beta) = 5 days
                Vd = 20-30 L

Recommendations: Two options are suggested. One, the breastmilk should be tested for platinum levels and not used as long as they are measurable. Two, without measuring platinum levels, breastfeeding should be permanently interrupted for this infant.

References:
1.   Pharmaceutical manufacturers prescribing information. 2005.
2.   Grochow LB, Ames MM. A clinician's guide to chemotherapy pharmacokinetics and pharmacodynamics. 1st ed. Baltimore, MD: Williams & Wilkins; 1998.

Carmustine - BCNU

Trade: BCNU, Becenun, Bicnu, Carmubris, Gliadel, Nitrumon

Carmustine is a alkylating agent of the nitrosourea type. Among its indications are brain tumors, gastric carcinoma, Hodgkin's lymphomas, and other syndromes. With a rather low molecular weight (214), it is best known for its ability to enter the CNS by crossing the blood-brain barrier.[1] This would suggest its ability to enter the milk compartment is significant. No data are available on its transfer to milk, however, initial transfer may be significant. The metabolism of this product is somewhat obscure, and may account to some degree for its lasting side effects. Further, the half-life is highly varied among patients (15-20 fold). Because of the prolonged and delayed side effect profiles (pulmonary injury) associated with this drug, mothers should delay breastfeeding for a minimum of 24-48 hours.

Kinetics: T½ (beta) = 12-45 minutes.
Vd = 2.59 L/kg

Recommendations: Withhold breastfeeding for a minimum of 24-48 hours.

References:
1.   Pharmaceutical manufacturers prescribing information. 2005.

Cetuximab

Trade: Erbitux

Cetuximab is a recombinant, human/mouse chimeric monoclonal antibody (152 kDa) that binds specifically to the human epidermal growth factor receptor, resulting in inhibition of cell growth, induction of apoptosis, and decreased matrix metalloproteinase and vascular endothelial growth factor production. Following a two-hour infusion of 400 mg/m^2 the mean elimination half-life was 97 hours (range 41-213 hours).[1] The volume of the distribution (Vd) for Erbitux appeared to be independent of dose and approximated the vascular space of 2-3 L/m^2. The manufacturer recommends mothers discontinue breastfeeding for 60 days, which would correspond with the longer half-life of this product.

Although no data are available on its transfer into human milk, some transfer into colostrum should be expected. The amount in mature milk would likely be exceedingly low as IgG levels in mature milk are low anyway (4mg/dL). When admixed and diluted with the plasma compartment IgG, few if any, molecules of cetuximab would enter mature milk.

Kinetics: $T\frac{1}{2}$ = 41-213 hours
                  Vd = 2-3 L/m^2

Recommendations: Withhold breastfeeding for less than 60 days.

References:
1.   Pharmaceutical manufacturers prescribing information, 2005.

Chlorambucil

Trade: Leukeran, Linfolysin, Alti-Chlorambucil

Chlorambucil is a derivative of nitrogen mustard with molecular weight of 304.[1] Administered orally, it is well absorbed (Oral= > 56%). Eliminated rapidly with a half-life of 1-2 hours. Only trace levels in CNS. Milk levels are unpublished, but probably low due to high protein binding, and amine structure.

Kinetics: $T\frac{1}{2}$= 1-1.9 hours

Recommendations: Withhold breastfeeding for at least 24 hours.

References:
1.   Grochow LB, Ames MM. A clinician's guide to chemotherapy
        pharmacokinetics and pharmacodynamics. 1st ed. Baltimore,
        MD: Williams & Wilkins; 1998.

Cisplatin

Trade: Cisplatin, Abiplatin, Bioplatino, Cis-Gry, C Platin, Placis, Platamine

Cisplatin is a platinum-containing anticancer agent. Platinum agents have high affinity for plasma proteins. Approximately 90% of cisplatin is covalently bound to plasma proteins within four hours. Following administration of radioactive cisplatin, cisplatin levels were eliminated in a biphasic manner. $T\frac{1}{2}$(alpha) was 25 to 49 minutes. $T\frac{1}{2}$(beta) was 58 to 73 hours. Other estimates of the terminal elimination half-life of total plasma cisplatin range between five to ten days. The volume of distribution is high, about 0.5 L/kg.[1] Platinum penetrates into tissues and is irreversibly bound to tissue proteins. Platinum can be found in these tissues for years afterward.

Plasma and breastmilk samples were collected from a 24 year old woman treated for three prior days with cisplatin (30mg/meter).(See monograph) On the third day, 30 minutes prior to chemotherapy, platinum levels in milk were 0.9 mg/L and plasma levels were 0.8 mg/L.   In another study, no cisplatin was found in breastmilk, following a dose of 100 mg/meter[2]. Other studies suggest that milk levels are ten-fold lower than serum levels in an older lactating woman.   These studies generally support the recommendation that mothers should not breastfeed while undergoing cisplatin therapy or withhold breastfeeding for many days (>20-30).

Kinetics: T½(beta) = < 130 hours
             Vd = 0.5 L/kg

Recommendations: Two options are suggested. One, the breastmilk should be tested for platinum levels and not used as long as they are measurable. Two, without measuring platinum levels, breastfeeding should be permanently interrupted for this infant.

References:
1.   Grochow LB, Ames MM. A clinician's guide to chemotherapy pharmacokinetics and pharmacodynamics. 1st ed. Baltimore, MD: Williams & Wilkins; 1998.
2.   DeConti RC, Toftness BR, Lange RC, et al: Clinical and pharmacological studies with cis-diamminedichloroplatinum (II). Cancer Res 1973; 33:1310-1315.

Cladribine

Trade: Leustatin, Leustat, Litak

Cladribine is an antimetabolitew, antineoplastic, purine nucleoside analog used for various forms of leukemia, multiple sclerosis, etc. Oral absorption ranges from 37-55%. The manufacturer reports a biphasic or triphasic elimination for this drug. For patients with normal renal function, the manufacturer reports the mean terminal half-life was 5.4 hours. Others report Cladribine plasma concentrations after intravenous administration declines multi-exponentially, with an average half-life of 6.7±2.5 hours.[1] In general, the apparent volume of distribution of cladribine is approximately <9 L/kg, indicating extensive sequestration in body tissues. Cladribine penetrates into cerebrospinal fluid which suggests it might enter milk as well. One report indicates that concentrations are approximately 25% of those in plasma. Other reports suggest that the terminal half-life is much longer, as high as 19 hours. Following a two-hour infusion in 12 adult patients receiving cladribine 0.14 mg/kg/day, cladribine has an alpha half-life of 35 +/- 12 minutes and a beta half-life of 6.7 +/- 2.5 hours. No data are available on its transfer into human milk, but the mother should pump and discard her milk for at least 48 hours.

Kinetics: T½ (beta) = 5.4 - 6.7 hours
Vd= 0.7 - 9 L/kg

Recommendations: Withhold breastfeeding for a minimum period of 48 hours. Adjust longer for patients with poor renal clearance.

References:
1.   Pharmaceutical manufacturers prescribing information. 2005.

Cyclophosphamide

Trade: Cytoxan, Cycloblastin, Carloxan, Cicloxal, Endoxana

Cyclophosphamide(CP) is commonly used in many treatments, including breast cancer. This family requires activation (metabolism) by the liver to produce the active cytotoxic agents. The oral bioavailability of CP is 75% and reaches a peak at one to two hours. The elimination half-life (T½ beta) is 7.5 hours.[1] The active metabolites stay in the plasma compartment with brief half-lives of four hours or less. Transport of CP and its metabolites into the CNS is exceedingly low. This would suggest milk levels will be low as well when they are ultimately determined. The kinetics of this agent are highly variable depending on renal function, creatinine clearance, liver function, etc. Waiting periods before returning to breastfeeding should be adjusted for this factor.

Kinetics: T½ beta = 7.5 hours
Vd = 0.7 L/kg

Recommendations: Withhold breastfeeding for a period of at least 72 hours.

References:
1.   Pharmaceutical manufacturers prescribing information. 2005.

Cytosine Arabinoside

Trade: Cytarabine, Alexan, Arabine, Cytosar

Cytarabine is an antimetabolite and antineoplastic agent commonly used in the treatment of acute lymphoid leukemia in adults and children. Cytarabine is rapidly metabolized by the liver and GI mucosa, and it is not effective orally: less than 20% of the orally administered dose is absorbed from the gastrointestinal tract.

Following rapid intravenous injection of cytarabine, the disappearance from plasma is biphasic. There is an initial distributive phase with a half-life of about ten minutes, followed by a second elimination phase with a half-life of about one to three hours.[1] After the distributive phase, more than 80% of the drug can be accounted for by the inactive metabolite 1-ß-D-arabinofuranosyluracil (ara-U). Ara C is essentially cleared from the body by conversion to ara-U. Within 24 hours about 80 percent of the administered drug is recovered in the urine, approximately 90 percent of which is excreted as ara-U. No data are available on its transfer to milk but levels would probably be quite low.

Kinetics: T½ (beta) = 1-3 hours
Vd = 0.6 L/kg
Oral=<20%

Recommendations: Withhold breastfeeding for at least 24-48 hours.

References:
1.   Pharmaceutical manufacturers prescribing information. 2005.

Dactinomycin

Trade: Cosmegen, Actinomycin D

Dactinomycin is one of the actinomycins, a group of antibiotics produced by various species of Streptomyces, and it is used to treat Wilm's tumor, Ewing's saarcoma, and many other malignancies.

After single or multiple IV doses, dactinomycin is rapidly distributed into and extensively bound to body tissues. Results of a study with radioactive actinomycin D in patients with malignant melanoma indicate that dactinomycin is minimally metabolised, is concentrated in nucleated cells, and does not appreciably penetrate the blood brain barrier (<10%). Approximately 30% of the dose is recovered in urine and feces in one week.[1] The terminal plasma half-life for radioactivity was approximately 36 hours. Dactinomycin is concentrated in nucleated cells. Concentrations are highest in bone marrow and tumor cells relative to plasma.

It has a molecular weight of 1255, which would probably reduce its entry into the milk compartment. No data are available on its transfer to human milk, but it is probably quite low. That withstanding, it is extremely cytotoxic. Mothers should abstain from breastfeeding for at least ten days.

Kinetics: T½= 36 hours

Recommendations: Mothers should abstain from breastfeeding for at least 10 days.

References:
1.   Pharmaceutical manufacturers prescribing information, 2005.

Daunorubicin

Trade: Cerubidin, Daunoblastina, Daunoblastin, DaunoXome

This is a typical anthracycline agent used in many forms of cancer, including: acute myelogenous, and lymphocytic leukemias, and others. As with doxorubicin, it is widely distributed to many body tissues. It is eliminated from the plasma compartment with a triphasic elimination curve. Its last elimination T½ (gamma) ranges from 11.2 to 47.4 hours, depending on the dose. It is rapidly metabolized to daunorubicinol which achieves a Cmax at 24 hours.[1] Daunorubicinol has a half-life of approximately 20-37 hours. No data are available on the transfer of this anthracycline into human milk. However, a close congener, doxorubicin, has been measured in milk, and the levels are low, but prolonged. Mothers should probably withhold breastfeeding for a minimum of seven to ten days.

Kinetics: T½ (daunorubicinol) = 20-40 hours.
                Vd= 1725 L/m²

Recommendations: Withhold breastfeeding for a minimum of seven to ten days.

References:
1.   Pharmaceutical manufacturers prescribing information. 2008.

Docetaxel

Trade: Taxotere

Docetaxel is an antineoplastic agent derived from the yew plant. It has a large molecular weight of 861 Da and acts by disrupting the mitotic and interphase cellular functions. Docetaxel's pharmacokinetic profile is consistent with a three-compartment kinetic model, with half-lives for the alpha, beta and gamma of 4 min, 36 min, and 11.1 hr, respectively. Oral bioavailability is just 8%. The initial rapid decline represents distribution to the peripheral compartments, and the late (terminal) phase is due, in part, to a relatively slow efflux of docetaxel from the peripheral compartment. Mean value for steady state volume of distribution is 113 L.[1] Within seven days, urinary and fecal excretion accounted for approximately 6% and 75% of the administered radioactivity, respectively. About 80% of the radioactivity recovered in feces is excreted during the first 48 hours, as metabolites with very small amounts (less than 8%) of unchanged drug. No data are available on its transfer into human milk. Due to its large molelcular weight and high protein binding, milk levels are probably quite low. However, mothers should be advised to withhold breastfeeding for a minimum of four to five days.

Kinetics: T½ (gamma) = 11.1 hours
Vd = 1.6 L/kg

Recommendations: Withhold breastfeeding for a minimum of four to five days.

References:
1.   Pharmaceutical manufacturers prescribing information, 2005.

Doxorubicin

Trade: Adriamycin, Adriblastina, Caelyx

A classic anthracycline, doxorubicin is one of a number in this family. Doxorubicin, when administered, reaches a rapid Cmax and disappears from the plasma compartment with a 3-exponential decay characterized by three differing half-lives, three to five minutes, one to two hours, and 24-36 hours.[1]   A fourth curve has been identified with a half-life of 110 hours which accounts for approximately 30% of the total AUC.   The last two elimination curves are probably due to this products high volume of distribution.   In essence, it is distributed and stored in sites remote from the plasma compartment and leaks into the plasma over many days thereafter. Levels of doxorubicin in milk have been published and are relatively low. However, the peak in milk occurred at 24 hours. Because this product is detectable in plasma (and milk) for long periods, a waiting period of approximately seven to ten days is recommended.

The kinetics of this agent are highly variable, depending on renal function, creatinine clearance, liver function, etc. Waiting periods before returning to breastfeeding should be adjusted for this factor.

Kinetics: T½ gamma = 24-36 hours
Vd = 25 L/kg

Recommendations: Withold breastfeeding for at least seven to ten days.

References:
1. Grochow LB, Ames MM. A clinician's guide to chemotherapy pharmacokinetics and pharmacodynamics. 1st ed. Baltimore, MD: Williams & Wilkins; 1998.

Epirubicin

Trade: Ellence, Epi-Cell, Farmorubicina, Pharmarubicin, Rubina

Epirubicin is an anthracycline similar to but less cardiotoxic than doxorubicin. It is used for the treatment of breast, lung, and bladder cancer. The terminal T½ (gamma) is 31.2 hours, even though the plasma levels are much lower than doxorubicin.[1] The volume of distribution is variable among studies, but is similar if not higher than doxorubicin. No data are available on its transfer to milk, but it is probably as low if not lower than doxorubicin. Mothers should be advised to discontinue breastfeeding for at least seven to ten days following the use of this product.

Kinetics: T½ (gamma) = 35 hours
Vd = 33 L/kg

Recommendations: Withhold breastfeeding for at least seven to ten days.

References:
1. Grochow LB, Ames MM. A clinician's guide to chemotherapy pharmacokinetics and pharmacodynamics. 1st ed. Baltimore, MD: Williams & Wilkins; 1998.
2. Pharmaceutical manufacturers prescribing information, 2005.

Erlotinib

Trade: Tarceva

Erlotinib is a human epidermal growth factor receptor inhibitor. It has a molecular weight of 429 and a pKa of 5.42.[1] Erlotinib is about 60% absorbed after oral administration, and its bioavailability is substantially increased by food to almost 100%. Its half-life is about 36 hours. Bioavailability of erlotinib following a 150 mg oral dose of TARCEVA is about 60%, and peak plasma levels occur four hours after dosing. Following absorption, erlotinib is approximately 93% protein bound to albumin and alpha-1 acid glycoprotein (AAG). Erlotinib has an apparent volume of distribution of 232 liters. No data are available on its transfer to human milk, but its entry into milk is likely minimal due to its size and pKa. However, because of its enormous volume of distribution, mothers should withhold breastfeeding for a minimum of 10-15 days.

Kinetics: T½ = 36 hours
                 Vd = 3.31 L/kg

Recommendations: Withhold breastfeeding for a minimum of 10-15 days.

References:
1.   Pharmaceutical manufacturers prescribing information. 2008.

Etoposide

Trade: Toposar, Abiposid, Celltop, Eposid, Eposin, Etopofos, Etopophos

Etoposide is an inhibitor of mitosis. It is commonly used to treat testicular, lung, and other cancers, and in bone marrow transplant. Oral bioavailability ranges from 50% to higher, and it is apparently associated with the dose, with lesser absorption at higher doses.[1] Etoposide is approximately 95% bound to plasma proteins. On intravenous administration, the disposition of etoposide is best described as a biphasic process, with a distribution phase half-life of about 1.5 hours and terminal elimination half-life ranging from four to eleven hours. No data are available on the transfer of etoposide into human milk; however, it is likely low. Mothers should withhold breastfeeding for at least two to three days following exposure to this agent.

Kinetics: T½ = 4-11 hours
Vd = 0.25- 0.41 L/kg

Recommendations: Withhold breastfeeding for two to three days.

References:
1.   Pharmaceutical manufacturers prescribing information, 2005.

Everolimus

Trade: Afinitor

Everolimus is a macrolide immunosuppressant intended for acute rejection prophylaxis after kidney transplantation. Everolimus blocks growth factor–driven transduction signals in the T-cell response to alloantigen. It is currently used as an immunosuppressant to prevent organ transplant rejections. It has a large molecular weight and is unlikely to enter the milk compartment at high levels. However it is very fetotoxic in pregnant women and its use in breastfeeding mothers with infants should be avoided.

Kinetics: T1/2 = 30 hours
Protein binding = 74%
Molecular weight = 958 daltons
Vd   =1.57 L/kg

Recommendations: Withhold breastfeeding for a minimum of 150 hours.

References:
1.   Pharmaceutical manufacturers prescribing information, 2010.

Exemestane

Trade: Aromasin

Exemestane is an irreversible, steroidal aromatase inactivator. It acts as a false substrate for the aromatase enzyme, causing its inactivation. Exemestane significantly lowers circulating estrogen concentrations in women, and it is useful in the treatment of estrogen-receptor positive breast cancer.[1]   After maximum plasma concentration is reached, levels decline polyexponentially with a mean terminal half-life of about 24 hours. It is 90% bound to plasma proteins. No data are available on its transfer to human milk. Steroids in general do not transfer significantly, so exemestane levels in milk are probably low. However, this product works irreversibly. Any present in milk could potentially suppress estrogen levels in a breastfed infant. It is not advisable to breastfeed an infant while consuming this product. A withholding period of five to seven days is recommended should the mother opt to discontinue taking this product and restart breastfeeding.

Kinetics: T½ = 24 hours.

Recommendations: Discontinue breastfeeding, if this product is used chronically. Withhold breastfeeding for at least five to seven days if discontinued.

References:
1.   Pharmaceutical manufacturers prescribing information, 2005.

Fluorouracil

Trade: Adrucil, Carac, Cytosafe, Efudex, Effluderm, Fluoroplex

Fluorouraci (5-FU) is a uracil analog used to treat a number of cancers. It is used topically for actinic keratosis, breast cancer, colorectal cancer, condyloma acuminatum, and many other cancers. Oral absorption is highly variable but averages less than 50-80%. Topical absorption through intact skin is less than 6-10%.[1] Ninety percent of the dose is accounted for during the first 24 hours, following intravenous administration.[2] Intravenous administration of fluorouracil, the mean half-life of elimination from plasma is approximately sixteen minutes, with a range of eight to twenty minutes, and is dose dependent. No intact drug can be detected in the plasma three hours after an intravenous injection. No data are available on the transfer of 5-FU to human milk. Mothers receiving injected 5-FU (IV, IM, IP) should be advised to withhold breastfeeding for a minimum of 24 hours after exposure.

Kinetics: T½ (parent) = 8-20 minutes
                 T½ (metabolites) = 52 minutes
                 Vd = 9 L/m^2

Recommendations: Mothers receiving injections of 5-FU should withhold breastfeeding for a minimum of 24 hours. Those receiving topical therapy would not need to discontinue breastfeeding, if the surface area is minimal.

References:
1.   Grochow LB, Ames MM. A clinician's guide to chemotherapy pharmacokinetics and pharmacodynamics. 1st ed. Baltimore, MD: Williams & Wilkins; 1998.
2.   Pharmaceutical manufacturers prescribing information, 2005.

Gemcitabine

Trade: Gemzar

Gemcitabine is a nucleoside analogue used for the treatment of metastatic breast cancer, non-small cell lung cancer, and pancreatic cancer.   Gemcitabine elimination follows a two phase elimination curve. The terminal elimination half-life is reported to be 49 minutes in females but can range to as high as 638 minutes following long infusions.[1] The volume of distribution following short infusions (< 70 min.) was 50 L/m^2, indicating that gemcitabine, after short infusions, is not extensively distributed into tissues. For long infusions, the volume of distribution rose to 370 L/m^2, reflecting slow equilibration of gemcitabine within the tissue compartment. Gemcitabine is metabolized to an active metabolite, gemcitabine triphosphate, which can be extracted from peripheral blood mononuclear cells. The half-life of the terminal phase for gemcitabine triphosphate from mononuclear cells ranges from 1.7 to 19.4 hours. Within one week, 92% to 98% of the dose was recovered, almost entirely in the urine. No data are available on its transfer to milk, but gemcitabine levels in milk are probably quite low, due to its low pKa(3.6). Women should be advised to withhold breastfeeding for seven days.

Kinetics: T½ (short infusions) = 49 minutes
T½ (long infusions) = 245-638 minutes
Vd (short infusions) = 50 L/m^2
Vd (long infusions)   = 370 L/m^2

Recommendations: Withhold breastfeeding for a minimum of seven days.

References:
1.   Pharmaceutical manufacturers prescribing information, 2005.

Hydroxyurea

Trade: Hydrea

Hydroxyurea is an antineoplastic agent used to treat melanoma, leukemias, and other neoplasms. It is well absorbed orally and rapidly metabolized to urea by the liver. In one study following a dose of 500 mg three times daily for seven days, milk samples were collected two hours after the last dose.[1] The concentration of hydroxyurea in breastmilk averaged 6.1 mg/L (range 3.8 to 8.4 mg/L). Hydroxyurea is rapidly cleared from the plasma compartment and appears to leave no residuals or metabolites. Approximately 80% of the dose is excreted renally with 12 hours.

Kinetics: T½ = 3-4 hours
Vd = 0.48 to 1.62 L/kg

Recommendations: Mothers receiving hydroxyurea should withhold breastfeeding for a minimum of 24 hours.

References:
1.   Sylvester RK, Lobell M, Teresi ME, Brundage D, Dubowy R. Excretion of hydroxyurea into milk. Cancer 1987; 60(9):2177-2178.

Ifosfamide

Trade: Holoxan, Ifex, Ifolem, Holoxane

Ifosfamide (IF) is structurally similar to Cyclophosphamide and is used in breast cancer. This family requires activation (metabolism) by the liver to produce the active cytotoxic agents. The oral bioavailability of IF is near 100% and reaches a peak at one to two hours.[1] IF is eliminated with a mono exponential curve. The elimination half-life (T½ beta) ranges from 3.8 to 8.6 hours. Active metabolites stay in the plasma compartment with brief half-lives of four to six hours or less. Transport of IF and its metabolites into the CNS is exceedingly low (approximately 1/6th of the plasma compartment). This would suggest milk levels will probably be low, when they are ultimately determined. The kinetics of this agent are highly variable depending on renal function, creatinine clearance, liver function, etc. Waiting periods before returning to breastfeeding should be adjusted for this factor.

Kinetics: T½= 3.8-8.6 h
Vd = 0.72 L/kg

Recommendations: Withhold breastfeeding for at least 72 hours.

References:
1.   Pharmaceutical Manufacturers Package Insert, 2007.

Imatinib

Trade: Gleevec

Imatinib mesylate (Gleevec) is a tyrosine kinase inhibitor used to treat several different types of tumors and leukemias. The metabolite half life is 40 hours, which means that 81% would be eliminated from the mother in seven days.[1] No data are available on the transfer of this medication into human milk, but due to the overt toxicity of this product, breastfeeding mothers should withhold breastfeeding for at least ten days after taking this medication. The milk should be pumped and discarded during this time.

Kinetics: T½ (metabolite) = 40 hours
T½ (parent) = 13 to 18 hours

Recommendations: Withhold breastfeeding for at least ten days following last use of this product.

References:
1.   Pharmaceutical Manufacturers Package Insert, 2007.

Ixabepilone

Trade: Ixempra

Ixabepilone is a microtubule inhibitor belonging to a class of antineoplastic agents, the epothilones and their analogs. It is approved for the treatment of aggressive metastatic or locally advanced breast cancer no longer responding to currently available chemotherapies.

No data are available on its entry into human milk but small levels should be expected in milk due to its chemistry.

Kinetics: T1/2 = 52 hours
Protein binding = 77%
Molecular weight = 506 daltons
Vd   =14.2 L/kg

Recommendations: Withhold breastfeeding for at least 260 hours. Discard milk.

References:
1.   Pharmaceutical manufacturers prescribing information, 2010.

Lapatinib

Trade: Tykerb

Lapatinib or lapatinib ditosylate is an orally active drug for the treatment of breast cancer (naive, ER+/EGFR+/HER2+ breast cancer patients) ("triple positive") and other solid tumors. It is a dual tyrosine kinase inhibitor. It has been approved as front-line therapy in triple positive breast cancer and as an adjuvant therapy when patients have progressed on Herceptin.   There are no data available on its use in breastfeeding mothers. Due to its high volume of distribution and high protein binding, milk levels will probably be exceedingly low once determined.

Kinetics: T1/2 = 24 hours
Protein binding = >99%
Molecular weight = 581 daltons
Vd   = 31.4 L/kg

Recommendations: Withhold breastfeeding for 120 hours. Discard milk.

References:
1.   Pharmaceutical manufacturers prescribing information, 2010.
2.   Medina PJ, Goodin S. Lapatinib: a dual inhibitor of human epidermal growth factor receptor tyrosine kinases. Clin Ther. 2008 Aug;30(8):1426-47. Review.

Letrozole

Trade: Femara

Femara is a non-competitive inhibitor of estrogen synthesis, and it is used for treatment of estrogen-dependent tumors, particularly breast cancer. Letrozole's terminal elimination half-life is about two days and steady-state plasma concentration after daily 2.5 mg dosing is reached in two to six weeks.[1] It has a high volume of distribution and is generally used for long periods. It is well absorbed orally. No data are available on its transfer into human milk. However, this product works irreversibly and any present in milk could potentially suppress estrogen levels in a breastfed infant. It is not advisable to breastfeed an infant while consuming this product.

Kinetics: T½ = 2 days
                  Vd = 1.9 L/kg

Recommendations: Discontinue breastfeeding while taking this product or for a period of ten days following its discontinuation.

References:
1.   Pharmaceutical manufacturers prescribing information, 2005.

Melphalan

Trade: Alkeran

Melphalan is an alkalating agent used in the treatment of multiple myeloma, rhabdomyosarcoma, and carcinoma of the ovary. Oral bioavailability in adults averages 61%, but it is highly variable by patient and even ranges from 9-58% in some patients.[1] Due to the wide variability, it is most commonly used IV at higher doses. The terminal elimination half-life is 1.5 hours but can vary to as high as three hours. Penetration into CNS fluid is low. No data are available on its transfer to human milk, but levels are probably quite low. Mothers should be advised to withhold breastfeeding for at least 24 hours following treatment.

Kinetics: T½ = 1.5 hours
                  Vd = 0.5 L/kg

Recommendations: Withhold breastfeeding for at least 24 hours.

References:
1.   Pharmaceutical manufacturers prescribing information, 2005.

Mercaptopurine

Trade: Purinethol, 6-MP

Mercaptopurine is an anticancer drug that acts intracellularly as an purine antagonist, ultimately inhibiting DNA and RNA synthesis.[1] It is the active metabolite of the drug azathioprine. See azathioprine.

Kinetics: T½ = 21 to 90 minutes
Vd = 0.9 L/kg

Recommendations: Risk is modest. See azathioprine.

References:
1.   Pharmaceutical manufacturer prescribing information. 1995.

Methotrexate

Trade: Folex, Rhedumatrex, Arthitrex, Ledertrexate, Methoblastin

Methotrexate is a potent and potentially dangerous folic acid antimetabolite used in arthritic and other immunologic syndromes. It is also used as an abortifacient in tubal pregnancies. Methotrexate is secreted into breastmilk in small levels.[1] Following a dose of 22.5 mg to one patient two hours post-dose, the methotrexate concentration in breastmilk was 2.6 ug/L of milk with a milk/plasma ratio of 0.08. The cumulative excretion of methotrexate in the first twelve hours after oral administration was only 0.32 ug in milk. These authors conclude that methotrexate therapy in breastfeeding mothers would not pose a contraindication to breastfeeding.   However, methotrexate is believed to be retained in human tissues (particularly neonatal GI cells and ovarian cells) for long periods (months).[2]   Oral bioavailability is apparently low in children approximating 33%.[3]   Elimination of methotrexate is by a two-compartment model with a terminal elimination half-life of eight to fifteen hours. Patients with poor renal function have prolonged methotrexate half-lives. It is apparent that the concentration of methotrexate in human milk is minimal, although due to the toxicity of this agent, it is probably wise to pump and discard the mother's milk for a minimum of four days. This may require extending if the dose used is quite high.

Kinetics: T½ = 8-15 hours.
Vd = 2.6 L/kg

Recommendations: Withhold breastfeeding for a minimum of four days.

References:
1.   Johns DG, Rutherford LD, Leighton PC, Vogel CL. Secretion of methotrexate into human milk. Am J Obstet Gynecol 1972; 112(7):978-980.
2.   Fountain, JR, Hutchinson DJ, Waring GB, Burchenal JH. Persistence of amethopterin in normal mouse tissues. Proc Soc Exp Biol Med 1953; 83(2):369-373.
3.   Pharmaceutical manufacturers prescribing information. 2005.

Mitomycin

Trade: Mutamycin, Mitomycin-C

Mitomycin is an antibiotic antineoplastic agent used for the treatment of cancer of the stomach, breast, pancreas, and numerous other cancers. Oral absorption is erratic due to its instability in aqueous media, so it is always used intravenously.[1] It is eliminated via a biexponential curve with a T½ (alpha) of two to thirteen minutes, and a T½ (beta) of 23-78 minutes. No data are available on its transfer into human milk. Mothers should be advised to withhold breastfeeding for a minimum of 24-48 hours.

Kinetics: T½= 23-78 minutes.
MW = 334
Vd= 11-48 L/m²

Recommendations: Withhold breastfeeding for a minumum of 24-48 hours.

References:
1.   Pharmaceutical manufacturers prescribing information. 2005.

Mitoxantrone

Trade: Novantrone, Formyxan, Genefadrone, Misostol, Mitoxal, Onkotrone, Pralifan

Mitoxantrone is used for various forms of cancer and even multiple sclerosis. It is similar to doxorubicin, but with less cardiotoxicity. Terminal elimination is described by a three-compartment model. The mean alpha half-life of mitoxantrone is six to twelve minutes, the mean beta half-life is 1.1 to 3.1 hours and the mean gamma (terminal or elimination) half-life is 23 to 215 hours (median approximately 75 hours).[1] Distribution to tissues is extensive: steady-state volume of distribution exceeds $1,000 \ L/m^2$. Tissue concentrations of mitoxantrone appear to exceed those in the blood during the terminal elimination phase. Levels in milk have not been reported, but mothers exposed to this medication should withhold breastfeeding for a minimum of 10-31 days.

Kinetics: $T\frac{1}{2} = 23$ to 215 hours. Median 75 hours.
                 $Vd = 14\text{-}24.7 \ L/kg$

Recommendations: Withhold breastfeeding for a minimum of 10-31 days.

References:
1.   Pharmaceutical manufacturers prescribing information. 2005.

Nilotinib

Trade: Tasigna

Nilotinib is used for the treatment of chronic myelogenous leukemia. Studies suggest it has a relatively favorable safety profile. Nilotinib is an inhibitor of the Bcr-Abl kinase. Nilotinib binds to and stabilizes the inactive conformation of the kinase domain of Abl protein. Nilotinib was developed as a second-generation inhibitor of BCR-ABL tyrosine kinase that would be effective in patients with imatinib-resistant or -intolerant CML.

The drug carries a black box warning for possible heart complications. No data are available on its transfer into human milk. Due to its high protein binding, levels in milk will probably be low. Further, its oral bioavailability is poor which would reduce oral absorption in infants.

Kinetics: T1/2 = 17 hours
Protein binding = 98%
Molecular weight = 529 daltons
Oral bioavailability = 30%

Recommendations: Withhold breastfeeding for 120 hours.

References:
1.   Pharmaceutical manufacturers prescribing information, 2010.

Ofatumumab

Trade: Arzerra

Ofatumumab is a humanized monoclonal antibody that binds specifically to both the small and large extracellular loops of the CD20 molecule. It is a cytolytic product indicated for the treatment of patients with chronic lymphocytic leukemia (CLL) refractory to fludarabine and alemtuzumab.

No data are available on its use in breastfeeding mothers. However, this product does not appear overly toxic to a fetus or older individuals. The major complication is heightened rate of pneumonia or infections due to depletion of B cells. Due to its large molecular weight and the fact that it is an IgG FAB product, milk levels are likely to be quite low. Oral bioavailability will be low as well.

Kinetics: T1/2 = 14 days
Molecular weight = 149,000 daltons
Vd = 0.07 L/kg

Recommendations: Withhold breastfeeding for one month.

References:
1.   Pharmaceutical manufacturers prescribing information, 2010.

Oxaliplatin

Trade: Eloxatin, Eloxatine, O-Plat, Oxalip

Oxaliplatin is a platinum compound. Its kinetics are similar to cisplatin with a biexponential model of elimination. The decline of ultrafilterable platinum levels following oxaliplatin administration is triphasic, characterized by two relatively short distribution phases (T½; 0.43 hours and T½; 16.8 hours) and a long terminal elimination phase (T½; 391 hours).[1] Check cisplatin for published milk levels. Oxaliplatin is extensively bound in peripheral tissues, which accounts for its extraordinarily long elimination half-life. While breastmilk levels are unavailable, but are probably low, breastfeeding is not advisable for many days (>20-30) and should probably be discontinued for this infant, unless milk platinum levels could be measured.

Kinetics: T½(beta) = 38.7 hours
                 Vd = very high

Recommendations: Two options are suggested. One, breastmilk should be tested for platinum levels and not used as long as they are measurable. Two, without measuring platinum levels, breastfeeding should be permanently interrupted for this infant.

References:

1.   Grochow LB, Ames MM. A clinician's guide to chemotherapy pharmacokinetics and pharmacodynamics. 1st ed. Baltimore, MD: Williams & Wilkins; 1998.
2.   Pharmaceutical manufacturers prescribing information, 2005.

Paclitaxel

Trade: Abraxane, Abitaxel, Biotax, Paxel, Paxene, Taxol

Paclitaxel is an antimicrotubule agent that inhibits reorganization of the microtubule network essential for mitosis in cells. It is commonly used in Kaposi's sarcoma, metastatic breast cancer and numerous other cancers. Paclitaxel is eliminated in a biphasic manner with a terminal elimination T½ (beta) of about 27 hours. It has a huge volume of distribution, which suggests extensive extravascular distribution/ binding to peripheral tissues.[1] This is potentially hazardous to breastfeeding infants. No data are available on the transfer of paclitaxel into human milk. Mothers should withhold breastfeeding for at least six to ten days following the use of paclitaxel.

Kinetics: T½ (beta) = 27 hours
                 Vd = 632 L/m^2

Recommendations: Withhold breastfeeding for at least six to ten days.

References:

1.   Pharmaceutical manufacturers prescribing information, 2005.

Pazopanib

Trade:

Pazopanib is a multi-tyrosine kinase inhibitor of vascular endothelial growth factor receptor (VEGFR)-1, VEGFR-2, VEGFR-3, platelet-derived growth factor receptor (PDGFR)-a and -b, fibroblast growth factor receptor (FGFR) -1 and -3, cytokine receptor (Kit), interleukin-2 receptor inducible T-cell kinase (Itk), leukocyte-specific protein tyrosine kinase (Lck), and transmembrane glycoprotein receptor tyrosine kinase (c-Fms). It profoundly blocks angiogenesis and could be profoundly hazardous to a newborn infant. No data are available on its transfer into human milk, but it should be expected to enter milk in low levels.

Kinetics: T1/2 =   31 hours
Molecular weight =   473 daltons
Oral = good

Recommendations: Withhold breastfeeding for 150 hours. Discard milk.

References:
1.   Pharmaceutical manufacturers prescribing information, 2010.

Pentostatin

Trade: Nipent

Pentostatin is indicated for the treatment of untreated and alpha-interferon-refractory hairy cell leukemia. It is poorly bound to proteins (< 4%).[1] In humans, the mean terminal half-life is reported to be 5.7 hours, but is increased to 18 hours in patients with poor renal function. No data are available on the transfer of this agent into human milk. Mothers should withhold breastfeeding for a minimum of two days, following exposure to this agent or up to five days if renal function is poor.

Kinetics: T½ = 3-18 hours (mean= 5.7 hours)
Vd = 0.5 L/kg

Recommendations: Withhold breastfeeding for two days or up to five days, if renal function is poor.

References:
1.   Pharmaceutical manufacturers prescribing information, 2005.

Raloxifene

Trade: Evista

Raloxifene is a selective estrogen receptor modulator (SERM) that has estrogenic actions on bone and anti-estrogenic actions on the uterus and breast. It blocks such estrogen effects as those that lead to breast cancer and uterine cancer. In addition, it also prevents bone loss and improved lipid profiles. It is used to prevent osteoporosis in postmenopausal women. It is poorly absorbed orally (2%). While we do not have data on its transfer into human milk, levels are likely probably quite low. That present in milk would not be orally absorbed to any degree in infants. While the manufacturer suggests it is contraindicated in breastfeeding women, short-term exposure may not be overtly hazardous. Long-term exposure should be avoided.

Kinetics: T1/2 = 27-32 hours
Oral = 2%
Protein binding = > 95%
Molecular weight = 510 daltons
Vd = 2348 L/kg

Recommendations: Probably Ok in short-term exposure, avoid long-term exposure.

References:
1.   Pharmaceutical Manufacturer Prescribing Information. 2010.

Rituximab

Trade: Rituxan

Rituximab, a large IgG antibody, binds to the CD20 antigen found on the surface of B lymphocytes.[1] It is used in the treatment of non-Hodgkin's lymphoma, rheumatoid arthritis, and lymphoid leukemia. There are no reported levels in human milk. Levels of IgG antibodies in human milk are generally low. In addition, oral bioavailability of this protein is likely to be nil.

Kinetics: T½ = 206 hours
                 Vd = 4.3 L/kg

Recommendations: Mothers who are less than two weeks postpartum should not breastfeed.   Because of numerous risks and the prolonged half-life of this product, mothers should probably not breastfeed following the use of this product.

References:
1.   Pharmaceutical Manufacturer Prescribing Information. 2007.

Temozolomide

Trade: Temodar, Temodal

Temozolomide is an alkylating agent used to treat refractory anaplastic astrocytoma and newly-diagnosed glioblastoma multiforme. Temozolomide is converted to MTIC spontaneously under physiologic conditions.[1] MTIC alkylates DNA primarily at the O6 and N7 positions of guanine, thus demonstrating its cytotoxic activity.[1] No studies have been performed regarding the transmission of the drug into milk, however, it is highly likely that temozolomide would transfer into the milk compartment, due to the low volume of distribution and molecular weight. Temozolomide would be orally bioavailable to an infant and thus should not be used in a nursing mother. In male infants, it could be genotoxic or cause damage to DNA.

Kinetics: T½ = 1.8 hours (parent drug)
                 Vd = 0.4 L/kg
                 MW=194

Recommendations: Temozolomide is an extremely toxic agent, and infants should be withdrawn from the breast for a prolonged period of at least seven days.

References:
1.   Pharmaceutical Manufacturer Prescribing Information. 2005.

Tamoxifen

Trade: Nolvadex, Tamofen, Tamone, Eblon, Noltam, Genox, Tamoxen

Tamoxifen is an nonsteroidal antiestrogen (See individual monograph). It attaches to the estrogen receptor and produces only minimal stimulation, thus it prevents estrogen from stimulating the receptor. Aside from this, it also produces a number of other effects within the cytoplasm of the cell, and some of its anticancer effects may be mediated by its effects at sites other than the estrogen receptor.

Tamoxifen is metabolized by the liver and has an elimination half-life of greater than seven days (range 3-21 days). It is well absorbed orally. It is 99% protein bound and normally reduces plasma prolactin levels significantly (66% after three months). At present, there are no data on its transfer into breastmilk; however, it has been shown to inhibit lactation early postpartum in several studies. One study describes complete interruption of postpartum engorgement and lactation. In a second study, tamoxifen doses of 10 mg four times daily significantly reduced serum prolactin and inhibited milk production as well. We do not know the effect of tamoxifen on established milk production. It has a pKa of 8.85, which may suggest some trapping in milk compared to the maternal plasma levels. This drug has all the characteristics that would suggest a concentrating mechanism in breastfed infants over time. Its potent effect in reducing maternal prolactin levels could inhibit early lactation, and may ultimately inhibit established lactation. In this instance, the significant risks to the infant from exposure to tamoxifen probably outweigh the benefits of breastfeeding. Mothers receiving tamoxifen should not breastfeed, until we know more about the levels transferred into milk and the plasma/tissue levels found in breastfed infants.

Kinetics: T½ = 3-21 days

Recommendations: Mothers receiving tamoxifen should not breastfeed.

References:
See individual monograph.

Teniposide

Trade: Vumon, Vehem

Teniposide is a semisynthetic derivative of podophyllotoxin. It is similar to etoposide chemically. Teniposide has a broad spectrum of in vivo antitumor activity against murine tumors, including hematologic malignancies and various solid tumors. Plasma drug levels declined biexponentially following intravenous infusion (155 mg/m^2 over 1 to 2.5 hours) of Teniposide given to eight children (4-11 years old) with newly diagnosed acute lymphoblastic leukemia (ALL).[1] The terminal elimination half-life was 5.4 hours. Mean steady-state volumes of distribution range from 8 to 44 L/m^2 for adults and 3 to 11 L/m^2 for children. Teniposide is highly (99%) protein bound and does not readily enter the CNS. These kinetics alone would suggest milk levels are probably exceedingly low. However, no data are yet available on the transfer of this product into human milk.

Kinetics: T½ = 5.4 hours
                  Vd = 8-44 L/m^2

Recommendations: Withhold breastfeeding for a minimum of 36-48 hours.

References:
1.   Pharmaceutical manufacturers prescribing information, 2005.

Toremifene

Trade: Fareston

Toremifene is a nonsteroidal agent that binds to estrogen receptors without producing an estrogenic response, hence blocking further estrogenic activity from that receptor. It is well aborbed orally (100%).[1]   The plasma concentration time profile of toremifene declines biexponentially after absorption, with a mean distribution half-life of about four hours and an elimination half-life of about five days. Toremifene has an apparent volume of distribution of 580 L and binds extensively (>99.5%) to serum proteins, mainly to albumin. No data are available on its transfer to milk, but its molecular weight of 580 and high protein binding will probably reduce its entry into milk. However, the potential for severe interruption of estrogen levels in breastfed infants would largely suggest this agent should not be used in breastfeeding mothers. Breastfeeding mothers should withhold breastfeeding for a minimum of 25-30 days.

Kinetics: T½ = 5 days
            Vd = 580 L/m^2

Recommendations: Withhold breastfeeding for a minimum of 25-30 days.

References:
1.   Pharmaceutical manufacturers prescribing information, 2005.

Trastuzumab

Trade: Herceptin

Trastuzumab is a therapy for women with metastatic breast cancer, whose tumors have too much HER2 protein. For patients with this disease, Herceptin is approved for first-line use in combination with paclitaxel. Trastuzumab is a recombinant DNA-derived monoclonal antibody that selectively binds to the extracellular receptor domain of the human epidemal growth factor protein (HER2). The antibody is an IgG1 kappa antibody that binds to HER2 receptor.

The manufacturer reports conducting a study in lactating cynomolgus monkeys at doses 25 times the weekly human maintenance dose of 2 mg/kg Trastuzumab, which demonstrated that Trastuzumab is secreted in their milk (no levels reported).[1] The presence of Trastuzumab in the serum of infant monkeys was not associated with any adverse effects on their growth or development from birth to three months of age. It is not known whether trastuzumab is secreted in human milk. IgG levels in collostrum are much higher, but IgG is normally present in mature human milk only at low levels, only 4 mg/dL. After a dose of 2mg/kg Trastuzumab, only 1 in approximately every 432 molecules of IgG would be this drug, thus the dose to infant daily would be infinitesimally small. It is unlikely that levels in 'mature' human milk will be high enough to produce untoward symptoms in human infants, but this has not yet been demonstrated. Caution is nevertheless recommended.

Kinetics: T½ = 5.8 days
            Vd = 44 mL/kg

Recommendations: The risk is low, but unknown at this time. Mothers should probably not breastfeed while taking this medication.

References:
1.   Pharmaceutical manufacturers prescribing information. 2005.

Vinblastine

Trade: Velban, Velbe, Velsar, Lemblastine

Vinblastine is an antineoplastic agent derived from the Catharanthus alkaloids familly. It is commonly used in numerous cancers including: breast, Kaposi's sarcoma, Hodgkin's, choriocarcinoma, and many others. Vinblastine has a triphasic elimination with half-lifes of 3.7 minutes, 1.6 hours, and 24.8 hours respectively.[1] No data are available on its transfer into human milk, but its levels are probably low due to a molecular weight of 909 Da.[2] However, mothers should be advised to withhold breastfeeding for a minimum of 10 days following treatment.

Kinetics: T½ = 24.8 hours (range=3-29 hours depending on dose)
                 Vd = 18.9-27.3 L/kg (dose dependent)

Recommendations: Withhold breastfeeding for a minimum of 10 days.

References:
1.   Grochow LB, Ames MM. A clinician's guide to chemotherapy pharmacokinetics and pharmacodynamics. 1st ed. Baltimore, MD: Williams & Wilkins; 1998.
2.   Pharmaceutical manufacturers prescribing information, 2005.

Vincristine

Trade: Oncovin, Citomid, Farmistin, Ifavin, Norcristine, Vincizina

Vincristine is an antineoplastic agent derived from the Catharanthus alkaloids familly. It is commonly used in numerous cancers including: breast, Kaposi's sarcoma, non-Hodgkin's, lymphoma, and many others. Vincristine has a molecular weight of 923 Da. The kinetic studies thus far are highly variable and exact data is lacking. Vincristine exhibits a large and variable volume of distribution and ranges from 8.4 to 10.8 L/kg.[1] Studies in patients suggest it has a triphasic elimination pattern with initial, middle, and terminal half-lives of five minutes, 2.3 hours, and 85 hours respectively. However, the terminal elimination half-live sometimes ranges from 19-155 hours depending on the individual patient. No data are available on its transfer into human milk, but its levels are probably low due to a molecular weight of 923 Da. However, mothers should be advised to withhold breastfeeding for a minimum of 35 days following treatment, as this product is slowly eliminated from the body.[2]

Kinetics: T½ (gamma) = 19-155 hours
Vd = 8.4-10.8 L/kg

Recommendations: Withhold breastfeeding for a minimum of 35 days.

References:
1.   Grochow LB, Ames MM. A clinician's guide to chemotherapy pharmacokinetics and pharmacodynamics. 1st ed. Baltimore, MD: Williams & Wilkins; 1998.
2.   Pharmaceutical manufacturers prescribing information, 2005.

Vinorelbine

Trade: Navelbine, Biovelbin

Vinorelbine is a close congener of vincristine. It is used for the treatment of advanced breast cancer, non-small cell lung cancer, non-Hodgkin's lymphoma, Hodgkin's disease, and ovarian carcinoma. In a number of studies, the terminal elimination half-life ranged from 31.2 to 80 hours. The volume of distribution in these studies ranged from 25 to 75.6 L/kg. No data are available on the transfer of this agent into human milk. Mothers should abstain from breastfeeding for a minimum of 30 days.

Kinetics: T½ (gamma) = 31.2-80 hours
Vd = 25-75.6 L/kg

Recommendations: Withhold breastfeeding for a minimum of 30 days.

References:
1.   Grochow LB, Ames MM. A clinician's guide to chemotherapy pharmacokinetics and pharmacodynamics. 1st ed. Baltimore, MD: Williams & Wilkins; 1998.
2.   Pharmaceutical manufacturers prescribing information, 2005.

Appendix B

Using Radiopharmaceutical Products in Breastfeeding Mothers

The use of radioactive products in breastfeeding mothers must be approached with great care. Invariably, the administration of a radiopharmaceutical to a lactating mother will result in some transfer of radioactivity into her milk. The relative dose received by the infant is dependent on a number of factors, but most importantly by the radioactive dose administered, the absorption and distribution of the radioisotope, the biological and radioactive half-life of the product, and the amount that enters milk. The following table presents data from some of the best sources in the world and provides their recommendations on interrupting breastfeeding to allow for the decay and/or clearance of the radiopharmaceutical. Most of their decisions were based on the probable radioactive 'dose' transferred to the infant, and whether or not it was considered hazardous. Please note that some of their recommendations conflict. Ultimately the mother and her radiologist will have to assess the relevancy of this data in their own situation.

- When evaluating radiopharmaceuticals, it is important to understand that all of these products have "two" half-lives. One is the radioactive half-life of the isotope. This half-life is set and invariable. While we prefer shorter half-life products like ^{99m}Technetium (6.02 h), many other isotopes have important uses in medicine. The second half-life is the 'biological' or 'effective' half-life of the specific product. Many of these products are rapidly eliminated from the body via the kidney, some within minutes to hours. Thus the 'biological or effective' half-life is critical and sometimes is so fast that the radiopharmaceutical is gone from body long before its isotope is decayed (see ^{111}In-Octreotide). However, some isotopes such as the radioactive iodides (^{131}I, ^{125}I) may be retained in the body for long periods and present extraordinary hazards to the breastfeeding infant. Lastly, two units of radioactivity are commonly used by differing sources. Just remember that one mCi (millicurie) is equal to 37 MBq (megabecquerel). Regardless of the unit you are given, you can now convert them easily.

1 millicurie = 37 megabecquerel

Some important points to remember about evaluating these products in breastfeeding mothers are:

- Use the shortest half-life product permitted such as ^{99m}Technetium. It's half-life is so short, and its radioactive emissions are so weak, that it poses little risk (but this depends on dose). While the table below often does not even require interrupting breastfeeding, I still suggest that waiting even 12-24 hours before breastfeeding would virtually eliminate all possible risks associated with this isotope.

- Regardless of the isotope used, if the dose is extremely high, then withholding breastfeeding for a minimum of five to as many as ten radioactive half-lives is probably advisable.

- Measuring the radioactivity present in milk is the most accurate way to determine risk. This often requires sophisticated equipment not available in most hospitals, but it is the "final" determinant of risk to the infant. If the isotope present in milk approaches 'background' levels, there is no risk.

- Use great caution before returning to breastfeeding if the Iodides are used. Iodine is selectively concentrated in the thyroid gland, the lactating breast (17% of dose), and breastmilk, and high doses could potentially lead to thyroid cancer in the infant. ^{131}I and ^{125}I are potentially of high risk due to their long radioactive half-lives and their affinity for thyroid tissues. ^{123}I has a much shorter half-life, and brief interruptions may eliminate most risks.

- Because radioactivity decays at a set rate, milk can be stored in the freezer for at least eight to ten half-lives and then fed to the infant without problem. All of the radioactivity will be gone.

Typical Radioactive Half-Lives

Radioactive Element	Half-Life
Mo-99	2.75 Days
TI-201	3.05 Days
TI-201	73.1 Hours
Ga-67	3.26 Days
Ga-67	78.3 Hours
I-131	8.02 Days
Xe-133	5.24 Days
In-111	2.80 Days
Cr-51	27.7 Days
I-125	60.1 Days
Sr-89	50.5 Days
Tc-99m	6.02 Hours
I-123	13.2 Hours
Sm-153	47.0 Hours

Activities of Radiopharmaceuticals That Require Instructions and Records When Administered to Patients Who Are Breast-Feeding an Infant or Child.*

Radiopharmaceutical	COLUMN 1 Activity Above Which Instructions Are Required		COLUMN 3 Examples of Recommended Duration of Interruption of Breast-Feeding*
	MBq	mCi	
I-131 NaI	0.01	0.0004	Complete cessation (for this infant or child)
I-123 NaI	20	0.5	
I-123 OIH	100	4	
I-123 mIBG	70	2	24 hr for 370 MBq (10mCi) 12 hr for 150 MBq (4 mCi)
I-125 OIH	3	0.08	
I-131 OIH	10	0.30	
Tc-99m DTPA	1,000	30	
Tc-99m MAA	50	1.3	12.6 hr for 150 Mbq (4mCi)
Tc-99m Pertechnetate	100	3	24 hr for 1,100 Mbq (30mCi) 12 hr for 440 Mbq (12 mCi)
Tc-99m DISIDA	1,000	30	
Tc-99m Glucoheptonate	1,000	30	
Tc-99m HAM	400	10	
Tc-99m MIBI	1,000	30	
Tc-99m MDP	1,000	30	
Tc-99m PYP	900	25	
Tc-99m Red Blood Cell In Vivo Labeling	400	10	6 hr for 740 Mbq (20 mCi)

Radiopharmaceutical	COLUMN 1 Activity Above Which Instructions Are Required		COLUMN 3 Examples of Recommended Duration of Interruption of Breast-Feeding*
Tc-99m Red Blood Cell In Vitro Labeling	1,000	30	
Tc-99m Sulphur Colloid	300	7	6 hr for 440 Mbq (12 mCi)
Tc-99m DTPA Aerosol	1,000	30	
Tc-99m MAG3	1,000	30	
Tc-99m White Blood Cells	100	4	24 hr for 1,100 Mbq (5 mCi) 12 hr for 440 Mbq (2 mCi)
Ga-67 Citrate	1	0.04	1 month for 150 Mbq (4 mCi) 2 weeks for 50 Mbq (1.3 mCi) 1 week for 7 Mbq (0.2 mCi)
Cr-51 EDTA	60	1.6	
In-111 White Blood Cells	10	0.2	1 week for 20 Mbq (0.5 mCi)
T1-201 Chloride	40	1	2 weeks for 110 Mbq (3 mCi)

* The duration of interruption of breast-feeding is selected to reduce the maximum dose to a newborn infant to less than 1 millisievert (0.1 rem), although the regulatory limit is 5 millisieverts (0.5 rem). The actual doses that would be received by most infants would be far below 1 millisievert (0.1 rem). Of course, the physician may use discretion in the recommendation, increasing or decreasing the duration of the interruption.

If there is no recommendation in Column 3 of this table, the maximum activity normally administered is below the activities that require instructions on interruption or discontinuation of breast-feeding.

*Source: Nuclear Regulatory Commission. For a more complete table see :   http://neonatal.ttuhsc.edu/lact/

Radioactive Diagnostic Procedures

Diagnostic Procedure	Radiopharmaceutical	Dosing Range (mCi)	Comments*
Brain Serotonin levels	^{11}C-WAY 100635	14.2	100 minute interruption
	^{11}C-RACLOPRIDE	10.3	100 minute interruption (see monograph). No interruption[8]
WBC scan	^{99m}Tc-WBC	10-15	12-24 hour interruption for 2-5 mCi or more
	^{99m}Tc-Ceretec	10-24	
	^{111}In-WBC	0.5	1 week interruption for 0.5 mCi[1]
Cystogram (voiding)	^{99m}Tc-SC, ^{99m}Tc-O$_4$-	0.5-1	6 hour interruption for 12 mCi[1]
Liver/spleen scan	^{99m}Tc-SC (sulfur colloid)	2-4	6 hour interruption for 12 mCi[1]
Bone marrow scan	^{99m}Tc-SC	<20	6 hour interruption for 12 mCi[1]
Lymphoscintigraphy	^{99m}Tc-SC	100-800 µCi	No interruption[1]
Liver SPECT (hemangioma)	^{99m}Tc-pyp-RBCs	20-30	12 hour interruption for 25-30 mCi[3]
Myocardial (MI) scan	^{99m}Tc-pyp	20-30	12 hour interruption for 25-30 mCi[3]

Radioactive Diagnostic Procedures			
Diagnostic Procedure	Radiopharmaceutical	Dosing Range (mCi)	Comments*
Meckel's diverticulum	$^{99}mTc\text{-}O_4$	10-15	24 hours for 30 mCi[1] 12 hours for 12 mCi[1]
Testicular scan	$^{99}mTcO_4$	0-25	24 hours for 30 mCi[1] 12 hours for 12 mCi[1]
Thyroid scan	$^{99}mTcO_4$	1-2	24 hours for 30 mCi[1] 12 hours for 12 mCi[1]
Bone scan	$^{99}mTc\text{-MDP, -HDP}$	<30	No interruption for 30 mCi or less[1]
MUGA scan	$^{99}mTc\text{-labeled-RBCs}$	20-30	6 hour interruption of breastfeeding for 20 mCi[1]
Lung ventilation imaging	$^{99}mTc\text{-DTPA}$ (labeled aerosol)	30	No interruption for 30 mCi or less[1]
Renal scan	$^{99}mTc\text{-DTPA}$	10-15	No interruption for 30 mCi or less[1]
Renal scan	$^{99}mTc\text{-DMSA}$	3-10	No interruption for 2-5 mCi or less[1]
Brain scan	$^{99}mTc\text{-}D_4\text{-, -DTPA, -GH}$	<20-30	No interruption for 30 mCi or less[1]

Radioactive Diagnostic Procedures

Diagnostic Procedure	Radiopharmaceutical	Dosing Range (mCi)	Comments*
HIDA (cholescintigraphy)	^{99}mTc-Choletec, Hepatolite,	3-5	No interruption for 4 mCi or less[2]
Brain scan-SPEC	^{99}mTc-Ceretec or Neurolite	20-30	24 hours for 30 mCi[1]
Parathyroid scan Subtraction:	^{99}mTc-Cardiolite	16-30	No interruption for < 30 mCi[3]
	^{201}Tl	2-3	2 week interruption for 3 mCi[1]
	^{99}mTc-D$_4$-	5-12	
Scintimammography	^{99}mTc-Cardiolite	20	No interruption for < 30 mCi[3]
CEA-Scan^R	^{99}mTc-arcitumomab	20-30	24 hours for 30 mCi[3]
Cardiac Studies	^{99}mTc, Cardiolite or Myoview	7- 30	No interruption for < 30 mCi[3]
Infections – labeled with HMPAO	^{99}mTc WBC	3-10	24 hour interruption for 5 mCi[1]
			12 hour interruption for 2 mCi[1]

Radioactive Diagnostic Procedures

Diagnostic Procedure	Radiopharmaceutical	Dosing Range (mCi)	Comments*
Gastroesophageal emptying time-liquids	99mTc Sulfur Colloid	1	6 hours for 12 mCi[1]
Gastroesophageal emptying time-solids		0.5	6 hours for 12 mCi[1]
		5	6 hours for 12 mCi[1]
SPECT Analysis – Liver		2	No interruption period[2]
Perfusion study –cardiac	99mTc Sestamibi Teboroxime	25	No interruption for < 30 mCi[3]
Adenoma- parathyroid		20	
MUGA Scan for cardiac gated ventriculography	99mTc RBC	20	6 hour interruption of breastfeeding[1]
Bleeding Scan of GI tract			
Liver Scan for Hemangioma			
Bleeding Scan of GI tract	99mTc RBC	20	6-12 hour interruption of breastfeeding[1,4]
Liver Scan for Hemangioma		20	

Radioactive Diagnostic Procedures

Diagnostic Procedure	Radiopharmaceutical	Dosing Range (mCi)	Comments*
Myocardial Infarct	99mTc Pyrophosphate	15	No interruption required[1]
		20	No interruption required[4]
	99mTc Plasmin	0.5	No interruption[2]
Diagnostic Imaging of thyroid	99mTc Pertechnetate	5	12 hour interruption of breastfeeding[1]
Meckel's Scan of GI tract		21	47 hour interruption[2]
		2	25 hour interruption[2]
	99mTc Microspheres	2.7	17 hour interruption[2]
	99mTc MIBI	27	No interruption[2]
Bone – osteomyelitis	99mTc MDP	20	No interruption for 30 mCi or less[1]
	99mTc Leukoscan	20.3	10 hour interruption[9]
Renal Blood Flow, Clearance	99mTc MAG3	10	No interruption for 30 mCi or less[1]
		11	Interruption for 5 hours[2]
		2.7	No interruption[2]

Radioactive Diagnostic Procedures

Diagnostic Procedure	Radiopharmaceutical	Dosing Range (mCi)	Comments*
Perfusion studies of Lung	99mTc-MAA (microaggregated albumin)		12.6 hours for 4 mCi[1]
Biliary Atresia - Cholecystitis -HIDA	99mTc IDA derivative	5	No interruption required[1]
SPECT Analysis of Brain Perfusion	99mTc HMPAO	20	No interruption required[1]
		13.5	No interruption required[2]
	99mTc Glucoheptonate	22	No interruption[2]
	99mTc HAM	8	No interruption[4]
	99mTc Sulfur colloid	12	No interruption[4]
	99mTc Ferrous hydroxide MA		Interruption with measurment[2]
	99mTc Erythrocytes	22	17 hour interruption[2]
	99mTc EDTA	10	No interruption[2]

Radioactive Diagnostic Procedures

Diagnostic Procedure	Radiopharmaceutical	Dosing Range (mCi)	Comments*
CNS Perfusion Renal perfusion/filtration	[99m]Tc DTPA	30	No interruption for 30 mCi or less[1]
		10 or 20	No interruption[2]
		22	No interruption[2]
	[99m]Tc DMSA	2.2	No interruption[2]
Kidney parenchyma imaging kidney DTPA + DMSA	[99m]Tc DMSA Glucoheptonate	5	No interruption required
		10	No interruption required
		2.2	No interruption[1],[2]
Unspecific uses	[99m]Tc DISIDA	4-8	No interruption[2]
	[99m]Tc Diphosphonate	16.2	No interruption[2]
	[75]Se Methionine	0.3	450 hour interruption or complete cessation[2]
Infections Tumors imaging	[67]Ga Citrate	5	1 month interruption for 4 mCi[1]
		5	2 weeks interruption for 1.3 mCi[1]
			1 weeks interruption for 0.2 mCi[1]
		4	20 day interruption[2]

Radioactive Diagnostic Procedures

Diagnostic Procedure	Radiopharmaceutical	Dosing Range (mCi)	Comments*
Gallium scan (tumor)	^{67}Ga	5-10	1 month interruption for 4 mCi[1]
Gallium scan for infections	^{57}Ga	5-10	1 month interruption for 4 mCi[1]
Schilling	^{57}Co- B$_{12}$	0.3-0.5	Feed infant following B12 loading. Avoid feeding at 24 hour peak if possible.[5]
Unspecified	^{51}Cr EDTA	0.1	No interruption[2]
	^{32}P Na phosphate	Any	Complete cessation of breastfeeding[2]
Cardiac perfusion and stress tests	^{201}Tl Chloride	3+1	2 week interruption for 3 mCi[1]
		2.2	No interruption[2]
Cardiac stress test	^{201}Tl	2.5-3.5	2 week interruption for 3 mCi[1]
		3	96 hours[4]
Brain Scan		3	48 hour interruption[7]
Glucose Metabolism Tumor Imaging	^{18}F-FDG	1.35-4.32	Risk from proximity to breast, not milk itself[10]

Radioactive Diagnostic Procedures

Diagnostic Procedure	Radiopharmaceutical	Dosing Range (mCi)	Comments*
Lung ventilation	[133]Xe Gas	10-30	1 hour interruption for washout[1]
Lung ventilation imaging	[133]Xe	10-15	1 hour interruption[1]
Renogram	^{131}I-OIH	0.15-0.3	No interruption needed[1]
MIBG (adrenal medulla)	^{131}I-MIBG	0.5	25 days interruption[3]
Adrenocortical Scan	^{131}I-Iodomethyinorcholesterol	2	Complete cessation of breastfeeding or until counts are baseline[3]
Thyroid hyperthyroid therapy	[131]I Sodium diffuse nodular	1-10 <30	Complete cessation of breastfeeding or until counts are baseline[1]
Thyroid ablation		30-300 108	Complete cessation of breastfeeding or until counts are baseline[1] 52 days[6]
Thyroid Diagnostic imaging – (post thyroidectomy)	[131]I Sodium	5	Complete cessation of breastfeeding or until counts are baseline.[1]

Radioactive Diagnostic Procedures

Diagnostic Procedure	Radiopharmaceutical	Dosing Range (mCi)	Comments*
Tumor Imaging	[131]I MIBG	1.5	Complete cessation of breastfeeding or until counts are baseline.[3]
	[131]I HSA		Complete cessation of breastfeeding or until counts are baseline.[2]
Renal Blood flow and clearance	[131]I Hippuran	0.25	
		0.05	34 hours interruption[2]
Thyroid scan (substernal)	[131]I	< 0.1	Complete cessation of breastfeeding or until counts are baseline.[1]
Whole-body ^{131}I carcinoma work-up	[131]I	1-5	Complete cessation of breastfeeding or until counts are baseline.[1]
	[125]I HSA	0.2	277 hour interruption or complete cessation[2]
	[125]I Hippuran	0.05	23 hour cessation[2]
	[125]I Fibrinogen	0.1	620 hour interruption or complete cessation.[2]

Radioactive Diagnostic Procedures

Diagnostic Procedure	Radiopharmaceutical	Dosing Range (mCi)	Comments*
Pheochromocytoma scan	[123]I	3-10	Complete cessation of breastfeeding or until counts are baseline.[3]
Thyroid Imaging Scans	[123]I Sodium	0.4	Complete cessation of breastfeeding or until counts are baseline.[1]
	[123]I Hippuran	0.5	27 hour interruption[2]
	[123]I MIBG	0.5	11 hour interruption[2]
		11	21 hour interruption[2]
Thyroid uptake and scan	[123]I	< 0.35	No interruption of breastfeeding[1]
OncoScint	^{111}In-satumomab pendetide	4-6	14 day interruption[3]
OctreoScan	^{111}In-pentetriotide	6	72 hour interruption[3]
Cisternogram	[111]Indium-DTPA	0.5-1.5	14 day interruption[3]
ProstaScint	^{111}In-CYT-356	5-17	14 day interruption[3]

Radioactive Diagnostic Procedures

Diagnostic Procedure	Radiopharmaceutical	Dosing Range (mCi)	Comments*
Infections	[111]In WBC	0.5	1 week interruption for 0.5 mCi[1]
CSF – imaging neuroendocrine tumors	[111]In Octreotide	5.3	<10 day interruption (see monograph)
CSF – cisternogram, shunt patency	[111]In DTPA	0.5	1 week interruption for 0.5 mCi[1]
	[111]In Leucocytes	0.5	No interruption[2]

The recommendations in the table above were derived by calculating the dose and time required to limit the ingested effective dose to the infant below 1 mSv. Please be advised, these recommendations still permit a minimal amount of radiation transfer to the infant that is considered safe by the authorities. The only way to totally avoid any radiation is to wait for all of it to decay (5-10 half-lives).

*Recommendations by the following sources:

1. Activities of Radiopharmaceuticals from the Nuclear Regulatory Commission.
2. Montford PJ. Textbook of Radiopharmacy. Third Edition. Gordon and Breach Publishers 1999.
3. T.W. Hale Ph.D.
4. Stabin MG, Breitz HB. Breast milk excretion of radiopharmaceuticals: mechanisms, findings, and radiation dosimetry. J Nucl Med 2000 41(5):863-73.
5. Pomeroy KM, Sawyer LJ, Evans MJ. Estimated radiation dose to breast feeding infant following maternal administration of 57Co labelled to vitamin B12. Nucl Med Commun 2005 Sep;26(9):839-41.
6. Robinson PS, Barker P, Campbell A, Henson P, Surveyor I, Young PR. Iodine-131 in breast milk following therapy for thyroid carcinoma. J Nucl Med 1994 Nov;35(11):1797-801.
7. Johnson RE, Mukherji SK, Perry RJ, Stabin MG. Radiation dose from breastfeeding following administration of thallium-201. J. Nucl Med 1996 Dec;37(12):2079-82.
8. Moses-Kolko EL, Meltzer CC, Helsel JC, Sheetz M, Mathis C, Ruszkiewicz J et al. No interruption of lactation is needed after (11)C-WAY 100635 or (11)C-raclopride PET. J Nucl Med 2005 Oct;46(10):1765.
9. Prince JR, Rose MR. Measurement of radioactivity in breast milk following 99mTc-Leukoscan injection. Nucl Med Commun 2004 Sep;25(9):963-6.
10. Hicks RJ, Binns D, Stabin MG. Pattern of uptake and excretion of (18)F-FDG in the lactating breast. J Nucl Med 2001 Aug;42(8):1238-42.

Appendix C

Radiocontrast Agents

Iodinated Radiocontrast Agents:

As a group, Iodinated Radiocontrast Agents are used as contrast agents in Computed Axial Tomography or CAT scans. In this procedure, X-rays are passed through the body, while the contrast agent is circulating. The iodine in the contrast agent absorbs the X-ray and thus appears white or dense, consequently highlighting hemorrhages or other lesions with high vascularity. With virtually all the iodinated contrast agents, the iodine is covalently bound to the molecule; hence, it is not free to move into other compartments like free iodine. As a result, these contrast agents generally are restricted to plasma and body water and are virtually excluded from the milk compartment. However, very small amounts of iodine may be metabolized and released as "free" iodine. This is usually very small and would not affect thyroid function in a newborn, other than transiently.

Gadolinium-Containing Radiocontrast Agents:

Gadolinium-containing contrast agents are used for Magnetic Resonance Imaging (MRI). As with the iodinated products, the gadolinium metal is tightly bound to the molecule and is unable to become free in the plasma. Just as with the above contrast agents, this product is largely restricted to plasma and body water, although it is able to penetrate tissues to a greater degree than the iodinated products. Unlike CAT scans, MRI uses a powerful magnetic field to align the magnetization of hydrogen atoms in the body which is detected by the scanner. To date, we have a few studies suggesting that gadolinium-containing contrast agents penetrate milk poorly and would be virtually unabsorbed orally. Therefore, they are of little risk to a breastfeeding infant.

The American College of Radiology has reviewed these agents and generally suggests that they are of little or no risk to a breastfeeding infant.[1]

Reference:
1. http://www.acr.org/MainMenuCategories/about_us/
committees/gpr-srp/AdministrationofContrastMediumtoNursing
MothersDoc1.aspx

Barium Sulfate

Trade: Baro-cat, Prepcat, Bear-E-Yum CT, Cheetah, Medescan, Enecat CT, Tomocat, EntroEase, Entrobar, Liquid Barosperse, Bear-E-Yum GI, HD 85, Imager ac, Flo-Coat, Medebar Plus, Epi-C, Liqui-Coat HD, EntroEase Dry, Barosperse, Tonopaque, Barobag, Baricon, Enhancer, HD 200 Plus, Intropaste, Anatrast

Barium sulfate is available in a wide variety of concentrations, from 1.5% to 210%, under many trade names. It is not absorbed orally; therefore, none will enter the maternal milk compartment or cause harm to a breastfeeding infant. No interruption in breastfeeding is necessary.

Kinetics: Oral Bioavailability = None

Lactation Risk Category: L1

References:
1.   Pharmaceutical Manufacturers prescribing information, 2008.

Diatrizoate

Trade: Angiovist, Cardiografin, Cystografin, Ethibloc, Gastrovist, Hypaque, Reno-30, Reno-60, Reno-Dip, Renografin, Reno-M, Retrografin, Sinografin, Urovist

Diatrizoate is an iodinated containing radiopaque medium used in a wide variety of x-rays. These radiocontrast agents range from 8.5 to 59.87% iodine.[1] However, the iodine is covalently bound to the molecule and is poorly released after injection, most being eliminated in the urine rapidly. Reported levels in breastmilk are very low. In a study of a single patient who received 18.5 grams of iodine in the form of sodium and meglumine salts of diatrizoate, diatrizoate levels were undetectable (LOD < 2 mg/L).[2] In another woman who received 93 grams of Iodine as diatrizoate, total iodine transferred into breast milk in the first 24 hours was 0.03% or 31 mg.[3]

Based on kinetic data, the American College of Radiology suggests that it is safe for mothers to continue breastfeeding after receiving iodinated x-ray contrast media.[4]

Kinetics: T1/2 = 120 minutes
Oral Bioavailability = 0.04-1.2%
Protein Binding = 0-10%
MW=614

Lactation Risk Category: L2

References:

1.   Pharmaceutical Manufacturers prescribing information, 2002.
2.   Fitz John, T. P., Williams, D. G., Laker, M. F., and Owen, J. P. Intravenous urography during lactation. Br. J Radiol. 55(656): 603-605, 1982.
3.   Texier, F., Roque, d. O., and Etling, N. [Stable iodine level in human milk after pulmonary angiography]. Presse Med. %19;12(12): 769, 1983.
4.   ACR Committee on Drugs and Contrast Media. Administration of contrast medium to breastfeeding mothers. 2004;42-43.

Gadobenate

Trade: MultiHance

Gadobenate is a gadolinium-containing radiocontrast agent used in MRIs. Although free gadolinium is neurotoxic, it is safe when bound to the parent molecule in the contrast medium. There have been no studies on its transfer into human milk, but it is unlikely that it would accumulate in therapeutic levels.[1] The American College of Radiology concludes that it is safe for a mother-infant dyad to continue breastfeeding after the administration of a gadolinium-containing contrast medium.[2]

Kinetics: T1/2 = 1.17-2.02 hours
Oral Bioavailability = Poor
Protein Binding = Low

Lactation Risk Category: L3

References:

1.   Pharmaceutical Manufacturers prescribing information, 2007.
2.   ACR Committee on Drugs and Contrast Media. Administration of contrast medium to breastfeeding mothers. 2004;42-43.

Gadodiamide

Trade: Omniscan

Gadodiamide is a gadolinium-containing nonionic, non-iodinated water soluble contrast medium commonly used in Magnetic Resonance Imaging scans.[1] It is quite similar to Magnevist, another gadolinium-containing agent. These agents penetrate peripheral compartments poorly, especially the brain. As such, they are extremely unlikely to enter milk as well. Data for gadopentetate (Magnevist) support this, as its transfer into milk is negligible (<0.04%). Neither of these compounds is well absorbed orally, and neither is metabolized to any degree. It is likely that gadodiamide will penetrate milk only minimally.

Kinetics: T1/2 = 77 minutes
             Oral Bioavailability = Nil
             Protein Binding = 0%

Lactation Risk Category: L3

References:
1.   Pharmaceutical Manufacturers prescribing information, 2007.

Gadopentetate

Trade: Magnevist, Magnevistan, Magnograf, Viewgam

Gadopentetate is a radiopaque agent used in magnetic resonance imaging of the kidney. It is non-ionic, non-iodinated, has low osmolarity and contains a gadolinium ion as the radiopaque entity. Following a dose of 7 mmol (6.5 gm), the amount of gadopentetate secreted in breastmilk was 3.09, 2.8, 1.08, and 0.5 μmol/L at 2, 11, 17, and 24 hours respectively.[1] The cumulative amount excreted from both breasts in 24 hours was only 0.023% of the administered dose. Oral absorption is minimal, only 0.8% of gadopentetate is absorbed. These authors suggest that only 0.013 micromole of a gadolinium-containing compound would be absorbed by the infant in 24 hours, which is incredibly low. They further suggest that 24 hours of pumping would eliminate risks, although this seems rather extreme in view of the short (1.6 hr) half-life, poor oral bioavailability, and limited milk levels.

In another study of 19 lactating women who received 0.1 mmol/kg and one additional woman who received 0.2 mmol/kg, the cumulative amount of gadolinium excreted in breastmilk during 24 hours was 0.57 μmol.[2] This resulted in an excreted dose of <0.04% of the IV administered maternal dose. A similar amount was noted in the patient receiving a double dose (0.2 mmol/kg). As a result, for any neonate weighing more than 1000 gm, the maximal orally ingested dose would be less than 1% of the permitted intravenous dose of 0.2 mmol/kg. According to the authors, "...that the very small amount of gadopentetate dimeglumine transferred to a nursing infant does not warrant a potentially traumatic 24-hour suspension of breastfeeding for lactating women."

Kinetics: T1/2 = 1.5-1.7 hours
            Oral Bioavailability = 0.8%

Lactation Risk Category: L2

References:
1.   Rofsky NM, Weinreb JC, Litt AW. Quantitative analysis of gadopentetate dimeglumine excreted in breast milk. J Magn Reson Imaging 1993; 3(1):131-132.
2.   Kubik-Huch RA, Gottstein-Aalame NM, Frenzel T, Seifert B, Puchert E, Wittek S, Debatin JF. Gadopentetate dimeglumine excretion into human breast milk during lactation. Radiology 2000; 216(2):555-558.

Gadoteridol

Trade: Prohance

Gadoteridol is a non-ionic, non-iodinated gadolinium chelate complex used as a radiocontrast agent in MRI scans. The metabolism of gadoteridol is unknown, but a similar gadolinium salt (gadopentetate) is not metabolized at all. The half-life is brief (1.6 hours), and the volume of distribution is very small. This suggests that gadoteridol does not penetrate tissues well and is unlikely to penetrate milk in significant quantities. A similar compound, gadopentetate, is barely detectable in breastmilk. Although not reported, the oral bioavailability is probably similar to gadopentetate, which is minimal to none. No data are available on the transfer of gadoteridol into human milk, although it is probably minimal.

Kinetics: T1/2 = 1.57 hours
             Oral Bioavailability = Poor

Lactation Risk Category: L3

References:
1.   Pharmaceutical Manufacturers prescribing information, 2007.

Gadoversetamide

Trade: Optimark

Gadoversetamide is a paramagnetic agent used as a contrast agent in magnetic resonance imaging (MRI). It does not enter most compartments and is confined to extracellular water with a low volume of distribution.[1] As with gadopentetate, this agent is very unlikely to penetrate milk or be orally bioavailable. However, no human data are available. Rat studies show some penetration of gadoversetamide into rat milk but rodent lactation studies do not correlate with humans.

Kinetics: T1/2 = 1.7 hours
             Oral Bioavailability = Nil
             Protein Binding = None

Lactation Risk Category: L3

References:
1.   Pharmaceutical Manufacturers prescribing information, 2003.

Iodamide

Trade: Isteropac, Renovue-Dip, Renovue-65

Not available in the US. Iodamide is an ionic contrast medium. No data are available on the transfer into human milk; however, levels would likely be quite low. Due to a poor oral bioavailability, it is unlikely that it would transfer to the infant during breastfeeding.

Kinetics: T1/2 = 1.3 hours[1]
             Oral Bioavailability = poor
             Protein Binding = 5%

Lactation Risk Category: L3

References:

1.   Difazio LT, Singhvi SM, Heald AF, et.al. Pharmacokinetics of iodamide in normal subjects and in patients with renal impairment. J Clin Pharmacol. 1978 Jan; 18(1):35-41.

Iodipamide

Trade: Cholografin, Sinografin

Iodipamide is an ionic radiopaque contrast agent used to view the gallbladder and biliary tract. It is used in both adults and pediatric patients.[1] No data are available on the transfer of iodipamide into human milk; however, it is unlikely when compared to other similar agents. It has a very short half life, and it is highly protein bound. Based on kinetic data, the American College of Radiology suggests that it is safe for a mother to continue breastfeeding after receiving iodinated x-ray contrast media.[2]

Kinetics: $T1/2 = 30$ minutes
Oral Bioavailability = 10%
Protein Binding = Very high

Lactation Risk Category: L3

References:

1.   Pharmaceutical Manufacturers prescribing information, 2003.
2.   ACR Committee on Drugs and Contrast Media. Administration of contrast medium to breastfeeding mothers. 2004;42-43.

Iodixanol

Trade: Visipaque

Iodixanol is an intravenous, nonionic, water soluble radiocontrast medium with iodine concentrations of 270 and 320 mg/mL.[1] It has been studied and approved in children one year of age and older, as well as adults. There are no studies on the transfer of iodixanol into human milk; however, it is unlikely that iodixanol would transfer into milk in any therapeutic level. Its poor oral bioavailability would further reduce any risk to an infant. Based on kinetic data, the American College of Radiology suggests that it is safe for a mother to continue breastfeeding after receiving iodinated x-ray contrast media.[2]

Kinetics: T1/2 = 123 minutes
Oral Bioavailability = Poor
Protein Binding = None

Lactation Risk Category: L3

References:
1.   Pharmaceutical Manufacturers prescribing information, 2006
2.   ACR Committee on Drugs and Contrast Media. Administration of contrast medium to breastfeeding mothers. 2004;42-43.

Iohexol

Trade: Accupaque, Myelo-Kit, Omnigraf, Omnipaque, Omnitrast

Iohexol is a nonionic radiocontrast agent. Radiopaque agents (except barium) are iodinated compounds used to visualize various organs during X-ray, CAT scans, and other radiological procedures. These compounds are highly-iodinated, benzoic acid derivatives. Although under usual circumstances iodine products are contraindicated in nursing mothers (due to ion trapping in milk), these products are unique, in that they are extremely inert and are largely cleared without metabolism. The iodine is organically bound to the structure and is not biologically active.

In a study of four women who received 0.755 g/kg (350 mg iodine/mL) of iohexol IV, the mean peak level of iohexol in milk was 35 mg/L at three hours post-injection.[1] The average concentration in milk was only 11.4 mg/L over 24 hours. Assuming a daily milk intake of 150 mL/kg body weight, the amount of iohexol transferred to an infant during the first 24 hours would be 1.7 mg/kg which corresponds to 0.23% of the maternal dose.

As a group, these radiocontrast agents are virtually unabsorbed after oral administration (<0.1%).[2] Iohexol has a brief half-life of just two hours, and the estimated dose ingested by the infant is only 0.2 % of the radiocontrast dose used clinically for various scanning procedures in infants. Although most company package inserts suggest that an infant be removed from the breast for 24 hours, no untoward effects have been reported with these products in breastfed infants. Because the amount of iohexol transferred into milk is so small, the authors conclude that breastfeeding is acceptable after intravenously administered iohexol.

Kinetics: T1/2 = 2-3.4 hours
Oral Bioavailability = Poor
Protein Binding = None

Lactation Risk Category: L2

References:
1.   Nielsen ST, Matheson I, Rasmussen JN, Skinnemoen K, Andrew E, Hafsahl G. Excretion of iohexol and metrizoate in human breast milk. Acta Radiol 1987; 28(5):523-526.
2.   Pharmaceutical Manufacturer Prescribing Information. 2006.

Iopamidol

Trade: Gastromiro, Iopamiro, Iopamiron, Iopasen, Isovue, Isovue-M, Jopamiro, Niopam, Pamiray, Radiomiron, Scanlux, Solutrast

Unilux Iopamidol is a nonionic radiocontrast agent used for numerous radiological procedures. Although it contains significant iodine content (20-37%), the iodine is covalently bound to the parent molecule, and the bioavailability of the iodine molecule is miniscule. As with other ionic and nonionic radiocontrast agents, it is primarily extracellular and intravascular, it does not pass the blood-brain barrier, and it would be extremely unlikely that it would penetrate into human milk. However, no data are available on its transfer into human milk. As with most of these products, it is poorly absorbed from the GI tract and rapidly excreted from the maternal circulation, due to a extremely short half-life.

Kinetics: T1/2 = 2 hours
Oral Bioavailability = None
Protein Binding = Very low

Lactation Risk Category: L3

References:
1.   Pharmaceutical Manufacturers prescribing information, 2004.

Iopanoic Acid

Trade: Biliopaco,   Cistobil,   Colegraf,   Colepak,   Neocontrast, Telepaque

Iopanoic acid is a radiopaque organic iodine compound similar to dozens of other radiocontrast agents. It contains 66.7% by weight of iodine. As with all of these compounds, the iodine is organically bound to the parent molecule, and only minimal amounts are free in solution or metabolized by the body. In a group of five breastfeeding mothers who received an average of 2.77 gm of iodine (as Iopanoic acid), the amount of iopanoic acid excreted into human milk during the following 19-29 hours was 20.8 mg or about 0.08% of the maternal dose.[1] No untoward effects were noted in the infants.

Kinetics: T1/2 = 33% eliminated in 24 hours
                   Oral Bioavailability = Well absorbed
                   Protein Binding = High

Lactation Risk Category: L2

References:
1.   Holmdahl KH. Cholecystography during lactation. Acta Radiol 1956; 45(4):305-307.

Iopentol

Trade: Imagopaque, Ivepaque

Not available in the US. There are no studies on the transfer of iopentol into human milk; however, it is unlikely that iopentol would transfer into milk in any therapeutic level. The poor oral bioavailability further reduces risk to an infant.[1]

Kinetics: T1/2 = 2 hours
                   Oral Bioavailability = poor
                   Protein Binding = 3%

Lactation Risk Category: L3

References:
1.   Pharmaceutical Manufacturers prescribing information, 2006.

Iopromide

Trade: Clarograf, Proscope, Ultravist

Iopromide is a nonionic, water soluble x-ray contrast agent. Its iodine content is 48.12%, and it is available in 150, 240, 300, and 370 mg iodine/mL.[1] No data are available on the transfer of ioversol into human milk, but others in this family transfer at extraordinarily low levels, and none are orally bioavailable. Therefore, iopromide use is not likely to pose a threat to an infant and should not be a contraindication for breastfeeding.

Kinetics: T1/2 = 2 hours
                 Oral Bioavailability = Poor
                 Protein Binding = 1%

Lactation Risk Category: L3

References:
1.   Pharmaceutical Manufacturers prescribing information, 2002.

Iothalamate

Trade: Angio-Conray, Conray-30, Conray-43, Conray-60, Conray 325, Conray-400, Cysto-Conray, Cysto-Conray II, Vascoray

Iothalamate is an iodinate contrast medium, available in iodine concentrations ranging from 81 mg iodine/mL to 400 mg iodine/mL.[1] No data are available on the transfer into human milk; however, levels in milk are expected to be low to undetectable, and oral bioavailability is low. Therefore, risk to the infant would be minimal. Based on kinetic data, the American College of Radiology suggests that it is safe for a mother to continue breastfeeding after receiving iodinated x-ray contrast media.[2]

Kinetics: T1/2 = 90-92 minutes
                 Protein Binding = Low

Lactation Risk Category: L3

References:
1.   Pharmaceutical Manufacturers prescribing information, 2003.
2.   ACR Committee on Drugs and Contrast Media. Administration of contrast medium to breastfeeding mothers. 2004;42-43.

Ioversol

Trade: Optiject, Optiray

Ioversol is a typical iodinated radiocontrast agent used in computed tomographic imaging (CT scans). The concentration of iodine varies from 16% organically bound iodine (160) to 35% iodine (350).[1] Ioversol is not metabolized, but it is excreted largely unchanged. Iodine is only minimally released; therefore, thyroid function tests remain unchanged with exception of iodine uptake studies (PBI, radioactive iodine uptake). The vascular half-life is brief, only 20 minutes. No data are available on its transfer into milk, but many others in this family have been studied and transfer to milk at extraordinarily low levels. Further, none of these agents are orally bioavailable.

Kinetics: T1/2 = 1.5 hours
Oral Bioavailability = Nil
Protein Binding = Very low

Lactation Risk Category: L3

References:
1.   Pharmaceutical Manufacturers prescribing information, 2003.

Ioxaglate

Trade: Hexabrix 160, Hexabrix 200, Hexabrix 320, Hexabrix

Ioxaglate is an ionic dimer that offers a lower osmolarity and consequently less pain upon injection. It contains 32% iodine and is approved for both pediatrics and adults. No data are available on the transfer into human milk; however, levels are expected to be below therapeutic levels, and oral bioavailability is low. Based on kinetic data, the American College of Radiology suggests that it is safe for a mother to continue breastfeeding after receiving iodinated x-ray contrast media.[1]

Kinetics: T1/2 = 60-140 minutes
Protein Binding = Low

Lactation Risk Category: L3

References:
1.   ACR Committee on Drugs and Contrast Media. Administration of contrast medium to breastfeeding mothers. 2004;42-43.

Ioxitalamic Acid

Trade: Telebrix

Ioxitalamic acid is available in both an oral solution and an injectable solution, in concentrations ranging from 12% to 38% iodine.[1] It is used in both adults and pediatrics. There are no data available on the transfer of ioxitalamic acid into breastmilk, although levels are likely to be low. Also, oral bioavailability is extremely low. As a result, any small ingested amount would pose little threat to a breastfeeding infant. Based on kinetic data, the American College of Radiology suggests that it is safe for a mother to continue breastfeeding after receiving iodinated x-ray contrast media.[2]

Kinetics: Oral Bioavailability = None

Lactation Risk Category: L3

References:
1.   Pharmaceutical Manufacturers prescribing information, 1999a.
2.   ACR Committee on Drugs and Contrast Media. Administration of contrast medium to breastfeeding mothers. 2004;42-43.

Ipodate

Trade: Bilivist, Biloptin, Oragrafin, Solu-Biloptin, Solubiloptine
Not available in the US. Ipodate is an oral contrast agent used for examining the gallbladder and bile ducts when gallstones are suspected. There have been no studies on the transfer of tyropanoate into human breastmilk. It is likely that minimal drug would transfer into the milk compartment; however, levels are unknown. Caution should be used.

Kinetics: T1/2 = 45% gone in 24 hours
               Oral Bioavailability = High
               Protein Binding = High

Lactation Risk Category: L3

References:
1.   Pharmaceutical Manufacturers prescribing information, 2008.

Mangafodipir Trisodium

Trade: Teslascan

Mangafodipir is a manganese-containing radiocontrast agent used in Magnetic Resonance Imaging. It is rapidly redistributed to liver and less so to other tissues.[1] The release of manganese is significant, and whole-body stores are approximately doubled with infusion of this product. Elevated plasma manganese levels drop rapidly, with a redistribution half-life of about 25 minutes, while the terminal elimination half-life of manganese is more on the order of 10.1 hours. Manganese is effectively transported into human milk, and milk levels are apparently a function of oral intake in the mother. Consequently, manganese levels in milk could temporarily be elevated. Infants are somewhat deficient in manganese and have higher oral bioavailability of manganese, due to the relative state of deficiency.[2] For this reason, it is reasonable to assume that the use of this product in a breastfeeding woman could conceivably elevate the levels of her milk significantly, although briefly. A brief interruption of breastfeeding for a few hours (four or more), followed by pumping and discarding, would significantly reduce any risk to the infant.

Kinetics: T1/2 = 10 hours
Oral Bioavailability = Low
Protein Binding = Nil

Lactation Risk Category: L3

References:
1.   Pharmaceutical Manufacturers prescribing information, 2003.
2.   Vuori E, Makinen SM, Kara R, Kuitunen P. The effects of the dietary intakes of copper, iron, manganese, and zinc on the trace element content of human milk. Am J Clin Nutr 1980; 33(2):227-231.

Metrizamide

Trade: Amipaque

Metrizamide is a radiographic contrast medium used mainly in myelography. It is water soluble and nonionic. Metrizamide contains 48% bound iodine. The iodine molecule is organically bound and is not available for uptake into breast milk due to minimal metabolism. Following subarachnoid administration of 5.06 gm the peak plasma level of 32.9 μg/mL occurred at six hours. Cumulative excretion in milk increased with time, but was extremely small with only 1.1 mg or 0.02% of the dose being recovered in milk within 44.3 hours.[1] The drug's high water solubility, nonionic characteristic, and its high molecular weight (789) also support minimal excretion into breast milk. This agent is sometimes used as an oral radiocontrast agent.[2] Only minimal oral absorption occurs (<0.4%). The authors suggest that the very small amount of metrizamide secreted in human milk is unlikely to be hazardous to the infant.

Kinetics: T1/2 = >24 hours
Oral Bioavailability = <0.4%

Lactation Risk Category: L2

References:
1.   Ilett KF, Hackett LP, Paterson JW, McCormick CC. Excretion of metrizamide in milk. Br J Radiol 1981; 54(642):537-538.
2.   Johansen JG. Assessment of a non-ionic contrast medium (Amipaque) in the gastrointestinal tract. Invest Radiol 1978; 13(6):523-527.

Metrizoate

Trade: Angiocontrast, Isopaque

Metrizoate is an ionic radiocontrast agent. Radiopaque agents (except barium) are iodinated compounds used to visualize various organs during X-ray, CAT scans, and other radiological procedures. These compounds are highly iodinated benzoic acid derivatives. While iodine products are generally contraindicated in nursing mothers these products are unique, because they are extremely inert and are largely cleared without metabolism.

In a study of four women who received metrizoate 0.58 g/kg (350 mg Iodine/mL) IV, the peak level of metrizoate in milk was 14 mg/L at three and six hours post-injection.[1] The average milk concentration during the first 24 hours was only 11.4 mg/L. During the first 24 hours following injection, it is estimated that a total of 1.7 mg/kg would be transferred to the infant, which is only 0.3% of the maternal dose.

As a group, radiocontrast agents are virtually unabsorbed after oral administration (<0.1%). Metrizoate has a brief half-life of just two hours, and the estimated dose ingested by the infant is only 0.2 % of the radiocontrast dose used clinically for various scanning procedures in infants. Although most company package inserts suggest that an infant be removed from the breast for 24 hours, no untoward effects have been reported with these products in breastfed infants. Because the amount of metrizoate transferred into milk is so small, the authors conclude that breastfeeding is acceptable after intravenously administered metrizoate.

Kinetics: T1/2 = 60-140 minutes
Oral Bioavailability = Nil
Protein Binding = Very low

Lactation Risk Category: L2

References:
1.   Nielsen ST, Matheson I, Rasmussen JN, Skinnemoen K, Andrew E, Hafsahl G. Excretion of iohexol and metrizoate in human breast milk. Acta Radiol 1987; 28(5):523-526.

Tyropanoate

Trade: Bilopaque

Tyropanoate is an oral contrast agent used for examining the gallbladder, when gallstones are suspected. It contains 57.4% bound iodine and is only used in adults.[1] Safety in pediatrics has not been established. There have been no studies done on the transfer of tyropanoate into human breastmilk. It is possible that minimal drug would transfer into the milk compartment; however, levels are unknown.

Kinetics: T1/2 = 45% gone in 24 hours
Oral Bioavailability = Well absorbed
Protein Binding = Moderate
MW= 641

Lactation Risk Category: L3

References:
1.   Pharmaceutical Manufacturers prescribing information, 1997.

Appendix D

Contraception Methods

Trade name	Type	Estrogen	Progestin	Formulation	Comment
Alesse, Avaine, Lessina, Levlite, Lutera, Sronyx	Monophasic	ethinyl estradiol 20 mcg	levonorgestrel 0.1 mg	Oral	Avoid
Angeliq	Monophasic	Ethinyl estradiol	Drospirenone	Oral	Avoid
Aranelle, Leena, Tri-Norinyl	Aranelle, Leena, Tri-Norinyl	ethinyl estradiol 35 mcg	norethindrone 0.5 mg (days 1-7), 1 mg (days 8-16), 0.5 mg (days 17-21)	Oral	Avoid
Brevicon, Modicon, Necon 0.5/25, Nortrel 0.5/35	Monophasic	ethinyl estradiol 35 mcg	norethindrone 0.5 mg	Oral	Avoid
Demulen 1/35, Kelnor, Zovia 1/35E	Monophasic	ethinyl estradiol 35 mcg	ethynodiol diacetate 1 mg	Oral	Avoid
Depo-Provera	Single Agent		medroxyprogesterone 150 mg every 3 months	IM Injection	Acceptable
Depo-SubQ Provera	Single Agent		medroxyprogesterone 104 mg every 3 months	SQ Injection	Acceptable
Estrostep 21	Triphasic	ethinyl estradiol 20 mcg (days 1-5), 30 mcg (days 6-12), 35 mcg (days 13-21)	norethindrone 1 mg	Oral	Avoid

Contraception Methods

Trade name	Type	Estrogen	Progestin	Formulation	Comment
Estrostep Fe	Triphasic/ Iron days 22-28	ethinyl estradiol 20 mcg (days 1-5), 30 mcg (days 6-12), 35 mcg (days 13-21)	norethindrone 1mg	Oral	Avoid
Femcon Fe	Monophasic/ Iron days 22-28	ethinyl estradiol 35 mcg	norethindrone 0.4 mg	Oral	Avoid
Gildess FE	Monophasic	Ethinyl estradiol 20 mcg	Norethindrone 1 mg	Oral	Avoid
Gildess FE 1.5/30	Monophasic	Ethinyl estradiol 30 mcg	Norethindrone 1.5 mg	Oral	Avoid
Implaron	Single Agent		etonogestrel 60-70 mcg/ day (year 1), 35-45 mcg/ day (year 2), 30-40 mcg/ day (year 3)	Subdermal Implant	Acceptable
Jolessa, Quasense, Seasonale	Monophasic, extended cycle	ethinyl estradiol 30 mcg	levonorgestrel 0.15 mg	Oral	Avoid
Junel 21 1/20, Loestrin 21 1/20, Microgestin 1/20	Monophasic	ethinyl estradiol 20 mcg	norethindrone acetate 1 mg	Oral	Avoid
Junel 21 1.5/30, Loestrin 21 1.5/30, Microgestin 1.5/30	Monophasic	ethinyl estradiol 30 mcg	norethindrone acetate 1.5 mg	Oral	Avoid
Kariva, Mircette	Biphasic	ethinyl estradiol 20 mcg (days 1-21), 10 mcg (days 24-28)	desogestrel 0.15 mg	Oral	Avoid

Contraception Methods

Trade name	Type	Estrogen	Progestin	Formulation	Comment
Leoestrin Fe 1.5/30, Junel Fe 1.5/30, Microgestin Fe 1.5/30	Monophasic/ Iron days 22-28	ethinyl estradiol 30 mcg	norethindrone acetate 1.5 mg	Oral	Avoid
Levlen, Levora, Nordette, Portia	Monophasic	ethinyl estradiol 30 mcg	levonorgestrel 0.15 mg	Oral	Avoid
Loestrin 24 FE 1/20, Junel FE 1/20, Microgestin Fe 1/20	Monophasic/ Iron days 25-28	ethinyl estradiol 20 mcg	norethindrone acetate 1 mg	Oral	Avoid
Lo/Ovral, Cryselle, Low-Ogestrel	Monophasic	ethinyl estradiol 30 mcg	norgestrel 0.3 mg	Oral	Avoid
LoSeasonique	Biphasic	Ethinyl estradiol 20 mcg (day 1-84), EE 10 mcg (days 85-91)	Levonorgestrel 0.1 mg (days 1-84)	Oral	Avoid
Lybrel	Monophasic	Ethinyl estradiol 20 mcg	Levonorgestrel 90 mcg	Oral	Avoid
Micronor, Camila, Errin, Jolivette, Nora-BE, Nor-QD	Progestin only		norethindrone 0.35 mg	Oral	Acceptable
Mirena	Single Agent		levonorgestrel 20 mcg/day for 5 years	Intrauterine Device (IUD)	Acceptable
Necon 1/35, Norinyl 1+35, Nortrel 1/35, Ortho-Novum 1/35	Monophasic	ethinyl estradiol 35 mcg	norethindrone 1 mg	Oral	Avoid
Necon 1/50, Norinyl 1+50, Ortho-Novum 1/50	Monophasic	mestranol 50 mcg	norethindrone 1 mg	Oral	Avoid

Contraception Methods

Trade name	Type	Estrogen	Progestin	Formulation	Comment
Next Choice	Emergency contraceptive		Levonorgestrel 0.75 mg	Oral	Available
NuvaRing	Combination	ethinyl estradiol 0.015 mg/day	etonogestrel 0.12 mg/day	Vaginal ring	Avoid
Ogestrel 0.5/50	Monophasic	ethinyl estradiol 50 mcg	norgestrel 0.5 mg	Oral	Avoid
Ortho-Cept, Apri, Desogen, Reclipsen, Solia	Monophasic	ethinyl estradiol 30 mcg	desogestrel 0.15 mg	Oral	Avoid
Ortho-Cyclen, MonoNessa, Previfem, Sprintec	Monophasic	ethinyl estradiol 35 mcg	norgestimate 0.25 mg	Oral	Avoid
Ortho Evra	Combination	ethinyl estradiol 20 mcg/day	norelgestromin 150 mcg/day	Transdermal Patch	Avoid
Ortho-Novum 7/7/7, Necon 7/7/7, Nortrel 7/7/7	Triphasic	ethinyl estradiol 35 mcg	norethindrone 0.5 mg (days 1-7), 0.75 mg (days 8-14), 1 mg (days 15-21)	Oral	Avoid
Ortho-Novum 10/11, Necon 10/11	Biphasic	ethinyl estradiol 35 mcg	norethindrone 0.5 mg (days 1-10), 1 mg (days 11-21)	Oral	Avoid
Ortho Tri-Cyclen Lo	Triphasic	ethinyl estradiol 25 mcg	norgestimate 0.18 mg (days 1-7), 0.215 mg (days 8-14), 0.25 mg (days 15-21)	Oral	Avoid

Contraception Methods

Trade name	Type	Estrogen	Progestin	Formulation	Comment
Ovcon 35, Zenchent, Balziva	Monophasic	ethinyl estradiol 35 mcg	norgestimate 0.4 mg	Oral	Avoid
Ovcon 50	Monophasic	ethinyl estradiol 50 mcg	norethindrone 1 mg	Oral	Avoid
ParaGard	Non-hormonal (copper)			Intrauterine Device (IUD)	Acceptable
Plan B	Emergency contraception		levonorgestrel 0.75 mg	Oral	Acceptable
Plan B One-Step	Emergency contraceptive		Levonorgestrel 1.5 mg		Acceptable
Prefest	Multiphasic	Ethinyl estradiol 1 mg (Days 1-6)	Norgestimate 0.09 mg (Days 4-6)	Oral	Avoid
Preven	Emergency contraception	ethinyl estradiol 50 mcg	levonorgestrel 0.25 mg	Oral	Avoid
Seasonique	Biphasic, extended cycle	ethinyl estradiol 30 mcg (days 1-84), 10 mcg (days 85-91)	levonorgestrel 0.15 mg	Oral	Avoid
Tilia FE	Triphasic/iron	Ethinyl estradiol (20 mcg for 5 days), (30 mcg for 7 days), (35 mcg for 9 days), 7 iron tablets.	Norethindrone 1 mg	Oral	Avoid

Contraception Methods

Trade name	Type	Estrogen	Progestin	Formulation	Comment
Tri-Lo_Sprintec	Triphasic	Ethinyl estradiol (25 mcg for 21 days	Norgestimate 0.18 mg (Days 1-7), 0.215 mg (Days 8-14), 0.25 mg (Days 15-21)	Oral	Avoid
Triphasil, Tri-Levlen, Enpresse, Trivora	Triphasic	ethinyl estradiol 30 mcg (days 1-6), 40 mcg (days 7-11), 30 mcg (days 12-21)	levonorgestrel 0.05 mg (days 1-6), 0.075 mg (days 7-11), 0.125 mg (days 12-21)	Oral	Avoid
Velivet, Cesia, Cyclessa	Triphasic	ethinyl estradiol 25 mcg	desogestrel 0.1 mg (days 1-7), 0.125 (days 8-14), 0.15 mg (days 15-21)	Oral	Avoid
Yasmin	Monophasic	ethinyl estradiol 30 mcg	drospirenone 3 mg	Oral	Avoid
Yaz	Monophasic	ethinyl estradiol 20 mcg	drospirenone 3 mg	Oral	Avoid
Zovia 1/50E	Monophasic	ethinyl estradiol 50 mcg	ethynodiol diacetate 1 mg	Oral	Avoid

Appendix E

Glossary

adipose	the fat tissue in the body
analgesic	drugs used to treat pain
androgen	drug that mimics the action of the male hormone testosterone
antiangina	drug used to treat the pain associated with reduced coronary flow in the heart
antidepressant	drugs that elevate or treat mental depression
antiemetic	compound used to treat nausea and vomiting
antihypertensive	drug used to treat high blood pressure
antimetabolite	drug generally used to inhibit the immune response, such as in arthritis or cancer
antineoplastic	drug used to treat neoplasms or cancers
antivertigo	compound used to treat dizziness, bradycardia, slow heart rate
anxiolytic	reduces anxiety, sedative drug
arthropathy	painful inflammation of joints
bronchodilator	drug that dilates the bronchi in the lungs
CCB	calcium channel blocker
candidiasis	fungal infection, candida, yeast, thrush
cholinergic	nerve transmitter, acetylcholine
d	day
diuretic	drug that induces excretion of water by kidneys
dL	deciliter, 100ml
DNA	deoxyribonucleic acid, chromosome, genetic components of human cells
estrogen	drugs that mimic the action of estrogens or female hormones
flora	bacteria normally residing within the intestine
GI	gastrointestinal
half-life	the time required for the concentration of a drug to diminish by one-half in the specified compartment (blood)
hepatoxic	drug that produces liver damage
hyperglycemia	elevated blood sugar (dextrose)
hypoglycemia	low blood sugar (dextrose)
hypotension	low blood pressure
immune	antibody system which fights infection, foreign protein, etc.
immunosuppressive	drugs that diminish or reduce the immune (antibody) response
L	liter, 1000 ml, 1000 cc, approximately 1 quart
lipid	fat
maternal	mother
mg	milligram, one thousandth of a gram
mg/L	milligram per Liter
milk-plasma ratio	ratio of drug in milk to plasma. Higher ratios indicate more drug penetration into milk. A ratio of 1 means that the amount of drug in milk is identical to that in plasma.
ng	nanogram, 1×10^{-9} gm
NICU	Neonatal intensive care unit

NSAID	Nonsteroidal anti-inflammatory
perineal	area between the anus and scrotum
progestational	drug that mimics the action of progesterone, a female hormone
prolactin	hormone that promotes breast milk production
pseudomembranous colitis	severe, sometimes bloody diarrhea caused by overgrowth of offending colonic bacteria
RNA	ribonucleic acid, genetic component of human cell
tachycardia	rapid heart rate
teratogenic	drugs or conditions that produce birth defects in pregnant women
μg	microgram, one millionth of a gram
μg/L	microgram per liter

Normal Growth During Development

Girls Growth Chart

Age	Weight (lb.)	Length (in.)
Birth	7.0	19.3
3 months	12.8	23.6
6 months	15.8	26.0
9 months	18.0	27.6
12 months	19.9	29.1
15 months	21.1	30.7
18 months	22.4	31.9
24 months	25.1	33.9

Close approximate values taken from WHO growth charts for breastfed infants, 2010.

Normal Growth During Development

Boys Growth Chart

Age	Weight (lb.)	Length (in.)
Birth	7.5	19.7
3 months	14.1	24.0
6 months	17.6	26.8
9 months	19.8	28.3
12 months	21.1	29.9
15 months	22.9	31.1
18 months	24.2	32.3
24 months	26.8	34.6

Close approximate values taken from WHO growth charts for breastfed infants, 2010.

Thyroid Function Tests

Test	Time	Normal Range
T_4(thyroxine)	1-7 days	10.1-20.9 µg/dL
	8-14 days	9.8-16.6 µg/dL
	1 month-1year	5.5-16 µg/dL
	>1 year	4-12 µg/dL
FTI	1-3 days	9.3-26.6
	1-4 weeks	7.6-20.8
	1-4 months	7.4-17.9
	4-12 months	5.1-14.5
	1-6 years	5.7-13.3
	>6 years	4.8-14
T_3 by RIA	Newborns	100-470 ng/dL
	1-5 years	100-260 ng/dL
	5-10 years	90-240 ng/dL
	10 years-adult	70-210 ng/dL
T_3 uptake		35-45%
TSH	Cord	3-22 µIU/mL
	1-3 days	<40 µIU/mL
	3-7 days	<25 µIU/mL
	>7 days	0-10 µIU/mL

Therapeutic Drug Levels

Reference (Normal) Values

Drug	Therapeutic Range	
Acetaminophen	10-20	μg/ml
Theophylline	0-20	μg/ml
Carbamazepine	4-10	μg/ml
Ethosuximide	40-100	μg/ml
Phenobarbital	15-40	μg/ml
Phenytoin		
Neonates	6-14	μg/ml
Children, adults	10-20	μg/ml
Primidone	5-15	μg/ml
Valproic Acid	50-100	μg/ml
Gentamicin		
Peak	5-12	μg/ml
Trough	< 2.0	μg/ml
Vancomycin		
Peak	20-40	μg/ml
Trough	5-10	μg/ml
Digoxin	0.9-2.2	μg/ml
Lithium	0.3-1.3	mmol/L
Salicylates	20-25	mg/dL

From Therapeutic Drug Monitoring Guide, WE Evan, Editor, Abbott Laboratories, 1988.

Pediatric Laboratory Values

Test	Age	Range	Units
pH	< 1 mo.	7.3-7.46	
pC0$_2$	2-5d	4.1-6.3	kPa(mmHg)
pC0$_2$	2-5d	5.6-7.7	kPa(mmHg)
Total C0$_2$	< 1 yr.	15-35	mmol/L
Albumin, Serum	< 1 yr.	3-4.9	gm/dL
Phenylalamine	Newborn	0.7-3.5	umol/L
Ammonia	< 1 yr.	68	µmol/L
Total Bilirubin	< 2 w	< 11.7	µg/dL
	< 10 yr.	< 0.9	mg/dL
Calcium	< 1 yr.	7.8-11.2	mg/dL
Chloride	< 2 yr.	100-110	mmol/dL
Cholesteral Total	< 1 yr.	93-260	mg/dL
Copper, Serum	1-5 yr.	80-150	µg/dL
Copper, Wiring	< 6 yr.	8-17	µg/dL
Creatine Kinose	1-3 yr.	50-305	IU/L
Creatine, Serum	< 10 yr.	0.2-1.02	mg/dL
Ferritin	1-4 yr.	6-24	µg/L
Fructosamine	5-17 yr.	1.4-2.2	mmol/L
Glucose	1-6 yr.	74-127	mg/dL
Hemoglobin A$_{1C}$	2-12 yr.	5.1	%HbA$_{1C}$
Cholesterol (HDL)	1-9 yr.	35-82	mg/dL
Iron	< 2 yr.	11-150	µg/dL
Magnesium	< 1 yr.	1.6-2.6	mg/dL
Osmolality	28d	274-305	mmol/dL
Phosphatose, alkaline	2-9 yr.	100-400	IU/L
Phosphorus, Serum	< 2 yr.	2.5-7.1	mg/dL
Potassium	< 2 mo.	3-7.0	mmol/dL
Prolactin	0-18 yr.	20 or less	ng/mL
Protein, Total	< 1 yr.	5-7.5	mg/dL
Protein, Urine	< 1 yr.	130-145	mmol/dL
Sodium, Urinary	1-6 mo.		
breast-fed		6.1	mmol/L
formula-fed		13.2	mmol/L

Drugs to Avoid in Lactation	
Generic name	**Brand name**
Dopamine Agonists	
apomorphine	Apokyn
bromocriptine	Parlodel
cabergoline	Dostinex
pramipexole	Mirapex
ropinirole	Requip
rotigotine	Neupro
selegiline	Eldepryl, Emsam, Zelapar
levodopa	Dopar, Larodopa, Sinemet
L5s (Contraindicated)	
acitretin	Soriatane
amiodarone	Cordarone
antipyrine	Antipyrine
blue cohosh	Blue Cohosh
borage	Borage
bromides	
busulfan	Myleran
cannabis	Marijuana
cocaine	Crack
comfrey	
cyclophosphamide	Neosar, Cytoxan
cytarabine	Cytosar
danazol	Danocrine
diethylpropion	Tepanil, Tenuate
diethylstilbestrol	Honvan
disulfiram	Antabuse
doxepin	Adapin, Sinequan
doxorubicin	Adriamycin
etretinate	Tegison
fluorouracil	5-FU, Adrucil, Efudex, Carac
gamma hydroxybutyric acid	Zyrem, Somsanit, GHB, Liquid Ecstasy
gold compounds	Ridaura, Myochrysine, Solganal
heroin	

Drugs to Avoid in Lactation

Generic name	Brand name
L5s (Contraindicated)	
isotretinoin	Accutane
kava kava	Awa, Kew, Tonga
kombucha tea	
lead	
leuprolide acetate	Lupron, Viadur
LSD	
mercury	
methotrexate	Folex
mifepristone	Mifeprex
mitoxantrone	Novantrone
oxaliplatin	Eloxatin
paclitaxel	Taxol
phencyclidine	PCP
strontium 89 chloride	Metastron
tamoxifen	Nolvadex
zonisamide	Zonegran

Drugs that are usually contraindicated in lactating women*

Drug	Nature of possible infant risk
Amiodarone	Relative infant dose 4-6% of maternal dose; may accumulate because of very long half-life; adverse cardiovascular and thyroid effects possible
Antineoplastic agents	Overtly toxic; avoid exposure; bone marrow suppression, damage to intestinal epithelial cells possible
Chloramphenicol	Relative infant dose 2% of maternal dose. Blood dyscrasias, aplastic anemia, etc. possible
Ergotamine	Symptoms of ergotism (vomiting and diarrhea) reported; potential to inhibit prolactin secretion
Gold salts	Relative infant dose varies from 1-7%. Long half-life in adults suggests potential for accumulation. Possibility of diarrhea, dermatitis, nephrotoxicity and blood dyscrasias
Lithium	Not recommended as relative infant dose is around 18-23% of maternal dose, and severe rash also reported. Caution if used
Phenindione	Relative infant dose calculated at around 18% of maternal dose and abnormal blood coagulation in an infant has been reported

Drug	Nature of possible infant risk
Radiopharmaceuticals	Temporary discontinuation of breastfeeding may be necessary. See Appendix B
Retinoids	Secretion into milk is unknown, but is likely to be significant as these drugs are usually very lipid soluble (e.g. isotretinoin). Contraindicated because if the wide range of adverse effects in adults and mutagenic and carcinogenic actions in animals
Tetracyclines (Chronic)	While the short-term use of tetracyclines for up to three weeks is OK, chronic use over many months may lead to staining of immature teeth, or changes in epiphyseal bone growth
Pseudoephedrine	Recently published data by the authors indicate that pseudoephedrine may inhibit milk production significantly

* Adapted from Hale TW, Ilett KF. Drug Therapy and Breastfeeding: From Theory to Clinical Practice, First Edition ed. London: Parthenon Publishing; 2002

Is It a Cold or the Flu?

Symptoms	Cold	Flu
fever	rare	characteristic, high (102-104F); lasts 3-4 days
headache	rare	prominent
general aches, pains	slight	usual; often severe
fatigue, weakness	quite mild	can last up to 2-3 weeks
extreme exhaustion	never	early and prominent
stuffy nose	common	sometimes
sneezing	usual	sometimes
sore throat	common	sometimes
chest discomfort, cough	mild to moderate; hacking cough	common; can become severe

(Source: National Institute of Allergy and Infectious Diseases)

Publication No. (FDA) 99-1264
http://www.fda.gov/fdac/features/896_flu.html

Neuromuscular Blocking Agents				
Agent (BRAND NAME)	Pharmacological Properties	Time of Onset (min.)	Clinical Duration (min.)	Half-Life (min.)
Succinylcholine (ANECTINE)	ultrashort duration	1 – 1.5	5 – 8	< 1 min
d-Tubocurarine	long duration	4 – 6	80 – 120	173 min
Atracurium (TRACRIUM)	intermediate duration	2 – 4	30 – 60	16 – 20 min
Doxacurium (NUROMAX)	long duration	4 – 6	90 – 120	120 min
Mivacurium (MIVACRON)	short duration	2 – 4	12 – 18	1.8 – 2 min
Pancuronium (PAVULON)	long duration	4 – 6	120 – 180	89 – 140 min
Pipecuronium (ARDUAN)	long duration	2 – 4	80 – 100	137 – 161 min
Rapacuronium (RAPLON)	intermediate duration	1 – 2	15 – 30	72 – 175 min
Rocuronium (ZEMURON)	intermediate duration	1 – 2	30 – 60	84 – 131 min
Vecuronium (NORCURON)	intermediate duration	2 – 4	60 – 90	80 min

Cold Remedies		
Trade Name	**Ingredients**	**Comments**
666 cold preparation, maximum strength liquid	Acetaminophen,Dexchlorpheniramine, Pseudoephedrine, Dextromethorphan	Probably safe but may suppress milk supply.
Actifed cold & allergy tablets	Triprolidine, Pseudoephedrine	Probably safe; observe for sedation and may suppress milk supply.
Actifed cold & sinus maximum strength tablets	Acetaminophen, Chlorpheniramine, Pseudoephedrine	Probably safe; observe for sedation and may suppress milk supply.
Advil Caplets Allergy Sinus	Chlorpheniramine Maleate, Ibuprofen, Pseudoephedrine HCl	Probably safe; observe for sedation and may suppress milk supply.
Advil cold & sinus tablets	Ibuprofen, Pseudoephedrine	Probably safe but may suppress milk supply.
Advil flu & body ache tablets	Ibuprofen, Pseudoephedrine	Probably safe but may suppress milk supply.
Advil Multi-Symptom Cold Caplets	Chlorpheniramine Maleate, Ibuprofen, Pseudoephedrine HCl	Probably safe; observe for sedation and may suppress milk supply.
Allerest PE Tablets	Chlorpheniramine Maleate, Phenylephrine HCl	Probably safe; observe for sedation.
Alavert	Loratadine	Safe
Alavert D-12	Loratadine, Pseudoephedrine	Probably safe but may suppress milk supply.
Aleve cold & sinus tablets	Naproxen, Pseudoephedrine	Probably safe but may suppress milk supply.
Aleve sinus & headache tablets	Naproxen, Pseudoephedrine	Probably safe but may suppress milk supply.
Alka-Seltzer plus cold & cough medicine effervescent tablets	Chlorpheniramine, Phenylephrine, Dextromethorphan	Probably safe; observe for sedation.
Alka-Seltzer plus cold & cough liquid-gels	Acetaminophen, Chlorpheniramine, Dextromethorphan	Probably safe; observe for sedation.
Alka-Seltzer plus cold & flu liqui-gels	Acetaminophen, Pseudoephedrine, Dextromethorphan	Probably safe but may suppress milk supply.

Cold Remedies		
Trade Name	**Ingredients**	**Comments**
Alka-Seltzer plus cold & sinus liqui gels	Acetaminophen, Pseudoephedrine	Probably safe but may suppress milk supply.
Alka-Seltzer plus cold & sinus tablets	Acetaminophen Phenylephrine	Probably safe
Alka-Seltzer plus cold medicine effervescent tablets	Acetaminophen, Chlorpheniramine, Phenylephrine	Probably safe; observe for sedation.
Alka-Seltzer plus cold medicine liquid-gels	Acetaminophen, Chlorpheniramine,Pseudoephedrine	Probably safe; observe for sedation and may suppress milk supply.
Alka-Seltzer plus flu medicine effervescent tablets	Aspirin, Chlorpheniramine, Dextromethorphan	Probably safe; observe for sedation.
Alka-Seltzer plus. liquid-gels flu medicine	Acetaminophen, Pseudoephedrine, Dextromethorphan	Probably safe but may suppress milk supply.
Alka-Seltzer plus nightTime cold liquid-gels	Acetaminophen, Dexchlorpheniramine, Pseudoephedrine, Dextromethorphan	Probably safe; observe for sedation and may suppress milk supply.
Alka-Seltzer plus night-time cold medicine effervescent	Dexchlorpheniramine, Phenylephrine, Dextromethorphan	Probably safe; observe for sedation.
Allegra-D tablets	Fexofenadine, Pseudoephedrine	Probably safe but may suppress milk supply.
Allerest maximum strength tablets	Chlorpheniramine, Pseudoephedrine	Probably safe; observe for sedation and may suppress milk supply.
Aprodine tablets	Triprolidine, Pseudoephedrine	Probably safe; observe for sedation and may suppress milk supply.
Benadryl allergy & cold tablets	Acetaminophen, Diphenhydramine, Pseudoephedrine	Probably safe; observe for sedation and may suppress milk supply.
Benadryl allergy & sinus fastmelt dissolving tablets	Diphenhydramine Pseudoephedrine	Probably safe; observe for sedation and may suppress milk supply.

Cold Remedies		
Trade Name	**Ingredients**	**Comments**
Benadryl allergy & sinus headache tablets	Acetaminophen, Diphenhydramine, Pseudoephedrine	Probably safe; observe for sedation and may suppress milk supply.
Benadryl allergy & sinus liquid	Diphenhydramine, Pseudoephedrine	Probably safe; observe for sedation and may suppress milk supply.
Benadryl allergy & sinus tablets	Diphenhydramine, Pseudoephedrine	Probably safe; observe for sedation and may suppress milk supply.
Benadryl maximum strength severe allergy & sinus headache tablets	Acetaminophen, Diphenhydramine, Pseudoephedrine	Probably safe; observe for sedation and may suppress milk supply.
Benylin expectorant liquid	Guaifenesin, Dextromethorphan	Probably safe.
Bromfed capsules	Brompheniramine, Pseudoephedrine	Probably safe; observe for sedation and may suppress milk supply.
Bromfed syrup	Brompheniramine, Pseudoephedrine	Probably safe; observe for sedation and may suppress milk supply.
Bromfed tablets	Brompheniramine, Pseudoephedrine	Probably safe; observe for sedation and may suppress milk supply.
Cardec DM syrup	Carbinoxamine, Pseudoephedrine, Dextromethorphan	Probably safe; observe for sedation and may suppress milk supply.
Cepacol sore throat liquid	Acetaminophen, Pseudoephedrine	Probably safe but may suppress milk supply.
Cheracol cough syrup	Guaifenesin, Codeine	Probably safe; observe for sedation.
Cheracol D cough formula syrup	Guaifenesin, Dextromethorphan	Probably safe.
Cheracol plus liquid	Guaifenesin, Dextromethorphan	Probably safe.
Chlor-Trimeton allergy-D 12 hour tablets	Chlorpheniramine, Pseudoephedrine	Probably safe; observe for sedation and may suppress milk supply.
Chlor-Trimeton allergy-D 4 hour tablets	Chlorpheniramine, Pseudoephedrine	Probably safe; observe for sedation and may suppress milk supply.

Cold Remedies		
Trade Name	**Ingredients**	**Comments**
Claritin-D 12 hour tablets	Loratadine, Pseudoephedrine	Probably safe but may suppress milk supply.
Claritin-D 24 hour tablets	Loratadine, Pseudoephedrine	Probably safe but may suppress milk supply.
Codiclear DH syrup	Guaifenesin, Hydrocodone	Probably safe; observe for sedation.
Codimal DH syrup	Pyrilamine, Phenylephrine, Hydrocodone	Probably safe; observe for sedation.
Codimal DM syrup	Pyrilamine, Phenylephrine, Dextromethorphan	Probably safe; observe for sedation.
Coldec D tablets	Carbinoxamine, Pseudoephedrine	Probably safe; observe for sedation and may suppress milk supply.
Coldmist LA tablets	Guaifenesin, Pseudoephedrine	Probably safe but may suppress milk supply.
Comtrex allergy-sinus treatment, maximum strength tablets	Acetaminophen, Chlorpheniramine, Pseudoephedrine	Probably safe; observe for sedation and may suppress milk supply.
Comtrex cough and cold relief, multi-symptom maximum strength tablets	Acetaminophen, Chlorpheniramine, Pseudoephedrine, Dextromethorphan	Probably safe; observe for sedation and may suppress milk supply.
Comtrex day & night cold & cough relief, multi-symptom maximum strength tablets	Acetaminophen, Chlorpheniramine, Pseudoephedrine, Dextromethorphan	Probably safe; observe for sedation and may suppress milk supply.
Comtrex flu therapy & fever relief day & night, multi-symptom maximum strength tablets	Acetaminophen, Chlorpheniramine, Pseudoephedrine	Probably safe; observe for sedation and may suppress milk supply.
Comtrex multi-symptom deep chest cold & congestion relief softgels	Acetaminophen, Guaifenesin, Pseudoephedrine, Dextromethorphan	Probably safe but may suppress milk supply.

Cold Remedies		
Trade Name	**Ingredients**	**Comments**
Comtrex multi-symptom maximum strength non-drowsy cold & cough relief tablets	Acetaminophen, Pseudoephedrine, Dextromethorphan	Probably safe but may suppress milk supply.
Contac day & night allergy/sinus	Acetaminophen, Diphenhydramine, Pseudoephedrine	Probably safe; observe for sedation and may suppress milk supply.
Contac day & night cold & flu tablets	Acetaminophen, Diphenhydramine, Pseudoephedrine, Dextromethorphan	Probably safe; observe for sedation and may suppress milk supply.
Contac severe cold & flu maximum strength tablets	Acetaminophen, Chlorpheniramine, Pseudoephedrine, Dextromethorphan	Probably safe; observe for sedation and may suppress milk supply.
Coricidin 'D' cold, flu & sinus tablets	Acetaminophen, Chlorpheniramine, Pseudoephedrine	Probably safe; observe for sedation and may suppress milk supply.
Coricidin HBP cold & flu tablets	Acetaminophen, Chlorpheniramine	Probably safe; observe for sedation.
Coricidin HBP cough & cold tablets	Chlorpheniramine, Dextromethorphan	Probably safe; observe for sedation.
Coricidin HBP maximum strength flu tablets	Acetaminophen, Chlorpheniramine, Dextromethorphan	Probably safe; observe for sedation.
Deconamine SR capsules	Chlorpheniramine, Pseudoephedrine	Probably safe; observe for sedation and may suppress milk supply.
Deconamine syrup	Chlorpheniramine, Pseudoephedrine	Probably safe; observe for sedation and may suppress milk supply.
Deconamine tablets	Chlorpheniramine, Pseudoephedrine	Probably safe; observe for sedation and may suppress milk supply.
Diabetic Tussin Cold and Flu Gel Caps	Acetaminophen, Chlorpheniramine Maleate, Dextromethorphan Hydrobromide	Probably safe; observe for sedation.

Cold Remedies		
Trade Name	**Ingredients**	**Comments**
Diabetic Tussin Maximum Strength DM Cough Suppressant Expectorant	Dextromethorphan Hydrobromide, Guaifenesin	Probably safe; observe for sedation.
Diabetic Tussin Night Time Formula Cold / Flu Relief	Dextromethorphan HBr, Acetaminophen, Diphenhydramine	Probably safe; observe for sedation.
Dihistine DH elixir	Chlorpheniramine, Pseudoephedrine, Codeine	Probably safe; observe for sedation and may suppress milk supply.
Dimetane-DX cough	Brompheniramine, Pseudoephedrine, Dextromethorphan	Probably safe; observe for sedation and may suppress milk supply.
Dimetapp cold & allergy elixir	Brompheniramine, Pseudoephedrine	Probably safe; observe for sedation and may suppress milk supply.
Dristan cold multi-symptom formula tablets	Acetaminophen, Chlorpheniramine, Phenylephrine	Probably safe; observe for sedation.
Dristan cold non-drowsy maximum strength tablets	Acetaminophen, Pseudoephedrine	Probably safe but may suppress milk supply.
Dristan sinus tablets	Ibuprofen, Pseudoephedrine	Probably safe but may suppress milk supply.
Drixoral allergy sinus tablets	Acetaminophen, Dexbrompheniramine, Pseudoephedrine	Probably safe; observe for sedation and may suppress milk supply.
Drixoral cold & allergy tablets	Dexbrompheniramine, Pseudoephedrine	Probably safe; observe for sedation and may suppress milk supply.
Duratuss GP tablets	Guaifenesin, Pseudoephedrine	Probably safe but may suppress milk supply.
Duratuss HD elixir	Guaifenesin, Pseudoephedrine, Hydrocodone	Probably safe; observe for sedation and may suppress milk supply.
Duratuss tablets	Guaifenesin, Pseudoephedrine	Probably safe but may suppress milk supply.
Dura-Vent/DA tablets	Chlorpheniramine, Phenylephrine, Methscopolamine	Probably safe; observe for sedation.

Cold Remedies		
Trade Name	**Ingredients**	**Comments**
Dynex tablets	Guaifenesin, Pseudoephedrine	Probably safe but may suppress milk supply.
Endal tablets	Guaifenesin, Pseudoephedrine	Probably safe but may suppress milk supply.
Entex HC liquid	Guaifenesin, Phenylephrine, Hydrocodone	Probably safe; observe for sedation.
Entex LA tablets	Guaifenesin, Phenylephrine	Probably safe.
Entex liquid	Guaifenesin, Phenylephrine	Probably safe.
Entex PSE tablets	Guaifenesin, Pseudoephedrine	Probably safe but may suppress milk supply.
Genac tablets	Triprolidine, Pseudoephedrine	Probably safe; observe for sedation and may suppress milk supply.
Guaifed capsules	Guaifenesin, Pseudoephedrine	Probably safe but may suppress milk supply.
Guaifed-PD capsules	Guaifenesin, Pseudoephedrine	Probably safe but may suppress milk supply.
Guaifenex PSE 120 tablets	Guaifenesin, Pseudoephedrine	Probably safe but may suppress milk supply.
Guaifenex-Rx tablets	Guaifenesin, Pseudoephedrine	Probably safe but may suppress milk supply.
Guiatuss PE liquid	Guaifenesin, Pseudoephedrine	Probably safe but may suppress milk supply.
Histex liquid	Chlorpheniramine, Pseudoephedrine	Probably safe; observe for sedation and may suppress milk supply.
Histex SR capsules	Brompheniramine, Pseudoephedrine	Probably safe; observe for sedation and may suppress milk supply.
Histussin HC syrup	Chlorpheniramine, Phenylephrine, Hydrocodone	Probably safe; observe for sedation and may suppress milk supply.
Hycodan syrup	Hydrocodone, Homatropine	Probably safe; observe for sedation.
Hycodan tablets	Hydrocodone, Homatropine	Probably safe; observe for sedation.

Cold Remedies		
Trade Name	**Ingredients**	**Comments**
Levall 5.0 liquid	Guaifenesin, Phenylephrine, Hydrocodone	Probably safe; observe for sedation.
Levall liquid	Carbetapentane, Guaifenesin, Phenylephrine	Probably safe; observe for sedation.
Lodrane liquid	Brompheniramine, Pseudoephedrine	Probably safe; observe for sedation and may suppress milk supply.
Motrin sinus headache tablets	Ibuprofen, Pseudoephedrine	Probably safe but may suppress milk supply.
Mucinex DM Expectorant / Cough Suppressant, Extended Release Bi-Layer Tablets	Dextromethorphan HBr, Guaifenesin	Probably safe; observe for sedation.
Mucinex Expectorant, Extended Release Bi-Layer Tablets	Guaifenesin	Probably safe.
Naldecon senior DX liquid	Guaifenesin, Dextromethorphan	Probably safe.
Nucofed expectorant syrup	Guaifenesin, Pseudoephedrine, Codeine	Probably safe; observe for sedation and may suppress milk supply.
Nucotuss expectorant syrup	Guaifenesin, Pseudoephedrine, Codeine	Probably safe; observe for sedation and may suppress milk supply.
Nuprin Cold Relief Cold and Sinus Caplets	Ibuprofen, Pseudoephedrine HCl	Probably safe; observe for sedation and may suppress milk supply.
Nuprin Cold Relief Cough, Chest and Nasal Liquid	Dextromethorphan HBr USP, Guaifenesin USP, Pseudoephedrine HCl USP	Probably safe; observe for sedation and may suppress milk supply.
OMNIhist LA tablets	Chlorpheniramine, Phenylephrine, Methscopolamine	Probably safe; observe for sedation.
PanMist JR tablets	Guaifenesin, Pseudoephedrine	Probably safe but may suppress milk supply.
PanMist LA tablets	Guaifenesin, Pseudoephedrine	Probably safe but may suppress milk supply.

Cold Remedies		
Trade Name	**Ingredients**	**Comments**
PanMist-DM syrup	Guaifenesin, Pseudoephedrine, Dextromethorphan	Probably safe but may suppress milk supply.
PanMist-S syrup	Guaifenesin, Pseudoephedrine	Probably safe but may suppress milk supply.
Percogesic extra strength tablets	Acetaminophen, Diphenhydramine	Probably safe; observe for sedation.
Percogesic tablets	Acetaminophen, Phenyltoloxamine	Probably safe; observe for sedation.
Phenergan VC syrup	Promethazine, Phenylephrine	Caution; observe for sedation.
Polaramine expectorant liquid	Dexchlorpheniramine, Guaifenesin, Pseudoephedrine	Probably safe; observe for sedation and may suppress milk supply.
Primatene tablets	Guaifenesin, Ephedrine	Unsafe.
Prolex DH liquid	Hydrocodone, K Guaicolsulfonate	Probably safe; observe for sedation.
Prometh VC w/ codeine cough syrup	Promethazine, Phenylephrine, Codeine	Unsafe.
Promethazine HCL with codeine cough syrup	Promethazine, Codeine	Unsafe.
Rescon-GG liquid	Guaifenesin, Phenylephrine	Probably safe.
Robitussin allergy & cough liquid	Brompheniramine, Pseudoephedrine, Dextromethorphan	Probably safe; observe for sedation and may suppress milk supply.
Robitussin CF syrup	Guaifenesin, Pseudoephedrine, Dextromethorphan	Probably safe but may suppress milk supply.
Robitussin cold sinus & congestion tablets	Acetaminophen, Guaifenesin, Pseudoephedrine	Probably safe but may suppress milk supply.
Robitussin cold, cold & congestion softgels & tablets	Guaifenesin, Pseudoephedrine, Dextromethorphan	Probably safe but may suppress milk supply.

Cold Remedies		
Trade Name	**Ingredients**	**Comments**
Robitussin cold, cold & cough softgels	Guaifenesin, Pseudoephedrine, Dextromethorphan	Probably safe but may suppress milk supply.
Robitussin cold, multi-symptom cold & flu softgels	Acetaminophen, Guaifenesin, Pseudoephedrine, Dextromethorphan	Probably safe but may suppress milk supply.
Robitussin cold, multi-symptom cold & flu tablets	Acetaminophen, Guaifenesin, Pseudoephedrine, Dextromethorphan	Probably safe but may suppress milk supply.
Robitussin cough & congestion formula liquid	Guaifenesin, Dextromethorphan	Probably safe.
Robitussin flu liquid	Acetaminophen, Chlorpheniramine, Pseudoephedrine, Dextromethorphan	Probably safe; observe for sedation and may suppress milk supply.
Robitussin honey cough & cold liquid	Pseudoephedrine, Dextromethorphan	Probably safe but may suppress milk supply.
Robitussin Honey Flu Multisymptom liquid	Acetaminophen, Pseudoephedrine, Dextromethorphan	Probably safe but may suppress milk supply.
Robitussin honey flu nighttime syrup	Acetaminophen, Chlorpheniramine, Pseudoephedrine, Dextromethorphan	Probably safe; observe for sedation and may suppress milk supply.
Robitussin honey flu non-drowsy syrup	Acetaminophen, Pseudoephedrine, Dextromethorphan	Probably safe but may suppress milk supply.
Robitussin maximum strength cough & cold syrup	Pseudoephedrine, Dextromethorphan	Probably safe but may suppress milk supply.
Robitussin night relief liquid	Acetaminophen, Pyrilamine, Pseudoephedrine, Dextromethorphan	Probably safe; observe for sedation and may suppress milk supply.
Robitussin PE liquid	Guaifenesin, Pseudoephedrine	Probably safe but may suppress milk supply.
Robitussin severe congestion liquid-gels	Guaifenesin, Pseudoephedrine	Probably safe but may suppress milk supply.

Cold Remedies		
Trade Name	**Ingredients**	**Comments**
Robitussin sugar free cough liquid	Guaifenesin, Dextromethorphan	Probably safe.
Robitussin-DM liquid	Guaifenesin, Dextromethorphan	Probably safe.
Rondec syrup	Brompheniramine, Pseudoephedrine	Probably safe; observe for sedation and may suppress milk supply.
Rondec tablets	Carbinoxamine, Pseudoephedrine	Probably safe; observe for sedation and may suppress milk supply.
Rondec-DM syrup	Brompheniramine, Pseudoephedrine, Dextromethorphan	Probably safe; observe for sedation and may suppress milk supply.
Rondec-TR tablets	Carbinoxamine, Pseudoephedrine	Probably safe; observe for sedation and may suppress milk supply.
Ryna liquid	Chlorpheniramine, Pseudoephedrine	Probably safe; observe for sedation and may suppress milk supply.
Ryna-12 S suspension	Pyrilamine, Phenylephrine	Probably safe; observe for sedation.
Ryna-C liquid	Chlorpheniramine, Pseudoephedrine, Codeine	Probably safe; observe for sedation and may suppress milk supply.
Rynatan pediatric suspension	Chlorpheniramine, Phenylephrine	Probably safe; observe for sedation.
Rynatan tablets	Chlorpheniramine, Phenylephrine	Probably safe; observe for sedation.
Rynatuss tablets	Chlorpheniramine, Carbetapentane, Ephedrine	Unsafe.
Singlet for adults tablets	Acetaminophen, Chlorpheniramine, Pseudoephedrine	Probably safe; observe for sedation and may suppress milk supply.
Sinutab non-drying liquid caps	Guaifenesin, Pseudoephedrine	Probably safe but may suppress milk supply.
Sinutab sinus allergy, maximum strength tablets	Acetaminophen, Chlorpheniramine, Pseudoephedrine	Probably safe; observe for sedation and may suppress milk supply.

Cold Remedies		
Trade Name	**Ingredients**	**Comments**
Sinutab sinus without drowsiness maximum strength tablets	Acetaminophen, Pseudoephedrine	Probably safe but may suppress milk supply.
Sinutab sinus without drowsiness regular strength tablets	Acetaminophen, Pseudoephedrine	Probably safe but may suppress milk supply.
Sudafed cold & allergy maximum strength tablets	Chlorpheniramine, Pseudoephedrine	Probably safe; observe for sedation and may suppress milk supply.
Sudafed cold & sinus non-drowsy liqui-caps	Acetaminophen, Pseudoephedrine	Probably safe but may suppress milk supply.
Sudafed Maximum Strength Non-Drowsy Nasal Decongestant 10 mg, Tablets	Phenylephrine HCI	Probably safe.
Sudafed maximum strength sinus nighttime plus pain relief tablets	Acetaminophen, Diphenhydramine, Pseudoephedrine	Probably safe; observe for sedation and may suppress milk supply.
Sudafed multi-symptom cold & cough liquid caps	Acetaminophen, Guaifenesin, Pseudoephedrine, Dextromethorphan	Probably safe but may suppress milk supply.
Sudafed non-drowsy non-drying sinus liquid caps	Guaifenesin, Pseudoephedrine	Probably safe but may suppress milk supply.
Sudafed non-drowsy severe cold formula maximum strength tablets	Acetaminophen, Pseudoephedrine, Dextromethorphan	Probably safe but may suppress milk supply.
Sudafed PE Severe Cold, Coated Caplets, Multi-Symptom	Acetaminophen, Diphenhydramine HCI, Phenylephrine HCI	Probably safe; observe for sedation.
Sudafed sinus headache non-drowsy tablets	Acetaminophen, Pseudoephedrine	Probably safe but may suppress milk supply.
Sudafed sinus nighttime maximum strength tablets	Triprolidine, Pseudoephedrine	Probably safe; observe for sedation and may suppress milk supply.

Cold Remedies		
Trade Name	**Ingredients**	**Comments**
Tanafed suspension	Chlorpheniramine, Pseudoephedrine	Probably safe; observe for sedation and may suppress milk supply.
Tavist allergy/sinus/ headache tablets	Acetaminophen, Clemastine, Pseudoephedrine	Unsafe.
Tavist sinus maximum strength tablets	Acetaminophen, Pseudoephedrine	Probably safe but may suppress milk supply.
TheraFlu cold & cough nighttime powder	Acetaminophen, Chlorpheniramine, Pseudoephedrine, Dextromethorphan	Probably safe; observe for sedation and may suppress milk supply.
TheraFlu flu & cold medicine for sore throat, maximum strength powder	Acetaminophen, Chlorpheniramine, Pseudoephedrine	Probably safe; observe for sedation and may suppress milk supply.
TheraFlu flu & cold medicine original	Acetaminophen, Chlorpheniramine, Pseudoephedrine	Probably safe; observe for sedation and may suppress milk supply.
TheraFlu flu & cough nighttime maximum strength powder	Acetaminophen, Chlorpheniramine, Pseudoephedrine, Dextromethorphan	Probably safe; observe for sedation and may suppress milk supply.
TheraFlu flu & sore throat nighttime, maximum strength powder	Acetaminophen, Chlorpheniramine, Pseudoephedrine	Probably safe; observe for sedation and may suppress milk supply.
TheraFlu flu & sore throat, maximum strength powder	Acetaminophen, Chlorpheniramine, Pseudoephedrine	Probably safe; observe for sedation and may suppress milk supply.
TheraFlu flu, cold & cough and sore throat maximum strength powder	Acetaminophen, Chlorpheniramine, Pseudoephedrine, Dextromethorphan	Probably safe; observe for sedation and may suppress milk supply.
TheraFlu flu, cold & cough nighttime maximum strength powder	Acetaminophen, Chlorpheniramine, Pseudoephedrine, Dextromethorphan	Probably safe; observe for sedation and may suppress milk supply.
TheraFlu flu, cold & cough powder	Acetaminophen, Chlorpheniramine, Pseudoephedrine, Dextromethorphan	Probably safe; observe for sedation and may suppress milk supply.

Cold Remedies		
Trade Name	**Ingredients**	**Comments**
TheraFlu maximum strength flu & congestion non-drowsy powder	Acetaminophen, Guaifenesin, Pseudoephedrine, Dextromethorphan	Probably safe but may suppress milk supply.
TheraFlu maximum strength flu, cold & congestion powder	Acetaminophen, Guaifenesin, Pseudoephedrine, Dextromethorphan	Probably safe but may suppress milk supply.
TheraFlu maximum strength nighttime formula flu, cold & cough medicine	Acetaminophen, Chlorpheniramine, Pseudoephedrine, Dextromethorphan	Probably safe; observe for sedation and may suppress milk supply.
TheraFlu non-drowsy flu, cold & cough maximum strength powder	Acetaminophen, Pseudoephedrine, Dextromethorphan	Probably safe but may suppress milk supply.
TheraFlu non-drowsy formula maximum strength tablets	Acetaminophen, Pseudoephedrine, Dextromethorphan	Probably safe but may suppress milk supply.
TheraFlu severe cold & congestion nighttime maximum strength powder	Acetaminophen, Chlorpheniramine, Pseudoephedrine, Dextromethorphan	Probably safe; observe for sedation and may suppress milk supply.
TheraFlu severe cold & congestion non-drowsy maximum strength powder	Acetaminophen, Pseudoephedrine, Dextromethorphan	Probably safe but may suppress milk supply.
Triaminicin cold, allergy, sinus medicine tablets	Acetaminophen, Chlorpheniramine, Pseudoephedrine	Probably safe; observe for sedation and may suppress milk supply.
Triotann pediatric suspension	Chlorpheniramine, Pyrilamine, Phenylephrine	Probably safe; observe for sedation.
Tussend syrup	Chlorpheniramine, Pseudoephedrine, Hydrocodone	Probably safe; observe for sedation and may suppress milk supply.
Tussend tablets	Chlorpheniramine, Pseudoephedrine, Hydrocodone	Probably safe; observe for sedation and may suppress milk supply.
Tussi-12 tablets	Carbetapentane, Chlorpheniramine	Probably safe; observe for sedation.

Cold Remedies		
Trade Name	**Ingredients**	**Comments**
Tussionex pennkinetic suspension	Chlorpheniramine, Hydrocodone	Probably safe; observe for sedation.
Tussi-Organidin-DM NR liquid	Guaifenesin, Dextromethorphan	Probably safe.
Tylenol allergy sinus nighttime, maximum strength tablets	Acetaminophen, Diphenhydramine, Pseudocphedrine	Probably safe; observe for sedation and may suppress milk supply.
Tylenol allergy sinus, maximum strength tablets, gelcaps and geltabs	Acetaminophen, Chlorpheniramine, Pseudoephedrine	Probably safe; observe for sedation and may suppress milk supply.
Tylenol cold complete formula tablets	Acetaminophen, Chlorpheniramine, Pseudoephedrine, Dextromethorphan	Probably safe; observe for sedation and may suppress milk supply.
Tylenol cold non-drowsy formula gel-caps and tablets	Acetaminophen, Pseudoephedrine, Dextromethorphan	Probably safe but may suppress milk supply.
Tylenol Cold & Flu Severe Daytime liquid	Acetaminophen, Dextromethorphan HBr, Pseudoephedrine HCl	Probably safe; observe for sedation and may suppress milk supply.
Tylenol Cold & Flu Severe Nighttime liquid	Acetaminophen, Dextromethorphan HBr, Doxylamine Succinate, Pseudoephedrine HCl	Probably safe; observe for sedation and may suppress milk supply.
Tylenol Cough & Sore Throat Daytime liquid	Acetaminophen, Dextromethorphan HBr	Probably safe; observe for sedation.
Tylenol Cough & Sore Throat Nighttime liquid	Acetaminophen, Dextromethorphan HBr, Doxylamine Succinate	Probably safe; observe for sedation.
Tylenol flu maximum strength non-drowsy gelcaps	Acetaminophen, Pseudoephedrine, Dextromethorphan	Probably safe but may suppress milk supply.
Tylenol flu nighttime maximum strength liquid	Acetaminophen, Doxylamine, Pseudoephedrine, Dextromethorphan	Probably safe; observe for sedation and may suppress milk supply.

Cold Remedies		
Trade Name	**Ingredients**	**Comments**
Tylenol flu nighttime, maximum strength gelcaps	Acetaminophen, Diphenhydramine, Pseudoephedrine	Probably safe; observe for sedation and may suppress milk supply.
Tylenol multi-symptom cold severe congestion tablets	Acetaminophen, Guaifenesin, Pseudoephedrine, Dextromethorphan	Probably safe but may suppress milk supply.
Tylenol PM extra strength tablets, gelcaps and geltabs	Acetaminophen, Diphenhydramine	Probably safe; observe for sedation.
Tylenol severe allergy tablets	Acetaminophen, Diphenhydramine	Probably safe; observe for sedation.
Tylenol sinus nighttime, maximum strength tablets	Acetaminophen, Doxylamine, Pseudoephedrine	Probably safe; observe for sedation and may suppress milk supply.
Tylenol sinus non-drowsy maximum strength geltabs, tablets and gelcaps	Acetaminophen, Pseudoephedrine	Probably safe but may suppress milk supply.
Tylenol Sore Throat Daytime Liquid	Acetaminophen	Safe.
Tylenol Sore Throat Nighttime Liquid	Acetaminophen, Diphenhydramine HCl	Probably safe; observe for sedation.
Vicks 44D cough & head congestion relief liquid	Pseudoephedrine, Dextromethorphan	Probably safe but may suppress milk supply.
Vicks 44E cough & chest congestion relief	Guaifenesin, Dextromethorphan	Probably safe.
Vicks 44M cough, cold & flu relief liquid	Acetaminophen, Chlorpheniramine, Pseudoephedrine, Dextromethorphan	Probably safe; observe for sedation and may suppress milk supply.
Vicks DayQuil Liqui Caps Multisymptom Cold/Flu Relief Capsules	Acetaminophen, 0, Pseudoephedrine, Dextromethorphan	Probably safe but may suppress milk supply.
Vicks DayQuil multi-symptom cold/flu relief liquid	Acetaminophen, Pseudoephedrine, Dextromethorphan	Probably safe but may suppress milk supply.

Cold Remedies		
Trade Name	**Ingredients**	**Comments**
Vicks NyQuil cough syrup	Doxylamine, Dextromethorphan	Probably safe; observe for sedation.
Vicks NyQuil multi-symptom cold & flu relief liquiCaps capsules	Acetaminophen, Doxylamine, Pseudoephedrine, Dextromethorphan	Probably safe; observe for sedation and may suppress milk supply.
Vicks NyQuil multi-symptom cold/flu relief liquid	Acetaminophen, Doxylamine, Pseudoephedrine, Dextromethorphan	Probably safe; observe for sedation and may suppress milk supply.
Vicodin Tuss syrup	Guaifenesin, Hydrocodone	Probably safe; observe for sedation.
Z-Cof DM syrup	Guaifenesin, Pseudoephedrine, Dextromethorphan	Probably safe but may suppress milk supply.
Zicam Cold Remedy RapidMelts Quick Dissolve Tablets	Zincum Gluconicum, Zincum Aceticum	Probably safe. Do not overdose.
Zicam Homopathic Cold Remedy Oral Mist	Zincum Gluconicum, Zincum Aceticum	Probably safe. Do not overdose.
Zyrtec-D 12 hour tablets	Cetirizine, Pseudoephedrine	Probably safe but may suppress milk supply.

Nasal Products		
Product Name	**Ingredients**	**Safety**
Nasal Spray	Sodium chloride 0.9%	Safe
Pretz Moisturizing		Safe
Afrin Saline, Extra Moisturizing		Safe
Simply Saline		Safe
Pretz Irrigation		Safe
SalineX	0.4% sodium chloride	Safe
Ayr Saline	0.65% sodium chloride	Safe
Breathe Free		Safe
HuMist Moisturizing Mist		Safe

NaSal		Safe
Nasal Moist		Safe
Ocean		Safe
Mycinaire Saline Mist		Safe
Rhinaris Lubricating Mist Solution	15% polyethylene glycol, 5% propylene glycol	Safe
Rhinaris Lubricating Mist Gel	15% polyethylene glycol, 20% propylene glycol	Safe
Nasalcrom Nasal Spray	Cromolyn sodium	Safe
Nasal-Ease with Zinc	Zinc Acetate	Unsafe
Nasal-Ease with Zinc Gluconate	Zinc Gluconate	Unsafe

Nasal Decongestants		
Oxymetazoline HCl	Oxymetazoline 0.05%	Safe: observe for nervousness, insomnia, excitation.*
12 Hour Nasal		Safe: see above
Twice-A-Day 12 Hour Nasal		Safe: see above
Neo-Synephrine 12 Hour Extra Moisturizing		Safe: see above
Neo-Synephrine 12 Hour		Safe: see above
Duration		Safe: see above
Afrin 12 Hour Original Pump Mist		Safe: see above
Afrin 12 Hour Original		Safe: see above
Afrin Severe Congestion w/ Menthol		Safe: see above
Afrin Sinus with Vapornase		Safe: see above
Afrin No-Drip 12 Hour		Safe: see above
Afrin No-Drip 12 Hour Extra Moisturing		Safe: see above

Nasal Decongestants		
Afrin No-Drip 12 Hour Severe Congestion w/ Menthol		Safe: see above
Afrin No Drip Nasal Decongestant Mist		Safe: see above
Afrin No-Drip Sinus w/ Vapornase		Safe: see above
Dristan 12 Hr. Nasal		Safe: see above
Duramist Plus 12 Hr. Decongestant		Safe: see above
Genasal		Safe: see above
Nasal Decongestant, Maximum Strength		Safe: see above
Nasal Relief		Safe: see above
Neo-Synephrine Nasal Decongestant, 12 Hour Spray, Extra Moisturizing	Oxymetazoline 0.05%	Safe: see above
Nostrilla 12 Hour	Oxymetazoline 0.05%	Safe: see above
Nuprin Cold Relief Nasal Decongestant 12 Hour Spray		Safe: see above
Vicks Sinex 12 Hour Long-Acting		Safe: see above
Vicks Sinex 12 Hour Ultra Fine Mist for Sinus Relief		Safe: see above
Zicam Extreme Congestion Relief No-Drip Liquid Nasal Gel		Safe: see above
ZICAM Intense Sinus Relief Liquid Nasal Gel		Safe: see above
Tyzine Pediatric	Tetrahydrozoline HCl 0.05%	Safe: see above
Tyzine	Tetrahydrozoline HCl 0.1%	Safe: see above
Otrivin Pediatric Nasal	Xylometazoline HCl 0.05%	Safe: see above
Natru-Vent		Safe: see above

Nasal Decongestants		
Otrivin	Xylometazoline HCl 0.1%	Safe: see above
Natru-Vent		Safe: see above
Dristan Fast Acting Formula	0.5% phenylephrine HCl and 0.2% pheniramine maleate	Safe: see above
Benzedrex	250 mg propylhexedrine	Unsafe
Vicks Vapor Inhaler	50 mg I-desoxyephedrine	Unsafe
Little Noses Gentle Formula, Infants & Children	Phenylephrine HCl 0.125%	Safe
Afrin Children's Pump Mist	Phenylephrine HCl 0.25%	Safe
Little Colds For Infants and Children		Safe
Neo-Synephrine 4-Hour Mild Formula	Phenylephrine HCl 0.25%	Safe
Rhinall		Safe
Neo Synephrine 4-Hour Regular Strength	Phenylephrine HCl 0.5%	Safe
Vicks Sinex Ultra Fine Mist		Safe
Phenylephrine HCl	Phenylephrine HCl 1%	Safe
4-Way Fast Acting		Safe
Neo-Synephrine 4-Hour Extra Strength		Safe
Zicam Homopathic Cold Remedy No-Drip Liquid Nasal Gel, Homeopathic	Zincum Gluconicum 2x	Unsafe
Zicam Homopathic Cold Remedy Swabs No Drip Liquid Nasal Gel		Unsafe
Adrenaline Chloride	Epinephrine HCl 1 mg/ml	Caution
Benzedrex Inhaler	Propylhexedrine 250 mg	

Nasal Decongestants		
Nuprin Cold Relief Nasal Decongestant Inhaler	Per Inhaler: Levmetamfetamine 50 mg	Caution stimulation possible
Pretz-D	Ephedrine Sulfate 0.25%	Unsafe
Privine	Naphazoline HCl 0.05%	Safe
Similasan Hay Fever Relief Nasal Spray	Cardiospermum HPUS 6X; Galphimia Glauca HPUS 6X; Luffa Operculata HPUS 6X; Sabadilla HPUS 6X	Probably safe
Similasan Sinus Relief Nasal Spray	Kali Bichromicum HPUS 6X; Luffa HPUS 6X; Sabadilla HPUS 6X	Probably safe
Simply Saline Nasal Mist Allergy and Sinus Relief	Purified Water; 3% Sodium Chloride	Safe
SinuCleanse Nasal Wash System	Sodium Bicarbonate, Sodium Chloride	Safe
SinoFresh Antiseptic Moisturizing Nasal and Sinus Spray	Cetylpyridinium Chloride 0.05%	Safe

*Products with Oxymetazoline, Tetrahydrozoline, and Naphazoline should only be used briefly in breastfeeding mothers, if at all. If overdosed, breastfed infants could potentially be agitated and tremulous. Do not use in infants with hypertension or cardiac syndromes.

Note: Nonprescription Drugs

For a more complete list of nonprescription medications or those sold over-the-counter in the USA, see *Nonprescription Drugs for the Breastfeeding Mother*, by Frank Nice.

Topical corticosteroids

Potency	Topical corticosteroid (Brand name)	Preparation	Comment
Low potency	Alclometasone (Aclovate)	0.05% cream/ ointment	Probably safe if not used in large amounts on the nipple.
	Desonide (DesOwen, Tridesilon)	0.05% cream	
	Fluocinolone (Synalar solution, Derma-Smoothe/FS)	0.01% cream/ solution	
	Hydrocortisone (Anusol-HC, Cortaid, Cortizone, Dermarest, Hytone, ProctoCream)	0.25%; 0.5%; 1% & 2.5% in various dosage forms	

Potency	Topical corticosteroid (Brand name)	Preparation	Comment
Intermediate potency	Betamethasone (Alphatrex, Betatrex)	0.025% cream/ gel/ lotion 0.05% lotion 0.1% cream	Probably safe if used in minimal amounts directly applied on the nipple. Some caution is recommended.
	Clocortolone (Cloderm)	0.1% cream	
	Desoximetasone (Topicort-LP)	0.05% cream	
	Fluocinolone (Synalar)	0.025% cream/ ointment	
	Flurandrenolide (Cordran)	0.05% cream/ ointment/ lotion/tape	
	Fluticasone (Cutivate)	0.005% ointment & 0.05% cream	
	Hydrocortisone butyrate or valerate (Locoid, Locoid Lipocream, Westcort)	0.1% ointment/ solution & 0.2% cream/ ointment	
	Mometasone furoate (Elecon)	0.1% cream/ ointment/ lotion	
	Prednicarbate (Dermatop)	0.1% cream/ ointment	
	Triamcinolone acetonide (Aristocort, Kenalog, Triderm)	0.025% & 0.1% cream/ ointment/ lotion	

Potency	Topical corticosteroid (Brand name)	Preparation	Comment
High potency	Amcinonide (Cyclocort)	0.1% cream/ointment/lotion	Do not use on nipple. Some caution is recommended if used on large areas on the body.
	Betamethasone dipropionate or valerate (Alphatrex, Betatrex, Diprolene AF, Diprolene, Maxivate)	0.05% cream/ointment & 0.1% ointment	
	Desoximetasone (Topicort)	0.05% gel & 0.25% cream/ointment	
	Diflorasone diacetate (Maxiflor, Psorcon)	0.05% cream/ointment	
	Fluocinonide (Lidex, Lidex-E)	0.05% cream/ointment/gel	
	Halcinonide (Halog, Halog-E)	0.1% cream/ointment	
	Triamcinolone (Aristocort, Kenalog)	0.5% cream/ointment	
Very high potency	Clobetasol (Clobex, Cormax, Olux, Temovate)	0.05% cream/ointment/lotion/foam	Never use on nipple. Caution is recommended if used on large areas on the body.
	Diflorasone diacetate (Maxiflor, Psorcon)	0.05% ointment	
	Halobetasol (Ultravate)	0.05% cream/ointment	

Herbal Drugs Contraindicated in Lactation*
Aloe
Buckthorn Bark and Berry
Cascara Sagrada bark
Coltsfoot leaf
Extract of Senna leaf, peppermint and caraway oil
Kava Kava
Petasites root
Indian snakeroot
Rhubarb root
Senna leaf
Uva Ursi
Blue Cohosh
Sage
Jin Bu Huan
Germander
Comfrey
Mistletoe
Skullcap
Margosa Oil
Mate tea
Gordolobo yerba tea
Pennyroyal oil

* Adapted in part from The Complete German Commission E Monographs. Ed. M. Blumenthal Amer Botanical Council 1998 and other literature.

Recommended Immunization Schedule for Persons Aged 0 - 6 Years   UNITED STATES - 2010

For those who fall behind or start late, see the catch-up schedule

Vaccine ▼ Age ►	Birth	1 month	2 months	4 months	6 months	12 months	15 months	18 months	19–23 months	2–3 years	4–6 years
Hepatitis B[1]	HepB	HepB	HepB			HepB					
Rotavirus[2]			Rota	Rota	Rota						
Diphtheria, Tetanus, Pertussis[3]			DTaP	DTaP	DTaP		DTaP	DTaP			DTaP
Haemophilus influenzae type b[4]			Hib	Hib	*Hib*[4]	Hib					
Pneumococcal[5]			PCV	PCV	PCV	PCV				PPV	PPV
Inactivated Poliovirus			IPV	IPV	IPV	IPV					IPV
Influenza[6]						Influenza (Yearly)					
Measles, Mumps, Rubella[7]						MMR	MMR				MMR
Varicella[8]						Varicella	Varicella				Varicella
Hepatitis A[9]						HepA (2 doses)	HepA (2 doses)			HepA Series	HepA Series
Meningococcal[10]										MCV4	MCV4

Range of recommended ages

Certain high-risk groups

This schedule indicates the recommended ages for routine administration of currently licensed childhood vaccines, as of December 1, 2007, for children aged 0 through 6 years. Additional information is available at **www.cdc.gov/vaccines/recs/schedules**. Any dose not administered at the recommended age should be administered at any subsequent visit, when indicated and feasible. Additional vaccines may be licensed and recommended during the year. Licensed combination vaccines may be used whenever any components of the combination are indicated and other components of the vaccine are not contraindicated and if approved by the Food and Drug Administration for that dose of the series. **Providers should consult the respective Advisory Committee on Immunization Practices statement for detailed recommendations, including for high risk conditions: http://www.cdc.gov/vaccines/pubs/ACIP-list.htm.** Clinically significant adverse events that follow immunization should be reported to the Vaccine Adverse Event Reporting System (VAERS). Guidance about how to obtain and complete VAERS form is available at **www.vaers.hhs.gov** or by telephone, **800-822-7967**.

CATCH-UP SCHEDULE FOR CHILDREN AGED 4 MONTHS THROUGH 6 YEARS

1. Hepatitis B vaccine (HepB). *(Minimum age: birth)*

At birth:

- Administer monovalent HepB to all newborns prior to hospital discharge.
- If mother is hepatitis B surface antigen (HBsAg)-positive, administer HepB and 0.5 mL of hepatitis B immune globulin (HBIG) within 12 hours of birth.
- If mother's HBsAg status is unknown, administer HepB within 12 hours of birth. Determine the HBsAg status as soon as possible and if HBsAg-positive, administer HBIG (no later than age 1 week).
- If mother is HBsAg-negative, the birth dose can be delayed, **in rare cases,** with a provider's order and a **copy of the mother's** negative HBsAg laboratory report in the infant's medical record.

After the birth dose:

- The HepB series should be completed with either monovalent HepB or a combination vaccine containing HepB. The second dose should be administered at age 1–2 months. The final dose should be administered no earlier than age 24 weeks. Infants born to HBsAg-positive mothers should be tested for HBsAg and antibody to HBsAg after completion of at least 3 doses of a licensed HepB series, at age 9–18 months (generally at the next well-child visit).

4-month dose:

- It is permissible to administer 4 doses of HepB when combination vaccines are administered after the birth dose. If monovalent HepB is used for doses after the birth dose, a dose at age 4 months is not needed.

2. Rotavirus vaccine (Rota). *(Minimum age: 6 weeks)*

- Administer the first dose at age 6–12 weeks.
- Do not start the series later than age 12 weeks.
- Administer the final dose in the series by age 32 weeks. Do not administer any dose later than age 32 weeks.
- Data on safety and efficacy outside of these age ranges are insufficient.

3. Diphtheria and tetanus toxoids and acellular pertussis vaccine (DTaP). *(Minimum age: 6 weeks)*

- The fourth dose of DTaP may be administered as early as age 12 months, provided 6 months have elapsed since the third dose.
- Administer the final dose in the series at age 4–6 years.

4. *Haemophilus influenzae* type b conjugate vaccine (Hib). *(Minimum age: 6 weeks)*

- If PRP-OMP (PedvaxHIB® or ComVax® [Merck]) is administered at ages 2 and 4 months, a dose at age 6 months is not required.
- TriHIBit® (DTaP/Hib) combination products should not be used for primary immunization but can be used as boosters following any Hib vaccine in children age 12 months or older.

5. Pneumococcal vaccine. *(Minimum age: 6 weeks for pneumococcal conjugate vaccine [PCV]; 2 years for pneumococcal polysaccharide vaccine [PPV])*

- Administer one dose of PCV to all healthy children aged 24–59 months having any incomplete schedule.
- Administer PPV to children aged 2 years and older with underlying medical conditions.

6. Influenza vaccine. *(Minimum age: 6 months for trivalent inactivated influenza vaccine [TIV]; 2 years for live, attenuated influenza vaccine [LAIV])*

- Administer annually to children aged 6–59 months and to all close contacts of children aged 0–59 months.
- For healthy nonpregnant persons (those who do not have underlying medical conditions that predispose them to influenza complications) ages 2–49 years, either LAIV or TIV may be used.
- Children receiving TIV should receive 0.25 mL if age 6–35 mos or 0.5 mL if age 3 years or older.
- Administer 2 doses (separated by 4 weeks or longer) to children younger than 9 years who are receiving influenza vaccine for the first time or who were vaccinated for the first time last season, but only received one dose.

7. Measles, mumps, and rubella vaccine (MMR). *(Minimum age: 12 months)*

- Administer the second dose of MMR at age 4–6 years. MMR may be administered before age 4–6 years, provided 4 weeks or more have elapsed since the first dose.

8. Varicella vaccine. *(Minimum age: 12 months)*

- Administer second dose at age 4–6 years; may be administered 3 months or more after first dose.
- Don't repeat second dose if administered 28 days or more after first dose.

9. Hepatitis A vaccine (HepA). *(Minimum age: 12 months)*

- HepA is recommended for all children aged 1 y¯ (i.e., aged 12–23 months). The 2 doses in the series should be administered at least 6 months apart.
- Children not fully vaccinated by age 2 years can be vaccinated at subsequent visits.
- HepA is recommended for certain other groups of children, including in areas where vaccination programs target older children.

10. Meningococcal vaccine. *(Minimum age: 2 years for meningococcal conjugate vaccine [MCV4] and for meningococcal polysaccharide vaccine [MPSV4])*

- MCV4 is recommended for children aged 2–10 years with terminal complement deficiencies or anatomic or functional asplenia and certain other high-risk groups. Use of MPSV4 is also acceptable.
- Persons who received MPSV4 3 or more years prior and remain at increased risk for meningococcal disease should be vaccinated with MCV4.

CATCH-UP SCHEDULE FOR CHILDREN AGED 7 YEARS THROUGH 18 YEARS

Vaccine	Minimum Interval Between Doses		
	Dose 1 to Dose 2	Dose 2 to Dose 3	Dose 3 to Booster Dose
Tetanus, Diphtheria[8]	4 weeks	6 months	**6 months** if first dose given at age <12 months and current age <11 years; otherwise **5 years**
Inactivated Poliovirus[9]	4 weeks	4 weeks	IPV[2,9]
Hepatitis B	4 weeks	8 weeks (and 16 weeks after first dose)	
Measles, Mumps, Rubella	4 weeks		
Varicella[10]	4 weeks		

1. **DTaP.** The fifth dose is not necessary if the fourth dose was administered after the fourth birthday.

2. **IPV.** For children who received an all-IPV or all-oral poliovirus (OPV) series, a fourth dose is not necessary if third dose was administered at age ≥4 years. If both OPV and IPV were administered as part of a series, a total of 4 doses should be given, regardless of the child's current age.

3. **HepB.** Administer the 3-dose series to all children and adolescents <19 years of age if they were not previously vaccinated.

4. **MMR.** The second dose of MMR is recommended routinely at age 4–6 years but may be administered earlier if desired.

5. **Hib.** Vaccine is not generally recommended for children aged ≥5 years.

6. **Hib.** If current age <12 months and the first 2 doses were PRP-OMP (PedvaxHIB® or ComVax® [Merck]), the third (and final) dose should be administered at age 12–15 months and at least 8 weeks after the second dose.

7. **PCV.** Vaccine is not generally recommended for children aged ≥5 years.

8. **Td.** Adolescent tetanus, diphtheria, and pertussis vaccine (Tdap) may be substituted for any dose in a primary catch-up series or as a booster if age appropriate for Tdap. A five-year interval from the last Td dose is encouraged when Tdap is used as a booster dose. See ACIP recommendations for further information.

9. **IPV.** Vaccine is not generally recommended for persons aged ≥18 years.

10. **Varicella.** Administer the 2-dose series to all susceptible adolescents aged ≥13 years.

EMERGENCY USE AUTHORIZATION of TAMIFLU®: FACT SHEET FOR HEALTH CARE PROVIDERS[1]

You have been asked as a health care provider to give TAMIFLU® (oseltamivir phosphate) to people who have been exposed to novel Influenza A (H1N1) (Swine Influenza A). TAMIFLU® is approved by the U.S. Food and Drug Administration (FDA) to treat and prevent influenza. Certain aspects of the emergency use are not part of the approved drug applications, such as use in pediatric patients less than 1 year old, use in patients who are symptomatic for more than 2 days, and use in patients who have complicated illness requiring hospitalization. **For more information**, refer to http://www.cdc.gov/h1n1flu or www.fda.gov.

Recommended Treatment Dosage

Adults and Adolescents 13 years and older: 75 mg twice daily for 5 days. Treatment should begin as soon as possible after symptom onset.

Pediatric Patients 1 to 12 year old: Dosage is shown in the following table. For pediatric patients who cannot swallow capsules, TAMIFLU® for Oral Suspension is the preferred formulation. If the oral suspension product is not available, TAMIFLU® Capsules may be opened and mixed with sweetened liquids such as regular or sugar-free chocolate syrup.

Body Weight (kg)	Body Weight (lbs)	Age (years)	Dose for 5 Days	# Bottles of Oral Suspension Needed for the 5 Day Regimen	# of Capsules Needed for the 5 Day Regimen
≤ 15	≤ 33	1-2	30 mg twice daily	1	10 capsules (30 mg)
> 15-23	> 33-51	3-5	45 mg twice daily	2	10 capsules (45 mg)
> 23-40	> 51-88	6-9	60 mg twice daily	2	20 capsules (30 mg)
> 40	> 88	10-12	75 mg twice daily	3	10 capsules (75 mg)

An oral dosing dispenser with 30 mg, 45 mg, and 60 mg graduations is provided with TAMIFLU® for Oral Suspension; the 75 mg dose can be measured using a combination of 30 mg and 45 mg. It is recommended that patients use this dispenser. In the event that the dispenser provided is lost or damaged, another

[1] In the event of an emergency, it is possible that public health officials or other volunteers might distribute TAMIFLU® products to recipients as authorized. In this fact sheet, the term "health care provider(s)" includes these individuals and is used for brevity here.

dosing syringe or other device may be used to deliver the following volumes: 2.5 mL (1/2 tsp) for children ≤ 15 kg, 3.8 mL (3/4 tsp) for > 15 kg to 23 kg, 5 mL (1 tsp) for > 23 kg to 40 kg, and 6.2 mL (1 ¼ tsp) for > 40 kg.

Pediatric Patients less than 1 year old:

Body Weight (kg)	Dose by Age	Recommended Treatment Dose for 5 Days (Dose in volume is based on the concentration (12 mg/mL) of commercially-manufactured TAMIFLU® Oral Suspension)
Dosing for infants younger than 1 year not based on weight	< 3 months	12 mg (1 mL) twice daily
	3-5 months	20 mg (1.6 mL) twice daily
	6-11 months	25 mg (2 mL) twice daily

*For more information regarding the basis for dose recommendations, see FDA's "Tamiflu Technical Review Document for H1N1 Influenza A" on www.cdc.gov/h1n1flu or www.fda.gov

For infants less than 1 year old, a different measuring device (such as a 5-mL oral syringe) must be used to correctly measure the dose.

Recommended Prophylaxis Dosage

Adults and Adolescents 13 years and older: 75 mg once daily for at least 10 days following close contact with an infected person. Therapy should begin as soon as possible after exposure. The recommended dose for prophylaxis during a community outbreak of influenza is 75 mg once daily. Safety and efficacy have been demonstrated for up to 6 weeks. The duration of protection lasts for as long as dosing is continued.

Pediatric Patients 1 to 12 years old: Dosage following close contact with an infected individual is shown in the following table. For pediatric patients who cannot swallow capsules, TAMIFLU® for Oral Suspension is the preferred formulation. If the oral suspension product is not available, TAMIFLU® Capsules may be opened and mixed with sweetened liquids such as regular or sugar-free chocolate syrup.

Special Dosage Instructions

No dose adjustment is recommended for patients with mild or moderate hepatic impairment (Child-Pugh score ≤ 9). No dose adjustment is required for geriatric patients.

Renal Impairment, Recommended Treatment Dosage: Dose adjustment is recommended for patients with creatinine clearance between 10 and 30 mL/min. Treatment dose should be reduced to 75 mg once daily for 5 days. No recommended dosing regimens are available for patients undergoing routine hemodialysis and continuous peritoneal dialysis treatment with end-stage renal disease.

Renal Impairment, Recommended Prophylaxis Dosage: Dose adjustment is recommended for patients with creatinine clearance between 10 and 30 mL/min receiving TAMIFLU®. In these patients it is recommended that the dose be reduced to 75 mg of TAMIFLU® every other day or 30 mg TAMIFLU® every day. No recommended dosing regimens are available for patients undergoing routine hemodialysis and continuous peritoneal dialysis treatment with end-stage renal disease.

Preparation of TAMIFLU® for Oral Suspension

TAMIFLU® for Oral Suspension may be constituted by a pharmacist or health care provider.

1. Tap the closed bottle several times to loosen the powder.
2. Measure **23 mL** of water in a graduated cylinder.
3. Add the total amount of water for constitution to the bottle and shake the closed bottle well for 15 seconds.
4. Remove the child-resistant cap and push bottle adapter into the neck of the bottle.
5. Close bottle with child-resistant cap tightly. This will assure the proper seating of the bottle adapter in the bottle and child-resistant status of the cap.

NOTE: SHAKE THE TAMIFLU® FOR ORAL SUSPENSION WELL BEFORE EACH USE.

Store constituted suspension under refrigeration at 2-8°C (36-46°F). Do not freeze. The constituted TAMIFLU® for Oral Suspension (12 mg/mL) should be used within 10 days of preparation; the pharmacist, health care official, patient, or patient's parent or guardian should write the date of expiration of the constituted suspension on the label. The Fact Sheet for Patients and Parents and oral dispenser should be dispensed to the patient.

Body Weight (kg)	Body Weight (lbs)	Dose by Age (years)	Dose for 10 Days	# Bottles of Oral Suspension Needed for the 10 Day Regimen	Number of Capsules Needed for the 10 Day Regimen
≤ 15	≤ 33	1-2	30 mg once daily	1	10 capsules (30 mg)
> 15-23	> 33-51	3-5	45 mg once daily	2	10 capsules (45 mg)
> 23-40	> 51-88	6-9	60 mg once daily	2	20 capsules (30 mg)
> 40	> 88	10-12	75 mg once daily	3	10 capsules (75 mg)

An oral dosing dispenser with 30 mg, 45 mg, and 60 mg graduations is provided with TAMIFLU® for Oral Suspension; the 75 mg dose can be measured using a combination of 30 mg and 45 mg. It is recommended that patients use this dispenser. In the event that the dispenser provided is lost or damaged, another dosing syringe or other device may be used to deliver the following volumes: 2.5 mL (1/2 tsp) for children ≤ 15 kg, 3.8 mL (3/4 tsp) for > 15 kg to 23 kg, 5 mL (1 tsp) for > 23 kg to 40 kg, and 6.2 mL (1 ¼ tsp) for > 40 kg.

Prophylaxis in pediatric patients following close contact with an infected individual is recommended for 10 days. Prophylaxis in patients 1 to 12 years of age has not been evaluated for longer than 10 days duration. Therapy should begin soon as possible.

Pediatric Patients less than 1 year old:

Body Weight (kg)	Dose by Age	Recommended Prophylaxis Dose for 10 Days (Dose in volume is based on the concentration (12 mg/mL) of commercially-manufactured TAMIFLU® for Oral Suspension)
Dosing for infants younger than 1 year not based on weight	< 3 months	Not recommended unless situation judged critical
	3-5 months	20 mg (1.6 mL) once daily
	6-11 months	25 mg (2 mL) once daily

*For more information regarding the basis for these recommendations, see FDA's "Tamiflu Technical Review Document for H1N1 Influenza A" on www.cdc.gov/h1n1flu or http://www.fda.gov

For infants less than 1 year old, a different measuring device (such as a 5-mL oral syringe) must be used to correctly measure the dose.

Expired TAMIFLU® for Oral Suspension

If you have been asked to distribute/dispense TAMIFLU® for Oral Suspension that is past its original labeled expiration date, please be aware that the expiration date may have been extended as part of the federal government's Shelf Life Extension Program (SLEP). Under SLEP, FDA conducts scientific testing to see if specific lots of TAMIFLU® can be used beyond the expiration dates originally printed on the label by the manufacturer. If the product passes testing, FDA determines that the shelf life of the product can be extended beyond the expiration dates originally printed on the label. **For any TAMIFLU® for Oral Suspension that is past its original labeled expiration date, you may look up the lot number at the following website to determine if the expiry date for this lot has been extended and for how long:** www.cdc.gov/h1n1flu/eua. **For TAMIFLU® for Oral Suspension whose expiration date has been extended, you may inform recipients of the new expiration date.**

What are the Possible Side Effects of TAMIFLU®?

The side effects reported most often in those people who took this drug were gastrointestinal (i.e., nausea and vomiting). Nausea and vomiting may be less severe if TAMIFLU® is taken with food.

Rare cases of anaphylaxis and serious skin reactions including toxic epidermal necrolysis, Stevens-Johnson Syndrome, and erythema multiforme have been reported in post marketing experience with TAMIFLU®. TAMIFLU® should be stopped and appropriate treatment instituted if an allergic-like reaction occurs or is suspected.

There have been postmarketing reports of delirium and abnormal behavior leading to injury, and in some cases resulting in fatal outcomes, in patients with influenza who were receiving TAMIFLU®. These events may occur in the setting of encephalitis or encephalopathy but can occur without obvious severe disease. Because these events were reported voluntarily during clinical practice, estimates of frequency cannot be made but they appear to be uncommon based on TAMIFLU® usage data. These events were reported primarily among pediatric patients and often had an abrupt onset and rapid resolution. The contribution of TAMIFLU® to these events has not been established. Patients with influenza should be closely monitored for signs of abnormal behavior.

Refer to the Package Insert for more safety information.
Make available to recipients the information in the Fact Sheet for Patients and Parents

Reporting And Monitoring Adverse Events

Health care providers and recipients that experience adverse events or medication errors are encouraged to report to MedWatch at www.fda.gov/medwatch, by submitting a MedWatch Form 3500 (available at http://www.fda.gov/medwatch/safety/FDA-3500_fillable.pdf) or by calling 1-800-FDA-1088.

TAMIFLU® EUA, Fact Sheet for Health Care Providers: July 14, 2009

Index

——— B ———

——— I ———

———— O ————

—— P ——

——— T ———

Ordering Information

Hale Publishing, L.P.
1712 N. Forest Street
Amarillo, Texas, USA 79106

8:00 am to 5:00 pm CST

Call » 806.376.9900
Sales » 800.378.1317
Fax » 806.376.9901

Online Web Orders
www.ibreastfeeding.com